PSYCHOLOGY: ITS PRINCIPLES AND MEANINGS

2ND
EDITION

PSYCHOLOGY: ITS PRINCIPLES AND MEANINGS

LYLE E. BOURNE, JR.
BRUCE R. EKSTRAND

UNIVERSITY OF COLORADO

HOLT, RINEHART AND WINSTON
NEW YORK CHICAGO SAN FRANCISCO ATLANTA
DALLAS MONTREAL TORONTO LONDON SYDNEY

Library of Congress Cataloging in Publication Data
Bourne, Lyle Eugene, 1932–
Psychology: Its Principles and Meanings.
　　Bibliography: p. 519
　　1. Psychology.　　I. Ekstrand, Bruce R., joint
author.
II. Title [DNLM: 1. Psychology. BF121 B775p]
BF121.B62　1976　　150　　　75-6072
ISBN: 0-03-089628-2

Printed in the United States of America

6 7 8 9 032 9 8 7 6 5 4 3

For permission to use copyrighted materials, the authors are indebted to the following:

Chapter 1

The Case of Anna O., p. 2, from B. Martin. *Abnormal Psychology.* Glenview, Ill.: Scott, Foresman, 1973, p. 32. Reprinted by permission.
Psychology: Hot Course on Campus, p. 3, from *Newsweek*,
May 21, 1973. Copyright Newsweek, Inc. 1973, reprinted by
permission.
Figure 1–1, p. 3, © National Geographic Society. Reprinted
by permission.
News story, p. 5, from *Time*, January 1, 1973. Reprinted by
permission from TIME, The Weekly Newsmagazine; Copy-
right Time Inc.
Alienation Revisited, p. 11, from *Time*, January 29, 1973.
Reprinted by permission from TIME, The Weekly Newsmaga-
zine; Copyright Time Inc.
The Psychic Scandal, p. 11, from *Time*, August 26, 1974.
Reprinted by permission from TIME, The Weekly Newsmaga-
zine; Copyright Time Inc.
Problem Solving, p. 13, from *Biomedical News,* May 1972.
Reprinted by permission.
The Hazards of Change (including Rating Life Changes), p.
15, from *Time,* March 1, 1971. Reprinted by permission from
TIME, The Weekly Newsmagazine; Copyright Time Inc.
Weber's Law, p. 17, data from E. G. Boring, H. S. Langfeld,
and H. P. Weld. *Foundations of Psychology.* New York:
Wiley, 1948. Reprinted by permission of Mrs. Lucy D. Boring.
Figure 1–3, p. 18, photo courtesy of The Bettmann Archive.
Figure 1–4, p. 20, photo courtesy of The Bettmann Archive.
Figure 1–5, p. 21, photo courtesy of James B. Watson.
Figure 1–6, p. 22, photo courtesy of UPI.

continued on page 524

PREFACE

Our purpose in writing this book originally was to provide a useful set of textual materials for the course in introductory psychology offered at most four-year colleges. The book treats a selection of major topics in psychology in some depth. Given our desire to be brief and concise, not all topics that might be covered in the traditional introduction are included. We did not want to write a superficial survey. While our selection of topics might, in the minds of some potential teachers and readers, leave significant gaps, we feel that our approach has allowed us to illustrate the problems of psychology and to communicate its method of inquiry. In the second edition we have concentrated mainly on updating our coverage and improving the general readability of the text. We hope that we have been successful in this effort and that you will enjoy reading and using the book.

CONTRIBUTORS

Douglas Bernstein
University of Illinois, Champaign-Urbana
Chapter 9

Roger Dominowski
University of Illinois, Chicago Circle
Chapter 5

Ralph N. Haber
University of Rochester
Chapter 3

William Hodges
University of Colorado
Chapters 11 and 12

Charles Tart
University of California, Davis
Chapter 8

Michael Ziegler
York University, Toronto
Chapter 10

ACKNOWLEDGMENTS

Because of their large number, it is impossible for us to name everyone who assisted us in producing this book. Several people, however, deserve special mention because of the importance of their contributions. Foremost among them are the six professors of psychology, each a teacher of college-level introductory psychology, who served as subject-matter experts and who drafted initial versions of several chapters in this edition. These psychologists are listed as Contributors elsewhere in the front matter of this book. We owe them thanks and apologies—thanks for telling us in written form about current developments in special areas of psychology and apologies for editing and revising their work in ways that may have distorted both their intentions and their scholarship.

In addition to the Contributors, several others made substantive contributions to sections of various chapters. Among these, we would name, in particular, Jane Dallinger, Los Angeles Pierce College; David Dodd, University of Utah; Philip Groves, University of Colorado; Ellin Scholnick, University of Maryland; Jay Trowill, University of Denver; and Rita Yaroush, University of Denver. Drs. Dodd, Groves, and Scholnick contributed whole chapters to the first edition. Dr. Groves, in addition, helped with the preparation of Appendix B.

The book has materially benefited from the comments and reactions of many reviewers. We would like to recognize the thorough, intelligent, and critical essays on our efforts provided by the following: Barry F. Anderson, Portland State University; Raymond W. Bennett, University of Illinois, Chicago Circle; John C. Brigham, Florida State University; Robert T. Brown, University of North Carolina, Wilmington; Edward C. Caldwell, West Virginia University; Charles N. Cofer, Pennsylvania State University; James F. Collins, University of Missouri, Kansas City; Martin V. Covington, University of California, Berkeley; Charles Dickson, Lenoir Ryne College; Richard Dolinsky, University of Toledo; Norman R. Ellis, University of Alabama; Roger S. Fouts, University of Oklahoma; Gary Greenberg, Wichita State University, Donald E. Guy, Central Washington State College; Robert A. Haaf, University of Toledo; Pryor Hale, Piedmont Virginia Community College; Teresa Hayden, Kansas State University; Wayne L. Hren, Los Angeles Pierce College; Donald M. Johnson, West Valley College; Frank J. Landy, Pennsylvania State University; Georgia Lanoil, Westchester Community College; Bibb Latane, Ohio State University; William Lawson, University of Illinois; Herschel W. Leibowitz, Pennsylvania State University; Astrid McHugh, University of Maryland; Barclay Martin, University of North Carolina, Chapel Hill; Jonpaul R. Martin, Ohio State University; Thomas O. Nelson, University of California, Irvine; Alan Pantle, Miami University; Hayne W. Reese, West Virginia University; Cecil Rogers, Augusta College; John Rosen, University of Miami, Coral Gables; Lee Ross, Stanford University; Zick Rubin, Harvard University; Len Schmaltz, Illinois State University; Lee Sechrest, Florida State University; Robert Solso, Loyola University; Elliot Weiner, Oklahoma State University; Eugene B. Zechmeister, Loyola University.

Also, there are the long-suffering companions who worked with us on many and varied tedious chores throughout this project. Their support and encouragement, typing and proofreading, ideas and stimulation, technical and emotional help, are too great to recount in detail. We are, however, eternally grateful to: Nancy Clemente, Deborah Doty, Mary Ann Gundel, Lyn Hart, Jeanette Ninas Johnson, JoAnne Naples, Stephen Rapley, Suzanne Reissig, Mary Ellen Stocker, and Roger Williams.

Finally, we owe special thanks to Norma for her continuing support.

L.E.B., Jr.
B.R.E.

CONTENTS

DEAR STUDENT . . .

Consider two stories in the Denver morning newspaper one day:

> Vatican City (Compiled from UPI and AP dispatches)—A man wielding a 12-pound sledgehammer broke off the left arm and disfigured the face Sunday of the Madonna in Michelangelo's Pieta, the priceless statue in St. Peter's Basilica depicting the mother of Christ holding Jesus in her arms after the Crucifixion. Damage to one of the world's greatest works of art may be irreparable.

> Washington (AP)—At ceremonies last night, the National Academy of Sciences, our country's most prestigious honorary scientific society, honored twelve new members for their significant contributions to human knowledge.

Newspapers report mainly what people do and say; that is, they report about the behavior of people. People damage statues, wage war, negotiate peace, assassinate political leaders, win awards, make discoveries, help others, etc. Everyone is interested in behavior—is amazed by how strangely people sometimes behave—is frustrated at times with his inability to modify his own behavior—wishes he could control the behavior of others—would like to be able to predict what others will do—is interested in describing behavior—wants to understand behavior—feels compelled to explain his own or someone else's behavior. In short, just about everyone is a student of psychology.

Psychology is the science of behavior. The goals of this science are to measure and describe behavior, to predict and control it, and to understand and explain it. While you have all been students of behavior, this book will introduce you to the study of behavior as a scientific enterprise and as a formal academic discipline. Our goal is to provide you with a broad overview of the field of psychology today. We aim for breadth (though not completeness), so the treatment will be somewhat superficial. We have attempted to simplify complex issues for this introductory survey—many will say that we have oversimplified, and in some cases this is undoubtedly true. We do not contend that behavior is simple and easy to understand, or that all psychologists agree with each other. Instead behavior is complex, and most of the current issues are hotly debated; there are at least two sides to every problem. In presenting you with an introduction to psychology, it is just not possible to avoid simplification and generalization.

We have emphasized two basic aspects of psychology in this book. First we have tried to present the basic knowledge about behavior—the facts, principles, and "laws." We have tried to present answers to the question:

"What do we know about behavior?" Secondly, we have tried
to spell out the significance of this knowledge, how it
can be applied, what implications it has for the future.
We have tried to present answers to the question: "What
does this knowledge mean?" Accordingly, with occasional
exceptions, each of the chapters has been divided into two
parts, the first telling what we know about a particular
aspect of behavior, such as memory or motivation, and the
second attempting to describe the impact this knowledge
has on our lives. We have not hesitated to speculate about
the potential usefulness and application of present
knowledge. We apologize for sometimes letting our
imaginations run away. We do not apologize, however, for
attempting to make psychology look important, exciting,
and fascinating, and of great applied significance,
because it is all that and more.

We hope that this book will convey to you what
psychology is about. Psychology, like other sciences, has
become highly specialized and diverse, and we can hope
only to cover the highlights. To give you an idea of the
diversity of specific problems that psychologists are
interested in, consider the following sample:

Ralph is a 27-year-old salesman for a large
insurance company. He has a promising career with
the company, makes a good income, is married with
two children. Yesterday he tried to commit suicide.
Why?

Mary is undergoing an operation for removal of a
brain tumor. She has received only a local
anesthetic, and while her skull is open and her
brain exposed the neurosurgeon stimulates her brain
with a tiny electrical current. Mary reports seeing
and hearing a past experience she had many years
ago as if it were actually happening again. Has
her brain recorded her entire life of experiences?
Is everything we have ever done stored in our
brains? How can we tap our stored memories more
efficiently?

Johnny is in the sixth grade but reads at only a
third-grade level. In one study of college
students, less than half could read and comprehend
at a level necessary to understand their
introductory psychology text. How do the eyes
perceive the words on this page and how are these
words understood by the reader? Can research on
visual perception lead to better methods of
teaching people to read?

In the heart of a New York City residential area,
a woman is attacked by a man. She screams loudly
many times, begging for help. Many residents hear
her scream, but no one even bothers to call the
police, much less come to her aid. How can we
understand this?

Psychologists devise tests of just about everything
—IQ, ability to assemble pickup trucks,
personality, etc. There are tests to predict your
success in college or in various occupations and
tests of your current state of mental health. Bill
is a young black high school graduate looking for a
job. He just finished taking a whole battery of
tests as part of a job interview at the local steel
factory. He thinks that the tests are specifically
designed by individuals who think that whites are a
genetically superior race to make sure that blacks
do poorly on them. Is there any truth in his
argument?

Gene is the successful mayor of a large city. His
backers want him to challenge the incumbent
governor in the upcoming primary election. Gene
wants to see the outcome of a local newspaper poll
before deciding. Will the poll be of any use to
him in predicting his chances of winning? Can
psychologists help him to be a more persuasive
speaker, a more attractive candidate? Can
psychology help him win the election?

As children grow up, do they acquire knowledge in
different ways? Should the method of teaching
change as children get older? Are there natural
stages in the development of a child that make it
impossible to teach some things such as reading,
until the child is at least, say, 6 years old?
How do people learn anything? Why can't we learn
while we are sleeping? Why can't we learn faster?
Why are some things easy to learn and others
difficult? Why do people forget what they once
learned?

Throughout the book you will see more examples of what
psychology is about. Many have been drawn from newspapers
and magazines. We present you with these clippings, not
because we believe everything that is said in each
clipping, but because they are thought-provoking,
interesting, exciting, and sometimes depressing. You should
not accept them as proven facts. Clippings are not a good
source of scientific information or of psychological
principles. They are, however, a fair reflection of what
is now going on in the world and of the problems
psychology must address. Use your common sense and think
about the ideas being expressed in the clippings—do not
hesitate to challenge the "facts" as well as the ideas.
And, incidentally, this applies as much to what we say in
the text as it does to what others are saying in the
newspapers and magazines.
We hope that you will maintain an open mind as you read.
When you get done with the book we hope that you'll be
asking for more—more facts and less speculation, more
precise knowledge and less oversimplification, and more
real answers to your questions about behavior. If so, we
will be satisfied with the book.

The book has twelve chapters, arranged in ascending order of the complexity of the behavior being discussed. The first chapter is an introduction, telling you in general what psychology is all about, including a little historical background. The next eleven chapters cover basic content areas in psychology: biopsychology, perception, learning and memory, cognitive processes, motivation and emotion, development of behavior, consciousness and its altered states, personality, social psychology, psychopathology (the study of deviant behavior), and finally psychotherapy (the treatment of disordered behavior). These eleven topics come nowhere near covering all the fundamental topics in psychology. We have tried to select those topics we feel are most important for the beginning student. With a good foundation of principles and applications in these eleven areas, we feel that you will be able to move on to more advanced study.

We hope that you enjoy reading this book. We aren't promising that you won't be able to put it down, but we will be satisfied if it turns out that when you do put it down, you will at least occasionally be thinking about what you read in it. And when you have finished with it, we hope you will have a better understanding and appreciation of psychology.

Sincerely,

PSYCHOLOGY: ITS PRINCIPLES AND MEANINGS

1

THE NATURE OF PSYCHOLOGY

This chapter gives a broad outline of psychology and of the work that psychologists do. In the most general sense, psychologists are people who systematically study behavior, and psychology is the knowledge that results from that study. Both psychologists and psychology cover an enormous range of topics: practically everything you experience in daily life, all forms of behavior, have come or will come under the scrutiny of psychologists; and the techniques of study that psychologists use vary greatly, ranging from simple observation to complex experimental manipulations. Therefore, giving a fair and accurate picture of what psychology is will be a difficult task. One way to explain what psychology is all about is to describe some of the things that psychologists do. This is the primary focus of the first chapter. But we will also consider the most important goals of psychology, look briefly at the history of the field, and present a definition of behavior suitable for use throughout the rest of the book.

What Psychologists Do

All psychologists study the behavior of living organisms. Still, as in other fields, there are many different specialties within psychology and thus many different types of psychologists. These differences can, for the most part, be described in terms of four dimensions: (1) the particular behavioral issues or problems examined, (2) the research methods used, (3) the focus or purpose of the study, and (4) the kind of employment circumstances under which the study is conducted. Table 1–1 summarizes these dimensions, which we will now discuss in some detail.

Issues

There are literally thousands of different problems under active systematic investigation within psychology today. The list in Table 1–1 is a crude classification of these issues, arranged in ascending order of complexity. It begins with the basic study of man as a biological organism in an environment of physical stimuli and culminates in topics that relate to the "whole person," his interactions with other people, and some abnormal aspects of his behavior. It is reasonable to assume that man's actions will be limited by his biological equipment and by the nature of his environment, and an understanding of these limitations provides a necessary background for further psychological analysis. The deeper, more complex questions have to do with how a person uses his biological equipment and operates within his physical circumstances.

The classification in Table 1–1 is such that issues at one level provide much of the background for understanding problems at higher levels. It is reasonable to try to understand the basics of psychology before considering the complexities of behavioral interactions; therefore, the chapters in our book reflect this ordering.

Table 1–1
What psychologists do

Issues

1. Relations between behavior and nonpsychological factors, such as chemicals (drugs), the physical properties of stimulation, genes, and the nervous system
2. Perception of stimulation from one's environment, the first psychological step in most behavioral episodes
3. Learning and memory: processes in the acquisition of knowledge and skill
4. Using one's knowledge and skill for purposes of problem solving, creativity, and other forms of thinking
5. Motivation, arousal, and intention, the driving forces behind our actions
6. The development, with age and experience, of perception, learning, thought, motivation, and other behavioral phenomena and processes
7. Human consciousness: what we are aware of, under both normal and atypical (altered) circumstances
8. Social interaction: the processes by which we influence each other's behavior
9. Personality traits and behavior patterns that make each of us unique and individualistic
10. Unusual or abnormal behavior patterns, behavior pathology, its causes and its treatment

Methods

1. Individual case study
2. Naturalistic observation
3. Tests and surveys
4. Experiments

Focus

1. Basic knowledge
2. Practical applications

Employment

1. Colleges and universities
2. Elementary and secondary schools
3. Clinics
4. Industry
5. Government
6. Private practice

Methods

Progress in psychology depends upon discovering new facts about the behavior of organisms. But knowledge does not materialize out of thin air. To find out about behavior, psychologists have invented new methods or adapted old methods of inquiry from other fields. Although learning about scientific methods tends to be tedious and involved, it is very important, because these methods are indispensable to the progress of psychology. You need to know something about methodology to decide between fact and fiction. The methods of psychology differ in both the kind of information about behavior that they yield and the type of behaviors to which they are best suited. We will discuss four major kinds of approaches to the study of behavior, as listed in Table 1–1.

Individual case study.   The case study or case history method is perhaps the simplest and most direct form of psychological investigation. One individual is examined intensively to find out as much as possible about a certain problem, question, or issue as it relates to that individual. A combination of procedures might be used, including collecting biographical data on the individual, administering psychological tests, and interviewing him, sometimes over a course of several weeks.

Case study procedure is most often used to investigate abnormal behavior patterns. Perhaps the best-known clinical case history in psychology is

The Case of Anna O.

Anna O. had a number of hysterical symptoms, including paralysis of the muscles of the neck, right leg, and right arm, as well as impairments in sight and hearing, and frequent altered states of consciousness. Under hypnosis it was discovered that she had nursed her dying father and was in constant attendance at his bedside. One night she had dozed off and dreamed that a snake was attacking her father. She attempted to knock it away with her right hand, but this hand had fallen alseep and would not move. The next day as she was reaching into some bushes for a quoit, she saw a branch which reminded her of a snake, and again her right arm became paralyzed. Breuer [Freud's collaborator] discovered that having her reexperience incidents of this sort with complete emotional expression often resulted in a remission of the symptom.   (Martin, 1973) intervention, no matter how subtle, might disrupt the basic behavioral pattern. Therefore, some animal psychologists use unobtrusive observational procedures, getting close enough to the animals in their natural habitat to be able to observe (with the help of equipment) but far enough away so that their presence goes undetected. The idea is to observe behavior without influencing it. The observations, of course, will be recorded as objectively as possible, for example, with tape recorders and cameras.

Naturalistic observation is also the best technique in cases where ethical considerations may prevent the scientist from creating the phenomenon in the laboratory. For example, all of us are concerned with relationships between countries and between races. From a scientific point of view, the

Figure 1–1
Chimpanzee searching for termites

© National Geographic Society.

In a now-famous naturalistic study, Jane van Lawick-Goodall observed the behavior of chimpanzees in their natural African habitat. Contrary to the generally accepted idea that only human beings are capable of tool making, Goodall's observations established that chimps can make crude tools. In this photograph, a female chimp is using a blade of grass as a "fishing rod" for termites. Evidence taken from animals in zoos or laboratories gives a quite different and more limited picture of their abilities.

that of a woman with three different personalities, popularized in the movie *The Three Faces of Eve*. Such case histories often have great impact both within and outside psychology, because of the detail of description they can provide and the unusual behavior they are concerned with. One of the earliest and most famous clinical case studies came about as a result of Sigmund Freud's investigations and concerned a patient, Anna O., who was paralyzed without apparent organic cause. By taking a detailed case history, Freud was able to discover the critical events in Anna O.'s life that contributed to her neurotic behavior.

Naturalistic observation.   As the name would suggest, naturalistic observation is a systematic method for observing and recording events as they naturally occur in the real world. It is used in those cases where artificial probes or manipulations might destroy some or all of the basic characteristics of the phenomenon in question or where there is no way of making a more controlled observation. Suppose we were interested in the mating or maternal behavior of wild elk. Any kind of human psychologist would like to know how relationships develop and how more cooperative relationships might be arranged. Some by-products of these relationships are destructive and unpleasant—for example, wars between nations and race riots. Because both wars and riots are a part of the basic phenomenon of interpersonal relationships, they cannot go without examination by the scientist. On the other hand, the scientist is in no position to influence the occurrence of either kind of tragedy. To investigate such behavioral phenomena he has to observe, record, and try to understand when the events occur naturally. While this may seem cold and inhumane, the scientist's position is that the knowledge he collects by this process might very well be helpful in solving later problems of the same sort.

Tests, interviews, and surveys.   Psychological tests have been developed and standardized for just about any aspect of behavior you can imagine. There are tests of general ability, called intelligence tests, and there are tests of specific traits, such as anxiety or leadership ability. All of these tests consist of a number of questions, and the pattern of answers a person gives is thought to reveal something about his level on the trait or ability being measured. The sum total of his answers gives a composite score that is taken to be a fair reflection of his typical behavior in everyday circumstances.

The psychological interview is often used in connection with the case study method. Generally, in that context, the interview is free-floating and unstructured. Its direction is guided by the responses of the individual being examined and any hypothesis that his examiner might have about the underlying rationale of these responses. But interviews can be highly structured, consisting, much like psychological tests, of a series of items to which the individual is asked to respond. A structured interview is most likely to be used when the purpose is collecting, from a group of people, data that will lead to general conclusions about the population, rather than when the purpose is intensive study of a single individual.

Surveys fall somewhere between structured interviews and psychological tests. Again, they consist of a series of questions or items to which individuals are asked to reply. The purpose is typically to determine general opinions, attitudes, or feelings on a specific issue. A candidate for political office, for example, might want to determine the general attitude of the public toward a particular

---

Table 1–2
Kinds of psychologists

Experimental psychologist.   Uses scientific methods to carry out experiments designed to develop a basic understanding of such processes as learning, memory, motivation, sensation, and perception in human beings and lower animals.

Biopsychologist.   Studies the contribution of biological factors—such as heredity, the sensory and nervous systems, drugs, and species differences—to various kinds of behavior.

Social psychologist.   Uses a variety of scientific methods to study the behavior of people in social situations, that is, in the presence of at least one other person.

Developmental psychologist.   Studies normal behavioral development from infancy to adulthood, including the development of learning, perception, social behavior, and motivation.

Educational psychologist.   Studies the educational process with the hope of developing better educational systems and is responsible for implementing these systems.

Personality psychologist.   Studies the whole person in an effort to discover the basic underlying dimensions of behavior, such as introversion-extroversion, and to find means of measuring and describing individuals on those dimensions.

Clinical psychologist.   Generally focuses on abnormal behavior in an effort to understand, diagnose, and change such behavior.

Counseling psychologist.   Offers expert advice for solution of personal or educational problems when there is no sign of serious mental disorder—for example, in marriage counseling and in student counseling and guidance.

Industrial psychologist.   Usually works for a business enterprise, applying psychological knowledge to such areas as personnel policies, working conditions, production efficiency, and decision making.

Education.   Most psychologists have a Ph.D (Doctor of Philosophy) degree, which requires 4 to 5 years of graduate study (beyond a bachelor's degree) in a specialty area. Most were psychology majors as undergraduates, although psychology graduate programs often take nonpsychology majors. There are also numerous graduate programs that lead only to the master's degree, usually requiring about 2 years of graduate study. Master's-level psychologists can be employed in most of the same jobs as Ph.D.-level psychologists, although the salary, responsibility, and opportunities for advancement are usually not as great.

---

issue in order to decide whether his campaign should stress or minimize that issue.

Testing, interviewing, surveying, and sometimes naturalistic observation are often combined under the general heading of a *correlational* approach to psychological issues. In general, this approach is used to discover the degree of relationship between two or more *variables*. A variable is any characteristic of an object, event, person, or whatever, that can take two or more values. A psychologist might hypothesize, for example, that a person's stand on welfare issues (one variable) is highly related to his annual income (a second variable). His hypothesis might then state the nature of this relationship. He might suppose that, in general, the more income a person has, the less likely he is to favor welfare payments to needy people. To check on this hypothesis, the psychologist tries to find data reflecting both income and attitudes toward welfare. He might interview or survey a cross section of the population at large. For each person in the study, there would be two scores, one for annual income and one reflecting both direction and degree of attitude toward welfare proposals, ranging from strongly opposed to strongly favorable.

To find out how strong a relationship there is between these variables, the psychologist would compute a numerical value, or statistic, called the *correlation coefficient* (see Appendix A). The correlation of zero signifies no relationship at all between the two variables. In the above example, a correlation of zero would mean that the amount of income that a person makes is not related to his attitude toward welfare plans. A positive correlation means that the two variables are related in a certain way: The higher the value of one score on the survey, the higher the value of the other. A positive correlation in this example would mean that the more money a person makes each year, the more likely he is to favor welfare plans. This, of course, would not confirm the original hypothesis. A negative correlation implies a relationship between the two variables that is opposite, or inverse: As the value of one variable increases, the value of the other decreases. In the example, a negative correlation would mean that the more a person earns, the less likely he is to favor welfare—and vice versa. Thus, a negative correlation *would* be consistent with the original hypothesis.

The experimental method. Case studies, naturalistic observation techniques, and the various correlational methods all suffer a major drawback. While they provide information about dependencies among psychological variables, they do not allow for a determination of direct or cause-effect relationships. For example, a case study of a psychologically disturbed person might reveal that he had a difficult childhood, but this does not mean that unhappy early experiences *necessarily* lead to abnormal behavior. Any number of other factors might also be involved. The fact that elk are observed to mate more frequently after a spring rain

Correlation Does Not Mean Causality

Time—Americans love coffee; they consumed 13.6 lbs. per person last year. But their taste for the brew may be dangerous. A team of physicians from Boston University Medical Center reports in *Lancet* that people who drink more than five cups of coffee a day are twice as likely to suffer heart attacks as people who drink no coffee at all. The researchers base their hypothesis on a study of 276 patients admitted to hospitals with acute myocardial infarctions. The team found that those patients and 1,104 others who were used as controls differed little in medical history or smoking habits. But when coffee comsumption was compared, the differences were dramatic. All the heart attack victims consumed appreciably greater quantities of coffee. The Boston group carefully avoids indicting coffee as a cause of heart attacks. Their findings suggest, however, that people already prone to heart problems would do well, when coffee-break time rolls around, to at least skip a second cup.

If two variables are correlated with each other, there is a tendency to conclude that one variable causes the other. Suppose variable A (the amount of coffee a person drinks each day) is correlated with variable B (the probability that the person will have a heart attack), such that the more coffee he drinks, the higher his risk of heart attack. There is a tendency to conclude that coffee (or caffeine anyway) causes heart disease. We cannot draw such a causal conclusion from correlations. By selecting people who are alike in drinking large amounts of coffee, we may quite inadvertently be selecting people who are also alike in other ways. Suppose that people who drink lots of coffee are, in general, highly anxious and nervous people. It could be that it is the anxiety that is responsible for the heart attacks, not the caffeine. We are saying that variable A is correlated not only with variable B, but with a third variable C (anxiety), and perhaps even several others. It might be C or some other variable, not A, that causes B.

cannot be taken as evidence for a direct relationship between humidity and the mating instinct. Perhaps the rains tend to occur in the late afternoon and the elk prefer evening as a time to get together. The fact that high income tends to be *correlated with* opposition to welfare does not necessarily imply that, if someone's income were suddenly to double, his opinion of welfare would automatically drop. Opinions toward welfare are commonly formed even before an individual has achieved permanent employment. Observational procedures are important, but the establishment of direct,

PEANUTS®   **By Charles M. Schulz**

© 1960 United Feature Syndicate, Inc.

For some reason, statistics has a bad name. Partly this is because statistics is a branch of mathematics and everybody "knows" that mathematics is a hard subject. We shall try to make it a little easier in Appendix A. Another reason is that statistics can be deceiving. Because statistics is a way of summarizing a lot of data, important results are occasionally overlooked. Be careful of this possibility as you read further in this book.

cause-effect relationships requires a different method of investigation, namely, the *experimental method.*

In addition to being an observer, the experimental psychologist also manipulates and controls his subject. He brings the phenomenon at issue into the laboratory, where he can rule out all extraneous and distracting variables and manipulate, with precise equipment and procedures, conditions that he wishes to explore. The experimental psychologist sets up a simplified version of what appears to be going on in the outside world and examines the process under conditions where only one thing at a time is changed. If whatever condition it is that changes is associated with a change in behavior, then he can be certain that there is a direct cause-effect relationship between the changing variable and the behavior in question.

For example, suppose we wish to know whether a person should study in relatively short periods over the course of, say, 2 weeks preceding an examination or whether it would be better to concentrate all study time during the evening before the exam. If the psychologist were merely to observe the study habits of people who happen to be available, he might have difficulty drawing a precise conclusion. The person who distributes his study time over 2 weeks preceding an examination might actually be studying more in terms of total time than the individual who concentrates his effort on the evening before. Furthermore, he might be a psychologically different type of individual, less secure about his ability to perform on a test or more intelligent than the individual who begins to study just before the examination. The observations would

tell us something, but they might not make all of the effective variables entirely clear.

An experimental approach to the question would be different. First, the experimenter would probably construct a simplified version of the problem for investigation in the laboratory. He selects a set of materials to be learned, similar though not necessarily identical to the kind of material a person might study for an examination. Suppose the test is to cover one's knowledge of foreign language vocabulary. A simplified version of this might be a list of about 12 to 20 pairs of words that a subject would try to memorize in such a way that given the first word of the pair he can respond with the second.

The psychologist now wants to find out how fast people learn these materials under different study conditions. He decides to have two timing conditions. In one condition, effort is concentrated. The pairs are presented to the student at a rate of 5 seconds per pair for study; immediately after presentation, the first member of each pair is shown and the subject is tested for his ability to respond with the second. Then the pairs are presented once again, followed by a second test. This procedure—study followed immediately by test, followed immediately by study, and so on—is repeated for, say, 20 trials. In the second study condition the same procedure is used, with the exception that the subject is allowed to rest for 30 seconds between each test and the following study period. The same number of trials will be given and the same amount of study time will be allowed, but practice is spread out over a longer period of time.

Independent and dependent variables.
Because observations of a subject's performance are taken within the laboratory or some other well-controlled situation, psychologists are in a position to hold constant most variables that might affect performance. All subjects perform as closely as possible under the same circumstances except for the variable the experimenter manipulates. A good investigator will try to control or hold constant

Two Common Pitfalls in Psychological Research

The Placebo Effect

The placebo effect refers to the fact that any kind of treatment may produce a behavioral change, perhaps due to suggestion. For example, suppose the hypothesis is that Drug A will relieve depression. The experimenter gives Drug A to a group of depressives and finds that they improve, so he concludes that Drug A is effective. His conclusion may be wrong—giving these depressives any kind of treatment might have resulted in equal improvement. He should have included a *placebo-control* group in his experiment. This group would have received a "fake," or placebo, "drug," one that contains no active ingredients. In order to conclude that Drug A is effective, the experimenter must demonstrate that it results in greater improvement than treatment with the placebo. Of course, subjects in the experiment must not know whether they are receiving the real drug or the placebo. In such cases the subjects are said to be *blind* to the conditions of the experiment.

Experimenter Bias.

While it is obvious that the subjects should be "blind" about the treatment they receive, it may also be important that the experimenter be uninformed about which group receives the placebo and which the real treatment. If both the subjects and the experimenter are blind, the study is called a *double-blind* experiment. You should be cautious about believing the results of treatment studies that are not double-blind.

   Robert Rosenthal has demonstrated that, in several different types of experiments, the experimenter, if he knows how the results are supposed to come out, can influence them in that

direction. The most startling demonstration of this was Rosenthal's study showing that teachers can influence their pupils' scores on intelligence tests (IQ scores). Rosenthal told a group of teachers that certain students in their classes had high intellectual potential as judged by psychological tests. Actually these students were randomly selected. At the end of the year, these pupils showed a much larger IQ gain than students not identified as high in potential. The teachers (the experimenters) expected these children to improve and probably took steps along the way, often unconsciously, to make sure that they did. We will have more to say about this phenomenon in Chapter 10.

"Not really . . . but you'd be surprised at the psychological effect."

all but the variable of interest. The variable of interest that the experimenter manipulates is called the *independent variable.* In our vocabulary-learning example, the independent variable is the time between the study and test periods, and there are two levels of this variable, 0 and 30 seconds. That is, half the subjects will learn while getting 0 seconds rest between study and test, and half will learn with a 30-second rest period. The experimenter then measures the subjects' performance to find out whether it is changed in any way by the difference in the independent variable. The measure of performance is called the *dependent variable.* The experimenter tries to determine whether the dependent variable depends in any way on the independent variable. In our example, the dependent variable might be the number of correct responses

made by the subject on each test trial. Thus the point of our illustrative experiment is to determine whether number of correct responses (the dependent variable) is influenced by the timing conditions during learning (the independent variable). Although in our example the experimenter manipulates only one independent variable and measures only one dependent variable, the logic of experimental procedure does allow him to study several of each type of variable within a single investigation.

Random selection.   Suppose performance by the spaced practice group (30-second rest condition) is better than performance by the concentrated practice group (0-second rest). What is there to assure us that subjects in our spaced practice

"NOW I WANT YOU TO RELAX COMPLETELY!"

Gahan Wilson Sunday Comics reprinted courtesy of The Register and Tribune Syndicate, Inc.

Simply by trying to observe or measure behavior, the psychologist can affect it and change it. If the psychologist uses equipment or techniques that affect the behavior he is trying to measure, his measurements are said to be *obtrusive*. The scientist in the cartoon is using obviously obtrusive techniques to study relaxation. Obtrusive measurement is one way an experimenter can bias his results, making them less useful. But developing *unobtrusive* methods for observing behavior is not always easy.

Independent and Dependent Variables

For each of the experiments described below determine what is the independent variable (the variable manipulated by the experimenter) and what is the dependent variable (the measure of performance he collects from each subject).

1. Subjects are asked to deliver a shock of 10, 20, 30, 40, or 50 volts to another subject (actually an employee who is working for the psychologist running the experiment). Just before this request, the employee has either insulted the real subject or has complimented him.

2. Two groups of mental patients (schizophrenics and depressives) are asked to tell stories about pictures they are shown. The psychologist counts the number of times in each story that the patient mentions anything that is connected with hostility or aggression.

3. A group of subjects is asked to rate paintings on a 7-point scale (where 1 = very poor and 7 = excellent). Actually, all the paintings are by the same unknown artist, but for half of the paintings the subjects are told the name of a famous artist and for half they are told a name made up by the experimenter.

4. Three groups of subjects are asked to read a short story and then take a multiple choice test on the content of the story. One group is given 10 minutes to read the story, a second is given 15 minutes, and a third 20 minutes.

5. A student goes to a shopping center, approaches people and tries to give them a penny. On half of the occasions he dresses in a suit and tie and is clean shaven; the other half of the time he puts on a fake beard and dresses in hippie clothes.

condition are not, in general, smarter than subjects in our concentrated practice condition? There might be unwanted effects in the experiment attributable to the fact that a different group of subjects participates under each of the two experimental conditions.

Our main assurance of unbiased effects comes from the manner in which subjects are selected for the various groups or conditions in the experiment; this is an important aspect of *experimental control.* The experimenter cannot hold individual differences among people constant in the same way he can control other variables operating in the laboratory situation. But he can take the following steps in order to equalize the groups: (1) select all subjects randomly from the population to which he wishes to generalize the results; (2) assign subjects randomly to the various experimental conditions; (3) use a large enough number of subjects in each group to average out random variations; and (4) take all possible precautions to avoid biasing subjects in any way. If the experimenter follows these simple steps, he should have comparable subjects participating in each condition.

Testing the hypothesis. With these considerations in mind the experimenter is now in a

position to test his hypothesis. Having no reason to believe otherwise, the experimenter might guess that the way a person distributes his study time has *no effect* on his performance on a test, if the total amount of time spent in study is comparable. A hypothesis stated in this form is called a *null hypothesis.* It is the prediction that the variable being manipulated, the independent variable, will have no effect on the behavior being measured, the dependent variable.

The results of the experiment provide a test of this hypothesis. If at the end of 20 study trials, both groups of subjects perform the same on their test, the experimenter would conclude that distribution of study time has nothing to do with degree of learning. The null hypothesis would be confirmed. If, on the other hand, he does observe a relationship,

The Control Group

The simplest and most common experimental design involves two groups, *the experimental group* and *the control group.* The control group is used to eliminate as a possible explanation for the results any variable which the experimenter does *not* want to influence his results. Suppose he wants to know if a particular treatment (treatment X) for mental illness is effective in helping patients. An experimental group of patients is given treatment X, and the experimenter observes their behavior and sees that there is marked improvement. He might conclude that treatment X is beneficial. But perhaps the patients would have improved anyway for numerous reasons. He needs a control group of patients that is treated the same way as the experimental group (same meals, same hospital, same diagnoses, etc.) with the *single* exception that no control patient is given treatment X. If the experimenter then observes greater improvement in the experimental group than the control group, he can safely conclude that the difference in improvement between the two groups must have been caused by treatment X, since treatment X was the only thing which the two groups differed on. Many experiments fail because the experimenter did not run an appropriate control group.

"Four years of research, and now you tell me you forgot which is the control group!"

G. Spitzer, APA Monitor, August 1971.

The following experiments should provide you with a better understanding of the need and use of control groups in psychological research.

1. A physiological psychologist surgically destroys a particular part of the brain, the hypothalamus, to see if this particular brain structure is important in controlling eating. He needs a control group of animals who undergo brain surgery procedures (anesthesia, cutting open the skull, etc.), but who do not have their hypothalamus destroyed or have some other area of the brain destroyed. If the hypothalamus is uniquely involved in controlling eating, the investigator should find greater eating disturbances in the experimental animals than in the control animals.

2. A psychologist wants to know if hypnotic suggestions can cause you to make your body become so stiff and rigid that it can be suspended between two chairs. He needs a control group of subjects that are asked to do the task without the induction of hypnosis. Both groups of subjects should receive the same instructions about their

ability to accomplish this feat if they try hard. The control subjects should be treated by the same experimenter, under the same conditions. The only difference between experimental and control subject should be whether or not a hypnotic induction procedure is used.

3. An industrial psychologist thinks that he can improve production at a factory by making the surroundings more pleasant—brightly colored rooms, better lighting, and music. So he sets up such a production line in a special room at the factory and selects a random group of the workers to come and work on this line. He finds that production is higher in this setting than at the regular line in the factory and concludes that the lighting, colors, and music were responsible. He needs a control group of workers selected from the regular lines and also asked to work in a "special" room, but this special room duplicates the regular working conditions. Merely being selected to work in a special room as part of an experiment may make people work harder, if only because they assume that someone is watching their work more carefully.

then he would reject the null hypothesis: For example, if performance improves as the length of rest between study periods is increased, he would conclude that distribution of study time has a favorable effect on learning.

The key advantage of the experimental method is that it allows for direct cause-effect conclusions from the data. If all of the variables are properly controlled, and it is observed that the dependent variable changes when the independent variable is

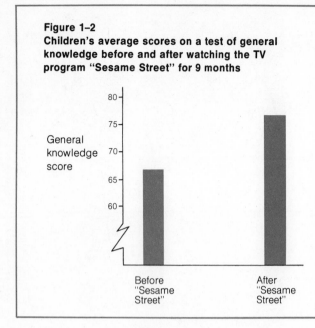

Figure 1–2
Children's average scores on a test of general knowledge before and after watching the TV program "Sesame Street" for 9 months

General knowledge score

What's Wrong with This Experiment?

An experimenter hypothesizes that watching "Sesame Street" on TV will increase children's general knowledge. He randomly selects 25 children to participate in his experiment. In September, with a special test, he measures the general knowledge of each child and finds that the average score is 67. Then every weekday for the next 9 months the parents bring the children to his laboratory, where he insures that they all sit and watch the 1-hour program. In early June, after the children have seen close to 200 different "Sesame Street" programs, he gives them the general knowledge test again. Now the children score an average of 77, which is significantly higher than the 67 average back in September. He concludes that watching "Sesame Street" results in increased general knowledge, so all parents should make their children watch the program.

changed, the experimenter can conclude that the relationship is *causal*. Because of this logic, psychologists have a distinct preference for experimental techniques over nonexperimental techniques in the study of behavior. The assumption is that understanding behavior comes down eventually to knowing what causes what, and the experimental method is our chief means of finding out.

How rigid are scientific methods?   The foregoing discussion of psychological methods may have given the impression that the accumulation of scientific knowledge is a very regular, systematic, and highly programmed process. It seems as if theories are logically formed, experiments are rigidly planned and executed, and the resulting data are precisely analyzed and interpreted. Every step is arranged in advance and followed exactly.

Of course, this concept is far from the truth. A lot of science is pure luck or serendipitous discovery. For example, a psychologist may discover something extremely important about human learning while investigating a minor question in a related area. Many times research is done with only a hunch or with the question "I wonder what would happen if . . ." in mind. For example, James Olds discovered the apparently pleasurable effects of direct electrical stimulation of the brain while studying the role that nerve centers in the lower brain play in learning (see Chapter 6). Ivan Pavlov happened upon the phenomenon of classical

conditioning in a project focusing on digestive processes in dogs (see Chapter 4). These important observations will be elaborated in later chapters. They are mentioned here only to illustrate that science is a flexible enterprise, with big discoveries often coming by luck and without design. Methods are *suggested* rules of procedure. They can be and are violated when circumstances indicate. What is really important is the question or issue under examination. The method must always be modified to fit the problem.

Focus

The focus of any psychological study is either basic knowledge, a practical application, or a combination of both. When the focus is on basic knowledge, the psychologist is searching for a verifiable principle that will help him to better understand some general psychological issue. Often, this work has an abstract, theoretical flavor to it. To an outsider, it may appear to make no contact at all with life's problems. For what practical reason, for example, might someone study the maze-running behavior of rats, the mating patterns of porpoises, the strategies people use in solving anagram problems? Studies like these seem too far removed from important problems in everyday life to be of any significance. Yet, psychologists do them, and with good reason: Studies of this sort are often the simplest and most direct way to get at general principles of behavior. For example, experiments on white rats in a two-sided shuttle box provided a basis for our

Alienation Revisited

Time—Is the American worker—blue-collar and white-collar alike—bored with his job and alienated? So it is often said, most recently by the Department of Health, Education and Welfare, which reported that only 25% of the workers it polled were satisfied and would choose the same kind of job again.

Actually, both the polls and the interpretation are misleading, according to Irving Kristol, Henry R. Luce Professor of Urban Values at New York University. "About 85% of American workers, when asked whether they are satisfied with their jobs, answer in the affirmative," he wrote in the *Wall Street Journal.* "[HEW] tries to show that they don't mean what they say. Thus if an employee tells an interviewer that he finds his work satisfying but also that he would like to change his job for something better, [HEW] concludes that he is 'alienated' from his work. One gets the firm impression that the authors of this study believe that to have unfulfilled aspirations, to daydream, to engage in wistful thinking, or to express regret for lost opportunities (real or imaginary) is less than human. It also apparently never occurs to them that it is utopian to expect ordinary working people to be as content as the most successful surgeon or lawyer. Why should they be? How could they be? Where and when have they ever been?"

The Psychic Scandal

Time—The world of parapsychology has more than its share of frauds, charlatans and opportunists. But even those critics who were openly skeptical about the phenomena reported by the Institute for Parapsychology in Durham, N.C., seldom questioned the sincerity or integrity of Dr. Joseph B. Rhine, the institute's founder, or his staff. Last week a shaken Rhine was preparing to acknowledge publicly a scandal that has already rocked the entire psychic establishment.

In the parapsychological equivalent of the famous case of the painted mice at Manhattan's Sloan-Kettering Institute (TIME, April 29 *et seq.*), Walter J. Levy Jr., 26, the bright, recently appointed director of Rhine's institute, resigned after admitting that he had falsified experimental data. . . .

Levy's research, elegantly computerized, was aimed at testing the ability of rodents to anticipate events (E.S.P.) or to effect physical changes by sheer will power (psychokinesis). He had electrodes implanted in the brains of rats in a zone where stimulation gave the animals intense pleasure. The stimuli were delivered at random intervals by a computer that in turn was keyed to the decay of atoms in a sample of radioactive strontium 90. Without any outside influence, the system would stimulate the rats' pleasure zones 50% of the time. If the rats could anticipate the computer by E.S.P. or influence the decay of the radioactive source by psychokinesis, their pleasure score would exceed 50%.

By early May, Levy was reporting 54% pleasure stimulus scores, indicating that the rats had psychic powers. Then one of Levy's assistants became suspicious when he noticed that the director seemed to be loitering needlessly around the equipment. With two colleagues, the assistant decided to check. From a hiding place one watched while the others helped Levy run a test. They saw him tamper with the recorder, causing his tape to score high. Another set of instruments—installed without Levy's knowledge—confirmed their suspicions by recording the expected 50% score. . . .

The three reported to Rhine, who confronted Levy. He confessed and resigned, later telling friends that he had been under great pressure to produce positive results and had been overburdened by administrative duties. He insisted that this was the only time he had falsified data; after failing to reproduce earlier positive tests, he had felt a need to force the data to reflect the results he expected. . . .

Don't Believe Everything You Read; or the Scientist Can Be Just as Wrong as the Man in the Street

Here are excerpts from two recent articles in *Time* Magazine. One illustrates the often forgotten principle in behavioral research that you can't believe everything that your subjects tell you. Some subjects when filling out questionnaires or answering pollster's questions may deliberately lie, or their responses may be heavily influenced by the wording of the questions. Thus, a factory worker might respond differently to "Are you satisfied with your job?" and "Are you completely happy with your job?" The "Alienation" excerpt indicates that 85 percent of workers will answer yes to the first question, but that a much smaller percentage will answer yes to the second. If you want data to show that workers are not alienated, ask the first question; if you want data to show that workers *are* alienated, ask the second. And in either case, remember that they may not be telling the truth.

The second excerpt demonstrates that scientists are, after all, merely human—they can deliberately lie and distort their data. It is always a tragedy when this type of behavior is exposed, but we must remember that these things do sometimes happen. We should also be aware that scientific conclusions occasionally are wrong not because of any deliberate action by the investigator, but because his results were merely due to chance. For these reasons, it is important to repeat experiments to make sure that the same results occur a second or third time and are not just a fluke. Repeating an experiment is called *replication,* and it is an important part of the scientific method. The next time you hear some surprising experimental results, ask, "Has the experiment been replicated?"

current understanding of anxiety as a motivating force in behavior. This is a major psychological principle, as we shall see. Many other illustrations of the same scientific process will emerge in our later discussions.

Basic scientific psychology depends on simple empirical results, which it pieces together in much the same way you solve a jigsaw puzzle. By looking at the available bits of information in a variety of ways, the psychologist searches for an overall orderly relationship—the "big picture." If he is successful, he arrives at a general *theory* that represents, organizes, and summarizes the facts and suggests some things about the yet-unknown factors and processes underlying them. The more general this theory is, the better our understanding of the issue and the more phenomena inside and outside the laboratory we will be able to describe, predict, and control.

Not all psychological research is focused on the development of basic knowledge. Some psychologists work directly on problems and questions of immediate practical importance. For purposes of developing a more useful school curriculum, a psychologist might want to find out which topics should be taught and in what order. Psychologists in industry might be given the task of finding the most readable layout of instruments on an automobile dashboard. In order to increase its sales, a cereal manufacturing company might ask a psychologist to determine the most attractive shape, color, and design for its new package. These are all practical matters in need of immediate data. Although behavioral theory might give a general idea of what to expect and some methods of finding out more, some questions demand a much more specific and quick answer. The majority of psychologists are no doubt engaged in solving specific practical problems.

Employment

Issues, methods, and focus all have something to do with where and how a psychologist might be employed, that is, with the nature of his job. Listed in Table 1–1 are six primary sources of employment. Psychologists in colleges and universities are generally concerned with the full range of issues outlined in Table 1–1. A well-rounded academic psychology department would try to provide training in each of these areas with as much depth as possible. Furthermore, psychologists engaged in teaching try to train new people to be competent in each of the methods that are available for research. When it comes to focus, however, psychologists in

---

What's Wrong with This Experiment?

An experimenter has a hypothesis that learning is impaired by loud noises, such as might take place when a student is trying to study in his dormitory room while his roommates and neighbors are playing poker. He sets up an experiment involving two groups of subjects. The experimental group wears earphones while studying a textbook for 30 minutes. Periodically, noises of all different sorts are played over the earphones to the subjects. The control subjects study the same textbook for the same 30 minutes with no earphones and noises. There are 20 subjects in the experiment, 10 randomly assigned to each of the two conditions, noise and no noise. After the 30-minute study period, both groups take a test on the material they were studying. The results show that the noise condition resulted in fewer correct responses on the test than the no-noise condition. The experimenter concludes, "As I hypothesized, noise interferes with learning."

---

colleges and universities are generally concerned with basic knowledge rather than with practical applications. The assumption is that with basic knowledge and skills in the methods, one would be able to engage, if he so desired, in psychology on a more practical level.

Other areas of employment, however, put a greater premium on practical application. In elementary and secondary schools, psychologists are concerned with the use of knowledge about learning and motivational processes and with student guidance and counseling. In hospitals, clinics, or private practice, the psychologist will generally be involved in diagnostics and therapy. That is, he will be concerned with trying to find out, by testing, by interviewing, or by the general case study method, what is wrong with a particular individual and why. He may then, if indicated, administer corrective or psychotherapeutic measures. Industries employ psychologists to answer particular questions about products, services, or personnel, such as how to design a product for efficient operation or improve employment conditions.

The Goals of Psychology

From the various activities carried on by psychologists, it is difficult to single out a simple set of goals. But remembering our definition of psychology as the scientific study of behavior and the systematic application of behavior principles, we

Problem Solving: Sometimes We Must Act Even in Absence of Experimental Proof

Biomedical News—Since the time of Francis Bacon, scientists have placed their faith in the power of the scientific method, especially the experimental approach. The procedures and techniques, especially recent statistical advances, have produced procedures that, while not always observed, nevertheless, are the regular guide for the development of conclusions from data.

However, as the complexity of knowledge has increased, certain practical problems have arisen that may prevent the development of conclusions about serious problems. Consider, for example, the relationship of crowding among humans to a decline in the birth rate. Hundreds of experiments using animals have been conducted so that procedures are clear and routine. For example, one may reduce the population to one-half, measure the pregnancy rates and other matters of the individuals removed, and then measure the birth rate for a suitable period of time as the population increases.

It is perfectly obvious that this procedure cannot be used on humans. Indeed, it has been impossible for purely practical reasons to apply this procedure to any species of primate. Furthermore, these practical considerations are such that it seems unlikely that a suitable experiment will be done on a primate species. Obviously other approaches are available, but again and again the practical or humane aspects prevent conducting a suitable experiment.

Let's ask the question as to whether we will ever have direct evidence of a causative effect of smoking on cancer. Any scientist can invent a protocol for an experiment which in some way or other would involve large groups of humans, some of whom would not smoke for a couple of decades, and others who would smoke a number of cigarettes for a similar period of time. Again, while there are many ways to develop experiments, in each case the practical limitations would prevent their performance. The important conclusion in this situation is that scientists should recognize that however powerful the experimental method may be, there are practical limitations to its use in solving human problems. Thus we must rely on indirect methods for drawing inferences, and in many cases we must go ahead with an action program even though we lack experimental proof.

It is also essential to tell the public that the scientific method cannot produce conclusions in every case, not because of theoretical deficiencies, but because of practical problems. In some cases large amounts of money will overcome these practical problems, as was the case in the experimentation on the use of polio vaccines. In other cases, it would be better to go ahead on an action program explaining to the general public that complete proof is unlikely to become available. Indeed, it seems possible that part of the current anti-intellectualism and disillusionment with the results of science arise from exaggerated expectations by the general public for results from the experimental method.

David E. Davis, Ph.D.

Dr. Davis is professor and chairman of the department of zoology, North Carolina State University, Raleigh.

Lest you be left with the impression that the experimental method is the method one should always use, consider what one prominent scientist—not a psychologist—thinks about the limitations of this approach. His position is probably acceptable to most experimenters.

can identify three basic goals: to measure and describe, to predict and control, and to understand and explain behavior. Let us consider each of these goals in more detail.

Measurement and Description

Before one can hope to understand or manipulate a phenomenon, he must first be able to describe and measure it. A good deal of a psychologist's work involves measuring and describing behavior. All the so-called psychological concepts and processes mentioned in the preceding pages—for example, IQ, anxiety, learning, attitudes, abilities, depression, and more—must be measured. A major goal, therefore, is to develop tests or techniques for measuring. Each measuring device must possess two characteristics: First, it must be *reliable,* which means that a person's score should not change much with repeated testing. A scale that registered a different weight each time you got on and off would be unreliable, and therefore not useful. Likewise, a test of intelligence that gave you a different score each time you took it would be worthless. But even if the test is reliable, that is not enough. Second, it must also be *valid,* which means that it must measure what it is supposed to measure. If a psychologist measured IQ by applying a tape measure to the circumference of your head, he might get the same score each time (indicating reliability), but the measuring technique would have little to do with intelligence.

The questions of reliability and validity of measurement and description apply, of course, not only to paper and pencil tests but to all techniques developed by psychologists for the assessment of behavior. You should keep these two criteria in mind when examining the experiments, surveys, observations, and clinical assessments reported in later chapters. These criteria are considered in greater detail in Appendix C.

Prediction and Control

The second goal of psychology is to be able to predict and thereby to control behavior. Success in this effort rests heavily on measurement. Indeed, as correlational methods imply, psychologists typically use present or past measurements of behavior as a primary basis for predicting what a person will do in the future. A psychologist can predict a student's performance in school with increased accuracy if he knows his general intellectual ability. From the factory worker's score on a mechanical aptitude test, the psychologist should be able to predict his success on an assembly line. College entrance exams help to determine who is admitted to college and aptitude tests help the personnel director decide whom to hire. Many prediction efforts include an assessment of interests rather than abilities. Vocational counselors give their clients tests to find out what kind of work might interest them most. Being able to predict your future bill-paying behavior would help a credit agency to decide whether or not you are a good risk for a loan. Psychological predictions of this sort have come more and more to affect the lives of just about every American. If you happen to be the one who is excluded from medical school, or denied a job or credit, it is difficult to think with kindness about the psychologist who produced these tests.

Prediction goes hand in hand with behavior modification and control. Assume that the knowledge to predict mental illness existed. We certainly would not want to stop there; good predictions alone would not satisfy us. Psychologists would want to try to do something to change or to modify the behavior of the potentially mentally ill person in a way that would help him. Indeed behavior change is often the practicing psychologist's primary aim. The psychotherapist tries to change his patient's behavior; the industrial psychologist is commonly engaged in an effort to modify the behavior of employees; the marriage counselor attempts to modify the behavior of husband and wife; and the prison psychologist is trying to control and modify the behavior of criminals. In all of these cases, an effort is made to improve the present or future circumstances of the individual in question and of society.

Many of the techniques of behavior modification that have been developed are remarkably successful, raising the possibility that someone who has mastered them may control others for his own ends. This implies the necessity of appropriate safeguards in society to insure the ethical use of successful techniques. A drug which will control cruelty or aggression does not exist now. Consider the problems that may arise if such a drug is discovered, however. Who is to decide when and where techniques and treatments of this sort will be used? What will be the role of society, the government, the individual himself?

Understanding and Explanation

The final goal of psychology is to *understand* and *explain* behavior, that is, to isolate the reasons for what is observed. This process involves not only the formulation of the theories, which are organized and are consistent with known facts, but also the development of hypotheses about relationships that are yet to be proved. A good theory will help us to make reasonable guesses when we do not know the correct answer.

Some have argued that explanation is really what basic research in psychology is all about. The psychologist may be able to describe and measure anxiety, to make predictions from these measurements about the likelihood of a person's suffering mental illness, and to intervene and modify the person's behavior in hopes of preventing the illness—all with little or no understanding of why his techniques work. In principle, almost anyone with reasonable intelligence and the necessary books can diagnose and treat a disease without knowing what causes the disease or why the prescribed medicine works. Science is motivated by the further desire to know and to understand, that is, to discover the causes or reasons for phenomena.

Psychologists seek to understand the most complex part of the world, namely, human behavior. This enterprise promises both excitement and reward, and potentially even greater practical achievements. Basic psychology is an attempt to understand in detail many significant issues, such as mental illness, the fundamental knowledge and skill involved in reading, and the basis of interaction between motivation and performance. The achievement of adequate explanations for these and other psychological phenomena has far-reaching implications.

Psychology in Historical Perspective

Some of psychology is ancient history. There is evidence of man's curiosity about himself as far back as historical records go. Despite the

Rating life changes

Life event	Value
Death of spouse	100
Divorce	73
Marital separation	65
Jail term	63
Death of close family member	63
Personal injury or illness	53
Marriage	50
Fired at work	47
Marital reconciliation	45
Retirement	45
Change in health of family member	44
Pregnancy	40
Sex difficulties	39
Gain of new family member	39
Change in financial state	38
Death of close friend	37
Change to different line of work	36
Change in number of arguments with spouse	35
Mortgage over $10,000	31
Foreclosure of mortgage or loan	30
Change in responsibilities at work	29
Son or daughter leaving home	29
Trouble with in-laws	29
Outstanding personal achievement	28
Wife beginning or stopping work	26
Beginning or ending school	26
Revision of personal habits	24
Trouble with boss	23
Change in work hours or conditions	20
Change in residence	20
Change in schools	20
Change in recreation	19
Change in social activities	18
Mortgage or loan less than $10,000	17
Change in sleeping habits	16
Change in number of family get-togethers	15
Change in eating habits	15
Vacation	13
Minor violations of the law	11

The Hazards of Change

Time—Any great change—even a pleasant change—produces stress in man. That is the implication, at least, of a study recently reported to the American Association for the Advancement of Science by Dr. Thomas Holmes, professor of psychiatry at the University of Washington in Seattle. Furthermore, Holmes found that too many changes, coming too close together, often produce grave illness or abysmal depression.

In the course of his investigation, Holmes devised a scale assigning point values to changes that often affect human beings *(above)*. When enough of these occur within one year and add up to more than 300, trouble may lie ahead. In Holmes' survey, 80% of people who exceeded 300 became pathologically depressed, had heart attacks, or developed other serious ailments. Of scorers in the 150–300 range, 53% were similarly affected, as were 33% of those scoring up to 150.

A hypothetical example: John was married (50); as he had hoped, his wife became pregnant (40), stopped working (26), and bore a son (39). John, who hated his work as a soap-company chemist, found a better-paying job (38) as a teacher (36) in a college outside the city. After a vacation (13) to celebrate, he moved his family to the country (20), returned to the hunting and fishing (19) he had loved as a child, and began seeing a lot of his congenial new colleagues (18). Everything was so much better that he was even able to give up smoking (24). On the Holmes scale, these events total an ominous 323.

To arrive at his scoring system, Dr. Holmes assigned an arbitrary value of 50 to the act of getting married and then asked people in several countries to rank other changes in relation to marriage. For example, a person who thought that pregnancy represented a greater change than marriage was to assign to pregnancy a number higher than 50. To correlate change and health, Holmes kept a watch on 80 Seattle residents for two years and then compared their personal-change histories with their physical and mental ailments.

Built-In Danger

To be sure, a method of predicting such ailments may well have a built-in danger; a self-rater using the scale could become depressed at the very prospect of depression. But Holmes is confident. Physical and emotional illness can be prevented, he says, by counseling susceptible people not to make too many life changes in too short a time.

An example of prediction. The investigator devised a means for predicting the likelihood that a person will develop emotional or mental disorder. Since there is a shortage of mental health professionals in many areas, efforts have been made to reduce the caseload by getting help to those who need it most *before* serious illness occurs. Accurate prediction can help prevent later behavior problems.

philosophical sophistication achieved as a result of this curiosity, however, psychology was essentially nonscientific until the nineteenth century. From that point forward, the field took on a new form, essentially empirical and scientific, possessing biological underpinnings and an experimental superstructure. The following section contains a brief review of some of the landmark achievements of the "new" scientific psychology on the assumption that some acquaintance with psychology's history is necessary to fully appreciate what psychology is today.

It may be well to note at the outset that the new psychology had rather modest beginnings. The problems addressed were simple, perhaps even naive, in contrast with the psychological issues that face modern man and today's scientist. Early psychologists, for example, studied the sensations aroused by simple physical stimuli. They were curious about how fast the human hand could react to a stimulus. They worried about how small a difference between two stimuli, such as pure tones, could be detected by the human ear. By modern standards early experiments in psychology were crude. The new discipline of "psychology," emerging in the late 1800's as an offshoot of philosophy, lacked coherence and organization. The few scholars who were interested in these psychological problems established their own individual schools of thought, and there were few psychological principles that they all agreed on. However, the impact of early scientific psychologists should not be minimized. Their accomplishments triggered many significant developments that are clearly identifiable in the field today.

Psychophysics

A key question among the nineteenth-century philosophers who were concerned with psychological issues was the relationship between the mind and the body, between man's physical and nonphysical aspects. Various positions were taken on the question, ranging from one that asserted a basic identity of mind and body to another predicated on their total independence. One of those concerned with the controversy was Gustav Fechner (1801–1887). Scientifically trained and experimentally minded, Fechner decided to collect data on the question of mind-body independence in hopes of settling what up to that time had been a completely speculative issue. To see, as Fechner did, that the experimental method could be used in psychology was an act of sheer genius. The present-day discipline of *psychophysics* was the eventual result of Fechner's work.

Psychophysics is defined as the study of the relationship between physical stimulation and the conscious sensations it provokes in a person. For example, a psychophysicist might study the way in which the mind translates the physical attributes of light waves—wavelength and amplitude—into the psychological attributes of color and brightness (see

"I'm not learning anything. I'm developing cognitive skills."

© Punch (Rothco).

Educational psychologists are now emphasizing the value of teaching students how to learn, think, and solve problems (cognitive skills) as opposed to cramming pure facts into their heads.

Chapter 3). Psychophysicists have found that some of the relationships between stimulation and sensations are predictable and can be expressed as "laws"; for example, Weber's Law states that the physical difference between two stimuli that is just barely noticeable is a constant fraction over the entire physical dimension. In the psychophysicist's view, the mind is assumed to consist of sensations lawfully produced by the physical world.

Early findings in the field of psychophysics are accepted as givens today. What is significant for our purposes at this point is that psychophysics was chronologically the first branch of the new psychology, the scientific study of the mind. It demonstrated the possibility of collecting objective, scientifically valid data on how the mind works. For his contribution, Fechner is often referred to as the father of modern psychology.

After Fechner, the activities of psychologists from approximately 1880 through 1940 were governed by a number of diverse viewpoints and beliefs about (1) the proper subject matter of psychology, (2) the basic questions to be asked about that subject

Weber's Law

One of the fundamental laws in psychophysics is known as Weber's Law, after its discoverer, Ernst Weber. It states that the amount of increase in stimulation that is just noticeable is a constant proportion of the starting level of stimulation. For example, suppose you determine that someone carrying a 50-pound load can detect the addition of 1 more pound to the load. Additions less than 1 pound are not noticed. So we say that the *just noticeable difference,* or *jnd,* is 1 pound. This is also called the *difference threshold*. It takes a change of 1 pound in 50 to produce a *jnd,* so the ratio is:

$$\frac{1}{50} = .02 \text{ or } 2\%$$

Weber's Law says that regardless of the starting weight, it will take a 2 percent increase in weight to be just noticeable. So if you were carrying 25 pounds, we would have to add 2 percent of 25, or .5 pounds, before you would notice the increase in weight. If you were starting with 100 pounds, we would have to add 2 pounds, and if you were starting with only a 1-pound box of candy, we would only have to add .02 pounds for you to detect it.

Weber's Law appears to hold quite well for middle ranges of starting values, but breaks down somewhat at extreme values—when the starting weights are extremely small or extremely large. It also applies to just about every dimension you can think of, including judging the height of a building, the loudness of a radio, the number of people in a crowd, and probably the price of merchandise. You could easily get away with a 10-cent increase in the price of a new car, but increasing the price of a roll of Life Savers by 10 cents would quickly be detected or noticed by customers.

The fraction above, 1/50 for weights, is called the *Weber fraction,* and it is a measure of how sensitive we are in various judgments. The smaller the fraction, the more sensitive we are. A fraction of 1/25 would mean we could detect a 4 percent change. Below are some actual Weber fraction values for different sense modalities. Note that the real Weber fraction for lifting weights is, more accurately, 1/53.

Dimension	Weber fraction	Percent change needed to notice a difference
Pitch	$1/333$	.3
Deep pressure	$1/77$	1.3
Brightness of a light	$1/62$	1.6
Lifted weight	$1/53$	1.9
Loudness of a tone	$1/11$	8.8
Smell—amount of rubber smell	$1/10$	10.4
Pressure on the skin surface	$1/7$	13.6
Taste—amount of salty taste	$1/5$	20.0

Note that Weber's Law states that within the same dimension the fraction is a constant, independent of the starting value. Between dimensions, however, the fraction can differ and represents how sensitive that sensory system is—the chart shows that our sense of pitch change is much better than our sense of change in salty taste. Thus, by this measure, your ears are more sensitive than your tongue.

matter, and (3) the appropriate methods for answering these basic questions. Several of the viewpoints and the schools of thought that evolved around them will be described briefly, for they are the ideas that shaped and are shaping psychology.

Structuralism

Psychophysics was essentially empirical and descriptive, focusing on facts and data. Psychology's first theoretical school followed closely on its heels, however. This school was *Structuralism,* primarily a product of the work of Wilhelm Wundt (1832–1920), a professor of philosophy who founded the first formal laboratory of psychology at the University of Leipzig, Germany, in 1879 (see Figure 1–3).

Wundt proposed that the subject matter of psychology was *experience,* the experience or knowledge one has of the content of his own conscious mind. Influenced by the rise of modern physical and medical science, Wundt argued that the fundamental approach of science, namely analysis, should be applied to psychological phenomena. To understand any problem, we need to break it down into its smallest component parts and then examine the parts themselves as fundamental building blocks. Structuralism, therefore, was an attempt to compartmentalize the mind into its basic parts, the so-called mental elements. The existence of these elements seemed, to Wundt, to be well established by philosophical study and examination, but he wanted to identify them *empirically* through a method called *introspection*. Introspection, according to Wundt, requires an observer who can dispassionately examine and report the contents of his own mind. He must give an objective verbal report of what he "perceives" to be going on in his mind. These verbal reports can then be analyzed

Figure 1–3
Wilhelm Wundt

The founder and leader of the structuralist movement felt that psychology should be concerned with studying the contents of conscious experience. By the method of introspection, he concluded that the mind consists of three basic elements—sensations, images, and feelings—from which the remainder of one's experience is compounded.

and categorized in an effort to decide how many and what kind of basic elements there are in the mind. Wundt's data led him to conclude there are three basic elements, which he called *sensations* (the direct products of external stimulation), *images* (sensationlike experiences produced by the mind itself), and *feelings* (the affective or emotional components of an experience).

The major fault of Structuralism was its failure to relate the concept of mind to human action. Psychology is still concerned today with mental activities, but its emphasis is on the way in which these activities influence performance. Psychologists attempt to explain the *hows* and *whys* of behavior, not just what is going on in one's mind. To do this, they must observe how a person acts, as well as his

thoughts and feelings. Also, note that Structuralism deals primarily with *private* experience. Later psychologists argued convincingly that private experiences alone can never be studied objectively. That being the case, they cannot provide the data of a scientific field, which by definition must be public and openly observable to all. What people *do* is publicly observable and can therefore legitimately be the subject matter of scientific psychology.

Functionalism

Partly because of its strong tradition in philosophy and partly because it was the first theoretical school of thought, Structuralism dominated psychology for years, both in Europe and the United States. But it was not without critics or competition, and after the turn of the century, three schools of thought became strong competitors. The first to be considered is *Functionalism,* primarily the product of early American psychologists. Among the foremost early functionalists were William James of Harvard University (1842–1910), James Cattell of the University of Pennsylvania (1860–1944), John Dewey of the University of Chicago (1859–1952), and E. L. Thorndike of Columbia University (1874–1949).

Structuralists tended to be concerned with what the mind is composed of, that is, the elements of consciousness. Functionalists, in contrast, studied *why* and *how* the mind works. Strongly influenced by the evolutionary principles of Darwin, functionalists argued that the mind is man's most important organ for adaptation to his environment. They emphasized the *use* of the mind rather than its contents. Thus, functionalists did not reject mind and consciousness as important concepts in psychology, but they took these concepts a step beyond the structuralists. They recognized the connection between mind and behavior and were determined to study mind-body interactions. They examined how the mind, envisioned as a sort of master biological organ, controls other bodily organs and systems in a never-ending struggle to cope with and adapt to one's circumstances. Rather than studying momentary glimpses of the structure or content of the mind, they proposed to investigate the continuous stream of consciousness that they

Functionalism placed great stress on the adaptive significance of behavior. The functionalists considered behavioral phenomena, such as learning, crucial because they allowed living organisms to adapt to their environments or rise above them.

said characterizes large segments of human life (see Figure 1–4). They did not reject introspection as a legitimate scientific method, but they did point out its limitations, especially in comparison with more objective observations of people functioning in the real world.

As the functionalists were among the first to see, man's most important way of adapting to the environment is *learning,* the acquisition of facts and skills. This ability is in large measure what sets man apart from lower animals and allows man, despite his relatively feeble physiological equipment, to adapt better to his environment than any other organism. The functionalists were among the first to subject the important concept of learning to psychological examination.

Behaviorism

Functionalism was a loose general orientation toward psychology. Its adherents studied a variety of psychological processes but never developed a coherent general psychological theory. In contrast, *Behaviorism,* the first truly American school of psychology, had a definite and explicit theoretical point of view. Behaviorism was largely a product of the thought of John B. Watson (1878–1958). Although trained as a functionalist, Watson argued that private mental states, those which we presumably study through introspection, cannot be the subject matter of a science. Only public events—that is, actions, responses, or performances that can be objectively observed and measured—fulfill the requirements of a scientific discipline. These events he called behaviors. (We will want to argue later that Watson was a little too narrow in his use of that term.) Responses or behaviors, according to Watson, are affected by specifiable stimuli in the environment (see Figure 1–5). Therefore, the major study of psychology is to identify those stimulus-response relationships that are lawful and predictable.

During the same period of time, in Russia, Ivan Pavlov (1848–1936) provided an impressive demonstration of the use of stimulus-response analysis in his famous description of classical conditioning. In the course of his physiological studies of digestion, Pavlov observed that his experimental subjects, dogs, came to salivate at the sound of a neutral stimulus—say, a bell—if food and bell were repeatedly paired together. Both Pavlov and Watson saw this conditioning phenomenon as evidence of the importance of learning and of stimulus-response connections in behavior. Watson saw Pavlov's research as confirmation of the lawful

Figure 1–4
William James

Stream of consciousness

One of the earliest and foremost American psychologists, William James founded the first laboratory of psychology in this country. For James the mind was a continuous, ongoing "stream of consciousness" that could not be analyzed into elementary building blocks.

nature of behavior and of the possibility that all forms of behavior, no matter how complex, can be reduced to learned stimulus-response units. Watson believed that *all behavior was learned,* no aspect of it was inherited. He once boasted that he could make any healthy baby into any kind of adult—doctor, lawyer, or thief—merely by controlling the conditioning of the child. Today we know, of course, that heredity is also an important determinant of behavior.

Behaviorism takes the subject matter of psychology to be stimulus-response relationships. These relationships are to be studied and understood by objective experimental and observational methods. A verbal report may be treated as an objective behavioral response (talking), but its status as a description of private mental

experience is rejected. For behaviorists, the problem of psychology is to predict what responses will be evoked by what stimuli.

Gestalt Psychology

Gestalt psychology was a different kind of reaction to Structuralism. The Gestalt movement began in Germany in the early part of the twentieth century, about the same time as Behaviorism began to dominate American psychology. The German word *Gestalt* has no exact English translation. Roughly speaking, it means form or organized whole, reflecting the emphasis of this school on organizational process in behavior. Whereas the focal problem of Behaviorism was learning, Gestalt psychologists chose primarily to work with perceptual problems, because they thought it best to prove Wundt wrong in the very area that Wundt himself chose to emphasize. As a result Gestalt theory is often identified as a theory of perception, although its principles are logically applicable to a broad range of psychological issues.

Behaviorists, like the structuralists, accepted the basic scientific idea that complex phenomena had to be analyzed into their simpler parts before they could be understood. The main proponents of Gestalt psychology, Wolfgang Köhler (1887–1967), Kurt Koffka (1886–1941), and Max Wertheimer (1880–1943), opposed the structuralists' efforts to reduce experience to a small set of fundamental component parts. They seized on other ideas from physical science, particularly the notions of field

theory, arguing that the whole of a phenomenon is different from the sum of its parts (see Figure 1–6). For example, from a series of still pictures, you perceive continuity of action in a movie. There is movement even in the neon lights on a theater marquee. Both of these effects are based on the phenomenon of *apparent movement,* or the *phi phenomenon,* identified by early Gestalt psychologists. Figure 1–7 shows another example of how perception of a whole can differ from perceptions of its parts.

Gestalt theory can be applied to nearly all important forms of behavior. Köhler, for example, argued that learning and problem solving, like perception, were largely a function of organizational

Figure 1–5
John B. Watson

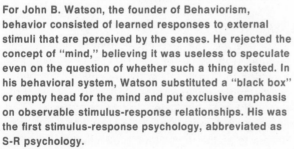

For John B. Watson, the founder of Behaviorism, behavior consisted of learned responses to external stimuli that are perceived by the senses. He rejected the concept of "mind," believing it was useless to speculate even on the question of whether such a thing existed. In his behavioral system, Watson substituted a "black box" or empty head for the mind and put exclusive emphasis on observable stimulus-response relationships. His was the first stimulus-response psychology, abbreviated as S-R psychology.

Figure 1–6
Max Wertheimer

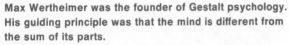

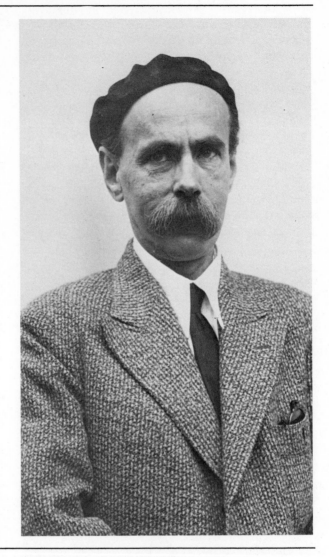

Max Wertheimer was the founder of Gestalt psychology. His guiding principle was that the mind is different from the sum of its parts.

processes. How to behave in a particular situation may elude the subject until he sees the various distinguishable components of the task in their appropriate relationship. The situation is a problem primarily because the correct or necessary relationship among the elements is not easily seen. The subject's behavior may take the form of overt trial-and-error or covert "thought." But he must take a variety of perspectives on the situation until the correct one emerges. When it does emerge, the subject experiences a "moment of insight." Finally the problem is solved and, in a flash, the subject knows what to do. Notice the persistent use of terms related to perception, such as seeing, perspective, and experience, in the foregoing description. This is a consistent theme within Gestalt attempts to explain behavior. Note also the implication that learning and problem solving are "all-or-none," insightful processes. This is another major principle

that distinguishes Gestalt psychology from other theoretical attempts to deal with learning.

From many examples like those given above, the Gestalt school argued against the utility of describing integrated human action by a mere analysis of component parts. They were concerned with the completeness, the continuity, and the meaningfulness of behavior as a whole.

Psychoanalysis

Psychoanalysis, the theoretical point of view identified with Sigmund Freud (1858–1939), was less a reaction to Structuralism than an effort to apply science and medicine to the study and treatment of abnormal behavior. (Several portraits of Freud appear in Chapter 9.) Psychoanalysis has been referred to as the third great intellectual blow to man's pride. First man found out that he was not at the center of the universe; then he discovered that

Figure 1-7
The Gestalt approach to perception

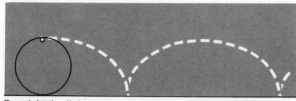

Panel A: rim light

Panel B: center light

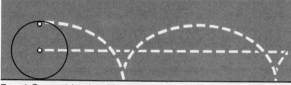

Panel C: combination (theory)

Panel D: what subjects actually see

Here is an interesting perceptual effect that demonstrates one of the basic principles of the Gestalt approach to perception. It suggests that we do not perceive a whole experience by just adding up the perceptions that we would have of the separate parts. A wheel is rolled from left to right across a table in a dark room. In the top panel, a light is attached to the rim of the wheel and the dashed line indicates what subjects perceive. In the second panel we have the perception of a light attached at the center of the wheel. Panel C indicates what the combination of the rim light and center light *should* be, but Panel D is what subjects *actually* perceive.

he was descended from the apes; and, finally, Freud argued that man was basically controlled by impulses, many of which are buried in the unconscious, below the level of awareness. The vision of man as a rational being in conscious control of his behavior dimmed when Freud described the behavioral impact of early childhood experience, anxiety, and conflicting unconscious motives.

Freud, whose theory we will discuss in detail in

Chapter 9, described the personality structure of a human being as consisting of three forces: the pleasure-seeking *id,* composed of basic biological impulses; the realistic *ego,* reacting to the stresses and strains of everyday life; and the idealistic *superego,* representing the dictates of one's conscience. His primary method of investigation was detailed case study during psychotherapy, which included the collection of autobiographical material, dream analysis, and free association. Psychoanalysis was primarily a *theory* of abnormal behavior, and its *techniques,* such as psychotherapy, were clinical. Today, psychoanalysis is primarily identified with a method of therapy for mental illness. As we shall see, its influence is mainly in the areas of personality function and clinical psychology.

Trends in the History of Psychology

The foregoing review is by no means exhaustive of all the historically important points of view in psychology. The few significant developments described here were chosen to illustrate trends that have characterized thinking in this field. One can abstract from these examples a number of important issues that have been frequently debated and that enter into psychological theorizing even today. Let us consider several of these dimensions briefly.

Holism versus atomism.   Points of view in psychology tend to be either *holistic* or *atomistic.* Structuralists and behaviorists were clearly atomistic in their thinking. They emphasized the importance of scientific analysis, and hypothesized the existence of a small number of fundamental building blocks out of which complex psychological processes were constructed. For the structuralists, these components were sensations, images, and feelings. Various combinations of these components, formed through a set of laws called the principles of association, were said to produce the wide range of complex conscious experiences of any individual. Behaviorists emphasized actions rather than experience, but, like the structuralists, thought that these complex activities were compounds of simpler ones, called conditioned reflexes. In contrast, functionalists, Gestalt psychologists, and psychoanalysts adopted a holistic orientation. Functionalists studied the continuity of consciousness, Gestalt psychologists felt that any experience was different from the sum of its individual parts and that no consideration of the parts alone could produce complete understanding, and psychoanalysts emphasized the dynamic processes of human motivation and personality.

The internal (mental) versus the external (performance).   Psychological theories also differ according to whether they emphasize *internal (mental) processes* or *external (performance) processes*. Structuralists, Gestalt psychologists, and psychoanalysts were primarily interested in mental life. Structuralists and Gestaltists emphasized mental events that derive from the perceptual systems, while psychoanalysts focused on the interaction of mental and motivational processes. But all studied the internal conscious experience of the individual. The behaviorists, in contrast, rejected the mind as a legitimate scientific concept. They refused to consider mentalistic ideas in any explanation of what a person does. They placed exclusive emphasis on the sensory and motor aspects of human performance, going so far as to assert that a person's most complex behavior—thinking and reasoning—was actually reducible to minute movements in the muscles and glands of the body. The functionalists' stand on the internal-versus-external issue is an interesting compromise. Psychologists of that persuasion neither rejected the mind as a legitimate concept nor placed exclusive emphasis on it. For the functionalists, what was important about the mind was its *function,* the role that it plays, for example, in governing performance. Thus, they accepted both a person's experience and his actions, both internal and external activities, as legitimate objects of scientific inquiry.

Nature versus nurture.   Psychologists differed in subtler ways with respect to their stand on the issue of *nature* (biological factors such as heredity) versus *nurture* (environmental factors such as conditioning) in behavior. Each school assumed certain physiological attributes as givens, or innate qualities. For example, Structuralism was strongly influenced by contemporary developments in biology, especially those having to do with the operation of the nervous and sensory systems. But for the structuralists, physiology was essentially a constant in the psychological equation. Biological systems, in their view, merely allowed for the occurrence of more important mental activities within the organism. As we have seen, behaviorists were even less impressed with the importance of biological factors in behavior, placing primary emphasis on learning (conditioning) and stimulus control of responses. Psychoanalysis, Functionalism, and Gestalt psychology placed different and, in general, heavier emphases on biological factors. Functionalists were struck by parallels between

biological adaptation and certain psychological processes such as learning. The Gestalt psychologists were convinced of a one-to-one relationship—that is, an isomorphism—between brain and mind. They viewed the processes occurring in the brain as surface indicators and determinants of parallel psychological phenomena going on in the mind. Thus, when one sees or imagines a triangle, there is at the same time a "triangular" configuration of neural activity. Freud, although clearly concerned with the effects of early experience on behavior, still considered basic psychological urges to derive from innate biological needs, such as hunger and sex.

The mechanistic view.   There is one characterization of psychological theory, both historical and contemporary, on which there appears to be nearly complete agreement. This is the *mechanistic view* of human beings. Seen this way, a person is unable to control his own fate. Rather, he is at the mercy of the stresses and strains imposed by his environment and by processes built innately into his nervous system and other biological structures. Stimuli are thought to impinge on a person much as they might impinge on an electronic computer or some simpler machine. According to the mechanistic point of view, what a person can do with these stimuli is a function of the way the machine is wired and what information has been stored from the past. His overt responses are programmed by earlier events in the sequence, and his reason and will exert little influence.

This assumption is not a logical requirement of psychological theory. It is just one form of theorizing, but one that most psychologists have accepted uncritically. It may be misleading and therefore inadequate. Contemporary research is beginning to reveal that a theory of this sort is too simple. It might be necessary to take a somewhat more humanistic view of the person. In fact, one of the major contemporary movements in psychology is basically a reaction against this mechanistic conception. This movement, usually referred to as *humanistic psychology,* has grown out of the writings of such noted psychologists as Carl Rogers, Abraham Maslow, Rollo May, and Fritz Perls. Briefly, this view holds that each person is unique and can determine his own fate by conscious exertion of his free will. The individual's exercise of his own reason and intuition is more important than environment and biological systems in determining the course of his development. You will read further about the ideas of humanistic psychology in later chapters.

Suffice it to say here that this school of thought presents a growing challenge to the prevailing psychological model of the person as machine. We shall not propose a view of the person in this book, but we do wish to alert you to the issue and to request that you keep an open mind before committing yourself too thoroughly to any particular point of view.

The Impact of Historical Events on Contemporary Psychology

The foregoing review of historical events has been sketchy, but it does illustrate some of the major trends in psychological thought. The schools of thought described earlier no longer exist intact, but they are not without impact on contemporary thinking. Psychophysics, which began as the study of the individual's reaction to simple stimuli, has progressed over the years into a powerful discipline in its own right. Today it is concerned with the precise scaling of psychological dimensions, from the brightness of lights to the impact of humor, and with the exploration of outer limits on all of the individual's sensory systems. With its emphasis on the way in which people perceive, process, and perform on the basis of physical stimulation, psychophysics today is as relevant to human and electrical engineering as it is to the behavioral sciences.

Structuralism, in its original form, never recovered from the penetrating counterarguments of other schools. Few psychologists would refer to themselves today as structuralists. Yet the concepts of Structuralism have not entirely disappeared. Jean Piaget, the famous Swiss developmental psychologist, has written volumes on changes with age in the structure of the human mind. American experimental psychologists study the way in which knowledge is organized and refer extensively to the structure of one's current memory for past events. The principles of association, originally applied by structuralists to the formation of complex mental events out of simpler elements, are still the basis of a viable learning theory. So Structuralism, too, makes its presence known in modern psychology.

Functionalism never was a coherent school, nor did it center on the thinking of any one psychologist. It was, rather, a vaguely stated set of principles about the pragmatic—that is, functional—significance of the mind. But, while there was no strong theoretical commitment, Functionalism left a strong legacy in the form of its emphasis on learning as humanity's most important adaptive process.

In a sense, Psychoanalysis has been the most persistent school. Strongholds of adherents can still be found. Its influence as a pervasive theory of human behavior has decreased, but it still has considerable importance in some areas of clinical psychology and forms the basis of a widely used psychotherapeutic technique.

Behaviorism and Gestalt psychology probably had the greatest role in shaping modern psychology. The basic ideas that both groups formulated and explored are clearly evident in contemporary psychology, though there are few psychologists today who identify themselves wholly as behaviorists or as Gestaltists. The behaviorists' emphasis on the role of learned responses as building blocks of behavior is a predominant principle in modern psychological theory. B. F. Skinner of Harvard University has developed both a theory and a technology for changing behavior based on observable responses and their subsequent rewards and punishments. Mentalistic ideas, rejected by Watson, are admitted into some modern versions of Behaviorism (called Neobehaviorism), though often disguised as implicit (nonobservable) responses. The insistence of Gestalt psychologists on the importance of organizational processes and continuity in behavior, as opposed to a simple analysis of content, persists in a lively form. The issue of content versus process analysis has a bearing on many aspects of contemporary psychology, perhaps the most important of which is learning. These relationships will appear throughout the book.

Schools of psychology disappeared because, as psychologists examined the issues more closely, explanations could not logically take the simple form offered by narrow versions of Structuralism, Behaviorism, or any other school. Psychologists came to realize that it takes a *mixture* of mental and performance, or innate and experiential, concepts to give a complete description of human activity. There are differences in emphasis and opinion in psychology today, but extremist thinking and close-minded groups are fortunately becoming rarer.

The Definition of Behavior

Psychology, as we said earlier, is the science of behavior. This definition has replaced an earlier definition of psychology as the study of the mind, because it is generally agreed that the mind is not entirely open to scientific analysis. It is not possible to examine the mind directly. The mind seems to be

". . . Over the rail, man, over the rail!"

Playboy, September 1968. Reproduced by special permission of PLAYBOY Magazine; copyright © 1968 by Playboy.

Being ill, like vomiting or having an epileptic seizure, might not be classified as behavior. One typically is not motivated to vomit and one does not have to have any particular knowledge or skill to vomit. Being ill is something that just happens to us at times. Running to the rail because you feel as if you are going to vomit, however, is clearly an example of behavior because you must know how to get to the rail (competence) and want to avoid vomiting into someone's stateroom (motivation).

knowable only through the behavior it controls, although some would argue that you can observe your own mind through introspection. In order to have an objective scientific discipline, however, we will have to resort to the study of behavior. Others can observe your behavior, study it, and attempt to understand it.

Our first step is to define behavior. It has become standard practice to define behavior as any observable action (or reaction) of the organism. In its broadest sense, behavior can refer to any movement of muscles anywhere in the body; even the electrical activity in the nervous system, such as brain waves, can be included in the broad definition of behavior. The various types of psychologists we have discussed would focus on different levels of behavior, some looking at the "behavior" of nerve cells or sweat glands or adrenal glands, others looking at "behaviors" at a much higher level, such as aggression, prejudice, or problem solving.

The common thread is that behavior is overt, observable movement, activity, or action, although it is obviously true that some behaviors will require very sophisticated procedures and equipment to make them observable, such as an EEG machine to observe brain waves. When behavior is defined in a way to include such diverse things as nervous system activity and prejudice, it is small wonder that psychology is such a loosely knit science with so many subspecialties.

As a starting point, we think that defining behavior as observable action or activity is reasonable. It allows for the inclusion of just about all aspects of human functioning and prevents psychologists from overlooking important areas of content that would shed understanding on the human condition. We must remember, however, that overt movement or activity is only a starting point, only the signal that behavior has occurred. Observing and describing behavior as movement is not the same thing as understanding it or explaining it. The psychologist wants to *understand* and *explain* behavior as well as describe it. To do this, it is necessary to go beyond merely reporting the movements, actions, reactions, activity, and the like of a given organism.

At least four major factors have to be taken into account to develop an adequate and complete description, explanation, and understanding of behavior. We shall have much more to say about each of them in later chapters but will introduce you to them briefly at this point.

The Organism

The first factor is the *organism* itself. The behavior we are interested in is carried out by a living biological entity, a human being or a lower animal. To understand its behavior, we need to know the biological characteristics and limits of this organism. We need to study the functioning of its brain, nervous system, endocrine system, and other biological structures. In addition, we will have to delve into its biological history and its heredity.

Motivation

The second factor is the *motivation* of the organism. Behavior is typically a product of wants, desires, needs, or intentions. To understand behavior, we need to examine its motivational underpinnings. To illustrate, suppose you are a juror in a murder trial. In part your task will be to decide whether the accused deliberately or accidentally killed the deceased. That decision about the accused's behavior hinges on what kind of motivation he had.

Knowledge

The third factor is *what the organism knows,* that is, his cognitions. Behavior depends in part on the concepts, thoughts, and facts called upon by a person in a given situation. We need to know how the behaving organism perceives his world as well as what he knows, thinks, and remembers. Take, for example, a multiple choice question on your psychology exam. Suppose one student gives the correct answer and a second does not. How do you understand the difference in their behaviors? Probably we would refer to a difference in knowledge or cognition processes. We say one

"Come on, Charlie, let me in on when you guys are making the break!"

Knowledge is a necessary component of most behaviors. This man cannot take part in the prison escape. Presumably he has the necessary motivation to escape and the necessary skills (climbing walls, picking locks, crawling through tunnels), but he lacks the appropriate knowledge.

student had learned and knew the correct answer and the other did not. Suppose there is a third student who selects the correct answer by chance—say, he just flipped a "mental" coin to decide on an answer and was lucky. He performed in the same way as the student who "knew" the correct response, but we explain his behavior differently if we explore the matter further. One student behaved in that way because he knew the answer; the other did not know the answer but "lucked out."

Competence

The fourth factor is the organism's *competence.* Behavior reflects the skills, abilities, or "knowhow" of an organism. Consider the difference between the first-string and the third-string quarterback on a professional football team. Differences in their playing are probably due to differences in competence. Both quarterbacks may know equally well what to do (they have equal experience and equal knowledge of the plays and of what to do in each play), but they differ in their ability or skill in doing it. The third-stringer knows what to do but not how to do it as well as the starter. This is what we mean by a difference in competence.

To summarize, when we see differences in behavior and we seek to understand or explain the differences, we will usually find ourselves employing one or more of four factors. We explain differences in behavior by identifying differences in (1) biological capacity, (2) knowledge, (3) competence, and (4) motivation. Understanding behavior involves more than describing the movement or activity of the organism. To explain what is really going on, we will need to know about the biological make-up and functioning of the behaving organism, its knowledge or cognition, its skills or competence, and its motivation.

Summary

1. All psychologists study behavior, yet they use a variety of approaches to a wide range of issues. There are many different kinds of psychologists, including experimenters, clinicians, counselors, and educational and industrial psychologists.

2. One way to describe the diversity within psychology and among psychologists is in terms of the issues studied, the methods used, the focus of the study, and the employment of the psychologist.

3. Issues in psychology range from those aspects of the physical organism that affect behavior, such as the genes, to the diagnosis and treatment of complex abnormal behavior patterns.

4. Psychology employs a variety of methods in its attempt to find out the whats, whys, and hows of behavior. Among them are (a) the case study, the intensive examination of one individual; (b) naturalistic observation, an investigation of interacting psychological processes as they occur in everyday circumstances; (c) surveys, tests, and correlational procedures—which are techniques for finding out what relationships exist between measurable variables and how strong these relationships are; and (d) experimentation, the establishment of arbitrary models of psychological situations in the laboratory and the examination of how manipulated independent variables affect the dependent variables (performance) in these situations under controlled circumstances.

5. The focus of a psychological study may be either the clarification of a basic general psychological principle or the answer to a practical question of immediate importance.

6. Psychologists in basic science are employed primarily at colleges and universities. Applied psychologists work in industry, government, clinics, schools, and in private practice.

7. Psychology is tentatively described as a science that studies behavior and systematically applies behavior principles. Three goals of psychology are: (a) measurement and description, (b) prediction and control, and (c) understanding and explanation of behavior.

8. Highlights of the history of psychology include the following important events: (a) the initial empirical efforts to get at mind-body interaction, exemplified by psychophysics, and (b) the formation of various major schools of psychological thought and theorizing during the late 1800's and the early 1900's, namely, Structuralism, Functionalism, Behaviorism, Gestalt psychology, and Psychoanalysis.

9. Certain psychological issues differentiate these schools, including (a) the distinction between atomism and holism, (b) the influence of nature or nurture in behavior, (c) the emphasis on external (performance) or internal (mental) factors in psychological explanations, and (d) the utilization of content or process analysis of behavior. Few of these early schools of thought have survived, but contemporary psychology was shaped by them.

10. Explaining behavior, as opposed to merely describing it, requires a consideration of at least four fundamental characteristics: (a) the organism, (b) its knowledge or cognition, (c) its competence or skill, and (d) its intention or motivation.

Recommended Additional Readings

For more on the methods of research psychology:
Arnoult, M. D. *Fundamentals of scientific method in psychology.* Dubuque, Iowa: W. C. Brown, 1972.
Johnson, H. H., & Solso, R. L. *An introduction to experimental design in psychology: a case approach.* New York: Harper & Row, 1971.
Plutchik, R. *Foundations of experimental research, 2d ed.* New York: Harper & Row, 1974.

For more on the history of psychology and an analysis of basic issues:
Wertheimer, M. *A brief history of psychology.* New York: Holt, Rinehart and Winston, 1971.
Wertheimer, M. *Fundamental issues in psychology.* New York: Holt, Rinehart and Winston, 1972.

If you are considering a career in psychology write to the American Psychological Association for a copy of their booklet:
A career in psychology. Washington, D.C.: American Psychological Association, 1200 17th Street, N.W., Washington, D.C. 20036.

For two other views of introductory psychology we recommend:
Harlow, H. F., McGaugh, J. L., & Thompson, R. F. *Psychology.* San Francisco: Albion, 1971.
Wallace, J. *Psychology: a social science.* Philadelphia: Saunders, 1971.

For a thoughtful analysis of the philosophical problems one encounters when studying and explaining behavior:
Mischel, T. (Ed.) *Human action: conceptual and empirical issues.* New York: Academic Press, 1969.

2

BIOLOGICAL FOUNDATIONS OF BEHAVIOR

Ralph has been in a state prison most of his life and is presently serving a life sentence for murder. He suffers from apparently uncontrollable episodes of rage during which he has committed several violent attacks against others, including guards and other prisoners. A group of neurosurgeons would like to operate on Ralph's brain to remove a structure called the amygdala.

Martha is taking a final examination in general psychology and is trying to remember the name of the psychologist who founded the school called Behaviorism—she is "racking her brain" for the answer. How is the brain involved in memory?

Since childhood Ray had suffered from severe attacks of a form of epilepsy. During these attacks he became violent and unreasonable, even homicidal. He was finally committed to a state institution, where several brain researchers became interested in his condition. Drug treatments were tried and found to be ineffective. The doctors decided to try a new experimental treatment. Small electrodes were surgically implanted in Ray's brain and attached to a stimulation device which he carried with him. His instructions were to press the button on his brain stimulator whenever he felt an attack coming on. Ray has not had a complete attack since the operation. He has been able to eliminate his violent obsessions by simply pressing a button and sending electrical impulses to the right place in his brain.

Louise was a chronic alcoholic for about half of her 62 years of age. She had a good job as a clerk and never drank enough during the day to ruin her ability to work. However, she had to retire early because her memory began to fail. She could not remember assignments, she forgot telephone numbers, and she even began to forget where she was. X-rays indicated that, as with many chronic alcoholics, a portion of her brain had undergone some deterioration. She can no longer drive and spends most of her time just sitting, trying to remember what she needs to do next.

All of these behavioral descriptions have something in common—they involve the operation of the nervous system. They are representative of the infinite number of ways that the brain is involved in the control of consciousness and behavior. People have long been intrigued by the question of how an organic mass of tissue such as the brain is capable of generating consciousness and behavior. How is it that the brain can translate its language of electrical and chemical activity into conscious perceptions, thoughts, and voluntary action? This is the classical "mind-body" problem and is considered by many to be the ultimate question in the search for the biological foundations of behavior.

The examples cited above raise many questions about the brain and behavior: What makes us violent, and which parts of the brain are involved? What is memory, and how and where are memories stored in the brain? How does the brain affect eating? Is alcoholism a disease, and if so is the nervous system involved? The answers to these questions are far from complete. However, a great deal is known about the functions of many parts of the brain and about the neural and chemical events that accompany such "psychological" processes as sensory perception and learning. The purpose of this chapter is to give an overview of what is known at the present time about the physiological underpinnings of behavior. We will also present some of the findings of the new field of behavioral genetics and conclude with a discussion of recent or potential applications of our knowledge in these areas.

The Neuron

If we are going to understand behavior from a physiological point of view, we must understand the physiology of the nervous system. If we are going to understand the functioning of the nervous system, we must understand the functioning of its most elementary unit, the nerve cell, or *neuron*. Actually the entire nervous system consists of only two types of cells, the neurons and the *glia,* or glial cells. We shall not discuss the glia except to note that there is some disagreement among investigators about their role. Some believe they merely provide support and support services for the neurons. Others argue that they might be involved in certain neural functions such as memory storage. In any case, it is the neuron that is at the heart of nervous system functioning.

The nervous system contains about 10 billion neurons. There are many different types in our bodies, but all have three basic structural features in common, illustrated schematically in Figure 2–1 (see also Figure B–1 in Appendix B). First, there is a cell body, or *soma*. The neuron is a biological cell and like any other cell it must carry out the life processes of oxygen utilization, energy production, etc. These activities are conducted mainly in the

Figure 2–1
Schematic diagram of the basic parts of a neuron

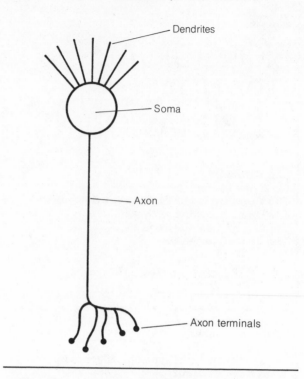

soma. The one difference between neurons and other cells is that neurons do not reproduce themselves—you are born with the full complement of 10 billion or so neurons and that is all you will ever have. But neurons do die. It has been estimated that we lose as many as 10 thousand neurons each day of our lives.

Second, each neuron has a series of short "fibers" or processes extending from the soma known as *dendrites*. The dendrites are like receiving stations that pick up signals coming from other neurons.

Third, each neuron has one *axon* extending from the soma. In some cases the axon may divide into several branches after leaving the soma. Some axons may be several feet in length, others very short. At the end of the axon there are many branches ending with *axon terminals*. These terminals are close to the dendrites or the soma of another neuron, and the signals generated by a neuron are transmitted from the soma, along the axon to the terminals, and then to the dendrites or soma of the next neuron.

Axon terminals do not actually touch the dendrites or soma of the next neuron in the communication chain. Instead there is a small space between them known as a *synaptic space*. The area where the terminals come close to the dendrites or soma of the next neuron is known as the *synapse*. A nerve impulse travels down the axon and into the terminals, where it causes the terminals to release *chemical transmitter substances*. These chemicals then travel the small distance across the synaptic space to the dendrites or soma of the next neuron and may excite that neuron into firing. In this way the nerve impulses are communicated from one neuron to the next, to some distant part of the body. Some transmitters are chemicals that inhibit or block firing in the next neuron. Thus the communication system of the nervous system can work by excitation or inhibition.

There is a great deal known about the generation and transmission of nerve signals, which are called *action potentials*. We have presented much of this information in Appendix B for the student who wishes to study these processes more intensively.

Coding of Information

The nervous system is a large communication system for transmitting information from one point in the body to another. For example, when we "see" something, information is being transmitted from the eye to the brain over a neural communication system, the optic nerve. The nervous system has two basic ways of coding information for transmission. First, individual neurons emit impulses or action potentials every once in a while—this is the base rate of firing, when nothing special is happening. A neuron can signal that something is happening by increasing the rate of impulse firing (turning the signal system on), or it can decrease the rate of firing (turning completely off). So the neuron can signal with "on" or "off" responses. The amount of increase or decrease in firing can convey additional information about what is happening. For example, if we have a visual neuron firing signals at a base rate, and then we shine a light in the eye of the subject, the neuron might increase its rate of firing. The brightness of the light might then be coded by the magnitude of change—small increases in firing rate would signal a dim light, and large increases would mean a bright light. In addition, the number of neurons which respond to a stimulus goes up as the strength of the stimulus is increased.

The second way of coding information concerns *which* neurons fire. This does not apply just to gross body areas such as the eye versus the ear or the ear versus the foot. It also applies within very specialized areas. For example, within the eye it makes a great deal of difference *which* neurons of the optic nerve are activated, and this difference helps us to tell the location, color, brightness, and other characteristics of the stimulus that is being observed. The same thing applies to the sense organs of the ear. It has been shown that tones of different pitches stimulate different neurons. Most amazing of all is the discovery that there are specialized cells in the visual system (and perhaps in other sensory systems too) that respond to particular types of stimuli and not to other very similar types. For example, there are cells in the visual system which respond (with an "on" response—an increase in firing rate over base rate) to a vertical line flashed before the eye but do not respond at all if the line is horizontal (see Chapter 3). If this neuron produced an "on" response, we would know a vertical line of some sort had been "seen."

In summary, just two factors characterize the way neurons transmit information about what is happening to the organism: (1) the rate of firing of impulses and the amount of change from the base rate, and (2) which particular neurons are doing the responding.

Neurons are organized into specialized groupings that constitute the main structures of the nervous system. Usually we find that large groups of neuron cell bodies cluster together in one place. Such a cluster of cell bodies is called a *nucleus* if the cluster lies within the brain or spinal cord. If the cluster of cell bodies lies outside the brain and spinal cord, it is called a *ganglion*. In similar fashion, the axons of the neurons tend to cluster together and travel in bundles from one place to another like the wires in an electrical system. Bundles of axons that run within the brain and spinal cord are called *tracts*. Outside of the brain and spinal cord, the bundles of axons are called *nerves,* for example, the optic nerve, which carries messages between the eye and the brain. Furthermore, several different nuclei may be organized into larger structures, the basic parts of the nervous system, such as the hypothalamus. It is important to remember that these structures are made up of neurons, and the neurons function by emitting impulses or action potentials. The neuron is the fundamental building block of the nervous system.

The Organization of the Nervous System

The nervous system consists of two general divisions: the *central nervous system,* which is contained within the skull and a bony spinal column; and the *peripheral nervous system,* which is comprised of all the nerves connecting the muscles,

Figure 2–2
The structural organization of the nervous system

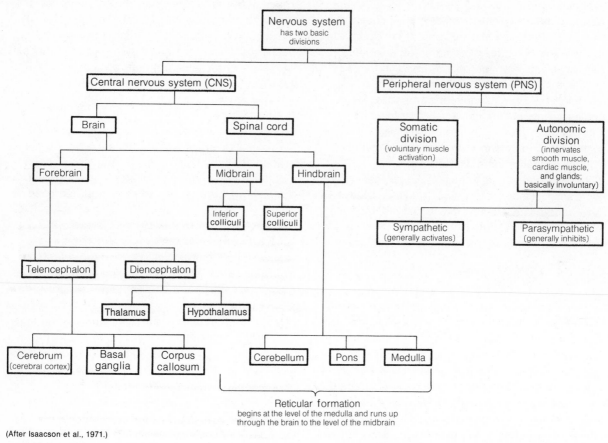

(After Isaacson et al., 1971.)

glands, and sensory receptors with the central nervous system (see Figure 2–2). The central nervous system, consisting of the *brain* and *spinal cord*, may be viewed as the integrating center for all bodily functions and behavior, while the peripheral nervous system simply brings information into and out of the central nervous system.

The Peripheral Nervous System

Without a peripheral nervous system (PNS) we would be unable to detect anything in the outside world and unable to command the functions of our muscles and glands. The peripheral nervous system is made up of bundles of nerve fibers and, in some instances, their associated cell bodies. Fibers that bring information to the central nervous system are called *sensory*, or *afferent*, fibers, while those fibers carrying information away from the central nervous system are termed *motor*, or *efferent*, fibers. These peripheral fibers usually run to and from the central nervous system in tightly packed bundles called *nerves*. Although a few nerves are either afferent or

efferent, most nerves contain both types of fibers and are, therefore, termed *mixed nerves*.

Most nerves enter or exit from the central nervous system by way of the spinal cord, the lowest division of the central nervous system. Information can easily be channeled up to or down from the higher parts of the nervous system by the connecting fibers found within the spinal cord. Although most nerves contain both sensory and motor fibers, these fibers segregate on entering the spinal cord.

The most important features of the spinal cord include the central *gray matter*, composed of cell bodies and short fibers, and the *white matter*, composed almost entirely of *myelinated* (covered with a fatty sheath) axon fibers (see Appendix B and Figure 2–3). Along the center of the spinal cord is a small canal called the *central canal*, which, like the other cavities of the nervous system, is filled with *cerebrospinal fluid*. Sensory information comes into the spinal cord through the large fiber bundles termed the *dorsal roots*. The cell bodies which give rise to these fibers are found in groups outside the

Figure 2–3
The organization of peripheral nerves and their relationship to the spinal cord

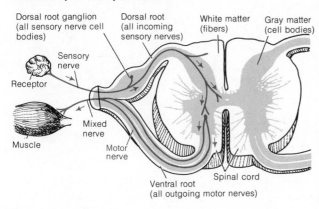

Dorsal root ganglion (all sensory nerve cell bodies)

Dorsal root (all incoming sensory nerves)

White matter (fibers)

Gray matter (cell bodies)

Sensory nerve

Receptor

Mixed nerve

Muscle

Motor nerve

Ventral root (all outgoing motor nerves)

Spinal cord

Only one-half of the cross section of the spinal cord is fully illustrated, but the arrangement is duplicated on both sides.

(After Thompson, 1967.)

spinal cord but running parallel with its length. They are called the *dorsal root ganglia.* All efferent fibers, passing out of the spinal cord to send information to the muscles and glands, leave by way of the *ventral roots.* Their cell bodies lie within the lower portions of the gray matter in the spinal cord. When a person has spinal cord damage, it is extremely important to understand the functions of the dorsal and ventral roots. Damage to the dorsal roots in the lower part of the spinal cord, for example, will produce a lack of sensation in the lower parts of the body. Damage to the central roots will produce paralysis, since the ventral roots relay commands to muscles for movement. Cutting all ventral roots would, therefore, produce complete paralysis below the neck.

Some nerves enter or exit from the brain directly, without using the spinal cord as a relay system. These are the *cranial nerves.* They carry sensory information to the brain from all the sense organs of the head, such as the eyes, ears, and nose; and they carry information from the brain to control the muscles and glands of the face and neck.

Subdivisions of the peripheral nervous system. The peripheral nervous system may be divided roughly into two main subdivisions. The *somatic division* includes the motor nerves that activate skeletal muscles—the muscles involved in bodily movement. The other major subdivision of the peripheral nervous system is the *autonomic division.*

This division is concerned with directing the activity of the *smooth* (involuntary) and *cardiac* (heart) *muscles* and *glands.* Smooth muscles are those muscles that line the blood vessels, activate the gastrointestinal system, and are often responsible for activating glandular secretion. The autonomic division of the peripheral nervous system is especially important in emotional behavior (see Chapter 6) and may be thought of as the *emotional response system.*

The autonomic system in turn consists of two subdivisions, the *sympathetic* division and the *parasympathetic* division (see Figure 2–4). Often, these two divisions will affect the same organ or gland in opposing ways. For example, the sympathetic division tends to speed the heart, slow down the stomach and gastrointestinal movements, dilate the pupils, decrease the activity of lacrimal (tear) glands, and increase sweating; while the parasympathetic division has precisely the opposite effect on each of these structures.

Activation of the sympathetic division prepares an organism for emergencies. (You have felt this if you have ever been in an auto accident or other frightening situation.) When the sympathetic division is activated, it produces activation of the *adrenal glands,* which then secrete *adrenalin* (epinephrine) into the bloodstream. Adrenalin produces by way of the bloodstream many of the same effects that activation of the sympathetic nervous system produces by neural connections. Thus, the adrenal glands are an essential aid to the general activation of the sympathetic division and its role in the mobilization of energy for emergencies.

The Central Nervous System

The central nervous system (CNS) is the collecting, integrating, and output center for all bodily functions and activities. In some instances, certain functions are controlled at a single level of the central nervous system, while in other cases, functions are controlled not in one place but rather by interconnected circuits at various levels of the brain. The human brain (shown in Figure 2–7) may be viewed as consisting of three major divisions: the *hindbrain,* which is the lowest level of the brain; the *midbrain,* lying above the hindbrain; and the *forebrain,* which includes the most highly developed part of the human brain, the cerebrum, or cerebral cortex.

The hindbrain. The major components of the hindbrain, depicted in Figure 2–7, include the medulla, pons, and cerebellum.

Figure 2–4
Schematic layout of the autonomic nervous system

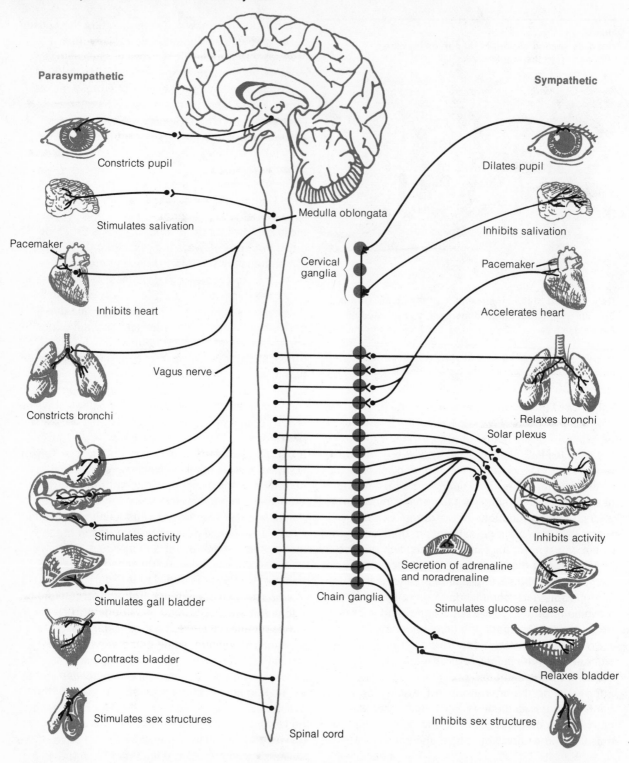

Parasympathetic

Sympathetic

Constricts pupil

Dilates pupil

Stimulates salivation

Inhibits salivation

Pacemaker

Medulla oblongata

Pacemaker

Inhibits heart

Cervical ganglia

Accelerates heart

Vagus nerve

Constricts bronchi

Relaxes bronchi

Solar plexus

Stimulates activity

Inhibits activity

Secretion of adrenaline and noradrenaline

Stimulates gall bladder

Chain ganglia

Stimulates glucose release

Contracts bladder

Relaxes bladder

Stimulates sex structures

Spinal cord

Inhibits sex structures

The sympathetic division is schematized on the right. The neurons are located in clusters or ganglia, which are lined up like a chain alongside the middle portion of the spinal column. In the parasympathetic system (shown on the left), communication with the spinal cord is at the top and bottom of the spinal column, and there are neuron cell bodies on the periphery (away from the spinal cord), often distributed near the organs being affected by this system. The end result is that each organ is "serviced" by two systems, one sympathetic and one parasympathetic, with opposite effects.

Figure 2–5
Recording the EEG

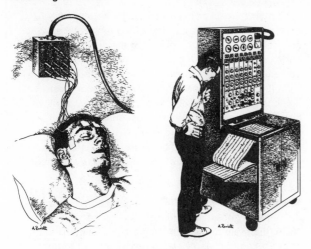

The EEG is recorded by small electrodes glued to the scalp that pick up the tiny electrical potentials generated by the brain. The EEG machine is basically a system for amplifying these potentials and converting them into a written record. The left panel shows a subject wired for a sleep recording. The wires from the electrodes are connected to a "terminal box" in his bedroom, which in turn is connected to the EEG machine in the next room. The right panel shows the EEG being printed out by the pens of the EEG machine.

Figure 2–6
Normal EEG records showing different patterns of electrical activity for different stages of sleep and wakefulness

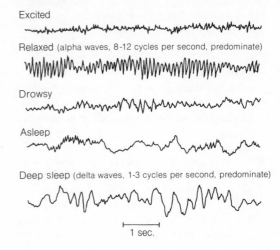

Excited

Relaxed (alpha waves, 8-12 cycles per second, predominate)

Drowsy

Asleep

Deep sleep (delta waves, 1-3 cycles per second, predominate)

1 sec.

From F. W. Penfield and T. C. Erickson (Eds.) *Epilepsy and Cerebral Localization,* 1941. Courtesy of Charles C Thomas, Publisher, Springfield, Illinois.

Note that for each level the EEG shows a characteristic frequency (the number of waves occurring during each unit of time) and amplitude (the height of each wave).

The *medulla* constitutes the portion of the brain closest to the spinal cord. It contains a number of important nuclei. Several of these serve as relays for the activities of certain cranial nerves, and others are important for certain vital bodily functions. For example, the medulla contains the nuclei that, in part, control heart rate and respiration. In addition to these important sensory and motor nuclei, all the fiber systems interconnecting the spinal cord with the rest of the brain are found within the medulla. Contained within the central core of the medulla, as well as the pons and a region of the midbrain, is the *reticular formation,* a lengthy network of neurons that will be discussed more fully later. Damage to the medulla could, therefore, produce malfunctioning of respiration, heart rate, and other vital processes. In addition, damage might involve the many ascending and descending fiber systems relaying information from the spinal cord to the rest of the brain. Damage to ascending systems might cause losses of sensation, and damage to descending fibers might result in partial or complete paralysis.

The *pons* lies just above the medulla and, like the

medulla, contains many ascending and descending fibers that connect higher and lower levels of the central nervous system. The pons contains other important respiratory nuclei as well as several of the important sensory and motor nuclei of the cranial nerves. Also, certain aspects of sleeping, such as triggering dreams, may be influenced by nuclei of the pons. The pons is depicted in Figure 2–7. It gains its bulging appearance from the large bundle of fibers that wraps around its periphery. These fibers connect the cerebellum with the rest of the hindbrain. In addition, some of the fibers of the pons originate in areas of the cerebral cortex that control certain aspects of body movement, and these add to the bulging appearance of the pons.

The *cerebellum,* also shown in Figure 2–7, lies on top of the pons. This structure developed very early in evolution. It possesses an outer cortex (covering) consisting primarily of cell bodies. The contour of the cortex is *convoluted* with regularly repeating lobules separated by fissures. Underneath the cortex is primarily white matter (myelinated nerve fibers). Buried at the center of the cerebellum are its nuclei, which control the input and output of the cerebellum, thus connecting it to the rest of the nervous system. Removal of the cerebellum

Methods for Studying the Brain

The first major goal of brain research is localization of function. We wish to know what areas or structures of the brain are involved in the control and regulation of particular behaviors. For example, is the hypothalamus involved in controlling food intake—eating? The following methods for studying the brain can add some information relevant to questions about localization of function.

The Lesion Method

A particular region of an animal's brain is destroyed, removed, or otherwise made inactive by a surgical procedure. The animal is then studied to determine if any behavioral effects have occurred. Perhaps the most famous lesion experiment deals with eating behavior. A lesion in one part of the hypothalamus can make a rat become extremely overweight, while a lesion in a different nucleus of the hypothalamus can cause the rat to stop eating, so that it eventually starves to death. This obviously suggests that the nuclei of the hypothalamus play an important part in regulating our eating behavior.

The Stimulation Method

A specific region of the brain is stimulated, either by electrical current or chemicals. Electrical stimulation and *excitatory chemicals* are used to elicit the behavior that is influenced by the area being stimulated. For example, if we electrically stimulate the hypothalamus, we can make a rat eat even though he has had his fill, or we can stop the eating behavior of a very hungry rat. The effect, starting or stopping, depends on which nucleus of the hypothalamus we stimulate. The effect of stimulation is also just the opposite of making a lesion. If a lesion in area A makes the animal overeat, then stimulating this area will make the animal stop eating, suggesting that the area controls the cessation of eating. Likewise, if a lesion in another area, B, causes the animal to starve itself, then stimulation in this area will elicit eating, suggesting that area B regulates the onset of eating.

We can also stimulate the brain area under investigation with *inhibitory chemicals*. These chemicals produce an effect opposite to the effect produced by excitatory chemicals. Inhibitory chemicals, as the name implies, inhibit the function of the area being stimulated—using these chemicals is like trying to produce a *temporary* lesion in the area by inhibiting its activity with a drug that will eventually wear off. By examining the behavior of an animal after we stimulate a particular area with both excitatory and inhibitory stimulation, we gain information about the function of that area.

Electrical Recording Techniques

When the brain is alive, it is electrically active. Presumably, the nature and number of electrical events taking place in various parts of the brain is a measure of the activity in that part. It has become a standard procedure to assess the electrical activity of the brain and there are several techniques for doing this.

Microelectrode method. A very small electrode is set in place inside or near a particular neuron to record the activity of a single cell. For example, a microelectrode might be placed in the occipital cortex in an area thought to be involved in vision. The animal's eye would be exposed to various visual stimuli and the scientist would watch the electrical response of the single cell. With this method, he might discover that some cells respond only to vertical lines, others only to horizontal lines, etc., and, in this way, he would begin to understand how the brain is involved in the perception of the external world.

Electroencephalogram (EEG). In human beings, it is not generally possible to implant an electrode deep inside the brain to measure single-cell activity. The scientist can only apply electrodes externally, to the scalp, and hope to record the gross electrical activity of the brain area lying under the electrode. The electrical activity is amplified and written out on paper by special equipment (see Figure 2–5), and this paper record of the brain in action is called an electroencephalogram, EEG for short. As you might expect, the method is not very precise, although it has proven to be very useful in diagnosing many types of brain injuries and abnormalities such as epilepsy.

Disappearance of EEG signals is now used as one of the criteria of death. The EEG shows a characteristic pattern during various levels of arousal, from alert wakefulness to deep sleep (see Figure 2–6) and is an important tool in research on sleep.

Evoked potential method. Finally, we mention the evoked potential method, which is a sophisticated refinement of the EEG technique. The EEG response of a particular region of the brain is not very precise—there is a lot of "noise" in the EEG measurement process since we must record with large electrodes and the signal must pass through the skull and scalp before our electrodes can pick it up. If we stimulate a subject's eye with a light, we might see no response at all in the raw EEG, because it is masked by the high noise level. Instead, we can use a computer to add up and average the electrical responses from many stimulations. The idea is that the noise in the system will be canceled out when we combine and average many stimulations, leaving a clear picture of the response. With this technique, we can measure the evoked response of the brain to different kinds of stimuli and we can measure the evoked potential the same stimulus causes in different areas of the brain. In this way we can develop a kind of map of the brain—we can find out what areas respond to visual stimuli, auditory and speech stimuli, and so on.

The Sex Testers

Newsweek—Neurologists have long used the electroencephalogram, which records patterns of electrical activity in the brain, to detect such disorders as epilepsy and brain tumors. Now, psychiatrists at Stanford University have found that the EEG may make it possible to read a person's mind. The California researchers have shown that brain waves produced in response to the sight of nude photographs seem to reveal an individual's sexual preferences. Ultimately, their findings may lead to new ways of treating scores of behavior problems, from sexual deviation to alcoholism.

These intriguing possibilities arose out of four years of research, by Drs. Ronald M. Costell, Donald T. Lunde, Bert S. Kopell and William Wittner, on the so-called E wave. Related to the four waves that register electrical potential on the standard EEG, the E wave is associated with anticipation or expectancy. Not unreasonably, the Stanford researchers suspected that an individual confronted with a preferred sex object or stimulus would show a heightened state of anticipation and that this could be objectively recorded in the form of intensified E-wave activity. To test their theory, they combined the EEG with a computer that averages E-wave changes over a succession of trials. The E-wave response can thus be made to stand out in bold relief against the background "noise" of other electrical activity in the brain.

In their first trials, Lunde and his colleagues recruited twelve male and twelve female Stanford students who were presumed to have normal heterosexual preferences. The volunteers were seated individually in a small, soundproof cubicle and EEG electrodes were attached to their scalps. They were then shown a series of photographs of naked men and women; while the pictures were not actively erotic, the genitals were fully revealed. Also included in the series was a "neutral" figure, a clothed young woman photographed in shadow so that her gender was not readily detectable. Each picture was flashed on a screen for half a second—to trigger a sense of anticipation at what was to come. Then, after a pause of one and a half seconds, the picture was displayed again for two full seconds. The E-wave levels during the interval between the showings were recorded and fed into the computer for analysis.

Female
The results were just what the researchers hoped for. The men showed a much stronger E-wave response to female nudes than they did to male figures. Precisely the opposite was true of the women in the study. Interestingly, over a series of trials, the males gradually showed increased E-wave activity in response to the so-called neutral picture, while the women showed a steadily lessening response. This, of course, reflected the fact that the volunteers had begun to perceive the picture as female as the experiment progressed. . . .

Lunde admits that recording E waves smacks of invasion of privacy. "It's a scary thing," he says, "and I do have a fear of its being wrongly used to find out what people are really thinking." But, he adds, the test doesn't seem to work unless the subject is willing. "They have to concentrate," says Lunde, "which is easy to avoid if you don't want to take the test."

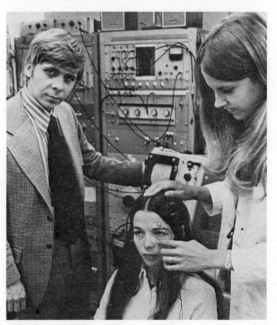

Photo by James D. Wilson—Newsweek.

produces severe disturbances of balance, movement, and muscle tone.

The midbrain. The midbrain represents the subdivision of the brain lying just above the hindbrain and contains a host of important systems and nuclei. Extending throughout the central core of the hindbrain and well into the core of the midbrain is the *reticular formation* (see Figure 2–8). This centrally placed network of cells has received a great deal of interest because of its alleged role in wakefulness and sleep. It is now well established

that the activities of the reticular formation may be critical to the maintenance of wakefulness and attentive behavior. In addition, it has been implicated as being at least partly responsible for sleeping and certain rudimentary forms of learning. The reticular formation has also been implicated in the control of certain aspects of movement and reflexive behavior.

Overlying and in front of the pons, but part of the midbrain, are the *inferior* and *superior colliculi*, which appear as four bumps on the surface of the midbrain in front of the cerebellum. These large

Figure 2–7
The lateral surface of the human brain is shown above, and a midline section below; the major subdivisions of the brain are indicated

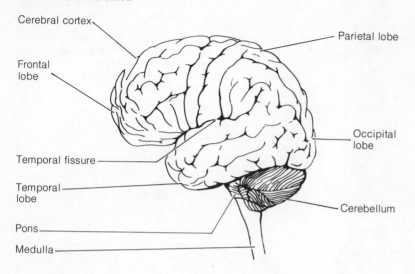

Cerebral cortex

Frontal lobe

Parietal lobe

Occipital lobe

Temporal fissure

Temporal lobe

Cerebellum

Pons

Medulla

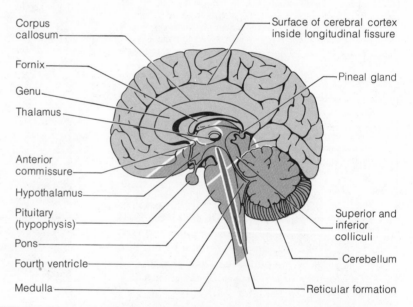

Corpus callosum

Fornix

Genu

Thalamus

Anterior commissure

Hypothalamus

Pituitary (hypophysis)

Pons

Fourth ventricle

Medulla

Surface of cerebral cortex inside longitudinal fissure

Pineal gland

Superior and inferior colliculi

Cerebellum

Reticular formation

nuclei are relay centers in the auditory (inferior colliculus) and visual (superior colliculus) systems. They are most clearly concerned with auditory and visual reflexes, such as turning the head toward a sound source, but may have other important functions as well.

The forebrain. There are two divisions of the forebrain. The first is the *diencephalon*—which divides into the *hypothalamus* and the *thalamus.*

The hypothalamus. The *hypothalamus* is a small but extremely important group of nuclei. This tiny

area of the brain has been shown to be involved in many behavioral functions, including many emotional and motivational aspects of behavior. For example, the hypothalamus contains nuclei that are involved in the regulation of hunger, thirst, body temperature, sexual behavior and reproductive cycles, activity cycles, expression of aggression, and sleep. This list is not exhaustive. One particularly striking feature of the hypothalamus is its intimate anatomical and functional connections with the *pituitary gland*, the master endocrine gland of the body (discussed in detail later in the chapter). Through its neural and circulatory connections with

Figure 2–8
Diagrammatic representation of the role of the reticular formation in the brain

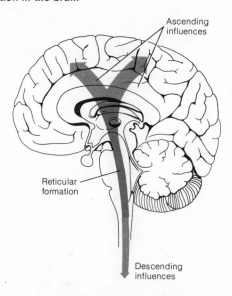

The reticular formation can influence higher structures, such as the cerebral cortex, by its "ascending projections," and it can influence the spinal cord by its "descending projections." The ascending influences of the reticular formation are believed to be intimately concerned with arousal and sleep, while the descending influences are believed to be primarily concerned with the excitability of reflexes and other types of movement.

the pituitary gland, the hypothalamus can directly control many hormonal secretions that regulate metabolism, the reaction to stress, and sexual development and behavior. It has also been found that the hypothalamus manufactures some of the hormones which had previously been believed to be manufactured by the pituitary gland. This fascinating and important interrelationship between the hypothalamus and the endocrine system is still an area of active and vigorous experimental research.

The thalamus.   Lying above the hypothalamus, the thalamus is shaped like two joined footballs and contains several important groups of nuclei. The best understood of these are the sensory relay nuclei of the thalamus. The visual, auditory, and somatosensory (sense of touch and position) systems all have relay stations in the thalamus. The information brought from receptors and lower relay centers to the thalamus is then projected by fibers from the thalamus to its appropriate destination in the cerebral cortex. The thalamus, therefore, performs an important relay function (see Figure

Figure 2–9
The functions of the thalamus

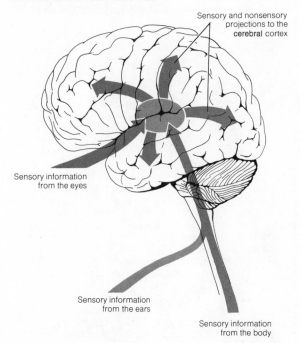

The functions of the thalamus include receiving sensory information from the receptors and their central relay stations and projecting it to the cerebral cortex. The thalamus also projects other information to the cerebral cortex, particularly to the association areas.

2–9). This is not the only function of the thalamus, however. There are many other nuclei contained within the thalamus that connect areas of the cerebral cortex not included in the classically defined sensory pathways, the so-called *association areas* of the cerebral cortex. The nonspecific nuclei of the thalamus have also been implicated in the control of sleep and attention, probably in collaboration with the reticular formation, hypothalamus, pons, and other areas of the brain.

The second division of the forebrain is the *telencephalon,* which includes such structures as the basal ganglia, the corpus callosum, and the cerebral cortex.

The basal ganglia.   Illustrated diagrammatically in Figure 2–10, the basal ganglia refer collectively to a group of nuclei buried deep within the cerebral hemispheres. They are concerned primarily with the control of movement and constitute a large contribution to the *extra-pyramidal system,* which includes all areas of the brain, outside of the motor

Pain and the Central Nervous System

"Gate Control" Called Key to Acupuncture

New York (UPI)—A Montreal psychologist believes the mysterious Chinese art of acupuncture works to block pain by instructing the brain to "ignore" pain messages from the nervous system, according to an article in the June issue of Psychology Today.

Psychologist Ronald Melzack of McGill University suggested that acupuncture works through the "gate control theory of pain," much like such folk medicine remedies as mustard plasters and ice packs.

"The theory proposes that a gate-like mechanism exists in the pain-signaling system," Dr. Melzack said in the article. "The gate may be open, partially open, or closed so that in certain circumstances, signals from injured tissues never get to the brain."

Dr. Melzack said he believes the key to acupuncture lies in the brainstem.

Activate Brainstem

"The nerve impulse produced by twirling the needles, or sending electrical pulses through them, activates parts of the brainstem that block pain signals coming from the site of the surgery," he said.

"The signals never reach the parts of the brain involved in pain perception and response, and the surgeon is free to begin his work," Melzack said.

The Chinese technique of pain control, which is centuries old but came to the attention of Americans after President Nixon's trip to China last year, also challenges a basic Western theory of pain—the so-called "specific theory."

This theory holds that pain is caused by a stimulus and is transmitted directly to the brain through the nervous system. The brain invariably perceives the stimulus as pain.

But according to Melzack, some nerves act to alter the brain's perception.

"Close the Gate"

"Large fibers in the sensory nerves running from the body's surface to the central nervous system tend to 'close the gate' when stimulated, and thereby diminish the level of perceived pain," Melzack said. "Small fibers in the same nerves tend to transmit signals that open the gate and produce increased pain. Acupuncture needles, then, may stimulate the large fibers."

Thalamic Lesions Give Pain Relief

By Lynn Payer
Biomedical News— . . . Lesions in specific regions of the thalamus and hypothalamus seem to be capable of relieving intractable pain without disturbing sensation, Dr. Keiji Sano told the International Symposium on Pain here. . . .

In reporting the results of stimulation performed before the lesions were made to localize the source of pain, and the results of experimentation on cats, Dr. Sano emphasized the interactions among the different regions of the brain in pain phenomena, with stimulation of one area often facilitating or inhibiting the sensation of another area. This indicates that pain is a summation of the various interactions, the same type that is explained by the "gate control theory" of pain, but at the level of the diencephalon instead of the spinal cord, he said.

The thalamus relays information from the sense organs to higher brain centers where perception of the stimulus takes place. Destroying parts of the thalamus (making a lesion) can thus block perception, in this example, pain perception. The thalamus may be the "gate" controlling whether or not a painful stimulus is perceived.

---

area of the cerebral cortex, that are concerned with movement. Recently, the basal ganglia have been shown to be involved in Parkinson's disease, a disorder characterized by jerky, uncoordinated movement produced at least in part by deterioration of the basal ganglia.

The cerebral hemispheres and the corpus callosum. In people and many other higher mammals, the most prominent feature of the brain is the *cerebral hemispheres,* illustrated in Figure 2–11. They represent the largest part of the brain. The most complex and perhaps uniquely human features of behavior, such as language, numerical ability, and the capability for abstract throught, lie in the activities of the cerebral hemispheres. The cerebral hemispheres consist of an outer cortex of cell bodies, called the *cerebral cortex,* and an inner core of white matter made up of myelinated axon fibers that connect areas of the hemispheres with each other and with other parts of the brain, including the projections of the thalamus.

The two cerebral hemispheres are connected by a great band of fibers running between them called the *corpus callosum.* As in most systems, there is a crossing over of fibers in the central nervous system such that the right hemisphere normally controls the left side of the body and the left hemisphere controls the right side. Surgically severing the corpus callosum removes the connections between the two hemispheres, which produces a striking effect. The two hemispheres are able, under appropriate experimental conditions, to function completely independently.

Figure 2–10
The basal ganglia

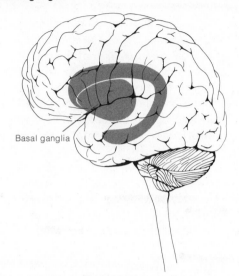

Figure 2–11
The cerebral cortex

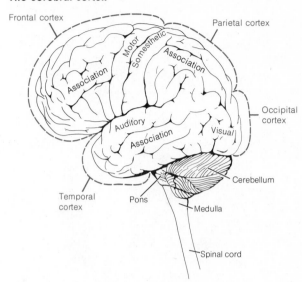

The basal ganglia are comprised primarily of three large nuclei, the caudate nucleus, globus pallidus, and putamen. These nuclei are involved in the regulation of gross movement.

Note that the cortex is often grossly described as consisting of four major lobes or areas: frontal, parietal, occipital, and temporal. Each of the major sensory systems feeds information to the cortex and to a specific receiving area in the cortex. This information is sent to the central nervous system from the peripheral nervous system. Once in the brain or spinal cord, the information is relayed from point to point until it reaches the primary sensory receiving area in the cortex. The figure shows the location of the receiving areas for vision, audition, and somesthesis (touch, pain, temperature). There also is a primary motor area responsible for the initiation of motor movements, which is located just in front of the somesthetic cortex. Stimulation in the motor area will cause a movement of muscles, and stimulation in the sensory receiving areas will cause the person to report that he saw or heard or felt something, depending on which primary sensory area was stimulated. Note that most of the cortex is association cortex.

Experimenters have performed the split-brain operation on animals and observed the behavioral results. Normally, in the unsplit brain, information from both eyes reaches both hemispheres by some crossing over at the *optic chiasm* (see Figure 2–12). When the corpus callosum and the optic chiasm are both severed in an experimental animal, there is no longer an exchange of information. If taught the solution to a problem with its left eye (right eye covered), the animal will be unable to solve it with its right eye.

Much information about the localization of various functions has been gained by studying individuals who, for medical reasons, have had the corpus callosum severed. It is known that the ability to describe objects verbally and other language abilities are in large part controlled by the left hemisphere, whereas recognition of geometrical forms and certain numerical abilities are largely controlled by the right hemisphere. When the split-brain operation is done on human beings (in some cases of epilepsy, for example), the corpus callosum is severed but not the optic chiasm. Thus information can still be exchanged at the chiasm, meaning that both hemispheres still get information from both eyes. So people are surprisingly unaffected by the operation. Only with careful

experimentation can deficits in human behavior be detected.

If a person who has had the split-brain operation is blindfolded and is asked to say the names of objects that are placed in his hands, he can name an object held in his right hand, but not one held in his left. The left hemisphere controls speech—his ability to say the names of the objects. If he is holding the object—say, a toothbrush—in his right hand, the information from his touch receptors in this hand is sent to the left hemisphere through the crossing-over organization of the nervous system. This information can be perceived and associated

Figure 2–12
The corpus callosum

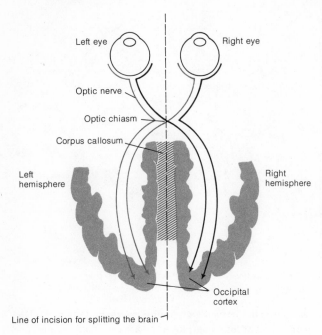

Line of incision for splitting the brain

This view looking down on the top of the brain shows the bundle of fibers, called the corpus callosum, connecting the two cerebral hemispheres. Studies have been done on the localization of brain functions by severing the corpus callosum and optic chiasm in experimental animals. The split-brain operation is performed on human beings in some cases of epilepsy. Amazingly little ability is lost when just the corpus callosum is severed.

with the correct name in the left hemisphere because "names" are stored there. And, as a result, the patient can say "toothbrush." In contrast, suppose you place the toothbrush in his left hand. Now the touch sensations are sent to the right hemisphere of the brain, and this hemisphere does not "know" the names of any objects. In a normal person, the information about the name could be retrieved from the left hemisphere via the corpus callosum, but the split-brain person has had his callosum destroyed, and so the name is not available—the right hemisphere has perceived the toothbrush but has no name available to associate with this perception. So it can be demonstrated that under special conditions the left hand does not know what the right hand is doing. There is even a suggestion that the two hemispheres can "experience" two different emotions at the same time. It really looks as if we have two brains and two minds.

The cerebral cortex.   The human cerebral cortex is highly convoluted, with as much as two-thirds of the area of the cortex buried within its own fissures. In lower organisms, such as the rat, the cerebral cortex has no fissures. As one ascends the evolutionary scale, convolution of the cerebral cortex becomes more and more pronounced. Because there are corresponding evolutionary changes in the complexity of behavior, it is commonly believed that the cerebral cortex is centrally involved in higher mental processes, such as language and thought.

The cerebral cortex may be arranged into functional areas (see Figure 2–11). Here we will discuss the three basic areas: the motor cortex; the sensory cortex, including the visual, auditory, and somesthetic cortexes; and the association cortex.

Motor cortex.   The particular portion of the cerebral cortex devoted to movement is called the *motor cortex.* Removal of the motor cortex in human beings will result in a loss of muscle tone as well as a loss of ability to perform fine, skilled movements. It does not usually produce complete paralysis because many other areas of the brain are concerned with movement and can to some extent take over the functions of the motor cortex following its removal. This is a common adaptive response in the nervous system called *recovery of function.*

Sensory cortex.   The sensory areas of the cerebral cortex may be regarded as the terminal receiving station for the classical sensory systems (vision, audition, somesthesis). A great deal of research has been done on the sensory areas of the cerebral cortex and much is known about the organization of these areas. For example, each of the sensory systems is represented in the cortex by at least one topographically organized area on the cerebral cortex, and in some cases by several. (Taste and olfaction are excluded since the organization of their cortical areas is still not fully established.) Topographical organization means that each point on the receptor surface for a given sensory system, such as the surface of the body for the sense of touch, is ultimately connected to some specific point on the surface of the cortex. Stimulation of one point on the body, therefore, would activate a particular point in the cortex. Stimulation of a particular point on the retina, the sensory structure at the back of the eyeball, would activate some specific point in the visual area of the cortex, and so forth.

In addition to this point-for-point representation

The Two Brains

Newsweek—Most people know that the actions of the right hand and the rest of the right side of the body are controlled by the left hemisphere of the brain, while the left side reacts to orders from the right hemisphere. Because nineteen people out of every twenty are right-handed, and because studies on patients with brain damage have shown that the faculty of speech is largely centered in the brain's left hemisphere, that side of the brain has long been regarded as dominant in controlling human actions.

But a series of research projects on brain-damaged subjects and normal people is revealing that a host of specialized functions, such as perception and artistic skill, are actually seated in the right hemisphere of the brain. This knowledge is contributing to a new picture of the human brain as an organ housing two entities—largely separate but equal—that think in different ways and can be applied preferentially to any task at hand.

In normal people, the brain's two hemispheres are linked by a large bundle of nerve fibers, known as the corpus callosum. The first scientific studies of differences between the hemispheres started about a decade ago, using as subjects patients who had had their corpora callosa surgically severed to alleviate epilepsy. Such patients behave perfectly normally except for one thing: their left hands literally don't know what their right hands are doing. One man in this condition, for example, attacked his wife with his left hand while trying to rescue her from the attack with his right hand.

At the California Institute of Technology, psychologist Roger Sperry has used a number of simple tests on such patients to determine the functional difference between their two hemispheres. In one, the subject is told to describe a pencil he is holding behind a screen, out of his sight. When he holds the pencil with his right hand he has no trouble, but when the pencil is in his left hand he is totally unable to describe it in words—his left hand is connected with his right hemisphere, which has virtually no capacity for speech. However, if the subject is then given a selection of objects and asked to select by feel the one he had previously held, he unerringly chooses the pencil.

These tests, and others showing that split-brain patients can draw much better with their left hands than with their right after the operation, suggest strongly that analytical skills such as language and arithmetic ability are based in the left hemisphere, while intuitive talents such as orientation in space, creative ability and appreciation of music lie in the right hemisphere.

In recent months, some brain researchers have tried to extend these findings to normal people. At the Langley Porter Neuropsychiatric Institute in San Francisco, for example, Drs. David Galin and Robert Ornstein are measuring the brain waves from both hemispheres as their subjects attempt a variety of analytical and intuitive tasks.

Alpha

In one experiment, scientists instructed their subjects first to show their analytical ability, by writing or mentally composing a letter, and then to exhibit their intuitive talent, by arranging colored blocks to match patterns and finding matches for specific shapes from a number of alternatives. The results provided clear proof that the specialization of the hemispheres in split-brain patients is shared by normal people. During the analytical tasks, the subjects' left hemispheres all showed electrical traces typical of mental activity, while their right hemispheres showed alpha waves, indicating total relaxation. On the tests of intuition, this was completely reversed, with the left hemispheres producing alpha. In effect, the hemisphere not called on to exhibit its specialist skills simply idled, leaving the other to do the work. . . .

HOW THE BRAIN DIVIDES ITS WORK

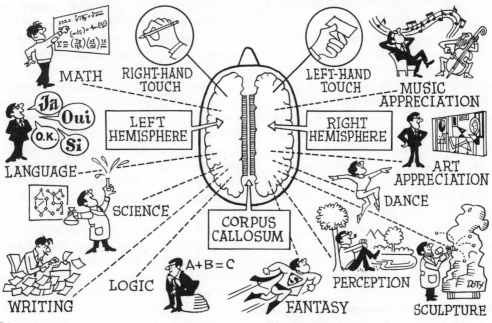

Drawing by Ray Doty.

found in all sensory systems, there are other features common to all sensory areas found in the cerebral cortex. For example, within each sensory area, there are cells that respond to particular aspects of the appropriate sensory stimulus. In the visual area of the cortex, for example, there are cells that will respond only if the individual looks at a line of a particular orientation. For example, one such cell might respond to vertical lines but not to horizontal lines. Other cells will respond only if the individual looks at two edges at a specific angle. Still others will respond to any kind of visual stimulus as long as it is in a particular place in the individual's field of vision. These are like single-cell analyzers of the external world, and they are crucial in our perception of the world around us (see Chapter 3).

Similar kinds of phenomena can be found in the auditory cortex. One cell might respond only to a particular frequency of tone, others only to a particular combination of tones. This kind of evidence suggests that the responses of different groups of cells might be an important means by which the brain codes and stores sensory information. Some preliminary evidence shows that many of these characteristic single-cell responses can occur at birth, which suggests that the neural mechanisms necessary to perceive many aspects of our sensory environment are present at birth.

Association cortex. The *association areas* of the cerebral cortex occupy the largest area of the cerebral hemispheres. They are most critically involved in the more complex aspects of behavior, including perception, language, and thought. Damage to specific parts of the association cortex will produce a loss of the ability to speak or understand language (aphasia). Damage to certain other areas will produce an inability to reproduce visual forms. Still other areas are involved in mathematical ability and other "cognitive" functions. The challenge of understanding the complex functions of the association cortex is immense. Some interesting experimental studies of people during thought processes have demonstrated that certain kinds of electrical and chemical events are correlated with learning and thought. But which, if any, of these correlations might yield the information needed to establish a basis for understanding the brain mechanisms of language, reason, and abstract thought is still uncertain.

The limbic system. The *limbic system* includes structures in both the forebrain and midbrain, and, rather than being a specific area, it is a circuit

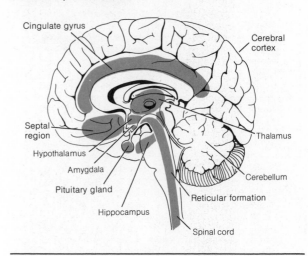

Figure 2–13
The major structures within or associated with the limbic system; this system is particularly involved in arousal, motivation, and emotion

including many areas and interconnections (see Figure 2–13). It includes the hypothalamus, portions of the cerebral cortex such as the hippocampus, the amygdala, and a number of other nuclei and pathways. The limbic system has been implicated in a number of functions, including motivation and emotion (see Chapter 6). Stimulation in certain areas of the limbic system, for example, may produce eating, drinking, or aggression. Damage to certain areas of the limbic system can produce docility and other "emotional" changes.

The limbic system in human beings seems to be very intimately concerned with memory storage. For example, surgical removal of the hippocampus in human beings, undertaken in an attempt to alleviate severe epilepsy, produces a particularly striking memory deficit. These individuals are perfectly capable of remembering all information that they acquired prior to the operation and can carry on a normal conversation and other functions requiring only short-term retention of information. However, they are completely unable to remember any new information for more than a few seconds; they are no longer able to store information over long periods. Those who have had the operation develop techniques to help them remember, such as carrying a note pad. Remember the case of Louise, cited at the beginning of the chapter, who had been a chronic alcoholic and lost some of her memory functions. Chronic alcoholism can result in deterioration of parts of the limbic system, providing additional evidence for the importance of this functional system for memory and other mental activities.

Physicians Told Results of Alcoholic Study

By James Crawford
Rocky Mountain News Writer

The common hospital practice of releasing alcoholics after a three or four-day drying-out period may foster continuation of the drinking habit, a Baltimore psychologist reported to doctors in Denver Friday.

At very least, the practice of releasing an alcoholic at this early stage of recovery returns him to the street in a highly vulnerable state, Dr. R. P. Allen told a gathering at the American College of Physicians' annual session at the Denver Convention Complex.

Physiological studies of alcoholics in remission at Baltimore City Hospital show that three days after their last drink they are at their weakest point in terms of ability to remember recent events and to deal with emotional stress, he said.

If released at this point, "he will be most comfortable in those situations in which he relies upon old and well-established habits," a state of mind which could "well contribute to a recurrence of drinking," said Dr. Allen.

Extended Spree

Full mental recovery from an extended drinking spree takes alcoholics anywhere from six to 13 days, the study suggested.

Dr. Allen, chief of psychological services at the Maryland hospital, teamed with Dr. L. A. Faillace, chief of the hospital's psychiatric unit, in a two-phase study which examined the short-term memory and sleep patterns of alcoholics brought to the hospital for "drying out."

Matched with a control group of nonalcoholics, five alcoholics were given a word-recall test both before and during the drying-out period. Subjects were asked to repeat a list of 12 words they had just heard read to them.

The short-term memory of the alcoholic is so poor on the third day of remission that he would often mention words not on the list, and often repeat the same word twice. "He apparently unknowingly repeats a word he has said less than 30 seconds before," Dr. Allen told the group.

Not until the 13th day of remission did the alcoholic's recall ability match up with the nonalcoholic control group. . . .

Chronic alcoholism can result in deterioration of parts of the limbic system, providing additional evidence for the importance of this system for memory and other mental activities. The study reported here indicates that the memory deficit of the alcoholic may drive him to resume his drinking habit if he is released from the hospital too soon after drying out.

Parts of the Nervous System

Many of the terms in the section on the anatomy of the nervous system may be new and unfamiliar to you. Below is a listing of the most important parts of the nervous system. These are the basic terms you will need to know to understand the biological foundations of behavior.

The Neuron

A. The cell body (soma)
B. The dendrites for receiving information
C. The axon for sending information on to other neurons; a nerve is basically a bundle of axons from many neurons

The Brain

A. The cerebral hemispheres
1. Sensory cortex: receiving area for information from sensory systems
2. Motor cortex: area that initiates motor responses
3. Association cortex: the undifferentiated remainder of the cortex that underlies all higher mental functions.
4. Corpus callosum: the band of fibers that connects the two cerebral hemispheres and constitutes a pathway for interhemispheric communication
B. Thalamus: the preliminary-processing and relay station for incoming information
C. Hypothalamus: a complex structure involved in regulating a wide variety of emotional and motivational behaviors
D. Medulla: involved in regulating involuntary behavior
E. Cerebellum: controls motor coordination
F. Reticular formation: regulates arousal level

The Spinal Cord

A. Dorsal roots—collects information coming into the spinal cord
B. Ventral roots—disperses information going out from the cord

The Peripheral Nervous System

A. Somatic division: the nerves that serve our voluntary muscles
B. Autonomic division: the nerves that serve our involuntary muscles
1. Sympathetic division: generally activates our bodies, as in emergencies
2. Parasympathetic division: generally inhibits or slows down involuntary functioning

Pleasure centers.   Another striking finding regarding the limbic system is that electrical stimulation of certain areas of the system (and other areas connected to it) produce what can only be termed a "pleasurable" sensation. James Olds and Peter Milner discovered in 1954 that rats could be

Figure 2–14
The endocrine glands and their products (hormones)

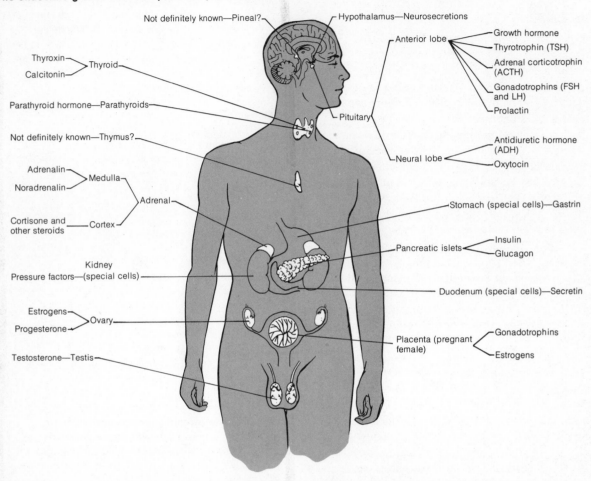

trained to press a bar for no other reward than having one of these "pleasure centers" stimulated with electrical current. In extreme cases, rats have starved to death when given a free choice between bar-pressing for food and bar-pressing for electrical stimulation. Other rats with electrodes in these rewarding areas of the brain have been known to jump over fire, swim through water, and undergo extreme exertion simply to obtain electrical stimulation. These fascinating findings suggest that these brain areas may be involved in the mechanisms that determine conditions of reinforcement or reward. As we shall see in Chapter 4, the control of reward is a powerful method of controlling behavior.

The Endocrine System

Another important biological system that is intimately involved in the regulation of behavior and that interacts in many important ways with the nervous system is the endocrine system. The endocrine system is composed of numerous glands distributed throughout the body, including two glands in the brain itself, the pituitary gland and the pineal gland. These glands execute their behavioral functions by secreting chemical substances called *hormones* directly into the bloodstream. In addition, a neural structure, the hypothalamus, is now known to manufacture hormones and thus to be a part of the endocrine system as well as the nervous system. Hormones travel by way of the bloodstream to other structures, including other glands and organs as well as certain sites in the central nervous system. Once these hormones reach their destinations, they act to produce a variety of effects.

The system is large and complex and involves many hormones. Figure 2–14 depicts the system, the location of the various glands, and the names of the hormones secreted by each gland. It is not possible to discuss the system in detail, so we will mention only a few of the major glands.

The Pituitary Gland

The *pituitary gland*, or *hypophysis*, may be characterized as the "master gland" of the endocrine system. The hormones secreted there not only control the functions of a number of other endocrine glands but also produce many separate effects on nonglandular tissues. In view of its importance, it may well be advisable to consider the functional and anatomical characteristics of the pituitary gland in some detail. A schematic diagram of the pituitary gland including its major categories of hormones is shown in Figure 2–15. Most readily apparent is that the hypophysis consists of two subdivisions or *lobes*. The *adenohypophysis*, or anterior lobe, secretes four important categories of hormones. The *thyroid stimulating hormone*, as the name implies, acts on the thyroid gland to stimulate the production of the thyroxin hormone of the thyroid gland. The *adrenocorticotrophic hormone* acts on the outer portion of the adrenal glands (the adrenal cortex) to stimulate the production of their hormones. The third category of hormones secreted by the anterior lobe is the *gonadotrophins*, which stimulate the reproductive organs. There are three major gonadotrophins. The *follicle stimulating hormone* acts on the ovaries to stimulate the development of the follicle, which contains the developing egg in the female. The *lutenizing hormone*, the second of the gonadotrophins, also acts on the ovaries and leads to the development of the corpus luteum, the small tissue body that develops from the follicle following the release of the egg. The third gonadotrophin, the *luteotrophic hormone*, also stimulates the development of the corpus luteum, and in addition it stimulates the breast to produce milk for the potential newborn.

The final category of hormone secreted by the adenohypophysis is the *growth hormone*. As its name implies, this important hormone serves a number of metabolic functions involved in growth and maintenance of the body, including the rate of growth of the bones and soft tissues of the body. Overproduction of the growth hormone may lead to grotesque increases in weight and body features.

The posterior lobe of the pituitary gland, also called the *neurohypophysis*, secretes two important hormones. The first, the *antidiuretic hormone*, acts on the kidneys to decrease the amount of water passed to the bladder, resulting in a decrease in urine output. The body uses this important mechanism when water loss has been excessive and

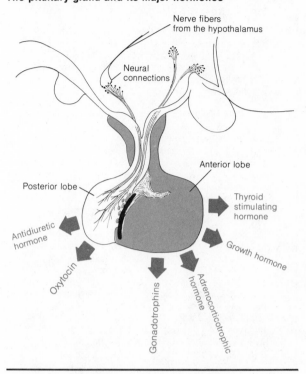

Figure 2–15
The pituitary gland and its major hormones

Nerve fibers from the hypothalamus

Neural connections

Anterior lobe

Posterior lobe

Thyroid stimulating hormone

Antidiuretic hormone

Growth hormone

Oxytocin

Gonadotrophins

Adrenocorticotrophic hormone

it must conserve water. The other hormone, *oxytocin*, acts on the mammary glands of the female to produce the ejection of milk and plays an important role in producing uterine contractions, which, of course, initiate the process of birth.

The Thyroid Gland

The *thyroid gland* secretes *thyroxin*, an important hormone in the regulation of growth and many metabolic processes. The effect of thyroxin is primarily to raise the metabolic rates of bodily tissues, which leads to an overall increase in the body's utilization of oxygen and heat production. Furthermore, proper thyroid activity is required for normal growth. Hyperthyroidism, which is characterized by greater than normal secretion of thyroxin by the thyroid gland, may lead to increased body heat production and its associated symptoms, such as excessive sweating, increased thirst, changes in heart rate, etc. Inadequate secretion by the thyroid, termed hypothyroidism, may lead to stunted growth, an inability to adjust to high temperatures, puffiness of the skin, and other symptoms. In infants, hypothyroidism is responsible for cretinism, characterized primarily by stunted growth and mental retardation. One other important effect of thyroxin is to inhibit the production of the thyroid stimulating hormone by the pituitary. This is

Hormones for Depression

Newsweek—Millions of Americans suffer from the crippling emotional disorder known as chronic depression. Most of them can be helped by some combination of medication, psychotherapy and electroshock therapy, but a small percentage will get no relief from these traditional treatments. Now scientists from Worcester, Mass., report promising results from giving a small group of "hard-core" depressive women massive doses of the female hormone estrogen.

Many antidepressant drugs work by lowering body levels of an enzyme called monoamine oxidase (MAO). This effect, known as MAO inhibition, results in increased activation of norepinephrine, a neurohormone associated with alertness, responsiveness and a high level of mental and physical activity. In the past, the Worcester researchers had observed that in normal women MAO levels are highest just before menstruation, when the effects of estrogen are diminished by the presence of the hormone progesterone. This is also the time when many women feel irritable and weepy—a sort of mini-depression. Furthermore, the scientists discovered that a group of depressed female psychiatric outpatients had abnormally high levels of MAO, which could be reduced—along with the patients' symptoms—by giving them large doses of estrogen.

To test this observation, two psychologists from Worcester State Hospital—Drs. Donald M. Broverman and William Vogel—collaborated with scientists from the Worcester Foundation for Experimental Biology in setting up a strictly controlled experiment. The researchers from the foundation were Dr. Edward Klaiber, an endocrinologist, and Dr. Yutaka Kobayashi, a biochemist. The subjects were 30 psychiatric inpatients, all with at least a two-year history of severe depression that had not responded to treatment.

Following an initial observation period, half the patients were treated for three months with daily oral doses of estrogen, and the other half got a placebo. The estrogen used is a natural substance that has not been linked with any serious side effects such as blood clots and strokes.

Changes

Some women in the depression study, reports Worcester's Dr. Broverman, had MAO levels 100 times higher than normal. Furthermore, the patients turned out to be highly "estrogen-resistant"—that is, they required more than five times the amount of estrogen needed by nondepressed patients to lower their abnormally high MAO levels. Some of the women needed to take 25 milligrams a day for more than two months before significant chemical or behavioral changes could be observed. Such estrogen resistance, the researchers point out, may be an important factor in causing depression in women.

After three months of treatment, says Broverman, MAO levels of the sixteen patients who had received estrogen were significantly reduced; those of the women on the placebo were unchanged. In addition, 80 per cent of the estrogen patients showed improvement of their symptoms, as measured on a standard psychological scale. Younger women responded particularly well to the estrogen therapy. No improvement of symptoms was seen in the women who had been administered the placebo. . . .

a familiar example of *negative feedback* of one endocrine gland on the functioning of another. Without this important negative feedback influence, the pituitary might produce more thyroid stimulating hormone than necessary, causing hyperthyroidism. Thus, these two endocrine glands interact in a way that properly regulates their overall activity.

The Adrenal Glands

The *adrenal glands* consist of two distinct anatomical divisions. The outer portion of each gland, the adrenal cortex, secretes a number of substances that may be collectively termed the *adrenal cortical steroids*. These substances regulate many metabolic processes, including metabolism of carbohydrates, balancing of sodium and potassium in body fluids, and influencing the reproductive organs.

The inner portion of the adrenal gland is called the *adrenal medulla*. It secretes epinephrine (adrenalin) and norepinephrine (noradrenalin). These two chemicals are intimately involved in the action of the nervous system. It is thought that they are "transmitter substances" that carry the neural message, which was coded in impulse form in the axon, across the synapse from one neuron to the next. The adrenal medulla is activated by the sympathetic branch of the autonomic nervous system, the branch that energizes your entire body in the face of an emergency. This emergency activation of the adrenal medulla will result in increased secretion of epinephrine, or adrenalin. The adrenalin secreted into the bloodstream then produces many of the same effects as are produced by direct stimulation of the sympathetic nervous system, such as increased heart rate, dilation of the pupils of the eyes, decreased tear production, increased sweating, and slower gastrointestinal motility. The emergency response system provided by the adrenal medulla and adrenalin is especially helpful in circumstances of prolonged or intense crisis or stress.

The Reproductive Glands

The final endocrine glands to be mentioned in our brief discussion are the reproductive organs, *ovaries* for females and *testes* in males. These structures secrete a variety of hormones that maintain and regulate sexual cycles and accompanying behavior; sexual characteristics of the male and female; and the functions that accompany mating and reproduction, such as the estrous and menstrual cycles, lactation (milk secretion), maintenance of the uterus, etc. Vigorous research on the endocrine bases of sexual behavior may well provide clues to many normal as well as abnormal sexual behaviors.

The endocrine system is clearly important in the regulation of many behavioral processes. Some of the effects of the endocrine system on behavior are direct, but many others are indirect; frequently the endocrine glands produce effects by acting on the central nervous system or other endocrine glands. It should also be clear that the effects of endocrine functions go far beyond their biological activities. The development of secondary sexual characteristics and body form and growth, as well as other aspects of physical development, have sufficiently obvious impact on the development of an individual's personality and attitudes to require little further amplification.

Behavioral Genetics

No discussion of the biological foundations of psychology would be complete without a discussion of the exciting new field of behavioral genetics. This field of study is concerned with the inheritance of behavioral characteristics, combining genetics and psychology. More precisely, behavioral genetics is that discipline concerned with the *degree* and *nature* of the inheritable causes of behavior.

It had been known indirectly, through the domestication of animals and the casual observations of many philosophers and scientists, that certain behavioral traits "run in families." Perhaps the most significant early scientific studies of this type were those of Sir Francis Galton, who studied eminence (genius) among families. In these classic studies of large populations, Galton was able to show that talents or behavioral traits were often passed along through many generations of the same family. The Bach family, for example, produced many extraordinary musicians, while other families were found to produce a disproportionate number of criminals. The work of Galton and others, though not as scientifically "rigorous" as later studies, did

suggest the possibility that *behavioral* traits are determined, at least in part, by genetic factors.

Genetic Structures

The mechanisms by which physical and psychological traits are transmitted to one's offspring involve what are called *genes.* These are carried by the organelles found within the cell's nucleus called *chromosomes.* Each chromosome contains many genes, and each gene is made up of a large and complicated molecule of hereditary material, deoxyribonucleic acid (DNA). Through a special process of cell division called *meiosis*, the human male sperm and the human female egg, or ovum, are provided with 23 chromosomes each. When the egg is fertilized by the sperm cell, it is thus provided with *23 pairs* (46 in all) of chromosomes. Each pair is distinct from all the others. One member of each pair is of maternal origin and the other of paternal origin. These genetic elements then direct the development and growth of every other cell in the body.

Chromosome pairs 1 through 22 are the same in male and female, but pair 23 differs according to sex. The normal female possesses two similar chromosomes in pair number 23 that are called X chromosomes. In the normal male, one of these is slightly different and is termed a Y chromosome (see Figure 2–16). Thus the normal female chromosome pair is represented by the symbol XX, and the normal male pair by the symbol XY. A number of genetically determined disorders are linked to abnormalities of this important pair of sex chromosomes.

Genetic Functions

Although we do not know the precise mechanisms by which the hereditary substance DNA directs the course of development and behavior, recent research provides some clues as to how this might take place. It is known, for example, that several forms of mental retardation are caused by the lack of specific genes and others by the absence of whole chromosomes.

One disorder resulting from the lack of a specific gene is *phenylketonuria,* abbreviated PKU. This disease is manifested in an inability to metabolize an important dietary building block, phenylalanine. One of the symptoms associated with this disorder is severe mental retardation. Although the precise mechanism that causes this symptom remains to be discovered, it seems likely that either the excess phenylalanine or some abnormal phenylalanine

Figure 2–16
Paired human chromosomes

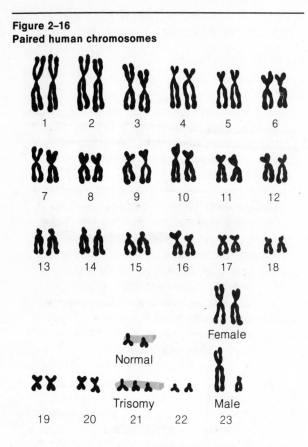

Males and females cannot be distinguished by the first 22 pairs of chromosomes. It is pair 23 where males and females differ. Females possess two similar chromosomes for pair 23, both called X chromosomes; thus the female genotype is XX. Males have two different types of chromosomes in the 23rd pair, one X and one Y chromosome, and thus have an XY genotype. Note pair 21 in the figure. Sometimes instead of there being a pair at this position, there are three chromosomes. This "trisomy" results in a form of mental retardation: Down's syndrome, or mongolism.

product is toxic to the nervous system and thus prevents normal development of intellectual functioning. Partial identification of the mechanisms responsible for this disease has made early diagnosis possible, and the appropriate special diet, free of phenylalanine, is prescribed for an affected individual. The diet seems to help the patient, although it may not provide a complete cure.

Normally, loss of an entire chromosome results in death to the developing organism. However, there are certain exceptions. For example, females having a single X chromosome instead of the normal XX complement have the condition known as *Turner's syndrome.* This disorder is characterized by retarded

sexual development and *visual agnosia,* a reduced ability to discriminate or recognize the form of objects.

Just as lack of specific genetic material may result in behavioral abnormalities, so an excess of genetic material may be associated with certain forms of behavioral pathology. Another form of mental retardation, *Down's syndrome,* or *mongolism,* involves the presence of three number 21 chromosomes instead of the normal pair. This condition is referred to as a *trisomy-21.* Trisomy of the sex chromosomes may result in a number of different behavioral syndromes. The condition XXY (a trisomy on the 23rd "pair"), for example, results in *Klinefelter's syndrome* in males and is associated with retarded sexual development, occasional mental deficiencies, and, commonly, physical abnormalities. Another sex chromosome trisomy in males, the XYY condition, has sparked intensive investigation recently. Early studies suggested that this condition resulted in abnormally large, aggressive males, and evidence was gathered which suggested that more XYY males were incarcerated for violent crimes than would be expected on the basis of chance. Although the evidence is still completely circumstantial, the XYY condition is receiving more than average interest and debate. In Australia, at least one individual with the XYY abnormality has been acquitted of criminal charges on grounds of insanity. In 1967 the female Polish track star Ewa Klobukowski was barred from competing in international track competition because she possessed an extra Y chromosome and was not allowed to qualify as a female. The moral and legal questions raised by the XYY condition are vast indeed.

Genetic Methods

Many experimental techniques are used to investigate possible genetic influences on behavioral traits. A particularly useful method for studying human inheritance has been the *twin study.* This involves the comparison of identical twins—those twins developing from a single fertilized egg and therefore possessing identical genetic make-up—with fraternal twins—who develop from different cells and are no more alike genetically than ordinary siblings (children of the same set of parents). Comparisons of this sort have provided evidence that traits such as intelligence, as measured by IQ tests, are partly determined by heredity (see Chapter 5). Many reports have confirmed the fact that identical twins are more similar with respect to IQ than normal siblings, and

X Marks the Manic

Newsweek—Manic depression is a remarkably common form of mental illness characterized by extreme mood swings, from intense excitement to deep despair. The disease usually appears in many members of the same family tree. For years, doctors have been trying to figure out just how the affliction is passed from generation to generation, and last week in Copenhagen a team of scientists from Columbia-Presbyterian Medical Center announced that they may have solved the riddle. Most cases of manic depression in their study, they reported, seem to be transmitted by a defective gene on the X chromosome.

A number of other genetic traits are also passed from parent to child on the X chromosome, one of two chromosomes that determine gender. For two of these traits, color blindness and a common blood group called XgA, geneticists have been able to determine patterns of inheritance so precise and predictable that they are known as genetic markers. Four years ago, researchers at Barnes Hospital in St. Louis observed that in two large families with a history of both manic depression and either color blindness or XgA blood type, members who had manic depression usually had one of the other traits as well.

Pool

Intrigued by these findings, Columbia psychiatrist Ronald Fieve decided to test the theory that manic depression really was, as it seemed, transmitted by a gene on the X chromosome. From a pool of 80 diagnosed manic depressives at the New York State Psychiatric Institute, Fieve, Dr. Julian Mendlewicz and their associates selected twelve patients with a family history of XgA blood type and seven with a family background of color blindness. Most

important, the relatives of these patients were either accessible for firsthand interviews and examinations or had reliably documented medical records. When the incidence of manic depression in these families was correlated with the incidence of XgA and color blindness, the researchers found just what the St. Louis group had reported: in most cases, the occurrence of manic depression was closely linked to the presence of one of the two traits known to be X-linked. . . .

In genetic research it is important to distinguish between the *genotype* and the *phenotype*. The genotype refers to the underlying genetic structures that each organism possesses. The phenotype refers to the surface manifestations of the genotype. For example, when we say that someone is male or female on the basis of his or her body structure and behavior, we are referring to that person's phenotype. As we have just seen, the typical genotype for a female is XX, whereas the typical male genotype is XY. Not all examples of the male phenotype have XY genotypes, incidentally, and not all examples of the female phenotype have XX genotypes. Occasionally, we find a phenotypically male person with an XYY genotype—he has an extra Y chromosome. Also there are cases of women with genotypes other than XX. Some such women have participated in the Olympic Games and have done so well that they have been called "superwomen" and have even been accused of not really being women at all.

---

that this is the case even for twins separated at birth by adoption and reared in different homes. Twin studies have also provided evidence of genetic influence in the mental disorder of schizophrenia.

Two other experimental methods used in behavioral genetics are worthy of mention—*selective breeding* and the development of *inbred strains*. Selective breeding is a particularly powerful technique. It involves selecting a behavior for study and then breeding animals according to how much of that behavior they exhibit. For example, consider the classic study by Robert Tryon at the University of California, Berkeley, in which rats were bred across many generations according to their ability to learn mazes. Animals that were particularly good at maze learning were bred together, and those that were very poor at learning mazes were bred together. This selective breeding was done for many generations, always mating the "bright" rats with other bright rats and the "dull" or slow learners with other dull rats. Two separate lines of rats eventually resulted,

the "maze-bright" line and the "maze-dull" line. As you can guess, the maze-bright rats were very good at learning mazes, while the maze-dull rats were unbelievably poor. Since the environments of both strains of rats were identical, the conclusion is that heredity must make a contribution to maze-learning ability in rats. It has been common for people to conclude that Tryon bred for "general intelligence," but subsequent research showed that this was not the case—the maze-bright rats were especially good at maze learning but they were not superior in performing all types of tasks that might measure rat intelligence, and in performing some tasks they were inferior to the maze-dull rats.

Many examples of selective breeding experiments exist. The important concept is that if the trait being bred for is influenced by heredity, selective breeding will be successful. If a characteristic cannot be influenced through selective breeding, then there is little evidence that it is differentially influenced by the genes.

Criminality and Heredity

"Criminal Chromosome" Debunked

By Don Kirkman
Scripps-Howard science writer
Washington—A panel of experts has dismissed as unproven the theory that a "criminal chromosome" drives some men to commit murders, rapes, robberies and other violent crimes.

They reported to the National Institute of Mental Health (NIMH) there is no conclusive evidence that men born with an extra male chromosome inevitably will become abnormal, deviate, violent or criminal.

The "criminal chromosome" idea gained coinage two years ago during a series of sensational murder trials in the United States, France and Australia when defense attorneys claimed their clients were innocent by reason of insanity caused by the extra chromosome.

These XYY chromosome men, the defense lawyer argued, were foredoomed to insanity because they were born with an extra Y chromosome and shouldn't be held accountable for their crimes.

An unusually large number of men with the extra Y has been found in prisons and mental institutions, the argument went, indicating these men almost invariably became criminals. . . .

"You can't talk to that crowd—they've all got extra Y chromosomes."

Inherited Criminality Supported by Rosenthal

APA Monitor—Dr. David Rosenthal, whose research has led him to embrace the hypotheses that behavior is integrally related to the genetic make-up, last month took the occasion of the AAAS meeting to cautiously support his genetic heterogeneity concept. . . .

In a paper entitled "Heredity in Criminality," Rosenthal brought to light some new research indicating that genetic factors shape the disposition toward criminality, and, at the same time he said, influence the form in which crime patterns will be expressed.

Drawing on his research into the associated hereditary variables influencing schizophrenia, Rosenthal presented some examples of variables which he links with criminality:

• "A number of studies have reported a higher incidence of EEG abnormalities in criminals than in the population at large. Such abnormalities often have genetic origin. The EEG abnormalities may be associated with poor impulse control and with bad judgement, which lead to crime.

• Many criminals have a low IQ. The IQ is well known to have high heritability. Many of us know examples of low IQ individuals who, placed in an environment where they can be readily influenced by smarter individuals with criminal intentions, are easily led into crime. . . .

• Many crimes are committed by individuals who are psychotic or near psychotic. We now have clear evidence that the major and most common psychoses are associated with some genetic factors. Therefore, such genes can indirectly contribute as well to criminality. . . .

• The case for XYY individuals being impelled to criminality because of the extra Y chromosome is much more in doubt than was originally thought. However, XXY individuals also manifest an increased tendency toward criminality. . . . It is possible that the XXY group is driven to criminality because of the psychological distress and personality disturbances accompanying the physical deviations resulting from the additional X chromosome.

• Many crimes are committed under the influence of alcohol, and evidence suggests an inherited factor in alcoholism. . . .

• It may be that most crimes in the U.S.A. today are committed by drug addicts. Who are these people who let themselves become hooked on hard drugs? Some clinicians believe that they are emotionally unstable individuals with a wide variety of personality disorders, at least some of which, such as borderline schizophrenia, are heritable. . . .

The third experimental method involves the use of *inbred strains.* These strains are derived by interbreeding animals related to each other. As successive generations develop, their genetic variability decreases. Animals in an inbred strain can be considered essentially identical to each other with respect to genetic make-up. There are many such strains, some having been inbred for several decades. When one animal in an inbred strain differs significantly from another, the most important determining factors must be environmental. Comparisons of behavioral traits in inbred strains provide important clues as to possible hereditary influences on these traits.

Genetic versus Environmental Influences

The modern work on behavioral genetics leaves little doubt that heredity plays an important role in behavior. Behavior is a function of living organisms, and genetic make-up must be taken into account if we are to understand why organisms behave as they do. However, we must not overlook or play down the effect of the environment on behavior.

Psychologists have typically been more interested in the environment than in genetics for the obvious reason that environment is more susceptible to experimental control or manipulation: One can *do* something about it. For example, several studies have shown that if rats are raised in an enriched environment (a cage with lots of rat toys, ladders, platforms, swings, and so on), their learning ability as adults is superior to that of rats raised in an empty cage with just food and water. Brain research on "enriched" versus "impoverished" rats has demonstrated that the enriched rats have thicker, more dense, and heavier layers of cerebral cortex than the impoverished rats. Enriched rats also appear to have brains with larger amounts of the neurochemicals involved in neural transmission, suggesting that they may have more efficient nervous systems. The most recent work has even demonstrated that an enriched early environment results in greater growth and density of the dendrites of neurons. Recall the two strains developed by Tryon: Research has shown that an enriched environment in infancy can compensate for a maze-dull heredity. Enriched maze-dull rats can catch up and perform as well as maze-bright rats. In short, we must remember that the behaving organism always has an environmental history as well as a biological or genetic history. An adequate understanding of behavior requires a consideration of both heredity and environment.

What Does It Mean?

Although knowledge of the brain and its relationship to behavior is still incomplete, there are attempts even now to apply research findings to the modification and control of behavior. A consideration of the biological control of behavior, therefore, holds an important place in the study of the biological foundations of behavior. Some of the methods used to study the nervous system have been successfully applied to the control of behavior, including surgery to cause brain lesions, electrical and chemical stimulation, and electrical recording techniques. In addition, the recent findings of behavioral genetics have had clinical application.

The use of these techniques and findings provides great hope for the elimination and control of unwanted behavior but also raises the possibility of misuse or abuse. There are many questions for future students of behavior to consider about the biological control of behavior.

Psychosurgery

The use of lesions or surgery to change behavior dates back to ancient civilizations. *Trephining*, a procedure for surgically opening the skull, was performed in Peru about 12,000 years ago, probably to free the patient of suspected demons. A type of psychosurgery called *lobotomy* was briefly popular in the United States during the 1940's and 1950's. In a lobotomy the nerve connections to specific areas of the brain, for example, the frontal lobe, were severed to alleviate certain emotional conditions, such as extreme anxiety. Sometimes, the surgeon totally removed the lobe of the brain (a *lobectomy*) instead of just cutting the nerve connections. Although the operation often resulted in remarkably improved behavior, just as often its effect was to make a human vegetable of the patient. Psychosurgery of such an extreme nature is no longer approved medical practice, but new surgical techniques are now being used in many hospitals across the nation on an experimental basis.

In cases of uncontrollable rage, the removal of an area that seems to control violent obsessions has provided relief for some individuals who, without psychosurgery, could not function in everyday life. First the surgeon locates the area of the brain that

Source: Playboy, April, 1970. Reproduced by special permission of PLAYBOY Magazine; copyright © 1970 by Playboy.

Psychosurgery Termed Partial Murder

Houston (UPI)—A Washington, D.C., psychiatrist describes psychosurgery as a partial murder of individuals and the first step to brain control through surgery.

Dr. Peter R. Breggin, in a paper delivered to the Houston Neurological Symposium, accused some surgeons of mutilating the brains of persons with no brain disease in order to pacify them.

Breggin, who said he is a former consultant for the National Institute of Mental Health, charged two participants in the symposium with masquerading under the guise of treating epilepsy while blunting the emotions of epileptics through psychosurgical procedures.

"There are certain kinds of things that can't be allowed even when people request them," Breggin said. "We are not allowed to murder someone at his own request."

He said psychosurgery should not be allowed because it destroys brain tissue and cannot be reversed. He said the United States is in a period of resurgence in the psychosurgery field. He said the first wave of psychosurgeries consisted of about 50,000 prefrontal lobotomies.

"Thus far the new wave has aimed largely at neurotic individuals who are often healthy enough to live and work at home," he said. "Often they are persons suffering from severe tension states or anxiety and depression, particularly women and old people.

"All psychosurgery . . . is a deadening operation, and is effective to the extent that a partially deadened or destroyed person is considered a suitable outcome."

effects of psychosurgery. Some psychiatrists and physicians feel that psychosurgery should never be performed because it deadens parts of the brain and creates irreversible personality changes. There is also the danger of using brain surgery indiscriminately to control unwanted behavior. Most of those who advocate the use of psychosurgery do so as a last resort—when other treatment approaches such as psychotherapy, shock treatment, and drugs have failed, and then only with patients who are considered a threat to themselves or others.

Brain Stimulation

Electrical stimulation of the brain has occasionally been used instead of surgery to prevent violent attacks in humans. José Delgado gave a dramatic demonstration of this method of controlling aggression several years ago when he used remote-control stimulation to stop a charging bull in its tracks. He carried a radio transmitter that sent an electric current through electrodes implanted in particular areas of the bull's brain (see Figure 2–17). The procedure is the same for humans. Following the surgical implantation of the electrodes in the appropriate areas, the individual simply carries with him a power source and presses a button to stimulate his brain whenever he feels an attack coming on. The stimulation blocks the rage response and appears to have a tranquilizing effect on the patient. Electrical stimulation is being used not only to control rage, but also to provide relief from pain in some nerve disorders.

The technique of "programmed movement" is another fascinating clinical application of the electrical stimulation of the brain. Lawrence Pinneo at the Stanford Research Institute has implanted electrodes in the brain stem of monkeys who have had their motor cortex destroyed. Using a computer, he has been able to program electrical signals that mimic the normal influences of the motor cortex on lower brain centers. Thus monkeys can be "programmed" to move limbs paralyzed by the loss of the motor cortex. It is possible that this kind of programming could be used in human patients whose motor centers have been destroyed in accidents or removed because of necessary surgery. Patients unable to move a limb voluntarily might then be provided with the necessary stimulation apparatus to move it artificially.

Biofeedback

There are literally hundreds of diseases that, while not directly caused by psychological stress, are precipitated by it. For example, ulcers have been

seems to be malfunctioning. This is done by placing electrodes into suspected regions and stimulating them with low-voltage electrical current. Electrical stimulation of the appropriate area will produce a violent rage response in the patient. Having located the critical area, the surgeon can then produce a lesion there by simply changing the electrical current and destroying the region.

The structures involved in the control of violent behavior are frequently part of or intimately connected with the limbic system. Removal of part of the amygdala, for example, eliminated or curbed attacks of rage in 5 of 13 patients who received the operation recently (recall the case of Ralph mentioned at the beginning of this chapter). A number of successes have also been reported following removal of part of the hypothalamus in cases of brain-damaged children who suffered from uncontrollably violent behavior.

Surgical removal of brain tissue is almost never the method of choice. Much more research is needed before we are sure of the possible adverse

Figure 2–17
"Fighting" a bull by radio

Dr. José Delgado of the Yale University School of Medicine faces a charging bull with cape and radio transmitter. The bull stops short when Delgado transmits a mild current to electrodes previously planted in the bull's brain.

produced in a laboratory monkey under stress in a famous experiment by Joseph Brady, in which two monkeys were exposed to a series of electrical shocks to the feet. One monkey could turn the shocks off by pressing a button; the other had no control at all over the shocks. Thus both monkeys received shocks when the button was not pressed in time. The monkey who had "control" developed stomach ulcers, while the other did not. The monkey in control of the shock button has been called the "executive" monkey, and his experimental condition is analogous to the psychological stress experienced by the many "executives" in the world who have

developed or will develop ulcers, heart attacks, or other forms of disease. Recent theory holds that even cancer is in part due to psychological conflict.

What is needed is a means for controlling the physiological processes, such as heart rate, that get out of hand when an individual is under stress for long periods. That such control is possible was first suggested by an extensive series of experiments by Neal Miller and Leo DiCara in which they showed that rats could be trained by techniques of operant conditioning (see Chapter 4) to slow their heart rates by as much as 20 percent. It had previously been believed that heart rate, blood pressure, and other physiological functions were completely involuntary and could not be so controlled. Miller and DiCara apparently demonstrated control of these functions when the voluntary muscles were paralyzed by the drug curare, although Miller's most recent experiments have failed to confirm this demonstration. Conceivably, the action of some voluntary systems is necessary to produce changes in involuntary functioning. That is, control of involuntary functions may be mediated by voluntary muscle effects. Nevertheless, subjects can learn some means and degree of control.

One hypothesis is that learning to control "involuntary" processes, such as blushing, is roughly comparable to learning to control the arms and legs. It involves learning to be attuned to fine nerve signals to and from the muscles and other parts of the body instead of to gross body movements. The secret to learning such control is to receive "feedback," that is, knowledge of the results of physiological changes as soon as they are made.

Some recent experiments have attempted to teach persons with a condition of irregular heart beats (called atrial fibrillation and currently treated with drugs) to control their own heart rates. Each patient receives training in a hospital setting, under medical supervision. The patient lies semireclined and observes a "traffic signal" at the foot of his bed (see Figure 2–18). A green light signals the patient to raise his heart rate, red signals to slow it down, and yellow indicates the desired rate. When the heart rate varies from that indicated by the yellow light, an electrocardiograph machine automatically changes the signal, which immediately informs the patient that he must either accelerate or retard the rate.

When working with rats, experimenters use rewards to facilitate learning. Often, the reward is stimulation of the brain's "pleasure centers." The stimulating current is simply made contingent upon the appropriate change in physiological function. Thus every time the heart rate, for example, of the rat changes in the right direction, the rewarding

Figure 2–18
Biofeedback

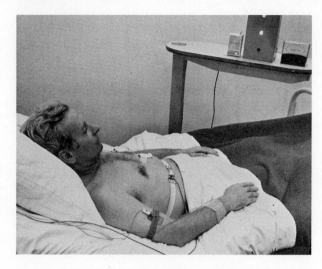

During a biofeedback training session to control heart rate the patient watches a "traffic sign" with red, yellow, and green lights that show him how he is doing. An intercom, on the left side of the table, enables him to communicate with the doctor and a meter, at right, shows him what percentage of the time he is accomplishing his task.

electrical current is turned on. For humans, the knowledge that the desired change in physiological function has taken place is reward enough.

Biofeedback training with heart patients is slow and must be done cautiously, but the results look promising. Four of the 8 patients in the first project learned to control their irregular heart contractions and have been able to maintain control. Some patients learn quickly, others need 10 to 15 training sessions. There are now several research centers and hospitals in the United States applying these techniques in an attempt to train individuals to control their own physiological states.

Another example of biofeedback training is the attempt to train individuals to control their own brain waves. You will recall that waves of different frequency and amplitude are associated with the various stages of sleep and wakefulness (see Figure 2–5). "Alpha waves" are associated with the physiological state best described by the term "relaxed wakefulness." By attending to feedback, human beings can learn to "control" their alpha waves, thus producing more or less of them in any given time period. This control is often associated with relaxation, easing of tension, and a general

feeling of restfulness and well-being. Imagine the benefit to patients suffering from hypertension, migraine headaches, and other forms of illness associated with psychological stress. The ability to control their own alpha waves, and thereby their own physiological state, could be of immense therapeutic value.

Applications of Electrical Recording from the Brain

The previous section discussed the potential importance of biofeedback as a means for preventing or possibly treating many kinds of physiological malfunctions through self-regulation of physiological processes. This is only one example of the more general significance of recording physiological activity. Many types of electrical responses generated by the brain can be recorded with the aid of computer and biomedical technology, and the technique of electrical recording has found several valuable applications.

Perhaps the best known form of electrical activity recorded from the brain is the electroencephalogram (EEG). As mentioned earlier, the EEG displays definite patterns during different stages of wakefulness and sleep and has been used in sleep research. In addition the EEG is used to diagnose brain-wave abnormalities of epilepsy. The pattern of electrical activity seen in the EEG during an epileptic attack is particularly unique. The EEG also shows abnormalities when there has been damage to a specific part of the cerebral cortex, from an accident or tumor, for example. The EEG recording technique has been used for many years to determine if brain damage exists, as well as to localize and characterize the form of damage.

There are other techniques of electrical recording that offer potential for clinical application; however, they are not yet widely used. One particularly exciting field of potential application involves the "evoked potential," an electrical signal recorded from the brain in response to external sensory stimuli. Within the last decade it has become possible, using computer techniques, to record evoked potentials from the human brain without having to place electrodes in direct contact with the brain. Electrodes can simply be placed on the surface of the scalp. Although the evoked responses occur relatively far away from the electrode (the skull and scalp lie between the brain and the electrode, causing some interference in the brain's response), devices called "averaging computers" are capable of taking many small and unclear responses and reconstructing them so that, added together, they look like the response that would otherwise have to be recorded directly from the brain's surface.

Now that this technology is possible, several applications have already been put into experimental practice and many others suggest themselves for clinical relevance. For example, a psychiatrist has suggested using the evoked response to identify hyperactive children. These children have numerous problems, particularly in school, because hyperactivity prevents them from settling down and concentrating on their schoolwork. Drug treatment for hyperactivity has been very successful, but therapists have felt the need for a test capable of screening large groups of school children to identify those who are hyperactive and will respond to treatment with drugs.

The evoked potential in such a screening test would be a characteristic "blip" on an EEG evoked by an auditory stimulus. Initial tests show that in 60 percent of a group of hyperactive children the blips evoked by a sound stimulus were less frequent and lower in amplitude than was the case for a control group of children. When the hyperactive group was given drug treatment, the ones who had shown the characteristic blip responded the best.

Addiction

There is hope that research in biopsychology will contribute to an understanding of the factors involved in addiction to narcotics and alcohol. In the case of alcoholism, there is clear evidence that heredity is a major factor, and similar suggestions have been made in the case of narcotics addiction. This evidence suggests that there are physical bases for these disorders over and above the role played by the environmental circumstances of the addict. Alcoholics may, for example, lack certain enzymes that are necessary for the metabolism of alcohol, and this lack may result in their systems being much more vulnerable to alcoholism. Individuals who are drug addicts may have inherited nervous systems that have unusually large numbers of receptors sensitive to the addicting drug, resulting in greater susceptibility to addiction.

One interesting hypothesis about the mechanism of addiction is known as the *disuse theory*. There is evidence from physiological experiments that prolonged periods of disuse of a muscle can result in that muscle's becoming supersensitive. It is likely that a similar phenomenon exists for nerves— prolonged inactivity of a nerve could result in its becoming so highly sensitive that when activity was resumed, the nerve would literally overrespond to

Alcoholism May Be Inherited

By C. G. McDaniel
AP science writer
Chicago (AP)—Five American and Danish psychiatrists say a study of adopted children who became alcoholics as adults suggests a tendency that the disease may be biologically inherited.

They studied 55 Danish men who had been separated from their biological parents during early infancy, and one parent had been diagnosed as alcoholic.

These were compared with 78 other adopted men whose biological parents had no known history of alcoholism.

The study found that "significantly more" of the first group had a history of drinking problems and psychiatric treatment.

And the offspring of alcoholics also had a divorce rate three times that of the second group. . . .

any stimulation, thus causing great disruption in nervous transmission. Since we know that narcotics are great pain killers, prolonged use of these drugs probably produces prolonged *disuse* of major parts of the nervous system. When the drugs are withdrawn and transmission resumes, the nervous system could be so sensitive from the period of disuse that smooth transmission of nerve impulses is impossible. The result is withdrawal symptoms, which, of course, are terrible for addicts.

Learning and Memory

Remember Martha, who was trying to remember the name of John B. Watson for her psychology exam? When she first learned that name, there might have been some physical change in her nervous system representing the storage in her brain of that fact. Physiological psychologists are intensely interested in determining the physiological and chemical bases for learning and memory and have already made some significant progress. Perhaps the most popular current hypothesis is that learning involves protein synthesis in specialized areas of the brain. That is, as a result of learning, chemical changes take place and new protein chains are manufactured in the brain. Somehow the learned information is stored in the protein, perhaps in a fashion analogous to the way information is stored in our genes. Experiments have shown, for example, that if animals are given a drug that blocks protein synthesis, memory for responses learned just before drug administration is severely impaired. If knowledge is stored in our brains as complex chemicals, then perhaps we can isolate these chemicals from the brains of trained or "bright" animals and inject them into the brains of untrained or "dull" animals to see if this improves learning or performance. Many such experiments have been tried and some have apparently succeeded in transferring knowledge this way. However, there have also been many failures (which do not get as much newspaper publicity as the successes), so we cannot at the present time conclude for certain that such gourmet learning is possible.

If drugs that block protein synthesis inhibit learning and memory, then perhaps there are other drugs that can facilitate memory. Indeed, there have been several successful experiments of this type. Drugs that excite the nervous system and that are thought to speed up nervous transmission have been administered to animals while they are learning and shortly after learning has taken place. The result appears to be that memory is improved. However, if these same drugs are administered well after learning has taken place, they have no such beneficial effect. This suggests that the brain processes involved in the storage of new memories are active for a short time after learning but then stop once storage is complete. At this point in time, drug injections would not help, presumably because the memory has already been stored—it is solidified or consolidated (see the discussion of memory consolidation in Chapter 4). Other researchers hope that memory-facilitating drugs will be discovered that work at any time, not just during or immediately after learning occurs. There is hope that such research will uncover the biochemical deficits that are presumably present in the brains of certain types of mentally retarded individuals and of old people, who often suffer severe learning and memory problems. Research on the physiological basis of learning and memory may eventually lead to new types of drug treatments that will alleviate these problems. Perhaps some day there will be special protein supplements we can all drink with our breakfast during finals week or just before taking the medical or law school admissions test.

Genetic Counseling

The findings of behavioral genetics have such important meaning for human lives that this knowledge is already being applied. For example, a new social-medical specialty, genetic counseling, has come into being just recently. Genetic counselors advise potential parents about their genetic histories and the probabilities that their children will be born normal—or mentally retarded, deformed, or with biochemical abnormalities that might be fatal. They use advanced biomedical technology to detect abnormalities in fetuses early in the prenatal period or to identify parents who are carrying defective genes.

Most typically, clients seeking genetic counseling are parents who have already had one or more defective children. They want to know whether to take a chance with another pregnancy. Others seek advice because they are pregnant and have been exposed to potentially harmful drugs, radiation, German measles, etc. Sometimes individuals ask for counseling before marriage, particularly those with a family history of genetic disease.

Take the example of a couple who have had one normal child and one mongoloid child. When the wife becomes pregnant again, they want to know what the chances are that the child will be mongoloid. There is now a test that can be given around the fourth month of pregnancy that involves drawing a sample of the fluid surrounding the fetus, growing the actual fetal cells in the laboratory, and then examining their chromosomal and biochemical make-up. If the test is positive, it is not too late for a therapeutic abortion if that is what the parents decide on.

The genetic counselor provides the best indication that he can of whether or not the child will be normal based on an analysis of the families' genetic histories and laboratory tests such as that just described. The counselor only advises, however; the decision is always made by the parents. Clearly, genetic counseling can help prevent many defective births and help provide understanding for parents who blame themselves for bearing a defective child.

Possible Uses of Biopsychological Knowledge

The potential areas of application of biopsychology are practically unlimited; a few of them are discussed here.

Obesity. Consider the control of obesity. Research has determined that certain nuclei of the hypothalamus are responsible for the control, both starting and stopping, of eating. It is possible that some day certain types of people with chronic overweight problems can be helped by electrical or surgical intervention in the hypothalamus.

Sleep. Insomnia is one of the most common symptoms in the American population. Since biopsychology has uncovered much of the neurological basis for control and regulation of sleep and wakefulness, there is little doubt that help for the insomniac will result. This could take the form of new drugs that affect the sleep system without the unwanted side effects of the barbiturates that are now commonly prescribed for insomniacs. Or there may be electrical devices for stimulating the brain in a way to induce sleep. There are devices in the research stage already that may some day eliminate the problem of insomnia.

Sleep research in biopsychology is progressing at a feverish pace, although we still do not really know why it is that we have to sleep. The most common theory is that sleep is a time for rejuvenation of the nervous system, a time when certain by-products or waste products are eliminated. When we discover why we need sleep, we can expect the immediate development of procedures that would make sleep unnecessary or less necessary. Again this could come in the form of drugs that would accomplish the necessary functions of sleep or in the form of electrical stimulation of the brain. Some claims have already been made that certain "sleep machines" can compress 8 hours of sleep into 4 or less. Consider the implications of discoveries that would eliminate the need for sleep.

Psychopharmacology.   The potential applications of psychopharmacology, the study of the effects of drugs on behavior, boggle the mind. A recent president of the American Psychological Association has called for the development of drugs to control violence. He would have political leaders be required to take such drugs in order to reduce the threat of world war. We have seen that the nervous system is based on chemical events, which means that the potential for drug control is enormous. We have already mentioned drugs for controlling obesity, insomnia, and sleep. Are there drugs that will increase intelligence, improve memory, increase creativity, and stop crime?

Knowledge of the mechanisms of drug action has contributed and will continue to contribute to the treatment of mental illness. Certain drugs, when taken in large amounts, can induce a reaction resembling that of psychosis. A basic understanding of the way in which the drugs produce these symptoms will possibly contribute to an understanding of psychosis. So basic research on the mechanisms of drug action involves payoffs, not only by discovering drugs for treatment, but also by discovering drugs that mimic the illness, which may lead researchers to find the ultimate causes and cures.

The work in behavioral genetics has far-reaching implications. Already there has been significant

The Right to Bad Genes

Time—Genetic engineering is just in its earliest tinkering stage, but it is already seen both as a great medical hope and a bugaboo. By learning the secrets of the genes, science is increasingly able to alert couples who run an unusually high risk of passing on crippling defects; sometimes a warning is possible even before children are conceived. Tests can also discover disabilities in the unborn as well as in infants and young children before symptoms appear.

Example: if both parents carry the genes for Tay-Sachs disease or sickle-cell anemia, there is great danger that their children will actually get the disease. Many geneticists and physicians are therefore enthusiastic about widespread genetic screening. They also support a new Massachusetts law—not yet put into practice—that would make sickle-cell examinations a requirement for school admission.

Others, however, argue that science and society must go easy not only in interfering with the genetic process, but even in mass screening. A 24-member team of scientists, lawyers and ethicists has been examining this question with the Institute of Society, Ethics and the Life Sciences at Hastings-on-Hudson, N.Y., for the past year. Now, in the *New England Journal of Medicine*, the group endorses the principle of helping people to make "informed choices regarding reproduction." But the authors are concerned that large-scale testing could violate people's rights to privacy and freedom of choice. Specifically, they argue that:

• There should be no attempt to impose a standard of genetic normality on any segment of the population. Virtually everyone carries a small number of harmful recessive genes. To eliminate these from the gene pool might require partners who both have similar "bad" traits to avoid parenthood entirely.

• No program should be made compulsory. "There is currently no public health justification for mandatory screening for the prevention of genetic disease. The conditions being tested for in screening programs are neither 'contagious' nor, for the most part, susceptible to treatment at present." People, the report says in effect, have the right to bad genes.

• Care should be taken to safeguard the privacy of participants in screening programs. The information obtained should be made available only to the individuals involved and their physicians. Otherwise, people might be stigmatized socially, and even perhaps denied life and health insurance. . . .

progress toward the development of a new type of engineer, the genetic engineer. It is not unlikely that, in the future, techniques for genetic manipulation of physical and psychological phenomena will be possible. In the future we may have techniques for actually affecting the chromosomes in ways designed to eliminate such things as mental retardation, schizophrenia, and alcoholism. This means that behavioral geneticists must pursue programs designed to determine the genetic contributions to various psychological disorders in the hopes that eventually application of genetic engineering techniques will contribute to their eradication. We can also envision engineering designed to produce offspring with more adaptive characteristics, such as great intelligence. Again, such knowledge will create new moral and ethical issues concerning their application. There is little doubt, however, that behavioral genetics represents a field of psychology that is certain to have an enormous impact on our future lives.

It is noteworthy that the study of the biological foundations of behavior cuts across disciplinary boundaries to include chemistry, anatomy, pharmacology, psychology, physiology, genetics, and many other disciplines. All of the techniques at the disposal of these diversified scientific disciplines are being applied in one way or another to the study of the nervous system. As we learn more about the functions of the nervous system and their relation to behavior, more and better clinical application of this knowledge to human behavior will be possible. The concomitant emergence of philosophical and ethical questions relating to the control of behavior seems inevitable. In his book, *Physical Control of the Mind*, José Delgado suggests that scientific information about behavior control should be shared with the population as a whole because of the power involved:

The fundamental question of who is going to exert the power of behavioral control is easy to answer: everybody who is aware of the elements involved and understands how they act upon us will have that power. It is therefore essential that relevant information not be restricted to a small elite but be shared by all. In this way, solutions will be the product of collective thinking, and more importantly, the individual will be provided with a critical sense which will diminish his dependence on group decisions and allow the search for new personal solutions and therefore greater individual freedom.

A new technology has been developed for the exploration of cerebral mechanisms in behaving subjects, and it has already provided data about the intracerebral correlates of learning, memory, drives, performance, and other aspects of mental functions. This methodology has proved that movements, sensations, emotions, desires, ideas, and a variety of psychological phenomena may be induced, inhibited, or modified by electrical stimulation of specific areas of the brain. These facts have changed the classical philosophical concept that the mind was beyond experimental reach.   (pages 256–257)

Summary

1. The biological foundations of behavior encompass the study of the nervous system and the many basic physiological processes that underlie behavior.

2. The neuron, the basic structural unit of the nervous system, possesses three basic parts: soma, axon, and dendrites. The neuron is specialized to conduct and transmit information.

3. Conduction is accomplished by the all-or-none action potential. Transmission occurs at the functional contacts between neurons, the synapses.

4. Neurally coded information is transmitted by the release of chemical substances from the axon terminals of one cell to the dendrites of the next neuron. This neuron may in turn "fire" an impulse to the next neuron. Transmission may result in either inhibition or excitation of the next cell. All nervous activity, and thus behavior, may ultimately be understood in terms of a balance between these two processes of neural excitation and neural inhibition.

5. The nervous system, composed of approximately 10 billion nerve cells as well as many other nonneural elements, is characterized by a number of functional circuits and divisions.

6. The peripheral nervous system (PNS) includes all nervous tissue outside of the skull and spinal column. It includes a somatic and autonomic division. Sensory and motor nerves of the somatic portion of the PNS bring information to and from the central nervous system. The two important divisions of the autonomic division of the PNS are the parasympathetic branch and the sympathetic branch.

7. The somatic division of the PNS is involved in skeletal movement and bodily sensation; the autonomic division is involved in emotional responses and glandular activity.

8. The central nervous system (CNS) may be conveniently divided into three major divisions derived from the study of evolution and development of the nervous system.

9. The hindbrain—the most posterior division of the generalized vertebrate brain—contains the medulla, cerebellum, and pons.

10. The midbrain, lying above the hindbrain, includes two important visual and auditory reflex centers—the superior and inferior colliculi.

11. The forebrain, consisting of the diencephalon and telencephalon, is most highly developed in primates. The diencephalon contains the hypothalamus—important in the control of sleep and wakefulness, eating, drinking, and many other motivated behaviors—and the thalamus, which

serves as an important relay center for sensory information. The telencephalon contains the cerebral cortex and several important motor nuclei, such as the basal ganglia.

12. In humans, the cerebral cortex has become extremely enlarged and convoluted so that it nearly covers the rest of the brain. An understanding of the unique functions of the cerebral cortex will make it possible to understand the higher mental functions of human beings, such as language and thought.

13. Another extremely important system involved in the control of behavior is the endocrine system, made up of the various endocrine glands. These glands take effect by releasing chemical messengers called hormones, which influence many aspects of physiological and behavioral functioning.

14. The close interrelationship between the endocrine system and the nervous system is partly illustrated by the neural control of the master endocrine gland, the pituitary, by the hypothalamus, lying at the base of the brain.

15. Another aspect of the biological foundations of behavior is the study of the inheritance of behavioral characteristics, a new field called "behavioral genetics." Using techniques of genetics, investigators in this field are discovering that inheritance plays an extremely important role in many behavioral characteristics.

16. As scientists approach greater understanding of the biological foundations of behavior, applications of this knowledge emerge for controlling and changing behavior. There is hope that brain surgery may someday be useful in relieving behavioral disturbances. Electrical stimulation of the brain is being used experimentally to alleviate epilepsy, excessive violence, and chronic pain.

17. Understanding the physiological functions involved in psychological stress is leading to remedial therapies for the untoward effects of stress, including the new technique of "biofeedback," which involves teaching individuals to control their own physiological responses such as heart rate or blood pressure.

18. Biopsychology research may also help us understand and treat drug addiction and alcoholism. There may also be applications of this type of knowledge to improvement of learning and memory abilities.

19. The findings of research in genetics and behavior have been applied by genetic counselors, who advise couples about the probabilities of their bearing normal offspring.

20. The wealth of information science is collecting about the biology of our nervous system suggests many future applications, including the control of obesity and insomnia and the prevention of mental retardation and other disorders.

Recommended Additional Readings

Barber, T. X., DiCara, L. V., Kamiya, J., Miller, N. E., Shapiro, D., & Stoyva, J. (Eds.) *Biofeedback and self-control, 1970.* Chicago: Aldine-Atherton, 1971.

Harlow, H. F., Thompson, R. F., & McGaugh, J. L. *Psychology.* San Francisco: Albion, 1971.

Hebb, D. O. *A textbook of psychology.* Philadelphia: Saunders, 1966.

Teitelbaum, P. *Physiological psychology.* Englewood Cliffs, N.J.: Prentice-Hall, 1967.

Thompson, R. F. *Foundations of physiological psychology.* New York: Harper & Row, 1967.

3
PERCEPTION

Have you ever noticed that the moon looks larger when it is near the horizon than when it is directly overhead? Yet the moon does not change size as it rises and falls. Our senses give us different information about the same object at different times. Why?

In contrast, how is it that some objects look the *same* to us regardless of how far away they are, or how much light illuminates them, or the angle or orientation from which we look at them? For example, doorway openings are usually physically rectangular and we usually perceive them that way. Our perception of rectangularity is not affected by the angle from which we view the doorway, despite the fact that the shape projected to the eye will be that of a trapezoid for all viewing orientations except the rare circumstance when we stand exactly in front of the doorway with our eyes equidistant from each of its sides. In fact, a painter must draw the doorway in the shape of a trapezoid if he wants us to perceive it as a rectangle. How is it that our visual-perception system takes input in the shape of a trapezoid and produces output, a perception, of a rectangle?

These are questions of perception. They represent the kind of problems psychologists must be able to solve if we are to understand how people take in and interpret information about the environment around them. These are not easy questions to answer. On occasion, as in our examples, the issues may seem on the surface to be contradictory. In the moon illusion, our perception is "fooled" by an object that remains constant. For doorways, which cast different images on the eye as we view them from different angles, our system is not fooled at all—they always look rectangular. But difficult questions are all the more challenging. We hope you will find the search for answers stimulating and interesting.

What Is Perception?

It is obvious that if you are going to behave in this world, you must know something about what is in it. Knowing the world begins with our sensory systems: vision, hearing, taste, touch, and smell. Knowing implies being able to sense the stimuli that make up our environment and to perceive meaning or information in these stimuli. Thus, sensing and perceiving play a crucial role in behavior. To the extent that your senses function abnormally (for example, if you are partially blind or deaf) or to the extent that you misperceive the world, your behavior will be different from the behavior of someone who has complete command of his senses.

The process by which we perceive the external world is one of the most fascinating and mysterious aspects of human behavior. When we talk about gathering information about something, such as the moon or doorways, we often seem to be talking as if the eye, or some other sensory receptor, "takes a picture" of the world and then passes it on to the brain to be interpreted. You might, therefore, expect a chapter on perception to cover the physical principles of how the brain receives copies of the physical world from our sense organs. But the topic is not nearly that simple. The eye has several features in common with a camera, but it does not work like a camera; neither does the ear work like a microphone. These analogies, implying a faithful "copying" of the outside world by our own sensory system, can be very misleading. An examination of the eye itself will show how poor a facsimile of the outside world is actually registered in this sensory receptor.

Furthermore, perception includes not only the registration of information but also its interpretation. The terms *sensing* or *sensation* are sometimes used to refer to the initial registration process, while *perception* is frequently reserved for the interpretation. Because the point at which sensation stops and perception begins is often difficult to determine, we will use the word *perception* in a general sense to refer to both processes. We receive information about the external world through the sensory receptors. But with our own knowledge, skills, and motivations, we use that information and construct from it meaningfulness about the world. This is very different from merely registering a faithful copy of the world. This interplay between the information in a stimulus and the construction of a perception is the primary concern of the present chapter. To understand this interplay is to understand perception.

Visual Perception as a Model

This chapter is largely about visual perception. For the normal person, vision is probably the most important and most completely used sensory system. Nearly all of our spatial information about the world comes to us via our eyes. Most of the principles of perception can be illustrated by the study of vision. For these reasons, we will use visual perception as a model for understanding the perception process. The other perceptual systems—those of hearing, taste, smell, and touch—will be briefly discussed to show how the general principles of perception apply to them.

An Analysis of Vision

Characteristics of the Stimulus

A brief introduction to the early stages of visual information processing is essential. *Light* is the name given to that portion of the electromagnetic spectrum of radiation that can affect the visual receptors (see Figure 3–7). Light has been thought of by physicists as having a dual nature. First, it is seen as bundles or packets of energies, called *photons*. Second, light is conceived of as *waves*, which are described by their wavelengths. Both of these characteristics are useful for the study of visual perception; we will need to consider the *intensity* (number of photons) of the light and the *composition* of the light (its wavelengths) when we examine color perception later in this chapter.

One of the simplest devices for measuring the intensity of light is the photographer's light meter, which transforms the physical light energy into a measurable electrical current. The eye is capable of responding to an enormous range of intensity, and the sensation received causes a variation in apparent brightness. Note that intensity refers to the physical characteristics of the stimulus—what would be measured by physical instruments. We use the term *brightness* to refer to the appearance of light. Hence, normally an intense light will look brighter than a less intense one. But there are some reasons why this relationship does not always hold, so it is important to distinguish between the physical input (intensity) and the perceived (psychological) result (brightness).

Sources of Stimulation

Visible electromagnetic energy is emitted from a light source such as the sun or a light bulb, but most of the light entering the eye is reflected from the surfaces of objects. The intensity and wavelength of this reflected light is determined both by the nature of the source and by the reflecting surface. The brightness of an object (whether it looks white, gray, or black) will depend *both* on how much light falls on it from a source and on the percentage of that light that the object reflects to the eye of the perceiver. Light objects are those that reflect virtually all of the light that illuminates them. Dark objects absorb most of the light, thereby reflecting little; thus, the eye gets a low-intensity

**Figure 3–1
The optic array**

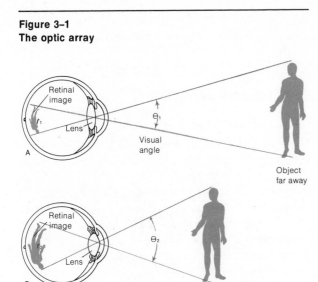

Two examples of optic arrays from objects with their retinal images. Only lines from the extremities of the objects are illustrated. In A the object is far away, so the visual angle is small with an accompanyingly small image projected on the retina. Notice that the lens inverts the image. In B the object is closer, so there is a larger visual angle and a larger retinal image. To provide a sharp focus on the retina the lens has to change its curvature, a process called *accommodation,* so that it is thicker for near objects and thinner for distant ones.

light from them and sees them as dark. Similarly, the colored appearance of a surface is determined by the particular wavelengths of light that fall upon it and by the ones that it reflects. A "blue" object appears blue because it reflects predominantly short (blue) wavelengths, absorbing any long wavelengths that happen to fall on it. Because many light sources emit the full range of visible wavelengths, the colored appearance of surfaces depends mostly on the reflecting qualities of the surfaces themselves.

If all surfaces reflected light of the same intensity and wavelength, we would see a homogeneous world, unbroken by contours or gradients. Most surfaces are uneven, however, so that the reflected light reaching the eye is patterned and varies in intensity and wavelength. The border between areas reflecting light of different intensity or wavelength is called a *contour.* Contours provide the variation in light coming to the eye that is used to perceive objects.

A pattern of energy reflected from the surface of

an object is called the *optic array.* This pattern can be illustrated by drawing lines or rays from every point on the surface of an object to the eye, as shown in Figure 3–1. A cross-section of the array will provide a pattern of intensities and wavelengths coming to the eye from the object.

The Eye

The organ that receives the pattern of light energy from a surface is the eye. The optic array passes through both the outer transparent coating over the front of the eye, called the *cornea,* and the transparent tissues of the *lens.* Both of these are curved and therefore bend and focus the light rays onto the photosensitive portion of the visual system, the *retina* (see Figure 3–2). To provide a sharp focus for the retina, the eye must adjust to changes in the distance between it and the object it sees. The cornea is fixed in shape and therefore cannot adjust to these changes in distance. This necessary adjusting is done by the lens, which varies in shape, thickening for near objects and thinning for distant ones. The process of changing lens shape is called *accommodation,* and is carried out by expansion or contraction of the ciliary muscles. (In cameras, the adjustment is made in a different way. Rather than changing the shape of the lens—difficult to do because it is made of glass—you change the distance from the lens to the photosensitive surface of the film. This is what happens when you change the focus control on your camera.) Two other important parts of the eye are the *iris,* the colored portion of the eye, and the *pupil,* the opening through which light passes to the retina. The iris is a muscular diaphragm that regulates the size of the pupil to adjust the amount of light entering the eye. The chambers behind the cornea and the large central portion of the eye are filled with clear fluids that help to maintain the shape of the eyeball and provide a medium for the collection of waste products.

Embedded in the retina of each eye are over 120 million photoreceptor cells. There are two types, labeled by their shape as either *rods* or *cones.* The rod receptors are found throughout the retina except in the small central region, called the *fovea.* They are extremely sensitive to light energy, though not equally sensitive to all wavelengths. The rods are especially useful in detecting small amounts of light energy, an ability that permits night vision. If you have ever tried to see a very dim star at night, you may have noticed that it is easier if you look slightly to one side of the star. This avoids focusing the image of the star on the fovea, which, because it has

Figure 3–2
The eye

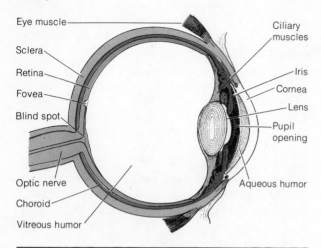

Figure 3–3
An enlargement of a section of the retina showing photoreceptor connections

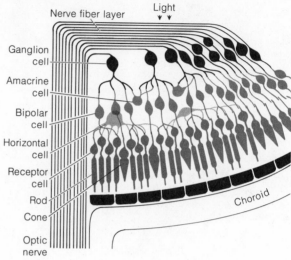

The rod and cone receptor cells are linked with the cerebral cortex by an intricate chain of neural interconnections.

no rods, is not very sensitive to small amounts of energy.

The cones are located primarily in the fovea, with decreasing numbers found further out in the retina. There are about 6 to 7 million cones altogether in each eye, and the cone photoreceptors require relatively large amounts of energy before they will be stimulated to respond. The cones are specialized to respond selectively to wavelengths. Because they respond differentially to light waves of different lengths, the cones give us the experience of color.

The Eye and the Brain

A complex series of connections between the photoreceptor cells and the brain allows the visual image or message recorded on the retina to be carried to the visual projection areas in the occipital lobes of the cerebral cortex. Figure 3–3 gives an example of the complexity of the neural interconnections between the receptor cells in the retina and the cerebral cortex. Each rod and cone is connected to one or more *bipolar* cells, which are in turn connected to one or more *ganglion* cells; furthermore, the bipolar and ganglion cells are interconnected by amacrine and horizontal cells. The axons of the ganglion cells form the optic nerve fibers, which communicate with the cerebral cortex through a relay station in the thalamus. As you can see in Figure 3–3, the rods undergo much more interconnection between the retina and the cerebral cortex than do the cones; more than 100 rods can connect to a single bipolar cell, which in turn may connect to a number of ganglion cells.

By contrast, the cones, located primarily in the fovea, undergo much less interconnection and are more densely packed together than the rods. This means that the ability to see fine detail, called *visual acuity,* is greater for cones than for rods and therefore is best in the fovea. The reason for this is as follows. Being able to distinguish one object or pattern from another depends on getting two (or more) different messages to the brain. Because of their density and directness of connection, cones (and therefore the fovea) are better able to communicate with the brain in these distinctions than the rods (or periphery of the eye).

What happens when light stimulates a photoreceptor? The process is not yet fully understood. In each photoreceptor there are several million molecules of a chemical known as a photopigment. When a photon of light hits one of these molecules, it is absorbed by it. The absorption produces a neurochemical change in the receptor, which results in a change in electrical potential of the output of the receptor. The greater this potential (that is, the more molecules in the receptor that absorb photons), the greater the likelihood that the bipolar cell or cells connected to the receptor will become active. This process is the first stage of visual perception.

Sensitivity to Light Intensity

How dim can a light be and still be seen? How fine can a line be and still be noticed? These questions are often of great practical significance, and to provide answers for them we need to know certain facts about the functioning of the visual system. Very careful measurements under *ideal* conditions have shown that a single rod receptor is capable of responding to the smallest unit of energy, a single photon of light. This is equivalent to detecting the presence of a lighted match on a dark night at a distance of nearly a million miles. The visual receptor is the most sensitive measuring instrument of its kind, far more sensitive than anything people have been able to build.

Of course, we do not see that well. Ideal conditions do not normally exist. First, even in an absolutely dark room where there is no visible energy, there is a substantial amount of spontaneous neural activity in the visual system. The cortex is continually being bombarded with nerve impulses. Thus, although a single photon might excite a single receptor, that excitation would surely be lost in all the "noise" of the system. Further, although a single photon can stimulate a receptor, it may take hundreds of photons entering the eye to guarantee that one will reach a receptor and excite it. Many of the photons are lost by reflection off the surface of the cornea, many are absorbed by the fluids and substances through which the light has to pass, and many are scattered all over the inside of the eye by errors of refraction in the lens. Finally, the rods are at their maximum level of sensitivity only if they have been in total darkness for at least half an hour prior to the stimulation, insuring a state of dark adaptation. These sensitivity changes involved in adaptation require further discussion.

Light and Dark Adaptation

Nearly everyone is familiar with what happens upon entering a movie theater from a bright street. At first it is difficult to see anything. After a short time you can see the screen, then gradually other relatively intense objects, and finally some fine details around you. This improvement in sensitivity to light as you sit in the dark is called *dark adaptation*. Roughly the reverse happens when you leave the dark theater and go into the light. Your eyes are overly sensitive relative to the high levels of illumination on the street. Your pupils will automatically contract to cut down the amount of light entering your eyes, but when this contraction is insufficient you may have to squint or even shut your eyes for a few seconds. Unlike dark adaptation, which takes about 30 minutes, *light adaptation* takes place relatively quickly, so that you can stop squinting usually in less than a minute.

Why should the visual system have to adjust its sensitivity in this way? Why can't we walk off an intensely lit street into a dark theater and be able to see immediately? The eye can respond to an extremely wide range of intensities, a ratio of about 10,000,000,000,000 (10 trillion or 10^{13}) to 1, from the most intense to the dimmest. But at *any one moment* the eye cannot be sensitive to the entire range; it can only respond to a fairly narrow range of perhaps 100 to 1. The eye adjusts to the prevailing light and you are sensitive to light levels within a limited range around that. If you go from a well-lighted room into darkness, the eye will have to readjust its sensitivity to a lower range. This is the process called dark adaptation, and it involves an *increase* in sensitivity of the eye. If you go from an inside room into intense sunlight, the eye again must adjust, in this case *reducing* its sensitivity so that it can comfortably operate at the higher light levels. This process is called *light adaptation,* or a *decrease* in sensitivity. It is easier to lose sensitivity than to gain it, apparently, which is why dark adaptation takes so much longer than light adaptation.

The mechanism by which dark adaptation and light adaptation occur involves two things: (1) changes in the photopigment molecules of each photoreceptor and (2) the transmission of excitation between the neural cells in the retina. The change in the photopigment is probably more important for the slower dark adaptation, while the neural transmission is more important for the faster light adaptation. We know much more about the changes in photopigmentation. When a photon is absorbed by a photopigment molecule, the molecule bleaches in color so that it cannot absorb another photon right away. It takes time to regenerate the photopigment, and it is this time that determines sensitivity loss. If the eye has been in high light levels, a substantial percentage of the photopigments will be bleached at any one time. New ones are being bleached as bleached ones are recovering the ability to absorb photons. The percentage bleached will determine the overall sensitivity. If the light levels are substantially reduced, fewer photopigment molecules will absorb photons and thus a smaller percentage of them will bleach. Therefore, sensitivity will increase.

Figure 3–4
Dark adaptation

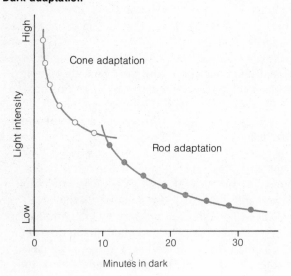

Cone adaptation

Rod adaptation

Dark adaptation is measured in terms of the lowest intensity of light that can be seen at a given time. As time in the dark passes, the lowest perceivable level decreases. A laboratory test shows that the process of dark adaptation takes a total of about 30 minutes. Adaptation of the cones produces an increase in sensitivity (shown by a drop in the curve) during the first 10 minutes. Subsequent sensitivity changes are due to adaptation of the rods.

Fire-Engine Yellow

Time—It may well be difficult to picture a black and white Dalmatian perched atop a screaming fire engine of bright lime yellow, but that peculiar color combination is beginning to appear in fire departments round the nation. Thanks to extensive research by such men as Dr. Stephen Solomon, an optometrist and a member of the Port Jervis, N.Y., volunteer fire department, more and more fire chiefs have been made aware of a stark physiological fact: people are red-blind at night. Says Dr. Solomon, who has published a number of articles on color research: "The color red is one of the least visible colors and rates next to black for getting attention."

Fire chiefs have seen the consequences of this principle. Chief Bernie Koeppen of Wheeling, Ill., has changed to lime yellow, even for the department's ambulance. "In accident after accident involving red wagons," he notes, "all you hear is, 'I didn't see it. I didn't see it.'" Adds Chief Ed Underwood of St. Charles, Mo.: "The majority of fire fighters killed or wounded catch it on their way to fires. Red is dead. Lime yellow is the coming color."

Fire engines have been red for so long (for no visible reason) that the switchover may create problems. Ted Haberman, manager of Pueblo West, Colo., points out that automobile drivers are accustomed to red as the danger color, and that since many Americans ride in air-conditioned cars with the windows rolled up, they may not hear the siren from approaching, unfamiliar lime yellow wagons. Simple tradition may also militate against a wholesale switch from red. But as Dr. Solomon accurately observes: "Firemen have one tradition that is stronger, and that is to stay alive."

This story illustrates a case in which not being able to see red in the dark is not helpful and may be dangerous.

The length of time needed for dark adaptation has been measured by determining how intense a small test spot must be in order to be detected after the eye has spent a period of time in darkness. As expected, the test spot can be made dimmer and dimmer and still be detected the longer the eye remains in the dark. But the change in sensitivity is not smooth (see Figure 3–4). There is a rapid initial increase in sensitivity due to the dark adaptation of the cones and a later, more gradual, increase due to the adaptation of the rods, which are sensitive to much smaller amounts of energy. It was evidence of the two parts of the sensitivity sequence that convinced visual scientists there must be two kinds of receptors in the retina, rods and cones, even before they found them anatomically.

Our knowledge about light and dark adaptation can be used to help persons who have to switch back and forth between the light and the dark, for example, a soldier on night patrol who occasionally has to read his map under bright light. The soldier can light-adapt to the flashlight to read the map quite quickly, but then will not be able to see the path for a number of minutes after he turns the light out. This problem was solved during World War II by using the knowledge that the rod photoreceptors are not very sensitive to long-wavelength light, which appears as red. If the soldier wears red goggles when the light is turned on the rod receptors will not undergo light adaptation and hence will not lose sensitivity. Thus, when the lights are turned off again his rods will still be at a high sensitivity level and he will be able to see the path. This principle is also useful to people who must go in and out of a photographic darkroom; if you wear red goggles in the light, you can see more quickly when you return to the dark.

Convex lenses are in order for "Mom." The lens in her eyes cannot sharply focus the visual image on her retina and so additional lenses are necessary for her to see close objects.

Pattern Acuity

Visual acuity refers to the perceiver's ability to notice fine detail in a patterned stimulus. How small can the print on the page be and still be read? How far away can one read which direction the arrow is pointing on a curve-warning road sign? How large would a satellite orbiting the earth 100 miles away have to be in order to be seen with the naked eye? These are all questions concerning the minimum size of detail that can be resolved.

The fovea, with its extremely high density of cone receptors, is specialized for perception of small detail, that is, high acuity. The convergent movement of the two eyes will normally bring the center of the optic array to focus on the fovea of each eye. Thus, when you fixate on an object, you are using the fovea and will see the finest possible detail. Because the cones are not very sensitive to low energy, acuity will be rather poor in low illumination. Thus we generally are pretty poor at reading or resolving small details at night or under poor lighting conditions.

As light intensity increases, visual acuity increases. Figure 3–5 shows this function. Notice that this function, like the one for dark adaptation, has two components, one for the small improvement in acuity produced by the rods and another, much larger, one for the improvement in the cones. The point here is obvious: If you need to notice very fine details in a visual display, make sure there is a lot of light.

Another major determinant of acuity is the *optical resolving power* of the eye. This is determined by the ability of the lens to focus the optic array sharply on the retina and not in front of or behind it,

conditions that would produce a blurred retinal image. When the lens fails to focus accurately, one can correct it with an additional lens placed in front of the eye—the familiar eyeglasses that 70 percent of the population wear or need.

Of course, different types of lenses are necessary to correct different visual abnormalities. Concave lenses, thin at the center and thicker on the periphery, are used by those who are nearsighted and can see only close objects with the naked eye. Convex lenses, thick at the center and thin on the periphery, are used to correct farsightedness, which makes close-up viewing difficult. Astigmatism is a third correctable defect and requires a lens individually tailored to match distortions produced by a cornea that is not perfectly spherical.

The standard clinical tests for glasses are acuity tests. Figure 3–6 shows some of the more familiar

Figure 3–5
Visual acuity as a function of light intensity

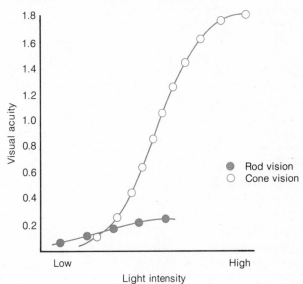

Figure 3–6
Vision tests

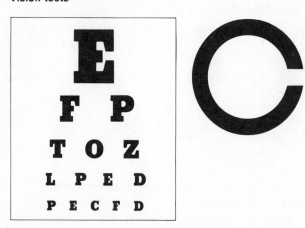

Above are two patterns commonly used for clinical tests of visual acuity. The Snellen letters (on the left) use lines and spaces that become progressively smaller as one reads down the chart. The Landolt C pattern (on the right) requires the viewer to locate the position of the gap—up, down, right, or left. The viewing chart consists of a series of C patterns of decreasing gap size. This test is somewhat more sensitive than the Snellen test, because the perceiver might be able to name a Snellen letter correctly even if he saw only part of it.

test patterns used clinically to diagnose defects of visual acuity. Tests have determined the size of print that the average person can read on the Snellen chart (see Figure 3–6) from a distance of 20 feet. If you can, at 20 feet, read the line on the chart with that size of print, but none smaller, your acuity is 20/20, which is normal. If you can read a line of finer print, which a normal person would have to stand at 15 feet to see, then your acuity is 20/15, or better than normal. Likewise, 20/30 visual acuity means that you have to stand at 20 feet to see what a normal person would see at 30 feet—that is, your acuity is below normal.

What is the minimum size of detail that can be resolved, if we assume the focus on the retina is as good as possible? Experiments have determined that under ideal conditions a person with normal vision can detect a fine line whose width is 1/2 second of arc, or 1/50 the diameter of a cone. This is equivalent to detecting a 1/4-inch black wire against a bright sky from more than a mile away. The human eye, then, is remarkably sensitive to detail under optimal conditions.

The eye depends primarily on brightness discriminations for its acuity. A stimulus like a black wire will cast a "shadow" on the retina. That is, there will be a line of cones that are not being stimulated by as much light as the cones on either side of the shadow, meaning that the cones will be differentially activated. Detection of this difference in stimulation would indicate the presence of a stimulus. Experiments have shown that a black wire will be detected if the line of cones in the shadow is receiving *only 1 percent* less light than the cones surrounding the shadow. The ability of the visual system to detect these very small differences in stimulation by light is responsible for our remarkable acuity.

Color Perception

In about 1600, Sir Isaac Newton discovered that a narrow slit of intense sunlight is somehow separated into a rainbow of colors when it passes through a prism. A prism refracts or bends the light falling upon it in such a way that short wavelengths are bent more than long ones. The color, or more correctly, the *hue* that we see is a function of the wavelength of light. Note that light itself is that band or range of electromagnetic radiation to which the eye is sensitive (see color insert, Plate 1). Wavelengths of electromagnetic radiation are measured in nanometers; one nanometer equals one thousandth of one millionth of a meter, or 1/1,000,000,000 meter. The longest visible wavelengths appear to us as red and the shortest as blue. Other hues are produced by intermediate wavelengths.

Early Theories

One early theory of color perception assumed that the eye contains many different receptors, each tuned to a different wavelength. Such a theory is too simple and is inconsistent with the facts. For one thing, people can discriminate a quarter of a million distinct hues. Thus, according to the theory, the eye must consist of a quarter of a million different types of receptors. Although there are a number of different receptor cells in the eye, there are nowhere near 250,000 different types. Furthermore, there are some hues that cannot be produced by a single wavelength, but result only from a *mixture* of wavelengths. Purple is an example of such a color. If receptors are tuned to single wavelengths, how can we perceive purple?

A far more adequate explanation of color perception was suggested early in the nineteenth century. This theory is based on the facts of colored light mixing. We have already seen that purple is a sensation derived only from the mixture of two (or possibly more) wavelengths. A general phenomenon is involved in this process. If you mix any two (or more) wavelengths, you get a new hue sensation, not the separate original hues. The mixture is so good, in fact, that you will not be able to tell with the naked eye what hues (wavelengths) are being mixed. If the two mixed wavelengths are not too far apart, the resulting sensation is an intermediate hue (see Plate 4). For example, if you mix wavelengths for red and orange, the resulting sensation will be yellow.

To carry this development one step further, if you take three wavelengths, properly chosen to represent the full color spectrum, and mix them in proper proportions, you will be able to produce any and all other hues that the eye can see. In other words, all color sensations can be created from just three different wavelengths of light. It was this discovery around 1800 that led to a new theory of color perception. Instead of thousands of different color receptors, each sensitive to a different wavelength, perhaps the eye contains only three. If only three wavelengths are needed to produce all color sensations, then perhaps the eye needs only three receptors to perceive any hue. If each of the three receptors was tuned to one of three basic wavelengths, the stimulation of each in proper proportions could result in any or all possible color perceptions.

Color Coding

The idea that only three receptors are needed to distinguish colors is *approximately* but not *precisely* correct. We have now discovered that there are three *types* of cones, each type maximally sensitive to a different range of wavelengths, one in the blue region, another in the green region, and a third toward the longer reddish wavelengths. The outputs of the three types of cones are combined in the brain and the resulting perception is just what we would expect from the facts of colored light mixing. Further experimentation, however, has added the following scientific elaboration: We *do not* simply add together the outputs of the three types of cones; they work in opposition to one another, and the combined signal, which we can call the *color code,* is forwarded to the brain.

To understand this, consider another facet of color perception: *color weakness.* Color weakness is the inability of some people to discriminate all the wavelengths from one another. The most common form of color weakness is red-green color blindness, in which a person sees both colors as gray and thus cannot distinguish between them. This effect seems to be due to the absence of cones sensitive to the medium and long wavelengths. According to the facts of color mixing, however, hues intermediate between red and green, such as yellow, should also be lost, because they are the result of mixtures of these two primary colors. But persons who are ''color-blind'' to red and green usually have no difficulty in seeing yellow. Therefore, it appears that such a color-blind person is not deficient in red and green cones, but rather does not *combine* the outputs of these cones in the normal way. It seems that for normal perceivers, the outputs from the three types of cones are connected to form two pairs of opposites, yellow-blue and red-green. It is the combined signals of these *opposites* that are sent to the cerebral cortex, not the separate activities of the three types of cones. There are still many unanswered questions about how the combined signal from the cone pairings is produced and how it is processed by the brain.

Detection of Visual Features

We have now considered some of the basic properties of the visual system and can begin to turn to how this system is used to perceive objects in the everyday world around us. We do not see patches of color or intensities of contours. We see things, objects, people in meaningful, organized perceptions. Our story has to start first with the basic representations in the brain of the visual features extracted from the information stimulating the retina. Then we must look at how these features are organized and constructed to be meaningful to us.

With the discovery of the numerous divergent and convergent interconnections between receptors and neurons in the retina and those in the brain (see Figure 3–3), any kind of straightforward *copy theory* of vision had to be discarded. But in some way these interconnections do make possible the transmission to the brain of some very specific information about the features of external objects. In fact, the visual system is probably far more efficient and precise than even a copy theory would predict. How do we know?

Visual Receptive Fields

In order to explore the interrelationships of the eye and the brain, experimenters have used the microelectrode recording technique (see Chapter 2). D. H. Hubel and T. N. Wiesel, who did the pioneer studies in this area, hoped to discover the stimulus

Figure 3–7
Mapping the visual field

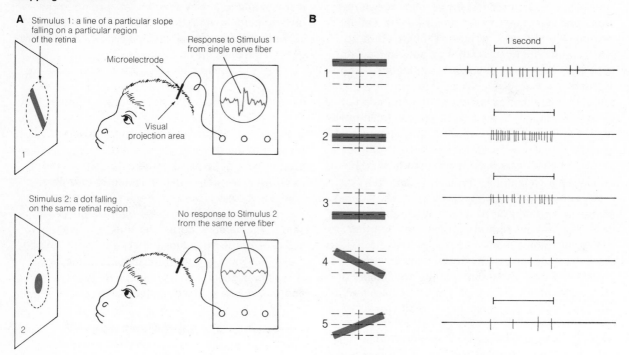

Mapping the visual field with a microelectrode implanted in the cortex—the Hubel and Wiesel technique. Panel A shows that single cortical cells are sensitive to stimuli of a particular type and from a particular area of the retina. In this case, only the slanted bar, and not the dot, elicits a cortical response. The responses of a single cortical cell to five different bar stimuli are shown in panel B. Note that the cell responds mainly to the horizontal bar and hardly responds at all to the slanted bars. Note too that the cell is also somewhat sensitive to location—it fires maximally when the horizontal bar is in the center of the field and responds less when the bar is higher or lower in the visual field. The bar was present for 1 second, indicated by the line above each of the five records.

that is *necessary and sufficient* to activate any particular cell in the area of the cortex where information from the retina is received. There are, of course, millions of such cells, and Hubel and Wiesel have never been able to sample more than 100 from any particular animal. Important generalizations can be made, however, even from these small samples.

The procedure Hubel and Wiesel followed is called *mapping* the visual receptive field of a neuron in the brain (see Figure 3–7). The receptive field for any given cell is defined as the set of receptors (rods and/or cones) that feed into it. A microelectrode is implanted in a single neuron in the visual projection area of the cortex of an experimental animal. Changes in the electrical activity in the electrode will indicate changes in the rate of firings of the cortical cell. The animal is then shown a wide range of stimuli, each over all parts of the retina, until one of

them produces a change in the cell's rate of firing. Now the experimenter has located the receptive field for that cell and can map the field by monitoring the cell's responses as he changes the location and orientation of the stimulus. If, for example, the stimulus to which the cell responds is a horizontal bar, as in Figure 3–7, the experimenter can map the receptive field by varying the position of the bar and recording the increase or decrease in the cell's firing that results from such changes in the stimulus. By trial and error with various stimuli, an experimenter can locate and map the receptive field of any cortical cell, and determine exactly what stimulus pattern will excite that particular cell.

Hubel and Wiesel's experiments led to two principal conclusions. First, individual cortical cells are sensitive to optic arrays falling over an *area* of the retina and not simply to single retinal receptors.

These areas are called *receptive fields.* A particular cortical cell will have a corresponding receptive field on the retinal surface. Receptive fields vary in size from less than a degree (smaller than the half-moon on your thumbnail at arm's length) to over 10 degrees. Receptive fields overlap so that the same retinal receptor may be a member of many receptive fields.

Second, and far more important, there is great specificity about the kind of optic array falling on a receptive field that will excite its corresponding cortical cell. Some receptive fields will produce a response in the cortex only from a narrow line. Others require that the line be at 45 degrees orientation (relative to the head); a line at 30 degrees or 60 degrees produces little or no response. Still others require that the line be at 90 degrees and moving horizontally across the receptive field. Finally, some cells have been discovered that respond only to a particular velocity of movement.

Visual Features and Their Organization

The discovery of visual receptive fields implies that relatively complex stimulus patterns are coded into a single *visual feature,* a discriminable and recognizable aspect of a visual stimulus. This feature is represented by the activation of a single cell in the brain. The stimulus pattern may affect millions of receptors in the retina, but the brain needs only one cell to represent it. This coding system, where one cortical cell represents all the receptors in a given visual field, is much more economical than a one-to-one correspondence of cortical cells and visual receptors would be.

The number of visual features that are detected in this manner is probably quite small. It is known, for example, that the presence of a contour or a line and its width, orientation, and velocity are represented by single cortical cells. There is also evidence that angles can be represented by simple cortical cells, and it is possible that even slightly more complex features are coded in this way as well. But these few known features are still a long way from "looking like" anything in the real world. More research is required before we can be sure of the relationship between visual information in the eye and in the brain.

Seeing what things really look like involves the *construction* of meaningful patterns from simple physical features. It is the perceiver's imposition of organization on physical stimulation that is at the core of the science of perception. For example, given only three lines of a certain orientation, we perceive a triangle. Perception of a meaningful pattern, then, can occur with just a short list of visual features. But to understand how we organize the visual features we see into a meaningful pattern, such as the triangle, we must consider the process in more detail.

Perception of Objects

One of the greatest controversies in psychology, extending back to antiquity and still pervading most theorizing today, concerns the degree to which prior familiarity with or knowledge of the visual world is required in order to see the objects in that world. Just what is the role of available *knowledge* in perceiving the real world? This argument is not yet resolved, either in perception or most of the other areas of psychology where it has left its mark. But it has helped pose some problems and questions in ways that have led directly to new discoveries.

At one extreme are those psychologists who argue that the optic array from the stimulus to the eye contains enough information for the viewer to construct a true and faithful representation of the world. This view stresses a correspondence between the objects in the optic array and the perceptions that arise from them.

The other extreme position argues that the stimulus information is always ambiguous and that therefore perception would also be ambiguous were it not resolved by our knowledge and expectations of what the stimulus *really* looks like. For example, if a hunter is expecting to see deer, he will be prone to misperceive ambiguous stimuli. He might shoot a cow, a scarecrow, or even another hunter, perceiving his victim to be a deer. This view pays relatively little attention to how much information is contained in the stimulus itself (because it is never sufficient) and focuses on tasks in which the perceiver's expectations are uppermost in importance.

Visual Gradients

In general, a three-dimensional world is immediately reduced to a two-dimensional one by the flat receptor surface of the retina. Yet we perceive a visual world of depth, occupied not by lines, planes, and gradients but by objects. It looks as if we have a sorting-out problem of such massive proportions that we would never be able to see. However, people *can* see, that is, interpret visual stimulation meaningfully, and it is the scientist's task to figure out how.

Figure 3–8
Texture gradients

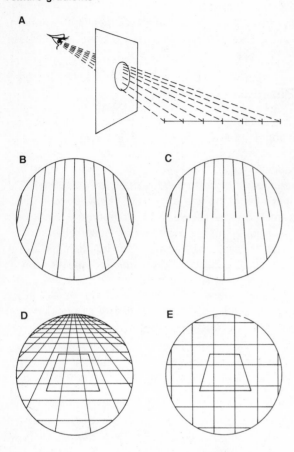

A

B   C

D   E

Some examples of texture gradients. A illustrates the
optic array from a uniformly textured surface, for
example, a tiled floor. Those parts farthest from the eye
subtend a smaller visual angle than those parts close to
the eye. There is, therefore, a texture gradient. This will
be true regardless of the nature of the texture or the
degree of slant. In B the texture is from a surface
stretching away that then rises at an angle. C shows a
discontinuity, where there is a step down to a lower level.
D and E show how the same trapezoidal retinal shape
can arise from two different real shapes, conveyed quite
differently by the texture. In D the actual figure is a
square on a floor stretching away, while in E it is a
trapezoid on a surface equidistant from the perceiver.

Texture.   One of the first steps is to find some way
of grouping together those visual features that arise
from the same or related objects. Take the simple
case of a single object seen in an otherwise empty
visual field; see Figure 3–8A. How can you tell what
is figure (object) and what is background? Are there
any characteristics in the optic array or in the

resulting visual features that would make this
possible to do? There are several. The figure seems
to stand in front of the background as if the
background continues behind the figure but is
partially blocked by it. This differentiation is made
possible in part by the differences in surface texture
between the area of the figure and that of the
background.

James J. Gibson has described the power of
texture gradients alone in organizing the visual field,
as shown in the examples in Figure 3–8 taken from
his work. These examples provide clear pictures of
depth—surfaces and objects organized in
space—even in the absence of contours (sharp
discontinuities of gradients) surrounding the objects
and surfaces. Thus, part of the sorting-out process
appears to rest simply on differences in the texture
of the surfaces.

Contour.   Contour is also very important. The vase
in part A of Figure 3–9, for example, is defined by
its contour as well as the dramatic difference in
color and texture between it and the background.
But the same contour can also define a different
organization, two white faces looking at each other,
as seen on a dark background. You cannot see both
of the "figures" at the same time, though it is
possible to alternate the two perceptions. In B and C
the figure-ground relationship is redrawn to reduce
the ambiguity. In B the vase is in front of the
background, and to see faces is much more difficult.
In C the vase is background, through which more
background is seen, and the two faces are a less
ambiguous figure.

Principles of Organization

Gestalt psychologists proposed a series of laws to
define which of several possible organizations would
prevail in the perception of ambiguous stimuli. They
suggested, for example, that separate elements will
be organized into a whole according to their
proximity to each other or their similarity to each
other. Another law states that a figure with gaps in it
will be filled in to be perceived as a whole.
Sometimes these laws are in conflict, as shown in
Figure 3–10.

The minimum principle.   Although each of the
Gestalt laws or principles has an intuitive logic to it,
early Gestalt psychologists were not successful in
translating them into quantifiable statements that
could be used to predict, ahead of time, the
organization of perception. In recent years, Julian

Figure 3–9
Figure-ground perception

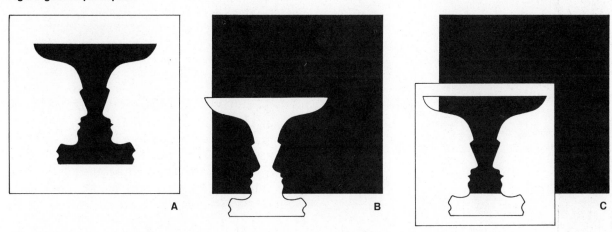

A   B   C

The Rubin vase, a reversible figure, is often used to point out the distinction between *figure* and *ground* in perception. In A the figure-ground relationship is ambiguous. Do the lines mark the edges of the center shaded space, in which case we see a vase, or do they mark the right and left edges of the white space, in which case we see two facing profiles? In the first case, the vase is figure and the surrounding white space is ground. In the second case, the shaded space in the center, which once was seen as figure, is now seen as background for the two faces. In B the ambiguity is reduced to accent the organization of the vase, and in C the profiles are accented.

Hochberg has taken several of these laws and reduced them to a single one, called the *minimum principle.* According to this principle, the organization that is perceived in an ambiguous stimulus is the one that keeps changes, discontinuities, and differences to a minimum. Hence, of two possible organizations we should see the simpler one. Hochberg then specified some physical measures of simplicity. A prediction of which organization would be seen could then be based on the simplicity ratings and tested against what perceivers actually see.

For example, it is possible to see each of the figures presented in Figure 3–11 as two-dimensional or three-dimensional. For each member of each series Hochberg counted the number of continuous lines (c), the number of angles (a), and the number of different angles (d). He then defined the simplicity of a figure as $2c + a + d$. Hochberg predicted that a member of any series will be seen as two-dimensional when the two-dimensional representation is the simpler one by the formula. He then gave each figure to a group of subjects and asked them whether they saw it as two- or three-dimensional. The results were entirely in accord with Hochberg's predictions. While there are undoubtedly other physical dimensions that enter into perception, Hochberg's success in prediction has provided convincing evidence for the hypothesis that *simplicity of organization is a determinant of what will be seen.*

This chapter so far has dealt only with outline drawings of simple figures. As already mentioned, a three-dimensional object would project only a two-dimensional image on the retina; yet most scenes one perceives are in depth, that is, they have three dimensions. Hochberg has tried to show that this minimum principle will also explain how the information in the optic array is used to determine three-dimensional depth perception. Next we will consider informational cues to depth.

Space Perception

Because the optic array is projected on an essentially flat retina, depth cannot be spatially represented. In fact, the optic array presents an ambiguous image on the retina, one that could be perceived as either a two-dimensional or three-dimensional scene. But since we do see in three dimensions, there must be enough informational cues to create a perceptual organization that is in depth. According to Hochberg's minimum principle, depth is seen

**Figure 3–10
Gestalt theory**

xx   xx   xx   xx   xx   xx   xx   xx

Proximity.

x   o   x   o   x   o
x   o   x   o   x   o
x   o   x   o   x   o
x   o   x   o   x   o
x   o   x   o   x   o

Similarity.

Closure.

xoxoxoxoxoxox
xoxoxoxoxoxox
xoxoxoxoxoxox
xoxoxoxoxoxox
xoxoxoxoxoxox

Proximity or similarity?

][ ][ ][ ][ ][ ][ ][

Proximity or closure?

because certain cues make a three-dimensional organization simpler than a two-dimensional one.

Monocular Cues for Depth

Monocular (one-eyed) cues for depth are those derived from information in the optic array that is

**Figure 3–11
The minimum principle**

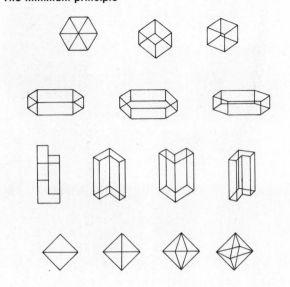

According to the minimum principle, the first member of each series of ambiguous drawings will be perceived as two-dimensional and the others as three-dimensional.

available to either eye alone. They are the cues one would use if one eye was closed. The most effective monocular cues appear to be *interposition* (or overlap), *size perspective, linear perspective, shading* and *aerial perspective,* and *texture gradients* (see examples in Figure 3–12).

To see how the minimum principle of perceptual organization might be applied, consider Figure 3–13. The figure illustrates four monocular depth cues, each of which could have arisen from a two-dimensional or three-dimensional spatial arrangement. In each case, the three-dimensional version seems simpler, more regular, and more familiar. This is especially true when all four appear in the same view. Clearly, the simplest organization is that of a scene stretching away from the perceiver rather than a two-dimensional surface in front of the eye.

Binocular Disparity

Because your two eyes are separated in space, the optic arrays reaching each eye are slightly different. This disparity of retinal image provides a powerful binocular cue for depth. Binocular disparity can be simulated by taking a photograph of a scene from the position of each eye and then viewing the left picture with the left eye and the right picture with the right eye. Although disparity is a powerful cue

Plate 1 The electromagnetic spectrum

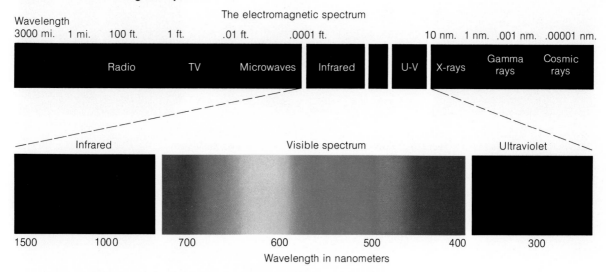

The electromagnetic spectrum

The full spectrum of electromagnetic radiation, of which the human eye can see only the narrow band extending from 400 to 700 nanometers in wavelength. A nanometer (abbreviated nm.) is a very small unit of length equivalent to 1/1,000,000,000 meter (a meter is 39.37 inches).

Plate 2 Interference

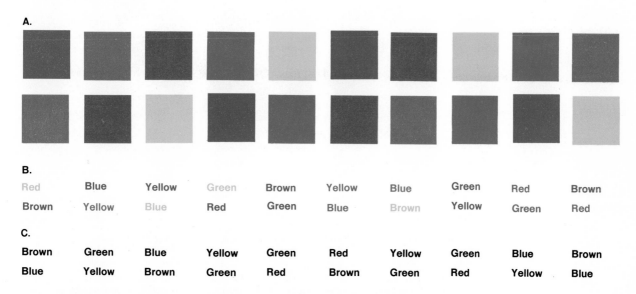

The Stroop Color Naming Test illustrates the effect of interference by irrelevant stimuli on attention. For A, name the color of each patch as rapidly as possible. For B, name the colors of the words, ignoring the meaning of the words. For C, read the color names. Try A, B, and C on your friends, timing each task.

Plate 3 Negative afterimage

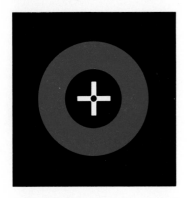  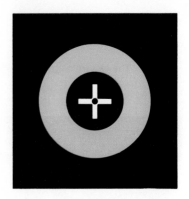

Look steadily for about 20 seconds at the dot inside the blue circle, then transfer your gaze to the dot inside the gray rectangle. Now do the same with the dot inside the yellow circle. What you see is a negative afterimage.

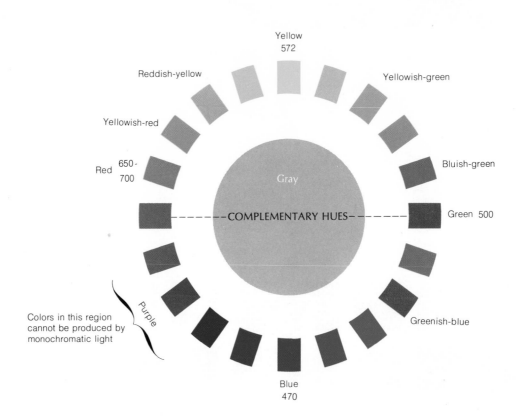

Plate 4 The color circle

The color circle is a device that helps us understand and remember the facts of color and color light mixture. Along the circumference of the circle are the color names and their corresponding wavelengths (in nanometers). Colors that are opposite each other in the circle, such as reddish-yellow and greenish-blue, are called *complements*. When you mix complements, the result is a gray (colorless) appearance. Mixing any two other wavelengths produces an *intermediate* color. Thus, mixing reddish-yellow and green in equal amounts will yield yellow. Yellowish-red plus blue will yield purple, a color that cannot be produced by a single wavelength, that is, by a *monochromatic* light. With three wavelengths, selected at roughly equal distances, such as blue (470 nm.), green (500 nm.), and reddish-yellow (580 nm.), we can produce all color sensations by proper mixing.

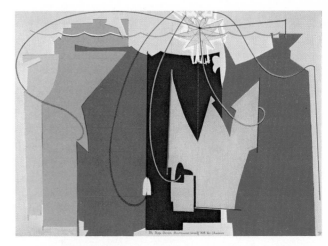

Plate 5 Colorblindness

The painting in the upper left panel appears as it would to a person with normal color vision. If you suffered from red-green blindness, the same picture would be seen as it is in the upper right panel. Similarly, the lower left and lower right panels show how the picture would look to persons with yellow-blue or total color blindness, respectively.

(Man Ray, "The Rope Dancer Accompanies Herself with Her Shadows," 1916. Oil on canvas, 52" x 6' 1⅜". Collection, The Museum of Modern Art, New York. Gift of G. David Thompson.)

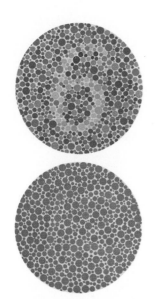

Plate 6 Tests for colorblindness

People with normal vision see a number 6 in the top plate, while those with red-green color blindness do not. Those with normal vision see the number 12 in the bottom plate; those with red-green color blindness may see one number or none. These two illustrations are from a series of 15 color-blindness tests necessary for a complete color recognition examination. (American Optical Corporation, from their AO Pseudo-Isochromatic Color Tests)

Plate 7   Color solid

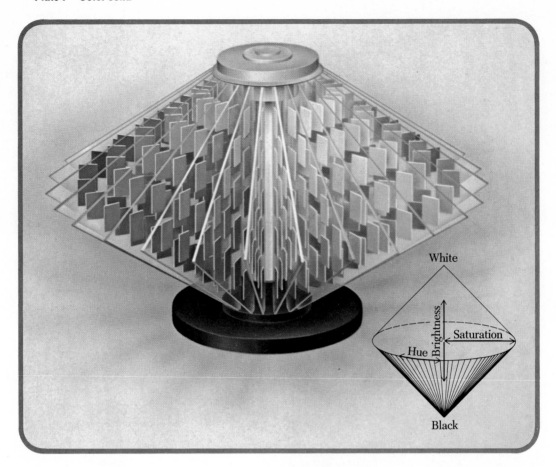

Three dimensions of color sensitivity—hue, brightness, and saturation—can be seen in this color solid. The gradual change in brightness from black to white along the central axis is illustrated by the diagram.

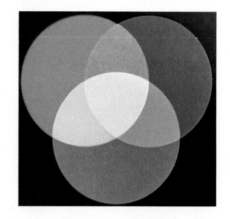

Plate 8   Additive color mixture

If a *light* of a single wavelength is shined onto a white surface, the perceived color will correspond to that wavelength, because the surface reflects only that wavelength to the eye. Now if two lights of different wavelengths are shined on the surface together, the resulting perceived color will be an *additive* mixture. The surface will reflect both wavelengths, and they will add together to produce a color sensation. As is shown in Plate 8, it is possible to produce the complete spectrum of colors by additive mixture if you mix three properly chosen wavelengths in the correct proportions.

Plate 9   Subtractive color mixture

In contrast to mixing lights, when paints are combined the resulting perceived color is produced by subtraction. For example, a yellow paint absorbs (subtracts) primarily non-yellow wavelengths. If you mix a yellow paint with a blue paint (which absorbs primarily non-blue wavelengths), the result is a subtraction which leaves wavelengths between yellow and blue, namely green. Plate 9 illustrates how you can produce a variety of colors by subtractive mixture given three appropriately chosen paints.

and probably contributes greatly to perceptual organization of depth, it is not a necessary cue, because depth can be experienced with only one eye.

Other Cues for Depth

All of the examples given so far have been of optic arrays emanating from stimuli and objects presented to the stationary eye, and this rarely occurs in nature. Our eyes, our heads, and our bodies are in motion with respect to the world around us, and the objects and the world move in relation to us. Each of these movements presents a different optic array to the eye. The succession of arrays of the same scene can be perceived as the same scene undergoing some transformation (such as moving away or to the side) or as an entirely different scene in each view. The minimum principle clearly suggests that perceiving the same scene undergoing a transformation is a far simpler perception, especially if we receive other cues that we are in motion.

Thus, while the optic array reaching the retina at each moment is continuously changing, the minimum principle makes it clear that little ambiguity should result in our perceptions. In fact, there would seem to be no way of fooling a perceiver about what he is seeing in the natural world around him. Perceptual organizations will almost always be true to nature. Only under certain contrived circumstances will perceptual illusions occur.

It is likely that the minimum principle operates as a biological given. Perceptual organizations of figures on grounds and objects in space are constructed from information in the optic array itself. No appeal need be made to our knowledge about what it is we are looking at.

But this does not mean that the perceiver's knowledge and expectations are irrelevant to perceptual organization. In fact, a number of circumstances exist where knowledge and expectation do contribute to perception. Consider, for example, Figure 3–14. The middle letter in each grouping has the same physical properties and so should have the same visual features transmitted to the brain. However, nearly all viewers perceive one as an A and the other as an H because of what they expect to be found in each "word." It thus seems reasonable to assume that an experienced perceiver will form constructions of his visual environment through an *interaction* of visual information and his expectations. This will be especially true when the environment is purposely ambiguous, as in the

Figure 3–12
Monocular depth cues

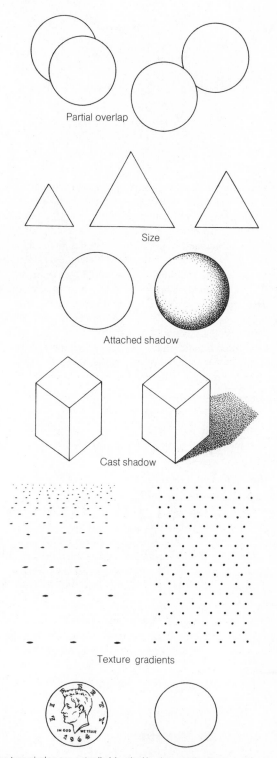

Partial overlap

Size

Attached shadow

Cast shadow

Texture gradients

The two circles are actually identical in size, yet the filled circle may appear both larger and closer as a function of the fact that the space is filled.

Figure 3–13
Depth perception

A

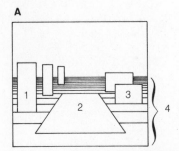

B

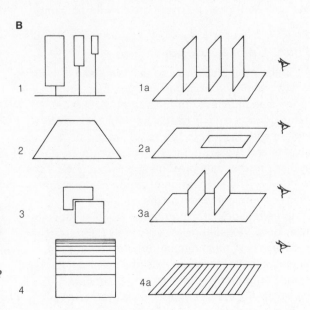

The minimum principle of organization as applied to perception of depth. A is a drawing of a surface that can be seen either as stretching away from the eye (in depth) or as a flat, two-dimensional surface. Parts A1–A4 illustrate monocular depth cues. In A1 the three posts could have been due to B1 or B1a. Which seems simpler? In A2 the shape could be a trapezoid (B2) or a square (B2a). Which seems simpler? In A3, one rectangle could be missing a corner (B3) or be behind the nearer one (B3a). Which seems simpler? In A4 the textured surface could be progressively finer near the top of the picture (B4) or could be stretching away (B4a). Which seems simpler? In each case, organizing the scene in depth permits the objects to be simpler in form; the posts are

all the same size, the shape on the floor is regular, the two rectangles are the same, and the textured floor is uniform. For these reasons, according to the minimum principle, the flat scene is perceived as three-dimensional.

difference between *bat* and *the* in Figure 3–17, or when our expectations are contrary to what we are trying to perceive.

Our discussion of perceptual organization has ranged from constructing figures on grounds to constructing objects in space. The same principles apply to each: The construction made is the simplest one possible given the information contained in the optic array. Our recognition of the richness of that information has been the most important contribution to our understanding of how we organize our perceptions of the external world.

Next we will examine two supposed anomalies of perceptual organization, constancies and illusions. These are situations in which the resultant perception does not, at first glance, seem to be determined solely by the information in the optic array.

Perceptual Constancy

One of the most impressive phenomena of visual experience is perceptual constancy. Most of us are hardly aware of instances in which our perceptual organization remains relatively stable even though

some aspects of the pattern within the optic array undergo great changes. For example, as we mentioned at the outset, doors and windows appear rectangular regardless of the angle from which we observe them, although it is easy to show that the pattern in the optic array should be trapezoidal for all angles except those viewed head-on. This kind of stability is referred to as *shape constancy. Size constancy* refers to the observation that heights of objects do not appear to shrink as we walk away, even though the size of the image on the retina does become smaller. *Brightness constancy* refers to the observation that an object maintains its brightness even when the amount of light reflected from it changes—for instance, coal continues to look black when viewed in intense light. Remember that reflected light intensity is the main physical determinant of brightness. There are a number of other kinds of perceptual constancy, all of which are typified by this apparent discrepancy between the varying physical dimensions in the optic array and the constant perceptual experience. How is it that we can maintain a constant perception of the constant world, even though the overall character of the optic array is undergoing great changes?

**Figure 3–14
Expectation and perception**

BAT TAE

Expectation, or knowledge about the world, affects perceptual organization. The middle letter is perceived as either an A or an H depending on which group of letters it is placed in.

Past Experience

Many explanations have been offered for the constancy phenomenon. One of the most widely held is that the perceiver "knows" what the object should look like, so he adjusts his perception or construction accordingly. Windows are always rectangular and never trapezoidal; consequently a trapezoidal window image on the retina is invariably organized as rectangular. Because we *know* the window is rectangular, even though it is producing a trapezoidal optic array, we see it as rectangular but at an angle. This type of appeal to prior knowledge has failed on a number of grounds, most notably because constancies occur just as easily for totally unfamiliar objects.

Constant Aspects in the Optic Array

J. J. Gibson has presented a more interesting and reasonable explanation than those based on past experience. He argues that the problem has been wrongly stated. We should not be asking how to account for constant perception in the face of changing stimulation. Rather we should be looking for those aspects of the optic array that are constant. Perhaps these are the factors the observer uses in his construction. Gibson has proposed several such constant aspects, the most important being based on texture density and changes in texture.

We have already discussed *texture gradients* as cues used to construct perceptions of objects located in space. The scene in Figure 3–15, for example, generates a clear sense of depth. Each of the objects appears to be about the same size, in spite of the fact that the retinal image of the object in the rear is one-half the size of the one "in front" of it. But if, instead of concentrating on the size of the retinal image of each object, you look at the ratio of the density of the surface texture near each

Four-letter Word Mystery

London Express Service
London—BBC Chairman Lord Hill spent an entire morning listening to a track from the Rolling Stones record "Exile on Main Street."

He was trying to hear a four-letter word. A word which offended clean-up TV campaigner Mrs. Mary Whitehouse when she says she heard it on British Broadcasting Corp.

Following a complaint from Mrs. Whitehouse, Lord Hill listened to the record but couldn't hear the word. In a letter to her later he wrote:

"I have this morning listened with great care to the tracks we have played on Radio. I have listened to them at a fast rate, at a medium rate, at a slow rate.

"Though my hearing is excellent I did not hear any offending four-letter word whatever.

"Could it be that believing offending words to be there, and zealous to discover them, you imagined that you heard what you did not hear?"

What we expect to perceive or are "set" to perceive often influences what we do perceive. Set effects are very prominent in speech perception. The cues in a speech stimulus, along with personal expectations of what the speaker will say, may determine what is heard. Speech has more clues in it than are necessary to help us perceive what is said. The redundant clues serve as insurance against the possibility of misperception. Rock songs lack many of these clues because they are usually not spoken but sung or screamed. As a result, it is often difficult to understand the exact words.

object to the size of the object, you find that the ratios for the two objects *are the same.* Therefore, according to Gibson, the two objects must be the same size. Another way to look at this is to consider how much of the texture is blocked out by each figure. Although the far one is smaller, the texture is also finer, and the number of squares covered is the same. This cue, the ratio of the size of the object to the size of the texture (or other nearby objects), *automatically* takes distance into account and yields a reasonable basis for the perception of size constancy. Hence, while the optic array contains objects of various sizes, they are perceived as identical in size if their true sizes are the same. Organization, for Gibson, is based on these ratios between components in the optic array.

The same type of explanation is used to cover the other constancies. For example, why does coal in a bin continue to look black when moved from dim

If you were a giant and thought everyone else was, too, then the simplest perception in this case would be that the man on the left is a giant who is far away.

light to sunlight? Although coal reflects a relatively small percentage of the light that illuminates it, which is why it looks dark in the first place, the total amount of reflected light will be substantial if the source of illumination is very intense. But coal still seems black. The reason is that the illumination usually also falls on the objects around the coal, such as the bin; in other words, there is always a background that is also reflecting the light. The ratio of the luminance (reflected light) of the coal to the luminance of the background remains constant when the illumination is increased or decreased. Thus, under increased illumination the coal reflects more light, but so does the bin in which it is sitting. The coal continues to look black because it is always so much darker than the objects around it. This can be verified by shining light only on the coal, but letting none of it touch the background. Then the coal will be judged much whiter.

It appears that each of the constancies can be explained by the perceiver's taking into account the constant relations among the optic array and using that information to construct a stable visual world,

Figure 3–15
Size constancy

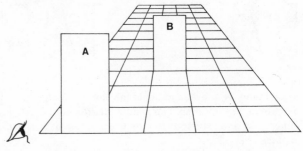

Size constancy is a function of a constant texture gradient ratio. While object B is physically smaller than object A, the two are perceived as equal. The reason, according to Gibson, is that the ratio of object to textured background is the same in both cases.

without the necessity of appealing to his prior knowledge, familiarity with the objects, or his expectations. Of course, he could use these latter sources in his constructions, and in most cases they will complement the information gained from the relationships in the optic array.

Illusions

As we saw in the beginning of this chapter, there are cases in which a normal perceiver can be fooled into making the wrong construction from an optic array. These perceptions are called *illusions* and are not to be confused with hallucinations and delusions, which occur only under abnormal circumstances. The important question that arises is: Can we find some cues or properties in the optic array of the illusory stimulus that lead us to construct a perception that does not correspond to the true stimulus?

We have known for hundreds of years that it is possible to draw two-dimensional pictures in which most perceivers will misperceive one of the attributes. They see it one way even after they take a tape measure and physically measure the line in question. See Figure 3–16 for three of these. Many psychologists have ignored these drawings as being contrived and trivial, because they are pranks of psychologists and not of nature. Even so, they are worth considering for what they can tell us about the way perceivers do construct perceptions of the visual world, even such a strange world as that of two-dimensional line drawings.

**Figure 3–16
Perceptual illusions**

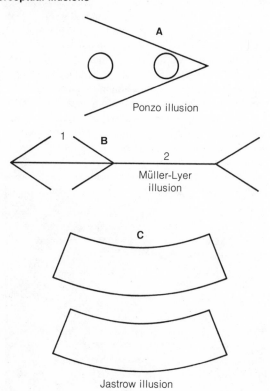

Ponzo illusion

Müller-Lyer illusion

Jastrow illusion

These flat line drawings all give the impression of depth, thus creating the illusion of size differences. In A the two circles are equal in diameter, although the converging lines suggest linear perspective, with the point farther away than the wide end. Thus the circle near the point appears larger. In B, lines 1 and 2 are the same length. The arrows suggest a linear perspective such that line 1 is nearer the observer than line 2 and hence shorter. In C the two sections are equal in size.

However, nature has provided a dramatic visual illusion that almost everyone sees frequently—the moon illusion. Nearly all perceivers judge the moon to be larger at the horizon than overhead, even though its real size and, hence, its visual angle, does not change with elevation. This illusion could occur if the moon is perceived, for some reason, to be more distant, presumably because of the intervening terrain. If the horizon moon looks farther away, yet casts the same size image on the retina as the moon overhead, the perceiver then constructs the horizon moon to be larger.

This explanation of the moon illusion is based on the *perspective theory,* one of the more promising attempts to explain how physically equal stimuli are frequently perceived as unequal. The perspective theory suggests that there are some aspects of the scene that induce a sense of depth, for example, proximity to the horizon in the moon illusion. Thus, if one part of the scene is perceived as being at a different distance from another part of *equal retinal image,* we perceive a difference in size in order to compensate for the equivalence of the images. In other words, we seem to judge depth or distance first and then take this factor into account when perceiving size.

The perspective theory is but one attempt to explain these geometrical illusions, and it is *consistent* with a few of them. We have no good evidence, however, that the theory actually accounts for the way those few cases are misperceived, and some of the illusions seem to have nothing to do with depth information. Some recent attempts have been made to explain these illusions by noting changes that occur in the retinal coding of the intersection of lines. For example, it is possible that an arrowhead is difficult to code precisely at the intersection, so that the shaft area is foreshortened. So far this idea has not been fully verified. Thus, no complete explanation of geometrical illusions has yet been found.

Other Sensory Systems

Vision is a sensory system ideally arranged to provide us with an awareness of things happening at a distance. We have other systems, however, that also play a role in acquiring information about remote environmental objects and events, namely, hearing and the sense of smell. In addition, we are able to sense external objects with which we come into contact through the skin senses. A special form of contact sensitivity is our sense of taste, which operates on objects or liquids in the mouth. Finally, we are equipped with internal receptors that are sensitive to the position and movement of the body as a whole and of various body parts. The system for detecting internal stimulation is by and large less well understood than the other senses. In fact, there is probably more than one such system. At present, however, in the light of inadequate knowledge, we refer to this entire group as the sense of *kinesthesis.*

Hearing

Characteristics of the stimulus.   The physical stimulus for hearing is mechanical vibration in an object, usually transmitted from the object to the ear

Impossible but Perceivable Shapes

Psychologists and artists have been especially ingenious at drawing forms that have impossible relationships among the components. Figure 3–17 illustrates three of these. None of the three drawings could be translated into touchable three-dimensional objects, but their interest resides in how perceivers can be fooled when looking at them as two-dimensional line drawings. Actually, of course, we are not fooled. We see the drawings as

Figure 3–17
Two-dimensional drawings of impossible three-dimensional forms

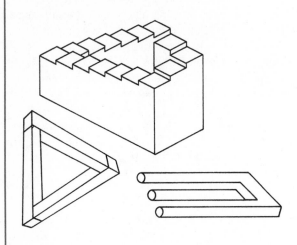

impossible. But it is hard to do so, because if we look at any one place on one of them, the information is quite consistent. It is as if we expect them to be a certain way based on one view, and then when we move our eyes to look at some other part, it is inconsistent with our expectations. Although nobody has fully explained how these are perceived, again we seem to have a case in which our expectations are important in telling us what we will perceive and how to construct it. When these expectations are not met, then we are fooled.

M. C. Escher, Relativity, collection Haags Gemeentemuseum—The Hague.

as rapid, minute changes in air pressure. Changes in air pressure are produced by slight back-and-forth movements of air molecules, in a wavelike motion. If there is no air (atmosphere), as in outer space or in a vacuum, then there is no medium for sound transmission, and consequently there can be no sound.

Sound waves vary along two fundamental physical dimensions, *intensity* and *frequency*. The simplest sound wave can be represented as a smooth, oscillating function. This function traces out the aggregate movement of molecules in the vibrating object or in the conducting medium from a zero or a resting position through a maximum deviation in either direction. In Figure 3–18, you see a tracing of molecular vibration; it moves smoothly from a zero point through a maximum deflection in one direction, back through the zero point to a maximum in the other direction, and then repeats. Repetition continues until the sound stops. The fundamental characteristics of sound are represented in this figure. Maximum deviation from the resting point, the *amplitude* of the wave, is a

measure of sound intensity. The number of complete cycles—zero point through maximum deviation in both directions and back to the zero point—in every second of time is a measure of frequency. *Hertz* is the currently used term for the measure of frequency. The number of Hertz for a sound, formerly called its *cycles per second,* is the number of complete cycles it makes every second.

Psychological attributes of sound.   Intensity and frequency are physical characteristics of objects in motion. When the vibrations coming from these objects fall within a certain range, they can be sensed by the human ear and therefore are heard. These physical characteristics of sound—intensity and frequency—correspond respectively to two psychological attributes of sound—*loudness* and *pitch*. Loudness and pitch are termed *psychological attributes* because they are a product of sound perception, not of the actual physical sound waves.

Loudness is measured in terms of a sound pressure scale relative to the *absolute threshold* for hearing. The absolute threshold for hearing is the

Figure 3-18
Representation of a sound wave

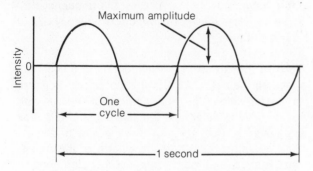

Intensity is measured by amplitude, the maximum
deviation from the zero point. Frequency is measured by
Hertz, the number of cycles completed each second. In
this example, the frequency is 2 Hertz.

Figure 3–19
The decibel scale

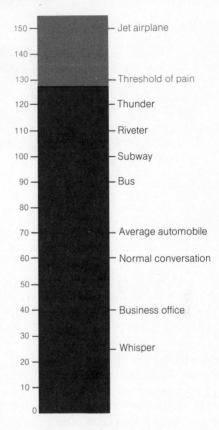

A scale of the loudness of various common sounds in
decibels (dB). The take-off blast of the Saturn V moon
rocket, measured at the launching pad, is approximately
180 dB. For laboratory rats, prolonged exposure to 150 dB
causes death.

lowest intensity level that can be heard by a normal
person in an otherwise absolutely soundproof room.
The scale uses a measure called *decibels*. The
absolute threshold is at zero on the decibel scale.
Normal conversation registers at about 60 decibels.
Figure 3–19 shows the decibel rating for a variety of
other common sounds.

Greater frequencies of vibration produce higher
pitches of sound and lesser frequencies produce
lower pitches. Thus the pitch of a soprano voice is
considerably higher in frequency than the pitch of a
bass voice.

There are individual differences among people in
hearing. Some people have tonal gaps such that
frequencies within a certain range are simply not
heard. Sensitivity to the higher frequencies (and
pitches) tends to degenerate with age. Human
beings with normal hearing, however, can hear
frequencies at some loudness level within the range
of 30–20,000 Hertz. For reference, middle C on a
well-tuned piano is 256 Hertz. Human voices range
up to 5,000 Hertz. We tend to be most sensitive to
the middle range, say 500 to 5,000 Hertz. The
minimum intensity necessary for hearing decreases
from 30 Hertz through the sensitive range of 500 to
5,000 Hertz, then increases again as frequency is
increased to 20,000 Hertz. Sounds can be so intense
that they will produce pain. When a sound is
delivered at sufficient intensity, it begins to cause a
tickling sensation and then pain.

Vibrations of the type represented in Figure 3–21
are called *pure tones*. A pure tone is actually an
idealization. By and large, what we hear are more
complex sounds. These are sounds that are made

up of a combination of two or more pure tones. For
example, different musical instruments, playing the
same fundamental note will differ in the sounds they
reproduce. This is so because each instrument
generates a unique set of *overtones*—tones of
frequency other than the fundamental and usually at
multiples of the fundamental. Overtones, when
combined with the fundamental frequency, give
each sound a characteristic *timbre*. The timbre of
sound is, then, determined by the *complexity* of the
wavelength combination. Timbre is the characteristic
that allows us to distinguish the piano from the
French horn. When many random frequencies are
combined, sounds lose their tonal characteristics,
and become atonal, or noisy. A special kind of
noise, white noise, which has a hissing sound, is the
sound produced by combining all audible
frequencies at roughly the same intensity.

Figure 3–20
The major parts of the ear

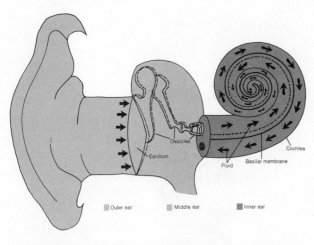

Outer ear   Middle ear   Inner ear

The ear. The human ear consists of three primary parts (see Figure 3–20). The outer ear, the part that we can see, is of little importance to human beings. The middle ear is a transmitter of sound. It begins with the eardrum, a thin membrane that is sufficiently sensitive to vibrate in reaction to oscillations in the air molecules adjacent to it. These vibrations are passed through the middle ear to the inner ear by an intricate interconnection of three small bones, called the ossicles. The inner ear is a fluid-filled cavity. Vibrations in the ossicles in turn set the fluid of the inner ear in motion. The part of the inner ear involved in hearing is the *cochlea*. The cochlea is a spiral tubular pathway that narrows toward the tip. The basilar membrane that passes through the center of the cochlea is covered with delicate hair cells. When the fluid of the cochlea moves, certain hair cells in the cochlea tend to be activated. Upon activation, these hair cells discharge nerve impulses in adjacent fibers of the auditory nerve. Electrical impulses originating in the cochlea are eventually interpreted by the brain as sounds.

Exactly how the membrane responds to different frequencies and intensities of sound is not clearly understood. There is some evidence that different places on the basilar membrane are sensitive to different frequencies of vibration and therefore underlie the perception of different pitches. There is also evidence that intensity of sound affects the amount of activity generated in the hair cells. But other findings indicate that some additional mechanisms are also involved in the detection of loudness and pitch. The best guess at the present time is that a place theory (a place on the basilar membrane specially sensitive for each frequency)

holds for high frequencies, say, those above 1,000 Hertz, while low-frequency sound may affect the entire membrane. In these cases, the frequency of nerve impulses may correspond to frequency of sound vibration.

Spatial localization. The location of objects in space on the basis of hearing is not nearly as good as it is for vision. Still, hearing does provide us with some ability to determine the distance and direction of a sound source. This ability, especially to detect distance, improves with the familiarity of the sound. The distance of an object is primarily determined by our familiarity with the loudness of the sound it emits, and knowing the loudness of a particular sound, for example, a cricket's chirp or a church chime, depends upon previous experience with the sound.

The detection of the position of a sound to the left or the right of our body is excellent. Detection of above versus below and back versus front, however, is poor. Sometimes we can tell whether a sound is above or below us on the basis of familiarity. For example, the roar of an airplane engine is unlikely to come from beneath us. Familiarity is of no help in determining whether a sound comes from the front or the back, however. Actually, we can detect accurately up-down and front-back differences only when we are allowed to move our heads in three dimensions. By moving our heads, we can get the sound into the right-left plane, where discriminability is better.

Right-left discriminability, and indeed all localization in space of a sound source, is possible only because we have two ears, positioned on either side of the head. Physically, a sound will reach the nearer ear sooner and with greater intensity. Although these differences are minute in a physical sense, our ears are sensitive to them. Of the two factors, the time of arrival of the sound appears to be more important. If the sound reaches the left ear first, the sound source is on our left side.

Location of objects on the basis of sound is, of course, especially important to a person without vision. A blind individual can learn to localize quite accurately on the basis of sound alone, even to the extent of using self-generated sounds that reflect back from an object in the form of echoes. In one experiment, it was shown that a blind person can detect large obstacles in his path at a distance of 10 to 15 feet in a large room. Blindfolded sighted people are initially poor at object localization. With practice, however, they improve. This suggests that the performance of a blind person depends upon

Flavor It with Vision

Newsweek—To a hungry man, the sight of his favorite foods increases the desire to eat them. But the visual appreciation of food, according to a recent study at Duke University, has more than merely esthetic or appetite-stimulating significance: many people, it turns out, are simply unable to identify the taste of food they eat unless they can also see it.

In an effort to learn more about the nature of taste, psychologist Dr. Susan Schiffman fed blindfolded subjects a variety of common foods, including bananas, lemons, beef and a coffee-flavored pudding. So that the subjects would not be guided by texture—which can be an important identifying factor—the foods were processed in a blender until they were of a uniform soft consistency resembling that of baby food.

Strained Bananas

The subjects best able to identify what they were fed were a group of obese patients from Duke's Dietary Rehabilitation Clinic. Those who scored lowest were a group of elderly volunteers, and in between fell the younger people of normal weight. In the obese group, for example, fully 69 per cent correctly identified strained bananas, while only 24 per cent of the elderly did so and 41 per cent of the normal-weight subjects.

"We know that older people often complain that most of the food they eat tastes bitter or sour," Schiffman says, "and one of the flavors they identified most readily in the experiment was coffee, which is bitter." From this and other experiments with similar results, Schiffman concludes that in older persons, the taste buds at the front of the tongue, which are responsible for identifying sweet and salty flavors, are the first to atrophy, while the taste buds associated with bitter and sour continue to function well into old age. . . .

In everyday situations, our sensory systems work together. Smell and taste are closely related, as you may have noticed when you have had a bad cold and found that food did not seem to taste just right. Here is some evidence that vision also plays a role in what we normally think of as just "taste."

considerable experience in exploring his environment acoustically. The blind person's ability to navigate successfully through a room with several barriers can be impeded by placing carpeting on the floor—reducing the sounds emitted by his own footsteps—or by requiring that he wear earplugs.

Smell and Taste

The senses of smell and taste are often discussed under a common heading because both are based on chemical reactions triggered by a stimulus. For something to have an odor, it must give off molecules in the form of a gas. Somehow, in a way not yet thoroughly understood, the gaseous molecules interact with sensory receptors at the top of the nasal cavity. The axons of odor receptors terminate directly in the brain. There are no intermediate neurons as there are for other senses. This fact suggests that, although smell is a relatively minor sense in human beings, it may have been the first and most important sense in the evolution of animals.

A taste stimulus must come in contact with the tongue, where it triggers a reaction in the taste buds. A taste bud, as the name would suggest, is a collection of taste cells (approximately 15 in number) clustered like a flower bud. Although most taste buds are on the surface of the tongue, about 10 percent are found elsewhere in the mouth. Nerve excitation occurs from an electrical exchange in the membrane of the taste cell, caused by a chemical reaction with substances in the mouth. The experience of taste, psychologically, is a composite of four primary sensations: sweet, sour, salt, and bitter. All tastes are some mixture of these, with a few substances producing more or less pure instances of each—sucrose, for example, gives a sweet taste.

Of the two chemical senses, smell appears to be the more important. Indeed, much of what we attribute to the sense of taste is really based on the odors that substances give off. There is no more dramatic evidence of this fact than the difficulty we have "tasting" food when our noses are stuffed and swollen from a cold.

Touch and Feeling

Objects that come in contact with the skin have four separate qualities. They may yield sensations of warmth, cold, touch, and pain. Each of these qualities appears to arise from electrical impulses triggered in a particular kind of receptor cell. Thus, an anatomical examination of regions just beneath the skin reveals a variety of different sensory cells and nerve endings. Some of these, when stimulated, yield a sensation of warmth, others a sensation of cold, still others the sensation of touch or feel, and finally some yield the sensation of pain. Most objects that we come in contact with produce a combination of sensations, not just one. Consider, for example, what it would "feel" like to touch, in the dark, a refrigerator, a cabinet, the arm of another person, or a hot stove. These objects are discriminable on the basis of touch alone because they give unique combinations of tactual sensations.

Body Position and Orientation (Kinesthesis)

We have sense organs in our joints and muscles that provide precise information about the position of our limbs and the forces being exerted on them, either externally or by our own muscles and tendons. Without this sensory information we would have great difficulty knowing where in space any part of our body was, and how much we would have to move to get into a desired new position. All of our fine skill movements are dependent on kinesthetic sensory feedback.

In addition, we have a keen sense of whole body position, orientation, and movement relative to gravity. The sense organs for body position are located in the inner ear, attached to the cochlea, where the receptors for hearing are found. Body motion is detected by three *semicircular canals* perpendicular to one another in three different planes of space. The canals contain a fluid that moves as the body moves, exciting separate sets of tiny hair cells in much the same way as the hearing sense does. Motion in one plane will create impulses from one canal, whereas motion in a direction across the planes of reference will cause impulses in all three canals. The perception of balance is provided by enlargements at the base of the semicircular canals, called the *vestibular sacs.* These organs respond to tilt even in the absence of motion or rotation, that is, a situation where the body is held still but tilted in relation to gravity.

To test your kinesthetic senses, close your eyes and extend one hand in front of you. Now with the other hand, alternately touch your nose and your extended forefinger. Move your extended hand around and see if your other hand can still find it. How do you know where your hands and your nose are? Think about the kinesthetic senses that must be operating. Incidentally, people who suffer damage to these sensory systems have difficulty with this and other motor tasks. Some can walk only by watching their feet (substituting visual for kinesthetic feedback).

So far we have discussed how the various sensory systems work, as if each functioned in isolation. In fact, of course, all systems are normally operating all the time, so that we perceive the world through all our senses simultaneously. Indeed, our senses cooperate with and supplement one another, giving us rich multidimensional sensations. We shall consider next some examples of this functional interplay among the senses.

Attention

Our senses are continually being bombarded with stimulation, most of it either insignificant for our activities or else repetitious. How good are we at selectively attending to significant aspects of stimulation? How good are we at attending to two or more inputs at once? Actually, human adults are fairly skillful at both activities, though the processes involved are quite complicated. Psychologists and others concerned with the phenomenon of attention have studied the conditions under which attention is most efficient and the factors that influence attention.

Divided Attention

Our attention is divided when we receive two or more different sensory inputs simultaneously. At a party or large gathering, for example, we may find ourselves trying to listen to two conversations at the same time, often one in each ear. Much experimental work has been done on the problem of divided attention. The usual method is to ask an observer to listen to and repeat a message coming into one ear (the primary message), while remaining attentive to some special target word or idea embedded in a similar message heard in the other ear (the secondary message). The results generally indicate that the target items in the secondary message are unnoticed unless those items alone are in a different voice or differ physically in some other very distinctive way from the rest of the message. One of the few exceptions to this rule is the ease with which listeners can hear their own name in the secondary message.

While we have little success dividing our attention between two similar types of stimuli, when the division is between dissimilar stimuli or tasks, very little interference occurs, and both tasks can be performed together nearly as well as either alone. For example, pianists have little difficulty playing even an unfamiliar piece of music while at the same time responding verbally to questions asked by another person. No more errors are made in either task together than when either is done by itself. When the tasks are similar it appears that there cannot be a true division of attention. Rather the stimuli must be treated in succession, one after the other. If, however, they both are continuous and arrive at the same time, the listener must either switch back and forth or ignore the secondary message.

It is important to note the possibility of storing

Everybody Has a Photographic Memory (Well, Almost)

There is now ample evidence that our brain continues to "see" a stimulus for some time after the stimulus has been physically removed. Unfortunately, this representation is available for viewing for only a fraction of a second. This memory system is sometimes called very-short-term memory. Instead of using the term *memory*, some prefer *sensory register*—the "picture" is registered for a short time in the sensory system involved. There is clearly an analogous phenomenon in the auditory system, often called the "echo box," because an auditory stimulus seems to be echoing after the stimulus has ceased.

George Sperling devised an important method for studying visual memory. (For more information see G. Sperling, The information available in brief visual presentations, *Psychological Monographs*, 1960, *74*, whole no. 498.) Subjects were shown three rows of four symbols (numbers and letters):

7 H T 9
P D 3 1
2 K 8 G

The matrix of symbols was briefly flashed (for less than 1/10 of a second), and then the subjects were asked to report what they saw. Presumably they would start reading off what they saw, reading from left to right and top to bottom. One subject might say, "7, H, T, 9, ah . . ." and fail on the remaining symbols because the sensory image had disappeared. But if he really had an image of the whole matrix, he should have been able to report any row, as long as he reported it first, before the image disappeared. Sperling demonstrated that if at the time of the flash, he inserted an arrow pointing to the row to be reported first, the subjects could report any row he asked for. This must mean that the subject had some kind of image of the array after it had gone off. Sperling's method is called *cued partial report,* because the subject is given a cue (the arrow) and asked to report only part of the array (the row the arrow points to). For example, the subject would see:

8 9 M F
$\longrightarrow$ 1 J 7 W
X V 6 2

Naturally, reporting was best if the arrow came on before the subject saw the array, because he could then focus his attention on the crucial row. But the subjects could report any row, even when the arrow came on *after* the array, provided it was immediately after. If presentation of the arrow was delayed until after the image had faded, the subjects could not report very well. So our visual perceptual system has a brief memory capability.

one message briefly while attending primarily to the content of the other, then switching attention to the stored one. Storage of visual stimuli in this way has been shown to be possible but limited. What is stored seems to be the visual features themselves, so that a constructed perception is still possible if attention is switched back to those features within half a second or so. Comparable auditory storage, equally limited in duration, has also been demonstrated.

Focused Attention

A different example of selectivity is *focused attention,* that is, attending to one aspect of a stimulus while ignoring all other parts. The usual reason for ignoring a part of a stimulus is that by attending to the irrelevant parts, we impede our perception or our response to the important aspect. One of the most dramatic demonstrations of interference by extraneous stimuli occurs in the Stroop Color Naming Test. The test stimuli are shown in Plate 2. Look at the top section and name the colors of the patches as fast and accurately as you can. Now do the same for the *colors* in the middle section, ignoring the meanings of the words. You should find that the middle section takes about 25 percent longer to read than the top, because of the difficulty of ignoring the meanings of the irrelevant words. Fortunately, nature does not design situations as diabolical as this one. Yet at times we all have been presented with unnecessary or conflicting information, part of which we could safely ignore while proceeding with the task at hand. But even though the conflicting information is irrelevant, we find it difficult to ignore.

Although many explanations have been proposed for the Stroop effect, the answer seems to lie in our inability to block responses to powerful irrelevant features. The words, which have to be looked at to perform the task, have meanings that name irrelevant colors. The irrelevant meaning of a word interferes with producing the name of the color it is printed in. This implies that all of the stimulus, both its color and the meaning of the word itself, is perceived, and that the interference occurs after the point of perception, that is, in making the required response. This suggests that focusing of attention is probably not a perceptual process per se, that is, not a failure to perceive the unwanted part of the stimulus. Rather, it is a process of response competition. In the Stroop test, the two "color" responses compete for output.

What Does It Mean?

The main goal of the study of visual perception is to understand some of the fundamental building blocks that make up more complex forms of human behavior. Most of the scientists who have concentrated on perception have not been as concerned with solving practical problems as they have been with unraveling the mysteries of how perception works. However, along the way they have worked out solutions to a number of everyday perceptual problems, such as tests for visual acuity to prescribe eyeglasses and tests for color blindness. Of course, there are other practical questions that can be answered by direct application of our knowledge about perception: How big should we make a highway sign placed at a specified distance from the road so that drivers can read it when traveling at the maximum speed? Can a baseball player catch a baseball when it is seen against the artificial sky of a domed playing field? Can an astronaut 100 miles away from the earth be at all useful in reconnaisance with his naked eye? And so forth. There are many other examples of instances in which principles we have been considering have been used outside of the laboratory or have been instrumental in leading to an understanding of more complex perceptual tasks. Let us consider some of them.

Subthreshold Advertising

Several years ago advertisers proposed that buying behavior could be influenced most effectively if people were unaware of being influenced. A number of attempts were made to influence buying behavior in movie theaters by flashing frequent repetitions of a message such as "Eat popcorn" on the screen during the show. The message would be flashed just briefly enough so that no one would consciously notice it. Although initial tests looked promising, in none of the carefully controlled experiments was any increase in popcorn consumption found when the message was flashed. Thus, it appears that this type of unconscious persuasion is ineffective. The

conclusion is not surprising, given the difficulty of demonstrating comparable effects in the laboratory. Even the few positive results that have been found have shown only very very small changes, and these tests never involved requiring the perceiver to act upon what he saw. Furthermore, these small effects may well be limited to quite minimal differences in detection or recognition that would have no significant influence on so complex a process as a decision to buy something. In any event, a "1984-like" process of unconscious persuasion through subthreshold visual presentations appears not to have been verified by careful scientific investigation.

Reading

Reading is undoubtedly one of the most complex perceptual cognitive skills routinely performed by human beings. Still, it can be taught to young children without too much difficulty with a variety of methods. Even adults who have been illiterate all of their lives can be taught to read. Although high levels of achievement in reading require special skill and ability, acceptable levels are obtainable by all but those who are severely below normal in intellectual capacity.

Only recently have scientists and educators explicitly recognized the extent to which reading depends on perceptual processes. Their first step in the analysis of reading as a perceptual process was to measure the movements of a person's eyes while he reads a page of print. The pattern of eye movements for an average reader shows that the eyes move in discrete jumps and then remain fixated briefly before jumping to the next fixation. The average reader remains fixated for an average of 1/4 of a second, and makes an average of four fixations a line. He has a reading speed of about 310 words per minute. Given the distance that the page is normally held from the eyes, the limits of good visual acuity would permit the reader to see clearly the letters of only slightly more than one word per line, though he typically notices gross details beyond that, such as extra large spaces denoting the end of a sentence and the ends of the lines of print.

Analysis of the fixation pattern indicates that typical readers do not look at every word, nor in fact do they need to see every word in order to read continuously. This should be expected, since reading is a very good example of constructive perception. The reader needs to develop some sense about what the sentence or passage is about. This implies that the fixations should be much closer together (almost on every word) near the beginning of a paragraph or when it is clear that the content is about to change. As the reader develops a sense of what it is he is reading, he can use this to guide his constructions. It is as if the reader forms a hypothesis about what he will find on the page and then checks every few words to verify it, revising the hypothesis as he goes along. If the content is quite predictable, less verification is needed and eye movements can be farther apart, allowing an increase in reading speed. If the writer should suddenly change content without warning, however, the reader may find that he cannot figure out the meaning, since his hypothesis is now inconsistent with the words he finds. He then has to look back to check the words that he missed.

This description of reading is inconsistent with the impression that the reader perceives every word on every line. What seems to happen is that he constructs all of the words because he "knows" (or assumes) that they are there, based upon a hypothesis, even though he does not actually fixate them. He probably can find some vague sense of word boundaries, the sizes of words, and perhaps even some visual features of the nonfixated words, particularly word shape. These features facilitate the construction of the nonfixated words, but they are not critical. We have somewhat the same problem in noticing typographical errors; most of them go completely unrecognized because our strong expectations or hypotheses about what letters are present in familiar words will override the actual visual features of an erroneous letter. Hence, we construct the correct letter even though the stimulus contained a different one, and we construct and perceive words that we did not actually see.

This view of reading places heavy stress on our abilities to construct sense (meaningfulness) out of partial sensory information. We know from experiments that if readers are given a text to read in which every third word has been removed, they have little or no difficulty in reading it with full comprehension. Hence, it should not be necessary to look at all the words. Further, studies with readers of different speeds show that speed is gained by making fewer fixations farther apart, not by making briefer fixations or moving our eyes more rapidly. In fact, the duration of fixations and the speed of eye movements in reading seem not to vary much with changes in reading speed or difficulty of the material. Thus, learning how to read faster is basically a task of generating larger and better hypotheses and trusting them, even as we check them against the actual text on a periodic basis.

Perceptual Distortion

If a person puts on a special pair of glasses that contain inverted prisms, the entire visual world will be inverted and reversed. What was up is now down, what was to the right is now to the left. How does a person perceive this transformed visual world? At first, as expected, everything looks upside down and reversed. If the person tries to walk or reach for things his movements are confused and very inaccurate. However, he improves rapidly, at first by consciously reminding himself to reach "right for things that appear on the left," etc. The need for consciousness itself soon drops out. Strikingly, after several days of wearing glasses, some subjects have reported that the world comes to look right side up again and not reversed. They perceive the entire visual world in its normal orientation, and they can move about the world just as they did before they put the glasses on. As further evidence that the world has become normal, if the observer now takes the glasses off again, the world temporarily reverses and inverts again. More visual experience is necessary before he sees it as normal.

Being able to perceive the world normally in the face of such distortion is not as surprising as it might at first seem. Remember, the brain does not receive a copy of the visual world. Rather, it constructs and organizes perception from a set of visual features. Distortions such as those produced by an inverting prism, which leave all stimulus relationships within the optic array unchanged, altering only the relation of the array to the body, should be easy to adapt to.

A longer adaptation period is needed if the prisms change the relations within the array, by producing curvature, for example. The construction of perception from the visual features itself has to be changed. But that change, too, can be made. It just takes some practice in extracting the new information from the optic array and comparing successive optic arrays that arise from eye, head, and body movements. The same principles discussed throughout this chapter for normal perception should apply in such cases of transformation of the visual world. Similar reasoning can be used to account for the fact that astronauts, living in a zero gravity environment, suffer no significant impairment of perceptual organization. They *do* lose the awareness of their own body's orientation with respect to the visual world, but that is only one relationship. Most are unaltered. Overall perception is essentially unaffected.

Another perceptual distortion that has been

Movement and Perception

Movement and interaction with one's environment are essential to developing the right "program" for the perceptual system. As we have seen, one's perceptual program is not inflexible; it can be modified to adjust to viewing the world through distorting prisms. However, development of the perceptual program and adjustments of it are greatly facilitated by self-initiated movement in the world, as an experiment by Richard Held and Alan Hein (1963) demonstrated.

Figure 3–21
The kitten carousel

The activity of one kitten (in harness) is transmitted into a free ride for the other (in box).

Held and Hein raised kittens in darkness to prevent them from having any visual experience until they were old enough to walk. Then a pair of kittens were placed in the apparatus shown in Figure 3–21. The device, called the "kitten carousel," forces one of the kittens to initiate all the movement while the other kitten gets a free ride around the environment. The object was to give both kittens the same visual experience, but for only one kitten to get this experience through self-initiated movement—the other one was to experience only passive movement. Later tests revealed that the active kitten had developed extensive *perceptual* abilities, while the passive kitten was *perceptually* retarded. These kinds of experiments show that experience and, presumably, learning are crucial in developing perceptual ability. Moreover, they suggest that the crucial kind of experience for *perception* is active, self-initiated movement in the environment.

analyzed is trying to read print that has been transformed. Turning this page upside down and trying to read it is equivalent to placing an

Figure 3–22
Transformed text

a. Each letter is inverted with left-right order unchanged.
b. Here the whole line has been turned through 180 degrees.
c. The letters run from right to left but they are not inverted.

inverting-reversing prism in front of your eyes. After only a small amount of practice (about half a page or so), your reading speed and accuracy will begin to approach your normal rate. The deficit is due primarily to the difficulty in learning how to make right-to-left eye movements, which are opposite to our learned reading habits. The transformations of print shown in Figure 3–22 are much more difficult to read, since they do not preserve the normal relationships among letters. But even these can be read. If you were to practice them long enough, you would begin to approach normal reading speed.

Improving Perceptual Abilities

Is it possible to make improvements in our perceptual abilities through practice, drugs, or concentration? Are there ways to discriminate details in unfamiliar patterns, to notice differences between two very similar stimuli, to read faster, or to be less distracted by irrelevant stimuli? Although the whole story is not known, there are partial answers to each of these questions.

The discrimination of small details can be improved with training, although only with extreme practice and patience as well as a carefully controlled set of learning conditions. Probably the most dramatic examples are those of the professional wine taster, the perfume smeller, and the chicken sexer. Such people are not born with extraordinary discrimination abilities. Consider the wine taster. Leaving aside the question of which wine is the best, how could you develop the ability to tell the hundreds of different wines apart and to recognize, by taste alone, the kind of wine, the type of grape, the year grown, and which valley and which country the grapes were grown in? The procedure is straightforward, though its execution is extremely difficult.

First you have to have a normal sense of taste and smell. Then you start tasting (generally no more than a sip), and at the same time you are given information about the origin and background of the wine you are sipping. You would probably start with a group of wines that taste quite different. For each, you would concentrate on those qualities that differentiated it from the others. After you develop a

The Electric Ear

Newsweek—One June afternoon in 1959, Charles Graser, a social-science teacher and weekend truck driver in Colton, Calif., was refueling his gasoline truck when suddenly it burst into flames. Graser was severely burned over 80 per cent of his body and for months took heavy doses of streptomycin to counter the infection that plagues burn victims. Eventually, Graser recovered from the effects of the fire—but not from the effect of the drug. The streptomycin had completely destroyed thousands of the delicate hair cells in his inner ear, and Graser found himself, at 34, unable to hear a sound.

His type of hearing loss, Graser soon learned, couldn't be reversed with surgery or even the most sophisticated hearing aids. The hair cells are an indispensable link in the chain of hearing, receiving signals from the middle ear and passing them on to the auditory nerve. But about the time of Graser's accident, investigators began trying to stimulate the inner ear directly with electrical impulses as a crude substitute for the missing hair cells. There were many problems—the rejection or corrosion of implanted electrodes, the fragility of the inner ear and the difficulty of reaching it (the protective bone is as dense as marble). But in 1970, one researcher, Dr. William F. House of the Los Angeles Foundation of Otology (now the Ear Research Institute), decided to attempt an implant on Charles Graser, who eleven years after his accident was still stone-deaf.

Wires: In an exacting operation, House slipped five platinum electrodes, each no wider than a hair, into the spiraling, snail-shaped cochlea of the inner ear. Wires from each electrode ran to a nickel-size plug inserted behind Graser's ear. The plug held an induction coil, to pick up signals from a tiny transmitter attached to the end of his eyeglass frame. A battery-operated receiver, to be carried like a pack of cigarettes in a breast pocket, would relay incoming sound to the transmitter.

After much trial and error, Graser's implant finally enabled him to hear. It wasn't normal hearing—more like "listening to your car radio in the middle of the desert and having trouble with a distant station," says Graser. But for the first time he could recognize a school bell, the sound of bowling pins falling, hands clapping, a cat meowing. He could even, with practice, carry on primitive phone conversations with his family. "I was exuberant," he says.

747 Level: House admits that today the implants are only "in the Lindbergh phase"; he predicts it may be more than ten years before they reach "the 747 level," where sounds can be heard without distortion. He and other otologists are working on ways to place a long array of electrodes in the cochlea to get better pitch perception, which is now poor at best. But certain investigators consider any cochlear implants on humans premature at present and possibly hazardous: some warn that constant electrical stimulation of the cochlea could cause serious deterioration of the auditory nerve. Dr. Robin P. Michelson of the University of California at San Francisco, who has performed six cochlear implants himself, thinks that further surgery should be suspended until a better device is available.

House counters by asking, "If a patient has his leg amputated, do I tell him to wait until I can graft on a real one—or do I offer him a peg leg now?" He also points out that Graser has used his implanted hearing aid almost continuously for two years with no apparent nerve damage....

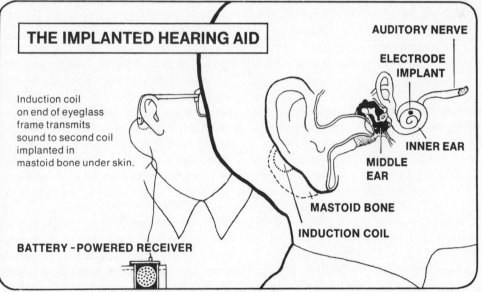

THE IMPLANTED HEARING AID

Induction coil on end of eyeglass frame transmits sound to second coil implanted in mastoid bone under skin.

AUDITORY NERVE

ELECTRODE IMPLANT

INNER EAR

MIDDLE EAR

MASTOID BONE

INDUCTION COIL

BATTERY-POWERED RECEIVER

Drawing by Don Mackay.

Bringing the sound closer: To hear bells, bowling pins and the cat's meow

good command of these wines, you would move to a group that are more similar. When you could begin to tell the difference in taste between, say, a fruity and a sweet wine, your trainer would tell you how these differences are produced—the kinds of grapes, the amounts of sun and rain, and so forth. Progressing in this way, through successively more similar groups of wines, with repeated tasting and a great deal of feedback on your reactions, you would become a skilled wine taster and the envy of your untutored friends. But it takes time (often years) to become a true expert. Learning fine sensory discriminations is a difficult and time-consuming process.

To our knowledge, no one has actually made a study of wine tasters. However, there have been laboratory studies of how subjects can learn to discriminate fine details of stimuli that they previously had not noticed. The assumption is that the sensory information is always there, but it has never been included in the constructions people typically make of the stimulus. Practice, with consistent feedback, helps the learner change his construction in the direction of emphasizing those details that are important in the discrimination. In the process, other parts of the construction may change too. In fact, many wine tasters report an aversion to wine after a while, even though they remain incredibly precise discriminators of it.

There is little evidence that drugs of any kind contribute to the development of better acuity or perception of detail. Usually the effects are quite the opposite (see Chapter 8). Some drugs may improve the ability to concentrate by making the user less distractable, but the ability to discriminate or perceive detail is not improved without additional training.

Helping the handicapped. One of the most important concerns of perceptual psychology has been to help perceptually handicapped persons. Is there any way a blind person can be helped to replace some of the information sight would normally provide? Most approaches have been to develop special sensitivities in one or more of the other senses to provide some of this information. We have already mentioned the blind individual's ability to increase his sensitivity to sounds, especially echoes, by training and practice. Physical devices can help him do this. The simplest is the cane that a blind person taps as he walks. He can hear the echo of the tap bounce back from walls in front of him, with the time from the tap to hearing the echo specifying the distance to the object. A

more sophisticated device for identifying the position of objects and discontinuities in the terrain involves a radarlike system. The subject wears glasses equipped with ultrasonic sensors and a transmitter. The transmitter sends out sound waves that bounce back to the receivers, allowing the subject to locate objects more accurately than with a cane.

Another system still in the experimental stage is even more dramatic. This has been developed by a number of psychologists and engineers in California and works by using the sense of touch on the skin. A small TV camera is mounted on the perceiver's head so that it receives a picture of roughly what is straight ahead. The perceiver can point it by moving his head, and he also has a zoom control available for close-up looks. The TV camera is connected to a matrix of vibrators that are strapped to the skin on the back or the stomach. Each of the vibrators represents a small part of the TV picture. Thus, if the upper right-hand corner of the picture is all dark, then none of the vibrators representing this area would vibrate. Areas that are light would vibrate, the more so the more intense the excitation reaching the TV camera in that area. Thus, the energy variation in the optic array reaching the TV camera is represented by differential activity in the vibrators placed over a small area of the skin.

So far we have been describing how the devices work rather than what the blind person perceives. What does he *"see"* or *feel* when the camera is turned on? Early work has been encouraging. Blind subjects who knew how to read before being blinded have been able to read at rates up to nearly 100 words per minute. Although this is slower than typical adult reading, it is impressive, and with some refinements now being made, the chances for improvement are good. Even more impressive, subjects are able to distinguish depth—to distinguish two-dimensional and three-dimensional objects and to perceive what is in front of what. Thus, they are able to move around without bumping into things.

Signs and Information

Most communities until very recently paid little official attention to the size and type of signs that could be used to inform the public or advertise products. This was left to the ingenuity and the pocketbook of the sign maker and user. Recently, William Ewald, an architect and city planner, wrote a book called *Street Graphics* (1971) in which he presented a number of principles that could be followed to determine reasonable standards for sign

**Figure 3–23
Cluttered signs**

How quickly could you figure out where to turn for
Armstrong vinyl and still drive carefully?

sizes, legibility, content or organization, and
placement. Many of these principles have been
drawn rather directly from concepts discussed in
this chapter.

One of Ewald's concerns was density of signs.
What are the chances of noting a particular sign
when there are no other signs around, when there
are a few others, when the street is cluttered with
them (see Figure 3–23)? Obviously the chances go
down as the number of signs go up, but laboratory
research has shown that they go down faster than
would be expected from the simple numbers alone.
Adding a second sign does not reduce your chances
of noting the first by half, but a third has a
substantial impact; and as soon as there are a lot of
signs, say 15, the chances of spotting a particular
one are much less than 1/15. Of course, an
individual owner could increase his chances of
having his sign read if he made his sign larger,
gaudier, brighter, and flashier. Judging from the way
some of our city streets look, all of the sign owners
have arrived at the same conclusion at the same
time.

Another concern is sign size, especially the size of
the display on the sign. Obviously, making it larger
should help make it more visible, up to some
limit—being too close to a large sign may prevent us
from seeing the message. But there are specific
principles that can help us determine some of the
factors influencing the readability or noticeability of
displays. You have to take into account the distance
of the viewer from the sign, how fast he is traveling
(meaning, how much time he has to look at the

sign), how much information there is on the sign
and how much of that information is predictable or
expected, and what else the viewer has to do at the
same time he is looking at the sign. For some of
these factors Ewald has developed standards based
on laboratory or field data. For others, psychologists
have not yet attacked the problem or provided a
clear enough theory from which to predict the
outcome. But we clearly know much more about
processing the information from the signs than the
viewing of our downtown world would suggest that
we know.

Summary

1. Visual perception begins when an array of light
reflected from objects and surfaces reaches the eye.
An external object is represented perceptually as a
set of visual features. From these features, a
meaningful organization of the world is constructed
by the perceiver.

2. Perception cannot simply be a copy of the optic
array coming from a stimulus. Neither the structure
of the eye nor the nervous system are designed in
this way.

3. Light enters the eye as it is reflected from
surfaces in the world around us. It varies in
wavelength, intensity, and complexity of
composition. Patterns are formed from variations in
these characteristics of light.

4. The optic array is focused on the retina, the
photosensitive part of the eye, by the lens. The rod
photoreceptors in the retina are very sensitive to
minimal amounts of energy, while the cone
receptors, packed closely together primarily in the
fovea, are more sensitive to differences in the
patterning and color of light.

5. The photoreceptors are organized into
receptive fields, with each receptive field signaling a
cortical neuron in the visual projection area of the
brain. Each receptive field will respond to only one
or a few visual features, such as a line of a specified
width, orientation, and color. Thus, nearly all of the
information about the patterning of stimuli is
automatically encoded.

6. The receptor cells of the eye adapt to the
amount of light in the immediate environment.
Sensitivity to light energy is determined primarily by
the adaptation state of the receptor.

7. The acuity with which we can discriminate
small differences in patterns is determined by the
accuracy with which the lens focuses the optic array
on the retina. Failure to focus properly can be
corrected by wearing eyeglasses.

8. Acuity arises as a brightness discrimination between adjacent cone receptors, which are capable of responding to a difference of less than 1 percent in the amount of light falling on two adjacent cones.

9. Sensations of color are mediated primarily by the cones. There is evidence to suggest a small number of different types of cones, which are maximally sensitive to different wavelengths and produce intermediate color sensations by combinations and mixtures.

10. To understand how organized perceptions can be constructed from the visual features received by the brain, it is necessary to recognize how much information about the stimulus is contained in those features. Especially important is the information in texture gradients, since clear perception of three-dimensional objects located in a three-dimensional visual world can ordinarily be achieved on the basis of texture cues alone.

11. Laws of organization have been specified to explain which perceptual organizations will occur, even from seemingly ambiguous information from the stimulus. A general statement, called the minimum principle, says that the perceptual organization achieved will be the one that uses the visual features to minimize discontinuities and maintain simplicity.

12. The perceptual constancies and some illusions are also examples of perceptual organization. The constancies, in which our perceptual experience does not vary even though the optical array changes, are explained by noting that ratios of features within the array are constant.

13. Visual illusions can occur because the organization seems to add a dimension of depth that results in corresponding changes in apparent size.

14. Vision is man's most important sensory system, but hearing, taste, smell, touch, and other systems make significant contributions to our awareness and knowledge of the world around us.

15. The stimulus for hearing is vibration in some object, a sound source, which carries to the ear through a conducting medium, usually air.

16. The physical dimensions of a sound source, intensity, frequency, and complexity of composition, determine three attributes of psychological experience, loudness, pitch, and timbre, respectively.

17. Although not as accurate as vision, hearing can be used to localize objects in the environment.

18. Studies on attention indicate that divided attention does not seem possible when two similar stimuli are presented simultaneously without a rapid switching or focusing of attention between them. Focusing is easy, however, when the stimuli are different. In that case, little interference is picked up from the unattended parts. But when the stimuli are similar, interference usually results.

19. Reading is one of our most complex perceptual skills. Reading speed and comprehension are partly determined by eye movements and constructive processes.

20. Distortion of perception caused by optical lenses lends strong support to the role of construction, because nearly all distortions disappear from perception as one learns to make consistent constructions out of the new arrangements of visual features.

21. Research in perception has led to the development of devices to aid the handicapped, especially blind and visually deficient people.

22. Studies of visual acuity have implications for the size, shape, and location of such things as traffic signals and road signs.

Recommended Additional Readings

Gibson, J. *The senses considered as perceptual systems.* Boston: Houghton Mifflin, 1966.

Gregory, R. *Eye and brain.* New York: McGraw-Hill, 1968.

Haber, R. N., & Hershenson, M. *The psychology of visual perception.* New York: Holt, Rinehart and Winston, 1973.

Hochberg, J. *Perception.* Englewood Cliffs, N.J.: Prentice-Hall, 1964.

Leibowitz, H. *Visual perception.* New York: Macmillan, 1965.

Mueller, C. G. *Sensory psychology.* Englewood Cliffs, N.J.: Prentice-Hall, 1965.

4

LEARNING AND MEMORY

Most of what human beings do is a product of learning. For present purposes we will define learning as *a relatively permanent change in behavior traceable to experience and practice.*

Questions about learning pervade every behavioral issue. Psychologists and others have asked: Do children learn to be aggressive from watching TV programs that contain violence? What kind of learning goes on in segregated versus desegregated schools? What is the best way to modify the behavior of criminals in prison? How is it that people learn prejudicial attitudes toward others, and what can be done to change this? Is stuttering a bad habit that children learn? What is the best way to learn to speak a foreign language? How can we train employees in order to maximize production? Every branch of psychology, indeed all areas of human concern, deal in a fundamental way with learning (see Table 4–1).

Learning and Behavior

Learning is intimately related to the basic behavioral characteristics of knowledge, skill, and intention. Generally, it is thought that knowledge and intention are acquired through experience, and skill through practice. A teacher might tell his or her class that Columbus discovered America in 1492, and from then on, as long as they remember, the students *know* and can respond to that fact. After an experience of pleasure from an event or activity, such as eating ice cream or drinking good wine, these activities become the objects of one's wants and *intentions.* Some activities, such as driving an automobile or playing baseball, involve *skills* as well as knowledge and intention. Repetition of these activities, or practice, leads to an improvement in skill. Note that each of these cases fits our definition of learning.

The relationship between learning and performance (the observed behavior in a particular situation) deserves special comment. Most learning theories, indeed most general theories of behavior, make note of this special relationship, drawing a strong distinction between the two. Traditionally, it is argued that learning is never really observed directly. In many theories, learning is given the status of an *intervening variable,* a variable that stands between (intervenes) and provides a relationship between some stimulus in the environment and some response or performance on the part of a person. Learning is not observed directly but is, rather, inferred from observation of a

Table 4–1
The central role of learning in psychology

Branch of psychology	Sample concerns dealing with learning
Physiological psychology	1. What changes take place in the nervous system when a person learns?
	2. Are there physiological defects in the learning mechanism of mentally retarded individuals? Are there any drugs that speed up the learning process or correct physiological defects?
Educational psychology	1. Will learning be improved or impaired in school buildings with no walls separating the classrooms?
	2. What is the best way to teach reading? Why do so many children fail to learn to read in school?
Developmental psychology	1. As a child grows, are there changes in the manner in which he learns that teachers should be aware of?
	2. Are there periods of readiness for learning (for example, reading readiness) before which attempts at teaching the child will be useless?
Industrial psychology	1. What is the best way to train employees to be safety conscious?
	2. What is the best way to retrain employees for jobs requiring new skills?
Social psychology	1. How do people learn attitudes?
	2. Will social facilitation (being in groups) speed the learning process?
Clinical psychology	1. How can a therapist teach a client not to be afraid of catching a fatal illness from the "germs" in his own home?
	2. What kind of reward or pleasure does a "peeping Tom" get from looking into his neighbors' windows?
Experimental psychology	1. What factors are important in determining the rate of learning?
	2. Does learning take place faster with rewards, punishments, or both?
	3. What is the best way to memorize (learn) a set of important facts?

"relatively permanent change in *performance*." We infer that learning has taken place from a change in performance.

Thus learning and performance are closely related but distinct concepts pertaining to behavior. Too often the distinction is not maintained, and performance is taken to be a direct and accurate measure of how much a person has learned. This would imply that if learning occurs, performance should improve; and if learning is reduced, for example by forgetting, performance should get worse. But performance is not always an accurate reflection of the amount learned. Consider the basketball team that does well throughout the season, only to be humiliated in the state tournament. The team *performed* poorly, but not because they forgot how to play or lost any of their skill. Other factors, such as tension or distraction, prevented the players from performing at the level of their true ability. Schoolteachers frequently report that a student does not perform as well as he is capable of. The student may have the necessary knowledge and skill, but for some reason they are not reflected in his performance. His poor performance is often attributed to lack of motivation.

Performance is also an inaccurate measure of the amount learned when it indicates more learning has taken place than actually has. A student might get a higher score on a multiple-choice test than his knowledge of the subject matter would indicate because of educated, but essentially lucky, guessing. Or you might have a fortunate day on the golf course so that your score is clearly an overestimation of the amount of skill you actually possess. The point is that we must be careful not to jump to rapid conclusions about the amount learned—that is, the true knowledge and skills of an individual—based on only a limited number of observations of performance.

Rudimentary Forms of Learning

It is possible to categorize most instances of learning into two basic types: *classical conditioning* and *instrumental* or *operant conditioning*. Indeed some investigators have suggested that there *are* just two types of learning. Incidentally, one might just as readily refer to these as classical and instrumental "learning" if it were not for a historical precedent favoring the term "conditioning."

Classical Conditioning

Pavlov's work. Ivan Pavlov, the Nobel-Prize–winning Russian physiologist, was among the first to report classical conditioning. During his studies of digestion, he examined the characteristics of dogs' salivary flow, a reflex response to food in the mouth. Pavlov's experimental method was to present food to the dog and measure the amount of saliva (see Figure 4–1). In the process he discovered that if a neutral stimulus, one that did not automatically elicit saliva, such as a bell, was paired repeatedly with the food, the dog would gradually "learn" to salivate at the sound of the bell alone, without any food. Learning to respond to a formerly neutral stimulus, because

Figure 4–1
Pavlov's work on classical conditioning

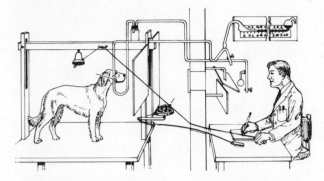

Pavlov's experimental set-up for measuring saliva flow responses in dogs. Food elicits saliva, measured by a tube connected to a cup placed over one of the salivary glands. The bell serves as the neutral stimulus.

that stimulus is paired with another stimulus that already elicits a response, is the essential characterization of classical conditioning.

The importance of Pavlov's work cannot be overestimated. Not long after it became known, some psychologists began to argue that all behavior is based on classical conditioning. Although this

extreme view is no longer popularly held in America, Russian psychology is still dominated by theories based on the principles of classical conditioning. It is agreed, at any rate, that a significant portion of our behavior can be better understood by noting the influence of classical conditioning.

Stimuli and responses. The conditioning situation involves four events, two pertaining to the stimulus and two to the organism's response. There is a neutral stimulus that, prior to conditioning, does not elicit the desired, to-be-learned, response. This is the *conditioned stimulus* (CS), the bell in our example from Pavlov. The second stimulus is the *unconditioned stimulus* (UCS). Prior to conditioning it reliably elicits the desired response. Presentation of meat, the UCS, elicits saliva flow before conditioning. The salivary response to the UCS is known as the *unconditioned response* (UCR). This is the response that occurs before any conditioning has taken place. The response that begins to happen as a result of conditioning is called the *conditioned response* (CR)—a salivary response to the bell alone in the absence of meat.

Conditioning occurs as the two stimuli are presented contiguously (close together in space and time) and repeatedly. Usually the UCS is presented just after the CS. Gradually, after several pairings of the CS and UCS, the CS begins to elicit the flow of saliva. Whenever this happens, the animal has made

---

Table 4–2
Basic features of classical conditioning (illustrated by salivary conditioning)

Before conditioning:

Meat
or ————————▶ saliva flow by reflex action, called the UCR
UCS

UCS = unconditioned stimulus, in this case the meat. The UCS already elicits the specific response of saliva flow.

Bell
or ————————▶ no saliva, only an "orienting response" (looking, pricking up ears, etc.)
neutral stimulus

UCR = unconditioned response made to the UCS, in this case saliva flow when meat is presented.

During conditioning:

Meat (UCS) +
bell (now CS) ————————▶ saliva flow

Bell and meat are presented together for several trials.

After conditioning:

Bell
or ————————▶ saliva flow or CR
CS

CS = conditioned stimulus, in this case the bell.

CR = conditioned response to the CS, saliva flow when the bell is sounded and no meat is present.

a CR. The once-neutral CS (bell) is now capable of eliciting saliva flow by itself. (See Table 4–2 for a summary of the events of classical conditioning.)

Note that in some respects the CR and UCR are identical. In this case, for instance, both the CR and the UCR consist of saliva flow. This fact has led to the *stimulus substitution* theory of conditioning: Conditioning is a process that results in the CS becoming a substitute for the UCS. The problem, however, is that on close examination we find that the CR and the UCR are not in fact identical in all ways. For example, it is common to find that the CR is not as large a response as the UCR is—more saliva will be elicited by the meat than by the bell. This is a difference in response amplitude (amount of saliva). The UCR and CR might also differ in other ways. These differences suggest the theory that the CR is a *response* in *anticipation* of the UCS. The CS is not a substitute for the UCS, but a signal that the UCS is about to be presented; and the CR, then, is a response designed to prepare the organism for the UCR.

A situation commonly used for the study of classical conditioning in human beings is the reflex action of blinking the eyes. The UCS is a puff of air delivered to the subject's eye that regularly and forcefully elicits a blink (the UCR). Experimenters use an apparatus that both delivers the air puff and measures the amplitude, latency (time to respond), and other characteristics of eye blinks. The eye-blink response can be conditioned to a neutral stimulus, for example, the word "psychology." Conditioning begins by pairing the CS *(psychology)* with the UCS (air puff). Usually it is arranged so that the CS occurs slightly in advance of the UCS, for research has shown that a .5-second interval between the two stimuli (the *CS–UCS interval)* will yield most rapid conditioning. Periodically, the experimenter tests for the occurrence of a CR, a blink in response to the word "psychology" alone. On test trials he might simply omit the UCS, or he might carefully observe eye movement records to determine whether the subject begins his blink before the air puff is presented. If the eye blink occurs following the CS (or before the UCS), conditioning has occurred. The subject blinks to a formerly neutral stimulus; he has acquired (learned to make) a CR.

If we introduce a longer time interval between the CS and UCS, conditioning is more difficult to produce and if the CS–UCS interval becomes very long, no conditioning at all will take place except under very special circumstances. In other words, normally it is necessary for the CS and UCS to be contiguous—close together in space and time—for

Figure 4–2
Classical conditioning of fear

A baby develops fear of an animal because that animal has become associated with a fear-eliciting stimulus. In panel 1 the rabbit is approached by the child, who shows no signs of fear before conditioning. Then the rabbit is presented contiguously with a loud noise that scares the child (panel 2). Panel 3: After conditioning, the rabbit alone is capable of eliciting fear in the child. Panel 4: Worst of all, the child may now be afraid of all furry things, such as rats, stuffed animals, or even a man with a beard. The fear, originally conditioned to the rabbit, has now *generalized* to similar stimuli. Can you identify the CS, UCS, CR, UCR, and the generalization test stimuli? How might a child or even an adult *learn* to be afraid of policemen? Of doctors and dentists? Of strangers? Of high places? Of taking examinations?

conditioning to take place. This principle is embodied in the *Law of Contiguity,* which states that two stimuli that occur together will automatically become associated. The CS and UCS become associated with each other in such a way that the CS signals the organism that the UCS is about to be presented.

Prevalence of classical conditioning. Examples of classical conditioning abound in the everyday life of animals and human beings. One important

YOU'VE GOT TO STOP RINGING THAT BELL EVERY TIME YOU FEED HIM, DR. PAVLOV... YESTERDAY HE ATE THE AVON LADY

1-28

Reprinted by permission of Newspaper Enterprise Association.

example is the conditioning of emotional responses. Some psychologists have argued that anxiety, perhaps the most common symptom of emotional disorder, is a case of classically conditioned fear. Suppose a person experiences terror from a wild automobile drive that ends in a crash and painful injury. The fear and pain (UCRs) have been elicited in the context of, and thus could become conditioned to, "automobile" stimuli. The mere sight of a car may elicit the vague emotional feeling of fear in the person following recovery. While the feeling of physical pain would be absent, "mental pain" or conditioned fear might occur. Some psychologists have argued that fear conditioned to specific neutral stimuli is the essence of anxiety (see Figure 4–2 and Chapter 6). This and other everyday examples of classical conditioning are diagrammed in Table 4–3.

Instrumental or Operant Conditioning

The second basic type of learning is called *instrumental* or *operant conditioning*. The term "operant" is used to emphasize the component of work involved on the part of the learner (he must "operate" on his environment), while the term "instrumental" indicates that the learner has some control over his own circumstances (what he does is instrumental to what happens to him). Thus instrumental conditioning involves more activity on the part of the learner than classical conditioning does. Whenever a person can be described as behaving so as to gain reward or avoid punishment, his behavior is an example of instrumental action. The emphasis in this form of behavior is on intention and achievement; the learner acts intentionally in a particular manner in order to bring about a specific state of affairs.

Key words in this type of conditioning are *contingency* and *consequences*. Instrumental learning can be characterized by saying that it

involves learning about the *consequences* of behaving in a certain way—learning that if a particular response is made it will be followed by a particular stimulus event. For example, a child might learn that if he cries, his mother will pay attention to him and comfort him, perhaps even giving him some candy to "make you feel better." The basic idea is simple: Learning consists of discovering that a particular response (R) is followed by a particular stimulus event (S)—R is followed by S.

Another way of looking at this kind of learning is

Table 4–3
Diagrams of classical conditioning

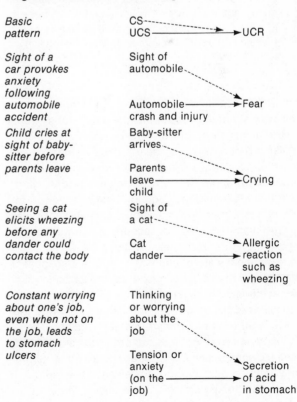

"Mommy, we keep saying 'go home, kitty-cat'—but she just keeps hanging around here!"

Reprinted courtesy of The Register and Tribune Syndicate, Inc.

If there is one thing that is certain about the behavior of animals and people, it is that they will repeat responses that lead to rewards. The cat will undoubtedly keep coming back as long as rewards are available. Likewise, assuming that the children like the cat and have fun (a reward) when they are feeding it, they will keep on bringing more food.

Figure 4–3
The Skinner box

Screen

Light

Water   Lever   Food tray

The experimental chamber called the Skinner box is used for many studies of operant conditioning. When the rat pushes the lever, a pellet of food automatically drops into the food tray.

in terms of contingency learning. The learner discovers that in order to make a particular stimulus event occur (say a piece of candy), he will have to make a particular response (perhaps crying). In such a case, we would say that getting the candy is *contingent upon* crying. The stimulus is contingent upon the learner's making a particular response. In short, responses have consequences; and if we want to produce particular consequences, we will have to make particular responses because the consequences are contingent upon the responses. A young boy might have to take out the garbage and mow the lawn in order to get his allowance; his behavior of taking out the garbage and mowing the lawn is an example of instrumental behavior. The consequences of doing his chores consist of getting his allowance, having his parents praise and thank him, and so on. Getting his allowance is contingent upon completing his chores. Whenever the occurrence of a particular stimulus event is

contingent upon the organism's behavior, or whenever a particular response leads to a particular set of consequences, we have the basic instrumental learning situation. This response-reward contingency is, of course, not present in classical conditioning. For example, in classical eye-blink conditioning, the air puff (UCS) is delivered regardless of whether the subject blinks when the CS is presented.

Historical antecedents.   Whereas classical conditioning is associated with the name of Pavlov, instrumental conditioning is associated with the names of E. L. Thorndike and B. F. Skinner (see Chapter 1). It was Thorndike who first did laboratory experiments using instrumental conditioning. His work led him to formulate the *Law of Effect,* which is the forerunner of the contemporary principle of reinforcement (see below). But it is Skinner who has made operant conditioning famous. He has studied the behavior of pigeons, rats, and human beings, including his own children. His work has led to the identification of the basic elements and laws of operant conditioning. He is the leading figure in the field of operant conditioning and almost singlehandedly has been responsible for the recognition of the importance of this type of learning in analyzing, predicting, and controlling behavior. His pioneering efforts have led to the

Table 4–4
The basic features of operant conditioning

The subject emits a response R	which leads to or produces →	a stimulus S
Hungry rat presses a bar R	→	experimenter presents food S+

development of an entire philosophy of behavior known as *functional analysis* for its emphasis on the functions (the consequences) of behavior. His discoveries have been the foundation for a whole new technology of *behavior modification* that is still in its early stages, but nevertheless has already had enormous success in its application and has been one of the most controversial developments in the history of psychology.

Reinforcement. A *reinforcer* is a stimulus event (a consequence) that increases the likelihood of any response with which it is associated. Reinforcement is the effective stimulus that makes learning of instrumental responses possible. Skinner used a device now known as the Skinner box to investigate the relationship between the events of instrumental conditioning. He placed a rat inside a glass box that contained a lever and a food tray (see Figure 4–3). The animal was allowed to explore the box freely. If he happened to press down on the lever, a pellet of food automatically dropped into the tray. A timer connected to the bar recorded the number of presses the rat made while in the box. Pressing the bar was the response to be learned (the operant response), and the food pellet was the stimulus consequence (or reinforcement). Skinner discovered that by rewarding the rat with food each time he pressed the bar, the rate of presses increased

dramatically. The rat learned the instrumental response by being reinforced.

There are two basic kinds of reinforcers: positive (symbolized S+) and negative (S−). A positive reinforcer is defined as *a stimulus event that when made contingent on a response will cause the frequency of that response to increase.* For example, food is a positive reinforcer because an animal will increase his rate of pressing a bar if food is withheld until he presses. Food delivery, the stimulus, is contingent on bar pressing, the response (see Table 4–4). In general it is convenient to think of positive reinforcers as things the organism would want or like, that is, *rewards.* A negative reinforcer is defined as *a stimulus event that causes an increase in response frequency when the contingency is a negative one*—that is, when making the response results in the removal or cessation of the stimulus. Thus, electrical shock is a negative reinforcer because its removal or cessation, if made contingent on a response, will cause the response to be made more often. If a rat presses a bar and this causes the shock to stop, then his rate of bar pressing will increase, and the shock is, thus, a negative reinforcer. In general it is convenient to think of negative reinforcers as things the organism would want to avoid or would dislike, that is, *punishments.*

Types of instrumental conditioning. By using instrumental conditioning we can teach someone to make a particular response or to withhold it, and we can do this with either rewards or punishments. There are four basic instrumental conditioning situations that result from combining the two types of consequences (rewards or punishments) with the two types of contingencies (either the consequence is contingent on making a particular response or it is contingent on *not* making it)—reward, omission, escape, and punishment training (see Table 4–5). In

Table 4–5
Basic instrumental conditioning situations

A. No cues available

	Train to elicit	Train to withhold
Use rewarding stimuli	Reward training	Omission training
Use punishing stimuli	Escape training	Punishment training (passive avoidance)

B. Discriminative cues present

	Train to elicit	Train to withhold
Use rewarding stimuli	Discriminated operant	Discriminated omission
Use punishing stimuli	Active avoidance	Discriminated punishment

"I'm getting him conditioned beautifully—every time I run through the maze, he throws me a bit of cheese."

© Punch (Rothco).

reward training positive reinforcement is used to elicit a desired response—a rewarding stimulus is contingent upon the occurrence of a particular response. Getting your allowance if you take out the garbage is an example of reward training. In *omission training,* rewards are used to get the learner to withhold a response that is not desired. For example, you make the purchase of a new car for yourself contingent on giving up cigarette smoking. The rewarding consequence is contingent on *not* making a particular response. In *escape training* negative reinforcement is used to increase the frequency of a desired response. If the learner gives the desired response, the consequence is that an unpleasant stimulus will be terminated. For example, you could train a dog to jump over a fence by giving him an electric shock until he makes the jumping response. Turning off the shock is contingent on making the jump. Telling a convict that he can have "time off for good behavior" is an example of escape training—he can escape imprisonment if he produces "good behavior." Finally, the fourth basic case is *punishment training* (also known as *passive avoidance*), and it is used to make the learner stop performing an undesired response. If the undesired response is made, the consequence is that a punishing stimulus is presented, and so the subject learns to withhold the

Experimental Diet Shocking

Miami, Fla. (AP)—Several overweight Miami women have discovered that the best way to take it off is to plug in.

A team of Miami psychologists is helping patients diet by attaching a portable electric "shocker" to their forks to discourage rapid eating.

"We're aiming for a change in eating behavior and we're even doing things like timing the intervals between forks to the mouth and the number of chews of food," said Dr. Michael S. Stokols of the Center for Psychological Services Inc.

"We may ask a patient to bring a portion of her usual dinner right here to our office and then we hook her up with electrodes and the shocking mechanism," he said. "One of us may sit opposite her and eat ourselves. If the patient picks up the fork too soon, she will get a shock."

Stokols said the psychologist sets a timed waiting interval for the patient after analyzing her eating behavior.

The patient soon begins to "chain together" non-eating behavior to take up time at the table instead of simply eating.

"She may take a sip of water, dab her mouth with a napkin, speak to us, instead of wolfing down the food," he explained. . . .

"We're not shocking the eating itself—just rapid eating. And often we shock only when the patient eats the 'wrong' thing—maybe cake, ice cream and so forth," he said.

The weight loss itself is usually the principal "reinforcer" to change the eating behavior, the psychologist said, noting that some women patients have lost as much as 80 pounds using the center's technique.

And in case a patient begins to backslide into her old "food addiction" approach, there are even portable shockers available. . . .

Here is an example of the use of punishment training to control eating behavior.

response. Telling a child that you will spank him if he says "dirty" words is an example; so is putting people in jail for breaking the law.

Discriminative stimuli (cues).   Suppose a child is punished by his parents for saying "dirty" words. We might expect that he would never say them again. But the child can only be punished if his parents are there to hear him say the words; that is, the punishment can only be delivered when a certain stimulus (his parents) is present. If the stimulus is absent, the response can be made without the threat of punishment. Thus whether or not the child says dirty words depends upon whether or not his parents are present. The child can discriminate between the presence or absence of his parents and he learns to make his behavior of saying dirty words contingent on this discrimination. There is a stimulus (the parents) that now controls whether or not the child says dirty words. This process is known as *stimulus control,* and the controlling stimulus is called a *discriminative stimulus* or *cue.*

In stimulus-control situations, there is a cue or stimulus that is presented to the learner to indicate that reward or punishment will take place contingent on his behavior. Reward or punishment is contingent on behavior only when this discriminative stimulus is present. When the critical stimulus is not present or some other stimulus is present, no rewards or punishments are delivered regardless of what the learner does. These cued situations are thus different from noncued situations, where reward or punishment is always available and contingent on behavior.

Stimulus-control learning (also called discriminative learning) can be demonstrated in the laboratory by training a rat to press a lever for food (reward) when a buzzer is sounded (cue present) and not to press when the buzzer is off (cue absent). The rat will learn to stop pressing the bar as soon as the buzzer stops and to start pressing again as soon as the buzzer comes back on. His pressing is then said to be under the (stimulus) control of the buzzer. In a real sense, his behavior is controlled by the buzzer.

Each of the four basic learning situations we have discussed has its counterpart involving a discriminative cue (see Table 4–5B). The rat's bar pressing for food only when the buzzer sounds is an example of a *discriminated operant.* The teenager who does not smoke *only* when his parents are around to reward his abstention exemplifies the *discriminated omission* response. The convict who works hard *only* when a guard is watching exemplifies *active avoidance* (he actively produces desired responses to avoid punishment from the guard). And the child who omits dirty words from his vocabulary *only* when his parents are present to punish him exemplifies the process of *discriminated punishment.*

Shaping. Because the desired response may be uncommon or difficult, the individual using operant training procedures may want to use an auxiliary technique called *shaping.* Shaping consists of learning in graduated steps, where each successive step requires a response that is more similar to the desired performance. It is often known as the method of successive approximations.

Punishment Is Not the Same as Negative Reinforcement

Punishment: an unpleasant stimulus is *delivered* contingent on the occurrence of a particular *undesired* behavior. This punishing stimulus terminates at some point in time, but the termination is in no way related to the behavior of the organism being punished.

Examples:
1. A child spills his milk and the parents administer a spanking.
2. A prisoner spits in the face of his captor and is beaten with a club.

Negative reinforcement: an unpleasant stimulus is *terminated* contingent on the occurrence of a particular *desired* behavior. The beginning of the unpleasant stimulus is in no way related to the occurrence of any particular behavior.

Examples:
1. A prisoner of war is tortured until he makes responses desired by his captors, such as confession; the torture is then terminated. This process strengthens the response of saying what the enemy wants to hear.
2. A rat is shocked continuously until it jumps over a barrier, at which point the shock is terminated. This strengthens the response of jumping.

In most everyday situations, punishment and negative reinforcement occur together and so are easily confused. The same stimulus event is used to punish one response and negatively reinforce another.

Example:
A child comes home and throws his coat on the floor. The parent yells at the child until he picks up the coat and hangs it in the closet, at which point the yelling stops.

Here the yelling is serving once as a punishment and once as a negative reinforcer. It is a punishment for throwing the coat on the floor because it is an unpleasant stimulus that is delivered contingent on the coat being thrown on the floor. It is a negative reinforcer because it is continuously delivered until the child picks up the coat and hangs it up, at which point the shouting is all over. The parent has *punished* throwing the coat on the floor and *negatively reinforced* hanging the coat in the closet. So you can see that punishment is used to *decrease* the rate of an undesired response, while negative reinforcement is used to *increase* the rate of a desired response.

BEETLE BAILEY

Suppose an experimenter wanted to train a pigeon to peck an illuminated response button. He might start by reinforcing the pigeon just for turning its head toward the response button. After the animal begins to orient toward the button consistently, the experimenter may then require him to move toward it before rewarding him. When the bird is trained to stand near the response button, the experimenter may withhold reinforcement until the animal makes slight head movements toward it. In the next stage, the animal may be reinforced only if he actually contacts the response button with his beak. Finally the animal is reinforced only when he hits the button with sufficient force to trip an automatic switch that controls the delivery of pigeon feed. After the bird has been shaped to peck forcefully at the button, the experimenter may introduce colored illumination as a discriminative cue.

Operant psychologists have claimed that training a child to talk is basically an example of shaping. The reinforcement in this case is probably praise and attention from parents and other adults. When the child is very young and preverbal, parents are likely to reinforce just about any babbling sound that the child makes. Gradually, response requirements become more rigorous, and the child must make sounds closer and closer to actual words before he gets a reaction from parents—the child's speech is shaped. Whether or not such behavior is actually acquired in this way is a matter of some debate among psychologists at the present time (see Chapters 5 and 7). This analysis, then, is a tentative proposal, by no means fully documented by fact.

Fading.   Another principle of operant conditioning, known as *fading,* allows for the gradual introduction of a new stimulus into a situation without disrupting the behavior that is already taking place. The stimulus is *faded in* gradually by making it increasingly louder, clearer, or more central—presumably making it more obvious. Instant, abrupt introduction of the new stimulus would ordinarily disrupt ongoing behavior. Fading in the stimulus allows the person to adapt to its gradually increasing presence without disruption.

A stimulus can also be *faded out* if you do not want it to be the only stimulus that controls behavior. Suppose you feel that you must have the radio on to be able to sit and study. However, the radio also distracts you. Studying is under the stimulus control of the radio, but this is not a desirable situation. You can gradually decrease the volume of the radio over successive study sessions (fading the stimulus out), until you can no longer hear it; then you can study without it.

Effects of Conditioning

Conditioning is a multifaceted phenomenon, and it has many effects on the subsequent behavior of the organism. In this section we will discuss several of the more important effects and by-products of conditioning.

Extinction and Spontaneous Recovery

Extinction is a process that takes place when (in classical conditioning) the UCS is no longer paired with the CS or when (in instrumental conditioning) reinforcement of a learned response is withdrawn. The response frequency declines toward zero. In classical conditioning, as the CS is repeatedly presented alone, it gradually loses its power to elicit the CR. In instrumental conditioning, extinction is brought about by eliminating reinforcement. An example of the value of extinction might be the elimination of a bad habit. All habits, good or bad, are learned presumably because a person has achieved something, reinforcement, for his action.

By permission of John Hart and Field Enterprises, Inc.

The dinosaur is responding to a discriminative stimulus: the verbal command "sit." This is not the most elementary form of operant conditioning. In the fundamental form the dinosaur would be rewarded whenever he sat down. From there we might progress gradually—the procedure known as shaping—to the situation where he sits only on command and does not sit if we say "roll over" or if we say nothing.

Man Hated Face—Then TV Did Trick

London (AP)—The man hated his face so much he couldn't bear to look at it.

Psychiatrists tried about everything—psychotherapy, insulin, LSD-25, electric shock, psychoanalysis, other drugs and even a brain operation. Nothing worked.

Then psychiatrists at Birmingham University hit on television.

Ages Given

The whole thing began when the unnamed man was 5. He overheard a neighbor telling his parents that he looked like a "proper boy." When he was 12 he became self-conscious about his face. He thought it was effeminate, and that others looked at him with contempt.

By age 18, he couldn't stand his reflection, was unable to look in windows or mirrors. At 22, he left work, lived alone in his room at his parents' home, eating alone and unable to talk to anyone without hiding behind a screen or at the back of the interviewer.

One time he permitted himself to enter a hospital. He wore a Ku Klux Klan-type of hood to hide his face.

Finally, over the years, he was enticed into an interview recorded by television tape. Then, the videotape was shown him, his face greatly out of focus and the light reduced. Seventeen times the process was repeated with focus sharpened and light increased. Finally, on the 18th showing his face was sharp and the light normal.

The man decided he didn't hate his face. . . .

An example of fading in.

By identifying the reinforcer of a bad habit and removing it, the habit would be extinguished and should disappear. Can you apply this principle to the elimination of temper tantrums in a child?

There is a process, however, that makes complete extinction difficult, if not impossible. This process is called *spontaneous recovery.* To illustrate, suppose a rat is trained to run a maze for food. On a certain day extinction is begun by removing food from the maze. The rat continues to run the maze, trial after trial, until finally he quits running. At this point, you may think that the rat will never again run the maze unless food is reinstated. But you would be wrong. If the rat is put back in the maze after a day, he will run again almost as rapidly as he did originally, for a few trials. Although he is given no food, his attraction to the goal box seems to recover without intervening training, that is, spontaneously. If the goal was to eliminate the running response,

Challenging the Law of Contiguity

The Law of Contiguity states that any two events experienced together in space and time will become associated with each other in the mind of the experiencing organism. It is often heralded as the most fundamental law of learning and the basic explanation of classical conditioning. In Pavlov's conditioning studies the CS and UCS were experienced close together in space and time; that is, the bell and food were spatially and temporally *contiguous*. Other studies have shown that the best conditioning occurs when the CS is presented about .5 seconds before the UCS.

But what happens if the CS is separated from the UCS by a long interval? For example, suppose the bell is sounded but the food is not presented until 30 minutes later. The food, of course, elicits salivating in the dog. But even after several trials in which both food and bell are presented, the dog does not salivate to the bell alone. Conditioning does not occur with such a long delay. Thus the Law of Contiguity seems well supported.

However, conditioning has in fact been demonstrated when the interval between the CS and the UCS was an unbelievably long 7 hours. S. H. Revusky (1968) did such an experiment using X-ray radiation as the UCS and a sweet solution as the CS. Earlier studies had shown that X-rays elicit the UCR of being sick (radiation sickness), which can be conditioned to the solution. Rats that were drinking the sweet solution while being radiated developed a firm dislike for the solution, which normally they enjoyed. Eventually the animals became sick at the sight, taste, and smell of the solution, even when no X-rays were given. Thus the rats had developed a conditioned aversion to sweets, as the Law of Contiguity would predict.

Revusky tried the same conditioning procedure, except that he changed the CS-UCS interval to 7 hours, so the stimuli were no longer contiguous. The rats drank the sweet water and were radiated 7 hours later. Yet even with such a long delay, the rats developed a dislike for the solution (see Figure 4–4). Either Revusky's demonstration is not an instance of classical conditioning, or the Law of Contiguity is not the only explanation of why conditioning occurs.

A possible explanation of this phenomenon is that some organisms have a built-in conditioning system, genetically based, that quickly acquires certain conditioned responses in particular. Thus there might be a special system that relates food stimuli, via taste perception, with feeling sick. Such a system would have survival value for the species because it would underlie the organism's ability to avoid eating things that might be poisonous.

Or Revusky's demonstration might be an instance of punishment training, one kind of operant conditioning. The response of drinking the sugar water is punished 7 hours later by the radiation sickness, and therefore the rats learn not to drink the solution (see Figure 4–5).

An important point to be emphasized here is that the distinction between classical and operant conditioning is often difficult to make. Indeed, the two types of conditioning often proceed simultaneously. There probably is no task that is purely instrumental or purely classical. The two basic types of learning are intimately related to each other.

Figure 4–4
It looks like classical conditioning, but is it?

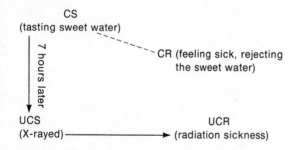

Figure 4–5
It looks like operant conditioning, but is it?

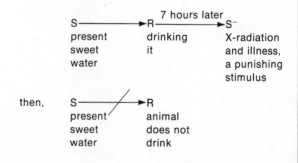

spontaneous recovery has worked against extinction.

Spontaneous recovery is likely to occur after each of several successive extinction sessions. Total extinction is likely to take a long time, as shown in Figure 4–6, and may never be attained. Spontaneous recovery is one reason that we all find it so difficult to eliminate bad habits. Ask anyone who has tried to stop biting his nails. One way to forestall spontaneous recovery is to overextinguish the habit

Figure 4–6
Extinction–spontaneous recovery sequence

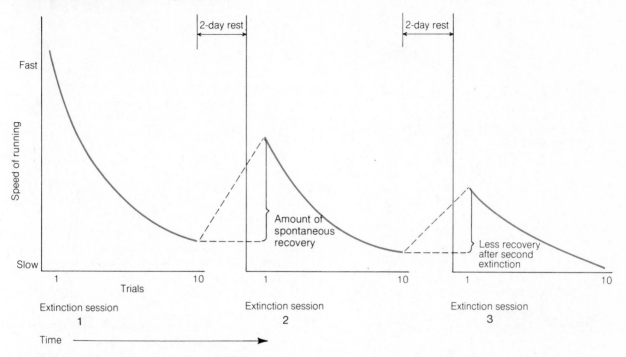

The three curves show the course of extinction of a maze-running habit in three successive extinction sessions, with a 2-day rest between sessions. Note that the strength of the habit increases between the end of one session and the start of the next. This is spontaneous recovery.

by carrying the extinction sessions on long after the response has ceased.

Generalization and Discrimination

The importance of two key learning processes, *generalization* and *discrimination,* has been implicit in the foregoing discussion. There are two kinds of generalization, response generalization and stimulus generalization. In response generalization, a person who has been trained to make a particular response will sometimes make a similar response if his originally learned behavior is somehow blocked or interfered with. Stimulus generalization pertains to the occurrence of a learned response under circumstances that are similar to but discriminably different from the original training situation.

As an example of response generalization, consider training a rat to press a bar in a Skinner box for food pellets. The first successful bar press might be quite accidental. Let's say the animal strikes the bar with sufficient force with his left paw while exploring the cage. The immediate delivery of a food pellet reinforces the left paw response. The animal will have a tendency to make that same response again. With successive responses and reinforcements the response gains strength. But that strength typically will not be limited to left paw presses just because the animal began that way. Rather, response strength will generalize to other similar responses. Indeed, it is typical of an animal in this situation to vary his response, sometimes using his left paw, sometimes his right, and even his nose and his rear end on occasion. The animal has learned a quite general response, or perhaps a set of equivalent responses, all of which produce reinforcement.

Now if the intention was to train an animal to press a bar with his tail only, a different procedure would have to be used. The animal would be rewarded only when he pressed with his tail and never when he pressed with his paw or nose; this method would effectively extinguish all responses except the tail press. The procedure would be called *response discrimination* or *differentiation,* resulting

"THIS IS A STICKUP!"

"THIS IS A STICKUP!"

"THIS IS A STICKUP!"

The New Yorker, March 4, 1961. Drawing by Opie; © 1961 The New Yorker Magazine, Inc.

Merely paying attention to someone's behavior can be reinforcing, particularly if the person is "starved for attention." Withdrawal of the reinforcing attention results in the elimination of the behavior.

generalization and response discrimination in human behavior. For example, in athletics, there is generally only one best way (or a very few ways) to perform a desired act, say high jumping or pole vaulting. Even slight deviations from the ideal, the response generalization phenomenon, may result in failure when jumping in a competition event. An athlete must undergo years of training in response differentiation until he can make the ideal response over and over again with little variation. Consider the problem of response differentiation as it pertains to playing a concerto on a piano, cutting a diamond, or disarming a bomb.

Stimulus generalization is likewise an important phenomenon and has received a great deal of attention from both experimental and theoretical psychologists. In this phenomenon, a response learned in one stimulus situation will tend to occur in other similar situations. For example, a child's fear of dogs after being bitten may generalize to similar stimuli, such as other animals or even stuffed animal toys. Experimenters frequently construct a *gradient of stimulus generalization* to indicate the degree of generalization to various stimuli. Suppose a group of pigeons were trained to peck a button illuminated with a light of 550 nanometers (a greenish-yellow color). Then, by testing the strength of their response to buttons of other colors, the experimenter can determine the gradient of generalization (see Figure 4–7). It is known that the more similar a test stimulus is to the original training stimulus, the greater the likelihood that the organism will respond to it in the way it has been trained. Thus it is no surprise that the curve in Figure 4–7 shows the greatest number of responses by the pigeons to buttons of illumination close to 550 nanometers.

Stimulus generalization can have both positive and negative consequences. On the positive side, note that it is unnecessary to teach an organism a desired response in each and every stimulus situation it will encounter. After training it to respond in one or at most a few situations, we can expect it to be able to respond in almost any similar situation. For example, a parent who has toilet-trained a child at home can reasonably expect him to generalize both his control and the appropriate behavior to the schoolroom, the neighborhood child's birthday party, his trip to the zoo, and just about everywhere else.

Negative effects of stimulus generalization are possible whenever the response in question is an undesired one, such as stuttering. Many speech pathologists believe that stuttering is a learned

in a highly specific, stylized response—pressing only with the tail.

There are many examples of response

Figure 4–7
Gradient of stimulus generalization

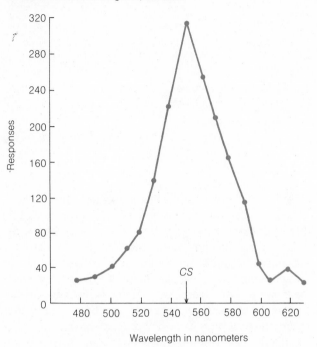

The gradient of stimulus generalization is shown for a group of pigeons trained to peck a button illuminated with a light of 550 nanometers and then presented with test buttons of several other colors, ranging from 480 to 620 nanometers. The graph shows that the closer the test stimulus was to the training stimulus of 550, the more the birds pecked.

Figure 4–8
The Lashley jumping stand

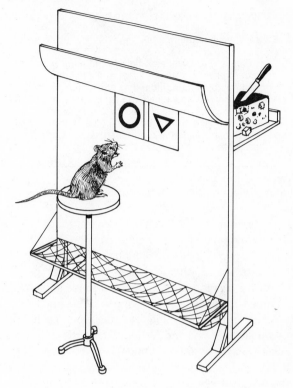

In discrimination studies, the rat must jump from the stand through one door or the other. If he selects the correct door, it opens and he lands on the platform, where he finds food. The wrong choice lands him unpleasantly in the net below.

response arising in parent–child interaction situations, especially when the parent is overly concerned with the child's speech behavior. Once stuttering is learned, however, the child stutters in almost all situations regardless of whether the parents are present. Problems arise also when we try to extinguish undesired behavior. It may be possible to extinguish stuttering in some situations but not all. Compounding the problem is some experimental evidence suggesting that the generalization gradient is heightened and broadened under conditions of anxiety. Since the extinction of undesirable responses is often accompanied by considerable frustration and anxiety, stimulus generalization may make extinction more difficult.

There are many responses that are acceptable in one situation but not in another. In these cases, stimulus generalization may cause mistakes that result in punishment. Thus it becomes necessary to learn a *stimulus discrimination* essentially the

opposite of stimulus generalization. The learner must be trained to discriminate among stimuli such that he responds to some but not to others. An essential aspect of learning to drive a car, for example, is learning to apply the brakes at the sight of a red light and not at the sight of a green one.

In the laboratory, discrimination learning is usually studied by training the subject to respond to one stimulus by rewarding him and not to respond to others by withholding reward if he does respond. A simple device, called the Lashley jumping stand, is used for studying discrimination learning in rats (see Figure 4–8). The rat is placed on a stool in front of the apparatus, which has two doors leading to a food platform. During discrimination learning, one door is open and the other is locked. The rat is forced to jump from the stand to the door in order to get to the reinforcement on the food platform, and he quickly learns to jump toward the unlocked

---

Table 4–6
Hypothetical sequence of events in mediated generalization

1. Condition a response (say an eye blink) to the word *big*

    Big– – – – – –Blink

2. Present test stimulus *large*

    Large

3. *Large* elicits *big* as an associate in the mind of the subject (makes him think of *big*) and since the subject has been conditioned to blink when he sees the word *big*, he now blinks to *large*. Note that the blink response is not directly elicited by the word *large*. Instead, the blink is mediated by the implicit associative response *big;* hence the term "mediated generalization."

    Large   Blink

    Big

---

door. Selecting the wrong door lands him in the net below.

The combination of stimulus generalization and differentiation can lead to quite complex learning tasks. Suppose a pigeon is taught to peck at a green response key as rapidly as he can, and after extensive training the response button is suddenly changed to yellow. If the response of pecking the yellow button is not reinforced, the pigeon will gradually stop pecking (extinguishing the response) and begin to form a discrimination. The green button is called the positive stimulus and the yellow the negative. The simplest theory of discrimination learning says that an organism, in this situation, builds up an approach or *excitatory tendency* to the positive stimulus and a corresponding avoidance or *inhibitory tendency* to the negative stimulus. Because of stimulus generalization, both excitatory and inhibitory tendencies will generalize to other, similar stimuli. The net tendency to respond to a particular stimulus will be determined by the difference between the excitatory and the inhibitory tendencies to that stimulus.

Secondary Effects of Conditioning

Mediated generalization. Most of the examples of stimulus generalization we have discussed are examples of *primary generalization* because they are based on *physical* similarity of stimuli, for example, color, size, sound, brightness, shape, or some other physical characteristic. *Mediated* or *secondary generalization,* on the other hand, is based not on physical similarity but on learned similarity.

Consider a special case of secondary generalization called *semantic generalization* because of its relationship to word meanings. Suppose we classically condition a person to blink his eyes whenever he is presented with the stimulus word *big*. After he begins to blink reliably to *big*, we

can present him with new words as test stimuli and observe whether the eye-blink response generalizes. If we presented the word *bag* as a test stimulus and the subject blinked his eyes, we would have an example of primary generalization because *big* and *bag* are physically similar stimuli. If, however, we present the word *large* and he blinks, we have an example of mediated generalization because *big* and *large* are not physically similar (see Table 4–6). The similarity between these two words, and therefore the basis of generalization, is word meaning. Generalization in this case is said to be mediated by something the learner knows, that is, has previously learned, about the two stimuli. A subject who spoke no English would be expected to show primary generalization between *big* and *bag,* but not secondary generalization between *big* and *large*. While this example may seem trivial, there is a good deal of evidence to suggest that our language system is the most important mediator of generalization. We will find that mediated generalization is an extremely important concept for understanding human behavior.

The hypothetical sequence of events in mediated generalization is as follows: A particular response becomes conditioned to a specific stimulus; for example, an individual is offended by the attitudes of a "hippie" and learns to dislike that person. Now when the hippie-hater meets people whom he associates in his mind with the hippie he was offended by, he will dislike them. The dislike is not directly elicited by these people. Instead the dislike response is mediated by the implicit associative response "hippie." Hence the term *mediated generalization*.

Secondary reinforcement. The kinds of reinforcement we have considered thus far are automatically effective. The subject does not need prior experience with reinforcers like food or electric shock for them to have the effect of increasing the subject's responses. Reinforcers like food for the hungry animal, water for the thirsty, and painful shock are all examples of "innate" or "unlearned" reinforcers. Technically they are referred to as *primary reinforcers.*

Other stimuli are capable of becoming reinforcers if the organism learns that they are associated with primary reinforcers or that they can be used to obtain primary reinforcers. Once the subject learns about them, they become *secondary reinforcers.* The most potent example of a secondary reinforcer for human beings is, of course, money. Consider the dollar bill and ask yourself why it is that we all learn and perform the extraordinary tasks that we do in order to get money. The dollar cannot be eaten or drunk. It becomes a reinforcer only because we have learned that money can buy food, drink, and many other things; that is, money will buy primary reinforcers (see Figure 4–9).

In our society, secondary reinforcers carry a major burden. Most people are not starving or thirsty or lacking oxygen. To be sure, the promise of sexual reinforcement may control a portion of human behavior, but, sex aside, most of our activity does not need to be motivated by primary reinforcement. Psychologists of all persuasions have postulated the existence of many learned secondary reinforcers. In addition to money, obvious examples are prestige, fame, security, and approval. There is, of course, a heavy emphasis on social factors in this list, implying the existence of a strong learned need to be liked by others. This, in turn, tends to make us dependent on the people who can deliver these reinforcers.

Many secondary reinforcers seem to develop through classical conditioning. The most important source of secondary reinforcement for a child is his parents. One or the other parent is almost always associated with the delivery of the infant's primary reinforcement—his food, diaper changes, water, and comfort. Thus the mere sight of his parents becomes rewarding, and the child will work (crawl around) just to maintain sight of them.

A possible unfortunate by-product of this state of affairs is that parents can inadvertently reinforce a bad habit merely by paying attention to the child at the wrong time. Suppose the child is playing with a friend and his mother overhears him saying or doing something bad. Running to him immediately constitutes secondary reinforcement of the undesired behavior, even if she scolds him when she gets there. Because attention has such a powerful effect, many psychologists recommend that a child's

Figure 4–9
Secondary reinforcement

Like human beings, chimpanzees can be trained to work for money (secondary reinforcement) that can be turned in later for primary reinforcement. The chimp shown here is about to put his money (a poker chip) into a "chimp-o-mat," which will dispense bananas or grapes. Chimps can be trained to work all day for poker chips, if they have first learned that the poker chips can be used to obtain food.

minor bad habits be ignored, at least as a first attempt at solution. Ignoring the child when he engages in "bad" behavior is a form of withdrawing reinforcement and should result in extinction of those habits. The picture is not this simple, of course, since attention is not the only reinforcer that is effective with children. In fact, it is important for anyone concerned with the rapid extinction of a response to remember to withhold not only primary reinforcement but also any secondary reinforcers that may be a natural part of the original learning situation.

Identifying reinforcers. In order to institute instrumental reward training, one must identify those objects or events that the learner values. Obviously, candy and other favorite foods can be used with children, but there are side effects that may be detrimental. What other reinforcers will be effective is sometimes hard to know. One general principle that may be helpful for the identification of reinforcers has been suggested by David Premack. The Premack principle is that *given two behaviors which differ in their likelihood of occurrence, the less likely behavior can be reinforced by using the more likely behavior as a reward.* For example, given free choice, many children will spend more time watching TV than studying. Watching TV is a more probable behavior. The Premack principle states that the amount of studying can be increased by making TV time contingent on study behavior. Again, children are more likely to eat candy than to do odd jobs, given free choice. Thus candy can be used to encourage work. In a prison, playing softball is more probable than learning a new skill, given free choice. To induce skill acquisition, the prison administration might use access to the softball field as a reinforcer. Thus from observation of an organism in a free-option environment, one can develop a list or hierarchy of preferred behaviors.

Chaining and higher-order conditioning.
Larger habits tend to be compounded of a number of smaller ones. In instrumental situations the compounding process is called *response chaining,* and in classical conditioning the corresponding process is *higher-order conditioning.*

Suppose a rat is trained to press a bar to get food. At this point the opportunity to press a bar should be secondarily reinforced because of its association with food. With further training, the rat can be taught to step on a pedal in order to open a door to the compartment where the bar is. Moreover, once he has learned to step on a pedal to get to the bar, the pedal should become a secondary reinforcer so that he could then be trained to stand on his hind legs before stepping on the pedal. By successive steps, working backward from the goal, a chain of responses could be built up that might consist of licking a spout that turns on a light, bumping the light to gain access to a string, pulling the string to produce a pedal, stepping on the pedal to open a door, running through the door to confront a bar, and finally pressing the bar to obtain food. Psychologists have made the rat do a lot of work for one small pellet of chow. The relation to human behavior is obvious. Generally, we are not rewarded for each response that we make. Rather, we are taught long chains of responses that eventuate in reward.

Higher-order conditioning is related to response chaining. Suppose a dog is trained to salivate at the sight of a light. Because the light now elicits saliva, it can be used as a UCS. Then a tone is presented, followed in half a second by the light, which elicits saliva because of initial training. Gradually, the tone will come to elicit saliva. When saliva is evoked by the original CS, the light, the response is called a first-order CR. When the tone elicits saliva, as a result of being paired with the light, the response is called a second-order CR. Next, the tone could be paired with a touch on the back of the animal. If the touch came to elicit saliva, it would be a third-order CR. It should be noted that higher-order conditioning is difficult to produce, even in the laboratory, and probably is not as powerful as chaining in human behavior.

Obviously, both response chaining and higher-order conditioning are dependent on secondary reinforcement. These and other examples stand as strong testimony to the crucial role played by secondary reinforcement in all behavior, human and animal.

Partial reinforcement and extinction. During learning, reinforcement might not be presented for each and every response that the learner makes. The learner's responses are only partially reinforced. *Partial reinforcement,* a reinforcement schedule in which less than 100 percent of all correct responses are rewarded, is a valuable aid in teaching new habits. For one thing, it saves money and effort if you do not have to give your dog a biscuit every time he brings your newspaper or slippers. At the outset of training, you would probably want to use *continuous* (100 percent) *reinforcement.* Once the animal is performing reasonably well, however, you can reduce the percentage gradually with the surprising effect that there is no deterioration in performance. In fact, there is some evidence that the partially reinforced subject actually comes to make the response faster and more vigorously than the continuously reinforced subject.

Now, suppose you institute extinction—no more rewards for the animal ever again. The effect here is also surprising. It will take much longer to extinguish an animal who has been trained on partial reinforcement than one trained on continuous reward. On an intuitive level, it is as if the partially reinforced animal does not realize that extinction has begun. He is used to not getting

Schedules of Reinforcement

There are four major types of partial reinforcement schedules that can be viewed as a 2 × 2 combination of two variables (see diagram below). First, the schedule can depend upon how many responses the subject makes (called ratio schedules) or it can depend upon how much time has passed since the last reinforcement (interval schedules). Second, the number of responses in the case of ratio schedules, or the time in the case of interval schedules, can be fixed and invariable, or it can be random and highly variable. This gives us the four basic combinations shown and described below.

	Ratio	Interval
Fixed schedules	Fixed ratio (FR)	Fixed interval (FI)
Variable schedules	Variable ratio (VR)	Variable interval (VI)

1. *Fixed ratio:* You reward after a fixed number of responses have been emitted. For example, you reward your dog every fourth time he performs the correct response.

2. *Fixed interval:* You reward the first response that occurs after a fixed amount of time since the last response. You might reward a rat for the first bar press emitted after 1 minute has passed since the last reward. Pressing during the 1-minute delay would do the rat no good. Note that getting paid every Friday is like a fixed-interval schedule.

3. *Variable ratio:* You reward such that, *on the average,* a reward is given after the fourth response, for example. Sometimes it is given after 1, sometimes after 6, after 3, after 9, and so forth on a random basis, the average being some specified value. The payoff schedule of a Las Vegas slot machine is a good example.

4. *Variable interval:* You reward the first response after *an average time interval* of, say, 1 minute. Sometimes only 5 seconds has to elapse, sometimes 2 minutes, sometimes 45 seconds, etc., but the average time interval is set at a specific value. Have you ever tried hitchhiking? Is that a good example?

In general, the variable schedules (variable interval and variable ratio) lead to much higher rates of performance. They also lead to much greater resistance to extinction. Pigeons and rats have been trained to perform at very high levels over very long periods of time for very little in the way of reward, provided the rewards are scheduled properly. They also will continue to perform for very long periods of time after you have ceased giving rewards altogether.

rewarded on some trials. In contrast, the continuously rewarded animal experiences an abrupt change in his circumstances on the first trial of extinction.

Any habit learned under partial reinforcement will be difficult to extinguish. Partial reinforcement is a pervasive phenomenon for human beings: Not every cigarette tastes good, only some of them; even the best gambler does not win on every play; temper tantrums do not always result in "getting your way." Because of partial reinforcement, we can expect our good habits to persist even in the face of adversity. But our bad ones will, too, and simple extinction is probably not the answer to getting rid of them.

Punishment and extinction.   An important but unusual observation is that a response that has been learned in the presence of mild punishment is often more difficult to extinguish than one learned on the basis of reward alone. In the laboratory, this can be demonstrated by training rats in a simple maze. Suppose the rat has to learn to choose between turning right or left. During training food is put on the right side and the rat is given a mild shock after he has turned right, just before he gets the food. The shock has to be mild enough, of course, that he still goes forward in the maze and gets his reward. After training, the food is switched to the left side. A rat who has learned under combined reward and punishment takes longer to learn the new response of turning left than does a control rat who did not experience punishment.

Remember the mother who ran to punish her child for being nasty to a friend. The attention of the mother is a reward for the child, and it is coupled with punishment, which the mother inflicts when she gets there. The inappropriate behavior of the child may be strengthened rather than weakened under these circumstances. A juvenile delinquent commonly gets both rewarded and punished for his activities. So does a cigarette smoker, a sex offender, a neurotic with a phobia, and so on. This fact may make these bad habits even more difficult to extinguish or to replace than they otherwise might be. The routine of replacing one habit by another, rather than simply extinguishing a habit

TRUDY

"Frankly, Ted—I think I liked it better before you quit smoking."

© King Features Syndicate, 1971.

If you are trying to quit smoking, *extinction* would involve simply stopping, whereas *counterconditioning* would involve substituting a new habit for the old one. In general, counterconditioning is a better procedure for eliminating bad habits, provided, of course, that the substitute habit is not worse than the original one.

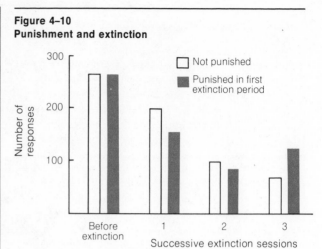

Figure 4–10
Punishment and extinction

☐ Not punished
■ Punished in first extinction period

Number of responses *(y-axis)*

Before extinction / 1 / 2 / 3

Successive extinction sessions

The data shown may cause you to think twice before using punishment as a means for facilitating extinction. Rats punished during the first of three extinction sessions made fewer responses during the first session; but by the third extinction session, they were responding *more* than animals not punished. If punishment is used in extinction, it should be carried out through the entire extinction, not just delivered early in extinction.

---

without replacement, is called *counterconditioning.* Research shows that counterconditioning is a better procedure than mere extinction for eliminating unwanted responses, particularly if the new, substitute response is incompatible with the undesired response.

An obvious alternative to extinction and counterconditioning for the elimination of a habit is severe punishment, probably the most popular, everyday method of response elimination. The use of punishment has been criticized frequently by psychologists on the grounds that punishment itself has undesirable side effects. To take an extreme example, your child may develop an aversion to you or even a neurosis if you use punishment excessively to control behavior. There is some experimental evidence that punishment during extinction may not accelerate the process. Punishment might cause an early suppression of undesired behavior, giving the impression that it is effectively extinguishing the behavior. The total time for complete extinction, however, may not be

affected at all (see Figure 4–10). Still, there are some situations in which punishment does work, particularly if the punishment is not overly severe. Frank Logan (1970) has summarized the available evidence into seven statements concerning the effective use of punishment, which are given in Table 4–7. As Logan himself cautions, his conclusions are not meant to encourage the use of punishment but rather to provide guidelines for its appropriate application.

Verbal Learning and Memory

The study of learning by human beings has focused heavily on language and verbal behavior for several reasons.

1. Human beings are verbal organisms, and verbal behavior (speaking, reading, listening, studying a textbook, etc.) is our predominant form of behavior.

2. Verbal materials are easy to work with experimentally. A researcher does not need elaborate conditioning or recording equipment.

3. Verbal learning problems can be arranged to require the subject to learn several responses—for example, memorizing several unfamiliar words more or less simultaneously—instead of focusing on a single response, as is typical of conditioning studies. The multiple-response task provides an ideal "next

Table 4–7
Principles for the effective use of punishment

1. *Avoid inadequate punishment*
   If the punishment is not strong enough to eliminate the behavior, the response is also being rewarded and fixation on that response may develop. Too small a fine for air polluting may in fact encourage pollution.

2. *If at all possible, the punishment should suit the crime*
   The punishment should by itself elicit a response incompatible with the undesired response. A jail sentence for a burglar is not necessarily incompatible with his committing future crimes, because he may use the time to learn more efficient techniques and to develop better plans.

3. *At least require an incompatible escape response*
   The person should be required to make an incompatible response to terminate the punishment. Jail sentences should be for indeterminate length—until the person has been rehabilitated or, in the case of vandalism, until the damage has been repaired.

4. *If at all possible, punish immediately*
   Since part of the punishing effects are a result of classical conditioning, and since classical conditioning is most effective with short intervals between CS and UCS, one should try to punish immediately after the undesired response has been emitted. Even better is to deliver the punishment just as the person is about to make the undesired response, but, of course, this is often impossible.

5. *If punishment cannot be delivered immediately, try to reinstate the circumstances*
   A child can be told or reminded about a past indiscretion that is now being punished. Even better is to "return to the scene of the crime." Make the person repeat the offense or simulate a repetition, which can then be punished immediately. If you are employing counterconditioning, make the person reenact the behavior sequence and perform the counter or incompatible response. If you walk into a party and immediately ask to borrow a cigarette when you are trying to quit smoking, go back outside and come in again with your hands in your pockets.

6. *Avoid rewards after punishment*
   If you feel sorry for your child after punishing him and then proceed to lavish affection and ice cream on him, the punishing stimuli will become secondary rewards (they get associated with rewards and are no longer effective). Masochism is a condition in which a person *wants* to be punished. It may result from always experiencing reward following punishment so that the punishment itself becomes rewarding.

7. *Always provide an acceptable alternative to the punished response*
   If a very strong drive is motivating the behavior, punishment will prevent the satisfaction of this drive, which leaves the person in a state of strong conflict—he wants to satisfy the drive but knows he will be punished. Prolonged conflict in important drive areas (e.g., sexual drive) can lead to neurosis. In such cases try to provide an alternative mechanism by which the drive can be reduced.

step" for testing the principles of learning found in the laboratory and extending them to more complex situations.

4. The complexity of the verbal learning situation leads naturally into the study of complex human behavior and thinking. Analyses of verbal behavior are often seen as fundamental in the explanation of human thought.

For these reasons the study of verbal learning is an enormously popular branch of experimental psychology today. Research on human learning and memory was initiated in the late 1880's by Hermann Ebbinghaus, who chose to work with an arbitrary form of verbal material, invented by him and called the *nonsense syllables.* These syllables are supposedly devoid of meaning and are therefore ideal for studying the complete learning process. The nonsense syllable is a three-letter nonword consisting of two consonants separated by a vowel, for example, GOF, ZIF, BER. Ebbinghaus used these materials because he thought they were meaningless and would allow him to study the learning process from its earliest stages.

Verbal Learning Tasks

There are several problems or tasks that researchers use to study verbal learning. As we noted, these tasks usually require very simple materials and equipment. We will discuss three major types of verbal learning tasks: free-recall, serial, and paired associate.

Free-recall learning.   In a *free-recall* task the subject is confronted with a list of items (words, nonsense syllables, sentences) and is asked to memorize them. The *study-test* or *recall method* is often used. First of all, the items are shown to the subject for a study trial, followed by a test trial during which the subject attempts to recall the items in any order they occur to him (see Table 4–8). After the test trial, there may be another study trial in which the items are presented to the subject in a different order, followed by a test, and so on for as long as the experimenter wishes to continue. One interesting thing about recall is that, despite the fact that the subject is free to recall in any order, he typically will adopt a fixed sequence across several study-test cycles. The subject will tend to give the items in the same order each time, a phenomenon known as *subjective organization.*

Subjective organization is important for several reasons. First, it shows clearly that subjects actively participate in the learning task, thinking and organizing as they learn. The learner is not passive in the process, waiting for items to be "stamped in" or conditioned, as some philosophical and theoretical positions would have us believe. The organizational phenomenon also indicates that there are limitations on our memories. Some evidence

Table 4–8
Sample verbal learning tasks

1. Free recall

Memorize this list of words—you may recall them in any order you wish.

Study trial: professor
book
library
study
test
memorize
learn
forget

Test trial: Write down the words in any order you wish.

2. Serial learning

A. Study-test method: Memorize this list of words in the order presented.

Study trial: man
sky
cat
big
dog
woman
blue
little

Test trial: Write down the words in the order presented.

B. Anticipation method: I will show you a list of words one at a time, always in the same order. As each word is presented, try to guess the next word and say it out loud before I show it to you.

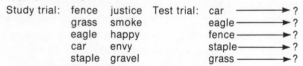

3. Paired-associate learning

A. Study-test method: Memorize the following pairs of words so that when I present the left-hand member of each pair (the stimulus), you can say the corresponding right-hand member (the response). First I'll show you the pairs for the study trial, then we'll have a test trial in which I'll present each stimulus and you try to give the appropriate response.

Study trial: fence   justice
grass   smoke
eagle   happy
car   envy
staple   gravel

Test trial: car ————→ ?
eagle ————→ ?
fence ————→ ?
staple————→ ?
grass ————→ ?

B. Anticipation method: As each stimulus is presented, try to guess the response, after which I will show you the correct response.

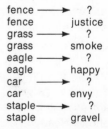

suggests that, actually, we can keep track of only about seven items at a time in our immediate memory; that is, we have a *limited capacity memory.* But what is an "item"? Surprisingly, the actual

Fitting the Crime

Newsweek—One night last winter, after drinking in a Miami tavern, 20-year-old Joe Fales drove to the home of an interracial couple and fired a rifle shot at the house. Fales was captured, pleaded guilty and faced a five-year prison term. But he has never spent a day in jail. Instead, every Saturday morning for six months, the young meat cutter traveled to St. John's Institutional Baptist Church in the heart of Miami's black ghetto. Once there he breakfasted on eggs, grits, sausage and homemade biscuits with a group of ministers. On other days, Fales would help children in a predominantly black Head Start program.

Fales was sentenced by Miami Judge Alfonso Sepe to spend his Saturdays in the ghetto program. Judge Sepe thinks that punishment should fit the crime. "He didn't seem like a bad boy," says the judge. "He was just misguided, and going to church was the best way to cure him. He can learn that there is no reason to hate anybody, something he wouldn't have learned in prison." Prisons, as penologists know, tend to turn young people and first offenders into hardened criminals—and at best a prisoner is a drain on the public till. Accordingly, law officers across the nation are groping for ways to combine punishment with rehabilitation and service.

When Phoenix, Ariz., physician Patrick Lorey was convicted of selling $40,000 worth of liquid amphetamine to a state undercover agent, he faced a life prison term. Instead, Lorey was sentenced to spend seven years practicing medicine in Tombstone, Ariz., which had not had a doctor of its own for four years. "He's a great asset to the town," says Mayor Jack Hendrickson, who doubles as keeper of the Lucky Cuss Saloon. "In Tombstone, what a man does before he comes doesn't matter a whit. It's what he does after he gets here that counts."

False Alarm

In Salem, Mass., District Judge Samuel E. Zoll has set up a schedule of penalties for juvenile offenders. For turning in a false fire alarm, 80 hours of polishing fire engines; for slashing trees, 40 hours of planting seedlings in town parks; for vandalizing a school, washing down school walls and writing an essay on citizenship. Under a two-year-old Alternative Community Service Program in Portland, Ore., a middle-aged first offender caught stealing a $4.95 blouse was sentenced to work 30 hours at an adoption center. In Florida's Dade County, Bertha Costas, 23, killed her husband with a butcher knife during a domestic row. Last week, she was put on probation and ordered to teach Sunday School for five years—or go to jail for fifteen. Mrs. Costas chose the Sunday-school assignment.

Some criminals balk at such unusual sentences. One Florida man chose a two-year prison term rather than spend several years helping teach black children to read. "I look at the person's background and what he did," says Miami's Judge Sepe, "and figure out what's good for him and the community." No one who has ever received one of his special sentences, the judge says proudly, has ever been in trouble with the law again.

Learned Helplessness

It is relatively easy to train an animal to escape shock and then to avoid shock by making the appropriate response before the shock comes on. This is called *active avoidance*. The classic example is a rat running in a shuttle box to avoid shock. We might say that the animal has learned to *cope* with a very unpleasant situation—he learned a response to avoid pain. But suppose before the experimenter tried to condition the avoidance response to shock, he deliberately tried to teach the animal the following fact of life: "There is nothing you can do that will allow you to escape or avoid this shock." This is done by placing an animal in a situation where shocks are unavoidable and inescapable. No matter what he does he still gets shocked. After giving several unavoidable shocks, the experimenter now introduces an avoidance contingency—now if the animal runs to the other compartment or jumps the barrier, the shock is turned off (he escapes), or if he runs or jumps at a signal, the shock is never delivered (he avoids).

Animals with the prior experience of unavoidable shocks have a very difficult time learning the avoidance response that now will solve their problem. Some animals actually never learn to avoid this situation. The animal learned to cope with the unavoidable shocks in the first phase by adopting a strategy of just sitting there and taking it. Now in the second phase where the shocks can in fact be avoided, he fails to learn how to cope more adequately. The animal simply endures the shock as if there were nothing he could do. He appears stupid to the outsider, who knows that normally avoidance learning is a rather easy task. He appears helpless because he does nothing to help himself out of this situation. Thus the phenomenon has been called *learned helplessness*. Students will find more information in M. E. P. Seligman, Can we immunize the weak? *Psychology Today*, June 1969, pages 42–44.

Many psychologists see clear parallels between the learned helplessness of experimental animals and neurotic or psychotic individuals, particularly depressed people. These individuals often appear to have given up trying to cope, as if they have learned that nothing can be done. The hope is that the study of learned helplessness in the laboratory will help us to understand the development of behavioral disorders. Experimental attempts to cure animals of learned helplessness will have some direct bearing on the treatment of behavioral disorders and perhaps lead to new preventive approaches.

amount of information in each item has little effect on this seven-item limitation. It is just as hard to remember seven unrelated single letters, for example, J R Y P D G W, as it is to remember seven words. When you remember seven words, you are actually remembering a very large number of letters. Thus, an important strategy for memory is to organize the individual items into larger units or "chunks." If, for example, a 21-letter string can be organized into seven 3-letter chunks, this will enlarge memory, facilitate recall, and speed up the learning process. An outline of a book can be thought of as an organizing or chunking device and should facilitate recall of the textual material.

The study of free recall is important because so much of our learning is of this variety. When you are memorizing facts for multiple-choice tests, order makes no difference. You just need to know the facts and recall them at the time of the test. Of course, if order is important, if there is an appropriate or correct order for recall, performance could suffer. This brings us to serial learning.

Serial learning.   Consider memorizing a list of things you want to buy at the grocery store. It would be convenient to have them ordered according to placement in the store. If you practiced learning the list in that order, then you would be engaging in *serial learning*. Experimental study of serial learning uses either the *study–test method* or the *anticipation method*. In the anticipation method, items are always presented in the same order and the subject must anticipate each succeeding item while looking at the item before it (see Table 4–8). Note that the anticipation method gives the subject immediate feedback about his recall attempt. For example, as he is shown the second item, he guesses what the third item is. Then, he is immediately shown the third item, which he can use to correct his guess.

In the study–test method, the experimenter shows the subject all the words on a study trial, after which the subject tries to write them down in the order given. In this case the subject will not find out whether he was correct or not until the next study trial. You might think that immediate feedback about the correctness of responses would facilitate learning and therefore that the anticipation method would yield more rapid learning than the study–test method. Most experimental comparisons, however, favor the study–test method. This has implications for educational practice. It is probably better to study a set of facts and then to test yourself on

Serial Position and the "Isolation" Effect

In studying a textbook, students often underline important points they want to remember, usually with bright colored "magic markers" that make the important points "stand out." Of course, some students underline so much that the entire book turns yellow or purple or orange. Do you think the underlining helps, and is there a limit to how much underlining is beneficial?

Here's a simple verbal-learning experiment you can try on your friends. At right is a list of 11 nonsense syllables. Copy each one onto a notecard so that you have a set of "flash cards" to show your subjects. Make three sets of cards: (1) none of the syllables are placed in a border of colored magic marker; (2) the middle or sixth syllable is "isolated" by surrounding it with a colored border; (3) all 11 syllables are surrounded with a colored border. Now test some people on each of the three sets, say 3 or 4 subjects on each set. Show them the cards one at a time at a reasonably slow rate. Say nothing about the borders; just ask them to learn the syllables in any order. After this study trial, hand them a slip of paper and ask them to write down as many of the syllables as they can in any order. Then tally the results and see which group remembered the most syllables altogether and which group did best on the middle syllable. In the second group with only one isolated item, was there any recall of the item before the isolate and the item after the isolate? Draw a graph, called a *serial-position curve,* in which you plot the number of people who recalled the syllable at each position. A sample curve is shown in Figure 4–11. In it you can see a *primacy effect* (syllables near the beginning of the list are remembered well),

and a *recency effect* (syllables near the end of the list are also remembered well). Did you find these two effects in your serial-position curve? This is a study dealing with what is known as the *von Restorff effect.* The von Restorff effect refers to better retention of an isolated item, in our example the single item surrounded with a colored border, than of other items around it. Was PIJ recalled better when it was isolated (in condition 2) than when it was not (conditions 1 and 3) in your experiment? If so, you demonstrated the von Restorff effect. The interested reader can consult the following reference: W. P. Wallace, Review of the historical, empirical, and theoretical status of the von Restorff phenomenon, *Psychological Bulletin,* 1965, *63,* 410–424.

Figure 4–11
Sample serial-position curve

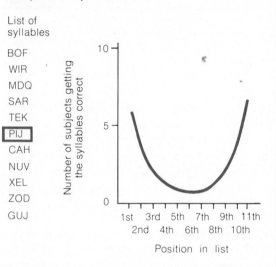

them, rather than to test on each fact repeatedly as you go along. In a self-test, you might try one item and then peek at the answer before going on to the next. This would be similar to the anticipation method. A better alternative would be to test yourself on all items, going back to check on answers only after you have completed them all.

Paired-associate learning. As the name would suggest, *paired-associate learning* requires the subject to learn a list of paired items. The left-hand member of each pair is considered to be the stimulus for the right-hand member, the response. The subject's task is to learn each pair in such a way that, when presented with the stimulus, he can produce the response. The learning procedure may involve either study–test or anticipation, as

illustrated in Table 4–8. As in serial learning, the study–test method involves alternating study and test trials. On a study trial, all pairs are presented and no response is required. By contrast, on a test trial only the stimulus terms are given, usually one at a time, and the subject attempts to produce the corresponding response term. No feedback for the response is provided until the next study trial. In the anticipation method the stimulus term is presented alone first, and the subject tries to guess the correct response. Immediately thereafter, the pair is shown, providing the subject with immediate feedback about his response. Comparisons of the two methods in paired-associate learning, as in serial learning, indicate that the study–test method leads to faster, more efficient learning.

The paired-associate procedure is probably the

most common task used in studies of verbal learning. One reason is the similarity between this procedure and classical conditioning. Some theorists have argued that a paired-associate list can be conceived of as an elaborate case of classical conditioning, in which a presentation of each stimulus-response unit is identified with a CS–UCS pairing in classical conditioning. Learning is said to take place when the subject anticipates the response term (a CR) before it is presented. Because of this basic similarity between learning situations, some psychologists argue that paired-associate learning is the natural situation to use to discover whether the principles of learning developed in the conditioning laboratory apply to complex human behavior. Obviously, this is not the only reason for studying paired-associate learning. The procedure is similar to conditioning, to be sure, but it is also similar to more familiar, everyday tasks that we do. For example, part of what is involved in mastering a new language is the learning of English equivalents for foreign words. Consider also learning the names for different kinds of rock samples in geology, the names for different chemical structures in organic chemistry, the names of various body structures in anatomy, or the names of plants and animals in biology. All of these cases involve a stimulus-response pairing that is at least partly verbal. All of them exemplify the paired-associate learning procedure.

Variables Affecting Verbal Learning

Meaningfulness.   Obviously, it is easier to learn meaningful than nonmeaningful materials. To take an extreme example, the pair JQM–ZJR is considerably more difficult to commit to memory than is the pair CAT–SKY. One question about this phenomenon that has proved difficult to answer, however, concerns why and how meaningfulness has its effect.

What is meaningfulness, and how can it be measured? Several possible answers have been offered.

1. The more similar an item is to an English word, the more meaningful it is. Note that JOK, while not an English word, is so much like one that it is easily connected with one. All other things being equal, this item would probably be easier to memorize than JQM.

2. Meaningfulness correlates with the frequency with which an item has been experienced in the past. The more familiar an item, the greater its meaningfulness. The letters JOK have been

experienced many more times by each of us than the combination JQM.

3. Meaningfulness depends on the number of associates elicited by an item "in your mind." Highly meaningful items elicit many associates, while items that are low in meaningfulness suggest absolutely nothing to you. JOK may elicit funny, comic, prank, and so on. But unless JQM happened to be your initials, the combination would probably suggest little or nothing. Moreover, highly meaningful items are more likely to produce images (JOK→an image of a TV comic) than are items low in meaningfulness.

4. In connection with verbal items, pronounceability also clearly relates to meaningfulness. JOK is easily pronounced, while JQM requires three separate responses, J-Q-M.

Meaningfulness is obviously a complex variable. No one of these four dimensions can account for its effect. If anything, meaningfulness is some combination of their effect, plus perhaps the effects of other variables that are as yet unidentified. More will be said about meaning and meaningfulness in Chapter 5.

How does meaningfulness influence learning in laboratory situations? Recall that when subjects learn a paired-associate list, they are given a stimulus term and are required to give a response (its associate). The effect of meaningfulness of the stimulus can be studied separately from that of the response term. In learning a paired-associate task, the effect of meaningfulness (similarity to English, familiarity, number of associates, or pronounceability) of the response item is strong. As the meaningfulness of response items increases, learning proceeds more rapidly. Increasing the meaningfulness of the stimuli, however, has relatively little influence on performance. Presumably, the increase in response meaningfulness has a twofold effect: The responses themselves become easier to master, and the association between each response and its corresponding stimulus becomes easier to form. Increasing the meaningfulness of stimuli can only facilitate the associative stage; it cannot make responses any easier to learn.

If meaningfulness facilitates learning, then a good technique for learning is somehow to make the material to be learned more meaningful than it is on the surface. For example, if you are faced with the task of learning the item JQM, you might use the letters to make up a sentence: "*Johnny quivered when Mary touched him.*" Under these circumstances, JQM becomes more meaningful. This

Meaningfulness Facilitates Learning: A Simple Test

Here are three lists of nonsense syllables that differ in rated meaningfulness. The rating procedure was to have the subject indicate whether or not a given syllable made him think of something—an association. If 100 percent of the subjects get an association to the syllable, the *association value* for that syllable is 100 percent, and so on. To prove that meaningfulness facilitates learning, ask a few friends to practice each of these three lists for a few trials of serial learning. Which one is easiest?

100%	*53%*	*7%*
NAR	NOH	NUX
CUS	CEG	CEJ
MEX	MIQ	MIB
HON	HUJ	HUC
BEC	BOZ	BOF
WOM	WOB	WOJ
PUF	PIV	PIW
DAR	DUP	DAQ
REG	RIK	XEZ
JUS	JIR	JEQ

Table 4–9
Different kinds of similarity

Formal similarity
The items to be learned are in some sense physically similar.

Orthographic similarity: They are similar because of identical letters.

High similarity:		Low similarity:	
	JZH		JZH
	ZJQ		MVQ
	QHJ		KPL
	HQZ		XTZ
	QJZ		BGN

Acoustic similarity: They are similar in sound when pronounced letter by letter.

High similarity:		Low similarity:	
	BIM		BIM
	TYN		XAF
	EPV		HUW
	GBQ		LOR
	DTU		SXB

Semantic similarity
The items are not physically similar, but they have similar or closely related meanings in English.

High similarity:		Low similarity:	
	large		black
	tremendous		hard
	gigantic		involved
	big		lovable
	whopping		quiet
	massive		distant

Conceptual similarity
The items are not physically similar nor do they mean the same or similar things. Rather they are instances of the same general concept.

High similarity:		Low similarity:	
	maple		maple
	oak		tango
	elm		diamond
	ash		doctor
	cherry		canary
	poplar		snake
	birch		priest
	aspen		valley
	pine		martini

technique is called *coding*. You code JQM to "*J*ohnny *q*uivered when *M*ary touched him," and, when asked to recall what you have learned, you decode from the sentence back to JQM. The major point to remember is that the more meaningful you can make the material, the easier it will be to learn. Three simple steps to faster learning and better memory, then, are: (1) familiarize yourself with the material over and over again; (2) pronounce each item until you can say it easily and identically every time; (3) invent associations for the material, including silly sentences or funny visual images.

Similarity.   There is a close relationship between similarity and generalization. When you learn a response to a stimulus, you simultaneously develop a tendency to make that same response to other similar stimuli. Therefore, when the stimuli of a paired-associate list are similar to each other, we can expect the learning task to be difficult because of interpair generalization. You will have trouble learning which response goes with which of the very similar stimuli, even though the responses themselves may be easily discriminated.

Like meaningfulness, similarity is a multidimensional variable. Some of the contributing factors, illustrated in Table 4–9, are formal similarity, semantic similarity, and conceptual similarity.

Formal similarity is based on physical features of words. There are two primary types: *orthographic similarity,* which means that the items to be learned share some number of identical letters; and *acoustic similarity,* which means that the items contain letters that sound alike, for example, T, B, C, D, E, G, P, V, and Z. A serial list of nonsense syllables that is high in orthographic similarity is practically impossible to memorize. Try the list given in Table 4–9 on yourself or your friends. Formal similarity, especially of nonsensical material, makes both response learning and the associative process of connecting these responses to different stimuli extremely difficult.

Semantic similarity refers to the fact that two words may have the same or similar meanings. Unlike formal similarity, semantic similarity may be used to *facilitate* the response-learning component of a paired-associate task. For example, if all responses of a list have something to do with "largeness," they will be easy to learn. Trouble may arise, however, when the learner attempts to associate these responses with their corresponding stimuli. Suppose the response *big* is paired with the stimulus *green,* and the response *large* is paired with the stimulus *dog.* It will be easy to learn the two required responses, *big* and *large,* but hard to remember which one goes with *green* and which one goes with *dog.* If you learn *green–big,* response generalization may introduce a tendency to say *green–large.* Semantic similarity, then, might facilitate response learning while inhibiting associative learning. In a paired-associate list, therefore, there should be little or no effect when the semantic similarity of responses is manipulated. The positive and negative effects will tend to cancel each other out. On the stimulus side, however, we will see only the negative effect, due to mediated stimulus generalization. Thus, in this case, semantic similarity will retard learning.

We will consider one other kind of similarity, called *conceptual similarity.* Its name derives from the fact that the items in question are interrelated as instances of a general concept, for example, names of animals, trees, birds, or professions. Conceptual similarity and semantic similarity have about the same effects on learning; they facilitate response learning but inhibit associative learning. Note that because conceptual and semantic similarity facilitate response learning, free-recall lists of items with high levels of these variables should be more easily learned. Moreover, if you want to memorize a list of names of objects, it will definitely help to begin by organizing the list into conceptual or semantic groupings. When similarity is likely to inhibit, you should try to develop a memory code for the material that minimizes similarity.

Imagery.   Another factor influencing verbal learning is the imagery value of words. Imagery is generally correlated with how concrete or abstract words are. Abstract words lack physical referents and typically fail to arouse images of any sort. Examples of abstract words are *injustice, envy, hate, moral,* and *peace.* Concrete words, on the other hand, refer to physical objects, for example, *table, book, door,* and *grass.* Concrete words readily evoke images for most people. Not all abstract words, however, are necessarily low in imagery value. *Peace,* for example, has frequently been symbolized by the dove, and dove may be the image aroused by

---

Imagery and Learning: A Simple Experiment

Here are two lists of words, one high in imagery value (concrete words) and one low in imagery value (abstract words). Look at each list for 30 seconds and then try to write down as many of the words as you can remember. You should find that imagery facilitates learning.

High-imagery concrete words	*Low-imagery abstract words*
nail	injustice
cloud	envy
house	happiness
tire	institution
ball	education
fence	fashion
cigar	modesty
rock	motive
truck	contempt
dress	depth
book	thought
table	void
milk	agreement
telephone	society
bed	temper

---

that word. Imagery and abstractness are highly correlated, but the correlation is not perfect.

Imagery facilitates learning. In paired-associate learning the facilitating effect is large when the stimulus rather than the response items are high in imagery. Consider the pair *football-happy.* Suppose the stimulus term, *football,* elicited the image of a large stadium, while *happy* elicited no image at all for the subject. His learning strategy might be to fill the stadium with whatever kind of thing the response term could be used to refer to, in this case, hundreds of *happy* spectators. When his memory is eventually tested for this pair, presentation of the stimulus term, *football,* should arouse this image and he should immediately be able to think of the response term, *happy.* The imagery of the response term is not nearly as important as that of the stimulus term because the response is not a cue or stimulus for recall, but instead is the word *to be* recalled.

Subjects who have been taught to make up strange visual images dealing with the material to be learned perform at a much higher level than subjects who do not use images. For hundreds of years, memory experts have used visual images

© 1966 United Feature Syndicate Inc.

Memory Aids (Mnemonics)

1. The Peg System

Memorize a set of "memory pegs" in advance of learning. A convenient peg system consists of numbers and words that rhyme with the numbers, the rhyme helping you to retrieve the word given the number. For example:

one is a bun
two is a shoe
three is a tree
four is a door
five is a hive
etc.

Suppose you now want to memorize a shopping list of things to buy at the grocery store. Each item to be purchased is "hooked" on to one of the memory pegs by using an interactive image involving the item and its peg word. If the first item to be bought is *milk* you hook *milk* on to the *bun* peg by conjuring up an image of a giant bottle of milk voraciously devouring a hot dog bun down the mouth of the bottle. Next, you hook, say, *peanuts* on to the *shoe* peg, perhaps by imagining a shoe with peanuts erupting from it like a volcano. You continue hooking each food item onto the next peg. When you get to the store, you recite the pegs to yourself, and each peg word should then call forth the image that will contain the desired item.

2. The Method of Loci (Locations)

This system is also a peg-type device, but the pegs consist of a sequence of locations that can always be recalled in order. For example, you might imagine yourself on a long walk from your home to a particular place in your city. Along the way, you will encounter locations, places, objects in a fixed order; and each of these becomes a peg on which you hang one of the items to be remembered. For example, you first might walk to the corner where there is a mailbox, so this mailbox is then used as a peg for, say, *milk*—you imagine the mailbox opening its "mouth" and spewing forth milk on innocent pedestrians. When it comes time to recall your shopping list, you just retrace your walk in your

mind, stopping at each location to recall the desired material. Another set of loci can be developed using the rooms and various objects in the rooms of your home or apartment—you develop a "walk" through your home, stopping at notable locations or objects, which then become the pegs on which you hang the material to be learned.

3. Verbal Elaboration

In this method, also known as narrative chaining, you make up a story centering on the items to be remembered. For example, Gordon Bower has suggested the following narrative for use in trying to remember the names of the 12 cranial nerves:

At the *oil factory* (olfactory nerve) the *optician* (optic nerve) looked for the *occupant* (oculomotor) of the *truck* (trochlear). He was searching because *three gems* (trigeminal) had been *abducted* (abducens) by a man who was hiding his *face* (facial) and *ears* (acoustic). A *glossy photograph* (glossopharyngeal) had been taken of him, but it was too *vague* (vagus) to use. He appeared to be *spineless* (spinal accessory) and *hypocritical* (hypoglossal).

4. Coding Numbers to Letters

This is a system that, unlike the others, can be helpful in remembering numbers such as dates, street addresses, etc. Each of the digits from zero to 9 is assigned a consonant and you memorize this code. For example:

0 = B	5 = H
1 = C	6 = J
2 = D	7 = K
3 = F	8 = L
4 = G	9 = M

The number is then coded into the letters, and vowels are inserted to make meaningful words, the theory being that meaningful words are easier to remember than meaningless numbers. Somebody who lives at 2908 Maple gets his address encoded into DMBL which in turn becomes DUMBEL. Try this with your own telephone number. Can you turn the digits into 1 or 2 words?

heavily to improve their performance. If your task is to remember a list of objects, you might try to imagine these items in a stack, one thing on top of another. Try to visualize what the stack would be like. Another technique is to contrive a picture to go with the words to be remembered. In the spinal cord there is a nucleus called the *substantia gelatinosa,* a difficult name for most people to remember. But imagine a strange midget sitting on your spinal column at the locus of this nucleus eating a *substantial* bowl of *gelatin,* and you may never again forget the name of this nucleus.

Why does imagery facilitate learning? The predominant interpretation at the present time is that human beings have two primary modes for remembering: a verbal mode and a pictorial, or visual, imagery mode. If we learn something in both modes of presentation, as is more likely for high-imagery words, for example, the chances for later retention are better than if we learned only in one mode. We shall have more to say about modes of memory in later chapters.

Imagery techniques are not only powerful, they can be fun. They not only improve your learning speed, but take some of the boredom out of what otherwise might be a dull memorization task.

Transfer of Training

When we learn something new, some knowledge or skill, we usually do so with the intent to use it at a later time. In some cases we are later asked to recall or remember the exact information we learned, as in a final objective examination in a college course. In such cases, we are concerned with *memory,* which will be covered in the next section. Closely related to memory is the phenomenon of *transfer of training,* which refers to the effect of prior learning on the subsequent performance of a different task. Driving a new car is an example of transfer. While the responses required are similar to those you've learned in earlier driving experiences, they are not exactly the same. You will find it necessary to adapt your old habits or learn some new ones. You may even find some of your old habits interfering with the smooth operation of the new car. The point is that there will be some effect of prior learning and that is what is called transfer of training.

To demonstrate transfer effects in the laboratory, we might construct two different paired-associate tasks. Two groups of subjects are used: (1) the experimental group, which learns Task 1 and then transfers to Task 2 and learns it; and (2) a control group, which has to learn the second task without the prior learning of Task 1. The control condition is

Table 4–10
Transfer of training

Experimental group———►learns Task 1——►learns Task 2

Control group————►does nothing———►learns Task 2

1. If the experimental group does *better* on Task 2 than the control, there is *positive transfer.*
2. If the experimental group does *worse* on Task 2 than the control, there is *negative transfer.*
3. If the experimental group and the control group do not differ, there is *zero transfer.*

similar to learning to drive a car for the first time, without any prior experience. We examine the performance of the two groups on Task 2 and ask which group did better. If the experimental group performed better than the control group, we assume that something about Task 1 benefited their performance—the prior learning of Task 1 transferred positively to the learning of Task 2. This would be a case of *positive transfer.* If the experimental group did worse than the control group on Task 2, we would have an instance of *negative transfer*—the prior learning of Task 1 actually hindered performance on Task 2. Finally, if there were no difference between the two groups on Task 2, we would have *zero transfer.* Zero transfer might mean that Task 1 learning has no effect whatsoever on Task 2 learning, or it might mean that learning Task 1 produces both positive and negative transfer effects on Task 2 that cancel each other out. The operations for measuring transfer are shown in Table 4–10.

The most important variable in transfer of training is the similarity of the two tasks. If Tasks 1 and 2 are highly similar, we can expect positive transfer. If they require opposite or conflicting habits, we can expect negative transfer. Suppose Task 1 is to memorize several pairs of words like *book–happy* and Task 2 is to memorize pairs like *book–glad. Happy* and *glad* are similar responses to the stimulus *book,* so similar that learning one is almost like learning the other at the same time, and positive transfer would result. If the subject has learned *book–happy* and is transferred to *book–dirty,* there might be interference. During Task 2, the stimulus *book* will elicit the competing response *happy,* which will slow down the rate of learning of the correct response, *dirty.* Negative transfer would probably result in this case, especially if there were a number of such pairs to learn. Finally, when the two tasks are completely unrelated, *book–happy* and

Why does a fireman wear red suspenders?
A. ☐ *The red goes well with the blue uniform.*
B. ☐ *They can be used to repair a leaky hose.*
C. ☐ *To hold up his pants.*

The New Yorker, March 25, 1974. Drawing by Dana Fradon; © 1974 The New Yorker Magazine, Inc.

The multiple-choice test is a test of recognition memory. One theory is that this test is easier than a fill-in-the-blank test (recall memory) because recall requires both retrieval of the correct answer and recognition of the fact that it is correct, whereas no retrieval is required on a recognition test because the correct answer is right in front of you. In short, this theory says that different processes are involved in the two types of test.

grass–old, for example, we would expect zero transfer.

Even if two tasks are related, we might find zero transfer because there is a combination of positive and negative transfer effects that cancel each other out. Analyses of transfer phenomena have suggested that this is usually the case. Transfer is usually a mixture of positive and negative effects, the particular balance determining whether the *net* transfer is positive, negative, or zero. The analysis of transfer has thus concentrated on breaking down the different tasks into various components and showing how, within the same task, some components might transfer positively and other components transfer negatively. To maximize positive transfer and minimize negative transfer, you would teach only those components that show positive transfer.

Memory

Most of us are plagued at one time or another with failing memory. We learned something just last semester but cannot remember it now. Having crammed the night before, we are frustrated by an inability to recall at the time of the exam. Just as interesting are cases of complete recall after many years. We have fairly vivid recollections of some events from childhood. We might be surprised by the fact that a poem or verse memorized in grade school reasserts itself verbatim when, as adults, we come across the title or author. These are the problems of memory. Why do we forget? Why do we selectively remember?

Storage, retention, and retrieval. Psychological analyses of memory have led to the identification of three stages or components: *storage, retention,* and *retrieval.* Storage is the assignment of items of information to be remembered to some hypothetical memory system. Retention is holding items in storage for later use. The interval between initial storage and eventual recall is referred to as the *retention interval.* The retrieval stage refers to the extraction of items, heretofore stored and retained, for use on some task. Memory failures can be traced to any one or all of these three processes. The to-be-remembered information might have been poorly stored or not really stored in the first place. Assuming proper storage, the information might somehow have been lost through the passage of time. Finally, the information might have been stored and retained, but for some reason it was unretrievable when needed.

Two commonly used tests for memory are the *recognition test* and the *recall test.* In a recognition test, the subject is presented with the correct response along with some "distractor" responses, and he merely has to recognize which of the several presented responses is correct. Does this remind you of a multiple-choice test? In a recall test, the subject has to produce the correct response on his own, as in a fill-in-the-blank or essay test. As you already know, recognition is normally easier than recall. The reason is probably that recognition tests eliminate one of the three stages of memory, namely, the retrieval stage. The response is provided in the test and the subject does not have to retrieve it from his memory as he does in a recall test. Compare the following two tests:

1. What was the name of the possessed child in the movie *The Exorcist?* _____
2. Which of the following was the name of the possessed child in the movie *The Exorcist?*
   a. Jennifer
   b. Susan

c. Regen
d. Damien

In the first item, you can fail because you never stored the name, or because you have failed to retain it since you learned it, or because you cannot retrieve it. In the second item, the name has already been retrieved for you, so a failure is probably due to poor storage or retention.

How many types of memory do we have?

Psychologists have formed two different theories about our memory system. The theory most widely accepted divides the memory system into three parts. The other, more recent, theory maintains there is only one kind of memory. We will examine both theories here.

Three types of memory.   Many psychologists have found it useful to distinguish between three different types of memory, based upon the length of time the memory persists. The briefest memories are products of our *sensory memory* storage system. We mentioned this type of memory in Chapter 3, where it was shown that our visual system has a very brief memory for visual inputs, lasting only a few tenths of a second. There is an analogous memory register in the auditory system. In this chapter, we are not concerned with transient sensory processes but with more lasting memories. Here it is necessary to distinguish between the other two memory systems that we all seem to possess. We appear to have two systems, one for remembering things for short time periods, and one for storing information for long periods of time. These two systems are called *short-term memory* (STM, also known as immediate memory or working memory) and *long-term memory* (LTM).

One simple model of the relationship of the three memory systems is shown in Figure 4–12. Incoming information is first registered in the sensory memory system. If this information is attended to, it is transferred or coded into the short-term memory system. As long as the information is maintained by rehearsal (repeating it) in the short-term memory, the subject can recall it as a response output. But the short-term memory system has a very limited capacity; perhaps only 7 chunks of information can be held in the system at any one time. If more than 7 chunks are put into the system, some are pushed out to make room for new ones. There are two things that might happen to a chunk that is pushed out of short-term memory. It might simply be eliminated (forgotten), as is usually the case when

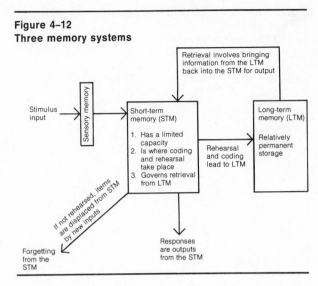

Figure 4–12
Three memory systems

you use a phone number you look up (enter into short-term memory) for the first time. Alternatively, you might say to yourself that you will want to remember that number for later use. You then keep the number in short-term memory, perhaps by repeating (that is, rehearsing) it or coding it in some way, for example, by making it into a word according to a number-letter code. This additional effort on your part then causes the number to be entered into the third memory system, the long-term memory. Thus, information passes from the short-term memory into the long-term memory for more permanent storage. The information is no longer in the short-term memory and so there is now room in the short-term memory for processing additional information. Now suppose that at some later time you want to use the phone number. First you retrieve the number from long-term memory, bringing it back into short-term memory, and then you proceed to dial it. Or if you used the memory device, you would retrieve the code words for the number from long-term memory and then you would retrieve the code itself. In short-term memory, you would decode the words into the number and begin dialing.

Levels of processing.   A recently suggested alternative to the three-store conception of memory says that there is really only one type of memory and that differences in how long and how well we remember a certain fact or experience have to do with how we process the information that experience provides. The idea is that we can process information at several levels, corresponding more or less to the amount of time, effort, and attention we invest. We may process an event

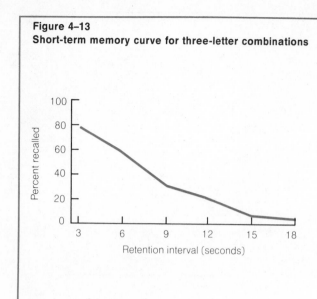

Figure 4–13
Short-term memory curve for three-letter combinations

y-axis: Percent recalled
x-axis: Retention interval (seconds)

Short-Term Memory

Do you think that you can remember a single 3-letter combination (e.g., HMK) for a period of 30 seconds? Of course you can if you rehearse the letters over the 30-second retention interval. But what if you could not rehearse? Suppose we do the following: We give you a syllable (XTK) and then immediately give you a number (291). You must start with 291 and count backward by three's (291, 288, 285, 282, etc.) until the 30 seconds are up. Then we ask you what the syllable was. A pioneering experiment by Peterson and Peterson (1959) on retention of 3-letter combinations used retention intervals of 3, 6, 9, 12, 15, and 18 seconds. As you can see in the graph in Figure 4–13, the startling results show that college students cannot remember a 3-letter combination for 18 seconds, much less 30.

superficially, attending only to its gross, physical, easily perceptible features. If so, we quickly forget the event. Sensory memory experiments are set up to allow only the barest degree of stimulus information processing, and sensory memories, as we know, have brief duration. If the material is important and time allows, we may engage in some rehearsal of the information, resulting in longer (though still short-term) retention. Consider the case of looking up the telephone number of a new restaurant in town.

But suppose the information is so vitally important that we spend considerable time and effort attempting to commit it permanently to memory. We look for relations between the new information and things we already know. We look at the information from various angles, searching for its truly significant features. We look for the deep semantic meaning of the information. We are processing the information at, essentially, the deepest possible level. Retention is likely to be correspondingly more permanent than results from superficial processing. This is the approach a successful student might use when preparing for an examination.

The levels-of-processing theory assumes only one kind of memory, not three. It accounts for different degrees of memory not on the basis of different storage locations but rather on the basis of how much information-processing capacity the learner invests in the stimulus material. This theory seems to explain many of the same aspects of memory as the three-store system does. Which theory helps more to understand all of memory is yet to be decided in the laboratory.

Why do we forget?   It is convenient to think of forgetting as happening for one of two basic reasons. The first is called *trace-dependent forgetting.* Some psychologists conceive of learning as setting up *traces* in the brain in some physiological fashion. Forgetting is then seen as basically due to the fact that the traces are not available at the time of recall. The reasons for the trace unavailability could be quite varied, but the basic underlying cause of the forgetting would be due to the loss of the trace. The information just is not in the brain any more.

The second reason or type of forgetting is called *cue-dependent forgetting.* Here the forgetting is seen mainly as a retrieval failure—the cues present at the time of learning are not present at the time of recall; or competing, interfering cues are also present and block memory. The traces, if any, are still in the brain, but the cues are not appropriate for "getting at" the traces, and so we have cue-dependent forgetting. The three theories involving memory and forgetting we are about to describe each involve one or the other of these processes.

Consolidation theory.   Corresponding most closely to the first stage of our memory scheme, storage, is the theory of memory *consolidation.* This theory postulates that every experience sets up some kind of trace. The trace may be thought of as a small electrical circuit that is formed in the brain, the circuit somehow coding the experience. According to the theory, this circuit must "consolidate" in order for the experience to be

Code-Specific Memory (Recognition Is Not Always Easier than Recall)

Normally, recall is aided by clues, that is, material closely associated with the material to be remembered. This is particularly true if the clues were present at the time of learning. For example, when you have forgotten someone's name, mention of the person's first name should help you remember his last name. But, amazingly, Endel Tulving has demonstrated that under some circumstances what should be very strong clues will not benefit recall.

Tulving's experiment confronted the subject with a list of to-be-remembered (TBR) words, each of which was paired with a *weak* clue, a weak associate of the TBR word. A few such pairs would be:

Weak clue words	TBR word
train	black
leather	chair
nose	cold
tiger	paper

The subjects were told that trying to relate each TBR word to its clue word would help them learn the TBR words. Then, at the time of recall, the weak clues were removed and strong clues were substituted. For example, *white* was substituted for *train* as a clue for *black. White* is so closely associated with *black* that you would think the subjects would still recall the TBR word, *black,* very well, but in fact they did very

poorly. Apparently *black* was *coded* into memory as being related to *train,* the weak clue. And this code was so specific to *train* that *white* would not "break the code" and result in recall of *black.* We call this *code-specific* or cue-dependent memory.

Most dramatic was the following demonstration by Tulving. After the subjects had failed to recall *black* when presented with *white,* he gave them a list of the strong clue words (hot, table, white, pencil) and asked them to free-associate to each one—to write down the first three or four words that came to mind. With these instructions, many subjects did in fact write down the word *black* (a TBR word) when free-associating to *white.* Then Tulving asked them to go back and circle any of the free associates that might have been TBR words. Believe it or not, most subjects failed to circle the TBR words that were staring them in the face. After their failure to recognize the TBR words in the presence of the strong clues, Tulving presented them with the weak clues, the clues that had been present during learning and that were used for coding the TBR words into memory. Presented with the word *train,* the subjects were now able to recall the word *black,* whereas they could not even recognize *black* when it was presented with *white* as the clue.

Apparently memories are coded in specific ways, and at the time of recall we must decode in the same "language" used during learning. If the cues or clues present at recall are not the same ones that were present during learning, recall may suffer.

---

permanently stored. When the circuit is first set up, it is not very stable and is subject to easy disruption. The "neuroelectricity" (or whatever it is that underlies storage) must travel around the circuit many times (a process called *perseveration)* in order to consolidate the circuit, making it final and lasting. After learning comes a period when the circuit can be destroyed easily, the time between the end of learning and the completion of the consolidation process. Once the circuit is consolidated, however, it has been stored in long-term memory and will be very difficult to destroy. According to the consolidation theory, the main reason for forgetting is that the memory was partly destroyed before it was consolidated. This theory focuses on the storage of information and states that memory failure is a consequence of inadequate storage.

What kind of events could affect the storage or consolidation process? Most research has studied the effects of electrical shock delivered to the brain shortly after learning. The shock is called *electroconvulsive shock* (ECS) whenever it is strong

enough to produce a convulsion in the subject. ECS has been used as a treatment for severe depression in human beings. Patients who receive ECS report a complete memory loss for events shortly preceding the ECS, a phenomenon known as *retrograde amnesia.* Their long-term memory, however, seems completely intact. The same is true for someone knocked unconscious by a blow on the head; he may not remember the events just prior to the blow. Effects of this sort support the consolidation theory. The strong electric shock and the blow on the head disrupt the consolidation of the memories that are at the time in the process of perseverating. Events that occurred earlier remain unaffected.

There is another side to the consolidation theory that is perhaps even more interesting. Consolidation is the process of laying down a permanent memory; therefore if consolidation could be facilitated, memory would be facilitated. Lengthening the time that perseveration continues might facilitate consolidation, and certain drugs, including strychnine, picrotoxin, and metrozal, are thought to have just this capability. These are drugs that excite the brain and might very well produce faster, more efficient, and more permanent memory storage. It has been shown that administration of these drugs to animals after each trial of a learning task does result in more rapid learning. The effect is strong support for the consolidation theory.

The theory might eventually lead us to a solution of problems related to mental retardation. Certain kinds of mental retardation may be caused by an inherited defect in the memory consolidation system. If drugs can be discovered that correct this defect or substitute for the chemicals that might be missing, it would be a fantastic development. Preliminary work is under way on this project.

Decay theory. Given that an item of information has been properly stored, what might account for its loss during the retention interval? *Decay theory* postulates a process by which stored information "wears out," or decays, over time. According to some versions of the theory, a biological process, metabolic or otherwise, produces the hypothesized decay and consequent forgetting.

There is a built-in circularity to decay theory. The theory states that forgetting is due to a process that breaks down stored memories. The only proof that such a decay process takes place, however, is that we forget. Since the physiology of the hypothesized decay process is not known, it cannot be directly manipulated (that is, the rate of decay cannot be changed) to test the effect on forgetting. The only variable that can be manipulated is the length of the retention interval.

On close examination, we may conclude that, as of now, decay theory sheds little light on forgetting. Still, the theory has great intuitive appeal. In the future, physiological investigations may indeed reveal the physiological correlates of memory, which will lead to some understanding of the physiological bases of forgetting. At that time we may be able to determine that a decay process exists, why it occurs, and how to prevent it. Memories may never be the same.

Interference theory. The most popular and best-developed theory of forgetting is based on the notion of *interference*. This theory deals primarily with the third aspect of memory, retrieval, or interference with the retrieval process. Interference theory focuses on certain interactions among different items of previously learned information. Failure to recall a particular item of information is attributed to the influence of other, usually similar,

Figure 4–14
Interference theory

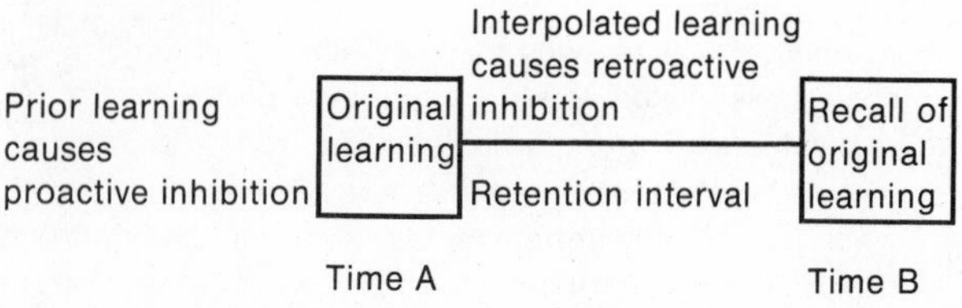

Material learned at Time A is tested for recall, after a retention interval, at Time B. Material learned prior to Time A (prior learning) produces proactive inhibition; things learned between Times A and B (interpolated learning) produce retroactive inhibition.

items of stored information.

To see how this works, let us call items of information that the subject is to recall the *originally learned* items. Prior to the time of original learning the subject may have learned one or more other things that are similar. Call this *prior learning*. If prior learning interferes with his recall of original learning, it is called *proactive inhibition*. Another source of interference arises from the subject's experiences between original learning and recall. Anything learned during the retention interval is designated as *interpolated learning*. When interpolated learning interferes with recall of original learning, the process is called *retroactive inhibition* (see Figure 4–14). Interference theory postulates that forgetting is produced by one of two factors: (1) proactive inhibition from materials learned prior to original learning and (2) retroactive inhibition from things learned during the retention interval (see Table 4–11).

Laboratory studies have provided strong support for the basic notions of interference theory. While it is now clear that interference *can* produce forgetting, it is not certain that *all* forgetting is due to interference. Empirically, we know that subjects remember more if they sleep during the retention interval than if they are awake. Since we are not learning interfering material while sleeping, this observation supports an interference theory. There are alternative interpretations, however. Sleep might have facilitated memory by slowing down the decay process, or it could have facilitated the consolidation of materials learned just before going to sleep. While the explanation of this experimental finding is vague, its practical implication is quite clear. It is better to go to sleep after studying for a

Table 4–11
Proactive and retroactive inhibition

Proactive inhibition
Experimental group
learns Task B   learns Task A <u>retention interval</u> recalls Task A
Control group
<u>retention interval</u> ➤ learns Task A - - - <u>rests</u> - - - recalls Task A

Here is the operational definition of proactive inhibition.
The experimental and control groups both learn and recall
Task A. But the experimental group also does some prior
learning, Task B, while the control rests. The control group
remembers more of Task A than the experimental group,
an indication of proactive inhibition.

Retroactive inhibition
Experimental
group   learns Task A   learns Task B   recalls Task A
Control
group   learns Task A ——————<u>rests</u>——————➤ recalls Task A

Here is the operational definition of retroactive inhibition.
The experimental group learns and recalls Task A, but
must do the interpolated learning of Task B. The control
group only learns and recalls Task A. The control group
remembers more, which is evidence of retroactive
inhibition.

test than to study for some other test, watch TV, or
engage in any other waking activity.

Can we say more about how interference operates
to produce forgetting? Two fundamental ideas have
been proposed. Consider the subject learning two
successive paired-associate lists. The first is
designated as a series of A–B associations, where
the A terms are the stimuli and the B terms are the
responses. The second list consists of the same
stimuli but different responses. Therefore, this list is
called A–C. After the subject has learned the A–B list
followed by the A–C list, his memory is tested for
A–B by presenting the A terms and asking him to
guess or remember what the responses were from
the first list. Failure to remember has been attributed
both to *response competition* and to *unlearning.*
Each A term should elicit two responses, the correct
response B and the interfering response C. B and C
compete with each other, and the subject may be
confused about which one to say. When A is
presented, the subject attempts to retrieve the
correct answer and comes up with two equally
strong possibilities which compete (cue-dependent).

In addition, the correct response, B, may have
been "unlearned" during A–C trials. If so, it is no
longer available to the subject (trace-dependent). At
recall, A is presented and the subject attempts to
retrieve the correct answer and finds nothing but C.
It is as if B had been removed from storage.

We might note that the A–B, A–C model in
paired-associate learning resembles
counterconditioning. After conditioning A–B we stop
"rewarding" B and begin to reward a new response,
C. Response competition and unlearning are not
mutually exclusive alternatives. Empirical evidence
suggests that both contribute measurably to the
forgetting process.

Context and State-Dependent Learning

Memory is best when the conditions of recall are
identical to those at the time of learning. This is
generally referred to as a context effect. If you are
going to take an exam (recall facts) in a particular
lecture hall, it would be to your advantage to study
the material in that lecture hall as opposed to
studying in the library or in your dormitory room.
The notion here is closely related to stimulus
generalization—the more similar the recall context
to the learning context, the better the recall.

Context, of course, refers to one's surroundings at
the time of learning and recall—the size and shape
of the room, the color of the walls, the amount of
noise, etc. More recently this idea has been
expanded to include the physiological state of the
learner at the time of learning and recall. One's own
body is, in some sense, a part of his context. Thus,
for best performance, one's bodily state should be
as similar as possible at the time of learning and
recall. To take a whimsical example, if you are drunk
when you learn something, you might be able to
recall it better at some future time under the
influence of alcohol. There are anecdotal reports of
alcoholics who hide things when drunk and are
unable to remember the location when they sober
up. This phenomenon has a special name,
state-dependent learning. Laboratory work on this
kind of learning has typically used drug-induced
states. Experimenters have found, for example, that
if a rat is taught to run a maze under the influence
of amphetamines, he performs better if given
amphetamines just before the recall trial.

Some writers have included state-dependent
learning in a list of dangers involved in drug usage.
Almost all learning takes place in the normal,
nondrug state. If a person takes a psychoactive drug
and enters a different state, some of this information
may become unavailable to him. He might, for
example, "forget" how to drive an automobile or
cope with anxiety, "forget" the laws of gravity or the
damaging effects of the sun's rays. As a result, we
might be able to explain the following drug-induced
behaviors: forgetting to yield the right of way to
oncoming traffic, committing suicide, jumping from

Can You "Remember" Something You Never Experienced?

Is it conceivable that a person could *remember* something that he had never even learned? A recognition-memory study by John Bransford and Jeffery Franks demonstrated just such an effect. Instead of the usual word list, Bransford and Franks used a group of sentences on a related topic. When we think of recognizing a sentence or a prose passage in a book, it does not seem that we recognize the exact words, but rather the general theme or the "whole idea" expressed in the sentences. Theories of memory, however, have emphasized memory for the specific words or elements, as if we memorized each word instead of learning an abstract "idea" that we "pull out of" the prose as we read it. The results of the Bransford and Franks study, however, mean that memory theories will now have to account for this abstraction process.

The group of sentences used in this study could be presented as a single sentence with four elements expressing a "whole idea."

Whole idea: The rock that rolled down the mountain crushed the tiny hut at the edge of the woods. *Four components:* (1) the rock rolled down the mountain; (2) the rock crushed the hut; (3) the hut was tiny; (4) the hut was at the edge of the woods.

During the study phase, the subjects never saw the sentence containing all four elements; they never saw or experienced the whole idea. Instead they saw sentences containing only one or two or three of the elements. For example, a three-element sentence would be: "The rock crushed the tiny hut at the edge of the woods." A two-element sentence would be: "The tiny hut was at the edge of the woods." And a one-element sentence would be: "The rock rolled

down the mountain." Several sets of sentences were mixed together for the study phase.

At the time of the test, the subjects were presented with several different kinds of sentences: three-, two-, and one-element sentences they had actually seen before; four-, three-, two-, and one-element sentences they had never seen before; and finally some sentences that were unrelated to the earlier materials. The basic finding was that the more elements of the whole idea a test sentence contained, the more confident the subjects were of having seen it before. They were most confident of having seen the four-element "whole idea," which had never occurred, as can be seen in Figure 4–15.

Figure 4–15
Degree of confidence that a sentence had been seen before

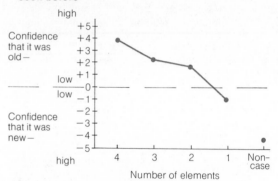

The results of the Bransford and Franks study strongly suggest that during learning, while hearing three-, two-, and one-element sentences, the subjects were actually abstracting the whole idea and storing it, even though it had never been presented in its entirety. Most learning and memory theories (particularly S–R conditioning-type theories) are not yet equipped to handle such findings, which makes the phenomenon all the more exciting.

a third-story window yelling "up, up, and away," and staring directly into the sun. Attributing these behaviors to state-dependent learning may be an exaggeration. Nonetheless, there is no doubt that this phenomenon does sometimes occur in drug-induced behavior.

Memory as Reconstruction

Finally, we wish to point out that most of what we have had to say so far about memory implies an underlying model that treats the brain as a copying machine. We learn something (copy it) and store it away in memory for later recall (retrieve the copy and "read out" what is in the copy). But, it is undoubtedly true that much of memory behavior is

not consistent with such a model, but instead is more in line with a *reconstruction* model. We do not simply copy events and store the copies; rather we store abstract representations of the events. In trying to recall an event, we retrieve the abstract representation and try to deduce (reconstruct) what the event must have been from this representation. This is perhaps most obvious when we consider trying to remember a conversation or something we read in a book or newspaper. We do not have word-for-word copies of the conversation or the prose stored in our memory; what we have are general ideas or facts about what was said or read.

This type of model makes it clear that an additional source of memory distortion can take place at the time of storage when we have to abstract the general idea of a conversation or a prose passage. We might misinterpret the incoming information and thus store general information that was not present in the conversation or passage. Consider the following passages and the distorted or elaborated information that might be stored by someone hearing the passages:

1. John was trying to fix the birdhouse. He was pounding the nail when his father came out to watch him and to help him do the work.
2. It was late at night when the phone rang and a voice gave a frantic cry. The spy threw the secret document into the fireplace just in time since 30 seconds longer would have been too late.

In the first example, chances are that you would store the general idea that John was using a hammer to fix a birdhouse with the aid of his father, when in fact the sentence does not say that a hammer was involved. In the second example, you would probably store the general idea that the spy burned a secret document just in time, when in fact the sentence does not say anything about burning. Johnson, Bransford, and Solomon (1973), in fact, asked subjects who had heard these examples if they had heard the following two test sentences:

1'. John was using the hammer to fix the birdhouse when his father came out to watch and to help him do the work.
2'. The spy burned the secret document just in time since 30 seconds longer would have been too late.

The subjects incorrectly judged that they had heard 1' and 2' when in fact they had heard only 1 and 2. Presumably they incorrectly interpreted 1 and 2 and stored general information, not word-for-word copies. At the time of the test they retrieved the general ideas (which included *hammer* and *burned*) and reconstructed from this information some notion of what it was they must have heard. This reconstruction was then similar enough to 1' and 2' that the subjects were fooled into believing that they had heard these exact sentences.

In short, memory is probably rarely based on having exact copies of the original experience available. When we learn and store information, we are not passive copy machines filing away perfect reproductions for later retrieval. Instead, we actively interpret information as it is received (we think as we learn) and may file away only general abstract

representations of this information. Later, if necessary, we can retrieve the general idea and reconstruct the original experience. As a result, our memories can be inaccurate because we misinterpreted the information in the first place, or because we did not retain sufficient general information to make a very accurate reconstruction, or because we commit errors in the reconstruction process itself.

Memory psychologists are only just beginning to explore the reconstructive aspects of memory in a systematic fashion. This is mainly because it has proved difficult to develop carefully controlled procedures and tasks that involve this type of memory. In the next few years we can anticipate that research will shed much new light on this important and crucial aspect of memory.

What Does It Mean?

Classical and operant conditioning techniques have been successful in many practical applications. Although the applications of learning principles have sometimes been called inhumane or degrading, the techniques have accomplished behavior changes that just about everyone would agree are of great benefit to individuals and society. It will be clear, however, that problems could develop if someone with a great deal of power decided to use these techniques to his own advantage. To the extent that these techniques are effective, their misuse could be detrimental to humanity.

We are only beginning to see what the application of learning principles might be. In the future we can expect the possibilities to expand to include all societal institutions—the family, the school system, and the prison and mental hospital. In order to reap the promised benefits of these programs, it will be necessary to have an informed public with some understanding of the benefits and dangers involved.

Classical Conditioning

Bedwetting.   The principles of classical conditioning have been used to cure children of bedwetting (called *enuresis*). Normally, bladder tension is the stimulus that awakens us in the middle of the night, but the bedwetting child has not learned the response of waking up. To stop the child from wetting the bed, then, requires conditioning the response of awakening to the stimulus of bladder tension. The UCS would be a stimulus that naturally awakens a person, such as a loud buzzer or bell. After repeated pairings of the bell with the

Figure 4–16
Conditioning cure for bedwetting

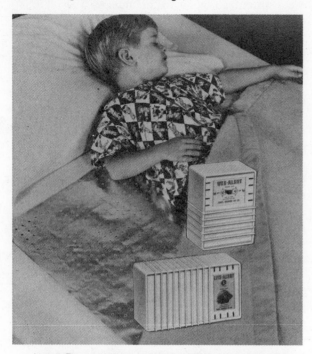

Children's Bedwetting Alarms
Helps keep sleeper dry by conditioning him to stop bedwetting. Each bedding pack has 2 foil pads with separating sheet between. Moisture passes from top pad to bottom . . . alarm goes off almost instantly. Units can't shock . . . use low voltage batteries. Not for organic disorders or baby training.

The principles of classical conditioning have been used effectively to cure bedwetting. The device sold by Sears, Roebuck, & Company is much less expensive than those sold by some enterprising people trying to capitalize on the fears of parents.

CS of bladder tension, bladder tension alone should be sufficient to elicit awakening.

In practice, though, how do the child's parents know when his bladder is full so that they should sound the bell? Obviously, the bladder is full at the time the child first starts to wet the bed, but how do the parents sleeping in the next room know when the child is wetting the bed? A psychologist has devised an apparatus that consists of a special sheet equipped with wires that detect urine the moment it starts flowing. The detection apparatus closes an electrical circuit that in turn sounds the bell to awaken the child. After a short period of training with this device, the child begins to awaken himself

in anticipation of the release of urine. Indeed, the unit works so well that some companies sell or lease it at extraordinarily high prices to desperate parents who are willing to pay. A functional unit, however, can be purchased for a small amount of money from most large catalogue companies (see Figure 4–16). Classical conditioning principles have also been applied to toilet training through the use of a buzzer circuit built into training pants.

Curing bad habits. A classical conditioning approach can be applied to just about any habit we wish to eliminate: gambling, smoking, overeating, etc. Evidence is accumulating that people who are overweight have developed habits that cause them to feel hungry and eat whenever they see stimuli associated with food—even if they have just eaten, their stomachs are full, and there are internal stimuli signaling satiation. Thus an obese person might start munching snacks right after dinner if he is provoked by a TV commercial for food. These people often do very well on starvation diets, if they are placed in a hospital or other surroundings devoid of food-related stimuli. Interestingly enough, although they might lose a considerable amount of weight in a sterile environment, they tend to return to their former voracious eating habits when released. Normal or underweight people presumably have not learned the hunger response to external, food-related stimuli. Instead their eating is more under the control of internal cues—for example, cues from the stomach—and they tend to eat only when their body requires food.

Conditioning taste aversions. Coyotes kill sheep. As a consequence sheep ranchers have taken up arms against them. The slaughter of coyotes has, in turn, become a matter of concern to environmentalists and naturalists. Thus a controversy has developed, and there is need for a solution that will be satisfactory to both naturalists, who want to stop the killing of the coyotes by ranchers, and to the ranchers, who want to stop the killing of their livestock. A direct application of long-delayed conditioning has been made to the problem by Gustavson, Garcia, Hankins, and Rusiniak (1974). Using principles derived from laboratory studies on conditioned aversions, these psychologists reasoned that coyotes could be conditioned to avoid killing and eating sheep flesh. If so, coyotes should then stop attacking sheep. The basic laboratory procedure consisted of feeding coyotes "free" sheep meat that was laced with lithium chloride, a chemical that makes the coyotes

Habits: The Cigarette Diet

Time—Beep. Tucked into a smoker's pocket or handbag, the small "Bellboy" paging device sounds. The smoker immediately stops whatever he is doing and lights up, interrupting his meal or stepping from his shower. A Pavlovian response? Posthypnotic suggestion? No. The smoker is so anxious to give up cigarettes that he is strictly following one of the newest and most unusual of the proliferating antismoking regimens.

To make the cure as painless as possible, the paging device initially beeps as often during the day as the smoker normally lights up, but in a random pattern. The patient agrees to smoke whenever it sounds. Secure in the knowledge that he can always look forward to hearing another beep, the smoker can control himself between signals. But soon the friendly beeper—triggered by radio signals sent out by the telephone company—lets him down, slowly decreasing his consumption by four cigarettes each week. The decrease is so gradual that withdrawal symptoms are minimal.

Substitute Signals

The automated weed-killer technique was developed by Psychologist David Shapiro and Psychophysiologist Bernard Tursky of Harvard Medical School. It was tried first on 40 people this spring.

Not everyone was able to keep down with the beeps; one participant had a relapse after his wife, unaware that he had left his Bellboy in the car, drove off on a shopping trip. But of the original 40, including a telephone man who set up the beepers, 34 stuck it out until the system had cut them down to as few as four cigarettes a day. Some have even quit smoking altogether.

Shapiro says that the system works on the theory that smoking is a simple habit set off by "cues"—tension, ending a meal or performing a task. To break the habit, he explains, "we put people on a diet and provide them with a substitute for the old signal. The old associations have to be broken down...."

Many psychologists feel that cigarette smoking is a prime example of a "bad habit" that should be curable by a treatment based on principles of learning. Here is one such treatment. As yet, however, no magic cure has been developed that works for everyone. Would you say that this treatment is based on classical or operant conditioning?

---

very sick. Despite the long delay between the CS (tasting the meat) and the UCR (getting sick), coyotes so treated develop an immediate dislike for the kind of food that contains poison. Significantly, only one or two "treatments" of this kind were needed to inhibit the coyotes' desire for killing and eating sheep. Furthermore, Gustavson and his associates showed that this treatment did not affect the coyotes' willingness to eat rabbit or other kinds of meat. In other words, the treatment results in a specific dislike for sheep. The authors concluded that a method based on their laboratory procedures could be used to stop coyotes from killing sheep and yet not deprive them of other prey. Sheep-meat baits, laced with a nondeadly but illness-producing chemical, could be distributed around the territory where the coyotes are known to prey on sheep. A coyote who happens on the trap would eat the sheep meat and automatically develop an instant aversion to sheep. It would then stop killing sheep but would be quite capable of surviving by preying on less-valued species, such as rabbits.

Instrumental Conditioning

In Chapter 2 we saw that psychologists have discovered how to use conditioning techniques to control physiological responses that are under the automatic control of the nervous system. Take the control of blood pressure, for example. To instrumentally condition blood pressure we need a device that will continuously monitor and inform the subject of his relative blood pressure at all times. To use the operant conditioning technique, we would, then, arrange a device such that a tone would sound whenever blood pressure rose above a specified level. The subject would be instructed to try to prevent the tone from sounding in any way that he could.

A shaping technique might be used. At the start the critical blood pressure level will be set fairly high and in such a way that only slight reductions will terminate the tone. The tone offset tells the subject that whatever he did in the preceding period was beneficial to his level of blood pressure. Those activities, whatever they might be and whether or not they are conscious, will be reinforced. If they are repeated, they will be reinforced again, and gradually the subject will learn to keep the tone off most of the time.

When the subject has learned to stay below the critical level, the setting will be adjusted, making him reach for even lower blood pressure. Gradually the critical level will be reduced to an acceptable range. Because of the advances in technology and

Classical and Instrumental Conditioning Usually Work Together

Novel Treatment

England (UPI)—Doctors have found a novel way to stop compulsive gambler David Smith from putting his money where his mouth is, Smith says.

"I pick out horses twice a day," Smith said of his treatment. "Then they let me listen to the race broadcast. When I get excited a doctor or nurse presses a button which gives me an unpleasant electric shock through the arms."

"It brings me down to earth every time," he said. "Already I am getting to hate racing and all that goes with it."

The Events

Listening to the races ⟶ getting excited

causes therapist to present

Shock ⟵ pain, discomfort

Classical Conditioning Component

CS (listening to the races)

UCS (shock) ⟶ UCR (pain and discomfort)

Results: Eventually the CS alone (listening to the races) should elicit a CR similar to the UCR—the subject will feel anxious (conditioned pain?) whenever he hears the races.

Instrumental Conditioning Component

R (getting excited) ⟶ S (shock)

Results: The subject learns that the consequences of getting excited are unpleasant. To avoid shock he learns to avoid making the "excitement response," which of course means that he would say he no longer enjoys (gets excitement from) listening to the races.

In most behavior modification situations, the therapy can be seen as consisting of a component centering on classical conditioning and another component involving instrumental conditioning. Usually, one of the two components is more obvious than the other (and perhaps more important), but both components are usually present.

the success of these techniques, we may expect in the future to see an even greater reliance on bioelectrical feedback devices for the control of undesired physiological responses. Use of these techniques will contribute to a longer and healthier life.

Behavior Modification

The application of operant conditioning procedures to behavior and the treatment of behavior defects has generally come to be known as *behavior modification.* Operant techniques have been applied with considerable success to such unwanted behaviors as stuttering, temper tantrums, poor study habits, smoking, excessive eating, and other problems (see Table 4–12 and Figure 4–17).

Teachers are presently being trained to use operant techniques for handling problem students. For example, the withdrawn child often gets reinforced for playing alone, because the teacher attends to him in an effort to interest him in group activities. Instead the teacher should reinforce him with her attention only when he shows signs of participating in group activities. The teacher who does not know or fails to apply reinforcement principles often encourages misbehavior and class disruption by her attention to it. Ignoring these activities in their initial stages is a much better cure.

Psychologists used operant conditioning procedures for an unusual task during World War II. They trained pigeons to guide missiles to their targets. The pigeon was placed in the nose cone of a rocket (see Figure 4–18, p. 141). As the missile approached the target, the pigeon would peck on a key, sending out signals that modified the direction of the rocket, until the pigeon "said" the missile was on target.

Pigeons have also been trained to function as quality control inspectors. A company that manufactures gelatin capsules for drugs had a problem in spotting defects that were difficult for the human eye to detect. Moreover, the inspection task was boring and human inspectors had to be spelled frequently. Pigeons, who have remarkable eyesight, were shaped to respond to defects. Their work was outstanding in contrast to the work of human inspectors. Nonetheless, the company decided not to use pigeons. Can you guess why?

The token economy. Reward training, derived from the principles of operant conditioning, has been applied on a large scale to shape the behavior of groups of patients living together in mental hospitals. The goal is to teach the patients to behave more in accord with the definition of normal behavior. The hospital staff and patients devise a miniature society based on a token economy. Tokens (poker chips) are used, like money, as

Table 4–12
Some examples of behavior modification

1. Elimination of crying episodes of a preschool boy by having the teacher ignore him when he cried and pay attention to him when he talked. Previously, the teacher had usually done just the opposite.
2. Elimination of the psychotic responses of a female schizophrenic who always talked about the "royal family" and called herself Queen. The nurses were instructed to reward her with social attention and cigarettes when she talked normally, and to ignore her when she talked about her delusions of royalty.
3. Elimination of a patient's obsessive thought about strangling his wife by having the patient punish himself whenever he had the thought. He did this by wearing a thick rubber band around his wrist that he snapped vigorously to inflict pain until the thought went away.
4. Reinforcement of standing and walking in a child who usually crawled around the classroom by having the teacher praise the child when she walked and ignore the child when she crawled.
5. Elimination of a child's tantrums and severe crying episodes at bedtime simply by having the parents stay out of the bedroom after the child was put to bed. Previously the child had cried and screamed until a parent returned to his room, and the parents had developed a pattern of staying with the child until he fell asleep.
6. Getting a patient to feed herself, instead of demanding spoon feeding by a nurse. The patient wanted to stay clean and neat, so the nurse was instructed always to spill some food on the patient during spoon feeding. In effect, the patient was taught, "If you want to stay neat, you will have to feed yourself." If self-feeding occurred, the nurse reinforced this with praise and social attention.

secondary rewards. The patients can earn tokens for certain behaviors and redeem them for special privileges.

At the outset the patient may earn points for only the slightest modification of behavior. Gradually the requirements are increased until the patient must behave normally to achieve rewards. In one project, tokens could be earned for the following behaviors: getting up quickly and at the right time every morning; good personal hygiene habits, such as bathing and wearing clean clothes; performing clean-up chores around the ward; and working at off-the-ward jobs, such as gardening or doing the laundry. The tokens could then be used to purchase a bed with an innerspring mattress to replace a cot, an opportunity to watch TV, and entrance to a fancy dining room rather than the customary undecorated hall.

Token economy programs have been extremely successful. Many long-term patients adopt model ward behavior, and sometimes the entire ward completely changes character. Follow-up studies are still in progress, but, on the basis of what is known so far, there is every reason to believe that techniques of this sort will speed up the reeducation

Figure 4–17
Conditioning cure for anorexia nervosa

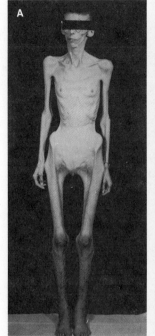

The individual above was suffering from a disorder called *anorexia nervosa,* characterized by an inability to eat. The photos show the patient before therapy (A); after 8 weeks of therapy that consisted of social attention, praise, access to radio and television, freedom to determine her menu and to invite others to dine with her, all made contingent upon her eating more and more (B); after 10 months as an outpatient (C); and after final discharge (D).

The A–B–A Design and Operant Control of Vomiting

Laura was a nine-year-old retarded child in an institution for retarded children. When she was enrolled in a class at the institution, she began to vomit in the class, and soon vomiting was an everyday occurrence. If she vomited on her dress, the teacher of the class had Laura sent back to her residence hall. No medical cause for the vomiting could be found and no medication seemed to help. Perhaps her vomiting was not a reflex action, as we usually think of it; in this case it might have been a response that Laura was emitting (*operant* behavior) because of its consequences (she could get out of the class).

In order to test this hypothesis, it was decided to measure Laura's vomiting under three conditions: (A) extinction—the reinforcement is eliminated, which in this case meant that Laura had to stay in class regardless of whether or not she vomited; (B) reinstatement—the original reinforcement is reinstated, which meant that once again Laura was returned to her residence hall if she vomited; and (A, again) a second extinction session, in which vomiting was not rewarded by allowing Laura to leave class. The results were quite dramatic. During the first extinction period Laura vomited a lot at first, but gradually the vomiting declined in frequency until it reached a zero level. Then reinstatement began (she could leave if she vomited). It was quite some time before she finally vomited again, but when she finally did, she was allowed to leave. In no time her vomiting reappeared; she vomited once a day and left class. Finally, during reextinction, she again was forced to stay in class despite her vomiting. Again, at first she vomited a great deal, but the vomiting gradually decreased to zero.

This case (Wolf, Birnbrauer, Lawler, and Williams, 1970) illustrates the application of operant conditioning to a behavior problem—once the reinforcing event is discovered, its elimination can be used to terminate the undesired behavior. The case also illustrates the A–B–A design (the reversal design) that operant psychologists use to make sure that they have discovered the relevant reinforcers for a behavior. The design involves three stages, where the first and third stages are the same (hence A–B–A) and going from one stage to the next involves a reversal of the contingency thought to be reinforcing the behavior. In this case, the design involved going from reinforcer absent (extinction stage one) to reinforcer present and then back to reinforcer absent. The ability to reverse the behavior (bring back the vomiting and then make it go away a second time) eliminates the alternate interpretation that Laura might have quit vomiting without any change in the reinforcement contingencies.

process for patients and produce more rapid discharge from hospitals. The program provides rewards to a patient for working on his own problems and encourages him to develop new skills that can be used upon release. The reaction to token economies, however, is not entirely positive. Many lay people and experts feel that these programs dehumanize patients, training them as if they were lower animals. This reaction is not unfounded, but it must be considered in light of the significant changes in patients in the direction of socially acceptable behavior.

Steps to a Better Memory

While there are no magic formulas for improving the ability to remember (newspaper ads to the contrary notwithstanding), research on verbal learning does suggest some steps you can take.

1. Maximize the degree of original learning, which is the single most important variable in memory. The better you learn the material initially, the more resistant it will be to forgetting. Subjects who are slow learners do not forget more than subjects who are fast learners, if the degree of original learning is equal. A slow learner might take 30 minutes to reach the same degree of learning as a fast learner attains in 15 minutes. But given that the two have learned the material equally well, they will remember equally well.

2. Use visual imagery and other coding techniques during the learning process. Make up bizarre and interesting images to relate the items of information to be retained. When learning someone's name, pick out some feature of his face or body and relate this to his name. If Mr. Bumstead has a nose that looks like a ski jump, think of him as a ''steady ski bum'' and imagine olympic skiers leaping off his nose.

3. Return to the scene of the ''crime.'' That is, reinstate the context and the cues of learning at the time of recall. At the very least, try to make the learning and recall context similar. Study in the place where you will have to perform. Practice under conditions that are similar to those under which you will have to perform. Note that a basketball coach should make his players practice under ''game conditions.''

4. Try to provide yourself with retrieval cues at the time of original learning. Select retrieval cues that you know will be present at the time of recall. Mr. Bumstead's nose is a retrieval cue. It will be present at the time you have to recall his name and so should be used in memorizing his name. In the case of an examination, try to find cues in the

Figure 4–18
Target practice

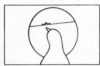

A pigeon trained to guide a rocket to its target is placed in the nose cone, where it pecks a key to direct the course of the missile. The signals created by the pigeon modify the direction of the rocket until it is on target.

examination room to use as "pegs" or "memory hooks" for the material you are learning. For example, there may be "no smoking" signs, a chart of chemical elements, or a map in the room. Try to form images relating these items to the material you are learning. Of course, while this technique may help you on the examination, you run the risk of being unable to remember certain items outside the examination room.

5. Repeatedly practice recalling the material. After studying a section, recite the important points to yourself or a friend. Get together with friends and test each other on the material. You must be able to retrieve what you have learned. If you do not practice retrieving, you run the risk of knowing more than you are actually able to show on an examination.

6. Do not take drugs to keep awake so that you can study more. With drugs you run the risk of state-dependent learning, unless, of course, you also take the drugs just before the exam. In that case, unwanted side effects, such as anxiety or confusion, may interfere with your examination performance.

These are just a few techniques that should improve your memory. The basic consideration throughout is type and degree of original learning. You should try to learn as completely and with as many retrieval cues as possible.

Summary

1. Learning is defined as a relatively permanent change in behavior traceable to experience and practice.

2. Many instances of learning can be classified into two basic types: classical conditioning (based on the work of Pavlov) and instrumental or operant conditioning (identified mainly with the work of Skinner).

3. In classical conditioning, a neutral stimulus (CS) comes to elicit a response (CR) that, prior to conditioning, was elicited as a response (UCR) only by some other stimulus (UCS).

4. Classical conditioning is thought to be mainly a function of contiguity between the CS and UCS during the learning trials.

5. In operant or instrumental conditioning, the subject must emit a response or withhold a response, this behavior being "reinforced" by the delivery of rewards or punishments contingent on what the subject does. There are eight basic types of operant conditioning.

6. The technique known as shaping (reinforcing successively closer approximations to the desired response) is also frequently used in operant training of a subject.

7. Several learning phenomena take place both in classical and operant learning situations: extinction, spontaneous recovery, generalization (both stimulus and response), discrimination, mediated generalization, and chaining of responses (or higher-order conditioning in the case of classical conditioning). Another phenomenon is the development of secondary reinforcement based on primary reinforcers.

8. Extinction is the process of eliminating a learned response. Partial reinforcement during learning retards extinction. Punishment can also make it more difficult to extinguish a response.

9. Studies of human learning have focused mainly on learning of verbal materials. Research has employed three major learning tasks: free-recall, serial, and paired-associate learning.

10. The meaningfulness of the material, the similarity level of the material, and the imagery level (abstractness versus concreteness) of the material are three factors that have strong effects on the ease of learning.

11. Memory is often conceived of as involving three basic steps: storage of the to-be-remembered information, retention of it over time, and retrieval of the information at the time of recall.

12. Forgetting may be analyzed into two types: trace dependent (is the information still intact in the memory system?) or cue dependent (are the recall cues sufficient to retrieve the stored information?).

13. Currently, there are two widely accepted, competing theories of memory. One assumes that

we have three separate and unique memory storage systems: sensory memory, short-term memory and long-term memory. The other proposes that the durability of a memory depends on the extent (depth) to which it is processed (rehearsed and organized).

14. Three major theories of memory and forgetting are: interference, decay, and consolidation. Memory is better when the conditions at the time of recall are similar to the conditions at the time of learning, including the physiological state of the learner (state-dependent learning).

15. Much of memory undoubtedly involves processes of reconstruction based on a stored abstract representation rather than a "verbatim" copy.

16. Learning principles have been widely applied to the solution of everyday problems, including the treatment of bedwetting and curing bad habits. Operant learning principles have been used to condition involuntary responses to bring them under voluntary control and shape the behavior of mental patients.

Recommended Additional Readings

Bolles, R. C. *Learning theory.* New York: Holt, Rinehart and Winston, 1975.

Bugelski, B. R. *The psychology of learning applied to teaching.* Indianapolis: Bobbs-Merrill, 1964.

Ellis, H. C. *Fundamentals of human learning and cognition.* Dubuque, Iowa: Brown, 1972.

Hill, W. F. *Learning: A survey of psychological interpretations* (2nd ed.) San Francisco: Chandler, 1971.

Lindsay, P. H., & Norman, D. A. *Human information processing: An introduction to psychology.* New York: Academic Press, 1972.

Logan, F. A. *Fundamentals of learning and motivation.* Dubuque, Iowa: Brown, 1970.

Skinner, B. F. *Walden two.* New York: Macmillan, 1948.

Skinner, B. F. *Beyond freedom and dignity.* New York: Knopf, 1971.

5

COGNITIVE PROCESSES

We use the term *cognitive processes* to refer to the ways in which an individual selects information from the environment, modifies that information, and uses his repertoire of knowledge and skills to meet the demands of the task at hand. Cognitive psychology characterizes people as active processors of information. This characterization does not mean that a person should be viewed as continuously and perpetually vigilant, taking in all of the information in his environment and constantly being aware of what he is doing. Rather, as we shall see shortly, people are selective in what they attend to and sometimes they process information unconsciously.

Cognition—or thinking, as we commonly call it—is a *problem-solving activity.* It is true, of course, that some cognitive processes are not well organized, clear, and problem directed. Dreams, fantasies, and hallucinations, for example, seem to be aimless activities with no specific purpose. Yet even these cases might represent problem-oriented activity, though of an ill-directed and inefficient sort. There is evidence to show that the tendency to daydream is correlated with the severity and frequency of everyday problems. People caught in conflict show an increase in daydreaming, especially when their overt attempts to solve the conflict have failed. In severe cases, unresolved conflict can lead to fantasy or hallucination as a means of reducing the conflict or temporarily shelving the problem. Moreover, numerous people have reported that the solution to an important problem occurred to them during sleep. Thus it is possible that such apparently aimless mental activities as dreaming do fulfill a problem-solving function.

Theories of Cognition

Motor Theory

One of the first theoretical analyses of cognition emphasized the basic concepts of stimulus and response. According to this theory, all knowledge and all skill is a matter of connecting particular stimuli with particular overt actions. Then, whenever a stimulus occurs, it will provoke the response with which it has been associated. If that stimulus is new, it will tend to provoke a response identical or similar to the response provoked by a similar stimulus. Thus all behavior is derived from conditioning and related processes, although in some cases these processes may involve the stringing together of a large number of responses.

These ideas are basic to the *motor theory* of thinking proposed by Watson and other behaviorists.

The New Yorker, December 9, 1974. Drawing by Herbert Goldberg; © 1974 The New Yorker Magazine, Inc.

record bursts of electrical activity (reflecting implicit movement) when people are instructed to think about a particular problem or situation. This muscular activity is the substance of their thought, according to Watson. Another example involved instructing a person whose forearms were covered with electrodes to think of being struck twice on the right arm with a hammer. Under these conditions, the subject shows two bursts of electrical activity in the right forearm and nothing in the left. Again, the thought has a definite muscular component.

There is also research to show that relaxation and thought tend to be mutually incompatible. People who have been taught techniques for progressive relaxation of the body find that, with relaxation, there is an accompanying reduction in the amount of mental activity, and relaxation has been used as a therapy for people whose thoughts are anxiety-arousing. Thus the behaviorists developed a strictly motor theory of thinking that eliminated mentalistic concepts altogether. They claimed that to think of something is to have that something (a stimulus) trigger low levels of activity somewhere within the body. The motor activity may or may not be followed by overt responses or a performance based on the thought.

Despite the supporting evidence and its attractive simplicity, the motor theory is not now widely accepted. Without going into detail, we can say that there are too many loopholes. First, it is unlikely that the processes of problem solving, creativity, language, and the like can realistically be described in terms of sequences of conditioned responses, no matter how long. But more important is the fact that there are other ways to account for the evidence that has been used to support motor theory. The muscular activity recorded in the experiments cited above could be merely an incidental by-product of thinking. It might be an overflow phenomenon resulting from activities in the brain that occur during thinking; the brain is so active during thinking that signals might "spill out" to the muscles over motor pathways (see Chapter 2). Moreover, there is evidence that both learning and thought occur in the absence of any recordable muscular activity, as, for example, when the body has been completely paralyzed by a drug. The motor theory simply cannot account for this finding.

Mediational Theory

A direct descendant of the motor theory is the *mediational theory* of cognition. As with the motor theory, the emphasis here is on learning and on

In their view, if there is no movement (muscular or glandular activity) there is no behavior. They held that strictly mental activity does not occur. Any activity of the organism, including thinking, involves movement. Sometimes the movement may be so fast or slight that special instruments are needed to record it; but, according to the motor theorists, if there is real thought, there is also real movement. Watson believed that most human thought was basically subvocal activity—the thinker speaking to himself, that is, moving the muscles of the voice apparatus.

Some ingenious experiments were devised by the behaviorists to support their position. Surface electrodes, placed on the skin above the muscles of the voice apparatus in the throat, characteristically stimuli and responses. We learn to think. Indeed, mediational theories are probably more properly described as learning theories (see Chapter 4) than as theories of cognition, although the application to cognition is direct and straightforward. At this point, you may want to refresh your memory of learning theories by rereading the discussion of mediated and semantic generalization in Chapter 4.

Basically, mediational theory holds that as a consequence of the formation of overt stimulus-response connections during learning, there may develop inside the organism miniaturized versions of these stimuli and responses, called *mediational stimuli* and *responses.* Mediational events provide a connecting link between the environment and the way one responds to it. They come about mainly through experience. Once a young child has learned several appropriate ways of responding overtly to his environment, he develops corresponding mediational processes that guide his actions in subsequent situations. When he encounters a new situation somewhat similar to one he has experienced previously, a number of mediational events may occur, representing ways in which he might behave. The child will select one of these ways, generally on the basis of its relative strength, and respond in accord with it.

As the child grows, experiences the world, and practices new skills, his repertoire of mediational responses increases. Consequently, hierarchies of mediators are formed. Any particular stimulus might elicit a number of possible responses ranked in the hierarchy by their strength. In attempting to solve a problem, then, the child proceeds to follow each elicited response in an order determined by its strength in the hierarchy. The theory includes both *divergent hierarchies,* in which a single stimulus elicits many responses, and *convergent hierarchies,* in which clearly different external stimuli all elicit the same response. The divergent hierarchy is the basis for problem solving because most problems require that we think of a variety of possible solutions. The convergent hierarchy supplies a basis for forming concepts that organize many different objects, such as tables, into the same category.

One weakness of both the motor theory and the mediational theory is that they view the organism as essentially passive and subject only to the influence of physical stimuli, whether external or internal. The purposeful aspects of performance, the ability of human beings to form and use rules, and the importance of language in thought are not adequately dealt with by these theories. Thus

The information-processing approach to cognition, based heavily on the principles of computer science, promises to have significant impact on our lives. Already there are very sophisticated programs for solving logic problems, playing bridge and chess, and even for directing psychotherapy. Computers will play an increasing role in teaching people how to think, reason, and solve problems in just about any area of knowledge. For example, computers are being used to teach medical students how to make diagnoses according to the principles used by specialists.

alternative theoretical explanations of cognition have been proposed. We shall now consider the theory that is perhaps the most widely accepted today.

Information-Processing Theory

While psychology was under the influence of strict Behaviorism, mental concepts such as memory, inference, reasoning, and others commonly used in reference to cognition were considered unscientific and therefore improper in psychological theory. With the advent of the electronic *computer,* most psychologists began to realize that one could speak

Talking Inhibits Thinking

By Dr. Leonard Reiffel
Boulder Daily Camera—In spite of its wonderful capabilities, the human brain has some definite limitations. There can be serious interference if two simultaneous tasks require the brain's attention, like trying to think and listen at the same time.

A scientific experiment on this subject was done recently in England. The tasks involved were trying to read something with an understanding of whether or not the material was correct and, at the same time, repeating a sentence that had been memorized. The sentence was familiar and didn't have significant information content. Thus, the simple act of talking and its effect on how accurately one could judge whatever he was reading, was studied.

Two groups of students from 19 to 26 years of age were asked to check off the correctness or incorrectness of a series of simple sentences. One group did so while repeating "Mary had a little lamb"; the other group did so silently. Various precautions were taken to mix the questions and the groups to avoid experimental errors.

The results were rather spectacular. The students who remained silent while they were doing these tests got about 28 correct answers on the average. Those who were speaking only got 17 correct answers. It was obvious, therefore, that the seemingly trivial act of verbalizing something like "Mary had a little lamb" slowed down the thinking ability of the people who were talking.

Psychologists have known for some time about the limited channel capacity of the human brain. They have known that a small load, even in a separate "output" channel such as speaking, can make a great difference in performance in another channel, like reading.

The psychologists who performed this test observed, however, that there are important applications. According to this experiment, compelling people to chant slogans would appear to be an excellent way of inhibiting and reducing their higher mental processes and judgements. Think about it. Doesn't it seem that the tyrants of the world have known this psychological fact for years? When people are busy chanting slogans, they can't think very well.

The mental requirements of two different tasks may be more than our limited capacity to process information can handle. Thus it is often impossible to do two things at once.

"mentalistic" processes in the computer, why couldn't one talk scientifically about mental processes in people?

The theories based on computer models are commonly known as *information-processing theories,* for they refer to the way people receive information from their environment, operate on it, integrate it with information available in memory, and use the product as a basis for deciding how to perform. Today we have information-processing theories that encompass nearly all levels of psychological concepts from basic sensory and perceptual activities through human personality. Among these theories are some that apply to human thought.

The general method for constructing a theory of this sort is as follows. Take a situation in which it is generally agreed that thought is involved, for example, playing a game of chess or solving logic problems. Write a program that will guide the computer in this activity, and then have the computer and one or more human beings solve a series of problems of the type in question. Compare the activities of the computer, as they are printed out, with the activities of the human beings, as they talk aloud during the problem-solving process. Compare also the eventual solution obtained by the computer and by the human beings. If it is impossible to discriminate the output of the computer from the output of human beings, we say that the computer *simulates* human behavior. If, however, there are discrepancies between the computer output and human behavior, the computer program is adjusted in hopes of getting a better approximation.

The theory eventually arrived at, written as a computer program, is a set of rules that operates on incoming information, transforms that information in appropriate ways, stores it, either momentarily or permanently, compares and integrates the information with previously stored information, makes decisions on the basis of the integration process, and executes some response (output).

Limits of human cognition.   One aspect of human cognition that computer simulations must make allowances for is the fact that human beings have a severely limited capacity for remembering and processing information. The mind can handle only a fixed amount of information at any given time. Limits on short-term memory have been noted in Chapter 4. In addition, there are limits on what can be done with information in short-term memory. Different kinds of information processing make

of these processes and not be accused of mysticism. After all, it was clear that the computer could remember, calculate, make inferences, and solve problems, to the point of doing these things in some ways better than people. The computer was built by people whose knowledge of science could hardly be criticized. If one could talk scientifically about different demands on this central processing capacity. Some mental operations can take place simultaneously—"in parallel" (that is, without mutual interference)—while others must be performed one at a time in a sequential fashion. One way in which this limited capacity has been studied is by having people attempt to "do two things at once."

The idea is that, if doing one task interferes with the performance of the other task, then both tasks must be making use of some common information-processing system that is incapable of handling them both at the same time. On the other hand, if the addition of a second task has no effect on the performance of a first task, then presumably the two tasks involve different systems. For example, the process of identifying a familiar stimulus (say, a word) does not seem to affect a person's reaction time to an auditory signal. Whatever processing is required by these two tasks can be done simultaneously. But most mental tasks do seem to interfere with each other—a person's reaction to a signal will be considerably slower if he is mentally adding numbers when the signal is presented.

This limited capacity affects performance in many cognitive tasks, including several that should be very familiar to you. If a person who has just looked up an unfamiliar telephone number and is trying to remember (rehearse) it long enough to complete dialing is asked a simple question, he is likely either to ignore the question or to forget the phone number. One of the difficulties in attending to lectures is that the demand to attend to the new information the lecturer is presenting competes with the activity of rehearsing or noting the just-presented information for later study. If you ask a person to add "in his head" the numbers 569, 148, and 452, he is very likely to reach for pencil and paper because he will be unable to remember what the numbers are, perform the arithmetic operations, and keep track of any subtotals "at the same time." When a listener says, "You lost me," it is often because the speaker has produced a long, complicated sentence that requires the listener to hold on to too many pieces of information before the idea expressed by the complete sentence is formed.

Assessment of the theory.   Information-processing theory is a popular way of viewing psychological processes today. It has the advantage of considerably more complexity and richness of description and detail than any of the other theories we have discussed. Although its implications have not been fully explored, it seems capable of a more

"Oh, you press the button down. The data goes 'round and around, Whoa-ho-ho-ho-ho-ho, And it comes out here."

The New Yorker, December 31, 1973. Drawing by Lorenz; © 1973 The New Yorker Magazine, Inc.

realistic account of the complex behavior of human beings. But we should not accept information-processing theory as a final explanation of cognitive processes. There are some questionable aspects, particularly the role of skills in human behavior, that remain to be satisfactorily handled. At this point, the best recommendation we can make is that a student should keep his mind open to a variety of theoretical possibilities and try to apply each of them to the various phenomena of cognition discussed in the following pages.

Problem Solving

A great deal of what we know about cognition comes from observations of what people do in well-structured problem situations. To illustrate some of the generally accepted principles of problem solving, we shall examine research findings about four types of problems: simple "one-shot" problems, tasks requiring original or creative solutions, conceptual problems, and reasoning problems. But first let's look at the stages involved in solving virtually any kind of problem.

Stages of Problem Solving

Although a number of different suggestions have been made as to what the stages of problem solving are, we shall concentrate attention on the proposal made by Donald M. Johnson. According to Johnson,

© 1974 United Feature Syndicate Inc.

Psychologists study thinking by examining the behavior of people attempting to solve problems of the kind mentioned in the cartoon, and by manipulating the **characteristics of the problem, the problem solver, and the nature of the information given to the subject (such as hints or strategies).**

the stages of problem solving are *preparation, production,* and *judgment.* Preparation refers to the activities of determining what the problem is, what information is available, and what constraints are imposed on its solution. Production involves thinking of alternative possible solutions. Judgment is the evaluation of alternatives. For some simple problems, these stages might follow each other in a neat, simple order. But for more complex problems, it may be necessary to reexamine the problem for new information, to repeat stages of production for different parts of the solution, or to evaluate possible solutions several times in the light of new information. Thus, although the general order of these stages is preparation, production, and finally judgment, there can be a considerable amount of recycling through them in the course of solving a problem. A diagram of the possible interplay among these stages is given in Figure 5-1.

Most studies of simple problem solving emphasize the production stage. That is, the researcher typically tries to prepare the solver completely by giving instructions. Because the problem is uncomplicated, solution attempts can usually be readily evaluated as either correct or incorrect. Consequently, the time a person spends in solving the problem reflects primarily the production of solution attempts, and the process the researcher seeks to describe is the process of generating alternative solutions. Other, more complex problems can involve different emphases. For example, in trying to solve the problem of selecting the best move in a game of chess, a considerable amount of effort is devoted to evaluating the consequences of a particular move.

Tasks requiring creative solutions involve all three stages in a fairly obvious fashion. Such a problem is likely to be somewhat ambiguous, which means that the statement of the problem is subject to different

interpretations and that no obvious "answer" can be readily identified. Suppose that a number of people are given the task of indicating "how to improve the distribution of wealth in the country." This problem is subject to many interpretations. One person might assume that the best distribution of wealth is one in which wealth is most closely tied to achievement, whereas another person might assume that the desired goal is to distribute wealth most evenly among the population. Two people who are generally working toward the same goal might make different assumptions regarding the constraints imposed on a solution—one might try only solutions allowable within the existing social-political framework, while the other might assume that modifying the form of government is an allowable alternative. The judgment of any proposed solution is likely to be very complicated, and people might not agree on the relative importance of various facets of the evaluation. We shall have more to say about these issues when we discuss creative problem solving.

A number of psychologists have proposed a fourth stage of problem solving called *incubation.* The general idea is that, if a person has worked on a problem for some time without finding a solution, he may temporarily (or in some cases permanently) withdraw from the problem. In severe cases this withdrawal process may involve pathological symptoms such as delusions or excessive daydreaming. Usually, however, it is simply a matter of going away and doing something else for a while. When the person returns to the problem, he sometimes finds the elusive solution quite easily. One suggested explanation of this incubation effect is that while the person is away from the problem he continues to work on it unconsciously. Another suggestion is that a rest period allows a person to "clear his mind," to get over any short-sighted or repetitive behavior that is preventing him from

Figure 5–1
The possible interplay between preparation, production, and judgment in problem solving

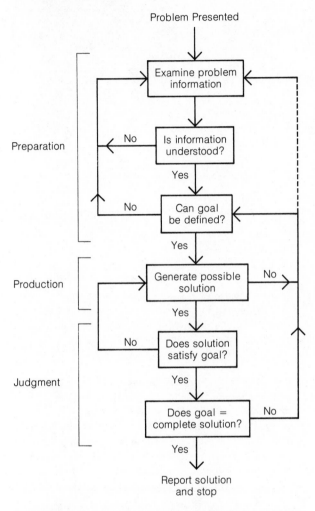

of uncomplicated steps. The term *one-shot* refers to the fact that the person receives all the information he needs or is going to get about the problem at the outset. In effect, the person is told what the problem is and goes to work. Furthermore, these problems all have a specific solution that the problem solver will easily recognize once he achieves it.

The major behavioral emphasis in experiments using simple problems is not on learning something new, but rather on utilizing the products of past experience and practice. The idea is to put together what you already know and are able to do in some simple but nonobvious way in order to bring about a solution. Of course, if a problem of this sort is new to you, you do learn something when you solve it. You experience the solution and how to derive it. Once you have experienced the solution, you will generally remember it, without further practice, for a fair amount of time.

Some simple problems emphasize the principles of perceptual organization (introduced in Chapter 3). Solving this kind of problem is often a matter of being able to visualize alternative solutions in the mind's eye. For example, consider the following problem:

Given the following array of sixteen matches, move three and only three matches to change the array into a sixteen-match array of four squares all the same size.

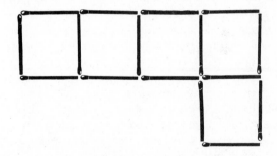

finding the solution. But there is no generally accepted account of incubation, in part because incubation does not always occur, and in part because researchers have had difficulty demonstrating incubation effects in laboratory studies of problem solving. Certainly, a rest period is no guarantee of a solution. What we can safely suggest is that if you find yourself in a situation that you cannot master, you have little to lose, and perhaps much to gain, by taking some time off, putting the problem out of your mind, engaging in some other activity, and only later returning to work on the problem.

Simple "One-Shot" Problems

"One-shot" problems are simple because the solution involves at most a relatively small number

Arriving at the solution to this problem (shown on page 155) depends on the ability to visualize different arrangements of the matchsticks. Imagery, especially visual imagery, is an important problem-solving thought process in perceptual problems. Misperception of the situation contributes materially to an inability to solve problems of this sort.

The majority of problems encountered probably rely more on language than they do on imagery as a problem-solving device. Word and anagram problems are good examples, although in neither case is perception or imagery entirely unnecessary. Some word problems require special knowledge and skills to solve them. Consider the following sample problem:

The ages of a man and his wife are together 98 years. He is twice as old as she was when he was the age she is today. What are their ages now? **(Johnson, 1944)**

Finding the answer to this problem (see page 155) depends on a knowledge of algebra and the techniques for solving simultaneous equations. Without that knowledge, it is unlikely that a person could arrive at an adequate solution except by trial and error or a lucky guess.

Algorithms and heuristics.   Generally speaking, there are two routes to the solution of any problem. Consider the following scrambled word or anagram problems.

Make five words out of the following five sets of scrambled letters:

```
CHIKT   _ _ _ _ _
EABLL   _ _ _ _ _
OANEC   _ _ _ _ _
HIGTR   _ _ _ _ _
IAFAM   _ _ _ _ _
```

There is a guaranteed route to each solution, though it typically takes a long time. This involves rearranging the letters in all possible combinations, of which there are 120 when 5 letters are involved. You then look at each separate rearrangement and decide whether it is or is not a word. When you find the first word, the problem is solved. A procedure of this sort, which will invariably pay off in a correct solution, is called an *algorithm*. Most people, however, would not use an algorithm to solve anagrams; they would adopt a more intuitive approach based on certain principles that might shorten the solution process. These short-cut methods are called *heuristics.*

A common heuristic for solving anagrams is to consider only letter combinations of reasonably high frequency and to rule out combinations that are unlikely in ordinary English words. Thus, in the first anagram it would be appropriate to consider the combination CH or TH at the beginning of the word and CK at the end. In contrast, KC, a combination of low frequency, can be ruled out. In this case, the heuristic works. Once TH and CK are put together, the solution is almost automatic. But solution is not

"If only he could think in abstract terms. . . ."

Imagery is a way of coding and remembering our perceptions of the world and our experiences. As such, imagery plays an important role in cognition. Often we solve problems "in our heads" by imagining the various aspects of the problem, and it is obviously much easier to conjure up images of concrete objects such as tables, chairs, and elephants than of abstract things such as love, mortality, and nth roots. Problem solution may be helped by translating abstract terms into concrete ones that can easily be visualized. Psychologists like to do this, for example, by devising mechanical models of psychological processes, as when cognition is treated as a computer program.

guaranteed, as is perhaps best exemplified by the third anagram, where NE, a frequent combination, is not correct, while OE, an infrequent one, is (see answers on page 155).

The role of past experience.   The major emphasis in research on solving simple problems has been investigation of the effects of past experience on current attempts to solve a problem.

Some investigators, such as the early Gestalt theorists, felt that a good deal of the problem-solving process was built into the organism. Finding a solution was mainly a matter of seeing things in the right way. Experience played a role, but a relatively minor one. Supporting this assumption were some studies showing insightful problem solving on the part of captive chimpanzees.

In one study, the chimp was given the problem of reaching a banana hanging from the ceiling of his cage, out of reach. There were several boxes inside the cage that could be stacked so as to provide a platform from which the banana could be reached. Wolfgang Köhler, the psychologist who conducted this study, observed that the chimp engaged for awhile in overt trial and error behavior without success. Characteristically, he then would retreat from the problem and enter a kind of incubation period. The solution finally appeared to come in a moment of insight, as if the animal realized all at once how to accomplish the goal. At that point, the animal would leap up, stack the boxes, and climb them to reach the banana.

It seems that Köhler's chimp solved his problem basically with insight, with little help from past experience. Köhler concluded that this problem-solving behavior occurs because of innate processes that force the animal (or person) to take different perceptual perspectives until, in a moment of insight, the solution automatically appears.

Later and more thorough examinations of this behavior, however, revealed that it rarely, if ever, took place in the absence of appropriate previous experiences. Animals who have had no experience with stackable boxes rarely, if ever, solve this kind of problem "insightfully." And, indeed, the more opportunity the animals have to play with boxes, examine them, and use them for one purpose or another, the more likely they are to solve the problem in this manner.

From these data and data of his own, Harry Harlow formulated a theory of problem solving in which prior experience is the *only* essential variable. Indeed, Harlow's point is that animals and people *learn* to think. According to Harlow, the ability to think is developed gradually through a process involving the acquisition of certain principles and skills that can then be applied to novel but similar problems. For example, studies have shown that monkeys can gradually acquire the ability to solve problems for which the solution principle is the same from problem to problem. A typical task used in these studies is the "oddity problem." The monkey must select one object from an array of three or more objects. All objects are identical except for one, the odd one. The odd member is always the "correct" choice. At the outset, inexperienced monkeys solve these problems slowly and with much trial and error. After experience with a number of problems of the same type, however, the animal's problem-solving behavior is immediate

American Scientist, January-February 1972. Reprinted by permission of Sidney Harris.

Coding or recoding a phrase as a set of initial letters (an acronym) may cause problems when you need to decode in order to solve a problem.

and "insightful." On each new problem most animals are then able to select the correct stimulus on the very first attempt.

Functional fixedness.   A special case of past experience getting in the way of effective problem solving involves *functional fixedness.* Here the function of a particular object is fixed, or determined, by its use in one way just before the problem is presented; thus the problem solver tends to overlook how the object can be used in a different way to solve the problem. Under these circumstances, the problem is more difficult than it ordinarily would be.

Functional fixedness can be demonstrated with a simple mechanical problem called the pendulum or two-string problem. To solve this problem, the subject must tie together the ends of two strings suspended from the ceiling. The strings are sufficiently far apart, however, that the subject cannot reach the second while holding onto the

Figure 5–2
The Maier two-string problem

This is perhaps the most famous task that has been used in laboratory studies of problem solving. The subject is required to figure out a way to tie two strings together, even though when he is holding onto one string the other is out of reach. A variety of objects are available for use in reaching the solution, such as a chair, tissue paper, a pair of pliers, and some paper clips. The solution involves tying the pliers to the string and setting it in motion like a pendulum so that it can be reached while the subject is holding onto the other string.

After W. J. McKeachie and C. L. Doyle. *Psychology*, second edition, 1970, Addison-Wesley, Reading, Mass.

The New Yorker, September 28, 1968. Drawing by W. Steig; © 1968 The New Yorker Magazine, Inc.

One long-standing issue in the psychology of cognition deals with the question of whether problem solution occurs gradually, through a process of *trial and error,* with the learner getting closer and closer to solution all the time, or whether it occurs suddenly, as if the solver had *"insight"* into the solution. This cartoon is a takeoff on the famous study by Kohler, who found that chimpanzees could solve problems on an insight basis—they could stack boxes and climb the stack to reach the bananas. However, it turns out that *prior experience* with the problem materials is important in determining whether chimps will solve the problem.

first. The solution is to find some weighty object, from a variety of possibilities lying on a table, attach that object to the end of one string, set it in motion like a pendulum, and then, while holding onto the other string, grab the pendulum at the nearest point on its arc (see Figure 5-2).

Suppose that prior to attacking the pendulum problem, the subject was given the task of wiring a simple electrical circuit. As part of that activity, he was required to use a pair of pliers. Subsequently, in the pendulum problem, the subject would be less likely to use the pliers as a pendulum weight, even

though the pliers were obviously the best object for that purpose. There is a stimulus generalization function, like those discussed in Chapter 4, that applies to this phenomenon. If instead of the pliers used in the wiring task, a new but identical pair of pliers is placed on the table, subjects show somewhat less resistance to using them as a pendulum bob, and more subjects eventually arrive at the solution. If instead of an identical pair of pliers, a similar but different pair is placed on the table, an even greater percentage will choose pliers to solve the pendulum problem. Finally, if a pair of scissors, similar to the original pliers, is available on the table, there will be an even greater tendency to use them to weight the string.

In other words, functional fixedness tends to be a response identified primarily with the particular tool or object used initially. The effect spreads, however, to other objects that bear some similarity to the initial one. Only when an object is sufficiently dissimilar is it recognized by most subjects as suitable for playing a second role.

There are many similarities between functional fixedness and other cases of learning that we have described in Chapter 4. Indeed, it is possible to conclude that functional fixedness is learned and, as such, is an example of the importance of past experience in the problem-solving process.

Mental set.   Sometimes, as a consequence of solving a series of similar problems, you fall into the use of certain procedures that might not be very efficient or might fail if even a simple change in the problem occurs. Consider the following problem. You have three empty jars and a water tap to work with. The jars, labeled A, B, and C, hold 10, 32, and 7 quarts, respectively. Your task is to use these jars in such a way as to measure out exactly 8 quarts of water. After some experimenting, the proper solution becomes clear. You fill the second container, pour off 10 quarts into the first, leaving 22, and then fill the third container twice, throwing out 7 quarts each time for a total of 14. This leaves you with 8 quarts in the second container. This is a relatively simple problem that requires knowledge and skills available to most of us.

Now, for further practice, solve successively Problems 1 through 5 as given in Table 5-1. You will find that each of them is solved by precisely the same formula: B − A − 2C. After you recognize the formula, getting the answer is trivial. Once you develop the *mental set,* that is, the tendency to use this formula, answers can be generated

Table 5–1
Jar problems

Problem number	Three jars are present with the listed capacity			Obtain exactly this amount of
	Jar A	Jar B	Jar C	water
1	21	127	3	100
2	14	163	25	99
3	18	43	10	5
4	9	42	6	21
5	20	59	4	31
6	23	49	3	20
7	10	36	7	3

Answers to Problems

Matchstick Problem

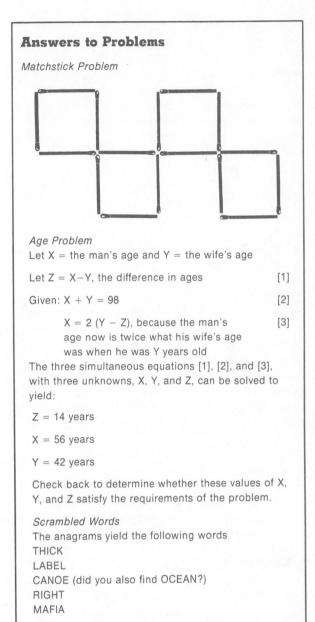

Age Problem

Let X = the man's age and Y = the wife's age

Let Z = X−Y, the difference in ages   [1]

Given: X + Y = 98   [2]

$\quad$ X = 2 (Y − Z), because the man's   [3]
age now is twice what his wife's age
was when he was Y years old

The three simultaneous equations [1], [2], and [3], with three unknowns, X, Y, and Z, can be solved to yield:

Z = 14 years

X = 56 years

Y = 42 years

Check back to determine whether these values of X, Y, and Z satisfy the requirements of the problem.

Scrambled Words
The anagrams yield the following words
THICK
LABEL
CANOE (did you also find OCEAN?)
RIGHT
MAFIA

---

automatically. But there is a potential disadvantage to developing a set way of solving problems. Sets are sometimes hard to break, and if a problem could not be solved by the formula, you might have more difficulty with it.

For example, continue on to Problems 6 and 7 in Table 5-1. Problem 6 you will find solves easily by the old familiar formula given above. Problem 7, however, may give you some difficulty, for the old formula will not work. Indeed, in a typical experiment, some subjects will fail to solve Problem 7 within a reasonable working period, say 3 minutes. Actually, the solution to Problem 7 is easier than the formula that applies to the other problems. All you have to do is subtract Jar C from Jar A to get the right amount of water. In addition, if you look back to Problem 6, you will see that the simpler formula works there also, although most people overlook it.

This example illustrates the potentially negative effects of a mental set. Sometimes we get so caught up in a particular way of doing something that we overlook other simpler ways that may also work. Our perspective on the problem becomes too narrow for us to see alternative possibilities. There are many examples of mental set acting as a blinder on our activities in everyday life.

In this example we again see the relevance of learning to the process of human thought and problem solving. The effect of training or practice on the first five problems is similar to the phenomenon of interference as discussed in Chapter 4. A particular way of responding is built up that then interferes with alternate ways of responding when they become appropriate or necessary. We could easily measure the *negative transfer* in this case by recording how long it takes a group to solve Problem 7 after solving Problems 1 through 5 and comparing that time to the amount of time it takes a group that has been given a different kind of training, or no training at all, to solve the problem. As you might expect, for the untrained subjects, Problem 7 poses no difficulty whatsoever.

Original and Creative Behavior

For the problems we have discussed so far, there is one clear-cut, generally accepted answer. In contrast, there are many problems, such as listing uses for a pair of pliers, for which many different answers are in some sense "correct," with some answers being "better" than others. The terms *originality* and *creativity* are used to refer to the behavior shown in solving such problems. Psychologists who study the responses to such tasks concentrate on evaluating the answers given.

For this purpose, it is useful to distinguish between original and creative responses. An original response is one that is simply infrequent. The maximum degree of originality is reached when only one person produces a particular response, but psychologists have been willing to deal with degrees of originality. The more original a response is, the fewer people there are who produce it. A creative act is one that meets some minimum criterion of originality *and* that is also relevant, practical, or feasible in some fashion. Suppose that people are asked to think of clever titles for a short story. If a person proposed the title "Q = Tor + WUG," this would very probably be original, but it would not be

judged creative unless it also captured the sense of the story. The distinction between original and creative behavior has two important implications. First, in any situation there are likely to be many more original responses than creative responses. Second, while originality can be defined in such a way that its measurement is straightforward and fairly reliable (one simply asks how infrequently the response is given), assessing creativity inevitably involves having someone *judge* the product. In everyday life, much of the controversy over what is creative stems from differences among judges. Two people might be looking at the same painting and agree that it is unique (= original), but they might differ substantially over whether or not it expresses some idea (whether or not it is creative).

Donald Campbell has proposed that creativity is the result of the production of a great many original ideas. If a mathematician discovers a previously unknown general proof, his success is a cause for enthusiasm, and there is a tendency to wonder what makes that mathematician different from all the others who have worked on the problem without success. Campbell suggests that it might be misleading to try to identify the peculiar characteristics of the successful mathematician because there might not be any. The idea is that, if the problem requires a truly creative solution, then it is likely that many, many attempts will have to be made before that solution is found. It is possible that the successful mathematician did nothing different from any of the others working on the problem, but simply happened to produce the attempt that proved successful. This idea does not mean that everyone is equally likely to produce a creative solution—quite the contrary. The person who has greater knowledge can restrict his efforts to those attempts that hold promise of leading to the solution, and the person who makes more attempts has a better chance. Campbell's essential point is that, if there are several people having equivalent knowledge and expending equal effort, it can be a matter of chance as to which of them will in fact find the solution.

As we noted earlier, Donald Johnson and his coworkers describe problem solving as consisting of three separate stages. Johnson has demonstrated that the distinction between the production and judgment stage is especially clear in the case of creativity. Johnson showed that, on the one hand, practice at producing solution ideas for a given problem increases the generation of ideas but does not necessarily lead to improved judgment of those ideas. On the other hand, practice at judging ideas improves a person's ability to discriminate better from worse ideas but does not necessarily lead to more production of ideas. These findings suggest that production and evaluation of creative ideas are entirely independent aspects of the creative process. Therefore, it is possible that two people who are equally capable of production can differ markedly in their problem-solving success, for the person who thinks of good ideas but has trouble deciding which one is best has less chance of being successful. The contribution of both production and judgment is sometimes mentioned in relation to team research, when it is suggested that a good combination might be an "idea man" and a colleague who is not particularly apt at producing ideas but has skill in evaluating them.

Conceptual Problems

A *concept* is a principle for organizing the objects and events that make up our circumstances into categories or sequences. A simple and familiar example of a category concept is "chair." Certain objects in our environment qualify as chairs and others do not. Concepts are generally not learned in a single experience. Typically, we have to see a variety of examples before we get the idea of what the concept is. After all, a concept does refer to a general category of things. It would be impossible to have a general idea of what all chairs are like from experience with only a single chair. So concepts develop over a series of experiences with several examples. Because each new experience will typically provide some additional information, we can gradually refine our knowledge of what the concept really is. In effect, we are accumulating information and integrating it with each new bit of information, all in an effort to figure out what the concept includes and excludes. As such, concept formation involves elements of both information processing and problem solving. But the relationship is reciprocal. Solving some new problem will often involve using concepts that are already known to us.

We can define any particular concept in terms of its *relevant* features, "Table," for example, has features like flat surface, supporting legs, used during meals, and the like. Instances of any concept usually also have *irrelevant* features, which are not involved in defining the concept. Tables, for example, can have any of a variety of surface shapes or heights. Learning a concept is mainly a matter of learning the defining as opposed to the irrelevant features. To study concepts and concept learning, psychologists set up tasks or problems in which a person must learn the defining features of some new

concept, usually an arbitrary concept that the psychologist has invented. For example, the person might be shown a series of nonsense drawings, some of which, according to the psychologist, are "DAX" and some of which are "non-DAX." DAX is a newly invented (arbitrary) concept. After seeing a large number of drawings, some of which are called DAX and some of which are called non-DAX, the person might discover that all DAXs have a curved (as opposed to an angular) shape with a squiggly line underneath. These are the defining features of DAX and all other features of the instances shown are irrelevant.

Complexity of the concept.   The number of relevant features a concept has determines, in part, the complexity of the concept. Furthermore, the more features there are, the more information we will have to deal with in learning or using the concept. It is not surprising to find, then, that concept complexity is directly related to the difficulty a subject has in using the concept. The number of different examples a person must see before he knows the concept increases significantly as the number of relevant features of the concept increases.

One possible reason for this effect is that, as we have noted, people have a limited capacity for processing information. As the number of relevant features of a concept increases, a subject will have greater difficulty attending to all the stimulus characteristics, remembering what they are, and performing the processing operations necessary to figure out what the concept is. Furthermore, these information-processing activities will compete with one another for access to the person's limited central capacity. Thus increasing stimulus complexity will lead to errors of various kinds and will increase the difficulty of the task much more than would be expected simply on the grounds that with more dimensions there are more possible answers.

Reducing the memory load.   There are several things you must do in solving a problem that requires you to figure out an unknown concept. You must attend to the stimulus features or attributes, make inferences, remember your decisions, and so on. Because of our limited processing capacity, these activities will interfere with one another. If you see each stimulus only once, it is virtually impossible for you to remember what the last three stimuli were like and what categories they belonged to while at the same time attending to the new stimulus and trying to figure out what information it provides about the solution.

One way to make the task easier is to reduce the memory load required. You will have much less difficulty if stimuli, for instance pictures or written descriptions, remain available for inspection throughout the task. Then you need not worry about remembering what "old" stimuli were like because you can look them up if you want to, and you can concentrate on the newest stimulus and the information it provides. Conceptual problems, because they necessarily require information to be extracted from a number of stimulus presentations, can rapidly overload a person's processing capacity, and providing a reminder of what has gone before reduces the stress and makes the task easier.

Time pressures.   Thinking takes time. If you are rushed through a series of instances in a conceptual problem, you will not be very efficient at utilizing the information. If you are given sufficient time to digest the information, you'll probably solve the problem more efficiently. Although each individual trial will take longer, the total time for a solution may be less. The most critical time interval is the time between feedback on one trial and the presentation of the next stimulus. During this "thinking period" you attempt to figure out what information you have just received. An interval that is too short will prevent you from completing this activity. If sufficient time is allowed, enabling you to complete the process, you can go on to the next trial knowing, for example, that some attributes are potentially relevant and others need no longer be considered.

Reasoning Problems and Logical Analysis

Our most sophisticated thought processes involve reasoning and logical analysis. *Formal logic* consists of a set of rules for analyzing an argument and deciding if the argument is internally consistent or not. Typically, unless people have studied formal logic, they will not follow the laws of logic in their arguments. If you stop and think about it, this finding should not be very surprising. If everyone were "automatically logical," there would be no need to teach courses in logic. Furthermore, if we were all logical, none of our arguments would ever be affected by anger or any other emotional factors.

Formal training in logic provides us with a set of intellectual skills (competence) that enables us to analyze our own and other people's arguments very thoroughly. But, what about the person who has not studied logic? How does this more typical person make arguments or in general solve reasoning

problems? In fact, studies have shown that people do make a lot of reasoning errors, but that these errors are predictable and understandable. There are several factors that help to understand how people typically reason. Before considering these ideas, let us examine some examples of logical problems.

Syllogisms.   A logical syllogism is a three-step argument consisting of two premises, both assumed to be true, and a conclusion that may or may not follow from the premises. Your task is to decide whether the conclusion is true, using only the information supplied by the two premises. Let's try some. Try to decide which conclusions are necessarily true, given the first two premises.

Syllogism 1
All As are Bs.
All Bs are Cs.
Therefore, all As are Cs.   True or false?

Syllogism 2
No As are Bs.
All Bs are Cs.
Therefore, no As are Cs.   True or false?

Syllogism 3
All As are Bs.
All Cs are Bs.
Therefore, all As are Cs.   True or false?

Syllogism 4
Some As are Bs.
Some Bs are Cs.
Therefore, some As are Cs.   True or false?

If you tried these four reasoning problems before reading on, you may be surprised to learn that only the conclusion of Syllogism 1 is *logically* true. Many people will accept all four conclusions as valid. To understand how this happens, let's consider briefly the difference between formal logic and one's own personal logic. Look at the first premise in Syllogism 1. Actually, this statement is ambiguous in the sense that it can apply to two different relations between A and B. These two meanings are illustrated in Figure 5-3, using diagrams that make it easier to understand the meanings of the statements. It can be seen that "All As are Bs" might refer to a situation in which there is only one set labeled AB; that is, "All As are Bs *and all Bs are As.*" On the other hand, "All As are Bs" can also refer to the things called As being included in the larger set of things called Bs, as in "All dogs are animals." The

Figure 5–3
Diagrams of possible meanings of "All As are Bs"

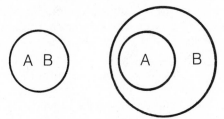

Figure 5-4
Diagrams of possible meanings of Syllogisms 1–4

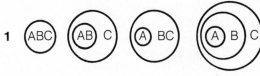

1

"All As are Cs" is true in every case.

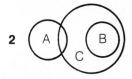

2

"No As are Cs" is false.

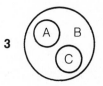

3

"All As are Cs" is false.

4

"Some As are Cs" is false.

point is this: Formal logic requires three things, that each premise be considered in all its possible meanings, that the various meanings of the premises be combined in all possible ways, and that a conclusion is valid only if it applies to every one of the possible premise combinations. In other words, if you can find a way of interpreting the premises and combining them such that a particular conclusion does not apply, then that conclusion is not logically valid. For Syllogisms 2 to 4, ways in which the premises can be combined to yield an A-C relation inconsistent with the stated conclusions are illustrated in Figure 5-4.

Reasons for errors in reasoning. It would not be surprising if you found that you really had to concentrate to understand the above description of formal logic. Quite clearly, formal logic requires a person to perform a considerable amount of information processing to analyze an argument or to solve a reasoning problem. The idea that we are somewhat limited information processors suggests ways in which errors can occur. Consider Syllogism 3 again. In this case, the conclusion is not logically valid because, as shown in Figure 5-4, the premises can be combined in such a way that the conclusion is not true. However, suppose you considered only one possible meaning of each of the premises, specifically the first meaning shown in Figure 5-4 for the "All As are Bs" statement. Thus you would interpret the first premise as also meaning that "All Bs are As" and the second premise as also meaning "All Bs are Cs." It is clear that, for these interpretations of the premises, the conclusion is absolutely valid. Your mistake would lie solely in your failure to consider other meanings of the premises.

Errors can also arise from the *atmosphere effect,* the tendency to accept conclusions consistent with the "atmosphere" or context established by the premises of the syllogism. For example, a set of premises all of the form "All ___ are ___," as in

Syllogism 3, establishes an atmosphere for a conclusion of the same form (see Figure 5-4). Alternatively, if one or more of the premises is negative, this sets up an atmosphere for a negative conclusion, as in Syllogism 2. Inability to ignore the atmosphere of a problem often leads to mistakes in reasoning. Sometimes the atmosphere accords with the correct answer, as in Syllogism 1. Nonetheless, it is important always to look beyond the atmosphere of a problem if you hope to reason accurately. The idea that people simply respond to the atmosphere created by the premises is used quite effectively in many political speeches to present illogical conclusions convincingly. The listener has little time for close analysis of the logic of the arguments being made, and is likely to accept the points the speaker makes without reasoning them through.

Perhaps the idea has occurred to you that people might simply have difficulty with syllogisms containing undefined terms, such as A or B, but

Did the Butler Do It?

One kind of problem used in research on reasoning is the "whodunit" problem, in which the subject is given information about a fairly complex set of relationships and must determine how they fit together. Such problems can be quite difficult. Although they involve some figuring out of "what follows from what" in a fashion similar to syllogisms, their solution depends heavily on appropriate hypothesizing (about what to figure out next). Because of this need for hypothesizing, performance on whodunit reasoning problems is not strongly related to performance on syllogistic reasoning problems. Try "playing detective" for this rather unrealistic mystery.

A murder had been committed. An examination of the fatal wound established that the murderer had used a dagger that made an unusual mark on the body. There were five suspects: the doctor, butler, cook, gardener, and accountant. Each had been alone in one of the five rooms in the apartment and thus had no one to vouch for his innocence. The rooms lie in a line down the single corridor: bedroom, den, living room, dining room, and kitchen, in order. The additional evidence, gathered from various sources, is as follows:

The butler was in the bedroom.
The man with the poison was in the room next to the man with the brown sweater.
The man with the dagger wore a gray jacket.
The man with the penknife wore a black jacket.
The cook wore a brown sweater.
The gardener was next to the dining room.
The man with the poison was in the living room.
The man with the pistol was in the room next to the man wearing the blue jacket.
The gardener had a rope.
The doctor was in the room next to the man with the black jacket.
The accountant wore a green sweater.

Sifting through the evidence, the crafty inspector deduced who the murderer was. Can you solve the crime? For the answer see page 163.

would reason more accurately when given arguments containing more meaningful concepts. For example, one might argue that the abstract statement "All As are Bs" is ambiguous, as indicated in Figure 5-3, but a meaningful statement like "All cats are animals" is unambiguous. Certainly, it is highly unlikely that a person could possibly interpret this statement to mean that "It is also true that all animals are cats." The fact of the matter is, however, that meaningful statements like "All cats are animals" do not always lead to more accurate reasoning. Syllogisms containing meaningful statements provide an opportunity for people's judgments to be influenced by a semantic factor, namely, the factual truth or falsity of the conclusion. People will tend to accept conclusions that are factually correct or that are consistent with their beliefs, whether or not the conclusions follow *logically* from the premises of the argument. For example, given the premises "All cats are carnivorous" and "All tigers are carnivorous," one has a strong tendency to accept the conclusion "all tigers are cats," a conclusion that is logically invalid. This argument is in fact like Syllogism 3; if you substitute "bears" for "tigers" you will see that the conclusion does not necessarily follow.

Language

Language is our greatest intellectual accomplishment. Languages differ from culture to culture, but the language of each culture provides members of that culture with an agreed-upon way of describing and remembering their experiences and communicating them to others. In a language, both visual and auditory, written and spoken, symbols represent various objects, events, actions, and relations that make up our circumstances. These symbols are combined in many different ways to express even larger ideas. Most language acquisition occurs during the early years of life; this process will be described in Chapter 7. In this chapter, we limit ourselves to a discussion of the structure and function of language and give some examples of the ways in which language is involved with cognitive processes.

Structure

One of the functions of language is to relate spoken sound to meaning. The speaker converts a meaningful experience into a series of vocalizations, and the listener in turn converts these vocalizations back into meaning. Let us assume that the speaker does his job well. Consider the task of the listener. To extract meaning from the vocalization, he must be able to identify the units and know the rules underlying their organization. It is quite common for travelers in foreign lands to fail to accomplish this task. We are inclined to attribute this failure to inadequate knowledge of "vocabulary," as in "How was I supposed to know that *strasse* means *street?*" Actually, the listener's task is much more complex than this. If you heard a language sufficiently different from your own, it is quite possible that you

The Syntactical Chimp

Newsweek—Over the last few years several researchers have demonstrated that chimpanzees can learn rudimentary language. At the University of Nevada, a six-year-old chimp named Washoe acquired a 140-word sign-language vocabulary and was taught to engage in complex sentence dialogue with humans. Bruno and Booee, two five-year-old males at the University of Oklahoma, used their sign language to converse with one another, actually preferring it to their natural means of communicating, which is a combination of chirps and gestures. Now, another remarkable demonstration of simian intelligence has been achieved. Researchers at the Yerkes Regional Primate Center in Atlanta, Ga., have taught a chimp named Lana to read and write simple but complete sentences in perfect syntax, and even to punctuate them accurately.

Lana writes her sentences, which convey her desires for food, movies or human affection, by punching plastic keys on a computer console. Each key of her large typewriter has a hieroglyphic-like symbol on it which stands for a word. The researchers say that there is no trick to what Lana does, as there is in teaching a dog to bark for a bone. "She understands the machine," says psychologist Duane M. Rumbaugh, "and she is very flexible in its use. Lana knows exactly what she is doing."

Lana's training began about two years ago when she was taught simple noun symbols such as apple, movie, drink and window. After she knew that pushing the picture key with the proper symbol—in this case a circle with two parallel lines in the center—would cause the computer to produce an apple, she was taught such verbs as give, make, open and tickle. But up to this point Lana's learning was merely rote association, similar to that of a human infant who learns that crying will get parental attention.

The breakthrough came about a year ago when Lana began using her 50-word vocabulary to make her own sentences, and to punctuate declarative ones with a period and interrogative ones with a question mark. To make sure that Lana had not become accustomed to a particular arrangement of the buttons on the computer console, the researchers scrambled the positions every day—the equivalent of randomly rearranging the keys on a secretary's typewriter. But even this shuffling did not interfere with Lana's performance.

Further verification that the chimp was actually using the keyboard to communicate with researchers (instead of merely following stimulus-response conditioning) came from a series of tests in which Lana had to complete valid or invalid sentences begun by a staff member. When Rumbaugh, for example, punched up the partial sentence *"Please machine open . . . ,"* Lana pushed the key for *"window,"* passing up such possibilities as "candy" or "banana." Semantics, in short, won out over the impulsive desire for a snack. When Lana was shown a meaningless sentence such as *"Please machine give a piece of window,"* she hit the erasure button in 90 per cent of the cases. Furthermore, in constructing her own sentences, if her fingers inadvertently hit a word which made no sense in the context of the sentence, she always caught the mistake and erased it. . . .

It is often said that human beings can be set apart from the rest of the animal kingdom because of two closely related capacities that only they possess: the ability to think and the ability to use language. Recently, there have been several experiments with chimpanzees designed to challenge human beings' unique status in this regard.

Groom   Give   Banana   Music   Water

Lana at the keyboard: Punch and you shall receive

would have no idea of what the vocal cues for units are, of when units begin and end; in other words, you might not have any idea of how to begin processing the vocalization. To state this differently, a language contains units and associated rules at several levels. The structure of language can be

"The thing to bear in mind, gentlemen, is not just that Daisy has mastered a rudimentary sign language but that she can link these signs together to express meaningful abstract concepts."

The New Yorker, October 7, 1974. Drawing by Lorenz; © 1974 The New Yorker Magazine, Inc.

described in terms of *sounds, words,* and *sentences,* and the rules that apply to determine what they mean. We will consider each of these briefly.

Sounds or phonemes.   The actual sound made by a speaker on any particular occasion is called a *phone,* but each phone is merely an instance of a general, conceptual class of sounds. These classes are called *phonemes.* For example, the b sound will not be exactly the same each time the word "boy" is spoken, even by the same speaker. Particular sounds vary from word to word and speaker to speaker. But the speakers of a common language will hear all of these sounds as members of the same phonemic class.

Each phoneme, generally designated by slashes, for example, /b/ as in *boy,* is considered to be the combination of several distinctive features associated with a particular language. In English the distinctive features include *voiced* (vocal chords vibrating) versus *voiceless* phonemes and *stopped* (the flow of air completely interrupted by the tongue or lips) versus *fricative* phonemes (a flow of air not

stopped but continuously flowing). To see the difference between voiced and voiceless phonemes make the /p/ and /b/ sounds (as in *pat* and *bat)* with your lips. Notice that /b/ uses the voice box and /p/ does not. These sounds are both stopped as well. Contrast them with the /f/ and /v/ phonemes (as in *fat* and *vat)*, which are fricatives; /f/ is voiceless and /v/ is voiced. Keep in mind that these are only two of many distinctive features of the English language.

Every language has many distinctive features, and, consequently, the possible number of different phonemes in any language is quite large. But not all phonemes that can be generated from these distinctive features will occur. For example, in English only 50 percent of the possible phonemes are actually used by native speakers. The explanation for this is related to an important psychological principle. While it is obviously critical to the language user to have phonemes organized into a predictable system, it is also essential for reliable communication that the system not be complete. If it were, errors of communication would probably increase and we would be quite likely to confuse one phoneme with others. We would constantly be asking, "What did you say?" The incompleteness of the system rules out some possibilities that are potentially confusing. This tends to guard against failure in the communication process that might be due to poor articulation on the part of the speaker, noise in the environment, or inattention on the part of the listener.

Words and morphemes. The language user deals not in sounds or phonemes but in larger units. The smallest meaningful unit of analysis in language is the *morpheme.* The value of using the morpheme instead of the word as the unit of linguistic analysis is best understood by example. In linguistic analysis the word "bat" is a single morpheme whereas "bats" consists of two morphemes, "bat" and "s," the second of which is the form for making a plural. Another example is the word "sadly," which is partitioned into "sad" plus "ly," the latter morpheme being used to produce an adverb from an adjective.

Phonemes combine to make morphemes. The combining process follows certain rules that we use in speaking English, although we may not know them in any formal sense. We use them, however, in the sense of being able to distinguish real English words from nonsense. Thus, certain combinations of sounds are allowable and certain others are not. For example, no English word could begin with "trv." We know immediately that "trvurs" cannot be a word. On the other hand, we might have to use a dictionary to find out about "dib" or "lut." Thus you can use your knowledge of the rules for combining sounds into English to judge whether unfamiliar combinations are real words or not.

Sentences and grammar. The morphemes and words produced by sound combinations are themselves combined to make sentences. Once again, the process obeys certain rules, known as the rules of grammar. The rules prescribe the ways in which words can be organized into phrases and phrases organized into sentences. For example, we recognize that "The red-haired boy threw the flat stone" is an acceptable English sentence, whereas "The stone red-haired flat the threw boy" is not. At a more fundamental level, there are transformational rules governing the relations between sentence forms and the underlying ideas they express. For example, we have no difficulty in determining that the sentences "The boy tossed the ball" and "The ball was tossed by the boy" express the same proposition even though they have quite different surface forms. The first sentence is in active form.

Solution to the "Whodunit" Problem

Room	Person	Clothing	Weapon
bedroom	butler	black jacket	penknife
den	*doctor*	*gray jacket*	*dagger*
living room	accountant	green sweater	poison
dining room	cook	brown sweater	pistol
kitchen	gardener	blue jacket	rope

The information given in the story can be sorted out and tabulated as shown above. The facts can then be used to deduce that the doctor, who wore a gray jacket, was in the den, had a dagger, and was the murderer.

The second is a passive transformation of the same underlying idea.

The functions served by such rules can be easily illustrated by presenting sentences that are ambiguous. One such example is "They are eating apples." We are not sure what this sentence means because we do not know whether the verb is "are" or "are eating"—that is, "They/are/eating apples" or "They/are eating/apples." The thought expressed clearly depends on the intended verb phrase. The same sequence of words expresses two different underlying ideas. For a different example, consider the sentence "The shooting of the hunters was terrible." This sentence is also ambiguous, but its noun and verb phrases are not—it is clear that the sentence is "The shooting (noun) of the hunters was (verb) terrible (adjective)." The ambiguity arises because "the shooting of the hunters" might have been generated by applying transformations to the underlying idea "the hunters shoot" or by applying different transformations to the underlying idea "they shoot hunters."

Meaning

It is a primary function of language to convey meaning, and the previously described structural components of language are intertwined with this function. Psychologists have not been especially successful in their attempts to understand linguistic meaning.

Most psychological theories have attempted to reduce meaning to associations between words (symbols) and the objects or things the words refer to (the referents). Thus, a word might be said to have meaning because it makes you think of the referent, elicits an image of the referent, or evokes reactions in you similar to those elicited by the referent. The meaning of a word *is* its associations.

Figure 5–5
Semantic differential ratings

Make your own ratings for the words "Mother" and "Tree"

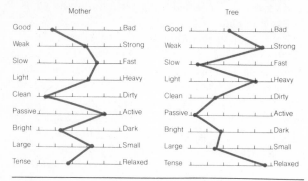

Mother

Good							Bad
Weak							Strong
Slow							Fast
Light							Heavy
Clean							Dirty
Passive							Active
Bright							Dark
Large							Small
Tense							Relaxed

Tree

Good							Bad
Weak							Strong
Slow							Fast
Light							Heavy
Clean							Dirty
Passive							Active
Bright							Dark
Large							Small
Tense							Relaxed

Compare your ratings with the averages obtained from a group

Mother / Tree

"I can't say I like the looks of that bunch."

The New Yorker, June 5, 1971. Drawing by Dana Fradon; © 1971 The New Yorker Magazine, Inc.

Words have both a *denotative meaning* and a *connotative meaning*. "Adolph Hitler" *denotes* a particular person but *connotes* many different unpleasant things to most people. The *semantic differential* measures the connotative or emotional meaning. How do you think "Hitler" would be rated on the three dimensions of connotation: evaluation, potency, and activity?

Furthermore, the meaningfulness of a word or nonsense syllable can be measured by the probability of an association or the number of associations elicited (see Chapter 4).

A variation of this approach is the idea of a *semantic differential,* proposed by Charles Osgood. According to Osgood, the meaning of a word is measured in terms of the ratings people give it on a number of different scales (see Figure 5–5). As many as 50 scales might be used, although it is typically found that the scales can be reduced to a basic set of three dimensions: *evaluation* (good-bad), *potency* (weak-strong), and *activity* (fast-slow). The adjective pairs in parentheses are those best illustrating these three dimensions. Notice that ratings on certain scales, like strong-weak and heavy-light, tend to come out pretty much the same. These pairs are related to the same dimension, potency. According to the theory behind the semantic differential, the meaning of any word can be indexed by its position on the three basic dimensions. Thus, "mother" is toward the positive end of evaluation, toward the strong end of potency, and toward the fast end of activity.

Clearly, the semantic differential approach does not measure meaning in its everyday sense. Usually, when we think of "mother," we do not imagine a point in three-dimensional space. Moreover, if a position in the space were designated, it would be unlikely to suggest a word or concept without further elaboration. What the semantic differential measures is called the *connotation* of a word, that is, what we feel about or associate with this word. The concept of mother is *defined* by its features, the most important being a biological and/or sociological relationship between one person, a female, and one or more other people. In this sense, we are talking about the *denotation* of the word.

In general, the above approaches provide only a very limited account of meaning, and much more work needs to be done before we will have a very full account of meaning. But we do know certain basic things about how words and concepts, words in sentences, and general knowledge convey meaning. Let us consider each of these briefly.

Words and concepts. Many of the words in our language are labels that identify concepts. The term "dog" may be used to refer to a particular furry, four-legged animal. But it is clearly a more general

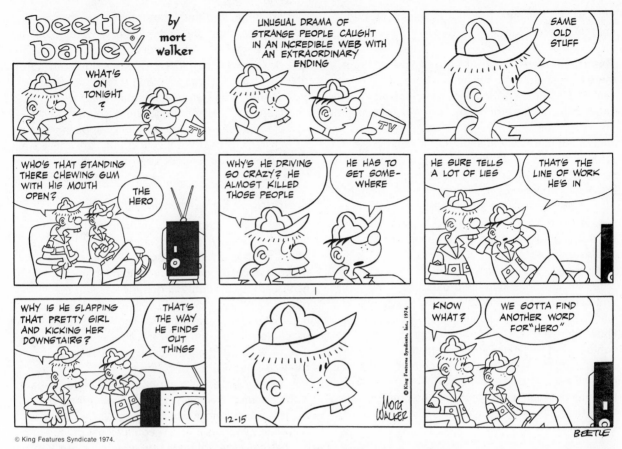

Words identify concepts. Sometimes the concept, an aspect of our culture, changes. Under these circumstances, we may indeed need a new word, at least for those of us who remember the old concept. Notice how the new concept of hero emerges from the series of descriptive sentences.

term than that. If we heard someone use the word "dog" but were unable to see what he was referring to, we could only surmise that one of a number of possibilities was in his presence. It might be *our* dog, it might be *his*, it might be a photograph, it might be a statue, and so on.

Many conceptual labels are learned without direct observation of instances. They are learned more or less by inference from the manner in which a word is used. Consider the following sentences. Almost everyone could get a good idea of what the nonsense word "corplum" means by considering how it is used in these sentences.

A corplum may be used for support.

Corplums may be used to close off an open place.

A corplum may be long or short, thick or thin, strong or weak.

A wet corplum does not burn.

You can make a corplum smooth with sandpaper.

The painter uses a corplum to mix his paints.

(After Werner and Kaplan, 1950)

The concept and the word become meaningful because of the context in which they are used.

Sentences.   Many words in our language are meaningless except for the functions they perform in sentences. For example, "but," "the," and "of" stand for no particular thing. Such words gain meaning in the *context* of sentences expressing some idea or ideas. As the Gestalt psychologists have told us, most of the messages we communicate are not completely analyzable into word components. Even though we know the words "the," "boy," "girl," and "hit," this knowledge alone does not enable us to account for the meaning of the sentence "The boy hit the girl." "The girl hit the boy" uses the same words but communicates an entirely different idea.

General knowledge. Actually, we may not get the full meaning of communication from the sentence alone. Most sentences interact with our "knowledge of the world," our memory for semantic meaning. Thus, through inferences, they provide us with much more information than looking at the sentence alone would suggest. For example, the sentence "Henry Aaron hit a home run and drove in three runs" describes a certain action. But it implies a great deal more: that a baseball game was being played, probably involving the Atlanta Braves, that a pitch was made, that two of Aaron's teammates were on base, and so on.

Usually we are unaware of how important our general knowledge is in the process of understanding language. Our ability to comprehend language is critically dependent upon this knowledge and not just on the information that is contained in the material we are trying to understand. If we are reading something and we do not possess the relevant knowledge to understand it, then the passage might appear to be nonsense. Read the following passage taken from Bransford and Johnson (1973):

If the balloons popped the sound wouldn't be able to carry since everything would be too far away from the correct floor. A closed window would also prevent the sound from carrying, since most buildings tend to be well insulated. Since the whole operation depends on a steady flow of electricity, a break in the middle of the wire would also cause problems. Of course, the fellow could shout, but the human voice is not loud enough to carry that far. An additional problem is that a string could break on the instrument. Then there could be no accompaniment to the message. It is clear that the best situation would involve less distance. Then there would be fewer potential problems. With face to face contact, the least number of things could go wrong.

This passage sounds like nonsense—it is difficult to comprehend because you do not have the relevant general knowledge necessary to understand the meaning of the sentences. The meaning, then, does not reside exclusively in the words and sentences that make up the passage—if that were so this perfectly grammatical material would be comprehensible. Rather, comprehending meaning is obviously an active process in which we interpret the information contained in the words, sentences,

and grammar, and this interpretation process must rely on other than purely linguistic knowledge in order to produce understanding. To get the relevant knowledge, turn the page and look at the drawing of the "electronic serenade"; then reread the passage. Now it should be quite meaningful—easy to comprehend. This should convince you that in comprehending language, written or spoken, cognitive processes are involved in a very active way and success is dependent upon the cognitions we have available.

Language, Culture, and Thought

It is generally accepted that thought and language are closely related, but the nature of that relationship is a subject of considerable debate. Is thought necessary for language? Is language necessary for thought? Is one the basis of the other? Are they identical? Do they have some material effect on each other? The fact is that psychologists do not know the answers to questions like these yet, and consequently there is a lot of room for theory and speculation.

A popular hypothesis about language and thought is the *linguistic relativity hypothesis* put forth by Benjamin Lee Whorf, which is often called the Whorfian hypothesis. It is a complex set of ideas, but basically the notion is that languages are organized differently, and, therefore, because language and thought are closely interrelated, speakers of these languages will think differently. Whorf argues that the way we perceive and think about the world is largely determined by the language we have for encoding the world.

Consider vocabulary richness. There is a tribe in the Philippine Islands whose language has names for 92 different kinds of rice. Arabs have about 6,000 ways of referring to camels in their speech. Naturally, we would expect these people to think more explicitly about rice or about camels than we can. But is this because they can think about camels or rice in ways we cannot, or is it because they just know more about camels and rice than we do? Their superior knowledge is surely based on the fact that camels and rice are more important in their culture and not on the fact that their language is different, as Whorf would argue. Most important, could they have a thought about camels or rice that we could not, in principle, have because we speak English? Basically no, because every language can probably express anything.

The evidence for the Whorfian hypothesis is highly anecdotal, with very little support for the notion that

Bilingualism and Information Processing

A very strong version of the linguistic relativity hypothesis would imply that a person's knowledge cannot be separated from his language. What then of the bilingual person who, say, is fluent in both English and French? One possibility is that some knowledge is stored in French and other knowledge is stored in English. A different, more nearly correct notion is that the person's knowledge is stored centrally and can be accessed equally well through either language.

In one experiment, French-English speakers were asked to read various short paragraphs and subsequently to answer questions about the information presented. A paragraph was either all in English, all in French, or in mixed English and French. An example of a mixed paragraph is given below:

His horse, followed de deux bassets, faisait la terre résonner under its even tread. Des gouttes de verglas stuck to his manteau. Une violente brise was blowing. One side de l'horizon lighted up, and dans la blancheur of the early morning light, il aperçut rabbits hopping at the bord de leurs terriers.

As long as the person could read the passage silently, it made little difference whether the paragraph was in one or two languages—for the same amount of study time, performance on the examination was the same.

Another test made use of the fact that when people see, one at a time, a long list of words and then are asked to recall as many as possible, words that are repeated more often in the list are recalled better. The question was whether or not "repetitions" in different languages would have the same effect on recall as repetitions in a single language. The results for French-English speakers indicated that, for example, experiencing "fold" twice and its French equivalent "pli" twice had the same effect on recall as four presentations of "fold." In other words, recall was a function of frequency of exposure to the meanings or concepts, not the linguistic forms expressing those meanings. This finding suggests that the subjects were utilizing a common meaning form that is accessible to either language.

they have single words to represent their discriminations. But there is little support for linguistic relativity when it comes to saying that language affects our overall outlook.

The Whorfian hypothesis is intriguing nonetheless, and of great significance if it is even partly true. What we need at this point is much better evidence on the subject than is provided by anecdotes about foreign phrases translated into English.

Intelligence

A variety of opinions have been expressed by psychologists about exactly what intelligence is. Some have argued that intelligence is a general ability to acquire and use knowledge and skills of any kind. Others have said that intelligence is the ability to get along in and adapt to one's environment. Still others have argued that, although there may be such a general factor, intelligence must be defined to include more specific mental abilities, such as word fluency, memory, reasoning, and the like, in order to reflect the concept adequately. An examination of the intelligence movement in psychology shows that all of these factors and perhaps others probably contribute to this complex behavioral trait.

Measuring Intelligence

The Binet test. The first general measure of intelligence was constructed for a simple pragmatic reason. Around the turn of this century, the Ministry of Public Instruction in Paris, France, decided it wanted to identify school children who were likely to have difficulty in school and could benefit from special programs. The Ministry commissioned Alfred Binet, a well-known psychologist of the time, and his colleague, Theodore Simon, to develop a test that could be used to sort out children with low intelligence. Since that time, the test, which for simplicity we will refer to as the Binet test, has been repeatedly and systematically revised, and versions of it are in common use today. Most recent revisions have been undertaken at Stanford University in California and are called Stanford-Binet tests.

Basic assumptions. Binet and Simon made two basic assumptions. First, intelligence is a composite of many abilities. Therefore, intelligence tests must contain a large number of different types of test items. Most items used in Binet tests are based on simple everyday tasks of the sort that almost anyone encounters. Binet wanted to construct a test that

language *determines* the general view we have of the world. Language does determine how efficiently we can code our experiences. Eskimos can talk more efficiently about snow than we can because

The Electronic Serenade

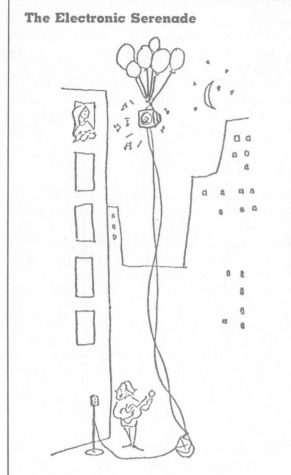

After you have studied this drawing of an "electronic serenade" go back and reread the passage on page 166 and see if the passage is easier to comprehend now that you have the relevant knowledge for understanding.

Taking the Chitling Test

Newsweek—It doesn't take a high IQ to recognize that intelligence tests have a built-in cultural bias that discriminates against black children. Tests designed to measure how logically a child can reason often use concepts foreign to the ghetto: a Harlem child who has never handled money or seen a farm animal, for example, might be asked a question that assumes knowledge of quarters and cows.

Adrian Dove, a sociologist and a Negro, for one, knows that black children have their own culture and language that "white" tests don't take into account. He saw this clearly when he worked with white civic and business leaders after the Watts riots. "I was talking Watts language by day," he says, "and then translating it so the guys in the corporations could understand it at night." Dove then designed his own exam, the Dove Counterbalance General Intelligence Test (the "Chitling Test") with 30 multiple-choice questions, "as a half-serious idea to show that we're just not talking the same language." The test has appeared in the Negro weekly *Jet* as well as in white newspapers, but mostly, says the 32-year-old Dove, "it has been floating around underground." Some samples (see end of story for the correct answers):

1. A "handkerchief head" is: (a) a cool cat, (b) a porter, (c) an Uncle Tom, (d) a hoddi, (e) a preacher.

2. Which word is most out of place here? (a) splib, (b) blood, (c) gray, (d) spook, (e) black.

3. A "gas head" is a person who has a: (a) fast-moving car, (b) stable of "lace," (c) "process," (d) habit of stealing cars, (e) long jail record for arson.

4. "Down-home" (the South) today, for the average "soul brother" who is picking cotton from sunup until sundown, what is the average earning (take home) for one full day? (a) $.75, (b) $1.65, (c) $3.50, (d) $5, (e) $12.

5. "Bo Diddley" is a: (a) game for children, (b) down-home cheap wine, (c) down-home singer, (d) new dance, (e) Moejoe call.

6. If a pimp is up tight with a woman who gets state aid, what does he mean when he talks about "Mother's Day"? (a) second Sunday in May, (b) third Sunday in June, (c) first of every month, (d) none of these, (e) first and fifteenth of every month. . . .

*Those who are not "culturally deprived" will recognize the correct answers are 1. (c), 2. (c), 3. (c), 4. (d), 5. (c), 6. (e). . . .

Most IQ tests have been criticized for a bias in favor of white, middle-class testees. Here's one designed to dramatize this fact. Much research is being done to develop IQ tests that are as "culture-free" as possible.

would not give any special advantage to children with cultural privileges. Despite his concern and careful selection of items, however, we know that Binet's test, even in its most modern version, is not free from special environmental influences. Indeed there is no test that is truly "culture-free," because the selection of items involves some assumption about what experiences people have had. The critical point is that, if people have had unequal exposure to these experiences, any differences in their scores cannot conclusively be attributed to differences in their ability to learn from these experiences. Some of the ramifications of this problem are illustrated by the extract from the "Chitling Test."

The second important assumption behind Binet tests is that the nature of intelligence changes with age. Therefore, items selected for Binet tests must be graded by age as well as difficulty. Items used for testing intelligence at age 3 are not appropriate at age 10. The same items will simply not discriminate low from high from average children at every age. Thus, Binet tests are actually a collection of subtests, one for each year of age. Some illustrative items at different age levels are given in Table 5-2.

Binet introduced the concept of *mental age* (MA). If a child can pass the items on which the average 9-year-old child is successful, that child is said to have a mental age of 9 years. Mental age is defined independently of *chronological age* (CA); thus, if a 6-year-old can pass the tests passed by the average 9-year-old, the child is considerably accelerated in his mental development. If an 11-year-old can manage to pass only the items passed by the average 9-year-old, his development is retarded. Binet felt that a dull child was retarded in mental growth and a bright child was advanced in mental growth.

It is important not to read too much into the concept of mental age, which is simply one method of scoring performance on an intelligence test. The items associated with age 7 are more difficult than those associated with age 6, which in turn are harder than those associated with age 5, and so on. Rather than earning "points" by passing items, the child earns months and years of mental age credits. Of two children tested, the child with the higher mental age has simply passed a greater number of and more difficult items on the test. Suppose a child passes all items up through age scale 7; passes 4 of

6 items, worth 2 mental age months each, on age scale 8; succeeds on 2 of 6 items on age scale 9; and fails everything on age scale 10 and above. His mental age score is then 7 years plus 8 plus 4 months, or 7 years plus 12 months, or 8 years.

IQ. The most useful score derived from the Binet test, and indeed any intelligence test, is the *intelligence quotient,* or IQ, which indicates how an individual scored relative to others of comparable age. Using mental age scores, one formula for the IQ is:

$$IQ = \frac{\text{mental age}}{\text{chronological age}} \times 100$$

The test is designed so that the average child will earn a mental age score equal to his chronological age, which means the average IQ is 100. An individual who passes more items than the average for his age group will have a mental age greater than his chronological age and thus an IQ greater than 100, while the child who does more poorly than the average will have an IQ less than 100. Using our earlier example of the child who earned a mental age of 8 years, we can see that, if the child were 6 years old, his IQ would be

$$8/6 \times 100 = 133$$

This ratio, the IQ, thus indicates a person's achievement on the test relative to the achievement of others of comparable age.

It is not necessary to use mental age units in order to calculate an IQ. The most general formula for the IQ, using the points scored on the test, is:

$$IQ = \frac{\text{the person's score}}{\text{the average score for his age group}} \times 100$$

Whenever a person scores higher than the average for his age group, his IQ will be greater than 100; should he score lower than average, his IQ will be less than 100.

Table 5-2
Test items for the fifth- and twelfth-year scales of the latest (1960) revision of the Binet test

Year 5
1. Completes a drawing of a man with missing legs
2. Folds a paper square twice to make a triangle, after demonstration by an examiner
3. Defines two of the following three words: ball, hat, stove
4. Copies a square
5. Recognizes similarities and differences between selected pictures
6. Assembles two triangles to form a rectangle

Year 12
1. Defines 14 words, such as haste, lecture, skill
2. Sees the absurdity in such items as: "Bill Jones's feet are so big that he has to pull his trousers on over his head."
3. Understands the situation depicted in selected complex pictures
4. Repeats five digits backwards
5. Defines several abstract words, such as pity, curiosity
6. Supplies the missing word in several incomplete sentences, such as: "One cannot be a hero _____, but one can always be a man."

Wechsler tests. Besides the Binet test, two other frequently-used tests of individual IQ are the Wechsler tests, named after their creator, psychologist David Wechsler. One version of the Wechsler test is designed for adults, the Wechsler Adult Intelligence Scale, and the other for children, the Wechsler Intelligence Scale for Children. Items on the Wechsler tests are quite similar to those on the Binet test, but, rather than being organized into age scales, the items are combined into subscales to test different abilities. Performance

Use of Computers for Mental Tests Urged

Lexington, Ky. (AP)—Because computers have no emotions, a psychologist-psychiatrist here thinks they might be better than people in evaluating the results of mental examinations.

They can be especially valuable, Dr. Joseph C. Finney said, in a criminal case where there is public outcry for vengance, such as in the assassination of a prominent figure.

To make his point, Dr. Finney fed his computer the results of mental tests given Sirhan Sirhan, convicted assassin of Robert F. Kennedy. It told him Sirhan was mentally ill.

In trials such as Sirhan's, Dr. Finney wrote in The American Journal of Psychiatry, "It is difficult for the expert witness to be sure of his objectivity."

The computer has no such problem, Dr. Finney said. In addition, it can make a far more complex evaluation than humans usually do because it can review more material. The average mental exam reviews about 13 scales of psychological evaluation, but the system he has developed scores more than 150.

Dr. Finney, a professor at the University of Kentucky, put into the computer the results of two extensive mental inventories given to Sirhan, one six weeks after Kennedy's death and the other five months after the crime.

In essence, Dr. Finney said, the computer diagnosis showed that Sirhan "was driven by the idea that it was up to him to do some dramatic act to right the wrongs of the world."

The analysis found "there was a high enough degree of psychosis or schizophrenia for him to be mentally ill," Dr. Finney said.

Psychologists are trained to give and to interpret IQ and other standardized tests in an objective, unemotional manner. Still, they are only human. It is possible to influence test scores in a variety of ways. Maybe the cold and calculating computer should give and score tests. Can you think of any reasons why not?

Table 5–3
Examples of test materials from the Wechsler Adult Intelligence Scale

Performance IQ
A. *Digit-symbol substitution*—a speeded test of ability to substitute symbols for numbers
B. *Block design*—a test of ability to build specified designs with colored blocks
C. *Object assembly*—a test of ability to assemble puzzle pieces to form a common object
D. *Picture arrangement*—a test of ability to arrange pictures in order for telling a logical, coherent story (such as reassembling cartoon panels)

Verbal IQ
A. *Digit span*—a test of ability to repeat a string of digits in forward and backward order immediately
B. *Similarities*—a test of ability to say how things are alike, e.g., a bus and an airplane
C. *Vocabulary*—a test of ability to provide word definitions
D. *Arithmetic*—problems that test arithmetic ability and general problem-solving skills
E. *General information*—a test of general knowledge items like: who invented the telephone, who wrote the *Canterbury Tales*, where does oil come from?

Individual and group testing.   The Wechsler and Binet tests are given to one person at a time and require a trained examiner for appropriate administration. One facet of the examiner's job is to try to insure that the person who is taking the test is allowed to perform to the best of his ability. Despite these efforts, there is no guarantee that an individual will achieve exactly the same IQ on the same test taken twice. It is not uncommon for a person to earn IQs that differ by as much as 10 points on two different administrations of a test. This is unlikely to be due to a change in his abilities, particularly if the two examinations occur close together in time. More probably, the difference reflects some simpler change, such as variation in alertness on the two occasions, a possible practice effect, or something similar. What this means is that, if a person achieves an IQ of 110, there is a reasonable chance that his "true" IQ lies between 105 and 115, or, if one wants to be more conservative, between 100 and 120. One lesson to be learned is that, if one person's IQ is 100 and another's is 95, the difference in their intellectual abilities may be negligible.

Because the Wechsler and Binet tests are administered individually, they are in a sense inefficient. Group tests are sometimes used when there are many people to be tested and not enough time to do it individually. In fact, group tests may be more familiar to you than individual tests. They have been devised for use in schools, for the military, as

on each subscale yields a score in points that can be converted directly into IQ. About half of the test is concerned with verbal abilities, involving definitions and similarities and differences among words. The other half assesses performance (nonverbal) abilities such as object assembly and picture arrangement. See Table 5-3 for examples. With the Wechsler tests, it is quite common to calculate both a performance IQ and a verbal IQ. Binet tests tend to emphasize verbal abilities more than Wechsler tests.

college entrance examinations, and for special industrial purposes. The existence of many different intelligence tests raises the question of how comparable they are. The answer is that it is reasonable to be cautious about their equivalence. Generally, people earn similar scores on the Binet and Wechsler tests. For many individuals, a group test will yield an IQ comparable to an IQ from an individual test like the Binet. However, a group test can result in a person's achieving an IQ quite different from that which he would earn on an individual test. Of necessity, group tests emphasize reading ability because the items must be read before they can be answered. It is thus quite possible for a poor reader to score much lower on a group test than he would on an individual test in which the questions are spoken to him by the examiner. A person with an average or high IQ who has great difficulty with reading has a condition called *dyslexia*. It is virtually impossible to identify a dyslexic person on the basis of a group test of intelligence. A quite sensible approach is to view a low IQ on a group test as a good reason to administer an individual test.

The distribution of IQ scores.

An IQ score of 100 is considered average. Half the population scores within the range of 90 to 110 (see Table 5-4). At the high and low ends of the distribution of IQ are exceptional people. At the high end, we speak of geniuses. Typically, people with high IQs are not only bright, but also eminent. Examination of biographical information on notable historical figures has allowed psychologists to make reasonable estimates of their IQs even though no tests were available. Invariably, this information leads to estimates of IQ in excess of 125, some ranging as high as 200. The following are estimated IQ scores derived in one study: J. S. Bach, 125; Napoleon, 135; Voltaire, 170. Although these numerical values are obviously just estimates and

Table 5–4
Variations in IQ scores

Range of scores	Approximate percentage of people
130 and above	2
120–129	7
110–119	16
100–109	25
90–99	25
80–89	16
70–79	7
Below 70	2

Who's Retarded?

Time—It is all too common for school systems to administer IQ tests and then confine the low scorers to "special" classes for the mentally retarded or emotionally disturbed. In San Diego, attorneys representing 20 black and Mexican-American student plaintiffs argued that the city's Unified School System had no right to make such placements on the basis of standard IQ tests designed for white middle-class students. Retesting by an outside psychologist indicated that all but two of the children were actually of at least average intelligence and the exceptions were borderline cases. The school district did not admit fault, but it did agree to a settlement, approved by the U.S. District Court, under which 2,500 improperly placed students will receive a token payment of $1 each. Moreover, the district promised to eliminate "racial, cultural, environmental or linguistic bias" from all future IQ tests administered to schoolchildren in San Diego.

How might it be possible for the San Diego school district to insure its promise of an unbiased test? Is it possible?

may be off by 10 or more IQ points in either direction, it is clear that individuals who make significant contributions to society or culture often have higher than average IQs. Biographical data of this sort have been largely substantiated by contemporary studies in which the growth and development of gifted children, those with IQs of 135 and above, have been followed throughout their life span. Contrary to common misconceptions, these children tend to be better than average in their adjustment to their environment, to enjoy good mental health, and to make use of their intellect in ways that often have a significant impact on society. Interestingly enough, however, genius is not always quick to develop. Albert Einstein did not talk until he was 4 years old, and he was 7 before he could read. On the other hand, Mozart composed his first piece of music when he was 6.

At the opposite end of the distribution are individuals who are in some sense mentally deficient. There are degrees, of course. The borderline range is about 70 to 90 IQ points, corresponding to an adult with a mental age of 12 years. These individuals are clearly dull, though not classifiable as retarded. Below IQ 70 are the mentally retarded, who used to be classified by terms such as moron, imbecile, and idiot. These terms have been replaced by adjectives describing

Hopkins Makes a Place for Childhood Geniuses

Baltimore (AP)—Two years ago, Colin Camerer was in the sixth grade. Now, he's a 14-year-old Johns Hopkins University freshman, enrolled in the school's program for math and science prodigies.

"What's an eighth-grade teacher supposed to do with a student capable of learning advanced college math?" asked Dr. Julian Stanley, one of the originators of the plan.

Stanley said the program began in 1969 when a 13-year-old computer student at Hopkins' night school wound up counseling his classmates—who were in their mid-20s.

Psychologists at the university, including Stanley, were so intrigued that they set up a pilot program for such mathematically gifted students.

Two years later, Stanley founded the Maryland Mathematics Talent Search, the Hopkins-sponsored program to help gifted children accelerate their education as quickly as possible.

The computer whiz whose activities helped spark the program is now an 18-year-old Cornell University student on the verge of finishing his doctoral work, Stanley said.

Yearly Search

The search for prodigies begins each winter when Stanley's three-man staff asks all public and private school systems in Maryland to submit names of seventh and eighth graders who rank in the upper two per cent of scores from standardized math tests.

Students in this group are invited to take the College Board mathematics exam, a test usually reserved for high-school seniors. Students scoring 640 or better out of a possible 800 on the test are eligible for the Hopkins program.

Last January, 1,519 qualifiers took the math test as part of the Hopkins' screening process; 111 scored 640 or higher.

"At this point, we confer with the student, his parents and school officials to see what will be best for the child," Stanley said. Depending on the results of the conference, the child could be advanced one or more grades in secondary school or could enroll for college-level math courses.

Ten of the program's discoveries are enrolled at Hopkins this semester, all working toward bachelors degrees. Camerer, who jumped from the sixth to the eighth grade and then to 11th grade at Dulaney Valley High School in suburban Timonium, Md., before entering Hopkins, is working on a B.S. in quantitative studies.

"It's helped me a lot," the young collegian said of the program.

"I've met a lot of people I wouldn't have met ordinarily, and that's given me a lot more confidence with myself."

Stanley says the 13- and 14-year-olds "fit right in" with older college students and experience no emotional problems because of their brilliance.

Contrary to common opinion, geniuses are not freaks. They adjust better than the average person to their circumstances.

---

the degree of retardation: *mild, moderate, severe,* or *profound.* Another way of classifying the amount of mental handicap is to indicate whether the person is educable or trainable. Those classified as mildly and moderately mentally retarded can usually be taught some basic skills. The severely retarded can be trained to acquire a few habits of self-maintenance (see Table 5-5). The profoundly retarded, however, need to be cared for, typically in an institution, although today parents are being trained to provide help at home. Special local school programs have been instituted for the educable retarded, and significant increases in IQ have been observed. Other programs attempt to provide employment for the trainable retarded in "sheltered workshops" where they can work at their own pace and get paid. The hope is to provide support services so that parents will be willing to keep the child at home instead of placing him in an institution. Institutions for the retarded are far too often "dumping grounds" for keeping the retarded out of sight of society. It is believed that many people classified as retarded could lead happier, more productive lives outside of an institution.

The Composition of Intelligence

As indicated earlier, there is some difference of opinion on what and how many abilities are involved in intelligence. The tests we have examined suggest that several abilities enter the picture. It seems reasonable that a person could be very good at the short-term retention of a series of digits and yet not have a particularly extensive vocabulary. Still, some have argued that there is but a single ability running through performances of all kinds, a general intellectual factor based largely on heredity. The rest of the individual differences in intellectual performance are attributable to special experiences that people have.

In contrast to the single-ability position is a theory proposed by L. L. Thurstone to the effect that intelligence consists of a cluster of seven *primary mental abilities.* Thurstone's argument is based on a good deal of empirical evidence. He observed that if

Table 5–5
Classifications of mental retardation

	Preschool age 0–5 Maturation and development	School age 6–21 Training and education	Adult 21 and over Social and vocational adequacy
Profound	Gross retardation; minimal capacity for functioning in sensorimotor areas; needs nursing care.	Obvious delays in all areas of development; shows basic emotional responses; may respond to skillful training in use of legs, hands, and jaws; needs close supervision.	May walk, may need nursing care, may have primitive speech; will usually benefit from regular physical activity; incapable of self-maintenance.
Severe	Marked delay in motor development; little or no communication skill; may respond to training in elementary self-help—e.g., self-feeding.	Usually walks, barring specific disability; has some understanding of speech and some response; can profit from systematic habit training.	Can conform to daily routines and repetitive activities; needs continuing direction and supervision in protective environment.
Moderate	Noticeable delays in motor development, especially in speech; responds to training in various self-help activities.	Can learn simple communication, elementary health and safety habits, and simple manual skills; does not progress in functional reading or arithmetic.	Can perform simple tasks under sheltered conditions; participates in simple recreation; travels alone in familiar places; usually incapable of self-maintenance.
Mild	Often not noticed as retarded by casual observer, but is slower to walk, feed self, and talk than most children.	Can acquire practical skills and useful reading and arithmetic to a 3rd to 6th grade level with special education. Can be guided toward social conformity.	Can usually achieve social and vocational skills adequate to self-maintenance; may need occasional guidance and support when under unusual social or economic stress.

different types of test questions were administered to a large number of people, one would find that scores on some test questions correlate highly while others do not. Correlation in this sense means that if you score well on one item, you will tend to score well on another item correlated with the first. However, if items are not correlated, it is impossible to predict your score from one item to another. Thurstone examined the scores that he obtained on a variety of items with a technique known as *factor analysis,* which is discussed in more detail in Appendix A. Briefly, factor analysis is a statistical device for finding out which kinds of measures correlate or cluster together and for identifying the variable or factor underlying these relationships. On the basis of measures derived from a large number of different intelligence tests, Thurstone concluded that there are seven primary mental abilities: number ability, word fluency (speed of thinking of the right word at the right time), verbal meaning, memory, reasoning, spatial relations, and perceptual speed (the ability to recognize similarities and differences in visual forms). Thurstone felt that he had a

complete characterization of human intelligence in terms of these seven abilities. The best possible intelligence test, therefore, would have one good measure of each one.

Others have extended Thurstone's argument. J. P. Guilford, for example, has proposed the possibility of as many as 120 different intellectual factors, representing *elements* of knowledge, skills for *operating* on elements, and knowledge of the *products* or outcomes of operations. Guilford, too, has used factor analytic techniques to verify a large number of these components of intelligence. Although we might disagree on the number of factors, there is no questioning the complexity of the human intellect. Most psychologists today are convinced that more than a general factor alone is involved.

Intelligence and Creativity

Measures of general intelligence, such as the Stanford-Binet test, are positively correlated with intellectual achievement. Some critics have argued, however, that IQ tests do not tap creativity or

The Drawing-Completion Test

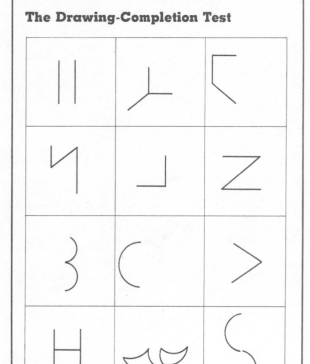

Use your pencil to elaborate on these simple figures in any way that you like. When you have finished, turn to page 177.

require a release from mental sets and inhibitions, allowing for the free flow of unusual ideas and a playful, permissive attitude toward those ideas. In one study, a number of "nonintellectual factors" were identified as being highly correlated with creativity. These included the individual's tolerance of disorder (the highly tolerant person is likely to be more creative), independence of judgment (the person who can make up his own mind, despite the opinions of others, is likely to be more creative), and uniqueness of ideas.

Thus creativity is more than just intelligence. Intelligence does not guarantee creativity, nor does creativity guarantee that the person in question is intelligent. It takes a combination of intellectual abilities and other factors for truly creative behavior to emerge.

Obviously, if creativity involves more than sheer intelligence, something other than an IQ test will be needed to measure it. A number of creativity measuring instruments have been developed, often using the factor analytic technique employed by Thurstone and Guilford to get at mental abilities. Several tests have been designed to elicit as many answers to a particular question as the subject can possibly give. In scoring such tests, it is important to consider both the number and the quality of a person's answers. Another kind of test measures the subject's flexibility. Here, what is at issue is the susceptibility of a subject to the effects of mental set and his ability to overcome that set when necessary. In addition, a test battery designed to measure creativity would also include one or more methods for assessing personality factors (see the discussion of personality inventories in Chapter 9).

What Does It Mean?

Mental Calculation

Our limited capacity for processing information places clear constraints on the kinds of unaided mental activities we are able to accomplish. It is perfectly understandable that a person reaches for pencil and paper when given anything but the simplest arithmetic problem. Imagine how surprising it would be to observe a person, asked to express the fraction 4/47 as a decimal, pause a few seconds and then say, "Point 0851063829787234042553191 4; that's about as far as I can carry it"! In fact, psychologist I. M. L. Hunter has witnessed such a remarkable event in his studies of Professor A. C. Aitken of Edinburgh University, who has been called perhaps the most expert mental calculator on whom detailed records exist.

originality in thinking. They measure the available knowledge and skills of an individual but have little to say about how he will put them to work in novel and unique ways. There are some research studies that seem to support such a conclusion. For example, Wallach and Kogan (1965) have constructed tests of children's creativity that do not correlate with traditional intelligence tests. Clearly, not everyone with an IQ over 140 is going to be creative. Moreover, some people make creative contributions with an IQ that is barely average. The general conclusion seems to be that a minimal amount of intelligence is required for creative work, but that amount is no more than an average IQ of 100. Beyond that, an individual might or might not be creative, depending upon other factors.

What other factors determine creativity? Some psychologists have suggested an ability to produce multiple and original associations to stimuli is involved. Earlier, we noted that an ability to evaluate one's ideas may be involved. Certain personality variables may be involved, for creativity appears to

How is Aitken able to accomplish such feats? Does he possess an unusually large information-processing capacity? Unlike the rest of us, can he do several things at once in his head? According to Hunter, the answer is no. Rather, Aitken has acquired a vast repertoire of number facts and calculating plans that make mental calculation problems much simpler for him than for the ordinary person. In other words, he knows things and knows how to do things such that much less mental effort is required, thus reducing the strain on his processing capacity, which is just as simple as our own. For example, most adults do not have to engage in obvious calculation to provide the answer to "What is 8 divided by 2?" The answer comes almost automatically. Aitken knows many more facts of the same general type. He knows that 1961 is 37 times 53, or 44 squared plus 5 squared, or 40 squared plus 19 squared. Furthermore, as a consequence of "playing with numbers" all his life, he has devised a variety of calculation schemes that enable him to break down a problem into simpler components and require him to remember less as he proceeds through the problem. Here is the way he calculated 4/47 as a decimal. First, he recognized the number fact that 47 is a prime number and thus cannot be broken down. Therefore, he transformed 4/47 into 68/799, which enabled him to use a familiar calculation plan. If he divided by 800, which is in effect by 8, he knew that his answer would be only slightly different from that obtained by using 799 (it would be off by an 800th). Thus he divided 68 by 800 making corrections to allow for the 1/800th error in each calculation. He reported the outcome of each division as a whole number, with the remainder from one step providing him with the number to be divided by 8 in the next step, and so on. The steps of this plan are represented as follows.

Dividend	Answer	Remainder	Next dividend
68 ÷ 800	0.085	0	85
85 ÷ 8	10	5	510
510 ÷ 8	63	6	663
663 ÷ 8	82	7	782
782 ÷ 8	97	6	697
etc.			

Each line represents the same sequence of events. The dividend is divided by 8 to give two digits of the answer and a remainder. The next dividend is formed by combining the answer and the remainder.

From the answer 10 and the remainder 5, the next dividend is 510. Repetition of the sequence generates the answer to 4/47, two digits at a time. In effect, Aitken carried out a series of divisions of three-digit numbers by 8, which does not seem that unwieldy.

To see how such knowledge and skills can simplify mental calculation, let us consider a simpler problem. If you ask the average person to multiply 36 times 72 "in his head," he will have some difficulty. But suppose you give the same problem to a person who (a) recognizes that $72 = 36 \times 2$ and (b) knows that 36 squared is 1296. For this person, the problem is translated into the relatively simple 1296×2! A person such as Aitken has available a much larger repertoire of knowledge and strategies that enable him to handle even larger problems with very little effort.

Problem Solving in Groups

Our earlier discussion of problem solving concerned the ways *individuals* attempt to solve problems; yet a great deal of everyday problem solving takes place in groups, whether it is a family deciding on a vacation, a legislative committee working on a new law, or a sandlot football team choosing its next play. What happens when a number of people work together on a problem? Are "two heads better than one" or do "too many cooks spoil the broth"? As you will see, the answer is complex, for there are both assets and liabilities associated with group problem solving.

Comparing group and individual problem solving is actually rather tricky. For example, suppose an individual solves a problem in 45 minutes while a group of 4 people solves the same problem in 20 minutes. In one sense the group did better, but in another sense, the group was less efficient. The individual required 45 "person-minutes" for a solution, but the group required 4 people × 20 minutes = 80 "person-minutes." To avoid this ambiguity, analyses of group problem solving usually compare a *real* group with a *statistical* group (which represents the statistically pooled efforts of an equal number of people, each of whom worked alone on the problem). Thus the question is whether it is better or worse to have, say, 5 people work together (as a real group) or to have each of the 5 people work alone with only their results subsequently pooled together.

The effect of group work depends strongly on the kind of problem involved. Suppose a simple problem requires for its solution a single idea that a person either knows or does not know. There is virtually nothing that a group can do, as a group, on such a problem; the group's achievement cannot be expected to be any better than that of the best individual in the group and might be worse if the group in some way interferes with the efforts of the person most knowledgeable about the problem to achieve the solution. In contrast, consider a problem that has several parts that can be worked on simultaneously. In this case, a group could allocate the parts to different group members and thus complete the problem much more quickly than if each of the people worked alone on the problem.

The major advantage a group possesses is that the group has available a greater amount of knowledge than any individual. In fact, it is possible for a group to solve a problem having a number of parts that no member of the group could solve alone. An individual member might not know the answers to all the parts, but each group member could contribute the answer to one part and thus together the group could solve the problem. On the other hand, the greater knowledge available might not be utilized in a group setting. Suppose a problem is best approached by considering many different ways of responding. To the extent that a group works as a group, there will be a "group direction" to its efforts. If that direction is inappropriate, everyone in the group will be "wasting his time" following it, whereas at least some of these people might try a different approach if everyone worked alone on the problem. Studies have shown that problems requiring the generation of creative ideas are best approached by having people work on them alone and subsequently pooling their ideas.

From the point of view of efficiency in problem solving, the major disadvantage of group work is that the group is a social setting. A person working in a group must not only contribute to solving the problem but also must get along with others in the group—cope with difficult personalities, listen agreeably to other members' ideas, and so on. To the extent that time and effort is spent in social interaction, the group will be less efficient in finding a solution to the problem.

Furthermore, if the problem has no obvious solution but allows many different solutions of varying quality, the group has to spend time agreeing on which solution to select. As the problem-solving session continues, the need to agree grows stronger—continued disagreement is *socially* unacceptable. Consequently, the group might adopt a solution primarily in order to reach agreement, even though that solution might not be

the best one they could think of. N. R. F. Maier has found that, if one asks a group that has just agreed on the solution to a complicated problem to produce a different solution, the second solution tends to be better than the first. This result seems to apply only to groups—multiple answers to a problem by an individual do not differ significantly in quality—and is presumably due to social factors.

From this discussion it is clear that before advocating group problem solving, one must assess the nature of the problem, the criteria of its solution, and the likely advantages and disadvantages a group would possess.

"Eyewitness" Testimony

You have already seen that, when people listen to a number of sentences all related to a general theme, they have, under some circumstances, great difficulty distinguishing between sentences they actually heard and sentences that were not presented but that "fit the theme." Furthermore, you know that the context in which a given sentence is spoken has a good deal to do with its meaning and interpretation. Such results indicate that a person may have difficulty distinguishing between what actually happened and what he infers to have happened. This inferential aspect of remembering is not limited to recalling the exact form of sentences but can affect the recall of "facts," as has been shown in experiments conducted by Elizabeth Loftus and her colleagues.

"Yes—that's the man!"

**Sample Responses to the
Drawing-Completion Test**

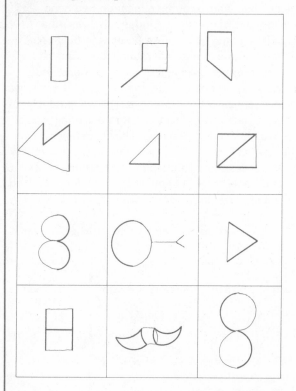
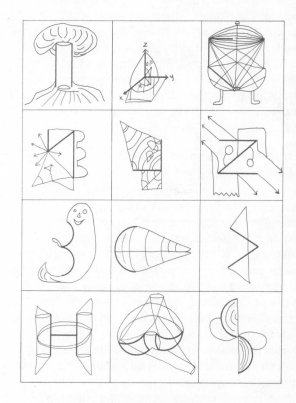

The drawings on the left illustrate the responses of the average person to the drawing-completion test, while those on the right exemplify the responses of creative individuals. The introduction of greater complexity and asymmetry is associated with creativity. Such differences are not limited to the actual production of drawings. When drawings or colored patterns of varying complexity and symmetry are shown to people, creative individuals show a greater tendency to prefer complex and asymmetrical presentations. Some psychologists have argued that a preference or "need" for complexity is an integral component of creative behavior.

In these studies, people watched a film of a traffic accident, having been told that they were participating in a memory experiment, and were subsequently asked questions about what they had seen. The critical variable concerned the way in which the questions were phrased. Some subjects were asked questions like, "Did you see *the* broken headlight?" The definite article "the" implies that there was a broken headlight, with the person only having to decide whether or not he noticed it. Others were asked, "Did you see *a* broken headlight?" The indefinite article "a" has no implication—indeed, it raises the question of whether or not there was a broken headlight as well as the question of whether or not the person saw it.

Several questions of both forms were asked about both things that had occurred in the film and things that had not. The form of the question did not affect the frequency with which people indicated that they had seen something that actually did occur. However, asking questions with "the" resulted in a much stronger tendency for people to say that they had seen something that had never occurred!

Similar effects of "suggestive questions" were reported by Loftus and John Palmer. People who had witnessed a traffic accident were asked either "How fast were the cars going when they bumped into each other?" or "How fast were the cars going when they smashed into each other?" Witnesses who were asked the first question estimated much lower speeds than those asked the second. These results are consistent with the view of memory as a reconstructive process and indicate that suggesting plausible inferences to a person at the time of recall can affect what he believes to have happened. Simply by asking the right questions, you can convince at least some people that they saw events that did not happen. The implications of such results for courtroom examinations or police investigations are fairly obvious. Such interrogations are intended to identify "the facts," with attorneys told not to "lead the witness." These findings suggest that the definition of a "leading question" may be very subtle indeed.

Language, Intelligence, and the Disadvantaged

In recent years, psychologists and educators have characterized the language of many "disadvantaged" (and primarily minority) children as deficient, undeveloped, and grammatically inadequate. At the preschool level, it was noted that many poor and minority children seemed to have no grammar at all. They occasionally generated two-word sentences, but these were really only "giant" words in their vocabulary. Presumably, these deficiencies arise from backgrounds that are particularly impoverished in language experience.

Arthur Jensen, a Berkeley educational psychologist, presented a different argument. Assuming that intelligence is heavily influenced by hereditary factors and observing that disadvantaged children—blacks in particular—score consistently lower on IQ tests, Jensen concluded that the intellect of nonwhite minorities must be *genetically* lower than that of whites. He provided an experiment that showed that black children were equal to white on a rote memory task but were inferior on a conceptual task. In short, Jensen proposed that blacks were generally deficient in the ability to abstract.

The many rebuttals to Jensen addressed various aspects of his claims. First, as you may recall from an earlier discussion, IQ tests are not (and probably cannot be) experience-free. If the experiences provided by one culture or subculture are more appropriate to the test, people from that culture will have higher IQs whatever their native intellectual endowment. Only to the extent that all of those measured have the same experiences may variations in IQ be held to be determined by genetic factors. Alternatively, if genetic factors are held constant, then variations in IQ may be attributed to experience. Unfortunately, in human beings, both factors vary in unknown ways, and it is difficult to be certain about the relative contribution of each.

In contrast to Jensen's position, some linguists,

especially William Labov, have emphasized the importance of complex social variables in controlling the speech of children. Labov tested a black child whose formal education had been limited and who could be judged to possess a deficient language because he uttered only one word at a time in a formal testing situation. However, in the presence of his best friend and given an appropriate topic, the same child produced highly sophisticated sentences. The white educator using a standardized test in a formal setting would "prove" the child to be linguistically deficient. To the contrary, however, Labov has shown that this child possesses adequate linguistic facility as well as considerable general knowledge. Take the following dialogue between the child and a trusted examiner.

JL: What happens to you after you die? Do you know?
Larry: Yeah, I know.
JL: What?
Larry: After they put you in the ground, your body turns into—ah—bones, an' shit.
JL: What happens to your spirit?
Larry: Your spirit—soon as you die, your spirit leaves you.
JL: And where does the spirit go?
Larry: Well, it all depends.
JL: On what?
Larry: You know, like some people say if you're good an' shit, your spirit goin' t'heaven . . . 'n' if you bad, your spirit goin' to hell. Well, bullshit! Your spirit goin' to hell anyway, good or bad.
JL: Why?
Larry: Why? I'll tell you why. 'Cause, you see, doesn' nobody really know that it's a God, y'know, 'cause I mean I have seen black gods, pink gods, white gods, all color gods, and don't nobody know it's really a God. An' when they be sayin' if you good, you goin' t'heaven, tha's bullshit, 'cause you ain't goin' to no heaven, 'cause it ain't no heaven for you to go to. **(Labov, 1970)**

Clearly the child is cognitively competent, though he may not or will not exhibit his knowledge in some contexts. Labov further suggests that Jensen's claim of deficient ability to abstract cannot be correct, since the language known by the young black child embodies some particularly abstract distinctions.

These kinds of differences do not generally change the meaning of the words or sentences; speakers of both dialects *can* quickly learn to understand each other. Black English is a complete language, systematic and rule-governed. It is clear that speakers of Black English can express abstract

Silent Speech

Time—Kari Harrington is seven years old and a victim of severe cerebral palsy. Thus she lacks the muscular coordination necessary for controlled movement and speech, and is virtually restricted to a wheelchair. Like many other victims of the disease, she will never be able to move around normally or speak well enough to be understood. Now an experimental training program that uses printed symbols to convey meaning has begun to draw her out of her isolated world.

The Ontario Crippled Children's Centre in Toronto, where Kari is a pupil, is successfully using a system of symbols as a substitute for spoken language. They are patterned after "Blis-symbols," devised some 30 years ago by an Austrian-born chemical engineer named Charles Bliss in the hope that they would be used to promote international understanding. Hardly anyone paid any attention, though, until last year, when Shirley McNaughton, a teacher at the center, came upon an account of them in a library and decided that they might be modified for use by the handicapped.

Currently the center is using about 200 symbols arranged on wooden trays attached to wheelchairs. With demonstrations and explanations from their teachers, six brain-damaged youngsters are learning to use their fingers or a special clock hand fastened to the trays to point to the symbol that expresses what they want to say.

Naturally there are symbols for such simple words as yes and no, hello and goodbye, man and woman. There is also a symbol for action that turns a noun into a verb. For example, a child who wants to say "Father sees mother" points first to the sign for father, the male symbol topped by the sign for roof or protection ⚣. Next the child points to the eye symbol ⊙ and then to the action indicator ∧, thus transforming the noun eye into the verb see. Finally, the youngster points to the sign for mother, combining the female and roof symbols ⚢.

The sign for animal is ⋀⋀; for needs ⟋, a slanting figure to suggest dependency; for food ⚇, a mouth over the earth. All these can be put together to say "The animal needs food." To express emotions, a youngster can point to the sign for happy ♡↑ or sad ♡↓.

The ability to communicate even such uncomplicated ideas as these has had remarkable effects. Less frustrated because they can finally express

themselves, the youngsters become more relaxed and can thus make better use of whatever slight physical—and in a few cases even vocal—abilities they may have.

The children, most of whom seemed mentally retarded, are being stimulated to read and to demonstrate other intellectual skills. Perhaps most important, their previous apathy and withdrawal have been replaced by a new capacity to share in family life. The mother of one child at the center was "thrilled" when her son used symbols to say that he was angry about some things but that he loved his family. Kari's mother voiced surprise and delight when Kari managed to convey her sadness over the fact that her guinea pig cannot think.

An understanding of language behavior and the interrelationship of language and thought is beginning to find application in planning therapy for individuals with language deficits. More basic knowledge in this field will result in more effective therapies.

Cerebral palsy victims learning to "speak" with printed symbols

ideas, make logical arguments, and so on. Probably, as we said earlier, any language has the capability for expressing any idea.

The implications of the linguists' arguments are important for educators. Many variant languages coexist with Standard English, serving as effective means of everyday communication. The teacher who suggests that the grammar book is the true source of correct English is mistaken. Educators must realize that spoken and written forms are not identical and that the appropriate variant or dialect

will depend on the speaker and the listener. Most of all, for blacks and others whose language is noticeably different from Standard English, the teacher should accept and understand the child's communication, teaching the child not only how to speak Standard English but also when it is appropriate to do so.

Cognition and Behavior Therapy

As we shall study in detail in Chapter 12, certain varieties of abnormal behavior are the target of a

Nurturing Intelligence

Time—Of the nation's 6,000,000 mentally retarded children and adults, 80% have no detectable abnormality of the central nervous system. How then to explain their inadequacy?

In the bitter controversy over the reasons for low IQs, some psychologists, notably Arthur Jensen and Richard Herrnstein (TIME, Aug. 23) put the blame largely on inferior genes. Others believe that environment—especially the environment of the ghetto—is of primary importance. A recent report on the first five years of an experiment with mentally retarded mothers and their children in Milwaukee supports the latter view. It also offers persuasive evidence that mental retardation in the offspring of mentally retarded mothers can be prevented.

To recruit subjects for their experiment, University of Wisconsin psychologists Rick Heber and Howard Garber went to a slum, which typically is the section of any city with the highest concentration of the mentally retarded. Initial testing showed that retarded mothers are likely to have retarded children, but did not reveal the reason. Heber and Garber suspected that it was the way in which the retarded mothers dealt with their children that made the critical difference between them and the children of equally impoverished mothers of normal intelligence.

The psychologists' aim was to wipe out that difference. Choosing 40 retarded mothers with newborn babies, all black, they assigned them randomly to two groups with 20 mothers and infants in each. For the control group, nothing special was done. In the experimental group, the mothers were given job training and taught homemaking and baby care. Their babies, beginning at three months of age, were picked up every morning and taken to the university. There, "infant stimulation teachers" fed, bathed and taught them until 4 p.m.

Tested at intervals, the 20 "stimulated" children have proved "distinctly superior" to the youngsters who stayed at home. They have IQs averaging about 125, compared with scores of 75 or less for their mothers and about 95 for untreated children of similar background.

Yet Heber and Garber admit that the experimental children have become "test-wise" and that the differences between the two groups could disappear as they grow older. Still, the psychologists conclude, the youngsters have accomplished so much that "it is difficult to conceive of their ever being comparable to the lagging control group."

New evidence points to the possibility that much of what appears to be mental retardation can be prevented by providing infants with stimulation.

form of psychotherapy known as behavior therapy, or behavior modification. One of the best-known procedures is called counterconditioning. It has received wide use in the treatment of phobias (strong irrational fears). We have seen some simple examples of behavior therapy used to counteract bad habits in Chapter 4.

At this point, we wish to emphasize the importance of cognitive factors in the counterconditioning process. Consider the patient with a fear of heights so severe that he is unable to go up in an elevator or climb a flight of stairs. A therapist might try to reduce or eliminate this fear in part through the use of imagery. The first step would be to determine, by interviews, what kinds of events are most fear provoking and which events are most pleasurable for the patient. Then the therapist would train his patient to relax throughout a series of *imagined* scenes, beginning with the least feared and proceeding through the most feared. The patient would be asked to imagine a pleasurable scene immediately after each fear-provoking image. With repetition of such encounters, paired fear and pleasure in imaginary form, the patient's fear of heights is counteracted and replaced by pleasant thoughts.

This kind of therapy is a direct extension of laboratory research on the conditioning of animals. But there are two notable differences that are related to material learned in this chapter. First, the behavior therapist deals with imagined scenes, which are much easier and quicker to produce than real ones in most circumstances. It is images and the behavior *they* produce that are counterconditioned. Sooner or later the patient must, of course, deal with real heights. But, in treatment, he generally only imagines. Incidentally, there is some evidence that people who have high imagery ability benefit more from this treatment.

Second, fear of heights is a conceptual classification. If the patient includes rising elevators in the class of high places, then the concept is somewhat different from ours. Being in a rising elevator provides no direct stimulation comparable to standing on a high place looking down. But to cure his patient, the therapist must countercondition the entire conceptual class by getting him to relax when faced with a wide variety of positive instances of the concept "heights."

Stimulating Environments

There are some current observations about stimulation that point to astounding possibilities in the future. For example, several experiments with animals have shown that early infant stimulation can accelerate the development of the brain. Animals raised in special enriched environments have developed what might possibly be described as

Maybe Exercise Does Expand Brain

Boulder Daily Camera—It used to be a tale with which old—and not so old—wives goaded their children to study: "You've got to exercise your brain," they would say. "The brain is like a muscle; it's got to be used or it will get flabby."

But for years scientists were unable to find any evidence that the old wives knew what they were talking about, that the physical brain benefitted from exercise. There was no evidence that the brain could be expanded or strengthened or changed in any way because it was used.

That is no longer the case.

Benefits of Exercise

Scientists now believe that there are detectable, measurable, physiological changes in the brain associated with learning. They also believe that someday they will be able to stimulate these changes either to enhance learning ability and memory storage or to correct learning disability.

It is not yet known what the mechanism of those changes is. But a team of West Coast researchers, with help from the National Science Foundation, has spent more than a decade measuring changes in the brain that are associated with experience, if not with learning. . . .

Chemical Clues

"What we were looking for then," recalls [Mark] Rosenzweig, "was effects of learning on the chemical activities within the brain."

As have other scientists, they found them. They found that short-term learning and experience seem to have some impact on the activities of enzymes—molecules that help chemical reactions take place—at the junctions—called synapses—where nerve cells meet and across which neural messages are flashed.

"It was while trying to check that finding," says the Berkeley psychologist, "that we made the unexpected discovery that the cerebral cortex (the nerve-cell-rich outer layer) of the brain changes in weight as the result of enriched experiences." The brain, indeed, develops as it is exercised. . . .

The Cortex Thickens

What they have found, broadly, is that in experimental animals exposed to an enriched environment there is a measurable thickening and enlargement in the gray matter—the cerebral cortex—that overlies much of the brain. The weight increase, at least in rats, seems to be concentrated in the area of the brain responsible for sensory perception.

The increase in weight, say Rosenzweig, Bennett and Diamond, does not seem to be the result of any increase in the number of nerve cells. The nerve cells of educated experimental animals do, however, grow larger than those of their environmentally deprived brothers. At the same time, there is an increase in the number of what are called glial cells. Those are non-nerve brain cells that perform a service and support function.

Though these brain changes seem to have some relation to increased problem solving ability, no one, least of all Rosenzweig, is at this point going to call that ability "intelligence." Nor is anyone suggesting what the mechanism is that enhances it. This is despite the fact that the effect has been detected and measured on several levels.

On Several Levels

On the biochemical side, the researchers have their original finding of increased enzyme activity at nerve junctions. Within the nerve cells themselves, there is evidence that the brains of more richly experienced rats produce more RNA (ribonucleic acid), a link in the cell's genetic and growth chains.

And more recently, thanks to the use of an electron microscope at their laboratory, the Berkeley scientists have discovered that learning appears to have an anatomical as well as a chemical effect on the nerve-linkages or synapses themselves.

At the sites they have probed so far, they are finding—with support beginning to come from other laboratories—that the brains of more richly experienced animals seem to have fewer interneural linkages, but that those synapses that do exist are considerably larger and more fully developed. The scientists have seen the phenomenon; they are not yet ready to interpret it fully.

The Memory Circuit

"But if one thinks," Rosenzweig hypothesizes, "of the brain as having circuitry on which learning and memory storage depend, then learning could be seen as being encoded by either making new or more secure connections (synapses) between nerve cells, or by the selective removal of unwanted synapses so that impulses can be channeled over specific pathways."

Whether the search for the mechanism of learning in the brain will ultimately concentrate on the selective expansion of synapses, on the interrelationships among RNA synthesis, protein production and enlarged neurons, or on some as yet unrecognized mechanisms, the Berkeley team, as do other researchers, see significant implications to their search.

"Increased knowledge of brain mechanism of learning and memory," they wrote recently, "could provide bases for application to many problems of health, such as these:

"How can ability be increased in the case of retarded learners? A clue may be present in our finding that cerebral responsiveness to experience can be modulated by . . . drugs.

"What accounts for cases of decreased ability to learn in old age? A suggestion comes from the finding that although middle-aged rats show 'normal' cerebral responsiveness to experience in terms of cortical weight, the changes in cortical enzymes occur more slowly than in young or young-adult rats.

"How can optimal types and amounts of early stimulation be determined in order to produce superior emotional and intellectual development? Working out these problems in detail for the rat should provide insights and methods that will be helpful in work with other species, including man."

The Berkeley group is more than cautious in concluding from its work so far anything more than an apparent connection between learning and the phenomena they have described. They will make no statement stronger than:

"We know that memory is stored in the brain. And we now know that the brain can be changed by experience. We now must determine whether or not the changes are related to memory storage."

more efficient brains. We are already cautioned by psychologists that in raising our own children we should provide them with an interesting and stimulating environment, beginning the moment they come home from the hospital, for example, by hanging brightly colored mobiles over their cribs. Discovery of new and better techniques for enriching the infant environment may significantly accelerate the growth of intelligence.

Along the same lines, much research is being done on the conditions that influence the acquisition of language. Because certain language deficiencies may be related to deficiencies in the language environment of the child, we can expect developmental psycholinguists to try to discover ways to accelerate language development and to combat language-deficient environments. Soon every crib may come equipped with a tape recorder for playing language materials or music to the infant, even while he or she is sleeping. Once psycholinguists discover the principles of language acquisition, we can expect accelerated language acquisition, better treatment for language deficiencies, and greatly facilitated acquisition of second and third languages. If there is anything to the Whorfian hypothesis of linguistic relativity, we would expect that certain kinds of problems are best solved while thinking in one language, whereas a different language is better for solving other problems. If techniques were available for the mass teaching of several foreign languages, so that everyone could speak at least three languages, we might find topics in mathematics being taught in English, physics in Russian, and chemistry in Japanese.

Much of our adult thinking is dominated by the linguistic mode. Although we certainly are capable of nonlinguistic thought such as images, we do not seem to have developed the facility for imagery to the utmost. We can expect psychologists interested in cognition to develop techniques for the training of more efficient visual thought, particularly in the area of visual memory. Is it possible that someday we may all have photographic minds, which we can turn on and off at will?

Summary

1. Cognitive processes are typically studied in problem-solving situations requiring a person to select and utilize environmental information, together with his knowledge and skills, to meet some task demand.

2. Several different theories of cognition have been proposed. Motor theory and mediational theory are based on stimulus-response ideas. Both imply that thought is action on an internal or implicit level.

3. Information-processing theory attributes to the organism a number of mechanisms capable of receiving, storing, transforming, and integrating information and of making decisions among possibilities that arise from these activities. Most contemporary research can be interpreted in terms of information-processing theory.

4. Consciousness is sometimes associated with a central information-processing system of limited capacity. A person's limited capacity for certain kinds of information processing affects his behavior in a wide variety of problem-solving situations.

5. The activities involved in problem solving can be categorized into stages. The preparation stage involves determining what the problem is, what information is available, and what kind of solution is required. The production stage refers to the generation of alternative possible solutions. The judgment stage involves the evaluation of the alternatives that have been produced.

6. Problems differ in the extent to which they emphasize one or another stage, and the solution of a problem can involve considerable switching among the stages. Sometimes, there is an additional stage, called incubation, which refers to a withdrawal from active work on a problem for a period of time. Such "time off" may aid solution of a problem under some circumstances.

7. For simple, "one-shot" problems, the person receives all the information he is going to get at the outset, and the solution involves a small number of simple steps. Performance on such problems is influenced by the way in which the problem is presented, and by the problem solver's past experience with similar problems.

8. Solving a series of problems having similar solutions will lead to the adoption of a mental set that can facilitate solving problems for which the set is relevant but can also prevent the solver from finding alternative, perhaps simpler, ways to solve the problem.

9. Functional fixedness occurs when experience with the ordinary use of an object prevents a person from discovering an unusual use for the object that would solve the problem at hand.

10. Tasks allowing many different responses are used to study originality and creativity. Original ideas are unusual or uncommon and tend to occur more frequently as a person continues working at a

task. Creative ideas are both original and useful. It is fairly easy to increase the production of original ideas, but increasing creativity is much more difficult.

11. Concepts involve principles that enable a person to respond systematically to the objects and events in his environment. Solving conceptual problems is affected by the complexity of the objects in the environment and by the kinds of information the person receives.

12. Conceptual tasks require considerable integration of information from a number of events distributed over time and can thus easily overload a person's limited capacity for processing information. Consequently, the amount of time a person is given to analyze information and the extent to which memory aids are provided have important effects on conceptual behavior.

13. Reasoning is the process of analyzing arguments and reaching conclusions, and formal logic is typically used as the criterion of proper reasoning. People ordinarily are not perfectly logical but rather follow a kind of personal logic that sometimes leads to correct conclusions but also results in systematic kinds of errors.

14. Two characteristics of ordinary reasoning are the failure to consider all possible interpretations and a tendency to seek confirmation of arguments rather than attempting to determine if an argument can be proved false.

15. Language is a complex, flexible, highly-organized symbolic system that is simultaneously something we acquire, something we know, and something we may use in performing a variety of tasks. The structure of a language includes sounds and phonemes, words and morphemes, and sentences and grammar, with each level having its own concepts and rules.

16. An important function of language is to convey meaning. Various approaches to measuring the meaning of words have been proposed. The semantic differential method is used to place word concepts on scales representing dimensions such as evaluation, potency, and activity.

17. The meaning of a sentence is not completely predictable on the basis of the meanings of its component words, and the most meaningful

sentences are those that make contact with our knowledge of the world and thus allow us to fill in information not explicitly stated in the sentence.

18. Intelligence refers to a number of cognitive abilities. However, there is disagreement over whether intelligence is an underlying general ability or simply a label applied to a set of relatively independent abilities.

19. Intelligence tests are used to compare a person to others of similar age with respect to whatever abilities a particular test involves. Different tests may be based on different assumptions regarding the nature of intelligence and do not necessarily yield similar scores.

20. Contrary to common opinion, intelligence and creativity are not closely related. It takes a certain minimum intelligence to create anything, but beyond that, intelligence is less critical than other variables.

21. The study of cognition is beginning to have visible impact on the problems of everyday life. These applications include the development of extraordinary feats of mental calculation through the mastery of certain basic skills and knowledge, the evaluation of performance by groups and individuals in problem-solving tasks, the role of language in intelligence testing, the use of cognitive processes in psychotherapy, and finally the contribution of stimulating environments to mental development.

Recommended Additional Readings

Biggs, J. B. *Information and human learning.* Glenview, Ill.: Scott, Foresman, 1971.

Bourne, L. E., Jr., Ekstrand, B. R., & Dominowski, R. L. *The psychology of thinking.* Englewood Cliffs, N.J.: Prentice-Hall, 1971.

Carroll, J. B. *Language and thought.* Englewood Cliffs, N.J.: Prentice-Hall, 1964.

Humphrey, G. *Thinking: An introduction to its experimental psychology.* New York: Wiley, 1963.

Slobin, D. I. *Psycholinguistics.* Glenview, Ill.: Scott, Foresman, 1971.

Wason, P. C., & Johnson-Laird, P. N. (Eds.) *Thinking and reasoning.* Middlesex, Eng.: Penguin, 1968.

Wickelgren, W. A. *How to solve problems.* San Francisco: Freeman. 1974.

6

MOTIVATION AND EMOTION

In recent months, readers of the newspapers in the Denver area have been confronted with the following kinds of news items: (1) a man tried to jump over a canyon on a motorcycle; (2) several high government officials, including the President of the United States, conspired to deny certain individuals their civil rights; (3) a couple decided not to let doctors administer insulin to their diabetic son, who subsequently went into a coma and died; (4) a city councilman was arrested for hit-and-run driving; (5) a young boy and his father designed an illegal car in order to win the Soapbox derby; (6) a religious group refused diphtheria inoculations after one of their members contracted the disease and died, leaving the whole group and possibly the state vulnerable to a diphtheria epidemic; (7) three young men were arrested for a "joy killing" of a 4-year-old girl; (8) numerous stories appeared about people of all ages, sexes, sizes, and shapes running nude in just about every place imaginable; (9) a young man was hospitalized after spending 4 1/2 days in the shower in an abortive attempt to break the world's record (more than 7 days); and on and on it goes. Why do people do such things as walk the high wire over the busy streets of New York or deliberately harm zoo animals? Another way to state this question is, "What *motivates* people to behave like this?"

This chapter is about motivation. Motivation raises the question of *why* people behave as they do. This is in contrast to *how* they do it, which is usually a question about the person's knowledge, skill, and performance. In this chapter, we assume that people have the ability to act in certain ways, and ask why they do what they do. We can assume that many teenage boys know how to drive a car and to shoot a shotgun. *Why* would three such youths use their knowledge and skills to murder a 4-year-old girl playing in her front yard? What motivates such a brutal act? And what motivates such seemingly senseless activities as streaking? Indeed, what motivates common, everyday behaviors, such as playing games, reading novels, eating, and the like? Obviously, in order to understand behavior, we will have to answer questions like these.

Motivation as an Explanatory Concept

The Variability of Behavior

Different people behave differently in the exact same situation. At the same cocktail party, some people eat the available food and others don't. This is a

The Daring Young Man On the Skyline Trapeze

Newsweek—"If I see three oranges, I have to juggle," said an overnight celebrity named Philippe Petit, a juggler and aerialist who has been earning a hand-to-mouth living—up to now—with impromptu performances on the sidewalks of New York. "And if I see two towers," Petit added, "I have to walk." The 24-year-old Frenchman took a historic walk last week on a tightrope high over downtown Manhattan between two of the world's tallest buildings.

About 7:15 one morning, early-to-work commuters stopped to gape at a black speck edging across the sky between the twin towers of the World Trade Center. With a balancing pole in his hands, Petit was serenely walking a high wire 1,350 feet above the street. For 45 minutes, he crossed back and forth between the towers—and even lay down on the wire. The unadvertised exploit ended when policemen burst onto the rooftops and a cop bellowed at the daredevil: "Get the hell off there or I'm coming out after you."

The police booked Petit for disorderly conduct and criminal trespass, but the case was promptly dismissed in exchange for his promise to entertain in a city park. Some of his confederates peddled photographs of the stunt—Associated Press paid more than $1,000 for a set of pictures—and Petit himself began asking for $200 for interviews. Just how he had engineered his death-defying feat was thus apt to be established only by checkbook journalism—if at all—but it appeared that Petit and several helpers had posed as construction workers, hauled equipment up the towers by freight elevator and settled in for the night. They arched the steel-cable tightrope from one roof to the other with a bow and arrow, then tightened the line with winches, turnbuckles and guy wires.

In Petit's apartment, a reporter saw blown-up photographs of the World Trade Center. There were also pictures of Niagara Falls and a notation: "Next?"

French daredevil Philippe Petit walking tightrope 1,350 feet above the sidewalks of New York.

difference in behavior *between* people. There is also variability *within* the same person. When you pass by a restaurant, sometimes you go in and eat and other times you don't. The same person behaves differently in an identical situation on different occasions—his behavior is variable. It is this variability in behavior, both between individuals and within the same person on different occasions, that psychologists are trying to understand. When we say motivational concepts help us make sense out of behavior, one important thing that we mean is that motivational concepts help to explain behavioral variability.

Circularity in Explanations

Consider the person who goes to lots of cocktail parties. Suppose we observe that this person eats lots of food at one party and eats nothing at another. There is variability in his behavior—he eats at one time and not at the other. Motivation is an obvious way to account for the difference in his behavior. We postulate the existence of a motive for food and "explain" the behavioral variability by saying that he was hungry on one occasion and not on the other. This explanation makes sense, but note the circular reasoning involved. The only way we had of knowing that he was hungry on the first occasion was the fact that he ate some food—the very behavior we are trying to explain. It goes like this: He eats food. Why? Because he was hungry. How do you know he was hungry? Because he ate the food.

Motivational Constructs

To get around this circularity, psychologists look for *independent* ways of defining a motive. Often this boils down to defining the strength of a motive as being the length of time since the motive has been satisfied. In our example, the existence and degree of hunger is determined by the number of hours it has been since this person has eaten—the hours of food deprivation. So the hunger motive is defined not by if and how much one eats (which would be circular), but by amount of deprivation. Now the reasoning is like this: He eats food. Why? Because he was hungry. How do you know he was hungry? Because it has been 5 hours since he has eaten any food.

Motivational constructs, such as hunger, are powerful explanatory devices because they can account for a wide variety of behaviors without having to have a new principle for each action we observe. People go shopping at grocery stores for food, work for food, steal money for food, beg for it,

Blue Streaks

Newsweek—It was rush hour in Tallahassee and the roads were clogged with motorists struggling slowly home through the late-afternoon Florida sunshine. Suddenly, four male Florida State University students sprang from the back seat of one of the cars—every one of them stark naked. Ignoring the incredulous stares of drivers and pedestrians, they dodged through the standing lines of traffic, sprinted across a crowded roadside tennis court and disappeared as quickly as they'd come into another waiting car which roared quickly out of sight.

"Streaking"—making *Blitzkrieg* runs through public areas completely in the buff—has become a fad of epidemic proportions among students from California to Maryland. In Detroit, two skinny male streakers recently collided while racing through a fashionable restaurant; one of them was knocked cold and had to be dragged from the scene by his fellow nudist. At the University of Maryland, a student who participated with 125 others in a coeducational streak has been suspended from school—not for indecent exposure, but for assaulting a college official who suggested that he cover up. For a time, one Los Angeles radio station broadcast "streaker alerts" to warn the populace that naked youths were on the loose. And at Florida State, the streaking incidents are now so common—at least three were reported last week alone—that the campus newspaper no longer bothers to report them.

Why do students streak? One coed at Florida State thinks it's just an exciting game. "It's like playing bank robber," she explains. "A guy jumps from the men's room without his clothes, runs across the campus and vanishes into a getaway car—just to see if he can get away with it. It's a challenge." It certainly is—just like swallowing goldfish, or munching phonograph records, or seeing how many of your fellow students you can jam into a telephone booth, or leading panty raids on the girls' dormitory, or . . .

"The crew is in excellent health and seems to be suffering no ill effects, with the exception of Commander Fenwick, who reports that he is hornier than a hoot owl!"

Commander Fenwick is suffering from a long period of sexual deprivation. Motives are often measured by the length of time since the person has engaged in the behavior that reduces the motive. In fact, motives are often defined by the fact that deprivation leads to increases in behavior designed to obtain the deprived object. For example, we infer the existence of a hunger motive because if we deprive people of food they will try harder and more often to get food.

Also note the variability—the other two astronauts are apparently not suffering. How would you account for the variability between these spacemen? Does Fenwick have a higher sex motive than the other two? Has he been deprived longer?

grow it in a backyard garden, stand in long cafeteria lines for it, kill animals for it, and so on. There are numerous different behaviors involved, all centering on food, and all understood by introducing one concept, namely motivation for food, or hunger. Instead of having a separate explanation for each of these behaviors, we can use the concept of hunger to account for all or many of them. You might try making your own list of things that people do because they are hungry. This should give you a good idea of the wide variety of behavior that one might ultimately account for with a single motivational construct, hunger or the food motive.

Motivation Is Not the Only Explanation

Motivational constructs are used in psychology because they account for some of the variability in behavior. They do so by reducing a large variety of acts to a much smaller number of motivational principles. In these aspects, motivational constructs are not different from other psychological principles. Take the concept of *learning,* for example. We use it also to account for variability in behavior—Jane is a good bridge player and Harvey is a lousy one because Jane has taken lessons and *learned* how to play. Or take heredity—Jane and Harvey differ in IQ,

© 1972 United Feature Syndicate, Inc.

Incentive refers to the *motivational* **properties of a reward. Two things, say, a hug and a kiss for Lucy, might be rewards in that she would learn something in order to get either one. But the kiss might motivate her more than the hug—she would try harder for a kiss reward than a hug reward. In that case, we would say that the** *incentive value* **of a kiss was higher than the** *incentive value* **of a hug.**

in part because they have different genetic backgrounds. Learning and heredity are two major concepts used to understand why people differ or vary in their behavior, but these two concepts cannot account for all the variability. Motivational principles fill in many of the remaining gaps in understanding.

How can we sort out the effects of motivation from those of learning and heredity? Consider the following example. Two rats that are known to have identical genetic make-ups (through extensive inbreeding, see Chapter 2) and an identical history of learning experiences have learned to run down a straight alley to a goal box for food. These two rats might differ greatly in the speed with which they run down the alley. Further, once they get to the goal box they might differ in the length of time before they start eating or in the amount of food they eat. We see, then, that these two rats differ on three *dependent* variables—running speed, time to eat, and amount eaten. Why? The reason cannot be heredity or learning because we have used scientific techniques to equate the rats on these two important dimensions. It *could* be motivation. Perhaps one rat was fed all the cheese he could eat just before being put in the alley and the other one had not eaten for 24 hours. The variability in all three dependent measures would then be understood in terms of variability in one factor: motivation, or hunger in this case.

Note that we could be sure that the rats were equal in learning experience and had identical genetic make-ups *only* because they had been raised in the laboratory, where these factors can be controlled. In studying everyday human behavior, we

can almost never be sure that two people have equivalent genetic make-ups or learning histories. Thus, behavior variability in human beings might be due to learning or heredity, not to differences in motivation. This means, obviously, that it is difficult to tell why people behave differently and difficult to conclude with any confidence that differences in motivation are responsible for behavioral variability. When the University of Colorado defeats an opponent in football, do we conclude that the CU team had a higher level of *motivation* to win, that CU players had done a better job of *learning* the skills of football, or that CU had better players because it recruited men with superior heredities for football? In order to isolate motivational factors from learning and from hereditary predispositional factors, psychologists have had to turn to the laboratory, particularly to studies of animal behavior. As we shall see, much of the evidence and theory about motivation is based on animal research.

Basic Concepts

Recall our example of the rats trained to run down a straight alley to a goal box containing food. The rats have learned that food is at the end of the alley. Now suppose we want to make the rats run faster—we want to motivate them to work harder. Basically, there are two ways to accomplish this. Crudely translated, they are (1) "push" the rats harder or (2) "pull" them harder.

To push them we can increase the level of their need for food, say, by increasing the amount of time since they have eaten. Rats that have recently eaten will not run as fast as rats that have not eaten for 24 hours. When we do this, we say that we have increased the drive level of the animals. The *drive level* corresponds to the amount of energy available for *pushing* behavior. The fact that the animal has not eaten in some time means that there is a *need* for food. This need is somehow detected or "felt" by the animal and results in an increase in his drive level. There is more energy available for pushing

Which Drive (or Incentive) Is Strongest?

The Columbia obstruction box, shown in Figure 6–1, was used in some classic studies designed to measure the strength of various drives. A deprived rat was placed in compartment A and the needed object was placed in compartment C. Unfortunately for the rat, in order to get to the reward, he had to go across an electrified grid, B. If he did not cross over, he was immediately picked up and returned to A for another chance. The strength of the drive was measured by the number of times the rat crossed the grid. Several rats were tested. The average number of crossings for five drives were: maternal drive, 22.4; thirst drive, 20.4; hunger drive, 18.2; sex drive, 13.8; and exploratory drive (empty compartment), 6.0. The maternal drive appears to be strongest—a mother rat will cross 22.4 times in order to get to her litter of babies.

A problem with studies like these is that the effects of drive are confused with the effects of incentives. The rats could see across the grid to compartment C and so they knew what was waiting for them when they crossed. Maybe they were not driven across by their deprivation state, but instead were attracted across by the incentive. Were they pushed or pulled?

Figure 6–1
Columbia obstruction box

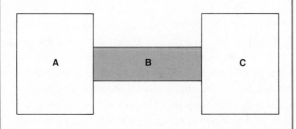

The Columbia obstruction box, two compartments separated by an electrified grid, is used to test drive strength in rats.

corresponding to pulling the rats harder, would be to increase the quantity or quality of the food reward in the goal box. Rats will run faster for a large reward than for a small one, and they too have preferred foods (such as Limburger cheese) that will cause them to run faster than they would for ordinary laboratory rat chow. By this technique we can motivate the rats by enticing or pulling them. When we do this, we say that we have increased the *incentive* for the rats.

These two concepts, drive and incentive, have long dominated psychologists' thinking about motivation. If we are in a state of need, a drive is aroused that energizes and pushes or goads us into action to seek the things that will satisfy the need. Some of these things are more attractive to us than others and so we will work harder to get them. The incentive value of each of these rewards represents their pulling power. *Motivation* is the combined action of drives and incentives, push and pull.

How much is push and how much is pull? Are we mainly *driven* to behave or *enticed* into it? The answer to that question reflects the history of motivational psychology. For a long time, drive theory predominated as the basic explanation for motivational phenomena, while incentives were treated as merely minor "extra attractions." In the last 10 to 15 years, as our understanding of the concept of drive grew, psychologists became less convinced of its importance. Now the main focus of attention is on incentives. Indeed, some incentive theorists have maintained that the entire concept of drive can be discarded, although most researchers still include it in their systems, especially when talking about basic biological needs such as food and water. Let us first take a closer look at the concept of drive as the energizer of behavior.

Motivation as a Pushing Force: Drives and Energy

Drive theorists emphasize the energizing aspects of motivation. Like a machine, a person must have energy in order to behave. The theory is that the arousal of a motive provides the energy or the drive necessary for executing some behavior. High motivation means high drive, which in turn means more energy for pushing behavior, which ultimately means more behavior, more vigorous behavior, and more persistence of behavior.

According to drive theory, deprivation of some needed substance such as food or water leads to a state of need, which in turn leads to increases in drive level. The result is an increase in the energy available for behaving (going to get food or water).

behavior, and thus the rat runs faster. Note that the need leads to the drive, but needs and drives are not the same thing. If you starve an animal long enough, the need for food will get very high. The drive level or available energy for pushing behavior to get food, however, will drop off as the animal becomes too weak to behave.

The second way of increasing motivation,

When someone manages to perform a "superhuman" act such as lifting a car off a child, we tend to think in terms of high drive or energy. Consider also the drug addict who will stop at nothing for a "fix" or the nicotine addict who will "walk a mile" for a cigarette—these behaviors seem best described by saying the person was driven or pushed into behavior by his addiction. As we will see in Chapter 9, Sigmund Freud believed in an energy concept and postulated the existence of sources of instinctual energy that he called *libido*. Often psychologists invoke such states as anxiety and frustration as sources of the energy needed for behavior. In short, much of our behavior gives the appearance of being pushed or driven and this has been recognized by motivational theorists and formalized into the drive-energy concept.

According to this drive-energy formulation, the motivated organism is aroused or energized. This implies that the motivated organism should be active, an organism bubbling with energy. And indeed, many early studies indicated that hungry or thirsty or sexually deprived animals were highly active—given the opportunity they ran around a lot in an activity cage. Female rats, for example, show activity bursts just at the time of peak sexual motivation. Hungry rats will explore a maze more quickly than rats that have just eaten.

Aroused or arousable?   The most recent available evidence questions this interpretation. Increases in activity may not be a *direct,* automatic result of deprivation. Several studies have shown that the animals' activity increases because they *expect* reward. The increased activity displayed when an animal is hungry seems to be more a reaction to stimuli that are associated with food than a reaction to a state of need. One study showed that hungry rats are not more active than satiated (full) rats unless there is a change in the stimulus situation. When the lights in the room were turned on (perhaps a signal that the experimenter was coming with food) or the fan was turned off, the hungry rats *reacted* with increased activity more than the satiated rats. But the hungry rats were not more active before the stimulus change. In another study, food odors were used as a stimulus and the hungry rats showed a great increase in activity, while the satiated rats hardly reacted at all to the smell of food. Again, when no stimuli were presented, the hungry and satiated rats did not differ in their activity levels.

The conclusion is that a deprived organism *is not necessarily* a more active organism. Motivation does

---

Woman Lifts Car Off Son

Kentucky (AP)—Mrs. Herbert Seaman, a 5-foot-5, 120-pound brunette, lifted a 2,000 pound automobile off of her trapped son following a traffic accident, then dismissed the feat as "nothing."

"I knew my boy was under the car and I had to get him out," Mrs. Seaman, 33, said Tuesday. "I didn't notice the weight of the Pinto."

Her son, Dana, 11, was recovering today in a hospital with head and shoulder injuries.

Mrs. Seaman, of Louisville, Ky., said she was driving home from a veterinarian's office and was distracted when the family Irish setter became sick in the front seat.

The car ran off the road and Dana was thrown out. He was trapped under the car after it hit a pole and rolled over.

"Dana was partially under the car and was complaining of his shoulder, and it was just a small car," said Mrs. Seaman, a part-time secretary.

Motivation as a source of energy.

---

not *directly* lead to increased activity as was once thought, and this finding casts doubt on a simple energy notion. Instead, the motivated organism appears to be more *reactive* to stimuli, especially stimuli that are associated with the motive being manipulated. Instead of thinking of the motivated organism as being simply energized or active, it is perhaps more accurate to speak of higher *arousability*. The motivated organism is more reactive to stimuli, more sensitive, more arousable. Stimulation will arouse the organism more easily when it is deprived, especially when the stimuli are associated with the deprivation state. Thus a hungry rat appears to be more sensitive to food-related stimuli and reacts with greater arousal to such stimuli. For that reason, he gives the impression of being more active. The activity is a function of being aroused by the stimulus situation, not a direct effect of being deprived of food. We might say that the motivated organism is *predisposed* to react to certain stimuli but is not automatically more active or energized.

Motivational functions of stimuli.   Donald O. Hebb has suggested that each stimulus can serve two functions, an arousal function and a cue function. The smell of food will arouse the hungry person (arousal function) and provide information about where to find the food (cue function). Physiological evidence indicates that the *reticular formation* (see Chapter 2) underlies the arousal function. Each sensory modality, such as smell or vision, involves inputs into the reticular formation, which then produces arousal of the higher brain centers. These centers then evaluate the information in the stimulus (cue function) for clues to the source of the stimulation and its significance.

Levels of motivation.   Our arousal level varies. Sometimes we are sleeping and not aroused at all; at other times we are highly excited, practically "crazy" or "climbing the walls." We cannot engage in behavior to satisfy our motives when we are sleeping, nor can we do a very good job of behaving appropriately when we are in a highly excited state. Presumably there is some optimal level of arousal for engaging in any behavior. The relationship between arousal and efficiency of behavior is an *inverted U function* (see Figure 6–2). At very low levels of arousal, such as when we are drowsy and near sleep, our performance will not be very efficient. At very, very high levels of arousal, our behavior will be disorganized and inefficient to the point that people might describe us as "wild" or "berserk." In between the extremes of sleep and frenzy are the moderate levels of arousal that are presumably optimal for behavior.

Exactly where the optimal level lies depends on the task at hand. With a very easy task to perform the optimal level will be high—the task is so easy that efficiency does not suffer until extremely high arousal takes place. With a very difficult or complicated task, the optimal level will be on the low side. You should be aroused somewhat but not very much. This principle is generally known as the *Yerkes-Dodson Law* and applies to motivation in general, not just to the arousal aspects of motivation. The principle says that the optimal level of motivation will depend upon task difficulty—the more difficult or complex the task, the lower will be the optimal motivational point (see Figure 6–3).

In summary, motivation does not automatically mean arousal, energy, and high activity. However, we must be aroused in order to behave, and so arousal, activity, and energy are a part of motivated behavior. Increasing motivation leads to an organism that is more sensitive, more reactive, or more easily aroused. This arousal is necessary in order for the organism to react to incoming stimuli, to process the information in these stimuli, and thereby to engage in behavior that will satisfy its needs. It probably will simplify our discussion if we continue to use the term "drive," but we should keep in mind that high drive does not automatically energize and push the behavior of the organism.

Figure 6–2
Arousal and performance: The inverted U function

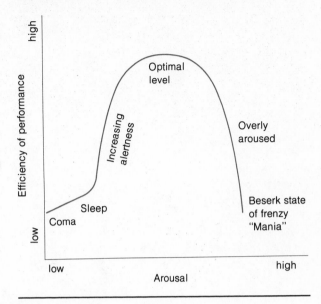

High drive will mean that the organism is predisposed or set or prepared to respond, but it will not respond in the absence of stimulation.

Motivation as a Pulling Force: Incentives

The incentive theory of motivation stresses the attracting or pulling power that rewards appear to exert on behavior. The emphasis is on rewards and the conditions of reinforcement for behaving (see Chapter 4). Incentive theory rests on the assumption that the behaving organism knows what the consequences of its behavior will be. Thus, it focuses attention on the circumstances that we are attempting to obtain (positive incentives) or those that we are trying to avoid (negative incentives). Incentive theory is primarily concerned with the objects, events, and states of affairs that people find rewarding or punishing and are thus motivated to achieve or avoid. The emphasis is on the goals of behavior. Such an analysis of motivation leads researchers to study what it is that people are trying to acquire—food, drink, love, fame, prestige, money—and what it is they are trying to avoid—pain, anxiety, frustration, starvation, poverty, and the like. Incentives not only are objects to be obtained, such as money, but may include complicated states of affairs, such as receiving a promotion, winning an election, feeling satisfied with one's accomplishments, earning the respect of a colleague, and so on.

Switching the emphasis away from drives and toward incentives is consistent with the facts of

Figure 6–3
The Yerkes-Dodson Law

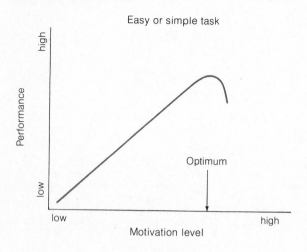

Easy or simple task

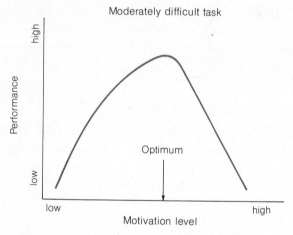

Moderately difficult task

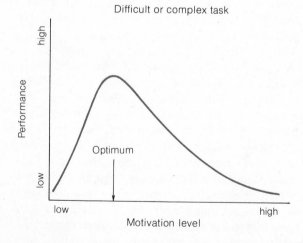

Difficult or complex task

Graphs showing the effect known as the Yerkes-Dodson Law of motivation and performance. With an easy task, increasing motivation increases performance. With increasing task difficulty, the optimum motivation level (that giving best performance) decreases.

human motivation. People do not seem particularly driven to behave, except in special circumstances usually centering on physical needs of the body. For example, our behavior with respect to getting food for our bodies is usually better described as behavior designed to prevent intense hunger from arising rather than behavior caused by an intense hunger drive. We engage in all sorts of behavior designed to prevent us from becoming hungry or thirsty. We go to the grocery store not because we are driven by an intense hunger drive, but because we know that food is necessary to prevent intense hunger and starvation. We know the consequences of not being able to eat and so we arrange our behavior in ways that are designed to keep food available. Thus, our behavior is usually best described as an attempt to achieve certain goals. We are primarily motivated by the consequences of our behavior. We seek positive incentives and we avoid negative ones.

Why incentives and not drives?   Many factors led to deemphasis on drives as motivators and increased emphasis on incentives as motivators. We have already mentioned one, the fact that deprivation states apparently do not automatically energize behavior. We have also indicated that drive theory does not contribute much to an understanding of human motivation because our behavior seems more appropriately described as a search for goals. Another major factor came from experiments showing that drives were not necessary to motivate behavior. In one study, it was found that animals will work to achieve rewards that have nothing to do with any known need state. Rats will perform in order to get to drink a sweet saccharin solution, even though they were not deprived of water and the saccharin, an artificial sweetener, does not provide any nutrients for the body. Monkeys will work and learn just for an opportunity to see out into the laboratory or to see novel objects (see Figure 6–4). Of course, human beings do lots of things that do not alleviate any known drives—they go to horror shows, read murder mysteries, play all sorts of games, run nude through school cafeterias, and try to break the world record for staying in the shower. It seems nearly impossible to explain such behaviors as attempts to satisfy some kind of drive. Rather they appear to be a result of the consequences of the behavior—excitement, pleasure, recognition, prestige, or whatever. They are motivated by incentives, not drives. A lot of research converged on one conclusion that more than any other led to the decline of drive theory—to motivate behavior it is not necessary to provide a

Figure 6–4
The curious monkey

One major problem with drive theory became obvious when various studies showed that animals would learn and work for rewards that did not reduce any known drive. Thus, it was difficult to maintain that it was a drive that motivated them in the first place. One of these studies showed that monkeys would learn to operate a lever that opened a door in the box just so they could see out into the laboratory or get to see novel objects such as a toy train. The monkey in the picture above, however, seems more interested in the photographer than the train.

reward that will reduce a drive. From this it follows that the behavior was not motivated by a drive in the first place.

To summarize, the emphasis, particularly in human motivation, has shifted from drives to incentives, from push to pull, from motivation as an attempt to reduce a drive to motivation as a search for goals. What is needed, however, is an understanding of how it is that incentives produce their motivational effects, and how we learn the incentive values of various things. Why is one person's positive incentive another person's negative incentive?

Predisposition and Precipitation

We can think of the motivated organism as being *predisposed* or set to behave in particular ways. Further, we can imagine that there are *precipitating* circumstances—circumstances that actually result in the organism behaving in those ways. As we mentioned earlier, depriving an animal of food does

Youth Is Slain Trying to Make His Dream True

Missouri (UPI)—For the past three years, 17-year-old Joe Allen Gray's dream was to attend the U.S. Air Force Academy.

He had won an appointment and passed every entrance examination but one, which he was to take Saturday.

Instead, he will be buried on that day, the victim of a police bullet fired while he was attempting to make sure his dream came true.

Gray ran when officers surprised him Wednesday in Center High School, where copies of the examination were stored in an office safe. Police said he was trying to cut wire mesh glass protecting the office. He carried a butane torch.

Patrolman Gordon Smith said he fired after the fleeing youth ignored commands to halt. The prosecutor ruled the shooting a justifiable homicide.

"They didn't have to kill him," Mrs. Georgette Gray, his mother, said Thursday. "He didn't resist. He didn't do anything but try to get away. He's been a good boy all his life and he must have just wanted so bad to get into the academy that he made a mistake.

"It's all he thought of for three years. Now he's dead."

His father, Joseph Gray, said his son had "never been in the least bit of trouble. He didn't have time. He studied and worked and thought about flying and that was it."

Most human behavior can be best described as attempts to achieve certain goals or incentives. Some goals have such high positive incentive value for particular people that they will do almost anything to obtain them. To understand motivation we will have to know about the incentive (what is desirable about getting into the Air Force Academy) and we will have to know about the incentive value for the particular person (why admission had such high positive incentive value for this young man). This will, of course, mean that we have to understand the personality and the learning history of the behaving organism.

not automatically cause him to become active. Instead deprivation appears to predispose or set him to behave, but in the absence of any stimulation he does not do much of anything. The stimulation is the precipitating factor. He starts behaving when he smells food or hears a noise that might be the laboratory assistant bringing food.

One can think of deprivation or drive states as *one way* of predisposing an organism to behave in particular ways. The hungry person is predisposed to eat or to behave in ways that will result in food and eating. The female dog "in heat" is predisposed to engage in sexual behavior. Likewise, one can think of the incentives as being the primary precipitating factor in getting an organism to behave. For example, rats, even if quite hungry, will not run very fast in a maze if there is no food for them at the end, but they will start running quickly as soon as they discover that the experimenter has placed food in the goal box. Moreover, if the experimenter switches the reward from a large amount to a small amount, the rats very quickly adjust to the lower incentive by running more slowly. If the amount of reward is increased, the rats immediately start running faster. This demonstration of switching reward size emphasizes the importance of incentives in controlling motivation. Furthermore, it shows that incentives precipitate behavior. The rats will not run without some incentive motivation.

It will be helpful in organizing your thinking about motivation to focus on the concepts of *predisposition* and *precipitation*. The advantage of these terms over *drives* and *incentives* is a matter of generality. Drive states are not the only source of predispositions and incentives are not the only precipitators. Predispositions can come from sources other than deprivation. The most important one is learning, particularly learning of the incentive value of various rewards. Consider the person who absolutely loves to eat snails. For this individual, snails have positive incentive value; but this is the same thing as saying that the person is predisposed to behave in ways designed to get snails. Obviously this person has learned to like snails—learning was the source of the predisposition, not deprivation of snails. In fact, most of the things we find rewarding, the things that have positive incentive value for us, have achieved this status through learning.

Another source of predisposition may be heredity. For example, in Chapter 2 we mentioned that heredity probably plays a role in susceptibility to alcoholism and perhaps drug addiction. People with certain inherited physiological features are thus predisposed to behave in certain ways. For example, strains of mice have been developed that have a strong preference for drinking alcohol instead of water. They are thus predisposed to be motivated by alcohol as an incentive and this predisposition comes from their genetic make-up. It has nothing to do with being deprived of alcohol, and so it is not an alcohol *drive* but a predisposition.

Later in this chapter we will see that most psychologists consider personality traits to be sources of motivation. Some people are said to be highly motivated by a trait called need for achievement. These people need to engage in

Fly Me Again

Time—Since National Airlines took off with its "I'm Cheryl. Fly me" campaign in 1971, the sexy—and sexist—slogan has enraged feminists. It has also pulled in business. National reported a 23% increase in passengers during the first year of the campaign, nearly twice that of the industry as a whole. Having succeeded that well with sex, National is now drumming up an even more suggestive campaign scheduled for television airing this summer. The new ads feature National stewardesses looking seductively into the camera and breathing "I'm going to *fly* you like you've never been flown before." The film makers coach them "to say it like you're standing there stark naked." A San Francisco-based group called Stewardesses for Equal Rights is considering complaining to the Federal Communications Commission and the Equal Employment Opportunity Commission.

Basically advertising does two things: it acquaints you with the product and it attempts to make the product have positive incentive value for you (tries to motivate you to buy the product). To create the positive incentive, the ad attempts to impart information or knowledge as to what will happen if you buy the product—in this case, the information is clearly aimed at male customers. All too often, the ads are designed to communicate knowledge that in no sense has anything to do with the consequences of buying the product. The stewardesses on National Airlines are not going to seduce all the male passengers.

behavior that will lead to recognized achievement; they have a strong desire to win, to be best at something, or to be better than the next person. Perhaps the need for achievement motivated the man who tried to set the world's record for continuous showering. Thus, one's personality can involve predispositions to behave in certain ways, to be motivated by some incentives (the opportunity to set a world's record) and not by other incentives (the opportunity to sit around and help someone else set the world's record). In turn, however, one's personality is obviously a result of other factors, especially the two we have already mentioned, learning and heredity.

One final point we need to make is that incentives themselves are not usually the immediate precipitators of our behavior. Most of the time, our behavior is precipitated by our *knowledge* that certain behaviors will lead toward positive incentives or away from negative incentives, and, of course, this knowledge is a result of our learning history. As an example, consider the laboratory rat who is motivated into activity when he hears the door open, or sees the lights come on, or smells food. The activity is motivated not by the food itself, but by the stimuli that serve to inform the rat that food might be forthcoming. The animal has learned that such stimuli are often followed by food, and this is the source of the action the rat displays.

To summarize, motivation is generated when a predisposed organism is subjected to precipitating circumstances. These circumstances result in the organism's utilizing its knowledge and skills to behave in ways designed to achieve positive incentives or avoid negative ones. Sometimes this behavior will appear to be pushed, or driven; at other times it will appear to be a matter of pulling.

Motivation and Biological Needs

We are biological creatures with bodies that require certain things to survive. The motivation for much of our behavior can be traced to this fact. We need food, water, air, sleep, and a certain amount of heat, and our behavior can often be described as an attempt to obtain these life-sustaining things. We have built-in physiological systems for regulating the intake of such things as food and water. It is because of these needs and the systems that regulate them that such items as food and water can reinforce behavior and become positive incentives. As an example, in this section we will discuss the regulation of eating, but first we must introduce the important concept of homeostasis.

Homeostasis

Complex physiological systems in our bodies determine the conditions under which a need for food or water exists, resulting in the organism's becoming predisposed to eat or drink or to engage in behaviors that have in the past led to food or water. Finally, when sufficient food and water have been ingested, the system detects this fact and the organism is no longer predisposed to eat or drink.

Basically, these physiological systems are designed to maintain a "steady state" in our bodies. As such, they are said to operate according to the principle of *homeostasis.* The best analogy for describing homeostasis is the heating system in the typical home. The system is designed to maintain a steady state, say a temperature of 70 degrees. In order to accomplish this, we have a thermostat (a homeostat for temperature) that detects the need for heat, turns on the furnace when the temperature is too low, and then turns off the furnace when the temperature has reached 70 or so again.

The physiological systems underlying our biological needs appear to operate in a similar fashion, that is, according to a homeostatic principle. Thus, we presumably have "sensors" that detect when we need food and water. When the need reaches some critical level, we become motivated to act in ways designed to obtain and ingest food or water. When we eat or drink, the system senses that the need is being reduced and modifies our behavior such that we stop eating or drinking at the appropriate time. Of course, we must remember that overlying this homeostatic system is an elaborate system of learned behaviors designed to make food and water available. We have learned to anticipate the need in order to prevent starvation or dehydration. Many of these behaviors have been learned because food and water reinforced them; part of the motivation for these behaviors stems from the fact that food and water are positive incentives. But given that we have learned how to find, buy, beg, or borrow food or water, the homeostatic systems regulate how much we consume.

Eating

We eat to satisfy bodily needs. How do we know when to eat, how much, and when to stop? We have a complicated homeostatic system for regulating food intake, much of which we still do not understand. But we do know a great deal about the system. First, we know that it works incredibly well if left to itself. Despite wide variations in our expenditure of energy, our body weight stays remarkably constant—the system obviously adjusts intake to outflow. Just imagine if the system were consistently off by as little as 1/2 ounce per day. In a year, that would amount to over 10 pounds gained or lost. Starting at age 15 with a 150-pound person, such a system would produce a 45-year-old person who weighed 450 pounds or, if you can imagine a negative weight, a person weighing −150 pounds.

Another thing about the system is that it is complex, involving multiple control factors that provide "fail-safe" back-up or auxiliary support should one aspect of the system fail. Thus, it is not nearly so simple as the home-heating system.

Predispositions—the set weight level.   Like the thermostat in the home set to a particular level, the body has a set weight level, and the homeostatic system is designed to regulate food intake in a way that maintains that level. We have little information

Trying to Stop Eating? Have Your Jaws Wired Shut

Chicago (AP)—Fat people are flooding oral surgeons with requests to wire their jaws shut, even though such action probably will not lead to permanent thinness, says an editorial in a dental journal.

"Persons who need a gimmick such as wiring of the teeth to lose weight are probably so poorly motivated in the first place that long-term success with weight control is extremely doubtful," Dr. Daniel M. Laskin writes in the September issue of the Journal of Oral Surgery.

Laskin, an oral surgery professor at the University of Illinois school of dentistry, says many oral surgeons are being "flooded with requests" to wire teeth ever since news accounts of a woman who lost 100 pounds that way.

Now oral surgeons are "thrust into the midst of the weight reduction craze" and faced with the moral and ethical question of whether to participate, Laskin says.

"For most people, weight control is even more difficult than weight reduction. New eating habits must be developed; most gimmicky diets are failures because an eating pattern that can be followed indefinitely is not established," he says.

Only highly motivated persons can make the transition from the liquid diet they must maintain with wired teeth to a solid diet later, he says.

And he cautions that in addition there is the potential for complications such as shifting of teeth, periodontal disease and tooth decay.

Food intake is closely regulated by the body in order to maintain a pre-set weight level that is apparently largely determined by the number of fat cells in the body. In order to prevent the system from doing its job, some people have gone to extraordinary lengths.

about the exact way this is accomplished, but research to date indicates that the culprit is fat—fat levels in the blood and the number of fat cells in the body as a whole. Here we are speaking of the long-term regulation of weight, not the hour-by-hour food intake, which, as we will see later, appears to be related to the level of sugar (glucose) in the blood.

Evidence is beginning to accumulate that supports the hypothesis that the number of fat cells in the body is a crucial determinant of the set weight level, although not all investigators are yet convinced. The general idea goes something like this. The body sets a weight level according to the number of fat cells in the body, in order to keep a relatively constant level of fat. For example, the overweight person

apparently does not have bigger fat cells, stuffed to the brim or overflowing with fat, but rather he has *more* fat cells stuffed to the same level as the weight cells of the normal-weight person. In other words, the system regulates food intake in a way to keep a constant level of fat in the cells, but if you have more cells than the next person, you will obviously have to eat more to keep your fat cells stuffed to the same degree. And, of course, because you have more cells for storing the fat, you will weigh more.

The hypothalamus in the brain is involved in regulating the set weight level over the long term. There is evidence that the hypothalamus may regulate fat levels in the cells by being sensitive to the levels of free fatty acids in the bloodstream. Investigators have long thought that the hypothalamus is the only regulator of food intake. Recent evidence, however, indicates that the hypothalamus is only part, though a crucial part, of a more complex system.

The evidence for the important role this structure plays comes from studies on surgical destruction and electrical stimulation or activation of two areas of the hypothalamus: the ventromedial nucleus and the lateral nucleus. Destruction of these areas is accomplished surgically by making lesions in them. Making a lesion in the ventromedial nucleus produces an animal with *hyperphagia,* an abnormally increased desire for food. The animal overeats and becomes enormous (see Figure 6–5). But the animal does not go on eating forever and ever until he explodes. Instead the animal levels off at a new, although very much higher, weight and then maintains that weight. It is as if the thermostat or "fatostat" has been reset at a higher level. In fact, if the animals are gorged and forced to become extremely overweight *before* the operation, then they will not overeat after the operation, but will actually eat less until they reduce down to the new weight level, which of course is now set higher than normal.

Making a lesion in the lateral hypothalamus produces the opposite effect, apparently resetting the fatostat to a lower level. Animals with this lesion exhibit *aphagia;* they will not eat at all. Such an abrupt and complete cessation of eating would normally lead to death, and so they have to be force-fed for a while. After recovery they eat on their own, but they maintain their body weight at a much lower level than normal. If the animals are gradually starved down to a very low weight *before* the operation, then after the operation they will eat to bring themselves up to the new weight level, which

Motivation and Emotion   **197**

Figure 6–5
Hypothalamic hyperphagia

A hyperphagic rat made obese by a lesion in the
ventromedial nucleus of the hypothalamus. This rat
weighs 1080 grams (the indicator has spun completely
around the dial and beyond). A normal rat the same age
weighs less than 200 grams.

Table 6–1

**Effects of lesions (destruction) and electrical stimulation
(activation) on two parts of the hypothalamus**

	Destruction	*Activation*
Ventromedial nucleus	Animal becomes hyperphagic and overeats	A hungry animal who is eating will stop eating immediately
Lateral nucleus	Animal becomes aphagic—it will not eat at all and will die unless force-fed	Animal will immediately start eating, even if it has just eaten all it wants

is much lower than normal but higher than the
weight they were starved to.

Electrical stimulation of these two areas of the
hypothalamus produces an effect opposite to that
caused by lesions. Stimulation of the ventromedial
nucleus will cause a hungry animal who is eating to
stop immediately. Stimulation of the lateral nucleus
will cause an animal to start eating immediately even
if the animal has just eaten all the food it wants (see
Table 6–1).

To summarize, the overall, long-term
predisposition to eat seems to be mainly a function
of the number of fat cells in the body. Long-term
food consumption is designed to maintain body
weight at some set level, and this seems to be quite
closely regulated by structures in the hypothalamus
that are sensitive to levels of body fat.

Precipitating factors.   In the short term,
day-to-day food intake seems to be more a function
of blood glucose (sugar) levels than of fat levels in
the body. The hypothalamus also plays an important
role in this phase of food-intake regulation.

Glucose is the body's basic source of energy, and
when we are using it up quickly, the blood glucose
levels are affected. Blood glucose levels are
obviously monitored by the body, because the level
is closely regulated to stay within certain limits. If
blood glucose levels drop, presumably we are using
energy and need food. This decrease in sugar levels
is somehow detected and results in our eating.

Taking insulin into the body results in decreased
blood glucose levels. People who take insulin
injections report feeling hungry soon afterward, and
animals given insulin injections will start to eat.
Reversing the process works too; giving glucose
injections to hungry animals will cause them to stop
eating. All this supports the idea that blood glucose
levels are crucially involved in regulating food intake
in the short term. Actually, the regulation may be
more complex than simply monitoring overall
glucose levels. Overall levels do not correspond very
well to hunger and the amount eaten; therefore, it
has been suggested that what is monitored is the
difference between the glucose levels in the arteries
and the levels in the veins. In any case, it is clear
that glucose levels are critically involved.

It has been suggested that there are specialized
cells (glucoreceptors) in the body to detect glucose

levels and communicate the need for food to the higher centers of the brain, which then initiate eating. There may be glucoreceptors in the stomach and the liver, and it is also assumed that the hypothalamus contains these cells. Remember that hypothalamic lesions can cause hyperphagia and aphagia. At one time it was thought that this was merely a result of destroying the parts of the brain that start and stop eating, presumably because these parts monitor the glucose levels. The picture is not so simple, however, because, as we have seen, the hypothalamus regulates not only short-term weight level, but also long-term weight level. Another problem is that the hyperphagic rats, while obviously prone to overeating, are not particularly *motivated* to eat. They overeat their favorite food if it is right under their noses, but if the food does not taste good or if they have to do the least bit of work to get it, they do not appear to be hungry.

It is perhaps the case that both the long-term weight level (based on fat levels) and the short-term system (based on glucose levels) have regulatory centers in the hypothalamus and that these two systems are complexly intertwined. Lesions in the hypothalamus cannot be made so precisely as to affect only one of the two regulatory systems, and so the effects of such lesions will be complex. For example, the lateral lesion results in a new lower weight level being set, but it also appears to disrupt monitoring of glucose levels. Rats with lateral lesions do not start eating if insulin injections are given, as normal rats do. Also, as mentioned previously, the hypothalamus is only one, though evidently a crucial, part of the complex system involved in regulating food intake. The manner in which the hypothalamus plays its role in regulating food intake is not completely known at this time.

Peripheral precipitators.   Blood fat and sugar levels and the hypothalamus are critical, but there are other factors that play a role, although it may be a small role compared to that of the blood and the brain. For example, consider the stomach. We have already mentioned the possibility of glucoreceptors in the stomach that would monitor glucose and send information to the brain. The stomach also contributes by monitoring the amount of food in the stomach. An empty stomach leads to hunger pangs, while a full stomach signals satiation to the brain. Ingested food is also monitored in the mouth by taste, smell, and muscle receptors involved in chewing and swallowing. All of this information is used by the brain to decide when to start or stop eating. But neither mouth factors nor stomach

factors alone are absolutely necessary. We can feed an animal working for food rewards by directly placing the food in his stomach, bypassing the mouth completely. The animal will regulate his weight within normal limits even though he never gets to taste or chew any of the food he has been working for. Likewise, we can surgically remove the stomach or cut the nerves from the stomach to the brain, and the animal will still be able to regulate his eating. Mouth and stomach factors play a role, but they are only part of the system.

Taste seems critically involved in regulating what we eat. This is shown by experiments on *specific needs.* We can create a specific need in an animal by feeding him a diet that is deficient in one particular item, say, salt. There appears to be a built-in system designed to detect and regulate sodium (salt) intake, and taste is critical to it. If you take a rat's favorite food and cut out all the sodium to produce a sodium deficiency, the rat, when given free access to several different foods, will immediately eat only the ones with sodium. But you can fool the rat with lithium, which tastes like sodium but does not satisfy his needs. So the reason that salted popcorn tastes especially good to you on some particular day may be that you have a momentary sodium deficiency. Of course, taste is also involved in the pleasurable aspects of food and much of human eating is centered on producing taste sensations that we have learned to enjoy.

External precipitators.   Take a chicken and give him all the food he wants until he stops eating. Then put the chicken into a cage with another chicken that is still eating. The first chicken will start eating again. Did you ever "stuff yourself" at dinner on the turkey and dressing and then somehow find room for the pumpkin pie with whipped cream? Did you ever eat something because it looked good or did you ever feel hungry all of a sudden because you smelled the pizza your dormitory neighbor just had delivered? It is obvious that stimuli outside the body also play a role in getting us to eat. The sight, smell, and anticipated taste sensations of food and even the presence of other eaters can induce us to eat.

Perhaps the most amazing fact about the external factors is that we regulate our food intake so well *despite* their continued presence. But there is also some impressive evidence that external stimuli can come to play a dominant role in food consumption for some people, overriding the internal regulatory systems we have been talking about. As you might guess, these are people with weight problems, the obese or overweight. We shall consider their plight in the "What Does It Mean?" section at the end of this chapter.

To summarize our discussion of eating, the key point is that the starting and stopping of eating is complexly controlled by many factors that work together. There is regulation of fat stores and the blood glucose level and monitoring of the sensations from the stomach and mouth. The hypothalamus is critically involved in the regulation process, but it is not the only crucial brain center, and it certainly is not the simple food thermostat we once thought.

Motivation as Instinct

The concept of motivation first entered psychology in the form of *instincts,* inherited patterns of behavior or predispositions to behave in particular ways. Thus, a man who fought a lot would be characterized as having a strong aggression instinct, and it was this instinct that motivated him to fight. The instinct conception of human motivation had its origins in the evolutionary theory of Darwin, which stressed the survival value of instinctive animal behaviors (particularly instincts centering on aggression, feeding, and reproduction) and which hypothesized that human beings are descendants of the lower animals. If animals are obviously creatures of instincts, then it followed that human beings are too. Freud also adopted an instinct-based theory of motivation. The instinct theory came to dominate psychology around the turn of this century, when two distinguished psychologists, William McDougall and William James, adopted the concept as the central explanatory construct in their theories.

But the popularity of instincts did not last long. Instinct theories were attacked as being useless for understanding behavior, basically because of the circular reasoning problem: He fights. Why? Because of a strong aggression instinct. How do you know he has such an instinct? Because he fights. Psychologists were also indiscriminate in their use of instincts. "Everything under the sun" was viewed as being caused by an instinct. At one point, a survey revealed that several thousands of instincts had been postulated by various theorists. The concept of instinct "explained" everything and nothing and so it gave way to another explanation.

What instinct gave way to was learning. Instinct theories imply that behavior is predominately a function of heredity. In the early years of this century, psychology turned radically away from such ideas, focusing instead on the concept of learning. Classical conditioning, Pavlov, Watson and the rise

of Behaviorism, to a large extent, were responsible for the decline of instinct theories. Behavior came to be viewed as primarily learned, not inherited. But learning theories quickly found that a motivational principle of some kind was necessary. Instead of instinct, they adopted the concept of *drive* as the central motivational force.

Ethology and the Resurrection of Instincts

The concept of instinct lay dormant until the 1930's, when it began to reappear in the writings of a small group of influential European zoologists studying animal behavior in natural settings. They called their science *ethology* and resurrected the concept of instinct in a new and scientifically acceptable form. The three most notable figures in ethology are Konrad Lorenz, Karl von Frisch, and Nikolaas Tinbergen. In 1973 they became the first scientists to win the Nobel Prize in physiology and medicine for work done strictly in the area of behavior.

Fixed action patterns. For the ethologists, an instinct is defined as an invariant behavior sequence that is universally observable in and unique to the members of a single species of animals. Furthermore, there is no learning involved—the behavior is innate to members of that species. In short, an instinct is an *innate fixed action pattern* uniquely characteristic of a particular species (species-specific). The crucial aspects of the behavior, then, are: (1) it is innate, (2) it is invariant from one time to the next, (3) it is universally found in all members of the species (if you look at the right time and place and at the appropriate sex), and (4) the pattern is unique to that species.

Of course, modern ethology theory consists of much more than just saying that the behavior is an instinct. The major concepts are illustrated in Figure 6–6. First, innate fixed action patterns do not just happen. Instead, they are triggered by stimuli known as *sign stimuli* or *releasing stimuli*. For example, the territorial defense action pattern of the flicker is "released" by the black "moustache" of the male flycatcher trying to intrude. For the squirrel, the action pattern of burying nuts is released by any object that is hard and round. Place a steel ball bearing on a concrete floor and the squirrel will go through all the motions (the fixed action pattern) of trying to bury it. Another example comes from Tinbergen's classic studies of a species of fish called the three-spined stickleback. Aggressive behavior in defense of territory in this fish is released by the red belly of the male intruder. Tinbergen used balsawood models of males in order

Learning From the Animals

Newsweek—In the 72 years since it was established, the Nobel Prize has honored nearly every milestone in the advancement of medicine and physiology, from the development of insulin, cortisone and antibiotics to the unraveling of the genetic code. Not once was the coveted award conferred for fundamental research in the field of psychology or behavior. Last week this omission was rectified. The $120,000 Nobel Prize in Medicine or Physiology for 1973 will be shared by the three major founders of the relatively new science of ethology—Konrad Lorenz, Karl von Frisch and Nikolaas Tinbergen.

Ethology (from the Greek word for "custom") is the scientific study of comparative behavior among animals in the wild, a field long mired in contentious debate among a number of theorists. There were the so-called "vitalists," who thought that instincts were mystical and inexplicable forces governing individual behavior. There were "reflexologists," who insisted that behavior was a purely mechanistic phenomenon. And then there were the behaviorists, who maintained with equal vigor that all behavior patterns could be explained by learning processes. What the ethologists did was to extricate the contestants from this muddle by showing that patterns of behavior among species are just as much the result of Darwinian natural selection as is the development of obvious anatomical and physiological features.

Fixed

In the process, the ethologists have also shown that life experience must be superimposed on genetically programmed patterns of behavior for normal development of the individual. Many of their observations of insects, fish and birds can be extended to man. In man, thanks to his superior cerebral cortex, learned behavior has largely replaced the mechanical, fixed behavior patterns of the lower animals. But the ethologists have also demonstrated that humans too exhibit a number of fixed patterns—such as the instinctive smile of the newborn infant in response to his mother's embrace—that have important implications for his well-being and, indeed, his survival.

Von Frisch, 86, a Vienna-born zoologist, carried out his most important research on bees while at the University of Munich. He showed that bees communicate by elaborate dancing movements of their bodies. For example, a scout bee that has found a source of nectar nearby performs a "round dance" on returning to the hive. The circular motions are imitated by the others until they interpret the signal and head for the source. If the nectar is situated farther away, the scout employs a tail-wagging dance, back and forth.

Von Frisch also found that each subspecies of bee has its own dance language; dances performed by the member of one subspecies turned out to be totally incomprehensible to a hive occupied by members of another subspecies. Von Frisch concluded that the language of the bees was inherited and not learned.

Energy

The importance of both instinctive and learned behavior to survival was demonstrated by Tinbergen, 66, a Dutch-born zoologist who has spent most of his career at Oxford. He discovered that a baby shore bird called the oyster catcher will first instinctively peck and chisel at any object it finds, as though trying to pry it open for food. Only by observing its mother will the young bird learn to focus its energy on opening shellfish. More recently, Tinbergen has applied his observations about animals to speculations about the nature of human violence and aggression.

Aggressiveness, he believes, evolved as an inheritable instinct in humans when man gave up the vegetarian existence he had shared with other primates and became a hunting carnivore. In doing so, humans evolved behavior patterns characteristic of wolves, including fierce group loyalties such as those that become manifest in nations going to war. Tinbergen points out that most animals seem reluctant to kill their own kind if confronted with demonstrations of peaceable intent. The development of long-range weapons, he fears, has freed man from such natural restraining mechanisms.

Like Tinbergen, with whom he once collaborated on studies of the egg-retrieving habits of the graylag goose, Lorenz also concluded that aggression in man has been programed into his genes and argued the theory forcefully in his celebrated 1963 book, "On Aggression." . . .

Follow

As an ethologist, the Vienna-born Lorenz is best known for his research on instinctive behavior among birds conducted at the Max Planck Institute for Behavioral Physiology in Seewiesen, West Germany. Lorenz showed that although animals are born with innate "fixed" patterns of behavior, certain key experiences early in life establish irreversible patterns of behavior. And his classic experiments in this field centered on the phenomenon known as "imprinting." . . . [See Figure 6.7.]

Round Dance

Wagging Dance

Von Frisch's bee language.

Lorenz with ducks and geese.

Figure 6–6
Important ethological concepts

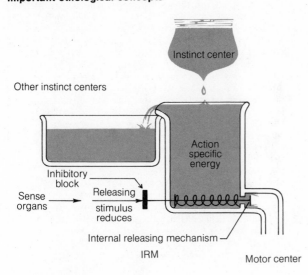

A hen searches frantically for a peeping chick she cannot see but ignores the chick in distress that she can see but not hear. Sound is the releasing signal for her maternal behavior. Can you suggest why sound rather than sight evolved as the releaser here?

Vacuum activity. Dr. Lorenz in his easy chair watching his fly catcher snap at an insect that is not there.

The male flicker's defense of territory instinct is released by the sight of another flicker in his territory provided the intruder has the black "moustache" that distinguishes the male from female. This black patch is the releaser stimulus.

Releasing stimuli are generally simple but specific and conspicuous so that in nature they would not be confused with other characteristics. For example, the herring gull's chicks peck at the red spot on the parents bill to get food.

Displacement activity. When one instinctual center is blocked from expression its energy may "spill over" to another center to produce displacement behavior. Thus ducks show preening and gulls show grass pulling as displacement behaviors.

to determine what would release the defensive aggression pattern. He found that a perfect replica of the male intruder would not release the pattern if the belly was not painted red, but that a very crude model with a red belly would release the pattern.

Even a floating beachball would release aggression if it was red.

Action-specific energy.   Figure 6–6 shows the general model that the ethologists developed to

Instinct or Intelligence?

Newsweek—Of all the crutch-words that modern scientists use to describe what they do not understand, "instinct" is probably the most pernicious. To evolutionary dogmatists, the concept of instinctive behavior has become a sacrosanct doctrine that reduces even the most advanced skills displayed by animals to mere mechanisms of genetic programming. To Austrian ethologist Karl von Frisch, however, the mysteries of nature are not so easily explained. A 1973 Nobel Prize winner for his research on the dance language of bees, von Frisch finds evidence in the behavior of insects, birds and other creatures suggesting that learning and individual experience play a greater role in the life of animals than evolutionary hard-liners care to admit. And in "Animal Architecture" *(306 pages. Harcourt Brace Jovanovich. $12.95)*, written in collaboration with his son, Otto, the 88-year-old scientist provides a loving, lavishly illustrated survey of nature's most ambitious animal constructions.

From the pebble-lined homes of the tropical jawfish to the simple tree-nests of apes, von Frisch explores the details of animal construction with an alert eye for craftsmanship. In his view, termites are the animal world's master architects and civil engineers. Some species build towering homes nearly 25 feet high—the equivalent, on a human scale, of a mile-high apartment building. In rainy climates, termites add roofs with overhanging eaves to protect their homes against torrential storms. In arid regions of the Australian outback, compass termites construct termitaries in the shape of axheads; the thin sides always point north and south so that the broad sides can catch the warming rays of the rising and setting sun. . . .

Equally impressive, though less complex, are the hanging nests of the penduline titmice, whose homes are so sturdily built that they are sometimes used as purses by the Masai of East Africa and even worn as slippers by children in eastern Europe. The nest of the knot-tying weaverbird is at once more delicate and more loosely plaited—and for a very good reason. The female of the species, it appears, is very fastidious. If she finds her mate's workmanship shoddy, she will spurn his sexual overtures, forcing him to unweave his handiwork and begin all over again. Obviously, von Frisch argues, the male is learning from his rebuff, not operating by instinct alone. Through repeated experience, individual birds learn how to build better nests, and through trial and error, they may also discover that some grasses make better materials for weaving than others.

Close observation of bowerbirds indicates to von Frisch that these amorous creatures exercise distinctive esthetic judgments in pursuit of sexual conquest. Unlike other birds, the males build their bowers exclusively for trysting, and they spare no effort in decorating their love nests. The bower is festooned with brightly colored flowers, berries and parrots' feathers, plus any bottle tops, bits of glass or other glittering baubles the male can steal from human habitation. As a finishing touch, a bowerbird may actually paint the inside of his arbor with the juice of blueberries that he has crushed in his beak. When all is ready, he stands back like a painter, scrutinizing his display. He will not hesitate to rearrange a blossom or a berry if the pattern does not please him. Courtship ends when a female slips into the bower and mates with her "decorator." Later, she builds a separate nest for the homely business of raising children.

If there is a lesson to be learned by humans from the bowerbirds' behavior, von Frisch theorizes, it is not that their antics merely resemble the seduction rites of suburban courtship. In fact, he suggests, the birds' activities—like those of other animals—actually anticipated "human behavior in comparable circumstances." Indeed, "Animal Architecture" offers several examples in which the birds and bees—not to mention whole colonies of wasps—have anticipated by thousands of years some of man's most useful artifacts.

Fishing nets, for instance, are nothing new to the larvae of caddis flies, who have been spinning them in ponds for untold generations. . . . Wasps were producing paper centuries before man learned how to write, and the American Indian, it is said, learned how to fashion clay jars by watching potter wasps at work.

For sheer craftsmanship and efficiency of construction, however, no one—not even *Homo sapiens*—has yet surpassed the skill of bees. The hexagonal shape of honeycombs, von Frisch declares, provides the most functional use of space the bees could have designed. The strength of the comb's thin, light construction is measured by the fact that only 1.4 ounces of wax are used for a comb that will hold 4 pounds of honey. And the precision of its design is demonstrated by the fact that the thickness of each cell wall is 0.073 millimeter, with a tolerance of no more than 0.002 millimeter. "None of these things just 'happen'," von Frisch insists. "They are the result of work directed to a purpose."

But directed by what? Among lower forms of life, especially social insects like bees, von Frisch is willing to concede that instinct is the governing force. But the more man learns about the subtle complexity of animal architecture, von Frisch believes, the less likely he will be to make a distinction between instinct and intelligence. Somewhere between the extremes of genetic programing and conscious rationality, animals reveal acquired skills that command respect even from mankind.

Potter-wasp nests: Models for man.

Australian termite towers: Master architects and civil engineers.

account for fixed action patterns. It is a drive-energy model that states that members of the species inherit action-specific energies to motivate specific fixed action patterns. The energy builds up (we might say the animal is becoming predisposed to respond) and is finally released (we might say precipitated) when the sense organs perceive the sign stimuli. If no sign stimuli or releasers are encountered, the energy will continue to build up, finally bursting forth and releasing the behavior in the absence of a releasing stimulus. When this happens, the behavior is called a *vacuum activity.* Another principle states that competing action patterns (say, both an aggressive pattern and a sexual pattern) can block each other, leading to a build-up and overflow of action-specific energy into other instinct centers, from which the energy is then released. Under these circumstances, the animal is said to be engaging in displacement activity, which might take a number of forms, grooming for example. The animal is neither aggressive nor sexy, but grooms (displacement activity) because the energy from the sexual and aggressive instincts has overflowed into the grooming instinct centers. The interpretations of vacuum activity and displacement activity have been among the most controversial aspects of ethological theory, with critics saying that such a theory does not really explain these behaviors in any but an after-the-fact fashion. This has led some to seriously question the concept of action-specific energy as a useful explanatory principle.

Imprinting

The phenomenon that has made ethology and Konrad Lorenz famous is known as *imprinting.* Lorenz demonstrated that there is a *critical period* early in life when newborn species members become attached or imprinted to members of that species in a way that probably underlies their social and sexual behavior later in life. Using graylag geese as his subjects, he noted that the young goslings follow their mother in a neat line behind her. His experiments showed that during the critical period in the early hours of life, the geese will follow any large moving object they encounter. Usually, of course, this is the mother, but Lorenz managed to imprint some young geese on himself (see Figure 6–7). In fact, these animals will follow a lawn mower if that is the object they see during the critical period.

Ethology and its revised treatment of instinct is not without its critics and problems. We have already mentioned the problem with displacement and

**Figure 6–7
Imprinting**

A group of young goslings follow the noted ethologist Konrad Lorenz. Goslings instinctively follow the first large moving object they encounter after birth (normally the mother), a phenomenon known as imprinting.

vacuum activity. Another major problem has been the tendency of ethologists to generalize their findings to human beings without adequate evidence. Lorenz, for example, has written a book, *On Aggression,* that implies that man's aggressiveness is basically instinctive. The ethologists have been helped in this endeavor by such authors as Desmond Morris *(The Naked Ape)* and Robert Ardrey *(The Territorial Imperative),* who have taken great liberties in applying instinctive concepts to humans. Do human beings have a personal territory that they instinctively will defend against intruders? Are such instincts responsible for world problems such as the Arab-Israeli conflict and war in general? The ideas are certainly provocative and worthy of study, but it is much too soon to decide. Perhaps a significant segment of human behavior is motivated by instinctual factors, but at present the evidence is merely suggestive and not complete.

Motivation as the Search for Optimal Arousal

As we have seen, for a long time psychologists emphasized the push aspect of motivation. The key

Do human beings have an instinct for territoriality? In many animal species the evidence for a territorial instinct is very convincing. Consider the "right to own property," fence building, and the rise of suburbia. Might human territorial instincts play a role in war?

New Yorker, May 29. 1971. Drawing by Ed Fisher; © 1971 The New Yorker Magazine,

concept was "drive"—our behavior was driven or pushed toward relevant goals. Deprivation led to drive, which led to arousal or energy mobilization, which pushed our behavior until we found the goal. Attaining the goal then satisfied the drive—that is, the goal object reduced the drive and with it the arousal and energy. In short, we were seen as being motivated to keep our arousal level at a minimum, to keep our drives down to nothing.

One of the main problems with this general formulation of motivation as drive is that it is perfectly clear that we do not always try to keep our level of arousal low. Much of the time we behave in precisely the opposite manner—we try to increase our arousal level. To do this, we seek rather than avoid sources of stimulation. On these occasions, external sources of stimulation become positive incentives that we will work to expose ourselves to. Consider the number of people who went out of their way to see the highly arousing movie *The Exorcist.* Think of mountain climbers, daredevils, race-car drivers, and ski jumpers. Consider the

things you might say you do for "fun," such as playing bridge or poker, watching TV, reading mystery stories, and playing tennis. A lot of these things share a common feature—they involve exposing yourself to external stimuli that will arouse you. These activities can hardly be described as attempts to keep your arousal level at a minimum. Obviously, then, a theory that implies that we try to keep arousal at a minimum is just plain wrong.

But it took some experimental evidence to put drive theory in its proper place. Some psychologists believe that drive theory is needed to account for our biological needs, but others argue that it can be completely dispensed with. In its place has come the notion of arousal level and the crucial assumption that we are motivated to keep our level of arousal at some optimal and nonzero point. Let us take a brief look at some of the studies that support this idea.

The Need for Stimulation

There were several lines of attack on the theory that we seek to minimize stimulation and drive. First, there were the studies of curiosity in animals, mentioned earlier, that showed monkeys will learn new responses and perform old ones just to get a chance to look out of a window to see the laboratory. Drive theory tried to account for this behavior by postulating a curiosity drive, but it never was clear what it was you deprived an animal of and what this did to his body that resulted in the activation of the drive.

In other studies, it was demonstrated that monkeys would work on and solve mechanical puzzles left lying around in their cages. The monkeys got no extrinsic rewards for playing with the puzzles or solving them; yet they kept on doing the latch problems over and over. Drive theory responded with the concept of a *manipulation* drive, although again there was no explanation of the manner of drive activation and the underlying source of the drive. And, of course, the only way we knew that animals had a drive to manipulate things was the fact that they manipulated things.

Next were the demonstrations of exploratory behavior. Rats will learn a new response apparently just to have the opportunity to explore. Say you have a two-choice maze in which a left turn leads the rat into another maze that is very complex and a right turn merely leads to the end of the corridor. Rats will learn to turn left apparently just for the opportunity to explore the complex maze, and if you reverse the two choices, the rat will learn to turn right to get to the complex maze. No food or water or sex or any other tangible reward is offered. Drive theory responded to these data with an exploratory drive.

But as drives proliferated, drive theory became less and less useful as an explanation. People would see an organism do something and to explain it would say that there was a drive to do that thing, which explained nothing. Remember the circularity in reasoning about motivation that we discussed earlier.

There were two more, quite startling demonstrations that we are not motivated to keep stimulation at a minimum. First, James Olds and Peter Milner made an extremely important discovery while studying the effects of electrical brain stimulation on behavior. Electrodes had been embedded deep into the brains of rats during surgery, making it possible to deliver electrical stimulation to certain brain areas. What Olds and Milner discovered was that the rats liked it! The rats would work hard to have their brains stimulated in certain areas. It has since been demonstrated that a rat will press a bar thousands and thousands of times a day to activate brain stimulation. There have

Figure 6–8
A sensory deprivation study

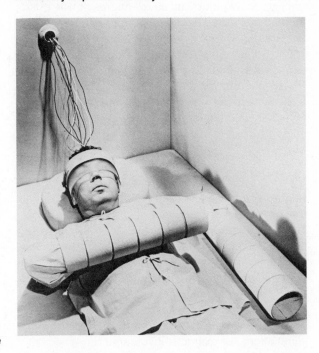

In a series of experiments at McGill University, students were paid $25 a day to stay in a room in which stimulation was reduced to a bare minimum. They wore an eyeshade that reduced vision to a dim haze and arm casts that kept their hands from feeling anything. They were placed in a soundproof room where they could hear nothing but the continual hum of a fan. Not many could stay for more than 2 days, and some very bizarre behaviors occurred, such as hallucinations.

been reports that, if the electrodes are in the right place, the rats will spend so much time pressing for stimulation that they do not have time to eat. Correspondingly, there are areas in the brain where the electrical stimulation is not pleasant, but extremely unpleasant. The rats will work hard to *prevent* the stimulation in these areas.

The second demonstration addressed the question of stimulation from the opposite point of view. If we are seeking to keep stimulation at a minimum, then the minimum state must be the most highly desired. What would be the consequences of being in a state of stimulus or sensory deprivation? The answer came from the work of W. H. Bexton, W. Heron, and T. H. Scott. These investigators paid undergraduate students up to $25 a day to participate in a *sensory deprivation* experiment. Subjects were to remain in a room under conditions designed to minimize sensory stimulation (see Figure 6–8) for as long as they possibly could. The subjects, of course, had adequate food, water, oxygen, heat, and toilet facilities. But every effort was made to cut off all other sensory input. The important result was that no students lasted very long in this environment despite the high rate of pay for those days (about 1953). Some of the students reported bizarre experiences, including hallucinations, after enduring the situation for several hours. All in all, the environment was not a pleasant one. The conclusion is that an environment designed to minimize stimulus input is not something we generally seek out.

Optimal Arousal Level

Studies like those just cited have led to the notion that arousal level is crucially involved in motivation. The idea is that we are motivated to maintain an optimal, presumably moderate, level of arousal. The arousal level at any moment is a direct function of the total amount of stimulation (from both external and internal sources) impinging upon the organism. If the current arousal level is above optimum, the organism will be motivated to reduce the level of stimulation. For example, if you are terribly frightened (and thus above the optimal level of arousal) when watching a scary vampire movie, you might cover your eyes or actually leave the theater during the most frightening parts of the movie to keep the arousal level from getting too extreme. On the other hand, if the current arousal level is below optimum, the organism will be motivated to do things that will increase the level of stimulation. This is why you might have gone to see the vampire movie in the first place, for example.

Note that what is involved here is basically a homeostatic system designed to keep the arousal level within some acceptable, moderate, reasonably optimal range. If we become overaroused or underaroused, we are motivated to alter things until the arousal level returns to the normal range. One implication of this is that any stimulus, if it is strong enough, will be a source of motivation. It will increase the arousal level so much that the person will be overaroused, resulting in behavior motivated to eliminate the stimulus or reduce its intensity. An extremely loud and continuous noise, for example, would motivate you to do something about it. Similarly, too little stimulation would result in the arousal level drifting below the optimal range, and you would be motivated to increase stimulation. When you are alone in your room and bored (too little stimulation), you might turn on the radio, or you might leave the room to go watch TV or play cards, or you might entertain yourself with a good murder mystery.

Fireman's Holiday

Time—In the firehouses of Norman Rockwell's bucolic America, firemen passed the hours between alarms playing checkers and showing off the polished brass and bright red trucks to wide-eyed young visitors. But for the volunteer firemen of Genoa, Texas, in suburban Houston, that was not enough. In the past three years, eight bored Genoa firemen have set about 40 fires in abandoned buildings and grass fields. As soon as the blazes were going, the arsonists would dash back to the firehouse and rush off to put out their own fires.

The Genoa firemen were quite busy until they made the mistake of setting fire to a barn owned by the brother of a Houston fire department official. An investigation of the blaze led to the Genoa firehouse, and the overeager fire fighters were exposed. Explained one of the firemen charged last week with arson: "We'd hang around the station on the night shift without a thing to do. We just wanted to get the red light flashing and the bells clanging."

There is strong evidence that lack of stimulation can be a source of motivation designed to increase the level of stimulation. Here is an example of this principle in action.

What constitutes the optimum arousal level will depend upon the task at hand, as we mentioned in the discussion of the Yerkes-Dodson Law. Listening to loud rock music on the radio might be a source of arousal that would move you toward the optimum if you are alone with nothing to do. However, the same radio program might move you away from the optimum if you are alone with a lot of difficult mathematics homework to do. It will also be true that the incentive value of a particular external stimulation will depend upon your arousal level at the moment. Listening to a tape-recorded listing of all the closing prices on the New York Stock Exchange might not be something you would want to do if you are already moderately aroused. But subjects in sensory-deprivation experiments, who are underaroused, are often quite happy to get to hear about the daily fortunes of IBM, AT&T, and GM. A quiet walk in the woods might be nice if you are troubled and worried about lots of things (overaroused), but it might not be so nice if you are lonely and bored with the world.

Motivation as a Personality Characteristic

When we think about human behavior and the factors that motivate it, we are likely to conclude that instincts, biological needs for food and water, a need for optimal stimulation levels, and related factors do not account for very much. Certainly our behavior does not look much like the fixed action patterns characteristic of instinctive behaviors. Moreover, most of us are fortunate enough to have ready access to adequate food and water. True, some of the things we do are probably motivated by these needs, but these behaviors seem to be rather minor and infrequent aspects of our behavior. Maybe we do most of the things we do largely for fun and excitement so as to maintain an optimal arousal level. But isn't there a lot more to human behavior than just maintaining optimal arousal?

Psychologists who have attempted to answer questions about the motivation for uniquely human behaviors have, in general, offered answers that treat the concept of motivation as a personality characteristic. Like motivation, personality is a concept that is used to account for variability in behavior, and many personality theorists have made motivational concepts central in describing personality. This is rather like saying that your personality can be described by describing your motives or, more specifically, your needs. In short, we might say, "You are what you need." If you need to be with people, we say you are friendly, extroverted, and gregarious. If you need to work hard in order to beat out the next man or woman, we say you are hard-driving or energetic. If you need to win so badly that you will do anything to achieve victory, we say that you are ruthless, dishonest, and heartless. To some extent, then, a description of the things you need is both a description of your personality and a description of the things that motivate you. In other words, to understand human motivation completely, we will have to understand personality.

Henry Murray's Work on Psychogenic Needs

The pioneer worker in this field was Henry Murray. For him the concept of need was central and he spent a great deal of time attempting to objectify the measurement of needs and to identify the various needs that human beings have. He is perhaps most famous for having devised the Thematic Apperception Test (TAT) with Christiana Morgan (see Figure 6–9). In this test, the subject is shown a picture and asked to make up a story about what is going on in the picture. The basic idea is that the subject "projects" into the story his own needs, and so a careful analysis of the stories will tell a great deal about the person who made them up. Murray also developed questionnaires for assessing needs in a more direct way. His intensive scrutiny of a

Figure 6–9
Measuring human motives and needs

The object in the TAT test is to write a short story about what is happening in a picture like the one above. You might try it with this picture. Tell in your story (1) what is happening and who the people are, (2) what led up to the situation shown in the picture, (3) what the people in the picture are thinking and feeling, and (4) what will happen in the future. Does your story tell you anything about yourself and your motives and needs?

small group of subjects led him to believe that there are many independent human needs. Table 6–2 lists 20 representative needs that Murray felt were present in various degrees in each of us. This list has been expanded and modified somewhat in his later writings, but it should give you a good idea of what Murray sees as the needs of humanity. The listing is primarily of the *psychogenic* (psychological or learned) needs, as opposed to what Murray called the *viscerogenic needs,* such as needs for food, water, and oxygen.

Murray made another important point, namely, that each person has a hierarchy of needs; some needs are more important than others, with the viscerogenic needs being most important because they are so directly tied to survival. The needs will be satisfied in order of their priority for each

Table 6–2
Twenty human needs identified by Henry Murray

Need	Brief definition
N Abasement	To submit passively to external force. To accept injury, blame, criticism, punishment. To admit inferiority, error, wrongdoing, or defeat.
N Achievement	To accomplish something difficult. To master, manipulate, or organize physical objects, human beings, or ideas as rapidly and as independently as possible. To surpass others and excel oneself.
N Affiliation	To draw near and enjoyably cooperate or reciprocate with others. To adhere and remain loyal to a friend.
N Aggression	To overcome opposition forcefully. To revenge an injury. To attack, injure, or kill another.
N Autonomy	To get free, shake off restraint, break out of confinement. To resist coercion and restriction. To be independent and free to act according to impulse.
N Counteraction	To master or make up for a failure by restriving. To overcome weaknesses, to repress fear. To efface a dishonor by action. To search for obstacles and difficulties to overcome.
N Defendance	To defend the self against assault, criticism, and blame. To conceal or justify a misdeed, failure, or humiliation.
N Deference	To admire and support a superior. To praise, honor, or eulogize. To conform to custom.
N Dominance	To control one's human environment. To influence or direct the behavior of others by suggestion, persuasion, command, or restraint.
N Exhibition	To excite, amaze, fascinate, entertain, shock, intrigue, amuse, or entice others.
N Harmavoidance	To avoid pain, physical injury, illness, and death.
N Infavoidance	To avoid humiliation by leaving embarrassing situations or avoiding conditions that may lead to belittlement. To refrain from action because of the fear of failure.
N Nurturance	To give sympathy to and gratify the needs of a helpless person. To feed, help, support, console, protect, comfort, nurse, heal.
N Order	To put things in order. To achieve cleanliness, organization, balance, neatness, tidiness, and precision.
N Play	To act for "fun" without further purpose. To like to laugh and make jokes. To seek enjoyable relaxation of stress.
N Rejection	To exclude, abandon, expel, or remain indifferent to an inferior person.
N Sentience	To seek and enjoy sensuous impressions.
N Sex	To form and further an erotic relationship. To have sexual intercourse.
N Succorance	To be nursed, supported, sustained, surrounded, protected, loved, advised, guided, indulged, forgiven, consoled. To always have a supporter.
N Understanding	To ask or answer general questions. To be interested in theory. To speculate, formulate, analyze, and generalize.

person—if two incompatible needs arise, the stronger need, which is higher in the hierarchy, will be satisfied first. If you need water and you need aggression, chances are you will drink first and fight later.

Finally, Murray also recognized that motivation is partly a function of environmental factors, which he called *press*. You may have, as a personality characteristic, a strong need for achievement (*n* achievement); particular environmental situations will arouse this need. For example, seeing a friend beat someone in a chess game might arouse your own achievement motive and cause you to challenge your friend. This would be a case of press for achievement (*p* achievement). Seeing a picture of a juicy steak would constitute p food, which, along with your viscerogenic need for food (n food), would motivate you to eat something. So motivation for

Murray is a result of the combined action of personal needs (characteristics of people) and press (characteristics of the environment). We would classify the needs as predisposing factors, and the press as precipitating factors.

The human needs we will discuss in this section are all based on a model like Murray's. During psychological development, each person acquires (learns) certain psychological needs. Different people acquire different strengths of the various needs and thus different hierarchies of needs. Initially, the psychological needs develop from the inherited, innate, biological needs, but later these needs somehow become independent of the biological needs and the goals that satisfy these needs become ends in themselves. Here is an example of how this might happen. We begin with a biological need for food and water that for a young

Abraham Maslow and the Hierarchy of Human Needs

The psychologist most often associated with the idea of a hierarchy of needs, arranged in order of importance, is Abraham Maslow. His writings have had tremendous impact in the modern movement known as humanistic psychology. Indeed he was one of the founders of this movement. Maslow grouped the various needs (like those postulated by Henry Murray) into five categories and arranged them in the order shown in Figure 6–10. With the exception of the highest need, self-actualization, the needs are self-explanatory.

It was his concept of self-actualization that made Maslow such an important figure in the humanistic psychology movement. Self-actualization is conceived of as a need to fulfill oneself, "to become whatever one is capable of becoming." It is a need to develop and utilize one's talents, abilities, and potential fully. It is a need that very few people have ever satisfied, and Maslow spent a great deal of his time studying people (such as Eleanor Roosevelt and Albert Einstein) who he thought had become self-actualized.

The ordering of the needs in the pyramid in Figure 6–10 reflects several features: (1) the relative potency of the needs—we will attempt to satisfy a lower need like safety before satisfying a need above it such as love; (2) the order in which the needs develop in our lifetime—we are born with only the physiological needs and then develop safety and security needs, then love, then self-esteem, and finally, much later, self-actualization; (3) the order in which the needs emerged in the evolution of human beings; and (4) the degree to which the need must be satisfied in order to survive.

The needs higher in the hierarchy will emerge only as the lower ones become satisfied. We will not need love-belongingness and self-esteem if we have not first satisfied our physiological and security needs. If we live in fear for our safety or in anxiety about where our next meal will come from, we will have no need for love and self-esteem. In our society, where safety and security and physiological needs are reasonably well satisfied for everyone, we appear to be motivated largely by needs for love and self-esteem. Maslow felt that our inability to satisfy these needs was the major cause of neurotic psychopathology in this country. Ideally, of course, a society would provide for all the lower needs and allow for the emergence of the need for

Abraham Maslow

self-actualization in everyone. Although few people may ever fully satisfy this need, everyone should be striving at this level in the pyramid, free of the lower needs. In fact, for Maslow, such persons are no longer "striving" but are "being"—being themselves rather than being people who are seeking something external to themselves.

**Figure 6–10
Maslow's hierarchy of needs**

According to Maslow's motivational theory, human needs form a hierarchy, and lower needs must be satisfied before higher needs are felt.

infant is satisfied by other people, mainly the parents. The infant is almost entirely dependent on other people and is likely to be most happy when other people are around, fulfilling the needs for nourishment, playing with and entertaining him, and so on. Because of this kind of continued exposure, the people who tend the infant become secondary reinforcers (see Chapter 4), having been continuously associated with his general state of well-being. As secondary reinforcers, people then become goal objects themselves, and the child will want to be with people and will want these people to be good to him, to like him and take care of him. The child will behave in ways designed to win the approval and affection of people. After a while, we might conclude that the child has developed a need to be with people and win the approval of people (n affiliation in Murray's list) and a need to be nursed, loved, and protected by people (n succorance). If the people in the child's life themselves value and reward achievement, the child may develop a strong need to achieve (n achievement) in order to win adult approval.

Although this is merely a speculative example, you can see how three of the human needs that Murray identified might develop and be learned by the child. Given certain kinds of experiences, the child will become predisposed to behaving in certain ways later on in life, when the circumstances arouse the need, or in other words, when the need-related behavior is precipitated by the circumstances. Of course, different children have different experiences and different parents, who themselves have different needs and different values. Out of these differences in environmental circumstances, each child learns a different set of priorities. Each child develops the human needs to various degrees or strengths and emerges into adulthood with his own hierarchy of psychological needs. It is this variation in the strengths of the various needs that largely accounts for the variation in adult personality, that is, for the fact that one person is a hard-driving, success-seeking fighter and another is an easy-going, introverted pacifist. We shall now turn our attention to some of the specific human needs that psychologists have found most interesting.

The Need for Achievement

Largely because of the efforts of David McClelland and J. W. Atkinson, the need for achievement (*n ach* in their shorthand) has been studied intensively. These investigators elaborated on Murray's TAT techniques for measuring needs and developed sophisticated scoring systems for the stories that subjects told in response to the carefully selected pictures. Their attention turned first to n ach, the need to excel, overcome obstacles, attain a high standard, accomplish the difficult. In the United States, we are so achievement oriented that for us, motivation "really" means achievement motivation.

Figure 6–11
Problem solving as a function of achievement motivation

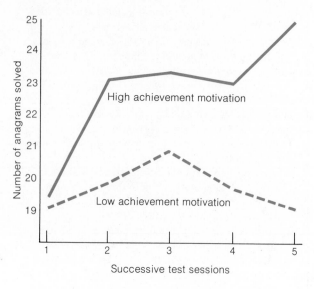

High achievement motivation as measured by the TAT *correlates* with success in solving a series of anagram problems. Why doesn't this study prove that increased achievement motivation *causes* better performance on the anagrams?

After developing a TAT scoring system for n ach, McClelland and Atkinson demonstrated that they could arouse the achievement motive (precipitate it) simply by telling subjects in an experiment that they had failed. The subjects took a group of tests and were told that they had done poorly and then were asked to tell TAT stories. The experience with failure aroused or precipitated the achievement motive, as measured by an increase in the number of achievement themes and elements in the stories. These psychologists went on to demonstrate that individuals vary in their need for achievement and that each person has a relatively stable level of n ach over time.

Performance differences due to n ach. Many studies have shown that people with high n ach as measured by the TAT procedure do better than people with low n ach on a variety of experimental laboratory tasks, such as solving anagrams and doing arithmetic problems (see Figure 6–11). It has also been demonstrated that high n ach people perform better in school than low n ach people with comparable intelligence. In the business world, high n ach people advance further than low n ach people

Figure 6–12
Parental influence on achievement motivation

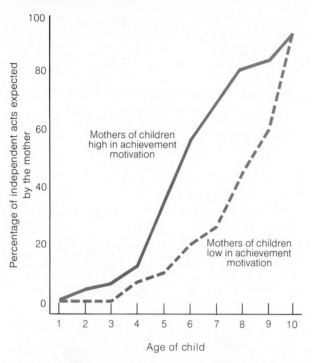

Achievement motives seem to be culturally instilled or learned and parents seem to be the major teachers. As the graph shows, mothers of children who score high in achievement motivation expect their children to accomplish acts of independence at an earlier age.

with the same training and opportunity for advancement.

As suggested earlier, achievement motivation is apparently developed during childhood and is determined largely by the cultural and parental emphasis placed on achievement. These values are transmitted to the children during their socialization into the culture. One study, for example, demonstrated that mothers who themselves were high in n ach behaved differently toward their children than mothers low in n ach (see Figure 6–12). High n ach mothers demanded that their children become independent and self-sufficient at an earlier age than low n ach mothers. Low n ach mothers were more protective of their children and placed greater restrictions on them for longer periods of time.

McClelland has looked at n ach in different cultures and found very stable cross-cultural differences. He developed techniques for scoring a culture's literature for themes relating to

achievement, particularly the readers used in the schools. He has demonstrated that the amount of achievement in the literature of a culture correlates with the rate of economic growth in that culture, as well as the emphasis the culture places on independence. In one study, children's readers were examined and scored for n ach. Taking the readers used in 1925, McClelland attempted to predict economic growth for the country in 1950, 25 years later, when the children who learned from those readers were now the adults responsible for the growth. Believe it or not, he was successful —countries with 1925 readers low in n ach showed less economic growth in the 1950's than countries with high n ach readers. More recently, McClelland has gone back in history and found many fascinating relationships between n ach and the growth and fate of various cultures, societies, and governments.

Success and failure.   More recently, it has been suggested that n ach is not a simple unidimensional personality characteristic, but a complex combination of factors. Atkinson, for example, has suggested that at least two factors are involved in achievement, a *need for success* and a counteracting *fear of failure,* and that different people have different combinations of these two tendencies. He has also stressed the importance of the situational factors operating at any given time, particularly the probability or chances of success or failure on a particular task and the incentive value of success or failure. If the task at hand is so difficult that nobody could possibly do it, then failing is nothing to be ashamed of and failing would have no negative incentive value. Likewise, if the task is so easy that anybody can do it, then achieving success is not worth much; success has little positive incentive value. Also, the goal itself (independent of the probability of getting it) has a positive incentive value that will determine the amount of motivation to achieve it. A person high in n ach will not indiscriminately attempt to achieve every conceivable goal. He might work very hard to achieve a goal of great value, but expend little effort to achieve a prize of no value.

In addition to suggesting that fear of failure can counteract the need for success, Atkinson also reminds us of the importance of precipitating factors in motivation. While a need to achieve (or a fear of failure) may be a stable predisposing feature, there will be no motivation without precipitation. You need both a task to be done (which has associated with it certain chances of success or failure) and

To Precipitate, Appeal to the Predisposition

We have emphasized in this chapter that motivation is a joint product of predisposition and precipitation. In the area of human motivation, this joint action is beautifully illustrated by an experiment done by Elizabeth G. French. From a large population, she selected large numbers of two types of people —achievers and affiliators. The achievers were selected because they scored high on n ach and low on n aff, meaning they are predisposed toward achievement but not affiliation. Just the opposite was true for the affiliators—they were high on n aff and low on n ach, meaning they are predisposed toward affiliation, not achievement.

French then set groups of four achievers and groups of four affiliators to work on a group problem-solving task that required the people to work together to get the correct solutions. The precipitating factor was introduced in the form of feedback to the groups about how they were doing. French used two different feedback techniques: (1) by telling the groups that they were working efficiently, achieving many correct responses, she could "appeal" to the achievement motive as a way to precipitate increased motivation to perform; or (2) by telling the groups that they were working well together, cooperating, she could appeal to the affiliation motive. But giving an achievement appeal should only work if the group is composed of people predisposed to achievement—it should fail with a group predisposed to affiliation. Likewise, the affiliation appeal should work only with the groups composed of people high in n aff, and not with groups with high n ach members.

Her results, shown in Figure 6–13, confirmed these predictions. When the work group was an

achievement group (all people high in n ach), performance on the task was better with the achievement feedback than with the affiliation feedback. Just the opposite was true with the affiliation groups (all people high in n aff). In short, an affiliation appeal will not precipitate much behavior in someone with a low level of predisposition toward affiliation (low n aff). It is like trying to get Howard Hughes to go through "hell week" so he can join the fraternity. Likewise, an achievement appeal will not work on people who are low in n ach. The motivation is a joint function of the predisposition and the precipitation.

Figure 6–13
Effects of the interaction of motivation and feedback on task performance

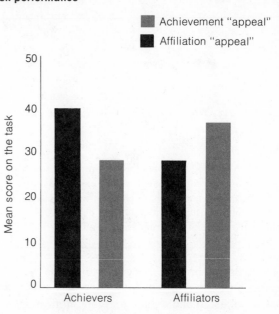

positive and/or negative incentives (goals to be achieved that have positive incentive value for the person or consequences of failure that have negative incentive value). As we have seen over and over again, motivation is a product of predisposing needs and precipitating incentives and conditions.

The Need for Affiliation

We are social creatures who derive much of our satisfaction from other people. We join clubs, sororities, fraternities, weight-watchers, and Gamblers Anonymous. We try hard to make friends and often become very dependent upon them. Henry Murray would say we have a need for affiliation (n aff), and that like n ach, this functions to motivate

us, making particular goals, such as being admitted to the local chapter of the Loyal Order of the Friends of Harvey Wallbanger, positive incentives. Likewise, other events, such as anything that would cause the defection of friends, will serve as negative incentives to the person with high n aff. Such a person will avoid hurting the feelings of his friends or avoid doing things that his friends would find shocking.

Elizabeth French has developed a special set of test items for measuring and distinguishing between n aff and n ach. She has shown that subjects high in n aff perform better on a simple task than subjects low in n aff under extremely pleasant and relaxed conditions designed to avoid arousing n ach instead of n aff. French concluded that the desire on the part of the high n aff subjects to please the experimenter, cooperate, and be friendly is what motivated them to perform better. In another experiment, French studied how people high in n ach and n aff go about picking partners to work with. People high in n ach choose partners who are competent at performing the task at hand (rather than choosing friends for partners), presumably because their goal is to succeed at the task. In contrast, people high in n aff tend to choose their friends as partners, as opposed to selecting partners on the basis of ability. When choosing sides for a game of volleyball, football, or charades, do you pick your friends for your team or the people who you believe will be the best players?

Like n ach, n aff is conceived of as a personality predisposition, presumably learned in childhood and possessed in varying degrees by different people. Like n ach, n aff is also subject to precipitation by the current circumstances. A person high in n aff will not be motivated by the goal of affiliating with a person or group of people who are extremely unpleasant and disliked. Instead, such people will be motivated by a friendly request to cooperate, to help out for the common good, given that the request comes from a person or group that has positive incentive value. Obviously, a dedicated member of the John Birch Society is not going to be motivated by a need to affiliate with the Communist party. Finally, it has been suggested that the desire to affiliate ourselves with others is not really a need, but that instead affiliation is a goal for some other need, either our need to escape or avoid anxiety or our need to have others approve of us, known as a need for social approval, our next topic.

The Need for Social Approval

Perhaps the most fundamental purely psychological need is the need for social approval—the need to have others approve of us and our actions. It is obvious, for example, that the need to affiliate with others could be based on a need for approval. Also, one could argue that the need to achieve is ultimately based on a need to win recognition and approval from others. If others did not approve of striving to achieve then people probably would not strive to achieve. The cross-cultural and family differences in achievement motivation suggest that approval from others is an important factor in determining the strength of the achievement motive. There is almost no limit to what some people will do to get certain other people to approve of and

therefore like them. Conversely, such people will often do almost anything to avoid creating the circumstances that will lead others to disapprove of and therefore dislike them.

The need for approval is an important motive for understanding much of our social behavior. Consider, for example, why people tend to be conformists, to do what others do or what they think others would do. The pioneer investigators of the need for social approval are Douglas Crowne and David Marlowe. Together these investigators have developed a test to measure social desirability, the need to be liked by others or to be socially desirable. They show that people who score high and low on the test and thus presumably have high and low motives for approval sometimes behave in vastly different ways. In one experiment, the subjects were asked to spend 25 minutes doing an incredible task: taking 12 spools and one at a time putting them into a small box, then emptying the box and starting over again. Afterward Crowne and Marlowe asked the subjects how much they enjoyed the task. Subjects with high approval motives, believe it or not, said they enjoyed the task, more so at least than subjects with low approval motives. In addition, high need-for-approval subjects said they learned more from the task, rated the experiment as more scientifically important, and had a greater desire to participate in similar experiments than low need-for-approval subjects. Would you pack and repack spools (and say that you enjoyed doing it) in order gain the approval of the person who asked you to do it?

In another study, Crowne and Marlowe showed subjects slides containing two clusters of dots, one clearly larger than the other. The subject was asked to indicate which cluster was larger, a very easy task indeed, except that there were other "subjects" in the room (actually not subjects but assistants to Crowne and Marlowe) who lied and said the wrong answer before the real subject could speak. The results showed that on 59 percent of these trials where the confederates lied, the high need-for-approval subjects lied also. The low need-for-approval subjects conformed and lied only 34 percent of the time. These results show that subjects with high and low approval motives behave differently, and they suggest that conformity (in this case, agreeing with the judgment of others) comes from the need to win the approval of others. It can be very sobering to stop and think of our own behavior and ask how much of it is motivated by a desire to be desirable.

A Final Note of Caution

The work on human motives as personality traits is very appealing and seems to contribute greatly to our understanding of human behavior. However, we must remember that there are pitfalls (see the section on dispositional theories of personality in Chapter 9). With a long list of needs, you can account for just about everything by saying that the person did what he did to satisfy such and such a need. It is the same problem we encountered with the long list of instincts that were once used to explain everything, or the long list of drives. A long list of needs may not be as much of an improvement as it first appears. We must remember that there will have to be independent ways of defining and measuring these needs to avoid saying circular things like: "She works so hard because she has a high need to achieve and I know this because I see her working so hard all the time." It is for this reason that so much time has been spent investigating ways to measure human needs with various kinds of tests, such as the TAT story-telling techniques. But there is still a lot of room for improvement. The tests are not highly reliable and they may be measuring other things besides the intended need. Another problem is that people are not as consistent in their behavior as such theories imply. For example, a person with a high need for approval does not always behave in a way designed to get approval—sometimes the person seems to be seeking approval, at other times just the opposite tendency appears. This may just mean that we have a long way to go in understanding the precipitating conditions for behavior; but it may also mean that it is not very useful to speak of enduring stable traits, such as a high need for approval. Behavior may be so much a consequence of the precipitating circumstances that personality predispositions are only modestly useful in predicting what a person will do in any given situation.

Note that most of the studies we have talked about in this section are basically correlational in character. If we pick out people who are high and low in achievement motivation and see that the highs do better on some task than the lows, we merely have a correlation between n ach and performance. This does *not* mean the n ach differences caused the performance differences. Perhaps high n ach people are more intelligent, or better coordinated, or stronger, or whatever, than low n ach people. If so, the performance difference could be due to that factor and not to n ach. It is not easy to reach unequivocal conclusions in this complex area of human motivation. Thus, we must remember to be cautious.

Emotion

People love and hate. They are afraid, anxious, and sometimes terrorized. They are happy and sad, angry and mad. People are emotional. They have feelings. Furthermore, there are motivational consequences associated with these emotions. People fight, we say, because they are angry and full of hate. People seek each other out because, we say, they are in love. People are motivated to do all sorts of things in order to escape or avoid unpleasant emotional states (fear, anger, anxiety) or in order to obtain pleasant emotional states (love, happiness, joy, pleasure). Clearly emotion and motivation are closely related topics.

In psychology, the concept of emotion has proved very complex and difficult to study scientifically. This is partly because so much of emotional experience is private personal experience that is not readily open to scientific scrutiny. Also, it is difficult to elicit emotions in controlled laboratory situations (particularly the positive emotions such as love, pleasure, and joy). But although there is still a long way to go, we can say that progress is being made.

Emotions and Incentives

A great deal of effort has been expended in an attempt to devise a classification system for emotions. There are hundreds of words in our language refering to different emotional experiences. Many of these overlap in meaning, however, or refer merely to slight differences in the intensity of the emotion. There are two primary dimensions of emotions: (1) the qualitative dimension of *pleasant-unpleasant* and (2) the quantitative dimension of *intensity*. Emotional states are basically pleasant or unpleasant, and they vary in the intensity of the feeling of pleasantness or unpleasantness. Thus the difference between anger and rage is primarily one of intensity, as is the difference between happiness and ecstasy.

These two basic dimensions also determine the motivational consequences of emotional states. First, we can expect that unpleasant emotional states (and the things we have learned will produce them) will act as negative incentives (we will be motivated to avoid or escape them). Likewise, pleasant states (and the things that will produce them) will be positive incentives (we will be motivated to achieve them). Because we learn about

Face Reading

Newsweek—Everybody knows that people's facial expressions contain clues to their moods. A smile is easy enough to recognize, but the face's subtler emotional indicators—tiny twinges and winces produced involuntarily by the facial muscles—are too fleeting to be noticed in all save the most expressive faces. Now, Harvard psychologist Gary Schwartz has devised a technique that picks up clues electronically and reliably reveals subjects' true feelings. The technique, known as facial electromyography, is already being studied to check the progress of clinically depressed patients receiving therapeutic drugs; eventually, it may come into its own as a direct form of biofeedback treatment for such victims.

Schwartz monitors the expressions of his subjects by attaching miniature electrodes to their skin above four facial muscles—generally the corrugator and frontalis in the forehead and the depressor anguli oris and masseter of the mouth and jaw. These electrodes pick up electrical signals that originate around the muscles. The signals are passed to an oscilloscope screen for interpretation.

Think

Schwartz and four colleagues at Boston's Erich Lindemann Mental Health Center set out to discover whether the device could detect moods self-induced by healthy volunteers. After wiring up his subjects' faces, Schwartz asked them to assume expressions of sadness, happiness and anger. He then told them to think about sad, joyful and enraging experiences without consciously adopting any give-away expressions.

By comparing the muscle readings from the overt and covert expressions, the psychologists were able to discriminate between happy, sad and angry thoughts, even when their subjects' expressions appeared to give nothing away. They also found that they could monitor the moods of patients who had been diagnosed as clinically depressed.

The 30-year-old Schwartz readily concedes that the device is far from foolproof, and can be cheated by any dedicated diplomat or poker player who makes a real effort to bury his emotions and adopt a stiff upper lip or a strained smile. "But the typical subjects we study come into the lab because they want to," he noted last week. "They're not interested in cheating the machine."

The development of techniques for objectively measuring emotional states would greatly improve research on emotion.

result in unpleasant emotional experiences. Of course, we cannot *avoid* everything unpleasant —sometimes we accidentally encounter an overbearing bore at a party. Under those circumstances, we will be motivated to *escape* (the bore) because we failed to *avoid* (him).

Second, we can expect that the degree of motivation will depend upon the strength of the anticipated or experienced state. The stronger or more intense the emotion, the greater the motivation to approach or avoid. In other words, the emotional intensity will determine the amount of incentive and whether the emotion is pleasant or unpleasant will determine whether the incentive is positive (approach) or negative (avoid).

Anxiety and Anger

Psychologists have been particularly interested in the motivational consequences of two emotional states, anxiety and anger. Anxiety is of interest because it appears to play a central role in the motivation of abnormal behavior (see Chapter 11) as well as everyday behavior. Anger is of interest because it is the standard emotion accompanying frustration, and anger probably underlies most acts of aggression. Together then, anxiety and anger represent two emotional states that may produce a great deal of undesirable behavior in people. Understanding these emotions may help us control or eliminate much of this behavior.

Anxiety. Anxiety is like conditioned fear. The anxious person is anticipating that fearful or harmful things are about to happen. The state that occurs when you encounter an armed robber is fear, whereas the state in which you think you might encounter an armed robber is anxiety. Presumably anxiety is an unpleasant experience with negative incentive value, meaning that we will be motivated to escape anxiety when it develops and to avoid it if at all possible. Much of psychopathological behavior is thought to be motivated by the desire to escape anxiety. Behaviors that allow a person to escape anxiety will be reinforced and thus repeated, and eventually will become habits for dealing with anxiety. Similarly, objects, events, and circumstances that we have learned will prevent or counteract anxiety become positive incentives, and we will direct our behavior toward achieving these goals.

The classic experiment demonstrating anxiety as a motivating force was done with rats by Neal Miller, using a shuttle box with two compartments, one

the world, we can usually anticipate the emotional states that specific objects, events, and states of affairs will elicit. Then we can seek as goals those things that we expect will elicit positive emotions and try to avoid those things that we expect will

Motivational Dilemmas

A person is in a state of conflict when he has two or more competing motives, all of which cannot be satisfied. There are two basic kinds of motives: *Approach motives* refers to situations in which there is a reward or positive incentive to be gained if the person approaches the goal. *Avoidance motives* refers to cases in which the incentive is negative—it is an object, event, or state of affairs that is unpleasant and is to be avoided. All cases of conflict between motives can be described in terms of approach and avoidance:

1. *Approach-approach conflict:* In this case two positive incentives exist but cannot both be attained—one or the other must be chosen. An example is trying to decide whether you should spend the evening at a movie or watching a favorite TV program. An approach-approach conflict is usually easily resolved (you can see the movie tomorrow), unless the motives for both incentives are very strong and the goals are indeed incompatible.

2. *Avoidance-avoidance conflict:* This conflict results when the choice is between two negative alternatives or incentives. For example, you may have to decide which of two dull courses to study for tonight. The most distinctive feature of avoidance-avoidance conflict is that it is usually difficult to resolve, especially if both incentives are strongly negative. Often the person fails to make any decision at all, attempting instead to remove himself from the conflict situation, for example, by watching TV and doing no studying at all.

3. *Approach-avoidance conflict:* Frequently a goal or incentive has both positive and negative aspects, resulting in both approach and avoidance responses. For example, foods that you find particularly tasty may cause weight gain and cavities. In this type of conflict, "distance" from the incentive appears to play an important role. At great distances, the negative aspects do not seem as important as the positive ones, and so you move toward the goal, for example, by making a dental appointment for 6 months in the future. As the time for the appointment gets nearer, however, the negative aspects increase in strength and may surpass the positive ones, causing you to retreat from the goal (you break the appointment). The reaction of two different patients to this approach-avoidance conflict is shown below.

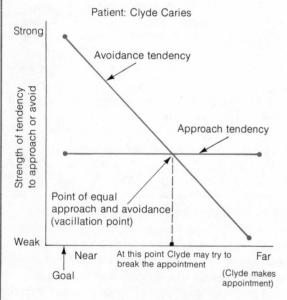

Patient: Clyde Caries

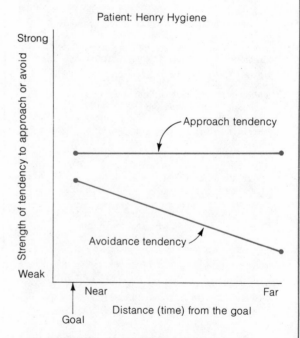

Patient: Henry Hygiene

The graph above diagrams the approach-avoidance conflict of a patient (Clyde Caries) who makes an appointment with his dentist a long time before he actually has to show up. There are two tendencies, one to approach (go to the dentist) and one to avoid (stay away from the dentist). In this example, the approach gradient does not change as the time for the appointment gets closer, but the avoidance tendency gets stronger and stronger (Clyde anticipates lots of pain) as the appointment gets closer. At first, the approach tendency is stronger than the avoidance tendency, and so the appointment is made. Later, as the time for the appointment draws near, the avoidance tendency gets stronger and at some time it becomes as strong as the approach tendency. This is the point of maximum conflict about what to do, the vacillation point. This is when Clyde may try to cancel or at least postpone the appointment. In any given conflict situation, what happens will depend on the strengths of the approach and avoidance gradients and how steep they are. For example, in the right graph, the avoidance tendency is not as strong as in the first graph because Henry Hygiene is not nearly as afraid of the dentist as Clyde. For Henry, the approach and avoidance tendencies never intersect, and so he does not try to cancel his appointment.

*"I'll tell you what's missing from
your game, Cowley—hate."*

New Yorker, October 24, 1974. Drawing by Lorenz; © 1974 The New Yorker
Magazine, Inc.

**Emotions are generally considered to be important
sources of motivation. This is particularly evident in
athletics.**

"Can I kick it for you this time, Daddy?"

Reprinted courtesy of The Register and Tribune Syndicate.

**In modern technological society, machines that do
not work properly are a common source of
frustration, as this cartoon suggests. A common
reaction, in line with the frustration-aggression
hypothesis, is an aggressive act directed toward
the machine. The cartoon also illustrates the fact
that children can learn aggression by imitation.
Presumably, the child has seen his father kick soda
machines many times in the past and is already
prepared to kick this one for him.**

black and one white. A rat was placed in the white
compartment and electric shock was turned on,
causing the rat to run into the black side of the box,
where he *escaped* from the shock. This routine was
repeated for several trials until presumably the fear
was conditioned to the white compartment. At that
point, no further shocks were given. Despite the
absence of shocks, the rat continued to show signs
of fear when placed in the white side—the rat was
"anxious." He continued to run into the black side
even though he was never shocked again. The white
side took on negative incentive value and the black
side probably took on positive incentive value. Next,
a door was put in place between the compartments
and a wheel was placed in the white compartment.
This wheel, if turned by the rat, would open the
door. The result was that the rats learned the
wheel-turning response to get out of the white
compartment, even though shock was not
administered. The rats were not escaping from real
shock, but from the threat of shock. They were
escaping from the white compartment because it
had been associated with shock. They were
evidently motivated by the conditioned fear or
anxiety produced by the white compartment. They
may also have been motivated by the positive
incentive of the black side of the box, because this
side had repeatedly been associated with relief from
the shock.

You might ask yourself about your own behavior
at this point. How much of your behavior is
motivated by the desire to *escape* or *avoid* an
unpleasant consequence? How often do negative
incentives (like the rat's white box) influence your
behavior? How often does the positive incentive
value of things (like the rat's black box) stem from
the fact that they allow us to escape anxiety,
although many of these things may simply be
temporary solutions to our anxiety. You may be
anxious about a test, and instead of studying, you
may find yourself watching TV, a momentary relief
from the anxiety. Or consider the alcoholic who may
find temporary relief from anxiety in alcohol (the
alcohol becomes a positive incentive). Because
there are so many maladaptive ways to deal with the
anxiety that is normal in life, anxiety can become a
devastating state. While it can motivate appropriate
behaviors such as studying for the exam, it can also
motivate behaviors that ultimately cause trouble. We

will have more to say about anxiety in Chapter 11.

Anger and frustration. Dollard, Doob, Miller, Mowrer, and Sears (1939) have suggested that all aggressive acts are caused by frustration, which is almost always accompanied by anger. This theory is known as the *frustration-aggression hypothesis.* Inflicting harm on others is a major problem in our society and the world, and so it is important to understand the motivation for this aggression. There is very strong evidence that frustration is *sufficient* to produce aggression, although it is almost impossible to determine whether frustration is also a necessary factor—that is, whether *all* aggression involves frustration. Consider just one study, in which a very hungry pigeon was trained to peck a key in a Skinner box in order to get grain. After the pigeon had learned this response, an "innocent bystander" pigeon was placed in the box with the trained pigeon and simultaneously the experimenter stopped giving grain for pecking (extinction). During this extinction period, the trained pigeon attacked the bystander by pecking at his head, throat, and especially his eyes. There is little doubt that this was an attack reaction, apparently elicited by the frustration that was caused by the termination of the grain rewards (compare this with Figure 6–14).

The same kind of attack reactions were elicited in birds that had been reared in isolation, suggesting that there is a biological, innate component to this behavior. This conclusion accords with the suggestions of the ethologists, who have argued that there is an aggressive instinct in human beings as well as in animals. However, although it may be true that there are aggressive instincts that result in predisposing us to fight when frustrated, it is clear that learning is also important. We learn aggressive tactics from seeing how others practice aggression, and limiting such observation may be one way of exerting some control on the development of aggression. This is why, for example, so many people are concerned about the violence on television.

Issues and Theories

The sequence of events. When you encounter a ferocious bear in your room, at least two things are very likely to happen: (1) you will run and (2) you will have an emotional experience (a feeling) that is usually called fear. Most of us would guess that we experience the fear first and run second. The first major psychological theory of emotional behavior postulated that we do just the opposite. This is

Figure 6–14
Aggression substitute

Two rats fight each other, ignoring the doll. When an appropriate object of aggression is missing, the lone rat displaces his aggression, attacking the innocent bystander. The most appropriate object for aggression is the object that is the source of the frustration. Often there are constraints against expressing the aggression against this source, as when a man is frustrated by his boss and hesitates to aggress against the boss for fear of his job. So the aggression is displaced onto an "innocent bystander" such as his secretary or his wife.

known as the *James-Lange theory* after William James and Carl Lange, who independently in the mid 1880's suggested that we run first and then are afraid. According to this theory, we are afraid because we observe that we are running. More specifically, the idea is that perception of the bear in the room leads simultaneously to running and to all sorts of changes in body physiology, such as increased blood pressure and heart rate. When we perceive these changes in our body, we experience the emotion (fear). This implies that we experience different emotions because the body produces a different set of physiological changes for each of the emotions. Fear is not the same thing as anger, presumably because the physiological activity in the

War Called Aid to Man

London (UPI)—Since scientists must be ruled by reason rather than emotion, Prof. Stanislav Andreski now states his belief that war has done as much for mankind as peace.

In an article in Science Journal, Andreski, who heads the Department of Sociology at Reading University, makes quite clear that he is not advocating war.

But he says it is worth remembering "that in this imperfect world everything has its disadvantages—even peace."

Professor Andreski believes the proto-hominids, forerunners of man, used weapons while they were still in the trees and thus acquired the capacity to kill—most animals restricted to claw and tooth seek only to disable or humble opponents.

One of the lethal effects of clashes in that prehistoric era would have been the extinction of "the missing link" between man and the apes. And war, he says, may explain why the human brain advanced so much more rapidly than that of the apes.

Professor Andreski says that population growing faster than resources has been responsible for most wars.

Although he doesn't state it as such, his recipe for peace is control and balance of world population and the provision of "attractive employment for the energy and aggressiveness of young men . . . which in most times and places found an outlet in war."

Did the violent use of weapons enable certain organisms to survive better than others? Have we inherited violent instincts?

body is qualitatively different during the experience of these two emotions. Whether or not this is true constitutes a critical issue to which we shall return shortly. For now, just remember that the James-Lange theory requires it to be true.

Other psychologists disagree with James and Lange. A prominent alternate view is commonly referred to as the *Cannon-Bard theory,* named after W. B. Cannon and P. Bard, who formulated the theory in 1915. Whereas James and Lange say, "We see the bear, we run (and our body physiology changes), and then we experience fear," the Cannon-Bard theory gives the commonsense argument: "We see the bear, we experience fear, and then we run (and our body physiology changes). Cannon and Bard thought that the thalamus (see Chapter 2) was the "seat of emotions" (the hypothalamus would have been a better guess). According to them, when an emotional stimulus is

presented, there is first strong stimulation of the thalamus. The thalamus then discharges electrical impulses upward in the brain, activating the cerebral cortex, and downward throughout the body, activating the autonomic nervous system. This produces an all-over state of arousal that prepares the person for "flight or fight." It is this state that is experienced as the emotion. After this comes the observable behavior, the running. So for Cannon and Bard, emotion precedes overt behavior and consists mainly of a general state of arousal or activation. There is only one basic physiological state in this theory, namely arousal, although obviously emotions differ in terms of degree of arousal.

Do different emotions correspond to qualitatively different physiological states?

The James-Lange theory required a yes answer to this question, while the Cannon-Bard theory said no, there are just differences in degree of arousal. The evidence on several fronts went against the James-Lange theory. Cannon criticized the James-Lange theory because the evidence available at the time did not show different physiological patterns for different emotions. Cannon also thought that the physiological changes out in the body's periphery took place too slowly to be the primary source of emotion. Further, in one study subjects were injected with adrenalin (epinephrine), which produces arousal in the autonomic nervous system, and yet these subjects did not report emotional experiences; the reason, according to Cannon, was that the central nervous system was not activated through the thalamus (there was no emotional stimulus). The overall picture is strongly against the James-Lange theory, although it is dying a slow death.

One reason the James-Lange theory still persists is that recent work has begun to demonstrate some differences in peripheral responses for different emotions. Most often cited is the work of A. F. Ax, who has demonstrated physiological differences between fear and anger. The adrenal glands secrete two different hormones, epinephrine and norepinephrine. Ax found that during fear epinephrine seems to dominate, while during anger both epinephrine and norepinephrine are implicated. Other studies have shown that animals that are preyed upon (and should thus be creatures of fear) secrete high amounts of epinephrine in contrast to the animals that do the preying. The preying animals (creatures of "anger"?) show predominately norepinephrine secretion. More recent work has centered on the biochemical substances that serve as neural transmitters in the central nervous system, which seem to be involved in different ways depending on the emotion. However, the evidence is not yet convincing, and so there is still a strong commitment to the notion that basically the emotional state is a general diffuse state of overall arousal or activation.

How important is cognitive appraisal of the situation?

If the emotional state consists mainly of general arousal and there is not a different physiological state for the different emotions, how do we know whether we are happy or sad, pleased or angry? The answer probably comes from analyzing the total emotional experience into two basic parts: (1) the *general arousal* and (2) the *cognitive appraisal* or *evaluation* of the situation—such as "there is a dangerous animal loose in my room and it is about to attack me." In a simplified sense, the appraisal is designed to answer the question "Why am I aroused to this degree?" There is a continual interplay between the arousal and the appraisal, out of which emerges the emotional experience. The experience is thus a joint product of the arousal (including the degree of arousal) and the ongoing evaluation of the situation. Which comes first is not of much concern in this theory, because arousal and appraisal are constantly changing and interacting with each other. Sometimes the arousal may precede the appraisal and sometimes it may come later.

The key new element in this interpretation is cognitive appraisal. The person is appraising the situation and at the same time is looking for something that the arousal can be attributed to (the bear is an obvious choice). This part of the theory comes from the *attribution theory* of Fritz Heider (see Chapter 10) and has been investigated and elaborated by Stanley Schachter. Having something to attribute the arousal to and having a cognitive evaluation of that thing (such as "it can harm me") are crucial. Without these components, there would be no emotional experience even if the arousal component has occurred. Thus, as mentioned earlier, subjects given injections of adrenalin, which produces the arousal, do not become emotional because there is nothing to attribute the arousal to other than the injection, which is nothing to be happy, sad, angry, or ecstatic about. Presumably the subjects attribute the arousal to the injection (the doctor told them they would experience arousal) and then are not emotional. On the other hand, if the subjects were misled about the injection ("this is

a vitamin shot") and were told that it would not produce arousal, then when they became aroused they would need an explanation, and would evaluate their predicament in seeking the explanation.

Schachter and Jerome Singer tricked subjects in just this way—the subjects received adrenalin but thought they were getting a vitamin shot. The subjects found their explanation for the experienced arousal (and thus their emotion) in the situation. Half the subjects, after receiving the "vitamin" shot, were asked to wait in a room with someone else who was pretending to be very angry. These subjects reported that they became angry. The other half waited in a room with someone who was acting very happy, and these subjects said they were happy. They thus falsely attributed the arousal they were experiencing to the situation and experienced an emotional feeling that was consistent with their evaluation of the situation.

To emphasize the back-and-forth interplay between arousal and evaluation, we can point out that there is evidence that persons evaluate the degree of arousal as well as the situation that is apparently producing the arousal. And the evaluation of the degree of arousal will be fed back into the system and can affect the evaluation of the situation. In an ingenious experiment, Stuart Valins demonstrated this feedback feature. Male subjects were led to believe that they were listening to their own amplified heartbeat over a loudspeaker, when in fact what they heard was a prepared tape recording. Valins then showed these men pictures of nudes from *Playboy;* for half the nudes, the fake heart rate sounds were speeded up when the picture appeared. This was designed to create the false impression in the subjects that they were especially aroused by these particicular nudes. Later the subjects were asked to rate the nudes on attractiveness, and, as predicted, they rated the nudes that had been associated with increased heart rate as more attractive than the other nudes. The reasoning is that the subjects, thinking they were aroused, searched for an explanation by more closely examining the nudes to find particularly attractive features in the photographs. Having found these features, the subjects would judge the photographs more attractive.

In fact, Valins has demonstrated that the subjects still rate these nudes as more attractive after they are told that the "heartbeats" were a fake. Fake or not, they caused the subjects to discover more attractive features. It has also been shown that the "heart-rate" effect does not take place if the nude photos are presented rapidly, presumably because the subject does not have time to find the explanation for his arousal—he does not have time to find attractive features in the playmate.

The currently most popular account of emotional experience stems from a combination of general arousal theory (similar to the Cannon-Bard theory) and attribution theory. The experienced emotion is a complex function depending on the interplay among several factors: (1) the arousal level—the degree of arousal (or more accurately the degree to which the arousal level is changed from some baseline) probably mediates the intensity dimension of emotion; (2) the cognitive evaluation of the situation producing the arousal change, which will at least partly determine the pleasantness-unpleasantness dimension; and (3) the evaluation of the arousal change, which may in turn affect the cognitive evaluation of the situation. A fourth factor is the specific physiological pattern of the arousal, which may partly determine the quality of the experience (is it fear or anger?). As yet, however, we know very little about what biochemical and physiological factors differentiate the various emotional states.

It is also possible that the degree of arousal change from the normal baseline may play a role in determining the pleasant-unpleasant dimension, in addition to determining the intensity dimension. If we assume that there is a homeostatic arousal system trying to keep arousal level in the moderate range, then we would guess that very large changes in arousal from this optimal level will, in general, be experienced as unpleasant. We might also expect that this homeostatic system will, in such cases, immediately attempt to counteract these large changes in arousal in an effort to return the arousal level to the moderate range.

The effect of opponent processes in emotions.
Richard Solomon and John Corbit have proposed just such an opponent-process model: Given a large change in arousal produced by either a pleasant or an unpleasant stimulus, the homeostatic system will immediately activate an opponent process to counteract the emotional reaction. The opponent process, in general, will have just the opposite effects of the initial process, meaning that the overall experience will be a combination of the opposing processes. If the initial experience is pleasant, it will be maximally pleasant only for a short while, because the opponent process, which is by definition unpleasant, will soon be activated and begin to counteract the pleasant process. As the unpleasant opponent process gathers strength, the experience will become less and less pleasant. If the

original stimulus situation that triggered the pleasant process were suddenly removed, we would experience only the opponent process in action. That is, we would experience an unpleasant emotion.

In contrast, suppose the initial state of arousal is unpleasant. Soon afterward, a pleasant opponent process will be activated to counteract the arousal. Such an experience will be maximally unpleasant only in the beginning because the opponent process will begin to temper or diminish the degree of unpleasantness. If at this moment the original unpleasant stimulus situation is suddenly removed, only the opponent process will be active and we will experience a pleasant emotion.

Solomon and Corbit use this theory to account for a variety of phenomena, among which they consider the following: Immediately after hatching, the newborn duckling gives every appearance of being quite satisfied with his new circumstances, though he may emit a few cries of distress. But then, according to imprinting studies, if the duckling is exposed to a white, moving object, he will stare at it intently. All movements and vocalizations tend to disappear. If the moving object is removed, there will be a burst of distress cries that may last for several minutes before subsiding. According to the typical ethological interpretation, the moving object has suddenly established a "following behavior" released by an adequate imprinting stimulus, a white moving object. In contrast, according to the Solomon-Corbit theory, the moving object is a stimulus that automatically releases in the duckling an affective state with *pleasant* emotional connotations. The stimulus-induced state is, however, opposed by an *unpleasant* process, of lesser intensity and designed to bring the organism back in the direction of emotional neutrality. When the triggering stimulus (the white object) is removed, only the unpleasant state remains, resulting in the distress reaction of the organism.

As another example, consider the studies by Epstein (1967) of the motivational bases and emotional accompaniments of parachuting. When the novice parachutist makes his first jump, he is terrified, judging by verbal reports, facial expressions, and changes in his autonomic nervous system. When he lands safely, he will appear stony-faced or stunned for several minutes, only gradually recovering composure. The initial fear-induced state of arousal is presumably opposed by a state of quiescence that persists for some period of time after the jump is complete.

A third example comes from the use of drugs,

such as opium. Upon first use, an individual is likely to report an intensely pleasurable feeling known as the "rush." With the passage of time, as the drug effect wears off, the user will suffer aversive pain and frightening withdrawal symptoms. There may also be a feeling of craving for the drug. Presumably, this is the opponent process in action.

Finally, consider the situation of a girl and boy falling in love. The initial state presumably experienced by both is characterized by pleasurable excitement, sexual highs, ecstasy, happiness, and, in general, good feelings. When the lovers are separated, the opponent process becomes evident. They feel lonely and depressed. Even when they anticipate reunion, loneliness may persist. Reunion does, of course, reinstate the initial stimulus circumstances and thereby overwhelm the negative opponent process.

If we are repeatedly exposed to the identical emotional situation, the character of the emotional experience changes. Solomon and Corbit suggest that this happens because the opponent process gets stronger each time it is elicited. With enough repetition, the opponent process may become so strong that it overwhelms the initial stimulus-induced state and comes to dominate the emotional experience. Imagine your favorite food, the thing that gives you that most pleasant taste experience. Now imagine eating that food all the time, morning, noon, and night. Do you think the pleasure would disappear?

For the examples mentioned above, consider what happens when repetition takes place. For the ducklings, if the imprinting stimulus is presented and removed several times, the frequency and intensity of distress crying by a duckling will increase (the opponent process has been strengthened). For the parachutist, after many jumps he or she no longer reports terror and is instead eager to jump, although there may be a little anxiety or tension. The opponent process has been strengthened, and this turns the terror into the milder state of anxiety. After landing, the jumper is no longer subdued, but exuberant. Parachutists claim that they love to jump because of this exhilarating after-feeling (the strong opponent process). For the addict, after several weeks of opiate use, the "rush" begins to weaken, and it takes more of the drug to produce it. Moreover, the aftereffects become more intense and turn into an intensely unpleasant state of craving. Indeed, the opponent process has become so strong that the addict must take drugs all the time just to maintain his normal feelings. The drugs no longer produce the pleasant state, but just maintain the normal one,

and the lack of drugs is what produces the abnormal state. Finally, consider the couple in love. After several weeks, months, or years of repeated affectionate interaction, the qualitative and quantitative aspects of their love will change. Being together is a state of "contentment," normalcy, and comfort, not the same as the excitement, joy, and enthusiasm of the young lovers. Now, separation can have highly intense aversive effects, and in extreme cases grief and severe depression. It is as if the partners have become addicted to one another; being together is "normal," not exciting, and separation will result in withdrawal symptoms.

What Does It Mean?

Increasing Motivation

If psychological research allows for the identification of the factors that determine motivation, it should be possible to bring these factors to bear on an individual or group in hopes of increasing motivation to behave in some particular way. The focus of such an effort would probably be on increasing achievement in one way or another. In industry, for instance, it is obviously important to management that the productivity of employees be increased, that the employees increase their motivation to produce. In fact, of course, industrial psychology has concerned itself with this issue for a long time, attempting to understand how principles of motivation can be applied in a work setting. Many studies of the effects of various incentive plans on productivity have been carried out, with the goal of identifying the optimal incentive conditions for the employees.

Recently, there has been a recognition of the fact that performance in an industrial setting is dependent on other than monetary incentives. Giving praise and recognition to employees is often equally important. Consider the following case. A few years ago, the management of the Emery Air Freight Corporation instituted a program to improve performance based on the motivational ideas of operant conditioning. The heart of the program consisted of setting specific goals for the employees and giving them a great deal of feedback as to how they were doing in reaching these goals. The first target for the program was shortening the time a customer had to wait for replies to questions about air freight shipments. The goal was to respond to all customer questions within 90 minutes. Although the employees thought they were meeting this goal most of the time, studies showed that in fact only about 30 percent of the time did the response to the customer come in less than 90 minutes. By keeping

"Why, thank you, sir, and I had it in mind to tell you what a bang-up job I think you're doing."

New Yorker, January 13, 1975. Drawing by Mulligan; © 1975 The New Yorker Magazine, Inc.

Giving praise and recognition is apparently a good way to motivate people.

accurate performance records, and by praising employees for improvements found in the daily records, management was able to increase performance dramatically in a very short time—in some offices it took only one day to meet the 90-minute criterion. After 3 years on the program, the response rate is now so high across the entire company that 90–95 percent of all customers receive a reply within the 90 minutes.

Next, the same techniques were applied to loading dock employees in order to motivate them to be more efficient in the use of "containers." The idea was to combine lots of small packages into one large package or container, which results in substantial savings in the air freight charges. If the dock workers could be motivated to increase their use of containers, the company could save a great deal of money. Again it was found that the employees thought they were making good use of the containers, but they were wrong. Containers were used in only about 45 percent of the shipments where they could be used. By keeping accurate records, the management could give feedback to the workers about how they were doing and could reward them, again with praise and recognition, whenever the rate of container use went up. The result was that container use shot up from the old 45 percent figure to over 90 percent, and 2 years later it was still at a very high level. In one month alone, the company saved $125,000 because of their container program.

Intrinsic and extrinsic motivation.   It seems rather obvious that the best way to increase motivation (and thereby performance) is to increase incentives. But increasing incentives is a very tricky business and can often have effects just the opposite of those desired.

Some recent research has demonstrated that it is possible to *decrease* motivation by giving rewards for performance. The reason is that people are self-motivated to do certain things. Some tasks are interesting and enjoyable and provide their own rewards to the people doing them. If a psychologist, a teacher, an employer, or a parent offers tangible rewards to a person for doing a task he would do well anyway, the person may develop a more negative attitude about the task. Where once the task seemed worth doing by itself, the new reward system makes the task take on the complexion of work. The task is now perceived as something that must be done in order to get the reward, rather than as something important in its own right. When a person does something for no obvious tangible reward, we say that he is *intrinsically motivated*. If, on the other hand, a person is doing something in order to receive a particular tangible reward, say, a paycheck, we say that he is *extrinsically motivated* by the external incentives. If the amateur photographer decides to give up his present job and become a professional photographer, the work may take on a different flavor and become much less fun and much more like drudgery.

Edward Deci has collected some very interesting data on this problem. He asked different groups of college students to solve 4 puzzle problems that required the subjects to construct various shapes from a set of three-dimensional pieces. One group of subjects were told they would get a dollar for each of the 4 problems they could solve and the other group were just asked to try the problems. The first group were presumably extrinsically motivated by the money reward, while the second group were supposedly intrinsically motivated by the challenge of the puzzle. Deci then left both groups alone for a while to do whatever they wanted. One of the things they could choose to do during the wait was to solve the 4 puzzle problems. During the free time, the money, or extrinsic, group played with the puzzles *less* than the no-money, or intrinsic, group. During the free time, of course, the subjects could not expect money for solving the puzzles, meaning that the extrinsic source of motivation was no longer present, and thus the money group did not work on the puzzles as long as the group that never received money. Deci also showed the same effect if the subjects were told that they must solve the puzzles in order to avoid punishment (a loud buzzer that came on to signal that time was up for that problem). During a free period after the 4 test problems, these subjects played less with the puzzles than a group that did not get the buzzer punishment. In short, both of these experiments demonstrated that if you provide extrinsic reward (money or an unpleasant buzzer) as the incentive for doing something that is intrinsically interesting, you can decrease intrinsic motivation. In a third experiment, Deci showed that these effects do not take place when the reward is praise for a job well done instead of money. One group of subjects were told that they did very well—solved the puzzle quickly considering its difficulty—for each of the 4 test problems. In the free period, these subjects showed high levels of intrinsic motivation to work on more problems. Deci has suggested that praise works differently than money because praise involves giving feedback to the subject about his competence and self-determination. Tasks that are intrinsically interesting are presumably tasks that, when completed, automatically give the person good feelings of competence. Perhaps this is why praise and recognition worked so well in the case of Emery Air Freight.

Tangible external rewards will not always have the desired effect of increasing motivation, and we must pay close attention to the types of incentives we use. In the classroom, for example, we might inadvertently turn the task of learning into a chore by promising the students all sorts of rewards. Many parents and grandparents have promised children money or special privileges for good grades. These promises may have contributed to an attitude about school that makes studying appear like work. In fact, our entire school system seems predicated on a tangible futuristic reward system—"if you go to school and learn a lot you will earn a lot of money." Does going to college seem like a chore to you or are you intrinsically motivated to learn? We hope that further research in the area of motivation will allow us to discover the best ways to motivate behavior, and this includes the best ways to develop intrinsic motivation for the most important tasks of our lives.

Changing the Personality Aspects of Motivation

As we have seen, motivation is often used as a personality concept, particularly when we are discussing human motives or needs. Earlier in this chapter, we focused on achievement motivation. Is it possible to alter such personality characteristics in

"I'll give it to you straight, Benson. We don't think you're maximizing your potential."

New Yorker, September 2, 1974. Drawing by Lorenz; © 1974 The New Yorker Magazine, Inc.

Knowledge of the principles of motivation may ultimately lead to techniques for improving our motivation, or "maximizing our potential." Research on motivation should find application in our educational system to help students learn more effectively and to develop intrinsic motivation for learning. Getting "chewed out" by the principal or guidance counselor is probably not going to do much for the student's intrinsic motivation to learn.

adults? Typically it has been assumed that, once a person has reached adulthood, it is quite difficult—if not impossible—to change personality characteristics such as achievement motivation. However, we can expect that an understanding of the principles of human motivation might eventually allow us to manipulate or change the personality aspects of motivation. There is not a great deal of research on this topic, mainly because we do not as yet have anything like a complete understanding of human personality. But as our knowledge grows we can expect that our ability to change human motivation will increase.

As one example, consider the work of David McClelland on achievement motivation. He has used the knowledge derived from his research on the development of achievement motivation and from other areas of psychology to develop a training course designed to increase the level of need for achievement in students. He has taught this course to numerous groups of businessmen, mainly in India, and has done careful follow-up studies of the effects of the course on students' later achievements in the business world.

The participants were thoroughly trained in the theory and measurement of achievement motivation. They all took the TAT test and scored their own stories for achievement motivation. They were taught to think about everything in terms related to achievement. They analyzed the achievement motivation level in their own culture by scoring such things as books, children's stories, and customs of the culture on achievement. They also played a business game in which each person had to think in achievement terms (for example, set goals for profits and productivity) and could get fast feedback about how he was doing in running the business. The results were measured by comparing students who had taken the course with control students who had applied for the course but had not been admitted. On a number of economic measures—starting new businesses, working longer hours, increasing the number of employees in existing businesses, and so on—the students in the course did very much better than the controls. This, of course, is taken as evidence that the course did indeed succeed in increasing the achievement motivation of the participants.

McClelland's course was specifically designed to increase only achievement motivation. McClelland believes, however, that the principles he used in setting up the course would be applicable to any personality aspect of motivation. In short, his results suggest that it would be possible to design training programs or courses that would affect all of the human psychogenic needs or motives, such as the need for affiliation, the need for power, and the need for social approval. He argues that the economic growth, development, and decline of a country depends heavily on the achievement motivation of its people. If this is true and if we can develop ways of increasing achievement motivation for businessmen, then it should be possible to design ways to bring about great changes in the economic conditions of an underdeveloped country by subjecting the inhabitants to these techniques. Does this sound a little frightening to you? Wouldn't it also then be possible to destroy the economy of a rather well-developed country by systematically attempting to decrease or undermine the achievement motivation of its inhabitants?

It is hardly necessary to mention that development of techniques to change aspects of someone's personality would have important applied consequences. Many beneficial things could be done with such knowledge, such as helping people

Perhaps Your Shrink Can Help You Peel Off Pounds

Chicago (AP)–Psychologists are succeeding where physicians have failed in helping fat people lose weight, a California psychiatrist says.

And, he said, they're doing it without special diets.

Dr. Albert J. Stunkard said that in the past three or four years effectiveness of weight reduction programs has improved 50 per cent through the use of what psychologists call behavior modification or operant conditioning.

Stunkard, chairman of the psychiatry department at Stanford University, told newsmen at the annual meeting of the American Medical Association Monday that the medical profession "has been very backward" in using this new, proven technique to help persons lose weight. He said "psychologists all over the map are doing it."

The psychiatrist, who described the technique at the AMA meeting, said he has been involved with about 130 obese patients at the University of Pennsylvania, where he formerly taught, and at Stanford.

Obese patients enrolled in these group therapy programs do not have to go on special diets and are not even told to restrict their food intake at first.

It begins with the patients keeping a diary of when, what and how much they eat and how they feel when they do it.

Stunkard said that just keeping records helps patients start losing weight as they become aware of how much they eat.

Patients are advised not to have a lot of food around their homes and to keep away from tempting situations. They are told to eat in just one place in the house.

Persons who eat while watching television, for example, become stimulated to eat in that situation, he said.

Fat persons also tend to eat faster than others, and the physiological signal that they are full is not triggered until after they've overeaten, the psychiatrist said. Therefore, they are advised to put down their knife and fork between bites.

"A lot of obese people are not aware of what they're eating—they don't taste their food," Stunkard said.

On the average, patients lose 1½ pounds a week during the 10 weeks of the group therapy sessions and continue to lose during a period of follow-up, and the weight loss is maintained, he reported.

to change in ways they want to change, as when a psychotherapist tries to help clients become better adjusted emotionally. But knowledge could also be used not to help people, but to control them. Some readers will already have reacted that way to the case of Emery Air Freight. Similarly, many people have strongly criticized the various types of "behavior modification" projects that have been tried in schools, mental hospitals, and prisons. The facts argue strongly for the conclusion that the people who control the incentives, whatever they may be, can use their power to control the behavior of the people who are seeking those incentives. The question is not so much whether we can apply this knowledge to affect behavior, but what kinds of behavior change are desirable and how the rights and wishes of the individual will be safeguarded.

We might also note that knowledge of the conditions that lead to certain adult personality-motivation characteristics could also be applied to raising children. If we can change the adult level of achievement motivation, as the results of McClelland's course suggests, we certainly should ultimately be able to raise children in such a way that as adults they possess more of those personality characteristics the parents value and fewer of those aspects their parents do not value. In other words, there will be knowledge that will allow parents to determine effectively the adult personality of children.

Controlling the Hand That Feeds You

One major area of concentration in motivation research is hunger and eating. A major application of knowledge derived from this research is body weight control. Obesity is a problem for millions of people in this country. It has been implicated as a major factor in heart disease, to say nothing of the personal pain and discomfort and rejection that the obese person so often feels. Presently we do not have very good techniques for controlling obesity. People go on diets and lose weight, but a disappointingly small proportion of them are able to keep the weight off. Most dieters gain back later what they lose and spend much of their lives losing the same 10 pounds over and over again. Recent research has begun to suggest reasons for this typical pattern. This knowledge may eventually lead to effective techniques for combating obesity permanently.

Numerous experiments by Stanley Schachter and his colleagues suggest the conclusion that obese people have difficulty in controlling their weight because they eat mainly in response to uncontrollable external cues in their environments. The experiments showed that normal-weight people, in contrast, eat mainly in response to internal, physiological cues. The normal person eats because his internal food-intake system "tells" him to eat, while the obese person eats whenever he encounters external stimuli that have something to do with food, such as when he walks by a doughnut shop or sees a TV commercial for frozen pizza. The

"I was reminded of the refrigerator by the installment I just paid on it."

According to Schachter's theory of hunger motivation, obese people are overcontrolled by external food-related stimuli and undercontrolled by internal stimuli related to bodily needs for nourishment. Thus, the fat person is likely to eat in response to food or food-related stimuli (such as the bill for the refrigerator installment) regardless of the internal state of his body. The normal person responds to food and food stimuli more in accord with his internal cues—he tends not to eat unless "physiologically" hungry.

normal-weight person encounters identical stimuli, but his food intake is not under external control and so he does not respond by getting something to eat. It follows that it will be easy for the obese person to lose weight if he isolates himself from these stimuli. And indeed it is. If obese people are put into the hospital and deprived of TV, magazines, and any stimuli that have to do with food, they can lose large amounts of weight without great pain or discomfort. But what happens when they leave the hospital and return to the world of refrigerators, restaurants, MacDonald's hamburger stands, and 31 flavors of ice cream? Yes indeed, they gain back what they lost.

Obese people are exceptionally sensitive to external food-related stimuli and insensitive to internal stimuli. It has been shown, for example, that normal-weight individuals report being hungry in a way that corresponds with the contractions in their stomachs, an internal stimulus. Obese people's reports of hunger do not correlate highly with stomach activity. In an ingenious experiment,

Hurrying a Heart Attack

Time—Do you explosively accentuate key words in your sentences when there is no real need to do so, or deliver the last few words of a sentence much faster than the first? Do you try to hurry someone else's speech by interjecting "Yes, yes!" or by finishing his sentences for him? Do you try to do more than one thing at a time—work out a problem while someone is talking to you, or dictate to a secretary while driving a car? Do you often clench your fist or pound the desk for emphasis? Do you feel guilty if you are idle for a few days or even hours?

Anyone who answers most of the above in the affirmative has what Drs. Meyer Friedman and Ray Rosenman of San Francisco call Type A behavior. If he has not already had a heart attack, then he may be hurrying toward one. That, at least, is the conclusion of their book, *Type A Behavior and Your Heart* (Knopf; $7.95). Just published, the book not only helps people to determine if their behavior is hastening a heart attack but also offers some practical advice for those who want to avoid coronary complications.

Chain Reaction

Friedman and Rosenman are fully aware of the plethora of factors that contribute to the 20th century epidemic of heart disease and premature deaths: obesity and diabetes, high-fat and high-cholesterol diets, smoking and lack of exercise, and hereditary tendencies. But the two doctors maintain that behavior patterns are at least as important as any of the other causes and may indeed underlie some of them. For example, the Type A's instantly aggressive response to trivial slights and threats may set off a chain reaction of hormonal changes that can impair the metabolism of fats or cholesterol, thus accelerating the buildup of these substances in the coronary arteries.

The two physicians base their conclusions on a ten-year study of patients who were asked, among other things, to work a maze-like game to determine their frustration levels. They found more Type A's among professional men—attorneys, editors, advertising men, dentists and physicians. But, they insist, it is not merely what a man does that distinguishes the hard-driving Type A from the more easygoing Type B. A factory worker can be just as strongly Type A if he is concerned only about how fast he gets his job done, and sets his goals in terms of time and numbers rather than quality.

Changing Patterns

Changing a behavior pattern from Type A to B is difficult, but Friedman and Rosenman believe that it is possible. First, Type A must recognize himself for what he is. Then he must consciously try to slow himself down. The authors advise the Type A to get up earlier in the morning to allow time for a relaxed breakfast and avoid rushing for the 8:14. He should also schedule fewer appointments, stroll in a park after lunch and take time to be alone once in a while. He might, as a macabre reminder of his mortality, even write his own obituary from time to time.

It will take Friedman and Rosenman many years to determine whether their advice will actually prevent premature death from heart disease. In the meantime, they can study each other. Rosenman has never had a heart attack and, being a relaxed Type B, is not likely to suffer one. Friedman worked on his personality theory with typical Type A drive until his heart attack at age 55. That and a later coronary-bypass operation seem to have persuaded him to slow down. Friends now describe him as a mercifully modified Type A.

Psychological factors, particularly emotion, have long been implicated in physical illness. Research on motivation and emotion may find application in the prevention of such problems as heart disease and cancer, as well as asthma and ulcers, where psychological factors have been implicated for a long time.

Schachter and Gross showed that obese people will eat if you fool them into thinking it is dinnertime (the clock being an external stimulus), while normal-weight people will not. Subjects were brought into the laboratory late in the afternoon to participate in an experiment. They worked in a room with a large clock that was set either to run faster than normal speed or slower than normal speed. When real time was 5:30, the clock was either set fast at 6:05 or set slow at 5:20. The experimenter entered the room munching on a cracker and carrying a box of crackers, which he set down on the table, inviting the subject to help himself. The obese subjects ate just about twice as much when the clock said 6:05 as when it said 5:20, while just the opposite was true for nonobese people. They ate less at 6:05 (fake time) than at 5:20, saying they did not want to spoil their upcoming dinner. In short, the obese people responded to the external stimulus of the clock by increasing their intake simply because they thought it was dinnertime. Since the real time was 5:30 in both cases, the internal stimuli were presumably the same, and if their eating were under internal control, they would have eaten the same amount regardless of whether the clock said 6:05 or 5:20.

If obese people are sensitive to external food-related stimuli, we can understand why it is so difficult for them to keep off the weight they lose. Another factor is the number of fat cells in the body and the pre-set weight level, which is probably controlled in the hypothalamus. These are apparently hereditary factors, which means that it will be difficult to modify them. Here we can surmise that if an obese person does lose weight, his internal regulating system will be signaling a food deficit and he will constantly be experiencing feelings of hunger and will be motivated to eat. Ultimately, research on the physiological regulation of food intake may uncover means by which we can modify the pre-set weight level and allow an obese person to lose weight and keep it off without suffering from constant hunger. In the meantime, we will have to use other techniques, such as behavior modification and social group pressures (for example, Weight Watchers), to modify eating habits.

Controlling Emotions

If we understood emotions fully we would be able to control and to express them in an appropriate fashion. Knowledge of emotion has potentially far-reaching application in the area of mental health. It is believed by many psychologists that inability to deal with and appropriately express emotions is the major source of psychopathology. The individual's attempt to escape anxiety is thought to be the primary motivation for pathological behavior. As we will see in Chapters 11 and 12, anxiety is a key concept for understanding mental illness, and teaching people to cope appropriately with their anxiety is a key concept in psychotherapy.

Complete knowledge of the physiology underlying emotion will also contribute to emotional control. We already have tranquilizing drugs and "mood-elevating" drugs, and as our knowledge of the physiology of emotion grows, additional techniques will be developed. As we saw in Chapter 2, there are now surgical procedures that can be used to destroy parts of the brain that control violence and aggression. The suggestion has been made that all world political leaders be given drugs to control their aggression. Perhaps we could ultimately control and eliminate all violence from child beating to war.

The ability to control emotions would have impact on our physical health as well as our mental health. Medical science has implicated emotional factors in many diseases, the so-called psychosomatic disorders. For example, asthma and stomach ulcers are usually thought to be partially caused by emotional factors. If our knowledge of emotion were sufficient, we should be able to teach people ways to control their emotions and in turn to improve their physical health. Recently there have been suggestions that emotional factors play a role in two diseases that are major causes of death, cancer and

heart disease. If this is true, then the ability to change our emotional habits could significantly prolong our lives. At the very least, it ought to be possible to identify people who because of their emotional habits are high-risk individuals. Perhaps these people could be given special medical treatment of a preventive nature.

Summary

1. Motivation is an explanatory concept used to answer questions about *why* organisms behave as opposed to how they accomplish the behavior. It is used to account for observed variability in behavior both within the individual (the same person behaves differently on two occasions when the situation is identical) and between individuals (in the same situation, two different people will behave differently).

2. Motives are often defined by the length of time the organism has been deprived of some goal object, such as food, and by the observation that such deprivation leads to increased attempts to achieve the goal.

3. Two fundamental concepts of motivation are drive and incentive. Drive refers to the "push" behind behavior—the energy. Incentive refers to the goal objects that entice or pull the behavior. In practice, drive is measured by length of deprivation and incentive is measured by the quality and quantity of the rewarding goal object.

4. In the past, most psychologists emphasized drive as the more important factor, implying we are mainly pushed into behaving by our drives. More recently, the emphasis has shifted to incentive as the most important aspect of motivation, especially in analyses of human behavior.

5. For some time it has been believed that deprivation leads to increased energy and more activity. Recent analyses, however, suggest that deprived animals are not automatically more active, but instead are more reactive to stimuli in the environment. Deprived animals are not more aroused, but more arousable when subjected to stimulation. This evidence casts doubt on the traditional drive-energy-activity concept.

6. A useful formulation for understanding motivation is based on the distinction between predisposition and precipitation. The motivated organism is predisposed to respond but will not do so until there are appropriate precipitating circumstances.

7. We have built-in physiological systems that regulate intake of such things as food and water.

These systems operate according to the principle of homeostasis, with the goal of maintaining a steady state within our bodies.

8. The homeostatic system regulating food intake is complex and involves a pre-set weight level determined largely by heredity and involving the monitoring of fat levels in the body. There is also a regulation of hour-by-hour intake of food, which is apparently accomplished by monitoring levels of sugar in the blood. The hypothalamus also plays an important role in regulating weight levels and food intake. Finally, the stomach and mouth play a role in food regulation, although a relatively minor one.

9. An instinct is an inherited, invariant behavioral sequence that is unique to the species. It is a fixed action pattern precipitated by environmental "releasing" stimuli. Instinct theories were once quite popular but were not very useful in explaining behavior. Ethology has revived the concept of instinct and has used it to account for feeding, reproductive, and defensive behaviors in animals. The role of instincts in human behavior is a subject of considerable controversy.

10. Much of our behavior appears to be motivated by a homeostatic system that is designed to keep our arousal level at some optimal point. We seek out sources of stimulation when our arousal level is lower than optimal and we attempt to reduce stimulation when we become overaroused.

11. Psychologists studying human motivation often treat motivation as a personality characteristic, dealing with the psychological needs of people. These personality characteristics can be viewed as predispositions to respond to particular incentives.

12. Some of the human needs and personality characteristics that have received attention from psychologists include need for achievement, need for affiliation, and need for social approval. Each person presumably learns a set of psychological needs as he grows up and these needs are of varying strengths. Variation in adult motivation is then accounted for by variation in the strengths of the needs.

13. There are two primary dimensions of emotion, the qualitative dimension of pleasantness-unpleasantness and the quantitative dimension of intensity. Emotions are generally considered to be important sources of motivation—we seek positive, pleasant emotional states and strive to avoid negative states.

14. Modern analyses of emotion suggest two basic components, a general arousal and a cognitive evaluation of the circumstances that led to the arousal. There is also an evaluation of the degree of arousal, which in turn can affect the evaluation of the situation. The emotional experience is an outgrowth of the interplay between the arousal and the cognitive evaluations.

15. Applications of motivational research have been made in order to improve or increase the performance of industrial workers. Also, it appears possible to increase the level of achievement motivation among businessmen.

16. A full understanding of motivation and emotion would allow us to help solve such problems as obesity and emotional disorders, including the psychosomatic illnesses.

Recommended Additional Readings

Bindra, D., & Stewart, J. (Eds.) *Motivation* (2nd ed.). Baltimore: Penguin, 1971.

Bolles, R. C. *Theory of motivation* (2nd ed.). New York: Harper & Row, 1975.

Cofer, C. N. *Motivation and emotion.* Glenview, Ill.: Scott Foresman, 1974.

Cofer, C. N., & Appley, M. H. *Motivation: Theory and research.* New York: Wiley, 1964.

Lorenz, K. *Evolution and modification of behavior.* Chicago: University of Chicago Press, 1965.

Malmo, R. B. *On emotions, needs, and our archaic brain.* New York: Holt, Rinehart and Winston, 1975.

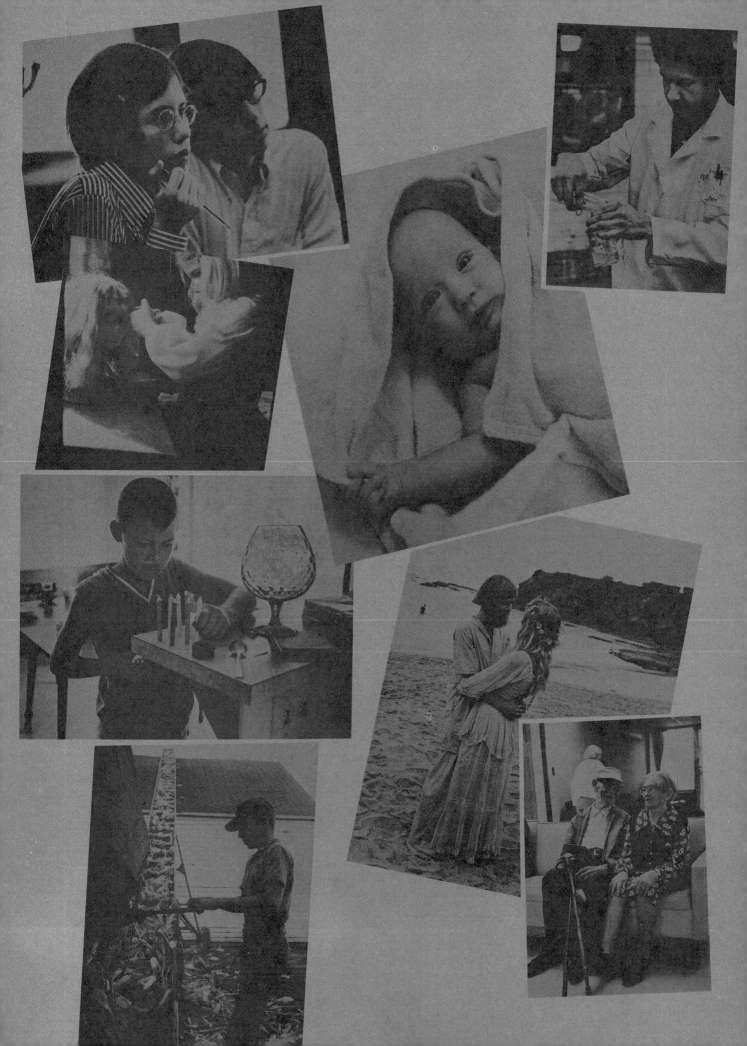

7

DEVELOPMENTAL PSYCHOLOGY

At what age does the normal infant begin to perceive his environment, to learn ways of reacting to it, or to express his emotions?

On the first day of school, some children seem calm, comfortable, and secure, while others are anxious and unhappy. What factors contribute to these differences?

What influence does watching violent or educational television programs have on the young child?

What effects do biological changes initiated at puberty, such as the change of voice in males or the appearance of breasts in females, have on the behavior and feelings of the 12- to 15-year-old?

On what basis can we judge when a person stops being an adolescent and becomes a responsible adult?

These are some of the many questions about human developmental processes that people commonly ask. Developmental psychology is an attempt to find out the answers. In a sense, developmental psychology is concerned with all the various aspects of behavior we have discussed in preceding chapters, as well as some topics yet to be treated in detail. Using scientific procedures, developmental psychologists attempt to understand how and why these behaviors change over the lifetime of an individual.

Developmental psychology is the study of changes in behavior that normally occur with increases in chronological age (Spiker, 1966). Developmental psychologists limit themselves to changes that are fairly pronounced and permanent and take place over periods of time. Changes in our mood are typically momentary. Some things that we learn are quickly forgotten. These short-term variations are not the primary concern of a developmental psychologist. But biological, intellectual, emotional, and social changes that take place over a period of weeks, months, and years are processes that the developmental psychologist tries to understand. We will concentrate our discussion on behavioral changes during infancy, childhood, and adolescence. It is during these years that the greatest change takes place and the basis for adult behavior is formed.

Some Major Issues of Developmental Psychology

Throughout this chapter, you should be aware of certain major issues that characterize both the research and the opinion of developmental psychologists about behavior changes.

*"Your manuscript exposing the Little League is
sensational, but I'm afraid it's a little
too hot for us to handle!"*

**A precocious child is one whose development,
intellectually or otherwise, is well ahead of the
norm. Such children are sometimes quite
troublesome (mischievous?) individuals for adults
and age-mates to handle.**

Heredity, Maturation, and Experience

A human being is what he is for a variety of reasons.
A person's future is partly shaped at conception,
when the male sperm and female ovum unite into a
single fertilized cell. This is because the sperm and
the ovum carry genetic material from both parents
that will determine, barring later unforeseen
circumstances, many of the biological
characteristics (such as hair color) and
psychological characteristics (such as general
temperament) of the organism to be. But that
certainly is not the whole story. If it were, our
eventual adult would be doomed to behave only in
ritualistic ways laid down at conception by *heredity,*
and we know that other processes affect behavior.

Biological *maturation* is also of crucial
importance. Some abilities not present at birth
nonetheless develop in a preprogrammed way with
age and growth. These maturational changes are
most obvious in behaviors closely tied to anatomical

growth. They tend to be the sorts of changes that
are more or less the same in children from various
cultures, and hence minimally dependent upon
individual experiences. They also occur at
approximately the same time in all individuals, and
are relatively independent of the effects of special
training. There are a variety of behaviors and
abilities that meet most of these criteria. Think, for
example, of the infant's ability to control his eyes,
especially their points of focus. This ability develops
only at a particular time after birth when the various
muscles controlling eye movement and the shape of
the lens (see Chapter 3) have fully matured. Other
examples are the ability to walk and the ability to
vocalize meaningfully. Both are dependent on
muscular growth and a capacity for coordination not
present at birth.

But not all behavior changes, obviously, can be
the product of heredity and maturation alone. The
human being begins to *experience* the environment
while still in the mother's uterus. The fetus (unborn
child) may well be capable of rudimentary learning
on the order of classical conditioning. Of course, the
environment expands immensely upon birth, and it
is at this point that the most dramatic changes in
behavior begin to unfold. Most of these changes will
be attributed to experience or learning.

Questions about the extent to which heredity,
maturation, and learning contribute to the behavior
of an adult have been asked and argued at least
since the time of Plato (400 B.C.). The issue is still
unsettled regarding many aspects of psychological
development and probably will continue to be for
some time to come.

The answer probably lies in a compromise
position. No matter what example we think
of—controlling the focus of one's eyes, learning to
vocalize meaningfully, giving a piano concert, or
whatever—it is probably the product of a process
extending through time that involves both biological
and experiential components. Sorting out the *extent*
to which each of them contributes, even if possible,
is probably less important than understanding the
mechanisms by which each contributes.

Individual Differences

Like other types of psychologists, developmental
psychologists are interested in both explanations
and descriptions of behavior. Many of the behavior
descriptions provided by a developmental
psychologist are *normative.* The developmental
psychologist will often talk about the average
performance of normal human beings in this task or
that at any particular age. We should recognize that

although the norm is meaningful and interesting, there will always be *individual differences* in development. The norms are based on large samples of people at various ages, only some of whom fall close to the *mean,* the arithmetic average of a set of scores. Others will deviate to the extremes (see Appendix A). Variation in both rate of development and kinds of development is to be expected. Not all of us will learn to walk, reach puberty, or achieve our intellectual peak at the same time or in the same way. Individual differences among us are an important fact of psychological life. The norms are helpful in spotting serious behavioral deviations (see Chapter 11), but are not to be interpreted as exact values for all normal people.

Stages versus Continuity in Growth

There is no question that behavior, like physiological changes, shows age spurts. How often have you heard it said, "It seems like Mary became an adult overnight," or "Johnny can't fit into the shoes I bought him just last month." The appearance of dramatic and permanent changes within a short period of time, coupled with the infrequency or lack of apparent changes before or after these major changes, suggests that growth may be a stagelike process. The individual enters the world at a particular stage of development. At some later time, triggered by some unspecified events, he makes the transition into a more mature stage. Then, later on, there is another transition, and so on. We all pass through a series of qualitatively different stages, each one building on the preceding stage. Our behavioral competence becomes increasingly greater. This observation has been taken as the basis of a number of theories regarding psychological development, called stage theories.

There is a contrasting theory that psychological growth is basically a continuous process, which may pick up speed or slow down at particular ages, but nonetheless involves no abrupt or discontinuous transitions from one state to another. Both our intuitions and our introspections tend to support this idea, for very few individuals claim to experience abrupt stagelike changes in their feelings or abilities.

Here again the answer no doubt is a compromise. It is naive to think that development must be *either* steplike *or* continuous. Quite probably, some aspects of development are continuous and sequential while others unfold in spurts. An important task of developmental psychology is to determine in detail the processes that underlie changes of both types.

Are Big Babies Brighter?

Newsweek—Pediatricians have known for years that a premature baby is more apt to have trouble with his school work than a child born at full term, but a new study now suggests that the determining factor in such a child's difficulties in school may be not prematurity itself, but rather the low birth weight that usually accompanies it. In a study of 241 children, a team of researchers at the University of Minnesota has shown that those who weighed less than 5½ pounds at birth—whether premature or not—have "significantly more school-related problems" than those born weighing more.

The twenty researchers, headed by educational psychologist Dr. Rosalyn Rubin, selected their subjects from infants born at the university's hospital during the early 1960s. In order to rule out any racial, environmental or socioeconomic variables, they concentrated on babies born of white, urban, middle-class families and classified them according to their birth weight and whether or not they had been born prematurely. Then the team followed the children's progress into elementary school.

Lower Scores

On every test measuring language development, readiness for school and academic achievement, the low-birth-weight children scored lower than those born weighing more. Their IQ scores averaged only 94, as compared to 104 for those of normal birth weight. And significantly, full-term babies born at low weights had a far higher incidence of trouble in school than premature babies weighing more than 5½ pounds.

The results of this study are still under close examination, but they do suggest another way in which biological factors can influence human behavior and abilities.

Kinds of Developmental Studies

A variety of research strategies are used by developmental psychologists. Some studies follow a particular group of subjects over several (sometimes many) years, while others, in contrast, investigate several different groups of differing age. In many cases the psychologist will manipulate variables to determine how they influence behavior, while in others he will look for correlations between chronological age and behavior. In all cases, of course, the general idea is to reveal the changes in performance and ability that occur as the organism develops.

When the same people are repeatedly observed or measured at regular intervals over a long period of time, the study is called *longitudinal.* We might wish

Deadend Street?

London Express Service
London (UPI)—A British Broadcasting Corp. (BBC) program director said Monday the state-owned television network turned down "Sesame Street" because of its "authoritarian aim."

Monica Sims, head of children's television at BBC, said she admired many aspects of the American series, which she termed a "kind of junior Laugh-In."

But she cited criticism by educators of "essentially middle class attitudes, lack of reality, and attempt to prepare children for school but not for middle life.

Despite the BBC rejection, British small fry will get a liberal helping this fall of Cookie Monster, Big Bird, and Oscar. British independent television has announced plans to screen 13 55-minute installments of "Sesame Street" beginning Sept. 25.

The famous children's program "Sesame Street" has used developmental research in planning educational programs. In fact, the program is so inventive and makes such heavy use of elaborate animation techniques that schoolteachers may have trouble competing. And not everyone is enthusiastic about the impact of this program on child development, as the clipping indicates. What kinds of knowledge, skills, and intentions do you think children might acquire from various kinds of TV programs? Just how important is television in shaping such things as personality, attitudes, values, or even spelling?

Figure 7–1
Types of developmental studies

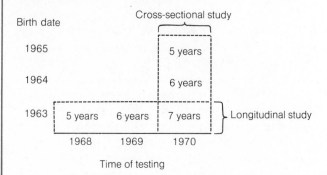

A format for hypothetical studies using the cross-sectional and longitudinal methods. The longitudinal study can use the same group of subjects at each time of testing but must run for a period of years. The cross-sectional approach has the advantage of requiring less time to gather the test data, but gives no information about the consistency of one subject's behavior.

to know, for example, whether a person's IQ at age 15 is predictable from his IQ at age 7. There is no way to execute such a study without testing the same individuals, at least at the two critical ages. The main advantage of longitudinal studies is that they allow us to determine the degree to which behavior is consistent over time. They are the only way of determining the effects of early experience on later behavior.

There are disadvantages to the longitudinal approach that limit its usefulness. First of all, this type of study tends to be expensive and time-consuming. The research can only be concluded when the required number of years between measurements has passed. In addition, modern cultures change quite rapidly. Longitudinal data, therefore, can become outmoded before the study is completed. It is easy to imagine the frustration of a researcher who began studying logical abilities in children in 1965, and who finds, after 10 intervening years, that new educational television programs such as "Sesame Street" have influenced intellectual growth processes in a unique way.

As a means of avoiding some of the difficulties and biases that can creep into longitudinal studies, many investigators of age changes use the *cross-sectional* method. In this method, children of different grades, stages, or ages are tested more or less simultaneously (see Figure 7–1). A psychologist might be interested, for example, in changes in the sociability of children between the ages of 5 and 7 years. To execute this study, the psychologist would test different samples of children at approximately the same time, one sample for each of the ages involved. The obvious advantage of the cross-sectional study is that data can be gathered in a relatively brief interval of testing. The major disadvantage, of course, is that it does not allow for an evaluation of performance consistency across time in the individual child.

Developmental studies differ along another dimension. One kind of study attempts to determine the way in which manipulations of the environment affect behavior. The experimenter sets up *antecedent* conditions and measures *consequent* outcomes. For example, 5-, 6-, and 7-year-old children might be examined to see whether they can learn simple arithmetic principles more efficiently through instruction and guidance by the teacher or through a "discovery" method that encourages them to solve problems on their own. The focus is on the way in which manipulations of the environment

"Tonight's special 'Why Junior Can't Spell' was brought to you by the makers of Kwik Koffee, Minit Pudding, Tastee-Ade, Choc Snax, Froot Bits, Korn Chips, Sweetie Treets, Jelli Muffins, and Sooper Soup."

Reprinted courtesy of The Register and Tribune Syndicate.

Figure 7–2
The startle reflex

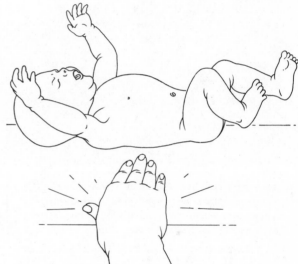

The startle reflex, sometimes called the Moro reflex, is displayed by all human infants. It is a fixed reaction to a startling event such as a loud noise or loss of support of the head. The reflex will disappear in the first 6 months of life, unless the child suffers a certain neurological impairment.

affect behavior at one or more stages of development.

More or less in contrast to this approach is the *normative-developmental* procedure, which is generally favored by those who are interested in maturational changes. This kind of study focuses on the behavior of groups of children at different ages, all performing in a single, tightly-controlled situation. The aim is to chart behavioral norms across a significant span of ages. Studies that provide the standardization or normative data for an age-scale IQ test (see Chapter 5) are a good example of this kind of research. In order to evaluate the performance of any given individual, we need to know how well children of his age do, on the average, on the test.

In reviewing these research strategies, be sure to keep in mind the advantages and disadvantages of each. For any particular problem that a psychologist might wish to explore, one strategy is probably better than the rest. But the choice will depend on the problem and the kind of information the researcher wishes to gather.

Intellectual Development

The newborn child is a challenge not only to his parents but to psychologists. He sleeps approximately 16 hours a day in 7 or 8 short cycles. When he is awake he demands attention. He can perform some physical actions, but he is undeveloped psychologically. He will respond to a loud noise, a sudden change in head position, or other unexpected events by throwing his arms out to the side, extending his fingers, and then curving his hands back toward the midline, a sequence which is known as the startle reflex (see Figure 7–2). But he will display little or no purposive behavior.

In 10 to 15 years, this helpless organism will normally become an independent, knowledgeable, and social human being who has a capacity for originality and creativity in thought and action. The transition is largely a matter of *intellectual*

*"Gee, it's still just the same as
when I was a little kid!"*

Playboy, May 1968. Reproduced by special permission of *Playboy* Magazine; © 1968 by Playboy.

Perhaps parents would have an easier time of it if they tried, at least occasionally, to see the world through their children's eyes or tried to remember how it was when they were very young.

**Figure 7–3
Measuring visual preferences in infants**

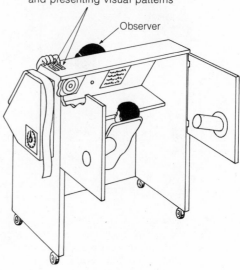

A device used to measure the interest value of different visual patterns in terms of time spent looking at them. The subject sits facing a "stage" where patterns are presented. His view is restricted to the inside of the illuminated chamber.

development, the growth and change in competence that enables one to interact and cope successfully with one's environment. The next section is devoted to a discussion of intellectual development, which we shall organize in four categories: perception, learning, cognition, and language.

Perception

Infant perception.   Even the newborn (under 1 month of age) infant exhibits certain perceptual skills. He is attracted to stimuli in the environment and can discriminate among some of them. He can hear differences in the pitch of sounds as small as one note apart on the piano when those sounds are presented at moderate loudness. He can differentiate among some odors and some tastes as well.

Sensory systems develop to full capacity over the years of infancy, 0–2 years. Interestingly, the most important of our senses, vision, is more immature than other systems at birth. Once the infant opens

his eyes, his visual focus is relatively fixed at about 9 inches from the cornea, which is the approximate distance between him and his mother's face during nursing. The coordination of his eyes is poor because his eye muscles are weak; indeed, the newborn infant often appears cross-eyed. Most evidence suggests that he cannot converge his eyes to change their point of focus until he is about 2 months old and that he cannot change the shape of his lens to bring near or far objects into focus until he is about 4 months old. The retina, too, is immature, but it does respond to changes in light and intensity. The infant will blink to an aversive stimulus and he can follow a moving target passing in front of him. Estimates of infants' visual acuity are generally placed at 20/150. This would mean that the child can see from 20 feet what an adult with normal vision could see at 150 feet. But, by the age of 2, the child's visual acuity will reach the adult level.

An infant spends much of his waking time just looking. In doing so, he exhibits definite visual preferences. A device used to measure looking behavior and visual preferences is shown in Figure 7–3. If you present the baby with a moving array of

Figure 7-4
Pattern preferences in infants

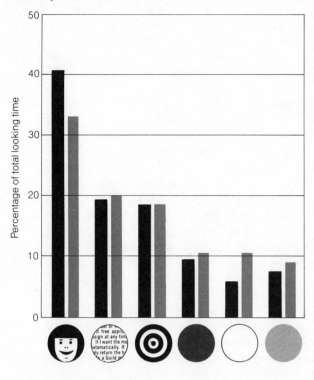

Importance of pattern rather than color or brightness is illustrated by the response of infants to a face, a piece of printed matter, a bull's-eye, and plain red, white, and yellow disks. Even the youngest infants preferred patterns. Black bars show the results for infants from 2 to 3 months old, orange bars for infants more than 3 months old.

lights versus a stationary pattern, you will find that he is more attentive to the moving stimulus. Another feature attractive to infants is patterns. Even a 1-day-old infant spends more time looking at patterns like a bull's-eye than at plain colored figures like a red circle. An example of the relative preferences of infants for various patterned stimuli is shown in Figure 7-4. These effects occur so early in a child's lifetime that many people have concluded that sensitivity to pattern is an innate phenomenon. In this connection, recall the discussion of receptive fields in Chapter 3.

One of the most interesting of the newborn's visual preferences is the human face. An infant will smile more at a line drawing of a face than at an equally complex, nonhuman pattern. He will attend more to a three-dimensional mask than to a line drawing of a face and pay more attention to real faces than to masks. After several months, natural,

familiar faces will elicit more smiling than unfamiliar ones. Then, at about 2 years of age, the child's preference for familiar and more realistic objects tends to wane. A 2-year-old confronting a face with eyes on its chin and a nose in the middle of its forehead no longer ignores it but appears to be fascinated. Unusual stimuli becomes attractive and appear to take on the character of problems in need of solution. Thus the child's perceptual activity develops from a point where attention is given primarily to movement and contrast, to a second point where what is familiar and meaningful is most attractive, and finally to a point where he searches for the unusual.

The perception of objects in depth, which we, as adults, take for granted, seems to develop by the time the child begins to crawl (6–8 months) and possibly even before. The existence of depth perception in young children has been verified by a device called the "visual cliff," shown in Figure 7–5. The illusion of a cliff is built into a level glass floor, and the child is urged to crawl across the floor, over the edge of the "cliff." Babies have refused to crawl across the surface beyond the cliff even to reach their mothers. There is some evidence that the heart rate changes in response to the cliff even in precrawling infants. These facts do not, of course, prove that depth perception exists at birth, but they do suggest that it develops early in life.

Later development of perceptual skills. Fully developed sensory systems allow the child, 2 years and older, to experience the world. Experience leads to behavior changes, and these changes reflect not only new knowledge but also new ways of gathering knowledge. Consider the following experiment. A child is blindfolded and given the chance to explore tactually a strangely contoured object. The object is then put on display with a number of other objects, and the child must identify the target object on the basis of touch only. If a 3-year-old is presented with this problem, he tends to hold the target object briefly in his palms. His contact with the object is minimal and uninformative. As a result, he typically fails to identify the test object. In contrast, 7- and 8-year-olds run their fingers around the edges and spread their thumb and forefinger in an apparent effort to gauge the length of the object. The even more experienced 10-year-old child efficiently touches just those features that are likely to distinguish the object from others. The organized search pattern of an older child allows him to identify objects more quickly and more accurately. Systematic, efficient, and thorough search patterns

Figure 7–5
The visual cliff

A mother testing her child on the "visual cliff." Above, the child eagerly crawls to the mother on the "shallow" side of the cliff, where the checkerboard pattern is placed right below the glass surface. Below, the pattern has been placed on the floor, giving the illusion of depth or of a cliff. Now the child refuses to crawl off the cliff despite his mother's inducements.

develop with age in all sensory systems, not just touch.

E. J. Gibson's analysis of reading shows that what is searched for as well as the search method itself

changes with age. When an adult scans a book, he uses highly refined reading skills that the typical 3-year-old does not possess. Asked to identify letters, the 3-year-old will correctly ignore line drawings but will incorrectly assume that unintelligible scribbles are letters. Even 5-year-olds, who know which marks are letters, often cannot isolate words because they ignore spaces between words (see Figure 7–6).

There are at least three features that distinguish letters from one another: open versus closed, as in *o* versus *c*; direction, as in *p* versus *d*; and curvature, as in *u* versus *v*. The distinction between open and closed figures is easy, even for 3-year-olds. Approximately 45 percent of 4-year-olds, however, regard figures varying in direction or curvature as identical. The problem stems from ignorance, not insensitivity. Training procedures, such as pointing in opposite directions for *b* and *d,* can quickly improve letter differentiation (Gibson, Gibson, Pick, and Osser, 1972).

By the time the child reaches the age of 10 or 12, his perceptual skills, including those involved in reading, are essentially mature and fully developed. There will be significant changes later, especially the commonly observed marked deterioration in one or more sensory systems brought on by the aging process. But the peak of these fundamental abilities underlying behavior is reached at a relatively young age. Only intense specialized training (see, for example, the discussion on wine tasting in Chapter 3) can bring about significant further improvement in perception.

Learning

Learning in infants. The newborn infant lacks the motor control to reach out and explore his environment directly. As a consequence, it was thought for many years that newborns could not actively learn. With the advent of new experimental procedures, however, researchers have begun to destroy that myth. In fact, there is even some evidence that learning takes place before birth. The newborn learns particularly well those responses that are important to the maintenance of life and that provide an opportunity to explore the environment.

Sucking is a very prominent behavior in infants. A common example of early learning is the classical conditioning of anticipatory sucking at the sight of a nipple. In one experiment, Kaye (1967) sounded a tone just before a nipple was presented. Babies only 3 or 4 days old quickly learned that the tone was a signal for the subsequent appearance of the nipple.

Figure 7–6
Which is writing?

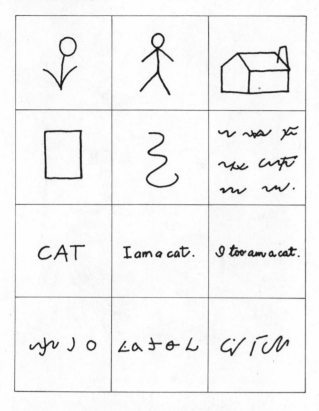

Because they do not distinguish scribbles from letters, 3-year-old children would have trouble telling which represents writing. Even 5-year-olds might have difficulty.

When the tone was sounded, they began to suck. Even during extinction, when the tone was no longer paired with the nipple, many babies persisted in sucking to the tone alone. Conditioning of the sucking responses is one of the first signs of learning that parents notice. A baby will, for example, typically recognize the position in which he is fed, and begin to suck as soon as he is placed in that position.

Instrumental conditioning can also be demonstrated. Siqueland and Lipsitt (1966) increased head turning in 3- and 4-day-olds by rewarding that response with a nipple filled with sugar solution. After 27 rewards, their subjects had increased head turning about three times over. A control group, not so reinforced for head turning, did not change their response rate at all.

The same investigators taught infants to turn their heads when a buzzer was sounded. Then the rewards were switched so that reinforcement was

Figure 7–7
Discrimination learning and discrimination reversal in infants

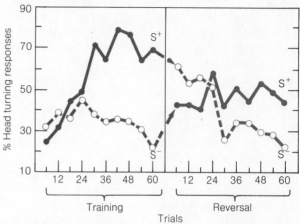

Comparison of percentage head-turning responses to a positive (S⁺) and a negative (S⁻) stimulus during 60 trials of training and reversal.

given when the baby turned at the sound of a tone instead of a buzzer. Babies 3 days old quickly reversed their behavior (see Figure 7–7). Hence, it is clear that infants are capable of learning discriminations as soon as we can test them.

Fairly young infants also show signs of the development of responsiveness to what are known in learning theory as secondary reinforcers. When the child is 3 months old, for example, vocalization and smiling can be increased when reinforced by a friendly pat or a bit of baby talk from the experimenter. Subsequent withdrawal of adult contact produces a decrease in vocalizing and smiling. Indeed, attention from parents or caretakers can facilitate learning during earliest infancy, a period of life when the child must learn a lot to equip himself for adolescence and adulthood.

Concept learning in early childhood. A good deal of a young child's behavior involves learning and using concepts. At first his concepts are rudimentary and based on concrete, perceptual examples. The child learns, for example, concepts such as dogs and cats. Having formed these concepts, he will on later occasions be able to classify correctly unfamiliar and entirely novel animals, such as a stray dog who happens to wander across his path.

Although his repertoire of concepts grows increasingly with experience over the years, the child apparently does not develop very abstract kinds of concepts until he reaches his fifth or sixth year. The young child probably learns most early concepts by rote memorization. It is as if he has to associate the same response (or category) with each of a large number of individual stimuli before he gets the idea of generalizing to novel instances. In contrast, the older child, say, 7 or 8 years of age, appears to learn in a different way. He can abstract the characteristics of objects that are the basis of a concept. He appears to analyze each stimulus into its constituent parts and to use only those parts that define the concept in making his decision about any stimulus object.

It is interesting to note that the transition point in this developmental sequence, from rote learning to an ability to abstract and deal analytically with stimulus features, comes at about the time that the child is developing an adultlike command of the language. This also seems to be the period of time during which the child develops an ability to talk and think to himself. Some theorists believe that internalized speech operates as a problem-solving device and as a mechanism for guiding and regulating overt speech and other forms of human behavior. The issue is not settled, however; other theorists, such as the psychologist Jean Piaget, believe that language does not determine but merely reflects cognitive processes, which develop first.

Cognition

The most detailed description of human knowledge and how it develops has been provided by the Swiss psychologist Jean Piaget. Piaget divides development into three major periods or stages: the *sensorimotor,* the *concrete operational,* and the *formal operational.* The sensorimotor period covers the time from birth to about 2 years of age. During this time the infant progresses from understanding the world only in terms of his own activities to the realization that objects have existence in a spatial and temporal framework independent of himself. In the period of concrete operations, from 2 to about 11 years, the child develops language as a system for symbolizing events and objects and learns to deal with fundamental physical concepts, such as quantity and weight. For this introductory treatment, we find it convenient to subdivide this stage into a *preoperational* (2–7 years of age) and a *concrete operational* (7–11 years of age) period. During the preoperational period, the child learns the rudiments of language, as a system for representing objects, events, and states of affairs in his environment. During the later concrete operational stage, the

"Oh, to dream once more the untroubled dreams of childhood!"

New Yorker, October 29, 1973. Drawing by Whitney Darrow, Jr.; © 1973 by The New Yorker Magazine, Inc.

One factor that makes research with infants difficult is their limited range of behaviors. We have no way of really knowing what a young child is thinking (or dreaming).

child begins to execute the logical operations of classification and order, which form a basis for more abstract operations in later life. At 11 or 12, the child enters the *formal operational* period. Formal operational thinking is the most abstract level of thought that a human being will achieve. It enables him to conceive of events beyond the concrete present, to imagine hypothetical situations, and to develop complex systems of logic.

Piaget asserts that all children go through all stages in the same order. According to his theory, human intellect is constructed over time by the individual's progressively more complex interactions with the environment. Each stage depends on and integrates previous stages. But the pace of development can be determined largely by the environment. A highly technological society, for

Figure 7–8
Object permanence

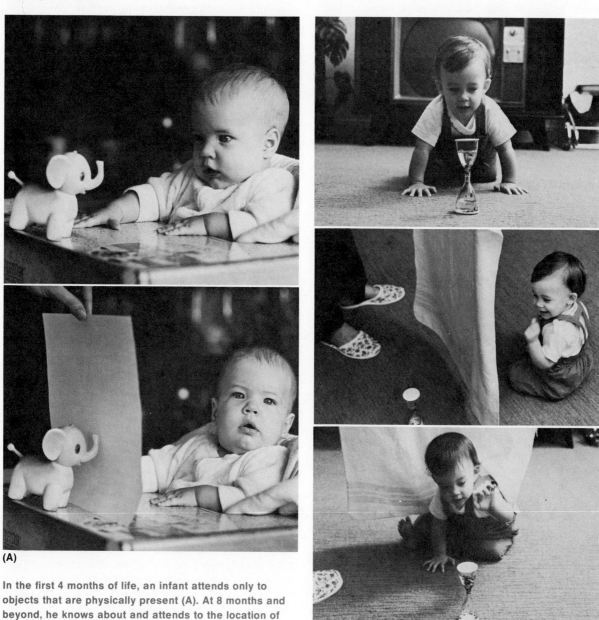

(A)

(B)

In the first 4 months of life, an infant attends only to objects that are physically present (A). At 8 months and beyond, he knows about and attends to the location of hidden or occluded objects (B).

example, provides more complex experiences and thus more rapid intellectual development.

The sensorimotor stage (birth to 2 years).
Piaget is famous not only for his theory but also for his naturalistic observations of the developmental process. Here are some of the things he reports about the development of cognition during the first 2 years of life, which he sees as requiring six steps

corresponding to the discovery of different environmental objects and their relationships.

During the first month of life (*Step 1*) the baby appears to be unaware of objects around him or even of himself. He does not realize that the bottle he grasps one minute and sucks the next is the same object. Neither does he know that objects exist when he is not looking directly at them. If something drops out of sight it also drops out of mind.

In months 1 through 4 (*Step 2*), the baby's motor activities become more coordinated. At this point, he begins to look at what he is grasping. He will move his hands to touch an object by alternating his gaze between hand and object, homing in on the object by successive approximations.

Between months 4 and 8 (*Step 3*), the child attempts to control and manipulate objects, though his efforts are often comical. He may hear an interesting noise and want to have it repeated. He does not know what causes the noise, so he tries to make the noise reoccur by repeating whatever he was doing when he heard the noise. Piaget calls this one example of "magical procedures to make interesting spectacles last." It is during this period that the child first begins to realize that objects exist when they are out of sight. If he drops a toy, he will search for it, but probably only for a short time.

In the final 4 months of the first year of age (*Step 4*), magical thinking gives way to more instrumental activity. Suppose you give a child a shiny object to examine, and then take it from his grasp and place it under a pillow. At about age 6 months the child is likely to cry or to repeat what he was doing at the time the object disappeared. At 8 months, he is likely to lift the pillow and feel around in hopes of retrieving the object. At this point, we can say that the child has definitely achieved *object permanence*; that is, something can exist even while it is not immediately available to the child's sensory systems (see Figure 7–8). The child at this stage must have some memory image of the object to help him recall it and its location. Moreover, he must have some sense of space and time, for his actions of lifting the pillow and searching for the object are organized and orderly. But the child is still quite limited intellectually. If you hide the object under one pillow and then move it in plain view to a second, the child will search under the first pillow and may or may not move subsequently to the second. He does not short-circuit the process by going directly to the second pillow.

Short-circuiting will appear in the first half of the second year of life (*Step 5*). The 12- to 14-month-old is likely to go directly to the second pillow to find the hidden object. More systematic exploration of the environment also emerges. Piaget sees much of cognitive growth as the formulation of more and more complex hypotheses about events and of the modification of these hypotheses in the light of experience. Hypothesis testing involves trying out variations of behavior and determining their results. For example, the child might systematically vary the position from which he drops a toy in order to discover where the toy will land. As we have seen, there are parallel developments in the infant's perceptual search processes during this time.

The final stage of sensorimotor development covers the last half of the second year of life (*Step 6*). The child makes his first inferences. In the preceding 6 months, the child appears to be stumped when an object is placed under one pillow and then moved in a closed fist to another pillow. The older child is not fooled by this invisible movement, because he infers what the moving hand holds. Likewise, he is not upset when a ball rolls out of sight under a table, because he can predict where and when it will emerge.

The first means the child has of symbolizing an event is by motor gestures. Piaget described one classical gestural symbol elicited from his young daughter in a game that involved a disappearing pocket watch. When he hid the watch in a partially closed matchbox, his daughter retrieved it by scooping the chain out through the opening. When Piaget replaced the watch leaving only a narrow slit of an opening, his daughter at first appeared puzzled. She stared intently at the box and then began to open her mouth wider and wider. Almost immediately, she put her fingers into the slit and with pincerlike movements opened the slit wider and wider too. This, of course, allowed her to reach in and to retrieve the watch. In later stages, of course, the child develops much more sophisticated ways of symbolizing and mentally representing objects and events.

The preoperational stage (2–7 years). The major advance made by the developing child during this period is the ability to represent the external world internally by means of arbitrary symbols that stand for objects. This is the period in which language develops and begins to reflect the cognitive activities, abilities, and limitations of the child. We shall have more to say about language development in the next section. At this point, we wish mainly to point out that the preoperational child is in a transitional period. The child's perspective on the world expands rapidly, but he is still confused in his use of physical concepts and in his evaluations of causality. The child's lack of understanding of the world is reflected in the way he deals with new information. He makes inappropriate generalizations. He attributes his own feelings to inanimate objects, assuming that clouds "cry" to make rain. He tends to explain the world in terms of human agents. If mothers make clothes and fathers make money, why can't parents be responsible for the origins of mountains and the weather? The child's limited conception of the world is revealed in the following interview:

Adult: Why is it dark at night?
Child: Because if you don't sleep, Santa Claus won't give you any toys.
Adult: Where does the dark come from at night?
Child: Well, bandits they take something or mother pulls down the blinds and then it's very dark.
Adult: What makes it day?
Child: God, he says to the dark, go away
           (Laurendeau and Pinard, 1962, pages 170–171)

Notice what Piaget would call *egocentrism* in this example. The child seems unable to imagine the world from any perspective other than his own. He cannot acknowledge alternative perspectives. This failure limits the kind and amount of new knowledge the child can acquire. Still, the child has a rudimentary system of logic which expands toward the end of the period to take into account other possibilities.

The concrete operational stage (7 to 11 years).   *Conservation* is Piaget's term for the idea that a property or attribute of an object remains the same despite an irrelevant transformation that may change the appearance of the object. Piaget found that when a preoperational child is shown two identical balls of clay and then sees one rolled into a sausage, he may claim that the sausage contains less clay because it is thinner than the ball. He takes only one aspect of the situation into account. Occasionally he will change his judgment, alternating between "less" because the sausage is thinner and "more" because the sausage is longer, without apparently noticing the contradiction. Because he focuses on the end state without considering how the sausage was produced, he arrives at the wrong answer. If he remembered that the sausage came from a ball that he knew was identical to the unchanged ball, he would arrive at a different answer. When the child understands these facts, we say he has the concepts of quantity and weight or that he is capable of *conserving* these concepts.

At about age 7, the child grasps the solution to conservation problems. He does this by developing three explanations that characterize *concrete operations*. The first is *compensation:* The sausage is thinner but that change is balanced by its increase in length. The second is *reversibility:* If you roll the sausage back you get the same ball you started with. Reversibility is important in arithmetic, where addition cancels subtraction and multiplication cancels division. Finally, there is the *identity* operation: Nothing has been added to or subtracted from the clay, so the sausage and the ball contain the same amount of clay.

In the concrete operational period, the child acquires and applies the notion of reversibility and identity through a wide variety of tasks. He learns systems of classifications and of number. Arithmetic is much easier when he realizes that $4 + 3 = 7$ is the same as $3 + 4 = 7$. And it follows that if $3 + 4 = 7$, then $7 - 3 = 4$. The ability to perform these mental operations in many different situations, with many numbers in any concrete problem, eliminates the need for rote memorization. The same laws are applicable across all situations. The child gives evidence of beginning to realize that arithmetic, as well as other disciplines, is based on a system of rules. He begins to make the transition from associative learning to rule learning and rule using.

The formal operational stage.   The complex, abstract, and mature logic of adults begins to manifest itself during adolescence. Teenagers develop what Piaget calls formal operational thinking: the systematic analysis, exploration, and solution of problems. Adolescents comprehend combinations, rearrangements, and permutations of objects and events, which most 10-year-olds cannot. Furthermore, they are capable of true symbolic logic.

The following fairly complex problem can be used to demonstrate how formal operational thought differs from earlier stages of cognitive development. Four similar glass containers of different colorless, odorless chemicals and another smaller container containing a fifth chemical, potassium iodide, are placed on a table before the subject (see Figure 7–9). A certain amount of chemical from two of the similar containers is poured into an empty glass. The experimenter then adds several drops of potassium iodide, and the liquid, consisting of two unknown chemicals, turns yellow. The subject is asked to reproduce this color, using any or all of the containers. The only thing he knows is that the glass that turned yellow contained chemicals from two out of the four containers.

There are distinct age differences in the approach to solving this type of problem. Infants up to 2 years old pay no attention to the problem situation and merely play with their toys. Children in the preoperational stage randomly combine chemicals,

Figure 7–9
The chemical problem

The chemical problem illustrates the different stages of cognitive development described by Piaget. Children of different ages are presented with four containers of colorless, odorless chemicals and a fifth beaker (g). Next, the children are shown a glass with a combination of two chemicals (unknown to the children, these are chemicals 1 and 3). When several drops of g are added to the glass, the liquid in the glass turns yellow. The children's task is to reproduce this color.

making no attempt to keep track of what they have done. Between the ages of 7 and 11 years, children begin to combine chemicals systematically, but tend to become confused after several steps. They too do not maintain a good record of what they have done. Children above 11 years, however, are able to approach the problem with a logical and complete plan. They take chemicals from the containers two at a time, keeping a record of those that do not work so that they do not repeat themselves. Piaget's explanation of these chronological differences in problem-solving ability is summarized in Table 7–1.

Teenagers differ in other ways from their younger counterparts. Most of them can deal skillfully with abstract questions or questions that are contrary to fact, like "What would have happened if the U.S. had not entered into the Vietnam war?" The more literal, concrete operational child insists that questions of this sort are invalid because the war did take place.

It is during the teenage years that a young person realizes that thoughts are private and that no one else knows what he is thinking. He values friendship and sincerity highly and spends much time trying to discern his and others' real motives. He is more aware than the younger child that events can be interpreted in many ways and that there is no final version of truth. He is also more sensitive to the discrepancy between reality and ideals. His

Table 7–1
Contrasting approaches to solving the chemical problem

Stage	Behavior	Explanation
Sensorimotor (birth–2 years)	Child ignores the request and plays with the toys.	Lacks the vocabulary and motor skills to understand what's required of him and to perform the task. Before 8 or so months lacks object permanence. Should one container drop from view he won't search for it.
Preoperational (2–7 years)	Child combines two containers at random.	Understands he is to produce the dye, but he does not order his tests (take one jar and "g," then the next, then the third). He cannot keep track of what he has done. He does not classify the results into combinations that produce a yellow color and those that do not. He is likely to think an irrelevant feature like the shape of the containers or the amount of the contents determines the color.
Concrete operations (7–11 years)	Child adds the fluid from each container in a systematic fashion. Then starts to combine "g" with pairs of containers and becomes confused.	Can order his tests, one container at a time, but has difficulty ordering two variables simultaneously. Can classify container combinations into those that make the yellow color and those that do not. Possesses logical operations of reversibility and identity. Understands conservation. Knows the problem has to do with the identity of the chemicals, not the shape of their containers.
Formal operations (11 years and older)	Child takes the containers and combines them with "g" one at a time, etc. Is able to keep track of system and identify both the chemicals making the dye and some of the others.	Possesses knowledge of permutations and combinations. Can go beyond data to describe in abstract terms the nature of his system of testing. Can figure out what would happen if new chemicals were introduced, since he can deal with hypothetical situations, laws of probability, etc., because he possesses the essentials of symbolic logic.

knowledge of politics and attitudes toward arbitrary rules of conduct are very different from those of a younger child. If a rule proves unworkable, he is likely to advocate change, while the younger child recommends increasing the punishment for disobedience as if the rule were inviolate, or sacred (Adelson, Green, and O'Neil, 1969). In summary, adolescent thinking is characterized by sensitivity to others, ability to handle contradiction, and ability to handle the logic of combinations and permutations. This mature system of thought allows the mastery of complex systems of literature, mathematics, and science. It makes possible the planning of future goals and the integration of past and present into a realistic self-identity, abilities that are necessary for adultlike socioemotional adjustment.

Language

The acquisition of language is a unique achievement, made even more remarkable by the speed with which it occurs. A child starts to speak intelligibly at about 1 year of age and goes on to master the fundamentals of language in about a 3-year span. By 4 years of age, the child has a vocabulary of well over a thousand words and can understand and produce most of the grammatical structures of his language. How this is accomplished and the stages of development involved are not as yet clearly known. We shall give a sketch of the evidence to date, followed by a brief consideration of the contributions of both biology and experience to this process.

Initial speech. Sound production can be divided into four periods: crying, cooing, babbling, and speaking words. The baby's first sounds are merely accidental by-products of the business of living—breathing, digestion, crying in distress. Most of the sounds he produces are vowellike. At about 12 weeks, cooing, which may be the first form of social communication, begins. The child now responds vocally to interesting sights in his environment, particularly faces. Consonants begin to emerge. At about 6 months of age, babbling begins. Consonants and vowels are combined into one-syllable utterances, as for example, "Ma," "Di." At about 8 months, the child begins to imitate his own speech and the speech of others, producing repeated syllables like "Di, Di, Di, Di, Di." Some of the syllables heard in babbling will be associated with objects or events, resulting in the child's first words at about 1 year of age.

These first words are usually only approximations consisting of a consonant and a vowel sometimes

Older and Wiser

Time—From the moment of birth the average human being loses brain cells. They die at a rate that can accelerate to as many as 100,000 per day by age 60, and unlike other cells they are not replaced. That dismaying loss would seem to ensure a substantial decline in mental capacity by middle age. But Psychologist Jon Kangas, director of the University of Santa Clara Counseling Center, believes that despite the diminishing number of brain cells, IQ may actually increase with age. In a recent study, Kangas found that the IQs of 48 men and women in the San Francisco Bay area went up about 20 points between childhood and early middle age.

First tested as preschoolers, members of the group had a mean IQ of 110.7. This rose to 113.3 ten years later and to 124.1 after another 15 years. By the time the subjects were in the 39-to-44 age group, their mean IQ was 130.1.

Kangas found an unexpected variation between IQ changes in men and women: among men, those with the highest IQs as children showed the greatest increase in IQ scores as adults. But among women, those who were brightest as youngsters made the smallest gains in adulthood. Most of the female subjects were housewives or held undemanding jobs, while all of the males had stimulating careers. For this reason, Kangas attributes the male-female IQ differences to his subjects' jobs— or lack of them. Though he admits that he cannot prove it, he theorizes that performing menial tasks may not only bore some women, but may even hold them back intellectually.

It is commonly thought that people become less intellectually capable with age and that contemporary cultural advantages contribute to greater mental ability among the younger members of our society. Recent data indicate that IQ probably *does not* decrease with age. Indeed, there may be significant increases under some circumstances.

produced repetitively. Although such a "word" is not, strictly speaking, a part of the English language, the presence of critical consonants and its consistent usage as a label for objects and classes of objects makes it function like a word. Some words do not even sound like English, such as "O'yoi" for water. The meaning of the word is likely to be less precise or perhaps more flexible than the corresponding word in adult speech. "Da Da" may describe father, mother, a baby sitter, or indeed any adult. Other examples of commonly heard first words and their meanings are given in Table 7–2.

For a few months, the rate of vocabulary acquisition is slow, then additions occur rapidly. The

Table 7–2
Commonly heard first words

Utterance	Age (months)	Probable meaning
eh?	8	An interjection. Also demonstrative "addressed" to persons, distant objects, and escaped toys.
dididi	9	Disapproval (loud) or comfort (soft).
mama	10	Food, tastes good, hungry.
nenene	10	Scolding.
tt!	10	Calls squirrels.
piti	10	Interest(ed)(ing).

typical child's vocabulary contains approximately 200 words at 18 to 21 months, 300–400 words by 24 months, and as many as 1,000 at about 3 years.

Although the 1-year-old child uses only single words, they have a certain sentencelike quality. One reason for claiming that these words are sentences is the child's intonation in using them. One word (for example, "milk") can be used to make a declarative ("Milk."), an emphatic ("Milk!"), or an interrogative ("Milk?") sentence on different occasions and in different contexts.

The production of speech sounds appears to lag somewhat behind speech comprehension. The 1-month-old child can hear the difference between *b* and *p,* although he cannot produce these two sounds (Eimas, 1971). A lisping child may call himself "Tham" but be irked by people who fail to call him "Sam." On infant intelligence tests, 9- to 10-month-olds are expected to respond accurately to "No" or "Where's Daddy," although they probably will not produce these words until at least a year later.

Childhood language period. Between 18 months and 2 years of age, the child begins to produce two-word sentences that are clearly based on a grammar. Among English-speaking children, the production of these sentences is systematic and regular, both in position (first or second) and in allowable combinations of words. Some people have described the child's language at this stage as a simplified or telegraphic version of adult speech. Recent evidence, however, suggests that the child's language is unique. Its systematic nature, for example, leads to unusual sentences that do not occur in adult speech and therefore cannot be direct imitations—for example, "All gone shoe," "Bye bye car." The following conversation between a 2-year-old and his father, who has arrived home

"Know how much I have? I have six moneys!"

Reprinted courtesy of The Register and Tribune Syndicate.

One of the most informative features of children's language is a study of the errors they make. Analyses of these humorous mistakes clearly indicate that language acquisition involves learning rules, and the errors come from misapplication of the rules.

from work and is changing his clothes, illustrates how a young child combines two words to form some short sentences.

Child: Hi, Daddy.
Daddy: Hi, Johnny. Did Mommy buy this truck?
Child: This truck.
Daddy: Can you make it go fast?
Child: Go fast. Hat off. Shirt off. Pants off. That blue.
Daddy: Yes, my pants are blue.
Child: Sweater on. See Mommy. Hear Mommy.
Daddy: I'll go and help her carry in the groceries.
Child: Groceries. Bye-Bye. Two bag. Chicken. That red. Bag fall. Close it.
Daddy: I can't close the box so we'll have pizza for dinner. **(Palermo, 1970, page 437)**

The child's mini-sentences lack many features of adult speech, such as noun-verb or adjective-noun agreement. In the example just given, Johnny says "Two bag" or "Bag fall." Tense is not marked through auxiliary verbs; Johnny deleted "is" in "That (is) red" and "Bag (is) fall(ing)." But the sentences are nonetheless recognizable, functional, and governed by some linguistic rules; and they do convey meaning.

Braine (1963) observed a 2-year-old child who had 14 different 2-word combinations in his vocabulary. Seven months later he knew 2500 words. With so many combinations learned in such a short time, it seems unlikely that the child was just memorizing each one independently. There must be a system of rules for forming sentences. Consider the following observations: Certain words appear very frequently, such as "off" in the utterances "hat off," "shirt off," "pants off," or "that" in "that red," "that blue." These might be called *pivot words* (P). They are few in number, but frequently used. Words from another more variable class, called the *open class* (O), seem to attach themselves to pivots. "Hat," "shirt," "pants," "red," and "blue" are open words. Pivot class words are generally adjectives, articles, and demonstration pronouns; new members are added slowly. Open class words are generally nouns, and the child acquires these words rapidly. Some pivots, like "that," occur only in the first position; others, like "off," only in the second position. Sentences may consist of two opens, but the combination of two pivots is rare. Pivot-open constructions are by far the most common (see Table 7–3).

For the 2-year-old child studied by Braine, the grammatical system can be described by using a simple notational system (S = sentence; P = pivot word, O = open word):

S → (P) + (O)
P → a, big, dirty, little, more, my, poor, that, the, two
O → Adam, Becky, boot, coat, coffee, knee, Mommy, tinker toy, etc.

This description of children's language emphasizes the syntax of utterances, as prescribed by the linguistic theory known as transformational grammar. It leaves out a factor of obvious importance, namely, semantics or meaning. Any complete description of children's language must consider the information the child is trying to represent, conceptualize, or communicate. Thus, more recent accounts of language development have tended to focus more on the content or substance of children's speech, even at the most rudimentary level of vocalizing. Although it is possible to give an abstract description of the language of a 2-year-old in terms of the syntactic rules followed, a complete explanation of the child's behavior must consider what he means when he says, "Hat off," "That blue," or "A celery."

Further development occurs through word additions and new combinations of words. The child learns that "A book" is correct but not "A celery." He combines two-word sentences like "That red" and "That flower" into "That red flower." He also learns some ordering rules. When he describes the number, color, and size of trains, he says "Two large, red trains," not "Large, red, two trains." He learns how to make himself clear to others.

The child soon goes beyond two-word sentences. From three-word sentences on, the process gets more complex. The syntax becomes more diverse, having a variety of optional constructions. At the same time, the classes of words differentiate into subclasses, eventuating in the parts of speech of adult language. The meanings a child can understand and express increase rapidly.

During his third year, the child begins to demonstrate transformations. For example, "You went there" is a simple declarative sentence that can be transformed into a question ("Did you go there?") or a negative ("You did not go there") by appropriate changes in word order and the insertion of auxiliary words. The child's early speech lacks transformational rules. The first negations simply attach "No" to the beginning or end of a sentence, producing "No cry" or "Wear mitten no." Then the child learns to insert the negative into the middle of the sentence ("I not crying"), and finally to insert the required "am" ("I am not crying"). This progression in the direction of adult sentence structure is taken as an indication of the child's gradual acquisition of the transformational rules thought to underlie most languages.

Language and the development of thought.
Language and thought are intimately related. In previous sections we have touched on this relationship. For example, we noted that the child's ability to use attributes or features of stimuli as mediators of his behavior probably corresponds to

---

Table 7–3
Early two-word sentences

A coat	More coffee
A celery*	More nut*
A Becky*	Two sock*
A hands*	Two shoes
The top	Two tinker toy*
My mommy	Big boot
That Adam	Poor man
My stool	Little top
That knee	Dirty knee

*Ungrammatical for an adult.

Look at How Child Learns Language

By Sandra Blakeslee
New York Times News Service
Menlo Park, Calif.—I goed there," the child said.

"I went there," his mother said, correcting him.

"No, no," the child protested, "I goed there."

So went a typical conversation between a small child and his mother. It illustrates one of the things that modern linguists are finding out about how children learn language.

Children have their own sets of rules for speaking any language. The rules change over time and they are not necessarily the same rules used by adults. Thus, the experts say, a parent can coax and coach a child to speak correctly all day long—but the child will not alter the way he speaks until he is innately ready to change.

Over the last two decades, but especially in the last few years, students of child language acquisition have come up with numerous new observations.

During the first stage of learning a language—when 1- and 2-word "sentences" are heard—children in every land speaking every language talk only about the same basic relationships. . . .

There are universal strategies which children use to learn language. Before children learn how to talk, they learn how to "mean."

Talking baby talk to a child seems not to retard his speech development.

Despite areas of wide agreement, there is a lingering debate underlying the field of child language acquisition.

One camp, represented by B. F. Skinner, Harvard behaviorist, says children are born as blank slates. They learn language by interacting with their environment. They learn from outside sources. They hear, imitate and are reinforced by other people.

The other camp, represented by Noam Chomsky, a linguist, of the Massachusetts Institute of Technology, claims a child is born already knowing the principles of language before he says his first words. A child uses so-called inborn mental structures to build an abstract rule system or grammar of his language.

Roger Brown, a Harvard psychologist, who tends to side with Chomsky, has written a soon-to-be-published book called "A First Language, The Early Stages" (Harvard University Press; $15). In it he has attempted to summarize much that is known about early language.

"The gist of it all is quite surprising," Dr. Brown said recently. "In all languages so far studied—in some very diverse languages—the earliest speech constructions are limited semantically to a single rather small set of relationships. Furthermore, the complications that occur are also everywhere the same."

Children everywhere begin talking in 1- and 2-word sentences such as "more cookie," or "go store."

"At this first stage of language development children talk about the location of things, the names of objects and actions, how things cause other things and about qualities," Dr. Brown said. "They do not yet talk about themselves or about social relationships. They don't use articles, prepositions or word endings."

This type of speech, which often comes when the child is about 18 months old, has been described as telegraphic in that children sound like talking telegrams.

First stage speech is alike across languages because it reflects the kind of intelligence most children have at this point, Dr. Brown said. It reflects the notion that all children develop perceptually along common lines. . . .

Most psycholinguists today believe that the pacesetter in linguistics growth is the child's cognitive growth. That is, there is a connection between how the child gradually integrates more and more details of the world around him and how he gradually builds a grammar of his own language.

Language, they say, is used only to express what a child already knows. Thought comes first. Language is merely a device for expressing thought. . . .

It is becoming increasingly clear that language reflects cognition and that language development is dependent on prior cognitive development. Language is the way human beings communicate what they know (that is, what the world means to them) to each other.

his ability to think to himself verbally. Also, we said that at the age of 2 years the child has learned object permanence and can deal with stimuli that are not immediately present. In this section we will discuss in more detail the impact of language on the development of thought.

The mental world model. There is reason to believe that, in addition to the concept of object permanence, thinking involves the development of a reasonable mental model of what the world is like.

And the final step in the development of the mental world model depends upon development of an adequate language.

The newborn infant has little in the way of an adequate world model and may be almost exclusively dependent upon and controlled by stimuli in his immediate circumstances. As the child develops and as he experiences external stimuli, he gradually acquires a more accurate, complete, and highly differentiated representation of the world. According to Piaget, almost all children develop

Figure 7–10
Conservation of volume problem

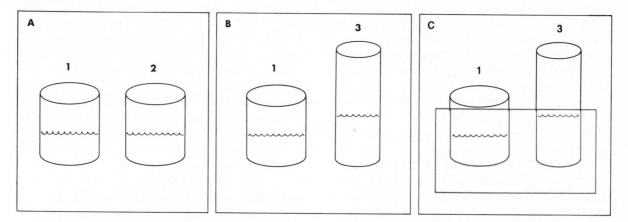

A child is shown two beakers of liquid (A) and asked, "Which contains more, 1 or 2?" A 5-year-old child will say that they contain equal amounts. Then the contents of 2 are poured into 3, a taller and thinner beaker (B), and the child is again asked, "Which contains more?" He answers, "3." **The child is said to be unable to conserve volume. However, if a screen is used to block his view of the water levels, so that only the tops of the beakers show (C), the 5-year-old does conserve; he will say that they still contain the same amount.**

several qualitatively different representations in a regular order, until they finally arrive at a universal conception of the way things are.

Jerome Bruner has identified three fundamental ways by which human beings convert the world of immediate experience into a cognitive or mental world model. The first to develop is called the *enactive mode* and is based upon action or movement. Within this mode, the world is constructed of bodily movements. The child knows no other way to "think about" the world. We have encountered an example of this in the attempts of Piaget's daughter to retrieve the watch from a matchbox. The idea of opening the box is represented by opening her mouth. For adults, familiar motor skills provide an example of how this mode works. Most of us know how to ride a bicycle and can, therefore, think about riding a bicycle. But riding a bicycle is largely a matter of nonverbal, motor abilities of which the mind is, generally speaking, not even conscious. Trying to teach someone how to ride a bicycle or play golf strictly by verbal instruction is difficult, if not impossible, because knowledge of these activities is so heavily stored in the enactive mode.

At a later stage of development, knowledge of the world is based heavily on pure sensory information stored as images. This is called the *iconic mode*, and the emphasis is usually on visual images, although other sensory images are possible. Think about the arrangement of furniture in your room, apartment, or house. You do not have to be there. Instead, you can imagine the scene and "read off" your image. In so doing, you are using iconic knowledge.

The third mode is linguistic, the truly *symbolic mode*. In this case, words and sentences are used as symbols of objects, events, and states of affairs. Probably most adult abstract thought is in the symbolic mode, which is why thinking may seem mainly like talking to yourself. Obviously, the chief milestone of cognitive development is the child's acquisition of language and his development of the ability to think in the symbolic mode.

Bruner illustrated a developmental sequence in modes of thought by showing how children of different ages approach a problem involving conservation of volume. A 5-year-old child is shown two identical beakers filled to the same level with water. When asked which contains more water, he replies they are the same. The water in one beaker is then poured into a third beaker that is taller and thinner so that the resulting water level is higher (see Figure 7–10). Now when the child is asked which beaker contains more water, he selects the tall beaker. Perhaps he is limited to the enactive mode of knowing. ("What is involved in drinking from the containers? Taller things require more drinking.") Maybe his thinking is bound by the stimulus situation, and he focuses too much on the level of the liquid. Symbolic thought seems to be necessary for the child to conserve, so that he is not inappropriately influenced by the distracting difference in water levels.

Bruner placed a screen in front of the beakers so that only the tops of the beakers could be seen and not the water level (the distracting feature). He studied the responses of children who were 4 through 7 years old. Without the screen, almost all 4- and 5-year-olds missed the answer, and even up to half the 6- and 7-year-old children responded that the taller beaker contained more water. With the screen blocking the view of the water levels, however, almost all the 5-, 6-, and 7-year-olds answered that the beakers contained the same amount, and even about half the 4-year-olds answered correctly. When Bruner removed the screen and confronted all children with the differing water levels, the 4-year-olds who had answered "equal" now changed their minds and chose the taller beaker. But the older children still stuck with their original answer. By this procedure, then, 5-year-old children, who almost always fail the test under ordinary circumstances, come to answer correctly and stick with their answer.

According to Bruner, the 5-year-old is capable of the symbolic thought necessary to make the proper judgment, but he is at a transition point between the iconic and the symbolic mode, and he feels unsure of himself. He relies heavily on enactive or iconic information, if it is available. The screen forces him to use the symbolic mode and blocks the iconic by preventing distracting information about the different water levels from reaching him. He thus answers correctly. The 4-year-old is even less sure of his symbolic abilities; he reverts to the dominant iconic mode when the screen is removed.

Inner speech.   Closely related to the acquisition of symbolic skills is the development of inner speech, a matter that has been emphasized by Soviet psychologists over the last 50 years. *Inner speech* refers to the description of thought as "talking to yourself." Thinking is seen by most Soviet psychologists as speech that has "gone underground," that has become implicit and mental. Thus inner speech guides and directs more overt behavior. In young children, outward speech serves the same function. Thus, we see 3- and 4-year-old children talking to themselves while playing or

otherwise engrossed in a task. Gradually, according to the theory, overt speech behavior breaks up, becomes abbreviated, perhaps whispered, until finally it becomes completely inaudible and only its indirect signs (such as minute physiological changes) can be detected. Recall the motor theory of thinking (Chapter 5) and notice how closely related to it the Soviet position is. Incidentally, it is interesting to note that implicit speech sometimes surfaces in an adult when he is concentrating on a very difficult problem. You may have observed someone who was deep in thought talking out loud to himself without being aware of it.

In contrast to this position, Piaget has taken a more cognitive perspective. He classifies children's conversations into one of two types: (1) *egocentric,* in which the child speaks, but is unable to assume the perspective of a listener—he appears to be talking out loud for his own sake, and no one else's; and (2) *socialized,* in which the main objective of communicating with someone else is achieved because the child can adopt the listener's perspective. Egocentric speech is viewed by Piaget as an important indicator of intellectual development. The gradual decline of these "conversations with oneself" is considered a sign of the development of a more sophisticated mental world model, one that is not centered exclusively on the child but allows for other perspectives. For Piaget, egocentric speech does not go underground to become inner speech and to control overt performance. Instead, it disappears because it is no longer a reflection of the child's cognitive abilities.

Psychosocial Development

Whereas the newborn infant seems to be caught up in the here-and-now of experience, with a limited range of expressions that are more or less common to all infants, each adult is a unique individual, behaviorally as well as physically. There appears to be only one major dimension to the emotions of a newborn, namely, comfort-discomfort. In contrast, the teenager is a bundle of confused and often conflicting emotions; he is not sure whether he is happy or sad half the time. A person develops from a newborn who is wholly dependent on, yet seemingly indifferent to, his circumstances into a social being who copes continuously and in most cases adequately with a very complex social structure. Clearly, vast changes occur during the early years of our social and emotional development. Much of what goes on is unique and contributes to the characteristic personality of an individual. We shall concern ourselves with the analysis of adult personality in Chapter 9. Other processes are more or less universal throughout a social group or culture. The contribution of these factors to behavior will be the primary topic of Chapter 10. In this chapter we shall try to summarize what is known about *psychosocial development:* the development of the newborn into an adult having a unique personality and capable of fulfilling his role in society.

Birth Order

Intuitively it seems likely that birth order affects personality and intellectual development. In many ways, the oldest child has the most difficult time, especially early in life. It is more difficult for him to pass through the birth canal; the mother is more likely to have long labor; there is usually greater head impression during birth; the first-born is less likely to survive childbirth; and he weighs less at birth than later-born children. But two or three years later, the first-born tends to weigh more and to be taller than later-born children at the same age. The initial physical growth of the first-born is probably due to the fact that his parents have no one else to care for and thus provide more intensive nurturance. Differences in size tend to disappear by adulthood, because eating at later stages of development is determined much less by parental attention.

Psychologists have studied possible relationships between birth order and personality but have found them very difficult to verify. Some generalizations do arise from this literature, and we summarize them in Table 7–4. But none of these relationships is especially strong, and questions have been raised about the identification of all the factors contributing to these relationships. Yet no one would wish to imply that birth order is completely irrelevant to any aspect of human development. Rather, it is probably the case that there are *so many* other factors involved that simple generalizations are not possible.

Consider a recent analysis of intelligence made by Robert B. Zajonc. Using data on intelligence from a study of close to 400,000 Dutchmen, Zajonc developed a model for describing birth-order effects on intelligence. First, the overall data did show a birth-order effect. The first-born child is in general slightly more intelligent than the second-born, the second-born is slightly more intelligent than the third, and so on down the line. But the data also show clearly that overall family size is a factor in this relationship. The larger the family, the lower the intellectual ability for all the children. Thus, the

Table 7–4
Some relationships between birth order and personality

Achievement. One of the strongest correlations between birth order and behavior is in the area of achievement. First-borns are much more likely to be prominent achievers—university professors, scientists, Rhodes scholars, research biologists, physicists, social scientists, and astronauts. First-borns are more likely to achieve better in school and be written up in *Who's Who.* It is assumed that this is the result of higher motivation, because the first-born is more adult-oriented, conscientious, and studious than later-born children.

Creativity. As with achievement, there is evidence to suggest that first-borns are more creative.

Aggression. In our society first-borns are taught to inhibit their aggression while younger siblings are taught to express it. For example, the older child is told to "pick on someone your own size," but the younger child is told to "stand up for your rights."

Sociability. It is the later-born siblings who are more often characterized as sociable, approachable, and comfortable with peers. The only child and the first-born child are characterized as being more uncomfortable in their interactions with others.

Self-esteem. Children without siblings have the highest self-esteem. In families that have more than one child, there is no relationship between birth order and self-esteem.

Psychopathology. There is no relationship between birth order and the probability of any particular child in the family being diagnosed as having emotional problems. However, if problems do occur, first-born children are likely to be timid, over-sensitive, and demanding of attention, whereas later-born children are more likely to be aggressive, negativistic, and destructive.

Favored by parents. Either the oldest or youngest child in the family is more likely to be favored by parents. Middle children are less likely, for example, to have affectionate nicknames.

first-born in a family of two is likely to be brighter than the first-born in a family of three. Also, the first-born in a very large family, say, nine children, is likely to be *less* intelligent than the second-, third-, or fourth-born in a family of only four children. Thus first-borns can be *less* bright than fourth-borns *when* the family sizes differ.

Zajonc's data also showed that these effects of birth order and family size on IQ depend also upon the spacing between children, such that the closer together the children come, the lower their intelligence tends to be. Thus, a third-born child in a family of three could conceivably be more intelligent than the second-born in some other family of three if the first family spread their children over 10 years and the second family had three children in 3 years. One final thing Zajonc discovered was that the last-born child in a family tended to be lower in intelligence than would be predicted from factors of

Mother-Child Attachment

A human infant, like most primate offspring, cannot satisfy his physiological needs by himself. Someone else must feed him, keep him warm, and so on. Satisfaction of these needs is pleasing to the infant. Because the mother is generally the agent of satisfaction, her presence comes to produce the expectation of pleasure. Studies with monkeys, however, show that the affective feelings of the infant toward his mother arise from more than just the satisfaction of physiological needs. In one such study, Harry Harlow examined newborn monkeys who were separated from their mothers within the first 12 hours after birth. These babies were given two substitute mothers, one made of wood and sponge rubber and covered with terrycloth and the other made of wire mesh. To test the importance of nursing per se versus the feel of contact with the mother, half the babies were bottle fed through a nipple inserted in the wire mother and the other half through a nipple in the terrycloth mother.

Harlow observed the amount of time spent in contact with each "mother." Even when babies were fed from the wire mother, they spent most of their nonfeeding time huddled against the terrycloth mother. If the baby monkeys were placed in a strange situation, they first clung to the terrycloth mother, then ventured out and explored. If the terrycloth mother was absent, the babies displayed emotional behaviors such as crouching, rocking, and sucking. There was no sign of curiosity or of exploratory behavior in the absence of the terrycloth mother.

The monkey's attachment to his terrycloth mother is not a temporary phenomenon. During 6 months of observation, Harlow found that these babies displayed the same attachment to terrycloth mothers as other infant monkeys showed their real mothers. Apparently, then, the infant monkey's love for his mother is not just a matter of being fed, but is also related to other satisfactions. Harlow calls the feel of the terrycloth mother—its warmth and softness—contact comfort. Contact comfort is not merely a source of pleasure; it also serves to reduce the fear of strange objects for the infant monkey.

The terrycloth mother, however, is not a fully adequate substitute for a real mother. Contact comfort may not be as important to youngsters raised with real, animate, responsive, active mothers as it is in Harlow's experiments, which involve no live mothers. Furthermore, later observations showed that monkeys raised with both a terrycloth mother and a wire mother failed to show normal sexual development, and were sexually inadequate even when paired with experienced partners. Because of a few persistent males, a number of formerly motherless monkeys did become pregnant. Those who had known only terrycloth and wire dolls as mothers did not care for their offspring. They avoided them, pushed them away, and even beat them. Apparently, a cloth to cling to, while it does provide some comfort, is no substitute for a live monkey.

These studies suggest the need for environmental stimulation and for social interaction if normal development is to occur. They are corroborated by naturalistic studies of human infants placed in institutions. Where the institution provides little stimulation (either tactual or emotional), the child's development, in even the more rudimentary motor and perceptual skills, is delayed.

Harlow's work clearly indicates that visual, tactual, and social stimulation in the first few months after birth are important factors in the perceptual and cognitive development in infants, in assuring their emotional security, and in determining later social responses.

The two artificial mothers—one made of wire, the other of terrycloth—that Harlow used in his study.

family size and spacing. He suggests that this is because the last child does not get the benefit of the intellectual challenge of teaching younger brothers and sisters.

Of course, there are many other factors in determining intelligence besides birth order, family size, and spacing of children. But Zajonc's analyses suggest the following for people who want to maximize the intelligence of their children: (1) keep the size of the family small—two children is best;

Babies Are People First

By Dee Wedemeyer

New York (AP)—Do pick up your baby when it cries. Don't childproof your home. Don't have a nurse for the baby; have a maid for you. And above all don't seek too much advice.

That's the sort of thing mothers are being taught in a new course on the emotional care of children under way at the New York Hospital-Cornell Medical Center. It is believed to be the earliest effort being made to prevent emotional disturbances.

"This is the one thing that has been neglected," said Dr. Lee Salk, head of the pediatric-psychology division at the hospital and director of the course for 3,000 mothers. "Hospitals have been giving courses in feeding and bathing babies for years.

"The whole focus in this course is on the prevention of emotional disturbances. When you start to think what it costs to care for one mentally disturbed person, this really helps in terms of cost, aside from saving a human being."

He said many new parents are overwhelmed with advice and have no one to turn to for professional help but their pediatrician who, he said, is not always qualified to help.

"For example, a lot of people will say, 'Don't pick up your child when he cries. You'll only spoil the child.' Well, you ought to spoil your child. Spoil the devil out of your child. Pick it up. What the baby is getting is stimulation. The whole world moves for him. It's fascinating." . . .

Salk, author of "How To Raise a Human Being," and the forthcoming book, "What Every Child Would Like His Parents to Know," said the question most often asked by parents of more than one child was about sibling rivalry.

He warns them that when a new baby comes into the home, an older child may regress to babylike habits and even express an interest in breastfeeding. His advice was to let the child try it and he will probably lose interest, preferring milk from a glass.

He also suggested telling the older child that the new baby was growing in "Mommy's uterus" because some children could get terrible misconceptions from hearing that the "baby was in Mommy's stomach."

"They have very peculiar ideas about what is going on," he explained. "It's very important not to say stomach. That's where food is." . . .

"But my dishwasher makes a terrible clamor," declared one mother at a recent session. "Won't it scare the baby?"

"You keep a child in a quiet room, the baby becomes conditioned to that," said Dr. Salk. "Later on a normal amount of stimulation becomes too much. A baby in that environment will get startled very easily. Babies are very adaptive. This is how they become used to stress. Babies who have stimulus now seem to be able to cope with stress later on. When we talk about mental problems we are talking about the amounts of stress a person can take."

Salk also suggests not getting a nurse or in-laws or anyone else to help with the baby, when the mother brings the child home from the hospital. Sometimes these people can separate the mother from the baby and undermine her confidence in her own abilities to care for the child, he said.

"If you can afford help, get it for you and your husband. You take care of the baby," he said.

Even the earliest experiences can have a tremendous impact on what kind of people we become.

(2) plan the family such that there are several years between children; and (3) try to find other younger children in the neighborhood for the last child to teach.

Child Rearing

Social and emotional behavior changes rapidly during childhood. The responsibility for the shape of this development lies mainly with the parent. Here we will discuss three of the most frequently studied areas of child rearing: feeding, toilet training, and how parents cope with their children's aggression.

Feeding. According to the best available evidence, neither breast nor bottle feeding has a clear advantage for a child at any early period. The only known relationship between breast feeding and personality is related to weaning. Here research indicates that the later and more abruptly the child is weaned, the more upset he is likely to be by the weaning. But even these effects tend to be shortlived.

Although the method of feeding seems to have little bearing on the child's personality development, there is a clear relationship between choice of feeding method and the personality of the mother. Close to half of the mothers in this country try breast feeding. Those who do show greater tolerance for sexual play and masturbation in children and seem to be more relaxed about nudity and sexuality in themselves. Mothers who indicate that they wish to breast feed their first child also tend to be high in maternal interests; that is, they like children and are interested in other people's children as well as their own.

Of those mothers who try breast feeding, more than half stop within 3 months. There are many reasons why a mother decides to stop, most of which have nothing to do with the personality of

Help for Exceptional Parents

Time—For the parents of the 6,000,000 U.S. children who are physically, intellectually, perceptually or emotionally disabled, life is what Clinical Psychologist Lewis Klebanoff of Boston describes as "a surrealist nightmare of anxiety, perplexity and fatigue." In the hope of easing that nightmare, Klebanoff and two other Boston psychologists, Stanley Klein and Maxwell Schleifer, have just published the first issue of a new bimonthly called *The Exceptional Parent*. The magazine offers advice to help "exceptional" children live full lives—not in segregated centers but "in the mainstream of their communities."

The psychologist-editors, who spent $30,000 of their own money to start the magazine, have put together a first issue of jargon-free articles, which supplement the knowledge of professionals with the special expertise of parents and of the disabled themselves. One piece, the first of a series on recreation, explains how to improvise active wheelchair games that are not only enjoyable, but good for letting off steam. Another details a system for teaching the use of public transportation. The same article deals forthrightly with a highly sensitive and seldom-mentioned topic: the intermittent and "very human" parental wish "to get rid of or lose their disabled child."

In a different vein, an adult quadriplegic writes about "Solving Hopeless Problems" (he types by striking the keys with a stick held in his mouth), and explains his philosophy: "One adjusts to realities. I try to forge ahead, aware that life may never be full but determined never to accept less than I must." With a similar emphasis on facing facts, an article titled "How Different Is My Child?" counsels against overprotection—which can deprive a youngster of the experiences he needs to become emotionally independent—and against overexpectation, which can make a child feel that "he cannot do anything, no one likes him, and he will never be any good."

Bold Goal

Beyond all this, Psychologists Klebanoff, Klein and Schleifer have a bold and touching goal: to alter the temper of the nation by influencing normal as well as abnormal children. Explains Klebanoff: "Maybe that's the mission of these disabled kids—if normal schoolkids see a child in braces struggling to overcome his problems, maybe things won't look so bad to them, and maybe they'll be inspired to help. I hope it might make a more gentle America. It sure can't hurt."

There are wide variations in development. Furthermore, some children are permanently retarded or disabled by accident or illness. What can a parent do to help himself and the child? Sound advice based on empirical psychological knowledge is apparently on the way.

either the mother or the child. For example, the mother might experience considerable physical discomfort or inconvenience. The best course for a potential mother who is uncertain about how to feed her baby is to choose the method she feels most comfortable with.

In infancy there is also the question of the feeding schedule. Should the baby be fed on demand or according to a rigorous schedule? The conclusion is that demand feeding is generally easier on everyone concerned. Furthermore, demand-fed babies develop physically and intellectually at least as well and possibly better than schedule-fed babies. In these and other aspects of feeding, we can generally conclude that parents who are well-informed and do what they believe is best for their children and for themselves obtain the best results. Actually, as we will see, this conclusion is probably applicable to just about all areas of child rearing.

Toilet training. Toilet training is perhaps the earliest significant effort by a parent to exercise control over a child's life and his behavior. The key question is: "When is the best time to begin toilet training?" A decade ago, a doctor heavily influenced by Freudian theory, Benjamin Spock, suggested in his best-selling book *Baby and Child Care* that children be allowed to enjoy the freedom of wetting and messing. Demands by the parent for achievement of self-control might be seen by the child as a threat to his freedom. Thus, determining the time to begin training should be left at least partly to the child himself. Current advice offered by Dr. Spock is less permissive and more cognizant of the needs of parents. The child who wets at will imposes restrictions on his parents. Children need to be taught to consider the needs of their parents and others as well as their own. Toilet training is one step in this process.

There is, however, rather strong agreement among experts that toilet training probably should not begin until well into the second year of life. Because early physical development progresses from the head on down, the bowels and bladder mature relatively late and the child may not be capable of controlling them until he is 18 months or older. In addition, toilet training is easier when the child knows how to undress and can communicate, at least roughly, what his needs are. The child must be able to judge when he needs to defecate and must be able to sit

And Now, Teaching Emotions

Time—The fifth-graders at Denver's Thomas A. Edison elementary school sit in a circle with their principal, Forest Fransen. Placing an empty soda bottle on the floor, Fransen and the kids spin it to choose the order of children who will "tell about themselves." After a few embarrassed giggles, a boy named Paul says: "I like to go fishing a lot. There's six in my family and two are babies. That's all." Don reveals that "I've got a sister in junior high; I had another sister but she had cancer." The children are fidgetless and fascinated. Finally the bottle points to Fransen, who tells of his pride in a father who came from Sweden to homestead in a sod house.

So goes the first class in "emotional skills," a new course that has spread to several dozen public and private schools in cities from New York to San Francisco. Increasing numbers of states are mandating some form of classroom instruction in mental health. The goal: helping children forestall the emotional scars that lead to drug abuse, delinquency and adult unhappiness.

Induced Jealousy

Based on the idea that neither guidance counselors nor existing hygiene courses meet the need, the Denver program uses one of the nation's first comprehensive guides for teaching mental health to the young: *Dimensions of Personality*, a new series of fourth- through sixth-grade textbooks published by Dayton's George A. Pflaum. The series was originated by Walter J. Limbacher, a Denver clinical psychologist, who started the program as a consultant to the U.S. Army and pilot-tested his ideas in Denver's Roman Catholic parochial schools.

To help young children cope with their feelings, Limbacher aims to show them what is normal for their age—"peer pressure," for example, or reluctance to associate with the opposite sex. Limbacher's guidelines for teachers call for gently provoking children into emotional experiences that they can discuss later on. The bottle-spinning game is designed to start the children discovering both their individual qualities and how much they have in common with others.

For one fifth-grade lesson, the teacher induces jealousy by repeatedly choosing the same bright, attractive youngster to do blackboard work. When the class balks at this favoritism, the teacher admits her ploy, then tries to coax the students into conceding that they feel jealous. "It is important," says the teachers' guide, "that no one feel he is strange or wicked if he is jealous from time to time. By admitting jealousy and talking about it, children are less likely to act out their aggressive feelings."

At four schools in Colorado Springs, where the courses have been taught for the past two years, about half the parents say their children have become more willing to discuss their problems. "Before," said one mother, "my daughter just threw a fit." Teachers report fewer discipline cases; social workers say they get more "self-referrals—kids with problems they sense they can't handle alone." Among the few criticisms, one parent said "these attitudes and insights are training I would rather my child received at home."

Despite this seeming success, no one is yet sure how much of the kids' improvement is due to normal growing up or merely the extra attention they get in the course. Noting that the Colorado teachers have been trained in special seminars, critics also fear that untrained or insecure teachers could easily confuse the kids they are trying to help. . . .

Emotional-skills courses are obviously well-intentioned efforts to forestall critical social problems. As the courses spread, though, mistakes seem inevitable. Thus sharp questions are likely to be raised about whether those efforts are pointed in the right direction.

As psychologists learn more about behavior, classroom instruction in "emotional skills" may become more common.

still while he does. Success is unlikely without these rudimentary skills. Research has shown that mothers who start training early tend to be more insecure and anxious about sex. The least successful mothers are those with the highest sex anxiety. They tend to use very severe toilet training techniques that produce significant emotional upset in the child.

In one training method (McIntire, 1970), the parent keeps a chart of the times the child eliminates during a 2-week span. If there is some regularity, the parent chooses the time the child most frequently has a bowel movement and takes the child to the toilet at that time. Success is immediately rewarded by praise, or something tangible like candy or a toy. The mother then keeps track of successes and failures and concentrates on those circumstances where the success rate is highest. The child is not punished for lapses, but each accident deprives the child of a chance for reward. A planned, gradual approach insures reward for the child and should produce a smoother training process for the parent.

Aggression.   Among middle-class American parents a permissive attitude toward aggression has generally predominated in recent years. The feeling has been that children should be allowed to express their anger openly, without fear of unfair retribution. This attitude suggests that pent-up anger and hatred is a bad thing and that the child should be encouraged to "let it out."

While acknowledging the possibility that extreme amounts of pent-up anger and hatred can be harmful, most psychologists do not advocate training children to be openly hostile and physically

Most Beliefs Called 'Myths': 'Psychology of Sex Differences' Probed

By Judith Martin
(C) 1974, Denver Post-Washington Post

Washington—What is the difference between boys and girls, anyway?

This emotion-laden question is the subject of a collection and evaluation of hundreds of studies on sex differences compiled by two Stanford University psychologists, Eleanor Emmons Maccoby and Carol Nagy Jacklin. Stanford University Press has just published their report, "The Psychology of Sex Differences," as a follow-up to the 1966 "The Development of Sex Differences," edited by Professor Maccoby.

It is full of warnings about the dangers of handling material in which everybody concerned is probably thoroughly acculturized and opinionated.

'Not Very Often'

A parent might report that a child cries "not very often," but really be thinking "not very often for a girl." A social scientist may only consider behavior worth reporting when it contradicts an expected stereotype.

Of course, a child may behave in ways patterned after adults of the same sex, or in ways that win approval from adults as being appropriate to the child's sex. Trying to separate this from inherent, biological differences is a chief task of this book.

Finally, they admit that two feminist psychologists may have their own bias. "Although we have tried to be objective about the value-laden topics discussed in this book," they say in the introduction, "we know that we cannot have succeeded entirely. We doubt, in fact, that complete objectivity is possible for anyone engaged in such an enterprise."

After all the reservations, the authors have concluded that most beliefs about learning differences and behavioral patterns between boys and girls are "myths," but that some do exist and cannot be accounted for by socialization.

Specifically, they concluded that:

—While there is a slightly greater tendency for boys to move in groups of their peers and girls in pairs or smaller groups, there is no basic difference in their sociability or social dependency.

—Neither sex seems more susceptible to the influence of others.

—During college years, men seem to have more of a sense of control over their fate than women, although this is not true earlier or later in life, and the self-esteem level generally is the same.

—The ability to do rote learning and that of doing higher-level work that reverses previously learned responses is equally distributed in boys and girls, as is analytic ability.

—Boys are more vulnerable to their environment

before and after birth, but in matters of learning, both sexes are affected by heredity and environment in the same fashion.

—In motivation to achieve, there are either no sex differences or, in some cases, researchers have found girls to be more highly motivated; however, boys are more challenged by competition.

—Responses to auditory and visual stimuli are the same in boys and girls.

Significant Differences

But the authors found what they considered significant differences in four areas:

—Girls, from age 11 on, have better verbal skills than boys.

—Boys are better at visual-spatial tasks from adolescence on, possibly because of a sex-linked gene.

—Boys' mathematical ability increases faster than girls' from adolescence on.

—Boys are "more aggressive both physically and verbally," than girls, from age 2, a finding they say goes contrary to culturalization that tends to try to restrain boys' aggressiveness because it is considered more dangerous than that of girls.

Areas that the psychologists decline to characterize on the grounds that the evidence is scant and ambiguous are tactile sensitivity, fear, timidity and anxiety; activity levels, competitiveness, dominance, compliance or even nurturing behavior.

Of the last, they say, "There is very little information on the responses of adult men to infants and children, so it is not possible to say whether adult women are more disposed to behave maternally than men are to behave paternally. If there is a sex difference in the tendency to behave nuturingly, it does not generalize to a greater female tendency to behave altruistically over varying situations."

Social Dominance

In evaluating their material, the psychologists suggest that the greater aggression found in males is what has given them social dominance—that it has not been "an historical accident." But, they say "it is a quality not necessarily linked to modern leadership ability."

They also state that many people have been handicapped in their sex roles because of social pressures toward "masculine" or "feminine" qualities.

"A man who adopts the 'machismo' image may gain prestige with his peers, or enhance his short-term attractiveness to women, at the expense of his effectiveness as a husband and father. A similar problem exists for the highly 'feminine' women. Effective caretaking of the young, for example, involves a good deal of assertiveness . . . Training a girl to be 'feminine' in the traditional nonassertive, 'helpless' and self-deprecatory sense actually may make her a worse mother."

aggressive under any circumstances. Among other things, children and young adults who are overtly aggressive are less popular with their peers. Children should, indeed, be taught that aggressive

and hostile feelings are natural and that guilt about such feelings is usually inappropriate. Those feelings should be expressed. But children should also be taught to deal with these feelings rationally, expressing them verbally rather than physically and considering the possibility of appropriate displacement. Extreme attitudes about aggression, either complete tolerance of complete suppression, are inappropriate.

The Development of Sex Roles

A most important part of psychosocial development is the acquisition of sex roles. Is the difference between a normal boy and a normal girl in our society mainly biological or is it a product of training and experience? As in most aspects of development, a little of each is involved. In a new book Eleanor Maccoby, a long-time student of sexual development, sex roles, and sex stereotypes, and her colleague Carol Jacklin have reviewed the available evidence about differences between the sexes. They concluded that many beliefs about differences in the sexes are unfounded and are clearly misconceptions. Where differences do exist, they attempt to evaluate the degree to which these effects are attributable to learning versus heredity.

Recent evidence suggests that many sex differences formerly thought to be inherent are probably due to learning. For example, 3 Tufts University psychologists questioned 30 pairs of parents within 24 hours of the birth of their first child. Parents were asked to "describe your baby as you would to a close friend." Parents also filled out a questionnaire, rating the baby on 18 scales such as firm-soft, big-little, relaxed-nervous, and so on. Finally, the psychologists obtained hospital records on each baby's weight, height, muscle tones, reflexes, heart rate, and so forth. None of the hospital data showed any difference between male and female babies. Parents, on the other hand, "detected" marked differences. Parents of daughters thought their babies were significantly softer, finer featured, and smaller than did parents of boys. Fathers went further than mothers in enumerating differences between boy and girl babies in looks and behavior.

These data show that sex stereotyping begins at the time parents first learn of the sex of a child. One might question, however, whether these immediate impressions stand up later in the face of an infant's actual looks and behavior. In another study, two groups of mothers of young children were observed as they played with a 6-month-old boy in a nursery. For the first group, the baby was dressed as a boy and named Adam; the mother thought the baby was a boy. For the mothers in the other group, the same baby was dressed as a girl and called Beth; these mothers thought the baby was a girl. A number of

toys were available. Women who thought the baby was a girl most often selected a doll for "her" to play with. Those who thought the baby was a boy most often handed him a train to play with. Mothers smiled more at "Beth" than at "Adam." The play behavior of mothers clearly differed depending on the apparent sex of the child. Mothers, and no doubt fathers as well, impose their own expectations on an infant and treat him or her accordingly. No wonder so many sex-role differences and sex stereotypes are learned!

At least two theories have been proposed to account for the learning of sex-role behaviors. One is based on reinforcement and imitation. A child receives rewards for "appropriate" sex-role behaviors and punishments for "inappropriate" ones from parents and peers. Same-sexed adults and peers provide models that the child can observe and imitate. We can see the effects of these processes by observing how mothers play with infants.

Another interpretation has emphasized the importance of physical differences between the sexes in size and strength. These physical differences permit the male greater access in general to positions of power and to opportunities for education and intellectual development. The achievement of power and knowledge leads to expectations of male dominance by both males and females alike. The influence of parents and peers is less important in this theory.

Probably both physical or biological and psychological factors are involved in sex-role development. Maccoby's studies argue strongly in support of both. The questionnaire experiment cited above, however, clearly shows that parental expectations about certain sex roles are *not* contingent on body size or strength, at least among newborns.

Adolescent Growth and Development

At puberty, the age at which a human being becomes sexually competent, there are many rapid physical changes. The most important of these is the appearance of secondary sexual characteristics. Accompanying the physical changes are an increase in the intensity and the diversity of the teenager's emotional feelings and a significant increase in the demands placed on him by society. During this period, parents come to have much less influence on their child's development. This may generate mixed feelings in the parents about the onset of adolescence. Wanting the child to be more independent, they may at the same time be reluctant to allow him to have his way. It is possible, also, that the adolescent embarrasses his parents by his behavior or makes them feel older and less needed because of his newfound responsibilities. The adolescent himself may feel uncertain about his independence. When both the parents and the adolescent are uncertain as to whether independence is appropriate, there are many opportunities for conflict. Research indicates that both boys and girls tend to resolve most of these issues, especially those concerning moral standards, in the direction of their parents.

Physical changes. Late in the first decade of life, there is a marked increase in the production of sex hormones, leading directly to a spurt in height and a change in the sex organs. During this growth spurt, other physical characteristics such as brain volume remain more or less stable and there is even a decrease in the size of certain endocrine glands. For girls, the average age of onset of major height changes is 11 years. The next notable change occurs when breasts begin to bud, followed by the appearance of underarm hair and then pubic hair (see Figure 7–11). Last comes the first menstrual period (*menarche*). The average age of menarche for American girls is 13 years, with 50 percent of the population starting between 12 and 14 years and 95 percent between 10 and 16 years (Meredith, 1967). The first ova produced by a teenager are probably immature, but she is fertile and essentially able to support pregnancy relatively quickly after menarche.

The adolescent growth spurt in boys begins around 13 years (see Figure 7–11). Marked height changes become apparent sometime between the ninth and fourteenth year. The average length of the penis doubles and the volume of the testes increases tenfold between the ages of 12 and 17 years. Growth of the genitalia is followed in rapid succession by the appearance of pubic, underarm, and facial hair, deepening of the voice, and the first ejaculation of semen (approximately 13.5 years).

There is enormous individual variability. One 14-year-old boy can be on the verge of physical changes, while a second is in the midst of them, and a third virtually mature. In a longitudinal study of late and early maturers (Jones, 1965), the late maturers, as teenagers, were less popular with their peers, more restless and attention seeking, and had poorer self-images. Early maturers were reserved, self-confident, and likely to make a good impression. In their early thirties the early maturing boys continued to be slightly more sociable, conforming, controlled, and successful, even though by this time the two groups did not differ in physique. In their late thirties, the two groups were

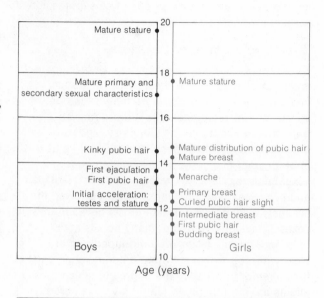

Figure 7–11
The typical sequence of sexual maturation in boys and girls

Age (years)

not distinguishable in occupational success, although their patterns of behavior continued to be somewhat different. The early maturers maintained their conforming image; the late maturers were more insightful and flexible. The effect of timing of physical maturity in girls is less clear-cut. Early maturing girls are initially at a disadvantage, because they are ahead of both girls and boys at a comparable age. But by the late teens, differences in personality traits between early and late maturing girls are practically nonexistent.

The clumsiness so often observed in early adolescence is not due to a lack of motor control of the new physical dimensions of the body, but rather to increased self-consciousness about bodily activities. Increasing and acute awareness of self characterizes much adolescent behavior. Boys may find that they have an erection at embarrassing or unexpected times. Girls who are not sure of their sexual changes may try to hide breast growth rather than being pleased at signs of maturation. While the wide fluctuations in voice tone in males (from low bass to high squawk) may produce a great deal of amusement for individuals around him, the adolescent is typically self-conscious about these variations to the point of embarrassment. Girls also go through a voice change, but the amount is not nearly as dramatic as it is in boys, and it tends to occur more gradually.

Psychosocial changes. The diminishing parental influence during adolescence is in part replaced by an increase in the influence of the teenager's peer group. The teenager strongly needs to be accepted, liked, and even loved by his peers. Mature interest in the opposite sex is aroused at this time. One reason why peers' friendships are so important is that they have a certain liberal quality generally unexpressed by parents. The teenager's friends will want him to experiment with new identities, while typically his family will not. The family frequently will not recognize that because a boy is now shaving he is a quite different person or that because a girl now wears a bra she wishes to take on new features in her personality.

The early adolescent may experience a resurgence of the egocentrism described by Piaget, a failure to differentiate between what others are thinking and what he is thinking. He believes that everyone else is just as preoccupied as he is with his appearance and his behavior. He assumes everyone else is aware of his pimples, for example. He constantly anticipates reactions from others and may even imagine different kinds of reactions in his fantasies. One of the most common fantasies involves the anticipation of one's own death. Almost half of all college students report that they remember having such fantasies, which usually involve observing the reactions of friends and relatives during or after the funeral and deriving a great deal of vicarious pleasure from finally being "appreciated."

An adolescent will commonly overdifferentiate his own feelings and assume that they have a unique quality and intensity. "But you don't know how it feels!" is a frequent adolescent comment. The overdifferentiation process may lead to the development of a *personal fable,* in which the adolescent assumes that his experiences and emotions are entirely different from anyone else's. One reflection of this fable is the popularity of diaries, especially among girls, during early adolescence. These diaries almost always reflect the felt importance and unique intensity of the person's own experience.

Surprisingly, research indicates that personality is remarkably stable during adolescence. There is a sharp drop in self-esteem at the beginning of adolescence, but nonetheless teenagers tend to use the same words to describe themselves throughout this period. The amount of stress and traumatic experience in adolescence is, in all probability, overemphasized. Much of what the general population knows about adolescence comes from magazine articles that discuss the rebellious or neurotic nature of adolescents. In fact, adolescence is marked by considerable stability and conformance to the norm.

Adolescent Suicide

Time—Every year about 1,000 U.S. young people between the ages of 14 and 21 take their own lives, and thousands more try unsuccessfully. Behavioral scientists have long believed that it mostly girls who make the unsuccessful attempts. Now a new study of female adolescent suicide based chiefly on 750 case histories confirms that impression. Among those who try to kill themselves and fail, says Boston University Psychologist Pamela Cantor, girls outnumber boys 9 to 1; among those who succeed, boys are in the majority by a 3-to-1 ratio.

The boys succeed because they really want to die, says Psychologist Cantor, which explains their choice of such failure-proof methods as hanging and shooting. She notes that society expects more of males than of females, so that boys who doubt their sexual prowess or career prospects may see death as the only way out. By contrast, a suicide try by a young girl may be less an attempt to die than "a cry for help, a reaching out for human contact, love and attention." The method chosen (sleeping pills, for example) often permits rescue.

Psychologist Cantor observes that the married teen-age girl is more apt to commit suicide than the unmarried girl, and the college student than those not in college. Her study suggests that two groups are especially likely to attempt suicide: those whose fathers have been either uncaring or long absent from home, and first-born girls, particularly those with younger brothers.

In both sexes, Cantor advises, there are several warning signals: insomnia, neglect of personal appearance, the giving away of prized possessions, or a long-lasting depression. Nor does the end of a depression mean danger is over. On the contrary, it is just then that a deeply unhappy youngster "is most likely to mobilize his energies and actually commit suicide."

Sometimes the pain of growing up is too much to take. Many teenagers fantasize about death, which may account in part for these suicide statistics.

The Development of Morality

Morality is a kind of knowledge that consists of the attitudes of human beings toward social practices and social institutions and questions of right and wrong or good and bad. The acquisition of morality begins early in life, but moral judgments change many times throughout a person's life. Lawrence Kohlberg has found clear evidence of a stepwise developmental process in the formation of morality. His technique for tracing the development of morality is as follows. He begins by telling a person a story such as the following:

A man wanted to buy a new drug that could save his wife from a fatal, incurable disease. The inventor of the drug, wanting a profit, tried to charge the husband much more than he could afford to pay. When the inventor refused to change his price, the desperate husband stole the drug.

After detailing the story, Kohlberg asks his subject what he thinks about the husband's act. Was it justified? If so, why; if not, why not? Kohlberg found that people take different moral approaches, make different judgments, and exhibit different attitudes depending upon age and experience.

Morality seems to develop in stages, with each successive level representing a more mature form of moral reasoning (see Table 7–5). There are three basic levels: *premoral, conventional role conformity,* and *self-accepted moral principles.* Within each level, there are two steps. At the first level, in *Step 1,* typical of early school-age children, being right or wrong is judged on the basis of the amount of damage or punishment. One justifies the theft because the drug did not cost much to manufacture or condemns the theft because the druggist lost a lot of money. At *Step 2,* judgment shifts to the intention that motivates the act. Selfish intentions are often condoned. Stealing the drug may be judged moral because the man needs his wife's companionship, or the thief may be branded immoral because the inventor deserves a profit. Moral acts, at this level, often are related to the satisfaction of one's needs.

In *Step 3,* the beginning of the second level, social needs and the consideration of other people enter much more forcefully into the picture. Altruistic intentions are highly valued. The thief may be

Figure 7–12
Mean percent of moral statements on Kohlberg's three levels made by boys aged 7 to 16

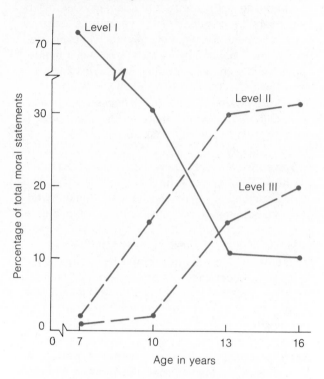

The figure illustrates the typical decrease from the first type of moral reasoning with advancing age and the accompanying increase in advanced moral judgments.

Table 7–5
Kohlberg's stages of moral development

Level one	*Premoral*
Step 1	Punishment and obedience orientation. Obey rules to avoid punishment.
Step 2	Naive instrumental hedonism. Conform to obtain rewards, have favors returned.
Level two	*Conventional role conformity*
Step 3	Good boy morality. Conform to avoid disapproval or dislike by others.
Step 4	Law and authority maintaining morality. Conform to avoid censure by authorities.
Level three	*Self-accepted moral principles*
Step 5	Morality of contract, individual rights, and democratically accepted law. Conform to maintain community welfare.
Step 6	Morality of individual principles of conscience. Conform to avoid self-condemnation.

excused because he is unselfish and protecting his wife. Alternatively, he may be condemned because his family will be ashamed of his acts. *Step 4,* generally occurring around ages 7 through 11, reflects the concrete operational child's concern with culture and cultural rule systems. Emphasis is placed on law and order. The child says the husband must be condemned because he broke the law, or in justification of the theft the child claims that the husband would have violated his vows to protect his wife if he had let her die.

The final two steps seldom appear before adolescence (see Figure 7–12). Then a system of reciprocity that balances the rights of the individual and of society begins to be recognized. Two points of view are acknowledged and weighed in every situation. Rules are recognized as compromises, even though sometimes the compromise works out to no one's advantage. Thus, at *Step 5,* there is an emphasis on contractual obligations and the rights of the majority. The theft is condemned on the grounds that one does not steal even when

Toward Moral Maturity

Time—A group of young inmates in a New England reformatory began meeting regularly last year to talk about a subject that normally receives little attention in prisons: ethics. They were participating in a novel experiment designed by Harvard Psychologist Lawrence Kohlberg to teach moral judgment—not by sermons, but through open discussions.

When the reformatory sessions began, many of the boys agreed with the philosophy of one teenage felon who insisted that "If I'm not gettin' nothin', I'm not givin' nothin." But now they share the outlook of another inmate who voices a concept that would have seemed alien to them before they began meeting: that it is important "to respect other people's feelings."

Wide Cross Section

This change in attitude seems to bear out Kohlberg's unique theories, formulated in the course of 15 years of research in the field of moral psychology. He believes that morality "is not a bag of virtues" (honesty, generosity, loyalty and the like) but an idea of justice that is primitive in young children and becomes more sophisticated as a child passes through distinct stages of moral development. . . .

Kohlberg's reformatory subjects were operating primarily at Stages 1 and 2 when the experiment began. Although most of them are now moving into Stage 4, their problems are far from over. As Kohlberg himself acknowledges, moral judgment does not ensure moral behavior; it is hard to act justly in an unjust world, especially for those too weak to resist temptation. Prison rules are often unfair, and prison staffers are not necessarily much more moral than inmates. Outside, released prisoners may find a society that may not help reinforce their new-found morality; although U.S. democracy is founded on Stage 5 thinking, Kohlberg estimates that fewer than one out of three Americans have reached that level.

Moral Nihilism

Yet Kohlberg does not despair, either for his delinquents or for society. He recalls that Socrates was put to death for trying to teach morality and observes that although "we now occasionally assassinate such people, it is not government policy to do so." Besides, as recently as a generation ago, "nobody would have raised an issue such as the Son My massacre." Kohlberg is also optimistic about the behavior of college students; he hopes that the moral nihilism displayed by some may actually mark "a developmental step forward." He cites as an example one study in which 20% of the students who left high school with a mixture of Stage 4 and Stage 5 morality regressed in college to Stage 2. But by age 25, they had again attained Stage 5, with a new tolerance for moral outlooks different from their own.

Times do change and so do the minds of psychologists. Kohlberg's recent writings indicate that college students do not regress to Step 2 as suggested in the last paragraph of this clipping. Rather they "progress" to an intermediate stage, between Steps 4 and 5 (Step 4.5?), that represents the transition between conventional and principled reasoning.

---

desperate because others also may be in great need. Or the theft is excused because the law was not set up for circumstances in which the individual would forfeit a life by obeying the rules. At *Step 6,* the individual's own conscience is his guide, and that conscience is based on abstract universal moral principles. The man steals because it is never justified to take a life no matter what the consequences for stealing might be. Or he refrains from stealing because of the value he sets on honesty. There is the recognition that both choices are justifiable, and one decides on the basis of his own personal, unique, internalized standards.

The progressive stages of moral development become less and less egocentric and involve changing perspectives of the role of the individual in society. A major task of adolescence is to decide how to mesh with the social order and how to change it, if necessary, to provide a more satisfactory life pattern. Those decisions become increasingly important as the individual reaches biological maturity and develops more complex and broader psychosocial perspectives.

Erikson's Theory of Psychosocial Development

Erik Erikson, an American psychoanalyst whose ideas are grounded in the principles of Sigmund Freud, has developed the most all-encompassing theory of psychosocial development. Erikson views behavior and personality as emerging from an interaction between our hereditary instincts and the teachings of our culture. He conceives of development as involving a series of stages that each person encounters during his existance. In each of Erikson's eight stages the individual is confronted with a basic crisis, consisting of two alternatives, one healthy and the other damaging. We have summarized these crises in Table 7–6. The crises are turning points that may involve conflict between an individual's own instinctual energy and the people and institutions he encounters during

Table 7–6
Erikson's developmental theory

Developmental stage	Crisis
1. Oral-sensory (birth to 1½ years)	Basic trust versus mistrust: learning to develop trust in one's parents, oneself, and the world.
2. Muscular-anal (1½ to 4 years)	Autonomy versus doubt and shame: developing a sense of self-control without loss of self-esteem.
3. Locomotor genital (4 to 6 years)	Initiative versus guilt: developing a conscience, sex role, and learning to undertake a task for the sake of being active and creative.
4. Latency (6 to 11 years)	Industry versus inferiority: receiving systematic instruction, developing determination to master whatever one is doing.
5. Adolescence	Identity versus role confusion: not "Who am I?" but "Which way can I be?"
6. Young adulthood	Intimacy versus isolation: study and work toward a specific career, selection of a partner for an extended intimate relationship.
7. Adulthood	Generativity versus stagnation: parental preparation for the next generation and support of cultural values.
8. Maturity	Ego integrity versus despair: development of wisdom and a philosophy of life.

Figure 7–13
Erik Erikson

that stage. Growth and development involve meeting and resolving each of the crises with some degree of success. Development in any stage is greatly influenced by the nature of the individual solutions achieved in earlier stages.

Stage 1: oral-sensory. During the first stage—in *infancy*—we develop a sense of *basic trust* or *basic mistrust,* depending on how we are treated. A newborn child is almost entirely dependent on others for the satisfaction of his needs. If he receives love, care, and stimulation, especially consistent attention from his parents, he develops a sense of trust. This sense includes trust in himself and his own ability to successfully deal with his needs. On the other hand, if no one comes when he cries for food, if wet diapers stay wet for long periods of time, if the handling he receives when his needs are met is harsh and cold instead of warm and caring, he then develops a basic mistrust. The world can*not* be depended upon to meet his physical and emotional needs in a consistent, nurturant manner, and so he mistrusts it and is cautious with other people. If the mistrust is severe, the child may become withdrawn and apathetic, giving up his hopes of getting what he wants. Those

who resolve this first stage in a healthy manner carry with them into adulthood a basic trust that becomes faith in the world and oneself, and finally develops into a belief in the ability to live a meaningful existence. A sense of basic trust is the foundation on which healthy personality development depends.

Stage 2: muscular-anal. During the second stage—*early childhood*—the formation of *autonomy* or *shame and doubt* is the issue being resolved. The child who has established a secure sense of basic trust is ready to begin to *separate* himself from his mother, to exercise his individuality by trying to do things on his own, by asserting his will and by developing an awareness of himself as a separate, autonomous being rather than the extension of his mother he sensed himself to be during the formation of basic trust. The child also begins to learn self-control of such bodily functions as bowel movement and walking. It is during this period that "No" becomes a favorite word for many children. In fact, it sometimes seems that children at this stage will try exactly the opposite of anything they are

AT SIXTEEN:

I WAS STUPID, CONFUSED, INSECURE AND INDECISIVE.

AT TWENTY-FIVE:

I WAS WISE, SELF-CONFIDENT, PREPOSSESSING AND ASSERTIVE.

AT FORTY-FIVE:

I AM STUPID, CONFUSED, INSECURE AND INDECISIVE.

WHO WOULD HAVE GUESSED THAT MATURITY—

IS ONLY A SHORT BREAK IN ADOLESCENCE.

© 1974 Jules Feiffer.

Dist. Publishers-Hall Syndicate

asked to do. If parents encourage exploration, allow the child to do some things on his own, are reasonably tolerant of the often irritating negativism, and help the child to gradually and smoothly gain control of his bodily functions, for instance, during toilet training, he develops a sense of separateness, independence, and individuality. This is autonomy. However, if parents constantly hover over the child and do everything for him, or make harsh, unreasonable demands that cannot be met in relation to learning bodily control, the child will begin to doubt his own ability to be a free, separate person. He will also begin to feel shame at his inability to meet parents' expectations. According to Erikson, those who resolve the issues of this second stage in a healthy manner carry with them into adulthood the courage to be independent individuals and the ability to guide and determine their own existence.

Stage 3: locomotor-genital. During the third stage—in *childhood*—we form *initiative* or *guilt*. During this period children become much more mobile, able to move into and explore previously unreachable places. Language becomes highly functional now also, and exploration in the form of questions about everything imaginable takes place. Here "why" and "how" become favorite words; imagination and make-believe are prevalent. Curiosity also leads children to explore their bodies and the differences between male and female bodies—this is an "infantile sexuality" that includes

an attraction to the parent of the opposite sex. If the child is allowed to be curious and to explore his world within reasonable limitations, he develops confidence and a sense of initiative. If his curiosity is generally met with "Don't bother me now," if he is given an environment with little to explore, or if he often encounters "Don't do that, it's bad!" then he develops a basic sense of guilt. This becomes the feeling that he has bad desires, that what he wants to do will not be liked by others. As a result he may stifle his explorations, his questions, and his basic curiosity, or he may express them but feel very anxious and unhappy in the process. Successful resolution of this crisis of childhood frees our initiative, imagination, and curiosity for use in dealing with life as an adult. It allows us to meet experiences in new, flexible ways without the constricting effects of excessive guilt.

Stage 4: latency. In the fourth stage of development—at *school age*—the focus is on the emergence of *industry* or *inferiority*. Children are in school now, learning to make and do things. They learn to get attention and praise by doing things well, for example, by building a model airplane, drawing a picture, baking cookies, or getting good grades on tests. If much of what an individual tries to accomplish is done fairly well, he receives encouragement and attention and develops a sense of industry. This involves actively pursuing tasks and feeling confident about being able to handle them well. If a child continuously experiences failure in

"Your mother and I had no idea you felt this way. Of course you may stay and get your doctorate."

New Yorker, June 5, 1971. Drawing by Robt. Day; © 1971 The New Yorker Magazine, Inc.

Which of Erikson's eight crises characterizes this man's plight?

his attempts, receiving criticism or a lack of attention for much of what he tries, then the feeling develops that "everything I try turns out wrong or not good enough, so I must be inferior." This in turn can cause the child to avoid taking on new tasks or to put little effort into his work because he feels doomed to fail regardless of how much effort he exerts. In contrast, from the development of a healthy sense of industry comes enjoyment of work and a feeling of pride in one's ability to do something very well; this attitude is then carried into adult life. Another characteristic of this stage is that children begin to identify very closely with what they do: "I am what I do." They think of their future selves in terms of occupations—lawyers, nurses, bricklayers, or teachers. Some people remain at this stage throughout life, with their entire being focused on the job they perform. Most move on to the next stage, where identity is defined in a more self-conscious fashion. A sense of industry is a necessary ingredient, however.

Stage 5: adolescence.   Erikson's fifth stage begins around *puberty,* during *adolescence,* and centers on the *identity crisis,* where the question is whether a *positive identity* or *identity diffusion* will be the outcome. The question "Who am I?" comes to the forefront, often creating much turmoil, confusion, and anxiety. For a while, the adolescent has no stable answers to this question. One day he is a "hippie," the next day he is "straight"; this week it's short curly hair, next week it's long straight hair. Typically adolescents are very fickle during the identity crisis because things that are pleasing and seem right for a while can suddenly become very unpleasant and no longer fit the individual's changeable self-image. Also characteristic of this stage is a need for consistency and stability to offset the confusion and decrease the anxiety. For some this involves attachment to a charismatic individual or a group that can provide seemingly ready-made answers to many of the questions that bother adolescents. Teenage gangs, political groups, social clubs, and religious organizations can be used to provide guidelines and stability for adolescents.

But if an adolescent relies too much on others in trying to resolve his identity crisis, a major problem will develop. For a while he can live comfortably with others' choices, but eventually he will begin to feel anger and resentment at being forced to do things—to see people, work at jobs, raise children, and so on—that are not really right for him. The identity of others is *not* his, so he begins to be displeased with his life when what he does is not based upon what his inner self really wants to do. The result is often a return to the identity crisis, and may be complicated by the presence of unwanted children, economic and social pressures, fears about the ability to find new friends, an unhappy marriage, or simply habits that are now harder to overcome.

If, on the other hand, an adolescent is given support by others but encouraged to answer his own questions and seek out what really feels best for himself, the identity crisis begins to move toward a more enduring resolution, a stable sense of personal identity. Experimentation is the key here. By trying things out, by really experiencing some of the alternatives that are available and discarding those that seem wrong, each person begins to find certain activities, people, attitudes, and values that fit his own life style and fill his own needs. This process can take a long time; in our current society it typically may extend into the mid 20s. Eventually it leads to consistent answers to the question "Who am I?" and development of confidence in oneself and one's way of life.

Stage 6: young adulthood. In *young adulthood,* the issue of developing *intimacy* or *isolation* comes to the fore. Here we become especially concerned about developing intimate, lasting relationships with others. If an individual has established a reasonably healthy and stable sense of identity he is prepared to be open with others, to share important parts of himself, and to respond with warmth and caring to the disclosures of others. On the basis of this sharing, close and personal relationships can evolve. On the other hand, if a person feels unsure of his identity or has developed an unhealthy identity (criminal or psychopathic, for instance), he is less likely to be truly open and caring and may become isolated from most other people. One type of isolated person that may emerge is the "hermit," who simply avoids most contact with others to protect himself from being hurt. Another type is the "pseudo-intimate," a person who has many superficial friends but never lets anyone close enough for true intimacy to develop. Both of these types of people feel vulnerable and unsure of themselves, and thus are unwilling to take the emotional risks involved in being close to others. Genuine intimacy occurs, according to Erikson, only between two healthy identities.

Stage 7: adulthood. After the first phase of adulthood, development focuses upon acquiring a broader sense of shared intimacy. An emerging concern for the next generation is the issue we face in the seventh of Erikson's stages. It is possible for an individual who has progressed through the first six stages to settle into a life of complacency, stagnation, and lack of growth. During this period people need more than intimacy. They strive for productivity and a true concern for others. The crisis involved in this stage, then, is the choice between *generativity* and *stagnation.* Assuming the role of parent, the individual must put together all the virtues and wisdom he has acquired in order to care for and to guide the next generation. Fulfillment involves the growth of a sense of love not only for one's spouse but also for one's children and the closer community. By maintaining meaningful contact with these others, the individual receives in return new stimulation and exciting ideas that prevent him from falling into ruts and growing stagnant.

Stage 8: maturity. The last of Erikson's stages involves the issue of *integrity* or *disgust and despair.* If an individual can look back and feel that he has lived his life in meaningful ways, that he has made mistakes but in the long run has been reasonably successful in his life, then he develops a sense of integrity. He feels good about his past, comfortable with his present existence, and generally acceptant of the value of his being. If, however, he feels his life has had no meaning, has been wasted, useless, and unsuccessful, then he may experience disgust with himself. In addition he may feel despair—"It's too late to change now, or too hard to change, so I'll never be any different." In contrast, a healthy resolution of this stage brings a feeling of wholeness and peacefulness as one lives out the rest of his life.

There are several other important features of Erikson's developmental scheme. First, how we emerge from the earlier stages is partly dependent on our parents. Thus, if parents are extremely doubting and mistrusting they will tend to overprotect their children, will insist upon doing everything for them, will incessantly warn them of all the dangers in life, and will probably pass on their own feelings of doubt and mistrust. Second, how we emerge from earlier stages greatly affects our growth during later stages. For example, a mistrusting child is likely to be so cautious that he avoids new experiences and stifles his curiosity out of fear. As a result, during the third stage he is less likely to form a strong sense of initiative than a child who is more trusting and willing to explore new situations. Third, children who progress fairly successfully through the first four stages have the best chance of resolving the identity crisis in a healthy, enduring way.

Finally, in our current society it is quite typical for healthy individuals to experience more than one identity crisis during a lifetime. A second one often occurs during middle age, and a third one is often triggered by retirement or the death of a spouse in later life, especially if much of one's past identity was dependent on the job or the spouse. Resolution of these later crises involves much the same process as resolution of the first one. There are periods of turmoil, exploration, and inconsistency that can lead to an entirely new series of answers to the question "Who am I?"

What Does It Mean?

There are many ways in which the products of developmental research affect our everyday behavior. We have chosen to present just a few where the connection between research and application is fairly obvious.

Death: The Vital Buoyancy of Optimism

Time—Literature and folklore abound with tales of people who cling to life as long as they have "reason for living," and mysteriously die within weeks after they feel that their purpose is accomplished. Now a young sociologist at Johns Hopkins University has suggested that this fictional behavior pattern is well founded in fact. More often than not, according to a study by David Phillips, people who are about to die seem to hang on until after a birthday, an election, a religious holiday or another event that they keenly anticipate.

Phillips, 26, who presented his findings to this week's convention of the American Sociological Association in San Francisco, initially checked the death dates of 1,251 famous Americans listed in *Who Was Who* and *Four Hundred Notable Americans.* He found that death came for them least often during the months before their birthdays and most frequently during the three months afterward. Turning to cities that have kept precise death records, he discovered that between 1875 and 1915 the death rate in Budapest, which had a large population of Jews, declined markedly during the months before Yom Kippur, the high holy day of atonement; the pre-Yom Kippur "death dip" also occurred during the years 1921–1965 in New York City, which also has a big Jewish population. In the dramatically expectant weeks before every U.S. election between 1904 and 1964, the nationwide death rate showed a marked decline.

Familiar Pressures

Phillips suspects that the quality of expectation is all-important. He suggests, for example, that a decrease in the death rate might not occur during the period of anticipation before Christmas—perhaps because of the familiar pressures that also accompany that season. Or it might not apply to ordinary people whose birthdays are not celebrated with the fuss that surrounds a man of fame. Still, the statistics that Phillips has gathered are convincing enough to impress the Russell Sage Foundation, which is oriented toward the social sciences; it has just given him an eleven-month grant for additional explorations of the vital buoyancy of optimism. Eventually he hopes to establish that anticipating significant events can help people to live longer, a finding that could lead to important changes in the psychological treatment of the elderly and the seriously ill. If further study bears out this hypothesis, Phillips says, it will prove that "dying can be a form of social behavior."

Beyond Erikson's eighth stage of development, but obviously having something to do with it, is the ability to put off death for strictly personal and pleasureful reasons. There is a force which we can identify as the will to live. Furthermore, there is a will to die, exemplified by old people in good health who die because they feel "unwanted."

Educational Toys

Manufacturers are selling, and parents are buying, a lot of toys that are supposed to hasten physical, social, and intellectual development. There are toys to stimulate infants' senses, develop their eye coordination, exercise motor control of limbs, and so forth. Toys for older children are designed to teach analysis, recognition of attributes, such as color, and spatial relations and shapes.

There is considerable disagreement among psychologists about the value of such toys. Some claim that the environment "enriched" with mobiles, mirrors, tape recordings, aquariums with live fish, and so on, may have the effect of depriving the baby of normal interaction with his parents—watching their faces and being held and talked to. Moreover, the child may be able to learn just as much by exploring a set of pots and pans as by playing with an expensive toy.

An elaborate educational machine called the "talking typewriter" has been developed to teach children how to read. The typewriters are used in some schools and institutions, often with children who need special instruction, such as the retarded. The typewriter has a conventional keyboard except that the keys are different colors corresponding to the finger positions skilled typists use. The child's fingernails are painted in matching colors. When the child presses the key, the machine prints the letter and pronounces it. After the child has explored the device, the typewriter takes the lead. A letter is printed and spoken, and only the matching key will work. Initially children search the keyboard, ignoring letter configurations, but eventually they learn to match the letters. After letters come words. Most children progress rapidly with the help of this intriguing machine. Even kindergartners come to be able to produce and type short stories, for example:

I paint at Sharon's house. I like Ricky. I like God. He makes us healthy.

My friend Susan squirted me with water on my new dress. Susan had to put her head down.

(Moore, 1966, page 182)

Some commercial toys use the same technique. One familiar toy has a dial with letters of the alphabet matched to appropriate pictures, for instance, "C," candy. When the dial is turned to C the machine pronounces the letter and names the object.

Educational Innovation

Jean Piaget's theory of intellectual development has sparked some recent educational reform, especially

Is This Crib Necessary?

Time—"A total responsive environment," the manufacturer calls it. That is the way one company describes its new three-level baby crib equipped with toys to grasp and pull, sand timers to watch, wheels to spin, voice-activated mobiles and sound tapes, plus a tank awash with live fish. According to the developers and to some child psychologists who have endorsed the environmental crib, almost every baby needs such a scientifically engineered corral for sleep and play. Parents who prefer the traditional, simple "containment crib," it has been argued, may end up with a child who is not too bright.

The claims for the gadget-laden crib typify a growing trend in child psychology toward forced early education and "programmed enrichment." Now Harvard Pediatrician Richard Feinbloom has strongly urged the American Academy of Pediatrics to take a stand against it. At the organization's recent annual meeting, he maintained that elaborate educational toys for infants are no better playthings than pots and pans. As a matter of fact, he said, their use, especially in the elaborate new "crib environments," may endanger normal intellectual and emotional development.

A follower of famed Swiss Psychologist Jean Piaget, Feinbloom believes that systematic infant training generally fails to speed learning—with or without special toys. Even when children do acquire some skills early—counting, for example, or understanding the principle of cause and effect—they soon forget them, and rarely can they apply this knowledge to new situations. In any case, knowledge gained unusually early has no value over the long run. Kittens, for example, understand "object permanence"—the idea that things stay the same even when they are out of sight—before human infants do, but "they cannot do very much with their precocious acquisition," Feinbloom observes.

Children and Chicks

Beyond that, Feinbloom believes that teaching babies is no substitute for playing with them: turning them over "to a machine wired up for sound and light" deprives them of the warm parent-child give-and-take that is crucial to emotional health and to eventual academic achievement.

In essence, the rationale for the new special equipment is that certain mental skills can be acquired only by "imprinting," a special form of rapid learning that generally occurs at certain critical periods soon after birth if it is to occur at all. That is the way newly hatched chicks learn to follow their mothers. But, observes Feinbloom, children are not chickens: they do not learn intellectual skills by imprinting, and if they miss one learning opportunity, they will get another later on. "Do we need any more anxiety than we already have about reaching milestones on time?" he asks rhetorically.

Also erroneous, Feinbloom insists, is the theory that everything that is learned must be taught. In fact, children pick up abstract concepts just by exploring the world around them and meeting new situations.

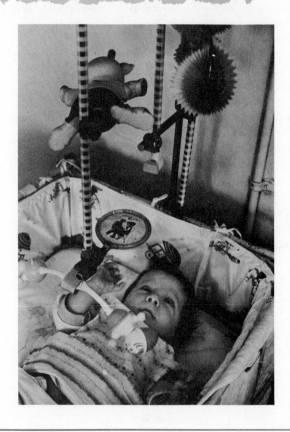

in the "open classroom" of the British school system. Piaget insists that children at different stages require different kinds of teaching. Most schools, unfortunately, instruct even the young child as if he were in the formal operational stage, using abstract lecture methods. Because they rely primarily on the enactive mode of symbolic representation, preschoolers learn best if they can manipulate things. According to Piaget, a 6- to 7-year-old child taught on a purely verbal level learns to mimic phrases but does not necessarily understand them.

Piagetian theory implies that young children learn best through active discovery. Thus classrooms in the early grades might be arranged in a series of centers stocked with intriguing materials to arouse the child's curiosity. In informal instructional laboratories set up to investigate discovery learning, the child is allowed to manipulate things and see results. He is asked to describe the outcomes and

Figure 7–14
Dienes balance

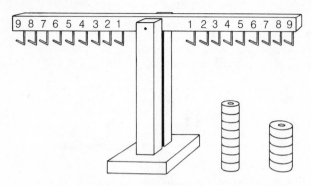

The Dienes balance is used to teach arithmetic and is a Piagetian way of teaching a child to organize his experience.

sometimes to write reports. Classmates are encouraged to question his procedures and explanations, forcing him to communicate his ideas more clearly.

A curriculum based on Piagetian principles stresses new ways to organize experience rather than the mere accumulation of knowledge. Specific tasks designed to teach conservation of concepts are sometimes included in the curriculum. The development of conservation of area, for example, might be facilitated by using the linoleum squares on the floor. The child might be given 12 squares and be asked to work out how many different shapes can be made from them. In this way he learns that area is independent of shape and depends on a square measurement unit. Fundamentals of arithmetic can be taught by a Dienes balance (see Figure 7–14). Each side of the balance rod contains numbered hooks placed at equal intervals from the center, starting with 1 and going outward to 9. The child must figure out where to place two rings on one side to balance one ring placed at 6 on the other. Following simple addition, he might place rings at 2 and at 4, or at 1 and 5. He will also discover he must multiply the number of rings by the number at which each ring is placed to achieve a balance. One ring at hook 6 is balanced by three at hook 2.

As we saw in Chapter 4, application of the principles of operant conditioning has led to a quite different but equally effective approach to classroom learning. Instead of discovering concepts through free exploration and manipulation, as Piaget recommends, in the operant approach the learner is led through a series of steps of increasing complexity, each building on the preceding, until the task has been learned. The structured steps may be presented by the teacher or by a programmed textbook. Whereas the Piagetian method of discovery learning involves instrinsic rewards from the pleasure of solving problems, external reinforcement (such as tokens) supply the motivation for learning in the operant approach. The two learning approaches are not necessarily incompatible. Some teachers can comfortably use a combination of approaches in the classroom.

Mental Retardation

You may be familiar with the current controversy over the reasons for low-level IQs. Some psychologists place the blame on heredity. They believe that low IQ is for the most part genetically determined. Other psychologists contend that the environment in which a child grows up is of fundamental importance. This is another case of the heredity versus environment debate. Recently two University of Wisconsin psychologists, Rick Heber and Howard Garber, have reported research that dramatically demonstrates the importance of the environment. Their study offers some important evidence that retardation in the child of a mentally retarded mother can be reduced if not entirely prevented. It has long been known that mentally retarded parents are likely to have retarded children.

Heber and Garber hypothesized that this phenomenon could be traced in part to the way in which retarded mothers raise their children, and they began to investigate differences between the child-rearing practices of retarded mothers and the practices of mothers of normal intelligence.

The researchers' goal was to eliminate differences in child-rearing practices and in other social-environmental conditions. They chose 40 retarded mothers with new babies, all the mothers coming from impoverished ghetto environments. They then assigned the mothers randomly to two groups. In the control group nothing special was done. In the experimental group, the mothers were given training on some job within their range of ability and were taught home-making and baby-care skills. Their babies were cared for at the university during the day. They were fed, bathed, and taught by special teachers and returned home in the late afternoon.

Both groups of children were tested at regular intervals. The IQ scores of the 20 stimulated children have turned out to be much higher than those of the children of the control group. The stimulated children scored well above average on IQ tests. In contrast the control children scored in the dull to normal range on IQ tests. Untreated children from the same impoverished background without a retarded mother generally have IQs just slightly below the nationwide average.

This program of research is still in its beginning stages. It is entirely possible that differences in behavior between the groups that now seem rather stable will disappear in time or with age. Still, the program is quite promising; the experimental youngsters have accomplished so much that it is hard to imagine them ever falling back to the level of their control counterparts. The results suggest the need for changing the inadequate and insufficiently stimulating relationships that develop between adults and children in impoverished environments. By so doing, it may be possible to eliminate some significant percentage of the mental retardation that afflicts our population.

TV Violence and the Development of Aggression

A recent report of the U.S. Surgeon-General examined evidence concerning the effect of the fictional violence portrayed on television on the development of social behaviors in children, especially aggression. Much of human conflict as portrayed on television programs is resolved by violent means. Furthermore, violent resolution is often shown to result in a good and a successful conclusion to an episode. More intellectual ways of resolving human conflict are rarely portrayed and even more seldom glorified.

Knowing what we do about the young child's tendency to imitate and the importance of imitation as a learning process, we may naturally expect violent and aggressive modes of behavior to be learned. Granted that portrayals of violence on television *may* have adverse effects on children, can we be sure they have any more effect than cases of violence in *real* human conflicts? Consider our recent involvement in Vietnam. Even if we could remove all fictional violence and aggression from television, surely an impossible task, the real cases would remain and provide plenty of opportunity for imitation learning by the young.

Most of the evidence for the relationship between television violence and aggressive behavior has been anecdotal. Recently, psychologists have begun to study the relationship with more rigorous scientific methods. Some of the preliminary findings are surprising. For example, the evidence of Dalmas Taylor is that viewing television violence *reduces* hostility in many people. Because hostile feelings usually precede aggression, TV viewing may remove the underpinnings of aggression. In other words, viewing violence on television may be a form of release, a way of working things out, that allows people to get rid of hostile feelings without expressing them openly to other people.

Other research has shown that the adverse effects of television viewing are not so much the imitation of violence as they are the tendency to produce a passive, nonintellectual child who is too tolerant of aggression in others. Television occupies much of the time in which a child might otherwise be actively expressing himself, as in sports or some productive activity. Instead, he whiles away those potentially productive hours sitting quietly in front of the TV. Television viewing also removes the opportunity of learning through some sort of outward action, whether it be reading or taking instruction. Viewing most of today's commercial programs is a distinctly nonintellectual activity that provides little chance for self-improvement.

Child-Rearing Advice

To the extent that disagreement and uncertainty exist in the area of developmental psychology, parents cannot get specific instructions on what is best for their child in every circumstance. Parents must make decisions every day about when to punish their children, when to toilet train, when to

THE WORLD IS LOOKING TO YOUTH TO SOLVE ITS PROBLEMS

AND YOUTH IS LOOKING AT TELEVISION.

Bill Yater 11-8

© King Features Syndicate 1973

TV Violence Does Not Create Violent Kids

Chicago (AP)—It isn't the violence on television which creates violent children but the way their parents rear them, two child development experts say.

However, they are critical of the passivity involved in hour after of hour of television viewing by children. . . .

One of them, Dr. Maria W. Piers, psychologist and dean of the Erikson Institute for Early Education in Chicago, said it is not television which makes young people violent, or keeps them from relating to others. It is the absence of other ingredients which make for a fulfilling life.

The other child expert, Joseph Palombo, social worker and director of the child therapy program at the Chicago Institute for Psychoanalysis, said children's personalities already are developed before they are able to understand what is happening on the screen.

Mrs. Piers said "violent people come in all shapes and sizes" but it does not matter what level of society they come from and they have the same things in common:

—They lack the capacity for empathy, the ability to put themselves in another person's shoes.

—They lack well-developed skills that satisfy in and of themselves. That is, there are no activities, such as cooking or playing golf, which give them pleasure.

—They lack imagination.

She said the dangers of television are the frequency with which parents place children before the set to sit passively for hours and the facile solutions television offers to many problems.

Palombo spoke against allowing children to watch television for long periods because, he said, "there is little warmth or empathy emanating from television."

Children watching a lot of television miss valuable human experiences, Palombo said, adding that the enforced passivity deprives children of opportunities to express themselves.

The Effects of Viewing TV

There are different opinions and conflicting evidence on the extent to which TV influences behavior. However, excessive viewing, especially of programs of violence, is unlikely to have much positive effect.

discuss sex, and a thousand similar decisions. Dr. Spock has proposed that the parents' *anxiety* about doing the right thing may be more detrimental to the child than using an "incorrect" child-rearing practice. Indeed, there is some research indicating that parental attitudes may have more impact on the child than the specific child-rearing practices used. Thus there is some support for the idea that if the parents treat the child as a valuable human being, the child will probably turn out all right. We tend to agree with that philosophy and, as psychologists, feel somewhat chagrined by our inability to make specific suggestions to parents in all cases. However, on the basis of what *is* known about child development, we will present here some tentative

answers to a few detailed questions that parents frequently ask.

Should I punish my child, and, if so, how?

Children differ in their response to punishment. The same child may react differently on different occasions or at different ages. There are some general principles of learning that do apply, however, to the use of punishment (see Chapter 4). For example, punishment should occur as close in time to the misbehavior as possible and should be of short duration. Delayed punishment, or punishment that lasts for several weeks, makes it more difficult for the child to associate the punishment with the misbehavior. In addition, the

It is clear that there are fads in child-rearing practices. On the one extreme is the "child-centered" technique involving great permissiveness on the part of the parents with a heavy emphasis on communication with the child ("meaningful dialogues"). On the other extreme is the severe disciplinarian who sets strict standards of acceptable behavior and demands that the child meet them, usually enforcing the demands with punishment for failures. As is typical in such disputes, extremes at either end of this dimension are probably harmful, and some combination or compromise seems most appropriate.

punishment should be only as severe as is necessary to change the behavior. Excessive punishment tends to increase the negative emotional response. The child in his anger is more likely to retaliate by continuing to misbehave. In addition, there is some evidence to suggest that severe punishment increases the desirability of the misbehavior in the eyes of the child (the importance of the behavior becomes consistent with the consequences).

Will an effeminate boy (aged 6 to 12) become homosexual?

This question reflects a major concern on the part of a large number of people in our culture. It also indicates a confusion between sex-role identification and the object of sexual desire. It is relatively rare for an effeminate boy to become homosexual. Effeminate behavior is more likely to reflect the absence of an adult male model in the home or an extremely close relationship between the boy and his mother. The occurrence of inappropriate sexual behavior should be of concern, however. As our society is presently constructed, inappropriate sexual behavior on the part of boys (less so for girls until after puberty) leads to poor peer relationships and low self-esteem. It may be desirable therefore to try to provide an adult male role model.

Is masturbation normal in young children?

Masturbation is a very common form of behavior in even very young children. However, if masturbation becomes very frequent or almost constant, parents should look for the possibility that the child is being affected by some unusual circumstances. For example, a mother concerned with cleanliness of the genitals may wash them frequently after urination or defecation, leading to direct stimulation of the genitals. Infection in the genital area requiring frequent handling may lead to an increase in masturbation. For the infant, the parent's best response under these conditions is nothing at all. In older children (age 3 years on) it may be desirable to tell the child that such behavior is inappropriate in public and should be performed in the privacy of the child's bedroom.

How do I get my child to internalize my own standards and values?

In this area, research supports common sense. Explaining to a child the reasons why a particular behavior is appropriate increases his development of a conscience. The most important factor in the development of parentlike behavior in children is love. Parental warmth and affection for the child increases strongly the identification of the child with the parents. Because the child loves the parents, he wants to be like them, and he tends to accept their values and standards. Most children do adopt the attitudes of their parents in most important respects.

Why are some children so aggressive?

The aggressive child tends to come from two types of homes: the home that uses excessive physical aggression as a form of punishment (thereby providing an aggressive role model for the child) and the extremely permissive home. There is a great deal of evidence to support the idea that aggressive behavior in children is self-reinforcing.

Sex Questions Valuable, Says Expert

By Gay Pauley
UPI Women's Editor
New York—Take time to talk with your children when they ask questions about sex.

Keep the channels of communication between parents and children open. This makes it easier to discuss all personal matters.

An authority on child development and parent education, Sadie Hofstein, conceded this often is difficult—"We lead busy lives today and in some families there is not much time for being together.

"Few children ask, 'Where do babies come from?' as they run out the door. We need to provide more time for talking. We also have to use the opportunity to talk whenever it arises."

She gives one example. "What's rape?" asks a 10-year-old with his head in the newspaper. "A simple honest reply can be given and the discussion then refocused on healthy sexual relationships," Mrs. Hofstein said.

Answer Simply

What if the questions come up around the dinner table with smaller children present? "Answer questions simply and encourage more talk when you're alone with the questioner," she said. "Of course, some questions may be perfectly appropriate for dinner talk for all ages. The younger ones will pick up what they can—the rest will go over their heads. . . ."

Mrs. Hofstein said information and misinformation are only one aspect of sex education. "More significant," she said, "are the attitudes consciously or unconsciously transmitted from parent to child."

Some parents may feel confused and embarrassed talking about sex to their offspring. This isn't necessarily harmful, she said, for it can convey to the child that sex and love are very special. . . .

Varied Stages

Parents also must realize, she said, that at each stage of development children have different questions and concerns about sex. They may forget quickly, or recall inaccurately, what has been taught them, but parents should be ready to reinterpret information over and over if necessary.

As for sex education in the schools, Mrs. Hofstein disagreed with those who want the schools to take over the full job just as she disagreed with those who feel the schools shouldn't be involved at all.

It is certainly appropriate for parents to ask "Who is to teach?" and "What are their qualifications?" But she said that "the day to day methods and techniques of good teaching are applicable to teaching about sex."

Mrs. Hofstein said all teachers should be expected to participate in training programs prior to classroom instruction and continue to meet together in professional seminars. A teacher shouldn't take sides in controversial matters, such as contraception or abortion, but should help students with the facts and encourage them to state their own opinions.

Therefore, if parents do not try to inhibit aggressive behavior on the part of the child, it will lead to even more aggressive behavior. The most aggressive child of all has parents who are very permissive but use extreme physical force when they do punish.

What can I do with a withdrawn child?

This is a difficult question to answer for a variety of reasons. There is some evidence to suggest that genetics may influence the degree of introversion that a child shows. More typically, however, such a child has low self-esteem. The parent should help the child to identify his feelings and indicate at the same time an acceptance of those feelings. While accepting the child's feelings, the parent does not have to indicate acceptance of how the child expresses them.

Why do adolescents work so hard at being different?

As Erikson has suggested, the adolescent is concerned about establishing his own identity. The use of idiosyncratic clothing, dress, music, and other interests is an attempt on the part of the adolescent to define himself as a person different from his parents. Note, however, that the adolescent does not work hard at being different from his peers. In fact, he is likely to conform completely to his peer group in matters of dress and speech.

How can a parent help a child to improve his motivation to learn?

First, a child needs some level of basic ability to cope in the normal classroom. Too many failure experiences can teach a child to avoid learning tasks. Piaget has suggested that the best approach for helping a child to learn is to provide him with tasks that are challenging to him and *just* above his current level of ability. With some extra effort the tasks can be accomplished. The intrinsic rewards of learning to cope with such tasks lead the child to be self-motivating and reduce his need for rewards.

When should a parent seek the help of a specialist in child rearing?

The answer is very simple—whenever the parent feels the need. There is no social stigma involved in seeking expert help, and the child can only gain from such help.

Summary

1. Developmental psychologists study behavioral changes that take place over a period of years in an individual's lifetime—from birth to death.

2. Both maturation (that is, natural changes in the body that take place with age) and experience contribute to the behavior of all children. It is difficult to determine which factor is more important, for both operate simultaneously and the relative contributions of each are different for different behaviors.

3. There are wide individual differences among children in their development and progress. Parents must learn to tolerate variations from the norm, although occasionally extreme deviations from the norm are signs of serious disorder.

4. There are several kinds of developmental studies. Longitudinal studies follow behavioral changes in the same children as they grow older. Cross-sectional studies test children of different ages. The antecedent-consequent type of research investigates factors affecting performance at a given age. In normative studies, behavior on the same task is examined in children of several different ages.

5. According to Piaget, intellectual development can be divided into four distinct periods: infancy (birth to 2 years), early childhood (2 to 7 years), later childhood (7 to 11 years) and adolescence and adulthood (11 years and beyond).

6. The infant is capable of learning at birth, and perhaps before, although his capacities are clearly limited.

7. Perception depends on the maturation of sensory systems, not all of which are ready to function at birth. Perception expands markedly in the first year of life.

8. In the first 2 years of life, the infant develops knowledge of the permanency of objects, the ability to represent internally stimuli that are not immediately present in his environment, and the beginning signs of language. Language develops from mere crying and babbling at the first few months of life to the ability to produce two-word sentences by age 2.

9. During childhood learning is largely a matter of forming concepts, the strategies for which become increasingly more sophisticated with age.

10. Perceptual skills for gathering information about the environment become increasingly more sophisticated. These skills relate directly to the ability to read.

11. During the preteen years, the child becomes capable of performing concrete, rule-following operations on objects of his environment. He learns the operational systems that are the basis of language and mathematics.

12. In the childhood years, the basis for full adult use of language is formed. The length of sentences spoken by the child increases, he learns the various parts of speech that adults use, and his speech begins to obey the complex transformational rules characteristic of adult speech.

13. Human children develop three forms of symbolic representation of the world. The first and most primitive is the enactive mode, wherein the environment seems to be represented in terms of movement tendencies in the muscles. Second is the iconic mode, which involves memory of the world in terms of images. Finally, the child develops the linguistic mode, using words and sentences of the language to characterize the objects, events, and circumstances in the world.

14. In adolescence the beginnings of adult logic and reasoning appear. Adolescents can solve complex abstract problems and deal with hypothetical questions.

15. Emotional, social, and personality development are all affected by parental child-rearing practices, particularly the patterns of feeding, toilet training, and aggression training.

16. Adolescence is a period of great change, marked by diminishing parental influence, by important physical changes including the appearance of the secondary sexual characteristics, by an intensity of emotion, and by new social interests and expectations.

17. A person's sense of morality passes through a series of steps that begins with materialistic considerations of punishment, obedience, and hedonism and progresses through the acquisition of universal principles of conscience.

18. Erikson has formulated a theory of psychosocial development that describes eight stages of life from infancy to maturity and the major

crisis an individual faces at each stage. Perhaps the most familiar of these is the identity crisis of adolescence, in which the question "Who am I?" comes to the forefront, often creating much turmoil, confusion, and anxiety. Growth and development involve meeting and resolving each life crisis.

19. The applications of knowledge of developmental processes are numerous and diverse. Piaget's theory has greatly influenced education in Great Britain, resulting in the reduction of the use of abstract, lecture methods for teaching young children and the increase of discovery-oriented and manipulative methods. The principles of cognitive development have also been applied to the designing of educational toys.

20. Child-rearing advice is difficult to give parents for each instance in which they must decide how best to handle their child. One general principle that psychologists propose is that parents should become as well informed as possible and apply their knowledge systematically.

Recommended Additional Readings

Ambron, S. *Child development.* Hinsdale, Ill.: Dryden, 1975.

Dale, P. S. *Language development: Structure and function* (2nd ed.). New York: Holt, Rinehart and Winston, 1976.

Developmental psychology today. Del Mar, Calif: CRM Books, 1971.

McCandless, B. R. *Children: Behavior and development* (2nd ed.). New York: Holt, Rinehart and Winston, 1967.

McCandless, B. R. *Adolescents: Behavior and development.* Hinsdale, Ill.: Dryden, 1970.

Munsinger, H. *Fundamentals of child development* (2nd ed.). New York: Holt, Rinehart and Winston, 1975.

Mussen, P. H. *The psychological development of the child.* Englewood Cliffs, N.J.: Prentice-Hall, 1963.

Wadsworth, B. *Piaget's theory of cognitive development.* New York: David McKay, 1971.

8

ALTERED STATES OF CONSCIOUSNESS

Consciousness is undeniably an important aspect of human behavior, yet very little is known about it. The fact that we have thoughts and feelings that we are aware (or conscious) of is perhaps one of the most distinctive qualities of human behavior. Thus the comprehensive study of behavior should attempt to understand what consciousness is and how it functions. The chief approach to the study of consciousness has been to study altered or abnormal states of consciousness in the hope that a complete analysis of altered states will shed light on the meaning of normal consciousness.

Any instance in which the overall functioning of one's mind takes on a pattern quite different from normal is called an *altered state of consciousness* (abbreviated SoC). In our normal, waking SoC there are many variations in function, aside from the particular thoughts that we are aware of at any moment. Some days our mental processes seem sharp, other days dull. Sometimes we sense the world in a very clear fashion, other times we feel isolated from it, as, for example, in the simple case of having a cold. Such quantitative variations are all within the normal or ordinary SoC. Yet when we wake up from a dream or if we have taken a powerful psychedelic drug, we feel that the overall functioning of our consciousness was in a *qualitatively different pattern*, not just as if we experienced a little more or less of some aspect of ordinary consciousness. Altered SoCs have attracted considerable interest and excitement because of the extraordinary psychological phenomena said to accompany them, such as profound insights, bizarre visions and perceptions, and incredible relaxation.

Knowledge about SoCs comes from a variety of sources, including commonsense assumptions based on personal experience, philosophical speculation, metaphysical and spiritual doctrines and observations, and (probably the smallest category) "hard" scientific data. The emphasis in this chapter will be on scientific knowledge, although this is often so fragmentary that knowledge from other domains is used to round out our discussion. The major kinds of altered states we will discuss are dreaming, out-of-body experiences, hypnosis, possession states, alcohol intoxication, marijuana intoxication, psychedelic experience, meditation, and biofeedback-induced states.

For each SoC discussed, we will look at a variety of psychological processes, including the subject's perceptions and awareness, emotions, cognitive processes, subconscious processes, memory functions, feelings of identity, perception of time, and motor functions. Often, however, some of these categories will be omitted, for our knowledge of most SoCs is far from complete. For convenience, we will diverge from our usual two-part chapter organization and mention applications and uses as each SoC is examined. Much of our knowledge about SoCs comes directly from anecdotes involving applications, and at this point there is no clear or sensible way to separate what we know from what it means.

It is difficult to know exactly where, in a book that plans to progress from simple to complex principles, to locate a discussion of altered states. We have chosen to undertake the discussion at this point, even though some of the topics covered are directly connected with later analyses of personality, because our information about altered states primarily concerns relatively simple behaviors involving perceptual, motor, and learning processes. But, admittedly, our decision was largely arbitrary.

Problems with Studying Consciousness

The study of consciousness has recently become a subject of renewed interest to psychologists. For some years past, the subject had received little scientific attention, primarily because the behavioristic viewpoint dominated psychological research for so long. Behaviorists, as we have seen, will accept only measures of overt performance as legitimate scientific data, and the primary data about SoCs come from subjects' *introspective* reports of their perceptions and experience. Behaviorists have continually warned against the use of self-reports in psychological studies because such reports are apt to be incomplete and biased. Still, self-reports are forms of behavior after all, and their potential scientific value cannot be entirely overlooked.

A more important problem in the scientific study of SoCs is the frequent report of many subjects that certain aspects of their experience are *ineffable*—that is, cannot be put into words. There are three ways this kind of data can be handled. First, the psychologist can investigate what can be readily investigated and simply note but not otherwise treat reports of ineffable experiences. Second, he may attempt to develop more adequate language for communicating the experiences of altered SoCs. Or finally, he may attempt to induce the same SoC in himself, and then, although the experience itself may not be expressible in words, he may be able to communicate *about* it with other people who have had the same experience. From

their combined discussions, a more adequate way of communicating to others might evolve. The latter approach is regarded with suspicion by many psychologists, although it is not necessarily incompatible with the basic tenets of science. The ambivalence about this approach was manifested during the peak of research on LSD in the early 1960's. Investigators who had *not* taken the drug themselves were accused of being basically ignorant of the phenomena they were supposed to be studying, while those who *had* taken the drug were accused of having lost their objectivity!

The problem of obtaining unbiased data about SoCs is further compounded by the fact that the particular content of many SoCs is highly responsive to what the subject expects to happen. For example, research has shown that hypnotic behavior depends on the instructions given the subject about what will take place when he is hypnotized. People's expectations can determine the specific experiences they have without their realizing it. When LSD was first extensively investigated by psychiatrists who conceived of it as a way of creating model psychoses, many psychotic symptoms were manifested by those taking the drug. In retrospect, it is clear that psychotic symptoms can be experienced with LSD *if* the expectations given to the subject call these forth, but they are not an inevitable effect. Thus the observer is a focal part of the observation process in studies of SoCs, and the characteristics of the investigator-observer must be taken into account in interpreting the data. At present there is no certain way of doing this, and as a result, much of the data that have been obtained are contaminated by the (unknown) biases of the observers.

Dreams

Ordinary Dreaming

Ordinary dreaming refers to the experience almost all of us have had of waking up and recalling scenes and events that seemed to take place in a nonphysical world, a world we retrospectively consider to be purely imaginary. Although there have been many laboratory and home studies of dreams, most people in our culture have not learned to be good observers of their dreams. Thus much of what is known about dreams has come from piecing together the reports of poor observers.

Sleep and Dreaming. As we saw in Chapter 2, different stages of sleep are associated with brain waves of different frequency and amplitude, which

Two Modes of Consciousness

Recent research indicates that there are two fundamentally different, but normal, modes of consciousness available to man, physiologically based on different modes of operation of the right and left cortical hemispheres of the brain.

The most dramatic evidence comes from patients who have suffered severe injury to one hemisphere, but not the other, and from split-brain patients—epileptic patients who have had the connecting fibers (the *corpus callosum*) between the two hemispheres surgically severed to control epilepsy, a technique pioneered by Dr. Joseph Bogen of the California College of Medicine (see Chapter 2).

The two hemispheres generally specialize in function, and control opposite sides of the body; the left hemisphere controls the right side of the body and vice versa. In one of Dr. Bogen's studies, a split-brain patient was allowed to feel a pencil (hidden from sight) with his right hand, and he could verbally describe and name it quite well. But if the pencil was placed in his left hand (connected to the right hemisphere), he could not name or describe it at all. The right hemisphere possesses little or no capacity for speech and, with the corpus callosum cut, it could not communicate with the left hemisphere speech functions. But, if the patient was allowed to feel a set of objects with his left hand, such as a key, a pencil, a book, and so on, he could correctly match it with the previously felt object, although he still could not state verbally what he was doing.

Effects in brain-damaged and split-brain patients are far more dramatic than in normal people, of course, but Drs. Robert Ornstein and David Galin of the Langley Porter Neuropsychiatric Institute, two of the leading investigators of the two modes of consciousness, feel that this duality is present in all people. Ordinarily we alternate rapidly between use of the two hemispheres, suiting ourselves to the task. The left hemisphere mode of consciousness is involved with analytical, logical thinking, especially verbal and mathematical thinking, and processes information sequentially and linearly. The right hemisphere mode of consciousness processes information more simultaneously than sequentially, dealing more with patterns than sequences. It is

more relational, and is more involved in artistic endeavor, spatial orientation, crafts, body skills, and recognition of faces.

Ornstein emphasizes that these two modes of consciousness are not opposed, but rather are complementary if used properly. Unfortunately, both individuals and cultures often overvalue the one or the other mode. Ours is a predominantly verbal-logical culture and undervalues the right hemisphere mode of consciousness. Because many of the characteristics of altered states of consciousness resemble increased right hemisphere functioning (for example, greater awareness of patterns), one of the motivations for experiencing altered states may be the satisfaction of a more balanced state or of functioning in neglected modes.

Many kinds of dichotomies (two-part divisions) have been made in literature, science, the arts, and religion that roughly reflect aspects of the right-left hemisphere duality. Many of these dimensions are shown in Figure 8–1 as opposite sides of the ancient Chinese yin-yang symbol. The dynamic form of the yin-yang symbol, the growing dot of white in the black (yin) and the growing dot of black in the white (yang), remind us of the complementarity of the two modes.

Figure 8–1
The yin-yang dichotomy

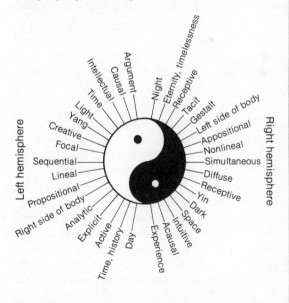

produce distinctive EEG patterns for each stage (see Figure 8–2). The subject who is awake but resting with his eyes closed shows predominantly *alpha* brain waves (a regular rhythm of about 10 cycles per second). As sleep comes on, the alpha rhythm is replaced by slower, irregular waves in what is called

Initial Stage 1 EEG. With the appearance of bursts of activity of about 14 cycles per second, called *spindles*, the EEG is classified as Stage 2 sleep. When larger, slower *delta* waves (1 to 2 cycles per second) are added to the irregular activity and spindles, the pattern is called Stage 3; and when

Figure 8–2
Brain waves, sleep, and dreaming

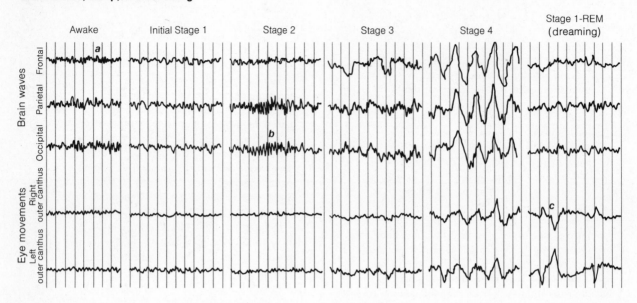

Recordings of brain waves from three cortical areas (frontal is on the forehead, parietal is over the ear, occipital is back of the head) and eye movements as a person goes to sleep. The regular alpha rhythm (a) in the awake subject is replaced by slower, irregular activity in Initial Stage 1. Spindles (b) appear in Stage 2, and delta waves are added to the irregular activity and spindles in Stage 3. The large, slow delta waves predominate in Stage 4. Rapid eye movements (REMs), measured by the electrooculogram (EOG), are associated with dreaming and occur in later Stage 1 periods of the night. They are indicated by synchronous but opposite deflections (c) on the eye movement channels.

delta waves predominate, the pattern is Stage 4. The cycle of Stage 1 through Stage 4 is repeated four to six times a night.

Eugene Aserinsky found that during Stage 1 EEG periods (after the initial Stage 1), an electrooculogram (EOG) recorded rapid eye movements (REMs) in sleeping subjects, and if he awakened the subjects during these periods, they recalled a dream about 80 percent of the time. It is now generally accepted that ordinary dreaming occurs in Stage 1–REM sleep, although dreamlike activity is sometimes reported to occur during other stages of sleep. If the Stage 1–REM periods are plotted, the first one occurs about 90 minutes after going to sleep and lasts 5 to 10 minutes. At the second 90-minute mark, a somewhat longer Stage 1–REM period occurs, and this stage of sleep reoccurs and gets somewhat longer at each 90-minute cycle. The last Stage 1–REM dream of the night may be from half an hour to an hour long, and awakening from it is common. This last dream, of course, is the one you are most likely to remember in the morning.

Psychological Effects

Perception.   Ordinary dreaming represents one of the most radical changes in perception of any altered SoC, for the external world is almost completely eliminated and replaced by an internal world. There are tremendous individual differences in how "real" the dream world is. At one extreme, some people report experiencing every sensory quality that they experience in a wakeful state. They see dream scenes clearly and in color, they hear and speak with dream characters, and they may taste, touch, and smell in the dream world. At the other extreme, some people report their dreams to be rather hazy black and white images.

Occasionally, stimuli from the external world make their way into the dream world, where they are usually distorted in some fashion to fit in with the action of the dream. The ringing of the alarm clock, for example, may be perceived as a church bell in the dream. Furthermore, there is selectivity in the perception of the external world during dreaming, as well as during waking (see Chapter 3). A familiar example is the mother who sleeps through and

© King Features Syndicate, 1971.

One interesting feature about dream sleep (REM sleep) is its depth. In animals, REM sleep is the deepest of all types of sleep, as measured by how loud a noise it takes to awaken the animal. In human beings, however, a strange system has evolved. If the noise is meaningful to the sleeper, such as his wife raiding the checkbook, he will awaken easily.

never hears the rumble of traffic outside her bedroom window, but who snaps wide awake at the slightest whimper from her baby three rooms away.

Performance.   Motor output is virtually eliminated during dreaming. Laboratory studies have shown that there is an active inhibition in the spinal cord of nerve impulses to the muscles. Impulses corresponding to the imagery experienced during dreaming may arrive at the muscles, but the inhibitory signal keeps the muscles from reacting. Occasionally the muscles of the limbs or face may twitch slightly, and occasionally there is some vocalization during ordinary dreaming. But for the most part the dreaming person is almost totally paralyzed. The paralysis of the dream state is adaptive in a sense, for if people acted out their dreams the world would be a rather dangerous place at night, for both the dreamer and anyone near him. On occasion, the paralysis may last into the waking state for a few seconds.

Cognitive processes.   Cognitive processes in dreams are often rather stupid. Not only does the dreamer fool himself as to whether he is awake or asleep, but he also accepts all sorts of incongruities and absurdities in the dream situation without the slightest question. In the normal SoC, the person would be immediately alerted by such incongruities and consider them in detail, but the dreamer ignores errors in his cognitive processes until afterward, during the waking state. Freud theorized that this was because subconscious desires and emotions

were actually responsible for the particular content of the dream, and not enough psychological energy was available to the "secondary processes," the intellectual functions, to allow observation of dream content. Other theorists view dream "stupidity" as a simple consequence of inadequate activation of higher brain centers during sleep.

Emotion.   Emotional processes have a greater effect on the dream experience than cognitive processes do. The range of emotional experience is as great as in ordinary waking consciousness, although the emotions may be evoked by rather different stimuli than would evoke them in the waking state. Emotions may also become extremely intense, possibly because the lowered level of critical processes no longer acts to inhibit the emotional systems. Even the amount of sleep and dreaming a person does has been partially tied to emotional factors.

Memory.   Memory systems obviously function at a very high level during ordinary dreaming. Almost the entire dream world is constructed from memory images of things the dreamer has seen or otherwise sensed or from new combinations of past memories. The memory quality of an experience is often missing during ordinary dreaming, and the dreamer often mistakes an intense scene constructed from memory for a real world of experience. As is typical in altered SoCs, visual memory seems particularly strong in dreams, much stronger than a person's ability to produce a visual image from memory in the normal state.

Recall that memory *for* dreams varies tremendously from person to person. Some people almost never remember a dream in the morning after waking. Other people remember all their dreams practically every morning. With those who do recall their dreams on awakening, the rate at which the dream fades from memory in the normal

Antidream Machine

Time—Dream when you're feeling blue? Not any more—if a machine reported in a recent issue of the *Naval Research Reviews* is put into use. By measuring brainwaves through the use of electrodes, a device no larger than a pack of cigarettes can gauge a person's level of concentration. If his mind begins to wander, a tone sounds, jolting him from his reverie. If he continues to daydream, another alarm goes off, notifying his boss, his teacher or some Big Brother who can promptly set the dreamer straight.

This instrument of wakefulness, designed by Scientist Karel Montor, was first tested on midshipmen volunteers at the U.S. Naval Academy. When their minds strayed from their assignment to thoughts about a girl friend or their next leave—bong! they were found out. Like the fear of being hanged, the machine wonderfully concentrates the mind. Hitched up to a truck or bus driver, an airline pilot or an air-traffic controller, it may prevent accidents. Generally, it could be used to teach people to keep their minds on the matter at hand. But the right to daydream—the right not to pay attention—should be rigidly respected and, if need be, fiercely fought for, even if it is not listed in the Bill of Rights. A machine that could banish idle reveries would be a nightmare.

Here is one potential application of brain wave technology. What do you think of this level of control of the human mind?

state also varies. Some people lose the memory of the dream within a few seconds, unless they make a conscious effort to rehearse it; others may remember a dream vividly for months or years. Sometimes a dream will be forgotten, but an incident later in the day will trigger a complete memory of it. Many people who claim they never remember their dreams begin to do so in great detail if they practice taking notes on their dreams as soon as they wake up. If you are interested in your dreams, you might start keeping a "dream diary."

Identity. A person's sense of identity is highly variable in a dream. The dreamer can be his normal self, he can completely identify with an entirely different character in the dream, or he can identify with a version of himself that is changed in a number of important ways. At times, a person may have no identity at all in a dream, simply perceiving the dream as an "outside" observer might. This is a striking example of the arbitrariness of our belief in a fixed personal identity. Unique combinations of characteristics and personality elements can be grouped as "the ego" quite readily during dreams. Note too that much of the cognitive activity and emotional reaction of a dream takes place with respect to *who* the dreamer is. If he becomes a *different* person in a dream, then events that might be important or evoke specific plans or emotions for his ordinary identity might not do so within the dream.

Time sense. Time in dreams generally seems to flow at about the same rate as normal waking activity. This has been established in the laboratory by timing the length of the brain-wave state associated with dreaming and then waking the person and having him estimate, in various ways, how long his dream was. Generally the subject's estimate is quite close to the actual amount of time elapsed. There still seem to be some dreams, however, in which the perceived time correlates very poorly with clock time. Thus, one might have a dream that seems to take a week, when the sleep stage associated with dreaming could not have lasted more than an hour or so. This may not mean that a week's worth of events actually occurred in the dream, but only that the *feeling* of time was of a week passing.

Physiological Correlates. As we mentioned, nearly all motor functioning is inhibited during dreaming, with two major exceptions. The first is the REMs that are characteristic of dreaming sleep. REMs have been related in some experiments to what the dreamer reports he is seeing. Thus, if the dreamer reported watching objects fall from airplanes to the ground, his electrooculogram might register large vertical REMs. Dreams of watching a ping-pong match would probably produce large horizontal REMs. The other exception to the complete lack of motor functioning in the dream state seems to be the autonomic nervous system. Heart rate, blood pressure, and respiration show great variability and can undergo large, sudden changes during dreaming. It is not yet clear whether this reflects the emotions of the dream or not.

In males the penis is partially erect throughout most of Stage 1–REM dreaming. This does not necessarily represent specific, overt sexual content of the dreams so much as some sort of physiological release phenomenon. The "morning erection," previously attributed to a full bladder, is now seen to result from the last dream of the night, which frequently occurs just before awakening.

Big Differences Seen in Short, Long Sleepers

New York (UPI)—According to scientific estimates, 5 to 10 per cent of young adults either sleep less than six hours or more than nine hours out of every 24 and are none the worse for it.

They're very special, these short or long sleepers. Most people find it necessary to sleep about eight hours in 24 in order to function effectively. They are groggy with less, loggy with more.

The tested young adults excited the curiosity of Drs. Ernest Hartmann and Frederick Baekeland, who respectively operate sleep laboratories at Boston State Hospital and the State University of New York in Brooklyn.

These scientists wondered if there were psychological differences between the short and the long sleepers which might account for their places on the two extremes of the usual (and therefore "normal") sleep pattern.

They advertised for volunteers in Boston and New York newspapers and got more than 400 responses. Of those, 260 were entirely authentic—the short night or the long night in bed was a firmly established way of life and the young men, all over 20, were healthy.

Hartmann and Baekeland put them through an exhaustive series of psychological tests and interviews. Twenty-nine slept eight nights in the laboratories, having their brain waves, sleep-depths and dreams analyzed.

For the shorts, the results were clear-cut, the scientists reported to an organ of the American Medical Association—"as a group they were efficient, energetic, ambitious persons who tended to work hard and to keep busy.

"They were relatively sure of themselves, socially adept, decisive, and were satisfied with themselves and their lives. They were somewhat conformist in their social and political views and they wished to appear very normal and 'all-American.' They were extroverted and definitely were not 'worriers'; they seldom left themselves time to sit down and think about problems."

The long sleepers did not fall so readily into a psychological group, the scientists reported. Among them was a wide variety of opinions on all subjects. They were inclined to be nonconformist and critical.

They were more uncomfortable than the shorts, "complaining of a variety of minor aches and pains and concerns. Although none of them was seriously ill psychiatrically, most had mild or moderate neurotic problems.

"Some were overtly anxious, some showed considerable inhibition in aggressive and sexual functioning, and some were mildly depressed. They appeared in general not very sure of themselves, their career choices or their life-styles."

An example of the possible relationships between dreaming and human personality and potential.

A large number of drugs have been investigated for their effects on the sleep cycle. Practically all drugs, particularly sedatives, cut down the amount of time spent in Stage 1–REM sleep. There is some evidence that psychedelic drugs such as LSD, taken just before going to sleep, may cause more Stage 1–REM time early in the night, without having much effect on the total amount of such sleep. The effects of drugs on the content of dreams have only begun to be investigated.

Theories of Dreams. Dreams have been the subject of inquiry and speculation for centuries. Until the development of psychoanalysis, however, psychology largely considered dreams to represent the meaningless refuse of mental life. It was, therefore, a major departure from contemporary thought when Sigmund Freud suggested that dreams are meaningful, purposive, and determined.

Freud's theory. Freud evolved psychoanalytic theory partly from reports of dreams, and he believed that the dream was the clearest example of unconscious processes. Very briefly, psychoanalytic theory states that during sleep the psychological energy ordinarily used in coping realistically with the world becomes available to the unconscious and to certain perceptual areas of the brain. These generate a special type of thought activity at hallucinatory intensity, and we perceive this activity as an "external" dream world. The particular content of the dream is controlled by the emotions aroused during the day and their associative connections with the primary drives of sex and aggression and repressed memories of earlier experiences centering on these drives.

Dreams fulfill or express repressed or unconscious wishes. This is perhaps most apparent in the dreams of children, which often include very explicit fulfillment of some nagging wish or motive that might otherwise become so intense as to awaken the dreamer. Hungry children, for example, frequently dream of eating sumptuous meals or desserts and thus remain undisturbed by their hunger pangs.

The motives underlying adult dreams, however, are usually more obscure. The content of dreams recalled by normal healthy adults is typically absurd, inconsistent, and confused. In this regard, Freud identified two distinct types of interrelated dream content. If a person is asked what he dreamed about last night, the material he might be able to report is called the *manifest content* of the dream, the

One interesting aspect of REM sleep is that it is accompanied by a loss of muscle tone. Falling asleep does involve a relaxation of the muscles, but it is not until one enters the REM state that muscle tone dramatically drops (and with it, beer cans). This fact has been used to "automatically" deprive animals of REM sleep. The animals are placed on a small pedestal surrounded by water. They can sleep on the pedestal but they cannot have REM sleep because the loss of muscle tone is so great in REM that the animals fall off the pedestal.

conscious dream experience. Freud suggested, however, that each dream also involves a *latent content*, which consists of the unconscious wish or impulse that seeks expression. Freud postulated that since most of this material (largely concerned with the drives of sex and aggression) is unacceptable to our waking consciousness, it generally cannot be *directly* expressed in the dream. A variety of special processes, the *dream processes,* exist for expressing this emotional material in a disguised form that does not directly arouse a person's conscience.

The first of the processes that Freud described for disguising unacceptable material is called *condensation*. A single character in a dream may look like one person we know, dress like another, bear the name of a third, and be engaged in the occupation of still a fourth. The dream composite would therefore be a condensed representation of all four people. Another technique involves a change of affective emphasis. Frequently, the least prominent element of the manifest dream represents the latent thought carrying the greatest charge of psychic energy. Conversely, the clearest, most central manifest feature may represent a latent impulse with very little impetus. This type of dreamwork is called *displacement*, because it involves a reallocation of psychic energy.

A third process is *symbolization*. Freud observed

that certain dream elements seem to have the same meaning from person to person, even though the individuals involved may not be able to interpret the symbols. The fourth method by which unconscious impulses are disguised in the production of dreams is *secondary elaboration*. This involves the imposition of a story line or logical framework, often incorporating events of the preceding day, that adds transitions between images and combines them into a coherent whole.

By distorting the expression of the latent dream thought, the dream processes produce a compromise between gratification and censorship of an unwanted impulse. Dreams are not, therefore, the "refuse of mental life" which psychologists once dismissed as meaningless. However, Freud's theory of dreams, while widely used as a guide to the therapeutic interpretation of dreams, is very controversial. A methodology has not yet been found to prove or disprove many of Freud's contentions.

Other theories.   A number of therapists working with dreams recognized the value of Freud's theories and methods of interpretation but felt that he was too restricted, that important aspects of man and his dream life were neglected. The most prominent of these people was Carl G. Jung, a Swiss physician. Jung's theory of dreaming indicated that underlying the purely *personal* elements in a person's dreams were forces and elements that were transpersonal, *archetypal*, characteristic of man as a species rather than only of a particular individual living in a particular culture at a particular time (see Chapter 9). For example, if a patient dreamed of crossing a river, Freud might link the river with some past event in the patient's life, but Jung would carry the interpretation further, because "crossing a river" is a basic symbol of surmounting obstacles. For Jung, dreams were also a time when aspects of

"I'd better not dream about you and that blonde hussy again tonight!"

Reprinted courtesy of The Register and Tribune Syndicate, Inc.

How would you interpret this woman's dream? A Freudian approach would expect dream content to be highly disguised examples of wish fulfillment —does she *wish* that her husband were having an affair with the blonde hussy? According to the continuity theory, however, the woman may be *worried* that her husband is having an affair. Clearly, we need more information about the wife's dream and about her life with her husband before we can develop an adequate interpretation of her dream.

"Dreams are just taped replays of your day."

Reprinted courtesy of The Register and Tribune Syndicate, Inc.

Much dream content can be related to recent past experiences of the dreamer, meaning that the "taped replay" hypothesis is not a totally facetious one. How would you test this hypothesis?

our personalities opposite to our waking personalities were dominant. The waking extrovert might be a dreaming introvert.

Another theory of dream content holds that dreams are basically continuous or congruent with normal waking thoughts, worries, needs, and desires. We worry in our dreams about the same things we worry about while awake. Most dream research supports this notion. For example, subjects who have been deprived of food report more food-related dreams than nondeprived control subjects. Thus, dreams seem to represent a continuation of waking cognition, as opposed to thoughts opposite to waking thoughts (Jung's position) or thoughts not allowed into waking consciousness (Freud's position).

One important starting point for the study of dream content is to find out what kinds of things people say they dream about. There are many so-called common dreams according to dream folklore, such as dreaming of being attacked or pursued, of failing an examination, or of being

buried alive. In one study, 250 college students were given a list of 34 dream actions thought to be "classic" dream themes and were asked to indicate whether or not they had ever dreamed about each of the actions. The results showed that indeed many college students had experienced these common dreams (see Table 8–1). However, the meaning of each dream remains a point of hot debate. Even the question of whether or not dreams have a hidden (or latent) meaning or content is being seriously argued.

Uses of Dreaming. There is little general agreement on the functions or uses of ordinary dreaming. In psychoanalytic theory, dreams are viewed as a safety valve that allows enough expression of unacceptable unconscious impulses to prevent them from disrupting daytime behavior. Some theorists see the content of dreams as reflecting some kind of information processing of the day's events. Others believe the function of dreaming is to help alert the cortex to prevent sleep

Table 8-1

Percentage of college students who have experienced common dream themes

Have you ever dreamed of . . . ?	%
1. being attacked or pursued	82.8
2. falling	77.2
3. trying again and again to do something	71.2
4. school, teachers, studying	71.2
5. being frozen with fright	58.0
6. sexual experiences	66.4
7. eating delicious food	61.6
8. falling with fear	67.6
9. arriving too late, e.g., missing the train	63.6
10. fire	40.8
11. swimming	52.0
12. dead people as though alive	46.0
13. being locked up	56.4
14. loved person as dead	57.2
15. snakes	48.8
16. being on verge of falling	46.8
17. finding money	56.0
18. failing an examination	38.8
19. flying or soaring through air	33.6
20. being smothered, unable to breathe	44.4
21. falling without fear	33.2
22. wild, violent beasts	30.0
23. being inappropriately dressed	46.0
24. seeing self as dead	33.2
25. being nude	42.8
26. killing someone	25.6
27. being tied, unable to move	30.4
28. having superior knowledge or mental ability	25.6
29. lunatics or insane people	25.6
30. your teeth falling out	20.8
31. creatures, part animal, part human	14.8
32. being buried alive	14.8
33. seeing self in mirror	12.4
34. being hanged by the neck	2.8

so deep that the organism could not be readily aroused in the event of danger. No theory has conclusive evidence to support it.

Interestingly, there does seem to be a physiological *need* to dream (or at least a need for REMs). If a person is deprived of Stage 1–REM dreaming by being awakened every time he shows this physiological pattern, he will have to be awakened more and more frequently as nights go on in order to prevent this kind of sleep. If he is then allowed some uninterrupted sleep, there will be a temporary increase in Stage 1–REM time, a partial compensation for the previous deficit. Some initial investigations of the effects of dream deprivation suggested that subjects became quite anxious and jittery the following day. Later experiments have failed to confirm this, however, in spite of prolonged periods (up to 10 days) of Stage 1–REM deprivation.

Dreamless Sleep. *Dreamless sleep* is a term commonly used to refer to Stages 2, 3, and 4 of the

EEG sleep pattern. They are not accompanied by REMs and are therefore commonly referred to as non-REM stages or non-REM sleep. The term "dreamless sleep" should be used with caution. While there are *seldom* reports of intense, emotional episodes of dreaming from stages other than Stage 1–REM periods, they do occur occasionally. Researchers have not yet been able to decide whether these vivid reports are dreams recalled from an earlier Stage 1–REM period or whether they actually happened in non-REM sleep.

If subjects are awakened in the laboratory from non-REM sleep and asked what was going through their minds just before awakening, the usual answer is "nothing." Either there is no mental activity during this kind of sleep, or else memory of it is extremely poor. On rare occasions, something is described by the subject that he labels a "dream." More frequently, reports from non-REM sleep are labeled by the subject as "thinking." The impression of experiences during dreamless sleep is that they are often a sort of sporadic thinking—brief, relatively logical, and pedestrian thoughts. Perception of the external world is generally nonexistent; either stimuli are not well incorporated into the ongoing experience or the ongoing experience is forgotten. Self-awareness also seems to be nonexistent.

The major exception to the notion that only occasional vague and dull thoughts occur during dreamless sleep is the finding that most *sleep talking*, *sleep walking*, and intense *nightmares* occur during non-REM sleep. Since the person is not in a state of peripheral motor paralysis as he is during Stage 1–REM, mental experiences may be expressed in physical action. The fact that most nightmares occur in non-REM sleep indicates that occasionally *exceptionally* intense dreamlike processes may occur, with maximal emotional arousal.

Hypnagogic and Hypnopompic States

The SoC that one passes through in going from waking to sleeping is called the *hypnagogic* state. It is similar, and possibly identical, to the SoC that one passes through in going from sleeping to waking, the *hypnopompic* state. The few laboratory studies that have been carried out have concentrated on the hypnagogic state, which varies tremendously from individual to individual. For some people, the period of falling asleep is filled with experiences as rich as the best nocturnal dreams. For others, it is very dull and usually forgotten almost immediately.

Much hypnagogic experience may be identical to later dreaming, although not enough investigation of similarities and differences has been carried out to make this comparison complete. Even for the best hypnagogic "dreamers," the experiences of the hypnagogic state are usually forgotten more rapidly than ordinary dreams, especially if the dreamer continues on into sleep.

You can observe your own hypnagogic state in detail by doing the following: When lying down to sleep, balance one arm vertically, with the elbow resting on the bed. You can go fairly far into a hypnagogic state and maintain the arm in a balanced, comfortable position with little effort. When you are deep in the hypnagogic state, your arm will start to fall. The action will usually startle you into wakefulness, and you can try to fix the memory of the hypnagogic experience in your mind before it fades. With the balanced arm technique, the hypnagogic state can be greatly prolonged.

Ego States in the Hypnagogic Period. In the most comprehensive recent study of the hypnagogic state, subjects were awakened from various stages of falling asleep (as defined by brain-wave recordings) and were asked to describe what was going through their minds just before the awakening. Reports were classified into three "ego states." In the *intact ego state* the subject maintained his contact with the external world (that is, he could control his mental processes, he knew where he was, and he could discriminate between internal and external events), and his perceptions and cognitions were reasonably plausible and logical. Reports were classified as indicating a *destructuralized ego state* if both contact with the external world and maintenance of plausible mental content were impaired. For example, the subject might report that his only experience was of a number hanging in mid-air or of gnomes making tunnels through his brain. He no longer was aware of his position in the external world, nor was his mental content plausible. Reports were classified as *restructuralized ego* if the mental content was relatively plausible even though contact with the external world was lost.

A review of subjects' reports showed that reports of intact ego states diminished rapidly as the subject went from alpha rhythm EEG to Stage 1 sleep (see Figure 8–3); the number of reports classified as destructuralized ego states increased through Stage 1 but fell off markedly in Stage 2; and restructuralized ego states increased steadily through all stages of falling asleep. Thus, in the course of going into the hypnagogic state and sleep, ordinary consciousness (the intact ego state) seems to break up and be replaced by rather bizarre and

Figure 8–3
Ego states in the hypnagogic period

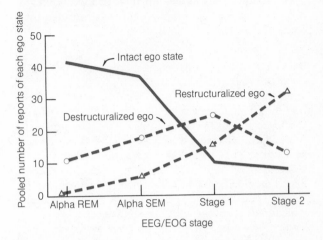

Reports of hypnagogic activity classified into different ego states as a function of brain wave activity (EEG) and eye movements (EOG) at the time of the report. Physiological test states are alpha wave EEG with rapid eye movement (REM), alpha wave EEG with slow eye movement (SEM), Initial Stage 1 sleep (without REMs), and Stage 2 sleep.

implausible content, but then content tends to become more plausible even though contact with the external world is lost.

Uses. Some spiritual development systems have attempted to teach people voluntary control of the hypnagogic state, that is, entering the "internal world" while falling asleep but maintaining full consciousness and willpower. This possible use has not been investigated scientifically yet. There have also been reports of people going from a Stage 1–REM dream state at the end of the night into the hypnopompic period and acquiring some control of the hypnopompic state. The purpose would be to get back into a full dream state in a more desirable position, by continuing the dreaming process in the half-awake hypnopompic state, correcting any unpleasant attributes of the dream, and then going into a more pleasant dream state.

The High Dream

The *high dream* is a special type of dream in which the dreamer feels that the functioning of his or her consciousness has changed to a pattern similar to that experienced when taking a psychedelic drug such as LSD or marijuana. This SoC has only recently been described, and, therefore, little is known about it. Our knowledge is based almost entirely on the reports of a few individuals.

The following example, in which a high dream develops from an ordinary dream, was reported by a young woman.

Someone had brought a tremendous amount of LSD into town and had been dispensing it freely. The cops were frustrated because they couldn't arrest everyone and they didn't know who to pin it on. In dispensing this there seemed to be a spirit of free giving and there were no strangers. Someone said to me that if you took the LSD with fish the way the Indians (American) do, it wouldn't make you sick, but if you took it medically, it might. I took some by itself, but I knew it wouldn't make me sick anyway. I continued walking, and noticed that I wasn't wearing my clothes. The other people in town were dressed, but my unclothed state didn't seem to bother them. I went into a room where there were a lot of young people and also a man I know who is associated with young people as a teacher and counselor. . . . As I went in, the whole room seemed to radiate life and color. The man was sitting on one end of a couch which was covered with a serape. The colors of the serape blended and moved in a free flowing maze. I went over and lay down on the couch with my head in the man's lap. He started stroking my hair as I looked up at the light. The light was shimmering with rainbow colors and seemed very close. . . . As I lay there looking up I felt the presence of all those in the room moving into my body as definite, discernible individual vibrations. I felt these vibrations in every cell of my body and I was raised to a state of ecstasy.   **(Tart, 1969, page 173)**

The beginning of the woman's dream report contains ordinary dream elements such as acceptance of incongruity (calmly walking about naked) and the rather bizarre sequence about taking LSD with fish. Then the dreamer dreamed of actually ingesting LSD (although this particular content is not essential to defining a high dream), and she experienced changes in perception characteristic of the effects of psychedelic drugs (intensified and flaming colors, rainbows, "vibrations," ecstasy).

In a high dream the qualities of perceived objects may undergo many of the changes characteristic of the effects of psychedelic drugs in a wakened condition, including a temporary loss of the split between perceiver and perceived. There may not be any self-awareness that one is *dreaming*. Emotions can apparently cover the same range of change as with psychedelic drugs, reaching a feeling of ecstasy, as in the example given. Cognitive processes may become more intuitive, with feelings

of immediate insight and significance. Nothing is yet known about the degree to which subconscious processes are manifest in or control the high dream. Memory can apparently be state-dependent (see Chapter 4) for previous psychedelic states; that is, qualities of experience of previous psychedelic states that are not recallable in the ordinary waking state may be recalled and recognized in the high dream. As in ordinary dreams, there is an almost complete paralysis of motor functions.

Previous experience with psychedelic drug-induced states is obviously necessary for a person to *recognize* that he is having a high dream. Whether a similar dream could occur without previous psychedelic experience is unknown, but it may be possible. Insofar as it duplicates many of the effects of an actual psychedelic experience, the high dream demonstrates the role of learning; once a person knows certain experiences are possible, he may then induce them without having to reingest any drug.

The Lucid Dream

In ordinary dreaming it is possible to have the dream thought "This is a dream" without in any way changing the functioning of the SoC. In rare cases, however, it is possible for a shift in consciousness to come about during dreaming such that the dreamer feels that: (1) he possesses his *normal* state of consciousness, that is, all his abilities to think and reason, while (2) still remaining experientially *in the dream world.* For example, if you *knew for certain right now* that what you were experiencing was a dream and that you would wake up in a few minutes, no matter how real it seemed, this would give you the feeling of a *lucid dream.*

Lucid dreams are apparently rare, and very little is known about them. The term "lucid dream" was first used by a Dutch physician, Frederick van Eeden, who gave the following description of this SoC: "In these lucid dreams the reintegration of the psychic functions is so complete that the sleeper remembers day life in his own condition, reaches a state of perfect awareness, and is able to direct his attention, and to attempt different acts of free volition. Yet the sleep, as I am able confidently to state, is undisturbed, deep and refreshing." The following is an example of one of van Eeden's lucid dreams:

On Sept. 9, 1904, I dreamt that I stood at a table before a window. On the table were different objects. I was perfectly well aware that I was dreaming and I considered what sorts of experiments I could make. I began by trying to break glass, by beating it with a stone. I put a small tablet of glass on two stones and struck it with another stone. Yet it would not break. Then I took a fine claret-glass from the table and struck it with my fist, with all my might, at the same time reflecting how dangerous it would be to do this in waking life; yet the glass remained whole. But lo! when I looked at it again after some time, it was broken.

It broke all right, but a little too late, like an actor who misses his cue. This gave me a very curious impression of being in a *fake-world*, cleverly imitated, but with small failures. I took the broken glass and threw it out of the window, in order to observe whether I could hear the *tinkling*. I heard the noise all right and I even saw two dogs run away from it quite naturally. I thought what a good imitation this comedy-world was. Then I saw a decanter with claret and tasted it, and noted with perfect clearness of mind: "Well we can also have voluntary impressions of taste in this dream-world; this has quite the taste of wine." **(van Eeden, 1913)**

Although it would be premature to say that all functions of our normal SoC appear in lucid dreams, it certainly seems that way to the people having the experience—a conviction that persists after awakening. Little more can be said about psychological functioning in lucid dreams, for our information about them at the present time consists only of occasional accounts by individuals who have managed to develop this ability.

Although it is apparently rare for individuals to have a complete lucid dream, a fair number of people when questioned will believe they have had moments of lucid dreaming once or twice in their lives. The main technique for developing lucid dreaming appears to be the diary method. A number of people who have started keeping detailed records of their dreams report that after several months they begin getting critical of their dreams *while* they are occurring. Eventually they begin to recognize that they are dreaming, which seems to be a transitional step for some from the ordinary to the lucid dream.

The possible uses and benefits of lucid dreams are intriguing. One of these is therapeutic. Psychologist-anthropologist Kilton Stewart reports on a tribe of people, the Senoi, in Malaysia, who teach their children to value dreams. Each morning, family members discuss their dreams in detail. Everyone is completely accepting of the others' dreams. The result is that practically all members of the tribe develop lucid dreaming on a regular basis. They then attempt to work out conflict situations *during* dreams, and Stewart reports that this seems

to be responsible for a uniquely high degree of maturity and mental health in these people. The possibility of therapeutic use for lucid dreaming has not yet been adequately tested in a Western setting. Another intriguing possibility is that lucid dreams may be used as a technique for achieving other SoCs. There are scattered references in some of the literature of Yoga to the development of lucid dreaming for this purpose. Furthermore, the lucid dreams can turn into out-of-body experiences, described in the next section.

Altered States of Wakefulness

Out-of-Body Experiences

Suppose that gradually during a dream you become certain that the world around you is not a dream world, existing only in your imagination, but the real world. The experience in which a person feels himself located at some point other than where he knows his physical body is, and yet feels he is in a perfectly normal SoC, is termed an *out-of-body experience* (OOBE). It is called an *astral projection* in occult and mystical literature. OOBEs may shade off, in some cases, into more mystical experiences. However, we will confine our attention to the typical nonmystical OOBEs.

The incidence of OOBEs is not known and is hard to estimate, because many people having the experience do not tell anyone about it for fear of being considered insane. It may be as low as one in a thousand ordinary persons, and it may be as high as 20 or 30 percent in certain groups, such as psychedelic drug users.

A typical experience may start during sleep, illness, or dreaming. The person suddenly finds he is in his normal SoC but floating near the ceiling of his bedroom. He often looks down and sees a body lying in his bed and is then quite shocked to perceive that it is his *own* physical body. He may or may not think of some distant place, but if he does he typically reports suddenly finding himself there, with or without sensations of flying or traveling to that distant place. The experience may last anywhere from a few seconds to what seems like hours. Although sleep or a prone position often precedes OOBEs, some people have experienced them while actively moving about or immediately following severe accidents that include being knocked out or otherwise coming close to death.

For most of the people who experience it, the OOBE is a once-in-a-lifetime phenomenon and has profound effects on them. Typically, people having the experience state that they no longer merely

Pilot Turns Minister after Out-of-Body Experience

Boulder Daily Camera—By Bob Keeler

The explosion ripped through the boat's engine compartment just as Burris Jenkins III was bending down to pick up a screwdriver a foot away from the engine.

The blast slammed Jenkins into the cabin's overhead, leaving a neat impression where his head hit. The flames left second-and-third-degree burns over 80 per cent of his body. A doctor at the hospital where Jenkins was taken after the explosion aboard his father's yacht told Doris Jenkins that her husband had only a 50-50 chance of survival.

After months in bed, first at Huntington Hospital, then at Manhattan's Roosevelt Hospital, Jenkins pulled through. It was during his recuperation that a profound spiritual experience turned his life upside down, nudging him along the twisting road to his current wind-and-prayer career as an international airplane pilot and a full-time minister. He flies for Trans World Airlines and preaches at Christ Community Church in Farmingville, L.I. . . .

Jenkins is still hesitant as he talks about the experience in the hospital, because it is so personal. "I was laying in bed, watching TV," he said, "and the next moment, I was looking back at myself in bed. It was as if I had no control over my movements. I rose out of the bed, above the courtyard. I was above New York City, in the clouds."

Soon, he said, he found himself accelerating through intergalactic space. "I became aware of an aura off to the right and a huge number of beings in communion with this great being, which you could only describe as light. I got to figuring, 'I must be dead.' I figured pretty soon my wife would die and she would join me. But then it hit me that I would always be alone. I would always be moving faster than anybody behind me and slower than anybody ahead of me. I was not destined to be one of them (the beings he had sensed). If the soul screams, my soul screamed. When I screamed, 'God help me,' I was back in bed and the TV commercial hadn't even completed itself yet."

No Explanation

"I've talked to various psychiatrists about it, and nobody could come up with any conclusion as to what kind of phenomenon it was. It was similar to what Carl Jung experienced—this disembodiment kind of thing. It had a profoundly moving religious effect on me, in that it shook my view that the universe is made up strictly of what we can see, touch and feel. . . ."

Cross-cultural Similarities.   Practically all of our knowledge of OOBEs comes from reports of spontaneous cases. As an SoC, the intriguing thing about the OOBE is that extremely similar reports come from people with entirely different cultural backgrounds. Descriptions of OOBEs found in ancient Egyptian records sound exactly like those of a modern American. People without any previous information about OOBEs often report identical experiences. For example, many people report that there is some sort of thin cord or cable connecting their physical body to their "projected" form while out of the body. Typically, the person finds himself possessing a second body that resembles his own normal physical body in all respects.

Paranormal Aspects.   Although OOBEs can be treated as an intriguing SoC, some of the well-documented reports possess characteristics that are difficult to deal with in conventional terms. Apparently, in some cases, what a person experiences seeing at some distant location corresponds to what was actually going on there and cannot be accounted for by previous knowledge. Thus one must consider either the possibility of coincidence or that some kind of extrasensory perception (ESP) is combined with the "imaginary" experience of being out of the body. Some have argued that human consciousness can exist and perceive at a location different from the physical body. Until a better-developed body of data becomes available, we remain skeptical about that possibility.

Physiological Correlates.   Because of its rarity, little has been done experimentally with the OOBE phenomenon. Two subjects who have had OOBEs repeatedly have been studied in the laboratory. One of them had a number of OOBEs in the laboratory while showing the brain wave patterns characteristic of ordinary dreaming (Stage 1–REM sleep). A second subject, a young woman who frequently experienced floating near the ceiling for a few seconds and looking down at her body during sleep, had several OOBEs in the laboratory in conjunction with brain wave patterns in which slow alpha waves predominated. Thus her experiences occurred neither in a waking state nor in the ordinary dreaming state.

Inducing OOBEs.   Although most OOBEs occur either spontaneously or as a result of accidents or illness that bring a person close to death, some writers have described techniques for inducing

believe in survival after death; they know that it exists, for they have experienced being alive and functioning outside their physical bodies. The logic may be shaky, but the reaction is typical. A small minority of people having the experience find it terribly frightening, but most find it ecstatic.

them. These techniques usually involve long and difficult training procedures, however, so few people have attempted to verify their effectiveness.

Uses and Dangers.   Some individuals claim to be able to receive important teachings or find out important information through deliberately induced OOBEs, although none of the claims has been verified by laboratory testing. As with other psychic abilities, there are many people who will make fantastic claims in order to inflate their own egos but who are not prepared to *demonstrate* their claims in a scientifically valid fashion. OOBEs can be quite frightening, and the student should not try to induce one out of simple curiosity without considerable reading in this area. There is little useful scientific literature available, but some descriptions can be found in the mystical literature and occasional autobiographical accounts.

Hypnosis

Hypnosis has been one of the most widely investigated SoCs in our society. We can define hypnosis as an SoC characterized by a kind of mental quiet, a lack of the ongoing thought processes usually associated with ordinary consciousness, and hypersuggestibility. In hypnosis, a wide variety of specific phenomena and experiences can be brought about by suggesting them to the subject.

Hypnosis is usually induced while the subject is sitting or lying in a relaxed position. The hypnotist asks the subject to relax, to be calm and quiet, and not to worry about anything. It is usually suggested that the subject is getting drowsy or sleepy, but the subject implicitly knows that this is merely a way to let his mind drift and become completely relaxed. Suggestions that are responded to positively by most people are given early in the induction procedure, and the skillful hypnotist uses positive responses to these to build confidence on the subject's part that he can go into an even deeper hypnotic state. Various types of "gadgetry" are sometimes used to induce hypnosis, such as fancy machines or crystal balls. These have no real function other than increasing the credibility of the hypnotist. The hypnotist using a machine to hypnotize his subject appears to be very "scientific," and so the subject has that much more confidence in him.

The hypnotist's long repetition of suggestions of sleep and drowsiness may lead to a state generally termed *neutral hypnosis,* the hypnotic state without specific suggestions that anything *in particular* will

happen. Subjects describe this as a state of detachment and mental quiet. They feel totally relaxed. If asked what they are thinking about, they usually answer "nothing." They describe their minds as blank, although alert and attentive to the hypnotist. This state contrasts markedly with our normal SoC, in which, as we discussed in Chapter 5, we are always thinking about something.

There are immense individual differences in response to hypnosis. About 5 to 10 percent of people do not respond at all, while another 10 to 20 percent can achieve very deep hypnotic states and experience almost all hypnotic phenomena. Most people fall on a normal distribution of susceptibility between these two extremes. In spite of an immense amount of research on personality characteristics of responsive and unresponsive hypnotic subjects, no solid findings have come to light. We have little knowledge of why one person is readily susceptible to hypnotic suggestion and another is not. Similarly, there has been a great deal of research on possible physiological changes during hypnosis, but no distinct changes have been identified other than those that can be attributed to physical relaxation.

Psychological Effects
Perception.   Under hypnosis, many aspects of perception can be totally restructured from the subject's point of view. Perception in specific sensory modalities can be reduced to various degrees, a state called *hypoesthesia*. A subject may be told, for example, that he cannot see clearly, and he will report that his vision is blurred or dim. Hypoesthesia can be carried to the point of total blocking of a sensory modality. Subjects may be told that they cannot smell at all, after which some will be able to take a sniff out of a bottle of household ammonia, show practically no reaction it it, and report that they smelled nothing. Since the sensation of pain can be completely blocked by hypnotic suggestion, hypnosis has been used as an analgesic (pain killer) in medical and surgical treatment.

On the other hand, *hyperesthesias* may be created by telling subjects that one sense is exceptionally keen. Most subjects will report "feeling" an increase in sensitivity, although there is no evidence that actual sensitivity changes. Suggestion can be carried to the point of illusion, or even hallucination, in which case the subject will see things which do not really exist around him. A very responsive subject can be told, for example, to see a friendly polar bear walking around the room, and he will "see" it. Note that the careful hypnotist is sure to

Hypnosis Use Helps To Relieve Terminal Cancer Patients' Pain

By Connie Skipitares, Ridder News Service
Boulder Daily Camera—The use of hypnosis to relieve pain in cancer patients may have a success rate as high as 50 per cent, Stanford University hypnotherapist Dr. Ernest Hilgard says.

Hilgard said laboratory experiments in recent months have shown that as many as half of the terminal cancer patients hypnotized lost all pain sensation related to their illness and refrained from taking pain-killing drugs.

The hypnotherapist-psychologist has been advancing his theories on pain reduction through hypnosis for several years and believes the therapy is the one last way of making life tolerable for a suffering terminal cancer patient.

He cautions that the treatment in no way pretends to be a cure for cancer but strictly an alleviation of pain.

Hilgard, addressing a University of Santa Clara audience, warned against viewing hypnotism as a theatrical act "where the subject is a zombie puppetted by the hypnotist."

"Hypnotism," he says, "is something a teacher teaches you to do that you didn't know how to do before."

Many subjects, he contends, learn how to put themselves under.

"There's no great mystery in it," he said. "We've got to take the hocus pocus out of it."

Guiding the audience through brief exercises,

Hilgard explained hypnosis is achieved through a state of "believed-in imagination."

He described how he treated a woman suffering from extreme pain in her right arm after a mastectomy proved ineffectual in curbing spreading cancer in the woman.

He said first he worked with the sensations in her "normal" left arm and through hypnosis, transferred the painless feelings to her suffering right arm.

In producing the feeling of "believed-in imagination" in patients, Hilgard said, he is able to relieve pain in subjects by helping them fantasize about being some place else or doing something else, or, in other words, displacing their feelings.

For instance, he said, he learned that one patient liked to watch television as a form of escapism, so he played on that and had the woman watch TV as a means of alleviating her pain.

During the TV viewing, he said, the pain was gone.

Another patient had enjoyed the horse races. So, unable to leave his hospital bed, he imagined for long periods of time under hypnosis that he was at the race track and the pain went away.

Hilgard also said the patient's imagined feelings at the track conjured up visions of hot dogs and soda pop, making him hungry enough to eat the food necessary to his diet.

One major use of hypnosis is to control pain.

specify a *friendly* polar bear to avoid frightening the subject.

Self-awareness.   Awareness in hypnosis may readily be focused on various external or internal processes. For example, subjects may feel able to become hyperaware of their internal bodily processes. Even more interesting, many processes that are ordinarily in the subject's awareness may become disassociated. Thus a subject may be told that his arm will keep moving around in circles without his awareness, and it will do so. A subject may be told that he is going completely blind, but that when the hypnotist makes a certain gesture with his hands the blindness will cease. The subject will report being completely blind and act appropriately, yet when the hypnotist makes a certain gesture with his hands the "blindness" disappears. "Seeing" the gesture takes place outside of conscious awareness.

Emotion.   In neutral hypnosis there are generally no emotional feelings at all. Emotions can be totally structured by suggestion; any particular emotion

can be elicted at any intensity and in conjunction with any stimulus object. The stimuli can be entirely inappropriate. For example, the subject may be told, "You are about to hear an extremely funny joke"; the hypnotist then tells him, "Pine needles are green," and the subject laughs uproariously.

The hypnotic state may allow a psychotherapist access to processes that are normally unconscious. Thus, hypnosis is a frequent adjunct to psychotherapy. Often when a subject is told to have a dream while in hypnosis, he reports material similar to that experienced in his ordinary nocturnal dreams, and thus his subconscious processes can be detected.

Memory.   Memory function can be drastically altered in hypnosis. If told he cannot remember certain things, the responsive subject cannot consciously do so. He may be told that after awakening from the hypnotic state he will not be able to remember anything that went on. Or he may be told that he can remember certain parts of the hypnotic experience and not other parts. Alternatively, a subject may be told that his memory

German "Bridey Murphy" Tale Surfaces

Elkton, Va. (UPI)—Evoking memories of the "Bridey Murphy" furor two decades ago, a middle-aged woman has described [under] hypnosis her life as a young girl in 19th century Germany.

Delores Jay's mystic trip to Bismarck's Germany began in 1970. Her husband, the Rev. Carroll Jay, said he hypnotized her "for a backache or something. When I finished I asked her if it still hurt.

"She answered something that sounded like 'nein,' but I couldn't make anything of it," said the Methodist minister. After she gave another answer in what appeared to be German, he said he "got out my tape recorder and began to tape her."

A language teacher confirmed the language was German, which Mrs. Jay, 52, never learned. Dr. Ian Stevenson, a psychology professor at the University of Virginia, became interested in the case, as did other German-speaking professors.

In three years of interviews under hypnosis, Mrs. Jay described her life as Gretchen Gottlieb, daughter of a Catholic burgermeister in a tiny village named Ebeswald.

"Gretchen was about 16 years old and lived during the 1870s," Jay said. "She is illiterate and can't read or write."

In a terror-filled voice she described her family's suffering at the hands of Bismarck's followers during his conflicts with German Catholics. Her father was jailed. Gretchen herself was captured and killed by a group of men in a forest where she had hidden horses to help her uncle escape his enemies.

The tale resembles that of a young Colorado housewife who used the pseudonym Ruth Simmons. Under hypnosis she described her life as "Bridey Murphy" in 19th century Ireland.

In 1956 Morey Bernstein, a businessman and amateur hypnotist, wrote in "The Search for Bridey Murphy" that many things which "Bridey" told him in her Irish brogue were subsequently checked and verified, including obscure place names and obscure Gaelic words.

However, the Denver Post sent a reporter to Ireland to check details she related. Reporter Bill Barker discovered names of streets given by Bridey never existed, there was no record of people she named and her geography was wrong. The story of Bridey was dismissed.

Stevenson has studied reported cases of reincarnations for 20 years. He believes Mrs. Jay may actually have lived as Gretchen Gottlieb, citing her use of German.

"Language is a learned skill," he said. "Anyone who has ever tried to learn one knows that you must practice and practice."

In Bridey Murphy's case, skeptics suggested that she was reliving early childhood memories.

Both Mrs. Jay and her husband are skeptics. "I have always believed that you have only one chance in this life," Mrs. Jay said.

Gretchen Gottlieb's life was hardly notable, despite her murder. And there are several towns and villages named Ebeswald in Germany.

Jay believes that he and his wife have become involved in "a scientific venture which now has to be completed regardless of the consequences." But the couple stopped the hypnotic interviews almost a year ago and Jay said there are not plans to resume.

"I wish it had never happened," he said.

Hypnotic age regression is one of the most controversial phenomena in the study of hypnosis. Almost all the evidence is consistent with an explanation centering on the subjects' ability to behave "as if" they were younger in age. Regression to a "previous life" is the most unusual claim in this area. Although reports like the one above make fascinating newspaper reading, there is little reason to believe in reincarnation on the basis of such anecdotes.

is exceptionally good for some sorts of events, and he may sometimes exhibit better memory than usual.

Identity and regression. The subject's sense of identity can be radically altered in hypnosis. It may be suggested that he will act like a different person, and he will do so. Secondary personalities, completely different from the subject's ordinary personality, have been created experimentally in the laboratory. Such secondary personalities may or may not be aware of the activities of the primary personality. Little research has been done on the creation of secondary personalities, however, because of very real dangers to the normal personality.

One of the interesting phenomena of hypnosis is a talented subject's ability to *regress* to an earlier period in his life. If he is told that he is only 5 years old, he will feel and act, in many cases, as he recalls himself to have been when he was 5. All memories of events subsequent to that age will be temporarily unavailable to consciousness. Experts are still undecided whether a regressed subject can generally recall events of that time that are normally inaccessible to consciousness, but this seems to be possible at times. Experientially, the regressed subject *feels* as if he is 5.

Sometimes hypnotized subjects have been told to regress back to before they were conceived, to a past life or previous incarnation. A fair number of responsive hypnotic subjects will then claim to recall a past life and will tell the hypnotist all about it. This may often be a psychologically meaningful experience to the subject, but its *objective* truthfulness is not determined by how much the subject is impressed. In most cases of past life regression, the subject gives no *verifiable* details of the past life that he could not ordinarily have known. Because reincarnation is not a generally accepted belief in Western society, it is reasonable to treat such past life recall as an interesting fantasy. In a *very few* cases the subject has given evidential detail. Even in these cases, however, it is not always possible to rule out normal channels of information—for example, the subject may have read a book about some historical personality but be unable to consciously recall having read it. Thus there is currently no strong scientific proof for reincarnation, although the topic deserves further research.

Performance.   The popular notion that a hypnotized subject looks rather like a zombie is partially correct; many hypnotized subjects *do* act like zombies at first because they think that is how they are *supposed* to act. What the subject expects to happen is crucial in determing what does happen. A hypnotized subject can act perfectly normal when it is suggested he do so, and it is frequently impossible for even an experienced hypnotist to tell whether a subject is hypnotized or not under these conditions. Thus motor functioning can be perfectly normal under hypnosis. There is some evidence that a subject may be somewhat stronger or more skillful in the hypnotic state. We have already mentioned that various kinds of motor acts can be done without conscious awareness of them, a phenomenon called *automatism.* One example is *automatic writing.* The hypnotized subject is given a pencil and paper and told that the hand will begin to write messages of one sort or another, without his having any idea of what his hand is doing. A talented subject may converse with someone else during this procedure and be greatly surprised by what he reads later.

It should be noted, however, that laboratory studies of hypnosis, done chiefly by T. X. Barber, have shown that many phenomena, which when elicited under hypnosis appear to be quite astounding, can actually be elicited readily *without* inducing hypnosis. This evidence has led Barber and others to attribute all hypnotic phenomena to motivational and social-psychological variables and

to conclude that there is no unique state called hypnosis that is qualitatively different from wakefulness.

The typical experiment by Barber involves two basic groups of subjects. One group is administered a hypnotic induction treatment, and the second group is highly motivated by the experimenter's instructions but is not hypnotized, as defined operationally by the fact that the subjects are not read the hypnotic induction procedure. The basic finding is that many of the acts accomplished by the hypnosis group can also be accomplished by subjects in the motivated control group, such as lying stretched between two chairs, supported only by the head and ankles. Barber uses such experiments to argue that hypnosis is not a real phenomenon. Therefore, he always puts quotation marks around the word "hypnosis."

Critics have countered that Barber's results are *misleading,* particularly to those who have never worked with hypnosis and do not understand hypnotic behavior. They feel that defining hypnosis as reading a set of hypnotic instructions is misleading, because many subjects in the hypnosis group do not respond and thus cannot be fairly described as being hypnotized. In the control group, some highly suggestible subjects might actually become hypnotized by the instructions for performing—they are so highly motivated that self-hypnosis might be induced. Furthermore, control subjects are often led to believe that everyone can perform these feats, and they might feel so compelled to perform that they would fake some of their responses.

Barber has responded to his critics' arguments, and the debate continues. It does seem clear, however, that the human mind and body are capable of doing some very strange things, with and without hypnosis, and that explanations of hypnotic phenomena will not require the invocation of mystical or magical powers on the part of the hypnotist or the subject.

Posthypnotic Effects.   A particulary interesting aspect of hypnosis is what are called *posthypnotic effects.* During hypnosis the subject is told that such and such a hypnotic phenomenon will happen later, after he is back in normal waking consciousness. For example, the subject may be told that 15 minutes after awakening he will become extremely thirsty and need to get a glass of water. About 15 minutes later the subject does become thirsty, but he does not remember that his thirst is the result of posthypnotic suggestion. Subjects will often rationalize posthypnotic behavior even when it is very bizarre.

Uses and Dangers.   Hypnosis can serve many important functions if *properly* used. In addition to being an experimental tool in psychology, hypnosis has important medical and psychiatric uses. As we mentioned, hypnosis was widely used as an analgesic in surgery before chemical anesthetics were available, and it is still used frequently today when chemical anesthetics are inadvisable. Hypnotic suggestions can also relieve tensions and sometimes speed the healing processes of wounds. Many special uses of hypnosis have also been developed in psychotherapy. Indeed, practically every branch of medicine has found applications of hypnosis.

On the other hand, hypnosis can be dangerous if misused. The dangers stem from two main factors. First, many mentally ill people expect hypnotists to provide them with a magic cure, and, because of the power of hypnosis to restructure experience, they can accidentally be led into experiences that could make them worse. The second factor is that the techniques of how to hypnotize are too easy to learn. People who do not have training in psychology or medicine easily pick up the techniques and begin practicing hypnosis because of a desire to control others (sometimes rationalized as a desire to help others). A combination of these two factors can seriously upset some people. The student should avoid offering himself as a subject to improperly trained hypnotists.

Possession States

A *possession state* is one in which an individual feels that his own personality or soul is temporarily displaced by some nonphysical entity or spirit. Most of our information about such states comes from cross-cultural studies or from accounts of the mentally ill. The possessing "entity" may be considered either good or bad by the subject. It may be perceived as an animal spirit, an elemental nature force, the spirit of a deceased human being, or, in Western societies, as a fragment of one's own unconscious mind. A person may like or dislike possession, may try to stop it from occurring or make it occur more frequently. He may or may not attribute great spiritual value to possession. Some Christian sects, for example, deliberately attempt to induce possession by the Holy Ghost, whereas others attribute possession to the devil and have

rituals for exorcizing the devil's spirit. Most of you have probably seen the movie *The Exorcist* or read the book on which it was based. In either case, you witnessed a powerful portrayal of this most startling religious practice.

Since the idea of independently existing spirits is not generally accepted in our culture, we usually explain a possession state as a split-off fragment of a person's own mind, an aspect of his unconscious mind. *Multiple personality* is a term frequently used in such cases. Multiple personalities can be temporarily induced by hypnosis, but, as mentioned earlier, this can be a dangerous process. The secondary personality or possessing "entity" may do things that are embarrassing or unacceptable to the ordinary personality.

We know very little about the SoC in possession states. If we ask a person about his SoC after the possession is over, he may be completely *amnesic* and not remember anything about it, or he may report being in a kind of dreamlike or mystical state that seems to have no relationship whatsoever to the actions of the possessing "entity." Occasionally he may report being aware of the actions of the possessing "entity" but unable to control his body or otherwise interfere with it.

Spiritualist Mediums.   Some spiritualist mediums claim to develop SoCs in which a highly evolved spirit will temporarily possess them and function as a guide to their spiritual activity. Most of the scientific knowledge of possession states has come from studies of spiritualist mediums, although the emphasis in these studies was not on understanding the SoC but on investigating whether the possessing spirit did indeed possess some kind of independent reality. This was, and still is, a serious scientific question, because many spiritualist mediums occasionally produce information about other persons that they could not have obtained through normal sense channels. They attribute this information to the ability of the possessing spirit to travel about and use its own extrasensory abilities. In these cases, however, parapsychologists have proposed a counterhypothesis that the possessing spirit is only a fragment of the medium's own mind, and the special information comes from the medium's own ESP abilities.

Uses and Dangers.   Possession states often occur as part of the course of mental illness. They may also be induced deliberately, through various combinations of prayer, dancing, drugs, techniques

"I can give you Samuel F. B. Morse, Mr. Wells, or Mr. Fargo right away, but there's a half hour's delay in getting through to Alexander Graham Bell."

The New Yorker, January 24, 1970. Drawing by Alan Dunn; © 1970 The New Yorker Magazine, Inc.

Some spiritualist mediums claim to be able to induce states of possession by the spirit of any deceased person the "customer" specifies. Mediums are reluctant to submit themselves to scientific investigations, however. The great magician Houdini is said to never have failed to expose the tricks used by some mediums to achieve the illusion of possession and to obtain the supposedly secret information they sometimes have about the deceased.

for inducing trances, or simply sitting quietly and trying to be open to being possessed by whatever comes along (a "good" spirit, one hopes). In some societies, possession states are said to be very valuable. Often, people in these cultures who show neurotic or psychotic illnesses undergo some major crisis that results in the stabilization of their personality such that they are occasionally possessed by what they believe to be spirits. They can serve a useful social and religious function and are generally happy and well-adjusted to their particular society.

In our culture, being subject to possession states is generally looked upon as "pathological," a manifestation of mental illness. However, some

subcultures within our larger culture, such as the spiritualist religion and certain Christian sects, encourage possession and maintain a social role for it, so that people who exhibit possession states can continue to function as useful members of society. Lack of cultural support usually results in possession states leading to psychotic deterioration.

Drugs

Alcohol Intoxication

Alcohol, in the form of wine, beer, or distilled liquors, is probably the most widely known and used drug in the world. Records of its use go back to the dawn of civilization. Attitudes toward it in various cultures have ranged from acceptance and glorification to total rejection. Cultural attitudes can apparently also affect what we think of as the basic "physiological" effects of drinking alcohol. In some cultures, for example, hangovers are almost unknown in spite of heavy drinking. Given the extent of use, alcohol intoxication is rather underresearched. There is a large literature on the effects of alcohol, but much of it seems intended to prove that "demon rum" is the devil's tool or that "a few drinks never hurt anybody." Given the ambivalent attitude toward alcohol in our own culture, this is understandable.

Not all drinking, of course, leads to an altered SoC. Degree of intoxication and the effects on behavior and functioning correlate with the concentration of alcohol in the blood (see Table 8–2). With low levels of alcohol in the blood we can pretty much talk about effects on ordinary consciousness, but once the level rises to .01 percent or higher, we may begin to speak of drunkenness as a distinct SoC.

Psychological Effects
Perception and self-awareness. At low levels of intoxication, there actually may be a slight increase in auditory acuity. Pleasant feelings, such as warmth, may dominate perception of the body. At higher levels of intoxication, sensory impairment occurs, such that a drunk person may not be able to read or otherwise perform fine visual discriminations. At very high levels the intoxicated person begins to see double. Nausea and vomiting may occur at very high levels, with a hangover the following day.

The primary effect of alcohol on self-awareness is extremely unfortunate; it tends to produce feelings of increased competence and ability rather than a realistic perception of the impairments of mental

Table 8–2
Effects of alcohol intoxication

Alcohol concentration in blood	Experiential and behavioral effects	Amounts of common beverages*
.50%	Death likely.	
.30%	Stupor likely.	1 pint whiskey
.15%	Intoxication noticeable to observers: clumsiness, unsteadiness in walking. Reduction of anxiety, fears. Impairment of mental functioning. Feelings of personal power. State-dependent memory (see Chapter 4).	5 cocktails, 28 ounces wine, or 10 bottles beer
.12%	Impairment of fine coordination, some unsteadiness in walking or standing. Feelings of social and personal power.	4 cocktails, 22 ounces wine, or 8 bottles beer
.10%	Legally defined as impaired driving in California.	
.09%	Amplified emotions, lowering of inhibitions.	3 cocktails, 1 pint wine, or 6 bottles beer
.06%	Relaxation, warmth, feeling "high," some impairment of motor acts that require a high degree of skill.	2 cocktails, 11 ounces wine, or 4 bottles beer
.03%	No obvious behavioral effects.	1 cocktail, 5½ ounces wine, or 2 bottles beer

*The alcohol concentrations in the blood for the shown quantities of beverages are based on 150 pounds of body weight. Concentrations would be higher for the same amount of beverage consumed by a lighter person and vice versa. A cocktail is specified as containing 1½ ounces of distilled liquor (whiskey, etc.). Wine refers to ordinary table wine, not fortified (dessert) wine.

and motor functioning that occur. Such an effect is responsible for the difficulty one has in convincing a drunk that he is incapable of driving and for the death and destruction that the drunk driver produces.

Emotions. Alcohol intoxication has long been known for its effects on emotions. The relaxation and lowering of inhibitions that accompany drinking have often been cited as a plus for successful parties, allowing people to feel sociable and interact more freely. It has been found that reduction of existing anxiety does not occur until rather high levels of intoxication and that a major effect of alcohol is to induce fantasies of *power* in users. At lower levels of intoxication these tend to be feelings of "socialized power," that is, of being able to do things to save the world and the like, but at higher levels they become fantasies of purely personal power. Thus a good deal of the aggressiveness that can result from drunkenness is understandable.

Alcohol is also widely touted as reducing sexual inhibitions, but there is some question as to how much of this (as well as other behaviors characteristic of alcohol intoxication) is actually a *direct* effect or simply a *culturally mediated* effect. That is, looser standards of conduct are applied to people defined as "drunk," and they are allowed to do things that normally they would be censured for.

Dangers. The drunken person's feelings of confidence and ability along with his serious loss of competence make him particularly dangerous when driving. He feels he is a *better* driver than usual and so may drive faster and more recklessly than he ordinarily would. As with other SoCs, there are very wide individual differences. Highly overlearned motor actions are somewhat less vulnerable to the effects of alcohol than recently learned ones. Some people have learned to distrust feelings of increased competence and thus handle their alcohol more adequately, but most do not.

Despite its wide social use, it is clear that alcohol and the state produced by it can be very dangerous, even if we disregard the danger of the drinker becoming an alcoholic. The effects of alcohol in small quantities are not of great consequence. But when large quantities of alcohol are consumed and/or when alcoholism has developed, the effects constitute one of our greatest social problems (see Chapter 11 for a discussion of alcoholism).

Marijuana Intoxication

Marijuana is the name given to preparations of the flowering tops or leaves of the Indian hemp plant, *Cannabis sativa.* Slang terms for marijuana include pot, grass, shit, dope, maryjane, and hemp. Marijuana has been known as an intoxicant for thousands of years, but research into its effects has

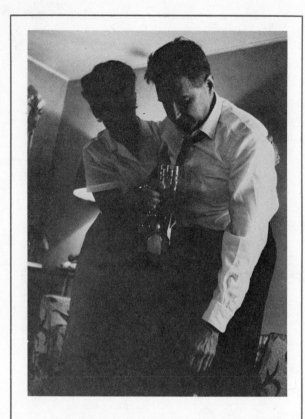

Among the victims of alcoholism we must include the alcoholic's family.

only recently begun. For example, the major active ingredient of marijuana, tetrahydrocannabinol (THC), was identified and subsequently synthesized only in the last decade. Despite the sometimes severe legal penalties for possession or sale of marijuana, a 1970 Gallup poll showed that about half of all college students have tried it and many use it fairly regularly.

In looking at marijuana intoxication as an SoC, we must remember that the particular effects achieved at any time are greatly determined by psychological factors in addition to the pharmacological effects of the drug itself. Indeed, aside from quality and quantity of the drug ingested, almost all other factors influencing the quality of the induced SoC—the "trip"—are psychological. These include the user's personality, expectations, mood, and desires (see Table 8-3). Other nondrug factors include the physical setting and the user's physical state. We can think of marijuana intoxication or psychedelic experiences as producing two kinds of effects. The first might be called a *pure drug effect*, almost inevitably resulting from the chemical action

of the drug on the human nervous system. The second is what we might call *potential effects*. The chemical action of the drug on the human nervous system creates the potential for certain kinds of experiences *if* various nondrug, psychological factors take on the appropriate values. The potential effects immensely outnumber the pure drug effects for marijuana. Taking these factors into account, we will describe the most common *experiential* characteristics of marijuana intoxication as it occurs in present-day college-educated users under ordinary social circumstances.

Psychological Effects

Perception.   Marijuana intoxication has a marked effect on perceptual processes such that the intoxicated person generally feels his perception is enhanced, that he is closer to the real, true qualities of perceptions he receives. The effects are usually very pleasing. The person may perceive new qualities in sound, taste, and touch; he may get more enjoyment from eating; understand the words of songs better; find his sense of touch becoming more sensual; find new and pleasurable qualities in sexual orgasm; and be able to see patterns in visual material that is ordinarily ambiguous. New internal bodily sensations are also frequently available, and generally the intoxicated user's awareness is captivated and pleased by these interesting and pleasurable sensory enhancements. There is no evidence to date indicating an actual lowering of the threshold for any sense receptors, so these effects may be primarily a matter of how incoming stimuli are processed. The marijuana user feels that there is *less* processing; he feels in touch with the raw sensory data rather than with an abstract representation of it.

Emotions.   Experienced users of marijuana almost invariably feel good when intoxicated, but they usually find both pleasant and unpleasant emotions considerably amplified. Naive users trying marijuana may find the experience stressful and have very unpleasant emotions. Although no exact figures can be obtained, given the illegality of marijuana, rough estimates indicate that somewhere between 5 and 10 percent of people trying it have an initial bad reaction and do not go on. Even experienced users occasionally have a bad emotional reaction, particularly if they are trying to escape from unpleasant emotions by using marijuana.

Cognitive processes.   Cognitive processes can change radically during intoxication. The user may

Table 8–3
Factors involved in maximizing the probability of a good or bad trip

	Variables	*Good trip likely*	*Bad trip likely*
Drug	Quality	Pure, known	Unknown drug or unknown degree of (harmful) adulterants
	Quantity	Known accurately, adjusted to individual's desire	Unknown, beyond individual's control
Long-term factors:	Culture	Acceptance, belief in benefits	Rejection, belief in detrimental effects
	Personality	Stable, open, secure	Unstable, rigid, neurotic or psychotic
	Physiology	Healthy	Specific adverse vulnerability to drug
	Learned drug skills	Wide experience gained under supportive conditions	Little or no experience, preparation; unpleasant past experience
Immediate user factors:	Mood	Happy, calm, relaxed, or euphoric	Depressed, overexcited, repressing significant emotions
	Expectations	Pleasure, insight, known factors and eventualities	Danger, harm, manipulation, unknown eventualities
	Desires	General pleasure, specific user-accepted goals	Aimlessness (repressed), desires to harm or degrade self for secondary gains
Experiment or situation:	Physical setting	Pleasant and esthetically interesting by user's standards	Cold, impersonal, "medical," "psychiatric," "hospital," "scientific"
	Social events	Friendly, nonmanipulative interactions overall	Depersonalization or manipulation of the user, hostility overall
	Formal instructions	Clear, understandable, creating trust and purpose	Ambiguous, deliberate lies, creation of mistrust
	Implicit demands	Congruent with explicit communications, supportive	Contradict explicit communications and/or reinforce other negative variables

feel that his thoughts are more intuitive, less bound by ordinary logic. Usually he feels in very good control of his thought processes, except at very high levels of intoxication. Characteristic experiences include the ability to turn off the effects of intoxication at will if necessary, feeling more childlike and open to experience, finding it difficult to read, having feelings of psychological insights about others and about oneself, giving little thought to the future and feeling more in the here-and-now, appreciating very subtle humor, and being more accepting of contradictions.

Memory. Marijuana intoxication produces both state-dependent memory and some overall loss of memory functioning. A characteristic effect is that the span of memory may be shortened, so the user forgets the start of a conversation, although he may feel able to compensate for this with special effort. Memories may come back as images in various sensory modalities rather than as abstract thought. At very high levels of intoxication, even the start of a sentence may be forgotten. This shortened memory span probably explains why performance on difficult tasks that require one to remember previous steps is impaired by marijuana intoxication. Experienced users are not particularly bothered by memory

deficits, however, because they do not usually use marijuana in situations in which they would be required to show extremely skilled memory performance.

Identity. One's sense of identity can change radically with marijuana. Being more childlike and open to experience has already been mentioned; this may be described as perceiving stimuli more as they are instead of as they are *valued* by the ordinary ego. Other characteristic effects are being more accepting of events, feeling less need to control them, finding it hard to play ordinary social games, and having spontaneous insights about oneself.

Time sense. Time usually seems to pass more slowly for the intoxicated, although occasionally the user feels that time passes more rapidly. A sense of being more in the present, more in the here-and-now, is also characteristic.

Performance. Marijuana intoxication makes experienced users feel relaxed and disinclined to move about. They also report being quieter than they are in their normal state or in a state of alcohol intoxication. If they do move about, though, they

"Hold it, mom, don't dig that up—those are my special Cannabis sativa plants!"

The technical name for marijuana is *Cannabis sativa* and the widespread use of the drug in this country by people of all ages, occupations, and social classes has created a real social problem due to the sometimes strict penalties involved. A national commission has advocated the abolition of penalties for private use of marijuana.

"I smoked pot, once. It made me want to rape and kill!"

Most people think that a drug, being a physical agent, has relatively invariant effects, but this is not at all true for drugs with profound effects on consciousness, like marijuana or LSD. The personality of the user and his expectations markedly alter how the physiological effects of the drug are going to be interpreted, and which kinds of effects are going to receive the additional energy of focused attention. Table 8–3 lists such nondrug variables systematically.

usually feel very coordinated and smooth. Laboratory studies have generally found that most motor tasks are not affected by marijuana intoxication in *experienced* users, although the probability of some impairment increases with the complexity of the skill required. Naive users sometimes experience great difficulty in performing simple tasks.

Uses and Dangers.   Proponents of marijuana use claim many benefits: relaxation, relief of tension, greatly enhanced sense of beauty, important psychological insights into oneself, and, sometimes, important spiritual or religious experiences. Some data collected suggest that marijuana may have value in the treatment of certain medical conditions such as high blood pressure and migraine

headaches. The primary proven dangers of marijuana intoxication are the adverse effects of being in jail.

The long-term effects of marijuana are still largely unknown. There is, however, no evidence that the psychological or physical effects of marijuana lead users to try more dangerous drugs, nor does any kind of addiction develop. Whether from ignorance or a desire to curb marijuana use, authorities in the past called marijuana "addicting" and today refer to it as producing "psychological dependence." Actually, the term *psychological dependence* refers to the fact that drug withdrawal produces psychological discomfort, mainly anxiety, as opposed to the real physical illness in physical addiction. However, many people believe that because a person repeats an experience he likes many times, he is psychologically addicted. Although any drug can be abused, the evidence

Pot Termed "Most Dangerous"

By Don Kirkman, Scripps-Howard Staff

Washington—A California research psychiatrist who once called marijuana harmless and urged its legalization has told Congress he now thinks it's "the most dangerous drug" sold illicitly in the United States.

He is Dr. David H. Powelson, former director of the Student Health Service Psychiatry Department at the University of California at Berkeley.

Dr. Powelson told the Senate Internal Security subcommittee Thursday he has found evidence that chronic marijuana use permanently impairs the user's ability to "think clearly."

He said he regrets his 1965 statement that marijuana should be sold openly and bases his new conviction on seven years of psychiatric research with Berkeley students and junior faculty members who were "injured" by prolonged use of the drug.

All of the injured were "potheads" who smoked marijuana or hashish, a stronger version of marijuana, for one to three years, he said.

He said the drug's effects on longtime smokers seem to follow a clearly damaging pattern in which the regular user first loses his ability to think sequentially, then part of his memory, and finally his ability to reason clearly. As the last stage, he sinks into a paranoid mental state during which he thinks everyone is picking on him, Dr. Powelson said.

Typical of what Dr. Powelson said he encountered during his research was a junior faculty member who smoked hashish daily for 18 months in the late 1960s. After suffering the full gamut of symptoms, the young man realized the drug was injuring his mental and physical health and stopped using it.

Two years later he tried to continue his education by working for an advanced degree in mathematics. However, he found he no longer was able to solve advanced problems, including some he had been able to solve before he began smoking hashish, Dr. Powelson said.

The damage has persisted for about three-and-one-half years, Dr. Powelson said, and the man fears he will be able neither to complete his education nor reach his former level of competence.

Dr. Powelson said he has seen a number of other students who tried to give up marijuana or hashish smoking and resume their academic careers. In each case the students found they no longer had the ability to think as clearly as they once did, he said. The students found the drug seems to cause a "loss of desire" to achieve, he said.

"All of these students simply found they couldn't use their minds in the way they did before," Dr. Powelson said.

The debate on the dangers of marijuana continues.

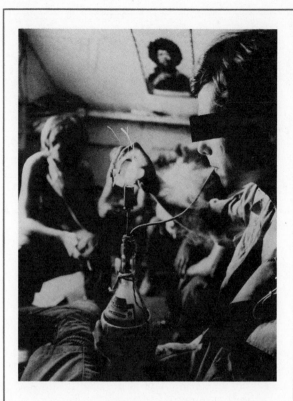

Getting high on chianti? A GI in Vietnam improvises a hookah from a wine bottle and a .45 caliber shell.

of misinformation about the alleged dangers of marijuana and has recommended that private use of the drug should not be considered a crime. Certainly marijuana is no *more* dangerous than alcohol. The fact that alcohol is legally available in most places, while there are often severe penalities for marijuana use and sale, makes it appear as if we have drastically overestimated the potential dangers of pot.

The Psychedelic Experience

The word *psychedelic* means "mind manifesting." It came into general use as a result of a contest between the Canadian psychiatrist and investigator of psychedelics Humphrey Osmond and the famous writer Aldous Huxley. Both men had had experience with such drugs and decided to see who could invent the best name. Huxley submitted the following verse:

To make this mundane world sublime,
Take a half a gram of phanerothyme . . .

Osmond replied with:

does not suggest that marijuana is particularly dangerous in this respect.

The most recent national commission on marijuana use has realized that there is a great deal

To sink in Hell or soar angelic,
You'll need a pinch of psychedelic.

The term *psychedelic* is now generally applied to any drug whose primary effect is to induce an altered SoC, including LSD (lysergic acid diethylamide), mescaline (the active ingredient of peyote cactus), psilocybin, and a large number of other drugs occurring naturally in plants. Knowledge of the effects of LSD and similar psychedelics comes from several sources: the personal experiences of at least a million Americans, a large number of artistic creations (popularly known as psychedelic art) that attempt to express aspects of the experience in a nonverbal way, and finally the more than one thousand laboratory studies of this class of drugs.

Psychological factors are even more significant in the experience of psychedelics such as LSD than in marijuana intoxication. Indeed, such an immense range of variability is seen in psychedelic states that we may be dealing with many transient SoCs triggered by the drug rather than with any single uniform state. Unfortunately, many laboratory studies have been conducted under the set of psychological conditions indicated in Table 8–3 that tend to maximize the probability of a "bad trip." Thus LSD was considered a *psychotomimetic* (mimicking a psychosis) drug when it was first studied. It is now clear, however, that an exceptionally wide range of experiences can be produced depending on the personality factors and the setting. Just about every effect reported for other states of consciousness has been reported at one time or another for LSD experiences.

Profundity of Experience. Certain regularities in what we might consider the profundity of the psychedelic experience have been noted by two of the leading investigators in this area, R. E. L.

Masters and Jean Houston. They distinguish four levels of psychedelic experience. The first they call the *Sensory* level, in which the subject's primary experience is that of marvelous and beautiful sensory changes. Colors take on vibrant new values, rainbows may form in the air, commonplace objects become magnificent works of art, and so forth. The second and more profound level is called the *Recollective-Analytic*. Here the subject experiences very strong emotions related to his own personal history and, with proper guidance, may have very important therapeutic experiences, resolving personal conflicts. Without competent guidance, most subjects' experiences stay at the Sensory or Recollective-Analytic levels.

The third level of profundity is called the *Symbolic,* and here the images and hallucinations the subject experiences deal with the general history of man, animal evolution, rituals of passage, and so forth. If dealt with successfully, usually after successful resolution of problems at the Recollective-Analytic level, the person working at the Symbolic level can have important insights and experiences dealing with the nature of being human.

The most profound level, seldom reached, is called the *Integral* level. Experiences at this level are religious and mystical, often dealing with a confrontation with God. The individual may experience the death of his own ego, a union with God, and being reborn. The feeling is profoundly religious and cannot be adequately dealt with in verbal terms. Because of the experiences at the Integral level, some people have proposed that LSD be made legal for supervised religious use.

Uses and Dangers. A number of research studies have shown that LSD and other psychedelics can be used profitably in psychotherapy, and two major psychotherapeutic applications have been

Psychedelic Drugs and Creativity

Many users of marijuana or the more powerful psychedelic drugs, such as LSD, feel that their thoughts are more original and creative when they are high. Often, though not always, this turns out to be an illusion; the "insight" is judged wrong or senseless on later evaluation in the normal state. One study investigated whether a preparation containing mescaline could, *under well-guided and otherwise optimal conditions*, enhance creativity in people who needed creative solutions to their real-life professional problems. Twenty-seven professionals (designers, architects, physicists, and so on), after adequate preparation, had a "psychedelic session" in pleasant surroundings. During part of this session they took some psychological tests measuring creativity and also worked on a professional problem of their own that they had brought to the session.

In addition to the psychological tests showing increased creativity, most of the participants reported solutions to their practical problems that were judged, in retrospect, to be professionally useful. Thus there are possibilities of using psychedelics for creative problem solving. Note, however, that the conditions of this study included subjects with creative abilities to begin with, a real-life need for creative solutions, an optimal setting, and experienced guidance—the conditions under which the drug was taken were carefully controlled.

developed. The first, called *psycholytic therapy,* uses small doses of LSD in the course of regular psychotherapeutic work. The drug loosens associations, bypasses some defenses, and purportedly enables the analysis to proceed much faster. With prolonged therapy, occasional clients begin to deal with material on the Symbolic or Integral level.

The second major therapeutic use of LSD is called *psychedelic therapy,* in which very large doses and single guided sessions are used to give the patient an overwhelming experience at the Symbolic or Integral level. The theory is that by contacting these extremely deep sources within oneself, a new sense of strength can develop and many ordinary neurotic problems can be successfully transcended or overcome. Psychedelic therapy has also been successfully used with people suffering "existential neurosis" (that is, suffering from a sense of loss of meaning of life) even though they are otherwise successful members of society.

Considering the immense psychological power of

psychedelic drugs, there are real dangers in the SoC produced. Subjects with neurotic or psychotic personality structures, or ordinary subjects who are not prepared for the drug experience, may have extremely bad reactions—sometimes, although rarely, leading to a psychosis. People who buy LSD through black market sources today also risk being poisoned by the many impurities that analyses have shown to be in black market drugs. For example, a wide variety of street drugs sold as mescaline, psilocybin, or THC (the active ingredient in marijuana) actually contain none of these substances. Often they consist either of inert ingredients or LSD, with various degrees of adulteration by highly dangerous substances like strychnine or amphetamines.

Another danger is the amateur therapist, a person who has only a little psychological knowledge and wants to cure people's hangups by giving them LSD. It is quite possible to get people into experiences that they are unprepared for and that contribute to further psychopathology instead of curing. The situation in which psychedelic drugs are taken is important too; unexpected interruptions, ugly surroundings, or being arrested can lead the user into extremely unpleasant, sometimes hellish experiences.

Although controlled studies of therapy have shown that the *proper* use of LSD (at *infrequent* intervals, under *trained* guidance, with lots of time devoted to *assimilating* the insights) can be valuable for personal and therapeutic growth, the *frequent* use of LSD generally seems to nullify any actual growth benefits and, instead, is likely to produce someone who *talks about* his great experiences but is otherwise a poorly adjusted, ineffective individual.

A good deal of propaganda about the dangers of LSD is false. First, LSD does not automatically make people go crazy. Indeed, experts have been surprised at the infrequency of psychotic breaks, given the impurities of the drugs generally used by individuals on their own. Second, experience with a psychedelic drug does not automatically lead to people "dropping out." In spite of their illegality, psychedelic drugs are used (not openly, of course) by many professional people occupying high status positions in society. Third, there is no solid evidence that LSD causes chromosomal damage. It should be noted, however, that this statement applies to the use of pure LSD; it is not known what effects the impurities in "street" drugs might have. Finally, although the belief that using LSD during pregnancy causes birth defects has not been clearly substantiated, most physicians suggest that it is

No One Told Them

Time—If there is a family in the U.S. with a just grievance against the CIA, it is the Olsons of Frederick, Md. The widowed mother, her married daughter and two grown sons felt compelled last week to call a press conference in the backyard of the mother's rural home to talk about what they had endured. They wanted everyone to know how an agency of their Government had driven Frank R. Olson—the man they knew as husband and father—to commit suicide, and then left them for 22 years to wonder why.

In 1953 Olson was a civilian biochemist employed by the Army at Fort Detrick, Md., the Army's supremely secret biological-warfare center, which was closed in 1971. Olson was working on a highly classified project for the CIA, which was interested in learning about the effects of new and powerful drugs that its agents conceivably could use—or have used on them. After spending a five-day period away from home engaged in the research, Olson returned in a state of unusual agitation. His wife was baffled and then alarmed by his moods of self-doubt and self-recrimination. He said nothing about what was bothering him, a fact that his wife attributed to the secrecy of his work. By Sunday he said that he had decided to quit his job.

The next day Olson seemed to get better, but on Tuesday morning he returned from work at 10 o'clock to tell his stunned wife that he had been advised to see a New York City psychiatrist—his colleagues feared he might have become a menace to her. Mrs. Olson accompanied her husband to the airport. She never saw him again.

Psychosis Delusions. Olson was taken to New York by two men, Army Colonel Vincent Ruwet, a colleague at Fort Detrick, and a man named Robert Lashbrook, who the Olson family later said they believed was a CIA agent. A psychiatric examination of Olson was conducted by Dr. Harold Abramson, now 75, who had done pioneering work on LSD. Abramson found that Olson was suffering from "severe psychosis and delusions," and recommended that he enter a sanitarium.

Olson returned to Washington with the intention of spending Thanksgiving with his family, but was so upset that he went back to New York without ever seeing them. This time, according to a New York City police report, he registered at the Statler Hotel along with Robert Lashbrook and went to Room 1018A. At 3:20 a.m., the police said, Lashbrook was awakened by the crash of shattering glass. The window on the Seventh Avenue side was broken, and Olson's body was ten stories below . . . .

The Olson family remained baffled and burdened by the death until last month, when the Rockefeller commission issued its report on the CIA. In Chapter 16 it revealed that the CIA in the late 1940s began studying drugs that change behavior, and tests were made on unsuspecting subjects; the practice was not stopped until 1963. The report referred to an incident in 1953: "LSD was administered to an employee of the Department of the Army without his knowledge while he was attending a meeting with CIA personnel working on the drug project." CIA agents had slipped the LSD into an after-dinner drink; 20 minutes later the subject was informed he had been drugged. LSD influences different people in varying ways. In this case, the man developed serious side effects. The Rockefeller report went on to tell how he had been taken to New York City for psychiatric treatment and had jumped from a tenth-floor window. The CIA had simply reprimanded the two men who were responsible for administering the LSD. . . .

probably not a good idea for a pregnant woman to take the drug because of its exceptionally powerful psychological effects.

Drug Use and Drug Abuse

The use of some drugs is automatically assumed to be deterimental to the user or society, while the use of others is casually tolerated. Indeed the topic of drug use is surrounded by much emotion and prejudice. From a "neutral" point of view, we might define acceptable drug *use* as a level of use that does not significantly impair the user's functioning or cause his actions to be harmful to others. Drug *abuse*, on the other hand, occurs when the user's functioning or health is significantly impaired or his actions harm others. Occasional social drinking, in small quantities, might then be considered drug use, while alcoholism or drunken driving would be abuse.

Some individuals can abuse any drug (or anything else, for that matter). Nevertheless, there exist important differences between various drugs in their *potential* for abuse. Almost no one, for example, can experiment with injections of amphetamines ("speed") without significant damage to his health and drastic impairment of functioning. Many people, on the other hand, can safely use alcohol or marijuana because the abuse potential of these two drugs is less than that of injected amphetamines.

Although too much emotional bias exists to allow an "objective" ranking of the danger of various drugs, experts would probably agree that the following drugs have a dangerous potential for abuse (because of immediate impairment of body functioning or neural damage, or the possibility of

Medics: LSD Evils Overstated

The Denver Post—The case against the hallucinogenic drug LSD may have been overstated, according to evidence accumulated by four California medical researchers.

While others have suggested that LSD causes chromosome damage, malformed offspring or cancer, the four Californians said the supporting evidence was insubstantial.

Their study was limited to genetic damage and cancer and didn't include the possibilities of brain damage or behavioral disturbances.

A report on the study is the lead article in a recent issue of Science, the journal of the American Association for the Advancement of Science.

Medical Men

The authors are Dr. Wendell R. Lipscomb, chief of research at Mendocino State Hospital, Talmage; Dr. Norman I. Dishotsky, a member of his staff; W. D. Loughman of the University of California at Berkeley, and Dr. Robert E. Mogar, psychology professor at San Francisco State College.

Other than during pregnancy, they suggest, there's no reason to abandon "the continued controlled experimental use of pure LSD."

The authors emphasize "pure" throughout their article. In previous studies, where evidence of chromosome breakage was found, nearly all the subjects used or abused drugs other than LSD, the researchers said.

The four conclude such results "are related to the more general effects of drug abuse and not, as initially reported, to LSD use."

Massive quantities of the drug—full name, lysergic acid diethylamide—can cause genetic defects in laboratory animals, but so can many other substances, the authors note.

Claims Unfounded

Moderate doses of pure LSD won't break human chromosomes, they conclude, and "there appears to be no definite evidence" that the drug causes cancer.

LSD may cause genetic mutations, they said, but it's a weak mutagen effective only in massive doses and "unlikely to be mutagenic in any concentration used by human subjects."

Research suggests LSD may cause birth defects in laboratory animals, but not conclusively.

"Case reports of malformed children born to users of illicit LSD are rare," the authors continue, "although there is some indication of an increased risk of spontaneous abortion.

"There is no evidence that pure LSD causes birth defects or fetal wastage in man," they said.

Here is some evidence refuting the commonly held notion that LSD causes damage to chromosomes. There is no doubt that all the facts about any of the drugs are not available and that a truly informed opinion will not be possible until much more research is done. An enlightened society should support such research efforts, but often the only result is conflicting evidence, which leaves the general public in a state of confusion. Just about every day, you can find more evidence reported in the press to add to your confusion; there are certainly opinions that drastically differ from those presented in this clipping. One thing that does seem clear is that street drugs are often diluted with dangerous other drugs that the unsuspecting buyer had not bargained for.

---

addiction): alcohol, amphetamines, barbiturates, cocaine, and "hard" narcotics like morphine, opium, and heroin (see Table 8-4). Major psychedelics, such as LSD or mescaline, might or might not be added to the list by various experts, but all would agree that the impurities frequently found in black market psychedelics are dangerous.

Techniques of Mind Control

Meditation

Meditation is a group of mental and physical exercises designed to produce relaxation, tranquility of thought and body, and profound insight into oneself and the meaning of worldly things. Little scientific research has been done on the wide variety of known meditative techniques and their associated SoCs. Most of our knowledge comes from religious sources, particularly Oriental. The best Western psychological approach to these techniques has been made by Ornstein and Naranjo (1971), and much of this section is drawn from their excellent analysis. We shall consider some general principles concerning meditation but will not be able to treat it in any detail.

Why do people practice meditation? A common theory underlying almost all schools of meditation is that people, because of the highly selective perception induced in the course of seeking pleasure and avoiding pain, have come to live in a world of illusion. A person cannot attain truth or permanent happiness because the illusions built up in the course of his lifetime cut him off from the outside world and himself. He may have a fair amount of success and happiness in terms of the culture he lives in, but he is inevitably subject to suffering and death. Meditation techniques are designed to eliminate the illusions constantly being

Addicted.

and/or (2) facilitate the eventual production of SoCs in which truth is more directly perceived.

Techniques of Meditation. The variety of techniques that can be used for meditation is enormous. One may, for example, sit up straight in one of the classical meditation postures and simply concentrate on being aware of the movements of the belly in breathing. Or, as in Yoga, the meditator may focus his attention on complex, artificial breathing exercises *(pranayama). Mantras* are sound patterns that one may meditate on; some of these are considered to have special qualities in terms of their effect on the mind, and others are regarded primarily as convenient focal points. The sound pattern may be audibly uttered, or it may be imagined in one's own mind. The ancient Indian mantra "Om mani padme hum" is well known. *Yantras* are visual patterns to meditate on. They may be as simple as a burning candle or a religious object, or as complex as diagrams symbolizing the nature of the cosmos, called *mandalas.*

Two major classes of meditation can be distinguished. One might be called *concentrative* or *restrictive meditation,* the other *opening-up* or *widening meditation.*

produced by the human mind and, by a nonintellectual process, allow the person to *directly* perceive truth.

We might define meditation, then, as *a special action and/or deployment of attention designed to (1) purify the ordinary SoC by removing illusion*

Concentrative meditation. The essence of concentrative meditation is "one-pointedness" of the mind, restricting attention to one designated object for long periods. In simple Zen meditation, for example, the meditator focuses on the movement of

Table 8-4
Some results of drug abuse (X = dangers or symptoms of abuse; O = symptoms of withdrawal)

| | Symptoms of abuse and withdrawal | | | | | | | Some dangers of abuse | | | | |
Drug	Drowsiness	Belligerence	Anxiety	Euphoria	Depression	Hallucinations	Distortion of space or time	Physical dependence	Psychological dependence	Tolerance	Psychosis	Death from overdose
Morphine	X		XO	X	O	X		X	X	X		X
Heroin	X		XO	X	O			X	X	X		X
Codeine	X		XO	X	O			X	X	X		X
Methadone	X		XO	X	O			X	X	X		X
Cocaine			X	X		X			X			X
Marijuana	X		X	X	X	X	X		X			
Amphetamines			X	X		X			X	X	X	X
Methamphetamine			X	X		X			X	X	X	X
Barbiturates	X	X	O	X	X	O		X	X	X		X
Lysergic acid diethylamide (LSD)			X	X	X	X	X		X	X	X	
STP			X	X	X	X	X		X			
Peyote			X			X			X	X		
Psilocybin			X	X	X	X	X		X	X		
Dimethyltryptamine (DMT)			X	X	X	X	X		X	X		

his belly in breathing. Whenever his attention wanders away from the sensation of breathing, he is to gently bring it back. He is not to *force* his attention back or strain to keep it there, because forcing actually shifts attention to distractions.

Concentrative meditation is extraordinarily difficult. The meditator often finds that he has become lost in flights of fancy or "important" thoughts for long periods of time and has forgotten all about meditating. Some people achieve great success with concentrative meditation in weeks or months; others spend years before they become very good at it.

What does concentrative meditation lead to? Successful practitioners insist that only part of the experience can be expressed in words, but it seems to lead to an SoC that can be characterized by words like *emptiness, clearness,* or *voidness.* All sensory input, all perception of the world, eventually ceases temporarily. Similarly, there is no internal mental activity (fantasizing, thinking, and so on) to replace it. Yet awareness remains—pure awareness, without any particular content. This state may or may not lead to other states in which the meditator feels that he has a direct perception of truth.

The aftereffect of reaching a state of voidness through concentrative meditation is a feeling of greatly freshened and enhanced perception of oneself and the world, a feeling that one is perceiving things directly rather than through all the selective filters affecting normal perception. Desire for objects or personal attachments is temporarily transcended following successful concentrative meditation. This transcendence and its effect on perception has been described by a Zen master, Suzuki Roshi, in the following words: "The perfect man employs his mind as a mirror, it grasps nothing, it refuses nothing, it receives but does not keep." One is supposed to perceive with absolute clarity, in much the same way a mirror reflects everything perfectly, without distortion. Some studies of the brain waves of meditating Zen monks may be interpreted as supporting this. The monks did not show the adaptation to repeated stimuli that is considered normal, and so they may have been responding to the actual stimulus *every time* instead of "classifying" it automatically as unimportant and no longer perceiving it fully.

Opening-up meditation.   The second major style of meditation, opening-up meditation, consists basically of paying *full* attention to everything that happens to one *continuously.* Usually this is found to be rather exhausting at first, and so is only done

"Larry, in case we don't find enlightenment, do you think we can still get back your Pontiac dealership?"

for periods of a few minutes to a half hour. No daydreaming or drifting off into comfortable thoughts is permitted. The meditator must pay complete attention to everything that happens to him and to his own reactions. Opening-up meditation supposedly results in greatly clarified perception of the world and oneself immediately, rather than as an aftereffect, as in concentrative meditation.

Self-remembering.   A process similar to opening-up meditation has been described by other writers as *self-remembering.* The rationale for self-remembering is the belief that the ordinary person is so identified with events that happen to him, including his own feelings, that he is a slave to them. He exists in a kind of "waking sleep," in which events mechanically catch him up and sweep him away. His own needs and desires have so distorted his perceptions, even of himself, that he lives in a kind of waking dream. The only freedom he has is an ability to direct a small portion of his attention. If this small amount of attention is directed toward *being aware of being aware*, it is believed that he can enter an SoC in which he is *not identified* with the events that happen to him, and thus he can eventually develop genuine freedom.

The technique for dissociating oneself from events requires the person to split his attention. While part of it is observing ordinary events and thoughts, another part is aware of being aware of these

Meditation in Action

Meditation tends to be thought of as a solitary escapist action, something done for a limited period in a quiet corner. Many meditative disciplines, however, stress the importance of making meditation a constant part of all life activity.

Aikido (pronounced ī kēy dō) is, on the surface, a Japanese self-defense art. Underlying all the physical techniques, however, is a comprehensive meditative practice that stresses sensing and control of spiritual energy (*ki*), harmony (*ai*) with the universe, and centering consciousness in the abdomen, the *hara*. The basic Aikido practice is thus meditative; the body is conceived of as a feedback mechanism, such that when one is properly centered and controlling spiritual energy, physical self-defense techniques are carried out with exceptional skill and power.

The founder of Aikido, Professor Morihei Uyeshiba, demonstrated the ability to resist attack by controlling spiritual energy. The fact that three young men were unable to move him, a man of 60 years, in spite of having strength and leverage advantages (see Figure 8–4) is considered due to his ability to direct ki rather than his physical strength. Indeed, after several seconds, in the film from which this drawing was made, Uyeshiba threw the young men to the mat.

Figure 8–4
Meditation and self-defense

The control of spiritual energy through meditative practice enables the late Professor Morihei Uyeshiba to resist the efforts of three young men to topple him.

---

events. It is as if one divided oneself into an actor and an observer. The observer is not the same thing we ordinarily think of as *conscience*, which is simply another aspect of oneself that has been mechanically programmed to approve of certain acts and disapprove of others. The observer has no characteristics other than the ability to observe. It does not approve or condemn, initiate or stop, action.

The practice of self-remembering is long and arduous, and few people succeed in it. If successful, the practice is supposed to lead to such total awareness of what is actually happening in the here-and-now that a person ultimately develops the genuine ability to overcome the deterministic nature of his behavior based on his upbringing and cultural biases. He develops the freedom to choose how he will react.

Physiological Correlates.   The few physiological studies that have been done on meditation suggest that there may be important brain wave and other physiological changes in experienced practitioners. Studies of Zen monks, practitioners of Yoga in India, and American practitioners of Transcendental

Meditation have all found increased amounts of alpha brain waves, occasional slowing of alpha waves, and occasional appearance of theta waves (4 to 7 cycles per second) in some practitioners. There are also reports of lowered metabolism and heart rate.

Uses and Dangers.   In addition to the use of meditation in seeking higher SoCs and a clearer perception of truth within various philosophical and religious contexts, there is some evidence that meditation may be therapeutic or an aid to development in ordinary people. Many people practice simplified forms of meditation and report that it calms them after a long day at work and generally keeps tension from building up. Meditation as a device for easing tension may assume increased importance as the steadily accelerating pace of our urban society imposes increasing pressures on each person. A number of meditative techniques have been incorporated as adjuncts to psychotherapy by various investigators.

There is some danger in meditative technique. For mentally ill or poorly balanced people, various forms of meditation may put them in contact with

Mind Control Seen As Big Future Force

By Andy Rogers, Denver Post staff writer
Mind control, like electricity and gravity, is one of those things we've discovered and put to use, but don't know what it is.

That was the view of mind control given by Glen Robinson, regional director of Silva Mind Control International, Inc., who was in Denver with Dr. Milan Ryzl, a leading expert and researcher on the subject.

Ryzl, a native of Czechoslovakia, where he began research into mind control, said he is "dealing with forces not known so far," but which he predicts will bring great changes.

"Replace Telephones"
"Practical applications (of mind control) may change all aspects of life. In the future, telepathy may replace telephones," he said. Or persons might be taught to see through opaque objects just as xrays do, "without instruments, just with the power of the mind.

"Don't ask me what the nature of this thing is," Dr. Ryzl commented. "Nobody knows."

Dr. Ryzl, who began his research into mind control or parapsychology 20 years ago, was in Denver to address an advanced group of Silva Members. Dr. Ryzl is director of parapsychological research for the Silva organization.

Robinson said mind control as taught by the Silva group is a scientific method of learning to utilize the latent abilities of the mind. When the mind, especially the subconscious mind, is func-

tioning properly, a person's health, happiness and everyday life are improved.

Parapsychology, Robinson continued, attempts to train persons to have greater control over more areas of their mind. "Just as you learn to ride a bicycle, you can learn to train the mind," Robinson explained.

"Scientists are beginning to realize the function of the mind in the health of the body," he said. People are sometimes "taught to be sick," he added, and some doctors estimate that 80 to 90 per cent of the illnesses they treat are psychosomatic.

Persons who experience stress in certain areas, for instance stress associated with job difficulties, often attribute the problem to the outside, physical atmosphere. However, Robinson said, the real problem may lie inside the individual and result from lack of understanding of other people or a breakdown in communications with others.

Help "Misapplications"
Such "misapplications of the mind" can be helped through mind control, he added.

Dr. Ryzl, who left his country for political reasons six years ago, said he has found Americans "fearful of hypnosis" and said they view it as mystical and mysterious.

In Czechoslovakia, the people have adopted hypnosis as a method of self-training and realize it is a specific state of mind "just as normal as sleep or being awake.

"Hypnosis, when used by an expert," he emphasized, "can be very helpful. But it doesn't belong on the stage" where its suspected dangers are often overinflated for theatrical purposes, he explained.

unacceptable parts of their mind and thus precipitate emotional crises or, in some cases, a psychotic break. Also, some techniques of meditation are extremely strenuous and may cause adverse reactions in people who are otherwise in good mental and physical health. Those who use the strenuous techniques usually point out that they are quite dangerous. They are designed for people who desire higher SoCs so much that they are willing to take severe mental and physical risks.

Biofeedback-Induced States

There have been reports of specially trained people, such as yogis, who have shown large degrees of control over their "involuntary" bodily functions. For example, there is a yogic practice of sitting in water and voluntarily drawing water up into the lower intestine to cleanse it. Another example is the Indian yogi who, in a laboratory at the Menninger Foundation, voluntarily threw his heart into *fibrillation* for 17 seconds; that is, he made it beat about 300 beats per minute for that time. At this rate the heart will not pump any blood, and so his pulse

disappeared. Reports of such unusual actions have been largely ignored in Western scientific literature but are now being looked at more intensely because of the rapidly developing field of biofeedback research.

As we saw in Chapter 2, biofeedback research centers on the finding that if instruments are used to inform a person of exactly what some part of his body (normally inaccessible to consciousness) is doing, he may find various ways of affecting it. If the electrical activity of a single muscle fiber is electronically amplified and displayed to subjects—for example, in the form of a sound whose pitch varies with the intensity of the muscle activity—many subjects can learn to totally relax that single muscle fiber or make it even more activated. Similarly, if a sound or light is used to indicate when the alpha rhythm of the brain is present, many subjects can learn to increase or decrease the amount of alpha rhythm in their brain wave pattern. The essence of biofeedback techniques is that they make available to consciousness information that ordinarily is not present; and, having the

G. DOLE

"You'd better start meditating on how to come up with this month's rent."

"Would you mind turning down your damn alpha waves a little? I'm trying to read!"

information, people can try various strategies to see what affects the involuntary process.

There are two major links of research with biofeedback to SoC. The first link is that when subjects learn an *extreme* degree of control over some things, such as producing profound muscle relaxation throughout their bodies or being able to produce very high levels of alpha waves, they report strong alterations in their states of mind, over and above that necessary for control *per se*, which suggests they may be in an altered SoC. Thus biofeedback techniques may be useful for some people in *inducing* altered SoCs, although much work remains to be done before we can adequately describe what sorts of SoCs can be induced.

The second link to altered SoCs comes from the studies of physiological changes during traditional meditation practices, such as increases in the amount of alpha rhythm and some slowing of its frequency. It would be naive to assume that the SoC Zen monks get into is *simply* a matter of increased amount and slowed frequency of the alpha rhythm. Still, if these physiological changes are *one* of the components of the state Zen monks get into, perhaps *that* component could be taught by biofeedback techniques, and thus be learned much more rapidly and efficiently than it is ordinarily learned in Zen meditation. Conceivably, biofeedback techniques can serve as technological aids to developing certain SoCs.

Note that the biofeedback area is quite new, and possibilities should not be confused with definite findings. Already much irresponsible reporting has appeared in the press, suggesting, for example, that

if you can learn to turn on your alpha rhythm continuously, you will reach a marvelous SoC or enlightenment. It is true that *some* individuals find the high alpha state very pleasant, but we are still a long way from electronic Zen.

States of Consciousness and You

A recent Gallup poll showed that some 50 percent of college students had tried marijuana, many had used more powerful psychedelic drugs, and many are practicing various kinds of meditation. Thus the topic of SoCs is not only of intellectual interest but also of great personal interest to many students. The question of "Should I try to alter my SoC by such-and-such a method?" is a real one for many students, and it must be answered by the individual himself. But the decision should be made in the light of available knowledge, which, at best, is very slim. We will briefly discuss some of the known advantages of experiencing altered SoCs and some of the disadvantages.

The advantages claimed for such SoCs as meditative states and drug-induced states are of two kinds, namely, *psychological* pleasure and insights and *spiritual* insights. For example, the experienced marijuana user not only reports greatly enhanced pleasure in all that he does but also commonly feels that he has obtained important psychological insights that contribute to his personal growth. Similarly, systematic use of some meditative SoCs is claimed by some to aid *spiritual* growth, a process extending beyond physiological or normal

Alpha Wave of the Future

Time—Alone in a semidarkened room, a young woman relaxed in an armchair before a blank screen, three electrodes fixed to her scalp and one grounded to an earlobe. Suddenly a pale blue light flickered on the screen and then steadied; a voice said quietly: "That's alpha."

The voice was that of Neurophysiologist Barbara Brown of the Veterans Administration Hospital in Sepulveda, Calif. She was demonstrating "biofeedback training," a new way of teaching human beings to control the kind of waves their brains emit—in this case, a rhythm called alpha, which usually accompanies a mood of relaxed alertness.

Letting Go

The brain's constant electrical activity produces wave patterns that can easily be measured with an electroencephalograph attached to the scalp. The patterns, recorded by the EEG as tracings on ribbons of paper, come in four main wave lengths: delta (.5 to 3 cycles per sec.), occurring in sleep; theta (4 to 7 per sec.), linked to creativity; beta (13 to 30 per sec.), identified with mental concentration; and the relaxed alpha (8 to 12 per sec.). It was only in 1929 that German Psychiatrist Hans Berger discovered alpha waves and not until 1958 that experimenters began working with alpha training. A tone or light activated by the EEG tells a trainee when he is producing alpha. Asked to keep the feedback (the tone or light) steady, most people can comply simply by relaxing.

If the system works as well as current research suggests, it may prove a boon for psychology, psychiatry, education and even industry. Already it has spawned a pop-alpha cult of profit-seeking trainers and fervent devotees in search of instant Zen.

The link between alpha and meditative states seems real enough. According to Psychologist Joe Kamiya of San Francisco's Langly Porter Neuropsychiatric Institute, an early pioneer in the field, Zen masters produce more alpha when they are meditating than when they are not, and they are quick to learn how to switch it on and off. Artists, musicians and athletes are also prolific alpha producers; so are many introspective and intuitive persons, and so was Albert Einstein. Alpha researchers report that subjects enjoy what Psychologist Lester Fehmi of the State University of New York at Stony Brook calls the "subtle and ineffable" alpha experience. Its pleasure, theorizes Kamiya, may come from the fact that alpha "represents something like letting go of anxieties."

It is partly this tension-relieving aspect of alpha that makes brain-wave control potentially useful in psychiatry. For example, scientists hope they can help claustrophobics by training them to produce alpha and thus relax in enclosed spaces. In Beaumont, Texas, the Angie Nall School for problem children has experimented with alpha training to relax stutterers and as a substitute for tranquilizers in hyperactive youngsters. At the Menninger Foundation in Topeka, Kans., Psychologist Elmer Green is training subjects not to raise but to lower their alpha while increasing theta. In a low-alpha, high-theta state, Green explains, deeply buried unconscious problems sometimes seem to float into awareness.

Alpha may also prove useful in other ingenious ways. Psychologist Thomas Mulholland, president of the Bio-Feedback Research Society, thinks it may be feasible to develop teaching machines controlled by attention. When concentration is high, alpha is low: notified by proliferating alpha that a child's mind is wandering, the mechanical teacher could win his student back by showing a few attention-getting pictures.

Keeping Secrets

Other researchers believe that in an alpha state a sleep-deprived person may become effective again. Defense Department researchers are said to be toying with the idea that captured U.S. intelligence agents trained to turn on alpha could foul up enemy lie detectors and keep military secrets. In industry, major companies like Xerox and Martin Marietta are investigating biofeedback training to spur creative thinking and reduce executive tension; some are already experimenting with one of the dozen brands of portable brain-wave trainers now available for $300 or less.

To scientists like Mulholland, commercial alpha machines and the "alpha training institutes" now proliferating on the West Coast attract chiefly "the naive, the desperate and the superstitious." Machines operated by amateurs may record little more than amplifier noise or scalp twitches. There is still no proof that alpha and special mental powers go together, though the possibility tantalizes even the scientists. The alpha machine is still a long way from becoming Walker Percy's "lapsometer," which allowed Dr. Thomas More in *Love in the Ruins* to probe people's minds. But research is too new for anyone to claim that alpha training is a shortcut to nirvana, Electronic yoga remains a faddist's dream.

psychological growth. In this context, spiritual growth is defined in terms of actualizing various human potentialities that supposedly put one in a more harmonious relationship with the universe or God.

On the other hand, the dangers of experiencing some SoCs are real. A person's knowledge of the possible dangers must be weighed against the possible advantages, and, if the person goes ahead, he should realize that he is taking a calculated risk. We can consider four broad categories of dangers: *physical*, *psychological*, *legal*, and *spiritual*.

Physical dangers may come about through the exertion required in some meditative techniques or through the deleterious side effects of some drugs. *Psychological dangers* may result from a person

He Who Tastes, Knows! Or Does He?

This all-too-relevant cartoon illustrates the problems of communication between a person who has experienced altered states of consciousness (marijuana intoxication here) and those who have not, compounded by the generation gap and the more dynamic conflicts between parents and children. If Ronnie tries to tell his parents about the lightness he is experiencing, they will worry that his mind has been affected, that he is going crazy. If they try to tell him that some of the "wonderful insights and ideals" he has are a function of his age and that he will get over them, he will protest violently that his ideas are his own and his generation, unlike all previous, stupid generations, really knows "where it's at."

Many sorts of experience in altered SoCs are *state-specific:* They do not translate well back into our ordinary state of consciousness. The style of thinking, sensing, remembering, and feeling is different in the altered state. In that sense, the old saying "He who tastes, knows," states an important truth.

But unfortunately, there is no guarantee that he who tastes knows. He who tastes, who experiences various altered states himself, *may* know something as a result. On the other hand, he may not pay very much attention to what he is tasting (his experiences), he may avoid tasting if there is any unpleasant or frightening quality to the taste, or he may have a very distorted, neurotic *interpretation* of what he tastes. People always have experiences, but often fail to learn much from those experiences, whether ordinary life experiences or more exotic ones in altered states.

Recently four books have been published by Carlos Castaneda (*The Teachings of don Juan, A Separate Reality, Journey to Ixtlan,* and *Tales of Power*), reporting his experiences as an apprentice to a Yaqui Indian shaman don Juan.

In his apprenticeship with don Juan, Castaneda experienced many states of nonordinary reality, often

"Ronnie, come and watch this program about the dangers of marijuana."

drug-induced. Many of them were confusing and incredibly frightening to him. His health was so ruined after a few years of his apprenticeship that he stopped it for several years in order to preserve his sanity. Learning from altered state experiences is not easy, and may be almost impossible. Look at the dialogue between don Juan (who presumably understands) and Castaneda the day after Castaneda has the experience of turning into a crow and flying through the sky while under the influence of a drug.

coming into contact with repressed aspects of his personality that he cannot defend himself against in the altered SoC, thus experiencing traumatic emotional difficulties. For some people who are already neurotic or prepsychotic, the experience of an altered SoC can act as a trigger to a psychotic episode. The *legal dangers* apply primarily to the use of drugs; most psychedelic drugs are illegal in the United States, and there are severe penalties for their possession. Regardless of whether one feels that such laws are just, spending time in jail is not only unpleasant but generally results in adverse effects on one's psychological health.

In traditional spiritual disciplines the systematic and supervised use of altered SoCs is considered necessary for certain aspects of spiritual growth, but the same techniques and SoCs are often considered highly dangerous if indulged in without proper guidance. A particular *spiritual danger*, especially with drug-induced states, is that a person will generate and become attached to a counterfeit of a real spiritual experience, thus blocking his further progress.

We conclude with an apology for the sorry state of scientific knowledge about psychological processes under altered SoCs. This lack of knowledge is

Dialogue between don Juan and Castaneda

. . . There was a question I wanted to ask him [don Juan]. I knew he was going to evade it, so I waited for him to mention the subject; I waited all day. Finally I had to ask him, "Did I really fly, don Juan?"

"That is what you told me, didn't you?"

"I know, don Juan. I mean, did my body fly? Did I take off like a bird?"

"You always ask me questions I cannot answer. You flew. That is what the second portion of the devil's weed is for. As you take more of it, you will learn how to fly perfectly. It is not a simple matter. A man *flies* with the help of the second portion of the devil's weed. That is all I can tell you. What you want to know makes no sense. Birds fly like birds and a man who has taken the devil's weed flies as such."

"As birds do?"

"No, he flies as a man who has taken the weed."

"Then I didn't really fly, don Juan. I flew in my imagination, in my mind alone. Where was my body?"

"In the bushes," he replied cuttingly [referring to where Castaneda found himself at the end of his experience], but immediately broke into laughter again. "The trouble with you is that you understand things in only one way. You don't think a man flies; and yet a brujo can move a thousand miles in one second to see what is going on. He can deliver a blow to his enemies long distances away. So, does he or doesn't he fly?"

"You see, don Juan, you and I are differently oriented. Suppose, for the sake of argument, one of my fellow students had been here with me when I took the devil's weed. Would he have been able to see my flying?"

"There you go again with your questions about what would happen if. . . . It's useless to talk that way. If your friend, or anybody else, takes the second portion of the weed all he can do is fly. Now, if he had simply watched you, he might have seen you flying, or he might not. That depends on the man."

"But what I mean, don Juan, is that if you and I look at a bird and see it fly, we agree that it is flying. But if two of my friends had seen me flying as I did last night, would they have agreed that I was flying?"

"Well, they might have. You agree that birds fly because you have seen them flying. Flying is a common thing with birds. But you will not agree on other things birds do, because you have never seen birds doing them. If your friends knew about men flying with the devil's weed, then they would agree."

"Let's put it another way, don Juan. What I meant to say is that if I had tied myself to a rock with a heavy chain I would have flown just the same, because my body had nothing to do with my flying."

Don Juan looked at me incredulously.

"If you tie yourself to a rock," he said, "I'm afraid you will have to fly holding the rock with its heavy chain."

---

regrettable, for the topic is both fascinating and important. Unfortunately, in the past there has been considerable resistance by the general public and reluctance by trained psychologists to undertake research on altered states. But, although the area has been an unfashionable one, all signs point to a rapidly changing awareness of and growing interest in these phenomena among psychologists. The immediate future promises much more penetrating psychological analyses of altered SoCs than can be offered at this writing.

Certainly the general public is now greatly intrigued by the phenomena of altered SoCs. In fact, the public often does not exhibit intelligent skepticism about the topics we have discussed here. We do not believe that the validity of all these phenomena has been adequately demonstrated. We wish to conclude this chapter by pointing out that there is ample reason to be skeptical about how to interpret the reality and uniqueness of many of the

topics in this chapter, particularly phenomena such as possession states, lucid dreaming, and OOBEs. Our knowledge in these areas is so minimal that there is reason to doubt whether the phenomena are qualitatively different from other more established and better understood behaviors. For example, is a possession state any different from what we typically refer to as mental illness (see Chapter 12)? Even the validity of hypnosis as a separate state of consciousness is doubted by some investigators.

The topics covered in this chapter are about as controversial as any topics in psychology. We hope that you will not blindly accept everything you hear and read about such phenomena. But it is probably just as foolish to decide blindly that any phenomenon you do not understand is not a real one. It is only through careful, tedious, objective analysis that an understanding of consciousness will emerge. Until then, retain a healthy skepticism and an objective, inquisitive mind.

Summary

1. An altered state of consciousness is defined by the subjective feeling that one's mind is functioning according to a pattern qualitatively different from the pattern of normal consciousness. There are still many difficult problems to solve about how to study these states scientifically. Much of the present knowledge about altered SoCs comes from sources other than scientific studies.

2. Ordinary dreaming is characterized physiologically by the Stage 1–REM EEG pattern and by the loss of muscle control. An enormous amount of research on dreams is being carried out, but analyses of the function of dreams remain largely theoretical, dominated by the theory of Sigmund Freud.

3. Non-REM sleep also has mental content, but it is more like ordinary thought than dreaming. Most sleep-walking and talking episodes take place during non-REM sleep.

4. The hypnagogic state occurs while one is falling asleep and the hypnopompic state while waking up. They are characterized by altered ego functioning.

5. Two special dream states have been reported: (a) the high dream refers to a dream with remarkable similarity to a psychedelic experience, and (b) the lucid dream occurs when the dreamer feels that he still possesses his normal state of consciousness, including the ability to direct the action of the dream.

6. One of the strangest states is the out-of-body experience (OOBE, or astral projection in the occult literature). In this rare experience the person feels that his mind has left his physical body, which he usually can still "see" as apart from himself. OOBEs usually have a profound effect on the individual involved.

7. Whether hypnosis is a unique SoC is a topic of great debate among psychologists. Hypnosis is usually characterized by a "mental quiet" and an increase in suggestibility. It has many uses in medicine and psychotherapy.

8. A possession state occurs when the subject feels as if his own personality or soul has been displaced by some nonphysical entity or spirit. Most of the research has dealt with spiritualist mediums. Such states may be associated with mental illness.

9. Alcohol intoxication is often accompanied by feelings of increased competence but a severe loss of motor control. Alcohol is the most widely used drug and can be very dangerous.

10. Marijuana intoxication is accompanied by feelings of enhanced perception, relaxation, well-being, and quiet. Complex motor functioning may be impaired. The dangers associated with long-term use of marijuana are largely unknown. The great rise in marijuana use in this country is creating a social problem, because possession of the drug is illegal.

11. Psychedelic drugs are drugs whose primary effect is to induce an altered state of consciousness. The most predominant ones are LSD, mescaline, and psilocybin. These drugs produce profound changes in mental functioning and have found some use in psychotherapy. The quality of the psychedelic experience depends on the psychological attributes of the user and the setting as much as on the pharmacological attributes of the drug itself.

12. Meditation refers to procedures designed to produce a state of consciousness characterized by less illusion in perception and a search for more directly perceived truth. The two basic types are concentrative and opening-up meditation. Practitioners report feelings of pure awareness, voidness, and a lack of internal mental activity. Aftereffects purportedly include heightened awareness, enhanced perception, and a feeling of profound refreshment of the mind and body.

13. Some altered SoCs seem to be induced by biofeedback techniques, which are used to make available to consciousness information about bodily processes that are not consciously controlled. There is great promise for the use of these techniques in modifying numerous "involuntary" functions of the body, such as blood pressure.

Recommended Additional Readings

Aaronson, B., & Osmond, H. (Eds.) *Psychedelics: The uses and implications of hallucinogenic drugs.* New York: Doubleday, 1970.

Barber, T. X. *LSD, marijuana, yoga, and hypnosis.* Chicago: Aldine, 1970.

Castaneda, C. *Journey to Istlan: The lessons of don Juan.* New York: Simon & Schuster, 1972.

Castaneda, C. *A separate reality.* New York: Simon & Schuster, 1971.

Castaneda, C. *The teachings of don Juan: A Yaqui way of knowledge.* New York: Berkeley: University of California Press, 1968.

Foulkes, D. *The psychology of sleep.* New York: Scribner, 1966.

Murphy, G. *The challenge of psychical research.* New York: Harper & Row, 1967.

Ornstein, R. E. *The psychology of consciousness.* San Francisco: Freeman, 1972.

Ornstein, R. E., & Naranjo, C. *On the psychology of meditation.* New York: Viking, 1971.

Tart, C. (Ed.) *Altered states of consciousness: A book of readings.* New York: Wiley, 1969.

Tart, C. (Ed.) *The spiritual psychologies.* New York: Harper & Row, 1974.

9

PERSONALITY

Imagine that, as part of a psychology experiment, you are spending an evening observing the behavior of shoppers in a large and busy supermarket. You are recording the approximate age and weight of persons who purchase candy, sour cream, and frozen pies (for later comparison with those who stick to melba toast and cottage cheese). Suddenly all the lights go out. Being an intrepid scientist, you attempt to continue your observations in the illumination provided by the store's emergency spotlights but find that conditions are not adequate for you to make accurate age and weight estimates. You therefore turn your attention to how individuals deal with the situation. In the produce department you spot a person calmly squeezing avocados as if nothing unusual were going on, while over by the green peppers, another individual is very frightened and begins to shout and scream. You arrive at the meat counter in time to see an opportunistic shopper put a standing rib roast under each arm and head for the exit. Nearby, you listen as an irate customer informs the manager that there is no excuse for this kind of situation and threatens to patronize a competitor's store in the future.

In short, you find that each individual handles the unexpected blackout differently. This is not particularly surprising; we expect great diversity in human behavior. Of course, we also expect that each individual will usually display some consistency in behavior in coping with different situations. Thus, a person who is quiet and shy at parties usually also behaves timidly and quietly in class, at public meetings, and on a date. Similarly, you expect a close friend to deal with you in a warm and interested manner in most situations and on a daily basis, not just once in a while.

How can we understand and explain these differences *between* individuals and consistencies *within* individuals, which we may take for granted as part of "human nature"? What makes each person so different from every other, yet so consistent within himself? For centuries philosophers, physicians, and religious leaders have wrestled with this very basic question about people and their behavior, and in recent years psychologists have studied and theorized about it.

Over the years, the most commonly used term to *describe and account for individual differences and behavioral consistencies* in human beings has been *personality*. In everyday situations we hear people's behavior *described* in terms of their personality: "He would be a nice guy if he didn't have such an aggressive personality," or "Your blind date is a bit on the heavy side but has a great personality," or "My psychology professor really knows his material but has no personality." In addition, the concept of personality is often used to *explain* behavior: "I think that my husband's depressions are caused by his basically insecure personality," or "Her stable personality allows her to handle any situation."

What Is Personality?

Even though almost everyone frequently uses the term *personality*, there is little agreement on what it actually means. To get some idea of the problem, jot down your own definition (before you finish this chapter) and then ask three of your friends for theirs. You will probably find that each of them has a somewhat different conception of the term and that the three definitions you collect from others differ from your own. Such differences of opinion result not from the fact that you and your friends are not experienced psychologists, but from the generality of the concept of personality.

Over the years, people have defined "personality" in various ways, including one's outward appearance, one's role in life, the totality of one's qualities or attributes, the way one really is, one's general behavior pattern, and many others. Today dozens of formal definitions exist (see the examples in Table 9–1), none of which is universally accepted. Like all definitions, those in Table 9–1 reflect the many different interests of their sponsors: prediction (Cattell), dynamics (Allport), predispositions (Eysenck), individual differences (Guilford), description (McClelland), uniqueness (Kolb). But each of these aspects is subsumed under our *general definition* of personality as a term used to *describe* (McClelland) and *account* (Allport) for

---

Table 9–1
Some definitions of personality

1. The dynamic organization within the individual of those psychophysical systems that determine his unique adjustments to his environment (G. Allport).
2. The more or less stable and enduring organization of a person's character, temperament, intellect, and physique that determines his unique adjustment to his environment (H. Eysenck).
3. That which permits a prediction of what a person will do in a given situation (R. B. Cattell).
4. A person's unique pattern of traits (J. P. Guilford).
5. The most adequate conceptualization of a person's behavior in all its detail (D. McClelland).
6. Each individual's characteristically recurring patterns of behavior (L. Kolb).

---

individual differences (Guilford, Kolb) and *behavioral consistencies* (Cattell, Eysenck).

It is somewhat easier to define personality as an area of psychological study than as a "thing" that people have. Because the concept of personality is so broad, its study involves more branches of psychology than any other specialty. A psychologist interested in personality may ask questions as diverse as: How do personality characteristics develop? Does the existence of one characteristic predict anything about the likelihood that the person will have certain other characteristics? What role do other people play in the development of an individual's personality? When and why do different people behave similarly and given individuals behave inconsistently? How do genetic and physiological factors influence personality? What causes the appearance of "abnormal" versus "normal" personalities? Can personality be changed and, if so, how?

The study of personality can involve all facets of human behavior and can encompass aspects of developmental, social, experimental, physiological, and clinical psychology. Thus, in a sense, any psychologist who deals with human behavior can be said to be exploring some segment of personality.

The Role of Theory in Studying Personality

If, as we have seen, there is no universally accepted definition of personality, on what do psychologists base their studies of human personality? Clearly, any investigator must proceed with some sort of guidelines. What the psychologist does is to use a *theory* of personality. The theory is important because it provides some basic *assumptions* about human behavior and a *working definition* of the concept.

For example, one could start out with the somewhat fanciful assumption that all human behavior is the result of the presence of thousands of tiny, invisible elves that reside in the pancreas. An abundance of depressed elves would produce lethargic behavior except when they were sleeping, when a smaller number of happier and more optimistic elves would take over the controls, producing less melancholy behavior. Personality could then be defined through a kind of census of the elf population in each individual. People hosting lots of anxious elves would be called neurotic, those with a preponderance of sociable elves would be labeled extroverted, and so on.

Suppose that the investigator elaborated this kind

Personality Description Is Not Hard—Just Deal in Generalities

It is pretty easy to make up a personality description of someone that the individual being described will judge to be quite accurate as a characterization of the way he "really" is. All you have to do is be vague enough and deal in generalities based on common sense. This has been demonstrated by experiments in which the participants were asked to take special personality tests and were told that a psychologist would review the tests and write a personality sketch of each person. Actually, all the participants were handed back the exact same sketch, which was as follows:

You have a strong need for other people to like you and for them to admire you. You have a tendency to be critical of yourself. You have a great deal of unused capacity which you have not turned to your advantage. While you have some personality weaknesses, you are generally able to compensate for them. Your sexual adjustment has presented some problems for you. Disciplined and controlled on the outside, you tend to be worrisome and insecure inside. At times you have serious doubts as to whether you have made the right decision or done the right thing. You prefer a certain amount of change and variety and become dissatisfied when

hemmed in by restrictions and limitations. You pride yourself as being an independent thinker and do not accept others' opinions without satisfactory proof. You have found it unwise to be too frank in revealing yourself to others. At times, you are extroverted, affable, sociable, while at other times you are introverted, weary, and reserved. Some of your aspirations tend to be pretty unrealistic. (Ulrich, Stachnik, and Stainton, 1963, page 832)

After having read the above "individualized" interpretation, the participants were asked to rate how accurately the psychologist had interpreted their personalities. Almost every participant said that the psychologist had done a good or excellent job. People who write horoscopes, or analyze handwriting, or read palms or tea leaves or bumps on your head know how to deal in generalities. There are lots of general statements that apply to just about everyone to some degree, so you can restrict yourself to making such statements and most people will believe that you are an expert in personality assessment. This will be particularly true if you preface your generalities by mentioning that you are a psychology major and if you go through some fancy, but useless, procedures designed to create an air of expertise, training, and scientific measurement of personality.

of thinking into a comprehensive set of statements or assumptions that could account for human behavior as we know it, generate accurate predictions about it, and suggest procedures through which it can be altered. He would then have a *personality theory* that might result in hundreds of experiments designed to test the validity of its assumptions and hypotheses. "Elf theory" would probably also foster the development of highly specialized procedures (such as extremely sensitive X-ray devices) for assessing the specific kinds of elves in each individual. In addition, the theory might suggest specific strategies for elf research.

   This fanciful example is meant only to make the point that, because human behavior can be interpreted in so many ways, personality can be approached, defined, assessed, and researched, from any one of a wide variety of theoretical points of view, each of which will have strengths and weaknesses. Literally dozens of such theories exist. Here we shall present a description and discussion of four major *classes* of personality theories: *dispositional theories*, *psychodynamic theories*, *social learning theories*, and *phenomenological*

theories. In considering each class of theories, you should not ask which are "right" and which are "wrong," but which come closest to providing an efficient, complete, and testable account of the development, maintenance, and modification of human behavior, "normal" and "deviant." Note that each of these four classes of theories forms what might be called a "strategy" of personality study (Liebert and Spiegler, 1974) in the sense that, like the "elf approach," they provide not only a way of thinking about personality, but also a set of procedures for measuring and investigating it. With the exception of dispositional theories, each class of approaches has also generated techniques designed to produce personality change; these are discussed in Chapter 12.

Dispositional Theories

When people say, "He is the nervous type," or "Kindness is one of her most outstanding traits," or "Some people are driven to work hard by their strong need for achievement," they are, usually without knowing it, adopting a *dispositional* theory of personality. Dispositional theories start with the basic assumption that personality is composed of *dispositions within the individual* to behave in certain ways. Further, they assume that these dispositions are relatively stable in time and generalized over a wide variety of circumstances. And from this they conclude that if you know about people's dispositions, you can make some predictions about their future behavior. The names given to these hypothesized behavioral dispositions are different in different theories.

Personality Types

Some dispositional theories assume that there are a few specifiable *personality types* and that each type is disposed to behave differently. One of the earliest personality type theorists was the ancient Greek physician Hippocrates. Working on the assumption that the human body contains four fluids, or humors (blood, phlegm, black bile, and yellow bile), he categorized people into four corresponding personality types: phlegmatic (a calm, apathetic temperament caused by too much phlegm), choleric (a hot-headed, irritable temperament due to an excess of yellow bile), sanguine (an optimistic, hopeful temperament attributed to a predominance of blood), and melancholic (a sad, depressed temperament based on black bile). Hippocrates' theory is no longer taken seriously, yet it survives as a way of describing people—you will still find his four personality types listed in your dictionary.

Since Hippocrates, several other *type* theories of personality have been proposed, most of which seek to relate behavioral dispositions to physical characteristics. For example, it was once thought that people's facial characteristics provided clues to the kinds of behaviors they would display. This "science" was called *physiognomy* and related factors such as head size, distance between the eyes, shape of the chin, and color of the hair to personality *type*. Although this theory has no scientific value, it has become a part of popular thinking about people—"Criminals have small, beady eyes set close together"; "Blondes have more fun."

The German psychiatrist Ernst Kretschmer had a different theory. He believed that the kind of mental disorder displayed by his patients was related to their overall physique. He identified four basic body types (see Figure 9–1) and reported that those he called asthenic, athletic, and dysplastic tended to be diagnosed as schizophrenic, while those labeled manic-depressive were more likely to have a pyknic physique.

**Figure 9–1
Kretschmer's four body types**

Asthenic

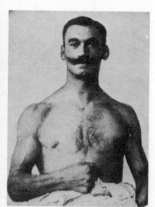
Athletic

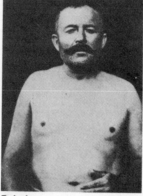
Pyknic

Dysplastic

According to Kretschmer, diagnosed manic-depressives tend to be pyknic, while schizophrenics are more likely to have any of the other three body types. This does not mean, you should take care to note, that all pyknics are manic-depressives.

Kretschmer's theory was obviously too simple. His general ideas have been picked up and extended by others, most notably an American physician, William Sheldon, who examined the relationship between body type and behavior in the general population, not just psychiatric patients. His system involved three primary body types: endomorphic, mesomorphic, and ectomorphic (see Figure 9–2). But instead of assigning individuals to one category, as Kretschmer had done, he characterized each person in terms of the *degree* to which that person displayed features of each primary type. (This approach contains features of *trait* theories of personality, to be discussed later.) Sheldon then examined the relationship between people's body

Figure 9–2
Sheldon's body types and their associated temperaments

Physique	Temperament
Endomorphic (soft and round, overdeveloped digestive viscera)	**Viscerotonic** (relaxed, loves to eat, sociable)
Mesomorphic (muscular, rectangular, strong)	**Somatotonic** (energetic, assertive, courageous)
Ectomorphic (long, fragile, large brain and sensitive nervous sytem)	**Cerebrotonic** (restrained, fearful, introvertive, artistic)

type and their behavior. He found that endomorphs tended to be what he called "viscerotonic" (relaxed, sociable, slow, and tolerant); mesomorphs displayed "somatonia" (an assertive, athletic, energetic, and bold temperament); and ectomorphs were "cerebrotonic" (introverted, restrained, fearful, and artistic). It is interesting to note that these relationships parallel popularly held stereotypes about physique and behavior (the jolly fat person, the bold athlete, the frail, sensitive artist). The influence of these stereotypes may account for the relationships Sheldon found, despite his use of highly trained observers. In any case, his theory has not received strong support and is not influential.

The convenience and simplicity of *type* theories has great popular appeal. It would be nice to know everything about a person by looking at his face, manner of dress, hair style, body type, or genetic makeup, but the behavior of human beings is just too diverse and complicated to be dealt with using a cut-and-dried, "pigeonhole" system of categorizing people. Thus, type theories are not generally valid because they are oversimplified and inadequate descriptions of behavior. Furthermore, they can be harmful because they tend to generate or maintain prejudices about people.

Traits of Personality

Trait theories of personality seek to avoid the limitations of type systems by accounting for both the diversity of human behavior and the behavioral consistencies shown by each individual. They start with the basic assumption that a given person's behavior is controlled not by the *type* of person he is, but mainly by the wide variety of stable personality traits (such as dependency, aggressiveness, gentleness, thoughtfulness, and the like) that each individual has to some degree or another. Thus, just as grade-point average is

Nixon Handwriting Reflects Pressure

New York [Aug. 14, 1974]—(AP)—Former President Nixon's signature tells it all, according to a handwriting analyst.

Felix Lehmann studied three examples of Nixon's signature—the first from shortly after Nixon took office in 1969, the second several months ago and the third shortly before he resigned from office.

"Tremendous capitals show pride, but the long thread at the end of his name shows he wants to leave room to maneuver," Lehmann said of the first signature. "The striving for recognition and ambition are overpowering in his handwriting."

The second example:

"He goes from an appearance of clarity to being wishy-washy . . . But in this signature there is still hope."

And Lehmann's analysis of the third signature:

"There's nothing left. Only a shadow. His ambitions are over. A shapeless stroke, ambiguity. A disintegration of personality, a person sinking within himself."

Examples of Richard Nixon's signature. Three examples were studied by handwriting analyst.

Some people think handwriting analysis, or graphology, provides clues to personality. You should note that, to date, there is *no* reliable scientific evidence to support any relationship between handwriting and personality.

determined by a student's academic performance in many separate courses, each personality is determined by the combination of traits, occurring

Phrenology, the study of head shape and its relation to behavior, was once a popular means of personality assessment. Snoopy seems skeptical and for good reason. Head reading is no longer taken seriously in scientific circles.

at varying strengths, present in each individual. The idea that many combinations of trait strengths are possible accounts for the uniqueness of each human being and the differences between them. The idea that the individual's traits are enduring explains the relative consistency in each person's behavior over time and in many different situations.

Like type theory, the trait approach has a clear appeal and, in fact, most of us employ it in describing others. If you ask a friend to tell you about her parents, for example, you will very likely be given a list of traits: "Dad is *hard-working*, *serious*, and *shy*, but overly *dependent* and *insecure* as well. Mom is *warm*, *outgoing*, *efficient*, and *optimistic*, but also *impulsive* and often *overbearing*."

The danger in the casual use of this approach to personality is that trait descriptions like "Integrity is Ralph's strongest trait" can too easily be used as *explanations*. If we use Ralph's trait of integrity to "explain" his honesty we end up making a statement that may be true but is not very useful in terms of understanding behavior: "Ralph is honest because he has integrity." This is like saying, "Ralph is 6 feet tall because he measures 72 inches from head to toe." Our *description* of behavior cannot also be its *cause*. We must use trait labels carefully so that we do not fool ourselves into thinking we have explained behavior when, in fact, we have merely described it.

Over the years, there have been many scientific attempts to avoid this problem. Some early efforts, such as those of Franz Gall (1758–1828), were temporarily influential but have ultimately been discredited. Gall believed that all behavioral dispositions and abilities existed neurophysiologically in the brain and that the better

developed a particular part of the brain was, the stronger the corresponding trait or ability would be. Gall thought that there were 37 basic traits and he developed a "map" of the head to locate each of them. Personality assessment then became a matter of feeling an individual's skull for bumps (well-developed traits) and depressions (poorly developed traits). This may be how the expression "having your head examined" got started.

Traits as Entities

Gordon Allport, one of the first and most influential of the modern personality theorists, also believed that traits actually existed within the person as "neuropsychic systems," but he went about describing them in a quite different and far more scientific way than did Gall. Allport discussed several kinds of traits, organized according to their generality: (1) *cardinal* traits, which determine behavior in the widest range of circumstances (describing someone as "a regular Albert Schweitzer" would be an example of the use of the cardinal trait of humanitarianism); (2) *central* traits, which are not as broad as cardinal traits but are still fairly general (our earlier descriptions of a hypothetical set of parents provide examples); and (3) narrow *secondary* traits, which appear only in certain circumstances (for example, "She is grouchy in the morning"). Further, Allport pointed out that while some traits appeared to some extent in everyone (*common* traits), others were unique to the individual (*individual* traits) and could only be studied on an intensive, long-term, case-by-case basis. Cardinal traits, in particular, apply only to relatively few people.

Allport's methods for describing common traits included asking people to tell how they would behave in certain situations. Their responses allowed him to do two things. First, he could measure the strength and stability of a trait in a single individual by determining how often and how generally a person displayed the trait. Second, he could measure the frequency of traits among people in general by totaling the answers he received from large numbers of subjects.

Allport's influence upon the development of modern trait theories has been enormous, but one of the problems with his approach is that one could spend several lifetimes describing and researching all of the 18,000 or so trait names in the English language, let alone the relationships among them. Some more efficient method of dealing with traits was needed, and a technique called *factor analysis* provided it.

Traits as Factors

Basically, factor analysis is a procedure that allows the personality researcher to look at large amounts of data relevant to the traits of many individuals and summarize what seems to "go with" what. Then he can group related traits together and classify them as personality *factors*. An example may help clarify the idea. Several days of close observation of one particular man might result in a long and varied list of highly specific activities, including: "places food in mouth," "rakes leaves," "plays tennis," "waxes car," "reads newspaper," "sits at desk," "chews food," "kisses wife," "drives to tennis court," "buys newspaper," "swallows food," "burns leaves," "writes reports," "sits on toilet," "removes clothes," "lies asleep for 8 hours," "washes dishes," "argues with supervisor," "sets alarm clock," "watches TV," "pets dog," and on and on. You could report on the man's behavior simply by presenting the entire list of everything he did during the period of observation (which is analogous to listing all of a person's personality *traits*) but this would be cumbersome and the report would be very difficult to deal with. Alternatively, you could summarize all the specific behaviors under a few categories (analogous to personality *factors*). You might see that certain behaviors are related to one another in some way. A group of behaviors such as "plays tennis," "pets dog," "walks to tennis court," "reads newspaper," and "watches TV" might be called "Recreation" or "Relaxation" (the name you give it is arbitrary; you could just as easily call it "behavior group A"). Several other behaviors may be unrelated to those called "Recreation" but highly related to one another—such as "washes dishes," "rakes leaves," "burns leaves," "waxes car"—and this group might be named "Household Chores." You could follow the same grouping and naming procedures with respect to all the other behaviors observed, and the result might be a report saying that the person spent his time engaged in 5

categories of behavior: "Housework," "Occupational Pursuits," "Recreation," "Sexual Activity" (which may or may not be the same as "Recreation"), and "Body Maintenance."

Factor analysis (see Chapter 1 and Appendixes A and C) allows the same kind of summaries as those in our example, but in factor analysis the relationships among specific traits are determined through sophisticated mathematical procedures, not just by human observation. We turn now to the work of two theorists who have used factor analysis in their investigation of personality traits.

Cattell's surface and source traits.   Raymond B. Cattell is one of the foremost proponents of factor analysis as a means of learning about personality traits. In his research on personality, Cattell has tapped three sources of information about human behavior: L-data, Q-data, and T-data. L-data come not directly from the person under study but from *life* records, generally supplied by individuals who have observed the subject and who can provide information about his behavior. Q-data consist of the subject's answers to *questions* about himself. T-data consist of scores on standardized, objective *tests*. Cattell argues that one cannot obtain a complete picture of personality without using these multiple data sources.

Like Allport, Cattell recognizes that some traits are broader and more pervasive than others. His extensive research has resulted in the grouping of human behavior into about 35 *trait clusters*. Cattell calls these clusters *surface* traits because they summarize the most obvious ways in which overt behaviors are related. For example, "honest" is a surface trait that summarizes a range of related behaviors that might include "returning a lost wallet," "telling the truth," "paying a parking fine," and the like. The other end of this surface trait dimension, "dishonest," summarizes an opposite set of related behaviors.

Because they describe only the *overt* reactions between people, Cattell regards these surface traits more as manifestations of personality than as the basic dimensions of personality itself. In order to identify these more basic elements, the sources of personality, Cattell used factor analysis to analyze the surface traits. With this procedure he isolated 16 *source* traits. He then developed a test called the 16 PF (personality factors) to measure their relative strength in individual subjects. Thus instead of describing personality in terms of specific behaviors or even clusters of behaviors (surface traits), Cattell

© 1959 United Feature Syndicate Inc.

provides a *profile* for each person in terms of his or her scores on source traits such as "reserved–outgoing," "shy–venturesome," or "relaxed–tense" (see Appendix C). Cattell views these source traits as the "building blocks" of personality and notes that they stem from either environmental influences (*environmental-mold* traits) or genetic-constitutional factors (*constitutional* traits).

Eysenck's three basic dimensions of personality. Cattell's research is confined mainly to the description of the so-called normal aspects of personality and has resulted in the isolation of 16 source traits. Hans Eysenck, a British psychologist, also has developed an approach using factor analytic techniques, but he outlines only three basic personality dimensions, and they relate to both "abnormal" and "normal" behavior. Eysenck began with the notion that personality traits are based on learning (conditioning) and that because of genetic-constitutional factors, some people are more easily conditioned than others. For example, one child may avoid a forbidden activity after having been punished for it only once; another might learn much more slowly, and a third might persist in the activity indefinitely. Eysenck found that, by using factor analysis to assess human behaviors and the traits they form, he could describe a given individual on three basic dimensions: neuroticism, psychoticism, and introversion–extroversion. (Note that Eysenck uses the terms *introvert* and *extrovert* in a sense different from the popular stereotypes of the extrovert as outgoing and the introvert as shy and withdrawn. In Eysenck's terminology, introverts are those who condition most easily and as a result develop behaviors that reflect this conditionability, such as anxiety and depression. Extroverts, on the other hand, condition less easily and tend to be more impulsive and unruly.)

On the basis of specially designed personality tests such as the Maudsley Personality Inventory (MPI), an individual can be given a score on each of these dimensions. Eysenck has found that particular combinations of personality factors (especially introversion–extroversion and neuroticism) are associated with particular patterns of behavior. For example, neurotic introverts are likely to display intense emotions involving anxiety, while neurotic extroverts will also be emotional, but their behavior will be antisocial or even criminal (see Figure 9–3).

It is interesting to note that, although Eysenck's theory does not contain suggestions for *new* personality change techniques, it does have clear implications for the way in which existing procedures should be used. Thus, if one is working with a neurotic introvert, the goal would be to help the person *reduce* overlearned reactions (such as fear of authority). By contrast, an *increase* in conditioned reactions might be desirable when dealing with an extrovert who has not learned to "play by the rules."

Need Theory

Another kind of dispositional approach to personality views behavior as driven by the individual's *needs* or *goals* rather than by his traits or personality type. This approach is exemplified by the work of Henry Murray (see Chapter 6), who postulated the existence of 12 *primary* human needs, such as air, water, food, sex, and 27 secondary or *psychogenic* needs, such as achievement, recognition, dominance, autonomy, aggression, affiliation, and nurturance. These needs, in combination with environmental influences (called *press*), shape the individual's personality and behavior. From Murray's point of view, measurement of personality involves assessment of both *manifest* (obvious) needs and *latent* (more subtle) needs.

Manifest needs can be measured directly by observing how often, how long, and how intensely a person engages in particular behaviors. A person who spends a lot of time pushing others around has a stronger need for aggression than a person who seldom if ever behaves assertively. Latent needs, however, are not overt—for instance, a person's

Figure 9–3
Characteristics of introverts and extroverts as neuroticism increases

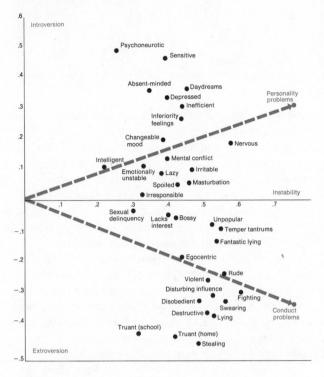

Points on the horizontal axis represent the degree of personality stability from a relatively normal condition on the left to highly neurotic at the right. The vertical axis represents the introversion–extroversion dimension. The graph suggests that someone who does a lot of fighting and swearing in public is probably quite extroverted and rather neurotic. In contrast, the person who daydreams a lot and tends to be a loner and depressed is probably an introverted person with a moderate amount of neuroticism. One can predict, on the basis of Eysenck's analysis, that relatively normal introverts and extroverts will, if they become neurotic, show completely different symptoms. As a result, they should be given different therapies.

latent need for affection might be expressed through romantic daydreams—and therefore they must be measured indirectly. To measure these needs, Murray developed the Thematic Apperception Test (TAT), in which the subject looks at an ambiguous stimulus, such as a picture; (see Appendix C), and tells a story about it. The content of the story is seen to reflect the individual's latent needs. Tests of this type are called *projective tests* because they allow the subject to ''project'' aspects of his personality onto relatively neutral stimuli. We shall mention other projective tests in discussing psychodynamic theories in the next section.

Some Problems with Dispositional Theories

Dispositional theories have been very influential in psychology and have generated massive amounts of research that has increased our ability to describe and make predictions about human behavior, but they have also been criticized on several points. For example, although dispositional theories *describe* personality (in terms of traits, types, or needs), they provide very little *explanation* of how it develops. This relative lack of attention to processes of personality development is a weakness of the dispositional approach.

In addition, one might question the assumption that personality is entirely a collection of stable, enduring, unchanging traits. Behavior and personality do not seem always to be independent of the individual's current circumstances or context—we do not always behave the same way. For instance, we may be generous most of the time, but downright stingy on occasions. Explaining the *variability* of behavior is often difficult for the dispositional theories.

Finally, dispositional theories have been criticized for their extensive use of self-report procedures in personality assessment and research. Asking someone about his behavior may be one of the most direct means of gaining information about personality, but it is also dangerous, because the data collected on a personality test may be biased or distorted in various ways. Subjects may try to present themselves in a particularly positive or negative way, or their responses may be influenced by factors such as the characteristics of the person giving the test, the situation in which they take the test, or events that occurred prior to it.

Psychodynamic Theories

Psychodynamic theories are based on the assumption that personality and personality development are determined by *intrapsychic* events and conflicts—that is, events and conflicts taking place within the mind—and that these events and conflicts can best be explored and understood through careful, in-depth study of individual subjects. The foundations for this approach were set down late in the nineteenth century primarily by one man: Sigmund Freud. A physician devoted to the

© 1957 United Feature Syndicate Inc.

According to psychodynamic theory, expressive activities such as drawing may reflect unconscious feelings. As the cartoon suggests, care must be exercised in interpreting such material.

principles of science, Freud evolved one of the most comprehensive and influential theories of personality ever presented.

Freud's Theory

Freud called his approach *psychoanalysis* and based his theorizing on a few fundamental principles. One of these was *psychic determinism*, the idea that human behavior does not occur randomly but instead occurs in accordance with intrapsychic causes, which may not always be obvious to an outside observer or even to the person displaying the behavior. This concept, that all of our behavior "means" something, even if we are not aware of its meaning, is one of the most significant and widely known features of Freud's theory. In the psychoanalytic perspective, few, if any, aspects of human behavior are accidental: Writing the word "sex" when you meant to write "six," calling your lover by another person's name, or forgetting a dental appointment could be interpreted as expressing feelings, desires, fears, or impulses of which you are not aware.

Freud called the part of mental functioning that is out of our awareness and to which we cannot readily gain access the *unconscious*. Thoughts, feelings, and ideas of which we are unaware but which we can bring into the *conscious* portion of the mind are said to be *preconscious*. For example, you can easily become aware of the feeling of your tongue even though, until you read this sentence, you were probably not thinking about it. Such thoughts are *preconscious*. By contrast, according to Freud, if you harbor *unconscious* hatred toward a close friend, you would claim that no such feelings exist because you do not experience them consciously.

Another of Freud's fundamental assumptions was that human personality is formed out of the continuous struggle between the individual's attempts to satisfy inborn instincts (primarily involving sex and aggression) while at the same time coping with an environment that will not tolerate completely uninhibited conduct. In Freud's view, every human being is born with instinctual sexual and aggressive impulses that demand immediate gratification but that the individual cannot always directly express without causing himself harm or other negative consequences. Thus, it becomes each individual's lifelong task somehow to satisfy instinctual urges while taking into account the demands, rules, and realities of the environment. For example, a man may desire sexual relations with a particular woman, but because he has been socialized by his parents and other agents of society, he knows that he cannot just walk up to her as a perfect stranger and attempt to attain his goal directly. Therefore, he may seek to meet her socially, develop a close relationship with her over some period of time, and ultimately reach his original objective. This solution to the man's problem is far more socially appropriate than a direct expression of sexual impulses and thus reflects a compromise between instinct and reality. For Freud, then, personality is a kind of arena in which what the person *wants* to do (instinct) conflicts with what he has learned he *should* or *can* do (morality and reason) and where some compromise is worked out.

It is important to note that Freud lived and wrote in a time of Victorian sexual repression. To argue and theorize as he did made him a rebel against society. His theory was truly dangerous to the existing social order, and his bravery in proposing such a position should not be overlooked.

Structure of personality. Freud called the unconscious, instinctual component of personality the *id*. In the id are all of a person's inherited sexual, aggressive, and other impulses that seek immediate expression. All of the psychic energy, or *libido*, that motivates behavior is part of the id at birth. Because the id seeks to gratify its desires without delay, it operates on the *pleasure principle* (this might be

Figure 9–4
The relationship of the id, ego, and superego to levels of awareness

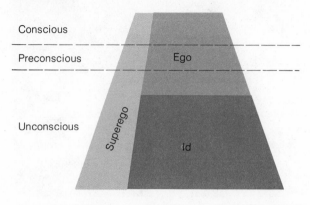

Conscious

- - - - - - - - - - - -

Preconscious   Ego

- - - - - - - - - - - -

Unconscious

Superego

Id

translated as "if it feels good, do it"). Because it is unconscious, the id is not in touch with the world outside, which, as the person grows, will impose more and more limitations on direct gratification of instinctual impulses.

Therefore, as a newborn child develops, a second aspect of personality, called *ego*, begins to take shape. The ego gets its energy from the id, but it is partly conscious and thus is in contact with external reality. Its function is mainly to find ways to allow satisfaction of id impulses while at the same time protecting the organism as a whole from danger. In our example of the man who wanted to have intercourse with a certain woman (id impulse), the ego planned and directed the implementation of a socially acceptable way of doing so. Because the ego takes reality into account while seeking to facilitate expression of id impulses, it operates on the *reality principle* (which might be translated as "if you are going to do it, do it quietly" or "do it later").

As the child grows, a third component of personality develops. It is called the *superego* and is roughly equivalent to the "conscience" in the sense that it contains all of the teachings of the person's family and culture regarding ethics, morals, and values—how one *should* behave. According to Freud, the development of the superego actually involves internalizing these teachings so that they function not as someone else's values, but as our own. Thus, this aspect of personality acts as a kind of internalized representative of society that seeks to influence us to behave in a socially acceptable fashion. Feelings of guilt are seen as the result of failing to follow the demands of the superego.

In Freud's system, then, personality is a three-part structure, partly conscious, partly unconscious (see Figure 9–4), that is constantly involved in conflicts within itself. The ego is involved in most of these intrapsychic conflicts because it must find a way to reconcile the impetuous impulses of the id, the perfectionistic demands of the superego, and the requirements of the outside world. Some examples of intrapsychic conflicts are presented in Table 9–2.

Ego defense mechanisms.   The result of conflict among various components of personality is *anxiety*. For example, if id impulses were to prompt a hungry person to take food from a neighboring restaurant table while waiting for his own lunch, the ego would recognize the potential danger of such action, the superego would point out that such behavior is "wrong," and the resulting feelings would be experienced as anxiety. Freud postulated that in order to prevent anxiety the ego employs a variety of *unconscious* tactics called *defense mechanisms*, which attempt to keep unacceptable id impulses or

Table 9–2
Possible conflicts among the aspects of personality

Conflict	Example
Id vs. ego	Choosing between a small immediate reward and a larger reward that requires some period of waiting (i.e., delay of gratification)
Id vs. superego	Deciding whether to return the difference when you are overpaid or undercharged
Ego vs. superego	Choosing between acting in a realistic way (e.g., telling a "white lie") and adhering to a potentially costly or unrealistic standard (e.g., always telling the truth)
Id and ego vs. superego	Deciding whether to retaliate against the attack of a weak opponent or to "turn the other cheek"
Id and superego vs. ego	Deciding whether to act in a realistic way that conflicts both with your desires and your moral convictions (e.g., the decision faced by devout Roman Catholics as to the use of contraceptive devices)
Ego and superego vs. id	Choosing whether to "act on the impulse" to steal something you want and cannot afford—the ego would presumably be increasingly involved in such a conflict as the probability of being apprehended increases

Figure 9–5
Sigmund Freud

Top left: Freud at 35 in 1891. At this time Freud was developing his abilities slowly and painfully. As he said, "I have restricted capacities or talents. None at all for the natural sciences; nothing for mathematics; nothing for anything quantitative. But what I have . . . is probably very intense" (Jones, 1961).

Top right: Freud at 50 in 1906, the year thought by many to mark the first recognition of Freud by English-speaking countries. Also this year Carl Jung, who later became author of his own system of personality, began a regular correspondence with Freud from Switzerland. Thus, "his researches of the past thirteen years, so scorned and despised elsewhere, were finding wider acceptance" (Jones, 1961).

Bottom left: Freud at 66 in 1922. This was one of Freud's most productive yet disappointing times. The Committee, a group of Freud's disciples that had existed for 10 years, was disrupted by dissension among its members. This event coincided with the first signs of cancer, from which Freud would eventually die. In 1920 he changed his original ideas of the unconscious and began a new theory of the ego, which is considered a great advance in the theory of psychoanalysis.

Bottom right: Freud at 82 in 1938. Because he was a Jew, Freud was forced to leave his lifelong home of Vienna, Austria, during the Nazi invasion. Here he is in England in the process of reading and writing his last work, the *Outline of Psychoanalysis.* He was still writing the manuscript a year later when he died.

other threatening material from reaching consciousness.

According to Freud, one of the most basic and primitive defense mechanisms is *repression.* In repression the ego devotes a great deal of its energy to keeping a particular thought, memory, feeling, or impulse at the unconscious level. (Note that repression, an unconscious process, is not the same as suppression, a conscious means of denying an impulse that you are aware of.) Thus, if a father has strong unconscious impulses to murder his children, his ego may prevent him from becoming aware of this. However, like trying to hold a fully inflated beach ball under water, repression takes a lot of constant effort. At times the repressed material may threaten to surface, or actually do so.

Complete and entirely successful repression without additional help is unlikely, and the ego often employs supplementary defenses to keep unacceptable material from consciousness. One of these is *reaction formation*, in which the individual thinks and acts in a fashion directly opposite to the unconscious impulse. Our hypothetical murderous

father might thus be extremely overprotective of his children and express great concern for their welfare. He might also employ (unconsciously, of course) the defense mechanism called *projection*, through which he would attribute his own taboo impulses to others. This might take the form of accusing other fathers of abusing their children. A defense mechanism called *displacement* actually allows some disguised expression of the id impulses. Here, the father who unconsciously wishes to harm his children may "take it out" on the family dog or some other target. If he justifies or explains inappropriate or unacceptable behavior toward his children without being aware of the "real" unconscious reason for it, he is using the ego defense mechanism called *rationalization*. Thus, he might point out that he punishes his children frequently because he loves them or "for their own good."

In Freud's view, one defense mechanism results in socially adaptive behavior. It is called *sublimation* and involves expressing taboo impulses within productive, creative channels. For instance, an individual's sexual impulses may be converted into artistic energy and result in the production of paintings or sculpture. Sublimation can provide a more or less permanent solution to the problem of protecting the person against anxiety. The other defenses, however, are less desirable alternatives that "tie up" large amounts of psychic energy and that may eventually break down, thus allowing a partial breakthrough of repressed material and forcing the person to fall back to even more primitive lines of defense. (This is why dependence on maladaptive ego defense strategies often indicates a need for psychotherapy; see Chapter 12).

What could be more primitive than repression? Freud believed that, when adult ego defenses fail, the person may to some extent *regress* or revert to behavior characteristic of earlier, less mature developmental stages. Partial regression may result in behaviors that are simply immature or otherwise mildly inappropriate. More profound regression can result in the appearance of severely disturbed, even psychotic behavior.

Personality development.   Freud postulated that as a newborn develops he passes through several *psychosexual stages* of development. Each stage is named for the area of the body most closely associated with pleasure at the time. Thus the first year or so of life is the *oral* stage because eating, sucking, and other oral activities are the predominant sources of pleasurable stimulation. If, because of premature or delayed weaning, oral needs are frustrated or overindulged, the child may *cling* to some behavior patterns associated with the oral stage after he has passed through the stage. Freud called this phenomenon *fixation*. The idea is that the personality fixates on some mode of gratification (in this case, oral gratification) because that is the only way it has of dealing with anxiety or lack of gratification at the time. For example, a baby can only reduce his tension orally (by crying and sucking). If the tension or lack of gratification is overwhelming to the developing ego, it will interfere with reality testing, and the personality will handle future tension (unrealistically) as it was earlier. Thus, an anxious adult may smoke cigarettes heavily. Oral stimulation might have helped him with his childhood problems, but will smoking relieve the problems at his office? Adults who display and depend upon patterns of behavior that are oral in nature, such as smoking, overeating, "biting" sarcasm, may be said to have oral personalities or to have some degree of oral fixation. Freud felt that the more strongly fixated an individual was at a given psychosexual stage, the more likely he was to

display behaviors typical of that stage, and the more likely he was to regress to that stage when he was under stress. Thus, Freud viewed forms of psychosis where the individual becomes totally dependent on others for his care and ceases to speak as conditions involving almost complete regression to the oral stage.

Freud assumed that the anus and the stimuli associated with eliminating and withholding feces were central to the second year or two of a child's development, and so he called this period the *anal* stage. The critical feature of this period is toilet training, and Freud thought anal fixation resulted from either overly rigorous or overly indulgent toilet-training practices. Fixation at the anal stage is indicated in adulthood either by excessively "tight," controlled behavior or by very "loose," disorderly behavior. Individuals who are (for example) stingy, obstinate, highly organized, and overly concerned with cleanliness and small details are characterized as *anal retentive* personalities. Those who are (for example) sloppy, disorganized, or overly generous may be labeled *anal expulsive*.

Following the anal stage (at about age 4), the genitals become the primary source of pleasure and the child enters the *phallic* stage. As the name implies, Freud paid more attention to psychosexual development in the male than in the female. He theorized that during the phallic stage the young boy begins to have sexual desires toward his mother and wants to eliminate his father so that he will not have to compete with him. Because these desires parallel the plot of the Greek tragedy *Oedipus Rex*, Freud characterized them as the *Oedipus complex*. Because the child fears that he will be castrated for having such incestuous and murderous desires, he normally resolves the conflict and its resultant anxiety by repressing his sexual desires toward his mother, attempting to imitate or *identify* with his father, and ultimately finding an appropriate female sex partner. Freud outlined a parallel though less clearly specified process for girls involving what he called the *Electra complex* (named after another Greek play). Here, the girl desires her father and rejects her mother. She must resolve this situation by repressing her incestuous feelings, identifying with her mother, and eventually finding an appropriate male sex partner.

Freud believed that successful resolution of the conflicts inherent in the phallic stage was crucial to healthy personality development. Identification with the parent is the beginning of superego development and of the incorporation of sex-typed behaviors. But conflict resolution at this stage is extremely difficult. Freud thought fixation at the phallic stage was very common and was responsible for a variety of later interpersonal problems, including aggression and various sex "deviations" such as exhibitionism.

Following the phallic stage, the child enters a sort of dormant period that lasts until the onset of puberty. This is called the *latency* period and is characterized by a lack of sexual interest.

During adolescence, the child matures physically and sexually and begins the *genital* period, which lasts through the adult years. Pleasure is again focused in the genital area, but the individual seeks more than the self-satisfaction characteristic of the phallic stage. If all has gone well in the earlier psychosexual stages, the individual seeks to establish stable, long-term sexual relationships that take into account the needs of others.

Freud assumed that, because so much of the individual's personality operates at the unconscious level, the individual cannot be relied upon to report his own personality accurately. Thus, he and others who followed him developed special methods of assessing the unconscious aspects of personality functioning. The main problem as Freud saw it was to get around the ego defense mechanisms that prevent unconscious material from surfacing. In his early attempts to do this, he interviewed patients while they were under hypnosis. Later he employed procedures such as free association, the analysis of "accidental" behavior, and the interpretation of dreams (see Chapter 12). In more recent years, projective tests such as the Rorschach Inkblot Test and the TAT have been developed and employed as another approach to exploring the unconscious (see Appendix C).

Variations on Freud's Theory

Freud's original ideas have gone through many changes over the years since he first enunciated them. In fact, Freud himself was constantly altering, editing, and supplementing his views, so that it is possible to speak of many editions of his theory. He did cling to a few of his basic principles, however, notably the instinctual basis of human behavior (emphasizing sex and aggression); and it was on this point that many of his prominent followers ultimately broke with him. Each of them took Freud's ideas and developed them in a slightly different way. The result is not only a multitude of neo-Freudian theories but also the evolution of new therapeutic emphases. Generally speaking, these variations on Freud's theory tended to deemphasize the instinctual basis of human behavior and pay more attention to environmental factors, especially the influence on the individual's social situation.

Here we will briefly consider a few of the many approaches that grew out of Freud's groundwork (see also "Recommended Additional Readings").

Erik Erikson.   In many respects Erik Erikson followed Freud, but Erikson saw the need to highlight the role of social factors in the development of personality. Accordingly, he outlined a sequence of *psychosocial* development that is more elaborate than Freud's psychosexual stages and also more socially oriented. Erikson's eight developmental stages, each characterized by a particular crisis or problem to be solved and each resulting in a particular psychosocial outcome, are discussed in detail in Chapter 7.

Alfred Adler.   One of the first of Freud's colleagues to reject the instinct theory of behavior was Alfred Adler. He developed instead an approach called *individual analysis*, which assumed that the most important factor in the development of personality is that each person begins life in a completely helpless, inferior position. Adler believed that the individual's subsequent behavior represents a "striving for superiority" (first within the family, then in the larger social world) and that the way in which each person seeks superiority constitutes his *style of life*. He thought adaptive life styles were characterized by cooperation, social interest, courage, and common sense, while maladaptive styles of life involved undue competition, lack of concern for others, and the distortion of reality. For Adler, maladaptive life styles and the behavior problems they cause are due not to unresolved conflicts but to mistaken ideas or basic *misconceptions* that the person has about the world. For example, a child may discover that a good way to exert control over others (and thus gain some feeling of superiority) is to be very dependent on them. Over time, he may develop the misconception that he is a "special case" who cannot deal with the world independently. Accordingly, a life style may evolve in which the person is always sick, hurt, frightened, or handicapped in some other way and therefore demands attention and special consideration from others.

Otto Rank.   Like Adler, Otto Rank disagreed with Freud's emphasis on sex and aggression as the bases of human behavior. But while Adler emphasized inferiority and striving for superiority, Rank focused on the developing person's basic dependency and inborn potential for growth and independence. Rank thought the *trauma of birth* was very significant because it involved an abrupt transition from the passive, dependent world of the fetus where no demands are made (the unborn child does not even have to breathe) to a chaotic outside world that requires ever-increasing independence. Thus, birth provides the first example of what Rank considered to be a basic human conflict between the desire to be dependent and the need to be independent. Rank felt that the appearance of behavior problems indicated that this conflict was not adequately resolved.

Some Problems with Psychodynamic Theories

Freud's influence is hard to overestimate. His concepts are so well known that they have become a part of our language and culture. It is not uncommon to hear people refer to "Freudian slips," unconscious motivation, the Oedipus complex, and psychoanalysis in everyday conversation. However, Freud's theory has also received strong criticism, mainly on the grounds that his concepts (such as id, ego, superego, defense mechanisms, and the unconscious) are elaborate abstractions that cannot easily be measured. The techniques designed to assess personality and personality functioning in Freudian terms have not shown themselves to be very reliable or valid. The fact that the entire basis for Freud's approach was his experiences with a relatively small number of case studies (a few patients and Freud himself) rather than experimental research has prompted the criticism that psychodynamic formulations are unscientific and do not apply to the bulk of the human population. Critics also point out that many of Freud's assumptions about personality are difficult or impossible to evaluate because the results of any test can be interpreted according to his theory. For example, if psychoanalytic interviews or projective test results lead to the conclusion that a person harbors strong unconscious feelings of hostility toward the whole world, subsequent hostile behavior would be interpreted as evidence for the breakthrough of unconscious impulses, thus confirming the original hypothesis. But *lack* of subsequent hostile behavior could also provide evidence for underlying hostility because it could be seen as a defense mechanism (reaction formation). It has also been argued that psychodynamic personality theories make it too easy to interpret behavior as indicative of pathology and thus create problems where none existed before. For instance, a person might be called anxious and insecure if he shows up for work early, resistant and hostile if he is late, and compulsive if he is right on time.

"Remember that foul mood I was in this morning?"

Some personality theorists, notably Walter Mischel, have downplayed the role of lasting, overriding traits in personality. Rather, they focus on the particular situation confronting an individual as being the major determinant of behavior. For example, rather than characterize the harried housewife as being hostile, they believe that it makes more sense to say that in the morning, when things were going badly, she behaved in a hostile manner, whereas in the afternoon, after a pleasant and rewarding day of shopping, she behaved more civilly. Thus, she is not a "hostile" person, characterized by a permanent trait of hostility, but her hostile behavior is under the control of the particular situation. As in most disputes of this kind, both the trait position and the situational position are probably at least partially correct.

Social Learning Theories

Instead of emphasizing intrapsychic conflicts, instincts, or dispositions (such as enduring traits), social learning theories focus on *behavior* and the environmental conditions that affect it. From this point of view, personality is the sum total of the individual's behavior rather than some hypothetical structure which that behavior reflects. Social learning theories also assume that behavior (personality) is determined primarily through *learning*, which takes place in a social context. These two basic assumptions have resulted in an approach to personality that accounts for both variation and consistency in behavior. This approach explains *differences among people* in terms of each person's unique learning history—for example, under stress conditions such as an exam, a person who has learned to deal with problems by depending upon others may seek to cheat while another who has been rewarded for self-reliance may not. Social learning theories view *consistencies* in a particular person's behavior as a function of generalized learning—for example, a person may learn to be calm and serious in most situations if that behavior has been consistently rewarded over many years and under a wide variety of circumstances. Further, these theories seek to understand *inconsistencies* in a particular person's behavior and other "unpredictable" behavioral phenomena in terms of the concept of *behavioral specificity*—the idea that behavior changes to fit particular circumstances. Walter Mischel summarizes this point well:

Consider a woman who seems hostile and fiercely independent some of the time but passive, dependent, and feminine on other occasions. What is she really like? Which one of these two patterns reflects the woman that she really is? Is one pattern in the service of the other, or might both be in the service of a third motive? Might she be a really castrating lady with a facade of passivity—or is she a warm, passive-dependent woman with a surface defense of aggressiveness? Social behavior theory suggests that it is possible for the lady to be *all* of these—a hostile, fiercely independent, passive, dependent, feminine, aggressive, warm, castrating person all in one (Mischel, 1969). Of course which of these she is at any particular moment would not be random and capricious; it would depend on discriminative stimuli—who she is with, when, how, and much, much more. But each of these aspects of her self may be a quite genuine and real aspect of her total being. **(Mischel, 1971)**

There are many social learning theories of personality. Although they often differ substantially among themselves with respect to certain specifics, all of them share several common characteristics: (1) an emphasis upon *measurable behavior* as the content of personality, (2) stress upon the importance of environmental as opposed to hereditary influences or other "givens" in personality and personality development, (3) attention to experimental research on the behavior

of both human and nonhuman organisms, and (4) use of scientific methods to evaluate hypotheses about behavior and personality change techniques. The main differences among these theories are the type of learning process emphasized (for example, classical versus instrumental; see Chapter 4) and the degree to which cognition (thinking) plays a role in learning.

Social Learning and Motivational Drives

One of the earliest social learning theories was developed as part of an attempt to translate or recast Freud's clinically derived concepts into a language that was consistent with experimental data on human and animal learning. The task of explaining Freudian phenomena in learning theory terms was undertaken in the 1940's by John Dollard and Neal Miller. They began with the assumption that human beings enter life not with instincts but with primary *needs*—for food, water, oxygen, and so forth—that must be satisfied. They further assumed that each person *learns* to satisfy these needs (and others based on them) in somewhat different ways, thus leading to the development of individualized patterns of behavior (personality). For example, an infant's need for food results in strong internal stimuli, such as hunger pangs. Dollard and Miller called such primary stimuli *drives* because they motivate or impel behavior aimed at satisfying primary needs. Such behavior is usually fairly diffuse and generalized—for example, crying and thrashing. This activity may bring a parent into the room with food, which reduces the hunger drive and *rewards* or *reinforces* the behavior leading to it. In this way, each child learns to repeat those particular behaviors that result in or are associated with reduction of primary drives.

Of course, Dollard and Miller did not assume that all human behavior is learned as a function of reduction of primary drives. The behaviors necessary to drive a car, for example, are reinforced by praise, encouragement, and other social rewards that do not involve primary drives in an obvious way. Dollard and Miller postulated that these kinds of rewards reduce *secondary* or *learned* drives. Citing much careful laboratory data, they asserted that humans can "learn to need" things (such as praise) and the resulting acquired drives can motivate behavior in the same fashion as primary drives.

Dollard and Miller dealt with many Freudian concepts, but instead of treating them as intrapsychic events they treated them as environmentally determined and experimentally researchable phenomena. For example, they saw

Social learning theorists contend that the best predictor of future behavior is past behavior in the same or similar situations.

conflict not as a clash between or among id, ego, and superego, but as the result of competition between incompatible behavioral tendencies. They divided these tendencies into two types: *approach* tendencies, meaning behavior the person wants to engage in, and *avoidance* tendencies, behavior a person wants to avoid. A person is *in conflict* when he must (1) choose between two positive activities (approach-approach conflict), such as going to a party or attending a film; (2) choose between two negative activities (avoidance-avoidance conflict), such as mowing the lawn or taking out the trash; or (3) choose whether to do something that has both positive and negative aspects (approach-avoidance conflict), such as deciding whether to be with someone who is sexually attractive but not very considerate.

Perhaps the most difficult situations to resolve are those known as double approach-avoidance conflicts. Here the person faces two alternatives, each of which has both positive and negative features. If you have ever had to make a choice about which of two restaurants to visit when one is nearby but expensive while the other is less costly but inconveniently located, you know how it feels to be in such a conflict. Choosing which college to attend often results in double (or triple) approach-avoidance conflicts because one school may be prestigious but very large and impersonal, while another is smaller and more friendly but less well-known for quality.

Much as Freud had done, Dollard and Miller emphasized the role of conflict and anxiety in the appearance of behavior disorders, but they employed learning theory terminology. Thus, in their terms, a "neurotic" conflict could be analyzed as follows: A person's approach tendency toward a member of the opposite sex may be thwarted by a simultaneous avoidance tendency, such as anxiety based on negative social experiences or parental teachings warning against the expression of sexual desires. The closer the person gets to contact with the feared-yet-desired situation, the stronger the avoidance tendency becomes, and he retreats, thus reducing anxiety but allowing the approach tendency to reappear. The individual in such a conflict may "seesaw" back and forth between approach and avoidance. In some cases he may experience such great psychological discomfort that he needs therapy to strengthen the approach tendencies, or reduce the avoidance tendencies, or both.

The Role of Operant Conditioning

Notice that although Dollard and Miller's system eliminated some of Freud's intrapsychic ideas, it retained other inferred constructs such as "drive" and "anxiety." Thus, their theory depended to some extent on hypothesized internal processes and mechanisms to account for personality. Quite a different social learning approach has been presented by the well-known American psychologist B. F. Skinner. He views personality as learned, but assumes that inferred constructs such as "anxiety," "drive," "motive," "conflict," "need," and the like are unnecessary to account for and understand the learning involved. Instead, Skinner asserts that careful observation of and experimentation with the learned relationships between environmental stimuli and observable behavior will ultimately allow for a complete picture of the development, maintenance, and alteration of human behavior (recall here the discussion in Chapter 4 of operant conditioning, which is central to Skinner's view of behavior). This means that, instead of theorizing about personality (behavior) and introducing unobservable constructs (such as ego, drive, or trait) to explain it, one should simply observe the ways in which behavior relates to its consequences and then describe these relationships. This method of learning about behavior is called *functional analysis* because it involves analyzing the causative, or functional, relationships between the environment and behavior.

As an example of how Skinner's functional analytic approach eliminates inferred constructs, let us consider the notion of motive or need. Dispositional theorists assume that individuals "have" needs or motives whose existence is inferred from behavior—for example, aggressive behavior reflects the need for dominance. Skinner would focus instead on the functional relationship between, say, aggressive behavior and its consequences. He would argue that a person's aggressive behavior simply reflects the fact that such behavior has in the past been rewarded or reinforced, that is, has been operantly conditioned. No further explanation in terms of internal dispositions is necessary. Thus, Skinner would say that the person in question has *learned* through operant conditioning to behave aggressively, not that he "has" a need to be aggressive.

The same approach can be used when talking about concepts like drive. Instead of saying that a person who has not eaten in 48 hours "has" a strong hunger drive, you could simply observe that after such deprivation food is a stronger reward than if no deprivation had occurred. "Hunger" can then be defined not in terms of "drive strength" but in terms of the number of hours since the person's last meal.

Similarly, behavior disorder may be understood without reference to inferred constructs. A person who spends the day silently staring into space, fails to maintain control over bowels and bladder, and must be fed from a spoon would not be considered "psychotic," "regressed," or "mentally ill." Instead, Skinner's version of the social learning approach to personality would assume that the individual had gradually developed these "disordered" behaviors

Figure 9–6
Albert Bandura

"During the past half century, learning-theory approaches to personality development, deviant behavior, and psychotherapy have suffered from the fact that they have relied heavily on a limited range of principles based on . . . studies of animal learning or human learning in one-person situations. . . . It is necessary to extend and modify these principles and to introduce new principles that have been established and confirmed through studies . . . of dyadic [two-person] and group situations" (Bandura and Walters, 1965).

as a function of various kinds of reinforcement, probably over a long period of time.

Like other versions of social learning theory, Skinner's approach to personality not only promotes understanding of the ways in which behavior is learned (how it relates to its environment), but also leads directly and logically to appropriate "treatment" procedures. As one might expect, these procedures tend to focus on observable behaviors

Figure 9–7
Learning aggression by imitation

In specialized situations, there is little doubt that children will imitate the aggressive actions of adult models. Here are some pictures from a study by Bandura, Ross, and Ross (1963) that is now a classic experiment. In the top row you see an adult model exhibiting four different ways to hurt a Bobo clown doll. The next two rows show a boy and a girl duplicating the model's efforts.

as "treatment targets" and on the use of operant conditioning principles in the production of behavior change (see Chapter 12).

The Role of Cognition and Imitation

Although Skinner's functional analytic approach is very influential and has attracted many ardent followers, it has also provoked a considerable amount of antagonistic reaction. Many theorists, even within the social learning camp, feel that Skinner pays too little attention to cognitive or symbolic processes in the development and maintenance of personality (behavior). One of the most prominent of these theorists is Albert Bandura, a psychologist at Stanford University who has produced a great deal of research evidence about the ways in which cognitive activity and social influences contribute to learning.

Bandura is probably best known for his work on *observational learning*, in which he has shown that human beings can learn new behaviors without obvious reward or reinforcement and even without the opportunity to practice. All that may be required is for the person to observe another individual (called a *model*) engage in the to-be-learned behavior; later, especially if the model was rewarded for his performance, the observer may also display the new response. For example, children may learn how to display aggression by observing someone else do so. In one well-known experiment (see Figure 9–7) Bandura and his colleagues arranged for preschool children to observe models either vigorously attacking or sitting quietly near an inflatable Bobo doll. In subsequent tests, the children who observed aggression tended to match the model's behavior quite precisely, while those who had seen a passive model tended to be nonaggressive.

Presidential Perceptions

Time—One of Richard Nixon's most persistent Watergate defense themes is that he will never do anything to weaken the institution of the presidency. A study of children's attitudes toward the office by Political Scientist F. Christopher Arterton of Wellesley College indicates, however, that the Watergate scandal already has profoundly altered at least one small group of the younger generation's perceptions of the presidency.

Writing in the current issue of *Political Science Quarterly*, Arterton cites a national 1962 study that indicated that children in the third, fourth and fifth grades overwhelmingly idealized the President, viewing him as "benevolent, omniscient, omnipotent, protective, infallible, diligent and likable." The professor's own much more limited current study of 367 children in the same grades in an upper-class Boston suburb (whose parents voted almost 2 to 1 for Nixon in 1972) shows a complete reversal. The President is now seen as what Arterton calls "truly malevolent, undependable, untrustworthy, yet powerful and dangerous." Where only 7% of the fourth-graders said of President Kennedy in 1962 that "he is not one of my favorites," 70% of Arterton's fourth-graders now hold that negative opinion of Nixon.

Attitudes as well as overt behaviors may be strongly influenced through modeling and reinforcement.

Thus, a major thrust of Bandura's theory is its emphasis upon *vicarious processes*, that is, processes involving observation and imitation of others. For Bandura personality develops not only as a function of what the individual learns directly (through reward or punishment) but also through observation of other people's behavior and its consequences and an understanding of how those consequences could apply to him. According to Bandura, vicarious processes can result in a wide variety of behavioral effects, including acquisition of new responses, as we saw in the Bobo experiment; inhibition or disinhibition of already learned behaviors, as when a person violates a "don't walk" sign after watching someone else do so; and facilitation or prompting of behavior, as when, during gasoline shortages, a long line of cars forms at a closed station after a single prankster pulls up to the pumps.

It is important to note that although Bandura's theory emphasizes the role of observational and cognitive processes in learning, it also recognizes the importance of both social and primary reinforcement as factors influencing the continued performance of new or altered behaviors. Thus, for example, a person may learn how to meet attractive members of the opposite sex by watching others do so successfully, but unless the approach actually leads to positive consequences (once in a while, at least), it will ultimately be abandoned.

Cognition and Expectancies

The role of cognitive variables has an even stronger place in the social learning theory of Julian B. Rotter, who places strong emphasis on the importance of expectancies in the development, maintenance, and alteration of behavior. In Rotter's system, the probability that a given behavior will occur is dependent on (1) what the person expects will happen following the response and (2) the value the person places upon that outcome. Thus, a person will pay for a ticket if he expects that this will result in admission to a movie theater (outcome) and if the film being shown is of interest (value). Rotter assumes that the expectancies and values that influence, organize, and alter behavior (personality) are acquired through learning. Therefore, in order to "have" an expectancy about an outcome or make a judgment regarding its value, a person must have some direct or vicarious experience with equivalent or similar situations in the past.

Social Learning Approaches to Personality Assessment

In our earlier discussion of dispositional and psychodynamic personality theories, it was clear that the various strategies they employed to measure personality, such as dream analysis and projective techniques, assumed that a person's responses to assessment procedures provide *indications* or *signs* of underlying personality traits or characteristics. Social learning approaches to personality measurement begin with radically different assumptions. Because they view behavior and personality as virtually identical, they do not seek to learn about presumed underlying traits or constructs but focus instead on careful, systematic attempts to assess (1) *how* the person in question behaves and (2) the environmental and other circumstances that influence that behavior.

Thus, an individual's response to Rorschach inkblot cards would be assumed to tell us not about unconscious processes but about how that person behaves during psychological testing. In other words, the social learning approach treats responses to any sort of personality assessment procedure as a *behavior sample* that is useful in making predictions about future behavior in similar or related

circumstances, not as a *sign* of broad, generalized personality characteristics (see Appendix C). Because of this orientation, social learning personality assessment procedures tend to focus on direct observation of behavior rather than traditional "paper and pencil" tests. Those questionnaires that are used tend to be direct and straightforward, asking the testees simply to provide information about the effects of environmental stimuli on their behavior. Examples of this sort of "test" are the Fear Survey Schedule (Geer, 1965; Wolpe and Lang, 1964), which simply asks respondents to rate the degree to which they fear a wide variety of objects and situations, and the Reinforcement Survey Schedule (Cautela and Kastenbaum, 1967), which asks respondents to rate the degree to which they enjoy a variety of activities, such as dancing, talking to friends, and eating.

There are several types of direct *behavioral observation* procedures employed by social learning theorists. Some of these ask the individual to act as his own observer. This is especially common when adult behaviors that typically occur in the natural environment are of particular interest. Examples include asking individuals to keep records of the number of cigarettes they smoke or the frequency and duration of sleep disturbances. A clinician who employs such assessment techniques may seek to understand a client's "depression" or "anxiety attacks" by asking that client to specify the behaviors and feelings that make up such states and to keep track of their frequency and the environmental conditions that precede, accompany, and follow them. This type of personality assessment leads to precise statements about behavior (such as "This person behaves in a depressed fashion on the average of three times per week") instead of labels ("This person is a depressive"). Further, this technique can provide clues to the factors contributing to the problem. For example, a careful behavioral analysis of "depression" often reveals that episodes of discomfort tend to be associated with periods during which the client does not have access to very many enjoyable activities. An increase in such activities might thus become part of an overall treatment program.

In other forms of social learning personality assessment, specially trained personnel make systematic observations of many aspects of the behavior of children or adults. This may involve simply watching a child in a large playroom containing a wide variety of toys, games, and other materials. Recording the relative amounts of time the child spends engaged in each of the various

"Hi, Jack."

Mechanix Illustrated, November 1971. Reprinted from Mechanix Illustrated Magazine. Copyright 1971 by Fawcett Publications, Inc.

In addition to its significance for the development of personality, social learning also influences many events in our daily lives. One of Bandura's examples of how modeling affects society is the rapid increase in the number of hijackings in recent years. Hijacking was almost nonexistent a few years ago, and Bandura feels that the mass media's reports of such incidents provide models of the behavior, which others imitate. It is noteworthy that this imitation occurs even though the models (previous hijackers) have often been punished by society. Thus, reporting of deviant behavior (often with pictures or films) leads to an increase of the same behavior, regardless of the consequences to the model.

activities available allows the observer to determine the kinds of things that interest the child (and that might thus be usable as rewards in a later behavior change program). Notice that, instead of attempting to identify the child's internal needs, traits, or motives, the social learning approach seeks to identify the external stimuli that influence behavior.

Direct observations in other settings are also used to specify the degree to which people display problem behaviors. For example, nurses, aides, and other personnel in mental hospitals often use *behavior rating scales* to describe with precision the nature of patients' difficulties. Typically, staff members record behaviors on a periodic basis (called time sampling); they note the presence or absence of various categories of patient behavior, such as sitting, talking to others, reading, fighting, shouting, and sleeping. The data gained from these observations, summarized in terms of the frequencies with which certain behaviors occur, may then be combined with other observations regarding the circumstances and consequences associated with the behaviors.

Similar observational techniques are used to assess less severe problems, such as fears. Paul (1966) employed a time-sampling observation system called the timed behavioral checklist to assess the behavior of college students while they gave speeches. The investigator recorded on this checklist the presence or absence of 20 fear-related

behaviors in eight 10-second observation periods (see Figure 9–8). These data, along with additional observations on other reactions to speech giving, such as pulse rate, were employed to decide whether subjects needed treatment for speech anxiety.

Some Problems with Social Learning Theories

Social learning theories of personality have been criticized mainly on the grounds that their emphasis on learning as the basis for behavior results in a narrowing of their perspective. Critics often note that these theories pay too little attention to the influence of hereditary, physiological, and constitutional factors in determining human

Figure 9-8
The timed behavioral checklist for performance anxiety

Rater . . . . Name . . . .

Date . . . . Speech No. . . . . I.D. . . . .

Behavior observed	Time Period								
	1	2	3	4	5	6	7	8	Σ
1. Paces									
2. Sways									
3. Shuffles Feet									
4. Knees Tremble									
5. Extraneous Arm and Hand Movement (swings, scratches, toys, etc.)									
6. Arms Rigid									
7. Hands Restrained (in pockets, behind back, clasped)									
8. Hand Tremors									
9. No Eye Contact									
10. Face Muscles Tense (drawn, tics, grimaces)									
11. Face "Deadpan"									
12. Face Pale									
13. Face Flushed (blushes)									
14. Moistens Lips									
15. Swallows									
16. Clears Throat									
17. Breathes Heavily									
18. Perspires (face, hands, armpits)									
19. Voice Quivers									
20. Speech Blocks or Stammers									

Comments: ΣΣ

This checklist illustrates the way in which the social learning approach seeks to assess specific behavior problems, not generalized traits.

behavior. Others point out that not all experimental evidence supports the principles of learning on which these theories are based and that therefore these principles are not as clearly established as the learning theorists would have us believe. Furthermore, even where learning phenomena in animals are well known through laboratory research, they may not be analogous to the ways in which humans learn. For example, a cat faced with an extremely difficult or insoluble task may display a bizarre pattern of behavior called "experimental neurosis," but human neurotic behavior may not be learned in the same way.

Phenomenological Theories

So far, we have discussed personality theories that view human behavior as being primarily influenced by (1) underlying traits or needs, (2) intrapsychic events and conflicts, and (3) direct or vicarious learning. A fourth group of theories, called *phenomenological* or *cognitive*, rejects many of the basic assumptions of the other three approaches and asserts that the behavior of each human being at any given moment is determined primarily by that particular person's *perception of the world*. In other words, phenomenological theories assume that each person is unique because his view of reality is just a little different from anyone else's and that each person's behavior reflects that view as it exists from moment to moment. Thus, when two people listen to the same political speech, one may react favorably and plan to vote for the speaker, while the other may decide to vote for the speaker's opponent. These divergent reactions are viewed by phenomenologists as due not to the listener's personality traits, ego development, or reinforcement history, but to his individual perceptions of the candidate while he was speaking.

From this perspective, human beings are not passive "carriers" of personality or mere recipients of reinforcement, but active, thinking organisms that are responsible for and capable of making plans and choices about their behavior. Although phenomenological theories recognize the existence of biological needs, these are deemphasized in considering personality and its development. Instead these theories assume that people are born with a potential for growth that provides the impetus for behavior. Each person is seen as having an innate tendency to grow and develop into a fully mature individual, just as the seed contains the potential to be a flower. In contrast to Freud, who saw people as motivated by crude instinctual desires,

phenomenological theorists view the individual as a basically good organism that will naturally strive toward attainment of love, joy, creativity, harmony, and other positive goals.

Perhaps the most important implication of the phenomenological view of personality development, assessment, and change is that no one can truly understand another person's behavior unless he can perceive the world through that person's eyes. Accordingly, phenomenological theories, like social learning theories, reject the concept of mental illness and other pejorative labels for behavior that appears strange, unusual, or unexpected. Instead, these theories assume that all human activity is normal, rational, and sensible *when viewed from the point of view of the person being observed*. Thus, people who are violently hostile toward others are seen not as "sick" or "disordered" but as simply acting in accordance with their perception of other people.

Phenomenological theories have evolved from several sources. In part, they represent a reaction against Freud. In their rejection of the importance of instincts and their emphasis on the uniqueness of the individual and his conceptions of the world, Adler and Rank anticipated phenomenological theories; their writings have influenced several modern phenomenologists. Attention to the individual's perception of reality was prompted, in part, by the existential philosophies of Heidegger, Kierkegaard, Sartre, and Camus, which assert that the meaning and value of life and everything in it is not intrinsic, but is provided by the perceiver. For example, a person is not "actually" beautiful or ugly; these qualities can only be assigned when someone else sees and reacts to the person in question. Thus, a different "reality" is in the eye of each beholder. This focus on the individual's view of reality was also sharpened by the writings of the Gestalt psychologists, who, as we saw in Chapter 3, emphasized that the human perceiver is an active participant in viewing the world, not just a "receiving station."

Rogers' Self Theory

Perhaps the best-known example of phenomenological approaches to personality is the *self* theory of the American psychologist Carl Rogers. Many of Rogers' basic propositions about personality are similar to those of other phenomenologists. For example, these statements from Rogers' writings (1951) are characteristic of all phenomenological theories: "Every individual exists in a continually changing world of experience of

**Figure 9–9
Carl Rogers**

"I have come to feel that the more fully the individual is understood and accepted, the more he tends to drop the false fronts with which he has been meeting life, and the more he tends to move in a direction which is forward" (Carl Rogers, 1961).

which he is the center." "The organism reacts to the field as it is experienced and perceived. This perceptual field is, for the individual, 'reality.'" "The organism reacts as an organized whole to this phenomenal field."

Rogers assumes that the one innate human motive is the tendency toward "self-actualization" and that this concept is sufficient to account for the appearance of all human behavior, from the most fundamental food seeking to the most sublime acts of artistic creativity. He has defined this innate quality as "the directional trend which is evident in all organic and human life—the urge to expand, extend, develop, mature—the tendency to express and activate all the capacities of the organism" (Rogers, 1961). Given this basic motive, Rogers views human personality (as reflected in behavior)

as the individual's efforts to actualize himself within the world as he views it.

As the person develops and interacts with the environment he begins to differentiate between the environment and the "self." In other words, each person becomes aware of a part of his experience that he recognizes as "I" or "me." According to Rogers, all of a person's experiences, including "self" experiences, are evaluated as positive or negative, depending on whether they are consistent or inconsistent with the self-actualizing tendency. The person evaluates experiences partly in terms of *direct* or *organismic feelings*, as when a child evaluates the experience of ice cream positively simply because of its taste, and partly through the *influence of others*, as when a young boy negatively evaluates the experience of touching his genitals even though it "feels good" because his mother told him that he was a "bad boy" to behave that way. Thus, the "self" or "self-concept" emerges not merely as a set of experiences but as a set of *evaluated* experiences, and the positive or negative value assigned to these experiences is influenced by the combination of direct evaluations and evaluations provided by other individuals.

Rogers postulates that human beings tend to act in ways that produce *positive regard* (evaluation) from others and that this allows them to have positive *self-regard*. When a person's behavior results in positive *direct* (organismic) experiences as well as positive regard from others there is no problem. For example, a child practices reading skills and experiences not only positive direct feelings based upon gaining competence, but also positive regard from a parent, such as "I am so proud of you." The result will probably be a positively evaluated self-experience, such as "I like to read." Here, the positive direct organismic experience is in accord with or, as Rogers puts it, *congruent* with the positive self-experience, and the child accurately perceives both his own behavior and his evaluation of it.

However, as in the example given above of the boy fondling his genitals, some behaviors may produce a positive organismic experience, but a negative reaction from others. When this happens, and especially when it happens early in life, the evaluations of others may overwhelm the individual's direct evaluation. Then, instead of developing a self-experience like "I enjoy masturbation but mother is opposed," the person may acquire the self-experience "I do not want to masturbate" or "I should not want to masturbate." Rogers theorizes that this uncomfortable discrepancy (or *incongruity*) between organismic experiences and self-experiences is caused by what he calls *conditions of worth:* feelings that one can only receive positive regard from others (and, ultimately, from the self) on a conditional basis, that is, when one behaves in certain prescribed ways. Conditions of worth are usually set up first by parents and others, but later by the person himself:

If an individual should experience only unconditional positive regard, then no conditions of worth would develop, self-regard would be unconditional, the needs for positive regard and self-regard would never be at variance with organismic evaluation, and the individual would continue to be psychologically adjusted, and would be fully functioning. **(Rogers, 1959)**

According to Rogers, recognition that one's feelings and/or behavior do not fulfill conditions of worth results in anxiety over potential loss of positive regard. To prevent this, the individual may seek to reduce incongruity by distorting or misperceiving reality or his own experience of it so that it fits the self-concept. For example, children are usually taught to behave in ways "appropriate" to their sex and may receive positive evaluations only when they display role-"appropriate" behavior. Thus, when a mother scolds her little boy for displaying emotional behavior (such as crying) and praises him for unemotional "masculine" reactions, she may be setting up conditions of worth. If the child actually feels better when expresses strong emotions than when he suppresses them, he may have to discount his experiences in order to conform to the requirements of the situation. Or he may distort his own personal reality—the fact that he feels better when expressing his emotions—by maintaining that anyone who is emotional is weak.

Rogers thinks that behavior disorders result from the individual's attempts to reduce incongruity by altering actual feelings and experiences so that they approximate the self-concept. The more incongruity and distortion, the more severe the disorder. Rogers' approach to treatment of psychological problems is aimed at helping people reduce incongruity without distorting reality.

Learning to feel feelings. Many of Rogers' notions about personality and personality change are similar to those present in the Gestalt therapy of Frederick S. (Fritz) Perls. Although Perls used terms and procedures that differ substantially from those of Rogers, and although he focused more on using

personality growth experiences than on articulating a formal, researchable personality theory, the basic ideas of Perls and Rogers are very similar. Perls believed that behavior problems arise when people deny or disown their feelings or experiences (that is, are incongruent, in Rogers' terms) or when they claim as their own feelings or ideas they have borrowed from others. Gestalt therapy, then, is oriented toward helping the person take responsibility for himself and experience or "get in touch" with genuine feelings. It is assumed that when this occurs, it is possible for individuals to face and resolve conflicts and internal inconsistencies of which they had been unaware. Application of the concepts and principles enunciated by Rogers and Perls (among others) has prompted widespread interest in and rapid growth of the wide variety of encounter and sensitivity groups available today.

Kelly's Personal Construct Theory

George Kelly developed a theory of personality that is of considerable interest, partly because it illustrates the ways in which aspects of the phenomenological approach are related to social learning formulations. Kelly's theory is extremely complex, but it is based on the single fundamental assumption that human behavior is determined by what he called *personal constructs*, or ways of predicting the world. In other words, Kelly believed that individuals act in accordance with their own unique set of expectations about the consequences of their behavior (note the similarity to Rotter). Thus, each person's set of personal constructs or predictions about life constitutes his personality and his reality, and guides his behavior. For example, a person may consider all power saws dangerous (as opposed to safe—constructs are always bipolar) and act accordingly by handling them with care. Such behavior reflects an accurate anticipation of the consequences of carelessness and thus *validates* the construct "Saws are dangerous."

For Kelly, human behavior is not "pushed or pulled" by instinctual desires, external reinforcement, or response tendencies, but instead reflects each individual's attempts to make sense of the world as he sees it. Kelly felt that, like the scientist who revels in the thrill of discovering why or how some phenomenon occurs and how that phenomenon can be controlled, each human being is seeking to be correct about the phenomenon called Life.

Like other phenomenologists, Kelly did not try to judge whether an individual's personality is "sick"

Figure 9–10
George Kelly

"It is only fair to warn the reader about what may be in store for him. The term *learning,* so honorably embedded in most psychology texts, scarcely appears at all. We are for throwing it overboard. There is no *ego*, no *emotion*, . . . no *reinforcement*. There are some brand-new psychological definitions. . . . Let us then, instead of occupying ourselves with man-the-biological-organism or man-the-lucky-guy, have a look at man-the-scientist" (Kelly, 1955, pages x–xi).

or "healthy" but attempted instead to understand things from that person's point of view. For Kelly this meant determining the set of constructs the individual uses to organize his behavior. To do this, Kelly developed the Role Construct Repertory (or REP) Test. The procedure involves asking the subject to provide a list of people and things that are important to him, to consider the items listed in groups of three, and to say, within each group, how two are like each other but different from the third. By carefully analyzing responses on this task, the skilled assessor can begin to see themes or constructs that underlie the way the subject sees the world. For example, if a person usually characterizes the similarities and differences between people in

terms of dominance versus submissiveness, that dimension may be one of his basic constructs, or ways of looking at others.

Kelly felt that behavior disorder results from faulty, inaccurate, or overly narrow construct systems. If a person has only a few broad constructs with which to anticipate and comprehend the vast number of events occurring around him, the behavior based upon those constructs may be inappropriate or ineffective in many situations. For example, a man who behaves on the basis of the construct that "all women are hostile" will probably deal with women in a fearful, disrespectful, disparaging, hostile fashion. The result may be similar responses from the women with whom the man comes in contact; these responses validate his construct but perpetuate problems in interpersonal relations.

Kelly believed that people are not helpless victims of their constructs but are instead capable of altering them in such a way as to allow their behavior to be more flexible, spontaneous, and adaptive. He therefore developed a therapeutic approach based on *constructive alternativism*. Basically, it involves asking the person in question to try to change disordered or maladaptive behavior by reorganizing and elaborating his personal constructs on an experimental basis. This usually involves two things: developing a description of the constructs and behavior of the person he would like to be and then spending time behaving on the basis of that ideal set of constructs. Therapy is a kind of experiment in which the client tries out and evaluates new constructs, roles, and behaviors. In this sense it resembles some procedures associated with the social learning approach to personality and personality change.

Some Problems with Phenomenological Theories

Critics of the phenomenological approach, like those of other approaches we have presented, argue that it is too narrow. They point out that by restricting attention to immediate conscious experience as the main determinant of behavior, phenomenologists fail to recognize the importance of unconscious motivation, reinforcement contingencies, situational influences, and the like. Another criticism is that phenomenological theories do not elaborate sufficiently on the ways in which personality develops; postulating an innate tendency toward growth or actualization that is assumed to "drive" the organism can account for development but it does not explain it. This brings up a related point of criticism: Phenomenological theories provide excellent *descriptions* of human behavior

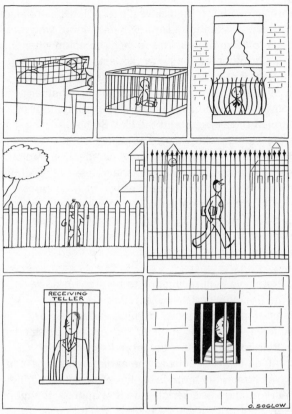

New Yorker, September 25, 1937. Drawing by O. Soglow; © 1937, 1965 The New Yorker Magazine, Inc.

The amusement of this cartoon lies in the absurdity of thinking that the man in the cartoon was a "victim of his biography." Kelly, too, had no use for such deterministic views and felt that man's behavior is greatly influenced by his ability to think, to judge, and, in so doing, to change. Thus Kelly thought that "no one needs to be completely hemmed in by circumstances."

but are not usually focused on scientific exploration of the functional causes of behavior. To say that people behave as they do because of their unique perception of reality or because they are seeking to actualize themselves is not very informative in terms of promoting understanding of the variables that are important in the development and alteration of human behavior. Finally, critics point out that many phenomenological concepts, like psychodynamic variables, are vague and therefore difficult or impossible to measure. Indeed, many phenomenological theorists (not including Rogers) see research on human behavior as relatively unimportant compared with activities designed to promote increased individual awareness. This emphasis on experiential rather than experimental

evidence has made phenomenological theories unpopular with those who favor a careful, controlled research approach. When human beings are described as "a momentary precipitation at the vortex of a transient eddy of energy in the enormous and incomprehensible sea of energy we call the universe" (Kempler, 1973), it is difficult to generate an easily testable hypothesis about their behavior.

What Does It Mean?

So far, we have looked at the ways in which psychologists of several theoretical persuasions conceive of the concept called personality. In this section, we shall examine the ways in which the concepts advanced by personality theorists affect the everyday behavior of other psychologists and the rest of society. As we shall see, personality is anything but an "ivory tower" concept. Personality theories have had significant impact on the lives of millions of people, whether they are aware of it or not.

Perhaps because some theorists conceive of personality as a collection of actually existing traits or because they talk about "personality structure" or the "distorted" or "disorganized" personality, the personality concept has achieved the status of an entity or thing in the minds of many psychologists and certainly in the minds of the general public. As noted at the beginning of this chapter, personality is commonly thought of as something that a person either does or does not possess and that he can turn on or off like a tap.

Of course, this view misrepresents and distorts the writings of many careful theorists, but the notion persists that we all carry around inside us a thing called personality that determines our behavior. On recommendation forms for some graduate schools, for example, there is an item asking the professor to rate the student's personality on a five-point scale from "poor" to "excellent." Presumably, this rating is thought to relate in some way to the student's potential as a graduate student.

Whether they conceive of personality in terms of traits, types, or intrapsychic events, people are very interested in attempting to assess the personality of other individuals, sometimes in order to describe them as they are and sometimes in order to make predictions about what they will do in the future.

Personality and Clinical Psychology

In clinical treatment settings, the therapist is interested in assessing the client's personality in order to understand the client's problems better.

Naturally, the clinician's overall approach to personality will dictate the kinds of diagnostic and treatment procedures he employs (see Chapters 11 and 12). Thus, when one chooses from among several sources of psychological assistance, it is important to know the personality strategy adopted by each practitioner.

However, the importance of personality in clinical psychology goes beyond attempts to assess the characteristics of individual clients. Considerable research activity focuses on exploring more general relationships between personality and the appearance of a variety of psychological and bodily disorders. For example, about 25,000 Americans kill themselves every year; about 1,000 of these are college students. Many were depressed prior to or at the time of suicide, but others apparently were not. Furthermore, countless thousands of people suffer depression but do not take their own lives. How can psychologists and others interested in suicide prevention tell who will commit suicide and who will not? Is there a "suicidal personality"?

Unfortunately, data from traditional personality tests, such as the Minnesota Multiphasic Personality Inventory (MMPI; see Chapter 12), provide no clear answer. For example, one study found that in terms of MMPI scores persons who had only thought of suicide were more deviant than either those who had actually made a suicide attempt or "controls" who had never even thought of self-destruction. In another study, MMPI data collected prior to successful suicides were not significantly different from those coming from nonsuicidal individuals.

Thus, if one thinks of personality as a collection of enduring traits or characteristics, an individual's personality can tell us little about his suicide potential. However, if one conceives of personality in terms of overt behavior and other observable information, the accuracy of predictions about suicide increases markedly. It is known, for example, that the greatest risk of suicide occurs among males who are over 50, divorced, living alone, have a history of suicide attempts and/or talking about suicide, are depressed or stressed, have no family or friends, and have worked out a clear and lethal plan for self-destruction. Of course, the presence of *all* of these factors is not necessary to prompt suicide, but knowing about them provides some guidelines for the professional and nonprofessional workers who deal with potentially suicidal individuals. In this sense, then, there is a "suicidal personality," but it can best be described in social learning rather than dispositional or trait terms.

In addition to being consulted about which people are likely to harm themselves, psychologists are also frequently asked to make judgments about who is likely to harm others. This is most common when a court or other legal agency requests advice on whether a criminal should be imprisoned or given treatment as an inpatient or outpatient, whether a convict or "criminally insane" patient should be paroled or released, and the like. Some professionals who view personality from a dispositional or psychodynamic perspective employ instruments such as the Rorschach test or the MMPI in the hope that test responses will provide clues about future criminal behavior. As was the case with suicide, however, no "criminal personality" has emerged from the use of such tests. Predictions based on them are often incorrect and can lead to tragic consequences.

Predictive accuracy tends to be greater, however, if the personality data collected relate to demographic and social learning variables. For example, the earlier in life an individual is arrested or tried for an offense, the more likely he is to continue criminal activity; the earlier in life a person leaves home, the more likely he is to continue a life of crime; the more serious the first offense, the more likely later crimes will be serious. Factors used to predict parole violation are also more closely related to overt behavior, that is, the actual crime a person has committed, than to personality traits. Murderers, rapists, and other violent criminals are least likely to violate parole; violations are most common among persons who have committed nonviolent crimes such as theft, burglary, or forgery.

Personality and Selection

Everybody will probably be subjected at some time to various kinds of selection procedures, for a job, military service, higher education, or other roles. Personality and personality assessment play a large role in such selection efforts because it is hoped that applicants' responses to various tests and interviews will allow accurate prediction of their future behavior. Some form of personality assessment is employed whenever one wishes to identify those individuals who will behave in some desired fashion.

On a college campus, for example, an informal but continuous process of selection-oriented personality assessment occurs. In fact, one study indicated that college students *say* that they choose social partners on the basis of personality, looks, and intelligence, in that order (however, tests have established that height, physical attractiveness, and proximity are actually the three major factors). Both

How To Tell Who Will Kill

Newsweek—On a warm August afternoon in 1964, Edmund Emil Kemper III, an unusually tall 15-year-old regarded by his classmates as a well-mannered but shy lone wolf, stood outside the screen door of his grandmother's house in North Fork, Calif., and calmly shot her to death with two bullets to the head. When his grandfather returned from the grocery store, the youth murdered him in similar fashion. Then he telephoned his mother to tell her what he had done. "I just wondered how it would feel to shoot Grandma," Kemper later told authorities. After examination by a court-appointed psychiatrist, the youth was duly committed to Atascadero State Mental Hospital.

Kemper proved to be a model inmate, and after serving five years he was remanded on the advice of staff psychiatrists to the California Youth Authority. In 1970, having turned 21, he was set free and dropped into obscurity in California's Santa Cruz County. Then last September, Kemper went to court to have his juvenile murder record permanently sealed, a formality that would make his acts of violence an official secret. Two court-appointed psychiatrists examined Kemper and declared him no danger to society. "He has made an excellent response to the years of treatment," one of them reported. "I see no psychiatric reason to consider him a threat to himself or any other member of society." Accordingly the records were ordered sealed.

But the psychiatrists were to be proved tragically wrong. Late last month, Kemper called Santa Cruz County authorities, and confessed that during a year-long reign of terror he had murdered and dismembered six young girls in the Bay Area—and that just three days before, he had slain his mother with a hammer and strangled one of her friends. As it happened, one of his victims, 15-year-old Aiko Koo, was murdered only four days before he reported for the examination that found him mentally well.

The Kemper case produced cries of indignation and outrage in the press and throughout northern California. Still vivid were memories of John Frazier, who murdered five Santa Cruz residents three years ago after his parents had unsuccessfully tried to get him committed. And just during the past year, Herbert Mullin, a youth who had been in and out of mental institutions much of his life, had been charged with ten killings.

Care
Inevitably, this latest epidemic of psychopathic slayings has set off a storm of virulent criticism—partly of the evolving trend toward releasing potentially dangerous mental patients and placing them in the care of community health centers, but particularly of the ability and competence of psychiatrists to judge when someone who has killed may be fit to return to society.

Most psychiatrists freely admit that the problem is almost unsolvable because specialists have no sure way of predicting antisocial behavior. "Kemper is a marvelous example of the fact that psychiatrists don't know everything," says Dr. Herbert McGrew, a staff psychiatrist at California's Napa State Hospital. "If you're right 75 per cent of the time, you're doing pretty well." For this reason, few of their colleagues would find fault with Kemper's as yet unidentified psychiatrists. "These guys weren't stupid," notes another Bay Area psychiatrist, "they were victims of the odds." "If a person appears to have changed to constructive behavior," says Dr. David Abrahamsen, a New York psychoanalyst and author of a new book on the subject, "The Murdering Mind," "you have no choice, you have to let him go." But Abrahamsen stresses that psychopaths should be followed up closely and for a protracted period after their release.

Hostility
Psychological tests like the Rorschach aren't much help in telling who will kill, most psychiatrists agree. "I get psychological test results all the time that say this guy is full of hostility and aggression," says McGrew, "so I let him go and he goes back to college and leads a perfectly normal life. The hostility and aggression are still there, and some time, under certain circumstances, they may come out. But when?"

Usually, court-appointed psychiatrists rely entirely on an interview, often cursory and seldom lasting more than an hour. And if the patient is clever enough, he can deceive the examiner. "All tests or examinations require a response," notes Dr. Bernard Diamond of the University of California, a founder of the American Academy of Psychiatry and the Law and one of the nation's outstanding forensic psychiatrists. "If a person lies or restricts his response, it may be impossible to determine whether he is mentally ill." "You develop a knack based on experience," adds Dr. Walter Rapaport, former California director of mental hygiene. "You interview the man knowing it's not what he says that's important, but how he responds, his attitudes, reactions and general behavior. You look for tender spots and probe them."

Diamond criticizes Kemper's psychiatrists not for their diagnosis, but for their willingness to go beyond this and suggest that the killer is normal. While one cannot predict that a person will commit violent crime, he notes, "there is no way, ever, that a psychiatrist can say that a person is *not* dangerous. If I find evidence of abnormality, I will say that. But I will not say that someone is normal." . . .

Personality theory has a long way to go before it can accurately predict antisocial behavior.

men and women collect personality data on members of the opposite sex from various sources. They observe the verbal and nonverbal behavior of individuals of interest by talking to them or watching them as they interact socially with others—Did she talk about her contraceptive pills? Did he talk about himself all the time? They listen carefully to the reports of those who know the "target" individuals—"Believe me, Jack, she is all show, no go!"; "Listen, that guy is a smooth talker but basically a real jerk." And they look for other clues, such as manner of dress, grooming habits, type of car owned, and the like. They then summarize this information in some fashion and use it to predict "target" persons' behavior and to guide decisions about initiating or accepting invitations for social contacts with them. Not surprisingly, selections made on the basis of this kind of personality assessment are not always satisfactory, especially when the predictions are based on presumably enduring personality traits. Anyone who has had to repulse unwelcome amorous advances or suffer through an evening filled with tense silences ("We always found things to talk about during class") knows that personality can be radically altered by situational factors.

Another option chosen by many (on or off the campus) is to allow a computer to collect and analyze personality data in a more formal fashion and "fix them up" with potentially compatible dates. The matching is usually based upon similarity of personality characteristics, interests, and attitudes, but at least two experiments have shown that such pairings do not result in any more satisfactory results than do random matches.

Selection errors in business and industry, where many decisions involving hiring and promotion are made each year, are far more costly than errors in selection of social companions. Accordingly, companies of many kinds and sizes spend significant amounts of time and money to develop employee selection procedures. Some kind of personality assessment usually plays a part in these procedures. For example, IBM requires potential employees to have an initial interview, fill out a formal application, take a variety of ability and personality tests, have a second interview, provide letters of reference, and pass a physical examination.

The personality tests most commonly employed in industrial selection procedures include projective tests like the Rorschach test (especially in executive selection, even though the evidence against their validity and usefulness is strong) and self-report inventories like the MMPI and the Guilford-Zimmerman Temperament Survey, which asks respondents to answer questions such as whether they start a new project with enthusiasm. By and large, self-report inventories of personality do not fare well in industrial settings:

A dismal history has been recorded by personality tests. There have been a few scattered successes with some modern techniques, but on the whole the typical personality questionnaire, test, or inventory has not proved to be useful. In many of them, the "right" answers . . . are so obvious that everyone comes out a model of healthy adjustment. **(Barrett, 1963)**

It should be noted that any test, psychological or otherwise, is only as good as the test administrator. Part of the problem in industry stems from the use of inexperienced and untrained examiners.

As usual, somewhat better results seem to come from test batteries that view personality not only in terms of traits but also in terms of overt behavior. For example, Sears, Roebuck developed a test battery for selecting executives based not on a theoretical measure of personality but on the characteristics of successful and unsuccessful executives. The company first decided how "good" executives behave, built a test that discriminated "good" from "bad" executives, and then used the test to hire or promote new executives. The results have been assessed as excellent.

As we might expect, part of the Sears test battery measures overt behavior under simulated job-relevant stress conditions. This "stress technique" is employed by other companies as well, such as AT&T, and is based on procedures developed during World War II by the Office of Strategic Services (OSS) in its officer selection program. Candidates may be tested individually or in groups, but the common characteristic of the approach is that individuals must attempt to accomplish work, such as solving a complex problem, while under some form of pressure and while being observed by testers. One group stress-testing procedure had the following results:

Some candidates panic and disrupt the group with frequent and unhelpful reminders of the deadline, some others lose their tempers, become hopelessly confused, or refuse to abandon obsolete plans. The visible contrasts sharpen between the steadier, more flexible, and even-tempered men and those who can't operate under pressure. **(Albrook, 1968)**

The purpose of this kind of personality assessment is not to make candidates uncomfortable but to identify behaviorally those who will be unlikely to handle stress well under actual employment conditions. This saves both the candidate and the company discomfort in the long run.

NFL Players Oppose Psychological Testing

Key Biscayne, Fla. (AP)—The National Football League Players Association called Friday for an end to personality and psychological testing of players by NFL teams because of questions involving the validity and use of such tests.

The association's board of representatives, consisting of one player from each NFL team, urged players not to participate in further testing programs.

In the cases where tests already have been given, the group's resolution asked that results be kept confidential and made available to the tested individual.

It also asked that players be given access to their entire personnel files when they leave football.

Executive Director Ed Garvey said that since professional football is such a short career, most players expect to seek other work after leaving the game.

"If there is damaging information in those files and it is available to employers or to government agencies . . . the player should have the right to see what is in that file to find out whether there are unsupported allegations against him as an individual."

Center Bill Curry of the Baltimore Colts, a member of the executive committee, said he could cite several instances in which coaches have misinterpreted information from the tests and mishandled players. He said many coaches weren't qualified to help in personality problems.

Association President John Mackey, also of the Colts, said test results should not be used to determine if a player makes a team. That should be determined by performance on the field, he said. . . .

Almost every conceivable type of employer has used personality tests in an effort to improve the productivity of the organization. Basically the idea is to select employees in a way that will maximize production by improving morale, decreasing turnover rates, decreasing absenteeism, and so forth. The factors involved for football players are of course different than for assembly-line workers. Because such testing procedures can have great impact on the employee, and because there is always a possibility of misuse of the techniques, such programs raise moral and ethical questions that are not easy to solve.

Personality assessment has begun to play a role in several other selection settings. For example, the personalities of prospective jurors and even football players are sometimes assessed in order to select those whose future performances match the goals of attorneys and head coaches. Whether this turns out

"I don't like the look of this at all."

New Yorker, October 24, 1964. Drawing by Richter; © 1964 The New Yorker Magazine, Inc.

to be a beneficial trend will depend largely on how carefully users of personality tests evaluate the validity and utility of their procedures. Assessment for the sake of assessment does no one any good, and because personality measurement can constitute an invasion of privacy, it should at least be restricted to spheres where it is clearly demonstrated to be useful.

Personality and Early Experience

As noted in Chapter 7, a child's early experiences, such as physical contact and other tactile and social stimulation, have an influence on personality. Thus, the parents of a developing child are faced with many problems and decisions. Should the baby be fed via bottle or breast? When and how should weaning take place? Should the child be toilet-trained early or late, rigidly or permissively? Should the child's every wish be granted or should some frustration be experienced? Would the presence of additional children be beneficial to the child's personality development? Some of these issues are discussed in Chapter 7. It should be noted here, however, that the advice parents receive about such concerns as handling toilet training or feeding is usually rooted in a particular theory of personality.

As an example, consider the question of dealing with aggression. Some theories (notably the psychoanalytic) argue that the child is born with aggressive instincts or needs that should be given some direct or indirect expression in order to avoid development of maladaptive defense mechanisms or other problems. In marked contrast, social learning theorists assert that, like reading, expression of

Birth without Terror

New Times—. . . In *For Birth without Violence*, [Frederic] Leboyer contends—like a great many psychiatrists—that birth is about the most traumatic of human experiences. The trauma is heightened, he claims, by contemporary birth procedures: the glaring operating-room lights, the noise, the instantaneous cutting of the umbilical cord, the shaking of the newborn infant, the drops in the eyes, the cleaning of the mouth and ears. "I had participated in the births of 7,000 babies," says Leboyer, a short, white-haired, soft-spoken man, "before I realized that the first cry that everyone is so pleased to hear is actually a frightful scream of terror. Hell does not come at the end of life but at the very beginning. The newborn comes into a strange and new environment after what for him has been an agonizing struggle. He leaves the world of warmth and silence and darkness and enters one of coolness and clamor and light. No wonder he screams! And we are so alienated from nature that we smile, and take the scream as a sign of health."

Dr. Leboyer's alternative method of performing births is staggeringly obvious. He simply eliminates those environmental factors which he sees as being upsetting to the infant. His births are performed under strictly controlled conditions; the aim, above all, is to assure the serenity of the newborn.

The doctor recently made a film of one of his "nonviolent" (or "gentle") births, and it provides a documentary record of precisely how the Leboyer method works. As soon as the baby's head becomes visible to the attending physicians, the overhead lights in the operating chamber are dimmed and voices drop to whispers. The baby is then pulled out very slowly and with very great care. Once he emerges completely, the infant is deposited on his mother's belly, where he remains while the nurse strokes him gently (Country veterinarians do much the same thing, Leboyer points out, to soothe newborn colts.) After a few moments, the baby, on his back, unfolds his limbs like a flower opening to the sun.

About ten minutes later, after the baby has begun breathing normally, the doctor cuts his umbilical cord and deposits the child in a lukewarm bath—a comforting return to the environment from which the child has just emerged. According to Leboyer, the newborn infant—no more than 15 minutes old—actually appears to smile with pleasure in his bath. In fact, the baby in the film doesn't cry at all during the entire birth process. . . .

Almost lost in the commotion about the method itself is a question of potentially far greater importance: what effect "gentle births" will have on the infants themselves as they mature.

Leboyer is emphatic on this point. He agrees with legions of psychiatrists who maintain that many aggressive impulses may be traced to the terrors of birth, and he claims that babies brought into the world by his method make healthier human beings. As evidence, he points to a bulging file of letters from grateful mothers, all thanking him for having delivered such stable, well-adjusted children. "The baby you delivered," reads a typical one, "is not like my other children. She is much more serene and much calmer. She is gay, relaxed. She never seems scared of life."

No comprehensive studies—starting from infancy and featuring control groups and all the rest of it—have yet been conducted to test the method's effectiveness in creating emotionally healthy children. But Leboyer has been at it for seven years now, and potential subjects for comparative tests abound. As a matter of fact, a pair of French psychoanalysts have been digging around, and they plan to issue a report shortly.

Some people think the procedures through which we are brought into the world play a role in determining how we behave afterward.

aggression is learned and that by allowing the child to observe and imitate aggressive behavior parents may actually be teaching the child to be belligerent.

Concern over the effects of early experience on personality even extends into the delivery room. When a child is born, he faces a rather abrupt transition from the uterine environment to the outside world. Some people think the circumstances surrounding this event have an influence on subsequent personality development, and they raise questions about the best way to deliver an infant. For example, some people believe that traditional delivery room procedures (involving noise, bright lights, and, of course, the slapping of the infant) result in harmful psychological consequences; they contend that less traumatic methods should be used to deliver babies.

Personality and Education

The educational environment to which the child is exposed may be another significant factor in the development of personality. This means that parents must exercise as much care as they can in choosing a school for their child. Educators must be acutely aware of their potent influence (see Chapter 7). Many parents fear that what they perceive as the overly rigid programs of the traditional public schools will have an adverse effect on their children's personalities. Therefore, they seek alternative educational settings that promise greater freedom and flexibility. The staff at many "traditional" schools have the same concerns and have pushed for innovations that go far beyond straightforward presentation of "the three Rs."

As an example of how personality theory can

The Personalized Instruction Approach

This is a course through which you may move, from start to finish, at your own pace. You will not be held back by other students or forced to go ahead until you are ready. At best, you may meet all the course requirements in less than one semester; at worst, you may not complete the job within that time. How fast you go is up to you.

The work of this course will be divided into 30 units of content, which correspond roughly to a series of home-work assignments and laboratory exercises. These units will come in a definite numerical order, and you must show your mastery of each unit (by passing a "readiness" test or carrying out an experiment) before moving on to the next.

A good share of your reading for this course may be done in the classroom, at those times when no lectures, demonstrations, or other activities are taking place. Your classroom, that is, will sometimes be a study hall.

The lectures and demonstrations in this course will have a different relation to the rest of your work than is usually the rule. They will be provided only when you have demonstrated your readiness to appreciate them; no examination will be based upon them; and you need not attend them if you do not wish. When a certain percentage of the class has reached a certain point in the course, a lecture or demonstration will be available at a stated time, but it will not be compulsory.

The teaching staff of your course will include proctors, assistants, and an instructor. A proctor is an undergraduate who has been chosen for his mastery of the course content and orientation, for his maturity and judgment, for his understanding of the special problems that confront you as a beginner, and for his willingness to assist. He will provide you with all your study materials except your textbooks. He will pass upon your readiness tests as satisfactory or unsatisfactory. His judgment will ordinarily be law, but if he is ever in serious doubt, he can appeal to the classroom assistant, or even the instructor, for a ruling. Failure to pass a test on the first try, the second, the third, or even later, will not be held against you. It is better that you get too much testing than not enough, if your final success in the course is to be assured.

Your work in the laboratory will be carried out under the direct supervision of a graduate laboratory assistant, whose detailed duties cannot be listed here. There will also be a graduate classroom assistant, upon whom your proctor will depend for various course materials (assignments, study questions, special readings, and so on), and who will keep up to date all progress records for course members. The classroom assistant will confer with the instructor daily, aid the proctors on occasion, and act in a variety of ways to further the smooth operation of the course machinery.

The instructor will have as his principal responsibilities: (a) the selection of all study material used in the course; (b) the organization and the mode of presenting this material; (c) the construction of tests and examinations; and (d) the final evaluation of each student's progress. It will be his duty, also, to provide lectures, demonstrations, and discussion opportunities for all students who have earned the privilege; to act as a clearing-house for requests and complaints; and to arbitrate in any case of disagreement between students and proctors or assistants. . . .

All students in the course are expected to take a final examination, in which the entire term's work will be represented. With certain exceptions, this examination will come at the same time for all students, at the end of the term. . . . The examination will consist of questions which, in large part, you have already answered on your readiness tests. Twenty-five percent of your course grade will be based on this examination; the remaining 75% will be based on the number of units of reading and laboratory work that you have successfully completed during the term.   (Keller, 1968)

The personalized instruction approach is an alternative to the use of the traditional grading approach to student evaluation. In this system, students use evaluative feedback to guide them in their studying; grades are not simply labels attached to performance. This system was first used at the college level but is gaining acceptance elsewhere as well.

relate to educational practices, ask yourself about the functions and effects of academic grades. At first glance, they seem to provide a standardized way of evaluating students, identifying problems, and singling out excellence. But what do grades mean for the personality development of individual students? In Rogers' terms, they may contribute to setting up conditions of worth, because very often a child confuses evaluation of his *performance in school* with evaluation of himself *as a person*. From this perspective, it is easy to see that an individual might become test-anxious or overly competitive if grades become more important to him than they were ever meant to be.

An alternative to the foregoing approach to grading has evolved from the social learning orientation. It is based on the notion that grades should provide more than final evaluation of performance and that learning should take place in an environment that maximizes rewards for progress, does not punish errors, and allows each student to proceed at his own pace. The most fundamental assumption of this approach is that a student's academic progress is not determined by enduring personality characteristics, but by the nature of the educational environment. A leading proponent of this "personalized instruction" view put it this way: *"The student is always right.* He is not asleep, not unmotivated, not sick, and he can learn a great deal if we provide the right contingencies of reinforcement" (Keller, 1968).

Personality and Advertising

Soon after infancy children come under the influence of advertising; its impact will be more or less continuous throughout their lives. Therefore, it is important to understand that those who would have us use a particular product or service do not rely solely upon a clear presentation of its assets and benefits to sway our decision. Using some version of the dispositional or psychodynamic approach to personality, advertisers seek to understand the motives and psychological needs of their target population and to pitch their messages so that they appeal to those motives and needs. "Motivation research" has become an important part of the advertising industry and results in ads whose psychological aspects are subtle but often powerful. The assumptions of this approach are spelled out in a statement by a well-known motivation researcher:

Motivation research is the type of research that seeks to learn what motivates people in making choices. It employs techniques designed to reach the unconscious or subconscious mind because preferences generally are determined by factors of which the individual is not conscious.... Actually in the buying situation the consumer generally acts emotionally and compulsively, unconsciously reacting to the images and designs which in the subconscious are associated with the product. **(Quoted in Packard, 1957)**

One way advertisers have found to exploit consumers' personalities is to give their product a "personality" of its own. They assume that people will buy products whose "personality" matches their own actual (or desired) traits. For example, the early "personality" of Marlboro cigarettes was described

as "Mild as May" and the product did not sell. Changing Marlboro's "personality" to reflect masculinity, independence, and the values of the American West placed them among the best-selling cigarettes in the country.

Advertisers point to such results as an example of getting consumers to "identify" with their products. To put it another way, the advertiser often attempts to sell you something you may not need (or that may not be any different from competitive items) by associating it with desirable personality traits or with the fulfillment of presumed needs and motives. Usually, these traits, needs, and motives are unrelated to the actual nature of the product sold. For example, food freezer ads often sell "security" by emphasizing the amount of food one can stash away. Various kinds of boxed cake mixes sell self-worth and creativity, not by telling consumers to bake the cake "from scratch" (which would be truly creative), but by telling them to put in the eggs or milk—mixes to which the consumer adds only water are not accepted well. One ad man went so far as to equate creation of a cake with the symbolic birth of a child. No wonder we hear slogans like "Nothin' says lovin' like somethin' from the oven"!

Most adult-oriented ads place strong emphasis on the sexual benefits of products (whether there are any such benefits or not), usually by having them demonstrated by attractive, high-status models whose opposite-sex partners are often nearby just about to ravish them. The implication, of course, is that people just like these will be climbing into the consumers' beds if only they will buy a particular brand of clothing, beer, cigar, or cosmetic. Why else would Connie Stevens show up in a slinky outfit on a TV commercial for hardware? Or Ricardo Montalban try to convince you to buy a new car?

Summary

1. Personality is a broadly defined term that is used to describe and explain individual differences and stylistic consistencies in human behavior.

2. Intensive studies by psychologists over the last 100 years show that personality pervades every aspect of human behavior.

3. Many diverse theories have been proposed to explain personality. Each of them begins with a working definition of the concept and some basic assumptions about human behavior. There are many theoretical disagreements about the proper definition and the necessary assumptions.

4. These theories fall into four general classes: dispositional, psychodynamic, social learning, and

phenomenological. Each approach has strengths and weaknesses, and each seeks to provide a way of understanding personality as well as a means of assessing, investigating, and changing it.

5. Some dispositional theories assume that there is a small number of personality types, each of which has a unique set of general behavioral tendencies.

6. Dispositional theories see personality as being made up of characteristics, such as traits or needs, within the person which guide the individual's behavior.

7. Psychodynamic theories derive largely from Sigmund Freud's writings about psychoanalysis. They assume that personality is shaped by events and conflicts (many of them unconscious) taking place within the mind through the action of hypothesized internal structures known as the id, ego, and superego.

8. Social learning theories base their approach on the assumption that personality is essentially the sum total of each individual's learned behaviors, and not an independent structure that is merely reflected in behavior. According to social learning theory, "personality" depends on, and therefore may change with, the social context.

9. Dispositional, psychodynamic, and social learning theories differ mainly in whether they emphasize internal needs, environmental contingencies, or imitation and expectancies as major determiners of the kind of personality an individual develops. In contrast, phenomenological theories view personality as that pattern of cognitions and perceptions of reality, unique to each

individual, which guides behavior. To understand someone's personality, you must view things from that person's point of view.

10. Each kind of personality theory has shortcomings. No complete or universally accepted description and explanation of personality has yet been provided.

11. Nonetheless, there are applications of personality research to a variety of everyday problems. For example, personality research has clinical applications. Suicidal, criminal, and other "personality" types have been partially identified. Knowing what behavioral characteristics to look for in people can help prevent possible tragedies later.

12. Other applications of personality research include better techniques for selecting jobs, juries, and even dates, for selecting child-rearing methods, and for evolving educational procedures.

13. Finally, whether we like it or not, advertising and public relations agencies make effective use of personality and motivational principles in influencing our buying habits.

Recommended Additional Readings

Hall, C. S., & Lindzey, G. *Theories of personality* (2nd ed.). New York: Wiley, 1970.

Liebert, R. M., & Spiegler, M. D. *Personality: Strategies for the study of man* (rev. ed.). Homewood, Ill.: Dorsey Press, 1974.

Mischel, W. *Introduction to personality.* New York: Holt, Rinehart and Winston, 1971.

Munroe, R. L. *Schools of psychoanalytic thought.* New York: Holt, Rinehart and Winston, 1955.

10
SOCIAL PSYCHOLOGY

Aristotle observed that man is a social animal. This characterization emphasizes the extent to which what is distinctly human is a social product. All culture, all language, all institutions, all social interactions, are affected by social experience. We are, largely, what others have told us and taught us, what others expect of us. It is the social aspect of human identity and action that social psychologists study; they study people in groups and people as affected by social experience. Social psychology is the study of *the effect on individual behavior of the presence of others*. This obviously applies to a very wide range of phenomena, some dramatic, others mundane. Perhaps the most convincing evidence for the significance of the presence of other persons on an individual is the consequence of the absence of others. When children are raised with little or no social stimulation, the result is disastrous. Every now and then we hear about parents who have isolated their children. The children are almost always socially disturbed and retarded in language and intellectual development. Occasionally we hear about cases of "feral children," raised in social isolation with only animal contact. These children never become normal in social or intellectual behavior. More rigorous conclusions in the area of behavior are based on the work of Harry Harlow, who reared infant monkeys in complete social isolation. When returned to a normal social environment as adults, these animals exhibited a variety of psychopathological symptoms, especially in their reactions to cage mates.

Areas of Social Psychology

The various areas that constitute social psychology can be categorized into two types, more or less representative of two basic traditions in the field. The first to be discussed focuses on the relatively long-term and enduring effects of culture, society, social institutions, and social learning on individuals' attitudes. *Attitude research* has been the most popular topic in social psychology. We shall consider various types of attitudes and how they enter into an individual's personality and serve as a general guide for his behavior toward others.

One of the major types of attitudes studied is *prejudice.* Its existence is expressed in thousands of different ways—from simple refusal to interact with specific individuals to mass murder. For several years there has been a raging conflict in Northern Ireland, ostensibly being fought on grounds of religious prejudice. Prejudice patterns social

Parents Held for Keeping Diapered Teen in Isolation

California (AP)—Sheriff's deputies have arrested the parents of a 13-year-old girl who doctors say can't talk and has the mind of an infant because she was kept in virtual isolation since birth.

Sandy X, wide-eyed and brown-haired, spent her time inside her parents' modest two-bedroom home in a Los Angeles suburb except for the brief periods when she played in the yard or sat on the porch, deputies said.

She walks with a stooped shuffle like an aged person and her arms and bone structure are extremely thin, doctors said.

They placed her mental development as equal to that of a 12- to 18-month-old infant, said she still wore diapers, and that her size was that of a 10-year-old.

The doctors said Sandy could become physically normal after treatment but that they were unsure about possible mental progress.

Deputies said Sandy has been hospitalized since Nov. 4. The case was made public after her parents were arrested Monday.

Bill X, 70, and his estranged wife Joan, 50, were booked for investigation of child abuse and released on $1,250 bail each.

Sheriff's investigators said a social worker brought the case to their attention when Mrs. X left her husband, took Sandy to live with the girl's grandmother and applied for welfare.

No motive for the girl's alleged treatment was advanced by authorities.

Clearly, lack of social contact has devastating, perhaps irreversible, effects on human development and functioning.

relations in commonplace circumstances—who gets a job, attends a particular school, is invited to a party, or joins a club. Probably everyone reading this text is affected continuously and personally by prejudice—if you are not directly the object or agent of prejudice, then you are indirectly affected by the influence of prejudice on what classmates you will have and what persons you will meet. We all have a social environment that is more homogeneous than it would be if prejudice did not structure and restrict our social relations. The problem of prejudice—its origin, correlates, and consequences—and the search for means to reduce it have long been a central concern of social psychologists.

A related area of investigation is *interpersonal attraction*—the issue of friendship and romantic involvement. Do we like persons similar to ourselves or different from ourselves? Beauty is only skin deep, but how important is it for mate selection or for determining who gets a particular job? How can a person make friends and influence people? Social psychologists have tried to answer questions like these by formal research.

The second tradition in social psychology focuses on the behavior of individuals in groups. We shall examine why it is that a person will do one thing in the presence of others and quite a different thing when he is alone. Why, for example, do bystanders or onlookers at the scene of an emergency often fail to help the person in trouble? Why is a person more apt to help or get involved if he is alone and not part of a group of bystanders?

When the social group becomes a crowd, individual behavior is even more noticeably altered. People seem more excitable, less rational, and much more conforming when in a crowd. Consider the violence of some crowds, for example, in race riots, at political rallies, and in burning buildings. How is it that perfectly normal, respectable citizens can be incited to form a fearsome, raging lynch mob? Why will people obey the commands of someone they perceive as being an authority, such as a gang or religious leader, to an often unbelievable extent?

Our two-part organization, attitudes and individuals in groups, should not be taken to mean that there is no relationship between these two research traditions or that they exhaust the entire field of social psychology. Because we lack the time and space to present a comprehensive survey of social psychology, we have elected to concentrate on a few of what we consider the foremost problems in the field today. Even if we are wrong in our evaluation of what is important, we think that our selection of topics and our analyses of them will give you the knowledge and skill you need to carry on into other issues when the occasion arises.

Research on Social Attitudes

A major concern of social psychologists has been the study of social attitudes. *A social attitude is a combination of feelings, beliefs, and action tendencies toward classes of persons or objects that are directly or indirectly social in nature.* Thus an attitude has three components: (1) beliefs or knowledge—the cognitive component; (2) feelings—the emotional-motivational component; and (3) tendencies to act in particular ways on the basis of knowledge and emotion—the performance component. For example, your attitude toward, say, the members of NOW (National Organization for Women) is a matter of what you know or believe about the functions, goals, and constituents of that group; the feelings (positive or negative) they arouse in you; and your tendency or disposition to take one or another action regarding the group or its individual members.

Social attitudes are a kind of concept. They are concepts about classes of people, concepts with a prominent evaluative character. Attitudes seem to function much like the concepts we discussed in Chapter 5. For one thing, they provide a way of responding to all members of a given class or category. A given object is responded to not as unique but on the basis of the object's class membership. This is not just a matter of economy (not having to learn a response to each individual object), it is a matter of necessity, because the human mind cannot contend with the welter of physical variations that make up the environment.

Furthermore, attitudes, like other concepts, serve as a guide to future behavior. They are an important basis for consistency, for we always respond in the same way to class members. A person who has a concept of or an attitude toward a particular class of objects or people has a basis for responding to any member of that class, even one he has never specifically encountered before.

Finally, attitudes, like other concepts, can be learned both by direct examples (actual contact with class members) or by instruction from others (being told about members of the class). The similarity of attitudes and concepts has not escaped the notice of social psychologists. Some believe that the same underlying processes are involved in both and that laboratory studies of concept formation will tell us quite a bit about how attitudes can be established or changed.

Organization of Attitudes

Most social psychologists now believe that attitudes and beliefs are organized basically according to the principle of consistency. The *consistency principle,* as applied to attitudes, states that the attitudes held by a particular individual are mutually supportive and do not conflict with one another. That is, they make sense to the person in a logical or psychological fashion. Consistency also refers to the tendency of individuals to segregate liked objects from disliked objects and to structure their thoughts in simple black-and-white terms. If a set of attitudes held by a particular person is viewed by him as consistent, it will be difficult to change any single member of the set, because changing one attitude will make it inconsistent with all the others in the set. The person, finding this inconsistency unpleasant, will resist attitude change.

As an example, suppose that you really like Bob Hope—your attitude toward him is totally positive—you view him as nice, warm, benevolent,

happy, funny, and interesting. Now suppose you see him interviewed on TV, and you find out that he is politically extremely conservative. If you are politically conservative, your attitude toward him will be consistent with your attitude toward conservative politics. It is as if you are saying to yourself, "I like Bob Hope, I like conservative politics, Bob Hope likes conservative politics." It makes sense to have this set of attitudes—they are consistent. But suppose instead that you are a liberal. Then you are faced with, "I like Bob Hope, I like liberal politics, Bob Hope likes conservative politics."

How can you have such fond admiration for a man whose politics are so different from yours, or how can you have such fond admiration for the kind of politics that your favorite performer dislikes so much? These attitudes are psychologically inconsistent. According to the consistency principle, you are likely to change one of them to bring about consistency. Inconsistency is seen as a primary reason for attitude change. Inconsistency must be resolved, because it is disturbing to see one's own attitudes as inconsistent with one another. You are now likely to change the attitudes in such a way as to bring about a state of consistency. You might conclude that you really do not like Bob Hope all that much, or that you really are not a political liberal, or you might even try to delude yourself into thinking that Bob Hope is really a liberal. Such delusional beliefs can happen when the other attitudes in a consistent set are extremely difficult for a person to change for other reasons (for example, if they are deeply held religious attitudes).

The basic prediction derived from this principle is that attitudes will be acquired and/or modified so as to bring about a state of mental and behavioral consistency. The basic law of attitude change is that change follows from a state of inconsistency and proceeds toward a state of consistency. If you want to change someone's attitudes, you should create a state of inconsistency in that person's mind (usually by presenting him with some new evidence against his beliefs). You hope that he will resolve the inconsistency (assuming he believes what you are telling him) by modifying the attitude you wish to change. We will have more to say about attitude change later.

There are several varieties of consistency theory, three of which we will briefly review: the balance theory of Fritz Heider, the A-B-X model of Theodore Newcomb, and the theory of cognitive dissonance developed by Leon Festinger.

Balance theory.   From an analysis of the psychological relationships expressed in everyday language, Fritz Heider (1958) formulated the first version of consistency theory. Heider's version, usually referred to as *balance theory,* states that objects perceived as belonging together will have the same dynamic quality—they will either be all liked or all disliked. Liked objects will not be associated with disliked objects.

The formulation of the theory involves the *p-o-x model.* The letters *p, o,* and *x* refer to the elements of a system where (1) p is the person having a positive or negative orientation toward o (usually another person); (2) p holds a positive or negative orientation toward x (usually an object); and (3) p perceives o as having a particular orientation toward x. Balanced (consistent) relationships are represented in the following diagrams:

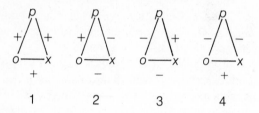

1   2   3   4

For example, diagram 2 represents the case of a person (p) liking another (o), as is indicated by the plus sign near the line joining p and o. The two other lines with the minus signs represent the fact that p dislikes x and he perceives that o dislikes x also. Thus diagram 2 could represent the fact that p likes Bob Hope, p dislikes liberal politics, and p perceives that Bob Hope also dislikes liberal politics. As an exercise, you might work out all possible combinations of p-o-x and imagine real examples for each. Note that a balanced state exists when there are two negatives or none; an imbalanced state exists when there are three negatives or only one.

Balanced states are psychologically comfortable —they are consistent. Imbalanced states are uncomfortable, motivating people to reduce or avoid ·the imbalance. For example, your continual disagreement with a friend (o), on some issue (x), say, an upcoming presidential election, may lead either to rejection of your friend or a change in your attitude on issue x. The case of rejecting your friend can be shown as:

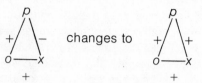

The case of your continued friendship at the cost of changing your attitude on issue x can be shown as

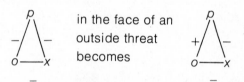

In either case, balance is restored, but you have lost a friend or changed an attitude.

In another case, suppose someone (p) has a neighbor (o) that he dislikes intensely. This is a balanced state as long as he *likes* everything and everyone that the neighbor *dislikes* or vice versa. But suppose he and the neighbor find out that they share the same attitude about someone (x) moving into the neighborhood, whom they both see as an outside threat. Now there is a state of imbalance that is likely to lead to a change in attitude toward the neighbor (assume that the threat is perceived as so great that attitudes toward *it* will not be changed instead). What we have is:

in the face of an outside threat becomes

and the two neighbors join forces and cooperate to fight the threat. As we will see later, one good way to reduce tension and hostility between two people (or two nations) who dislike each other is to subject both of them to a common threat. The imbalance thus created motivates the two people or nations to cooperate, which creates further imbalance unless they change their attitudes about each other. Of course, the principle can have either good effects (for example, the Soviet Union and the United States might cooperate to fight pollution and learn to live with each other) or bad effects (neighbors who do not get along well might form a strong group to oppose integration).

Considerable evidence has been collected supporting the general proposition that the cognitions, attitudes, opinions, and beliefs of people tend toward balance. We are motivated by states of discomfort brought on by cognitive imbalance and behave in ways designed to eliminate imbalance. Note the homeostatic character of this principle. As in other forms of motivation (see Chapter 6), the goal is to bring all operative factors into harmony, or a state of homeostasis.

A-B-X model.   An alternative consistency model, usually called the A-B-X model, was developed by Theodore Newcomb. While Heider's balance theory refers to how one person perceives others, Newcomb's model refers to both subjective belief and actual interaction. Thus Newcomb's model gives a better account of interpersonal attraction and interaction. The elements of the model refer to persons A and B, A's and B's attitudes toward X (typically a nonperson object), A's perception of B's attitude toward X, and B's perception of A's attitude toward X. In other words, there are two systems analyzed by Newcomb, one as A sees it and the other as B sees it. Newcomb postulates that both systems will tend toward balance.

The main suggestion added here is that interaction will tend to increase balance. This means, for example, that as people get to know one another, they will tend to choose as friends those who are similar to themselves (who have the same attitudes); thus "birds of a feather flock together." In one study children in grades 4 through 12 were asked to evaluate strangers whose opinions on issues from comic books to religion had been described. The results showed a strong, linear (straight-line) relationship between liking and attitude similarity (see Figure 10-1). The more the stranger thought like the child about some issue, the more the child liked him. This relationship is established by age 9 or even earlier.

Newcomb (1961) investigated interpersonal attraction by bringing university students, strangers to one another, together for a term and offering them room and board in exchange for their cooperation in an extensive psychological study. At the outset there appeared to be little or no relationship between degree of liking and similarity of feelings and beliefs on various issues. This relationship did develop over the term, however, and at the end of the experiment a strong relationship existed between attraction and attitude similarity. The more common the opinions between two people, the more they liked each other. What was especially important in mutual attraction was the degree to which two students shared the same attitudes toward each of their fellow house residents. If you have lived in a dorm or other group housing facility, you have probably seen and experienced friendships that develop in this manner. To what extent do you think attitude similarity enters into your relationship with others?

Dissonance theory.   Leon Festinger's consistency theory, known as *cognitive dissonance*

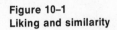

Figure 10–1
Liking and similarity

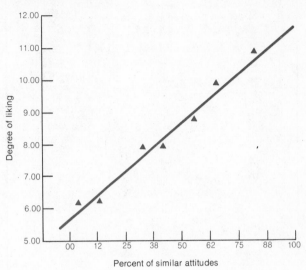

Children's ratings of strangers as a function of similarity or dissimilarity of their attitudes and opinions.

theory, has been particularly influential. The theory of cognitive dissonance concerns the relationship between two or more cognitive or mental elements (ideas or beliefs). A consonant relationship exists when one of the elements implies the other in some psychological sense. A dissonant relationships exists when one cognition a person holds follows from the *obverse* of another cognition he also holds. If a person holds cognitions A and B, and A implies not B, the cognitions are in a dissonant relationship. Some of the cognitive relationships said to be consonant include smoking (A) and believing it is harmless to health (B), reading in a car magazine that the kind of car you just bought has been judged best by a panel of experts, and observing your chosen team winning by a landslide. On the other hand, if you smoke and know it is bad for your health, or if you bought the type of car that experts say is the most dangerous one on the road, you probably have experienced dissonance. Because dissonance, like inconsistency, is in general uncomfortable, you probably have resolved or reduced the dissonance by now. Perhaps you have said to yourself, "I like smoking and I'll quit before it starts to affect my health" or "This car was a good buy and I'm a very careful driver."

If you pay a lot for something or work hard for it, it should be of high quality. If something is cheap or

"It can't be very scary."

free, you should not expect much. These situations are characterized by consonance. But if you work hard or pay a lot of money for something that is of very poor quality, that is dissonance. Suppose you undergo a severe initiation procedure to become a member of a fraternity or sorority, only to find out that you do not like the members very much. Dissonance theory would predict that you would search for a means of reducing the dissonance, perhaps by denying that the initiation was severe or by coming to believe that the group is actually a pretty good one. Thus, we might deduce that the more severe the initiation, the greater the perceived liking of the group members. This prediction, which is not one we would make on the basis of common sense, has been verified by laboratory research (Aronson and Mills, 1959). Much of our behavior can be viewed or described as attempts to reduce the dissonance that has arisen from our experiences.

The amount of dissonance is a function of the importance of a cognition and the number of dissonant elements. In general, dissonance can be reduced in two ways, either by increasing the ratio of consonant to dissonant elements or by decreasing the judged importance of the dissonant elements. A smoker, for example, could accomplish the former by adding the belief that smoking reduces tension and gives him great pleasure (increasing the consonant to dissonant ratio). Or he could reduce the importance of the problem by saying that he plans to quit or by belittling the risk of cancer.

When Prophecy Fails

What happens when you vehemently make a prediction, such as telling your friends over and over that you are never going to have another cigarette or that George Foreman is going to beat Muhammad Ali, only to have the prediction fail miserably? The result is dissonance that you must somehow reduce. Leon Festinger, H. W. Riecken, and Stanley Schachter did a study on this kind of problem, which we might call "when prophecy fails." (For further information see their book, *When prophecy fails: A social and psychological study of a modern group that predicted the destruction of the world.* New York: Harper & Row, 1956.)

The investigators studied a group of religious followers of a woman who, some years ago, predicted the end of the world in December of that year. She and her followers believed that only they would be saved, because a spaceship would rescue them. Some of the members made considerable financial sacrifices to join the group, and all of them were strongly committed to their belief in the woman's prophetic powers and the test of their beliefs with the impending disaster. The situation was set up for a monumental cognitive clash between prophecy and outcome. The hour was set, the world was to end, and it didn't.

The experimenters, following the situation closely (even to the point of joining the group), made a curious prediction. They said that instead of disbanding and trying to live down and forget the affair, the followers would maintain their beliefs and their group commitment and would seek even more support. The experimenters were right. As the hour of destruction passed, apprehension within the group grew. But soon the leader received a "message" that the group's devotion had been the world's salvation. Thanks to their devotion, destruction had been avoided.

At the critical moment, two facts were in dissonance. The followers believed in their prophet and her prophecy failed. Choosing to maintain their beliefs, the followers then wholly accepted a reinterpretation of the events. That the world was not destroyed they saw as an even greater sign of the prophet's power. Now the cause was redirected. Whereas before the prophecy failed, the group had avoided publicity, now they actively sought more followers. They purposely exposed themselves to public ridicule in the belief that this would increase their popular support. In short, they did what they could to increase the number of consonant elements and decrease the dissonant ones.

Dissonance theory has survived extensive critical evaluation to remain a major formulation of consistency theory. It applies to any situation in which there is cognitive conflict. Dissonance is a source of discomfort and therefore has important application to such areas as decision making and attitude change. Perhaps its more important contemporary application is in the area of the relationship of attitudes to behavior. Dissonance theory suggests that if a person is induced to behave in a fashion contrary to his present attitude (such as giving a speech or writing an essay in favor of something he is against), his attitude will tend to move in a direction consistent with his behavior (he begins to believe what he is saying, writing, or doing). There is considerable evidence to support this hypothesis.

This suggests that the old line "You can't legislate morality" may not always be true. If the law leads people to change their behavior—as with desegregation in the United States—at least some attitudes should follow suit.

However, not all attitudes change with behavior. People often hold attitudes that are inconsistent with their public acts. This is especially so when they feel coerced by some real or imaginary external force. The more they perceive an external cause, the less they need to accept responsibility and readjust their internal views. Dissonance studies indicate that minimal external pressure or reward is most effective in achieving lasting change. The child who is threatened with a beating for eating a cookie is less likely to view the act as inherently wrong than the child who is mildly coerced into abstention; the college student who is rewarded with a large check for good grades is less likely to value study for its own sake than is the student who is simply complimented.

Prejudice

Prejudice is a kind of attitude and thus consists of a combination of feelings, beliefs, and action tendencies. As the word itself suggests, prejudice is often a matter of prejudgment. The implication is that one has made up his mind too soon, before all the facts are in or have come to his attention. This, of course, further implies that the conclusion arrived at with the inadequate set of facts is the wrong one—which means that prejudice is seen as a wrong attitude or a bad one.

There is no single, overall definition of prejudice that all social psychologists would agree with. Most would agree, however, that prejudice is an attitude that is basically intergroup in character; members of one group have this type of attitude toward members of another group. Prejudice is usually, though not always: (1) highly emotional in character, (2) rigidly or inflexibly felt and acted on by group

Figure 10–2
Race consciousness

Although earlier studies indicated that both black and white children preferred white dolls, a recent study has shown a shift in the attitude of black children, with a majority of them now preferring black dolls.

members (meaning they will not listen to reason), and (3) negative (the object of the prejudice is disliked and the group's tendency is to mistreat or *discriminate against* members of the disliked group).

Racial, ethnic, and religious prejudice develop at an early age. Kenneth and Mamie Clark, in a classic demonstration of the insidious nature of racial prejudice, found that black children of preschool age showed an awareness of racial identity and a markedly higher evaluation of whites than of blacks, as indicated by their characterization of white dolls as "good" and as preferable to black dolls (see Figure 10-2). Originally reported in 1941, this study has been replicated several times, with the preference for white dolls expressed by both black and white children. Times are changing, however. A recent study by Hraba and Grant (1970) has, for the first time, shown a majority of black children preferring a black doll. This shift undoubtedly reflects the development of racial pride among blacks, which is summed up in the phrase, "Black is beautiful."

Like attitudes in general, *prejudices are learned,* but usually indirectly rather than through contact with the objects of the prejudice. Prejudice has been demonstrated in persons who have no firsthand knowledge whatsoever of the objects they are prejudiced against. Prejudice has been demonstrated even against social groups that do not exist. In one study, 3 fictitious names—Danerians, Pirenians, and Wallonians—were included within a list of 32 other ethnic labels presented to a group of college students for evaluation. The students were asked to rate all groups. The fictitious groups were generally rated negatively!

Many interrelated and mutually supporting factors are involved in the development, expression, and perpetuation of prejudice; this means that modifying prejudice is not an easy job—and you do not have to be a social psychologist to know that. Let us examine the many factors that have been suggested as contributing to prejudice. For convenience we will divide these factors into two classes: (1) those that operate at the level of the specific individual who is prejudiced and (2) those that operate at the level of social institutions such as clubs, fraternities, unions, and even society in general. These are the social-cultural aspects of prejudice.

Prejudice at the individual level. Psychologists have been prone to interpret prejudice differently than they interpret attitudes in general, probably because in prejudice there is an implication that the belief is held in the face of overwhelming contradictory evidence. If a person believes something that to an "objective" observer is clearly false, then one tends to feel that this person is benefiting in some way from his false beliefs. For example, holding a prejudiced attitude may make one more popular among people who also hold the same attitude.

Prejudice as a defense against anxiety. One way to see prejudice as benefiting an individual is to suggest that he is using the prejudice as a way of dealing with his emotional problems. Such an explanation is often based on the Freudian principle of projection, one of the ego's defense mechanisms. The prejudice is seen as a means by which the prejudiced person can defend himself against the anxiety that is part of his own inner conflict. In projection, a person attributes to others the very things that he is worried about in himself. For example, the prejudiced person who believes that blacks are sloppy, dirty, and immoral might be defending himself against the realization that certain aspects of his own behavior suggest he is sloppy, dirty, and immoral. According to this explanation, the prejudiced person (1) is bothered by (feels anxiety about) some characteristic he perceives in himself; (2) projects this onto some other person and says that the other person possesses this characteristic; (3) emphasizes how different he is from the other person, even to the point of identifying the person as a member of various groups and then showing how he himself could not be part of these groups; and (4) denies that the

---

U.S. Charges Two Cities with Hiring Bias

Washington, D.C. (UPI)—The Justice Department filed two civil suits Monday charging the city of Los Angeles with discriminating in the hiring of firemen and the city of Montgomery, Ala., with discrimination in public employment.

The suits are the first to be filed under the 1972 Equal Employment Opportunity Act, which removed an exemption in the 1964 Civil Rights Act for state and local employees.

Atty. Gen. Richard Kleindienst said that the suit filed in Federal Court in Los Angeles accused the city of discriminating against blacks, Mexican Americans and Orientals in recruitment and hiring.

Kleindienst has said that many cities in the United States are guilty of similar discrimination. . . .

48 of 3,150 Are Black

The Los Angeles Fire Department employs about 3,150 firemen of whom 48 are black—1.5%—and 94 are Mexican American—3%. It has no Orientals. The minority group population of the city is 18% black, 18% Mexican American and 3.5% Oriental.

The government said that the city pursued policies and practices that discriminated against members of the minority groups, such as using tests and educational and height requirements that disproportionately excluded minority applicants. . . .

Blacks Paid Less

The suit filed against Montgomery said that blacks there were hired as unclassified laborers even though they performed work similar to that done by whites with classified status. It also said that blacks hired in the classified service got lower pay than whites with less experience doing the same work.

The suit also charged that Montgomery and its agencies had used employment tests and educational standards that discriminated against blacks and were not related to job performance. . . .

This news story was written in 1972. Suits like these have become relatively popular—and successful. The statistics reported here have no doubt changed somewhat as a consequence.

"bad" characteristic applies to himself, because he now sees himself as being so different from the object of his prejudice that he could not possibly have any of the same feelings, attitudes, or characteristics as any member of these groups. By coming to this conclusion, the prejudiced person defends himself against anxiety. Thus, prejudice can be seen as an unfortunate result of the application of a defense mechanism designed basically to cope with anxiety. Appealing as this hypothesis may be, research suggests that projection is a relatively

Are There Any Faces in a Crowd?

Social psychologists have suggested that crowd violence may, to a large extent, be a function of the fact that crowd members typically lose their individual identity. They may feel less personally responsible for their behavior, less likely to be punished because they cannot be identified, and, as a result, more prone to behave violently. Phillip Zimbardo (1969) has done an ingenious experiment to demonstrate the importance of the deindividuation, or loss of personal identity, that takes place in groups. Groups of four female subjects listened to recordings of interviews with potential "victims." Some groups were given a deindividuation treatment—the women wore gowns and hoods to disguise themselves and the experimenters never used their names. In other groups, the women were not disguised; they wore name tags, and everyone referred to everyone else by name—these were the identifiable groups. Each group listened to interviews with pleasant and unpleasant "victims," and later each group member was induced to deliver shocks to the victims, whom they could now see through a one-way mirror. The victim was, of course, a coinvestigator in the study, and she acted as if she were being shocked, although no shocks were delivered. The key finding

was that women in the deindividuation groups delivered longer shocks than women in the identifiable group, and this was true regardless of whether they perceived the victim as a pleasant or an unpleasant person.

**Figure 10–3
Deindividuation treatment**

The experimental group in which individuals were devoid of personal identity wore gowns and hoods and were never called by name.

minor factor in prejudice, being limited to specific individual cases.

The scapegoat theory.   A more likely hypothesis is that prejudice is a way of dealing with frustration. This hypothesis is a derivative of the frustration-aggression hypothesis we encountered in Chapter 6. The typical prejudiced person is seen as a frustrated individual who cannot readily identify or aggress against the sources of his frustration. Instead he selects "out-groups" and their members as displacement objects and proceeds to attack them, either verbally or physically. This has been called the *scapegoat theory,* because the object of the prejudice is serving as a scapegoat for personal feelings of hostility, frustration, and aggression. Research has demonstrated that frustrated individuals will displace aggressive feelings onto innocent bystanders, but this holds true only when the bystander is someone who is already disliked; that is, dislike precedes displaced aggression. This suggests to many social psychologists that the scapegoat factor is involved in the expression of already existing prejudice but that scapegoating is not the reason the prejudice was learned in the first place.

The operation of scapegoating as a means of expressing already prejudiced attitudes is perhaps best and most dramatically illustrated in the behavior of people in violent crowds. Usually such crowds have leaders whose main function seems to be to identify the scapegoat and convince the crowd members that indeed this person or group is responsible for all their frustrations. Once the scapegoat is identified, all that remains is for the social constraints that normally inhibit aggression to be removed. Perhaps the most important factor in weakening the social inhibition against aggression is that the crowd situation seems to reduce feelings of responsibility. The individual tends to lose his identity in a crowd; he cannot easily be singled out by others as being personally responsible for *the acts of the crowd.* Phillip Zimbardo has called this phenomenon *deindividuation* (see Figure 10-3). Did you ever wonder why the Ku Klux Klan members wear sheets?

The authoritarian personality.   The final individual hypothesis to be discussed deals with the relationship between prejudice and personality structure in general. The hypothesis is that prejudice is only one aspect of a particular personality type

Authoritarian Social Climates

An intriguing study of the relationship between social-economic stress and authoritarian responses was done by Stephen M. Sales (1972). He contrasted the peaceful 1920's with the period of the Great Depression, the 1930's. In the 1920's, 22 comic book series were started, 2 of which had powerful central characters. During the Depression, 21 new comic series were started; 12 had powerful central characters. Also, in the thirties there was a strong increase in membership of authoritarian churches, in sales of astrology books, in budgets for police (but less crime and lower budgets for firemen), and in sales of machismo magazines.

In a follow-up study, contrasting periods of economic recession in Seattle, Washington (1961, 1964, and 1969), with times of relative prosperity (1962, 1965, and 1966), Sales found a higher success rate in attracting converts to authoritarian churches during periods of economic stress.

Sales has confirmed his hypothesis that failure-induced threat increases authoritarianism in laboratory studies that replicate his naturalistic observations. For example, in one experiment, subjects were led either to fail or to succeed at a gamelike task (a "computer skill task" requiring the decoding of anagrams and solving of algebra problems). Failure increased authoritarianism scores; success led to decreased authoritarianism scores. The observed changes were greatest for those persons who indicated their success or failure was internally caused (Sales and Friend, 1973).

called the *authoritarian personality* (Adorno, Frenkel-Brunswik, Levinson, and Sanford, 1950). The hypothesis grew out of a study of anti-Semitism conducted immediately following World War II. The general conclusion was that prejudiced people tended to share a common core of attitudes. They tended to be (1) ethnocentric, having a strong identification with their in-groups and a strong dislike of out-groups; (2) politically and economically conservative; and (3) antidemocratic or authoritarian. The scores on several different measures of these factors tend to correlate with one another. For example, the prejudiced person will usually agree with all of the following statements:

1. It is wrong for Jews and gentiles to intermarry (an item from the anti-Semitism scale).
2. We are spending too much money for the pampering of criminals and the insane and for the education of inherently incapable people (an item from the ethnocentrism scale).

3. Men like Henry Ford or J. P. Morgan, who overcome all competition on the road to success, are models for all young people to admire and imitate (an item from the political and economic conservatism scale).
4. Obedience and respect for authority are the most important virtues children should learn (an item from the Implicit Anti-democratic Trends scale, known as the F scale).

The authors of the study suggest that these attitudes go together because they are rooted in some underlying personality factor. Thus, prejudice may be an outgrowth of a personality syndrome, and prejudiced people may have a lot in common in addition to their shared prejudices.

For many persons, prejudice is only one aspect of a more general attitude-belief-personality system. In such cases, it may follow that reduction of prejudice will take place only when there is a change in the person's basic personality structure—meaning, of course, that prejudice in such people will be very difficult to eliminate.

Social-cultural aspects of prejudice. Now we turn to the factors in prejudice that arise from the individual's membership in social groups and institutions.

Conformity. Often prejudice seems to be simply a matter of *conformity* to the norms of the social groups to which one belongs. Thomas Pettigrew has demonstrated a strong relationship between prejudice and conformity. The most prejudiced people are most likely to conform in other areas of behavior. They are most likely to be joiners; for example, they are typically members of a political party as opposed to being independents. This relationship between conformity and prejudice holds most clearly in the South, where strong social norms "dictate" that a person should be prejudiced. This suggests that many people express overt prejudice just because it is the thing to do. The need for approval probably plays a strong role, causing people to conform to the prejudiced norms in order to be better liked by their friends and associates.

Realistic group conflict. A second social factor has been called the *realistic-group-conflict* theory (Campbell, 1965). If two groups are actually in conflict with each other for some reason, members of one group will tend to develop prejudice against members of the other group. For example, if Jewish and Gentile businessmen are both competing for the

Copyright, 1971, G. B. Trudeau. Distributed by Universal Press Syndicate.

same business, the Gentiles might develop prejudice against the Jews and vice versa. If the United States and the Soviet Union are competing for world supremacy, we would expect prejudice to exist as a natural outgrowth of this competition. The competitor is seen as a threat, and it is only natural to feel hostile toward sources of threat against one's own security. Such a theory also implies that removing the conflict will reduce or remove the prejudice.

History supports the realistic-group-conflict theory. Anti-Russian attitudes were not prevalent during World War II, when Russians and Americans were on the same side, but there was a good deal of prejudice against the Germans and Japanese. Now there is significant anti-Russian feeling, although it is being held in check somewhat by the fact that both Russians and Americans tend to see a common threat in China. American efforts to normalize relations with China might serve to keep things in balance, because both China and America see the Soviet Union as a potential threat. What would you predict about the attitudes of Americans, Russians, and Chinese if the earth were under attack by people from another planet?

Realistic-group-conflict theory has also been supported by experimental research such as the Robbers Cave study, described in detail later. In this study boys were divided into groups and put in conflict with one another; prejudice in all its forms developed. By later arranging things so that the groups had to cooperate in order to achieve a common goal, the prejudice and intergroup hostility was reduced.

The kernel of truth hypothesis.

A major source of prejudice is the opinions and actions of institutions. *Institutional prejudice* is reflected in segregated schools, houses, jobs, roles,

communication patterns—in the many ethnic, religious, racial, and sexual divisions whereby one group is disadvantaged. The observer is aware of differences because differences are institutionally imposed; he becomes aware of the ranking of groups because one group is institutionally disadvantaged.

Institutionally based prejudice is the basis for what is called the *kernel of truth* or *putting 2 + 2 together* hypothesis. The unfortunate facts of the matter are that blacks are underpaid, hold inferior jobs, and are less well educated. A child seeing these harsh realities may ask himself why this is true and may reach the wrong conclusion. He puts "2 + 2" together and concludes that blacks must be inferior because they are black, completely failing to realize that there are other explanations for the unfortunate situations that blacks are in. This conclusion would be most likely to occur to a child with prejudiced parents, who would do nothing to correct the child's erroneous conclusion. And this would account for the fact that prejudiced parents have prejudiced children, without having to resort to Freudian principles about early childhood experiences. In this regard, seemingly trivial things such as making sure that black people are represented in television commercials or are given such TV roles as doctors and lawyers may be very important. These simple steps will serve to counteract the 2 + 2 phenomenon even if the parents do not.

Stereotypes.

The final social factor to be mentioned is closely related to *social learning* and *imitation,* as discussed more fully in Chapter 9. The argument is that the prejudiced person learns, mainly through social learning principles, that all members of a particular group hold to certain beliefs or have certain attitudes or characteristics. Thus, the prejudiced person is said to hold social *stereotypes.* Social stereotypes are generalizations about other groups. Examples include beliefs that Scots are thrifty and miserly, that blacks are naturally athletically gifted, that the Japanese are industrious. Such generalizations are usually but not always negative; they are almost always inadequate. Donald Campbell has identified the following kinds of inadequacies:

1. People falsely tend to assume that their view of others (the out-group) is unquestionably accurate.
2. Differences between in-groups and out-groups are much exaggerated.
3. Attributes are strongly believed to be innate ("racial") and unchangeable rather than environmentally caused.
4. Perceived differences between the out-group and the in-group are believed to cause the felt hostility toward the out-group when in fact the hostility precedes the discovering of differences.

Even when there are no differences between oneself or one's group and others, the evaluation of the in-group and out-group may differ sharply.

The content of stereotypes is relatively stable over time but it also changes in response to differing social climates. On three occasions, Princeton students have been questioned on their social stereotypes. Students were much more likely to make stereotyped judgments in 1931 than in 1951 or 1967; more recently, they have criticized stereotypes as unreasonable. At all three times, of the 10 groups listed, the Turks were the most negatively characterized. An interesting shift has taken place in the evaluation of Americans; in 1933 and 1951 they were quite positively evaluated, but in 1967 they dropped to fifth place (the Japanese were first, the Germans second, the Jews third, and the English fourth). Table 10-1 presents the characterizations for 3 of the groups. Dramatic shifts have occurred in the rating of blacks. There was a general reduction in group consensus between 1931 and 1951; but consensus increased between 1951 and 1967, which suggests that group stereotypes endure to the extent that students share a common awareness of such generalizations even though they are reluctant to express them.

Stereotypes form the cognitive component of prejudice. This component is quite complex, consisting in some cases of many beliefs that can have positive, neutral, and negative evaluative implications. There is no simple relationship between prejudice and the willingness to make a particular generalization. John Brigham (1971) reports a positive correlation between *percent* of persons attributing the trait "irresponsible" to blacks and prejudice—persons high in prejudice are more likely to say blacks are irresponsible. He found a negative correlation between attribution of the trait "intelligent" and prejudice. For many traits, there was no relationship between prejudice and stereotyping. Overall, however, there is a significant relationship between racial prejudice and the tendency to generalize about blacks.

We should note that not all stereotypes are

Table 10–1
Comparison of stereotype ratings by Princeton students

AMERICANS				GERMANS				BLACKS			
Trait	1933	1951	1967	Trait	1933	1951	1967	Trait	1933	1951	1967
Industrious	48	30	23	Scientifically minded	78	62	47	Superstitious	84	41	13
Intelligent	47	32	20	Industrious	65	50	59	Lazy	75	31	26
Materialistic	33	37	67	Stolid	44	10	9	Happy-go-lucky	38	17	27
Ambitious	33	21	42	Intelligent	32	32	19	Ignorant	38	24	11
Progressive	27	5	17	Methodical	31	20	21	Musical	26	33	47
Pleasure-loving	26	27	28	Extremely nationalistic	24	50	43	Ostentatious	26	11	25
Alert	23	7	7	Progressive	16	3	13	Very religious	24	17	8
Efficient	21	9	15	Efficient	16	—	46	Stupid	22	10	4
Aggressive	20	8	15	Jovial	15	—	5	Physically dirty	17	—	3
Straightforward	19	—	9	Musical	13	—	4	Naive	14	—	4
Practical	19	—	12	Persistent	11	—	4	Slovenly	13	—	5
Sportsmanlike	19	—	9	Practical	11	—	9	Unreliable	12	—	6
Individualistic	—	26	15	Aggressive	—	27	30	Pleasure-loving	—	19	26
Conventional	—	—	17	Arrogant	—	23	18	Sensitive	—	—	17
Scientifically minded	—	—	15	Ambitious	—	—	15	Gregarious	—	—	17
Ostentatious	—	—	15					Talkative	—	—	14
								Imitative	—	—	13

In-group Heroes, Out-group Villains

The sociologist Robert K. Merton has cleverly illustrated how the in-group virtue becomes the out-group vice:

We begin with the engagingly simply formula of moral alchemy: the same behavior must be differently evaluated according to the person who exhibits it. For example, the proficient alchemist will at once know that the word "firm" is properly declined as follows:

I am firm,
Thou art obstinate,
He is pigheaded.

There are some, unversed in the skills of this science, who will tell you that one and the same term should be applied to all three instances of identical behavior. Such unalchemical nonsense should simply be ignored.

   With this experiment in mind, we are prepared to observe how the very same behavior undergoes a complete change of evaluation in its transition from the in-group Abe Lincoln to the out-group Abe Cohen or Abe Kurokawa. We proceed systematically. Did Lincoln work far into the night? This testifies that he was industrious, resolute, perseverant, and eager to realize his capacities to the full. Do the out-group Jews or Japanese keep these same hours? This only bears witness to their sweatshop mentality, their ruthless undercutting of American standards, their unfair competitive practices. Is the in-group hero frugal, thrifty, and sparing? Then the out-group villain is stingy, miserly, and penny-pinching. All honor is due the in-group Abe for his having been smart, shrewd, and intelligent and, by the same token, all contempt is owing the out-group Abes for their being sharp, cunning, crafty, and too clever by far. Did the indomitable Lincoln refuse to remain content with a life of work with the hands? Did he prefer to make use of his brain? Then, all praise for his plucky climb up the shaky ladder of opportunity. But, of course, the eschewing of manual work for brain work among the merchants and lawyers of the out-group deserves nothing but censure for a parasitic way of life. Was Abe Lincoln eager to learn the accumulated wisdom of the ages by unending study? The trouble with the Jew is that he's a greasy grind, with his head always in a book, while decent people are going to a show or a ball game. Was the resolute Lincoln unwilling to limit his standards to those of his provincial community? That is what we should expect of a man of vision. And if the out-groupers criticize the vulnerable areas in our society, then send 'em back where they came from. Did Lincoln, rising high above his origins, never forget the rights of the common man and applaud the right of workers to strike? This testifies only that, like all real Americans, this greatest of Americans was deathlessly devoted to the cause of freedom. But, as you examine the statistics on strikes, remember that these un-American practices are the result of out-groupers pursuing their evil agitation among otherwise contented workers.

negative and not all generalizations are made in the service of prejudice. But the general view of students of prejudice is that for prejudiced persons, stereotypes serve to rationalize hostile opinions and feelings. These hostile views are shared with others to yield group stereotypes.

Attitude Change

Much of what we can say about attitude change follows from what we have already suggested about attitude formation. For example, if it were true that strict child rearing is the basic cause of the "authoritarian personality" and if it were true that this in turn causes prejudice, then the obvious way to change things would be to convince people to change the way they raise their children. But are you going to be successful if you tell a prejudiced person that if he raises his children differently, the children will not be prejudiced? This is just what the prejudiced person does not want to do; he wants his children to have the same values, attitudes, and beliefs that he has.

In a similar vein, we have seen that conformity to group norms is a major factor in prejudice. So you set out to convince people that they should not conform. And yet if they believe you and do not conform, they are likely to suffer somewhat for their newfound individuality; they will be cast out of their favorite social groups, lose their friends, and so on. Finally, we have emphasized realistic-group-conflict as a major source of prejudice. So you say, "Eliminate group conflict" and "Make everyone work together to achieve some superordinate goal," and theoretically this will eliminate prejudice. Easier said than done, unless you can get someone on another planet to attack us so that we all have to pull together to fight a common enemy.

Suppose we wanted to convince someone to be

Protection from Propaganda

Persuasion and propaganda are methods for bringing about attitude change. Of course, the term *propaganda* implies that the message is not really true and should not cause a person to change his attitudes, but the method is often effective nonetheless. What might one do to "inoculate" himself against propaganda? W. J. McGuire has proposed a psychological inoculation model based on the medical model of inoculation as a preventive treatment. The basic idea is to expose the person to small amounts of propaganda before he is hit with a big propaganda campaign. This, of course, is like giving someone a minute quantity of live virus in a vaccination. The assumption in medicine is that the small amount of live virus will cause the development of antibodies to fight off the disease itself at some later time. In psychological inoculation the assumption is that a lot of attitudes are learned without critical examination of the reasons why one should hold them. It is as if they are acquired and are surviving in a "germ-free" environment. If you have an attitude but are not aware of sound reasons to support it, you might be particularly vulnerable to propaganda that attacks your attitude with apparent reason. You are at a loss to produce good reasons for maintaining your attitude, and so you give in.

Suppose, however, that your views are opposed on several different occasions. Not enough information is given on any occasion to change your attitude, but you do hear enough to cause you to think of and examine your reasons for believing as you do. Now you have developed antibodies that should help you fend off propagandist attacks. This may be why hearing a two-sided presentation of an issue provides good inoculation against later counterpersuasion. Suppose you decide on the basis of a two-sided presentation (after you have heard both sides of the story) to believe A instead of B.

Later you are subjected to propaganda implying that A is wrong and B is right. Because you already know the arguments in favor of B and have chosen A despite this, you have inoculated yourself against the arguments in favor of B. Thus propaganda favoring B should have less of an effect on you.

**Figure 10–4
Propaganda**

Is there a "vaccine" that will protect you from persuasion and propaganda?

more permissive in rearing his children, or we wanted to change people's attitude about the number of children they should have, or about driving their cars downtown to work instead of taking the bus. What would we do? First, we might assume that the person in question has the wrong attitude and that, if only he knew all the facts, he would change his attitude to the correct one. This implies that we have all the facts and that he does not. All we have to do is tell him our facts and convince him that they are true. In short, attitude change may be conceived of as a process whereby someone (the *source*) communicates the true facts (a *message*) to someone (the *recipient*), thus persuading him to a new point of view.

The basic process in attitude change is the familiar principle of cognitive consistency. Presumably the recipient's present attitude is consistent with facts or cognitions available to him. The source introduces inconsistency into the picture by communicating a new view or different position. If the recipient is persuaded that the new position is true, then he must change his attitude to be consistent.

Variables influencing attitude change.   There are many variables, other than consistency, that affect the attitude change process. Here we will present some of these variables. Ask yourself why each of the variables changes attitudes. Does it

*"Some of you used to call us 'boy,'
and that's why now some of us
like to call you 'mother.'"*

Playboy, November 1971. Reproduced by special permission of PLAYBOY Magazine;
copyright © 1971 by Playboy.

When attitudes change, previously suppressed
behaviors may emerge.

10. the source speaks last when two opposing
messages are delivered (as in a debate);
11. the message is repeated on several occasions;
12. the recipient is induced to express the desired
attitude publicly.

These statements are, of course, subject to
qualification. They do not hold in every possible
instance. They are simplified conclusions from a
research literature that clearly shows that attitude
change is the result of very complex interactions of
many such factors.

As a final variable for our list, we suggest that
more attitude change will occur if you can get the
recipient to change his behavior, even if his attitude
has not yet changed. This relates to the question of
"legislating morality," mentioned earlier. If you can
induce someone to behave in a way that is
inconsistent with his present attitude, he might
change that attitude to return to a state of
consistency. But you must not use extreme force to
induce the behavior change because then there will
be no inconsistency, and no attitude change.
Getting someone to stand up and give an
improvised speech on the dangers of overpopulation
will change his attitudes against birth control more
than passing a law and forcing him to go to the
family planning center.

Interpersonal Attraction

Although psychologists have been perhaps most
concerned with the study of people's unfavorable
attitudes and prejudices, there is curiosity also
about people's favorable attitudes toward one
another, attitudes of liking. Thus, some attitude
research has centered on the topic of interpersonal
attraction and friendship.

Variables affecting liking.   What is the primary
basis for interpersonal attraction? Before you come
to like someone and develop a friendship, it is
obvious that you must have the opportunity to
interact with that person. Thus *physical proximity* is
important in determining friendship. Living near
someone or working near someone is likely to
produce interaction. A study of friendship patterns
within a housing project for married university
students showed that the students chose the
occupants of the nearby apartment units as friends
(see Figure 10-5). Another factor appears to be
frequency of interaction. The more frequently you
interact with someone, the more likely it is that
friendship will develop. Again physical proximity is
likely to produce more frequent contact and thus

affect whether the message is received, attended to,
understood, or believed? Or does it affect the
amount of inconsistency produced by the message?

In general, *other things being equal,* there will be
more attitude change if:

1. the recipient inadvertently hears the message;
2. the person delivering the message (the source)
is of high status and prestige;
3. the source begins the message by stating
attitudes that are similar to the recipient's views;
4. the message gives both sides of the argument if
the recipient is intelligent and gives only one
side of the argument if the recipient is not very
intelligent;
5. the recipient perceives that the source has
nothing personal to gain by the attitude change
the source is trying to produce;
6. the source clearly states the facts and the
conclusions;
7. the source has a lot in common with the
recipient;
8. the source is perceived as an expert on the
issue;
9. the recipient does not feel compelled or forced
to change but perceives that he is changing
freely, as a matter of choice;

Figure 10–5
Distance and attraction

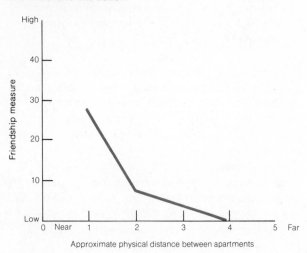

The relationship observed between friendship (sociometric choice) and physical distance in a student housing project.

more friendship. Indeed, any variable that increses the likelihood and the frequency of interaction between two people is likely to increase the degree of friendship between them.

But frequent interaction is not the only basis for friendship and liking. You all know individuals whom you have interacted with frequently, probably because you had to interact with them, but whom you do not like or regard as friends. Frequent interaction does not *guarantee* liking, although it is perhaps a starting place.

Given that two people frequently interact, what determines that a friendship will develop? Friendship is more likely if two people share the same race, sex, occupation or career objectives, socioeconomic status, age, attitudes, and so on. The evidence overwhelmingly supports similarity as a characteristic of friendship. We must be careful, however, not to conclude that similarity causes friendship in an automatic fashion. Similarity may affect friendship indirectly by affecting physical proximity and frequency of interaction. There are likely to be people with similar attitudes near you frequently; thus the important effect on friendship could be frequency of contact, which in turn is caused by similarity. If you like to go to the library, the chances are that the people you frequently meet at the library and perhaps become friends with share

this feeling about the library. *Actual* similarity may not be the *direct* cause of liking; studies show that it is *perceived* rather than actual similarity that is important. If you *think* that someone is similar to you even if he is not, attitudes of liking are more likely to happen. Thus, although it is true that your friends are likely to be similar to you in many ways, this similarity is only part of the reason for your friendship.

Friendship may come about and be maintained through the satisfaction of complementary needs. For example, a dominant person may like people he can dominate, and a submissive person may like people who dominate him. The needs of these two people would be described as complementary. The simplest way to see how complementary and similar needs might influence liking is to suggest that friendship is heavily determined by the mutual benefits that people can deliver to one another. In most cases, we would expect that we would benefit most from people with similar attitudes and needs (for example, we would get the most social approval from such people). However, we would also expect that in special cases two people with nearly complementary needs would gain a great deal by associating with each other, and these benefits could be the basis of their friendship.

One theory suggests that initial attraction between dating partners is based on fairly superficial characteristics like physical attraction, then proceeds to an exploration of belief, attitude, and value similarity, and continues with a concern for mutual and complementary satisfaction. Finally, some of the variables that seem related to a successful marriage include empathy with the marriage partner, open communication, and tolerance for differences.

Social exchange theory. Elaborating on the notion of mutual benefit as a factor in friendship, Thibaut and Kelley (1959) proposed that interpersonal attraction could be analyzed in terms of *rewards* and *costs* of each event or type of interaction. Suppose two strangers meet. They may find each other interesting, witty, helpful, and comforting. If so, they will certainly have a strong basis for friendship. Or they may find each other boring, antagonistic, and discomforting. At any rate, some level of satisfaction or reward results from the encounter. That reward is always at some cost, some effort expended, sacrifice made, risk taken, or obligation incurred. The attraction to each other is based on the interplay of these two factors, reward and costs.

Study Shows Beauty Beats Inner Traits

By Arthur J. Snider
© 1972, Denver Post-Chicago Daily News

Most people consider it vulgar to judge a person's character by physical appearance. Inner attributes are said to be much more important in determining who wins or loses our affection and esteem.

But two attractive female psychologists have concluded after a number of studies that for all the talk about inner-personality traits . . . we tend to give the best to beauty.

Prof. Ellen Berscheid of the University of Minnesota and Prof. Elaine Walster of the University of Wisconsin find in their collaborative studies that the influence of physical attractiveness begins making an impact early in life.

The teacher's pet in kindergarten is likely to be the attractive youngster. The one blamed for breaking the vase or creating the disturbance is the unattractive one.

A Test at Dance

The psychologists sponsored a dance for college students, but instead of permitting a computer to select the dates on the basis of shared interests, as the students believed, they were paired on a random basis.

They filled out a questionnaire to determine how the students liked their dates. Instead of shared interests, the most important determinant of how much each liked his or her date, wanted to see the partner again, and actually did, was how attractive the date was.

Not only is physical attractiveness the crucial standard by which we form our first impressions, the psychologists said, but also we tend to assign to pretty people attributes that may not exist.

Possible Reason

One of their studies finds students think good-looking persons generally are "more sensitive, kind, interesting, strong, poised, modest, sociable, outgoing and exciting than less attractive persons," Professors Berscheid and Walster report in Psychology Today.

"These findings suggest a possible reason for our nearly obsessive pursuit of suitably attractive mates. If we believe that a beautiful person embodies an ideal personality and that he or she is likely to garner all the world's material benefits and happiness, the substantial lure of beauty is not surprising."

What is the basis of our stereotyped image of beauty and virtue?

"It seems possible that in earlier times physical attractiveness was positively related to physical health," the authors conjecture. "It might be the instinctive nature of any species to want to associate and mate with those who are the healthiest of that species. We may be responding to a biological anachronism, left over from a more primitive age."

What determines whether two people will like each other? Is it similarity in personality? Does physical beauty play a more important role than most of us would care to admit?

Consider the fact that friendships are typically between similar individuals. According to social exchange theory we can understand the similarity effect by realizing that rewards in a social encounter are more likely to occur if the individuals have similar attitudes. If you encounter someone and mention in the discussion that you do not feel that abortion laws should be liberalized, what happens when he responds with, "I wholeheartedly agree" as opposed to "I think you're all wrong"? In the first case, the response is very much like a reward, a positive reinforcer of your attitude. In the second case, you may find yourself in a heated debate (high cost factor in the encounter) with very few rewards. So similar people are likely to deliver more rewards at lower costs than dissimilar people. Social exchange theory suggests that this is one reason why similarity is such a predominant characteristic of friendships.

The costs and rewards, according to Thibaut and Kelley, are based not on any absolute level but on a comparison level. Comparison level refers to the standard by which persons evaluate what they feel they deserve. It is modified by experience, so that past outcomes raise or lower the comparison level depending on whether the outcomes were positive or negative. If a person has recently experienced a series of inadequate outcomes (costs are higher than rewards), he will lower his expectations and raise his evaluation of future outcomes. A future encounter for this person may be judged to be adequate, while for someone with a higher comparison level the same personal encounter would be judged inadequate.

Social exchange theory has a basis in learning theory and decision-making theory, both of which propose, in one form or another, that behavior is a function of possible reward and the probability of achieving that reward. This formulation—people choose what they like best and avoid what they dislike—has great intuitive appeal as well as empirical support. It is a quite general formulation and can encompass other simpler formulations based on single factors such as complementary of needs, similarity of attitudes, and frequency of contact.

"I'm awfully sorry, Dick, but we've all just had a little meeting, and we've agreed that perhaps it's best that you leave the commune."

New Yorker, May 12, 1973. Drawing by Weber; © 1973 The New Yorker Magazine, Inc.

Individuals within Groups

The discussion in the previous section has focused on the attitudes of individuals, which are generally viewed as relatively permanent products of social experience. The major concern was with the rather pervasive effects of attitudes on an individual's treatment of or response to another person or group. This section is concerned with somewhat more immediate and probably more transitory phenomena. Its purpose is to review research in a different social psychology tradition, involving how the actual presence of other people can and does influence our behavior. Research shows that the personal, social, and physical characteristics of other people who are present in a situation can forcefully affect the manner in which a person responds in that situation.

Social Influence

The mere presence of others, as audience or as coworkers without any verbal exchange, affects individual performance, a phenomenon known as *social facilitation.*

The first social psychological experiment, conducted by Norman Triplett in 1897, demonstrated social facilitation. Triplett, a fan of bicycle racing, noticed that when racers were bicycling against one another, their times were faster than when they raced against the clock. His observation prompted him to conduct the following experiment. He had children wind kite string under two conditions—either while alone or with other children. Triplett found, as he expected, that children performed the task more slowly when they were alone.

Since Triplett's study, many other investigators have conducted experiments on social facilitation. In all these the presence of others seems to enhance performance of simple, well-learned skills, such as winding string, but inhibits the acquisition of new skills, such as memorizing a list of nonsense syllables. Robert B. Zajonc (1965) has suggested that the presence of others increases arousal or drive level in such a way that the dominant (or most probable) response becomes even more dominant. Because old response patterns take precedence over new responses, new learning is inhibited. Zajonc's interpretation, diagramed below, seems to take into account most of the data.

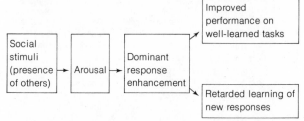

Conformity. The effect of others is more dramatic when pressure is placed on the individual to conform. People tend to feel uncomfortable when they are alone in their actions, out of step with the crowd. The effect of a conflict between individual judgment and group decisions has been cleverly studied by Solomon Asch (1956), among others. Asch required subjects to make perceptual judgments of the length of two lines in the presence of a group of confederates (see Figures 10-6 and 10-7). (Confederates are collaborators of the experimenter who pose as subjects.) First the confederates reported, publicly and in turn, that what was clearly and objectively the shorter of two lines was the longer. Then it was the subject's turn to respond. He was in a state of conflict, since he saw that the group was wrong. Asch found that approximately one-third of the subjects' responses were in conformity with the group, an indication of succumbing to social pressure (see Figure 10-8). Compare this with the lone jury member who disagrees with all the others. Asch suggests that the subjects' conformity reflects their reasonable reliance on the judgment of others. Subjects have two sources of information, their own and others'

Guidelines for Building a Happy Marriage

Every couple and every relationship is different, so there are no infallible rules for selecting a mate with whom you can maintain a happy and satisfying relationship. However, on the basis of problems encountered by marriage counselors and the research discussed in this chapter, some general guidelines can be suggested.

Before Marriage

1. Try to *distinguish sexual attraction from love.* Obviously, sexual attraction is an important component of love, but it is not enough to base an enduring relationship on.

2. Examine your reasons for wanting to marry this particular person. If you are marrying to escape from an unhappy homelife, to "reform" the other, to solve your own personal problems, or because all of your friends are marrying, don't. Analyze what you would gain and what you would lose should you marry.

3. Keep the lines of communication open. Discuss areas that will be important after marriage, such as the relationship between the two of you and your in-laws, money, religion, children, and the role of husband and wife. There should be no surprises in basic areas after the wedding ceremony. *Really get to know the other person.*

4. Be analytical about the relationship you now have with the other person. Patterns of interaction before marriage are your best clue as to what life with the other person will be like after marriage. Don't delude yourself that the other person will "change" after marriage. *What you see is what you're going to get.*

5. Think about the characteristics of the other person. Are you compatible in areas that are important to you? Complete similarity could lead to a boring relationship, but dissimilarity in important areas—such as attitudes about sex, religion, children, the husband and wife roles, and so forth—can be irritants after marriage.

After Marriage

1. Be as concerned about the happiness, growth, and well-being of the other as you are about your own.

2. Keep the lines of communication open. Don't store up grievances. Air important differences openly, but in a way that will not wound the self-esteem of your partner.

3. Be tolerant. Nobody is perfect. Accept the imperfections of the other that you can tolerate. Before criticizing the other, think about some of your own imperfections, and decide whether the issue is important enough to discuss.

4. Don't try to make your partner into a carbon copy of yourself. You married your partner because you liked and loved what was there; give the other person some breathing room. You'll both be more interesting to the other if you don't have total togetherness.

5. Be aware of the other person's moods and guide your reactions accordingly. Don't bring up an irritating subject when the other person is feeling tired or irritable.

6. If you do get into an argument, keep the discussion limited to the issue at hand. Hurtful remarks about areas irrelevant to the issue at hand will only interfere with the discussion. If you sense that the argument is escalating, break off the discussion. When tempers have cooled, resume the discussion.

7. Be your partner's best friend. Act in such a manner that the other person knows he or she is deeply loved. Be receptive to discussions of the other person's problems, but don't dwell exclusively on them. A marriage is not psychotherapy. Be sure you share pleasant events as well as problems.

8. Be analytical about the meaning of your patterns of interaction. Say what you mean and not what you think you should say. Be honest with one another.

9. Make "marital rules" explicit. Bargain openly and negotiate contracts about duties, obligations, and privileges. There are some unpleasant duties that must be performed, and how the chores are to be allocated should be made explicit.

judgments, both of which have proved reliable in the past and neither of which is necessarily superior. Asch suggests that conformity is in large part a *rational process* reflecting a recognition of the validity of other viewpoints. Asch's formulation is important because it points to the complexity of social influence. Social influence is not simply a blind following of others, an instinctive response to group pressure or social dominance. Rather, it is the result of a complex set of factors, including the

informational value of other responses as well as a need for social approval.

Is Asch right in asserting that conformity results from reinterpretation of perception as a result of information? If others only provided additional information, people who conformed publicly would also do so privately. However, when simple judgments of line length are given privately, conformity drops markedly. Thus it seems that expressing disagreement with others publicly is, in

Figure 10–6
To conform or not to conform?

Figure 10–8
Asch's results

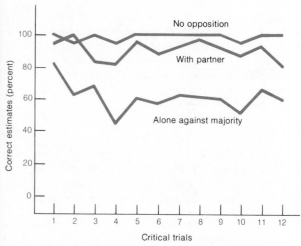

The number of correct responses of subject Number 6 under three conditions: when the group did not lie (no opposition), when they all lied together (alone against majority), and when one confederate agreed with Number 6 against the majority (with partner). Note that all it takes is one other person to counteract the conformity effect.

In the classic study of conformity, Solomon Asch had seven subjects sit around a table and judge which of three lines was equal in length to a standard line they had seen earlier. The only real subject was Number 6; the others were paid confederates of Asch. Although the task was very easy, in one of the experimental conditions the confederates all lied about which line was correct. When it was Number 6's turn to respond, he usually showed signs of conflict (straining, double-checking, etc.) over whether to conform to the group judgment or give the response that he perceived was correct.

Figure 10–7
Asch's task

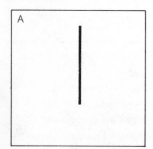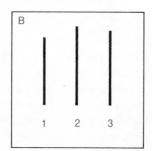

After viewing card A, the subjects must pick the line from B that matches.

itself, disagreeable and is probably a major factor contributing to conformity.

Limits? The most dramatic demonstration in the social psychological literature of willingness to obey—to comply with the demands of another—has been reported by Stanley Milgram (1965). Milgram had subjects help him run an experiment where the subjects were to administer electric shocks to another person—presumably to investigate the effect of punishment on learning. In fact, Milgram was concerned with how far subjects would go in shocking another when told to do so by an authority figure. No one actually was shocked. The shocking apparatus was disconnected, although the subjects did not know this.

The setting of the experiment was as follows. A middle-aged victim was strapped into a chair. Subjects, who had been led to believe that the victim had a heart ailment, were told to give increasingly intense electric shocks, ranging from 15 to 450 volts (15 more volts with each "mistake" the victim made), labeled "mild" to "danger-severe" shock. (The "victim" was, of course, a confederate; his "mistakes" were deliberate.) At 75 volts, the victim grunts; at 100 volts, he complains; at 150

Social Influence in Action

One obvious place where social influence can have literally "life and death" implications is in the process of deliberation by juries. Consider the following case.

Newsweek—Across the country in Fairfield, Calif., 61-year-old Naomi Underwood wasn't so stubborn. After holding out for a week against the conviction of Juan Corona on charges that he was the killer of 25 migrant farmhands (NEWSWEEK, Sept. 25), Mrs. Underwood capitulated. Gripping the table in front of him but otherwise stoic, Corona, a 38-year-old labor contractor and father of four, was declared guilty on each of 25 counts of murder. Then he was taken back to the state prison hospital in Vacaville, where he has suffered two heart attacks and a "coronary insufficiency" in the last eighteen months. His lawyer, Richard Hawk, moved immediately for a retrial. Mrs. Underwood said that Corona's failure to take the stand himself in his four-month trial "bothered me very, very much," but she added: "I don't think they had enough evidence. I still doubt I made the right decision."

volts, he demands release; at 285 volts, he screams and refuses to answer. When subjects objected to the experiment's continuation, they were encouraged or ordered to go on (with phrases like "You must continue; the experiment requires you to continue"). Many subjects did strongly protest but nevertheless obeyed the experimenter. In fact, 62 percent of the subjects in the experiment (20- to 50-year-old males of varied occupations, all of whom had voluntarily responded to a newspaper ad promising $4.50 to take part in a psychological experiment) obeyed completely. They went all the way to 450 volts!

Milgram's results are frightening. They can be related to such things as the behavior of Lieutenant Calley at the My Lai massacre and the obedience of the Germans under Hitler. They also raise the moral question of who is responsible for the behavior—the person behaving or the authority demanding obedience. Subsequent studies in varied conditions have confirmed the willingness of a large proportion of perfectly ordinary persons to obey authority when requested to mistreat another in cruel and potentially harmful ways. Milgram concluded that:

The results, as seen and felt in the laboratory, are to this author disturbing. They raise the possibility that human nature, or more specifically the kind of character produced in American democratic society, cannot be counted on to insulate its citizens from

brutality and inhumane treatment at the direction of malevolent authority. A substantial proportion of people do what they are told to do, irrespective of the content of the act and without limitations of conscience, so long as they perceive that the command comes from a legitimate authority. If, in this study, an anonymous experimenter could successfully command adults to subdue a 50-year-old man and force on him painful electric shocks against his protests, one can only wonder what government, with its vastly greater authority and prestige, can command of its citizenry.   **(Milgram, 1965)**

Leadership

Many persons hold that there are natural-born leaders, or at least those who are leaders in all circumstances. Much time and money has been spent by government and industry on trying to identify the qualities that distinguish such leaders. The evidence now strongly indicates, however, that a general leadership trait does not exist. Leaders in one group are followers in another; different situations require different leaders. To put it another way, nearly everyone can and might become a leader in some groups or situations. There are some important characteristics of demonstrated leaders, such as higher intelligence, better adjustment, and greater self-confidence. But these characteristics alone are not sufficient or strongly enough associated to define a leadership syndrome.

Several different styles of leadership have been identified, but the evidence on which is most effective is at this time still confusingly unclear. In one case, for example, authoritarian and democratic leaders were compared for their effectiveness in a variety of tasks and situations. Authoritarian leaders directed most of what went on, were inconsiderate of group members, and differentiated sharply in their evaluations of the most and least preferred coworkers. Democratic leaders, on the other hand, were considerate of group members, were concerned with group morale, allowed for group decisions, and evaluated least and most preferred coworkers similarly.

The results of this study show that authoritarian leaders are more effective under some circumstances, democratic leaders under others. For example, authoritarian leaders get the most out of a group when leader-member relations are good and the task at hand is highly structured or mechanical—or if the task is unstructured, but the leader is powerful. They are also more effective when leader-member relations are poor, the task is unstructured, and the leader has little power. A democratic style of leadership is most effective under two conditions—when relations are good, the task is structured, and the leader has little power, and when relations are not good, the task is structured, and the leader is powerful.

Thus, it is difficult to arrive at a general conclusion or recommendation. Leaders differ in style. But which style will work best depends so much on the people and situation involved that predictions are hazardous. Group-leader relations are complicated, and we will need a lot more information from research before the principles of leadership become clear.

Group Performance and Organization

"Too many cooks spoil the broth." But, "Two heads are better than one." These two common sayings are potentially conflicting descriptions of the relative excellence of individual versus group performance. But in the area of problem solving both statements are sometimes right. With some problems, for some groups, a group solves problems more accurately than any individual. For others, group performance is lower. Like our evidence on leadership, the evidence here is by no means clear or straightforward.

Group problem solving. Although conclusions about group problem solving are far from final, it seems that group performance is particularly superior on moderately difficult problems but inferior on very difficult ones requiring a series of cumulative steps for solution. Groups have *not* been demonstrated to be clearly superior to the sum of attempts of individuals working separately, and sometimes they are clearly inferior. Furthermore, a group decision frequently takes longer and uses more total hours than individual ones. Whether the improvement in performance shown by groups in solving some problems makes up for their frequent inefficiency is an open question (see Chapter 5 for further discussion).

In part, group forces may inhibit a creative approach. The social facilitation literature suggests that the presence of others inhibits new and unique responses. In addition, fear of the reaction of others may inhibit the expression of unusual responses. Such self-censorship may prevent expression of very useful solutions. To counter this inhibition the technique of brainstorming has been developed. This technique requires group members to respond freely without evaluation either by themselves or others. The intent is to discover as many approaches as possible that may be productive of an original

and superior solution. Systematic evaluation, however, suggests that brainstorming itself is often inferior to individuals working alone, because groups tend to concentrate on one line of thought and do not move as readily to other perspectives or themes. Moreover, when individuals are given instructions to avoid self-criticism, their creativity and problem solving improve whether or not they are part of a group.

Group decision making. Who will be more likely to recommend a risky course of action—an individual or a group, a brain surgeon or a committee of brain surgeons? This problem first came to the attention of social psychologists in 1961, when a student in the School of Business Administration at MIT, J. Stoner, reported in his master's thesis that group recommendations were in general more risky than the average individual recommendations. Stoner asked subjects to indicate the chances of success they would require before recommending that a risk be taken in several problem situations (see Table 10-2). He found that groups tended to require lesser chances of success than individuals did—the *risky shift.*

Several interpretations of this phenomenon have been offered. One emphasizes the diffusion of responsibility that can occur in groups. Because individuals in groups share the potential burden of being wrong, each individual has less to lose. He is willing to risk *partial* blame for an error for the chance of being right, which he can represent as a personal success.

Table 10–2
Two sample problems used by Stoner

Problem A

A college senior planning graduate work in chemistry may enter University X where, because of rigorous standards, only a fraction of the graduate students manage to receive the Ph.D.; or he may enter University Y, which has a poorer reputation, but where almost every graduate student receives the Ph.D. What chance of success would you require before recommending that the student enter University X?

Problem B

Mr. M is contemplating marriage to Ms. T, a woman whom he has known for a little more than a year. Recently, however, a number of arguments have occurred between them suggesting some sharp differences of opinion in the way each views certain matters. Indeed, they decide to seek professional advice from a marriage counselor as to whether it would be wise for them to marry. On the basis of the meetings with a marriage counselor, they realize that a happy marriage, while possible, would not be assured. What chance of success would you require before recommending that the couple marry?

But there are other factors. Some data suggest that in a group people who are naturally riskier in their decisions are also more influential. The risky person tends to talk more and louder and to be more impelled by immediate practical possibilities than the conservative person. The risk takers, then, might effectively pull the group as a whole toward the decision they favor.

Finally, Roger Brown has pointed out that most Americans evaluate themselves as being *at least as risky as the average person.* Even objectively conservative people tend to appraise themselves as daring and willing to take a chance in most situations. Risk appears to be a general cultural *value* in this country. Thus, when a person hears other members suggest riskier positions than he was thinking about, he shifts his thinking toward greater risk to prove to himself and the group that he is at least as risky and daring as the next person.

A complication with these explanations is that there are some problems for which groups are more cautious than individuals. Problem B in Table 10-2 is an example of one of the Stoner problems that consistently elicits a more cautious group response.

Any explanation of the difference between individuals and groups should apply to both greater riskiness and greater caution. Groups are not always more risky; sometimes they are more conservative than individuals. Fortunately, the risk-as-value hypothesis can be modified to fit the cases where groups are more conservative. For certain kinds of issues, there are cultural values implying that conservatism is "right." In such cases the individual values his conservatism and feels that he is at least as conservative as the next person. He may see that some group members are more conservative and so he shifts toward a greater degree of caution—*the cautious shift*

It seems that the initial definition of the problem—that is, whether it calls for riskiness or caution—determines the relative position of the group response. By their very nature, most problems entail an element of risk, and risk is the only means of attaining a valued outcome. This fact, combined with the influence of "risky as thou" group members, means that, on the average, groups will conclude in favor of more risky action than individuals. However, when the potential payoff to a risky course of action is not seen as equivalent to the cost even by the risk takers, caution is indicated and the risky group becomes the cautious group.

Groupthink.   What happens when powerful decision makers get together to decide important courses of action potentially leading to historic events? What are the possible sources of error? How is it that brilliant people may make stupid decisions? After analyzing a number of historic decisions, Irving Janis formulated the concept of *groupthink* to describe what happens in such situations. Groupthink occurs in highly cohesive groups where the members are strongly oriented toward maintaining group unanimity, with the result that critical responses are reduced and rendered ineffective. Janis identifies the characteristic of groupthink as: (1) a sense of invulnerability, (2) extensive rationalization, (3) moral self-righteousness, (4) simplistic stereotypic description of the opposition, (5) strong conformity pressures, (6) self-censorship of divergent views, (7) suppression of divergent information from others, and (8) an illusion of unanimity.

Janis has analyzed the decision by President Kennedy and his advisors to support the Bay of Pigs invasion of Cuba by Cuban dissidents in groupthink terms. The events leading up to the final decision have been widely documented; important intelligence information was ignored, misinformation was attended to, and the results were disastrous. The President and his advisors formed a highly cohesive group. Everything seemed to fall right for them. Moral questions were not raised; self-censorship and the censorship of others have been documented. The Cuban government was characterized as stupid and ineffective. Because serious doubts were not expressed, the illusion of unanimity was maintained.

Many other events seem to fit Janis' model. Consider as an example the events preceding the disastrous decision of the Israeli leaders in the 1973 Arab-Israeli war not to mobilize. There are strong suggestions that elements of groupthink were operating. Can you think of any other instances? What about the "Watergate affair" and the White House plumbers unit?

Social psychologists are now working on ways of preventing groupthink.

Cooperation and Conflict

The problem of conflict between individuals and between groups is one of obvious importance. Psychologists have tried to analyze and understand the processes underlying the problem in order to find ways of reducing conflict and its accompanying hostility and to induce cooperation in its place. Perhaps the most important factor uncovered in this research is the overwhelming tendency to overvalue one's own groups (either those we belong to or those we identify with) and to undervalue others. This is perhaps the major component of the dynamics of intergroup hostility. It is clearly at the heart of the stereotypes involved in prejudice that we discussed earlier.

The Robbers Cave experiment.   A classic social psychology experiment on group conflict called the Robbers Cave experiment (named after the site of the study) was published in 1961 by Sherif, Harvey, White, Hood, and Sherif. Here are the facts of the Robbers Cave experiment.

The subjects were 12-year-old boys selected to be good examples of typical middle-class American children. They were normal, healthy, well adjusted, happy, fun-loving, and energetic. The experimenters divided the boys into two groups designed to equate the members on such attributes as intelligence and size.

The boys understood they were going to summer camp, and each group was taken separately to an isolated Boy Scout camp.

The camp was actually being run by the experimenters, who hired the camp counselors. The couselors observed the boys' behavior and reported on it to the experimenters (the measurement was unobtrusive because the boys merely thought of the counselors as counselors). The experimenters and counselors conducted camp activities according to a preconceived experimental plan that had three stages.

In the first stage the two groups of boys were treated separately in such a way as to develop a feeling of group identification and belongingness. This was done by having the boys work on projects designed to achieve goals that they all would value and that they all would have to cooperate to attain. Sample projects were improving the swimming hole and building a rope bridge. Each group was treated so that the end result would be two groups of boys, each with a high level of within-group cohesiveness. One group of boys decided to call themselves the Rattlers, and the other group took the name Eagles. At this stage, each group was separated from the other and worked independently on different projects. By the end of the first stage, the experimenters had succeeded in creating two real groups as opposed to just a collection of boys. Within each group there were definite feelings of belonging to the group.

In the second stage the counselors began to create conflict between the two groups, pitting one group against the other in a series of contests, such as baseball and tug-of-war. The competition

between groups produced intergroup hostility, expressed in name calling, fighting, and raiding each other's camps. The Rattlers did not like the Eagles, and the feeling was mutual. Prejudice against out-group members and in favor of in-group members clearly existed.

The third stage consisted of efforts to reduce the intergroup hostility. Simply bringing the two groups together (for example, having them eat together) had no effect on the hostility. Providing the boys with a common enemy (a third group of boys) did reduce hostility between the Rattlers and the Eagles, but the boys were still hostile. The groups merely displaced their hostility to the common enemy.

What did reduce the total hostility was the same thing that was responsible for developing the feelings of "group belongingness" in the first stage. The experimenters set tasks that required both groups to work together to achieve the goals, and the goals were designed to be of value to members of both groups. For example, it was arranged for the camp truck to break down while it was taking both groups on a camping trip they both were looking forward to. All the boys in both groups were needed to pull the truck up a hill to get it started again. Because the goal was positive in character, hostility was not elicited. Because cooperative effort between the groups was necessary, intergroup hostility was no longer appropriate. A series of such cooperative ventures eventually led to intergroup friendliness to the point that the boys requested that they go home together in one bus. In fact, with their prize money one of the groups treated the other to milkshakes on the way home.

The trucking game study.   Deutsch and Krauss (1960) studied conflict in a situation analogous to the cold war arms escalation. Each of a pair of subjects was given a set of switches that controlled an imaginary truck. The two trucks were owned by competing trucking companies. Each truck could reach its destination by taking either a long route or a short shared route (see Figure 10-9). If both persons could use the short route, by cooperating with each other, they could gain the most—the faster the time, the greater the prize. In the first situation both participants controlled a gate that would block progress of the other along the short route; in the second situation only one person had a gate; and in the third neither had a gate. Players did best when no threat existed (no gate could be closed). They did next best when only one person controlled the threat; the player with the threat gained the most. They did worst when both had the

Figure 10–9
The trucking game

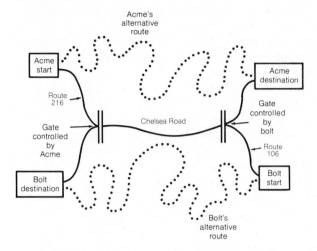

Subject's road map showing the long routes and the
short route that both trucks had to share.

gate as a weapon. Thus when a person was faced
with a threat, it was better for him in terms of
personal gain to be without a weapon!

The analogy is crude. It is a long way from the
Acme Trucking Company to the Kremlin or
Pentagon, from gates to bombs. But the
experimental results are intriguing and suggestive of
possible applications in international affairs.

Helping victims of accidents and crimes.
When will you help a stranger? Who can be counted
on? Why were Kitty Genovese's screams, ending in
her murder after half an hour of torment,
unanswered by 38 onlookers in New York City? Why
did no one even bother to call the police?

Bibb Latané and John Darley (1968) suggest that
help may be *least likely* when there are *many
possible helpers.* Two experiments on the reaction
of people to accidents support this idea. In one
study smoke was pumped into an experimental
room. When subjects were alone, 75 percent
reported the smoke to a nearby experimenter within
6 minutes. When others were present, 38 percent at
most (and in one condition only 10 percent)
reported the smoke.

In another study an attractive young woman gave
subjects some questionnaires, then went into an
adjoining room, made some noises as though she
had fallen, and screamed, "Oh, my God, my
foot . . . I . . . I . . . can't move . . . it. Oh . . . my

Motorists Ignore Girl's Pleas

New York (AP)—Why didn't at least one of 100 or
more motorists stop to assist a 10-year-old girl who
stood along a busy expressway, partially clad and
pleading for help?

Police in the county sought the answer today, as
they looked for clues in the rape and strangulation
death of Lydia Cox.

To help find the killer, the town's two newspapers and other groups have offered rewards totaling more than $4,000 for information leading to the
arrest of the girl's slayer.

The two newspapers said they received more
than a dozen calls Sunday, but few seemed related
to the case. Some came from motorists who said
they saw the girl or a "suspicious" man on Inter-
state 490 last Tuesday.

Police said the girl disappeared that day while on
a shopping errand for her mother. They theorized
the child was kidnapped, escaped and ran along the
highway hoping for help.

Her body was found by two teen-agers on Thursday along a rural road in a suburban town. A
medical examiner said she had been raped and
strangled.

Motorists who contacted police after the girl's
body was found and reported seeing the child along
the superhighway said traffic was heavy and moving at upwards of 60 miles an hour. Some said they
could not have stopped to aid her because of the
traffic.

Social psychologists are grappling with the problem
of bystander apathy, the refusal of bystanders to
help in an emergency. One theory is that the more
bystanders there are, the more everyone tends to
assume that someone else in the group will take
the responsibility.

ankle, I . . . can't get this . . . thing . . . off me." Of
the persons waiting alone, 70 percent offered help.
When two subjects were waiting together, 40
percent offered help. When a confederate was there
with a subject, and remained impassive, only 7
percent of the subjects intervened.

Who will help the victim of a crime? Latané and
Darley devised an ingenious experiment to test their
proposition that the more persons present when a
victim needs help, the less help will come forth.
They staged a robbery of a liquor store 96 times in a
two-week period. The robberies were planned so
that there were either one or two customers present
during the robbery. The liquor store was real, the
customers were real customers, the robbers were
experimental accomplices. The robber would enter
the store and ask the manager for his most

"They said they don't want to get involved."

©Punch (Rothco).

expensive beer. While the manager was in the back room, the robber would pick up a case of beer and walk out, saying, "They'll never miss this," and he would drive off. A minute later, the store manager would return to the counter, and if the customers did not report the theft spontaneously, the manager would ask, "Hey, what happened to that man who was here? Did you see him leave?" Twenty percent of the customers reported the theft without prompting; 51 percent of the remainder reported it after the manager's questions. Of the 48 single customers, 65 percent reported the theft. The theft was reported in only 56 percent of the cases when two customers were present, a significantly smaller percentage than statistically expected for two-customer groups. It seems that, in the case of a liquor store robbery at least, two customers are less likely than one customer to report a theft.

City life and social crowding. Most Americans live in or work in cities. Despite the flight to suburbia, cities continue to grow. It is impossible today for most of us to avoid almost continuous contact and interaction with other people, most of whom are strangers or at best mere acquaintances. Psychologists have become increasingly interested in the effects of crowded conditions and city life in general on the social and individual behavior of human beings.

This interest is prompted, in part, by the large number of socially pathological incidences in recent years that seem to be unique to cities. A prominent example, of course, is the slaying of Kitty Genovese in New York City, while literally dozens of people sat by passively and observed. Some writers have been quick to interpret facts like these as a result of the

evils of crowding and urban living. Highrise apartments, tenements, condominiums, housing projects, and other similar living arrangements that promote crowding have been indicted as the major modern cause of social grief. The general underlying factor is said to be urbanization and the expansion of modern cities.

One social psychologist, Stanley Milgram (1970), has offered a psychological interpretation for the unique social behaviors of city dwellers in terms of an information-overload hypothesis. He argues that people who live in large cities are subjected to an often overwhelming influx of stimulation and information. As a consequence, these people develop strategies to protect themselves against this overload. Among the commonly observed acquired strategies are a norm of noninvolvement in the affairs of others, respect for privacy, tolerance for diverse life styles, and distrust. Milgram has conducted a number of experiments to demonstrate the existence and function of these strategies. In one study, for example, experimenters attempted to gain entry to the dwelling of a selected sample of residents of New York City and a similar sample from a small town outside New York City. The results were interesting and consistent with Milgram's idea (see Table 10–3). Male experimenters could gain entry some three to five times more often in a small town than in a city. Female experimenters were more likely to gain entry than males, succeeding nearly 100 percent of the time in small towns. Still, even females could gain entry in less than half their attempts in the city. Apparently, city dwellers have a greater distrust of strangers than do residents of small towns.

Another example of the same sort of effect comes from a study in which a social psychologist arranged to leave an automobile for 64 hours either near the New York University Bronx campus or near the Stanford University campus in the suburban community of Palo Alto, California. The New York

Table 10–3
Percent of entries achieved in city and town dwellings

Experimenter	Percent of entries achieved	
	City*	Small town†
Male		
No. 1	16	40
No. 2	12	60
Female		
No. 3	40	87
No. 4	40	100

*Number of requests for entry, 100.
†Number of requests for entry, 60.

The Stanford Prison Study

To study the social psychology of imprisonment, Phillip Zimbardo and his colleagues devised an experiment in which they could observe behavior in a simulated prison environment. The inmates were male college student volunteers, as were the guards. Members of both groups received $15 per day for their participation. The expected duration of sentence was 2 weeks. The simulated jail, in the basement of the psychology building at Stanford University, was divided into cells with bars on the doors and equipped with the minimum amount of furniture; the toilets were public. The mock prisoners were "arrested" in realistic manner by the local police department, booked, stripped, examined, given prison clothes and a number, and incarcerated. The guards were in uniform with silvered sunglasses, billy clubs, and handcuffs. The atmosphere was oppressive.

The results of this experiment were dramatic; seemingly typical college students began to behave in strange ways. The pseudo-prisoners became increasingly disturbed; the pseudo-guards became quite brutal. After three days, the first prisoner was released because he showed signs of severe emotional disturbance. Before the experiment was prematurely terminated after 6 days, 3 other prisoners of the total of 10 had to be released because they were seriously disturbed. The guards also were affected. They relied heavily on physical force and harassment. For example, one of the guards commented: "I was surprised at myself . . . I made them call each other names and clean the toilets out with their bare hands. I practically considered the prisoners cattle, and I kept thinking I have to watch out for them in case they try something."

The investigators were surprised by the relative ease with which sadistic behavior could be elicited from normal, non-sadistic people, and the extent of the emotional disturbance which emerged in young men selected precisely on the basis of their emotional stability. The pathology observed in this study cannot be attributed to any pre-existing personality differences of the subjects. Rather, their abnormal social and personal reactions were a product of their transaction with an environment whose norms and contingencies supported the production of behavior which would be pathological in other settings, but were "appropriate" in this prison.

Findings such as these could have considerable impact on the administration of prisons and prison-reform efforts.

---

car was completely stripped within 24 hours. Within three days, it was reduced to a heap of rubble. In contrast, the California car was untouched over the entire period. There are many differences between New York City and Palo Alto, California, other than mere density of residence. Nonetheless, the results of this experiment do fit the pattern described by Milgram and give one reason why city dwellers are likely to develop protective strategies.

What Does It Mean?

Social psychology has application in many diverse areas. For example, consider the industrial work setting. Employee attitudes toward fellow workers and toward the company will influence production and product quality, as well as playing a large part in employee morale. There are group norms about how to work, how much work to do, how to behave on the job, and who to associate with. There are problems of picking and training leaders. Virtually every aspect of social psychology can be applied to the industrial setting, for the industrial setting is itself like a small society. Other areas where social psychology has useful applications include educational institutions, mental hospitals, and prisons. There is also a social psychology of sexuality, which ranges from studies of sexual promiscuity to studies of love and platonic friendship. There is a social psychology of organizations, of the family, of prejudice, of altruism, of obesity, of many other topics. In short, because social behavior is so prevalent, social psychology has wide applicability. What follows are descriptions of some applications of social psychology often practiced by more specialized professionals.

Aggression

Social psychologists have long been interested in aggression, both when legitimized, as in Milgram's study of obedience, and when illegal, as in explosive, individual acts of violence. For our purposes, we will consider only the latter case. Explanations for violent acts have included: (1) instinctual or quasi-instinctual mechanisms, (2) physical bases in hormonal imbalance and genetic predispositions, (3) rage resulting from severe repression, (4) aggression following from frustration, (5) learned patterns of response, and (6) group conflict patterns.

Several prominent social psychologists have focused on imitative aggression, investigating the extent to which people, especially children, imitate aggressive acts they observe others perform. Foremost in the study of imitative aggression has been Albert Bandura (see Chapter 9). He and his colleagues investigated aggression as a product of *social learning.* They set up experiments to determine how young children respond when they observe aggression by adults. In their studies, children watched adults playing with toys either in an aggressive manner or not. Then the children were subsequently observed playing with the same toys, and their behavior was described and coded as aggressive or not. These studies showed that there is a marked increase in aggression following observed aggression. Bandura's research, presented here in its simplest form, strongly supports the view that aggression is learned through observation of others (see Chapter 9 for a more thorough treatment of social learning theory).

This view of the origins of aggression is further supported by the clustering of aggressive acts. For example, political assassinations often occur in clusters, as do hijackings, kidnappings, and mass murders. Suicide also may cluster; for example, when Marilyn Monroe took an overdose of sleeping pills, the suicide rate briefly jumped.

But in order to employ the social learning hypothesis as a major explanation for violent acts, people must have wide opportunity to observe violence. Where are the opportunities? How often do we view violence? Consider films. Leonard Berkowitz has addressed the question "Does viewing violent acts in film presentations increase, decrease, or have no effect on violent behavior?" The standard experimental procedure has been to show one group of subjects a movie with much violence, such as a boxing movie, while showing the other group an innocuous film. Then, under the pretext that they were taking part in another study, the subjects were asked to administer an electric shock to another person (who in fact received no shock). Berkowitz found that viewing violent films increases the likelihood of shocking another and increases the magnitude and duration of administered shocks. He concludes that media protrayals of violence can indeed lead to violent acts, although, as we discussed in Chapter 7, the effects are undoubtedly no more pronounced than those attributable to real or natural violence, as in war, crime, and some sports.

These findings on imitative violence do not constitute a total explanation of violence; there are other important contributing factors, other plausible explanations, and even some contradicting evidence. But these studies do provide some information about the way certain kinds of behavior probably develop.

Persuasive Communication

Persuasive communication is a big business in the United States, and persuasion is mainly an application of the principles of attitude change. The most obvious example is advertising. An advertisement or TV commercial is basically a message designed to change your attitudes about some product or service, particularly the action tendency component of attitudes—advertisers want you to buy their product.

We can apply the principles of attitude change to advertising and see what an effective (persuasive) ad would look like. The fact that such an advertisement might not be one we would like in the esthetic sense is irrelevant, as you can well appreciate if you have ever watched television.

The effective ad, say for a new cereal, might have the following characteristics.

1. It would be catchy or lively or loud—you want your ad to stand out and be seen or heard.

2. It would be fairly simple-minded—you want your message to be clear and understandable to all who are to receive it.

3. It would repeat the message over and over, for example: "Buy Zappo! Zappo, the best cereal you ever tasted. Remember Zappo, Z-A-P-P-O, that's Zappo. Get Zappo today."

4. It might have a famous football player saying that he eats Zappo every day, implying that this is why he is such a good football player. A football player would be used, of course, only if the people you were trying to impress considered football players to be high-prestige and high-status individuals—people they would like to be like. You would adjust your choice of the actor in the ad according to the audience you wished to persuade. A roller derby star would probably not help you sell Cadillacs.

5. It would demonstrate for the audience the value of eating Zappo, perhaps by showing all the beautiful, rich, sexy, and completely happy people who eat Zappo.

How do you think the advertising business is doing with respect to the use of these principles? Have you ever seen a TV commercial that fits this description?

Actually, persuasive communications, such as speeches, TV commercials, and newspaper articles, sometimes fail to change attitudes, despite what seem to be optimal conditions. The best example of this is the failure of the antismoking campaign to decrease cigarette consumption in this country —despite some very clever and dramatic TV spots, a barrage of newspaper and magazine articles, warnings on cigarette packages, and a ban on TV cigarette ads. One major problem, obviously, is getting the audience to attend to the message; smokers probably pay less attention to the antismoking ads and obtain less information about the harmful effects of smoking. As for the warning on the cigarette pack, the odds are that it is perceived rarely, if at all.

With regard to cigarette smoking, one technique of persuasion that has shown some promise is *role playing*. In one study, smokers were required to assume the role of a patient who had just been diagnosed as having lung cancer. The technique was similar to psychodrama (see Chapter 12), with each subject acting out the role of the dying cancer patient and with the experimenter playing the doctor role and repeatedly giving antismoking information. Role playing significantly reduced smoking in this study. Other similar studies have shown significant attitude change resulting from giving speeches in favor of the desired attitude, especially if the subject must improvise his speech. Thus, getting a bigot to stand up before an audience and improvise a speech favoring equality, integration, and civil rights will produce more attitude change in the bigot than in the group of people who merely listen to what he has to say. Can you see how consistency theory would account for this? Why is it better to have a person improvise his speech as opposed to just reading a prepared speech?

The use of psychotherapy in behavior disorders is, in many cases, conceived of by the therapist as a process of attitude changes. Usually the goal of this type of therapy is self-insight, which is basically a matter of changing attitudes about oneself. Group psychotherapy obviously involves social psychology and attitude change. The sensitivity training —encounter group movement got its start in Bethel, Maine, at the National Training Laboratory, where students of the distinguished social psychologist Kurt Lewin pioneered the basic techniques. We will have more to say about psychotherapy in Chapter 12.

Persuasive communication is involved in just about all aspects of our lives. Consider political campaigns and the massive advertising involved. Consider sermons delivered at churches. Consider government propaganda on drugs and alcoholism.

Attitude formation and attitude change is a major aspect of education. We hope that some of your attitudes about behavior will be changed by reading this book.

Reducing Racial Prejudice

The nature and origins of racial prejudice have been an enduring concern in society. Roughly four major approaches to reduction of prejudice have been investigated by psychologists. The first involves treating prejudice as a symptom of internal conflict. Group psychotherapy and self-insight training (that is, pointing out how prejudice is related to and is in the service of unconscious needs) have been used successfully to reduce racial prejudice on a small scale. Such an approach, however, is expensive and inefficient.

A second approach is based on evidence suggesting that certain child-rearing practices, especially parental practices that emphasize status and power and involve harsh physical punishment, are the basis for prejudice. Although there is correlational evidence supporting this conception, achieving massive changes in child rearing and family structure is probably impractical.

A third approach is based on the status of prejudice as an attitude. Persuasion and education can be used for attitude change, but propaganda in an open society is limited in its effectiveness, since racial bigots can and do avoid contact with it; they may attend only to sources compatible with their views, and they may still distort or otherwise disregard what they hear. (Totalitarian states, on the other hand, can employ propaganda with extreme success, as is exemplified by Nazi Germany.)

As for education, better educated persons are less prejudiced, but that does not mean education per se reduces prejudice. For example, it is now known that northern students attending southern universities become more prejudiced, while southern students attending northern universities become less prejudiced. Clearly the *content* of educational experience is an important contributory factor.

The final approach is based on the observation that most prejudiced whites have little contact with blacks except when blacks are in a subservient position. Equal-status contact does tend to reduce prejudice, especially when individuals are working together and are dependent on one another for the achievement of group goals.

In summary, reduction of prejudice is not easy to accomplish. In terms of social economy, it is probably best achieved by increased integration accompanied by reduction of status differential

Generations Closing Gap In Life-Styles

Bellingham, Wash. (AP)—Fairhaven College is closing the generation gap.

A federally funded experimental program is bringing people of all ages together for multigenerational living and learning in a college environment.

Eight senior citizens, ranging in age from 60 to 80, have moved into the college dormitory; another 21 are to arrive this month; and a day-care center has been set up for preschoolers.

The program is known as "The Bridge." The senior citizens pay from $62.50 to $75 a month for housing and some meals at the college. Accommodations range from single rooms to two-bedroom apartments shared by two senior citizens.

Didn't Waste Time

"When I heard about the program I hot-footed it up here," says Violet Dail, 60. Mrs. Dail said she had been segregated into a senior-citizen environment at her previous home in a mobile home park.

"I like it here very much," she said after about two weeks. "Already I've audited some classes, gone to a concert and an operetta, attended some lectures and two parties . . . It's absolutely fascinating."

None of the senior citizens is required to take classes, but all say they want to enroll in both the regular college courses and in special programs geared for them.

Mary Yotter, 80, Seattle, says she joined the program at Fairhaven, a branch of Western Washington State College, because "I don't like the separation of generations you find nowadays. I like the idea of all ages together. And we all go on a first-name basis here—I really like that.

"Talking to the students here today is a revelation and an education in itself. They are just as lovely as we were when we were kids."

Planners of the program hope the senior citizens will be able to use their experiences to help their juniors. Mrs. Yotter has spent several hours working with a Fairhaven student on a paper dealing with nutrition and the elderly, and she's looking forward to working with the preschoolers in the day-care center.

There are no academic qualifications for admittance but all applicants are screened carefully and interviewed to insure they will be comfortable in the program.

The arrival of the senior citizens has helped the young and the old, says Blair Kirchner, a student. Fairhaven "isn't a youth ghetto anymore. It feels like a different community."

Here is a social psychological experiment aimed at reducing intergroup tensions and easing social change.

(reducing intergroup conflict) and continued efforts at achieving social norms favorable to social equality.

Easing Social Change

Important social changes of many sorts are taking place in the United States. What we will discuss here is related to prejudice—desegregation. Legal segregation has been slowly diminishing for about 20 years. Areas of change have included educational and other public facilities (buses, restaurants, and so on). Segregation, however, continues in many areas, even in public facilities. Efforts at increasing integration in the North as well as in the South continue to occupy attention. How can desegregation be facilitated?

Experience with integration as well as with psychological theory suggests that integration need not wait for an absence of prejudice; it can proceed readily and *peacefully* despite widespread and deep-seated prejudice. In fact, desegregation is generally *followed* by social support. Changing behavior, as consistency theory suggests, can lead to changing attitudes.

Attitude change resulting from behavioral change

may, however, be quite limited. For example, white soldiers in World War II who initially opposed integration of their units came to accept and even highly praise black soldiers who joined their units. However, their acceptance was restricted to blacks as soldiers, and they maintained social segregation outside the armed services. Similarly, integrated schools may be readily accepted (where no organized resistance opposes them), but social equality does not necessarily spread beyond that institution. In other words, both the opponents and proponents of integration exaggerate its effects; integration of one institution does not lead to widespread social change.

Attitudes toward black people in the United States have undergone dramatic change as a result of the many complicated social forces that have operated in the last 30 years. On the school question, when asked in 1942 if black and white children should attend the same school, 2 percent of the southerners and 40 percent of the northerners replied positively. In 1963, 30 percent of the southerners and 75 percent of the northerners replied positively. Pettigrew (1965) reports that between 1963 and 1965, "would not object" responses to sending white children to school with a few black children changed from 87 to 91 percent in the North and from 38 to 62 percent in the South. With regard to a more general question, in 1942 only 21 percent of white southerners and 50 percent of white northerners believed blacks to be as intelligent as whites; in 1963 the figures were 59 percent and 80 percent, respectively. Although more recent data are not yet available, there is every reason to believe that the trends reflected in these statistics have continued. We have, no doubt, a long way yet to go. Still, significant progress in attitude change has clearly been accomplished.

Social psychology literature suggests that if desegregation could somehow be achieved, its maintenance would be relatively easy and would lead directly to attitude change. But how can it be carried out initially? Advantage can be taken of another important finding. There is or can be a considerable discrepancy between attitude and action. Attitude and action are inconsistent when: (1) social support for the attitude is lacking or contradicts the attitude; (2) persons or groups that are respected by the individual take a position contrary to his; (3) the attitude is inconsistent with other attitudes or values; (4) the opportunity for expression of the attitude is absent; and (5) the attitude (in this case prejudice) is isolated or compartmentalized so that it is not connected to concrete behavior (for example, picketing an integrated school). In concrete terms, this might mean that integration can take place when: (1) no counter-propaganda efforts develop (perhaps because of insufficient time); (2) the mayor, police chief, churches, and other influential people and institutions support integration; (3) other attitudes, such as respect for the law and social justice, are appealed to; (4) no active, concrete, and organized resistance occurs; (5) it is made clear that the attitude is not compromised by lack of action (as in the statement, "I'm as opposed to integration as anyone, but the law has to be respected"); or (6) the change comes about quietly and hence does not seem glaringly important.

Public Opinion Polling

In order to study attitudes and opinions, psychologists have developed techniques for measuring attitudes accurately and efficiently. The development of these measurement techniques has had an enormous impact on our lives, and in the case of public opinion polling this impact has not always been beneficial. It is possible, by *sampling techniques*, to measure a small number of people

© Washington Star Syndicate, Inc.

Many people feel that politicians pay too much attention to public opinion polls and make decisions accordingly. On the other hand, the use of polls at election time is frequently attacked by politicans whose images might be damaged by a bad poll. Psychologists nevertheless find polling an enormously efficient technique for getting answers to many of their questions.

and determine the attitudes of the entire group from which the small number was sampled. Thus, one could get a fairly good idea of how all people in the United States feel about a particular issue or event by *randomly sampling*—asking just a few hundred people.

Public opinion polls are valuable sources of data on the beliefs, opinions, attitudes, and values of representative samples of large populations. Although most psychologists recognize the importance of generalizing to a large population, seldom do they have the opportunity to collect data on more than very restricted and rather peculiar groups such as college sophomores or white rats. Increasingly, social psychologists are recognizing the possibilities of using poll data to test hypotheses. Being interested and involved in attitude assessment, social psychologists have contributed extensively to the design of public opinion polls.

The technique of polling public opinion is much abused, as you probably know. But when properly conducted, polls are exceedingly accurate estimators of public opinion. Their impact as a contributory factor to democratic processes has been reflected as much in their misuse as in their proper application. Two factors, which we discussed in Chapter 1, are of great importance in evaluating polls: (1) that the data are based on random selection of respondents from the appropriate population and (2) that the basis for the data collection is not biased (leading questions, for example, are to be avoided). Few polling organizations meet these two criteria, which has led to some lack of confidence on the part of the public. Clearly, just because an organization calls itself an "independent research firm" does not insure either its independence (lack of bias) or research competence.

Improving Personal Attractiveness

With some misgivings and with apologies to Dale Carnegie, we suggest a few conclusions about "how to make friends and influence people." As already indicated, there is a strong relationship between similarity and liking. Similarity is important in mate choice not only with respect to attitudes but also with respect to physical characteristics (for example, short men tend to marry short women), intelligence, educational level, family background, religion, happiness of parents' marriage, drinking and smoking habits, and numerous other factors. In general, the basic problem for people who want to be liked is to find persons similar to themselves. The solution does not involve much changing of *yourself* (unless you are in jail or otherwise severely restricted in access to potential friends); rather it involves selecting potential friends.

Social distance is another important factor. Simply increasing the number of persons that you are physically or socially close to will result in more friends. Joining a club or church or bowling league or any social organization will help just because it will increase the number and variety of people you come in contact with. This can also be troublesome, however, since physical closeness can lead to negative evaluation. After all, you are much more likely to be hurt (or even killed) by a friend, relative, or acquaintance than by a stranger. In general, the closer you are, the more intense the relationship —either positively or negatively speaking.

Fulfilling the needs of others increases one's social worth. In particular, providing companionship for persons who are anxious, under stress, lonely, or insecure should increase those persons' liking for you. The problem is to become aware of the relevant needs of others.

Praising others will increase one's popularity. Praise is reward, and, as we have seen, reward-cost ratios influence liking. The ancient philosopher Hecato stated this proposition succinctly: "I will show you a love potion without drug or herb or any witch's spell; if you wish to be loved, love." One problem with praise, however, is credibility. If the person being praised has high self-esteem, then the praiser will be well received for showing such insight. However, if the person has low self-esteem, the praise will be relatively ineffective, since it will be seen as inaccurate and undeserved.

Social skills themselves—how to be clever and popular—are very complicated affairs. They are the product of a long socialization procedure and are not reducible to a simple formula. It seems unlikely that they ever will be formalized, and hence it is unlikely that they can ever be taught in a school-like setting. At any rate, popularity is probably no more general a characteristic than leadership. A person who is popular in one group may be unpopular in another. An optimal strategy seems to be to choose one's group carefully if popularity is the goal. Finally, a word about physical attraction. This appears to be quite important (at least for romantic relations) for men as well as women—probably more important than we would like. But even though physical attractiveness appears important in relatively superficial relationships, it is not necessarily of major importance in more enduring ones.

Applying Principles of Social Influence

International conflict.   The problems of generalizing from psychological studies of conflict between game players or young children to studies of conflict between nations are many and difficult. Nevertheless, social psychological analysis of international conflict can be illustrated by an impressive interpretation of a partial reduction in Russian-American tension accompanying what has been called the J.F.K. experiment. On June 10, 1963, at the American University in Washington, D.C., President Kennedy delivered an important policy speech that took a conciliatory tone toward Russia. He indicated that constructive changes had taken place that could lead to solutions to world problems, and he urged the American people to reexamine their attitudes toward Russia and the cold war. *Izvestia*, in turn, published the speech in full, and Russia reversed its objection to the Western proposal that United Nations observers be sent to war-torn Yemen. The United States then lifted its objection to full status for the Hungarian delegation to the U.N., and Russia announced it had halted production of strategic bombers. During the course of these events, there were clear signs of a cold war thaw. By November 22, 1963, additional tension-reducing events included: (1) signing of the limited nuclear test ban treaty, (2) discussion of joint space exploration, (3) consideration of new consular facilities, (4) sale of U.S. wheat to Russia, and (5) continuing meetings between the two sides to explore other matters of interest. The experiment slowed down with the approach of a new election campaign and ended with Kennedy's assassination.

Considerable reduction in conflict occurred

largely because of improved communication, which in turn helped correct the false images both sides held of each other. This allowed them to pursue matters of mutual interest and concern. The initial friendly overture by Kennedy reduced tension, which in turn enhanced communication, helped correct biased stereotypes (thus increasing social support for change), and initiated a decreasing cold war spiral. In addition, the improved communication and continuing reciprocity led to mutual dependence for attaining common goals. As we saw in the Robbers Cave experiment, cooperation in solving common problems is an important condition for reducing conflict.

We conclude that four factors are important in reducing international conflict: (1) a unilateral gesture toward conflict reduction, (2) increased communication, (3) heightened awareness of mutual dependence in order to identify the opportunities that exist for the nations to pursue common goals, and (4) actual cooperation between nations to achieve these goals. Perhaps the joint space mission involving Russian and American astronauts was not as trivial an event as it may have seemed at first glance.

Social influence and conformity.   In this brief section we will mention instances of social influence and conformity in action. This is not really an application of social psychology principles but is rather a small set of illustrations of these principles.

Consider the influence of a single person over another person. How many times have you done something just because someone in authority told you to do it, even to the point (in some cases) of doing things you felt were wrong? Lying to someone is a good example, and the whole notion of a "white lie" suggests the operation of the consistency principle. There are many examples of crimes being committed by people who were "under the influence" of another person, usually a loved one. Occasionally, in rare instances, there is the accusation that hypnosis was used to make the person commit a crime, but the fact is that hypnosis is an instance of social influence between two people, and the hypnotic procedures themselves are not necessary in order to get people to behave in unusual, even illegal, ways (see the discussion of hypnosis in Chapter 8).

It is obvious that conformity is everywhere. Think about what you are wearing right now and how it fits in with the style of dress of the groups you belong to. Think of a time when you and several friends went to a movie or a lecture and all your

"A word to the wise, Benson. People are asking why they don't see Old Glory on your bike."

Playboy, June 1971. Reproduced by special permission of PLAYBOY Magazine; copyright © 1971 by Playboy.

friends said they liked it, but you didn't like it. What did you do in this case? Have you ever been with a group of friends who wanted to do something that you found offensive, immoral, or just simply distasteful? What did you do? How do you think people get started drinking, smoking, taking drugs, stealing, and so on? Why is it that a drug addict who is cured or a paroled criminal who is rehabilitated cannot stay "clean" when he returns to his old social habits and his old friends? Why do parents so often fail to appreciate how it is that their children can behave the way they do—wear long hair and "strange" clothes and speak a "strange" language? And why do children see their parents' behavior as equally strange? Is there a generation gap? Is it because the social norms are different for different generations?

Social influence in the psychology experiment.   Now we turn to an analysis of the psychology experiment itself. As social psychologists have learned about the behavior of people in a social setting, they have suggested that more may be going on in an experiment than the experimenter realizes. And if an experiment is inadvertently influenced by social factors that the experimenter is unaware of, then the conclusions of the experimenter may be entirely wrong.

Work by Rosenthal (1966) demonstrates, on the one hand, the ease with which experimenters communicate their hypotheses to subjects and, on the other hand, how willing subjects are to fulfill the experimenter's expectations. In general, the research suggests that the typical subject wants to behave in a way that the experimenter considers appropriate. Cues are available to the subject in any experiment that suggest or even demand that he behave in particular ways. If some of these cues or "demand characteristics" give information about the hypothesis being tested, then subjects may produce data that support the hypothesis, not because the hypothesis is correct, but because they want to please the experimenter. Thus, an experimenter has expectations about how the subjects should behave (his hypothesis), and he can inadvertently or otherwise get his subjects to behave in this way. In short, he gets the kind of behavior he predicts, an effect called the "self-fulfilling prophecy."

In one experiment, Rosenthal recruited undergraduate students as experimenters for a study of learning in rats. The study was described as a replication of earlier work comparing the performance of inbred "dull" and "bright" rats on an operant conditioning task. Each student experimenter was assigned to work with a pair of rats, one "dull" and one "bright." They were told to expect rapid learning from the bright animals but little or no evidence of learning from the dull ones. Actually, the two groups of rats, "brights" and "dulls," were selected at random from the laboratory rat colony. Yet, the student experimenters observed and reported consistent differences in learning speed between the two groups of rats. In nearly every case, the subjects reported that the animals designated as "bright" performed better than those labeled "dull." The results provide convincing evidence of the biasing effects of experimenter expectations on observed subject behavior.

Worse yet, Rosenthal has demonstrated that the expectancy effect occurs outside the psychology laboratory in real-life situations. A study by Rosenthal and Jacobsen (1968), conducted at an elementary school, provided a dramatic demonstration of the effect of a teacher's expectations on students' academic performance. They found that children the teacher thinks will do well do indeed perform well, which implies that children the teacher expects to do poorly may indeed do poorly.

In the experiment, the students were given a standard test of nonverbal intelligence (see Chapter 5), which was represented to the teachers at the school as a measure of intellectual "blooming." About 20 percent of the children (who, unknown to the teachers, were chosen randomly) were said to be capable of marked intellectual growth as measured by the test. Thus, the difference between the "bloomers" and the other children was entirely in the minds of the teachers. The IQs of all the children were tested periodically, and the results showed that the "bloomers" had a clear advantage over the other

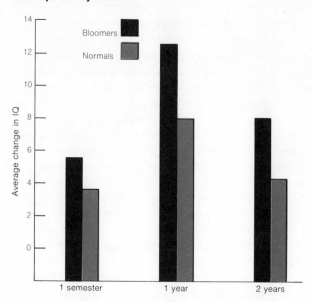

Figure 10–10
The expectancy effect

Mean change in IQ for "bloomers" and normal children after teacher expectations were established.

children in test score and test score gain for as long as 2 years after the teacher expectations had been established (see Figure 10–10). The evidence suggests that, because they expected "bloomers" to show marked intellectual improvement, the teachers worked more closely with these children, gave more encouragement and help, and unwittingly motivated them to greater achievements. Again we see the significant effects that one's expectations have on one's own behavior and the behavior of others. Consider the undesirable results of the expectancy effect when: (1) parents are told that their child's IQ is below normal, (2) people are told that someone, say a candidate for high office, has been hospitalized for mental illness, (3) parents are told their child has cerebral palsy, (4) people are told that a dog is vicious, or (5) people expect members of certain racial groups to behave in strange ways.

Social principles and self-understanding.
The major application of social psychological literature may well be its role in increasing our understanding of ourselves as social beings. Take as an example the implications of the social psychological findings on social prejudice and stereotyping. The insidious effects of prejudice have been extensively documented in social psychological laboratories. We have become

increasingly aware of the psychologically harmful effects of the hostility of prejudice, which, when combined with the binding force of social stereotypes and the destructive force of the corresponding self-fulfilling prophecies, produces social and psychological pathology. This awareness has contributed to concrete actions, such as the 1954 ruling by the Supreme Court ordering school integration.

Along a different line, social psychologists have shown an increasing interest in the effects of sexual discrimination. Evidence is accumulating that characteristics once thought simply innate and characteristically female or male are really social products. From an early age females and males have different socializing experiences. They learn what is *considered* sex-appropriate behavior. They then tend to conform to those expectations (see Chapter 7). We do not claim that *all* sex differences are psychological. Many of them are, however, and these can lead to unfortunate and unwarranted forms of sexual discrimination.

Understanding prejudice and how it might work within us, understanding sexual differences and their source, understanding our social motives, our capacity for social development, our morality and our concept of social justice are important for getting along with other human beings. What insights we have at present are at least in part a product of social psychological research. It is reasonable to expect a fuller understanding of ourselves as social beings as this research continues to progress.

Summary

1. Social psychology is the study of the effect on individuals of other persons. As a discipline it has been concerned with two major problems—social attitudes and group behavior. Some of the area's basic concerns originate in such dramatic phenomena as social deprivation, crowd behavior, social prejudice, and friendship.

2. Many social psychological phenomena demonstrate the validity of two principles—the need for consistency in behavior and the need for social approval.

3. Racial prejudice, which partially involves assumed dissimilarity of other racial groups on many dimensions, has been a dominating concern.

4. Social stereotypes and prejudice are closely related. Both phenomena can be associated with a highly defensive, potentially fascistic, personality syndrome labeled the *authoritarian personality*.

5. Social psychologists have established that most persons show a strong tendency toward cognitive simplicity and intolerance of both ambiguity and ambivalence in cognitions and attitudes.

6. Research on the simplicity-complexity dimension of cognition has been guided primarily by Heider's balance theory, Newcomb's A-B-X model, and Festinger's cognitive dissonance theory.

7. Similarity of attitudes, personality, and many other characteristics has been identified as the most powerful basis for friendship.

8. Some investigators have suggested additional factors in friendship, such as need complementarity and rewards or costs of the relationship. Physical attractiveness is strongly related to initial evaluation for romantic relations.

9. The presence of others and what they do—social influence—is an extremely powerful factor affecting individual behavior. We usually try to do what others do.

10. The investigation of group dynamics has included evaluation of the relative efficiency of groups versus individuals, leadership identification, and group decision making.

11. Studies of intergroup conflict have revealed the ease with which it is created and the difficulty with which it is dissolved, especially when the "warring" parties are armed with offensive weapons. One effective means of conflict reduction is joint pursual of superordinate goals.

12. Some additional problems of current interest to social psychologists include investigation of conditions that affect the likelihood that one person will help another in distress and the study of communication, both verbal and nonverbal.

13. The principles of social psychology have already been applied in many areas of psychology, including clinical, educational, and industrial psychology. Additional areas of potential application include altering aggression, reducing prejudice, easing social change, reducing international conflict, and improving social relationships.

Recommended Additional Readings

Aronson, E. *The social animal.* San Francisco: Freeman, 1972.

Berkowitz, L. *A survey of social psychology.* Hinsdale, Ill.: Dryden Press, 1975.

Brown, R. *Social psychology.* New York: Free Press, 1965.

Middlebrook, P. N. *Social psychology and modern life.* New York: Knopf, 1974.

Wrightsman, L. S. *Social psychology in the seventies.* Monterey, Calif.: Brooks/Cole, 1972.

PSYCHOPATHOLOGY

A Definition of Psychopathology

The term *psychopathology* covers a tremendous range of behaviors, including all of the following: a college student who gets violently ill before every final exam; a man who cannot quit gambling even though he does not enjoy it; a 22-year-old girl who believes she is the Virgin Mary; a woman who consumes a fifth of vodka every day; and a man in his late thirties who believes his mind is being controlled by creatures from Mars using invisible laser beams.

The extreme diversity of psychopathological behaviors, indicated by the examples above, has made it difficult to formulate a single definition that fits all cases. Some psychologists have tried to define the group of behaviors traditionally labeled psychopathological as behaviors that are characterized by *subjective discomfort,* that is, feeling anxious, depressed, or otherwise dissatisfied without apparent cause. The person's discomfort seems to be "all in the mind," as in the case of a person who claims he feels chest pains but has no physical signs of disease. However, in some cases the *lack* of discomfort may indicate psychopathology, as when a person responds to the death of a loved one or flunking out of school with no signs of grief or depression. Thus, this definition does not cover all instances.

Psychopathological behavior has also been defined as behavior that *deviates from the norm.* This definition is also unsatisfactory because it includes positive abnormalities such as great intelligence or creativity, which are seldom considered pathological. In addition, some deviant behaviors are considered more significant than others—eating peas with a knife might be more unusual than suicide in our country, but it would be considered much less pathological.

Others have defined psychopathological behavior as *maladaptive behavior,* that is, behavior that has adverse effects for either society or the individual. This definition clearly covers many of the conditions we described, such as compulsive gambling, alcoholism, and suicide, and it comes closer to what we mean by psychopathology. However, it fails to designate why the undesirable behavior occurred or how to modify it.

Using the characteristics of behavior discussed in Chapter 1, we define psychopathology as *the inability to behave in a socially appropriate way such that the consequences of one's behavior are maladaptive for oneself or society.* Thus, inability

Psychological Distress Common In U.S.: Report

By Frank Carey, AP science writer

Washington (AP)—The Public Health Service has reported evidence suggesting nearly one in five American adults has experienced a nervous breakdown or felt one coming on.

In disclosing some findings it termed surprising, the agency reported nearly 60 per cent of the adult population is fidgety and tense at times to the point of being bothered.

The agency questioned 6,672 adults representing the nation's 111-million population of civilian, non-institutional persons between 18 and 79. Eighty-eight per cent were white; 10 per cent black.

Persons interviewed were questioned not only on their history of actual, or threatened, nervous breakdowns, but also on whether they had ever been bothered by:

Nervousness, psychological inertia, insomnia, trembling hands, nightmares, perspiring hands, fainting or blackouts, headache, dizziness or heart palpitations.

In one of its major findings, the report declared:

"The over-all per cent reporting having had a nervous breakdown was 4.9 per cent and an additional 12.8 per cent reported having felt an impending nervous breakdown . . . without its actual occurrence . . . for a combined rate of 17.7 per cent for almost one out of five, with an estimated 20 million adults having experienced such severe psychological distress."

The survey found proportionately more women than men reported nervous breakdowns. Black women had a significantly higher rate than white women.

Women reported breakdown threats almost twice as frequently as did men, and had significantly higher rates for the 12 distress symptoms.

But the report found only two symptoms with significant differences by race for the same sex for both men and women.

"These were nervousness, with white men and women having a rate more than 15 per cent higher than Negroes; and dizziness, wherein Negro men and women had slightly higher rates than whites. . . ."

The survey found more symptoms of distress among less-educated and lower-income groups. On a geographic basis, Northeastern adults had lower rates, while Southerners had higher rates than average.

Among unexpected findings, the Public Health Service reported lower rates of breakdown among persons who had never married—especially white women—and among working men and women compared with retired men and women housekeepers, respectively.

Farmers and service workers tended to experience more nervous symptoms than did professional, clerical and operating workers.

The experience of anxiety and tension is much more common than most people realize. The average person thinks he is above average in anxiety.

might reflect *organic deficiency* (such as brain damage), *functional deficiency* (lack of knowledge, competence, or motivation), or *a combination of both.* In short, a person might fail to behave appropriately or adaptively for any of four reasons; he might not have the necessary physiological equipment, knowledge, or competence, or he might not want to behave appropriately.

The word *appropriate* is important in our definition because labeling behavior as abnormal is necessarily a culturally determined act. A woman from a rural area who thinks she is hexed may be behaving quite appropriately in her community, although her behavior would be considered abnormal by a psychologist or psychiatrist in the city. The anthropologist Ruth Benedict notes that trances and seizures, which most cultures consider pathological, may be a sign of prestige and power in some Indian tribes of California. The daily life of the people who live on an island in northwest Melanesia is based on suspicion and paranoia. They are preoccupied with being poisoned by a neighbor, and the person who failed to be suspicious would be viewed as behaving inappropriately and maladaptively. Thus there is no single set of behaviors that is considered appropriate in all societies and cultures.

Models of Psychopathology

Part of the problem psychologists face in defining psychopathology is due to the fact that they lack a complete understanding of maladaptive behavior and its causes and cures. Thus much of our discussion in this chapter will be based on *theories of psychopathology.* As we saw in our discussion of personality, psychological theories are typically based on a framework or structure, a *model,* which provides a way of conceptualizing behavioral observations. A model provides the basic assumptions from which various theories are derived. We will examine five major models that serve as the basis for most theories of psychopathology: the medical model, dynamic model, behavioral model, ethical model, and existential model (see Table 11–1). Like a theory, a

Table 11–1
Models of psychopathology

Model	Theoretical cause of abnormality	Theoretical cure	Therapist
Medical	A process similar to that underlying physical illness	Medication, rest, physical treatment	Physician
Dynamic	Unconscious conflicts	Insight into conflicts	Specially trained physician or mental health professional
Behavioral	Maladaptive learning	Learning or relearning	Behavior modifier
Ethical	Lack of responsibility	Acceptance of responsibility	Reality therapist
Existential	Lack of meaning in life	Development of purpose	Existential therapist

model is neither true nor false but only useful or not useful. A model is useful if it leads to valid explanations and effective therapies.

Medical Model

In the medical model, pathological behaviors are viewed as symptoms of a disease or a process *like* a disease. Hence the term *mental illness.* One basic assumption of the medical model is that emotional problems, like physical diseases, can be fitted into diagnostic categories that have implications for cause and treatment. The use of the medical model is historically very important. During the nineteenth century, people who behaved inappropriately but who claimed that they had no control over their behavior were seen as malingerers or fakers. They were either ignored or sent to prison. In an effort at reform, some physicians claimed that these people should be thought of as sick in the mind. Thus, people with emotional problems came to be defined as ill rather than loafers, and they were transferred from prisons to hospitals.

The medical model is still in common use today, although many people both outside and within the medical profession are disturbed by its unfortunate consequences. If an emotional problem is truly an illness, then one might argue that physicians are the only people capable of helping the emotionally disturbed. Although such restrictions may be appropriate in cases in which there is a known organic involvement (such as psychosomatic illness), there are many other cases in which other kinds of treatment are clearly called for. A person who is anxious and cannot get along with others

typically does *not* have a physical illness. His disorder could perhaps be viewed as analogous to physical illness, but this does not automatically make it a "medical" problem. His problem is not so much something that he *has* as it is something that he *is* or *does*.

Furthermore, the medical model has led people to feel no sense of responsibility for their behavior. It is common for a person to ask the therapist to "cure" him of emotional problems in the same way he asks a physician to cure his cold. Typically, the therapist has no "cure"—the patient must assume some responsibility for changing his own behavior.

Finally, although the term "mentally ill" was thought to be a more humane label for people with emotional problems than terms such as "insane" or "lunatic," few people view the mentally ill with the same compassion they feel for the physically ill. The negative attitudes and fears associated with the irrational, unpredictable, and sometimes dangerous behaviors of the emotionally disturbed have become associated with the term "mental illness." Thus, although the medical model provided the impetus for hospital care and medical treatment of people with emotional problems, it did not lead to much attitude change, as the "jokes" about "men in white coats" perhaps indicate.

In spite of its negative consequences, the medical model has been exceedingly useful in the treatment of psychopathology. As we shall see, much of the terminology, explanation, and therapy to be discussed in this chapter reflects the conception of psychopathology as a disease process.

Dynamic Model

In the dynamic model the basic assumption is that abnormal behavior reflects a "dynamic" battle or conflict occurring between parts or aspects of a person's personality rather than any physical or organic deficiencies. Ironically, it was Freud, a physician by training, who pioneered the dynamic model. He found the medical model unsuitable for treatment of abnormal behavior and developed in its place the first truly dynamic theory.

Freud believed that behavior is partially determined by psychological conflicts of which the individual is *totally* unaware. He proposed that mental processes occur at three levels: the *conscious,* the *preconscious,* and the *unconscious.* The conscious is made up of the ideas, thoughts, and images that a person is aware of at any given moment. The preconscious consists of ideas, thoughts, and images that he is not aware of at the moment but that can be brought into awareness with little or no difficulty. Finally, the unconscious is that part of his mental process that the person resists being aware of—the unacceptable drives of sex and aggression, and the memories, thoughts, impulses, and ideas that were once conscious but were removed from awareness because they made the individual anxious or tense.

Freud proposed that anxiety grows out of socially unacceptable impulses, the expression of which would lead to punishment or disapproval from one's self or others. For example, a child might find that his mother is terribly hurt and disapproving of the anger he feels and expresses toward her. He might then try to forget that he has angry feelings; although he is still unconsciously angry toward his mother, he consciously tries to convince himself and others of his devotion. If the process ended here, there would be no problem; the child would have rid himself of all unpleasant or unacceptable thoughts and feelings. However, as we will see, Freud felt that these thoughts persist, causing unconscious conflicts, and that they tend to be expressed behaviorally in ways that are often socially inappropriate. According to the dynamic model, therapy should make the person aware of his unconscious processes.

Theoretically, the medical model and dynamic model are independent of one another. One can accept the basic assumptions of one of the models without accepting the assumptions of the other. Historically, however, the two models are closely related. In the United States, some of the strongest proponents of the dynamic model have been psychiatrists, who are themselves trained in medicine. But recently many mental health workers have come to accept the idea that one can view mankind as functioning in a dynamic way without assuming that the process is similar to physical disease.

Behavioral Model

Behaviorists, as we have seen, believe that because the unconscious is by definition unavailable for direct study, it is neither a scientific nor a useful concept. On the contrary, the behaviorists assume that a person's observable actions are what determines whether he is normal or abnormal; one is abnormal if he *acts* abnormally. And it follows that the way to treat psychopathology is to change the person's behavior.

According to the behavioral model, all behavior, normal or otherwise, is a product of learning about the environment. Behavior is determined by one's history of reinforcement. Thus, one can change

abnormal into normal behavior by retraining (reeducating or reconditioning) the individual (that is, teaching him new and appropriate responses to stimuli in his environment) and/or by changing his environment in certain ways. Bandura's social learning theory (see Chapter 9) is typical of the theories based on the behavioral model. The application of learning principles to emotional problems is fairly recent, but the behavioral model poses a strong challenge to the medical and dynamic models and has provided the basis for several effective therapeutic approaches generally known as behavior modification.

Ethical Model

Thomas Szasz (1960), in an attack on the medical model, suggested that having "problems in living" is the most appropriate way of looking at those who suffer from emotional problems. He proposed that life is *not* essentially harmonious and satisfying but rather is filled with stresses (economic, social, biological, and political) that one must cope with. Individuals who need professional help are those who cannot handle these problems by themselves.

Szasz proposed that the medical "myth" of abnormal behavior allows people to avoid the *moral* responsibility of their actions. This same idea that people are responsible for their actions underlies Glasser's (1965) concept of reality therapy. For Glasser, abnormal behavior is behaving irresponsibly. Only when people are ready to accept responsibility for the consequences of their behavior can they adequately cope with their problems.

Existential Model

Carl Rogers, Abraham Maslow, and Fritz Perls propose an "existential" model to emphasize the importance of the person's existence in the here-and-now and his efforts to actualize his own potential. The existential model focuses on the need for each person to develop his own meaning for life, to take responsibility for guiding his personal growth. Existential anxiety is experienced when life seems meaningless. Rather than assuming that a person's behavior is determined by his past experiences, the existential model assumes that his behavior is determined by the choices he makes in life.

It is important to realize that the ethical and existential models are the only ones that assume that the person has responsibility for his own behavior rather than attributing the behavior to illness, unresolved childhood conflicts, reinforcement, or other governing factors. The

Comparative Approaches to Psychodiagnosis

John is a compulsive eater who weighs 350 pounds. Seeking help, he sees a psychodiagnostician, who might conceptualize his problem in the following ways.

Medical Model
The psychodiagnostician sees the behavior as a medical problem, perhaps a disorder in the neural systems controlling appetite.

Dynamic Model
The psychodiagnostician assumes that the compulsive eating is a symbolic expression of an unconscious conflict or wish. He might look for unresolved conflicts associated with the oral stage of development in which John is seeking reassurance for unmet dependency needs. He might also focus on aggressive or sexual conflicts and the way in which the eating behavior might be providing John with an opportunity to express anger or avoid sexual behavior.

Behavioral (Learning Theory) Model
The psychodiagnostician assumes that the overeating is reinforcing for John in some way. The behavior modifier might focus on the strong reinforcing nature of food. He might explore whether anxiety reduction occurs as a function of eating.

Jane is a 25-year-old graduate student with a severe stuttering problem. Seeking help she sees a psychodiagnostician, who might conceptualize her problem in the following ways.

Medical Model
The psychodiagnostician assumes that Jane's stuttering is the result of a neurological problem involving perceptual-motor areas.

Dynamic Model
The psychodiagnostician looks upon the stuttering as the expression of unconscious repressed hostility, particularly toward Jane's parents.

Behavioral (Learning Theory) Model
The psychodiagnostician assumes there are no underlying conflicts and proposes that the behavior *is* the disorder. This model might assume that stuttering results from a negative feedback loop in which Jane's monitoring of her own speech interferes with talking. Such a disorder might result from her parents' excessive attention to Jane's speaking patterns at an early age.

Existential Model
In both cases, stuttering and overeating, the psychodiagnostician makes no diagnostic assumptions at all. He would focus on the meaning of being-in-the-world for the client, not the symptoms of stuttering or overeating.

---

question of responsibility for individual behavior has far-reaching social implications. For example, our courts of law are currently having difficulty resolving the issue of personal responsibility. If a person's behavior is determined by his reinforcement history, how can he be held responsible for illegal behavior?

Classification of Psychopathology

The forms that psychopathology can take are many and varied, as our examples thus far indicate. In order to simplify and make sense of these diverse behavior forms, classification systems have been developed. There is no single classification system that all workers in this field agree on. For one thing, there is usually disagreement among psychologists and other professionals about the diagnosis (classification statement) of any one case. From their independent diagnoses, one might legitimately wonder whether two psychologists are talking about the same case. Diagnoses are usually highly reliable

on gross classifications such as whether a person is neurotic or psychotic, but not when a more specialized analysis is attempted. If there is no agreement on the diagnosis, of what value is it to make one in the first place?

Advantages and Disadvantages of Classification

The chief advantage of any classification system is communication. Diagnostic labels convey in a single word a lot of general information about a person's behavior and enable therapists, researchers, and others to discuss psychopathology in general and specific cases in particular. Knowing that an individual has symptoms similar to those of other patients also helps a psychologist form reasonable expectations about the individual's future behavior and his chances for improvement. In turn, this knowledge allows the psychologist to plan and conduct the most suitable therapy. However, since no two cases are exactly alike, the gain in communication and treatment planning can be costly, for it inevitably obscures the unique features of the individual's case.

Still another problem is that labeling someone may have the effect of making the person conform to the way he thinks the therapist expects him to behave (e.g., suicidally). The therapist, if anxious to prove that his diagnosis is correct, may pay special attention to aspects of the person's behavior that support his diagnosis and completely fail to notice other important aspects that do not fit it. Thus, the diagnostic prophecy becomes self-fulfilling.

Classification is important for communication, and thus we spend considerable time on it in this chapter. But we should not be fooled into thinking that classification is the same as understanding and treatment. No classification system should be regarded as explanatory. There is a tendency to feel that behavior can be explained by attaching a label to it, but labeling is neither explanation nor cure.

With all these drawbacks, it is no wonder that the trend in clinical psychology today is away from an emphasis on diagnostic classification. The clinical psychologist is primarily interested in changing behavior. He will use all the therapeutic tools available to him without an undue emphasis on the name he happens to apply to the disorder. And given the state of the diagnostic arts, this is only appropriate.

Major Diagnostic Categories

The most commonly accepted classification scheme for abnormal behavior is based on grouping people according to similar *behavioral symptoms*. (Note the use of medical terminology.) The assumption is that behaviors can be grouped together in meaningful and reliable ways. Thus everyone who behaves in a certain way would be given the same label. The term *symptom* is commonly used because of the assumption that the behaviors classified as abnormal are indications of underlying conflicts in the way that a fever is a symptom of various illnesses, such as a cold or infection.

The classification system presently in wide use is based on the medical and dynamic models, so it is not surprising that people who subscribe to other models of psychopathology are not happy with it. Other classification schemes could be based on dimensions such as the causes of emotional problems, the preferred treatment, the person's reinforcement history, the social environment, or the type of life choices the person has made. However, there is presently no evidence that any one of these classification schemes would be more useful than the one in common use now.

The procedure of deciding how to classify a person is known as *diagnosis*. Several kinds of evidence are typically taken into account in making a diagnosis, including family history and biographical information, descriptions of the problem behavior, and assessments of the person's intellectual, emotional, and personality characteristics. This information is usually obtained by having a relative or friend fill out a questionnaire giving the person's medical history and other data, interviewing the person himself, and administering appropriate tests. Assessment techniques such as personality inventories and projective tests are discussed in detail in Appendix C.

The major diagnostic categories of the present system are neurosis, psychosomatic illness, personality disorders, and psychosis. We will briefly define each of these classifications before discussing them and the various subcategories in detail. One thing to keep in mind throughout this discussion is that most, if not all, forms of psychopathology result from or are most commonly and strongly manifested during stress. Thus, psychopathology can be seen as an abnormal or inappropriate reaction to stress.

The primary defining characteristic of *neurosis* is anxiety, which can be described as the experience of fear in the absence of, or disproportionate to, the objective danger. Neurosis refers to behavior designed to avoid or reduce the anxiety. In neurosis there is no gross distortion of reality. The straight "A" student who is petrified of making a "B" (exaggerated fear) or who is constantly concerned about failing (unfounded fear) might very well be neurotic. (The term *nervous breakdown* is often used by the general public to describe a person whose emotional problems are so severe that he can no longer cope with a job or home responsibilities. It is not a description of the physical state of the person's nerves, nor is it synonymous with *neurosis*.)

The defining characteristic of a *psychosomatic illness* (the latest term is *psychophysiologic reaction*) is the presence of a physical illness in which psychological processes have played an important causative role. Asthma, peptic ulcers, hives, arthritis, and to a lesser extent the common cold all have possible psychosomatic elements. More recently, psychological factors, particularly emotional stress, have been strongly implicated in heart disease and even in cancer.

The primary defining characteristic of a *personality disorder* (formerly called *character disorder*) is a dominant personality trait leading to maladaptive behavior that the individual typically has no motivation to change, such as alcoholism, drug addiction, and sexually deviant behavior. The person's behavior is maladaptive from society's viewpoint, not his. He experiences little or no anxiety about himself and exhibits no gross distortions of reality other than his failure in self-appraisal.

The defining characteristic of *psychosis* is gross distortion of reality or loss of reality testing. The psychotic person can no longer tell the difference between his fantasy and what is actually happening. He loses voluntary control over thoughts, feelings, and actions. Psychosis is usually accompanied by *delusions* and *hallucinations*. A *delusion* is an unshakable idea or belief that is held in the face of contradictory evidence, simple logic, or common experience. For example, a person may insist, despite all objective evidence to the contrary, that he is Jesus Christ or the President. *Hallucinations* are a form of bizarre or distorted perception without corresponding sensory stimuli. The person perceives visual images, hears voices or sounds, and feels things over his body when no such events are occurring in the objective world. Hallucinations thus differ from illusions, which are misperceptions of sensory information. In short, the primary defining characteristic of psychosis is *faulty cognition.*

Another major distinction typically made is between *functional* and *organic* disorders. A *functional disorder* refers to an emotional problem that is the result of psychological variables rather than biological ones. For example, a person who has a phobia about going outdoors may be thought of as unconsciously avoiding the anxiety associated with failure in his job or some other anxiety-provoking situation. On the other hand, *organic disorders* are those caused typically by impairment of brain functioning. There is an interesting case history of a man who drank a bottle of insect killer because he thought it would make him sick and his girl friend would feel sorry for him. His behavior would be considered *functionally* abnormal, though not necessarily psychotic. However, as a consequence of his behavior, he was poisoned and developed a psychosis that would be called *organic.* Chronic alcoholism is perhaps the most common cause of organic psychosis today. With organic psychosis, the behavioral problem is usually resolved if the underlying biophysical malfunctioning can be corrected.

An assumption of this diagnostic scheme is that people whose behavior is psychopathological will fit neatly into one of the major diagnostic categories.

This assumption is not entirely correct, because people exist on continua within all these classes of behavior. One label is seldom an accurate description of any particular person's problem. But even though the present scheme is unsatisfactory, no better alternative has been presented, and the widespread use of the present system makes many therapists and researchers reluctant to change it.

Reactions to Stress

People are likely to have more difficulty behaving in a socially appropriate way when they are under stress. We frequently find that people are diagnosed as abnormal at a particularly stressful time in their lives—when they experience major life changes such as a death in the family, flunking out of school, or even positive events such as getting married or being promoted. Anxiety has far-reaching effects on behavior, even for apparently well-adjusted people. Given the many possibilities in one's life for fear conditioning, it is probably not surprising that the majority of college students report having at least one serious emotional problem during each school year. Most students report feelings of anxiety, and the average student thinks he is more anxious than the "average student."

Thus there seems to be a continuum of behavior, with no clear point separating normal from pathological. Indeed we all exhibit one or even several symptoms of psychopathology at times, and this does not necessarily indicate a serious behavior problem. People who usually function in a socially appropriate way may occasionally experience sleeplessness or loss of appetite when worried about something, have a periodic burst of temper, or get a "tension" headache.

Some students report that anxiety makes it impossible for them to study, that they go blank on exams and generally perform poorly in school for this reason. It is useful to make a distinction between two types of anxiety. *State anxiety* refers to momentary, consciously perceived feelings of apprehension and tension, whereas *trait anxiety* is defined as anxiety proneness or the predisposition to respond with high state anxiety when under stress. The distinction allows us to avoid a semantic problem presented when someone says, "John is anxious." Such a statement does not make it clear whether it is being said that "John is anxious right now" (state anxiety) or "John is generally an anxious person" (trait anxiety).

State anxiety is often appropriate; there are situations in which the normal, appropriate response

Copyright, 1971, G. B. Trudeau. Distributed by Universal Press Syndicate.

In Freud's theory there are three basic types of anxiety: (1) reality anxiety, which is anxiety about dangers in one's life; (2) neurotic anxiety, which is fear of being punished when attempting to satisfy some basic need such as sex; and (3) moral anxiety or guilt. Michael's mother is attempting to inflict moral anxiety on her son. It is as if she were saying, "I am suffering so I am going to make you suffer too."

is anxiety. However, to have a permanent tendency to respond to stress with great anxiety tends to become pathological. High trait anxiety is often inappropriate and tends to disrupt performance. In general, trait anxiety (presumably leading to high levels of state anxiety in the learning situation) facilitates the performance of simple tasks and interferes with performing difficult tasks (the Yerkes-Dodson Law—see Chapter 6). If the task is simple, anxiety increases the probability of the correct response being given. In a highly anxious state, the average person faced with a difficult task will become confused and will be likely to make mistakes. Thus it is easy to see how the highly anxious person could fail to behave appropriately or adaptively in tense situations.

Not all stress is generated by external sources. Freud proposed that even in normal circumstances a person must defend against internal stress in the form of dangerous thoughts or ideas. There are various techniques for coping with stress. The rational approach is a conscious, active attempt to understand the source and gain new knowledge or skill to overcome it. But many of us defend against stress on an unconscious level, according to Freud, with the defense mechanisms of the ego (see Chapter 9). Defense mechanisms are processes for handling stress in everyday life and are quite normal. When the anxiety is excessive and/or ways

of coping with it prove ineffective, however, neurotic behavior can result. According to the dynamic model, repression and denial are the two primary defenses against internal stress. Others include intellectualization, projection, reaction formation, fixation, and regression. You should review at this point our discussion of defense mechanisms in Chapter 9.

Laboratory Studies of Reactions to Stress

Because defenses are defined as unconscious, the area is difficult to investigate. Several attempts have been made, however, to study their effects in the laboratory. Lazarus and his colleagues (Lazarus, Opton, Nomikos, and Rabkin, 1965) examined the reactions of subjects to stressful motion pictures. One film was a safety movie designed to stop carelessness in a woodmill. Several realistic accidents occur, one in which the fingers of an operator are lacerated, another in which an operator loses a finger (spurting blood), and a third in which a plank is driven through the stomach of a bystander, killing him. The film is exceptionally stressful to watch, apparently because of the viewer's identification with the "actors."

The experimenters tried to manipulate the way in which people would cope with the stress of watching this movie by varying the preliminary instructions. One group of subjects heard only a short statement about the fact that there were some woodmill accidents in the film—they were given a *neutral orientation.* Another group of subjects were provided with a *denial orientation* in which it was pointed out that the events were not real, that actors played the roles and were not hurt, and that the "blood" spurting was a liquid used to create the illusion of blood. A third group was given an *intellectualization orientation* in which they were

Figure 11–1
Measuring defense mechanism effects

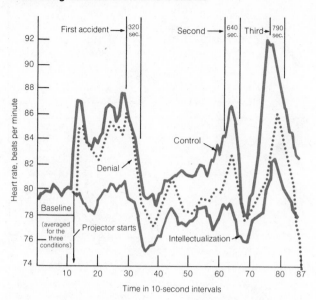

The effects of preliminary instructions on the heart rate of subjects observing a movie involving violent accidents.

Figure 11–2
Changes in stress with experience

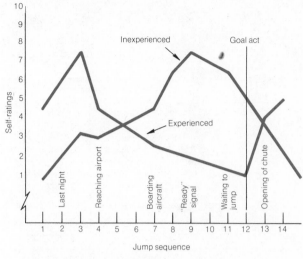

Self-ratings of the intensity of fear and tension for new and experienced parachutists as a function of the time before the jump.

asked to take a detached view of the situation. They were asked to focus, for example, on how the foreman was trying to get his point across to the workers. The experimenters recorded subjects' heart rate (an index of stress level) while watching the film, and they found that the groups given intellectualization or denial orientations had a lower heart rate than the group given a neutral orientation. The intellectualization condition produced the least stress of all (see Figure 11–1).

Reactions to Stress in Natural Situations

Another approach to studying the way people handle stress is to observe people in naturally occurring stressful situations rather than situations created in the laboratory. Epstein (1967) studied fear among sky divers. He found that inexperienced parachute jumpers used extreme, inappropriate defenses to handle their fear of jumping. Once these defenses broke down, the jumpers were overwhelmed with anxiety. Epstein described two young women, novice jumpers, whose denial defense was so strong that they appeared completely at ease on their first jump. Once they got into the plane, however, the defenses broke down; one began trembling and shaking and the other vomited.

With practice, the novice parachutists developed new defenses against anxiety that were more effective and more appropriate. With the new defenses the peak of anxiety was experienced earlier, allowing the parachutist to make the jump itself with relatively little anxiety (see Figure 11–2). Experienced parachutists are most anxious the morning before the jump, when they decide that they will parachute that day. Inexperienced jumpers are the most anxious just before they jump. Interestingly enough, no one seems to be very anxious at the point of maximum danger, that is, when the chute opens. Inexperienced jumpers frequently report more anxiety about the social embarrassment of not jumping than about the jump itself. (See Chapter 6 for an alternate interpretation of the changes in the emotions of parachutists based on opponent processes.)

The above studies tell us something about the strength and effectiveness of defense mechanisms different people employ when faced with the same threat. But it should be remembered that the stress in these situations derived primarily from the threat of physical harm and may involve very different kinds of processes and reactions than threats to self-esteem or fear of unacceptable impulses. Therefore, we cannot assume that the way a person

An example of a secondary gain.

handles one type of stress necessarily predicts how well or in what way he will handle another type of stress.

Neurosis

The neurotic has perfect vision in one eye, but he cannot remember which.
The Neurotic's Notebook

According to the dynamic model, neurosis is a special pattern of behavior that is instigated and maintained for the purpose of contending with stress and avoiding anxiety. What are the indications that a pattern of behavior is neurotic? First, if the person is prevented from performing the behavior, he will become anxious. Second, the behavior has a rigid, driven quality about it; the person cannot perform the behavior in a relaxed manner. Finally, the need being served by the behavior is insatiable; the person never seems to relax and give up the behavior. Thus it is easy to see why neurosis is a

problem for the individual. Defending against the anxiety takes up a tremendous amount of energy that the person could usefully spend elsewhere. In addition, the time spent avoiding the anxiety prevents the person from ever dealing effectively with its cause. Thus he never learns new behaviors that would allow him to get out of the anxiety-provoking situation altogether. This self-perpetuating aspect of neurosis is called the *neurotic paradox.*

The neurotic paradox refers to the fact that the neurotic individual persists in his maladaptive behavior even in the face of unpleasant consequences. Actually, the unpleasantness may not occur for some time after the behavior has taken place, whereas the immediate consequence is that anxiety is reduced, providing positive reinforcement of the neurotic behavior. The immediate reduction of anxiety is called the neurotic's *primary gain* for behaving the way he does. The primary gain is so great that later negative consequences, if they arise, do not have much effect in changing the behavior.

Neurotic behavior is extremely persistent because it often has other positive consequences in addition to the relief from tension, or primary gain. The additional benefits are the *secondary gains* of neurosis. For example, the neurotic may receive sympathy and support from his friends or special dispensations that allow him to avoid responsibilities or activities he dislikes. The fact that neurosis has both primary and secondary gains makes behavior change more difficult. In some cases the therapist may have to detect and remove the sources of secondary gain in addition to working on the neurotic's primary source of anxiety.

The various subcategories of neurosis can best be understood if they are grouped according to how people cope with anxiety. Neurotic defenses or coping behaviors fall into five classifications: (1) failure to defend against overwhelming stress, (2) repression or displacement of anxiety, (3) defenses against anxiety by behavioral inactivation, (4) defenses against anxiety by behavioral activation, and (5) neurotic depression.

Failure to Defend against Overwhelming Stress

An individual faced with repetitive, intense stress or a single traumatic incident will sometimes fail to develop any successful defense. He tries to cope but is unable to. He reacts as if he is under stress at all times, even when there is no obvious stressor. A common symptom is overreaction to minor stress, irritations, and noises. In war, soldiers who are under constant strain at the battle line sometimes lose their ability to cope. They develop poor appetites, are constantly nervous, and have insomnia with repetitive nightmares. This condition is referred to as a *traumatic neurosis.*

Repression or Displacement of Anxiety

One means of neurotic defense involves removing the anxiety-provoking thoughts from awareness and focusing the anxiety, which is still present, on another, less threatening stressor. An *anxiety reaction* is a neurotic episode in which a person has repressed the cause of his anxiety but not the anxiety itself. He is anxious without knowing why. He reports feeling nervous or jittery throughout the day but is unable to report anything occurring in his life that should make him nervous. He may displace the anxiety by attaching it to a less relevant and therefore less threatening stressor. In this way he may react with overwhelming anxiety to an objectively mild stress.

Phobias are intense irrational fears that, according to psychoanalytic theory, arise from the displacement of anxiety onto a situation that could

"How long have you had this fear of heights, Mr. Winthrop?"

© Punch (Rothco).

be mildly dangerous. Thus the woman who has a fear of heights (called acrophobia) might be symbolically expressing her anxiety over an overwhelming anger toward her parents. By displacing her fear, she is prevented from acting directly on her anger, which she has repressed. Other common phobias are fear of small enclosed spaces (claustrophobia), fear of water (aquaphobia), and, for young children, school phobia.

There is a subclassification of phobias not easily conceptualized as neurotic. These phobias are best explained by learning theory and might be called *traumatic phobias.* The young girl who develops a fear of dogs after being bitten is not displacing a fear; she has learned in one trial that dogs are dangerous. This conditioned fear response is durable. Even if the girl is not bitten again, as long as she can reduce the fear (reinforcement) by escaping from dogs, the fear will persist.

A third type of problem arising from displaced anxiety is *hypochondriasis,* a preoccupation with one's physical health. For example, the hypochondriac may read the health columns in the newspapers and magazines and rush to his doctor with all the latest symptoms. He may distort the meaning of minor aches and pains, imagine discomfort in various parts of his body, and constantly complain of ill health, although the physician can seldom find anything physically wrong. Physicians have estimated that as many as 60 percent of their patients express anxiety about their lives in their physical symptoms. The "medical student's syndrome," in which students working and studying in a hospital develop whatever illness they

"I don't know what's the matter with me, doctor —I've been feeling good!"

Source: "Berry's World," by Jim Berry. Reprinted by permission of Newspaper Enterprise Association.

Figure 11–3
"Glove" anesthesia

In the conversion reaction known as "glove" anesthesia the person loses all feeling in his hand in a pattern that follows the outline of a glove, stopping short at the wrist. However, because the nerve pathways for the hand go up the arm, as shown on the right, it would be impossible to have a *physically* caused glove pattern of anesthesia, as depicted on the left, unless there were also anesthesia of the arm.

read about or are exposed to that day, is probably a response to the extreme pressures of medical school training. Some male students express great relief when on duty in the obstetrics ward.

Defenses against Anxiety by Behavioral Inactivation

A person can defend against anxiety-provoking thoughts by selectively cutting off certain experiences. One subclassification of this response is the *conversion reaction,* in which the person reduces his anxiety by inactivating part of his body (as in paralysis, blindness, deafness, or the like). Thus the person converts his psychological problem into a physical one that prevents him from behaving in a way that would be anxiety provoking. For example, the student who suddenly became "blind" would be unable to do his class assignments. There are no actual physical changes; the inactivation is due to unconscious psychological factors.

One of the most famous conversion reactions is that of "glove" anesthesia, in which the person loses all feeling in his hand. The pattern of loss of feeling follows the outline of a glove (see Figure 11–3). Physicians are immediately able to identify this symptom as nonphysical because the nerve pathways for the hand mark off narrow strips of sensitivity that go up the arm, and it would be impossible to have a glove pattern of anesthesia unless there were also anesthesia of the arm. Conversion reactions were fairly common in Freud's day (and prompted him to move from neurology to psychiatry), but today people are better informed about biophysical processes, and their reactions to

anxiety usually take other forms, such as pain and simulation of bodily disease. Simply reading this chapter may prevent you from ever developing a glove anesthesia.

The second type of defensive inactivation is called a *dissociative reaction,* in which the person blocks off large parts of his memory as a way of avoiding anxiety-provoking associations. All of the dissociative reactions are rare, but they have a dramatic flavor that results in their frequent use in books and movies. The simplest is *amnesia,* which refers to partial or total loss of memory about one's past identity. The amnesic person may forget his name, family, job, and home. However, he will retain memory for nonthreatening aspects of life. He will remember how to speak, how to drive, and other perceptual-motor skills unrelated to any psychological danger. Amnesia can also be caused by physical trauma such as a blow to the head, but this form differs from neurotic amnesia in that the memories of the neurotic can often be recalled under hypnosis.

More complex and much rarer is the *fugue state,*

© 1960 United Feature Syndicate Inc.

Displacement phobias are ineffective means of controlling anxiety. The phobia tends to expand to include greater and greater aspects of a person's life until with serious phobias the person may be completely incapacitated.

in which the person has amnesia for his past but avoids the anxiety associated with such loss of identity by developing a new one and fleeing from the situation he could not tolerate. He may function as a completely new personality, remarry, have more children, get a new job in another city, all without any memory of his previous (and undivorced) wife and his children. Such states may last for a long or relatively short period of time, and when the old memories return, the individual may forget all of the events that occurred in the fugue state.

Finally, the rarest form of dissociative reaction is the *multiple personality.* There are fewer than 100 recorded cases of multiple personality in this century. In these cases the person has two or more complete but alternating personalities; at one point in time he is one personality and at another point in time he is the other. Frequently, the two personalities exress two aspects of a conflict that the person is experiencing. Usually, one personality is dominant and is unaware of the existence of the other personality. In the famous case about which the book *Three Faces of Eve* was written, Eve White was unaware of Eve Black, although Eve Black continued to be aware of what Eve White was doing. Jane, the third personality, seemed to be a more satisfactory resolution of the dissociations of aspects of personality. Later in life, Eve developed other personalities in spite of psychotherapy. Multiple personality is not to be confused with schizophrenia—literally, split personality—which is a much more common and more severe disorder.

Defenses against Anxiety by Behavioral Activation: The Obsessive-Compulsive

The final class of neurotic defenses involves behavior in which the person repetitiously thinks

about or performs a behavior against his own wishes. Most of us have obsessions (repetitive thoughts) from time to time, such as a song that keeps running through our heads. And we frequently feel compulsive about performing some act. Obsessions and compulsions are neurotic only when the thought or action interferes with the person's ability to behave appropriately. Obsessive thoughts and compulsive behavior tend to go together in the same individual, thus the term *obsessive-compulsive syndrome.*

Obsessive-compulsive behavior functions in two major ways. First, it prevents the individual from thinking anxiety-provoking thoughts. The obsessive may fill his mind with constant trivial thoughts (counting his heartbeats, for example) as a way of avoiding awareness of ideas or memories that would be threatening. A person who keeps to a rigid schedule or who maintains an extremely neat home may be structuring life so as to avoid any possible upsets. Sometimes the obsessive thinking or compulsive behavior bears a symbolic relationship to the anxiety-provoking thought. In one case, for example, a woman had an obsessive fear that she would harm herself if she picked up a kitchen knife. This fear so frightened her that she was unable to prepare meals. Therapy led to the interpretation that her obsession was covering up a desire to kill her husband (felt in a primitive way at the unconscious level and consciously unacceptable to her). By obsessively avoiding knives, she was also able to protect herself from overtly acting out her conflict. In addition, obsessive-compulsive behavior may be an expression of guilt and fear of punishment. The classic example of this is the compulsive hand washing of Shakespeare's Lady Macbeth. Compulsive hand washing has also been associated with conflicts over guilt about masturbation.

Neurotic Depression

The increasing incidence of depressive neurosis in our society has led some to suggest that we are facing an epidemic of depression. Neurotic

A Case of Obsessive-Compulsive Behavior

The following case description illustrates how the obsessive-compulsive individual successfully avoids anxiety-provoking situations. His defensive behavior, however, also prevents him from trying and learning new behaviors that would enable him to cope with his anxiety.

Eliot H., a college student, went to a telephone booth to call up a wealthy girl whom he had recently met, to ask her for a date. He spent an hour there, anxious and indecisive, unable to put the coin in the slot and unable to give up and go home. Each time his hand approached the telephone he anxiously withdrew it because he felt that telephoning her might ruin his chances with her. Each time he withdrew his hand he seemed to be throwing away a golden opportunity. Every positive argument for telephoning her he matched with a negative argument for not doing so. He went into all the ramifications of his ambivalent motivations. He imagined to himself what the girl and the members of her family—whom he scarcely knew—might think of his attentions to her; and then he had to picture to himself what they would think if he neglected her.

His whole future seemed to Eliot to hang on the outcome of this little act. Had he any right to put his coin in? If he did so would the girl respond favorably? If she did, what would happen next? Eliot fantasied every conceivable consequence as he sat there sweating in the booth, consequences to him and to her, on and on into remote contrasting futures. He was helplessly caught in an obsessive dilemma, as he had been caught before hundreds of times. The more he tried to be sure of what he did, the more things he imagined going wrong, any one of which might ruin everything. In the end he gave up the anxious debate and went home, exasperated and worn out. Later he became convinced that in not making the call at that particular time he had missed the chance of a lifetime for winning security and happiness.

This absurd little episode sounds like the mere exaggeration of a shy suitor's hesitancy, but it was much more than this. It was a condensed symbolic expression of an intensely ambivalent personality, one that was volatile, impulsive, and unpredictable. Almost every enterprise upon which Eliot had embarked since early adolescence had involved similar obsessive rumination. Into each decision he funneled all of his ambivalent conflicts—conscious, preconscious, and unconscious—and then he found himself unable to follow through to a decision. The same thing unfortunately happened to his search for therapeutic help. He began with despair, switched quickly to great optimism, and then got bogged down in endless doubting and rumination over whether to continue. In the end he withdrew from therapy without ever becoming really involved in it. (Cameron, 1963, page 396)

depression is characterized by an excessive reaction of depression, usually accompanied by significant anxiety feelings. The disorder usually involves feelings of fatigue, weakness, exhaustion; and yet the individual has difficulty falling asleep. He almost always considers himself a worthless person who has accomplished nothing in his life and who expects to accomplish nothing in the future; often the depressive neurotic feels guilty. Despite all these symptoms, the depressive neurotic does not suffer from loss of contact with reality, although some reality distortion is often present. He typically maintains a reasonable level of functioning in his life, a fact that distinguishes neurotic depression from the much more severe psychotic depression, which we will discuss later in this chapter. There is probably a continuum involved in depression, from the milder neurotic depression to the deep psychotic depression, which can be so severe that the person completely stops functioning.

Neurotic depression is often attributable to a personal loss such as the death of a loved one or a serious financial setback. Occasionally, depressive neurosis follows the achievement of an important goal in the person's life. At least three other factors have been suggested as important in neurotic depression, each having a different theoretical orientation. According to Freudian theory, depression is a result of the person's inability to express outwardly his hostility and anger, even when this expression would be perfectly appropriate. He turns his anger inward against himself and becomes angry and hostile toward his own self-image. He convinces himself that he is a no-good, worthless bum who does not deserve any of the good things he has earned.

Second, there is Carl Rogers' idea that depression arises because the person has an image of an ideal self that he views as different from the real self. The ideal self-image is so completely perfect that the real self seems impossibly far from attaining any of the qualities of the ideal self. If, as Rogers claims, one of a person's major goals is to strive for self-actualization, such a conception of the distance between one's real and ideal selves would lead the person to be depressed and anxious about his life.

Psychiatrists Fear Epidemic of Depression and Hopelessness

By Arthur J. Snider
Copyright, 1972, Chicago Daily News
Never have so many people been so unhappy. A public poll has shown one out of two people said they are depressed much or some of the time.

Doctors are confirming this in their offices. Even though patients don't use the word "depression," the nature of their symptoms tip it off.

Some psychiatrists are calling this the age of depression in contrast to the age of anxiety a generation ago.

The symptoms of anxiety were a pounding heart, troubled breathing, trembling, giddiness, nervousness, hot and cold spells.

Now the predominant symptoms are fatigue, inability to sleep, inability to eat, restlessness and boredom.

Patients say they "can't concentrate" on their daily tasks or have a feeling of "going to pieces." Crying spells are common.

"There's a loss of appetite for food, for sex and for pleasures in life," says Dr. Jan Fawcett, chief of the depression and suicide unit, Illinois State Psychiatric Institute.

Some complaints are physical. The patients come with a backache, a muscle ache, a skin condition.

The physician begins to suspect an emotional problem, such as a depression, when he can't find any organic basis for the symptom.

Body Language Tipoff
Body language may be a tipoff—the tone of voice, the clenched fist, the shifting glance, half-finished sentences.

Depression can masquerade under a variety of disguises. Some masked depressives even come in smiling.

But there's no mistaking the problem when the patient has "no interest in living" and talks of wrist slashing, jumping from a window or in front of a train.

This is a red flare and calls for emergency steps, such as hospitalization. . . .

What's the reason for the rising tide of hopelessness, a primary ingredient of depression?

Urban tensions, racial tensions, crime on the streets, rampant pollution, Vietnam and inflation have been cited, but special studies have shown that depressions are largely triggered by personal events—a personal illness, an argument with a spouse, a change in working conditions—rather than global affairs.

Another reason for the increasing incidence is the alarming rise of unhappiness among youth.

"Many young people have a hopeless outlook for the future and feel frustrated in trying to cope with problems," Dr. Fawcett comments.

Dr. [Harold] Visotsky [chairman of the department of psychiatry, Northwestern University Medical School] adds: "Both the increasing incidence of suicides among youth and the widespread use of mood-elevating drugs, such as amphetamines, indicate that depressions and depressive illness are more common than even our statistics have revealed.

"We're seeing significant numbers of young people as new cases, depressed for the first time. It signifies the illness is becoming epidemic."

Dr. Visotsky is concerned about the implications of the "downward shift in age level" of depression. It may mean recurring epidemics in the years ahead.

"When a person has responded to stress early in life with a specific type of emotional illness—in this case, depression—he tends to respond to future stresses, disappointments and adverse circumstances later in life with the same type of emotional illness.

Nobody Escapes
"Thus, today's youth, who constitute a greater proportion of the total population, will be disposed to react to depressive illness in the future."

No one escapes sadness. In many cases it is normal, such as the grief that follows the loss of a close relative or friend.

Most people also suffer from "the blues."

"People will say, 'I'm depressed today,' meaning that their mood is down. They have lost their job or their girl friend," explains Dr. Fawcett. "But in the midst of their describing their mood, it is quite clear they are going to feel better soon.

"They are not the clinical type cases. As long as the depression is of short duration and the individual is functioning and stays on the job, physicians have no concern about such people."

Everyone has his own prescription for beating the garden-variety blues. The solution for many is simply a new hairdo, a cheerful movie, a hot bath or lively music. Cheer'em-up books and articles abound.

But lifting one's self up by his own bootstraps doesn't apply to the persistent depression that affects everything he does.

One cannot talk, walk, sing or dance himself out of a depression that keeps him in a black mood most of the time. He needs therapy.

A third possible factor, based on behavioral theory, is that one becomes depressed because there is a lack of positive reinforcement in one's life, a view similar to the idea of personal loss. Feelings of happiness, freedom, and self-worth are seen as basically due to consistent receipt of positive rewards for one's behavior. If a person finds himself in a life situation in which his behavior is controlled mainly by negative reinforcement (he does what he does to avoid punishment), then his emotional responses will be depressive.

In summary, there are at least four possible factors in depression: (1) personal loss, (2) anger turned inward, (3) an unusually large discrepancy

A Case of Psychosomatic Asthma

Patricia M., a Baraboo school girl, fourteen years of age, was admitted to a general hospital because of severe attacks of bronchial asthma. The nurses reported that she entered the ward flanked by her frightened parents, the mother supporting her on one side and the father walking on the other side, carrying a syringe with adrenalin ready for instant use. This entrance was a dramatic representation of the attitudes which all three had developed during the four months of her asthmatic attacks. At home the father, after work, had been devoting himself entirely to a task of diverting Patricia, so as to minimize her attacks. Actually, the attacks had increased in frequency and severity following his arrival at home, but neither the parents nor the child seemed to suspect that there might be some connection involved. By the time she was brought to the hospital, her activities had been restricted to those of a person in imminent danger of collapse and sudden death.

Although a respiratory hypersensitivity to bacterial proteins was clearly demonstrated, it was obvious to everyone that the extreme anxiety of the child and her parents presented a major problem. At first, parental visits to the child, but not to the hospital, were limited. Both parents and the child received psychotherapy during the period of her being desensitized to her specific allergens. When Patricia had asthmatic attacks they were treated competently and without anxiety on the part of the staff. When it was observed that she had an increase of attacks on "Protein Clinic" days, the allergist made arrangements to have her treated on the psychiatric ward, and the increase disappeared. Because of her long period of inactivity, it was necessary to schedule increasing activity until Patricia had regained the confidence that she had lost because of everyone's extreme anxiety. After four months, she was well enough to go home and resume a normal life. When asthmatic attacks then occurred, which they did at infrequent intervals, both the parents and the girl were able to handle the situation without alarm. Patricia was seen in office treatment for some time after discharge so that some of her personal problems could be worked through. (Cameron, 1963, page 693)

probably impossible to account for all depressive reactions with only one of these factors.

Psychosomatic Illness

A psychosomatic illness (or psychophysiologic reaction) is a physical illness that has psychological causes. The psychosomatic is actually physically ill, in contrast to the person with a conversion reaction and the hypochondriac, who suffer no real physiological change or tissue damage. The word *psychosomatic* is a misnomer, because in all illness there is an interaction of psychological and physiological processes. But in the cases under discussion here, psychological variables play a greater role than usual.

Early in the history of the dynamic theories, specific conflicts were proposed for each of the psychosomatic illnesses. Thus, the person with asthma was described as someone whose dependency needs are threatened. The person with an ulcer was said to be in conflict between a wish to be fed and cared for and a wish to be independent and competent. The person with essential hypertension was assumed to be consciously inhibiting angry feelings. Attempts to validate the relationship between specific conflicts and specific psychosomatic illnesses have seldom been successful. Furthermore, in cases where the predicted relationship is found, there is often some question as to which is cause and which is effect. For example, it is a common finding that asthmatics *are* unusually dependent, but it is just as possible that asthma produces dependency as it is that dependency produces asthma. If a child is in chronic danger of suffocating, as the asthmatic child often is, it is understandable that he would become very dependent.

Factors Contributing to Psychosomatic Illness

A variety of factors are now believed to contribute to the development of psychosomatic illness. For any given individual, one or more of these factors may play a decisive role. Some of the more important ones are outlined below.

Physiological response stereotypes. People tend to have reliable physiological patterns of response to stress. For example, some people may show significant changes in heart rate, others may breathe rapidly and perspire freely, whereas still others may show changes in four or five

between the real and ideal self, and (4) the lack of positive reinforcement. The depressive reaction may often be triggered by personal loss, but the other factors are probably all important in maintaining the depression, although in any particular case only one or two of these factors may be operating. It is physiological modalities. One often sees in very young infants a response pattern (stereotype) that, regardless of the type of stress, persists into adulthood. It is not unreasonable to propose, as some psychologists have, that if a person tends to respond to stress in a particular physiological modality, and if he is exposed to chronic stress, he is especially likely to develop a physical illness in that modality.

Stimulus-response specificity.   The theory of stimulus-response specificity proposes that the pattern of physiological responses is dependent on the *type* of stimulus. For example, it is known that the response pattern for anger is different from the pattern for fear. When a person is angry, the stomach lining becomes red, contracts, and secretes hydrochloric acid. When a person is anxious, the lining is pale, contractions decrease, and acid levels go down. Thus, if the stress a person experiences leads to chronic anxiety, he will tend to develop problems in different physiological modalities than if he is chronically angry.

The stimulus-response specificity proposal lends some support to the theory that certain personality conflicts are associated with certain psychophysiological disorders. For example, because blood pressure goes up when a person is angry, if he is chronically angry (*and* if he typically responds to stress with changes in blood pressure), he may develop chronically elevated blood pressure.

Associational specificity.   The theory of associational specificity proposes that through learned mediation or accidental conditioning an association between a physiological response and an emotion, thought, or idea may become established. In the *ideational form* of associational specificity, a specific conflict may become associated with a particular physiological response. For example, we all learn to associate feeding with being cared for. Thus if a person wishes to be cared for and is at the same time intensely angry or frustrated, he may respond with increased stomach acidity (through association of being cared for with being fed) and physiological constriction of the blood vessels in the intestines (a direct physiological reaction to anger) and develop an ulcer.

New associations between a thought, feeling, or action and a physiological response can be obtained through both classical and instrumental conditioning; this is called *conditioned specificity*. If

---

A Case of Anxiety Displacement Involving Both Psychosomatic Symptoms and Hypochondriasis

An ambitious but overdependent patient . . . developed typical anxiety attacks in which gastrointestinal symptoms were prominent. One day at work, just after his convalescence from a severe attack of "grippe," he learned that he had not been granted an expected salary increase. To this information, which he angrily considered evidence of unfair discrimination, he reacted characteristically with nausea and diarrhea. Shortly afterward he had another attack of nausea and diarrhea, which he attributed to food poisoning; and because of his heightened anxiety level, the gastrointestinal symptoms persisted. The patient then became greatly concerned over the possibility that he had a gastric ulcer, or perhaps cancer of the stomach. He consulted one physician after another, tried innumerable sorts of medication, and insisted upon repeated gastrointestinal investigations, in spite of the discomfort they entailed. The consistent medical reassurances he received that there was no evidence of organ pathology gave him no lasting relief. Finally, he left work and stayed at home in bed for a period of nine weeks, convinced that he was suffering from an obscure but fatal illness.

This man, of course, had misinterpreted the visceral reactions of his own anxiety as signs of organ pathology. To these signs, which to him meant invalidism and death for him, and poverty and disaster for his family, he reacted with intensified anxiety. But the intensified anxiety brought him more intense and more frequent gastrointestinal distress, and this only served to reinforce his conviction that he was dying. When he finally appealed for psychiatric help, he reported that during the past ten years he had spent a total of eight thousand dollars for medical aid to combat his gastrointestinal symptoms. Therapy aimed, not at the symptoms of anxiety, but at the conflict between passive and aggressive reactions which had induced them, brought him eventually to full social recovery.   (Cameron and Cameron, 1951, pages 311–312)

---

a person is having a severe emotional upset at the time of a physical illness, it is possible that the next time the person is upset in that way, the same physiological illness will occur. It has been learned that asthmatics (who may have specific allergens to which they are sensitive) very easily associate asthma with previously neutral stimuli that then become capable of eliciting the asthma response.

For example, if the person is allergic to cat hair, it is possible that the sight of a cat will elicit the asthma response even before any of the specific allergens come into contact with the person.

Cause and Treatment

Determining the cause of specific cases of psychosomatic illness is very difficult, given all of the different pathways by which a person can develop an illness. Treatment of psychosomatic disorders may involve psychotherapy to resolve the conflict that leads to the excessive and prolonged physiological response under stress. However, if the emotional conflict and the physiological response were associated through conditioning, insight into the conflicts that the person has will probably not resolve the conditioned link. Through research, psychologists are now learning techniques to recondition the individual to produce a new pattern of physiological responses (such as those associated with relaxation) in the presence of the stimuli that previously provoked the physiological reaction (see Chapter 12).

Personality Disorders

"You agreed to fix the screen door!"

"I know, I know. I will. I just haven't had a chance to do it yet."

"But I asked you to fix it over two months ago."

"Look, I said I would do it and I will. I will get it done in the next couple of days."

(Two weeks later.)

"Dear" (said with controlled anger), "I thought you said you were going to get the screen door fixed!"

"You are absolutely right, dear. I don't have time right now, but I'll get right to it. You don't have to nag about it."

That was two years ago and the screen door is not fixed yet!

You might ask what the above example has to do with abnormal psychology. Certainly the importance of getting the screen door fixed is minor compared to the distress and lack of functioning that we see in severe neurosis or psychosis. However, this interaction illustrates a maladaptive relationship that leaves one member of the couple with extreme levels of frustration and anger and the other with a self-righteous indignation over being nagged after having agreed to the reasonableness of the demands.

This section describes a class of behavior referred to as *personality disorders*. People with personality disorders are defined as individuals with *dominant personality traits that lead to behavior that is seen as maladaptive to society*. There are many different types of personality disorders, but we will discuss only five major types: antisocial and dyssocial personalities, alcoholism, drug addiction, and sexually deviant behavior.

The Passive-Aggressive Personality

The procrastinating spouse described above is a passive-aggressive personality who illustrates an extraordinarily effective technique for manipulating other individuals. Passive-aggression is typically seen in individuals with deep dependency needs that prevent the direct expression of anger, because of fear that the dependency needs will no longer be met. Because overt anger or even behavior that might lead to unpleasant disagreement must be avoided, the person develops a pattern of behavior that involves *apparent* agreement and compliance, but that in fact displays passive resistance. The example demonstrates easy agreement over the assignment of chores, but *procrastination* as a way of avoiding a chore that obviously is unpleasant. Other strategies of the passive-aggressive involve stubbornness and *passive obstructionism*. Passive-aggressives can also behave in a passive-dependent manner, acting *helpless, indecisive,* and *clinging.* The passive-aggressive strategy is effective because it blocks any discussion about the trouble that arises from its use. All the passive-aggressive person has to do is agree readily with all the criticisms, apologize profusely, and continue to avoid doing whatever is asked *or* self-righteously assume the martyr role, pointing out that he has always been agreeable and that the demands reflect an intolerance on the part of the other person.

Theorists of both the dynamic and behaviorist schools agree that passive-aggressive behavior is the result of faulty development rather than unconscious responses to internal or external stress. Passive-aggressive individuals frequently are quite satisfied with themselves and would be content to persist in their behavior if society would just leave them alone.

The Antisocial Personality

The antisocial individual, often called a *sociopath*, is pleasure-oriented (hedonistic) and indifferent to the needs or concerns of others. He exploits others for his own selfish ends and does not feel guilt or anxiety except when it is clear that he might be

The Criminal Sociopath

Below are excerpts from a summary of Truman Capote's *In Cold Blood* by R. W. White and N. F. Watt (1973), with quotations from Capote's book. This is a good description of two criminal sociopaths who killed a family of four in an attempt to steal some money from their home.

Through most of his childhood Dick was no trouble to anybody, a cheerful boy who got along well in school, was popular with his classmates and obedient to his parents. The first inkling of criminal tendencies came at 17, when he was arrested for breaking into a drugstore. The next year he suffered head injuries in an auto accident that left his handsome face slightly askew and, according to his father, changed his personality so he "just wasn't the same boy." Now he became sulky and restless, ran around with older men, drank and gambled. Not everyone agreed with his father's testimony, which after all was given at his son's murder trial, where evidence for brain damage might have swayed the jury to recommend a milder sentence. A neighbor claimed that Dick would "steal the weights off a dead man eyes"; he would have gone to jail "more times than you can count, except nobody around here ever wanted to prosecute. Out of respect for his folks." . . .

He got deeply into debt from gambling and imprudent living shortly after his first marriage at 19. Though he was working, he began stealing things and writing fraudulent checks. Eventually he served seventeen months in prison for stealing a neighbor's hunting rifle, and the experience soured him, making him feel the whole world was against him. When he returned home he was contrite, promising his father he would never do anything more to hurt him because he had been a "pretty good old dad" to Dick, and he seemed to mean it sincerely. But this mood did not last.

Even as a hardened criminal Dick was personable, clean-cut, and affable, "a fellow any man might trust to shave him." He was a likable extrovert with a wonderful smile that really worked, sane but not too bright (though his I.Q. was tested at 130). He was fastidiously attentive to personal hygiene and the condition of his fingernails. There was also a hard side to his personality. To Perry Smith, his partner in crime, Dick was authentically tough, pragmatic, invulnerable, "totally masculine." Less appealing were his lack of aesthetic appreciation and his callous insensitivity to the feeling of others. He felt no guilt about making empty promises of marriage to ensure the seduction of a teen-age Mexican girl, and it thrilled him to run over mongrel dogs on the highway. He was an expansive, dominant type who spent his money freely for vodka and women after a windfall from passing bad checks. Dick had a way with women and boasted conceitedly of his amorous conquests.

While in prison Dick learned from another inmate, Floyd Wells, of a prosperous farmer named Clutter who usually had about $10,000 in a wall safe, and an attractive 16-year-old daughter. Dick began to devise a "flawless" plan to steal that money and leave no witnesses, even if there should be a dozen people in the home that night. To this end he chose as his partner Perry Smith, a "cold blooded killer" who claimed to have beaten a "nigger" to death with a bicycle chain, just for the hell of it. (In fact, he had never killed anyone.) Incredible as it sounds, Dick seems to have reckoned that he would be less vulnerable to prosecution in the event of capture if Perry did the killing, but there would be no capture if, as he insisted over and over again, they left no witnesses. At the scene of the crime Dick was brutal and sadistic to the victims; he obviously gloried in having them tied up at his mercy. It was Perry who put pillows under their heads to make them comfortable and reassured them that everything would be all right, and it was Perry who prohibited Dick from raping the girl. Dick was angry that there proved to be no safe and no $10,000; they found less than $50 altogether. Yet despite all his bluster and threats, Dick only held the flashlight while Perry slit Mr. Clutter's throat and finished off all four helpless victims with shotgun blasts to the head.   (White and Watt, 1973, pages 328–329)

prevented from satisfying his need for pleasure. At this point he will become anxious but will not regret his past behavior or learn from punishment to avoid this behavior in the future.

It was thought in the early twentieth century that antisocial personalities were "moral imbeciles" who were incapable of differentiating right from wrong. It has become clear, however, that these people are above average in intelligence and especially adept at manipulating others. They also tend to be physically attractive, which gives them a head start in learning to manipulate others. Punishment seems to have less impact on these individuals than is normal. The presence of an antisocial parent within the home is one of the chief factors in the development of a sociopath. The child is often used for family prestige and learns at an early age how to win social approval.

Treatment for the antisocial personality is difficult. The individual sees nothing wrong in his behavior and will seek help only to manipulate his way out of trouble. It is clear that his maladaptive behavior is a failure of *motivation* to behave appropriately, and psychotherapy is seldom effective in changing him. If it were not for the fact that many seem to "burn out" around the age of 30 and less actively pursue their manipulations of others, they would present a much more serious social problem than they already do.

The Dyssocial Personality

Dyssocial individuals hold values that conflict with the usual mores of the society. For this reason, they might more appropriately be called "cultural deviants." However, they do exhibit intense loyalty to one or, at most, a few subgroups, usually on the periphery of society. Some juvenile delinquent gangs and drug-oriented individuals fit into this classification.

Alcoholism

An alcoholic is defined as an excessive drinker whose dependence on alcohol is so strong that it interferes with his performance of socially appropriate behavior. Alcoholism occurs in all social classes and occupational groups, although the incidence appears to be higher in the middle and upper socioeconomic levels. Skid-row bums are estimated to constitute only 5 percent of the over 9 million alcoholics in the United States. Alcoholism is fourth among the major health problems in the United States and is considered a major social problem as well. Long-term consumption of alcohol can lead to damage to the central nervous system and susceptibility to other diseases, such as tuberculosis and liver disease. Alcohol dependence may also be the cause of family disruption, poor job performance, and social isolation for the individual. Society suffers from the high crime rate associated with alcoholism and the tragic consequences of drunken driving.

Contrary to popular belief, alcohol is not a stimulant but a depressant. Its first effect is to inhibit processes in the higher levels of the brain and reduce inhibitory control over lower levels. Thus, sexual activity might increase under mild intoxication because sexual controls are reduced more than sexual drive. At more extreme levels of intoxication, however, sexual desire is also reduced. Excessive drinking invariably results in some degree of motor incoordination and inability to make fine discriminations (see Chapter 8). More important in

Table 11–2
The pattern of development for alcoholism

1. Prealcoholic phase	→Social drinking →drinking to reduce tension →Daily drinking
2. Prodromal (beginning) phase	→Blackouts with no memory the next day →morning drinking to offset hangover or to face a difficult day
3. Crucial phase	→Loss of control over drinking →loss of family and job
4. Chronic phase	→Prolonged bouts of drinking→ impairment of thinking

the development of alcoholism is the fact that perception of discomfort (both physical and psychological) is dulled.

Many people are capable of restricting their intake to social drinking, but for others this is the first phase in the development of alcoholism (called the *prealcoholic* phase—see Table 11–2). In the second or *prodromal phase* the person drinks in the morning and experiences blackouts. In the *crucial phase* he loses control over his drinking behavior. The *chronic phase* is marked by long "binges" of drinking and impairment of thought processes.

Causes of alcoholism. There is probably no single cause of alcoholism. Although there is some evidence of a genetic component in alcoholic behavior, most psychologists still feel that the alcoholic has learned to drink to reduce anxiety generated by personal problems. There is no evidence that alcoholics are under unusual stress. They tend to be immature, impulsive individuals with low self-esteem and feelings of not living up to their own goals and standards, and they display an inability to tolerate failure.

Treatment of alcoholism. Alcoholics are extremely difficult to treat. The dependence on alcohol is evidently a result of a deeply embedded personality trait. Insight-oriented psychotherapy has not been successful in treating alcoholism. Alcoholics tend to see therapists as unsympathetic and nonunderstanding. Many do not return after the first session and most have left therapy before a month has gone by.

Some drugs have been used to reduce the typically rather mild withdrawal symptoms of craving for alcohol—tremors, sweating, and nausea. *Antabuse* is a drug frequently given to alcoholics; it causes intense nausea if a person drinks alcohol while the chemical is in his bloodstream. The knowledge that drinking will lead to a severe illness helps some alcoholics refrain from impulsive drinking. But because taking the drug each day requires the cooperation of the alcoholic, such a treatment program helps only the alcoholic who sincerely wants to control his drinking and needs a "crutch" to eliminate impulsive drinking.

Alcoholics Anonymous (AA), a mutual aid organization with a strong religious orientation, has had perhaps the greatest success in treating alcoholics. AA groups provide social support and reassurance from recovered alcoholics who understand alcoholics' problems. AA members help new members withstand the trials of "drying out" and provide social events to prevent them from returning to their drinking habits, especially during nonworking hours. The alcoholic must learn new ways to spend his time in place of his drinking activities. Part of the difficulty in treating alcoholism is that alcoholics frequently do not accept the fact that they have a drinking problem, rarely seek treatment voluntarily, and in most states cannot be forced to seek treatment.

Drug Addiction

Some people cope with life's problems by the excessive use of drugs other than alcohol. Drug addiction is considered primarily a personality disorder, although like alcoholism it can occur in combination with neurosis and psychosis. Heroin, the most commonly used addicting drug in the United States, constitutes a major social problem because of the large amount of illegal behavior associated with addiction; the loss of socially appropriate behavior like working and maintaining a family; and the "contagion" effect—it is estimated that each addict introduces an average of *6* others to narcotics.

There are several differences between drug addiction and alcoholism. Psychologically, drugs frequently produce euphoria rather than just the reduction in tension that alcohol produces. Furthermore, while the alcoholic shows an initial slight increase in his tolerance for alcohol, followed later by a decrease, the drug addict finds that an increasing amount of the drug is required in order to maintain the same "high." For this reason addiction becomes tremendously expensive, and the addict may need $50 or more a day to maintain his habit. For many, antisocial behaviors such as stealing or prostitution are the only means for attaining the necessary funds. Because the addict cannot be sure of the quality of the drugs, overdoses (ODs) are common and often result in death.

Whereas the chronic alcoholic may experience only mild to severe illness when withdrawn from alcohol, the heroin addict becomes severely ill within 2 days after withdrawal from the drug. The symptoms of withdrawal may begin anywhere from 4 to 12 hours after the last dose, depending on the level of addiction. Restlessness, depression, and irritability may begin the withdrawal, followed by vomiting, diarrhea, cramps, pains, severe headaches, tremors, and possibly hallucinations and delirium. The symptoms peak in 3 to 4 days and decline after the fifth day. The tolerance built up before withdrawal disappears after the addict goes "cold turkey" (so called because of the common "goose bumps" seen during withdrawal), and people have died from taking a dose as heavy as the ones they were taking before withdrawal.

Causes of addiction. Many drug addicts are more like the sociopathic personality than the impulsive, immature, and dependent person who becomes an alcoholic. One indication of the personality-disorder aspect of these addicts is the fact that many of them take the "cure" not to be cured but in order to start over again with a less expensive habit. Although the withdrawal symptoms are severe, it is not fear of withdrawal that maintains a drug habit, as is commonly believed. The sociopathic drug addict finds that drugs are an easy way to maintain a pleasure-oriented approach to life.

However, not all drug addicts are sociopathic. About 20 percent of the patients at the federal hospital for drug addiction in Lexington, Kentucky, used drugs originally to relieve anxiety. These people feel unsure of themselves and gain psychological support from the drug subculture. Another group of addicts come from middle-class liberal backgrounds. These addicts become users during adolescence and frequently try their first heroin out of curiosity. Often they are rebelling against their family's life style and start using drugs as one way of experimenting with alternative life styles. These individuals are rarely involved in criminal activities.

Treatment of addiction. Treating drug addiction is even more difficult than treating alcoholism. The addict's lack of *motivation* to behave in socially appropriate ways is a major problem. Psychotherapy is typically not successful. Enforced treatment in a government hospital has produced cure rates varying from 1 to 15 percent. Drugs have not been extensively applied, although *methadone* is increasingly being used. Maintenance on methadone prevents withdrawal symptoms from heroin addiction, and when taken orally, methadone does not produce the intense "high" that prevents the drug user from functioning in society. (Interestingly, methadone does produce a mild "high" of its own, which has led to a methadone black market.) Although methadone tends to block a heroin high, thus reducing the pleasurable (reinforcing) aspects of heroin, this treatment technique has been severely criticized because methadone itself is addicting. It is probably well to remember that, years ago, heroin was touted as the "cure" for morphine addiction. On the other hand, methadone is cheap and legal when used in a medically supervised treatment program. At the very least, it reduces the probability that an addict will have to steal or become a prostitute to get drugs. Methadone is not a cure-all, however, as demonstrated by the fact that when an addict withdraws from methadone, the craving for *heroin* returns.

The most successful form of treatment to date follows the model of *Synanon*, a residential group-treatment approach run by ex-addicts. The addicts live together as a group and attend group meetings or seminars. (The word *synanon* comes from an addict who tried to say the word *seminar*.) The approach is somewhat similar to that of Alcoholics Anonymous. However, we should remember that whereas the alcoholic is a dependent, immature individual, the drug addict is frequently a sociopath, adept at manipulating others. Synanon meetings are aggressive and punitive; the only rule is one prohibiting physical abuse. The group attacks the manipulative approaches of the addict and tears down his maladaptive, self-centered approach to life. The Synanon method and similar approaches have had success in an area in which numerous other programs have failed, but the Synanon approach can only work if the addict *wants to change his behavior.*

Sexual Deviations

The final classification of personality disorders—sexual deviations—is broadly defined as any method of obtaining sexual satisfaction or participating in sexual relationships that is disapproved of by the community. Sexual deviations can be grouped into three categories. The first is deficient sexual activity or desire, for psychological rather than physiological reasons. The most obvious example is sexual impotence or frigidity—the inability to engage in sexual intercourse with an opposite-sexed partner or the lack of any enjoyment

Figure 11-4
Homosexuality

Homosexuals are now militantly protesting their unequal treatment by society.

from this activity. Usually impotence and frigidity are traceable to personal (possibly unconscious) conflict with the partner that leads to remoteness, lack of emotional love, or even anger. But beyond interpersonal conflict, latent or overt homosexuality, excessive concern with the morality of sex, and situational stresses may all preclude normal heterosexual relationships.

A second form of deviation involves apparently normal sexual activity carried out in extraordinary antisocial conditions. Promiscuity, prostitution, and rape are examples of this category. The rapist has a fairly typical antisocial character structure. He seeks his own pleasure at the expense of others and feels no guilt about his behavior. He is clearly and coldly indifferent to the feelings of others. Rape is just a way of taking what he wants, and the rapist frequently rationalizes his behavior by claiming that his victim probably enjoyed it (Kopp, 1962). He learns nothing from punishment and does not cooperate with psychotherapy attempts unless the alternative is confinement.

The third form of deviation focuses on inappropriate sexual objects. This is a difficult category to discuss, mainly because of a lack of widespread agreement among experts as to what constitutes an appropriate or inappropriate object. Most people would agree that a person who can achieve orgasm only when masturbating against the foot of another person is sexually deviant.

But other conditions are not so easy to categorize. Consider the *homosexual,* a person who has overt sexual interests in or receives sexual satisfaction from members of the same sex. Homosexuality was for a long time commonly categorized as a sexual

Homosexuality Dropped as Mental Disorder

APA Monitor—In a historic move that has been hailed by both psychiatrists and leaders of the gay liberation movement, the American Psychiatric Association voted in mid-December to strike "homosexuality" from its official list of mental disorders.

The unanimous vote (with two abstentions) by the APA Board of Trustees thus erases a medical definition that goes back nearly 100 years and brings the psychiatric association into step with other mental health organizations.

Although the National Association for Mental Health (in 1970), and the Group for the Advancement of Psychiatry (in 1955) have publicly recommended that homosexuality not be defined as an illness, it has continued to be classified as such in the American Psychiatric Association's Diagnostic and Statistical Manual of Mental Disorders (DSM-II). Notably, the American Psychological Association has never taken an official position on this issue, but has followed the DSM-II.

Since the DSM-II is the official nomenclature followed not only by psychologists but by all North American medical groups, the recent APA decision is certain to have considerable impact not only here, but in other countries as well.

In addition to dropping the "illness" designation, the APA trustees adopted a resolution deploring all public and private discrimination against homosexuals in employment, housing, and other areas. They also urged the repeal of sodomy laws (currently on the books in 42 states and the District of Columbia) and other legislation making criminal offenses of sexual acts performed by consenting adults in private. The APA position on such laws echoes a similar statement made last year by the American Bar Association, and earlier recommendations by the American Law Institute, the National Institute of Mental Health, and others.

The APA trustees, however, stopped short of declaring homosexuality normal. Instead, they have substituted a new diagnostic category, "sexual orientation disturbance," for those homosexuals who are in conflict about their sexual orientation and who want either to change it or learn better how to live with it.

Despite the qualifier, leaders of the organized homosexual community termed the APA actions "the greatest gay victory" and a "major sociohistoric change." According to Dr. Franklin Kameny, President of the Mattachine Society of Washington, D.C., the psychiatric about-face represents a major breakthrough in the long struggle to end social prejudice against homosexuals. A statement to the press by the National Gay Task Force called the APA decision an "instant cure" for 20 million gay Americans. Dr. Robert L. Spitzer, head of the APA Task Force on Nomenclature and Statistics and principal author of the revised nomenclature, concedes that political pressure by the gay liberation movement had a lot to do with the APA's articulation of the new policy, but he insists that the shift in diagnostic categories is psychiatrically sound.

Both gay leaders and their new psychiatric allies agree that while some psychiatrists will no doubt continue to regard homosexuality, in and of itself, as pathological, the majority will begin to modify their views and, accordingly, their practices, as a result of the APA actions.

---

deviation. Recently, however, the American Psychiatric Association removed homosexuality from its lists of diagnostic categories. Also, several sections of society have become more accepting of homosexuality, but there is still much opposition to overt homosexuality from some groups and individuals who consider homosexual relationships distasteful (see Figure 11-4). As a result of changing attitudes toward homosexuality, it is impossible to explicitly categorize it as a sexual deviation. Most mental health professionals have adopted a flexible approach. If a homosexual is comfortable with his or her sexual adjustment and does not show maladaptive behavior in interpersonal relationships, a mental health professional is likely to accept the homosexuality. But if a homosexual is dissatisfied with this sexual interest and wants to become heterosexual, the professional tries to discover the causes of the homosexuality and to eliminate them if at all possible.

Although research has not given a clear picture of the causes of homosexuality, the literature tends to implicate four factors:

1. Lack of identity with the same-sexed parent. Female homosexuals report poor relationships with both parents. Males frequently have distant, cold fathers and possessive, domineering mothers who may be almost seductive in their behavior with their sons.

2. Seduction. There is some disagreement as to how frequently homosexual seduction in childhood causes homosexualism. Most homosexuals have emotional attachments with a same-sexed peer fairly early in adolescence, which suggests that homosexual interests begin early.

3. Fear of the opposite sex. A pathological home life may develop a fear of the opposite sex, or a child may lack the opportunity to learn social skills that would encourage normal heterosexual attachments.

4. Lack of opportunity. Homosexuals are frequently

The anguish of psychosis.

found in the armed forces and prisons, where normal sexual outlets are not available. Some of these individuals revert to normal sexual behavior after return to "civilian" life.

A person may develop a sexual deviation for a wide variety of reasons, from fear of appropriate sexual outlets to conditioned responses during the developing stages of sexual behavior. When treatment is sought for sexual deviations, successful behavior changes, as with the other personality disorders, are relatively rare. Conditioning therapy has shown some promise, but the gains here are minor compared with those obtained for other types of problems. It is more likely that sexual deviation will be controlled through prevention rather than treatment of individual cases.

Psychosis

If an individual can no longer differentiate between reality and fantasy, if he sometimes experiences hallucinations and delusions, or if he occasionally loses conscious control of his thoughts, feelings, and actions, he is considered *psychotic.* These behavioral characteristics often have dramatic effects on the individual's observable behavior as well as his internal processes. The person may lose awareness of who and where he is, talk aloud to himself, conduct nonsensical conversations with strangers, or withdraw and say nothing for days, months, or years. The normal workaday world is usually unprepared to understand or accept the bizarre behavior of the psychotic. Indeed, psychotic

behavior is apt to elicit fear, repugnance, or ridicule, because its effect is so disrupting to society. Psychosis, unless organically caused and treatable, is most often a chronic illness that may affect the greater part of an individual's lifetime. Spontaneous recovery is rare, although a person may have psychotic episodes alternating with periods when he is able to function independently and maintain a somewhat normal life style. The current emphasis in treating psychosis is to help the patient to do this, using long-term hospital care only as a last resort.

There has been a long and persistent search for physical causes of psychosis, with some suggestive findings but no definitive answers as yet. The fact that many of the symptoms of psychosis can be reduced or alleviated with drugs is also suggestive of organic causes. Indeed it is with psychosis that the medical model is most useful. In some of the disorders there is evidence of a genetic link. However, most psychologists agree that, even if there is a biochemical or genetic foundation for the psychosis, environment still plays an important role. The two major classifications of psychosis to be discussed are the affective disorders and the schizophrenias.

Affective Reactions

During the nineteenth century, Emil Kraepelin, the father of the present psychiatric diagnostic system, identified two emotional problems with opposite characteristics, depression and mania, as part of the same "disease" process. Deep or psychotic depression involves feelings of profound sadness and loneliness and lack of self-worth. Thought processes are slowed down, and the person has a very low level of energy. In contrast, mania involves feelings of optimism and the speeding up of thought processes and motor behavior. The person is loud and energetic. He is involved in all sorts of activities. The assumption is that the person who is manic is using a defensive mechanism, reaction formation, to escape feeling depressed. For some individuals, the mania and deep depression seem to alternate in a fairly regular pattern. These circular variations in mood, called *manic-depressive psychosis*, are relatively uncommon, however. Of those individuals exhibiting psychotic depressions, only 10 to 15 percent show the switch to mania and back again.

Depression reaches psychotic proportions when the person loses contact with reality. The manic may develop delusions of grandeur or consider himself to have unusual powers. The depressive may have hallucinations and delusions involving depressive thoughts. An example is the psychotic depressive who feels that his insides are rotting and filled with insects. There is evidence for a continuum of severity in depression from normal depression (with the normal disappointments of life) through neurotic depression to the most severe psychotic depression. All depressions, whether severe or mild, involve systems of fantasies that may become delusional. For example, it is not unusual for the depressed adolescent to have fantasies of committing suicide, an act that so upsets people that he imagines himself finally appreciated at his funeral. If the depression is severe the person may "live" this fantasy.

Suicide. Most people believe that suicide occurs in the depths of depression. With severe depression, however, the person seldom has enough energy to

Suicide, the ultimate act, can occur for a variety of reasons and take many forms.

Suicides Among Top 12 Causes Of Death; Rates Higher In West

Boulder Daily Camera—Accurate figures on suicide rates have always been difficult to determine because of the general stigma attached to taking one's own life in most societies.

However, suicide has ranked among the 12 leading causes of death in the United States for a number of years—this despite the reluctance to report suicide, as a cause of death, and the difficulty in many cases in distinguishing suicides from accidents, according to Metropolitan Life Insurance Co. statisticians.

When account is taken of unsuccessful suicide attempts—estimated at four to ten times the number of reported suicides—the magnitude of the suicide problem is clearly very much greater than indicated by the official statistics.

Higher in West

The statistics show that in 1972 the suicide rate was estimated at 11.7 per 100,000, slightly above the 11.1 per 100,000 recorded in 1971. In general, the rates of suicide have been highest in the Pacific and Mountain States; the lowest rates have usually been registered in New England and the Middle Atlantic States.

The Metropolitan Life study of 1968 suicide figures shows that two-thirds of the suicides in the United States occur at ages 35 to 74. Suicides among males in that age group averaged about 30 per 100,000 on a countrywide basis.

The highest rate—40 per 100,000—was recorded in the Mountain States, followed closely by a rate of 39 per 100,000 in the Pacific States and 37 per 100,000 in the South Atlantic area. The lowest rates were registered in the New England and Middle Atlantic regions—19 and 20 per 100,000, respectively.

The national suicide rate for women aged 35 to 74 that year was 11 per 100,000. The Pacific region reported the highest rate—21 per 100,000—while the lowest rates were 8 per 100,000 in the middle Atlantic and 9 per 100,000 in the New England, East South Central and West South Central regions.

More Men

Self-inflicted deaths are much more frequent among men than among women; although this disparity has narrowed somewhat in recent years. As already indicated, the study showed that the suicide rate among males in the age range 35 to 74 was nearly three times that of females. At age 35 to 54 the ratio was about two to one, rose to three to one at ages 55 to 64, and to four to one at ages 65 to 74.

However, according to Metropolitan Life statisticians, considerably more women than men attempt suicide, but are less successful in killing themselves. This is probably attributable to the methods usually used by men (shooting or hanging) which ensure a greater certainty of death.

The level of suicide rates is associated with a number of factors, such as season of the year, marital status and economic conditions. Although the incidence of suicide is not significantly related to climate, self-destruction is more frequent in the spring and early summer and is at the lowest point in the winter months.

Other Factors

The frequency of suicide also varies markedly with marital status, being lowest for the married, somewhat higher for the single, and highest for the widowed and divorced. Increased suicide rates have also been observed during periods of unemployment and economic recession. Suicide rates among males reached their highest point in 1932, coincident with the highest unemployment during the depression of the 1930s. Suicide rates also vary widely among those of different religious denominations, and in different social and cultural groups.

try suicide. It is during the swing out of depression that the risk of suicide is the most dangerous. The person is still depressed but now is active enough to do something about it. Indeed, the lifting of the deepest depression may indicate that the person has found one solution to his problems, death. Deep depression and suicides tend to occur during holidays, pleasant weather, and the first day of spring rather than in dreary weather, apparently because of the discrepancy between how the person feels and how he thinks he ought to feel. The expectation that everyone should be happy at Christmas causes the depressed person to feel even more depressed.

Suicide is the ninth greatest cause of death in the United States, with about 200,000 attempts each year and about 25,000 successes. Three times as many men as women successfully complete suicide attempts, but three times as many women attempt suicide. Suicide attempts are highest among professional groups. During national crises like war and earthquakes, suicide rates decrease; they increase during economic depression. The prevention of suicide will be discussed in Chapter 12.

Heredity.   Population statistics are often used to document the role of heredity in manic-depressive psychosis. Kallman (1953) noted that 25 percent of the brothers, sisters, parents, and children of manic-depressives were also manic-depressive, whereas the expectancy rate in the general population is around .5 percent. In a later study (1958) Kallman compared the *concordance rate* of

Genes and Depression

Time—Manic-depressive illness, or psychosis, is . . . one of the most baffling of emotional disorders. The victim may seem normal for months, then enter a period of mania in which, as one imaginative psychiatrist described it, he "comes in swinging from chandeliers that aren't there." Back to normal for a while, he may next become depressed, sometimes suicidally.

Psychiatrists have argued for generations about the cause of manic-depressive illness, although it is known to run in families. Is it "functional," meaning that it is acquired as the result of life experiences, or is it "organic," involving some abnormality in the body's biochemistry? Last week, at a conference in Copenhagen, a New York City team of researchers suggested that a tendency or predisposition to manic-depressive illness might be deeply rooted indeed: in the genes that determine heredity.

The suspected villain is the female or X chromosome, which carries hundreds of genetic instructions to offspring of both sexes. Three years ago, investigators at Barnes Hospital in St. Louis reported "presumptive evidence" that an anomalous gene on the X chromosome is associated with the emotional disorder. The new and more definite evidence comes from Dr. Ronald R. Fieve and colleagues at the Columbia-Presbyterian Medical Center.

The evidence is admittedly indirect. The Columbia researchers studied 19 manic-depressive pa-

tients. In the families of seven there was red-green color blindness, which is known to result from a defective gene on the X chromosome. The other twelve families displayed the blood-group pattern known as Xg , also transmitted on the X chromosome. The Mendelian pattern of inheritance for both these traits is known. Manic-depressive illness is associated with them, says Fieve. So the disorder is probably—in some cases, at least—transmitted by a nearby defective gene.

Fieve does not claim that his hypothesis accounts for all manic-depressive illness, or that all people with the abnormal gene will develop the emotional disorder in severe form. But with the refinement of testing for abnormal genes, it may eventually be possible to detect early in life those individuals in greatest danger of developing the illness, and thus to treat them earlier and more effectively.

F. J. Kallman presented data that indicated that manic-depressive psychosis is largely determined by heredity. Now we know that Kallman's work with identical twins suffered from numerous deficiencies and that he overestimated the role of genetics in psychosis. Nevertheless, there is agreement, based on studies similar to the one above, that heredity is an important factor.

manic-depressives in fraternal and identical twins. The concordance rate is defined as the probability that one of a pair of twins is manic-depressive, given that the other twin is so diagnosed. Fraternal twins have the same overlap of genes as any two brothers or sisters, whereas identical twins have identical genetic make-up. Kallman reported that the concordance rate for fraternal twins was .265 and the rate for identical twins was .957. He concluded that manic-depressive reactions result from a genetic defect in the neurohormonal mechanisms that control emotion.

These findings, while impressive, are not as conclusive as Kallman suggests. First of all, being from the same family, all siblings, including twins, have a much more similar environment than randomly chosen members of the population at large. Thus, if the nature of the environment is such as to produce depression in one family member, others subject to the same circumstances might be affected in the same way. Furthermore, identical twins, just because they look very much alike, will have even more similar environments than fraternal twins or ordinary siblings. For example, since it is difficult to tell one from the other, identical twins

will tend to elicit the same responses from people. Thus, the higher correlations noted by Kallman among identical twins as contrasted with fraternal twins or ordinary siblings could be environmentally rather than genetically based.

In addition, there are methodological problems with Kallman's work. At the time of his studies, techniques for distinguishing between identical and fraternal twins were imperfect. A fraternal pair might be incorrectly classified as identical if they looked and behaved enough alike—for example, if they were both depressed. Nowadays, blood serum studies make it possible to categorize twin types with little error. Furthermore, it should be noted that medical diagnoses of depression are not made blindly. A physician who finds in the family history that the identical (or fraternal) twin of a patient has been diagnosed as depressive is more likely to apply that label to his patient. These factors, too, tend to inflate the estimates of depression among family members.

All things considered, then, we cannot safely conclude that manic-depressive reactions are entirely or even largely genetic. While there is no question about the importance of heredity, psychological, especially learning, processes are at least as critical.

Biochemical causes. Because of current research there is increasing interest in the role of biochemical factors in affective disorders. One theory proposes that a state of well-being is maintained in the body by hormones produced in the brain called catecholamines (epinephrine and norepinephrine). Deficits of these hormones may lead to severe emotional disruption and the mood swings of the manic-depressive. The evidence to support this theory is indirect. A group of drugs that lift depression in some people is known also to increase the level of norepinephrine in the brain, while a drug that tends to produce depression reduces the amount of this hormone in the brain.

Psychological causes. There is some evidence that is difficult to fit into any strictly biological theory of manic-depressive psychosis. For example, a disproportionate number of manic-depressives tend to come from upper socioeconomic groups, and income is unlikely to be heavily biologically determined. Some researchers and clinicians have reached the conclusion that severe depression may be rooted in rejection in early childhood. The manic-depressive seems to be trying to win approval from parents who are constantly finding fault. Frequently, the precipitating event for the depression is loss of a loved one or loss of status. Behavior theorists have proposed that depression results from the lack of positive reinforcement within a person's life, a view that has a slightly different focus than the dynamic point of view but is consistent with it.

Treatment. One of the unique aspects of depression is the spontaneous remission of symptoms; that is, depression tends to lift after a period of time without the benefit of treatment. If a person in a severe depression is kept from committing suicide, the depression will lift. It may take weeks, months, or even years, but the state is self-limiting. This does not mean that the person will not experience depression again in the future. The one exception to the self-limiting aspect of depression is the involutional depression of middle age, which is usually attributed to a person's realization that some of life's important goals are unattainable. This type of depression is more likely to continue if treatment is not received. Treatment is important even for the self-limiting depressions, in

order to reduce the suffering of the depressed person and his family.

How to understand and treat affective disorders is still very much unresolved. Many factors are involved and no single set of circumstances has been found in the history of all manic-depressives. The treatment of psychotic depressives is difficult. Drugs are only partly successful, and psychotherapy tends to be a slow, up-hill climb. Supportive therapy, with attempts to understand the cause of the depression and to help the person change his life so as to eliminate the cause, is the most common strategy used today.

Schizophrenia

Schizophrenia refers to a group of psychotic disorders in which there are disturbances in thought processes as well as emotions and a marked distortion of reality. Conscious thought processes are often unpredictable, following a chain of associations that is difficult for others to understand. Generally there is a withdrawal from interpersonal relationships and a blunting or flattening of emotional responses, which may change to extreme, inappropriate emotional responses. Another frequent symptom is depersonalization, the loss of personal identity. There may be preoccupation with bodily functions, which are attributed to nonhuman causes. The schizophrenic may feel that his hand has turned to stone or that his body is full of bugs so that he is no longer human. There seems to be a preoccupation with inner fantasies. The schizophrenic is probably of normal intelligence, but his lack of attention to the external environment leads to low scores on IQ tests.

In some cases, schizophrenic breakdown is highly dramatic and is described by the person as something happening to him rather than something that he is doing. Schizophrenia in which there is a sudden onset of symptoms is sometimes referred to as *reactive schizophrenia,* and the probability of recovery (*prognosis*) is good in such cases. Schizophrenia characterized by slow onset of symptoms over a period of years with progressive withdrawal from others, increasing deterioration of thought processes, and slow onset of hallucinations and delusions is referred to as *process schizophrenia* and has a very poor prognosis.

Types of schizophrenia. There are four main subtypes of schizophrenia: simple, hebephrenic, paranoid, and catatonic. The *simple schizophrenic* is generally a process type, characterized by a

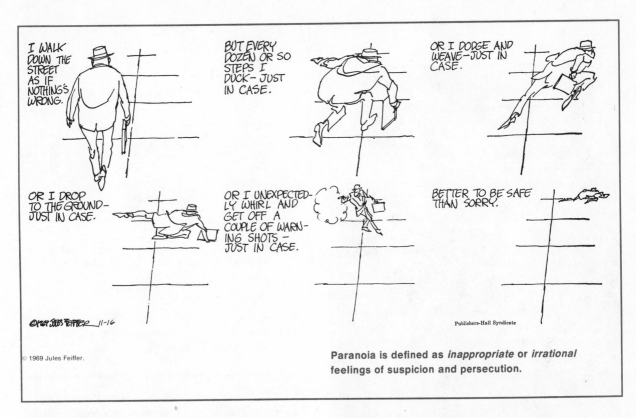

© 1969 Jules Feiffer.

Paranoia is defined as *inappropriate* or *irrational* feelings of suspicion and persecution.

reduction in interpersonal relationships, apathy and indifference, but seldom many delusions and hallucinations. He has difficulty in focusing on anything in the outside world. The simple schizophrenic rarely causes much trouble because his symptoms do not intrude on the lives of others.

The *hebephrenic schizophrenic* is characterized by inappropriate affect and silly, giggling, and childish behavior. Frequently hallucinations occur. Behavior is grossly inappropriate; the hebephrenic may break out into laughter for no apparent reason or have a burst of rage without provocation. Hebephrenic schizophrenia is usually a process type involving gradual symptom onset, and the prognosis is poor.

Paranoid schizophrenia is frequently a reactive problem, and there is a reasonable chance of recovery. This subtype is characterized by delusions of persecution and suspicion of others. The feeling of being singled out for persecution leads the paranoid to conclude that he is a special person, selected because of unusual powers or qualities. Thus, the paranoid schizophrenic is often characterized by *delusions of grandeur.* For example, in one case, a youth attacked a total stranger who was standing near him at a baseball game. When asked later by the police why he had done this, he responded that it was well known that

he was sexually attractive to women and this man was trying to steal his sexual attractiveness by electrical waves. It is assumed that the paranoid uses projection, denying his unacceptable anger and ascribing it to others. Paranoid schizophrenia should not be confused with the paranoid personality, a personality disorder characterized by suspiciousness and jealousy but no loss of contact with reality.

Catatonic schizophrenia may be a reactive or a process type. The reactive catatonic probably has the best prognosis of any of the schizophrenics. The catatonic is characterized by a *waxy flexibility* of body and limbs, loss of motion, and a tendency to remain motionless for hours or days. He may allow his arms to be placed in uncomfortable positions without resistance and remain in that position far longer than the normal individual would tolerate. The dynamic theorists see the catatonic as handling hostility by immobility (see Figure 11-5). The catatonic may have episodes of furious rage from time to time that alternate with the rigid withdrawal.

While these four types of schizophrenia are carefully described in diagnostic manuals and books of psychopathology, it is important to note that individuals seldom fit into such neat patterns. The two most common diagnoses made within the schizophrenic classification are *paranoid* and

Figure 11–5
Catatonic schizophrenia

The patient in this picture is in a position that he might typically hold rigidly for long periods.

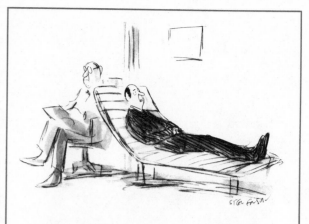

"All that political paranoia you helped me get rid of, Doctor—what do I do now that it turns out I was right?"

New Yorker, July 16, 1973. Drawing by Stevenson; © 1973 The New Yorker Magazine, Inc.

Sometimes it is difficult to determine whether *mild* paranoia is an emotional problem or a relatively accurate perception of reality.

chronic-undifferentiated. The latter diagnosis is a wastebasket term indicating that the person has characteristics belonging to more than one subtype. *Schizophrenia* itself is frequently a wastebasket term used when the person is psychotic but not depressed. The lack of clarity in the use of the term

schizophrenia and its different designations from one mental institution to the next has complicated the extensive research conducted on the causes of schizophrenia.

Causes of schizophrenia. We shall briefly consider research on genetic, biochemical, and environmental factors.

Genetic factors. There is little doubt now that there is a genetic component in schizophrenia, although different investigators have found widely different concordance rates for sets of identical twins. For example, Kallman, whose research is most well known in this area, found that of 174 pairs with one member who had already been diagnosed as schizophrenic, the other twin was also

Table 11–3
Schizophrenia rates in identical twins

Investigator	Number of twin pairs studied (one twin already diagnosed as schizophrenic)	Number of pairs in which the other member of the pair also has schizophrenia	Number of pairs in which the other member of the pair is abnormal but not schizophrenic
Kallman	174	103	62
Essen-Moller	9	0	8
Slater	37	18	11
Tienari	16	1	12
Kringlen	45	14	17
Inouye	53	20	29
Gottesman and Shields	24	10	8
Total	358	166 (46.4%) Concordance rate = .46	147 (41.1%) Concordance rate = .41

The Case of a Paranoid Schizophrenic

I, LPK, had a few days to spend with Long Island relatives before returning to work for the War Dept., Wash., D.C. One day I went to reconnoitre in N.Y. City's East Side. Being a stranger I was surprised to hear someone exclaim twice: "Shoot him!", evidently meaning me, judging from the menacing talk which followed between the threatener and those with him. I tried to see who the threatener, and those with him were, but the street was so crowded, I could not. I guessed that they must be gangsters, who had mistaken me for another gangster, who I coincidentally happened to resemble. I thought one or more of them really intended to shoot me so I hastened from the scene as fast as I could walk. These unidentified persons, who had threatened to shoot me, pursued me. I knew they were pursuing me because I still heard their voices as close as ever, no matter how fast I walked . . . Days later while in the Metropolis again, I was once more startled by those same pursuers, who had threatened me several days before. It was nighttime. As before, I could catch part of their talk but, in the theatre crowds, I could see them nowhere. I heard one of them, a woman, say: "You can't get away from us; we'll lay for you, and get you after a while!" To add to the mystery, one of these "pursuers" repeated my thoughts aloud, verbatim. I tried to allude [sic] these pursuers as before, but this time, I tried to escape from them by means of subway trains, darting up and down subway exits, and entrances, jumping on,

and off trains, until after midnight. But, at every station where I got off a train, I heard the voices of these pursuers as close as ever. The question occurred to me: How could as many of these pursuers follow me as quickly unseen? Were they ghosts? Or was I in the process of developing into a spiritual medium? No! Among these pursuers, I was later to gradually discover by deduction, [there] evidently were some brothers, and sisters,[1] who had inherited from one of their parents, some astounding, unheard of, utterly unbelievable occult powers. Believe-it-or-not, some of them,[2] besides being able to tell a person's thoughts, are also able to project their magnetic voices—commonly called "radio voices" around here—a distance of a few miles without talking loud, and without apparent effort, their voices sounding from that distance as tho heard thru a radio head-set,[3] this being done without electrical apparatus. This unique, occult power of projecting their "radio voices" for such long distances, apparently seems to be due to their natural, bodily electricity, of which they have a supernormal amount. Maybe the iron contained in their red blood corpuscles is magnetised. The vibration of their vocal chords, evidently generates wireless waves, and these vocal radio waves are caught by human ears without rectification.[4]   (Kaplan, 1964, pages 133–135)

[1]Maybe some were half brothers, or half sisters, or both.
[2]There is little doubt but what more than one of them can read minds.
[3]Hence the term "radio voices."
[4]The other day I read about a man who could hear radio broadcasts of a local station thru his teeth without a receiving set. In the plant where he worked the air was filled with tiny carborundum crystals, and some of these had collected on his teeth.

schizophrenic in 103 cases (see Table 11–3). On the other hand, Essen-Moller found no pairs of twins in which both members were schizophrenic. It is generally agreed now that Kallman's data significantly exaggerate the degree of heredity involved in schizophrenia. We reviewed some of the general problems with his methods in our discussion of affective disorders, but additional questions have arisen in connection with his work on schizophrenia. For example, Kallman's sample of patients has been criticized as having involved only the most severe cases and as having a preponderance of females. There is some evidence (Gottesman and Shields, 1966) that the degree of concordance between twins is higher as severity of affliction increases. This in turn suggests that schizophrenia is not a unitary disorder and that process forms may be more genetically based than reactive forms.

Perhaps the best estimate of the degree of genetic

determination of schizophrenia can be obtained by pooling the results of several different studies. On the basis of the results of the seven studies shown in Table 11–3, we conclude: Given that one twin is schizophrenic, the chances are 46/100 that the other twin will be schizophrenic (the probability that the other twin will be schizophrenic = .46). The value for ordinary brothers and sisters would only be around 10 to 15 percent, so these data strongly suggest a genetic component in schizophrenia. Even if the other twin is not schizophrenic, the odds are quite high that he will have some significant behavior abnormality. Thus, if one of a pair of identical twins is schizophrenic, about 88 percent of the other twins either will be schizophrenic or will suffer from some other behavior disorder (the sum of columns two and three in Table 11–3).

It is probably true that in all cases of schizophrenia, as in the affective disorders, both heredity and environment are important, a notion

Most research studies that find that children have problems similar to their parents' assume that the parents' behavior led to the children's problems. However, the possibility is frequently ignored that the parents' behavior may be a reaction to having an emotionally disturbed child.

formally called the *diathesis-stress* theory of psychosis. According to this theory, schizophrenia develops because there is a genetic predisposition to the disorder (called *diathesis*) *and* because there are environmental factors (*stress*) that trigger the disorder. If either factor is missing, the disorder will not appear. This theory is a better approximation to our current knowledge than a model that suggests that one type of schizophrenia is genetic (say, the process type) and the other is environmental (say, the reactive type).

Biochemical factors.   Are there biochemical factors in schizophrenia? At times chemicals have supposedly been found in the blood of schizophrenics that are not found in normal blood. However, no single chemical has been consistently found by all research groups. It has also been proposed that a neural transmitter, called serotonin, produces the symptoms of schizophrenia, but our understanding of how neural transmitters work is still far from complete.

All the studies implicating biochemical factors suffer the same difficulty in interpretation—it is never clear if the biochemical change is a cause or a result of the disorder. For example, many mental hospitals are nonhygienic and overcrowded. Most patients are on medication of some kind, taking drugs that often have unknown biochemical side effects. The eating habits of psychotics may be poor, since they often withdraw from all activity in the external world. All these factors may lead to biochemical imbalance. Although it is tempting to think of biochemical abnormalities as the cause of

schizophrenia, these conditions suggest that they might really be the result.

Environmental factors.   In an effort to isolate environmental factors, extensive research has been done on the family life of the schizophrenic. Lidz et al. (1963) have proposed that there is a *marital skew* in the family, in which serious psychopathology in one parent is accepted or supported by the other parent. In other families, the problem is one of *marital schism*—there is open warfare between husband and wife. Bitter arguments are so common that the marriage is in constant danger of breaking up. There may be a serious lack of understanding and cooperation between parents, resulting in

---

Table 11–4
Summary of psychopathic disorders

A. Neurosis
   1. Traumatic neurosis
   2. Anxiety reactions, phobias, hypochondriasis
   3. Conversion reactions
   4. Dissociative reactions
     a. Amnesia
     b. Fugue state
     c. Multiple personality
   5. Obsessive-compulsive
   6. Neurotic depression

B. Psychosomatic illness (psychophysiological reaction)

C. Personality disorder
   1. Passive-aggressive personality
   2. Antisocial personality (sociopath)
   3. Dyssocial personality
   4. Alcoholism
   5. Drug addiction
   6. Sexual deviation

D. Psychosis
   1. Manic-depressive reaction
   2. Schizophrenia
     a. Simple
     b. Paranoid
     c. Catatonic
     d. Hebephrenic
     e. Chronic undifferentiated

distrust and rivalry. The father is frequently seen as insecure and weak, and the mother as domineering and hostile. Bateson et al. (1956) describe a conflict situation known as the *double bind,* in which a parent presents to the child ideas, feelings, and demands that are contradictory. At one level of communication the parent may express love and at another rejection. At the third level of communication, the parent prevents the child from commenting on the paradox. The parent may say "I love you" but provide no physical contact, indicating rejection. Uncertain as to whether or not he should respond to the parent's expressions of affection, the child withdraws and establishes no relationships.

Still, there is a great deal of overlap between schizophrenics and normal people in family background. Also, people from completely different types of families become schizophrenics. Of two people from relatively similar backgrounds, one can be schizophrenic while the other is quite normal. Thus, as in the case of biological factors, the role of family and other social influences in schizophrenia is far from clear.

What Does It Mean?

Most of the meaning of our scientific knowledge of psychopathology is best illustrated by our discussion of psychotherapy in Chapter 12. Indeed, the techniques of psychotherapy can be seen as an outgrowth of the application of personality theory (Chapter 9) to the problems of pathological behavior described in this chapter. Therefore, this section will be somewhat briefer than comparable sections of earlier chapters. We will concentrate on only a few general issues.

Has the World Gone Mad?

We have already made it clear that psychopathology is to some extent a culturally defined activity. Behavior that is accepted in one society may be considered seriously deviant in another. Szasz (1963) was one of the earliest psychologists to ask the important question, "Who defines the norms and hence the deviation?" On the one hand, the person himself may decide that he deviates from the norm. Alternatively, someone other than the sufferer may decide that he is deviant in some important respect. When a psychiatrist is hired by the court to decide whether a person is sane or insane (and whether he should be held responsible for his behavior), the psychiatrist is not given the alternative to testify that the accused is normal, but the legislators are "insane" for passing the law that made that

*"I'm sure he's the one, Sarge.
He's a sociopathic personality with
clearly indicated schizoid and
depressive tendencies."*

Playboy, September 1967. Reproduced by special permission of PLAYBOY Magazine; copyright © 1967 by Playboy.

Diagnosing an individual patient by assigning a label to him may cause him considerable harm, including legal repercussions and the danger that the diagnosis will become self-fulfilling. The mental health professional should keep labels away from those who might misuse them, as well as avoid misusing them himself.

behavior illegal (Szasz, 1963, pages 14–15)! Obviously, society's laws and rules are not infallible. With respect to psychopathology, one need only consider the recent decision by the American Psychiatric Association to remove homosexuality from the list of categories of abnormal behavior.

R. D. Laing (1967, 1969) has gone even further than Szasz in attacking labels and diagnostic categories. Schizophrenia is not a "mental illness" but an adaptive response to an insane world, according to Laing. Diagnostic labels are "straightjackets" that keep us from communicating with the disturbed person. Society and particularly the family in the society are destructive forces that attack the self. Laing's approach is strongly anticognitive, and he sees feelings and intuition as the hope of mankind. Yet when we look at the behavior of a suffering neurotic or psychotic, it is difficult to defend the idea that such behavior is always a creative way of adapting to a disordered world, as implied by Laing.

Study Reveals Psychiatrists Can't Tell Sane From Insane

Stanford, Calif. (AP)—Who's sane? Who's insane?

The psychiatrists and staffs of mental hospitals cannot be trusted to tell the difference, declares Prof. David L. Rosenhan, a Stanford University psychologist.

Rosenhan says he and seven other sane investigators arranged as a test to be admitted as schizophrenic patients in 12 different mental hospitals, yet none of the eight was found to be sane by hospital professionals.

But Rosenhan says it was "quite common" for actual psychiatric patients to correctly identify the "pseudopatient" imposters.

Important Questions

"The fact that patients often recognized normality when staff did not raised important questions," Rosenhan observes. . . .

Rosenhan said he and his seven colleagues eventually were released as "schizophrenics in remission," despite their best efforts to convince the hospital staff of their sanity.

"We now know that we cannot distinguish insanity from sanity," Rosenhan declared.

"We continue to label patients 'schizophrenic', 'manic-depressive', and 'insane' as if in those words we had captured the essence of understanding," he wrote.

"The facts of the matter are that we have known for a long time that our diagnoses often are not useful or reliable, but we have nevertheless continued to use them."

Rosenhan, who also teaches law at Stanford, said he and the other pseudopatients were shocked and horrified by their experiences.

But, he said, they did not blame the hospital staffs.

"By and large, they were well-intentioned people, and in no way do we want to malign them," he said.

"The hospital itself imposes a special environment in which the meanings of behavior can easily be misunderstood."

Rosenhan said the pseudopatient group included a psychiatrist, a pediatrician, a painter, a housewife, a Stanford psychology graduate student and three other psychologists.

Feigned Symptoms

He said they gained admission to hospitals in California, Oregon, Pennsylvania, New York and Delaware by feigning symptoms of schizophrenia.

"The uniform failure to recognize sanity cannot be attributed to the quality of treatment facilities. While there was considerable variability between them, several are considered excellent," Rosenhan reported.

"Nor can it be alleged that there simply was not enough time to observe the pseudopatients. Length of hospitalization ranged from seven to 52 days, with an average of 19 days."

"All pseudopatients took extensive notes publicly. Under ordinary circumstances such behavior would have raised questions in the minds of observers, as in fact it did among patients.

"Nursing records for three pseudopatients indicate that the writing was seen as an aspect of their pathological behavior."

This article demonstrates clearly the danger of diagnosis. Once a person is labeled abnormal, any subsequent behavior is likely to be seen as additional evidence of emotional disturbance.

However extreme their positions in some respects, both Szasz and Laing remind us that societies as well as people can be disordered. Of course, all societies label some behaviors unacceptable. The range of behaviors is simply too great to permit all behaviors to exist in a society without some form of control. But societies that permit a greater range of nonharmful (a value judgment!) behaviors —behaviors that do not endanger the safety or well-being of others, for instance—can be viewed as healthier or more adaptive. As well as being willing to confront their personal ethical and social conflicts, people must be open to recognizing when the social structure needs changing.

The Danger of Diagnosis

As we said in Chapter 10, psychologists' expectations about the results of an experiment can influence (through their own behavior) the results that are obtained. The diagnosis of an individual— assigning a label to him—can have the same effect.

Although it is important to recognize that behavioral problems do exist and to know which symptoms indicate significant disorder, there is a danger that diagnostic labels will become self-fulfilling prophecies of the person's behavior. For example, there is some evidence that teachers who assume that minority students will do poorly in school lower their standards and demands for excellence, leading the students to perform at a lower level than they might have otherwise. A person who is labeled a mental retardate can be treated in such a way that he is effectively no longer allowed to learn. The juvenile labeled as delinquent starts to behave in such a way that he realizes society's expectations. With psychopathology, the same problem exists. There is a strong moral responsibility for the diagnostician to keep labels away from people who might misuse them. Thus, a diagnosis is seldom given to the person or family of the person who is diagnosed for fear that the diagnosis will be self-fulfilling.

The Danger of Diagnosing Your Own Problems

A little learning is a dangerous thing. It is not unusual for someone reading about abnormal behavior for the first time to raise questions about himself and his own level of adaptive or maladaptive functioning. The "medical students' syndrome" (where the medical student imagines he or she has every disease studied about) often occurs in students reading about abnormal psychology. One could suffer needlessly thinking that every symptom he showed similar to those described here was an indication of a behavior problem. As we noted, everyone shows one or more of these symptoms from time to time. It is best to keep in mind the definition of psychopathology given at the beginning of this chapter; psychopathology is a failure, for either organic or psychological reasons, to behave in a socially appropriate and acceptable way, such that the person or society suffers adverse consequences. Suppose you were unhappy and worried about poor school work. No one would think it unreasonable for you to feel anxious about the consequences of flunking out of school, and psychotherapy would not be indicated. However, if your poor work could be traced to a panic state you experienced before each exam, your anxiety would appear to be inappropriate and you might benefit from a therapy designed to replace fear responses with more functional behavior.

To be overly sensitive to minor anxiety or depression could lead you to worry more about the normality of feelings than about the stress that caused those feelings in the first place. Yet to ignore strong feelings of distress because of fear of being abnormal could lead you to settle for a much less rewarding life than you could obtain. All too often people are more concerned with knowing whether they can be labeled with a diagnosis of neurotic, psychosomatic, or psychotic rather than with asking and answering much more basic questions: *Am I functioning appropriately under the circumstances? Am I behaving responsibly? Am I happy or am I working toward goals that will allow me to be happy?*

Once you have determined that life is not as happy as it might be or that your behavior is not as responsible as you would like, you are faced with the question of what to do about this decision.

How Do You Solve Your Problems?

Psychotherapy is not the only way of resolving emotional problems. Most frequently, people are able to handle their problems on their own. It was mentioned earlier that two primary approaches can be used to handle a stressful situation. First, you can actively and directly confront the source of stress. This may involve obtaining new information through reading or talking to others or by trying out new behaviors. In addition, you can obtain new skills by practice, trying successively closer approximations to the behavior you would like to perform, a procedure similar to the method of shaping discussed in Chapter 4. When you lack motivation to behave the way you think you should, the problem becomes more difficult. Although artificial motivation can be produced by providing yourself with rewards and punishments (for example, by going to a movie after studying hard all day), behavior is difficult to change unless the new behavior leads to its own intrinsic rewards (for example, good grades). A person may also lack motivation because he has not clearly defined his goals. Each person has to make some decisions about the goals that will give meaning to his life.

Friendships also provide means for changing behavior. Friends will, as we saw in Chapter 7, allow you to try out new behaviors that parents are unlikely to permit. It is difficult to try out new behaviors when the people around refuse to recognize the change, actively resist the new personality, or ridicule it. Many students who go away to college find themselves changing in ways that result in their liking themselves better.

When these approaches do not result in a satisfactory resolution of the problem, professional aid may be indicated. Counseling may be available from a college counseling center, university adviser, or local mental health center, from people with a variety of training backgrounds. The next chapter will discuss the major techniques of psychotherapy and give some indication of what it is like to experience it.

What Is Good Personality Adjustment?

All too often psychologists focus on what is wrong or deviant and do not spend time describing good personality adjustment. The absence of symptoms cannot be used to describe optimal growth and development. A person can be totally devoid of any behavioral problems or emotional disturbance and still be an empty shell without purpose. To experience the full richness of life, the excitement of sharing experiences, of communicating, of caring

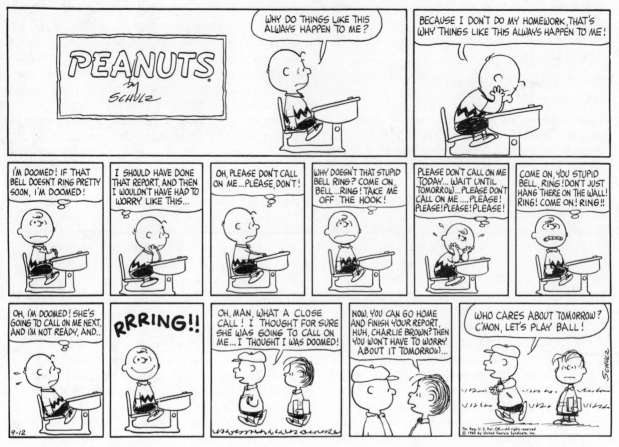

Linus suggests an appropriate strategy for coping with the *cause* of the stress. Charlie Brown decides to reduce the anxiety by avoiding the situation completely.

and being cared about requires much more than the avoidance of defense mechanisms or disordered behavior.

To some extent any definition of normality or of growth and maturation is arbitrary and is guided by the particular model of personality adhered to by the definer. Below are some principles of growth based primarily on the existential model, the area of psychological theory that has been most concerned with positive development.

1. The ability to experience feelings in the here-and-now. Good personality adjustment implies that a person does not cut off or postpone his feelings, but fully experiences them at the time they are evoked. Such a person is capable of experiencing the full range of human emotions and responds readily with either positive or negative emotions at the time the emotion-evoking stimuli are present. Such emotional responses are not

indulgences but controlled and appropriate responses to the situation.

2. The ability to experience the self in a positive way and to accept negative experiences as part of the self. If a person feels bad about himself, he can either revise his goals or change his behavior. Self-regarding attitudes are determined by careful self-evaluation and are relatively unaffected by the opinions of others.

3. The ability to develop a meaning for life. According to existential theory, to have a meaningless life is to live in a vacuum. Each person must develop his own individual meaning that gives zest to life. The process of developing meaning may take several years, but even the search can give meaning to life.

4. The ability to cope with problems or crises in an adaptive way. Some believe that the ideal life would be one without stress. But although we might be successful in eliminating some of the stresses in life, it is probably well to realize that life is inherently stressful. To develop as a person, to learn to communicate, to experience feelings fully, to learn to trust (and *when* not to trust)—all these require

trial and error. Growth does not occur without risk and risk does not occur without pain. To learn to face anxiety, to deal with the cause rather than to try to reduce the anxiety itself, is a skill that comes with practice. A person must also learn how to generate a variety of possible solutions to a problem and how to evaluate which solution is likely to be the most effective.

Summary

1. Psychopathology is defined as the inability to behave in a socially appropriate way, with maladaptive consequences. This inability might reflect either organic or functional deficiencies.

2. The medical model views psychopathological behaviors as symptoms of an underlying process that operates like a disease.

3. The dynamic model assumes psychopathology results from a conflict between the conscious and unconscious aspects of the personality.

4. The behavioral model proposes that psychopathology is the result of positive and negative reinforcements in a person's environment.

5. The ethical model assumes that psychopathology results when an individual makes irresponsible choices in life.

6. The existential model attributes psychopathology to a lack of purpose or meaning in life.

7. The experience of anxiety is unpleasant, and people try to cope with the stress of being anxious. The two primary defenses against anxiety are repression and denial.

8. Neurosis develops out of attempts to avoid anxiety. The neurotic paradox refers to the fact that while people find anxiety unpleasant, their defenses prevent them from learning new ways of dealing effectively with the cause of the anxiety.

9. Neurosis is divided into five classifications, according to how a person defends against anxiety: failure to defend against overwhelming stress, repression or displacement, behavioral inactivation, behavioral activation, and neurotic depression.

10. Psychosomatic illness (psychophysiologic reaction) refers to a physical illness that has psychological causes. Psychosomatic illnesses are explained by the theoretical constructs of response stereotypes, stimulus-response specificity, and associational specificity.

11. Personality disorders, such as alcoholism, drug addiction, and sexually deviant behavior, are defined as failures to behave in socially appropriate ways due to lack of motivation or lack of skill in coping with the normal stresses of everyday life.

12. Psychosis refers to behavior characterized by loss of contact with reality, frequently accompanied by hallucinations and delusions.

13. A depression becomes diagnosed as psychotic when the person has lost contact with reality. Mania, with feelings of great optimism and the speeding up of thought processes, is a form of reaction formation against depression. In manic-depressive psychosis, states of mania and depression occur alternately in a fairly regular cycle.

14. In schizophrenia there are marked distortions of reality and disturbances in thought processes and emotions. The four main subtypes of schizophrenia are: simple, hebephrenic, paranoid, and catatonic.

15. On the basis of twin studies, researchers have pretty well agreed that there is a genetic component in schizophrenia, although environment is also an important factor.

16. Psychopathology is defined in terms of the society, but the society itself can sometimes be considered disordered.

17. Diagnosis can be dangerous if the diagnostic label becomes a self-fulfilling prophecy.

18. Psychotherapy is only one strategy for resolving emotional problems. People can also solve problems on their own or with the help of friends.

19. Good personality adjustment implies experiencing feelings fully in the here-and-now, accepting oneself, evolving a meaning for life, and learning to cope adaptively with stress.

Recommended Additional Readings

Alvarez, A. *The savage god: A study of suicide.* New York: Bantam, 1973.

Elliott, D. W. *Listen to the silence.* New York: Signet, 1969.

Goldstein, J. J., & Palmer, J. O. *The experience of anxiety: A casebook.* New York: Oxford University Press, 1963.

Green, Hannah. *I never promised you a rose garden.* New York: Signet, 1964.

Kaplan, B. (Ed.) *The inner world of mental illness.* New York: Harper & Row, 1964.

Kesey, K. *One flew over the cuckoo's nest.* New York: Signet, 1962.

Plath, S. *The bell jar.* New York: Harper & Row, 1971.

Schreiber, F. R. *Sybil.* Chicago: Regnery, 1973.

Sechehaye, M. *Autobiography of a schizophrenic girl.* New York: Signet, 1951.

12
PSYCHOTHERAPY

I know you believe you understood what you think I said but I am not sure you realize that what you heard is not what I meant. **Anonymous**

The odds are surprisingly high that someday each of us will feel the need to seek professional help in solving a mental or emotional problem of our own or of someone close to us. Most families experience some maladjustment at some time whether it be a psychosomatic illness such as asthma or ulcers, a neurotic depression following divorce or loss of job, a strong dependence on alcohol or drugs, or a more serious disorder such as schizophrenia. There are those who feel, in fact, that the vast majority of American adults are neurotic to some degree. Divorce rates and suicide rates are skyrocketing in some areas, as are crime and delinquency. There is little doubt that psychological distress and disorder are common in our society and that psychopathology constitutes a major social problem.

Indeed, serious disturbances in psychological functioning are so common that it is absurd to attach any particular stigma to them. For a long time, the mentally ill were treated as criminals, witches, or worse, and even today there is a significant tendency for people to "look down on" those who have sought professional help for their psychological problems. They are often regarded as weird, "funny," or weak in some way, although some problem behaviors, such as alcoholism, seem to be more acceptable in our society than other problems, such as sexual exhibitionism.

Of the many different ways of responding to psychopathological behavior, only some are therapeutic. Others, such as imprisonment, cruelty, or rejection obviously are not. When mental illness was viewed as possession by the devil, drilling holes in the person's head to allow the evil spirits to escape was perhaps an appropriate "therapy." And when mental illness was considered a symptom of character weakness or moral degeneracy, chains and whipping were perhaps appropriate attempts to correct it. But given our conception of psychopathology as the failure, for organic or psychological reasons, to behave in a socially appropriate way, what is psychotherapy today?

A Definition for Psychotherapy

Psychotherapy can be defined as *a corrective experience leading a person to behave in a socially appropriate, adequate, and adaptive way.* The therapy will focus on the lack of knowledge, the lack

There are many different "schools of thought" about psychotherapy, only a few of which are represented in this parade and this chapter.

of skill, or the lack of motivation to behave appropriately, or on the abnormal behavior itself. In most cases, a combination of these factors would be involved in the pathology, and the therapy would be adjusted accordingly. When we speak of therapy we usually imply that it is delivered by a professional—a psychologist, psychiatrist, psychiatric social worker, or psychiatric nurse (see Table 12–1). This does not mean, however, that all corrective experiences are professionally arranged. Close personal friends probably do a great deal of psychotherapy unwittingly. Here, however, we will be concerned mainly with formal psychotherapy administered by professionals. Finally, it is important to note that all those concerned with correcting maladaptive behavior are equally concerned with *preventing* it. Although in the past prevention has not been a major focus of therapists' efforts, it may be increasingly so in the future.

One of the first questions in the therapist's mind when he is confronted with a person seeking psychotherapy is: Why is the person here? The most common motivation for seeking therapy is that the person is uncomfortable with the way he is handling life. He may be frequently anxious when interacting with others or find that he is having trouble coping successfully with his job or marriage. Other reasons may enter into the decision to seek therapy, however. The person may be blackmailed into therapy, such as when a man threatens to leave his wife unless she seeks help. Or a physician may tell the person that his ulcer or arthritis is of psychosomatic origin and that psychotherapy is recommended. Or the person may be experiencing anxiety, anger, or depression without knowing why, so that self-knowledge and control is the goal.

In general, the relationship between a person's ideal self-concept and his behavior is important in therapy. If the person's ideal self-concept and his behavior are consistent with each other, the symptoms (or inappropriate behaviors) are said to

Table 12–1
Mental health professionals

Name	Degree	Specialization	Education
Clinical psychologist	Master of Arts, Doctor of Philosophy	Research, therapy, diagnostic testing	Graduate education in a department of psychology
Psychiatrist	Doctor of Medicine	Therapy, psychosomatics, medication	Residency training in psychiatry
Psychoanalyst	Usually, Doctor of Medicine	Psychoanalysis	Usually psychiatrist with additional training in psychoanalysis
Psychiatric social worker	Master of Social Work	Individual and family therapy and counseling, community orientation	Graduate education in school of social work
School psychologist	Master of Arts, Doctor of Philosophy, or Doctor of Education	Counseling, or educational testing	Graduate work in psychology or education
Counselor	Same as school psychologist	Counseling, therapy, vocational counseling, rehabilitation	Graduate work in psychology or education
Psychiatric nurse	Registered Nurse	Counseling, therapy, care of hospitalized mental patients	Training in nursing and psychiatry
Paraprofessional	None necessary	Ability to communicate with people in own community	Short orientation in service facility

be *syntonic.* If the ideal self-concept and behavior are inconsistent, the symptoms are said to be *dystonic.* If the person is comfortable with his behavior (a syntonic relationship), he has little reason to change. He is likely to be brought to therapy by someone else (parents, spouse, courts) and is likely to be difficult to treat. In such cases the therapist has an ethical responsibility to make clear to the client his own goals in therapy and how they might differ from the client's.

Guidelines for the Therapist's Behavior

There are two considerations that guide the therapist's behavior: his model of psychopathology and professional ethics. While initially what the client says in therapy is based on the way he sees his problems, the therapist selectively responds to some comments, remembers others for future reference, and dismisses the rest. The therapist will ask questions and make comments that arise from his understanding of what causes psychopathology. Thus the five models of therapy discussed in Chapter 11 may lead to different types of interactions with the client.

In the medical model the assumption is that psychopathology is a process similar to physical illness. The therapist is likely to be a physician; he will have a tendency to use hospitals as a place for treatment and regard the use of medication as appropriate. (Incidentally, the term *patient* is usually used by therapists who follow a medical model or practice in a medical setting, whereas the term *client* is more frequently used by psychologists, psychiatric social workers, and others who hold nonmedical degrees and prefer other models of therapy.) If the therapist follows a dynamic model, he will view the goal of therapy as developing the client's self-knowledge of repressed memories that serve as the cause for anxiety symptoms. The behaviorist will focus on maladaptive behavior and show little concern for past experiences except to determine the relationships between stimuli. His goal is to try to change skills or reasons for behaving. Ethical models may lead the therapist to try to get the client to accept responsibility for his own behavior. The existential therapist may help the client develop a philosophy of life that aids him in making choices about the direction in which his life will go.

Actually, after a therapist has been in practice for a while, he probably develops his own ''model'' of psychopathology based on experience. He is then apt to make a more eclectic approach, borrowing

Nonverbal Communication in Therapy

While the therapist bases his understanding of his client on what the client says in therapy, he also gains information from the client's nonverbal behavior. Martha first came into therapy to talk about her difficulty in studying for exams. When she walked into the therapist's office for the first time, she picked up the chair that was beside his desk and moved it to the corner of the room. Although the therapist noted the unusual behavior, he did not comment on it for fear of increasing her anxiety about coming to therapy. In the second session, she again moved the chair away from the desk but seemed less concerned with placing it in the corner. The third session began with Martha sitting in the chair in its normal position without bothering to move it. Not until several sessions later in therapy did Martha feel comfortable about bringing up her interpersonal problems and concern about the therapy. She expressed in a nonverbal way her wish for psychological distance from the therapist and her fear of closeness with the therapist. Her concern about studying for exams became discussed less and less as she focused on what was for her a much more basic problem.

Joan's behavior also revealed how she felt about therapy. After about six sessions the therapist noticed that Joan seemed to fluctuate widely in her motivation to work during the therapy hour. Some days she was intensely interested in understanding her behavior; other days she avoided talking about anything significant and only complained about her irritating neighbors. The therapist soon learned that Joan gave nonverbal cues about how she felt that day even before she began talking. On days she wanted to work, she would dress informally in a blouse and shorts, and on days she wanted to avoid talking about her problems, she would dress in a formal suit. Once the therapist was aware of her communications he was able to comment on them and work through the feelings she had about therapy.

Note that clients who chronically forget appointments or always arrive late may be expressing, in their behavior, their feelings about therapy. Therapists also make note of hand movements, eye contact, facial expression, cigarette smoking, and many other nonverbal cues that might indicate topics of conversation that arouse anxiety, anger, or other feelings that the client is not expressing verbally.

theories and techniques from several different models. In fact, for experienced therapists, there may be a great deal of similarity in what they talk about in therapy even when the therapists have been trained in different models. Furthermore, even when comparing learning theory (behavioral) and dynamic models, we find similarities. There is some evidence, for example, that there is a great deal more talking that occurs in learning models than might be expected and that the therapist's warmth can be important even when learning theory is the basis for treatment.

The second consideration guiding the therapist's behavior is his sense of professional ethics. A therapist's feelings about drugs, premarital sex, political affiliation, and religion may all shade his opinion of the problem and influence his behavior in therapy. Should he try to cure a person of Catholicism or atheism? Should he express his opinion of his client's use of drugs? Because such questions are sometimes difficult to answer on an individual level, ethical standards have been developed by the profession as a whole. The following statements about appropriate ethical behavior for psychotherapists are taken from nineteen guidelines set forth for psychologists in practice by the American Psychological Association (1967).

1. Client welfare. The psychologist protects the welfare of any person receiving psychotherapy from him, and when conflicts of interest arise he resolves the conflict in the direction of the welfare of the client.

2. Competence. A psychologist recognizes the limits of his competence and does not offer service that is outside his ability. If there is a relevant medical problem associated with problems that he is treating, he will make referral to appropriate specialists. The psychologist discourages unqualified persons from practicing psychology and attempts to correct unethical behavior on the part of other psychologists.

3. Confidentiality. The psychologist safeguards information received by him from clients in his practice. He may not communicate confidential information unless there is a "clear and imminent danger to an individual or to society." The psychologist may break confidentiality if he feels that he must protect the person from committing suicide and he must tell others (for example, by hospitalizing him). A psychologist can break confidentiality if he thinks the person might kill someone if not prevented. In some states the psychologist is protected by law in a confidential relationship as are doctors and lawyers, and he cannot be directed to reveal information even under court order.

4. Client relationships. The psychologist informs his client of important aspects of the therapeutic

Patient Wins $170,880 in "Torture" Suit

San Francisco—(AP)—A Superior Court jury has awarded $170,000 to a former university coed from San Jose for injuries suffered in a 13-hour therapy session with a psychologist.

The award went to Anita Beekman, 22, who was a student of psychologist John Indorf when she attended California State University at San Jose.

Miss Beekman, who was advised by physicians not to testify in her suit, said in the formal complaint, "I was tortured, including choking, beating, holding and tying me down and sticking fingers in my mouth."

Indorf called his technique "rage reduction" and said it caused the patient to "reduce pathological resistance."

Miss Beekman said she came out of Indorf's $400 therapy course with near-fatal kidney damage, severe bruises about the hips, chest and legs and a lacerated mouth.

During the 17-day trial, a tape of the 13-hour session was played and the jury heard screams and pleading. During the trial, three medical doctors testified that Indorf's technique "exceeded the bounds of customary medical practice."

Indorf told investigators for the district attorney's office, "I think I did her a lot of good."

Ethical standards are an important part of professional psychotherapy, although this is not to say that the standards of the American Psychological Association are adhered to or interpreted in the same way by all licensed therapists.

relationship that might affect the client's decision to enter the relationship. He does not normally enter into a professional relationship with members of his own family or friends or associates, since the dual role he plays might jeopardize the welfare of the client.

5. Announcement of services. A psychologist does not directly solicit clients, advertise services, refer to testimonials, or promise results.

Finally, the psychologist must respond to the social and moral expectations of the community in which he works. Violating these norms may place him and his client in conflict with the community and may undermine the confidence of the community in him and the profession.

What are the ethical considerations in the following situations? A client says he has some doubts about his religious beliefs; a client says he has some doubts about his strong liberal beliefs; nude group psychotherapy; a client wants to be a more effective heroin pusher or more effective bigot;

a student is very shy and the therapist feels that she needs more socializing experiences and so he decides to ask her for a date; as a student you hear of a therapist who is on drugs.

The types of psychotherapy to be discussed in this chapter can be divided into two broad categories: (1) insight-oriented therapies, which have as their focus change in motivation and knowledge, and (2) noninsight-oriented therapies (often referred to as behavior therapies), which have as their focus change in motivation, skills, and performance. We will also discuss several other general approaches that might be based on any of several models but are distinctive enough to justify discussion alone, including the biological therapies, group approaches, and community mental health.

Insight-Oriented Therapy

Insight-oriented therapy is based on the assumption, similar to that of the dynamic model of psychopathology, that emotional problems stem from the conflict between conscious and unconscious processes. To resolve this conflict the person must be made aware of his unconscious processes, and thus the goal of therapy is insight or self-knowledge. The insight-oriented therapies can be divided into two types: (1) those focusing on the repressed memories of the past, such as psychoanalysis, and (2) those focusing on denied aspects of present feelings, such as client-centered therapy, Gestalt therapy, and transactional analysis.

Insight into Past Experiences

Psychoanalysis is the therapeutic technique Freud developed on the basis of his psychoanalytic theory. Freud, as we know, assumed that emotional problems are in part the result of repression of drives, feelings, and memories and that an awareness of these unconscious mental processes will resolve most emotional problems. However, not only must the client achieve insight into the cause of his symptoms, but he must also experience the emotion associated with the original memory.

> . . . we found, to our great surprise at first, that each individual . . . symptom immediately and permanently disappeared when we had succeeded in bringing clearly to light the memory of the event by which it was provoked and in arousing its accompanying affect (emotions), and when the patient had described that event in the greatest possible detail and had put the affect into words. Recollection without affect almost invariably produces no result. **(Breuer and Freud, 1957)**

**Figure 12–1
Psychoanalysis**

In classical psychoanalysis the patient lies on a couch, and the therapist sits out of the client's direct line of sight.

Because the open expression of sexual and aggressive feelings is generally thought unacceptable for children and adults in our society, we are taught to inhibit or repress these feelings. Thus sexual and aggressive feelings are a main focus of the psychoanalyst's attention. Sexual mores have been changing in the last 10 years and are still changing dramatically in the direction of greater freedom. If this is a mentally healthy change, psychoanalysis should in the future focus less on sexual feelings and more on aggressive feelings.

The aim of psychoanalysis is to overcome the client's unconscious resistance to remembering anxiety-provoking thoughts and impulses. Freud developed a variety of techniques to help the client overcome his resistance. One feature of psychoanalysis designed to facilitate these techniques is the *couch*, the subject of numerous jokes. In psychoanalysis the patient typically lies down on the couch on his back, facing the ceiling, and the analyst sits behind the client out of direct sight (see Figure 12–1). Some reasons for the use of the couch may have nothing to do with technique. First, Freud discovered the importance of recollection of repressed memories through hypnosis, and the couch is in part a carryover from the use of hypnosis as a technique. Second, it is rumored that Freud preferred sitting behind the patient because he felt uncomfortable having people look at him all day. Thus, the couch may be attributable to one of Freud's own hang-ups! Most

Copyright, 1971, G. B. Trudeau. Distributed by Universal Press Syndicate.

According to Freudian theory, anxiety-arousing thoughts, such as a hatred for one's father (the Oedipus complex), are often handled by repressing them into the unconscious. Freud believed that these repressed feelings may still seek expression in everyday behavior and may break through into consciousness in such unguarded moments as slips of the tongue.

important, however, is the fact that the couch reduces external stimulation and encourages the client to turn inward to focus on his own associations. Furthermore, it frees the analyst from the responsibility of controlling his own reactions. He can show surprise or dismay without the client seeing his facial expression.

It should be noted that some analysts who prefer face-to-face contact with the client want the client to be aware of their reactions on the assumption that one of the client's problems might be a lack of sensitivity to the reactions of others around him. However, the psychoanalyst is more interested in an inward focus of attention to facilitate the remembering of repressed memories. The following techniques are used to help the patient understand the contents of his own unconscious mind.

Free association.   The client is instructed to say anything and everything that comes into his mind. He is told to express his thoughts as freely as possible and hold nothing back no matter how trivial or shocking. This basic rule of psychoanalysis sounds relatively easy, but, in fact, most people find it extremely difficult to give up their concern over the impression they are making on someone else, including the analyst. Resistance to the basic rule of free association at the unconscious level will therefore often lead to blocking—the person simply cannot think of any association. Such resistance helps the analyst understand what areas of the

person's memories are repressed and enables him to help the client overcome such resistance to remembering.

Symptomatic acts.   The behavior of the patient during analysis may lead the analyst to understand areas of repression. Slips of the tongues, changes in behavior toward the therapy hour, forgetting therapy appointments, and unusual behavior during therapy may all be symptomatic of deeper and more significant unconscious processes.

Dream analysis.   In his book *The Interpretation of Dreams,* Freud maintained that it was useful to consider dreams as representing, in a symbolic way, the unconscious conflicts or desires of the dreamer (see Chapter 8). The purpose of the symbolic nature of the dream message is to avoid anxiety that would wake the person up. The symbolic meaning of elements of a dream cannot easily be interpreted without knowing the associational links of the individual who had the dream. There have been ''dream books'' published that propose to interpret the symbols in dreams. The authors tend to interpret every pointed object in a dream as a symbol of a phallus and every open space as a symbol of a vagina because Freud believed that sexual conflicts determined most symbols. Although Freud proposed that such general symbolism may be involved, he felt that each person tends to have idiosyncratic associations that lead to unique symbols as well. It is the therapist's task to discover the meanings of such symbols.

After the patient has related his dream in analysis, the analyst asks him to free associate to various elements of the dream. He may also ask for information about the previous day in an effort to understand the *manifest content* (the superficial story of the dream), and the *latent content* (the symbolic meaning of that story). For example, a

The Clinical Use of Dreams

An intellectual businessman of thirty-seven, married, a father, busy in such community work as PTA, and an avid reader of serious literature, came for sporadic consultations every few months over a period of two years. He was an exaggeratedly kind and considerate man, a "do-gooder." His chief difficulties were in his marriage, which was characterized by a coolness and strain that did not seem at all to reflect the qualities with which he sought to invest this and all other relationships. Among his friends were many who had been or were being psychoanalyzed. He felt, however, that he had derived so much insight from his occasional visits (more, in his view, than a number of his friends had achieved over extended periods of a continuous analytic process), that he had never seriously contemplated intensive therapy for himself. Finally, however, because of the increasing emotional distance between himself and his wife, he came to seek treatment on a regular basis.

He brought to the first session a dream that he had the preceding night. "I was at an ice-skating rink. All the skaters were going around in a circle. I was skating in a circle, too, but I was going in the opposite direction. I was having a good time."

The interpretive hypothesis was suggested to him that he had finally entered into analysis like many of his friends, but that he was still trying to maintain his special status, as represented by his skating in a different direction from the rest of the crowd. The session was devoted to exploring his secret sense of uniqueness. The discovery of this trait was extremely surprising to him, because he had always felt himself to be notably modest.

The importance of discerning his real feelings was emphasized. He was amazed at the course the session had taken.

He came to the next hour with the following dream: "I was at a beach and in the water, bathing. The waves were small, and I waded in deeper and was enjoying myself. Then the waves began to get bigger and bigger and I kept bathing, but I was worried. I wasn't sure I'd be able to keep from being overwhelmed."

He was puzzled because he loved swimming and had no fear of the water. He was asked how he felt about coming to the second session. He said he was a little afraid of what might come up. The

interpretive hypothesis was suggested that the prospect of "wading in deeper" to look at his true feelings was very frightening to him. He was afraid of the emotions he might find welling up in himself, afraid that he might be overwhelmed by his feelings. The hour was occupied with exploring his attitude toward emotions. He despised those who were carried away by emotions, particulary such feelings as anger and self-importance. When there was a conflict, he always tried to be understanding and reasonable. He tried always to do more than his share, and he never looked for credit. In the course of examining these attitudes, it began to appear that he secretly felt that his humility itself, as well as his maintaining calm when others became angry, placed him in a category above other men. His supposed humility, in fact, concealed a marked grandiosity. (This theme had been suggested by the work with the Skating Rink dream.)

He had complained also that in his marriage he wished merely to have credit where credit was due, that he was very helpful around the house and felt he was deserving of more affection from his wife. It was then suggested that his disdain for people might include some disdain also for his wife, and that perhaps this tended to stifle his wife's affection.

He left feeling somewhat shaken, but expressed gratitude that he was being helped to see himself more realistically.

He came to the third hour with another dream: "I was in a large tank like a swimming pool. There was also a shark in the water. I was swimming frantically to get away from him."

He could offer no explanation of the dream, and had no awareness of waking fear. His association with the swimming pool was that it was about "the shape of this office." The interpretive hypothesis was suggested that he frantically wished to elude the analyst, that he was extremely fearful that the analyst, who could navigate more skillfully in the therapeutic medium, would destroy him by destroying the illusions about himself. His illusion that he was a humble man had been shaken after the first dream. After the second dream he began to see more deeply into his disdainfulness and to embrace the concept that he had significant feelings of which he was unaware. His self-concept of humility, of self-effacing solicitude, of an unqualified, fearless desire to examine himself, were seriously challenged.   (Bonime, 1962, pages 125–126)

woman reported dreaming that a man unknown to her stole her car and was killed in an accident—the manifest content. The latent content of her dream was not obvious and could be clarified only with free association and the therapist's knowledge of

some of the personality dynamics of the client. However, the latent content became clear when the therapist discovered that the unknown man could be considered a symbol for her husband. The woman did not know or understand her husband very well ("unknown to her"), he frequently took advantage of her ("stole her car"), and she was very angry at him for this manipulative behavior ("he was killed"). Her anger toward him was unacceptable to her, and she feared expressing it because she felt he would leave her. The anxiety-provoking latent content of the dream was expressed symbolically.

Interpretation.   The basic work of the analyst in therapy is interpretation, explaining to the patient the unconscious meaning of what he says. The purpose of interpretation is to help the patient overcome his resistance to remembering repressed memories. Not infrequently the symbolic meaning of what is being said is not obvious, and the analyst must maintain a free-floating attention for many sessions, looking for cues to the content of the unconscious mind.

Once he develops a degree of certainty about his interpretation, the analyst must decide when to present it to the client. If the interpretation is given before the patient is capable of accepting it, anxiety will be generated and the repression will become more severe. It is desirable to lead the patient slowly so that he can gradually arrive at his own interpretations and work at overcoming his own resistance.

A single proper interpretation does not resolve the problems of the patient. The repression of unconscious material shows up in various aspects of the person's life and repeated interpretations are required to help the person give up the repression in all aspects of his life. The process of repeated interpretation and continued efforts on the part of the patient to resolve his conflict is called *working through.*

Transference.   According to the theory of psychoanalysis, the patient must *transfer* to the therapy relationship the conflicts from early life that interfere with his capacity to live normally. As a consequence, however, the analyst becomes a unique person in the eyes of the patient. Freud first noticed transference when he realized that patients ascribed to him characteristics of God and the devil or professed mad love for him even though their meetings were brief and infrequent. Transference is necessary and desirable, but it is only a temporary goal of psychoanalysis. As the significant unconscious processes affecting his behavior are made conscious to the patient, he gives up his neurotic defenses. As defenses are lowered, transference is resolved. The patient comes to respond more appropriately to the analyst, no longer exhibiting a need to defend against unconscious

"Yes, what is it? I'm very busy . . ."

© Punch (Rothco).

One criticism aimed at psychoanalysis is that relatively few people can be helped through this technique. Therapy typically lasts for 45 to 50 minutes 4 or 5 days a week and may go on for several years. Not only is the procedure enormously expensive, but the analyst is limited in the number of patients he can see at a particular time in his life.

conflicts. Problems that brought him to analysis are resolved and the problem of transference itself disappears.

Recent changes in psychoanalysis.   Although the basic techniques of Freudian psychoanalysis have remained the same, some variations have been tried. For example, analysts who follow the school of ego psychology place less emphasis on sex and aggression and more emphasis on the integrative functions of the ego. Most analysts still use the techniques of free association and dream interpretation, although with greater caution and less frequently than did Freud. Some analysts have given up the use of the couch and have a more spontaneous face-to-face interchange with the patient. Many psychoanalytically trained therapists place more emphasis on the "here-and-now" and less on what happened in the past. Chief among these therapists is Rollo May, one of the pioneers in a new technique called *existential therapy.*

Disadvantages of psychoanalysis.
Psychoanalysis is inefficient by today's standards. The analyst can treat only one patient at a time, and each patient is seen sometimes as frequently as 5 days a week for a 45- or 50-minute "hour" over a period of months or even years. Because analysis takes such a long time, the analyst can treat only a

very small number of people in his entire lifetime. Furthermore, since the analyst is so highly trained and treatment is so time-consuming, the total cost to the patient is very high. The cost alone excludes many potential users of psychoanalysis. For some people, such as children, analysis is ineffective or inadequate because they are not equipped for the highly verbal nature of the technique, and some potential patients are too disordered to benefit from it. Thus most persons in psychoanalysis are middle- or upper-class neurotics, although psychoanalysts have made some attempts to broaden their scope of treatment.

Primal therapy.　A new type of insight-oriented therapy, based on assumptions somewhat similar to psychoanalysis, is *primal therapy,* developed by Arthur Janov. Its theoretical strategy focuses on one particular conflict, the cutting off of feelings experienced as a young child in response to an accumulation of hurts and rejections from the parents. The major primal scene results from the accumulation of such small hurts. Eventually the hurts make sense to the child as indications that the parents do not like the child as he is. The recognition of this fact is so traumatic that the child cuts off the feelings and develops an unreal self that protects him from knowing that he is suffering. However, the pain associated with these hurts, the *primal pain,* still exists and continues to manifest itself in everyday life in subtle ways. The neurotic symptoms express the pain.

　In primal therapy, the therapist probes and attacks the defenses and confronts the client to help him reexperience the pain. This experience of the pain is called a *primal.* One indication that a person is experiencing a primal is the primal scream, the release of the primal pain that was stored up from childhood.

Insight into Present Experiences

Client-centered psychotherapy.　Rather than attempting to provide insight into repressed memories of the past, the client-centered therapist tries to help his client accept all aspects of himself in the present. Emotional problems are seen as stemming from a lack of self-knowledge, a denial of certain feelings, and an inability to experience all feelings fully. In order to describe how the therapist tries to help the client in therapy, it is necessary to outline the progress that client-centered psychotherapy has made over the years.

　Carl Rogers, whose ideas we encountered in Chapter 9, first wrote about the theory of

*"Oh, good Lord, no!
It was just a primal scream."*

New Yorker, July 2, 1973. Drawing by Whitney Darrow. Jr.; © 1973 The New Yorker Magazne, Inc.

In primal therapy, one indication that a person has experienced the pain of hurts accumulated during childhood is the expression of the primal scream, an agonizing scream of pain.

present-oriented therapy in 1942. His early views focused on recognizing and clarifying the client's expressed feelings. At that time the technique was called *nondirective psychotherapy* because a basic rule was that the therapist should respond only to the stated feelings of the client and never direct the conversation himself. The purpose of clarifying the client's feelings was to facilitate the appropriate expression of feelings, to help the person understand how he felt, and to help him use feelings as a basis for action. The term *nondirective* was dropped as it became clear that the therapist was indeed directing the course of treatment with his clarifying comments.

　Client-centered therapy is based on Rogers' theory of personality, in which, as we know, the main concept is self. The *self-concept* is defined as *a relatively consistent and enduring framework of self-regarding attitudes.* The disturbed person is one who finds some of his experiences or feelings to be inconsistent with his self-concept and so he denies that they apply to him. If the person denies part of his own experience, he cannot use these feelings and experiences as a guide for action. For example, one woman in therapy responded to every question about how she felt about a negative event in her life

Yes Begins with a No

Time—In my 30s I contracted tuberculosis, and the next ten years of my life were spent not being sure if there would be a tomorrow. All of a sudden the important projects, relationships, criteria, values by which I defined myself lost their worth. I learned quickly to tune in on my being, my existence in the now, because that was all there was—that, and my tubercular body. It was a valuable experience to face death, for in the experience I learned to face life.

Half a lifetime has passed since that experience befell Rollo May. He took from it the principle that illuminates his life and unites the psychotherapeutic school of which he is perhaps the most prominent and certainly the most articulate American member. The principle—that awareness of death is not opposed to, but essential to life—runs like a spine down May's latest work, *Love and Will.* Published last September [1969] by Norton, the book languished for months before popping up on the bestseller list in February. Today, 89,000 copies later, *Love and Will* is still there.

Disturbing Alternative

This feat is all the more remarkable because May, now a vigorous 61, espouses a theory that is unpopular in his professional field and almost unknown beyond it. He is an existential therapist. This practice, which claims only a few hundred adherents in the U.S., is dismissed in some quarters as either trivial or derivative. For ordinary travelers, the theory makes heavy going indeed. *Love and Will* demands of even the most persistent reader the same emotional and intellectual commitment that the author made three decades ago.

The old values—the myths and institutions with which civilization consoles itself and explains the unexplainable—are everywhere under attack and crumbling. Bereft of their support, says May, contemporary man faces a deeply disturbing alternative. He must either look to himself for the meaning of life, or he must decide that he and life have no meaning. All too readily, man takes the latter course.

Airless Refuge

"We cling to each other and try to persuade ourselves that what we feel is love," writes May. "We do not will because we are afraid that if we choose one thing or one person we'll lose the other, and we are too insecure to take that chance." The individual retires to what May calls "feelinglessness," from which it is only a short step to apathy. And from apathy it is only another step to violence. . . .

Love and Will invites its readers to embark on an even more hazardous and painful course: to recover the lost sense of self by accepting the shadow of death. To May and the existentialists, life is a moving sliver of time between what was and what will be. Man, too, is ever in motion: a process rather than a product, of which all that can be said with any certainty is that it will one day end. But to this school it is the inevitability and awareness of death that defines life and liberates the human will to act and to be. Writes May: "Abraham Maslow is profoundly right when he wonders whether we could love passionately if we knew we'd never die."

Self-Imprisoned

It is just here that existential thought seemingly departs from the mainstream. To Freud, man was the hapless prisoner of his past. The best that he could hope for in the present was a truce with those stern and deterministic taskmasters whom Freud called the Super Ego and the Id. The goal of life was "adjustment." Hence it followed that unhappiness, anxiety and guilt were usually pathological states—a measure of the struggle against those dynamic and contradictory forces.

May contends that man is a prisoner only if he chooses to be, and that life is more than a sentence imposed by the past. To accept this much is to break out of confinement into a self-awareness in which anxiety, guilt and unhappiness are not necessarily symptoms of maladjustment. They can count among the unavoidable costs of being. Existential therapy stresses the vital importance of accepting the pain as well as the pleasure, which, like life and death, are complementary. To be anxious, says May, may be merely to live within the awareness of death. To be unhappy may be only the free will's demand for expression.

Existential therapy is not so much a new school as a new interpretation of Freudian analysis. It is less interested in the past simply as past; indeed, May defines the past as "having been," a state that survives. Existentialists also quarrel with the common interpretation of the Oedipus complex as the guilt and fear engendered by the male child's attraction to his mother. May and others say that the conflict actually signifies man's refusal to face the truth of his own being. They ask pointedly: What does Oedipus do when he confronts the awful knowledge that he has loved his mother? He puts out his eyes—the organs of sight, not sex.

People and Things

. . . Born in Ada, Ohio, Rollo Reese May studied psychoanalysis under Alfred Adler, who was one of Freud's apostates. He also studied art in Poland and Greece and, after returning from Europe in the 1930s, enrolled in New York's Union Theological Seminary—"to ask questions, ultimate questions about human beings—not to be a preacher." He did serve briefly in a Congregational parish in Verona, N.J. The years he spent as a tuberculosis patient brought this varied background into focus. There, face to face with death, he discovered what he took to be its true relation to the human will.

The message he has since steadily proclaimed is that people happen to things; things do not happen to people. He does not deny man's limitations; he says only that within those limitations there is more freedom to move than most men realize. Everything, even apathy, is an act of will. . . .

Existential therapy, pioneered by Rollo May, is based on the existential model of psychopathology. The existential therapist tries to help his client accept the circumstances of his present life and assume responsibility for his behavior. By exercising his will, that is, making choices and accepting the consequences, the individual asserts that he is more than the sum of past experiences and repressed drives. Existential therapy takes a more optimistic view of human beings than psychoanalysis, although it is perhaps a more difficult form of therapy for the client to conceptualize.

Self-Exploration in Client-Centered Therapy

C: Well ah, I've been th-thinking about my ag-aggression. I'm beginning to feel more that I might be showing a lot of aggression in my st-stuttering toward other people because I know now ah, the other person suffers even more than I do sometimes. I mean this is something I could never—I could never admit before. I mean, I mean it would—if I just said it, it would just be a lie, but I'm beginning to see now maybe it isn't a lie, maybe I do have a lot of aggression in myself. That's the way I'm showing it toward other people. . . . I rather enjoy talking now. And I can also be quiet and sort of enjoy it (slightly laughing). But before I didn't want to talk and I didn't want to be quiet either (very loud). Boy, That was terrible! (raising voice) I was completely licked.

T: What a fight you were having about your speech; talking or no talking, it was still a fight.

C: Boy, it was, it was a terrible fight. I never realized it. I guess it was too painful to admit that fight. I mean, it's, I mean, I'm just beginning to feel it, to feel it now. Oh, the terrible pain. I mean it was terrible. I never realized how terrible it was. I'm just beginning to, I just have a little feeling now. I'm now just beginning to sort of get a hold of a small, small bit now, yeah, right now. I'm just trying to feel it now, trying to get hold of it here right now. It was *terrible* to talk, I mean you wanted to talk and then I didn't want to. M-hm.

T: It hurt you so much all these years that you didn't really know that it hurt you that much.

C: That's right. I'm just beginning to feel it *now* after all these years of that. Gee I don't know what to do. I don't know what to do; it's terrible (pause) (sigh). I can hardly, I'm having a time getting my breath now too, just all choked up inside.

T: You've let yourself feel it so much. . . .

C: I'm all *tight* inside, I'm all tight in the lungs. I mean I don't feel like crying. I'm just tight! All this heavy burden I've been bearing. I just feel like I'm crushed. Like I've been hit by a truck. . . . (pause) Do you know, I just can't realize, I just can't realize that I had a lot of aggression in me. Gee, I mean it's so

new yet. (sounds surprised) I mean I have to go back and talk about it again and again. It's just, boy! I'm aggressive. Even now, no, I'm not aggressive. Yes I am. I mean I just said I was, but I just don't want to *quite* accept it yet. I am aggressive—or am I? I'm beginning to doubt. . . . I'm beginning to enjoy this now, I'm getting a big kick out of it. Even about all these old negative things, I don't want to make progress, that I'm aggressive, I'm, I'm, I'm, joyful with my aggression. Sad and mo-mo-mournful, mournful, mournful about it (keeps repeating the word voluntarily). There the third time, why I'll do it, you just give me plenty of time (laughs). That's something I wasn't able to do before; I would have just said mo-mournful once and hurried to something else. But. . . .

T: Now, you're saying to me, OK, so I'll let you know I have trouble with my speech and I'm going to keep on working, right in front of your face.

C: Right! That's right! I don't care what you think about it. Maybe I'm showing ag-ag-aggression like that. Maybe I am. Maybe I'm, I'm just gonna make you hurt (leans very close to therapist, voice raising). I'm just gonna hurt you all I can with this stuttering. That's some-hmm. I'm surprised I said that. I'm just going to hurt you all I can with my speech. I'm just gonna st-st-st-stutter all I c-c-c-can (voluntarily imitates stutter). That wasn't an actual block, I imitated those, but I'm able to do it and I'm able to s-s-show ag-ag-aggression (real stutter) towards you like that. Gee! I showed quite a bit of aggression even toward my therapist, toward my therapist. Boy this is surprising.

T: You never knew you felt that?

C: I never knew I could do something like that. I'm surprised you're not klopping me on the head or something. "Mustn't do that, man, mustn't do that." I'm surprised you're not rejecting me, you're not punishing me. I'm surprised.

T: Surprised that I'm not giving. . . .

C: (Talking at the same time) I am, I'm terribly surprised (slightly laughing).

T: Surprised that I'm not coming back at you.

C: Yeah, that you're not. I can't believe it. (softly) I can't (slightly laughing) I can't, I can't believe it . . . (Seeman, 1957)

---

with the comment that she was "upset." When asked by the therapist what she meant by "upset," she said she did not know. Later it was discovered that, in her formative years, her mother had denied her the implications of any negative feelings. She would say, "You aren't angry at me, you're upset." The woman had learned to cut off feelings of anger, depression, jealousy, and anxiety. She responded to situations that would normally have elicited such

feelings with vague reactions of apprehension and uneasiness. Therapy led her to understand and accept the fact that she had these feelings and to experience them in appropriate situations. Instead of being confused and disoriented in unpleasant situations, she could respond spontaneously and openly with her feelings. Openly expressing one's feelings is more apt to help resolve the situation causing the negative feelings. For example, people are likely to avoid saying things that make you angry if they know how you feel about such things.

Client-centered therapy promotes self-exploration. The therapist tries to develop an environment of acceptance in which the client can take the chance of facing his denied feelings. The client is encouraged to move to an internal frame of reference in which *he* decides how worthwhile he is rather than always looking to others for evaluation. Emphasis is placed on the development of a *real* relationship in therapy rather than on role playing for the therapist.

Rogers proposed that three basic characteristics of the therapist are necessary before he can successfully use the client-centered technique: empathic understanding, unconditional positive regard, and congruence. *Emphatic understanding* means that the therapist accurately understands the immediate feelings of the client. *Unconditional positive regard* means that the therapist cares about his client. He does not put conditions on his caring, nor does he care less when the client reveals aspects of himself about which he is ashamed and anxious. This does not mean that the therapist agrees with the view that the client presents; but it does mean that he cares about him as a person regardless of his viewpoints. *Congruence* means that what the therapist is experiencing inside and how he presents himself to his client are consistent. Thus the therapist is genuine.

Rogers outlined several stages of development of the integrated person in the therapeutic process. The first stage is characterized by rigidity and remoteness of experiencing, with no self-relevant communication to others. As the client comes to accept his feelings, he may progress to the point where he can admit to feelings that are still removed from experience. For example, a client in therapy may be able to tell the therapist about how angry he was the previous week in therapy, while denying any annoyance at the present time. Eventually, through therapy or other positive experiences, the client is able to express his immediate feelings and to integrate his self-concept with his present everyday experiences.

Gestalt therapy. As we have seen, Gestalt psychology emphasizes the perception of patterns or totalities rather than separate elements of a stimulus. Gestalt therapy, founded by Fritz Perls, developed from attempts to help a person look at the entirety of his immediate experience. According to Perls, people with emotional problems tend to focus their attention only on part of what they feel

and only on part of what they do, especially in their communications with others. The focus of Gestalt therapy is not *why* the client is behaving the way he is but rather *what* he is feeling and *how* he is behaving. The therapist helps the client overcome barriers to self-awareness. The goal is for the client to become aware of what he is doing from moment to moment and to accept responsibility for that behavior. Theoretically, the client will then be able to attend to all aspects of his experience. Attention and awareness become integrated.

Notice in the following excerpt of a Gestalt therapy session how the therapist points out all aspects of the client's behavior—the tone of her own voice and the shaking of her leg. The client had been describing a dream in which her dead mother appeared, and the therapist, noticing that she was beginning to sound whiny and complaining, asked her if she had any "unfinished business" with her mother. The client replied:

Mrs. R: Well . . . if only she had loved me, things would be different. But she didn't and . . . and I've never had any real mother love (crying).

S (Steve Tobin): Put your mother in that chair and say that to her.

Mrs. R: If only she had cared for me, I'd be much better today.

S: I want you to say this to her, not to me. Can you imagine her sitting there in front of you?

Mrs. R: Yes, I see her as she looked when she was still alive. Mother, if you had only loved me. Why couldn't you ever tell me you loved me? Why did you always criticize me? (almost a wail, more tears)

S: Now switch over to the other chair and play your mother. (She moves over to the other chair and doesn't say anything.)

S: What do you experience as your mother?

Mrs. R: I-I-I don't know . . . I don't know what she would say.

S: Of course you don't know. She's not around any more. You're playing the part of you that is your mother. Just say whatever you experience there.

Mrs. R: Oh, I see. Well, I don't know what to say to her.

S: Say *that* to her.

Mrs. R M (Mrs. R as Mother): I don't know what to say to you. I *never* knew what to say to you. I really did love you, you know that. Look at all the things I did for you, and you never appreciated it. (voice sounds defensive and whiny)

S: Now switch back and reply as yourself.

Mrs. R S (Mrs. R as Self): Loved me! All you ever did was criticize me. Nothing I ever did was good enough! (voice beginning to sound more whiny). When I got married to J. you disapproved, you were always coming over and telling me what I was doing wrong with the kids. Oh, you never came right out and said anything, but you were always making snide remarks or saying, "Now, dear, wouldn't it be a good idea to put another blanket on the baby." You made my life *miserable;* I was always worrying about you criticizing me. And now I'm having all this trouble with J. (breaks down and starts to cry.)

S: Did you hear your voice?

Mrs. R S: Yes.

S: What did you hear in it?

Mrs. R S: Well, I guess I sounded kind of complaining, like I'm feeling sor—iike I'm feeling mad.

S: You sounded more like feeling self-pity. Try this on for size: say to your mother, "Look what you've done to me. It's all your fault."

Mrs. R S: Look what you've done. Everything's your fault.

S: Now let yourself switch back and forth as you find yourself changing roles.

Mrs. R M: Come on, stop blaming me for everything. You are always complaining about something. If you had been better—if you had been a *decent* daughter, I wouldn't have had to criticize you so much.

Mrs. R S: Oh, oh, (under her breath) Damn. (She's swinging her right leg slightly.)

S: Notice your leg.

Mrs. R S: I-I'm shaking it.

S: Exaggerate that, shaking it harder.

Mrs. R S: (shakes leg harder, it begins to look like a kick)

S: Can you imagine doing that to your mother?

Mrs. R S: No, but I-I-I-I'm sure feeling pissed at her.

S: Say this to her.

Mrs. R S: I feel pissed off at you! I hate you!

S: Say that louder.

Mrs. R S: I hate you! (volume higher, but still some holding back)

S: Louder!

Mrs. R. S: I HATE YOU, YOU GODDAMNED BITCH. (She sticks her leg out and kicks the chair over.)

S: Now switch back.

Mrs. R M: (voice sounds much weaker now) I-I guess I didn't show you much love. I really felt it, but I was unhappy and bitter. You know all I had to go through with your father and brother. You were the only one I could talk to. I'm sorry . . . I wanted you to be happy . . . I wanted so much for you.

Mrs. R S: You sure did! . . . I know you did love me, Mother, I know you were unhappy (voice much softer now, but sounding real, not whiny or mechanical). I guess I did some things that were ba— wrong, too. I was always trying to keep you off my back.

Mrs. R M: Yes, you were pretty sarcastic to me, too. And that hurt.

Mrs. R S: I wish you had told me. I didn't think you were hurt at all.

Mrs. R M: Well, that's all over now.

Mrs. R S: Yeah, it is. I guess there's no use blaming you. You're not around any more.

S: Can you forgive your mother now?

Mrs. R S: Mother, I forgive you . . . I really do forgive you. (Starts crying again, but not in the whiny way of before. She sounds genuinely grieving and cries for a couple of minutes.)

S: Now switch back.

Mrs. R M: I forgive you too, dear. You have to go on now. You can't keep blaming me forever. I made my mistakes but you have your own family and you're doing okay.

S: Do you feel ready to say goodbye now?

Mrs. R S: Yes. I-I think so (starts to sob). Goodbye, Mother, goodbye. (breaks down, cries for a few minutes)

S: What do you experience now?

Mrs. R: I feel better. I feel . . . kind of relieved, like a weight is off my back. I feel calm.

S: Now that you've said goodbye to her, to this dead person, can you go around and say hello to the live people here, to the group?

Mrs. R: Yes, I'd like that.

(She goes around the room, greets people, touches some, embraces others. Many in the group are tearful. When she reaches her husband, she starts crying again, and tells him she loves him, and they embrace.) **(Tobin, 1971, pages 154–155)**

Transactional analysis. Transactional analysis (T.A.) is a tremendously popular form of therapy espoused in best-selling books such as Eric Berne's *Games People Play* (1964) and Thomas Harris' *I'm OK—You're OK* (1967). The focus of the therapy is the transactions that people have with one another and how those transactions express three basic aspects of the personality known as the *Child*, the *Parent*, and the *Adult*. According to T.A., in each of us there is a Child that is made up of the residuals of our childhood way of behaving and thinking; a Parent based on the controlling behaviors, judgments, and attitudes derived from our parents' treatment of us as children; and an Adult, the mature, reasoning, adaptive part of personality. The Child is the recording from early childhood of internal events: the child's reactions to what he sees and hears. The situation of childhood leads the child to experience feelings of frustration, rejection, or fear of abandonment, leading the child to feel "not OK." There are many positive sides to the Child as well. Creativity, curiosity, exploration, the ability to touch, feel, and experience, and the excitement of new discoveries are all stored in the recording of the Child. The Parent is the recording from early childhood of external events during the first 5 years of life. Much of what is recorded at this time is

T.A.: Doing OK

Time—In the 1960s it was encounter groups. In the 1970s it is transactional analysis, or T.A., the pop-psychological path to happiness charted by Sacramento Psychiatrist Thomas A. Harris in his bestseller *I'm OK—You're OK*. T.A., or close facsimiles of it, is now practiced by some 3,000 psychiatrists, psychologists, social workers and ministers in the U.S. and 14 foreign countries. In fact, it may be the most widely used and fastest-growing form of treatment for emotional distress in the world. . . .

The central thesis of T.A., as Harris teaches it, stems from Psychiatrist Alfred Adler's concept of a universal "inferiority feeling." Most people, Harris says, never stop thinking of themselves as helpless children overwhelmed by the power of adults. For that reason they go through life believing that they are inferior, or "not OK," while they view everyone else as superior, or "OK." The aim of T.A. therapy is to instill the conviction that "I'm OK—you're OK," meaning that no one is really a threat to anyone else. . . .

More specifically, transactional analysts believe that what makes a person unhappy is an unbalanced relationship between the three parts that constitute every human personality: Parent, Adult and Child. Harris rejects any suggestion that these are the equivalent of Freud's superego, ego and id. "The Parent, Adult and Child are real things that can be validated," he insists. "We're talking about real people, real times and real events, as recorded in the brain." Be that as it may, the theory is that unless the mature, rational Adult dominates the personality, or, in the language of T.A., is "plugged in," the overly restrictive Parent and the primitive, self-depreciating Child will foul up most "transactions," or relationships with others.

To put his Adult in charge, Harris says, the troubled person must "learn the language of transactional analysis and use it in examining his everyday transactions." He must also learn to diagram these transactions, using three circles to represent the personality components of each person and drawing arrows to show how two people interact. Parallel lines depict "complementary transactions," which occur, for instance, when a hus-

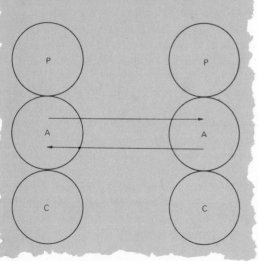

band's Adult speaks to his wife's Adult and gets a response in kind. In that type of exchange, the husband might ask, "Where are my cuff links?" and his wife might reply, "In your top left dresser drawer"—or, perhaps, "I'm not sure, but I'll help you find them."

Crossed lines like this denote uncomplementary

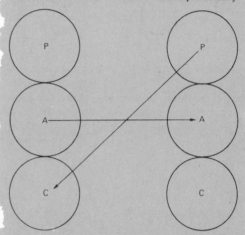

transactions, and bode trouble. For example, the Adult-to-Adult question about the cuff links might be answered with a sharp "Where you left them," a reproof that comes from the wife's Parent and is addressed to what she sees as the inept Child in her husband's personality.

T.A. therapy sessions usually involve eight to 15 participants and often begin with one member trying to describe why "I'm not OK." The group responds by giving him all the reasons that he should be OK. Therapist and group members alike try to help each member analyze, and change, his "life script"—the blueprint that, according to T.A., a child unconsciously draws up to shape his whole life. Bad scripts may include self-defeating "games" such as "Kick Me," a gambit of the self-pitying, and "Blemish," the ploy of people who compensate for inferiority feelings by pointing out the failings of others.

All Adults

As a way of inspiring group members, T.A. therapists usually make "contracts" with them to achieve specific goals like giving up alcohol or such amorphous ones as "to get more OK," "to be able to give myself to others" or "to exercise more control over my Parent." . . . Harris, who now does more teaching and training than therapy, usually begins his lectures with a few jokes to loosen things up. Sometimes he asks a listener to come forward and stand at the foot of the speaker's platform, thus demonstrating what it is like to have to look up at a parent and feel like a "not OK" child. Often, members of Harris' staff surprise the audience by interrupting him with comments of their own. The purpose is to suggest that Harris and his listeners are all adults together, and that he is no parent proclaiming infallible truths to obedient children. Occasionally, he writes out advice on a prescription pad: "I want you, John, to smile and greet ten new people every day." . . .

examples and pronouncements from the child's parents. Since the child is relatively incapable of interpreting the meaning of what is happening to him at this age, these recordings are made without editing (or question). The source of all rules and judgments or how-to-do-it instructions is in the Parent and the child is unable to determine where the rule is good (don't play with that knife!) or poor (never get dirty!). The replaying of the Parent ''tapes'' later in life has a powerful influence on personality. The Adult is that part of the personality which gathers information, processes and files it, and makes decisions based on that information.

Transactional analysis therapy involves using the above vocabulary to analyze the type of interactions (transactions) that people have with one another and to help them understand the difficulties of inappropriate interactions. People can communicate Parent to Parent, Parent to Child, Parent to Adult, Child to Parent, Child to Child, Child to Adult, Adult to Parent, Adult to Child, and, finally, Adult to Adult. It is this last type of transaction that is ideal and very difficult to achieve.

Transactional therapy allows a person to understand the communication interactions that he is having, to listen to and appreciate the Child and Parent in himself, and to train the Adult to make conscious decisions that allow the Child and Parent to be expressed in behavior in reasonable and controlled ways.

Behavior Therapy

The insight-oriented therapies are the traditional forms of psychotherapy; indeed the popular notion of psychotherapy is of developing insight into one's behavior. Self-knowledge is certainly a worthwhile goal, but many people have worked out an adequate understanding of their behavior only to discover that they still have difficulty changing it. Self-knowledge alone is seldom sufficient to change behavior. For example, a young man may understand that the reason he has difficulty asking girls for dates is that he had few opportunities to date in high school, he felt that he was not physically attractive, and he did not know how to ask for a date or what to say on a date. He understands perfectly well the reasons for his difficulty, but that does not change the fact that he still does not have the skill of appropriate dating behavior.

In contrast to insight-oriented therapy, behavior therapy focuses on changes in skill, motivation, and performance. *Behavior modification,* as the behavior therapies are called, uses the relatively well-established principles of learning and

Symptom Substitution

One of the battles that has raged between psychoanalytically oriented psychotherapists and behavior modifiers has centered on the problem of *symptom substitution.* According to psychoanalytic theorists, symptoms are visible signs of underlying, unconscious conflicts. Behavior modifiers assume that the symptom *is* the problem (or at least a major part of it) and show no concern for unconscious ''causes.'' According to psychoanalytic theory, if the therapist treats the symptom without corresponding treatment of the cause of the disorder, *symptom substitution* will result; that is, the person will develop new symptoms that still reveal the presence of underlying, unconscious conflict. This substitution process may be one reason why hypnosis is not very effective in permanently curing conversion reactions, such as paralysis. Hypnosis might eliminate a problem temporarily (for example, the patient is given a posthypnotic suggestion that he or she will be able to walk after having paralysis), but new symptoms show up later.

The behavior modifiers have responded to the challenge of the psychoanalysts in two ways, one empirical and the other theoretical. Their empirical argument is the most convincing. Long-term follow-up studies of clients treated by behavior modification reveal few relapses or transfers of conflict to new areas. Studies as much as 2 years later reveal that most clients continue to show effective functioning and do not seem to have been the victims of symptom substitution. The theoretical argument would probably not satisfy the psychoanalyst. The behavior modifier claims in fact to be treating the ''cause'' of the problem by eliminating the underlying anxiety associated with the behavioral symptom. It may not be necessary to find out why the anxiety exists in order to eliminate it.

It should be noted that there is some semantic confusion here that muddles the arguments: Is anxiety a cause or a symptom? Is the cause of a disorder the link between an external stimulus and an anxiety response or a link between an internal conflict and an anxiety response? If a psychoanalytically oriented therapist can accept the idea that the cause of a problem is the link between the stimulus and the anxiety response, there would be no real disagreement between the two approaches.

conditioning to help the person change (see Chapters 4 and 9). The behavior therapist makes no assumption of unconscious motivations and indeed proposes that such assumptions are irrelevant to therapy. The focus may be on the extinction of undesirable behaviors, such as compulsive eating or stuttering, or the learning of alternative positive behaviors. Since the early 1920's there has been interest in the use of conditioning techniques for psychotherapy, but it is only recently that the techniques of classical and instrumental conditioning have actually been successfully applied to individuals with emotional problems.

Systematic Desensitization

One of the more recent innovations in the use of learning techniques in psychotherapy was developed by Joseph Wolpe in the late 1950's. He proposed that neurotic habits are learned in anxiety-provoking situations by the association of neutral stimuli with anxiety responses. The anxiety response is made up of subjective feelings and physiological tension. Wolpe proposed that if a response incompatible with anxiety, such as relaxation, sex, or assertiveness, occurred in the presence of the anxiety-provoking stimuli, the connection between the stimulus and the anxiety response would be weakened. He called this process *reciprocal inhibition.*

Wolpe developed the technique of therapy called *systematic desensitization* based on the process of reciprocal inhibition. The first step in desensitization therapy is to gain an understanding of the type of stimuli that leads to anxiety responses. Based on interviews with the client, a hierarchy of fear-provoking stimuli is constructed ranging from situations involving very mild fear to ones in which the fear is quite intense. While the hierarchy is being constructed, *relaxation training* begins. Wolpe focuses on muscle relaxation techniques in which the client is taught to become aware of and control specific muscle groups throughout the body by successively tensing and relaxing each muscle group. Deep and slow breathing coupled with the relaxation of more and more muscle groups can lead to very deep relaxation. While deeply relaxed, the client is asked to imagine a scene involving the least threatening stimulus in the hierarchy. If any anxiety is felt while imagining the scene, the person raises a finger and he is told to immediately remove the scene from his mind. Deeper relaxation is induced. When the person can imagine the scene without anxiety several times, he is asked to move up the hierarchy and imagine the scene that is the next most anxiety-provoking. The relaxation response slowly generalizes to other items on the list, making the next item less stressful. Once relaxation to the entire list of scenes is complete, the client finds that freedom from anxiety to an imagined stimulus generalizes and results in freedom from anxiety to the real event.

Systematic desensitization can be used easily for anyone who finds himself anxious in a particular situation. Test anxiety, fear of speaking in front of large groups, and phobias have all been successfully treated with desensitization training. This type of therapy was effective with Mr. J, a talented basketball player attending college on an athletic scholarship (Katahn, 1967). Just before coming into therapy, Mr. J began to feel that his game was falling apart. His anxiety was so great that he lost 8 pounds in 1 month. He was tired and sluggish on the court. Although the intensity of the anxiety was new, he had felt anxiety about playing for a long time. Nausea and vomiting had occurred on the day of a game since he was 12 years old. Although his father did not seem to have a heavy involvement with his playing, his mother's avid interest in his achievement made him even more nervous.

Three therapy sessions were devoted to the construction of an anxiety hierarchy and training Mr. J in muscle relaxation. The following hierarchy, in order from least to most anxiety-provoking, was established:

1. Mr. J meets an assistant coach in the gym, and the coach doesn't say "hello" to him.
2. He is in the gym changing for practice, and he notices his hands beginning to sweat.
3. He is trying to study, and he can't get the day's practice out of his thoughts.
4. He finishes practice, and the "drugstore coaches" (his term for spectators who have passes for practice) speak to the other players and ignore him.
5. He is on the court and gets a tired, draggy, no-good feeling.
6. He is on the court and notices that the coaches are keeping a record of each player's performance.
7. He is visiting at home, and his mother makes some remark about another player.
8. He is eating dinner with his mother when she asks him something about how his game is going.
9. It is time for the late afternoon pre-game dinner, and he is on the way to the cafeteria.
10. He is in the cafeteria line, and the sight of food makes him feel sick.
11. He is in the gym changing for a game, and he is sick to his stomach.

After about 14 more sessions the anxiety hierarchy had been completely worked through and the client stopped vomiting before games. The nausea and tired, sluggish feeling during the games had also disappeared. The counseling that accompanied the desensitization focused on study habits and the role of basketball in his life. As a result of the combined therapeutic techniques, his grades rose from a "D" to a "B" average. Basketball plays a less overwhelming (although still important) part in his life, and he has been accepted as a student in law school.

Implosive Therapy

Systematic desensitization can be thought of as counterconditioning of an undesirable response (anxiety) by substituting an alternate response (relaxation) to the same stimulus. Another type of therapy, which uses imagination of fear-provoking situations, accomplishes the same goals by direct extinction. In *implosive therapy,* developed by Thomas Stampfl, the client is instructed to imagine, without any build-up, the very thing that he fears most. No hierarchy is constructed; only the most unpleasant scenes are imagined, and they are to be imagined as vividly as possible. The therapist spends his time describing the feared stimuli in great detail for the client, who is not given any relaxation training and typically finds such images extremely anxiety-provoking. The image descriptions are continued and repeated with more detail until the client's level of anxiety declines, which invariably it will in time with sufficient repetition. The client is not allowed to escape from the anxiety he feels during the description of the images. Crying, covering up one's ears, and refusing to continue are all considered attempts to escape and are not permitted. One girl in implosive therapy got so anxious she fainted; the therapist got down on the floor near her and immediately continued the description of the feared stimulus. He interpreted the fainting as an avoidance response, the very kind of response he was trying to extinguish.

Implosive therapy works with many people. One might wonder why, in view of the fact that it seems to be the exact opposite of systematic desensitization. Logically it should make the anxiety worse, not better. Actually, the difference between desensitization and implosion is more apparent than real. Both processes rely on extinction through stimulus repetition. Systematic desensitization is merely a more gradual extinction procedure than implosion.

The most important element in the technique of implosive therapy is the fact that the feared imagery is repeated, over and over, *until the anxiety response is eliminated.* In effect, the imagery of the

Afraid to Sleep?

Parade—An enterprising Miami psychologist is experimenting with new techniques for combating one of man's oldest enemies: insomnia.

Using complex questionnaires, psychologist Jeffrey Elenewski tested a hypothesis first advanced by Sigmund Freud—that insomnia is caused by an unconscious fear of dying. He concluded that insomniacs indeed fear death more than do normal sleepers. Therefore, the insomniac, while consciously yearning for sleep, unconsciously resists it because he thinks that to sleep is to die.

If so, it should follow that insomnia can be treated by reducing the fear of death. Elenewski set out to do this through a drastic, often frightening technique called "implosive therapy." Implosive therapy is based upon the principle that the best way to overcome fear is to expose the patient repeatedly to the things that frighten him.

In the case of death-obsessed insomniacs, Elenewski accomplishes this by causing them to imagine themselves dying, often under horrifying circumstances. He even subjects them to a 40-minute tape-recording of a vividly described death experience.

The first few sessions induce intense anxiety in the listeners. But after the procedure is repeated often, the anxiety lessens. And later, men and women who had needed at least an hour to fall asleep drop off in approximately 25 minutes. They report that they are still sleeping better a full month after their "counterfeit death" experience.

One interesting feature of implosion therapy is that it can be used as a technique by therapists with different theories of psychopathology. Although implosion is usually thought of as a *behavior modification* technique based on principles of learning and extinction, here we see it being used with a rationale derived from Freudian theory. The technique is for treating fear and may be useful regardless of why the fear developed.

feared stimulus is paired with a *reduction* in anxiety rather than an increase in anxiety. For example, consider the case of a young boy who would not go to bed because he had developed a fear of monsters he imagined were in his closet. Stampfl cured the child in one evening by repeatedly telling him the most horrifying stories about the monsters, who certainly were going to attack, murder, and devour him. The first story elicited intense anxiety in the child, but by the fourth repetition the child exhibited no fear at all. Now the child has no difficulty in going to bed and boasts of being able to make up his own horror stories.

There is probably one other reason why implosive therapy works as often as it does. The client is prevented from making escape responses and is forced to learn that his thoughts and fears cannot harm him. Research done with dogs has shown that they will learn to jump over a barrier on the signal of a light in order to avoid a shock. The dogs will continue to jump over the barrier when the light comes on, long after the shock has been turned off. The way to get the dogs to extinguish this response is to force them to stay on the starting side of the barrier so that they have an opportunity to learn that shock no longer occurs. In a similar way, people learn escape responses that prevent them from ever having the opportunity to learn that escape is no longer necessary.

Other Conditioning Therapies

Both desensitization and implosive therapy involve complex and specialized applications of the principles and techniques of classical and instrumental conditioning described in Chapter 4. Other, more direct uses of these principles have been successful in relatively simple forms of psychopathology.

Instrumental conditioning. The technique of *shaping,* which is based on the principles of instrumental conditioning, has been applied to the problem of short attention span, a frequent cause of classroom disruption and poor academic performance. The child with a short attention span can be rewarded for paying attention to his studies for even short periods of time. If the longest period of time a child can attend to studying without his mind wandering is 1 minute, then he is initially rewarded at the end of every minute that he successfully studies. After this habit is well established (maybe after several days), the requirements are increased. Now he is rewarded only when he studies for 2-minute intervals. Then the length of the intervals is gradually increased until he is able to study for half an hour or more without interruption. Through the judicious use of reinforcement, a therapist can shape the desired behavior from modest beginnings. After the new behavior is established, the external rewards can be withdrawn, because new rewards will maintain the behaviors. The rewards of easier studying, increased feelings of competence, and (one hopes) better grades will all help to maintain the behaviors.

Instrumental conditioning has been surprisingly effective with some severe cases of psychopathy. Withdrawn children can be trained to speak with others if properly rewarded. The behavior of severely schizophrenic adults who are hospitalized can be modified by rewarding them for talking to other patients on the ward, grooming themselves, or making their beds. The hospital staff may use cigarettes and candy for rewards, or it may use tokens that can be traded for things that the patient wants or privileges on the ward. As we saw in Chapter 4, some mental hospitals use treatment programs, called token economies, that are based completely on instrumental principles. The patient is put in a situation in which he must use tokens he has *earned* to gain any but the barest essentials of life. Although such treatment may seem cruel, it is probably kinder to require socially acceptable behavior than it is to provide total care of individuals who are capable of developing some degree of self-care.

Institutionalism refers to the passive, dependent behavior of the "model" mental patient who bothers no one and always does what he is told. Some patients are so disturbed and withdrawn from the real world that they must wear diapers and be spoon fed. In one such case the nurses complained about having constantly to change a man who stayed in bed all day and was cared for like a baby. As a final attempt at therapy, the patient was told that he would no longer be cared for, and he would have to get up and go to the restroom. For 3 days the man lay in bed, soiling himself, until the stench became intolerable. On the third day he got up and went to the restroom and continued to do so from then on. There is a tendency for hospitals to be more concerned with efficient administration than with the encouragement of appropriate behaviors. The programs based on operant learning principles have shown that patients do not starve when social behaviors are required before feeding occurs.

Punishment. Although the judicious use of rewards seems to be quite effective in changing behavior, the approach is sometimes difficult to implement. For example, how can the desired behavior be rewarded if it never occurs? Or what if the maladaptive behavior that does occur is self-reinforcing? One example of self-reinforcing behavior is stealing. The only way positive reinforcement could be used to eliminate stealing is to reward the person for *not* stealing with things of greater value than the things that could be stolen. This approach could become expensive, and a therapist is unlikely to be in a position to reward a person for not stealing. Social approval may help maintain nonstealing behavior, but people usually do not reward others for *lack* of a behavior. As almost everyone realizes, we typically ignore a child

Training to Be Sober

Time—It seems, at first glance, to be a conventional cocktail lounge. There are soft lights, a polished mahogany bar and the murmur of drinkers' voices rising above unobtrusive music. But there is more to the scene than meets the eye. The drinks are free, a TV camera is video-taping the activities and electronic equipment under the bar is administering shocks to the patrons, most of whom are alcoholic patients at Patton State Hospital in San Bernardino, Calif., where the lounge has been installed.

Journey to Sobriety

Most doctors believe that the only alternative to alcoholism is abstinence. Yet the former Skid Rowers are encouraged to frequent the lounge. They are being conditioned either to give up liquor or become social drinkers. Their therapeutic imbibing was suggested by Psychologists Halmuth Schaefer and Mark Sobell, who disagree with the widely held belief that alcoholism is based on a physiological craving. Instead, they say, it is a psychological ailment, a learned response to stress. Unlike normal drinkers, who may react to anxiety by overeating, taking a walk around the block or hitting someone, the alcoholic has learned to find relief by reaching for a drink. What has been learned can be unlearned, Schaefer and Sobell insist. As proof, they point to their high cure rate, which is achieved with the aid of a harmless but painful technique: electric shocks for those who drink too much too fast.

At Patton State, alcoholics begin the five-week journey to sobriety by getting smashed. In the company of normal drinkers, they are allowed to order as many as 16 one-ounce drinks. Then they are given a nonelectric shock: a video-tape presentation of their drinking behavior. Most are dismayed to watch themselves ordering their drinks straight instead of mixed, gulping instead of sipping, and still tossing them off long after the normal drinkers have stopped.

Once a choice is made between working toward total abstinence or social drinking, the patients begin training. Each has electrodes attached to his hand. They can produce a shock when the bartender-therapist pushes a control button. Those who are to be abstainers know that they may receive a jolt every time they order drinks and a continuous shock as long as they have a glass in their hand; they are willing to risk the punishment to effect a cure. The would-be social drinker can consume as many as three mixed drinks without a shock—as long as he takes sips and makes each drink last at least 20 minutes. The shocks come at random—the drinkers never know when they will feel pain, but they do know that it could come after any infraction of the drinking rules. Sometimes, despite the pain, they continue to drink; at other times they put their drinks down.

Preliminary Results

Six months later, from 50% to 70% of the alcoholics trained to drink socially will do so or will abstain entirely. By comparison, only 10% to 20% of a group treated by conventional therapy could do the same. For the new abstainers, the apparent cure rate is 50%, compared with 20% to 25% in a control group. The researchers admit that their results are preliminary and that more patients may relapse as time goes on. But they have high hopes that many of the former alcoholics—having learned to associate drinking with real physical pain—will stay cured.

Punishment training can be used to stop undesired behavior. Later, patients can be rewarded for *not* performing the undesired behavior. (This would constitute omission training; see Chapter 4.)

---

until he misbehaves, and attention at that point can increase the very behavior we would like the child to stop.

When reward does not work, punishment may be helpful. Alcoholics have been treated with some success in this way. In one such program, a bar was set up in a ward for alcoholics, but the bar stools were wired for electricity. Some alcoholics were shocked if they requested a drink and had one. Other alcoholics, under a different program, were allowed to have a drink but were shocked if they asked for a drink that was not diluted with a mixer, if they drank their drink in less than 20 minutes, or if they asked for a fourth drink. The theory behind this approach is that alcoholics are not physiologically dependent on alcohol but have maladaptive drinking patterns that can be relearned. The therapy consisted of using shock to punish inappropriate drinking behavior. Some alcoholics have been helped in an enduring way with this technique. (See Chapter 4 for a discussion of appropriate and effective uses of punishment.)

Classical conditioning. In Chapter 4 we saw how the principles of conditioning have been applied to the treatment of emotional problems such as enuresis (night bedwetting) in elementary school children, which was for a long time considered a sign of emotional disturbance. We know now that enuresis can be treated by training the child with classical conditioning techniques. An alarm is set off, waking the child so that he can go to the bathroom, whenever the slightest amount of urine begins to flow. The stimulus of the full bladder becomes conditioned to the response of awakening and inhibiting urination. The technique is effective,

Resolute Prisoners Struggle Against Behavioral Modification

By William Claiborne

Boulder Daily Camera—In a solitary confinement cell behind two locked corridor grills in a remote wing of the medical center for federal prisoners here, Forest G. is engaged in a desperate struggle of wills with the U.S. Bureau of Prisons.

For Forest G., a 34-year-old convicted bank robber serving 15 years, solitary confinement has become a way of life. He has been sitting alone in what amounts to a walk-in closet for more than eight months, and in all likelihood he will remain there at least until next February.

From Forest's point of view, what is at stake in the struggle is his pride and his right to control of his own behavior, even if it is regarded by others as belligerent and recalcitrant.

From the prison authorities' point of view, what is at stake is the right of the state to promote change in the behavior of the most hardened inmate, even if the only alternative is to let the inmate vegetate indefinitely in maximum security incarceration.

Sunshine Street

The struggle will ultimately be resolved in a U.S. District Court in Kansas City, but for now the drama is being painfully acted out at the massive, 40-year-old prison hospital here, which is incongruously located on Sunshine Street, on the outskirts of town.

At issue in the court test brought by a group of inmates and supported by the American Civil Liberties Union (ACLU) is a year-old behavior modification program called START, an acronym for Special Treatment and Rehabilitative Training.

The controversy over START has spread beyond Forest and the eight other prisoners currently enrolled in the experimental program, reaching out to many of the federal prison system's 22,500 inmates and beyond to the hundreds of penal reform groups around the country. . . .

START is based on a deceptively simple system of programmed rewards in which a prisoner begins a fixed term at the most severe level of incarceration and then "earns" some freedom of movement and a few privileges by adapting to various rules of behavior.

During a minimum of 7½ months and a maximum of a year, the inmate can move through eight different levels of confinement, depending on his willingness to adapt to rules.

The first level is round-the-clock "deadlock" in which the inmate is allowed out of his cell two hours a week for exercise and twice for showers. The rest of the day he sits in a tile-walled room approximately 6-by-19 feet behind a steel door with a small window.

If the inmate goes 20 days without a "bad day," he moves to the second level, at which he is allowed to work three hours a day, eat meals out of his cell and have 1½ hours of recreation a day.

Time Off

Gradually, the inmate is allowed more privileges, is allowed to earn money in an adjacent factory six hours daily and begins to have sentence time off for good behavior restored.

In 7½ months, he is "graduated" from the program and is returned to the general population of the penitentiary that referred him to START in the first place. If the inmate rebels, refuses to follow rules or becomes verbally abusive to staff members, he is returned to the solitary confinement level for a designated period. If he refuses to participate, he remains in solitary for a year, and is then returned to a segregation unit of his home institution.

Forest G. was in the "hole" (segregation unit) at the Leavenworth penitentiary for two years when he was notified that he was to be sent to Springfield's START program. . . .

Forest did briefly participate in the program, earning points for good behavior. Then, he said, he saw several other inmates being beaten by guards during a disturbance in the tier opposite his cell, and he decided to lay down and finish his year in solitary.

Hole with Factory

"After you look at it a while, all this is a hole with a factory, and somebody calling it behavior modification. There's nobody here who's going to modify me," said Forest.

Asked if he had considered faking a change in his behavior long enough to learn privileges and graduate from the program, Forest replied, "It wouldn't be no act, it would be for real. They're trying to get a program going smoothly by bribing guys. If you are playing a game on them, you are playing it on yourself, because they want you modified, and they don't care what makes you do it.

"They're treating me like a kid, like they're saying, 'If you don't cut the grass, you can't go to the movie,'" Forest said. "I'm refusing to let them impose their will on me. It's a matter of pride and principle, when you know that the guy you are dealing with is not fair."

The use of behavior modification in corrective institutions has led to a strong controversy about the ethics of forcing people to behave in "socially appropriate" ways. Do criminals have the right to resist such treatment? Does such a program constitute cruel and unusual punishment?

with from 75 to 90 percent of children so treated obtaining night control of their bladder in a matter of a few weeks.

Although many people now think homosexuality should not be considered abnormal (see Chapter 11), some homosexuals do wish to change. In these cases, classical conditioning techniques have been used with some success. The sexual response of male homosexuals is handled in the following way. In order to reduce the positive sexual response to men, the homosexuals are shown pictures of nude males and simultaneously given an emetic to induce vomiting. The idea is that the UCS of vomiting and nausea will become conditioned to the CS of the stimulus of a nude male. To condition a positive sexual response to females, the homosexual is injected with testosterone, a male sex hormone (the UCS), and then shown pictures of nude females (the CS). In one study, 12 of 67 male homosexuals showed changes in the direction of relatively long-term heterosexual behavior (Freund, 1960). Although this is a small proportion, insight-oriented therapies have typically been even less successful with homosexuals.

Unique Features of Behavior Therapy

Behavior modification has been criticized for being a cold, unfeeling, even inhumane approach to helping others. This is not entirely an accurate description. Any therapist, regardless of his theoretical approach, can fail to foster a warm relationship; being cold and unfeeling will interfere with the effectiveness of any therapeutic approach. There is a good deal of evidence suggesting that behavior modification techniques will not be very effective unless the therapist is highly motivated, displays a warm, friendly attitude toward the client, and is honestly concerned about the client's welfare. These therapist qualities are important for all types of therapy, including behavior modification. There are, however, some central ways in which behavior modification does differ from other approaches:

1. Focus of responsibility. The behavior modification therapist assumes much more responsibility for the content of therapy than therapists using other techniques.

2. Definition of cure. Overt changes in behavior rather than reports of feeling better define resolution of the problem. Thus the behavior therapist can more easily define the conditions under which he considers his client "cured."

3. Developmental history. There is little or no concern during therapy about the history of problems except to determine the stimuli that lead to the maladaptive responses. If the behavior therapist does collect a history of the problem, it is usually used for his own understanding of the development of such disorders or to help him develop methods of prevention in the future. Even then, his understanding of the reasons for the behavior does not enter centrally into therapy.

4. Insight. The behavior therapist does not care

whether the client develops self-understanding or insight into the reasons for his problems.

Although behavior modification may seem "too simple," considerable skill is required in observation in order to be able to specify the relationships between stimuli and responses. Moreover, the therapist must develop a learning program that is of the correct level of difficulty, and he must convince the client of the potential worth of the program. Furthermore, he must keep the level of motivation high to prevent the client from giving up before the anxiety and the behavioral symptoms are eliminated.

Biological Therapies

Chemotherapy

The use of drugs as a means of treating psychopathology has existed for at least as long as recorded history, although many of the drugs used for treatment today were originally used for other purposes and their psychological effects were discovered accidentally. Even now, in many cases, scientists have only a vague idea as to *why* some drugs work. The drugs used in chemotherapy can be roughly divided into three categories: sedatives and tranquilizers, antidepressants, and antipsychotics (see Table 12–2).

Sedatives and tranquilizers. Sedatives and tranquilizers have been used to help highly anxious people under transient stress or those showing early manifestations of neurosis and psychosis. Although tranquilizers have been in use only since the middle

---

Table 12–2
Drugs used in chemotherapy

Major tranquilizing drugs
1. Meprobamate (Miltown)
2. Chlordizepoxide (Librium)
3. Diazepam (Valium)

Major sedatives
1. Alcohol
2. Barbiturates
   a. Phenobarbital
   b. Secobarbital (Seconal)
   c. Sodium pentobarbital (Sodium Pentothol)
3. Bromides

Major antidepressants
1. Lithium
2. Imipramine
3. Nialamide
4. Pargyline

Major antipsychotics
1. Reserpine (Serpasil)
2. Chlorpromazine (Thorazine)

Comparative Approaches to Psychotherapy

John is a compulsive eater who weighs 350 pounds. Seeking help, he sees a therapist, who might approach his problem in the following ways.

Physician (Medical Model)
The therapist assumes that the behavior is the result of a physiological illness. He might use amphetamines to reduce appetite or tranquilizers to reduce anxiety associated with stress in John's life.

Psychoanalyst (Dynamic Model)
The therapist explores early childhood memories, the content of dreams, free association, and slips of the tongue to determine the symbolic meaning of the eating behavior. The psychoanalyst would look for the possibility that John is symbolically expressing strong needs for love and aggression.

Behavior Modifier (Behavioral or Learning Theory Model)
The therapist explores the rewarding aspects of overeating and determines whether such behavior allows John to avoid other anxiety-evoking situations. The therapist may set up a conditioning form of treatment in which John is punished for overeating or thinking about eating or is rewarded for noneating behavior. The therapist might try to increase behavior incompatible with eating or change John's eating patterns. If eating leads to anxiety reduction, relaxation techniques may be used to lower anxiety levels.

Jane is a 25-year-old graduate student with a severe stuttering problem. Seeking help, she sees a therapist, who might approach her problem in the following ways.

Physician (Medical Model)
The therapist assumes that stuttering is a neurological problem in the perceptual-motor areas of the brain. The physician might prescribe medication (tranquilizers) or recommend perceptual-motor training.

Psychoanalyst (Dynamic Model)
The therapist assumes that the stuttering behavior is an expression of an unconscious conflict associated with hostility, particularly toward Jane's parents. Therapy would involve trying to bring into awareness this underlying conflict through the interpretation of free association, dreams, slips of the tongue, and repressed memories.

Behavior Modifier (Behavioral or Learning Theory Model)
The therapist explores the possibility that the stuttering behavior was a classically conditioned response. Techniques to treat stuttering might involve negative practice, a technique requiring a person to stutter repeatedly on purpose. Rhythmic speech patterns and operant conditioning involving rewards for appropriate speech might also be used. Finally, if stuttering increases as anxiety increases, then relaxation training might be used.

Existentialist
In both cases, stuttering and overeating, the therapist makes no assumption about the underlying meaning of symptomatic behavior. Therapy would focus on helping the client clarify values, goals, and feelings. The client would be helped in understanding how he or she feels and would be led in a nonjudgmental, accepting atmosphere to experience those feelings in the here-and-now.

1950's, sedatives have been known for a long time. A sedative is defined as a drug that reduces anxiety and tension by inducing muscle relaxation, sleep, and inhibition of the cognitive centers of the brain. Although they do reduce severe anxiety responses, sedatives have a major disadvantage; the sedated individual cannot function well in activities involving complex cognition. The most common sedative is alcohol; others include barbiturates (a common type of sleeping pill), bromides, and chloral hydrate (also known as "knock-out" drops).

In the middle 1950's, a new group of drugs—the tranquilizers—were introduced. They had the advantage of reducing anxiety in neurotics and psychotics (as well as people under unusual stress) without the severe sleep-inducing side effect of the sedatives. Tranquilizers have become tremendously popular. Under moderate doses a person can cope with stresses of life without debilitating anxiety.

Both sedatives and tranquilizers have a major drawback that also applies to the antidepressant and antipsychotic drugs; once the person quits taking the drug, the emotional problems return. Severe dependence on tranquilizers and sedatives is far too common in our country. However, the drugs can be used effectively to help a person under transient situational stress and to help the neurotic or psychotic reduce his anxiety to the point at which he can work on his problems in therapy.

Antidepressants.   Although tranquilizers do not help individuals who are depressed, a group of

The Most Common Mental Disorder

Time—Depression is such a commonly used term and such a frequently experienced mood that there probably would have been no great national concern if it had been learned that Thomas Eagleton had merely sought medical help to shake such a state of mind. But the revelation that his condition had been considered by some doctors clinically serious enough to require electric-shock treatments twice sounded alarming. To many people, that smacks of a radical, frightening assault on the brain that would only be used in desperate circumstances. In fact, both the illness and the remedy are surprisingly commonplace. A panel of experts convened by the American Psychiatric Association to help handle press queries after Eagleton's medical history was revealed calls depression "the most common form of mental disorder." Every year doctors treat some 4,000,000 to 8,000,000 Americans for it; about 250,000 of the cases require hospitalization. No one knows how many undergo shock therapy, which, like the illness, remains in some ways mysterious. . . .

There is no clear-cut medical definition of depression (which used to be known as melancholia). No consensus exists on whether it is merely an aggravated degree of the sadness or "blues" that everyone feels at times, whether it stems from some deeply rooted inner psychological condition, or whether it has a biochemical origin in the body. Pragmatically, it tends to be defined by its symptoms: feelings of worthlessness, guilt and anxiety; an inability to find pleasure in normal activities; early-morning sleeplessness; fatigue and change of weight; and occasionally, serious consideration of suicide. When a person's feelings do not seem to be justified by his actual circumstances, and when they interfere with his functioning, he is considered ill. . . .

As practiced today, shock treatments are administered through electrodes attached to the patient's temples. A device the size of a file-card box is used to send an alternating current of about 400 milliamperes through the brain at roughly 100 volts for seven seconds (electric chairs employ a seven-ampere current at 50,000 volts). The resulting convulsion lasts less than a minute. The patient is protected by both muscle-relaxant drugs and anesthesia against one of shock treatment's early hazards: the possibility of arm or leg fractures. The patient experiences loss of recent memory when he regains consciousness, but memory returns quickly to all but elderly patients.

No one knows why the treatment helps, but it usually does. Boston Psychiatrist Robert Arnot theorizes that "when an intense, hard-driving person overdrives himself, the nervous system just won't turn off; shock turns off the mind and stops the patient from thinking about whatever it is that he is preoccupied with." Other experts suggest that the shock somehow shakes up the brain so that "things fall back into their normal places." It is largely because of the lack of scientific understanding about its workings that many psychiatrists distrust the treatment.

There has been a general decline in the use of shock therapy since the 1950s, when various antidepressant drugs such as Marplan and Thorazine came into wide use. Although their effect generally takes place more slowly, they do not present the doctor with the problem of first having to combat his patient's fear of the treatment, as in the case of shock. In treating depression, psychotherapy is always used by psychiatrists, sometimes in combination with shock or drugs. Prevailing medical sentiment seems to have shifted to the idea that shock therapy ought to be only an emergency measure or one of last resort, on the theory that psychotherapy alone can get at the underlying causes of the depression, however elusive they may be. This was not as much the case in 1960, however, when Eagleton first underwent treatment, and it has still not persuaded many doctors and hospitals.

Shock therapy in Massachusetts (1949)

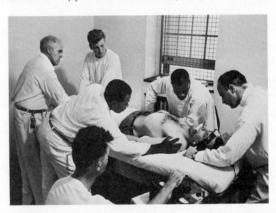

Shock treatment can be an effective method of treating depression, although many people object to the procedure because (1) it is a violent and distasteful treatment, (2) it may produce unknown changes in the brain, and (3) the reason for its effectiveness is unknown.

drugs referred to as "mood elevators," the antidepressants, are useful. The first drug discovered to have this effect was iproniazid. Originally designed for the treatment of tuberculosis, iproniazid was observed to have an unexpected side effect. The patients became less depressed and more happy about life. Other drugs belonging to the same chemical family or having similar biochemical properties were subsequently found to have some antidepressant function. Antidepressants apparently affect the amount of certain biochemical transmitters within the brain, which in turn affects synaptic transmission. Although the manufacturers claim tremendous success with antidepressant drugs, they are generally less effective for their purpose than are tranquilizers.

Antipsychotics. The first antipsychotic drug was extracted from a plant, *Rauwolfia serpentina,* mentioned in Hindu writing over 2500 years ago. The root of this plant was used in India to treat snake bites (which it did not affect), epilepsy and dysentery (which it made worse), and insomnia and insanity (which it helped). Not until the later 1940's were the therapeutic effects of this plant noticed in the Western world, and the active ingredient, called reserpine, was isolated in the early 1950's.

Although reserpine markedly helps to calm agitated psychotics, it occasionally produces undesirable side effects such as severe depression. For that reason, reserpine has largely been replaced by another group of drugs that dramatically calm agitated psychotics, the phenothiazines. The first phenothiazine to be used to treat psychosis, chlorpromazine, was, like the antidepressants, discovered by accident. It was originally used in anesthesia for surgical patients, in whom it produced profound calm before the operation. Many hospitalized psychotics have been discharged under chlorpromazine treatment, but the symptoms tend to reappear if the patient quits taking the drug.

We know relatively little about how these drugs work. However, antidepressant and tranquilizing drugs may affect a person's level of motivation by altering the process of synaptic transmission in the central nervous system. They probably also have peripheral effects, such as producing muscle relaxation. Antipsychotic drugs also affect CNS transmission and may work by inhibiting bizarre psychotic cognitions that interfere with applying more realistic knowledge and skills. Until more is known about the nature of the action of these drugs, however, we can only speculate.

Shock Therapy and Lobotomy

Two types of therapy or treatment that have become less popular since the advent of chemotherapy involve direct nervous system intervention. One of these, *frontal lobotomy,* involves cutting through nerve pathways in the frontal lobe of the brain. Different parts of the frontal lobe are cut depending on the technique. The operation usually has dramatic effects on agitated psychotics. They calm down, relax, and become more cheerful, although they still have psychotic thoughts. The main advantage of lobotomies is an administrative one. The patient is still psychotic but no longer violent, and he is therefore easier to care for (although he

150 Years in Asylum: Ohio Frees Forgotten Five

Lima, Ohio (UPI)—Five inmates of a state hospital for the criminally insane, confined for a total of 153 years and apparently forgotten by the courts, were ordered released Friday. ·

Judge David Steiner of Allen County ordered the five inmates freed after ruling they were not criminally insane as defined by Ohio law.

Dr. T. J. Reshetylo, acting director of the hospital, said there were about 100 to 150 other inmates in the hospital under the same circumstances and he hoped to have them released within a month.

Reshetylo said the five inmates ordered released were "mentally ill" but were never convicted or sentenced for the crimes with which they were charged. They were being held for observation, he said.

The five inmates were identified as Harry Haller, 71, Bert Grundy, 70, Lewis Ash, 55, Gregory Jones, 50, and Carl Kurtz, 49, all of Ohio. They have been confined from 22 to 41 years. All charges have been dropped against them.

Haller was sent to the hospital 41 years ago after he had been charged with attempted rape. Ash has been confined for 22 years after passing a bad check and Kurtz for 31 years after he admitted he stole three gallons of gasoline.

Jones was sent to the hospital 24 years ago after being charged with assault to commit rape. Grundy was confined 32 years ago after he allegedly had killed his wife.

As this article demonstrates, it is possible to be committed to a state mental hospital without trial and perhaps without being guilty!

now has irreversible brain damage). With the discovery of antipsychotic drugs, however, lobotomies were largely discontinued and today are used only in the most severe and intractable cases. Still, as we noted in Chapter 2, because drug therapy has its own weaknesses, psychosurgery may be on the upswing again.

Electroshock therapy (EST) has been demonstrated to be effective for people with particular problems and symptoms. In EST the patient is placed on a bed, given muscle relaxants, and while lightly held by attendants, is given an electric shock across the temples of sufficient intensity to produce a convulsion. The convulsion lasts up to a minute and is followed by unconsciousness for about half an hour. Although scientists do not actually know how EST works, both convulsion and resulting coma seem to be necessary for effective treatment. The patient cannot remember anything about the shock or convulsion. Surprisingly, EST has been found to be effective in reducing or eliminating depression (after several treatments), but it is not effective in treating other problems. Although the treatment may seem drastic, it can eliminate months of suffering and possibly prevent a suicide. Unfortunately, EST does not reduce the possibility of future depressions.

Hospitalization

If a person is not competent to handle everyday life requirements, if psychotherapy and/or medication do not help him to function effectively, if by his behavior he might be dangerous to himself or others, or if he needs more intensive treatment than can be provided by a therapist in his office, then hospitalization may be necessary. Each year about a quarter of a million people are admitted for the first time to mental institutions in this country. At any given time, around three-quarters of a million people are hospitalized for emotional problems—at least as many as are hospitalized for all physical illnesses combined. Fortunately, the average length of confinement today is roughly 2 weeks, a drastic reduction from earlier years. Still, 1 out of 5 will remain hospitalized for a year or more, and about 50 percent will be hospitalized again later in life.

Most of the hospitalized mental patients have been *involuntarily committed* by civil court procedures for a specific period of days or months or perhaps for an indefinite period, to be released only at the discretion of hospital officials. Commitment is a serious step and is presently quite controversial. In most states the involuntarily committed person is denied most of his civil rights; he may not be able to vote, marry, or obtain a divorce. Some states have put civil rights for patients into law, but in many states there is no protection. If a patient is disliked by the people in charge, he has few legal pathways available to him for freedom. All too frequently, the mentally ill are committed and "forgotten." Steps have been taken only recently to try to ensure that those who are committed to mental hospitals for treatment do in fact receive treatment.

A few years ago, most state mental hospitals were little more than rest homes for the emotionally disturbed, with little or no treatment. Frequently, the patient population numbered in the thousands while the professional staff was a mere handful. In recent years, we have come to realize that it is more expensive *not* to provide treatment than it is to help individuals leave the hospitals. "Back" wards, where some people spend all their lives, are becoming less

New Right to Treatment

Time—Even Alabama mental health officials admit that Tuscaloosa's Bryce Hospital is little more than an almshouse for many of its patients. All but 5% of the hospital's 4,800 patients are confined there involuntarily through civil court orders; almost half are geriatrics cases or mental retardees who receive only custodial care. The rest get scant medical treatment. Bryce is so backward that it does not even qualify for federal Medicare funds. The state spends only $6.80 a day on each patient, the second lowest (after Mississippi) such rate in the nation.

Recently a patient's guardian sued the state mental health board to protest the hospital's deficiencies. In a pioneering decision, last month, U.S. District Court Judge Frank Johnson provided a remedy. Alabama's involuntarily committed patients, he ruled, have a constitutional right to adequate medical treatment. "To deprive any citizen of his or her liberty upon the altruistic theory that the confinement is for humane therapeutic reasons," said Johnson, "and then fail to provide adequate treatment violates the very fundamentals of due process."

Though the District of Columbia Court of Appeals has issued similar rulings, Johnson's decision is the first to insist on adequate treatment for mental patients as a constitutional right. Even Alabama's mental health commissioner, Dr. Stonewall Stickney, another defendant in the suit, agreed with the decision. "I think the order is basically benevolent for the patients," said Stickney. "We feel we can live up to it."

To help Stickney keep his word, Judge Johnson has given the state six months to submit evidence that it has established appropriate treatment programs. If the state fails to take such steps, Johnson says that he will appoint a panel of mental health experts to show Alabama how to improve its dismal performance.

Therapeutic Friendship

Time—Suffering from a cancer that had left a gaping wound in her leg, 13-year-old Karen was sent home from an English hospital for a last visit with her family a few days before her expected death. Karen's mother, changing the girl's dressing, vomited over her child in horror when she saw what lay beneath the bandages. A week later, Karen died. But her mother lived on with her crushing sense of guilt that Karen's last thoughts had been of rejection. To ease her grief, the mother turned to the Society of Compassionate Friends, a rapidly growing organization that brings together parents of dead and dying children for what Founder Simon Stephens calls a therapeutic friendship.

Breached Defenses

From others in the group, Karen's mother gained what she most needed: a chance, as Stephens puts it, "to talk through her dreadful experience with a parent who had experienced something similar, so that she could begin to absolve herself of blame"—and eventually accept the loss of her child. Without the society, she probably would not have found anyone able to share her sorrow, because, he believes, society quarantines the bereaved exactly as it does people with contagious diseases.

"The death of a child was commonplace in Victorian days," explains Stephens, a curate trained in psychiatry and psychology. "Now it is so rare that we try to pretend it never happens. When it does, society turns away from those who are suffering, because their tears can breach our defenses."

Betty Edwards, a member of the Compassionate Friends, encountered those defenses. "A few weeks after my 22-year-old son was killed racing," she recalls, "a friend talked to me about everything under the sun; and I wanted to scream because she didn't mention John. She thought she was doing me a kindness, but I didn't want my son forgotten. The trouble is, most people have this little bit of fear that what has happened to your child could happen to theirs, and they don't want to face it."

This fear affects others besides friends, Stephens has discovered. He points out that doctors, unable to face the tragedy, will sometimes stop visiting an incurably ill child, and that nurses may try not to become emotionally involved. Clergymen frequently abandon bereaved mothers and fathers as soon as the funeral is over. Even close relatives, trying to be helpful, often remove every trace of the dead child—his books, clothes and toys and games—and encourage parents to forget at a time when their real need is "to work through their grief by talking incessantly and by remembering. . . ."

The society aims not just at softening grief but at preventing its most damaging results. Explains Stephens: "Parents who cannot share their sorrow sometimes come to reject their remaining children. Or they have another child in the hope of re-creating the one they have lost."

If the later child's sex is different, however, he may be rejected; in any event, he is likely to suffer from not being wanted for himself. In other families, says Stephens, a father may try so hard to "keep a stiff upper lip, because it's the British thing to do," that he shows his wife little warmth, and the marriage itself breaks down. The grief over the loss of a child is universal and inevitable. But Stephens insists that the consequences are not.

common, and antipsychotic drugs have helped to reduce patient loads. Hospitalization is now seen primarily as an aid to therapy and not a therapy itself. The federal government has a policy of trying to reduce the size of mental hospitals by keeping the afflicted person in his community, functioning as best he can under drugs if necessary and with some outpatient form of treatment. Some states are experimenting with a procedure called *voluntary commitment,* in which a person may sign himself in and out of a hospital. Under this procedure, he can be held involuntarily for only a few days at a time.

Group and Social Approaches to Emotional Problems

Group Therapy

Most of the treatment approaches discussed thus far have involved trying to help the individual in a one-to-one setting with the therapist, but since World War II, a number of different methods of group psychotherapy have become popular. Group therapy is a more efficient use of the therapist's time and talents, and it can therefore be offered with less expense to more people. The size of a group can vary from 3 to 20, although 8 to 10 seems optimal.

Group psychotherapy, moderated by an effective leader, can frequently provide a person with experiences that are difficult to duplicate in a one-to-one setting. First of all, people typically feel that their problems are unique and worse than anyone else's. In a group, people frequently find that others have similar problems. Second, a group member can get feedback from several points of view about how he affects others, and this feedback carries a weight that the therapist seldom can provide. The group can pool their own experience and encourage a member to try new solutions to problems. Third, group members frequently fulfill the needs of other people in the group. And helping someone else is often therapeutic for the helper. Finally, the individual may try out new behaviors on others in a relatively safe, accepting environment.

Sensitivity training. Some special therapeutic techniques have arisen from the group therapy movement. Among them is the *sensitivity training* group (sometimes called T-group for "training" group), which has increased in popularity since the mid-1940's. Sensitivity training originated as a series of group exercises for the business community (see Chapter 10) to improve managerial skills, human relations, and productivity. People were taught in an actual group experience how interpersonal relationships work, how to understand organizational behavior, and how to facilitate group functioning. In the clinical setting, these exercises focus on the need for interpersonal warmth and honesty and the requirement of self-disclosure for improved group functioning. T-groups serve to confront the individual with feedback about how others see him and to pressure him to change socially unacceptable interactions with others.

Encounter groups. In an *encounter group* the goal is not to work on specific problem areas of the members but rather to sensitize each member to the feelings of others. Members are placed in a face-to-face encounter under instructions to say what they feel and "pull no punches." Theoretically this procedure enables each member to experience and express his own feelings more forcefully.

The encounter group process varies tremendously from one group to the next. All encounter groups focus on here-and-now feelings, negative *and* positive feedback to each member of the group, and the removal of facades that interfere with honest, open communication. Most group leaders use a variety of techniques that are designed to make the participants communicate honestly. Some of those techniques are:

1. Self-description. Each person writes down the three adjectives most descriptive of himself. The slips of paper are mixed and the group discusses what kind of person is being described.

2. Eyeball-to-eyeball. This technique involves two participants staring into each other's eyes for a minute or two, communicating as much as possible, and discussing the feelings afterward.

3. The blind walk. All group participants pair off, and with one person leading and the other blindfolded, the "blind" person walks around the room or outdoors and sensitizes himself to the environment. One variant of this exercise is for the "blind" persons to try to communicate by touch alone.

4. Trusting exercises. Participants take turns

"Ever since his 'sensitivity training,' he's been overrelating!"

Reprinted by permission of Newspaper Enterprise Association.

being lifted and passed around a circle formed by the group members.

5. Hot seat. One group member sits in a special chair and others give him honest feedback about how he affects them.

6. Positive and negative bombardment. In this method, similar to the hot seat technique, the group member is given feedback that focuses only on positive or on negative feedback.

Some groups may not use any formal techniques at all. Instead the group is allowed to develop its own strategies for encouraging honest and open interactions.

The majority of participants in encounter groups report positive changes as a function of participation, but one study (Yalom and Lieberman, 1971) reports that 16 of 170 students who had participated in one or another of several different encounter groups reported significant psychological damage as a result of participation. Other studies also report possible psychological damage. These studies indicate that anyone entering an encounter group should be careful to choose one with an experienced, nondemanding, and open leader.

Marathon groups. A *marathon* is an encounter group in which members meet for many consecutive hours. Weekend marathons may start on Friday night and continue until Sunday night. Short breaks for eating and sleeping may be taken but usually

Copyright, 1971, G. B. Trudeau. Distributed by Universal Press Syndicate.

One overpublicized aspect of encounter groups is that the participants are encouraged to be completely frank with each other and reveal their true feelings and sometimes their innermost secrets and desires. Many participants in group encounters report that this was one of the most meaningful experiences of their lives and feel that the group experience has made them more effective individuals. On the other hand, many find no enjoyment or benefit from such experiences, and some have even suggested that the experience can be harmful to certain types of individuals. If you decide to participate in an encounter group, make sure that it is being supervised by a competent mental health professional.

only in the location of the marathon. Because the weekend defines the entire encounter for the group, there is no time for group members to be supportive and tactful toward one another. There is tremendous group pressure for self-disclosure and genuine open interactions with others. The fatigue of constant group interaction tends to break down defenses, making it more difficult to play those roles that often get in the way of honest communication and self-knowledge.

One special type of marathon therapy, *nude marathon therapy,* has received a lot of attention from the press. The idea of a group of mixed sexes interacting in an intense interpersonal encounter without wearing clothes has been seen by many in the general public as an excuse for perverted sexual behavior. However, those who have developed this technique are very serious about the therapeutic aspects. Clothes help define the roles we tend to hide behind. In addition to the rejection of some of our experiences and feelings, many individuals tend to be ashamed and nonaccepting of the physical aspects of their being. To give up one's clothes is really to be open and defenseless!

Family therapy. Many of the benefits of therapy sessions with a group of strangers hold true for that familiar group, the family. But there are other benefits of family therapy as well. In family therapy all members of a particular family meet together with a therapist to learn how to communicate honestly, to be sensitive to one another's needs, and to resolve conflicts satisfactorily. Sometimes the therapist will bring together families with similar problems, such as the families of alcoholics, who have all faced similar situations and can give one another support.

Conducting therapy with the family as a group

Hazardous Encounters

Time—At 24, Steve had a long record of success. Unusually enterprising, he was already making money at the age of 13 by importing and selling Japanese toys at Christmas time. He had done well in college and also in business, so well that he used to spend $300 for his suits and could quit work and go to California with $25,000 in ready money. While there, he decided to experiment with encounter groups at Esalen and soon became absorbed in the movement full time. He went into the "millionaires' group" where they had parties and burned $50 bills as part of their therapy. He later became a group leader, built a cabin in the mountains near by, took occasional acid trips, and wrote in his diary: "This is such a weird place . . . Somehow I'm still not dead, although for the first time in my life I've begun to look carefully at the possibility." On Feb. 9, 1971, in a craft shop on the grounds at Esalen, Steve picked up a Hawes .357 Magnum revolver and killed himself.

Steve's story, recounted in a new book, *The Encounter Game* (Stein & Day; $7.95), is one piece of the evidence assembled by Manhattan Psychotherapist Bruce Maliver to make a case against the human potentials movement. . . . Maliver, who has degrees in psychology from Yeshiva University, blames Steve's death largely on his experiences at Esalen, although he admits that the man had problems and took drugs before he went there. Arrested for possession of marijuana and chemicals for LSD, for example, Steve had spent a few days in jail.

Whether or not it is fair to blame Steve's suicide (and the six others that Maliver mentions) on encounter groups, Maliver makes a reasonably strong case that the movement often promotes "the artificial, the shoddy and the absurd" as if they were significant and holds out the "false promise of psychological nirvana." Considerable support for Maliver's view (framed in more temperate language) is to be found in *Encounter Groups: First Facts* (Basic Books; $15), written for professional readers by University of Chicago Psychologist Morton Lieberman, Stanford University Psychiatrist Irvin Yalom and State University of New York Psychologist Matthew Miles. After systematically evaluating more than a dozen varieties of encounter groups, the three scientists found that a third of the participants gained nothing, while another third reaped "negative outcomes" and in some cases sustained "significant psychological injury."

However, Lieberman, Yalom and Miles also report that a third of their subjects showed "short-run positive changes." Although the researchers believe that encounter groups sometimes offer "momentary relief from alienation," they warn that the groups can be dangerous and that their "danger is not counter-balanced by high gain."

Maliver himself admits that "there seem to be clear-cut positive effects for some participants." But he believes that "the encounter house" is badly in need of a cleanup. Although the growth centers where encounter flourishes often insist that their aim is not to treat emotional disturbances but to enrich life for normal men and women, the groups in fact attract many people in need of therapy. Nevertheless, there is rarely any screening to keep out those most likely to be harmed when buried problems surface.

Even more dangerous is the fact that most leaders, Maliver says, are either amateurs whose only "training" was their own participation in groups, or "marginally trained" professionals such as psychologists who dropped out of graduate school. These leaders are ill-equipped to deal with serious emotional problems, take no responsibility for what they do, and are unwilling to let trained investigators take a close look at their results. Their methods, moreover, tend to be either useless absurdities or destructive assaults on the often fragile psyches of encounter enthusiasts—or victims. . . .

Summing up his own view of encounter, Maliver cites a position paper issued by the American Group Psychotherapy Association. Its key statement: "A much lower incidence of adverse side effects produced by a drug would cause its immediate withdrawal from the marketplace by federal authorities."

Encounter group in action at Esalen Institute, Big Sur, Calif.

helps the therapist understand the family dynamics and patterns of interaction. It is particularly helpful in child therapy. Frequently a child who is brought to therapy by his parents or referred by the schools or a juvenile court cannot completely solve his problem until the parents face theirs. Resolution of the parental conflict may go a long way toward solving the child's problem.

Psychodrama. A technique called *role playing* is used to work through interpersonal problems in *psychodrama.* One member of the group agrees to

The Family as Patient

Time—In almost all traditional forms of psychotherapy, the patient meets alone with his therapist and is expected to tell no one—even his closest kin—about what goes on in his sessions. A major exception to that rule is family therapy, a fast-growing new specialty in which the patient is a whole family. Several relatives spanning two or three generations see their psychotherapist together for treatment, which does not always probe as deeply as individual therapy but costs less in both time and money.

Of the 1,000 or so psychiatrists, psychologists and workers in the U.S. who now practice family therapy, one of the most innovative is Psychiatrist Norman Paul of Cambridge, Mass. His theory: family troubles are frequently caused not by a generation gap but by a communication gap, which family members can bridge by sharing their innermost feelings with each other. . . .

Crippling Grief

In one case, a 39-year-old journalist named Lewis, about to divorce his wife to marry a young girl, had broken down in sobs as he recalled his grief over the death of his beloved Aunt Anna. "She was always accepting me as I am. Being with her was like peace," he explained. Reviewing his childhood sorrow as his wife listened, Lewis recognized that his girl friend represented the goal of his lifelong search for another Aunt Anna. This led him to return to his wife, now more understanding because she had shared his secret feelings.

Since then, Paul has used the Lewis tape to diagnose hidden, crippling grief in other families. A brusque father whose son William was in emotional trouble got "a feeling of being half lost" when he heard Lewis' sobs. Then, says Paul, "he recollected the time when he himself had felt intense grief"—when his father remarried. Then, Paul helped him reconstruct what he knew but had blocked off: that when he was four, his mother had killed both his nine-month-old sister and herself. Because he had repressed his sorrow instead of facing it, he had never recovered from the experience. Under Paul's guidance, he saw that he was jealous because his son still had what he himself had lost so early—a mother. That hidden jealousy, it soon became clear, was the real cause of the boy's emotional disturbance.

When divorce threatens to split a family, Paul often uses the "freeze-split technique," advising husband and wife to live apart for a while to find out what emotional problems left over from their premarriage days still need to be solved. In one instance, a woman who nearly broke up her marriage—by beginning a series of affairs just as her daughter turned four—revealed in therapy that she had lost her mother when she herself was four. To Paul, the somewhat fanciful conclusion was inescapable: the first affair "was an attempt to remove herself from her daughter just as her own mother had left her."

The reward for facing the reality of envy and other painful emotions during family therapy, Paul concludes, is "a sense of oneself, a sense of self-esteem and expectant mastery over whatever might be coming down the pike."

be the *protagonist* (the main actor in the drama), who typically describes a problem in interpersonal relationships. Other members of the group (including the therapist) play other roles in the drama, play aspects of the protagonist's personality, or merely observe as the audience. Because the situation is not real and the people with whom the protagonist is having trouble are not usually present, he feels less threatened and is capable of freer expression of feelings and greater spontaneity. Alternative solutions to problems can be tried out in the drama without danger. Not infrequently, spectators with similar problems become just as emotionally involved in the drama as the protagonist.

Group psychotherapy has become so popular that many "groups" have arisen relatively spontaneously. Individuals who have participated in a single group experience sometimes feel competent to lead another group. If nothing unusual happens the results may be minimally dangerous; however, the intensity of emotion experienced in groups generally requires an experienced leader to insure that negative experiences do not occur. A person

interested in participating in a group should get information about the level of competence of the leader before volunteering. It should go without saying that the same caution applies to all forms of psychotherapy.

Community Mental Health

The field of *community mental health* has developed out of two concerns: (1) the need for more efficient and comprehensive provision of mental health services and (2) the attempt to prevent mental illness by "treating" a community or a whole social system rather than each individual in the community.

President John F. Kennedy, just before he was assassinated in 1963, proposed to Congress that comprehensive community mental health centers be set up to provide treatment for the emotionally disturbed *within* the community. By so doing, Kennedy shifted the focus away from treatment in state hospitals, which were originally built in isolated rural areas usually miles away from the home of the disturbed individual. Under President Lyndon B. Johnson, the Comprehensive Community Mental Health Centers Act was passed, providing federal aid to states for the construction of community mental health centers. The centers were required to provide short-term hospitalization; outpatient care, usually traditional psychotherapy; 24-hour emergency service, including suicide prevention and crisis therapy; day care for people who need a structured setting during the day but can return home at night; night care for people who need a sheltered place to stay at night but can work at jobs during the day; and consultation to community agencies.

Although community mental health centers have not eliminated the need of many individuals for long-term care in a state or other hospital, they have provided more convenient treatment and a wider range of services than was previously available. Ultimately, these centers aim at broadening their activities so they can intervene in community crises before emotional disturbances occur. One center, for example, has already been able to prevent a potential race riot by sending a team of crisis workers into a school riddled by racial disturbances.

Community mental health programs tend to divide into three kinds of services: primary, secondary, and tertiary.

Primary services.

Primary services (often referred to as primary prevention) are directed toward eliminating the basic causes of a problem. The eradication of poverty and disease, of racial discrimination and injustice, and of other stresses might be taken as examples of primary prevention, for these conditions are probably significantly involved in the incidence of emotional problems. The theory of primary prevention is that by identifying potential crises in a person's life and preparing him in advance to handle these crises, abnormal reactions can be prevented. It is in primary prevention that the most important gains can be made in the control of psychopathology, but very little work toward this end is being done in our society as yet.

Secondary services.

In *secondary services* (also called secondary prevention) the focus is on existing psychopathological problems. Traditional psychotherapy is the major form of secondary treatment, although other approaches designed to help a wider group of people have evolved in the community mental health movement. *Crisis intervention* is an example of one of these more recent approaches. A *crisis* can be defined as a point in a person's life that is unusually stressful and may be handled in a maladaptive way. Crisis intervention is based on the assumption that a

© Punch (Rothco).

Psychologists do a great deal of marriage counseling. Many states, by the way, restrict the use of the word *psychologist* to licensed graduates of approved programs. As a result, many "therapists" call themselves marriage counselors. When seeking help, one should consult the local mental health association for the names of qualified practitioners.

person can best be helped when there is an immediate crisis in his life, when his marriage or romance has just broken up, for example. At this time a person is more willing to accept help from a mental health worker and is able to change more in a shorter period of time. Crisis therapy involves helping the person define the immediate problem and seek alternative solutions to it, because people panic when they see no way out of the problems they are facing. Crisis therapy tends to be more directive and confrontative than traditional insight therapy. Receiving short-term psychotherapy during crisis situations can frequently prevent the need for hospitalization, medication, or psychotherapy at other times in life. Students who are in danger of flunking out of school, individuals who have lost their jobs, or people in any of a thousand other crisis situations may need a therapist for four or five sessions to help them over that crisis, although they can function normally at other times.

A specific example of crisis intervention is *suicide prevention.* In many cities across the country, phone numbers are available that will connect a potentially suicidal person with a counselor at a suicide prevention center who will help him find solutions to his problems. Prevention centers are effective because people who are suicidal usually are ambivalent about dying, wanting to die but also wanting to live. It is well known that most people who are considering killing themselves communicate these feelings either in their behavior or by talking about suicide sometime before any attempt is made. Finally, suicide attempts occur when a person is in a crisis and therefore is more receptive to help.

One of the first things a suicide prevention counselor will try to do when on the phone with a suicidal person is to determine the risk. The following factors help determine how likely death is:

1. Age. The older the person the greater the risk of death. The exception is among male blacks, for whom the greatest risk is from age 20 to 24.

2. Sex. Men are about 3 times as likely to commit suicide as women, although women are about 3 times as likely to attempt suicide as men.

3. Plan for suicide. The more specific the plan and the more deadly the method, the greater the risk. Guns are a greater danger than pills or wrist cutting.

4. Resources. People who have fewer resources to turn to for help in a crisis are a greater risk for suicide. Those who are isolated from family, relatives, and friends and are not in a position to turn to physicians or clergymen for support and help are a greater risk. Divorced people have a suicide rate 3 to 4 times the national average.

If the risk of death is high, the counselor will be more active in trying to intervene. If the risk is low, the counselor will first try to establish a relationship over the phone in order to maintain contact and obtain information. The counselor first tries to communicate interest and optimism about finding a solution to the crisis. The second step is to identify and clarify problems. The suicidal person is often confused and unsure as to precisely what problems he faces. At this point alternative solutions to the problem might be suggested. The resources of the person will be taken into account and attempts will be made to bring the person in contact with mental health professionals within the community.

In an attempt to make mental health services more available to the poor, *storefront clinics* or outreach centers have been set up in the middle of poverty areas. These clinics are usually staffed by people from the community who act as problem solvers, sympathetic listeners, and community facilitators. Trying to obtain services from community agencies, for example, can be very frustrating if a person does not know what is available, which agency is appropriate, and what the eligibility requirements are. Sometimes mental health professionals work in conjunction with community service programs such as Model Cities.

Tertiary services.   *Tertiary services* (also called tertiary prevention) are concerned with the aftereffects of having emotional problems. This type of treatment is generally referred to as *rehabilitation.* People who have had severe emotional problems may have lost their job or family and need counseling to get back into the community. This may involve job training, counseling as to how to get a job, and development of social skills.

Social Action

As we have seen, psychologists have strong feelings about possible changes in the structure of society that could reduce the frequency of mental disorder and mental suffering, as well as correct social wrongs. However, such changes may involve expensive programs that the taxpayer is not willing to support, and there is frequently disagreement about the type of changes needed. Not infrequently a redistribution of power is required and those in power are not willing to give it up. Because a political activist orientation implies the direct confrontation of incompatible social values, such activities are controversial, and an activist orientation is not shared by all mental health professionals. However, almost all mental health professionals *are* concerned about social change.

Some psychologists have been active in redefining for society what is abnormal. Several states have removed or are considering removing laws pertaining to sexual behavior between consenting adults, because there is no victim and no crime. Homosexuality would then no longer be a crime. Psychologists have tried to institute changes in the punishment techniques used in prisons on the basis of modern reinforcement principles. Some have tried to remove bail as a requirement for release from prison prior to trial. The belief is that the poor should not be penalized by imprisonment simply because they cannot pay bail.

In the schools some psychologists concerned with social change have worked, not to produce a better curriculum content, but to change the focus of teaching from the memorization of facts to the process of problem solving. Working in such areas of concern is frustrating, however, because large institutions build up considerable inertia and change very slowly.

What Does It Mean?

What Is It Like to Be in Therapy?

Once a person has decided that he needs help to straighten out his life, he has to do something about

Families for Psychotics

Time—Most mental health specialists think that there is no alternative to hospitalizing psychotics and other mentally disturbed patients whose actions endanger others—and often themselves. Honolulu Psychologist Patrick DeLeon takes an entirely different view. "The worst thing you can do to a patient," he says, "is admit him to a hospital." Instead, DeLeon has a theory which advocates placing small groups of chronic mental patients in "family living units" in which they live as brothers and sisters in rented private apartments, hold jobs if they can, and solve day-to-day problems with almost no outside guidance.

Last week, at a convention of the American Psychological Association in Honolulu, DeLeon described his own experiment with five "families" that consisted of some of the "worst patients* he and his colleagues had encountered at Hawaii State Hospital and other institutions. Most of them had been hospitalized from one to eleven times and seemed in need of recommitment when DeLeon suggested to them that they might prefer a house to a hospital.

The patients were given food for the first weekend, but no support beyond that. They were told that money to pay living expenses would have to come from welfare, savings accounts and any jobs that they managed to find and hold. They got no advice except the admonition that "families should solve their own problems." For the first month, hospital staffers usually visited them twice a week; then the visits dropped to about one a week and finally to one a month.

At first, real and fantasied crises led the "brothers and sisters" to make frantic telephone calls to the hospital therapists. In one instance, when they asked what to do about a family member who was running around the house waving a knife, they were simply advised: "Do whatever you think right. Call the cops if necessary." Says DeLeon: "No one ever got hurt. Once a guy got drunk and

busted up the whole house. The police picked him up, let him out the next day, and he went back and repaired the house." Eventually, each group took to solving most of its own difficulties. They held family councils and adopted a policy of talking things out with each other before crises could erupt.

After a year, only one family member had been rehospitalized, and then only for a few days on two occasions. The rest stayed out of real trouble, and some even gained so much confidence that they moved into apartments of their own. One woman, proud of her new stability, recently wrote DeLeon, "I just got an A in a religion course at the community college. Next semester I'm taking two courses."

The theory behind the idea for the experiment, which was originally proposed not by a professional but by a hospital aide, is that chronic mental patients are dependent personalities who do not have much motivation to change their behavior as long as they have other people to look after them. DeLeon's goal was not to cure their dependence but to transfer it to the family group. "Once you switch your attitude toward these people and assume they are in control of themselves," he says, "they no longer go out of control."

*Included in the group were an alcoholic drug addict, a suicidal male homosexual and psychotics of several types.

Institutionalism, as we have seen, refers to the tendency of patients in a mental hospital to give up trying to learn to cope with their problems and accept the passive life of the institution. This article describes a community-oriented approach aimed at getting mental patients out of the hospital and into an environment where they have to accept responsibility.

it. Unfortunately, in many cases in which the problem is severe, it is someone else who decides that the individual needs treatment and involuntary commitment is sought. Indeed, some people have the misconception that one must be obviously psychotic or nonfunctioning before it is legitimate to ask for help. Actually, just the desire to *change* is sufficient reason to seek professional help. Dissatisfaction with his present existence was the client's motivation in the following case:

This [psychotherapy] is something I've been thinking about for a long time. I've known that it was something I've needed and wanted, but I just haven't done anything about it. Recently though, I've been realizing more than ever that I'm just not the way I want to be. I'm not sure what I am, and I'm not sure I want to know, but I sure don't like this. I'm not even

sure what I want to be—sometimes it's one thing, sometimes something quite different. I don't know where I am or where I'm going, but I've at last decided to try to find out. **(Fitts, 1965, page 16)**

It can, of course, be frightening to ask a strange person for help with one's problems, taking a chance that he will understand and not criticize or consider the problem trivial. Finally, the client must feel that he can trust the therapist, or he surely will not be frank and open with him. The client in the following case was probably not ready to benefit from therapy until he got over some of his initial doubts about therapy and the therapist:

The first few visits I felt uneasy, tearful, embarrassed, ashamed, guilty, and depressed, and constantly reminded myself: "surely I could have done better than this; why did this have to happen to me?" What does my Doctor think of me? How could he know what I'm going through? Why should he care? Why should he spend his time with me? (Someone else maybe, but I should be capable of straightening this out myself!)

As I sat in that chair choked with emotion, and ashamed that I was, it was hard for me to say anything. When I did have a feeling and wanted to express it, it was so vague I couldn't find the words. After these sessions of saying so little, I felt like I wasn't getting anywhere, and was wasting the Doctor's time. I wanted the therapist to be proud of me. What he thought of me was always important. **(Fitts, 1965, page 26)**

Therapy is difficult under the best of circumstances. There are times when the process of trying to understand oneself can be almost physically painful, and the effort is always tiring. People develop feelings of anger and affection for the therapist that can get in the way of clear thinking. Sometimes people get annoyed at the one-sided nature of the relationship, for the client learns little or nothing about the therapist. If therapy takes a long time, a person can become bitter about it. His high hopes, unfulfilled, make for considerable disappointment. It is known that some therapists can never empathize with some clients. Therefore, to prevent extreme disappointment, it is best to try several therapists before giving up therapy as a way of solving one's problems.

How Effective Is Psychotherapy?

In the early 1950's, Hans Eysenck challenged psychology to demonstrate whether psychotherapy was effective or not. In summarizing 19 experimental studies involving 7,000 cases of psychoanalytic and nonpsychoanalytic types of treatment (behavior modification had not become popular at that time), Eysenck concluded that people who did not receive psychotherapy (but who may have gotten custodial care or care by a general practitioner) improved as much as or more than those who underwent psychotherapy! Using successful social and work adjustment as the criterion, Eysenck found that 66 percent of the patients who completed psychoanalysis improved, 64 percent of those who received nonpsychoanalytic therapy improved, and those who received no formal psychotherapy improved at the rate of 72 percent (Eysenck, 1952).

As you can imagine, Eysenck's report was a blow to mental health professionals, since it seemed to demonstrate that psychotherapy was useless. Subsequently, however, it became clear that there

"Because of you, my darling, I've never had an ulcer. I've never needed a psychiatrist. When I poured out my troubles, you listened. When I ranted and raved, you listened. Thank you, my angel, for listening."
"Who listened?"

New Yorker, June 5, 1971. Drawing by Frascino; © 1971 The New Yorker Magazine, Inc.

Many psychologists feel that much good "psychotherapy" is done by close friends and relatives who simply listen. When personal problems are not too serious or disturbing, such "therapy" may be very helpful. Just having someone to talk to who will not be highly critical and rejecting can be very comforting in times of stress. Cynics have even characterized psychotherapy as "the purchase of friendship."

were several things wrong with Eysenck's conclusions. First, the people who improved without formal psychotherapy were frequently receiving help from some other source. Second, people who seek help are different from those who do not, and there is some evidence to suggest that those who seek help are the kind of people who do not improve without it. In several respects, such as severity of problems, Eysenck's treatment and nontreatment groups were not comparable. Also, he used different criteria of improvement for the two groups. Finally, some kinds of problems simply do not get better without professional intervention; for example, the symptoms of neurosis do not commonly disappear spontaneously. It is apparent, however, that many people improve without the aid of a psychotherapist. Those who conclude that nearly everyone needs a

Mental "Patients" Don't Like Treatment

By C. G. McDaniel, AP science writer

Elgin, Ill. (AP)—"Just because I was sick," the young woman asked, "did this mean I had to be treated like an animal?"

The woman, Christine Ruiz, is a mental health worker. She posed her question after spending a weekend recently as a "patient" at Elgin State Hospital. The weekend was an experiment to show mental hospital employes what it is like to be one of their charges.

"So many times I was ignored just as if I didn't exist," Miss Ruiz said. "The lost identity and dehumanizing, inferior feeling is all felt by the patients and so forgotten by the staff."

Twenty-nine employes were selected at random to be "patients" in a mock ward. Another 21 were selected to staff the ward. Observers took notes and filmed the proceedings.

The "patients" went through regular admitting procedures and were given showers and issued ill-fitted clothing. They were searched and all personal belongings were confiscated.

They ate in a dining room with actual mental patients.

The "staff" treated the "patients" just as they would treat patients in their wards. They gave tokens as rewards and took away tokens as punishment.

Interviews afterward showed the experience was realistic and often frightening. A questionnaire filled out by participants also demonstrated its realism.

"It was scary to me," said Nancy Klein, a DePaul University sociologist who was an advisor to the experiment. She said she feared the employees who became "patients" would regress in their behavior.

The patients were anxious, angry and restless. Dr. Donahue Tremaine, a Roosevelt University psychology professor who was an advisor, said the experiment also showed mental hospitals can cause people to react in ways which are considered abnormal.

The observers said the "patients":—Sat together but did not react to each other.

—Lied and cheated to get what they needed.

—Complained of having no place to be alone.

—Moved about constantly to reassure themselves that "everything is OK because I can feel something happening."

Tom Richardson, a hospital psychologist who helped design the experiment, said: "It has gotten people to see ways to change some things."

One "patient," who complained about the "horrible soap," lack of privacy and noise in the ward, said after the experiment:

"My God, my God. If it's that bad in our own wards we ought to run back right now and fix it."

"I don't think I've screamed at a patient since I got back," one woman said. And now, no matter how ridiculous the patient's request, she said, she has tried to honor it.

Steve Piser, a "patient" who escaped several times during the experiment, told an interviewer he did it because "things just got a little intense." For him, "the atmosphere changed from hospital to jail."

Sandra Kinser, a worker who as a "patient" became "extremely depressed and upset," said one of the first things she noticed was a "fantastic loss of energy."

"It took a great deal of effort just to walk to lunch," she said. "A lot of things I used to attribute to paranoid problems in patients are real. I now understand why people don't have feelings."

Steve Wendorf, a "staff" member in the experiment, said all mental health workers, including administrators, would benefit from having to be "patients." Training programs for mental health workers should include a program patterned after the experiment, he said.

A questionnaire answered by the "patients" after the experiment showed that 75 per cent did not feel they were being treated as real people.

All said they especially felt a lack of freedom, 89 per cent said they felt at times that they were being deprived of their identity and 93 per cent said they felt as though they were in prison.

Frequently staff members do not realize the effects of hospitalization on mental patients. Having mental health professionals spend a weekend in a hospital as patients is an excellent idea. Perhaps more guards and wardens should spend a weekend as prison inmates.

therapist sometime in his life are vastly underrating the ability of people to solve their own personal problems, although often with the help of relatives and of close friends.

People use different criteria for "cure" in therapy. The psychoanalyst will evaluate whether transference is resolved, the Rogerian will look at the quality of expression of feelings and experiencing, and the behavior modifier will be concerned with changes in the specific behavior that led to the request for therapy. So it is difficult to find a simple criterion for improvement for all kinds of therapy. Why not ask the client himself if he is better? The following evaluation of psychotherapy by a client indicates several criteria of improvement he considered important, such as reduction of anxiety in certain situations, a decreased dependence on relaxants, and increased self-knowledge:

I am much more at ease among groups of people than I was before my therapy. I now feel capable of accomplishing certain goals which I formerly regarded as desirable, but unattainable, dreams. I rarely need tranquilizers (or beer) to cope with tension.

I feel confident, have no guilt feeling and feel very capable and have a deeper rich meaning to life as a result of psychotherapy.

I have accepted "me." I know now everyone experiences anxiety and uses an individual mechanism to accommodate this. I understand my own particular pattern and can adjust accordingly. **(Strupp, Fox, and Lessler, 1969, page 69)**

Even more objective criteria, such as job advancement and ability to make decisions, are used by the following client:

I do not feel so gloomy, worried, and undecided as I did before. I am more self-confident, and I have gained much strength in standing for what I think best.

1. Ability to accept myself. 2. Ability to accept others and try to understand them. 3. Ability to give and accept love. 4. Willingness to try new things. 5. Development of confidence and independence (found a job, have been steadily advanced in job since—and I make decisions during a day without consulting husband). **(Strupp, Fox, and Lessler, 1969, page 69)**

A common problem that shades the client's evaluation of his therapy is the *hello-goodbye effect.* When the client says "hello" to the therapist at the beginning of therapy, he presents himself as unhappy and troubled; in fact, he may exaggerate to convince the therapist he is really "sick." At the end of the therapy, the "goodbye" effect is apt to occur. The client tries to present himself as strongly improved in order to resolve any dissonance about wasting his time and money and to express appreciation to the therapist for his efforts. Thus it would be easy to mistake the *hello-goodbye effect* for real improvement, although the effect did not seem to enter into the client's evaluation of his therapy in the following case:

I have experienced a few changes, both positive and negative, since leaving psychotherapy, but I do not believe the changes resulted from the psychotherapy experience. In the four years since psychotherapy, I have proven to myself that I can make it on my own, financially at least; and this has given me a measure of self-confidence. My job brings me into contact with many people, and I have learned to be less self-conscious and more at ease in dealing with people. On the other hand, I have made no progress

Mental Illness Needs Multiple Factor Approach

Biomedical News—Scientists with the Yale University Medical School have concluded that no single factor can serve as a reliable criterion for the success of treatment for mental illness.

Working under the small grants program of the National Institute of Mental Health in the Department of Health, Education, and Welfare, Drs. Kenneth Keniston, Sandra Boltax, and Richard Almond studied 65 psychotic or severely depressed patients admitted to the inpatient service of the Yale-New Haven Hospital.

Each patient was evaluated at admission, discharge, and 15 months after discharge following treatment which consisted primarily of milieu therapy.

Nurses, psychiatrists, social workers, and others involved in the treatment process were found to be greatly influenced by how well the patient adapted to expected hospital attitudes and behavior.

While such changes could be a genuine reflection of improvement, the researchers said, they also could have been feigned to expedite discharge; on the other hand, the ability to recognize and pretend to adopt staff values also could be a sign of improvement.

Improvement ratings by staff were based more on patient condition prior to discharge than on the degree of change since admission, the study found.

Improvement ratings frequently had little or no bearing on the patient's condition at the time of the long-term followup.

An outside interviewer's ratings were found to be influenced by how cooperative the patient was during the interview; extent to which the hospital stay was regarded as a positive experience; ease of contacting the patient for a followup interview, and the extent to which the patient felt the hospital experience had changed his views about life, himself, and the world.

Unfortunately, the scientists noted, these attitudes appeared unrelated to objective measures of functioning.

socially. Four more years of anxieties and frustrations concerning my original symptoms have added bitterness, sadness, and a growing feeling of hopelessness to an already pessimistic outlook on life. **(Strupp, Fox, and Lessler, 1969, page 109)**

The ideal situation would seem to be to determine the type of therapy that is most effective for each type of problem and refer people to the appropriate therapist, much in the same way that a physician writes a prescription for an illness. However, there is as yet little evidence that the various insight-oriented therapies differentially help different problems. Although there may be differences not yet found in research, present evidence suggests that all therapies tend to help the same types of problems.

(The single exception worth noting is that psychoanalysis has not been particularly effective in treating phobias.) Behavior modification has been demonstrated to be effective with phobias and anxiety states in which there is a specific anxiety-provoking stimulus. Typical reports suggest that as many as 90 percent of clients with such problems are helped with systematic desensitization or implosion. The learning of new responses is aided by instrumental conditioning, but the levels of improvement are not as high. As behavior modification techniques have been extended and applied to more complex problems, such as very diffuse anxiety, the improvement rate has not been as high. Thus, it is apparent that the question of the best therapy for a particular problem is still far from being resolved.

Psychotherapy—a Stigma?

Many personnel questionnaires ask if a person has ever been in psychotherapy or hospitalized for psychiatric reasons. The act of asking such a question prior to the decision of hiring someone raises some serious questions about the attitude of employers toward mental illness. Many people are embarrassed about seeking help from a "shrink" and avoid at all costs letting anyone know about it. Others seem perfectly comfortable telling anyone interested that they are in therapy. People differ in their acceptance of the information that someone is in therapy and make different judgments about the person as a result of that knowledge. A naive individual might assume that a person in psychotherapy is crazy or unpredictable and therefore would be nervous in that person's presence. A "self-made" individual might look with distain on a person who was not able to work out problems on his own. One who understands therapy might admire a person in psychotherapy for having the courage to face up to his problems and the energy to work them out. For some, psychotherapy might even be a source of prestige—the client can brag about having someone who will listen and care about him.

What Kind of Therapist Is Best?

For some reason there has been little research isolating the personality characteristics of good therapists. Many training programs in clinical psychology place considerable weight on intellectual attributes such as grade and test scores in deciding which applicants to accept for training. But do high intelligence and outstanding grades mean that a person will make a good therapist? Most of us

Psychiatric "Stigma" Is Feared in Reports

By Arthur J. Snider
© 1974, Denver Post-Chicago Daily News
Chicago—Psychiatric patients are becoming concerned that their privacy is being violated by disclosure of their medical records in group health-insurance plans, a psychiatrist said Wednesday.

Dr. Melvin W. Seglin said an increasing number of patients are asking whether their visit to a psychiatrist will appear on their company personnel record. They fear job security or a chance for advancement will be impaired.

"Patients may be treated for a transitory situational stress, for marital problems or for problems unrelated to their work capabilities," said Seglin, of suburban Skokie.

"Yet it is possible that the stigma they fear as a consequence of having the insurance report presented to their employer is real and not merely to be dismissed as evidence of paranoia."

He called on the medical profession to insist that an employer should not participate in any way in the processing of individual claims.

The psychiatrist's comments appeared in a letter in American Medical News, published by the American Medical Association.

A check of corporation personnel departments in Chicago showed great effort is made to maintain confidentiality of a patient's treatment under health insurance plans.

Even minor paper work like insurance claims for psychotherapy can be a source of violation of confidentiality. The strong need for keeping such records confidential reflects a growing concern about how information pertaining to a person's therapy would be interpreted by others.

would agree that other personality characteristics are also crucial to the effectiveness of a therapist. Even in the case of behavior modification therapies, which in some sense seem pretty impersonal, therapist "warmth" probably plays a role in determining the effectiveness of therapy.

It is clear that therapists do differ widely in their success rates. One factor contributing to this variability is the amount of experience the therapist has. It has been found that effectiveness in establishing an ideal therapeutic relationship with the client increases with experience. In fact, experience is a much more important factor in a therapist's success than the school of therapy to which the therapist belongs.

In addition, three personality characteristics of the therapist (all derived from Rogers' theory of therapy, see Chapter 9) seem to be important for positive change in therapy: *accurate empathy, nonpossessive warmth,* and *genuineness.* Accurate empathy means that the therapist is sensitive to the feelings of the client and is able to communicate that awareness to him. Nonpossessive warmth is basically caring for the client as a person without demanding changes in feelings and experiences as a precondition to acceptance. Genuineness is defined as a lack of defensiveness on the part of the therapist, who must present himself in an uncontrived, honest way. In one study it was shown that when therapists ranked low on the three characteristics, a 50 percent rate of improvement in their clients was found, but when therapists ranked high on the three personality characteristics, a 90 percent rate was found. The combined rate of 70 percent for the two groups is near the level of improvement found by Eysenck for untreated controls (Truax et al., 1966).

An interesting hypothesis regarding the relationship between personality and therapeutic effectiveness is that certain personality characteristics may make a therapist ideally suited to treat one type of behavioral disorder but poorly suited for treating other types of disorders. Many therapists realize this implicitly and will refer clients who have problems with which they have had little success to therapists who have had better results in treating such cases. The most actively researched hypothesis along these lines is called the *A-B variable hypothesis,* suggested by Whitehorn and Betz in 1954. "A" therapists were operationally defined as those who had the highest "success" rates with schizophrenics, while "B" therapists were those who did poorly in treating schizophrenics. In later studies comparing the effectiveness of the two types of therapists in treating neurotic disorders, the Bs tended to do better.

In assessing the personality characteristics of the A's and B's, the following has been suggested: A's are more trusting and tolerant of the client, more personally involved with the client, less coercive, and more flexible in helping the client to define acceptable behavior (they give the client more leeway). The B therapists are stricter in defining right and wrong, tend to see things more in black and white terms, and are more rigid about making the client conform to "socially acceptable" norms of behavior.

It is still too early to tell if the A-B variable is crucially important, but enough data have accumulated to suggest strongly that it is, although many methodological problems exist in these studies. It does seem fair to conclude that A therapists "get along" better with schizophrenic

". . . and I'd like something nice for my therapist."

APA Monitor, December 1971. Reprinted by permission of Al Johns.

patients and may thus be better equipped to persuade them to change their behavior. The main lesson to be learned, however, is that therapist characteristics are probably very important and that different characteristics may be desirable for handling different types of disorders. A great deal of additional research must be done, however, before psychologists can conclusively advise someone to seek out a particular personality type when looking for a therapist. At the present time clients select a therapist on a rather random basis, by asking a friend or looking in the phone book, or they are assigned to the therapist who happens to be free when they come to a mental health center or hospital.

Shortage of Therapists

There are simply not enough therapists to aid everyone who needs psychological help, and the population is growing faster than the number of psychologists and psychiatrists. Thus the movement toward community mental health has developed, as well as other alternative ways of providing help to those who need it. One approach that has developed out of the community mental health orientation to problems has been the use of *paraprofessionals.* Paraprofessionals are interested individuals in the community who can with a minimum of training serve as temporary therapists. Housewives, bartenders, and beauticians have successfully served this role. Individuals from poor neighborhoods, ghettos, and foreign-language-speaking areas of a city are all frequently alienated from the middle-class,

New Mental Health Program: They Tell It to Bartenders and Beauticians

By Theodore Irwin, Bismarck, N. Dak.
Parade—In most American communities, people with emotional problems can go to a psychiatrist. But in North Dakota, with only 19 psychiatrists in the entire state, this is not always feasible.

To help solve the problem, the state's Mental Health Association has enlisted the aid of bartenders and beauticians (the nation's unpaid psychiatrists).

Says Sally Speidel, who runs Sally's Beauty Boutique in Bismarck: "A woman may be in our stylist chair for an hour and a half. All this time she is usually unburdening herself by confiding in the beautician."

"A bartender," says Ken Habiger, who owns the Red Baron Lounge here, "can sense that a customer is begging for help. The guy may become belligerent, start an argument, but sooner or later, he'll tell the bartender what's wrong."

As a board member of the Mental Health Association, it was Habiger who suggested last year that the Association reach out to bartenders as "mental health helpers."

Bartenders Coached
The association explained the idea to bartenders, and provided them with "Help" booklets listing agencies for referral, including social service centers, alcoholism clinics, and the like. Over 60 bartenders became involved.

Meanwhile, Mrs. Gerridee Wheeler, Association president at the time, was in the beauty parlor one morning for a manicure when she overheard an operator advising another woman who was having marital problems.

With the bartending experiment fresh in mind, Mrs. Wheeler was struck with an idea. Why not beauticians, too?

"Troubled people are usually reluctant to go directly for professional aid," she explains, "perhaps because they feel it creates a stigma. I thought we should use trained citizens who are in constant contact with people as a bridge or conduit into available services. They could encourage those in distress to get the help they need."

In the case of beauticians, however, Mrs. Wheeler went about things a little differently, by approaching the state's 12 beauty colleges and urging them to provide training in mental health care. North Dakota Governor William L. Guy did his part, writing a letter to the state Board of Hair-

dressers in which he called for "broader understanding of mental health problems."

To Help Customers
As a result, students at all 12 colleges now take a week-long intensive training course in how to be "mental health helpers." In addition, Mrs. Joyce Robson, an experienced beautician and one of the instructors, plans courses for already-licensed operators. As for the bartenders, they were sufficiently impressed by the beauticians' experience to institute training sessions of their own. Soon they will meet on holidays to listen to a psychiatrist, a priest who does counseling, and a recovered alcoholic who teaches on a college faculty.

The idea, of course, is not to replace the psychiatrist's couch with a barstool or beautician's chair. Mental health helpers are reminded, however, that "you can do a lot of good by guiding patrons, and encouraging them to get professional help if they seem to need it. . . ."

Projects Praised
Already, North Dakota has received awards from the American Psychiatric Association and the Department of Health, Education and Welfare for its pioneering achievements in mental health. Moreover, its approach may catch on. Inquiries have come in from 15 states, and the National Institute of Mental Health (NIMH) has filmed training sessions at Bismarck's beauty colleges.

How come North Dakota, one of our most rural states, is setting the pace for the rest of the country? The answer, says Mrs. Wheeler, is citizen involvement. "We've made mental health so exciting," she declares, "it's caught the imaginations of volunteers all over our state."

To which NIMH official Herbert L. Rooney adds: "We're beginning to recognize that people are a natural resource for helping other people."

---

traditionally trained clinician. Paraprofessionals can communicate with these people better and are more aware of the cultural pressures surrounding them. Paraprofessionals are particularly useful in crisis intervention and community action.

One of the more recent interesting attempts to compensate for the shortage of therapists is the use of computers. Although the definition of the problem usually requires a skilled clinician, once the problem

is defined, many behavior modification approaches are relatively automatic. It is possible to program a computer to provide rewards and punishments in a systematic desensitization routine in much the same way that a programmed textbook or computer-assisted instruction works. A human therapist has to construct the hierarchy of anxiety-provoking situations, but the list can then be turned over to the computer, which will teach a person how to relax. Although lacking the warmth, genuineness, and empathy of the effective insight-oriented therapist, computers do work with some people. Instrumentally and classically conditioned problems can probably also be treated with computer-assisted psychotherapy. Psychology is just beginning to explore alternative means of helping people, and many scientists are working hard to develop more efficient means of providing help.

Where Do We Stand?

If you view these two chapters on psychopathology and psychotherapy superficially, you might arrive at the following oversimplified view. The clinical psychologist, confronted with a case of behavior disorder, first makes a diagnosis of the disorder, then applies a treatment or a therapy (psychotherapy) to remove the disorder or "cure" it, and finally helps his patient resume his normal activities within the community. In other words, the procedure appears quite similar to the medical model of treating physical illness (diagnosis-treatment-cure-rehabilitation)—a nice, neat, and simple picture. However, the picture is not nearly so neat in reality, and we would like to close this chapter by emphasizing that fact.

In Chapter 11 we saw that diagnostic classification is a difficult task, and clinical psychologists frequently disagree about diagnoses in particular cases. More important, we saw that with present knowledge of psychopathology, psychologists are rarely certain of the causes or "cure" for a particular disorder, even if they have been able to agree on what to call it. In this chapter we have seen that there are many different types of psychotherapy and that each type can be applied to a wide variety of diagnostic categories. Any particular therapist is likely to be "sold" on one school of thought in which he is a highly skilled and knowledgeable student. He then applies this method of therapy to just about all the cases he encounters. However, the state of the psychotherapeutic art is such that mental health professionals cannot now claim that they are doing an outstanding job in treating many kinds of behavioral disorders.

But there are some promising trends emerging that we would like to highlight in this concluding comment. First, as we stated in Chapter 11, there is much less emphasis today on the problem of diagnostic classification—the psychologist now attempts to determine what the client's problems are and does not worry too much about being able to fit each client into a neat category of mental "illness." Second, psychotherapists are more likely today to

be trained in a variety of techniques than they were 10 years ago. The hope is for more adaptable behavior *on the part of the therapist* in the future. Third, the new methods of behavior modification have great promise for specific disorders, and more and more psychologists are becoming sophisticated in the application of these techniques. Fourth, we see a greater realization among psychologists of the fact that traditional psychotherapy is not the answer to every problem for several reasons—it costs too much, it cannot be given to enough people, not everyone benefits from it, and the delivery system as it now stands discriminates unfairly. As a result of all these factors, we see a fifth trend emerging—a trend away from individual psychotherapy delivered after someone has developed a disorder to a community mental health system oriented around preventive mental health, crisis intervention, short-term psychotherapy, and minimal hospitalization. We see the continuing rise of community psychology with its attempts to delineate and attack the social-cultural sources of behavioral disorders.

We do not mean to conclude that psychology will shortly discover all the answers to mental illness. We do mean to suggest, however, that the next 20 years will result in more progress than the last 20 years. We do not feel that this progress will necessarily consist of the discovery of great new "cures" for neurosis (although we would hope that this would be the case for the psychotic disorders). Rather, we expect there to be an entirely new set of working assumptions about mental health, and we expect these assumptions to conflict dramatically with the "diagnosis-treatment-cure" model that has characterized the work of the clinical psychologist for such a long time.

Summary

1. Psychotherapy is defined as a corrective experience leading a person to behave in a socially appropriate way.

2. The therapist's behavior is guided by his model of psychopathology (e.g., medical, dynamic, behavioral, ethical, or existential) and professional ethics.

3. The types of psychotherapy can be divided into two broad categories: insight-oriented therapy, focusing on change in motivation and self-knowledge, and noninsight-oriented therapy (behavior therapy), focusing on change in motivation and skill.

4. Insight-oriented therapy assumes that emotional problems stem from conflicts between conscious and unconscious processes. The two

major types are those focusing on repressed memories of the past, such as psychoanalysis and primal therapy, and those focusing on denied aspects of present experiences, such as client-centered therapy, Gestalt therapy, and transactional analysis.

5. In classical psychoanalysis, the patient, lying on a couch to reduce external stimuli, is asked to free associate, to say anything and everything that comes to mind. Dream interpretation and interpretation of slips of the tongue help the therapist evaluate the contents of the unconscious mind.

6. The resolution of the transference, in which the patient treats the therapist like other significant people in his life, is a major goal of psychoanalysis.

7. Primal therapy focuses on the release of blocked pain due to perceived rejection by the parents. The expression of this pain leads to the primal scream.

8. Client-centered psychotherapy has as its focus helping the client move from denial of certain feelings and experiences to acceptance and experiencing of all feelings and thoughts in the here-and-now. The client-centered therapist develops an atmosphere of empathic understanding, unconditional positive regard, and congruence to encourage the client to risk facing his denied feelings.

9. Gestalt therapy is another therapy that focuses on insight into present experience. This form of therapy tries to help a person become aware of what he is feeling and how he is behaving from moment to moment.

10. Transactional analysis focuses on the way in which the Parent, Child, and Adult aspects of each person's personality are expressed in interactive communications.

11. The behavior modification therapist uses well-established principles of learning in order to change behavior. Wolpe's systematic desensitization pairs relaxation training with the fantasy of feared stimuli, moving slowly from the least to the most feared. Implosive therapy involves encouraging the client to visualize the most feared situation imaginable until anxiety responses are no longer produced.

12. In instrumental conditioning therapy, the client is rewarded for appropriate behavior or punished when he behaves inappropriately. However, if the desired behavior never occurs or if the inappropriate behavior is self-reinforcing, instrumental conditioning may be difficult to use.

13. Classical conditioning has been used in the treatment of neurosis, homosexuality, and alcoholism.

14. Drugs used in psychiatry for the treatment of emotional problems can be divided into three categories: sedatives and tranquilizers, antidepressants, and antipsychotics.

15. Lobotomies (cutting nerves in the frontal lobe of the brain) and electroshock therapy (in which a person has a convulsion induced by electric shock across the temples) are techniques that have become less common since the use of drugs in psychiatric treatment.

16. Hospitalization may be used as an aid to therapy when therapy and medication alone are not sufficient to help a person function effectively.

17. Group therapy offers group members the opportunity to understand others, get feedback, share solutions, be a therapist for others, and practice new behaviors.

18. Forms of group therapy include sensitivity training groups, encounter groups, marathon groups, family therapy, and psychodrama.

19. Community mental health is concerned with the more efficient delivery of mental health services, particularly to the poor, and treatment of a community or social system rather than each individual.

20. In primary services, the focus is on eliminating the cause of emotional problems. Secondary services center on problems that already exist. Tertiary services deal with the aftereffects of having emotional problems.

21. Community psychology works toward changing the structure of the culture to solve social problems.

22. Eysenck claimed that psychotherapy was no more effective than leaving people alone, but research indicates that "good" therapists have a reasonable rate of success.

23. The shortage of therapists, which is acute in many areas, has led to alternative approaches such as the use of paraprofessionals and computers.

Recommended Additional Readings

Axline, V. M. *Dibs: In search of self.* New York: Ballantine, 1964.

Bandura, A. *Principles of behavior modification.* New York: Holt, Rinehart and Winston, 1969.

Duke, M. P., & Frankel, A. S. *Inside psychotherapy.* Chicago: Markham, 1971.

Fitts, W. H. *The experience of psychotherapy.* New York: Van Nostrand, 1965.

Freud, S. *A general introduction to psychoanalysis.* New York: Washington Square Press, 1920.

Lindner, R. *The fifty-minute hour.* New York: Bantam, 1954.

A
ELEMENTARY STATISTICS

The single most commonly used tool in psychology is statistics. All areas of psychology rely on one or both of the two basic types of statistics: (1) *descriptive statistics,* which are used to describe and summarize the results of research, and (2) *inferential statistics,* used to infer the meaning of and to reach conclusions about the results. Descriptive statistics provide a summary of data. The main function of inferential statistics is interpretation of experimental findings by providing a method of testing alternative hypotheses about data.

Descriptive Statistics

Measures of Central Tendency

Suppose a teacher gives an IQ test to the 10 students in his class. How would he describe the test results? One way would be to name each student and his IQ score—10 names and 10 scores. That would probably work nicely in a small class. But it would certainly be inefficient with a class of 500. Moreover, a listing of numbers does not indicate much of anything about the group as a whole. It would be helpful to know the average, typical, or more representative score. What is needed is a measure of *central tendency* in the group of scores. We will describe three commonly used measures.

The arithmetic mean.   The *mean* is the number you arrive at when you add up all the scores and divide by the number of scores. In the above example, you would add up the 10 IQ scores and divide by 10. We have made up a set of 10 scores and computed the arithmetic mean in Table A–1, which also introduces some elementary statistical symbols. Any score for an individual subject is an X. It could be an IQ score, an anxiety score, a measure of height, or anything. In Table A–1, X is an IQ score. We add up the 10 Xs. The capital Greek letter sigma (Σ) is a shorthand symbol for "add up these scores." So, Σ X means add up the X scores. Table A–1 also gives each student's height in inches. To keep height distinct from IQ scores, we signify height by Y. Very often a problem involves 2 scores for each subject, as in this case, and we use X and Y to keep them separate. So Σ Y tells us to add up the heights, which is also done in Table A–1.

   The final step in computing the arithmetic mean is to divide by the number of scores added (symbolized by N). There are 10 IQ scores, so we divide Σ X by 10 and get the mean IQ: 107.5. Likewise, we divide Σ Y by 10 and we get the mean

Table A–1
Computation of the mean IQ and height of a class of 10 students

Student's name	X (IQ)	Y (height in inches)
Rita	115	65
Norma	120	60
Lyle	105	66
Bruce	100	68
John	130	72
Jane	95	64
Linda	90	62
Ralph	110	74
Frank	85	70
Polly	125	67
	$\Sigma X = 1075$	$\Sigma Y = 668$
	$N = 10$	$N = 10$

Then, the mean of the X scores is:

$$\bar{X} = \frac{\Sigma X}{N}$$

or

$$\bar{X} = \frac{1075}{10} = 107.5$$

Likewise, the mean of the Y scores is:

$$\bar{Y} = \frac{\Sigma Y}{N}$$

or

$$\bar{Y} = \frac{668}{10} = 66.8$$

height: 66.8 inches. The shorthand way of indicating that a particular number is a mean and not a single score is to put a bar over the letter. Thus, the arithmetic mean of the X scores is symbolized as $\bar{X}$ (read "X bar"), and the mean of the Y scores is $\bar{Y}$ (read "Y bar"). Thus, we arrive at a shorthand formula for finding the arithmetic mean of a set of X scores:

$$\bar{X} = \frac{\Sigma X}{N}$$

And, of course, the arithmetic mean of a set of Y scores is calculated by the formula:

$$\bar{Y} = \frac{\Sigma Y}{N}$$

Now if students ask the teacher how the class performed on the IQ test, he could simply report the value of $\bar{X}$; and if they ask about how tall his students are, he could report $\bar{Y}$. This is obviously much simpler than listing all the X and Y scores. It gives a better idea of the general level of ability of the students and a general idea of how tall they are.

The median.   The arithmetic mean of the scores is not always a good way of determining what is the *most representative* score. In these cases, two other measures of central tendency are often used. The *median* is the *middle-most score* in a list of scores

that have been arranged in increasing order. If there is an odd number of scores, then there will be one score exactly in the middle. Thus, if the class had 11 students, the score of the 6th student in order would be the median—there would be 5 scores higher than his and 5 scores lower than his. Or if there were 27 scores, the 14th score in order would be the median.

With an even number of scores, there is no single middle score. Instead there are 2 scores that determine the middle; 1 is above and 1 is below the theoretical midpoint. In a set of 10 scores arranged in order, the 5th score from the bottom is not the median—there are 5 scores above it, but only 4 below it. In the same fashion, the 6th score is not the median, because there are 4 higher scores but 5 lower scores. So we compromise and take the halfway point between the 5th and 6th scores as the median of a set of 10 scores. The median of 28 scores would be the mean of the 14th and 15th scores. Table A–2 shows the 10 IQ scores from Table A–1, but this time we have arranged them in order. The middle point is somewhere between the 5th and 6th score, somewhere between 105 and 110. So we take the mean of these 2 scores and use this as the median. The answer is 107.5. This is the same score we got for the arithmetic mean in Table A–1.

The mean and the median are not always the same, however. Furthermore, when they differ, the median may be more representative of the set of scores as a whole. Consider the set of "salary scores" in Table A–3. Here we note that most of the

Table A–2
Computation of the median IQ score of a class of 10 students

Name	X	
John	130	
Polly	125	
Norma	120	
Rita	115	
Ralph	110	←— the middle is in here, somewhere between
Lyle	105	105 and 110
Bruce	100	
Jane	95	
Linda	90	
Frank	85	

The median here is the mean of the 2 scores nearest the middle point, in this case, 105 and 110. We take the mean of 105 and 110:

$$\frac{105 + 110}{2} = 107.5$$

This is the median. Note that the median would not be changed if we changed John's score from 130 to, say, 160. What would the mean be in this case?

Table A–3
Comparison of the mean and median monthly salaries of the Zappo Cereal Company employees

Employee number	Monthly salary X (in dollars)
1	10,000
2	600
3	550
4	500
5	450 ←—midpoint
6	400
7	375
8	375
9	350
10	350
	$\Sigma X = 13,950$
	$N = 10$

We can see from the midpoint that the median salary is the mean of 400 and 450, which is $425.

Yet the mean salary is:

$$\bar{X} = \frac{\Sigma X}{N} = \frac{13950}{10} = \$1,395$$

Which value, the mean or the median, do you think is more representative of Zappo wages?

Table A–4
A frequency table of the anxiety scores of 200 mental patients

Score (X)	f or frequency
20	10
19	10
18	12
17	15
16	20
15	27
14	15
13	21
12	22
11	12
10	10
9	8
8	7
7	5
6	3
5	0
4	2
3	1
2	0
1	0
	$\Sigma f = 200 = N$

The mode, the score which occurs most frequently, is equal to 15.

10 people working for the Zappo Cereal Company are not making a lot of money. One employee, obviously the president, is making a bundle. The mean monthly salary is $1,395, which might lead you to believe that the company pays its employees very well. But the median is only $425, which would make you think a little differently about Zappo. The median will be unaffected if the president gives himself a big raise, but the mean will go up. You can see that in this case the median is more representative of the group as a whole than the mean is. Furthermore, the median is *unaffected* by extreme scores such as the salary of the president.

The mode.   The third measure of central tendency is called the *mode.* The mode is a quick but crude measure defined as the *most frequently occurring* score. In a small set of scores, as in Tables A–1, 2, and 3, there is the possibility that no score occurs more than once. Thus there is no mode. But suppose a psychologist gives an anxiety test to a group of 200 mental patients. With such a large group, it is convenient to set up a *frequency distribution* showing the various possible scores on the test and, for each possible score, how many people (f or frequency) actually got that score (see Table A–4). Suppose, for example, that 27 people got a score of 15 on the anxiety test. Looking down the frequency column in Table A–4, we see that 27 is

the highest value. This means that 15 is the *mode* or the *modal score,* because it is the score that happens most frequently. Note that the sum of all the frequencies in the f column is equal to N, the number of people taking the test, in this case 200.

Frequency distributions can also appear in graphic form. Figure A–1 shows a frequency distribution using the data from Table A–4. The horizontal axis of the graph gives the value of X, the anxiety score, and the vertical axis gives the frequency of the score.

The frequency distribution is a very important concept in statistics. More advanced techniques are heavily based on the frequency distribution principle, so make sure you understand just what it is.

Measures of Variability

Scores typically vary; not everyone gets the same score or has the same height. There are *individual differences* among people. People may vary a lot when it comes to anxiety or IQ scores but little when it comes to the number of fingers they have. Is there a convenient and accurate way of measuring the degree of variability in a set of scores?

The quickest and least informative measure of the variability in a set of scores is the *range*. The range is defined as the *highest score minus the lowest score*. In Table A–4 we see that the anxiety scores of

Figure A–1
A frequency distribution based on the data in Table A–4

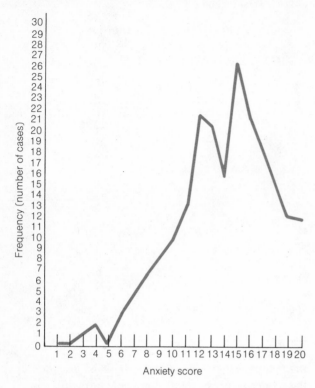

Anxiety score

Table A–5
Two sets of scores that have the same mean but differ in variability

Set A	Set B
22	36
22	32
21	28
21	24
20	20
20	20
19	16
19	12
18	8
18	4

$\Sigma X = 200$ $\Sigma X = 200$
N = 10   N = 10

$\bar{X} = \dfrac{200}{10} = 20$ $\bar{X} = \dfrac{200}{10} = 20$

Range = 22 − 18 = 4   Range = 36 − 4 = 32

the patients "range" from a low of 3 to a high of 20, so the range would be 20 − 3 = 17. The main reason for using the range as a measure of variability is that it is very easy to compute. But because it is based on only two scores, it reflects very little about the distribution. A better and more commonly used measure of variability is the *standard deviation,* which reflects the actual spread or fluctuation of scores *around the mean.*

Suppose we have a set of 10 scores that have an arithmetic mean of 20. Two such sets are shown in Table A–5. The scores labeled Set A consist of only 5 different numbers that are all close to the mean of 20 (19, 19, 20, 21, and 22). Obviously, the variability in Set A is low. In Set B we have the same mean, 20, but the variability is much higher. There are 10 different scores, and some of them are a long way from the mean. If we described both sets with a central tendency measure, we would not be communicating the fact that the two sets are different in a quite basic way. To be more complete, we need to provide a measure of variability.

The *standard deviation* is the *square root of the mean of the squared distance from the mean of the scores.* That's complicated, so let's analyze it in steps. First take each individual score, X, and

subtract the mean from it, as we have done in Table A–6. You should be able to see that these new scores, symbolized by the lower-case x, are merely measures of the distance each score is from the mean. Now why not just calculate the average or mean of these distance scores? A glance at Table A–6 should convince you that if you add up the distance scores to get a mean distance score, you will always get a sum of zero. For every score that is above the mean (a positive distance score) there is another score below the mean (a negative distance score) that cancels it out, meaning that the sum of the distance scores will always be zero. Instead, we square each score, which eliminates the negative numbers, and we have a new concept—the squared distance score, x^2. The x^2 scores are also shown in Table A–6. Now we can add these scores up and take the mean of them:

$$\frac{\Sigma x^2}{N}$$

This gives us the mean squared distance from the mean.

The mean squared distance from the mean has a special name, the *variance,* and a special symbol, the lower-case Greek letter sigma, squared (σ^2). The square, of course, serves to remind us that it is the mean *squared* distance score. The variance is a very good measure of variability, as you can see by comparing this value for Set A and Set B scores; σ^2 is much higher for B (96.0) than for A (2.0). This is as it should be because the Set B scores vary more than the Set A scores.

The variance can be used by itself as the variability measure, but it is usually more convenient

Table A–6
Computation of the variance and standard deviation for two sets of scores

Set A (ages of 10 people at a college dance)			Set B (ages of 10 people at the park)		
X	$X - \bar{X} \ (x)$	x^2	X	$X - \bar{X} \ (x)$	x^2
22	2	4	36	16	256
22	2	4	32	12	144
21	1	1	28	8	64
21	1	1	24	4	16
20	0	0	20	0	0
20	0	0	20	0	0
19	−1	1	16	−4	16
19	−1	1	12	−8	64
18	−2	4	8	−12	144
18	−2	4	4	−16	256
	$\Sigma x = 0$	$\Sigma x^2 = 20$		$\Sigma x = 0$	$\Sigma x^2 = 960$

$$\sigma^2 = \text{variance} = \frac{\Sigma x^2}{N} = \frac{20}{10} = 2.00$$

$$\sigma = \text{standard deviation} = \sqrt{\sigma^2} = \sqrt{2.00} = 1.414$$

$$\text{or } \sigma = \sqrt{\frac{\Sigma x^2}{N}} = \sqrt{\frac{20}{10}} = 1.414$$

$$\sigma^2 = \text{variance} = \frac{\Sigma x^2}{N} = \frac{960}{10} = 96.0$$

$$\sigma = \text{standard deviation} = \sqrt{\sigma^2} = \sqrt{96} = 9.798$$

$$\text{or } \sigma = \sqrt{\frac{\Sigma x^2}{N}} = \sqrt{\frac{960}{10}} = 9.798$$

to take the square root of the variance. We squared the distance scores before we added them up, so now we take the square root of the variance to get back to the original scale of measurement. The square root of the variance is the *standard deviation* (symbolized σ). The larger the value of the standard deviation, the larger the variability.

The Normal Frequency Distribution

Take a look at the frequency distribution in Figure A–2. It is sort of bell-shaped and is known as the *normal distribution.* Scores near the mean are most frequent, and frequency drops off smoothly as we move to the extremes. The normal distribution is the most important distribution in statistics because so many psychological factors are "normally distributed" in the population. IQ is a good example. IQ is normally distributed with a mean of 100 and a standard deviation of 15. This means that if we obtained IQ scores for everybody and took the mean of them, it would be 100, and the standard deviation would be 15. Furthermore, if we drew a graph representing the frequency of each of the possible IQ scores, it would be bell-shaped—normal—and would look like the one in Figure A–2.

If we know that a characteristic is normally distributed and if we know the mean and the standard deviation, we can use the theoretical properties of the normal distribution to deduce more information about the characteristic. We can do this because in any normal distribution the standard deviation can be used to divide the distribution into sections containing fixed percentages of the cases.

Figure A–3 shows a normal distribution divided up in this way—again we have used IQ scores. The fixed percentages are printed in the various sections of the frequency distribution. For example, about 34% of the people lie between the mean and 115—that is, 34% of the people have IQs between 100 and 115.

Figure A–2
The normal distribution of IQ scores

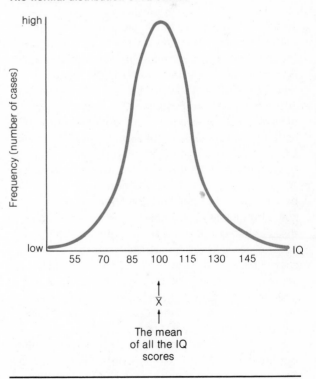

Figure A–3
The normal distribution divided into standard deviation units

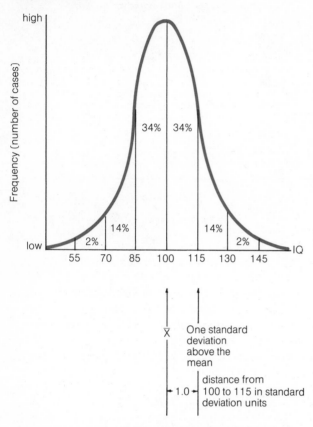

Figure A–4
The normal distribution and z scores

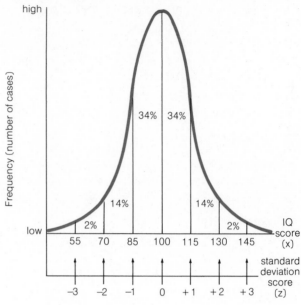

Because the standard deviation is 15, we can see that a score of 115 is one standard deviation above the mean (115 − 100 = 15 = the standard deviation). Remember that the standard deviation is a distance measure, so the "distance" from 115 to the mean of 100 is one standard deviation unit. Two standard deviation units above the mean would be the distance up to 130, and three units would be to 145. Of course, we can go in the other direction also, below the mean. One unit below would be an IQ of 85, two units of standard deviation distance would be 70, and three units below is 55. From three standard deviation units *below* the mean on up to three units *above* the mean (from 55 up to 145), we cover essentially all the scores. Very few people score below 55 or above 145. So the range of scores, as measured in standard deviation units, goes from a low of −3 to a high of +3. It is very convenient to convert the IQ scores into standard deviation scores, called *z scores.*

Figure A–4 again shows the IQ normal distribution, but this time we have two horizontal axes displayed. The upper one shows IQ scores and the lower one

shows standard deviation scores, or z scores. Thus you can see that an IQ score of 115 is one standard deviation above the mean, so the z score corresponding to 115 is +1.0. If someone tells you that his z score in IQ is +2.0, you can see that he has an IQ of 130. If he tells you that his z score is +4.0, he is either very brilliant or he is pulling your leg. Note that the mean of the z scores will always be equal to zero.

Looking at Figure A–4, suppose we ask you to figure out what percentage of the people have IQs between 85 and 115, which is the same as asking how many people have z scores between −1.0 and +1.0. The answer is 68%; 34% between 85 and 100, and another 34% between 100 and 115.

An important thing to remember is that these percentages and the z score procedure apply to *any* normal distribution, not just to the IQ distribution. The only difference between the IQ distribution and any other normal distribution is that they probably have different means and different standard deviations. But if you know that something has a normal distribution and if you know the mean and standard deviation of it, you can set up a figure like the one in Figure A–4.

Suppose, for example, that we told you that waist size in American men is normally distributed with a mean of 34 inches and a standard deviation of 4. You could now set up a normal frequency distribution, as is shown in Figure A–5. The waist size scores run from a low of 22 inches (z score of

Figure A–5
The normal distribution of waist size in American men (hypothetical)

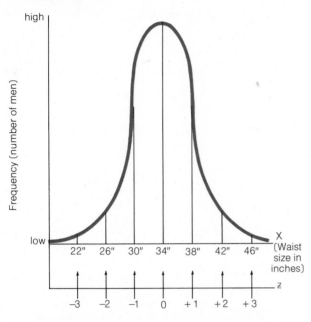

−3—22 is three standard-deviation units *below* the mean) up to a high of 46 (z score of +3—three units *above* the mean). Now you can fill in the percentages and answer the following questions:

1. What percentage of men have waist sizes less than 30 inches?

2. What percentage of men have waist sizes greater than 38?

3. If Joe's waist size is 47, is he unusual?

4. If we randomly selected one man from the American population, what is the probability (how likely is it?) that his waist size is equal to or greater than 38?

This last question brings us to the notion of *probability*. *Probability* refers to the *proportion of cases that fit a certain description*. In general, the probability of A (the likelihood that a randomly drawn object will be an A object) is equal to the number of A objects divided by the total number of all possible objects. The number of A objects divided by the total number of objects is, of course, the proportion of objects that· *are* A, so the probability is just a proportion.

Suppose that an A is someone with a waist size equal to or greater than 38. To find the probability of selecting an A-man at random from the population, we have to know what proportion of all men are A-men. Figure A–5 tells us that 14% of the men are between 38 and 42 and an additional 2% are greater than 42, so we add 14% and 2% and we see that

16% of the men are A-men. In proportion terms, this becomes .16 (we move the decimal two places to the left to translate a percentage into a proportion). In summary, the probability of selecting a man with a waist size equal to or greater than 38 = .16. This means that 16 out of every 100 selections would yield a man who fits this description.

Suppose that scores on an anxiety scale are normally distributed in the population of all American people with a mean of 50 and a standard deviation of 10. You should be able to calculate the probability that a randomly drawn person has an anxiety score that is equal to or *less* than 40. Can you do it?

Correlation

The final descriptive statistic to be discussed is the *correlation coefficient,* which was introduced in Chapter 1. The correlation coefficient does not describe a single set of scores as the mean or standard deviation does. Instead, it describes the degree of relationship between two sets of scores. It is basically a measure of the degree to which the two sets of scores vary together, or *covary*. Scores can vary together in one of two ways: (1) a *positive covariation,* in which high scores in one set tend to go with high scores in the other set (and low scores go with low scores), or (2) *negative covariation,* in which high scores in one set tend to go with *low* scores in the other set (and low scores go with high scores). When there is a positive covariation, we say the two sets are *positively or directly correlated,* and we say they are *negatively, indirectly, or inversely correlated* when there is a negative covariation. A common example of positive correlation might be the relationship that exists between height and weight—the taller you are the more you tend to weigh. A common example of negative correlation might be the relationship that exists between the amount of alcohol a person has drunk in an evening and his ability to drive an automobile. The more the person has drunk, the less his ability.

Note that we used "tend to go with." Correlations are almost never perfect—not all tall people are particularly heavy and not all short people are lightweights. Of course, there is the third possibility too, namely, *no* correlation between two sets of scores, or *zero correlation.* Thus, for example, we probably would expect there to be a zero correlation between your height and your ability to learn psychology. So two variables (two sets of scores on different measures) can be *positively or negatively correlated or not correlated at all.* And the degree of correlation can be great or little. What we need is a statistic that conveniently measures the degree and the direction (positive or negative) of the correlation between two variables. This is what the coefficient of correlation does for us.

Table A–7 shows the scores of 10 people on two tests. Each person took both a test of anxiety and a test of "happiness." The possible scores on each test ranged from 1 to 10, with 1 meaning low anxiety and 10 very high anxiety for the anxiety test. For the happiness test, 1 means a low degree of happiness and 10 means a high degree of happiness. Intuitively we would expect a negative correlation between the two variables of anxiety and happiness; the happier you are, the less should be your anxiety, and vice versa.

For convenience we arranged the anxiety scores in order in Table A–7. What this does is to cause the happiness scores to fall in *perfect reverse order*. In other words, it is obvious in this table that there is a perfect negative correlation between anxiety and happiness. This is best displayed by making a *scatter plot* of the data, which we have done in Figure A–6. Here the horizontal axis is the anxiety score, and the vertical axis is the happiness score. Each person is represented by a point on the graph that locates him on the two tests. For example, Clint had an anxiety score of 4 and a happiness score of 7. So we go over (to the right) to 4 on the anxiety scale and then up to 7 on the happiness scale, and we place a dot at that point to represent Clint on the graph. All 10 people are represented in the graph. You can see that the 10 points all fall on a straight line, which means that the correlation is perfect. You can also see that the line slopes down to the right, and this means that the correlation is negative

Figure A–6
"Scatter plot" of the data from Table A–7, relating anxiety to happiness

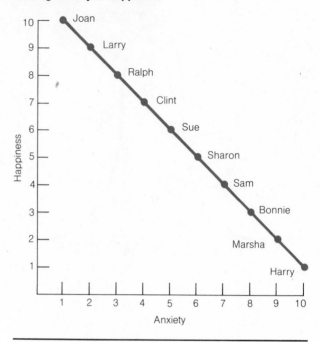

in direction—as you go up the anxiety scale the happiness scores go down.

As we have said, however, correlations are almost never perfect. This means that the points are likely to be scattered all over the graph, hence the term "scatter plot." The closer the points are to lying on a straight line, the higher the degree of correlation. So the procedure is to make a scatter plot and then try to draw a straight line that *best fits* the points in the plot. If all the points are close to or on this *line of best fit,* then the correlation is high. If the points are widely scattered and not close to any line you could draw, then the correlation is zero. Finally, if the line of best fit slopes downward to the right, then the correlation is negative, as we saw in Figure A–6. If the line slopes upward to the right, the correlation is positive. Figure A–7 shows three scatter plots. In panel A the two variables in question are highly negatively correlated; the points are all pretty close to the straight line, which slopes downward to the right. In panel B we have the case of a high positive correlation; the points are again all pretty close to the line, but this time the line slopes upward to the right. In panel C there is no correlation; the points are scattered all over and there is no line that fits them very well.

The *Pearson product moment correlation coefficient* is a measure of the correlation. It can take on any numerical value from −1.0 through 0.0

Table A–7
The correlation between anxiety and happiness

Name	Anxiety (X)	Happiness (Y)
Joan	1	10
Larry	2	9
Ralph	3	8
Clint	4	7
Sue	5	6
Sharon	6	5
Sam	7	4
Bonnie	8	3
Marsha	9	2
Harry	10	1

Here we have arranged the anxiety scores in order and we see that this causes the happiness scores to be arranged in *perfect reverse* order. This is a perfect negative correlation. The coefficient of correlation would be −1.0.

Figure A–7
Scatter plots of three correlations

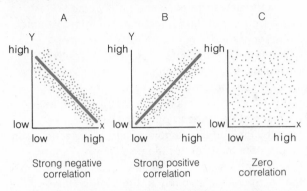

Strong negative correlation

Strong positive correlation

Zero correlation

up to +1.0. A perfect negative correlation, as in Table A–7, would be −1.0, and a perfect positive or direct correlation would be +1.0. Correlations close to zero would mean there is little or no relationship between the two variables, X and Y. The value of the correlation between 0.0 and 1 (ignoring the sign) would represent the degree of relationship. The sign of the correlation (positive or negative) does not tell you the degree of the correlation, only the direction. Thus a correlation of −.77 is just as strong a correlation as is a correlation of +.77; the only difference is the direction. Table A–8 shows the steps for calculating the Pearson product moment correlation coefficient in case you want to see exactly how it is done.

In all the examples so far, we have been correlating the scores of a person on two different tests. It does not have to be that way. We might correlate the scores of a person on the same test

taken at two different times. Then we would be asking if the test is reliable, that is, does a person tend to score about the same on the test if he takes it on two different occasions? If it is a good test, it should be reliable (see Appendix C). Another common use of correlation is to determine the validity of a test; does the test measure what it is supposed to measure? If we make up a test of intelligence, we would hope that it would correlate positively with performance in school. If it did, it would help us argue that our test really did measure intelligence. (See Appendix C for a discussion of validity.)

Regression

One very important use of the correlational statistics is in a procedure called *regression.* In determining the correlation we had a person's score on *both* of two tests, and we were asking if the scores were related. In the regression procedure we have only one score, and we try to make a prediction about what the other score will be. Suppose we try to predict your weight. We have no idea what to guess, because about all we know about you is that you are reading this book. If we knew that the average person reading this book weighs 142 pounds, then that is what we would have to guess, and we would make the same guess for every reader. But if we knew your height, and we also knew the correlation between weight and height, then we could make a much more accurate guess about your weight. For example, if we knew you were 4 feet, 10 inches or that you were 6 feet, 6 inches, we would hardly guess 142 pounds in either case. We would adjust

Table A–8
Calculating the Pearson product moment correlation coefficient

Name	Anxiety (X)	X^2	Happiness (Y)	Y^2	XY (X times Y)
John	2	4	9	81	18
Ralph	5	25	6	36	20
Mary	9	81	4	16	36
Sue	1	1	3	9	3
Jim	3	9	2	4	6
Harvey	7	49	2	4	14
Jane	8	64	4	16	32
Joanne	6	36	5	25	30
N = 8 people	$\Sigma X = 41$	$\Sigma X^2 = 269$	$\Sigma Y = 35$	$\Sigma Y^2 = 191$	$\Sigma XY = 169$

$$r_{xy} \text{ (the correlation between X and Y)} = \frac{N\Sigma XY - (\Sigma X)(\Sigma Y)}{\sqrt{[N\Sigma X^2 - (\Sigma X)^2][N\Sigma Y^2 - (\Sigma Y)^2]}}$$

For these data: $r_{\text{ANXIETY·HAPPINESS}} = \dfrac{(8)(169) - (41)(35)}{\sqrt{[(8)(269) - (41)^2][(8)(191) - (35)^2]}} = \dfrac{1352 - 1435}{\sqrt{(2152 - 1681)(1528 - 1225)}}$

$$= \frac{-83}{\sqrt{(471)(303)}} = \frac{-83}{\sqrt{142713}} = \frac{-83}{377.77} = -.219$$

our weight guess according to what we know about your height. Regression is a fancy, complex, but accurate way of making this adjustment.

Finally, a moment's thought should convince you that the higher the correlation (in either the positive or negative direction), the better job we can do at predicting your weight—the closer we will come to your true weight. If the correlation between the two variables is perfect ($+1.0$ or -1.0), we can predict perfectly the value of one of the variables if we know the value of the other. But because correlations are almost never perfect, our predictions are somewhat off, and the lower the correlation, the greater the likely error.

Regression is used in many different settings. Most of you probably took the College Board examination for getting into college. From past research we know there is a positive correlation between your score on the College Board and your success in college. Therefore, the College Board test can now be given to college applicants, and on the basis of their scores, a prediction can be made for each applicant about how he will do in college. These predictions are used to help decide whom to admit.

Similar procedures are used to process applications for law school, medical school, graduate school, or a job. Using regression techniques, the psychologist predicts the applicant's success on the job or in school, and he uses these predictions to determine whether or not to hire or admit the applicant. It is a serious business, and the decisions made on this basis are extremely important to the people involved.

Inferential Statistics

Inferential statistics are used to make inferences about data or draw conclusions about a hypothesis that we have tested. Two of the basic concepts in inferential statistics are *estimation* and *hypothesis testing.*

Estimation

One use of inferential statistics is to make estimates of the actual value of some population characteristic. Suppose, for example, we wanted to know how intelligent Americans are on the average. We *could* test all 208 million Americans and compute a mean. But it would be handy to have a shortcut method, even though it is just an estimate.

In order to estimate the mean and standard deviation of a population, we take a *sample* of the population and test the members of the sample. We then compute the statistics on the sample scores and use these statistics to estimate what the mean and standard deviation would be if we *could* test every member of the population. We might sample 200 people from America and use their scores to estimate what the whole population looks like. Obviously, this is what public opinion polls and the TV rating services do.

It is important to make sure that the sample is *representative* of the population. This is usually done by making the sample a random selection from all possible members of the population. *Random* means that everyone in the specified population has the same chance of being in the sample. It would not be a fair sample for estimating American intelligence if we measured only white female citizens of La Mirada, California. The second factor in sampling is sample size. The larger the sample size, the more accurate the estimates are going to be. If you randomly chose one person from the phone book, scheduled him for an IQ test, got his score, and then estimated that his IQ was the mean IQ for all Americans, you would almost certainly be off the mark. More than one score is needed. But how many should there be in the sample? The amazing thing about sampling is that the size of the sample necessary to get a pretty accurate idea of the population is much smaller than you might guess. A sample of 30 or 40 Americans out of the 208 million, if properly drawn, would give a very accurate estimate of the entire population. Of course, if the sample is not properly drawn, is not representative, then increasing the sample size would not help our estimation much at all.

Hypothesis Testing

When we set out to do an experiment in psychology, we always begin with a hypothesis. For our brief discussion, we will use the example of a psychologist who wants to know if Zappo cereal increases intelligence in people who eat it. His working hypothesis is: "People who eat Zappo will show an increase in IQ compared with people who eat Brand X." He gets 20 subjects to volunteer for his experiment, and he randomly assigns them to one of two groups, 10 per group. The random assignment is designed to create two groups that at the start of the experiment are equal in IQ, scoring 100 points on the average. The Zappo group eats Zappo for 1 year and the Brand X group eats Brand X for 1 year. At the end of this time, the psychologist tests all 20 subjects on intelligence and finds that the mean IQ of Zappo eaters is 105 and the mean IQ of Brand X eaters is 100. What can the psychologist conclude or infer about his hypothesis? If the Zappo group and the Brand X group were very close—say, 99.5 and 100.1 were the means—he would probably conclude that Zappo does not increase intelligence. If they were very far apart—say, 125 for Zappo eaters and 96 for Brand X eaters—he would probably conclude that eating Zappo increases intelligence. But what does he conclude about results in between these extremes?

There has to be an objective way to decide whether the psychologist's hypothesis can be accepted or not; he cannot leave it up to his intuition or, worse yet, the intuition of the owner of Zappo cereal. This is where hypothesis-testing statistics come into play. There are many different kinds of these statistics. Here we will consider only one, the *t test,* which is probably the most common statistical technique for hypothesis testing.

We want to decide if the difference between 100 (the mean of the Brand X eaters) and 105 (the mean of the Zappo eaters) is a real difference. Is it a *significant difference?* A difference is said to be significant if it is very unlikely that it would happen by chance, that is, if the chance probability is small for a difference this large. The difference between Zappo and Brand X means is 5.0 IQ points. We say the *mean difference* is 5.0 (105 − 100 = 5.0). For a moment, let's assume that Zappo has no effect on intelligence. This is called the *null hypothesis* (remember that the psychologist's working hypothesis was that Zappo increases IQ). What we need to know is *if the null hypothesis is true* (Zappo does not affect IQ), what is the probability that the two groups would differ by 5 IQ points or more. If Zappo is not different from Brand X, then any difference we find between our two groups is just a chance difference. After all, we would not expect two *random* groups of 10 people to have exactly the same means either. Sample means will differ, and every once in a while there will be a difference of 5 or more IQ points just by chance alone, with no help from Zappo. The question is: How often will we get a difference this large? Or what is the probability of the difference occurring by chance alone?

In order to answer this question, we must know the standard deviations in the two groups. We have to know how much variability there is in the IQ scores. To understand this, look at the three panels in Figure A–8. Each panel shows two frequency distributions, one for a Zappo group and one for a Brand X group. Note that in each panel the mean of the Zappo group is 105 and the mean of the Brand X group is 100. But the three panels display quite different pictures when it comes to IQ variability. In

Figure A–8

Three experimental outcomes differing in variability and overlap, but each with the same mean (100 and 105) and the same mean difference (105–100)

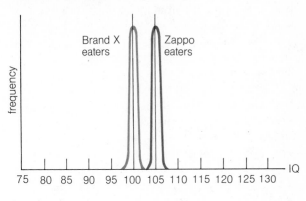

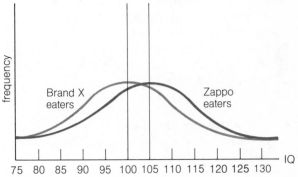

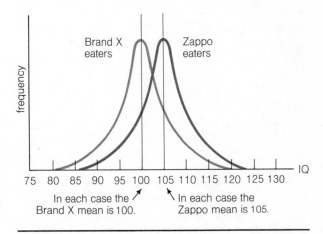

In each case the Brand X mean is 100.   In each case the Zappo mean is 105.

the top panel the variability is very small (all Zappo eaters score about the same, near 105, and Brand X eaters are all close to 100), and the two distributions do not overlap at all (all Zappo eaters have higher IQs than all Brand X eaters). In this case, it looks like the 5-point difference between the means is a significant one.

In the middle panel the IQ scores are highly variable (Zappo eaters do not all score near the mean of 105, and Brand X scores do not cluster close to 100). This means that there is a lot of overlap in the two distributions. Some Zappo eaters are lower in IQ than some Brand X eaters, and some Brand X eaters are higher in IQ than some Zappo eaters. In fact, there is so much overlap in the two distributions that we would tend to bet that the difference between 100 and 105 (the two means) is just a chance difference. The two distributions look almost identical. In neither the top nor the middle panel would we need a statistical test to help us decide whether or not to accept the null hypothesis.

Situations like those depicted in the top panel are very rare indeed. Unfortunately, the middle panel is a more frequent outcome of an experiment—the experiment is a flop! The bottom panel represents the most common outcome of all, and the only one of the three in which the conclusion is unclear. The two distributions overlap somewhat, much more than in the top panel but much less than in the middle panel. There is a moderate amount of variability. Do we conclude that the 105 to 100 mean difference is a real one or not? Is there a significant difference between the means?

The t test is basically a ratio. It is the *ratio* of the *mean difference to an estimate* of the *variability* involved in this difference. In the top panel the difference is 5 units, but the variability is very small. So if we take 5 and divide it by this very small variability number, we will get a large number for an answer. The t ratio will be large, and we will declare the difference to be significant. In the middle panel the same difference between means, 5, will be divided by a very large variability number to give us a t ratio that will be very small. We declare the difference insignificant. In the bottom panel we have the borderline case, where we will divide 5 by a moderate variability estimate, meaning the t value obtained will be moderately large. What do we conclude? Fortunately for us, mathematical statisticians have prepared *tables of the probability* of various values of t happening by chance. We compute the t ratio in our experiment and then look it up in the statistical tables to find the chance probability of a t as large as the one we found. If the table tells us that our t ratio is unlikely to happen by chance, we assume that what we have is not a chance effect but a real difference. Conventionally, this probability is .05. This means that if our obtained t ratio is likely to happen only 5% of the time or less by chance, then the odds are that this is *not* one of those times. The odds are that it is not a chance effect but a real one, which is called a significant effect.

The null hypothesis says, "There is no difference between Zappo and Brand X," and if we obtain a significant t ratio we infer or conclude that the null hypothesis is wrong. Statistical inference is basically a procedure for drawing conclusions about the null hypothesis. What the t test procedure allows us to do is to reject the null hypothesis when we get a t ratio that is very unlikely to occur by chance. If we set up the null hypothesis such that it is the opposite of our working hypothesis (Zappo improves IQ), then rejection of the null hypothesis will be evidence in support of our working hypothesis.

We will not go into the details of actually calculating a t ratio. You can find the information in any elementary statistics book (for example, Wike, 1971). Simply remember that when an experiment is done, the results will always indicate some differences between the conditions in the study. The t test as well as many other types of inferential statistics are used to help the experimenter decide if the differences are large enough, relative to the variability, to allow him to reject the null hypothesis and support his working hypothesis.

This reasoning applies to the correlation coefficient as well as to the difference between two means. If we get two sets of numbers by randomly drawing them out of a hat and correlate them, the correlation will almost never be exactly zero, even though the numbers are clearly unrelated (we drew them by chance from a hat). Suppose the correlation is very high, say, .80. It is obvious we would conclude that the correlation is significant. Suppose it is very low or close to zero, say −.07; obviously we would say there is no significant relationship or correlation. But what if it is .30 or −.42 or −.28? Where do we draw the line and say that it is highly unlikely that a correlation this high would happen by chance? At what point can we infer a real relationship between the two variables? Again, there are procedures in inferential statistics that decide objectively whether the correlation is significant or not. The null hypothesis would be that the correlation is zero, and we would then test this hypothesis to see whether it can be rejected.

Advanced Statistical Techniques Commonly Used in Psychology

Analysis of Variance

The t test is used when testing the difference between two groups and only two groups. But most experiments have more than two groups, and the t test is not useful in such cases. A very complex statistical procedure called the *analysis of variance* is used instead. As the name implies, the *variance* or *variability* in the data is *analyzed and compared to* the *mean differences* in much the same way as in a t test. In fact, the analysis of variance procedure reduces to a t test when there are only two groups. The test in analysis of variance is known as the *F test,* named after the famous English statistician, R. A. Fisher. Basically, the procedure is just like that for the t test. It allows the experimenter to make inferences or conclusions about the differences among a set of means. It is a very common technique now, so you are likely to encounter the F test if you read any modern psychology journal.

Factor Analysis

Factor analysis is a highly sophisticated correlational procedure that is used to identify the basic factors underlying a psychological phenomenon. The technique boils down to finding clusters of tests that correlate with one another. Suppose an experimenter administers the following 6 tests to 100 young men: (1) vocabulary, (2) ability to play basketball, (3) ability to write an essay on philosophy, (4) speed at running the 100-yard dash, (5) ability to understand statistics, and (6) ability to climb trees. Each man takes all 6 tests, and then the experimenter intercorrelates the tests. He correlates test 1 with 2, 1 with 3, 1 with 4, and so on. Suppose he finds that tests 1, 3, and 5 correlate highly with one another and that 2, 4, and 6 correlate highly with one another, but 1, 3 and 5 do not correlate at all with 2, 4, and 6. Why would this be the case? Look at the tests, and it is easy to see that 1, 3, and

5 all involve thinking or knowledge—they all involve "mental ability." On the other hand, 2, 4, and 6 all involve physical skill. So it probably is the case that 1, 3, and 5 are all measuring something in common, which we might call Factor A. Wouldn't you guess that Factor A has something to do with intelligence? Tests 2, 4, and 6 also seem to be measuring something in common. We call it Factor B. Because 1, 3, and 5 do not correlate with 2, 4, and 6, we conclude that Factor A, which we now have decided to call intelligence, is not the same thing as Factor B. Looking at tests 2, 4, and 6, we decide to call Factor B "athletic ability."

In short, we have isolated two factors that are involved in performance on our 6 tests; one we call "intelligence" and one we call "athletic ability." Factor analysis is basically a correlational technique that allows us to analyze performance on a large number of tests into factors by isolating clusters of tests (where the clustering is not as obvious as it is in the foregoing example). Correlations are high within a cluster but low between clusters. We assume that the clusters then "represent" and measure psychological factors.

This technique has been used extensively in two areas of psychology, intelligence testing and personality assessment (see Appendix C). Intelligence consists of many factors and so does personality. With factor analysis, we can identify these factors and hope to learn from them what intelligence and personality are.

NEURONS: THE BUILDING BLOCKS OF THE NERVOUS SYSTEM

Much of the complex structure and functioning of the nervous system depends on its basic component, the nerve cell or neuron, and the processes by which the neurons receive and transmit information. Until late in the nineteenth century, it was believed by many that the nervous system was one *continuous* network of neural tissue. Subsequently it became clear that the nervous system is composed of individual cells called neurons. This discovery has been called the "neuron doctrine" and has received virtually complete support by all those studying the structure of the nervous system. There are around 10 billion neurons in man's nervous system, all present at birth although not completely interconnected. Somewhere around 10,000 of these die each day and are not replaced.

Structural Properties of the Neuron

Like all cells, the neuron must carry on all those processes involving the use of oxygen and the use and production of energy. However, unlike the other cells of the body, the nerve cell is specialized for the important functions of *excitability* and *transmission.* Neurons are able to receive and transmit information. The means by which these processes take place depend on the special structural features of the neuron, as well as the neuron's ability to alter certain of its structural characteristics when given appropriate stimulation.

The Cell

The nerve cell body contains many of the components found in other animal cells (see Figure B–1). The *nucleus* serves as the control center for all cellular activities and many other *organelles* ("little organs") responsible for maintaining the structural and functional properties of the cell. In addition to these common cellular elements, the neuron possesses some unique features. The most prominent are the fibers that extend from the cell body, including the *dendrites,* which are generally short and quite numerous; and a single *axon.* The axon may divide into one or more branches *(collaterals).* The nerves running throughout your body are basically bundles of axons from many neurons.

The point at which the axon is connected to the cell body is called the *axon hillock.* In some neurons the axon is covered by a sheath made of fatty material called *myelin.* This *myelin sheath* always has gaps in it at short intervals along the length of

483

Figure B-1
The neuron

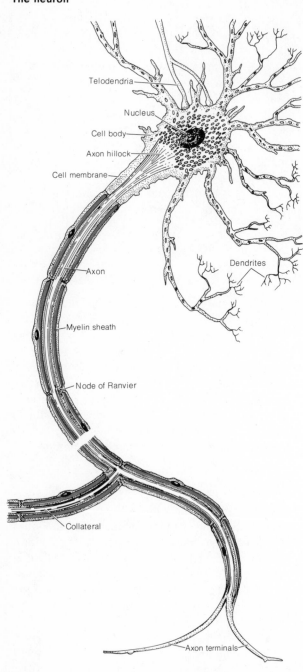

Telodendria

Nucleus

Cell body

Axon hillock

Cell membrane

Dendrites

Axon

Myelin sheath

Node of Ranvier

Collateral

Axon terminals

Diagrammatic representation of the common structural features of a neuron. The telodendria and axon terminals shown at the top are coming from another neuron and are synapsing with this neuron.

the axon, called *nodes of Ranvier.* In other neurons, the dendrites may look virtually identical to the axon. The most important difference between a

cell's dendrites and its axon is that *dendrites conduct information toward the cell body, while the axon always conducts information away from the cell body.* Thus the dendrites could be considered to be receiving stations and the axon a transmitter.

As an axon approaches its destination, which is most commonly the cell body or dendrites of another neuron some distance away, it divides into many fine branches called *telodendria.* The telodendria terminate very close to the dendrites or cell body of another neuron in the form of a small swelling that is called variously a *synaptic bouton, synaptic terminal,* or *axon terminal.*

The Synapse

The point at which an axon terminal and a dendrite almost join is called a *synapse* and is the area where transmission of impulses from one neuron to the next takes place. Note that the synaptic connection, including the axon terminal of one cell and the dendrite of another cell, does not violate the "neuron doctrine." A clear space, called the *synaptic cleft* or *synaptic space,* exists between the parts of the two cells. The important structural components of the synaptic junction are shown in Figure B-2.

The portion of cellular membrane that lines the synaptic space on the side of the axon terminal is called the *presynaptic* (before the synapse) membrane. That portion of cellular membrane of the next neuron lining the opposite side of the synaptic space is termed the *postsynaptic* (after the synapse) membrane. In addition to the larger organelles found occasionally within the synaptic regions of the two cells, one finds *synaptic vesicles* in the axon terminal. These are suspected to be the storage places for a chemical substance used to convey information from the axon terminal across the synaptic space to the dendrite or cell body of the next cell.

Functional Properties of the Neuron

The most important functional property of neurons is their electrical capacity. It is the electrical charge of each individual nerve cell that makes the transmission of nerve impulses possible. Electricity and chemistry do the work of the nervous system. We will describe several different electrical states of the neuron.

The Resting Membrane Potential

The neuron, like all living cells, possesses an electrical characteristic called the *resting membrane*

Figure B–2
The synapse

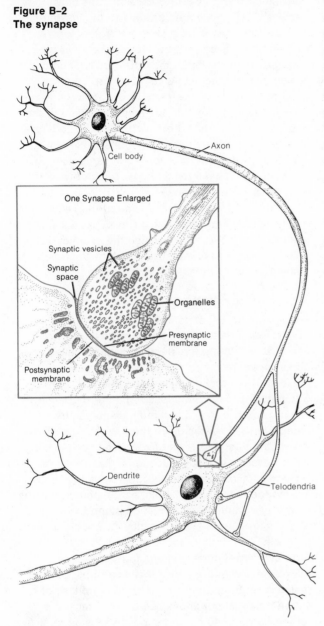

One Synapse Enlarged

Synaptic vesicles

Synaptic
space

Organelles

Presynaptic
membrane

Postsynaptic
membrane

Cell body

Axon

Dendrite

Telodendria

A single synaptic connection is enlarged to illustrate the structural details.

potential, which signals that it is alive and functioning normally. The resting membrane potential can be detected by means of a voltage measuring device, such as a voltmeter. One lead from the voltmeter is placed outside the cell; the other is connected by means of a fine wire, called a microelectrode, to the inside of the cell. When this is done, a voltage difference between the inside and outside of the cell is detected; it amounts to around

70 millivolts (thousandths of a volt), with the inside of the cell electrically negative with respect to the outside of the cell. It should be emphasized that this potential difference exists only *across* the cell membrane. The relative separation of electrical charge, with relatively more negative charge inside the cell membrane (or more positive charge outside the cell), is referred to as a state of *polarization.* Thus the resting membrane potential is analogous to a battery. The inside of the cell represents the negative pole and the outside of the cell represents the positive pole of the battery, with the voltage of the battery being approximately 70 millivolts. It is important to consider the mechanisms that generate and maintain the resting membrane potential before we consider the potentials that occur in active, nonresting neurons. The reason for this is that the electrical activity of all active neurons may be ultimately understood in terms of alterations in the resting membrane potential.

Before explaining the details of the resting membrane potential, it is necessary to deal briefly with several physical and chemical principles. Salt water will serve to illustrate several of these important concepts. When salt crystals dissolve in water, they break up into two elements, sodium (Na^+) and chloride (Cl^-). The positive and negative signs associated with the chemical symbols of sodium and chloride indicate that when they are in the dissolved state they possess an electrical charge—positive in the case of sodium and negative in the case of chloride. This is the case for many different types of molecules in solution. Any molecule fragment possessing an electrical charge is termed an *ion.* Thus sea water is composed of sodium and chloride ions.

The fluid that bathes the cells of the nervous system is very much like sea water and contains sodium (Na^+), chloride (Cl^-), and potassium (K^+) ions, as well as calcium (Ca^{++}) and magnesium (Mg^{++}) ions and more complicated molecules such as negatively charged protein ions. Simply stated, the resting membrane potential is due to an unequal distribution of ions across the cell membrane. This unequal distribution results in a more negative charge inside the cell than outside. Thus a 70-millivolt potential can be recorded that is negative inside relative to outside.

The unequal distribution of charged particles results from the operation of two physical–chemical principles relating to charged particles in solution. The first of these is the principle of *diffusion,* which states that substances in solution will tend to move from a region of higher concentration to one of lower concentration. The second factor determining the distribution of ions across the cell membrane is their *electrical charges.* The principle states that *unlike charges* tend to *attract one another* while *like charges repel.* Thus, two charged particles will tend to be drawn near each other if their charges are opposite (such as sodium and chloride) but will tend to repel each other if their charges are the same (such as sodium and potassium). The final factor resulting in an unequal distribution of ions across the cell membrane has to do with the structure of the membrane itself. The cell membrane is *semipermeable,* that is, the membrane "discriminates"—it will allow certain particles to pass through relatively unrestricted (such as potassium and chloride ions), but will not allow certain other particles to pass through at all (such as sodium and certain large protein ions).

Let us consider the situation surrounding each ion. The cell membrane is impermeable to the large negatively charged protein ions, which are consequently trapped inside the cell (see Figure B–3). Similarly, the membrane, when at rest, is impermeable to the positively charged sodium ions, which are therefore trapped *outside* the cell. The membrane is almost completely permeable to

potassium ions. Because potassium ions possess a positive charge they are attracted to the inside of the cell by the negatively charged protein ions, a movement assisted by repulsion by the positively charged sodium ions on the outside. The membrane is also almost completely permeable to chloride ions. Although they are free to move in and out of the cell, most of the chloride ions are forced to the outside, because they are attracted by the sodium ions and repelled by the protein ions, In keeping with the principle of diffusion, however, some potassium still manages to move to the outside of the cell (the region of lower concentration), while some chloride moves to the inside of the cell (where it is least concentrated). The net result is a slight excess of negative charge inside the cell, hence a −70-millivolt resting membrane potential, negative inside relative to outside.

The Action Potential

The means by which neurons conduct information to some destination within or outside the central nervous system are the electrical signals called *action potentials.* An action potential is a brief reversal of the resting membrane potential that originates at the axon hillock region of the nerve cell in response to some stimulus input to the neuron. It then travels down the axon, ultimately to invade the telodendria and axon terminals. As the input travels, it provides the signal that starts the process of synaptic transmission across the synaptic cleft to the next neuron. Thus, action potentials are means of conducting information along the length of a single neuron. Note that they do not cross the synapse.

An action potential is characterized by an initial *depolarization* (movement toward zero) of the resting membrane potential. This rising phase of the action potential continues past zero voltage to a value of around 40 millivolts, positive inside relative to the outside of the cell—a clear reversal of the resting membrane potential. This means that positively charged particles have broken through the discriminating membrane and invaded the inside of the cell. Following this +40-millivolt peak in the action potential, the voltage across the membrane begins to fall until it reaches a value slightly greater than its original resting value (about −75 millivolts, negative inside relative to outside), and after a brief period of time the membrane potential returns to its normal resting value. The period immediately after firing of an action potential is known as the *refractory period* because it is difficult to fire the neuron again during this time.

Figure B–3
Ion distribution

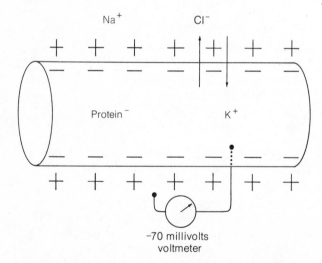

−70 millivolts
voltmeter

The relative distribution of ions across the cell membrane of a neuron. The membrane is almost completely permeable to potassium (K^+) and chloride (Cl^-) but impermeable to sodium (Na^+) and the large protein molecules. The result of the electrical and diffusional forces acting on these ions is a −70-millivolt resting membrane potential, negative inside relative to outside.

Once an action potential has begun at the axon hillock, it will travel down the axon in somewhat the way a wave travels on the top of a lake. But unlike a wave, it will maintain its amplitude, shape, and speed for the entire length of the axon, because the nerve impulse is generated anew at each stage of its progress. This is called the *all-or-none principle* of action potential travel (propagation). The action potential propagates down the axon all the way to the telodendria without changing any of its characteristics, somewhat like a burning fuse.

The actual mechanisms of the action potential are quite simple. The initial rising phase, during which the membrane voltage moves from −70 (inside) to +40 millivolts, is due to a temporary increase in the permeability of the cell membrane to sodium ions. You will recall that under resting conditions, the cell membrane is essentially impermeable to sodium. This temporary breakdown of the membrane barrier to sodium results in a rapid but brief influx (inward movement) of sodium ions into the interior of the cell because of the tremendous electrical and diffusional forces acting in this direction.

The alteration in permeability lasts only a brief time (around 1 millisecond), and then the membrane permeability to sodium is restored to normal—the membrane recovers, the sodium is "pumped" outside the cell, and the resting potential returns to −70 millivolts. This event begins the falling phase of the action potential. The falling portion of the action potential is caused by a temporary but complete increase in membrane permeability to potassium. Although the membrane is almost completely permeable to potassium in the resting state, there still exists a slight barrier that is broken down only during the falling phase of the action potential. The resulting efflux (movement outward) of potassium causes the membrane potential to fall from its peak of +40 millivolts (inside) to about −75 millivolts (the relative refractory phase), a value slightly more negative than the resting membrane potential. When the membrane permeability to potassium is restored to normal, the normal resting membrane potential returns. These events are illustrated schematically in Figure B–4.

One final point should be mentioned. We have described generation and propagation of action potentials as they occur in an unmyelinated axon. Action potentials are generated in the same way in myelinated axons—a change in the membrane potential by alterations in membrane permeability to sodium and potassium. Propagation, however, is different. The fuse does not just burn its way to the synapse. Instead, the action potentials occur only at

Figure B–4
The action potential

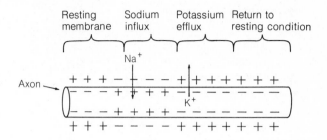

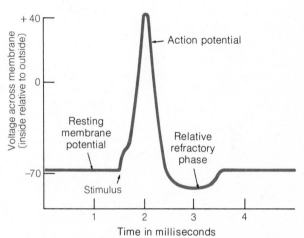

The graph (below) shows the change in voltage across the cell membrane during the rise and fall of the action potential. The voltage changes are produced by the events occurring across the membrane (illustrated above). Thus the rising phase of the action potential is caused by a brief influx of positive sodium ions, and the *hyperpolarization* (movement of the membrane potential away from zero) is produced by the efflux of positive potassium ions. Note that the entire action potential is of relatively short duration.

the nodes of Ranvier, the small gaps in the myelin sheath. Thus the action potential, instead of moving down the axon, "jumps" from one node of Ranvier to the next. This kind of action potential conduction is called *saltatory conduction,* and the most important feature of it is that propagation down the axon is much faster than that occurring in unmyelinated fibers. Myelination is a relatively recent development in evolution. It provides large organisms, like human beings, with very rapid conduction of nerve impulses from one place to another. This, of course, is particularly important as the axons of neurons become extremely long (some axons extend from the cortex to the lower spinal cord, a distance of several feet). Without myelination, a much longer time would be required to conduct information over such long distances.

Synaptic Transmission

The all-or-none action potential is the mechanism by which a neuron conducts information from its cell body (actually the axon hillock region) to the distant reaches of its axon terminals. But the transfer of information across the synaptic space between neurons is by means of *synaptic transmission.* The sequence of events that defines synaptic transmission may be summarized as follows:

1. An action potential traveling down the axon invades the telodendria and axon terminals.

2. This produces a release of a chemical transmitter substance from the axon terminal into the synaptic space (refer to Figure B–2 to review the structure of a synapse).

3. The chemical transmitter substance moves across the synaptic space in accordance with the principle of diffusion, discussed earlier.

4. The transmitter substance comes in contact with the postsynaptic membrane and alters the permeability of the postsynaptic membrane to one or more ions.

These events are essentially the same for all synapses, except that the chemical transmitter substance may be different for different neurons, and the change in permeability of the postsynaptic membrane may be different for different kinds of synapses. There are essentially two functional categories of synapses in the nervous system, *excitatory* synapses (the next neuron is excited) and *inhibitory* synapses (the next neuron is inhibited).

Excitation.   Although we have discussed the mechanisms that generate and carry action potentials, we have not yet dealt with how action potentials are initiated. Some are initiated by external stimuli. The eye, for example, is a specialized device that converts (transduces) light energy into electrical energy, which can give rise to action potentials. Within the nervous system, however, action potentials are initiated most commonly by the process of excitatory synaptic transmission. Excitatory synaptic transmission is the means by which one cell is able to increase the probability of an action potential in another cell.

Following invasion of the telodendria by an action potential, synaptic transmitter substance is released into the synaptic space, diffuses across the space to the postsynaptic membrane, and produces a change in the permeability of the membrane to the sodium, potassium, and chloride ions. The ions that have the

most potent effect in this instance are the sodium ions, because they are characterized by the most unequal distribution across the cell membrane during the resting state. The result of increasing the membrane permeability to these ions is, therefore, a net *depolarization* of the membrane, that is, a movement of the resting potential toward zero.

Unlike the depolarization that characterizes the rising phase of the action potential, the depolarization produced by excitatory transmitter action is dependent upon the strength of the input stimulus. Thus, synaptic activation results in a *graded* response (its size is proportional to the strength of the stimulus) in the postsynaptic cell, rather than an all-or-none response. The depolarization produced by excitatory synaptic activity is termed an *excitatory postsynaptic potential,* or more commonly an EPSP. The relationship between the EPSP and production of an action potential is depicted schematically in Figure B–5.

Whether the cell will fire an action potential as a result of excitatory synaptic activation is entirely dependent upon whether the EPSP reaches the critical level of depolarization necessary to initiate an all-or-none action potential. This critical level is termed the *firing threshold* of the neuron. If the size of the EPSP is below the firing threshold, then the postsynaptic cell will simply return to a quiescent state. If the EPSP reaches the critical firing threshold, an action potential will be initiated at the axon hillock and will then travel down the axon in an all-or-none fashion to the axon terminals of the cell and start the process of synaptic activity once again.

An analogy is usually made between excitatory synaptic activation and pulling the trigger of a rifle. The trigger may be pulled gently and returned to its resting position without firing the rifle. The pull of the trigger represents an EPSP. If the trigger is pulled to some critical level (representing the firing threshold), the rifle will fire a single, all-or-none discharge, analogous to the action potential. The threshold can also be reached by *summation* of EPSPs that occur close together on the dendrite (spatial summation) or close together in time (temporal summation).

Inhibition.   If all synapses in the nervous system were excitatory, it would be easy to start some neural activity but extremely difficult to stop it. Fortunately, there are many neurons in the nervous system that perform an inhibitory function. The processes of inhibitory synaptic transmission are

Figure B-5
Excitation and inhibition

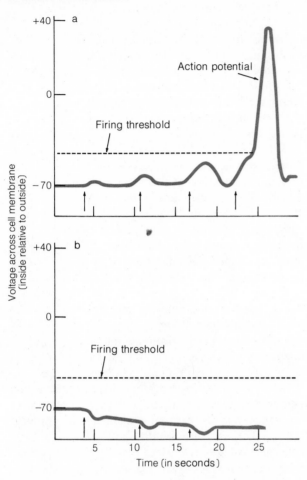

Activation of excitatory synapses results in excitatory postsynaptic potentials, shown in the top graph. Each arrow indicates activation at the synapse. Each successive activation is by a stronger stimulus. The last stimulus produces an EPSP large enough to reach the firing threshold and fire an action potential. Inhibitory postsynaptic potentials are illustrated in the bottom graph. Each arrow represents activation of an inhibitory synapse. Each activation is stronger than the preceding one. Notice that the resting membrane potential is pulled away from the firing threshold by inhibitory synaptic activation.

essentially the same as those outlined above except that the transmitter substance is often different and the change in the permeability of the postsynaptic membrane is different. The result of inhibitory synaptic activity is essentially the opposite of excitatory synaptic activity. The membrane voltage becomes *hyperpolarized* (that is, it is moved away from zero to become more negative inside than

normal). The trigger is now harder to pull—it will take more effort, meaning a stronger stimulus, to excite this hyperpolarized cell. The hyperpolarization (called an inhibitory postsynaptic potential, or IPSP) is probably caused by an increase in membrane permeability to potassium ($K+$) and chloride ($Cl-$) ions. This allows potassium to flow out of the membrane and chloride to flow in, making the inside more negative relative to the outside of the membrane. Some examples of inhibitory postsynaptic potentials are shown in Figure B-5.

Neurotransmitter Substances

Excitatory and inhibitory postsynaptic potentials in neurons in human brains are generated by the actions of chemical messengers released from the small endpoints of axons, called *synaptic boutons*. A general description of the process of synaptic action was given at the beginning of this section. We will now describe two chemical substances believed to act as major synaptic transmitters.

Acetylcholine.   Scientists have discovered that *acetylcholine* is the synaptic transmitter at the synapse between peripheral motor neurons, that is, those neurons that have connections with muscles and muscle tissue. It is by the release of acetylcholine that muscular activity is generated and maintained. It can be safely assumed that acetylcholine serves as the excitatory transmitter substance in these cases. That is, acetylcholine generates excitatory postsynaptic potentials and action potentials to produce muscle contraction. There is also abundant evidence that acetylcholine is found in the vesicles of presynaptic endings in the central nervous system. However, it is not clear whether acetylcholine serves as an excitatory or an inhibitory synaptic transmitter in these cases. The most probable answer is that it performs both functions in different parts of the brain.

   Acetylcholine is often considered inhibitory with regard to *behavioral excitability* or reactivity to sensory stimulation (measured, for example, as the overall activity level of an animal). Drugs that increase the level of acetylcholine in the brain often produce a reduction in activity, while drugs that destroy or inactivate acetylcholine often lead to hyperexcitability. The inhibition of activity could be entirely indirect, however. Acetylcholine might be excitatory at synapses in the central nervous system, but subsequent neurons on which it acts might be inhibitory, resulting in indirect behavioral inhibition. Interestingly, curare, the drug used by Amazonian Indians on the tips of penetrating hunting weapons, blocks the action of acetylcholine at the neuromuscular synaptic junction, thus blocking the ability of the animal to move its muscles. Curare is broken down in the stomach so that eating the prey does not result in paralysis.

Norepinephrine.   The second major transmitter substance, *norepinephrine,* was also first identified as acting in the peripheral nerves. But recently norepinephrine has been identified in the brain and is believed to be a synaptic transmitter there as well. The evidence suggests that norepinephrine, and several related chemicals, may play a role in behavioral excitability. If the levels of norepinephrine in the brain are increased slowly, behavioral excitability and reactivity increase, which suggests that it may function antagonistically to acetylcholine.

A particularly interesting theory of certain forms of behavior pathology has arisen through work on the *biogenic amines,* as norepinephrine and its related compounds have been called. The theory, called the biogenic amine theory of mood, suggests that the biogenic amines may control or produce changes in a person's mood, even to the extreme levels of mania or depression. Although preliminary, the theory is exciting because it relates human behavior pathology to naturally occurring substances in the brain.

Control of neurotransmitters.   It may be beneficial, before ending our discussion of synaptic activity, to describe the fate of neurotransmitters once they have done their job. As described earlier, the substance is released from the presynaptic ending, diffuses across the synaptic space, and activates or inhibits the postsynaptic neuron. After this important function either the substance may be broken down by special enzymes within or near the synapse, or it may be taken back into the presynaptic terminal for future use, a process called "reuptake," similar to recycling.

For example, in the *cholinergic system* (based on

transmission by acetylcholine) there is a chemical, *cholinesterase,* that "inactivates" acetylcholine that has been released from the synaptic vesicles. Without this inactivation mechanism, the acetylcholine would continue to affect the postsynaptic membrane for some time. In the *adrenergic system* (based on norepinephrine) the transmitters seem to be inactivated by the "reuptake" route—they are reabsorbed in the presynaptic terminal and probably stored again in the vesicles.

Drugs and neural transmission.   Many important behavioral effects of drugs are believed to take place at the level of synaptic events. To oversimplify, we can divide these effects into three categories. First, the drug might just mimic the transmitter. It may be a chemical so close in structure to the transmitter that it can "impersonate" the transmitter and have the same effect—excitation or inhibition. Second, the drug might "impersonate" the *effects* of the chemical that inactivates the transmitter. For example, some drugs appear to work by inactivating cholinesterase (the inactivator of acetylcholine), thus allowing the acetylocholine to have a greater effect.

The third way drugs can affect neural transmission and ultimately behavior is by directly interfering with the transmitter. Of course, the effect will be opposite to the effect of the transmitter. Such drugs are called *blocking agents*—they block the action of the transmitter and produce the opposite effect. If the transmitter is excitatory, the blocking agent will produce inhibition, and if it is inhibitory, the blocking agent will produce excitation. Thus, blocking agents are like substitutes for the inactivators of the transmitters.

With at least three different means of action, two basic systems (cholinergic and adrenergic), and several transmitters, it is no wonder that many different drugs can have profound effects on the nervous system.

C

PSYCHOLOGICAL TESTS AND ASSESSMENT TECHNIQUES

Test Construction

How are psychological tests constructed? Where do personality and behavioral assessment techniques come from? Does a psychologist just sit at his desk and decide arbitrarily on what will work? How can he be sure that what he makes up will measure what he says it measures? Are test scores meaningful? These questions may have arisen in your mind as we discussed several different kinds of psychological tests, including tests of intelligence, creativity, personality, and so on. Our description of the process of test construction and use appears as an appendix because the subject is technical and complex and therefore probably not of general interest in an introductory course. This appendix will be useful if, for some special reason, you want or need to know more about the origin and the development of tests.

Selecting Test Items

A psychological test is made up of a set of individual items—questions, commands, or stimuli—that the test subject must respond to. The particular form of the items depends on the purpose of the test. For example, to measure verbal fluency, the subject may be asked for the definitions of words; to measure short-term memory, he may be asked to repeat five digits backwards; and to measure creativity, he may be asked to name as many unusual uses for a brick as he can.

In many cases, the constructor of a new test will analyze available tests and select his items from those that have been successful in the past. If he is working in a new area, he may have no recourse but to make up his own items, perhaps asking colleagues and students to help. In either case the test constructor must gather an abundance of various types of items, for in the process of refining his test he is bound to find many items that are poor or worthless and therefore must be discarded.

The first hurdle that a test item must pass is *face validity;* that is, does the item appear on the surface as though it will correlate with the trait or variable being measured? After a large pool of items has been gathered, it is almost always found that some appear more valid than others. To measure the IQ of a 14-year-old, it seems intuitively clear (even theoretically clear, if we consider Piaget's theory discussed in Chapter 7) that defining abstract words is a better test item than building a stack of blocks. So some items in the pool are quickly rejected on grounds of appearance alone. The test constructor should be sure to have many more items than he will need in the final form of the test, because there are other reasons besides lack of face validity for eliminating items.

Trial Administration

After the test constructor has compiled an initial set of test items, the next step is to administer the test to a sample of people. The sample should be representative of those to whom the final test is meant to apply. For example, if the test is for children between 3 and 12 years old, then the sample should be likewise composed. Sometimes several samples are needed, as, for example, when there are too many items for one group to handle in a reasonable time period.

After the tests have been scored, individual items are examined to see how well they performed. Suppose, for example, that a psychologist wants to develop an age scale for intelligence. He wants items that discriminate ages—that are failed by all up to a certain age and passed by all beyond that age. An item that is passed by roughly the same percentage of subjects at every age is a poor item for his purpose and must be rejected. For example, an item that no 3-year-old passes and no 5-year-old fails would be kept and used in the 4-year-old scale (Item A in Figure C–1). Item B in Figure C–1 is likewise very good, although at an older age level. It too would be kept. Item C is marginal and would be rejected if the psychologist had enough other items to replace it. Item D is an unusable item and must be eliminated under any circumstances.

There are two other main criteria for evaluating an item. First, is the item *reliable?* Item reliability means that a given subject will perform at the same level on the item on two different occasions. Second, is the item *valid* beyond mere face validity? Validity means that the item should measure what it is supposed to measure. The tester rates items on reliability by correlating the scores obtained from a group of subjects who have taken the test twice and have thus been tested on the same item on two different occasions. He rates items on validity by correlating the item scores with some other known measure of the characteristic in question, in this case intelligence. These considerations apply not only to individual items, but also to the test as a whole, and they are more easily discussed in that context.

Standardization

On the basis of item analysis, the test constructor arrives ideally at a final form for his test. He assigns

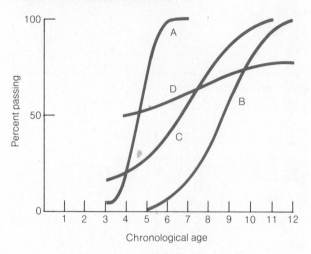

Figure C–1
Usable and unusable test items

Functions showing percentage of subjects who pass four different test items at each chronological age. Items A and B would be usable in a test to develop an age scale for intelligence. Item C could be used although it does not discriminate as well. Item D should not be used.

items to scales, selecting comparable numbers for each. For an age test, he groups items according to the age of maximal discrimination. For a point scale, he groups items according to type, for instance, vocabulary items and current events items, and arranges them in order of difficulty. He keeps only the best items. Then he administers the final form to a large sample of subjects for standardization purposes.

One purpose of test standardization is to work out the final details of the test procedure. To be fair to every individual, the test must be administered under comparable conditions and in a reasonably constant way. For example, test scores might not be comparable if the test were given under favorable conditions—good lighting, quiet room, period of alertness—to some individuals and unfavorable conditions—dark and noisy room, period of fatigue—to others. In intelligence testing particularly, even minor and seemingly unimportant variations, such as the time between items, can have significant effects. The aim is to identify the test conditions that maximize performance and then make sure that all subjects are tested under these conditions.

A second function of the standardization phase of test construction is to provide *test norms*. This is a complex issue and not easily described in general

"We had intelligence tests today. Boy!
Were they HARD!"

In constructing tests, we must remember that a test item that everyone gets correct is not worth very much if the goal is to discriminate among people in terms of the amount of knowledge or ability or intelligence they possess. Likewise, an item that is failed by everybody taking the test is not very helpful. Try to remember this important feature of test construction the next time you have a test in your psychology class.

terms. The norms for a personality test are fundamentally different from the norms for an intelligence test. Establishing norms involves determining the *average* or *typical level of performance* on the test and devising a measure of score variability. Therefore, the relevant statistics are measures of central tendency, such as the mean, and measures of variability in the frequency distribution of test scores, such as the standard deviation.

Consider, for example, a point scale IQ test. Each item passed in each subscale is awarded a certain number of points, and the total score is the sum of all earned points. In order to understand the score of any particular subject, the tester needs to know how it compares with the scores of similar people. Knowing that 16-year-old Billy earned a score of 75 points on the test is not particularly informative. To make sense of that score, the tester needs to know the average score for people like him. It makes considerable difference whether that mean is 100 or 70. Likewise, it is helpful to have an idea of the

variation in scores. A score of 75 in a distribution with a mean of 70 and a standard deviation of 2 is indicative of much better performance than a score of 75 in a distribution with a mean of 70 and a standard deviation of 15 (see Appendix A).

The norms of a test usually consist of means and standard deviations for all relevant subgroupings of subjects. Indeed, the better-developed tests provide this information for various classifications, such as different age, different subscales, and so on. To simplify interpretations, many norms are converted to some standard scoring across subclassification. For example, it has become conventional to transform intelligence test scores in such a way that, regardless of age of subject or subscale of test, the mean score is 100. For all subclassifications of the Wechsler test, the standard deviation in IQ points is 15.

Reliability

Standard test conditions and normative data are important in psychological testing, but the primary objective signs of a good test are *reliability* and *validity*. A rigorous check on reliability can be made in any of three ways, and occasionally all three are used. In the *test-retest method,* the same test is administered twice to some subjects. When there are two comparable forms of the test, which is especially desirable if there is the possibility of some transfer with repeated administrations of the same test, the *alternate forms method* can be used. In this method, reliability is indexed by the correlation between the sets of scores obtained by subgroups of subjects who took the different forms of the same test. The *split-half method* is the easiest and most economical check. Here the items of the test are divided into two comparable groups or halves, and the resulting two sets of scores are correlated.

In any case, the higher the correlation between the two sets of scores, the more reliable is the test and, by implication, all items within it. The best known tests of intelligence have reliability coefficients of .90 and above, which are extraordinarily high correlations. Such a high correlation indicates that a person is very likely to score approximately the same every time he takes the test.

Validity

Validity is the degree to which a test correlates with some accepted criterion of the behavior being measured. We shall consider briefly three kinds of validity. A test of *concurrent validity* is made when the new test is compared with existing tests designed to accomplish the same purpose. A psychologist might, for example, correlate scores on his IQ test with scores obtained by the same subjects on the familiar Wechsler-Bellevue test. If the correlation is high, he can conclude that his test measures what the Wechsler test measures, presumably intelligence.

Predictive validity is based on somewhat less circular reasoning. Here the tester asks if his test can predict later performance. Using subsequent school achievement to validate an IQ test is an example. If a psychologist has designed a test to select students with high engineering aptitude, later grade-point average in engineering school would be his criterion. Again, validity is measured by the magnitude of the correlation between test and the criterion it is used to predict.

Finally, when the test is designed to measure a theoretical idea or construct, its validity is judged by the extent to which it conforms to the requirements of the theory. *Construct validity* is a matter of logical analysis, not correlation. An "unusual uses" test is a valid measure of the construct of creativity according to theories that describe creativity in terms of divergent thinking and remote associative processes. But if one's theory emphasized personality traits, such as permissiveness, in creativity, a personality inventory (see Chapter 9) would be a more valid measure.

The validity of psychological tests varies with the type of behavior or construct measured. IQ tests are extremely valid, as measured in both the concurrent and predictive sense. We find correlation coefficients up to .90. Tests of less well-known processes such as creativity are acceptable with validity correlations of .50 to .60. In some cases of personality assessment, validity might be lower or not even rigorously established. The higher the validity, the better and more useful the test, but validity should not be taken as an overriding requirement. A test with low validity is often better than none at all, especially in a new research area.

Personality Assessment

Describing the personality of friends, relatives, or strangers is one of the oldest and most popular forms of entertainment. To a psychologist, however, it is a very serious business. Over the years, people have developed many different ways of arriving at statements describing a person's personality. At one time, for example, it was believed that analyzing the bumps on a person's head would reveal his personality. Others felt that different personality

types had different body shapes. Personality has been assessed by analysis of handwriting (graphology), the planets (astrology), the lines in your hands (palmistry), and the tea leaves at the bottom of your cup. Developing ways to describe other people's personalities appears to be important to everyone.

Personality assessment is the process of objectively measuring the fundamental properties of an individual's personality. To the professional psychologist, the personality assessment techniques are major tools for understanding people and for describing, predicting, and helping them change their behavior. Psychological assessment and measurement has become a highly sophisticated enterprise. Many of the assessment procedures can be administered and interpreted only by people with considerable mathematical and statistical training in addition to a thorough knowledge of personality theory, although some of the tests can be given and scored by trained assistants. The development of new assessment procedures and modification and refinement of techniques already in use is an ongoing interest of psychologists who study personality.

Uses of Personality Tests

Personality tests are used for two basic purposes: to make a diagnostic decision or to further understanding of the concept of personality. There are two distinct types of diagnostic decisions made on the basis of test results: (1) mental health decisions, that is, whether or not the person is sane, what kind of therapy to use, what aspects of his personality are abnormal, and the like; and (2) prediction decisions, that is, predictions about whether or not a person will be successful in some area, say school or on the job.

The most important and most frequent use of psychological tests is to diagnose mental disorders. You probably know that psychologists and psychiatrists are often called upon by the courts to determine if someone is "legally" sane or not. But not every person with a behavior disorder is involved with the courts. Usually it is the therapist who administers psychological testing in order to understand his client's problem and develop rational ways of proceeding in therapy. For many clinical psychologists, behavior or mental disorder means personality disorder, and personality measurement is the first step in diagnosis and therapy. The therapist must be able to measure personality if he is going to base his treatment on the notion that something is abnormal about the personality of his clients. The decisions made on the basis of these assessment procedures have incredibly important implications for the client. The results may determine whether or not he is committed to a hospital, sentenced to a prison, allowed to continue on his job or keep his children, and so on. Thus the measures of personality, the procedures used to make these judgments, must be the best that psychologists can devise. It may be fun to read handwriting, or tea leaves, or palms, or the stars, but these assessment techniques are not acceptable means for deciding whether or not a person should be declared insane.

Assessment procedures are also used to make nonclinical decisions and predictions about future behavior. In education, psychologists use the principles of psychological assessment to develop ability, aptitude, and achievement tests. Intelligence testing is used to diagnose mental retardation, reading difficulties, discipline problems, grade level, who gets into college, medical school, law school, and so on. In industry, personality assessment has become an important aspect of executive hiring. There are also tests of manual ability that determine who gets hired at a factory. The military uses psychological tests in planning the training programs of new recruits and in deciding who is qualified for what service. The government uses psychological tests to make hiring decisions. Just about every area of our lives has been invaded by people using behavioral tests to make decisions about us, decisions that have great impact on us.

Despite the importance of the topic, psychologists do not agree completely on what personality is or how it is to be measured. There is a lack of understanding of the concept of personality, and therefore a great deal of research effort is being devoted to the topic. In order to do research on personality, it is necessary to have personality tests that can be used to test hypotheses about what personality is. For example, psychologists who believe that personality is made up of a set of traits need ways to demonstrate this in a rigorous fashion. New conceptions of personality mean developing new ways of assessing personality; thus personality tests play a crucial role in the development and refinement of the concept of personality.

Types of Personality Assessment

Basically, there are three types of assessment procedures: interviews, objective tests, and projective tests. In an *interview* the subject is engaged in a conversation with a psychologist for the purpose of informing the psychologist about the subject's personality. This is an informal procedure and one of the oldest methods of finding out about a person.

The second technique, the *objective test,* is sometimes called a *personality inventory* or *self-report measure.* The procedure is to ask the person to answer, usually in writing, a number of objective questions about himself and his behavior. It is *assumed* that he will report the true facts about himself, or perhaps the test might be developed in such a way as to determine if he is being truthful. As you might suspect, this is an area of great debate —can an *accurate* measure of personality be arrived at from self-report measures?

The final technique is the *projective test,* a much less objective procedure. The "questions" on these tests are unstructured and not clearly stated. A trained psychologist is required to score and interpret projective tests, and there is considerable room for disagreement about the meaning of the responses. Those who use and defend these tests argue that their value lies in the vagueness that others criticize. The situation is so unstructured for the subject that there is no way he can "fake" his responses. For example, he would have no way of knowing how "sane" as opposed to "insane" persons would answer. These tests are limited primarily to clinical diagnosis of behavior disorders. In fact, the name *projective* derives from the clinical idea of projection. The test is so ambiguous that the subject will have to *project* his own personality into it to provide some structure and a way of responding. The basic problem with these tests is the difficulty of developing reliable and universally accepted ways of analyzing the highly unusual and idiosyncratic responses of the subject.

Interviews. The most obvious way to assess a person's personality is to talk and interact with him, the technique we all use in everyday affairs. It is the most common way of "getting to know" someone else. A somewhat more formalized version of this procedure is the psychological *interview,* which can be thought of as a form of social interaction, a conversation, with the definite purpose of diagnosis. The interviewer wants to know some particular behavioral fact or facts about the interviewee.

Structure. In contrast to other personality assessment procedures, the interview is relatively informal and can be conducted in a variety of ways. A completely unstructured interview takes whatever direction the interviewee wishes to pursue. The interviewer acts merely as a sounding board and tries not to guide or direct the conversation. The classical example of an unstructured interview is that conducted by a client-centered therapist, who responds infrequently and neutrally to whatever his client says. Usually, however, the interviewer imposes some structure, for time is limited and there are particular facts that he must learn. Interviews can be so highly structured and programmed that there may be no need for the interviewer at all; the interviewee merely fills in a questionnaire. Personality inventories are often described as completely structured interviews.

Control. In most cases the interviewer controls the session in fairly obvious ways. He has particular questions to ask, he allows the interviewee to answer only in certain ways, and he cuts the interview off at his own discretion. The interviewer's behavior also has subtle effects on the conduct of the interview. First, interviewers typically subscribe to a particular personality theory. For example, a psychoanalytically oriented psychologist might ask questions about the person's childhood or questions that are indicative of unconscious processes. An existential theorist might concentrate on the present existence of the interviewee. An interviewer with leanings toward learning theory might be curious about the important stimulus situations in a person's life and the reinforcers, especially social, that control his behavior. Thus the theoretical orientation of the interviewer may lend subtle structure to a session beyond any stated purpose or procedural principles that might be involved.

Research has demonstrated even more subtle effects of the interviewer's behavior. By a simple nod of his head the interviewer may greatly increase the amount of talking by the client. A frown may lead the interviewee to drop the current topic of conversation. The fact that interviewers are often unaware of their reactions to the conversation means that an interview can fail or proceed along relatively unproductive lines.

Field observation. A variation on the interview is a field test procedure. The subject is interviewed or observed, usually without his knowledge, as he performs in real life settings. A psychologist watching a problem child in the school classroom from behind a one-way vision screen would be an example. During World War II the United States government selected candidates for secret and hazardous missions by observing their reactions to threats, stress, and pain. These examples might give you the impression of a 1984 society with "Big Brother watching," which many people find

objectionable, if not intolerable. But whether you condone them or not, field observation techniques are used. Furthermore, given the fact that a person's behavior is greatly determined by the specifics of his immediate situation, these procedures turn out to be especially powerful and successful.

Rating scales. Interviews and related assessment procedures sometimes move at a fast pace, and thus the interviewer needs a way of quickly and accurately recording responses and events for later analysis. He may try to remember everything and write it down later, but if he has many interviews to conduct during the day, his memory is bound to be fuzzy for specifics at some later time. Even if he tape records every interview, the feelings or reactions *he* had at the time of the interview may be forgotten.

For convenience the interviewer may resort to a shorthand form of note taking known as a *rating scale.* A rating scale is a device by which an interviewer can rapidly and at any convenient time record his judgment of the subject according to several dimensions. The most common form is the *graphic rating scale.* Each dimension of the subject's personality that is considered critical, such as friendliness or industriousness, is represented by a segmented line. One end represents one extreme of the dimension (usually friendly or industrious) and the other end is the opposite extreme (very hostile or lazy). The interviewer places a checkmark at the appropriate place on the line to represent his judgment of the person's position relative to all other people that he knows. Ratings can be made either during or immediately after an interview. With a sufficiently complete list of scales, the interviewer can create an accurate description of the subject's personality or some components of his personality in a quick and relatively reliable way.

Inventories. A personality inventory generally consists of a large number of objective questions about one's behavior. The test taker is asked about his attitudes, hobbies, personal habits, friends and family, and so on. Usually the inventory is designed to measure his personality on several different scales. The test might have 10 subscales, each one presumably measuring a different aspect of personality, and for each subscale there might be 10 to 20 questions designed to get at that factor or subscale.

The MMPI. The most famous and widely used objective personality instrument is the Minnesota Multiphasic Personality Inventory, known simply as the MMPI. It consists of 550 statements that the subject must judge as being either "true" of himself, "false," or "cannot say." The items were selected because they are answered differently by normal people and psychiatric patients. The MMPI was developed by testing people with known behavior disorders and is used mainly as a diagnostic instrument for detecting psychiatric problems, although it can be used to assess individual differences in normal personality as well.

Statements on the MMPI are of this variety:

1. I have trouble making new friends.
2. I am seldom troubled by nightmares.
3. At times, my mind is very confused.
4. My parents often punished me physically.
5. I seldom get headaches.

The 550 items are usually analyzed into 10 basic "clinical" scales and 4 "validity" scales (to determine whether the subject has answered the test validly and truthfully). The 10 clinical scales are:

1. Hypochondriasis (HS)—a scale of how often the subject complains about his physical health.
2. Depression (D)—a scale of how depressed and pessimistic the subject is.
3. Hysteria (Hy)—a measure of neurotic reaction to stress by denial of problems with accompanying medical complaints.
4. Psychopathic deviation (Pd)—a measure of the subject's feelings about rules, laws, moral conduct, ethics, and so on.
5. Masculinity-femininity (Mf)—a measure of the orientation of the subject toward the traditional masculine or feminine behavior roles.
6. Paranoia (Pa)—a measure of how suspicious the subject is, particularly in the area of interpersonal relations.
7. Psychasthenia (Pt)—a measure of how obsessed the person is with certain thoughts and how compulsive (rigid) he is in his behavior.
8. Schizophrenia (Sc)—a measure of how withdrawn the subject is from the real world and the degree to which his thinking could be described as bizarre.
9. Hypomania (Ma)—a measure of how excited and active the subject is, particularly his tendency to show unusual elation and excitement.
10. Social introversion (Si)—a measure of introversion-extroversion.

As an example of how the MMPI differentiates between specified groups of individuals, consider

Figure C–2
Differentiating groups with the MMPI

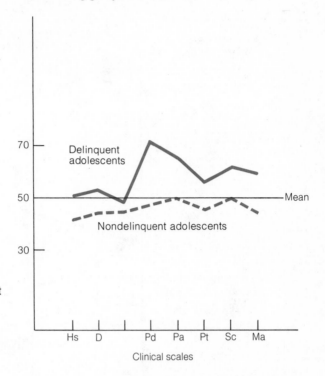

Scores for a group of delinquent adolescents and a group of nondelinquent adolescents on 8 of the 10 clinical scales of the MMPI. The largest difference between the two groups appears on the Pd (psychopathic deviation) scale.

the results of a study in which the test was administered to delinquent and nondelinquent adolescents. As you might guess, the largest difference between the two groups was on the psychopathic deviation (Pd) scale (see Figure C–2). The MMPI has proven to be a very useful clinical tool and has also contributed notably to research on behavior disorders. However, its use as a screening device, say, for job applicants, has been severely criticized. Would you think it appropriate for a large company to require all its workers to take the MMPI?

The 16 PF (16 personality factors). Another major inventory, the 16 PF, was developed by using only normal subjects. This is the test devised by Raymond Cattell in order to assess the basic factors of normal personality. Recall that Cattell's factor analytic studies indicated that human personality could be adequately characterized by 16 source

Figure C–3
A 16 PF test profile

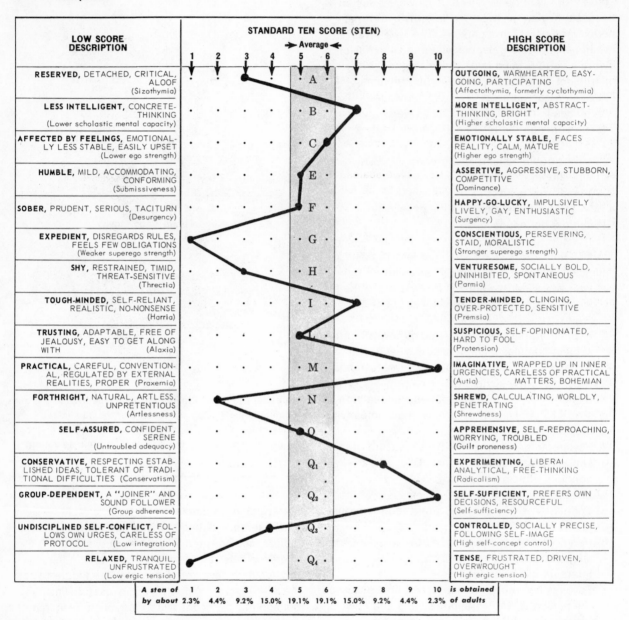

LOW SCORE DESCRIPTION	STANDARD TEN SCORE (STEN) → Average ←										HIGH SCORE DESCRIPTION
	1	2	3	4	5	6	7	8	9	10	
RESERVED, DETACHED, CRITICAL, ALOOF (Sizothymia)			A								**OUTGOING,** WARMHEARTED, EASY-GOING, PARTICIPATING (Affectothymia, formerly cyclothymia)
LESS INTELLIGENT, CONCRETE-THINKING (Lower scholastic mental capacity)				B							**MORE INTELLIGENT,** ABSTRACT-THINKING, BRIGHT (Higher scholastic mental capacity)
AFFECTED BY FEELINGS, EMOTIONAL-LY LESS STABLE, EASILY UPSET (Lower ego strength)					C						**EMOTIONALLY STABLE,** FACES REALITY, CALM, MATURE (Higher ego strength)
HUMBLE, MILD, ACCOMMODATING, CONFORMING (Submissiveness)					E						**ASSERTIVE,** AGGRESSIVE, STUBBORN, COMPETITIVE (Dominance)
SOBER, PRUDENT, SERIOUS, TACITURN (Desurgency)					F						**HAPPY-GO-LUCKY,** IMPULSIVELY LIVELY, GAY, ENTHUSIASTIC (Surgency)
EXPEDIENT, DISREGARDS RULES, FEELS FEW OBLIGATIONS (Weaker superego strength)						G					**CONSCIENTIOUS,** PERSEVERING, STAID, MORALISTIC (Stronger superego strength)
SHY, RESTRAINED, TIMID, THREAT-SENSITIVE (Threctia)					H						**VENTURESOME,** SOCIALLY BOLD, UNINHIBITED, SPONTANEOUS (Parmia)
TOUGH-MINDED, SELF-RELIANT, REALISTIC, NO-NONSENSE (Harria)					I						**TENDER-MINDED,** CLINGING, OVER-PROTECTED, SENSITIVE (Premsia)
TRUSTING, ADAPTABLE, FREE OF JEALOUSY, EASY TO GET ALONG WITH (Alaxia)					L						**SUSPICIOUS,** SELF-OPINIONATED, HARD TO FOOL (Protension)
PRACTICAL, CAREFUL, CONVENTION-AL, REGULATED BY EXTERNAL REALITIES, PROPER (Praxernia)					M						**IMAGINATIVE,** WRAPPED UP IN INNER URGENCIES, CARELESS OF PRACTICAL (Autia) MATTERS, BOHEMIAN
FORTHRIGHT, NATURAL, ARTLESS, UNPRETENTIOUS (Artlessness)					N						**SHREWD,** CALCULATING, WORLDLY, PENETRATING (Shrewdness)
SELF-ASSURED, CONFIDENT, SERENE (Untroubled adequacy)					O						**APPREHENSIVE,** SELF-REPROACHING, WORRYING, TROUBLED (Guilt proneness)
CONSERVATIVE, RESPECTING ESTAB-LISHED IDEAS, TOLERANT OF TRADI-TIONAL DIFFICULTIES (Conservatism)					Q_1						**EXPERIMENTING,** LIBERAL, ANALYTICAL, FREE-THINKING (Radicalism)
GROUP-DEPENDENT, A "JOINER" AND SOUND FOLLOWER (Group adherence)					Q_2						**SELF-SUFFICIENT,** PREFERS OWN DECISIONS, RESOURCEFUL (Self-sufficiency)
UNDISCIPLINED SELF-CONFLICT, FOL-LOWS OWN URGES, CARELESS OF PROTOCOL (Low integration)					Q_3						**CONTROLLED,** SOCIALLY PRECISE, FOLLOWING SELF-IMAGE (High self-concept control)
RELAXED, TRANQUIL, UNFRUSTRATED (Low ergic tension)					Q_4						**TENSE,** FRUSTRATED, DRIVEN, OVERWROUGHT (High ergic tension)

A sten of	1	2	3	4	5	6	7	8	9	10	*is obtained*
by about	2.3%	4.4%	9.2%	15.0%	19.1%	19.1%	15.0%	9.2%	4.4%	2.3%	*of adults*

This is a profile of an actual subject. Note that he is quite high on scales M and Q_2, fairly high on Q_1, fairly low on A and H, and very low on G, N, and Q_4. On the remaining scales his scores are all about average. From the verbal descriptions labeling the endpoints of the 16 scales, try

writing a personality "sketch" of this person. What kind of a person do you think he is? Do you think this test allows you to know a lot about him? For starters, he is a 21-year-old college student at the University of Colorado.

traits. The test is called the 16 PF (16 personality factors) because it consists of separate scales for each of these traits. A sample test profile describing the 16 scales developed by Cattell is shown in Figure C–3.

Suppose a psychologist felt that something was missing from these scales, perhaps that they failed to measure how introverted or extroverted someone's personality was. He might devise his own test of introversion-extroversion and give it along with the 16 PF to a group of subjects. Factor analysis would involve correlating his test with each of the existing 16 tests (the 16 factors). If his test did not correlate with any of the 16 factors, then presumably his test was measuring something that the 16 factors had missed. Chances are, however, that his test would correlate highly with one of the existing factors, probably factor H (Threctia-Parmia), meaning that his test was not measuring anything new. Through extended application of this process, the personality theorist can narrow the field down to a minimal number of scales necessary to describe personality. Each of the scales would measure something different, meaning that no two scales would correlate highly with each other. So he would end up with a small number of scales (16 for Cattell).

No new scales are needed unless they measure something new, something the 16 existing factors fail to describe. In other words, new scales are not useful unless they fail to correlate with any of the 16 existing ones. The psychologist's description of personality would not be enriched by adding his introversion-extroversion test as a seventeenth factor if his test correlated highly with factor H or any other factor. Thus factor analysis helps to minimize the number of scales; it allows the psychologist to describe personality adequately with the fewest possible tests.

The 16 PF test (which is actually 16 tests rolled into one) consists of multiple-choice items. Four sample items are:

1. I like to watch team games:
   a. yes   b. occasionally   c. no
2. I prefer people who:
   a. are reserved   b. are in between   c. make friends quickly
3. Money cannot bring happiness:
   a. yes (true)   b. in between   c. no (false)
4. Woman is to child as cat is to:
   a. kitten   b. dog   c. boy

Projective Tests

Rorschach Inkblot Test.   The most famous projective test, the *Rorschach Inkblot Test,* was developed in 1921 by Hermann Rorschach. The test consists of ten inkblots similar to the one shown in Figure C–4. Five of the blots are printed in shades of black and 5 contain varying degrees of color. The final set of 10 blots was derived from a large group of blots that was administered to psychiatric patients who had already been classified by type of disorder.

Figure C–4.
The Rorschach Inkblot Test

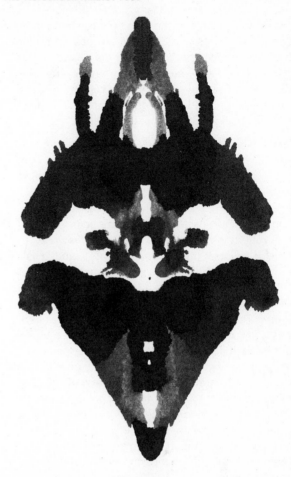

This inkblot is similar to those used in the Rorschach test. Typical responses would involve seeing animals or humans, whereas a psychotic might respond with a bizarre comment of little relevance to the shape of the blot, such as "pools of blood pouring out of a tree."

Normal people were also tested. The final 10 blots were the ones that best discriminated the reactions of normal people from the reactions of patients and, further, showed some evidence of discriminating among the various disorders within the patient population.

The subject is shown the Rorschach cards one at a time in a specified order and is asked to describe what he sees. Instructions are simple in order to keep the situation as unstructured as possible and not to restrict the kind of response the subject might give. In addition to recording what the subject says, the interviewer notes other features of the subject's behavior, such as the length of time it takes him to respond, facial expressions, the way the subject holds the card, and so on. All descriptions are then scored on such dimensions as the form of the description, color responses, perceived movement, the figures seen, and the details of the blots that the subject responds to. Scoring is obviously a problem because it depends so much on the opinion of the psychologist, who must decide whether a response really signifies movement, animal reference, color, or whatever. Clearly, in such an ambiguous situation the psychologist's personality as well as the subject's may influence the outcome.

TAT.   The other most commonly used projective test is the *Thematic Apperception Test,* the TAT. We encountered this test in Chapter 6 because it has been used successfully to measure achievement motivation. In the TAT, the subject is shown a picture, such as the one in Figure C–5, and is asked to tell a story about it. His story is supposed to tell what is happening in the picture, what led up to the scene in the picture, and what will happen in the future. There are 18 black and white pictures and one blank card (the subject must imagine a picture on the card and then tell his story). A popular shortened version of the test contains only 10 cards.

The stories are scored along several dimensions. A critical one is the person in the picture whom the subject identifies as the central character. Other considerations are how the story reflects certain needs and concerns of the subject and what factors seem to be aiding or hindering the satisfaction of personal needs. There are "norms" of typical responses that may serve as guidelines for the psychologist, but the test is basically *interpreted* and not quantified. This means that the scoring procedure is highly subjective and is perhaps easily affected by extraneous variables, just like the Rorschach test.

Other tests.   Other basically projective assessment techniques include dream analysis or interpretation, word association tests, analysis of subjects' artwork, and the sentence completion test. In a sentence completion test, the subject is given a stem of a sentence such as "The main trouble with people is . . ." and is asked to complete the sentence in a way that indicates how he really feels. This test is the most objective of the projective tests, because the subject's response is structured in advance by the stem of the sentence. The subject is also much more aware of the implications of what he says than he is when he responds to an inkblot or TAT card. As a consequence, attitudes and beliefs rather than unconscious processes (which are presumably best

**Figure C–5
The TAT**

This photo by Dorothea Lange, is similar to the kind of pictures used on the TAT. The event in the picture is ambiguous, permitting individuals to "project" their own conflicts and problems onto the picture. Subjects are asked: What is going on in the picture? What are the people feeling? What happens next?

revealed by the Rorschach or TAT) are the focus of measurement in sentence completion. Nevertheless, as with the TAT, distortions, themes, and unusual responses can give clues to a person's thought processes.

Projective tests represent a compromise between the free-floating character of some therapeutic interviews and the rigid structure of an inventory. The stimulus materials provide some guidelines and determinants of the client's behavior, but the therapist is free to pursue, with leading questions, the various potential trouble spots as the client may reveal them. Indeed, many diagnosticians do not rely at all on standard scoring methods that have been developed for projective tests but rather use them simply as a way to get a person to speak freely about various issues that he might otherwise repress or disguise. Nonetheless, there are ways of scoring a person's performance and of comparing him with others with known psychopathology. These comparisons are then used to make a classificatory diagnosis.

Rationale in Test Construction

Both empirical and theoretical rationales are used in the construction of psychological tests.

Diagnosis by Drawing

Time—"Draw a picture of everyone in your family *doing* something." Those are the simple instructions that Psychiatrist S. Harvard Kaufman and Psychologist Robert C. Burns give to children sent to them for treatment. In their new book, *Kinetic Family Drawings* (Brunner/Mazel; $8.95) the two therapists show some of the kinetic, or action, pictures drawn by their young patients and explain how the crude art reveals more fully than thousands of words what is troubling the children.

The idea of evaluating the intellectual and emotional makeup of a child by analyzing his drawings did not originate with Kaufman and Burns. Ever since the 1920s, psychologists have been measuring intelligence by asking children to draw a person (the D-A-P test). For the past two decades, clues to children's emotional problems have been found in their drawings of a house, a tree and a person (the H-T-P technique). By requiring children to draw their families in action, however, Kaufman and Burns believe they have opened new avenues of investigation. In fact, they say, kinetic family drawings "tell us more than we can decipher."

Isolated Children

What the therapists find most intriguing are some of the recurring themes that reveal how children feel about their families. Kids who feel neglected will time and again draw their mothers cleaning house and their fathers driving off to work, while "tough or castrating" fathers are often pictured mowing the lawn or chopping wood. The cat, soft and furry but armed with claws—a creature symbolizing ambivalence—turns up frequently in pictures by girls who both love and hate their mothers.

Youngsters who feel isolated, like Mike, 17, frequently draw family members doing things alone in separate rooms instead of together. Mike also showed his mother at work in the kitchen with her back turned, and he drew himself "'stealing' food (love) from the cold refrigerator." When they first took him to Psychiatrist Kaufman, Mike's parents insisted that the family was close. But they finally admitted to Kaufman what their son's drawings made painfully clear—that they "didn't give a damn what happened to Mike."

Sometimes children leave out of their pictures the very things that bother them most. Mary, 12, who had been raped by her brother, drew him sitting in a chair that concealed his body below the waist. Tim, 16, who suffered severe asthma attacks because he felt utterly unloved by his alcoholic mother, showed himself running after an elusive butterfly. On his picture he wrote: "Can't draw mother."

In a picture that the authors call typically oedipal, seven-year-old Tom drew himself as a powerful speedboat, dragging his naked mother behind him. Relegating his father and the dog to the reverse side of his picture, Tom saved "the whole front page for himself and his mother."

In another drawing, Billy, 14 revealed how he felt when his mother remarried. Her new husband had children of his own, and the family was polarized into two camps. Write Kaufman and Burns: "The boy must be aware of the sexual relationship between the stepfather and the mother, as the sword between the stepfather's legs is the largest weapon in the drawing." Billy, obviously jealous, drew himself throwing darts at his stepfather. The darts were very small and could do no harm; the boy must therefore have realized how powerless he was. That feeling of impotence, the authors say, may have accounted for Billy's "bad" behavior at home and at school.

"The ironing-board syndrome" is also a familiar motif in kinetic family drawings. Kaufman and Burns think it may represent the heat of mother love, longed for but dangerous. In what some therapists will consider a far-fetched interpretation, the authors attribute the X shape of the ironing board's legs—and other X shapes in the drawings—to the child's X-ing out or saying no to his sexual impulses.

Allan, an adolescent who was sometimes terrified of being at home, showed in his drawing that he feared both his mother and his seductive eleven-year-old sister. He drew himself eating from a lunch box marked X set on a table with X-shaped legs, and he drew his mother behind the X of an ironing board. Barely able to cope with his impulses, he showed his sister holding up a stop sign to keep him away and his brother pointing a gun at him. The father was apparently of no help to his troubled son. Allan pictured him racing away in a speedboat.

Assessing intelligence, personality, and emotional disorders in children is very difficult. A common technique is to analyze artwork they have already done or to ask them to draw particular objects or scenes.

Psychological Testing For Federal Applicants

By Art Buchwald

Washington—Psychological testing in the U.S. government has come under fire from several congressional committees, who feel that asking job applicants a series of questions to gauge their personalities is an invasion of privacy.

The test that has come in for the most criticism is the Minnesota Multiphasic Personality Inventory, a 566-question true or false quiz.

As an answer to the MMPI, one of its critics has developed the North Dakota Null-Hypothesis Brain Inventory, which the reader is invited to take right now. Answer true or false:

1. I salivate at the sight of mittens.
2. If I go into the street, I'm apt to be bitten by a horse.
3. Some people never look at me.
4. Spinach makes me feel alone.
5. My sex life is A-okay.
6. When I look down from a high spot, I want to spit.
7. I like to kill mosquitoes.
8. Cousins are not to be trusted.
9. It makes me embarrassed to fall down.
10. I get nauseous from too much roller skating.
11. I think most people would cry to gain a point.
12. I cannot read or write.
13. I am bored by thoughts of death.
14. I become homicidal when people try to reason with me.
15. I would enjoy the work of a chicken flicker.
16. I am never startled by a fish.
17. My mother's uncle was a good man.
18. I don't like it when somebody is rotten.
19. People who break the law are wise guys.
20. I have never gone to pieces over the week end.
21. I think beavers work too hard.
22. I use shoe polish to excess.
23. God is love.
24. I like mannish children.
25. I have always been disturbed by the size of Lincoln's ears.
26. I always let people get ahead of me at swimming pools.
27. Most of the time I go to sleep without saying goodbye.
28. I am not afraid of picking up door knobs.
29. I believe I smell as good as most people.
30. Frantic screams make me nervous.
31. It's hard for me to say the right thing when I find myself in a room full of mice.
32. I would never tell my nickname in a crisis.
33. A wide necktie is a sign of disease.
34. As a child I was deprived of licorice.
35. I would never shake hands with a gardener.
36. My eyes are always cold.

Now for the results. If you have answered more questions true than false, you should work for the Labor Department.

If you have answered more questions false than true, you should try for the Peace Corps.

If you answered 18 true and 18 false, you should apply for work with the Voice of America.

If you refused to answer some of the questions, you might work for the White House.

If you held your hand over the questions while you answered them, you should go into the FBI.

If you talk about this test to anybody else, then you could never get a security clearance and you'd better stay where you are.

The MMPI was designed not for use in job selection but for use in diagnosing emotional problems. The above parody of the MMPI indicates how ridiculous it is to ask personal questions that have nothing to do with job success or are so personal that the employer has no right to ask.

The Empirical Approach

Suppose a psychologist wishes to measure human anxiety. One way of proceeding would be to develop a set of *reference groups.* He might, for example, attempt to isolate one group of people high in anxiety, one medium in anxiety, and one low in anxiety. He would determine these groups by using existing tests or other available anxiety indicators. Then he would make up a set of test items, give these items to the three groups, and use their responses to eliminate items that do not discriminate. He would thereby supposedly arrive at a test that could tell him whether any newly tested person is high, medium, or low in anxiety. He would have an empirically derived test of anxiety.

Many tests have been developed in this way. The MMPI was developed by using many groups of people with different psychiatric diagnoses as the reference groups. Rorschach used a similar method in developing the inkblot test. In the most famous test of vocational interest, the Strong Vocational Interest Blank, successful doctors, lawyers, businessmen, and so on served as reference groups. If you take the vocational interest test your answers are scored to see how they correlate with the answers given by various occupational reference subjects. If you answer the items in a manner similar to that of a group of successful lawyers but different from that of successful doctors, the prediction is that you would do better as a lawyer than as a doctor. The reference group approach in various forms is probably the rationale underlying most psychological tests.

Another empirical approach would be to use the statistical tool known as factor analysis. This is the procedure used by Cattell to develop the 16 PF test.

In this approach, the psychologist who wished to develop a measure of anxiety would select a large number of existing tests, administer them to a large group of people, and then factor analyze to identify the basic underlying factors. Say, for example, that there are two clusters of tests, one more indicative of arousal and another related to compulsive movement. The last step is to select the two individual tests that best measure these factors. In this case, a statistical procedure rather than a set of reference groups is used to decide on the eventual measure.

The Theoretical Approach

In the empirical approach, no assumptions are made in advance about what anxiety "really" is. The outcome of the psychologist's work with reference groups or with factor analysis tells him about anxiety. In the theoretical approach, the steps are reversed. The test constructor first develops a theory about anxiety, based on past research and already known factors, and then proceeds to design a test that will measure anxiety as defined or characterized by his theory. Suppose, for example, his theory says that anxiety is a drive, a motivating force that impels people to act. The implication is that people high in anxiety should show evidence of a high level of motivation. This might be called the drive theory of anxiety. Alternatively, the psychologist might theorize that anxiety has little to do with motivation level but instead is a personality trait that has to do with a person's ability to cope with or deal with stress in an adequate fashion. High-anxiety people have trouble dealing with stressful situations and low-anxiety people do not. He might call this the stress theory of anxiety. Note that the stress theory says that anxiety is independent of drive level or motivation. A person could be highly anxious and still have low motivation, or he could be low in anxiety and still have high motivation.

One's theoretical conception of what anxiety really is will determine the kind of test he constructs to measure anxiety. A person who believes in the drive theory of anxiety will obviously develop a different kind of anxiety test than one who believes in the stress theory. The stress theorist is likely to develop a test designed to measure how people handle stressful situations. He might have an item like: "Suppose you are chewed out by your boss in front of several other employees—which of the following things would you most likely do: (a) break down and start crying, (b) tell the boss off, (c) explain to the boss that you have not been feeling well lately, or (d) say nothing to the boss, but, after he leaves, tell him off behind his back." The drive theorist, on the other hand, might have a test item that aims at assessing level of motivation, such as: "Which of the following statements fits you best: (a) I am constantly on the go—I can't sit still, (b) I always take my time, (c) I work hard and I play hard, (d) I am basically a lazy person."

After a test has been constructed and found to be reliable, the psychologist must determine if the test measures what it is supposed to measure, *according to his theory*. As you know, a test that measures up to its guiding theory is said to have *construct validity*. To determine if a test has construct validity, the psychologist would use his theory to deduce predictions about how people who score high and low on this test behave differently in some situations. He would then get a group of people who score high and another group who score low and test them in the situation to see if his prediction is supported. If it is, his test has construct validity. He would want to make many such predictions and tests and have them heavily supported before he reached a final conclusion about construct validity; establishing construct validity is a long, detailed research process.

Let us illustrate with predictions based on the two different theories of anxiety just described. The stress theorist might use the following situation to make predictions about the behavior of people who score high and low on his test of anxiety: The two groups of subjects are put in a learning situation, say, memorizing a list of words. At some point in the learning process, a stressful event is introduced, such as telling them that they are doing so poorly that they will begin to receive shocks when they make errors. This is stress, and the theory of anxiety as inability to cope with stress predicts that the learning rate of the high-anxiety group will go down, whereas the low-anxiety group will be unaffected or will actually improve. If the experiment confirms the prediction, the stress theorist gains a bit of construct validity for his test.

The anxiety-as-drive theorist might instead make the following experimental prediction: Take two groups, one high and one low in "drive-anxiety," and put them to work sorting different colored and different shaped objects into compartments. Because of their higher drive, high-anxiety people will get more objects sorted than low-anxiety people. If this prediction is confirmed, then his test gains a little in construct validity.

Although we have divided this rationale section into two parts, empirical and theoretical, in actual practice the two approaches are almost always combined. Sometimes the psychologist does not have a formal, completely specified theory to guide him, and we say he is using the empirical approach. But he always has his own personal hunches, guesses, and ideas, which serve as a theory to guide his efforts. In the case of the theoretical approach, the psychologist may have a very formal theory to go by, but he will also make great use of the empirical approaches of reference groups and factor analysis to refine his test procedures, establish construct validity, and modify his theory to account for the new facts brought out by his research.

Critique

In this final section, we wish to raise two hotly debated issues about psychological testing. No simple answers are possible, but it is important that you be aware of the issues.

Behavior as Sign or Sample?

Is the behavior of a person taking a test (his score or answers to the test) a *sign* telling the psychologist what the person really is (he really is sane, or he really is anxious, or he really is mentally retarded), or is his response on the test just a small sample of his behavior? We can all be anxious, crazy, or stupid at times. If a psychologist catches us at the wrong moment, we might appear worse (or better) than we really are. In fact, are we *really* anything for all time? Or does our behavior change radically with the situation such that sometimes, in some situations, we act silly and stupid, in others we are anxious, and so on? When the psychologist says that a person is anxious, he is using the test as a sign that the person is something (trait anxiety), rather than as just a sample of the way the person behaves in a particular test situation (state anxiety). "Diagnosing" a person attaches a label to him, and this label seems to dominate the thinking about this person in such a way that the unique features of his behavior are obscured. Just because he was anxious when he took the test, does this mean he is always and forever *an anxious person?* Who would not be "anxious" if he desperately needed a job and had to face a psychologist who would *determine* his qualifications? The tradition in psychology has been to use tests as signs, but there is a growing awareness of the sampling aspect of psychological testing and the situational determinants of test behavior, which can only lead to fairer and more appropriate test use and interpretation.

Projective versus Self-Report Measures

The final issue deals with whether or not it is better to use projective or self-report measures of

personality. Projective tests usually receive the most criticism because there is a great deal of subjective judgment and interpretation involved on the part of the psychologist. The projective tests therefore have lower reliability and validity measures, which suggests that these kinds of tests are dangerous to use when crucial decisions are to be made. Self-report, inventory-type tests are objective by comparison. They can be more easily validated (although this does not mean they are necessarily more valid), more impersonally administered, and more objectively scored.

On the other hand, the self-report measures rely heavily on the subject being honest when he responds. Many of the items in some self-report measures suggest to the subject what the "best" response is, and therefore these tests can easily be faked. An honest person might be penalized by not faking. A less intelligent person might be discriminated against because he cannot deceive the psychologists as well as a smarter person. For this reason, testers have added to many self-report tests special test items to detect faking.

Finally, even if the subject is honest, and even if he clearly understands the questions, is he likely to be aware of all the aspects of himself that are important? This is the issue of unconscious motivation—are there aspects to personality that he is unaware of, and if so, how can he be expected to report on himself in these areas? Projective tests presumably allow these features of personality to manifest themselves in a way that is presumably impossible in a self-report test. In response to this criticism, some self-report, objectively scored tests of unconscious processes have been developed. It is unfortunately too early to judge their adequacy.

We hope that you now have a better appreciation of why psychological testing is an emotional issue. It represents one area in which psychology intrudes into the lives of just about everyone in one way or another. When testing is used to decide who gets hired, who gets into a particular school, who goes to jail or to a mental hospital, then emotions are bound to run high. People who are affected by these intrusions in negative ways are bound to question the right of anybody to assess their personalities. All that psychologists can do in such cases is to develop fair tests, administer them under fair conditions, and interpret them with extreme caution. As long as decisions like these must be made by someone, then it is probably best to proceed in the light of as many facts as possible. We expect that many of these facts will come from continuing research in personality.

GLOSSARY

Absolute threshold for hearing Lowest amplitude level of sound that can be heard by a normal person in an otherwise absolutely soundproof room.

A-B variable Variable describing the effectiveness of therapists with schizophrenics or neurotics. "A" therapists work best with schizophrenics, and "B" therapists work best with neurotics.

A-B-X model Model of consistency relationships in balance theory developed by Newcomb. Persons A and B have attitudes toward X; A perceives B's attitude toward X and B perceives A's attitude toward X; both A's system and B's system will tend toward balance.

Accommodation In vision, the process of changing lens shape or curvature so as to focus the optic array on the retina.

Achievement motivation Need one feels to perform successfully on any task that is undertaken.

Acrophobia Fear of heights.

Action potential Nerve signal in the form of an electrical impulse that travels through the axon of a neuron.

Action-specific energies According to Lorenz, motivating energies that impel only very specific sequences of behavior; motivating energy for instinctual behaviors.

Adolescence In human beings, the period from 11 to 18 years of age.

Adrenal cortex Outer layer of the adrenal glands; during emotional arousal it releases hormones called corticosteroids into the circulatory system.

Adrenal glands Produce many hormones, including adrenalin (also called epinephrine). Especially important in regulating bodily responses to stress, the adrenal glands are partially controlled by the sympathetic division of the autonomic nervous system.

Adrenalin See "epinephrine."

Adrenal medulla Inner core of the adrenal gland, which secretes the hormones epinephrine and norepinephrine into the circulatory system.

Adrenal steroids Hormones secreted into the circulatory system by the adrenal cortex during emotional arousal; also called *corticosteroids.*

Adulthood In human beings, the period from the late teens or early twenties to death.

Affective reactions Category of psychotic reactions involving emotional behavior and variations in mood.

Affective state The positive, negative, or neutral feelings one is experiencing at a given moment.

Aggression Behavior directed toward another person that is intended to injure or harm that person.

Alcoholic Excessive drinker whose dependence on alcohol is so strong that it interferes with his performance of socially appropriate behavior.

Alcoholism Disorder marked by addiction to alcohol and inability to control drinking behavior.

Algorithm Method of problem solving in which one performs a single repetitive operation until a solution is reached. Some problems can be solved only by an algorithm procedure.

Alpha waves Particular brain wave pattern that occurs when the subject is in a state of "relaxed wakefulness." People can be taught to control the presence of alpha waves through biofeedback training.

Altered state of consciousness State that occurs when the overall functioning of the mind takes on a pattern that is qualitatively different from normal.

Altruism Looking after or doing things for the benefit of others.

Amnesia Neurotic dissociative reaction that involves partial or total loss of memory about one's past identity while retaining memory of nonthreatening aspects of life.

Amphetamines Class of drugs characterized by presence of $C_9H_{13}N$. A characteristic effect of these drugs is stimulation of the central nervous system. They are also characterized by a high potential for abuse.

Antabuse Drug that causes intense nausea if a person drinks alcohol while the chemical is in his bloodstream.

Antecedent-consequent research Research strategy that studies subjects of the same age to determine how different environmental conditions affect performance.

Antidepressants Drugs that elevate moods and counteract depression.

Antipsychotics Drugs that calm and increase the lucidity of psychotics.

Antisocial character Person who is pleasure oriented (hedonistic) and indifferent to the needs or concerns of others; person who exploits others for his own selfish ends and does not feel guilt or anxiety except when it is clear that he may be prevented from satisfying his need for pleasure.

Anxiety Experience of fear in the absence of, or disproportionate to, the objective danger.

Anxiety reaction Neurotic episode in which a person has repressed the cause of his anxiety but not the anxiety itself—a situation where he feels anxious without knowing why.

Aphagia Condition in which an animal refuses to eat, ignores food, and starves to death unless treated. Aphagia has been produced experimentally by surgical removal of the lateral hypothalamic nucleus.

Aphasia Loss or impairment of one's ability to use language, usually resulting from brain damage.

Aquaphobia Fear of water.

Archetypes Jungian concept referring to the basic elements that form the foundation for the collective unconscious and that often show up symbolically in dreams.

Arousal (activation) theory In motivation and emotion, a theory postulating a general continuum of physiological arousal, governed by the central nervous system and varying from extremely low arousal (coma and sleep) to extremely high arousal (panic and euphoria). Variations in arousal level are thought to underlie the intensity and quality of motivation and emotion.

Associated specificity Theory of psychosomatic illness stating that through learned mediation or accidental conditioning an association between a physiological response and an emotion, thought, or idea may become established.

Association cortex Largest portion of the cerebral hemispheres, most highly developed in human beings. The more complex functions like perception, language, and thought are centered here.

Astral projection See "out-of-body experience (OOBE)."

Atmosphere effect A term referring to errors made in reasoning that are the result of the atmosphere surrounding the problem, namely, the subject's attitude or the way the problem is presented. Affirmative premises tend to create an affirmative atmosphere and, thus, imply an affirmative conclusion.

Attitude Combination of feelings, beliefs, and tendencies to act in particular ways directed toward persons, objects, or events.

Authoritarian personality Personality type characterized by, among other traits, high ethnocentrism, conservatism, antidemocratism, and prejudice.

Autonomic nervous system Part of the peripheral nervous system, it contains neurons that connect to glands, smooth muscles, and the heart, and it is central to emotional behavior.

Autonomy Sense of independence, of being an individual separate from other people.

Axon A relatively long structure extending from the cell body of a neuron, it sends messages to other cells.

Balance theory   Theory of consistency in social behavior stating that objects perceived as belonging together will have the same dynamic quality—they will be either all liked or all disliked.

Basal age   In the Binet intelligence test, the highest age level at which a subject passes all items. Used in computation of mental age.

Behavioral model   Model of psychopathology in which all behavior, normal or otherwise, is a product of learning about the environment.

Behavioral symptoms   Classes of behaviors that are indicative of underlying psychopathology.

Behaviorism   Strong American school of psychology that viewed psychology as the study of observable, objectively measurable behavior and the way in which stimulus-response relationships are formed; the objective of psychology is to predict what responses will be evoked by what stimuli.

Behavior modification   Applying the principles of learning to achieve changes in behavior. See ''behavior therapy.''

Behavior therapy   Type of psychotherapy that emphasizes change in motivation, skills, and performance.

Belief prejudice   See ''stereotyping.''

Binet test   See ''Stanford-Binet Test.''

Binocular disparity   Difference in optic arrays reaching each eye caused by the slightly different location of the two eyes; powerful clue for depth.

Biofeedback   A technique used to teach organisms to control ''involuntary'' functions like blood pressure and brain waves, it involves giving the subject immediate feedback, or knowledge, of the results of bodily changes as soon as they occur.

Bipolar cell   Neuron in the retina connecting rods or cones to ganglion cells.

Birth-order effects   Various consistencies in personality that seem to be tied to whether a person was the first-born child in his family, the second-born, etc.

Blind spot   Point in the retina, containing no receptor cells, at which the optic nerve leaves the eye.

Brainstorming   Procedure used in generating new and creative ideas. Subject is encouraged to suggest any idea that has not been suggested before and might work. Evaluation of ideas is delayed until after as many suggestions as possible are made.

Brightness   Psychological sensation corresponding to the physical property of intensity of light stimulation, see ''intensity.''

Brightness constancy   Observation that objects maintain their brightness even though the amount of light reflected from them changes.

Case study   Simplest and most direct type of psychological investigation; in-depth examination of a single person to find out about a certain problem, question, or issue.

Catatonic schizophrenia   Subtype of schizophrenia characterized by a waxy flexibility of body and limbs, loss of motion, and a tendency to remain motionless for hours or days. See ''schizophrenia.''

Catecholamines   Epinephrine and norepinephrine, the chemical transmitter substances in the adrenergic division of the nervous system.

Cell body   The soma; the central part of a neuron, which is responsible for carrying out the cell's life processes.

Central nervous system (CNS)   Includes the brain and the spinal cord and is contained within the skull and spinal column. It is the integrating center for all bodily functions and behavior.

Cerebellum   Portion of the brain that controls balance, muscle tone, and motor coordination in general.

Cerebral cortex   The outermost layer of the cerebral hemispheres, it contains motor, sensory, and association areas.

Cerebral hemispheres   The largest parts of the brain in human beings and other higher mammals, they are the seat of the more complex functions like language, numerical ability, and abstract thought, in addition to being responsible for sensation, some aspects of bodily movement, and many other functions.

Chaining   Type of instrumental conditioning whereby one learns to exhibit a series of behaviors in order to obtain reinforcement.

Character disorder   See ''personality disorder.''

Chemical transmitter substances   Chemicals that are released from the terminals of a neuron when that cell has carried a nerve impulse. The chemicals then travel to the soma or dendrites of a second, connecting neuron and may excite or inhibit activity in the second cell.

Chemotherapy   Use of drugs as treatment for psychopathology.

Childhood   In human beings, the period from 2 to 11 years of age.

Chromosome   A structure composed of many genes found in the nucleus of cells, it contains the hereditary information of organisms. The normal human being has 23 pairs of chromosomes.

Chronological age   Actual age, in years and months, of a person; used in computation of IQ.

Classical conditioning   Learning of a new response to a stimulus caused by pairing this stimulus with another stimulus that already elicits the response.

Claustrophobia   Fear of small enclosed spaces.

Client-centered therapy   Developed by Carl Rogers, this type of psychotherapy is insight oriented and focuses on the present. Emphasis is on regaining the ability to experience all feelings fully. Also called ''nondirective'' therapy.

Cochlea   Structure in the inner ear containing fluid that vibrates with sound stimulation and auditory receptor cells that are stimulated by vibrations in the fluid.

Codability   Ease with which a stimulus can be assigned a language label.

Cognitive dissonance theory   Leon Festinger's consistency theory, which states that a person acts to reduce the inconsistency between two or more ideas or beliefs.

Cognitive theory   Approach to personality that emphasizes the cognitive processes such as thinking and judging and is thus highly rational in its outlook.

Collective unconscious   Concept proposed by Carl Jung, referring to an inherited aspect of personality that all people share owing to their common ancestry and that has accumulated over the generations.

Color blindness   Inability to experience all the colors in the spectrum.

Community mental health   Approach to mental health that emphasizes the prevention of mental illness and the need for broader and more effective mental health services based within communities.

Comparison level   In the social exchange theory of interpersonal attraction, the standard by which persons evaluate what they feel they deserve; similar to adaptation level.

Concentrative meditation   Meditation that involves ''one-pointedness'' of the mind, or focusing one's attention on a specific object for some period of time.

Concept   Unit of knowledge; principle for systematically responding to the objects and events that make up one's circumstances. Concepts can be classes or categories of things, sequential principles, or relational principles that specify a particular arrangement of things.

Conceptual problems   Problems that can be solved by recognizing or learning the concept the solution is based on, by the use of systematic strategies.

Concordance rate   Probability that one of a pair of twins will show a given characteristic, given that the other twin has the characteristic.

Concrete operational period   The third stage of cognitive development as proposed by Piaget; it occurs from 7 to 11 years of age; the child learns to use the logic of classification and numbers to relate and order events.

Condensation   Dream process that disguises material by having one aspect of a dream (a person, object, etc.) actually represent or be a composite of several things in real life.

Conditioned response (CR)   In classical conditioning, the response that occurs after training has been completed, upon presentation of the conditioned stimulus.

Conditioned stimulus (CS) In classical conditioning, the neutral stimulus that does not elicit the desired response prior to training.

Cone Photoreceptor cell shaped like a cone, located mainly in the center of the eye, not sensitive to low light intensities, responsible for color vision.

Confederates In research, collaborators of the experimenter who pose as subjects.

Conformity Adherence to the norms of the social groups to which one belongs.

Congruence Rogerian term meaning that what is experienced inside and what is expressed outwardly are consistent.

Conjunctive concept Concept in which two or more relevant attributes must be present in a stimulus for it to be a positive instance.

Connotation Characteristic of a word; how one reacts emotionally to or feels about the word.

Conscience A concept developed by Freud, it is part of the superego and contains the moral values, attitudes, and rules people learn from their parents and society.

Conscious In Freudian theory, the ideas, thoughts, and images that a person is aware of at any given moment.

Consciousness State of awareness generally accompanied by thoughts in human beings.

Conservation Idea that a property remains the same despite an irrelevant transformation that may change the appearance of the object.

Conservative focusing Systematic approach to solving conceptual problems in which the subject uses a positive instance of the concept as focus and then compares it with other single instances, each differing in one and only one dimension from his focus. In this way irrelevant dimensions are eliminated one at a time until only the relevant dimension remains.

Consistency principle The idea that people strive to be consistent in their behavior. As applied to attitudes, this means that attitudes held by a particular individual are mutually supportive and do not conflict with each other. Tendency to segregate liked objects from disliked objects and to structure thoughts in simple black-and-white terms.

Consolidation theory Theory that every experience sets up a circuit in the brain that must be allowed to consolidate or strengthen in order for the experience to be stored permanently in long-term memory.

Consonance In cognitive dissonance theory, the situation where one idea or belief implies another in some psychological sense.

Context effect Ability of the surroundings to affect the ease of learning, and the idea that the more similar the recall context is to the learning context, the better recall will be.

Contour In perception, sharp discontinuity of gradients; a sharp break in stimulus characteristics.

Convergent hierarchy According to mediational theory, a hierarchy of different external stimuli all of which can elicit the same response. Seen as the basis for forming concepts.

Conversion reaction Neurotic reaction in which one reduces anxiety by inactivating part of his body; person converts psychological problem into physical one that prevents him from behaving in a way that would be anxiety provoking.

Cornea Outer coating of the front of the eye.

Corpus callosum Structure that connects the two cerebral hemispheres to each other; severing the corpus callosum prevents the hemispheres from communicating with each other.

Correlational approach Research method used to discover the degree of relationship between two or more variables.

Correlation coefficient Numerical value or statistic that represents the degree of relationship between two or more values; can vary from −1 to +1, with 0 meaning no relationship and + or −1 indicating a perfect relationship.

Corticosteroids See "adrenal steroids."

Counterconditioning Eliminating unwanted behaviors using extinction, or punishment, while simultaneously replacing them with more desirable behaviors.

Crisis Point in a person's life that is unusually stressful and could be handled in a maladaptive way.

Crisis intervention Short-term type of therapy aimed at helping people handle crises in effective ways.

Critical period Very brief period early in life during which imprinting is possible; any limited period in development in which the organism is especially susceptible to a given developmental process.

Cross-sectional research Research strategy that tests subjects of different ages simultaneously in order to examine the relationships between age, experience, and behavior.

Cue-dependent forgetting Inability to remember learned information due to retrieval failure; cues present during learning are not present during recall, see "trace-dependent forgetting."

Dark adaptation Increase in sensitivity to light resulting from the reduction or complete absence of light energy reaching the eye, attributable to changes in the level of light-sensitive pigments in receptor cells.

Decay theory Theory that we forget things because the memory trace for them wears out over time.

Deindividuation Loss of one's identity in a crowd so that a person feels he cannot be singled out by others as being personally responsible for the acts of the crowd.

Delusion Unshakable idea or belief that is held in the face of contradictory evidence, simple logic, or common experience.

Dendrites Short structures that extend from the cell body of a neuron and pick up signals from other cells.

Denial Removal from consciousness of an external threat; a defense mechanism.

Denotation Characteristic of a word: the specific object, concept, or "event" to which the word refers.

Deoxyribonucleic acid (DNA) Molecules of hereditary material that direct the growth and development of every part of the body. Genes (and thus chromosomes) contain DNA.

Dependent variable In psychological research, the variable that the psychologist measures—some characteristic of behavior or performance.

Depersonalization Loss of personal identity; frequent symptom in schizophrenia.

Depression Condition marked by sadness, loneliness, and dejection. In neurosis, excessive depression is usually accompanied by anxiety, feelings of worthlessness, and fatigue, although adequate contact with reality is maintained. In psychosis, profound depression is marked by loss of contact with reality.

Deprivation Withholding of stimulation that could satisfy a need; lack of need-satisfying stimulation. Deprivation increases motivation.

Developmental psychology The area within psychology that is concerned with discovering the principles of behavioral change in the individual from conception to death. All the topics in psychology—personality, learning, etc.—as they relate to the dimension of age are studied by developmental psychologists.

Diagnosis Procedure and process of deciding how to classify a person, using information gained from tests, interviews, and other observations; usually used in the context of identifying psychopathology.

Diathesis Genetic predisposition to a particular psychotic disorder.

Diathesis-stress theory Theory of what causes schizophrenia; states that schizophrenia develops when there is a genetic predisposition (diathesis) present *and* there are environmental factors (stress) that trigger the disorder.

Displacement Rechanneling instinctual energy from an unacceptable object to one that is of neutral value to society. Also, a dream process by which material is disguised. It involves changing the affective emphasis of something in a dream so that if it is very important in real life it is seemingly unimportant in the dream, or vice versa.

Dissociative reaction Neurotic defensive behavioral inactivation in which a person blocks off large parts of his memory as a way of avoiding anxiety-provoking associations.

Dissonance   In cognitive dissonance theory, the situation where one idea or belief a person holds follows from the obverse of another cognition he also holds.

Divergent hierarchy   According to mediational theory, a hierarchy of responses all of which can be elicited by a single stimulus. Seen as the basis for problem solving in most situations.

Dream   Experience that occurs during the sleeping state and that involves having an awareness of scenes and events that take place in a nonphysical, imaginary world.

Dream analysis   Technique used by Freud and other analysts based on the idea that dreams are symbolic representations of our impulses and conflicts and that by understanding the symbols we can learn about ourselves.

Dream processes   Various methods used to disguise material so that when it is presented in a dream it is not too emotionally threatening.

Drive   Energy available for behavior; psychological correlate of a physical need (for example, the hunger drive results from the need for food).

Drug abuse   The use of drugs to the point where the user's functioning or health is significantly impaired or his actions harm others.

Dynamic model   Model of psychopathology in which abnormal behavior reflects a "dynamic" battle or conflict between parts or aspects of a person's personality rather than any physical or organic deficiencies.

Dyssocial character   Individual who has no personality disorganization but rather has values that conflict with the usual mores of the society; cultural deviant.

Eclectic   In psychology, a psychologist who uses the theories and techniques of several approaches or models, rather than specializing in one.

Ego   One of the basic structures of the personality as proposed by Freud. The ego maintains a balance between biological impulses and society's demands; it attempts to maintain a realistic approach to life.

Egocentric speech   Speech observed in preschool children, where they seem to be talking out loud for their own sake, rather than attempting to communicate to someone else. Proposed by Piaget.

Egocentrism   Lack of differentiation between one's own point of view and that of others. As used by Piaget, it refers to the early adolescent's failure to differentiate between what he and others are thinking about.

Ego ideal   Freudian concept referring to the part of the conscience that tells us the right things to do, as learned from our parents and society.

Eidetic imagery   Ability to retain an image of a picture or a scene with great clarity for a fairly long period of time. Sometimes called "photographic memory."

Electra complex   Proposed by Freud, this is the attraction a girl has for her father and its accompanying anxiety and guilt.

Electoconvulsive shock (ECS)   See "electroshock therapy (EST)."

Electroencephalogram (EEG)   Instrument used to sense and record electrical activity originating in the brain.

Electroshock therapy (EST)   Delivering an electric shock that produces a brief coma in a patient; sometimes used to treat depression.

Empathic understanding   Rogerian concept referring to the importance of a therapist actively understanding the immediate feelings of his client.

Enactive mode   The most primitive (or basic) way human beings convert immediate experiences into a mental model; as proposed by Bruner, it is based upon action or movement and is nonverbal.

Encounter group   Group experience aimed at increasing an awareness of emotions and an ability to communicate them accurately and effectively. Generally aimed at improving interpersonal relations.

Endocrine system   Composed of glands which produce hormones, it is central in the control and regulation of behavior. It interacts closely with the nervous system.

Enriched environment   Generally refers to an environment that contains an above-normal number of interesting and/or educational stimuli.

Enuresis   Bedwetting.

Epinephrine   Also called adrenalin, it is a hormone produced by the adrenal medulla. This chemical is especially important in mobilizing the body to meet emergencies.

Eros   Freudian concept referring to half of the id's instinctual energies—specifically those dealing with the life instincts and sexuality.

ESP   See "extrasensory perception."

Ethical model   Model of psychopathology in which psychopathology comes from guilt over immoral behavior; assumes that individual has responsibility for his own behavior.

Ethology   Study of animal behavior in the natural environment.

Existential neurosis   Feeling a loss of meaning in life even though one is a successful member of society.

Existential therapy   A type of psychotherapy developed by Rollo May and other existentialists, based on their existential model which emphasizes the here-and-now, or one's present being, and the uniqueness and separateness of each individual.

Experience   Learning, or the effects of the environment on development.

Experimental method   Research procedure in which the psychologist manipulates one variable and tests to see what effects the manipulation has on a second variable. Controls are used to eliminate the effects of all extraneous variables. This procedure can establish a cause-and-effect relationship between manipulated and unmanipulated variables.

Extinction   In classical conditioning, presenting a conditioned stimulus repeatedly without the unconditioned stimulus; gradually, the conditioned response disappears. In instrumental conditioning, eliminating a learned behavior by withholding all reinforcement of it.

Extrasensory perception (ESP)   Acquisition of knowledge about the world or another person's thoughts when no known sense modality could have picked up that information.

Extrinsic rewards   Candy, money, and similar objects that can be given to organisms and have the effect of increasing the frequency of behaviors that precede them.

Factor analytic approach   One type of trait theory approach that seeks to understand personality by using various types of psychological measurement and summarizing the findings of the testing in terms of the basic factors or dimensions of personality.

Fading   Gradually introducing or taking out a stimulus so that ongoing behavior is not disrupted. An instrumental conditioning technique.

Family therapy   Psychotherapy with all members of a family meeting together with the therapist.

Fear   Response to an object or situation perceived as threatening and that the individual believes he cannot cope with; a primary emotion.

Fetish   Preference for an object rather than a person as a source of sexual satisfaction.

Figure-ground   In perception, the tendency to perceive things as objects or events (figure) against a background.

Fixation   Stopping one's development at a particular stage and remaining there; a defense mechanism.

Focused attention   Attending to one aspect of a stimulus while ignoring all other parts.

Formal operational period   The fourth stage of cognitive development as proposed by Piaget, it occurs during early adolescence, 11 years and beyond, as the teenager learns to conceive of events beyond the present, imagine hypothetical situations, and develop a complex system of logic.

Formal operational thinking   Proposed by Piaget, it involves the systematic exploration and solution of problems and includes abstract thought and symbolic logic.

Fovea   The central region of the retina, containing cones but no rods. It is the area of greatest visual acuity.

Free association   Technique developed by Freud for use in psychoanalysis. It is basically saying anything and everything that comes to mind in an attempt to discover what things are being repressed and to understand the things that are being said.

Free recall   Learning some items and then trying to remember them in any order.

Frigidity   Lack of any enjoyment from sexual intercourse with an opposite-sexed partner.

Frustration   Prevention or blocking of ongoing, goal-directed behavior.

Frustration-aggression hypothesis   States that all aggressive acts are caused by frustration.

Fugue state   Neurotic dissociative reaction in which a person has amnesia for his past but avoids the anxiety associated with such loss of identity by developing a new one and fleeing from the situation he could not tolerate.

Functional disorder   Emotional problem resulting from psychological variables rather than biological ones.

Functional fixedness   Type of mental set occurring during problem solving in which an object critical to a solution is perceived as having one and only one function different from that required by the solution.

Functionalism   Early school of psychological thought that emphasized how behavior helps one adapt to his environment and the role learning plays in this adaptive process.

Ganglion cells   Neurons in the retina connecting bipolar cells to relay areas in the brain; axons of ganglion cells from the optic nerve.

Gene   One unit, composed of DNA (deoxyribonucleic acid), that determines hereditary traits. Many genes together make up one chromosome.

Genetic counseling   Using knowledge about genetics to advise people about genetic histories and the likelihood that they will have children free of inherited abnormalities.

Gestalt psychology   German school of psychology that opposed reductionistic psychologies such as Structuralism and Behaviorism and emphasized the completeness, continuity, and meaningfulness of behavior as a whole.

Gestalt therapy   A type of psychotherapy developed by Fritz Perls, it focuses on the immediate present and helps the client increase awareness of his experiences in their totality.

Gland   Bodily structure whose function is to manufacture chemicals, called hormones, that are secreted into the bloodstream and regulate bodily activities.

Gradient of stimulus generalization   Mathematical curve that illustrates the degree of generalization between various stimuli.

Group therapy   Psychotherapy of any type conducted with 3 to 20 clients at once. Most often 8 to 10 members are in a group.

Hair cells   Auditory receptor cells located in a membrane in the cochlea that are stimulated by vibrations in the cochlear fluid.

Hallucination   Form of bizarre or distorted perception without corresponding sensory stimuli.

Heart rate   Number of heartbeats per minute.

Hebephrenic schizophrenia   Subtype of schizophrenia characterized by silly, giggling, and childish behavior, frequent hallucinations, and grossly inappropriate behavior.

Heuristic   Principle or strategy used in problem solving that serves as a device for shortening the solution process; often used when there are many different ways to solve a problem.

High dream   Special type of dream in which the dreamer feels that his consciousness is functioning in a way similar to that experienced when under the influence of a psychedelic drug.

Higher-order conditioning   Type of classical conditioning that uses a conditioned stimulus—previously learned—as the unconditioned stimulus in a new conditioning situation.

Homeostasis   Tendency of the body to react in such a way as to maintain a particular, perhaps optimal, state; process of maintaining equilibrium.

Homosexual   Person who has overt sexual interests in or receives sexual satisfaction from members of the same sex.

Hormone   Chemical manufactured and secreted into the bloodstream by an endocrine gland, which may then activate another gland or help to regulate bodily functioning and behavior.

Hue   Color; property of light stimulation (wavelength) corresponding to the sensation of color.

Hyperphagia   Condition in which an animal eats abnormally large amounts of food and shows no satiation of hunger, produced experimentally by destruction of the ventromedial hypothalamic nucleus.

Hypnagogic state   State of consciousness experienced when passing from wakefulness to sleep.

Hypnopompic state   State of consciousness experienced when passing from sleep to wakefulness.

Hyponosis   State of consciousness characterized by mental quiet, lack of many normal ongoing thought processes, and a state of hypersuggestibility.

Hypochondriasis   Neurotic preoccupation with one's health.

Hypothalamus   Group of nuclei in the forebrain. The hypothalamus is involved in many behavioral functions, especially the emotional and motivational aspects of behavior. It controls much of the endocrine system's activities through connections with the pituitary gland.

Iconic mode   Way to convert immediate experience into mental models using images in the form of sensory information. Proposed by Bruner, this mode generally involves visual images.

Id   One of the basic structures of personality as proposed by Freud. The id pushes the individual to seek pleasure and avoid pain; it is the seat of human instincts.

Ideal self   The way a person would like to be, which may not match the way he actually is.

Identification   The incorporation into one's personality of some qualities or behaviors of another person.

Identity crisis   As proposed by Erik Erikson, coming together of or clarifying one's sense of self and direction in life that is marked by much confusion, experimentation, and emotionality. It generally occurs first during adolescence and may reoccur once or more often during adulthood.

Idiosyncratic   Unique to a particular person or situation.

Image   Sensorylike experience in the absence of any external stimulus. May have any sensory quality—vision, audition, touch, smell, etc.—or a combination of qualities.

Implosive therapy   A type of behavior therapy developed by Thomas Stampfl, it uses direct extinction to get rid of fears and anxieties.

Imprinting   Formation of sexual and social attachments to members of one's own species; confined to a very brief period early in life, it depends on exposure to one's own species during the period shortly after birth.

Incentive   Circumstance or stimulus situation that one attempts to obtain or avoid.

Incongruence   Behaving in ways that are different from the way we see ourselves or the way we feel. This results in much anxiety and sometimes psychopathology.

Incubation stage   Rest period in which one withdraws temporarily from a problem situation. Frequently, a solution is easier after an incubation period.

Independent variable   In psychological research, the variable, which the psychologist manipulates.

Individual differences   Refers to the uniqueness of organisms, the fact that all individuals vary and are different from other individuals even though they may have some things in common.

Infancy   In human beings, the period from birth to 2 years of age.

Inferiority complex   Proposed by Alfred Adler, it involves setting one's life goals around overcoming the feelings of inferiority that have developed during childhood.

Information-processing theory   Theory of problem solving that refers to the way a person receives information from his environment, operates on it, integrates it with other information available in memory, and uses it as a basis for deciding how to act.

Insight   In Gestalt psychology, the sudden achievement of understanding that arises from a change in perspective. Insight is viewed as the most appropriate description of human problem solving.

Insight-oriented therapy   Type of psychotherapy that emphasizes change in motivation and knowledge. It focuses on increasing self-knowledge or insight.

Instinct   Invariant sequence of complex behaviors that is observed in all members of a species and that is released by specific stimuli in the apparent absence of learning; an innate behavior that is unaffected by practice, an innate fixed action pattern.

Instrumental conditioning   Type of learning that uses reinforcers to change the frequency of a behavior. Also called operant conditioning.

Insulin   A hormone secreted by the pancreas, its presence allows sugar to be used by the body.

Intellectualization   Reducing anxiety in a threatening situation by turning it into an abstract problem or by explaining it in such a way as to remove the threat; a defense mechanism.

Intelligence Quotient (IQ)   An index of intelligence allowing for comparison of subjects across all chronological ages. IQ is calculated by dividing mental age by chronological age and multiplying by 100.

Intensity   Strength or amount of energy in a stimulus or response; in light stimuli, the amount of physical energy reaching the eye corresponds to the psychological sensation of brightness.

Interference theory   The theory that we forget things because our recall of them is interfered with by other usually similar items of stored information.

Interpersonal attraction   Issue of friendship and romantic involvement, and attitudes of liking; subject of social psychological research.

Intervening variable   Factor that stands between and provides a relationship between some stimulus in the environment and some response on the part of an organism.

Intrinsic rewards   Pleasurable internal feelings that result from accomplishments or behaviors and make it more likely that these behaviors will occur in the future.

Introspection   Observing one's own private, internal state of being, including one's thoughts and feelings.

Introversion   Personality dimension developed by Carl Jung and used to describe how outgoing and other-directed versus ingoing and self-directed a person is. At the two extremes are the extroverts and introverts.

Iris   Part of the eye surrounding the pupil that gives the eye color; diaphragm that regulates the size of the pupil to adjust the amount of light entering the eye.

Kernel of truth hypothesis   See "2 + 2 phenomenon."

Kinesthesis   Sense of body position and orientation.

Lashley jumping stand   Device used to study discrimination learning.

Latent content (of dreams)   Unconscious wishes or impulses that seek expression through dreams; symbolic aspect of dreaming.

Learning   Relatively permanent change in behavior traceable to experience and practice.

Learning strategies   Methods for forming concepts and generally for acquiring and using information about the environment. Children gradually develop more sophisticated and efficient strategies.

Lens   Transparent structure in the eye that changes shape to focus the optic array on the retina at the back of the eye.

Lesion   Damaged or destroyed part of the body. Lesions are often made in the nervous system by cutting out or electrically burning tissue in order to study the physical and psychological effects that occur.

Leveling   Cognitive style whereby one ignores differences and emphasizes similarities in perceiving the world.

Libido   According to Freudian theory, the source of instinctual motivating energy.

Light adaptation   Decrease in sensitivity to light resulting from an increase in light energy reaching the eye; see "dark adaptation."

Limbic system   A circuit of many structures in the midbrain and forebrain, especially important in emotions and motivation; it also contains several "pleasure centers."

Lobotomy   Type of psychosurgery that involves severing the connections between the frontal lobes and the rest of the brain. It has been used to treat extremely hyperemotional mental patients but is infrequently used today.

Logical syllogism   Three-step argument that consists of two premises, assumed to be true, and a conclusion that may or may not follow from these premises.

Longitudinal study   Research strategy that involves observing the same subjects at repeated intervals in order to examine the influences of age and experience on behavior.

Long-term memory   Memory for learned material over a relatively long retention interval (generally an hour or more). A hypothetical memory system for permanent storage of learning.

Loudness   The psychological attribute corresponding to amplitude of a sound wave.

Lucid dream   Special type of dream during which the dreamer is aware that he is dreaming and possesses his normal ability to think and reason.

Lysergic acid diethylamide (LSD)   Psychedelic drug that can be psychotomimetic. Its primary effect is to alter one's state of consciousness.

MA   See "mental age."

Mandala   Complex diagram symbolizing the nature of the cosmos. It can serve as a yantra.

Mania   Psychotic affective reaction involving speeding up of thought processes and motor behavior and exaggerated feelings of optimism.

Manic-depressive psychosis   Circular psychotic reaction marked by fluctuation between psychotic depression and mania.

Manifest content (of dreams)   Aspects of a dream that are recalled by the dreamer; concrete objects and events of the dream.

Mantra   Sound pattern that can be meditated upon.

Marathon group   Usually refers to an encounter group that meets for 8 or more hours with few, if any, breaks.

Marijuana   Substance prepared from the flowers or leaves of the Indian hemp plant *Cannabis sativa.*

Marital schism   Family structure in which there is open warfare between husband and wife; common in families of schizophrenics.

Marital skew   Family structure in which serious psychopathology in one parent is accepted or supported by the other parent; common in families of schizophrenics.

Maturation   Process involving growth or change over time, with heredity being the main determinant of the change.

Mean   Arithmetic average; the sum of all scores divided by the number of scores.

Means-end analysis   Problem-solving process in which one tests for difference between the present situation and a solution situation and continues to perform operations until no difference is detected. Applicable whenever there is a clearly specifiable problem situation and a clearly specifiable solution.

Median   An average, defined as the middle-most score in a set of scores; an equal number of scores are higher and lower than the median.

Mediated generalization   Generalization based upon learned similarities.

Mediational theory of thinking   Holds that as a consequence of external stimulus-response associations, the individual may form internal miniaturized versions of these stimuli (mediational stimuli) and responses (mediational responses) that serve as the connecting link between the environment and the way one responds to it.

Medical model   Model of psychopathology in which pathological behaviors are viewed as symptoms of a disease.

Meditation   Special action and/or deployment of attention designed to purify the ordinary state of consciousness by removing illusions and to facilitate the production of states of consciousness in which truth is more directly perceived.

Medulla   Part of the brain that is closest to the spinal cord, it regulates the body's vital functions, such as heart rate and breathing.

Menarche   First menstrual period in females. In human beings, this generally occurs in the early teens.

Mental age (MA)   In the Binet intelligence test the age level at which a child can successfully pass subtests. Computed by adding basal age plus the number of age units corresponding to items the subject passes at successively higher levels. Independent of chronological age.

Mental set   Tendency to respond in a given way irrespective of the requirements of the situation. Sets sometimes facilitate performance and sometimes impair it.

Mescaline   A psychedelic drug derived from the peyote cactus.

Methadone   Drug used in treatment of heroin addiction that prevents withdrawl symptoms and blocks the heroin "high" but still is addictive.

Minimum principle   In perceptual organization, the organization that is perceived in an ambiguous stimulus is the one which keeps changes, discontinuities, and differences to a minimum; simplicity of organization is a determinant of what will be seen.

Model   In psychological theory, a framework or structure that provides a way of conceptualizing behavioral observations.

Mongolism   Also called Down's Syndrome, it results from the presence of an extra chromosome and is characterized by mental retardation.

Monocular cues for depth   Cues for depth perception derived from information in the optic array that is available to either eye alone—interposition, size perspective, linear perspective, shading, aerial perspective, texture gradients.

Morality   Type of knowledge that involves the attitudes of human beings toward social practices and institutions.

Moro reflex   See "startle reflex."

Motor   Refers to information being carried out from the central nervous system. *Efferent* is a synonym.

Motor cortex   Part of the cerebral cortex from which messages leading to bodily movement originate.

Motor sequence   Series of events involving the development of posture, crawling, and walking in infants. These events tend to occur in a set order and at approximately the same age in most infants of a particular culture.

Motor theory   Early stimulus-response theory of thinking espoused by behaviorists and proposing that thinking always involves muscular or glandular activity of some kind. According to this theory, most human thought is basically subvocal speech activity.

Multiple personality   Neurotic dissociative reaction in which a person has two or more complete but alternating personalities; often different personalities express different aspects of a conflict that the person is experiencing.

Naturalistic observation   Systematic method for observing and recording events as they naturally occur in the world.

Need for achievement   See "achievement motivation."

Negative afterimage   After staring at a colored stimulus for a period of time, a person sees the same stimulus in complementary colors against a neutral background.

Negative reinforcement   A reinforcement that increases the probability of a response when removal of the reinforcement is contingent on the response.

Neo-Freudian   Also called "neoanalytic." Refers to a large number of psychologists who agree with some of Freud's ideas but have modified his theory to develop their own, more modern theories.

Nerve   A bundle of axons from many neurons, it runs from one point in the body to another and carries nerve impulses.

Nervous breakdown   Commonsense term usually used to describe a person whose emotional problems are so severe that he can no longer cope with home or work responsibilities; not a description of a physical nervous condition and not synonymous with *neurosis*.

Nervous system   The brain and spinal cord, plus all of the neurons traveling throughout the rest of the body. It is a communication system, carrying information throughout the body.

Neuron   Nerve cell. The most elementary unit of the nervous system, its function is to send and receive messages.

Neurosis   Special pattern of behavior that is instigated and maintained for the purpose of contending with stress and avoiding anxiety; diagnostic category of psychopathology characterized by anxiety, rigid and unsuccessful attempts to reduce it, and an inability to totally satisfy the need being served by the behavior.

Neurotic   Person who is experiencing a neurosis.

Neurotic anxiety   In Freudian theory, anxiety or fear that occurs when there is no rational reason for it; in learning theory, conditioned fear.

Neurotic paradox   Refers to the fact that the neurotic person persists in his maladaptive behavior even in the face of unpleasant consequences.

Nondirective therapy   See "client-centered therapy."

Nonsense syllable   Three-letter syllable, consisting of two consonants separated by a vowel. It is used to study verbal learning.

Norm   A rule, established and maintained in a social context, identifying desirable behavior.

Normative developmental research   Research strategy that compares the behavior of children at different ages in one situation. It tends to be used by psychologists who stress the role of maturation in development and aims to chart behavioral norms for different ages.

Nucleus   Structure containing hereditary information and other things, found in the center of most cells. Also, a cluster of cell bodies of neurons.

Null hypothesis   Prediction that the variable being manipulated will have no effect on the behavior being measured.

Nurture   Socialization, education, training, and other environmental influences that affect the development of the organism.

Obsession   Persistent, repetitive thought that cannot be pushed out of consciousness.

Obsessive-compulsive syndrome   Neurotic pattern in which obsessive and compulsive behavior tend to go together in the same person; the syndrome prevents a person from thinking anxiety-provoking thoughts and from doing anxiety-provoking things.

Oedipal conflict   Proposed by Freud, this is the attraction a boy has for his mother and its accompanying anxiety and guilt.

One-shot problems   See "simple-one-shot problems."

Opening-up meditation   A form of meditation that involves paying full, continuous attention to everything that is happening to one.

Operant conditioning   See "instrumental conditioning."

Opponent process theory   In motivation and emotion, a theory proposed by Solomon and Corbit which says that for every pleasant feeling and approach tendency there is an opponent or opposing process with the opposite characteristics, i.e., an unpleasant feeling and an avoidance tendency. The net motivation or emotion at any time is the sum of the strengths of the two opposing processes.

Optic array   Pattern of light energy, reflected from the surface of an object, that enters the eye.

Optical revolving power   Ability of the lens in the eye to focus the optic array sharply on the retina and not in front of or behind it.

Organic disorder   Emotional problem resulting from biological causes, usually from impairment of brain functioning.

Out-of-body experience (OOBE)   Experience during which a person feels that he is located at a point other than where his physical body is, and still feels he is in a normal state of consciousness.

Ovaries   Reproductive organs in females; they are also endocrine glands that secrete many hormones, regulating sexual cycles and behavior and supporting pregnancy.

Overtones   Multiples of a given frequency of sound, they combine with basic frequency to produce the psychological attribute of timbre.

Paired-associate learning   Learning a list of paired items such that one member of the pair can be recalled given the other member as a stimulus.

Pancreas   Produces the hormone insulin and thus regulates the use of sugar in the body. Below-normal production of insulin by this gland leads to diabetes mellitus, or too much sugar in the blood.

Paranoid personality   Personality disorder characterized by suspiciousness and jealousy but no loss of contact with reality.

Paranoid schizophrenia   Subtype of schizophrenia characterized by delusions of persecution, suspicion of others, and delusions of grandeur.

Paraprofessionals   Individuals from the community who are given minimum training and can then serve as temporary therapists.

Parapsychology   Study of topics that are related to psychology (such as ESP) but are not fully accepted as belonging under the heading of "psychology."

Parasympathetic nervous system   One part of the autonomic nervous system involved in controlling involuntary behavior, such as digestion; it works in opposition to the sympathetic system and conserves body energy.

Partial reinforcement   A reinforcement schedule in which less than 100 percent of all correct responses are rewarded.

Perception   The reception of information through sensory receptors and interpretation of that information so as to construct meaningfulness about one's world.

Perceptual constancy   The fact that perceptual organization remains relatively stable even though some aspects of the pattern within the optic array change: size constancy, shape constancy, brightness constancy.

Performance   One's observable responses or behavior in a given task.

Peripheral nervous system   Contains all the nerves which are the communication lines connecting muscles, glands, and sensory receptors with the central nervous system.

Personality assessment   Administering and evaluating a variety of tests (and perhaps interviews) in order to develop an understanding of an individual's personality.

Personality disorder   Diagnostic category of psychopathology marked by failure to behave in socially appropriate ways due to lack of motivation or lack of skill (competence) in coping with normal stresses of everyday life; such individuals are pathological by society's definition, not in terms of their own personal discomfort.

Perspective theory   Explanation of how physically equal stimuli are perceived as unequal by proposing that one uses perspective clues to judge depth and then uses this depth information in perceiving size.

Phi phenomenon   Apparent movement; an illusion of movement produced by the sequential illumination of two or more stationary lights, as in a theater marquee.

Phobia   Neurosis characterized by an intense, irrational fear of something; according to analytic theory, it involves displacement of anxiety onto a situation that is not dangerous or only mildly dangerous.

Phonemes   General classes of sounds common to a given language (basic sounds of a language); considered to be the conjunctive combination of several distinctive features associated with a particular language. In English, features include voiced versus voiceless and stopped (air flow interrupted) versus fricative (air flow sliding over articulator).

Phonology   Study of the sounds of a language.

Pitch   Psychological attribute corresponding to frequency of a sound wave.

Pituitary gland   The "master gland," it is activated by the hypothalamus and releases hormones that are responsible for activating many of the other glands, in addition to regulating bodily growth, water loss, and many other functions.

Pleasure centers   Areas in the brain that, when electrically stimulated, produce very strong, pleasurable sensations. May be involved in determining what is rewarding for animals in everyday life.

Pleasure principle   A concept originated by Freud, it is the idea that man strives to avoid pain and seek pleasure.

Positive reinforcement   A reinforcement that increases the probability of a response when the reinforcement is contingent on the response.

Positive instances   All stimuli in a population that have the characteristics that illustrate a given concept. For instance, if *red* is the concept, objects that are red in color are positive instances.

Possession state   State in which the subject feels as if his own personality or soul has been taken over or displaced by some nonphysical entity.

Posthypnotic effects   Behavior that occurs after a subject has been brought back to normal consciousness following a hypnotic state. The behavior is caused by suggestions given to the subject while he is hypnotized.

P-O-X model   Descriptive model used to diagram relationships according to balance theory; P (person) has an orientation toward O (another person); P also has an orientation toward X (usually an object); and P perceives O as having an orientation toward X. The nature of the orientations determines whether a balanced state exists.

Preconscious   In Freudian theory, the ideas, thoughts, and images that a person is not aware of at a given moment but that can be brought into awareness with little or no difficulty.

Prejudice   Attitude held toward members of another group that is emotional, rigidly or inflexibly felt and acted on, and negative. The object of the prejudice is disliked and the group's tendency is to mistreat or discriminate against members of the disliked group.

Premack principle   Given two behaviors which differ in their likelihood of occurrence, the less likely behavior can be reinforced by using the more likely behavior as a reward.

Preoperational period   The second stage of intellectual development, occurring from 2 to 7 years, proposed by Piaget; it is a transitional period during which children learn to use language as a way of representing events and knowledge.

Primal therapy   A type of psychotherapy developed by Arthur Janov; it focuses on the fact that people have cut off their feelings from childhood with respect to the rejection they have received from their parents, the goal being to reexperience these feelings and the associated pain.

Primary gain   For neurotic behavior, the immediate reduction of anxiety.

Primary mental abilities   According to Thurstone, the basic separate abilities that make up intelligence, including number ability, word fluency (speed of thinking of the right word at the right time), verbal meaning, memory, reasoning, spatial relations, and perceptual speed (ability to recognize similarities and differences in visual forms).

Primary reinforcer   Stimulus or event that is innately reinforcing.

Proactive inhibition   A situation where recall of learned information is made more difficult because of something learned earlier.

Process schizophrenia   Schizophrenic reaction in which there is a slow onset of symptoms over a period of years, with progressive withdrawal from others, increasing deterioration of thought processes, and slow onset of hallucinations and delusions; sometimes called *chronic schizophrenia.*

Prognosis   Probability of recovery.

Projection   Process of denying the presence of unacceptable impulses or characteristics and then seeing these qualities in another person (who may or may not actually have them); a defense mechanism.

Proximity   Nearness in physical location or occurrence.

Psilocybin   Psychedelic drug derived from a certain type of mushroom.

Psychedelic   "Mind-manifesting." In reference to drugs, it denotes any drug whose primary effect is to induce an altered state of consciousness.

Psychedelic therapy   Type of psychotherapy using one or a few large doses of LSD or other psychedelic drug.

Psychoanalysis   Insight-oriented therapy developed by Freud and based upon his psychoanalytic theory.

Psychoanalytic theory   Theory of personality developed by Freud out of his work with the unhealthy personality. It is a dynamic theory that sees personality as being based in biological needs.

Psychodrama   Therapeutic technique involving the acting out of parts or roles with others, under the supervision of a therapist.

Psychology   Scientific study of behavior and systematic application of behavior principles.

Psychopathology   Inability to behave in a socially appropriate way such that the consequences of one's behavior are maladaptive for oneself or society.

Psychopharmacology   Study of the effects of drugs on behavior and application of such knowledge in order to change behavior.

Psychophysics   Study of the relationship between physical stimulation and the conscious sensations it provokes in a person; historically, it was the first form of psychological study to appear.

Psychophysiologic reaction   See "psychosomatic illness."

Psychosexual stages of development   Series of stages, proposed by Freud, through which all people pass as they develop their personalities; they are the oral, anal, phallic, latency, and genital stages.

Psychosis   Diagnostic category of psychopathology characterized by gross distortion of reality or by loss of reality testing, inability to distinguish between reality and fantasy, hallucinations, and/or delusions.

Psychosomatic illness   Physical illness that has psychological causes.

Psychosurgery   Use of lesions or surgery on the nervous system, especially the brain, for the purpose of changing behavior.

Psychotherapy   Corrective experience leading the client to behave in socially appropriate, adequate, and adaptive ways.

Psychotic   Person who is experiencing a psychosis.

Psychotic episode   Sudden experience, generally triggered by some specific stimuli in the environment, during which a person develops a psychosis.

Psychotomimetic drug   Any drug that produces a state of being similar to a psychosis.

Puberty   Time of onset of sexual maturity; average age of onset for boys is 14, for girls, 12 years.

Punishment   Event or stimulus that tends to decrease the frequency of behaviors that it follows.

Random sampling   Selecting a sample in such a manner that each person in the population has an equal chance of being chosen for the sample.

Rapid eye movement (REM)   Activity of the eye muscles that occurs during one stage of sleep and that seems to indicate the occurrence of dreaming.

Reaction formation   Denial or masking of one's own unacceptable impulses by stating or emphasizing qualities that are the opposite to one's true feelings; a defense mechanism.

Reactive schizophrenias   Schizophrenic reactions in which the onset of symptoms is relatively sudden; sometimes called *acute schizophrenias*.

Realistic-group-conflict theory   Theory of prejudice stating that if two groups are in conflict with each other, members of each group will tend to develop prejudice against members of the other group.

Reality principle   A concept originated by Freud, it involves the idea that in order to exist, people must behave in ways that are consistent with the real world. The ego is the part of the personality that oversees and carries out this need.

Real self   The concept of *I, me,* or *myself* as one really is; one's own awareness of his existence.

Receptive field   Area of the retina corresponding to a single cell in the visual projection of the brain.

Reciprocal inhibition   Learning to decrease the presence of a response like anxiety by increasing the presence of an incompatible response like relaxation while the original anxiety-producing stimulus occurs.

Redundancy   Presence of distinctive stimulus features or cues in each of several stimuli that differ from each other in other ways. Redundancy reduces the chance of miscommunication or misperception.

Referent   Object or thing to which a word refers.

Refractory period   Time interval, usually following a response, during which almost no stimulus will produce another response.

Regress   In relation to hypnosis it involves taking a subject back in time, until he psychologically experiences the past. It may even be possible to take a person back to a past life.

Regression   Interrupting one's development at a particular point and retreating back to an earlier stage that is less threatening; a defense mechanism.

Reinforcer   Event or stimulus that increases the frequency of a response with which it is associated.

Relational concept   See "concept."

Relaxation training   Learning to relax the body by becoming aware of and controlling the muscles of the body; one part of systematic desensitization.

Releasers   See "sign stimuli."

Relevant attributes   Characteristics of a stimulus that make the stimulus a positive instance of a given concept.

Relevant dimension   Stimulus dimension along which a concept is defined. For example, color is a relevant dimension along which the concept *red* is defined; size is not a relevant dimension for the concept *red*.

Reliability   The degree to which a person's score on some variable does not change on repeated testings; it is a critical characteristic of every measuring device.

Repression   Act of keeping highly threatening impulses or memories in the unconscious far away from awareness, because they are very likely to produce much anxiety or other negative consequences; a defense mechanism.

Response (R)   Any behavior that results from a stimulus.

Response discrimination   Learning to give one, and only one, particular response in a given situation.

Response generalization   Learning one response, then giving a similar but slightly different one under the same stimulus conditions.

Response integration   Several independent responses gradually become unified into a single smooth response.

Restrictive meditation   See "concentrative meditation."

Retention interval   The time between initial learning of something and its recall.

Reticular formation   Structure extending through the central core of the hindbrain and midbrain that maintains wakefulness and attentive behavior.

Retina   Photosensitive surface at the back of the eye upon which the optic array is focused; it contains visual receptor cells.

Retinal disparity   See "binocular disparity."

Retroactive inhibition   Difficulty in recalling learned information because of something learned after the information one is trying to recall.

Retrograde amnesia   Loss of memory for events just prior to the event that caused the memory loss. Long-term memory remains intact.

Reward   Stimulus or event that increases the frequency of behaviors it follows.

Rod   Photoreceptor cell shaped like a rod, located throughout the retina, with greatest concentration near its edges; it is extremely sensitive to low intensities of light—not equally sensitive to all wavelengths of light.

Role playing   Technique involving the acting out of specific roles in order to work through problems.

Sampling techniques   Procedures for selecting a small number of cases from a large population such that the sample that results is representative of the larger population.

Scanning   Strategy for solving conceptual problems which uses a hypothesis-testing approach. Successive scanning involves testing possible solutions one at a time. Simultaneous scanning involves testing more than one hypothesis at a time.

Scapegoat theory   Theory that prejudice serves as an outlet for personal feelings of hostility, frustration, and aggression; that it is a displacement of aggression.

Schizophrenia   Group of psychotic disorders in which there are disturbances in thought processes as well as emotions and a marked distortion of reality; often characterized by emotional blunting, disturbances in interpersonal relationships, depersonalization, and preoccupation with inner fantasies.

Secondary elaboration   Dream process that disguises material by combining separate events or objects into one cohesive unit.

Secondary gain   For neurotic behavior, other positive consequences in addition to the relief from tension or anxiety.

Secondary reinforcer   Stimulus or event that becomes a reinforcer only after being paired with a primary reinforcer.

Secondary sexual characteristics   Physical features—such as growth of beard and change of voice in males and enlarging of breasts in females—that appear during puberty and remain for most or all of one's adult life. They are indications of sexual maturity.

Sedative   Drug that reduces anxiety by inducing muscle relaxation, sleep, and inhibition of the cognitive centers of the brain.

Self-actualization   Highest level need in Maslow's theory of motivation; the drive to develop and realize one's fullest potentialities; the need for self-fulfillment.

Self-concept   Fairly consistent and enduring framework of self-regarding attitudes.

Self-fulfilling prophecy   In research, an experimenter may have expectations about how the subjects should behave, and he may inadvertently or otherwise get his subjects to behave that way. By making a prediction one acts to insure that the prediction comes true.

Self-remembering   A process similar to opening-up meditation, it involves being aware of being aware.

Self theory   Approach to personality that focuses on the individual as a whole, unified self. It takes a fairly positive view of man and is a part of the humanistic approach to psychology.

Semantic differential   Procedure developed by Charles Osgood that uses the ratings that people give to words to derive the basic dimensions of meaning and the location of any given word on those dimensions. Measures word connotation.

Semantic generalization   Type of mediated generalization whereby language is the mediator.

Semicircular canals   Sense organs for body motion; three fluid-filled canals, in the inner ear, perpendicular to each other in three different planes, that respond to movement in any direction.

Sensations   In Stucturalism, the direct products of external stimulation.

Sensitivity training   Group experience aimed at improving human relations, skills, and honesty and understanding of oneself and others; also called *T-group*.

Sensorimotor period   The first stage of cognitive development proposed by Piaget, it occurs during infancy, 0-2 years, as the infant comes to realize that objects have an existence independent of himself.

Sensory   Refers to information being brought into the central nervous system. *Afferent* is a synonym.

Sensory cortex   Areas of the cerebral cortex that are the final receiving stations for sensory information.

Sensory deprivation   Prolonged reduction of external stimulation, either in intensity or variety; produces boredom, restlessness, and disturbances of thought processes.

Sequential concept   See "concept."

Serial learning   Learning a list of items in a particular order.

Sex-role identification   An organism's tendency to learn and display behaviors appropriate for males or females of the species.

Sexual deviations   Any method of obtaining sexual satisfaction or participating in sexual relationships that is disapproved of by the community; impotence, frigidity, homosexuality, fetishism.

Sexual impotence   Inability to engage in sexual intercourse with an opposite-sexed partner.

Shaman   A tribal medicine man who is thought to have extraordinary spiritual knowledge and powers.

Sham rage   Ferocious, undirected rage behavior provoked by very mild stimulation; experimental condition produced by surgical removal of the cerebral cortex.

Shape constancy   The fact that objects appear to maintain a constant shape regardless of the angle from which we observe them.

Shaping   Process that uses instrumental conditioning in gradual steps to develop an uncommon or difficult behavior.

Sharpening   Cognitive style whereby one ignores similarities and emphasizes differences in perceiving the world.

Short-term memory   Memory for learned material over a very brief retention interval. Hypothetical memory system for transient information.

Shuttle box   Device with two compartments separated by a door, used to study learning and motivation.

Sibling   Brother or sister.

Sibling rivalry   Jealousy or competition between brothers and/or sisters, which often develops in a child upon the birth of a new brother or sister.

Sign stimuli   Environmental cues that trigger instinctual behavior.

Simple one-shot problems   Lowest level of problems studied by psychologists. All these problems have specific, known solutions that can be found relatively automatically by following a simple series of steps. May emphasize perceptual or verbal factors.

Simple schizophrenia   Subtype of schizophrenia characterized by reduction in interpersonal relationships, apathy, indifference, and difficulty in focusing on anything in the outside world; but seldom many delusions and hallucinations.

Size constancy   The observation that heights of objects do not appear to shrink as we move away from them even though the size of the image on the retina does become smaller.

Skinner box   A box containing a lever that, when pushed, causes a food pellet to appear in a tray. This, and variations of it, is used to study learning.

Social attitude   Combination of feelings, beliefs, and action tendencies toward classes of persons or objects that are directly or indirectly social in nature.

Social concept   Concept about classes of people; attitude.

Social exchange theory   The idea that interpersonal attraction can be analyzed in terms of rewards and costs of each event or type of interaction.

Social facilitation   Phenomenon in which the mere presence of other persons, as an audience or as coworkers, without any verbal exchange, affects individual performance.

Social learning theory   Attempt to explain personality in terms of learning, based on the assumption that much of what we call personality is learned behavior involving imitation. Albert Bandura is a social learning theorist.

Social psychology   Study of the effect on individual behavior of the real or implied, immediate or past, presence of others.

Social speech   Speech with the purpose of communicating to someone else. Proposed by Piaget.

Sociopath   See "antisocial character."

Somatic nervous system   Part of the peripheral nervous system, it contains the neurons that connect to sensory organs and skeletal muscles.

Spiritual medium   Person who claims that highly evolved spirits sometimes possess him and serve as a guide to his spiritual activity.

Split-brain operation   Cutting of the corpus callosum, which connects the two halves of the cerebral hemispheres, so that the hemispheres are then unable to communicate to each other.

Spontaneous recovery   Following extinction training, the return of a learned behavior even though it has not been practiced.

Standard deviation   In statistics a measure of the variability or spread of a set scores around the mean.

Stanford-Binet test   A revision of the Binet intelligence test made by psychologists at Stanford University, it is an individual test using age-level subtests. Most widely used children's intelligence test.

Startle reflex   An automatic response shown by most normal infants to a startling stimulus, it involves throwing the arms to the side, extending the fingers, and then curving the hands back to the midline. Also called Moro reflex.

State anxiety   Momentary, consciously perceived feelings of apprehension and tension.

State-dependent learning   Ability of the learner's internal physiological state to affect learning; the more similar this state is during learning and recall, the better recall will be.

Stereotyping   Adopting the belief that all members of certain groups hold to certain beliefs or have certain attitudes or characteristics; treating all members of this group in the same ways, as if they belonged to a rigidly bound conceptual class.

Stimulus (S)   Event capable of affecting an organism; specifically, anything that can activate a sensory neuron.

Stimulus control   Instrumental learning process whereby a cue in the environment comes to control the behavior of an organism.

Stimulus discrimination   Learning to respond differently to various stimuli that may have some similarities.

Stimulus generalization   Learning a response to a stimulus, then showing the same response to a similar, but slightly different, stimulus.

Stroop effect   Difficulty in attending to or responding to a given stimulus due to an inability to block responses to irrelevant features in the stimulus situation, a response competition phenomenon.

Structuralism   Early school of psychological thought that held that the subject matter of psychology was conscious experience, that the object of study was to analyze experience into its component parts, and that the primary method of analysis was introspection.

Sublimation   Rechanneling instinctual energy from an unacceptable object to one that is highly valued by society.

Subvocal activity   Behavior of speaking to oneself (that is, moving the muscles of the voice apparatus at very low levels without speaking overtly). According to the motor theory of thinking, subvocal activity is the basic behavioral component of thinking.

Superego   One of the basic structures of the personality, as proposed by Freud. The superego contains people's values, morals, and basic attitudes as learned from their parents and society.

Suppression   Act of keeping an impulse or memory just below the level of awareness, in the preconscious, because it is likely to provoke anxiety or other negative consequences.

Symbolic mode   The most sophisticated method for converting immediate experiences into mental models. As proposed by Bruner, it involves using words and sentences as symbols of objects, events, and states of affairs.

Symbolization   Dream process that disguises material in the dream so that something in the dream represents or stands for something else in real life.

Sympathetic nervous system   Part of the autonomic nervous system, it prepares the organism for emergencies, making much bodily energy available for use.

Synapse   Area where the end of one neuron connects to the next neuron in a communication chain. Specifically, the axon

terminals of the first cell come close to (but do not touch) the dendrites or soma of the second cell.

Systematic desensitization   Type of behavior therapy developed by Wolpe to help people overcome fears and anxiety.

Taste buds   Taste receptors, each containing taste cells, located primarily on the tongue.

Territorial instinct   An organism's innate desire for complete control of the physical area in which it lives; territoriality.

Testes   Reproductive organs in males; endocrine glands that secrete many hormones that regulate sexual behaviors and characteristics.

Tetrahydrocannabinol (THC)   Major active ingredient in marijuana.

Texture gradient   Difference in surface textures or characteristics between the area of a figure and that of the background.

Thalamus   Portion of the brain that receives information about most of the senses and relays it to the cortex. It also is involved in sleep and attention.

Thematic Apperception Test (TAT)   Projective test requiring the subject to write stories about a number of ambiguous pictures; the story content reveals unconscious motivation. Also used to measure achievement motivation.

Theory   Set of principles and statements that represent, organize, and summarize facts and suggest an explanation of what lies behind them.

Thyroid gland   Produces the hormone thyroxin and thus regulates metabolism and growth.

Timbre   See "overtones."

Token economy   Reward training, based on operant conditioning, that uses tokens as rewards for certain behaviors. The tokens can be redeemed for special privileges, or primary reinforcers.

TOTE unit   Test, Operate, Test, Exit. A series of steps in problem solving, emphasizing the discrimination process. See "means-end analysis."

Trace-dependent forgetting   Loss of learned information due to the loss of a memory trace, see "cue-dependent forgetting."

Trait   Relatively permanent characteristic of an individual that he tends to show in most situations.

Trait anxiety   Anxiety proneness; predisposition to respond with high anxiety when under stress.

Trait cluster   Group of traits that tend to go together, so that if a person has one of the traits he will probably have all of them.

Transcendental meditation   One type of concentrative meditation, as taught by the Maharishi Mahesh Yogi.

Tranquilizer   A drug that reduces anxiety without inducing sleep.

Transactional analysis   A type of psychotherapy originated by Eric Berne and popularized by Thomas Harris. It focuses on the transactions people have with one another and analyzes these into interactions between the various parts of each person's personality (Parent, Adult, Child).

Transference   A concept developed by Freud, it generally refers to the tendency of a person in therapy to transfer to the therapist perceptions, feelings, etc., that he has about other people in his life, rather than seeing the therapist as he really is.

Transfer of training   The effect—positive or negative—of prior learning on the subsequent performance of a different task.

Traumatic neurosis   Inability to successfully cope with stress, brought on by a single traumatic incident or by prolonged, intense stress from which there is no escape, such as battle stresses in war.

Trucking game   Decision-making game used in research on cooperation and competition. Subject is asked to make a decision between cooperating for a steady reward or competing for a large but risky reward.

2 + 2 phenomenon   Adoption of a prejudiced attitude from an erroneous conclusion about facts (for example, concluding that blacks are innately inferior because they score lower on IQ tests and overlooking the fact that often tests are biased against blacks).

Unconditioned positive regard   Rogerian concept involving the idea that a therapist must care about his client without any conditions put on the caring, even when the client reveals things that the therapist is uncomfortable about.

Unconditioned response (UCR)   In classical conditioning, the response that automatically occurs whenever the unconditioned stimulus is presented, without any training.

Unconditioned stimulus (UCS)   In classical conditioning, the stimulus that automatically elicits the desired response, without any training.

Unconscious   In Freudian theory, that part of a person's mental process that he resists being aware of; unacceptable drives and impulses and material that were once conscious but were removed from awareness because they were anxiety provoking.

Vacuum activity   Occurrence of an instinctual behavior in the absence of any releasing stimulus.

Validity   Degree to which a measuring device measures what it is supposed to measure.

Variable   Any characteristic of an object, event, or person that can take two or more values.

Vestibular sacs   Sense organs for perception of balance; enlargements at the base of the semicircular canals that respond to tilt.

Visual acuity   Ability to notice fine detail in a patterned stimulus.

Visual cliff   Device used to study depth perception in infants. The illusion of a cliff is built into a level glass floor, and infants are urged to crawl over the edge of the "cliff."

Wechsler-Bellevue   Intelligence test battery, in adult and children's versions, composed of tests for different abilities. Divided into performance tests and verbal tests, it yields a point score that can be converted into an IQ.

Yantra   Visual pattern that can be meditated on.

Yerkes-Dodson Law   The fact that increased motivation will improve performance up to a point, beyond which there is deterioration. The easier a task is to perform, the higher the drive level for optimal performance.

The authors wish to thank Daniel L. Smith of University of Southern California and Jane Dallinger of Contra Costa College for their help in preparing the glossary.

BIBLIOGRAPHY

Adamson, R. E., & Taylor, D. W. Functional fixedness as related to elapsed time and to set. *Journal of Experimental Psychology,* 1954, *47,* 122–126.

Adelson, J., Green, B., & O'Neil, R. Growth of the idea of law in adolescence. *Developmental Psychology,* 1969, *1,* 327–332.

Adorno, T. W., Frenkel-Brunswik, E., Levinson, D. J., & Sanford, R. N. *The authoritarian personality.* New York: Harper & Row, 1950.

Allbrook, R. C. How to spot executives early. *Fortune,* 1968, *78,* 106–111.

Aronson, E., & Mills, J. The effect of severity of initiation on liking for a group. *Journal of Abnormal and Social Psychology,* 1959, *59,* 177–181.

Asch, S. E. Studies of independence and conformity: I. A minority of one against a unanimous majority. *Psychological Monographs,* 1956, *70* (9, whole no. 416).

Aserinsky, E., & Kleitman, N. Regularly occurring periods of eye mobility and concomitant phenomena during sleep. *Science,* 1953, *118,* 273–274.

Atkinson, J. W., & McClelland, D. C. The projective expressions of needs. II. The effect of different intensities of the hunger drive on thematic apperception. *Journal of Experimental Psychology,* 1948, *38,* 643–658.

Azrin, N. H., Hutchinson, R. R., & Hake, D. F. Extinction-induced aggression. *Journal of the Experimental Analysis of Behavior,* 1966, *9,* 191–204.

Bach-y-rita, P. *Brain mechanisms in sensory substitution.* New York: Academic Press, 1972.

Bandura, A., & Walters, R. H. *Social learning and personality development.* New York: Holt, Rinehart and Winston, 1965.

Barber, T. X. *Hypnosis: A scientific approach.* New York: Van Nostrand Reinhold, 1969.

Bard, P., & Mountcastle, V. B. Some forebrain mechanisms involved in expression of rage with special reference to suppression of angry behavior. *Research Publication Association Nervous and Mental Disorders,* 1948, *27,* 362–404.

Barrett, R. S. Guide to using psychological tests. *Harvard Business Review,* 1963, *41,* 139.

Bateson, G., Jackson, D. D., Haley, J., & Weakland, J. H. Toward a theory of schizophrenia. *Behavioral Science,* 1956, *1,* 251–264.

Bonime, W. *The clinical use of dreams.* New York: Basic Books, 1962.

Boring, E. G., Langfeld, H. S., & Weld, H. P. *Foundations of psychology.* New York: Wiley, 1948.

Bourne, L. E., Jr. *Human conceptual behavior.* Boston: Allyn and Bacon, 1966.

Bower, G. H. The influence of graded reductions in reward and prior frustrating events upon the magnitude of the frustration effect. *Journal of Comparative and Physiological Psychology,* 1962, *55,* 582–587.

Brady, J. V. Ulcers in "executive" monkeys. *Scientific American,* 1958, *199,* 95–100.

Braine, M. D. S. The ontogeny of English phrase structure: The first phase. *Language,* 1963, *39,* 1–13.

Bransford, J. D., & Franks, J. J. The abstraction of linguistic ideas. *Cognitive Psychology,* 1971, *2,* 331–350.

Bransford, J. D., & Johnson, M. K. Considerations of some problems of comprehension. In Chase, W. G. (Ed.) *Visual Information Processing.* New York: Academic Press, 1973.

Breuer, J., & Freud, S. Studies on hysteria. In Strachey, J. (Trans.) *Standard Edition of the Complete Works of Sigmund Freud.* New York: Basic Books, 1957.

Bruner, J. S. *Toward a theory of instruction.* Cambridge, Mass.: Belknap Press, 1966.

Butler, R. A. Discrimination learning by rhesus monkeys to visual-exploration motivation. *Journal of Comparative and Physiological Psychology,* 1953, *46,* 95–98.

Butler, R. A. Incentive conditions which influence visual exploration. *Journal of Experimental Psychology,* 1954, *48,* 19–23.

Byrne, D., & Clore, G. L., Jr. Predicting interpersonal attraction toward strangers presented in three different stimulus modes. *Psychonomic Science,* 1966, *4,* 239–240.

Campbell, D. T. Ethnocentric and other altruistic motives. In Levine, D. (Ed.) *Nebraska Symposium on Motivation.* Lincoln, Nebr.: University of Nebraska Press, 1965.

Cannon, W. B. *Bodily changes in pain, hunger, fear and rage.* New York: Appleton-Century-Crofts, 1929.

Casebook on ethical standards of psychologists. Washington, D.C.: American Psychological Association, 1967.

Cattell, R. B. Concepts of personality growing from multivariate experiment. In Wepman, J. M., & Heine, R. W. (Eds.) *Concepts of Personality.* Chicago: Aldine, 1963.

Cattell, R. B., & Ebel, H. W. *Handbook for the sixteen personality factor questionnaire.* Champaign, Ill.: Institute for Personality and Ability Testing, 1964.

Cautela, J. R., & Kastenbaum, R. A reinforcement survey schedule for use in therapy, training, and research. *Psychological Reports,* 1967, *20,* 1115–1130.

Clark, K. B., & Clark, M. P. Racial identification and preference in Negro children. In Newcomb, T. M., & Hartley, E. I. (Eds.) *Readings in Social Psychology.* New York: Holt, 1947.

Deci, E. L. Work: Who does not like it and why. *Psychology Today,* 1972, *6,* 56–92.

Delgado, J. M. R. *Physical control of the mind.* New York: Harper & Row, 1969.

Deutsch, M., & Krauss, R. M. The effect of threat upon interpersonal bargaining. *Journal of Abnormal and Social Psychology,* 1960, *61,* 181–189.

DeValois, R. L., Abromov, I., & Jacobs, G. H. Analysis of response patterns of LGN cells. *Journal of the Optical Society of America,* 1966, *56,* 966–977.

Dollard, J., Doob, L., Miller, N., Mowrer, O., & Sears, R. *Frustration and aggression.* New Haven, Conn: Yale University Press, 1939.

Dollard, J. & Miller, N. E. *Personality and psychotherapy.* New York: McGraw-Hill, 1950.

Eimas, P. D., Siqueland, E. R., Jusczyk, P., & Vigorito, J.

Speech perception in infants. *Science,* 1971, *171,* 303–306.

Engberg, L. A., Hansen, G., Welker, R. L., & Thomas, D. R. Acquisition of key-pecking via autoshaping as a function of prior experience: "Learned laziness"? *Science,* 1972, *178,* 1002–1004.

Epstein, S. Toward a unified theory of anxiety. *Progress in Experimental Personality Research,* 1967, *4,* 1–89.

Erikson, E. *Childhood and society.* New York: Norton, 1950.

Evans, R. M. *An introduction to color.* New York: Wiley, 1948.

Ewald, W. *Street graphics.* Washington, D.C.: American Landscape Architects Association, 1971.

Eysenck, H. J. The effects of psychotherapy: An evaluation. *Journal of Consulting Psychology,* 1952, *16,* 319–324.

Fantz, R. L. The origin of form perception. *Scientific American,* 1961, *204,* 66–72.

Fantz, R. L. Visual perception and experience in early infancy: A look at the hidden side of behavior development. In Stevenson, H. W., Hess, E. H., & Rheingold, H. L. (Eds.) *Early Behavior: Comparative and Developmental Approaches.* New York: Wiley, 1967.

Festinger, L. *A theory of cognitive dissonance.* Stanford, Calif.: Stanford University Press, 1957.

Festinger, L., Riecken, H. W., & Schachter, S. *When prophecy fails: A social and psychological study of a modern group that predicted the destruction of the world.* New York: Harper & Row, 1956.

Fitts, W. H. *The experience of psychotherapy.* Princeton. N.J.: Van Nostrand, 1965.

Foulkes. D. *The psychology of sleep.* New York: Scribner's, 1966.

Freedman, J., & Haber, R. N. One reason why we rarely forget a face. *The Bulletin of the Psychonomic Society,* 1974, *3,* 107–109.

Freud, S. *An outline of psychoanalysis (1940).* New York: Norton, 1949.

Freud, S. *The interpretation of dreams.* New York: Random House, 1950.

Freud, S. Some problems in the treatment of homosexuality. In Eysenck, H. J. (Ed.) *Behavior Therapy and the Neuroses.* Oxford, Eng.: Pergamon, 1960.

Freud, S. *The interpretation of dreams.* New York: Science Editions, 1961.

Freud, S. Introductory lectures on psychoanalysis (1917). In *The Complete Introductory Lectures on Psychoanalysis.* New York: Norton, 1966.

Freud, S. New introductory lectures on psychoanalysis (1932). In *The Complete Introductory Lectures on Psychoanalysis.* New York: Norton, 1966.

Gardner, R. A., & Gardner, B. T. Teaching sign language to a chimpanzee, *Science,* 1969, *165,* 664–672.

Gibson, E. J. The ontogeny of reading. *American Psychologist,* 1970, *25,* 136–143.

Gibson, E. J., Gibson, J. J., Pick, A. D., & Osser, H. A. A developmental study of the discrimination of letterlike forms. *Journal of Comparative and Physiological Psychology,* 1962, *55,* 897–906.

Gibson, E. J., & Walk, R. D. The "visual cliff." *Scientific American,* 1960, *202,* 67–71.

Gibson, J. J. *The perception of the visual world.* Boston: Houghton Mifflin, 1950.

Gibson, J. *The senses considered as perceptual systems.* Boston: Houghton Mifflin, 1966.

Glasser, W. *Reality therapy.* New York: Harper & Row, 1965.

Goldstein, K. *The organism.* New York: American Book, 1939.

Gottesman, I. I., & Shields, J. Contributions of twin studies to perspectives on schizophrenia. In Maher, B. A. (Ed.) *Progress in Experimental Personality Research.* Vol. 3. New York: Academic Press, 1966.

Green, R. F. Age-intelligence relationship between 16 and 64: a rising trend. *Developmental Psychology,* 1969, *1,* 618–627.

Griffith, R. M., Miyago, O., & Tago, A. The universality of typical dreams: Japanese vs. Americans. *American Anthropologist,* 1958, *60,* 1173–1179.

Guilford, J. P. *The nature of human intelligence.* New York: McGraw-Hill, 1967.

Gustavson, C. R., Garcia, J., Hankins, W. G., & Rusiniak, K. W. Coyote predation control by aversive conditioning. *Science,* 1974, *184,* 581–584.

Harlow, H. F. The nature of love. *American Psychologist,* 1958, *13,* 673–685.

Harlow, H., & Harlow, M. Learning to think. *Scientific American,* 1949, *181,* 36–39.

Harlow, H., Harlow, M. K., & Meyer, D. R. Learning motivated by a manipulation drive. *Journal of Experimental Psychology,* 1950, *40,* 228–234.

Harris, T. A. *I'm ok—you're ok.* New York: Harper & Row, 1967.

Heider. F. *The psychology of interpersonal relations.* New York: Wiley, 1958.

Held, R., & Hein, A. Movement-produced stimulation in the development of visually guided behavior. *Journal of Comparative and Physiological Psychology,* 1963, *56,* 872–876.

Helson, H. Adaptation level theory. In Koch, S. (Ed.) *Psychology: A Study of a Science.* Vol. 1. New York: McGraw-Hill, 1959.

Hess, E. The relationship between imprinting and motivation. In Jones, M. R. (Ed.) *Nebraska Symposium on Motivation.* Vol. 7. Lincoln, Nebr.: University of Nebraska Press, 1959.

Hess, E. Ethology: An approach toward the complete analysis of behavior. In Brown, R., Galanter, E., Hess, E., & Mandler, G. (Eds.) *New Directions in Psychology.* New York: Holt, Rinehart and Winston, 1962.

Heston, L. L. The genetics of schizophrenia and schizoid disease. *Science,* 1970, *167,* 249–256.

Hochberg, J. E. *Perception.* Englewood Cliffs, N.J.: Prentice-Hall, 1964.

Holt, J. *How children fail.* New York: Pitman, 1964.

Horney, K. *Neurotic personality of our times.* New York: Norton, 1937.

Hraba, J. G., & Grant, G. Black is beautiful: A reexamination of racial preference and identification. *Journal of Personality and Social Psychology,* 1970, *16,* 398–402.

Hubel, D. H., & Wiesel, T. N. Receptive fields of single neurons in the cat's striate cortex. *Journal of Physiology,* 1959, *148,* 574–591.

Isaacson, R. L., Douglas, R. J., Lubar, J. F., & Schmaltz, L. W. *A primer of physiological psychology.* New York: Harper & Row, 1971.

Janov, A. *The primal scream.* New York: Dell, 1970.

Jellinek, E. M. Phases of alcohol addiction. *Quarterly Journal of Studies on Alcohol,* 1952, *13,* 673–684.

Jensen, A. R. How much can we boost IQ and scholastic

achievement? *Harvard Educational Review,* 1969, *39,* 1–123.

Johnson, D. M. A modern account of problem solving. *Psychological Bulletin,* 1944, *41,* 201–229.

Johnson, M. K., Bransford, J. D., & Solomon, S. Memory for tacit implications of sentences. *Journal of Experimental Psychology,* 1973, *98,* 203–205.

Jones, M. C. Psychological correlates of somatic development. *Child Development,* 1965, *36,* 899–911.

Jung, C. G. *Analytical psychology.* New York: Moffat, 1916.

Jung, C. G. *Psychology of the unconscious.* New York: Dodd, 1925.

Kallman, F. J. The use of genetics in psychiatry. *Journal of Mental Science,* 1958, *104,* 542–549.

Kallman, F. J. *Heredity in mental health and disorder.* New York: Norton, 1953.

Katahn, M. Systematic desensitization and counseling for anxiety in a college basketball player. *Journal of Special Education,* 1967, *1,* 309–314.

Kaye, H. Infant sucking behavior and its modification. In Lipsitt, L. P., & Spiker, C. C. (Eds.) *Advances in Child Development and Behavior. Vol. 3.* New York: Academic Press, *1967.*

Kelly, G. A. *The psychology of personal constructs.* New York: Norton, 1955.

Kelly, G. A. Man's construction of his alternatives. In Lindzey, G. (Ed.) *Assessment of Human Motives.* New York: Holt, Rinehart and Winston, 1958.

Kelly, G. A. *A theory of personality: The psychology of personal constructs.* New York: Norton, 1963.

Kempler, W. Gestalt therapy. In R. Corsini (Ed.) *Current Psychotherapies.* Itasca, Ill.: Peacock Publishers, 1973.

Kohlberg, L. The development of moral character and moral ideology. In Hoffman, M. L., & Hoffman, L. W. (Eds.) *Review of Child Development Research. Vol. 1.* New York: Russell Sage, 1964.

Kohler, W. *The mentality of apes.* New York: Harcourt, Brace 1925.

Kolers, P. A. Bilingualism and information processing. *Scientific American,* 1968, *218,* 78–86.

Kopp, S. B. The character structure of sex offenders. *American Journal of Psychotherapy,* 1962, *16,* 64–70.

Krech, D., Crutchfield, R. S., & Livson, N. *Elements of psychology.* New York: Knopf, 1969.

Labov, W. The logic of nonstandard English. In Alatis, J. E. (Ed.) *20th Annual Round Table Meeting on Linguistics and Language Studies.* Washington, D.C.: Georgetown University Press, 1970.

Laing, R. D. *The divided self.* New York: Pantheon, 1949.

Laing, R. D. *The politics of experience.* New York: Pantheon, 1967.

Latane, B., & Darley, J. M. Group inhibition of bystander intervention in emergencies. *Journal of Personality and Social Psychology,* 1968, *10,* 215–221.

Laurendeau, M., & Pinard, A. *Causal thinking in the child.* New York: International Universities Press, 1962.

Lazarus, R. S., Opton, E. M., Nomikos, M. S., & Rankin, N. O. The principles of short-circuiting of threat: Further evidence. *Journal of Personality,* 1965, *33,* 622–635.

Lehman, H. C. *Age and achievement.* Princeton, N.J.: Princeton University Press, 1953.

Lidz, T., Alanen, Y., & Cornelison, A. Schizophrenic patients and their siblings. *Psychiatry,* 1963, *26,* 1–18.

Liebert, R. M., & Spiegler, M. D. *Personality: Strategies for the study of man* (rev. ed.). Homewood, Ill.: Dorsey Press, 1974.

Lilly, J. C. Mental effects of reduction of ordinary levels of physical stimuli for intact healthy persons. *Psychiatric Research Reports,* 1956, *5,* 1–9.

Lindner, R. *The fifty-minute hour.* New York: Holt, Rinehart and Winston, 1955.

Loftus, E. F., & Palmer, J. C. Reconstruction of automobile destruction. *Journal of Verbal Learning and Verbal Behavior,* 1974, *13,* 585–589.

Loftus, E. F., & Zanni, G. R. Eyewitness identification: Linguistically caused misreflections. Unpublished paper, 1973.

Logan, F. *Fundamentals of learning and motivation.* Dubuque, Iowa: Brown, 1970.

Lorenz, K. Der Kumpan in der Umwelt des Vogels. *Jour. Ornith.,* 1935, *83,* 137–213, 324–331.

Lorenz, K. Vergleichende Verhaltensforschung. *Zool. Anz. Suppl.,* 1939, *12,* 69–102.

Maier, N. R. F. Reasoning in humans. II. The solution of a problem and its appearance in consciousness. *Journal of Comparative Psychology,* 1931, *12,* 181–194.

Maslow, A. H. A theory of human motivation. *Psychological Review,* 1943, *50,* 370–396.

Maslow, A. H. Some basic propositions of a growth and self-actualization psychology. In *Perceiving, Behaving, Becoming: A New Force for Education.* Washington, D.C.: Yearbook of the Association for Supervision and Curriculum Development, 1962.

Maslow, A. *Motivation and personality.* New York: Harper & Row, 1970.

Masters, R., & Houston, J. *The varieties of psychedelic experience.* New York: Holt, Rinehart and Winston, 1966.

McClelland, D. C., Atkinson, J. W., Clark, R. A., & Lowell, E. L. *The achievement motive.* New York: Appleton-Century-Crofts, 1953.

McClelland, D. C., & Friedman, G. A. A cross-cultural study of the relationship between child-training practices and achievement motivation appearing in folk tales. In Swanson, G. E., et al. (Eds.) *Readings in Social Psychology.* New York: Holt, 1952.

McClelland, D. C., & Winter, D. G. *Motivating economic achievement.* New York: Free Press, 1969.

McIntire, R. *For love of children.* Del Mar, Calif.: CRM Books, 1970.

Meredith, H. V. A synopsis of puberal changes in youth. *Journal of School of Health,* 1967, *37,* 171–176.

Merton, R. K. *Social theory and social structure.* Glencoe, Ill.: Free Press, 1957.

Merton, R. K. *On the shoulders of giants.* New York: Free Press, 1965.

Milgram, S. Some conditions of obedience and disobedience to authority. *Human Relations,* 1965, *18,* 57–76.

Miller, G. A., Galanter, E., & Pribram, K. L. *Plans and the structure of behavior.* New York: Holt, Rinehart and Winston, 1960.

Miller, N. E. Learning of visceral and grandular responses. *Science,* 1969, *163,* 434–445.

Mischel, W. *Introduction to personality.* New York: Holt, Rinehart and Winston, 1971.

Moore, O. K. Autotelic responsive environments and exceptional children. In Harvey, O. J. (Ed.) *Experience, Structure, and Adaptability.* New York: Springer, 1966.

Murray, H. A. Techniques for a systematic investigation of fantasy. *Journal of Psychology, 1936, 3,* 115-143.

Murray, H. A. *Explorations in personality.* New York: Oxford University Press, 1938.

Neisser, U. Selective reading: A method for the study of visual attention. A paper presented at the 19th International Congress of Psychology, London, August 1969.

Newcomb, T. M. *The acquaintance process.* New York: Holt, 1961.

Nisbett, T. E. Determinants of food intake in human obesity. *Science,* 1968, *59,* 1254-1255.

Ogden, C. K., & Richards, I. A. *The meaning of meaning.* New York: Harcourt Brace, 1923.

Olds, J., & Milner, P.M. Positive reinforcement produced by electrical stimulation of septal area and other regions of rat brains. *Journal of Comparative and Physiological Psychology,* 1954, *47,* 419-427.

Ornstein, R., & Naranjo, C. *On the psychology of meditation.* New York: Viking, 1971.

Osgood, C. E. The nature and measurement of meaning. *Psychological Bulletin,* 1952, *49,* 197-237.

Packard, V. The hidden persuaders. New York: Simon & Schuster, 1957.

Palermo, D. S. Language acquisition. In Reese, H. W., & Lipsitt, L. P. (Eds.) *Experimental Child Psychology.* New York: Academic Press, 1970.

Paul, G. L. *Insight vs. desensitization in psychotherapy.* Stanford, Calif.: Stanford University Press, 1966.

Pavlov, I. P. *Conditioned reflexes.* New York: Oxford University Press, 1927.

Pervin, L. A. *Personality: Theory, assessment, and research.* New York: Wiley, 1970.

Peterson, L. R., & Peterson, M. J. Short-term retention of individual verbal items. *Journal of Experimental Psychology, 1959, 58,* 193-198.

Pettigrew, T. F. School desegregation. In *White House Conference on Education.* Washington, D.C.: U.S. Government Printing Office, 1965.

Piaget, J. *The language and thought of the child.* New York: Harcourt Brace, 1926.

Pishkin, V., & Burn, J. M. Concept identification in the brain damaged: Intertrial interval and information complexity. *Journal of Abnormal Psychology,* 1971, *77,* 205-210.

Premack, D. Reinforcement theory In Levine, D. (Ed.) *Nebraska Symposium on Motivation.* Lincoln, Nebr.: University of Nebraska Press, 1965.

Premack, D. Language in chimpanzee? *Science,* 1971. *172,* 808-822.

Revusky, S. H. Aversion to sucrose produced by contingent x-irradiation: Temporal and dosage parameters. *Journal of Comparative and Physiological Psychology, 1968, 65,* 17-22.

Rogers, C. R. *Client-centered therapy.* Boston: Houghton Mifflin, 1951.

Rogers, C. R. *On becoming a person: A therapist's view of psychotherapy.* Boston: Houghton Mifflin, 1961.

Rosenthal, R. *Experimenter effects in behavioral research.* New York: Appleton-Century-Crofts, 1966.

Schachter, S. Some extraordinary facts about obese humans and rats. *American Psychologist,* 1971, *26,* 129-144.

Schachter, S., & Gross L. P. Manipulated time and eating behavior. *Journal of Personality and Social Psychology,* 1968, *10,* 98-106.

Schachter, S., & Singer, J. E. Cognitive, social and physiological determinants of emotional state. *Psychological Review,* 1962, *69,* 379-399.

Schooler, C. Birth order effects: Not here, not now! *Psychological Bulletin,* 1972, *78,* 161-175.

Seeman, J. *The case of Jim.* Tape recording and transcript. Nashville, Tenn.: Counselor Recordings and Tests, 1957.

Seeman, J. Self-exploration in client-centered therapy. In Wolman, B. B. (Ed.) *Handbook of Clinical Psychology.* New York: McGraw-Hill, 1965.

Selfridge, R. G. Coding a general-purpose digital computer to operate as a differential analyzer. *Proceedings of the Western Joint Computer Conference. Los Angeles, March, 1955.* New York: Institute of Electrical and Electronics Engineers: 1955.

Seligman, M. E. P. Can we immunize the weak? *Psychology Today,* June 1969, pp. 42-44.

Sherif, M., Harvey, O. J., White, B. J., Hood, W. R., & Sherif, C. W. *Intergroup conflict and cooperation: The Robbers Cave experiment.* Norman, Okla.: Institute of Group Relations, University of Oklahoma, 1961.

Shuttleworth, F. K. The adolescent period. *Monographs of the Society for Research in Child Development,* 1938, *3,* 3.

Siqueland, E. R., & Lipsitt, L. P. Conditioned head-turning in newborns. *Journal of Experimental Child Psychology, 1966, 3,* 356-376.

Skinner, B. F. *The behavior of organisms.* New York: Appleton-Century-Crofts, 1938.

Slobin, D. I. *Psycholinguistics.* Glenview, Ill.: Scott, Foresman, 1971.

Solomon, R. L., & Corbit, J. D. An opponent-process theory of motivation: II. Cigarette addiction. *Journal of Abnormal Psychology,* 1973, *83,* 158-171.

Sperling, G. The information available in brief visual presentations. *Psychological Monographs,* 1960 (74, whole no. 498).

Spock, B. *Baby and child care.* New York: Simon & Schuster, 1957.

Standing, L. G., Conezio, J., & Haber, R. N. Perception and memory for pictures: Single trial learning of 2500 visual stimuli. *Psychonomic Science,* 1970, *19,* 73-74.

Stewart, K. Dream theory in Malaya. In Tart, C. (Ed.) *Altered States of Consciousness: A Book of Readings.* New York: Wiley, 1969.

Stone, L. J., & Church, J. *Childhood and adolescence.* New York: Random House, 1968.

Strupp, H. H., Fox, R. W., & Lessler, K. *Patients view their psychotherapy.* Baltimore: Johns Hopkins University Press, 1969.

Szasz, T. S. *Law, liberty, and psychiatry.* New York: Macmillan, 1963.

Szasz, T. S. *The myth of mental illness.* New York: Harper & Row, 1961.

Tart, C. The "high" dream: A new state of consciousness. In Tart, C. (Ed.) *Altered States of Consciousness: A Book of Readings.* New York: Wiley, 1969.

Tart, C. *On being stoned: A psychological study of marijuana intoxication.* Palo Alto, Calif.: Science and Behavior Books, 1971.

Terman, L. M., & Merrill, M. A. *Stanford-Binet intelligence* scale: Manual for the third revision form L-M. Boston: Houghton Mifflin, 1960.

Thibaut, J. W., & Kelley, H. H. *The social psychology of groups.* New York: Wiley, 1959.

Thigpen, C. H., & Cleckley, H. M. *The three faces of Eve.* New York: McGraw-Hill, 1957.

Thurstone, L. L. *Primary mental abilities.* Chicago: University of Chicago Press, 1938.

Tinbergen, N. *The study of instinct.* London: Oxford University Press, 1951.

Tobin, S. A. Saying goodbye in Gestalt therapy. *Psychotherapy: Theory, Research, and Practice,* 1971, *8,* 150-155.

Truax, C. B. Wargo, D. G., Frank, J. D., Imber, S. D., Battle, C., Hoehn-Sarie, R., Wash, E. H., & Stone, A. R. Therapist empathy, genuineness, warmth and patient therapeutic outcome. *Journal of Consulting Psychology,* 1966, *30,* 395-401.

Tryon, R. C. Genetic differences in maze-learning ability in rats. In *39th Yearbook, National Society for the Study of Education.* Chicago: University of Chicago Press, 1940.

Tulving, E. Retrograde amnesia in free recall. *Science,* 1969, *164,* 88-90.

van Eeden, F. A study of dreams. *Proceedings of the Society for Psychical Research,* 1913, *26,* 431-461.

Wallace, W. P. Review of the historical, empirical, and theoretical status of the von Restorff phenomenon. *Psychological Bulletin,* 1965, *63,* 410-424.

Wallach, M. A., & Kogan, N. *Modes of thinking in young children.* New York: Holt, Rinehart and Winston, 1965.

Warden, C. J. *Animal motivation: Experimental studies on the albino rat.* New York: Columbia University Press, 1931.

Wechsler, D. *Wechsler adult intelligence scale, manual.* New York: Psychological Corporation, 1955.

Werner, H., & Kaplan, E. Development of word meaning through verbal context: An experimental study. *Journal of Psychology,* 1950, *29,* 251-257.

Whitehead, A. N., & Russell, B. *Principia mathematica.* Cambridge, Eng.: Cambridge University Press, 1925.

Whitehorn, J. C., & Betz, B. A study of psychotherapeutic relationships between physicians and schizophrenic patients. *American journal of Psychiatry,* 1954, *111,* 321-331.

Whorf, B. L. *Language, thought, and reality.* New York: MIT Press—Wiley, 1956.

Wike, E. L. *Data analysis: A statistical primer for psychology students.* Chicago: Aldine-Atherton, 1971.

Winterbottom, M. R. The relation of need for achievement to learning experiences in independence and mastery. In Atkinson, J. W. (Ed.) *Motives in Fantasy Action and Society.* Princeton, N.J.: Van Nostrand, 1958.

Wolf, M., Birnbrauer, J., Lawler, J., & Williams, T. The operant extinction, reinstatement, and re-extinction of vomiting behavior in a retarded child. In Ulrich, R., Stachnik, T., and Mabry, J. *Control of Human Behavior: From Cure to Prevention.* Glenview, Ill.: Scott, Foresman, 1970.

Wolpe, J., & Lang, P. J. A fear survey schedule for use in behavior therapy. *Behavior Research and Therapy,* 1964, *2,* 27.

Yalom, I. D., & Lieberman, M. A. A study of encounter group casualties. *Archives of General Psychiatry,* 1971, *25,* 16-30.

Yarrow, M. R., Campbell, J. D., & Burton, R. V. Recollections of childhood: A study of the retrospective method. *Monographs of the Society for Research in Child Development,* 1970, *35* (5, whole no. 138).

Zajonc, R. B. Social facilitation. *Science,* 1965, *149,* 269-274.

Zajonc, R. B., & Markus, G. B. Birth order and intellectual development. *Psychological Review,* 1975, *82,* 74-88.

Zimbardo, P. G. The human choice: Individuation, reason, and order versus deindividuation, impulse, and chaos. In *Nebraska Symposium on Motivation.* Lincoln, Nebr.: University of Nebraska Press, 1969.

right Newsweek, Inc. 1974, reprinted by permission.
Figure 3–23, p. 95, photo courtesy of Wide World Photos.
Plate 1, The Electromagnetic Spectrum, after P. H. Lindsay
and D. A. Norman. *Human Information Processing: An Introduction to Psychology.* New York: Academic Press, 1972,
figure 4–1. Reprinted by permission.
Plate 2. The Strocp Color Naming Test,

Plate 3, Negative Afterimage, from Evans, R. M. *An Introduction to Color.* New York: Wiley, 1948. Reprinted by permission.
Plate 4, The Color Circle, after Munsinger, Harry. *Fundamentals of Child Development.* Copyright © 1971 by Holt, Rinehart and Winston, Inc. Reprinted by permission of Holt,
Rinehart and Winston.
Plate 7, Color Solid, from Munsinger, Harry. *Fundamentals
of Child Development.* Copyright © 1971 by Holt, Rinehart
and Winston, Inc. Reprinted by permission of Holt, Rinehart
and Winston.
Plate 8, Additive Color Mixture, courtesy Inmont Corporation.
Plate 9, Subtractive Color Mixture, courtesy Inmont Corporation.

Chapter 4

Figure 4–1, p. 101, after C. T. Morgan and R. A. King. *Intro-
duction to Psychology.* New York: McGraw-Hill, 1966. Re-
printed by permission. Also after Pavlov, 1928.
Figure 4–2, p. 102, after J. B. Watson and R. Rayner. Conditioned emotional reactions. *Journal of Experimental Psychology,* 1920, *3,* 1–4.
Experimental Diet Shocking, p. 106, from *Boulder Daily
Camera,* June 13, 1972. Reprinted by permission of AP.
Man Hated Face—Then TV Did Trick, p. 109, from *Denver
Post,* August 30, 1970. Reprinted by permission of AP.
Figure 4–7, p. 113, reprinted with permission of author and
publisher from: Guttman, N. The pigeon and the spectrum
and other perplexities. *Psychological Reports,* 1956, *2,* 449–
460.
Figure 4–8, p. 113, after K. S. Lashley. The mechanism of
vision: I. A method for rapid analysis of pattern-vision in the
rat. *Journal of Genetic Psychology,* 1930, *37,* 453–460.
Figure 4–9, p. 115, photo courtesy of Yerkes Regional Pri-
mate Research Center, Emory University.
Figure 4–10, p. 118, after Ernest R. Hilgard and Gordon H.
Bower, *Theories of Learning,* 3rd edition © 1966. Reprinted
by permission of Prentice-Hall, Inc., Englewood Cliffs, New
Jersey. Data from W. K. Estes. An experimental study of
punishment. *Psychological Monographs,* 1944, *57.*
Table 4–7, p. 119, after Frank A. Logan, *Fundamentals of
Learning and Motivation,* 1970, Dubuque, Wm. C. Brown
Company Publishers.
Fitting the Crime, p. 120, from *Newsweek,* December 23,
1974. Copyright Newsweek, Inc. 1974, reprinted by permis-
sion.
Meaningfulness Facilitates Learning, p. 124, ratings for lists
of nonsense syllables from J. A. Glaze. The association value
of nonsense syllables. *Journal of Genetic Psychology,* 1928,
35, 255–267. Reprinted by permission of Journal Press.
Figure 4–13, p. 130, after L. R. Peterson and M. J. Peterson.
Short-term retention of individual verbal items. *Journal of
Experimental Psychology,* 1959, *58,* 193–198. Copyright 1959
by the American Psychological Association. Reprinted by
permission.
Figure 4–15, p. 134, after J. D. Bransford and J. J. Franks.
The abstraction of linguistic ideas. *Cognitive Psychology,*
1971, *2,* 331–350. Reprinted by permission.
Figure 4–16, p. 136, photo courtesy of Sears, Roebuck and
Co.
Habits: The Cigarette Diet, p. 137, from *Time,* August 22,
1969. Reprinted from TIME, The Weekly Newsmagazine;
Copyright Time Inc.
Novel Treatment, p. 138, from *Daily Chronicle,* DeKalb, Ill.,
October 10, 1973. Reprinted by permission of UPI.
Figure 4–17, p. 139, from A. J. Bachrach, W. J. Erwin, and
J. P. Mohr. The control of eating behavior in an anorexic by
operant conditioning techniques. In L. Ullmann and L. P.
Krasner (Eds.) *Case Studies in Behavior Modification.* Copy-
right © 1965 by Holt, Rinehart and Winston, Inc. Reprinted

by permission of Holt, Rinehart and Winston. Photos courtesy of A. J. Bachrach.
Figure 4–18, p. 141, from B. F. Skinner. Pigeons in a pelican.
American Psychologist, 1960, *15,* 28–37. Copyright 1960 by
the American Psychological Association. Reprinted by permission.

Chapter 5

Talking Inhibits Thinking, p. 148, from *Boulder Daily Camera,* November 17, 1970. Copyright, Los Angeles Times. Reprinted with permission.
Problem of "The ages of a man and his wife . . ." from D. M.
Johnson. A modern account of problem solving. *Psychological Bulletin,* 1944, *41,* 201–229.
Table 5–1, p. 155, adapted from p. 109 of Abraham S.
Luchins and Edith H. Luchins. *Rigidity of Behavior.* Eugene:
University of Oregon Press, 1959, which describes experiments that minimized and maximized Einstellung effects and
recovery in arithmetic problems, anagrams, and mazes, as
well as other material. Reprinted by permission of the authors.
The Syntactical Chimp, p. 161, from *Newsweek,* January 7,
1972. Copyright 1972 by Newsweek, Inc. All rights reserved.
Reprinted by permission. Photo courtesy of Ron Sherman.
Bilingualism and Information Processing, p. 167, excerpt
from P. A. Kolers. Bilingualism and information processing.
Scientific American, March 1968, pp. 78–86.
The Electronic Serenade, p. 168, drawing from J. D. Brans-
ford and M. K. Johnson. Considerations of some problems
of comprehension. In W. G. Chase (Ed.) *Visual Information
Processing.* New York: Academic Press, 1973. Reprinted by
permission.
Taking the Chitling Test, p. 168, from *Newsweek,* July 15,
1968. Copyright 1968 by Newsweek, Inc. All rights reserved.
Reprinted by permission.
Use of Computers for Mental Tests Urged, p. 170, from
Rocky Mountain News, January 26, 1974. Reprinted by per-
mission of AP.
Table 5–4, p. 171, adapted from D. Wechsler. *The Measure-
ment and Appraisal of Adult Intelligence.* 4th ed. © 1958 the
Williams & Wilkins Co., Baltimore. Reprinted by permission.
Who's Retarded?, p. 171, from *Time,* September 4, 1972.
Reprinted from TIME, The Weekly Newsmagazine; Copyright
Time Inc.
Hopkins Makes a Place for Childhood Geniuses, p. 172, from
Denver Post, September 26, 1972. Reprinted by permission
of AP.
Table 5–5, p. 173, after a report of the President's Commis-
sion on Mental Retardation, 1963, by F. H. Sanford and L. S.
Wrightsman, in *Psychology: A Scientific Study of Man.* 3rd
ed. Monterey, Calif.: Brooks/Cole Publishing, 1970.
The Drawing-Completion Test, p. 174, and Sample Respons-
es to the Drawing-Completion Test, p. 177, after F. Barron.
The psychology of imagination. *Scientific American,* Septem-
ber 1958. Reprinted by permission of the author.
Silent Speech, p. 179, from *Time,* June 26, 1972. Reprinted
from TIME, The Weekly Newsmagazine; Copyright Time Inc.
Photo courtesy of Symbol Communication Programme, On-
tario Crippled Children's Centre, Toronto, Canada.
Nurturing Intelligence, p. 180, from *Time,* January 3, 1972.
Reprinted from TIME, The Weekly Newsmagazine; Copyright
Time Inc.
Maybe Exercise Does Expand Brain, p. 181, from *Boulder
Daily Camera,* April 4, 1972. Reprinted by permission of the
National Science Foundation.

Chapter 6

The Daring Young Man on the Skyline Trapeze, p. 186, from
Newsweek, August 19, 1974. Copyright 1974 by Newsweek.
All rights reserved. Reprinted by permission. Photo courtesy
of Wide World Photos.
Blue Streaks, p. 187, from *Newsweek,* February 4, 1974.
Copyright 1974 by Newsweek, Inc. All rights reserved. Re-
printed by permission.
Figure 6–1, p. 189, after C. J. Warden. *Animal Motivation:
Experimental Studies on the Albino Rat.* New York: Colum-
bia University Press, 1931.
Woman Lifts Car Off Son, p. 190, from *Boulder Daily Cam-
era,* January 16, 1972. Reprinted by permission of AP.
Figure 6–2, p. 191, from D. L. Hebb, *Textbook of Psychology,*

3rd ed. Philadelphia: W. B. Saunders Company, 1972, p. 199. Reprinted by permission.

Figure 6–4, p. 193, photo from R. A. Butler. Incentive conditions which influence visual exploration. *Journal of Experimental Psychology*, 1954, *48*, 19–23. Copyright 1954 by the American Psychological Association. Reprinted by permission. Photo courtesy of University of Wisconsin Primate Laboratory.

Youth Is Slain Trying to Make His Dream True, p. 193, from *Rocky Mountain News*, March 3, 1972. Reprinted by permission of UPI.

Fly Me Again, p. 194, from *Time*, June 24, 1974. Reprinted by permission from TIME, The Weekly Newsmagazine; Copyright Time Inc.

Trying to Stop Eating?, p. 196, *Rocky Mountain News*, August 24, 1972. Reprinted by permission of AP.

Figure 6–5, p. 197, photo courtesy of Neal Miller.

Learning from the Animals, p. 199, from *Newsweek*, October 22, 1973. Copyright 1973 by Newsweek, Inc. All rights reserved. Reprinted by permission. Drawing of bees by Robert Ritter, Newsweek. Photo of Lorenz by Harry Redl—Black Star.

Figure 6–6, p. 201, from *A Biology of Human Concern* by William Etkin, Robert M. Devlin, and Thomas G. Bouffard. Reprinted by permission of the publisher, J. B. Lippincott Company. Copyright © 1972.

Instinct or Intelligence?, p. 202, from *Newsweek*, January 13, 1975. Copyright 1975 by Newsweek, Inc. All rights reserved. Reprinted by permission. Drawing of potter-wasp nests from Karl and Otto von Frisch, *Animal Architecture*. New York: Harcourt Brace Jovanovich, 1975. Reprinted by permission. Also reprinted by permission of Hutchinson Publishing Group Ltd., London, England. Photo of Australian termite towers courtesy of Australian Information Service.

Figure 6–7, p. 203, photo by Thomas McAvoy, Time-Life Picture Agency.

Fireman's Holiday, p. 206, from *Time*, December 27, 1971. Reprinted by permission from TIME, The Weekly Newsmagazine; Copyright Time Inc.

Table 6–2, p. 208, from C. S. Hall and G. Lindzey. *Theories of Personality*. New York: Wiley, 1957. Reprinted by permission. Also from *Explorations in Personality* edited by Henry A. Murray. Copyright 1938 by Oxford University Press, Inc. Renewed 1966 by Henry A. Murray. Reprinted by permission of the publisher.

Photo of Abraham Maslow, p. 209, courtesy of Bertha Maslow.

Figure 6–10, p. 209, after A. H. Maslow. A theory of human motivation. *Psychological Review*, 1943, *50*, 370–396.

Figure 6–11, p. 210, after E. L. Lowell. The effect of need for achievement on learning and performance. *Journal of Psychology*, 1952, *33*, 31–40. Reprinted by permission of Journal Press.

Figure 6–12, p. 211, after M. R. Winterbottom. The relation of need for achievement to learning experiences in independence and mastery, from *Motives in Fantasy, Action, and Society*, edited by J. W. Atkinson, © 1958 by Litton Educational Publishing, Inc. Reprinted by permission of Van Nostrand Reinhold Company.

Figure 6–13, p. 212, after E. G. French. Effects of the interaction of motivation and feedback on task performance, from *Motives in Fantasy, Action, and Society*, edited by J. W. Atkinson, © 1958 by Litton Educational Publishing, Inc. Reprinted by permission of Van Nostrand Reinhold Company.

Face Reading, p. 215, from *Newsweek*, August 5, 1974. Copyright 1974 by Newsweek, Inc. All rights reserved. Reprinted by permission.

Figure 6–14, p. 218, from Neal Miller. Theory and experiment relating psychoanalytic displacement to stimulus-response generalization. *Journal of Abnormal and Social Psychology*, 1948, *43*, 155–178. Copyright 1948 by the American Psychological Association. Reprinted by permission. Photo courtesy of Neal Miller.

War Called Aid to Man, p. 219, from *Rocky Mountain News*, January 22, 1972. Reprinted by permission of UPI.

Perhaps Your Shrink Can Help You Peel Off Pounds, p. 225, from *Boulder Daily Camera*, June 26, 1974. Reprinted by permission of AP.

Hurrying a Heart Attack, p. 227, from *Time*, April 15, 1974. Reprinted by permission from TIME, The Weekly Newsmagazine; Copyright Time Inc.

Chapter 7

Are Big Babies Brighter?, p. 233, from *Newsweek*, February 18, 1974. Copyright 1974 by Newsweek, Inc. All rights reserved. Reprinted by permission.

Deadend Street?, p. 234, from *Rocky Mountain News*, January 7, 1971. Reprinted by permission of UPI.

Figure 7–2, p. 235, after L. T. Taft and H. J. Cohen. Neonate and infant reflexology. In J. Hellmuth (Ed.) *The Exceptional Infant. Vol. 1. The Normal Infant.* New York: Brunner/Mazel, Publishers, 1967. Reprinted by permission.

Figure 7–3, p. 236, after R. L. Fantz. Visual perception and experience in early infancy: A look at the hidden side of behavior development. In H. W. Stevenson, E. H. Hess, and H. L. Rheingold (Eds.) *Early Behavior: Comparative and Developmental Approaches.* New York: Wiley, 1967. Reprinted by permission.

Figure 7–4, p. 237, from "The origin of form perception" by R. L. Fantz. Copyright © 1961 by Scientific American, Inc. All rights reserved. Reprinted by permission.

Figure 7–5, p. 238, from E. J. Gibson and R. D. Walk. The visual "cliff." *Scientific American*, April 1960. Photos courtesy of William Vandivert.

Figure 7–6, p. 239, after E. J. Gibson. The ontogeny of reading. *American Psychologist*, 1970, *25*, 136–143. Copyright 1970 by the American Psychological Association. Reprinted by permission. Taken from research by Linda Lavine.

Figure 7–7, p. 239, after E. R. Siqueland and L. P. Lipsitt. Conditioned head-turning in newborns. *Journal of Experimental Child Psychology*, 1966, *3*, 356–376. Reprinted by permission of Academic Press.

Figure 7–8, p. 241, from A. T. Jersild. *Child Psychology.* (6th ed.) Englewood Cliffs, N.J.: Prentice-Hall, 1968. Photos by Zimbel of Monkmeyer Press.

Figure 7–9, p. 244, after Figure 6 from *The Growth of Logical Thinking: From Childhood to Adolescence* by Barbel Inhelder and Jean Piaget, translated by Anne Parsons and Stanley Milgram. © 1958 by Basic Books, Inc., Publishers, New York. Reprinted by permission.

Older and Wiser, p. 245, from *Time*, February 26, 1973. Reprinted by permission from TIME, The Weekly Newsmagazine; Copyright Time Inc.

Table 7–2, p. 246, after D. McNeill. *The Acquisition of Language.* New York: Harper & Row, 1970. Reprinted by permission. Data from W. F. Leopold. *Speech Development of a Bilingual Child.* Vol. 4. Evanston, Ill.: Northwestern University Press, 1949. Reprinted by permission.

Table 7–3, p. 247, from Roger Brown and Ursula Bellugi, "Three Processes in the Child's Acquisition of Syntax," *Harvard Educational Review* 34, Spring 1964, 133–151. Copyright © 1964 by the President and Fellows of Harvard College.

Look at How Child Learns Language, p. 248, from the *Kansas City Star*, April 17, 1973. © 1973 by The New York Times Company. Reprinted by permission.

Photo, p. 252, courtesy of the University of Wisconsin Primate Laboratory.

Babies Are People First, p. 253, from *St. Petersburg Times*, February 14, 1972. Reprinted by permission of AP.

Help for Exceptional Parents, p. 254, from *Time*, June 28, 1971. Reprinted by permission from TIME, The Weekly Newsmagazine; Copyright Time Inc.

And Now, Teaching Emotions, p. 255, from *Time*, February 22, 1971. Reprinted by permission from TIME, The Weekly Newsmagazine; Copyright Time Inc.

Most Beliefs called "Myths," p. 256, from *Denver Post*, December 31, 1974. Copyright, The Washington Post. Reprinted with permission from Los Angeles Times/Washington Post News Service.

Figure 7–11, p. 258, after F. K. Shuttleworth. The adolescent period. *Monographs of the Society for Research in Child Development*, Vol. 3, No. 3, 1938. Reprinted by permission.

Adolescent Suicide, p. 259, from *Time*, January 3, 1972. Reprinted by permission from Time, The Weekly Newsmagazine; Copyright Time Inc.

Table 7–5, p. 260, table of moral development from Lawrence Kohlberg. The development of moral character and moral ideology. In *Review of Child Development Research*, Volume 1, by Martin L. Hoffman and Lois Wladis Hoffman, Editors, © 1964 by Russell Sage Foundation. Reprinted by permission.

Figure 7–12, p. 260, figure of mean percent of total moral

statements of each of six moral judgment types at four ages, from Lawrence Kohlberg. The development of moral character and moral ideology. In *Review of Child Development Research*, Volume 1, by Martin L. Hoffman and Lois Wladis Hoffman, Editors, © 1964 by Russell Sage Foundation. Reprinted by permission.

Toward Total Maturity, p. 261, from *Time*, June 28, 1971. Reprinted by permission from TIME, The Weekly Newsmagazine; Copyright Time Inc.

Figure 7–13, p. 262, photo courtesy of Wide World Photos.

Death: The Vital Buoyancy of Optimism, p. 266, from *Time*, September 5, 1969. Reprinted by permission from Time, The Weekly Newsmagazine; Copyright Time Inc.

Is This Crib Necessary?, p. 267, from *Time*, November 8, 1971. Reprinted by permission from TIME, The Weekly Newsmagazine; Copyright Time Inc. Photo by Leonard McCombe, Time-Life Picture Agency.

Figure 7–14, p. 268, after J. S. Bruner. *Toward a Theory of Instruction*. Cambridge, Mass.: Belknap Press, Harvard University Press, 1966. Copyright 1966 by the President and Fellows of Harvard College.

Learning Tests Given, p. 268, from *Rocky Mountain News*, September 22, 1971. Reprinted by permission of UPI.

TV Violence Does Not Create Violent Kids, p. 270, from *Boulder Daily Camera*, September 18, 1973. Reprinted by permission of AP.

Sex Questions Valuable, Says Expert, p. 272, from *Denver Post*, June 8, 1972. Reprinted by permission of UPI.

Chapter 8

Figure 8–2, p. 280, after N. Kleitman. Patterns of dreaming. *Scientific American*, November 1960. Reprinted by permission of Dr. William Dement.

Antidream Machine, p. 282, from *Time*, June 11, 1972. Reprinted by permission from TIME, The Weekly Newsmagazine; Copyright Time Inc.

Big Differences Seen in Short, Long Sleepers, p. 283, from *Denver Post*, June 26, 1972. Reprinted by permission of UPI.

Table 8–1, p. 286, from R. M. Griffith, O. Miyago, and A. Tago. The universality of typical dreams: Japanese vs. Americans. *American Anthropologist*, 1958, *60*, 1172–1179. Reproduced by permission of the American Anthropological Association from *American Anthropologist*, Vol. 60, No. 6, 1958.

Figure 8–3, p. 287, after G. Vogel, D. Foulkes, and H. Trosman. Ego functions and dreaming during sleep onset. *Archives of General Psychiatry*, 1966, *14*, 238–248. Reprinted from the Archives of General Psychiatry, March 1966, Volume 14, Copyright 1966, American Medical Association, by permission.

Pilot Turns Minister after Out-of-Body Experience, p. 290, from *Boulder Daily Camera*, February 13, 1972. Copyright, Los Angeles Times. Reprinted with permission of Los Angeles Times/Washington Post News Service.

Hypnosis Use Helps to Relieve Terminal Cancer Patients' Pain, p. 292, *Boulder Daily Camera*, December 20, 1974. Originally from San Jose (Calif.) *Mercury and News*. Distributed by Ridder News Service. Reprinted by permission.

German "Bridey Murphy" Tale Surfaces, p. 293, from *Rocky Mountain News*, January 22, 1975. Reprinted by permission of UPI.

Photo, p. 298, by Werner Wolff, Black Star.

Table 8–3, p. 299, chart "values of variables for maximizing probability of 'good' or 'bad' trip" from Charles T. Tart. *On Being Stoned: A Psychological Study of Marijuana Intoxication*. Palo Alto, Calif.: Science and Behavior Books, 1971. Reprinted by permission.

Pot Termed "Most Dangerous," p. 301, from *Rocky Mountain News*, May 10, 1974. Reprinted by permission of Scripps-Howard Newspapers.

Photo, p. 301, courtesy of UPI.

No One Told Them, p. 304, from *Time*, July 21, 1975. Reprinted by permission from TIME, The Weekly Newsmagazine; Copyright Time Inc.

Medics: LSD Evils Overstated, p. 305, from *Denver Post*, May 23, 1971. Reprinted by permission.

Photo, p. 306, courtesy of UPI.

Table 8–4, p. 306, adapted from a chart prepared by the Bureau of Narcotics and Dangerous Drugs, U.S. Department of Justice.

Figure 8–4, p. 308, photo on which drawing is based courtesy of Robert Nadeau.

Mind Control Seen as Big Future Force, p. 309, *Denver Post*, July 8, 1973. Reprinted by permission.

Alpha Wave of the Future, p. 311, from *Time*, July 19, 1971. Reprinted by permission from TIME, The Weekly Newsmagazine; Copyright Time Inc.

He Who Tastes, Knows!, p. 312, from Carlos Castaneda. *The Teachings of don Juan: A Yaqui Way of Knowledge*. Berkeley: University of California Press, 1968. Copyright © 1968 by the Regents of the University of California; reprinted by permission of the University of California Press.

Chapter 9

Figure 9–1, p. 320, from E. Kretschmer. *Physique and Character: An Investigation of the Nature of Constitution and of the Theory of Temperament*, trans. W. H. J. Sprott. New York: Harcourt, 1926. Reprinted by permission of Routledge & Kegan Paul Ltd.

Figure 9–2, p. 321, from W. H. Sheldon. *The Varieties of Temperament: A Psychology of Constitutional Differences*. New York: Harper & Row, 1942. Reprinted by permission.

Nixon Handwriting Reflects Pressure, p. 321, from *Denver Post*, August 14, 1974. Reprinted by permission of AP.

Figure 9–3, p. 325, after H. J. Eysenck. *The Structure of Human Personality*. (3rd ed.) London: Methuen & Co., Ltd., 1970. Reprinted by permission of Associated Book Publishers Ltd.

Figure 9–4, p. 327, reproduced with permission from R. M. Liebert and M. D. Spiegler, *Personality: Strategies for the Study of Man* (rev. ed.; Homewood, Ill.: The Dorsey Press, © 1974), p. 67.

Table 9–2, p. 327, reproduced with permission from R. M. Liebert and M. D. Spiegler, *Personality: Strategies for the Study of Man* (rev. ed.; Homewood, Ill.: The Dorsey Press, © 1974), p. 73.

Figure 9–5, p. 328, photos courtesy of Sigmund Freud Copyrights Ltd.

Figure 9–6, p. 334, photo courtesy of Albert Bandura.

Figure 9–7, p. 335, photos from A. Bandura, D. Ross, and S. A. Ross. Imitation of film-mediated aggressive models. *Journal of Abnormal and Social Psychology*, 1963, *66*, 3–11. Copyright 1963 by the American Psychological Association. Reprinted by permission. Photos courtesy of Albert Bandura.

Presidential Perceptions, p. 336, from *Time*, July 1, 1974. Reprinted by permission from TIME, The Weekly Newsmagazine; Copyright Time Inc.

Figure 9–8, p. 338, reprinted with permission of the publishers from *Insight vs. Desensitization in Psychotherapy* by Gordon L. Paul (Stanford: Stanford University Press, 1966), p. 109.

Figure 9–9, p. 340, by John T. Wood, courtesy of Carl Rogers.

Figure 9–10, p. 342, by Ralph Norman, courtesy of Gladys T. Kelly.

How to Tell Who Will Kill, p. 345, from *Newsweek*, June 4, 1973. Copyright 1973 by Newsweek, Inc. All rights reserved. Reprinted by permission.

NFL Players Oppose Psychological Testing, p. 347, from *Denver Post*, January 29, 1972. Reprinted by permission of AP.

Birth without Terror, p. 348, from Dominique Torres. Birth without terror. *New Times*, 1972, *2* (8), 28–30. Reprinted by permission.

The Personalized Instruction Approach, p. 349, from Fred S. Keller. Good-bye teacher . . . *Journal of Applied Behavior Analysis*, 1968, *1*, 79–89. Copyright 1968 by the Society for the Experimental Analysis of Behavior, Inc. Reprinted by permission.

Chapter 10

Parents Held for Keeping Diapered Teen in Isolation, p. 354, from *Boulder Daily Camera*, November 18, 1970. Reprinted by permission of AP.

Figure 10–1, p. 357, after D. Byrne and W. Griffitt. A developmental investigation of the law of attraction. *Journal of Personality and Social Psychology*, 1966, *4*, 699–702. Copyright 1966 by the American Psychological Association. Reprinted by permission.

U.S. Charges Two Cities with Hiring Bias, p. 360, from *Milwaukee Journal*, August 8, 1972. Reprinted by permission of UPI.

Figure 10–3, p. 361, photo from P. G. Zimbardo. The human choice: Individuation, reason, and order versus deindividuation, impulse, and chaos. *Nebrasks Symposium on Motivation,* 1969, by permission of the University of Nebraska Press.

Table 10–1, p. 364, from M. Karlins, T. L. Coffman, and G. Walters. On the fading of social stereotypes: Studies in three generations of college students. *Journal of Personality and Social Psychology,* 1969, *13,* 1–16. Copyright 1969 by the American Psychological Association. Reprinted by permission.

In-group Heroes, Out-group Villains, p. 365, from R. K. Merton. *Social Theory and Social Structure.* Revised and enlarged edition. Glencoe, Ill.: Free Press, 1957. Reprinted by permission of Macmillan Publishing Co., Inc.

Figure 10–4, p. 366, photo courtesy of Wide World Photos.

Figure 10–5, p. 368, adapted with permission of the publishers from *Social Pressures in Informal Groups* by Leon Festinger, Stanley Schachter, and Kurt Back. Stanford: Stanford University Press, 1950, p. 44.

Study Shows Beauty Beats Inner Traits, p. 369, from *Denver Post,* March 29, 1972. Reprinted by permission of the Chicago Daily News.

Text diagram, p. 370, after Robert Zajonc. Social facilitation, *Science,* 1965, *149,* 269–274. Copyright 1965 by the American Association for the Advancement of Science. Reprinted by permission.

Guidelines for Building a Happy Marriage, p. 371, from *Social Psychology and Modern Life,* by Patricia Niles Middlebrook. Copyright © 1973 by Alfred A. Knopf, Inc. Reprinted by permission of the publisher.

Figure 10–6, p. 372, from S. Asch. Opinions and social pressure. *Scientific American,* November 1955. Photos courtesy of William Vandivert.

Figure 10–7, p. 372, after "Opinions and social pressure," by Solomon Asch. Copyright © 1955 by Scientific American, Inc. All rights reserved. Reprinted by permission.

Figure 10–8, p. 372, after "Opinions and social pressure," by Solomon Asch. Copyright © 1955 by Scientific American, Inc. All rights reserved. Reprinted by permission.

News story, p. 373, from *Newsweek,* January 29, 1973. Copyright 1973 by Newsweek, Inc. All rights reserved. Reprinted by permission.

Table 10–2, p. 374, after M. A. Wallach and N. Kogan. Sex differences and judgment processes. *Journal of Personality,* 1959, *27,* 555–564. Copyright 1959 by the Duke University Press. Reprinted by permission. Also reprinted from N. Kogan and M. A. Wallach. *Risk Taking.* Copyright © 1964 by Holt, Rinehart and Winston, Inc. 1964, Appendix E. Reprinted by permission of Holt, Rinehart and Winston.

Figure 10–9, p. 377, after M. Deutsch and R. M. Krauss. The effect of threat upon interpersonal bargaining. *Journal of Abnormal and Social Psychology,* 1960, *61,* 181–189. Copyright 1960 by the American Psychological Association. Reprinted by permission.

Motorists Ignore Girl's Pleas, p. 377, from *Boulder Daily Camera,* November 22, 1971. Reprinted by permission of AP.

Table 10–3, p. 378, after S. Milgram. The experience of living in cities. *Science,* 1970, *167,* 1461–1468. Copyright 1970 by the American Association for the Advancement of Science. Reprinted by permission.

The Stanford Prison Study, p. 379, quotes from pages 9 and 21 of P. G. Zimbardo, G. Haney, W. C. Banks, and D. Jaffe. The psychology of imprisonment: Privation, power and pathology. Mimeographed paper.

Generations Closing Gap in Life-Styles, p. 382, from *Denver Post,* January 4, 1974. Reprinted by permission of AP.

Figure 10–10, p. 386, after R. Rosenthal. *Experimenter Effects in Behavioral Research.* New York: Appleton-Century-Crofts, 1966. Reprinted by permission of Irvington Publishers, Inc.

Chapter 11

Psychological Distress Common in U.S., p. 390, from *Boulder Daily Camera,* November 5, 1970. Reprinted by permission of AP.

Figure 11–1, p. 397, after R. S. Lazarus, E. M. Opton, M. S. Nomikos, and N. O. Rankin. The principles of short-circuiting of threat: Further evidence. *Journal of Personality,* 1965, *33,* 622–635. Copyright 1965 by Duke University Press. Reprinted by permission.

Figure 11–2, p. 397, after W. D. Fenz and S. Epstein. Gradients of physiological arousal of experienced and novice parachutists as a function of an approaching jump. *Psychosomatic Medicine,* 1967, *29,* 33–51. Reprinted by permission of Harper & Row Medical Department.

A Case of Obsessive-Compulsive Behavior, p. 402, excerpt from *Personality Development and Psychopathology,* by Norman Cameron. Houghton Mifflin Company, 1963. Reprinted by permission of Houghton Mifflin and of H. K. Lewis & Co.

Psychiatrists Fear Epidemic of Depression and Hopelessness, p. 403, from *Denver Post,* April 11, 1972. Reprinted by permission of the Chicago Daily News.

A Case of Psychosomatic Asthma, p. 404, excerpt from *Personality Development and Psychopathology,* by Norman Cameron. Houghton Mifflin Company, 1963. Reprinted by permission of Houghton Mifflin and of H. K. Lewis & Co.

A Case History of Anxiety Displacement, p. 405, excerpt from *Behavior Pathology,* by N. Cameron and A. Margaret. Houghton Mifflin Company, 1951. Reprinted by permission of Houghton Mifflin.

The Criminal Sociopath, p. 407, excerpts from Robert W. White and Norman F. Watt. *The Abnormal Personality,* fourth edition. Copyright © 1973 The Ronald Press Company, New York. Quotes in excerpt are from Truman Capote. *In Cold Blood.* New York: Random House, 1965.

Table 11–2, p. 408, after E. M. Jellinek. Phases of alcohol addiction. *Quarterly Journal of Studies on Alcohol.* Reprinted by permission from *Quarterly Journal of Studies on Alcohol,* Vol. 13, pp. 673–684, 1952. Copyright by Journal of Studies on Alcohol, Inc., New Brunswick, N.J. 08903.

Figure 11–4, p. 410, photo courtesy of Wide World Photos.

Homosexuality Dropped as Mental Disorder, p. 411, from *APA Monitor,* February 1974. Copyright 1974 by the American Psychological Association. Reprinted by permission.

Photo, p. 412, courtesy of Esther Bubley.

Becoming Psychotic, p. 412, from Anonymous. An autobiography of a schizophrenic experience. *Journal of Abnormal and Social Psychology,* 1955, *51,* 677–689. Copyright 1955 by the American Psychological Association. Reprinted by permission.

Photos, p. 413, top courtesy of Wide World Photos, bottom courtesy of UPI.

Suicide among Top 12 Causes of Death, p. 414, from *Boulder Daily Camera,* October 24, 1973. Reprinted courtesy of Metropolitan Life Insurance Company.

Genes and Depression, p. 415, from *Time,* August 28, 1972. Reprinted by permission from TIME, The Weekly Newsmagazine; Copyright Time Inc.

Figure 11–15, p. 418, photo courtesy of Esther Bubley.

Table 11–3, p. 418, based on an analysis by L. L. Heston. The genetics of schizophrenic and schizoid disease. *Science,* 1970, *167,* 249–256. Copyright 1970 by the American Association for the Advancement of Science. Reprinted by permission.

The Case of a Paranoid Schizophrenic, p. 419, from B. Kaplan (Ed.) *The Inner World of Mental Illness.* New York: Harper & Row, 1964. Reprinted by permission of Robert W. White.

Study Reveals Psychiatrists Can't Tell Sane from Insane, p. 422, from *Boulder Daily Camera,* January 18, 1973. Reprinted by permission of AP.

Chapter 12

Excerpts, pp. 430–431, of guidelines for ethical behavior, from *Casebook on Ethical Standards of Psychologists.* Washington, D.C.: American Psychological Association. Reprinted by permission.

Patient Wins $170,880 in "Torture" Suit, p. 430, from *Denver Post,* July 4, 1972. Reprinted by permission of AP.

Figure 12–1, p. 431, photo by Lee Lockwood, Black Star.

The Clinical Use of Dreams, p. 433, from *The Clinical Use of Dreams,* by Walter Bonime, M.D., with Florence Bonime, © 1962 by Basic Books Publishing Company, Inc., New York. Reprinted by permission.

Yes Begins with a No, p. 436, from *Time,* June 22, 1970. Reprinted by permission from TIME, The Weekly Newsmagazine; Copyright Time Inc.

Self-Exploration in Client-Centered Therapy, p. 437, from J. Seeman. *The Case of Jim.* Tape and transcript. Nashville, Tenn.: Counselor Recordings and Tests, 1957. In B. B. Wolman (Ed.) *Handbook of Clinical Psychology.* New York:

McGraw-Hill, 1965. Reprinted by permission of Julius Seeman.

Excerpt, pp. 438–439, from Stephan A. Tobin. Saying goodbye in Gestalt therapy. *Psychotherapy Theory, Research, and Practice*, 1971, *8*, 154–155. Reprinted by permission.

T.A.: Doing OK, p. 440, from *Time*, August 20, 1973. Reprinted by permission from TIME, The Weekly Newsmagazine; Copyright Time Inc.

Excerpt, pp. 442–443, adapted from M. Katahn. Systematic desensitization and counseling for anxiety in a college basketball player. *Journal of Special Education*, 1967, *1*, 309–314. Reprinted from the Journal of Special Education by permission of the publisher.

Afraid to Sleep?, p. 443, from *Parade*, March 5, 1972. Reprinted by permission of Jeffrey Elenewski.

Training to Be Sober, p. 445, from *Time*, March 15, 1971. Reprinted by permission from TIME, The Weekly Newsmagazine; Copyright Time Inc.

Resolute Prisoners Struggle against Behavioral Modification, p. 446, from *Boulder Daily Camera*, January 5, 1974. Copyright, Washington Post. Reprinted with permission of Los Angeles Times/Washington Post News Service.

The Most Common Mental Disorder, p. 449, from *Time*, August 7, 1972. Reprinted by permission from TIME, The Weekly Newsmagazine; Copyright Time Inc. Photo by Herbert Gehr, Time-Life Picture Agency.

150 Years in Asylum, p. 450, from *San Jose Mercury*, April 24, 1971. Reprinted by permission of UPI.

New Right to Treatment, p. 451, from *Time*, April 5, 1971. Reprinted by permission from TIME, The Weekly Newsmagazine; Copyright Time Inc. Photo courtesy of Tommy Giles.

Therapeutic Friendship, p. 452, from *Time*, May 3, 1971. Reprinted by permission from TIME, The Weekly Newsmagazine; Copyright Time Inc.

Hazardous Encounters, p. 455, from *Time*, April 30, 1973. Reprinted by permission from TIME, The Weekly Newsmagazine; Copyright Time Inc. Photo by Ted Streshinsky; Time Magazine © 1973 Time Inc.

The Family as Patient, p. 456, from *Time*, May 31, 1971. Reprinted by permission from TIME, The Weekly Newsmagazine; Copyright Time Inc.

Families for Psychotics, p. 459, from *Time*, September 18, 1972. Reprinted by permission from TIME, The Weekly Newsmagazine; Copyright Time Inc.

Mental "Patients" Don't Like Treatment, p. 461, from *Boulder Daily Camera*, July 13, 1972. Reprinted by permission of AP.

Excerpts, pp. 461–462, from H. H. Strupp, R. W. Fox, and K. Lessler. *Patients View Their Psychotherapy*. Baltimore: Johns Hopkins University Press, 1969. Reprinted by permission.

Mental Illness Needs Multiple Factor Approach, p. 462, from *Biomedical News*, December 1971. Reprinted by permission.

Psychiatric "Stigma" Is Feared in Reports, p. 463, from *Denver Post*, March 13, 1974. Reprinted by permission of the Chicago Daily News.

New Mental Health Program, p. 465, from *Parade*, July 30, 1972. Reprinted by permission of Theodore Irwin. Photo courtesy of Ben Ross.

Appendix C

Figure C–2, p. 499, after Gregory A. Kimble and Norman Garmezy. *Principles of General Psychology*, third edition. Copyright © 1968 The Ronald Press Company, New York. Reprinted by permission. Data from Starke R. Hathaway and Elio D. Monachesi. *Analyzing and Predicting Juvenile Delinquency with the MMPI*. University of Minnesota Press, Minneapolis, © 1953 by the University of Minnesota. Reprinted by permission.

Figure C–3, p. 500, profile sheet for the 16 PF © 1954, 1969 by IPAT, Champaign, Ill. Reproduced by permission.

Figure C–5, p. 502, photo courtesy of Dorothea Lange Collection, The Oakland Museum.

Diagnosis by Drawing, p. 503, from *Time*, February 1, 1971. Reprinted by permission from TIME, The Weekly Newsmagazine; Copyright Time Inc. Drawings from S. H. Kaufman and R. C. Burns. *Kinetic Family Drawings*. New York: Brunner/Mazel, Publishers, 1970. Reprinted by permission.

Psychological Testing for Federal Applicants, p. 504, from *Nashville Tennessean*, June 20, 1965. Copyright, Los Angeles Times. Reprinted with permission.

Chapter Opening Photographs

Chapter 1, Rick Smolan; Chapters 2 and 5, Gordon E. Smith; Chapter 3, Arthur Tress; Chapter 4, George Roos; Chapter 6, Walter Iooss/The Image Bank; Chapter 7, newborn by Wayne Miller, Magnum; girl with doll by Abigail Heyman, Magnum; boy with candles by Burk Uzzle, Magnum; farm boy by Bob Adelman; students by Erich Hartmann, Magnum; wedding on beach by Hiroji Kubata, Magnum; man in laboratory by Burk Uzzle, Magnum; couple on couch by Sepp Seitz, Magnum; Chapter 8, Charles Gatewood; Chapter 9, Suzanne Szasz; Chapters 10 and 12, Fred Weiss; Chapter 11, Alfred Gescheidt/The Image Bank.

Cover Portraits

Association for the Advancement of Psychoanalysis of the Karen Horney Psychoanalytic Institute and Center—Horney; The Bettman Archive, Inc.—Freud, Jung, von Helmholtz, Wundt; Alice Boughton—James; Brown Brothers—Watson; Liss Goldring—Fromm; The Granger Collection—Adler; Radio Times Hulton Picture Library—Köhler, Pavlov; Townsend Wentz, Jr.—Wolpe; World Wide Photo—Piaget.

NAME INDEX

SUBJECT INDEX